A

THEOLOGY

FOR THE

CHURCH

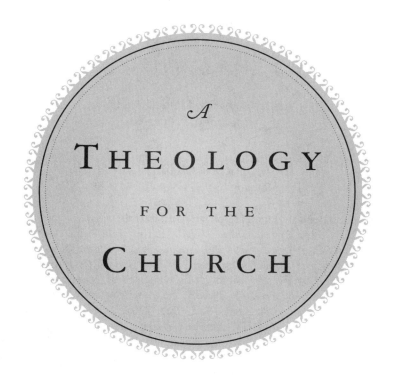

A

THEOLOGY

FOR THE

CHURCH

Daniel L. Akin
Editor

David P. Nelson and Peter R. Schemm, Jr.
Associate Editors

NASHVILLE, TENNESSEE

Published by B&H Publishing Group
Nashville, Tennessee

Dewey Decimal Classification: 230
Subject Heading: SYSTEMATIC THEOLOGY

Scripture quotations are identified by acronym as follows:
ESV, The Holy Bible, English Standard Version, copyright © 2001 by Crossway
Bibles, a division of Good News Publishers. Used by Permission. All rights
reserved. HCSB, the *Holman Christian Standard Bible®* Copyright © 1999,
2000, 2002, 2004 by Holman Bible Publishers. Used by permission. KJV, the
King James Version of the Bible. NASB, the New American Standard Bible,
© the Lockman Foundation, 1960, 1962, 1963, 1968, 1971, 1972, 1973, 1975,
1977; used by permission. NIV, the Holy Bible, New International Version,
copyright © 1973, 1978, 1984 by International Bible Society. NKJV, New King
James Version, copyright © 1979, 1980, 1982, Thomas Nelson, Inc., Publishers.
NRSV, New Revised Standard Version of the Bible, copyright © 1989 by the
Division of Christian Education of the National Council of Churches of Christ
in the United States of America, used by permission, all rights reserved. RSV,
Revised Standard Version of the Bible, copyrighted 1946, 1952, © 1971, 1973.

Unless otherwise noted, quotations from the church fathers are from the follow-
ing collections: *Ante-Nicene Fathers* (10 vols; New York: Christian Literature
Publishing Company, 1885–1897); *Nicene and Post-Nicene Fathers, Series 1*
(New York: Christian Literature Publishing Company, 1886–1890); *Nicene and
Post-Nicene Fathers, Series 2* (New York: Christian Literature Company, 1890–
1900). These volumes are available in reprint editions and at www.ccel.org.

1 2 3 4 5 6 7 8 9 10 11 12 • 15 14 13 12 11 10 09 08 07
LB

CONTENTS

Preface

The church of the Lord Jesus Christ is given the mandate "to contend for the faith that was delivered to the saints once for all" (Jude 3 HCSB). It is to that end that *A Theology for the Church* is written. "The church of God, which He purchased with His own blood" (Acts 20:28 HCSB) should be able to define and defend that body of truth committed to its care by God. The people of God must be equipped to distinguish truth from error, good theology from bad theology. Each contributor to this volume has a passion for a revival of theological knowledge and understanding in the church, that the church as a whole would regain a love for the great doctrinal truths of God's infallible and inerrant Word.

We believe it is crucial to wed doctrine and life—to recognize the unity of faith and practice. The Apostle Paul was exemplary in this manner. He was a great theologian as well as a great missionary. He saw no dichotomy between the theology of the church and the mission of the church. In Romans 12:1–2, Paul affirmed the importance of the mind in the life of the believer, calling for a daily renewing which results in a transformed life.

R. Albert Mohler, Jr., one of the contributors to this volume, states well:

> There is no room for antiintellectualism in the Christian life, nor intellectual egotism and pride. The frame of God's glory reminds us that all we know of God and his ways is given us by grace. We are absolutely dependent upon revelation, for God's ways are unfathomable and his judgments are unsearchable. Theological education exists, at least in part, to equip believers with the ability to think, to reason, to analyze, to learn, and to synthesize biblical truth, so that this truth may be imparted to others through preaching and teaching and ministry. We dare not lose sight of this great purpose. Disciples of the Lord Jesus Christ must be thinkers whose minds are captive to the Word of God and whose entire intellectual structure is shaped and determined by biblical truth. Our captivity to the Word of God is a scandal in the secular culture and among the Christians enamored with that culture. The secular intellectuals are blind to their own intellectual captivity to the spirit of the age. We, on the other hand, must wear our captivity to the Word of God as a badge of intellectual honor and integrity.

A Theology for the Church follows a distinctive pattern and a definite strategy. Each chapter is organized around four main questions, the order of which is significant: (1) What does the Bible say? (2) What has the church believed? (3) How does it all fit together? and (4) What is the significance of the doctrine for the church today?

First, *what does the Bible say?* Primacy is given, as it should be, to biblical revelation. Scripture is foundational for the development of Christian theology. Biblical illiteracy is a great enemy of the church. While many people revere the Bible, they do not read or study it. As a result, they are ignorant of its wonderful truths, and they do not see how the great doctrines of the Bible are defined and developed. Our prayer is that through this book God's people will grow to know more of the Bible and to know it better. We have this goal for the whole of the body of Christ. If we can teach our children and teens science, math, history, and a number of other disciplines, we are convinced we can teach them the Bible and theology as well.

Second, *what has the church believed?* If knowledge of the Scriptures is anemic in our day, a familiarity with church history and the history of doctrine is almost nonexistent. *A Theology for the Church* intentionally highlights the importance of doctrinal development in the various periods of church history. The great events and major participants are examined and critiqued to help God's people see how we arrived where we are today.

Third, *how does it all fit together?* Here we demonstrate the unity and coherence of biblical teaching as we consider each doctrine in light of the entire canon. The greatness of God will necessitate that we live with varying degrees of tension and mystery in the formulation of doctrine. Because of our finitude and sinfulness, we readily admit the limitations of our knowledge of God. Although we cannot know him exhaustively, we can know him truly. We are his image bearers, created to receive divine revelation. We can know propositional truth about our God, and we can know personally and intimately the God who is the Father of our Lord Jesus Christ.

Fourth, *what is the significance of the doctrine for the church today?* God's truth is eternal and unchanging. Yet it is the task of every theologian to demonstrate the relevance of the Bible for the contemporary audience. Each generation asks particular questions that are often characterized by unique concerns. Here we attempt to address the more significant questions and concerns of our day.

This is a unique approach to a systematic theology text with multiple participants, so a special word of gratitude is extended to each of the contributors. I am appreciative of their theological convictions and competencies. Each participant in this project is a confessional theologian and churchman. They are evangelical and baptistic in their commitments, and they believe, as do I, that the task of theology must be recovered in the church if it is to have vitality and health in the twenty-first century.

A number of people helped this project become a reality. Debbie Shugart, my administrative assistant, was invaluable to the process, collecting, typing, and correcting various manuscripts. Brian Sandifer, Lance Johnson, and Jon Horner were also instrumental in their assistance to

Drs. Nelson and Schemm as associate editors as they came alongside to see the project brought to completion. I also want to thank Jimmy Draper and Thom Rainer who gave us their full support in pursuing this project. I am also thankful for Tim Grubbs and Len Goss in whose heart God first put the idea of this project. John Landers and his staff at B&H Publishing Group are to be commended for their excellent assistance every step of the way.

Like any work done by finite and fallible humans, this project will have shortcomings, oversights, and mistakes. However, I believe it is the intention of every person involved that *A Theology for the Church* glorify our great God and edify his church. If that indeed comes to pass, then we rejoice that God in his grace has chosen to use our feeble and inadequate efforts to accomplish his sovereign purposes to the praise of his name.

"Now to the King eternal, immortal, invisible, the only God, be honor and glory forever and ever. Amen" (1 Tim. 1:17 HCSB).

Daniel L. Akin
Southeastern Baptist Theological Seminary
Wake Forest, North Carolina

Abbreviations

AB	Anchor Bible
ANF	*Ante-Nicene Fathers*
BEB	*Baker Encyclopedia of the Bible*
BEC	Baker Exegetical Commentary
BDB	Brown, F., S. R. Driver, and C. A. Briggs. *A Hebrew and English Lexicon of the Old Testament.* Oxford, 1907
BDT	*Baker's Dictionary of Theology*
BECNT	Baker Exegetical Commentary on the New Testament
BHH	*Baptist History and Heritage*
BSC	Bible Student's Commentary
CHB	*Cambridge History of the Bible.* Cambridge University Press, 1970
CT	*Christianity Today*
CTJ	*Calvin Theological Journal*
CTR	*Criswell Theological Review*
DJG	*Dictionary of Jesus and the Gospels.* Edited by J. B. Green and S. McKnight. Downers Grove, 1992
DPL	*Dictionary of Paul and His Letters.* Edited by G. F. Hawthorne and R. P. Martin. Downers Grove, 1993.
EBC	Expositor's Bible Commentary
EDNT	*Exegetical Dictionary of the New Testament.* Edited by H. Balz, G. Schneider. ET. Grand Rapids, 1990–1992
EDT	*Evangelical Dictionary of Theology,* ed. W. A. Elwell. Grand Rapids, 1984,
GTJ	*Grace Theological Journal*
HTR	*Harvard Theological Review*
ICC	International Critical Commentary
IDB	*The Interpreter's Dictionary of the Bible.* Edited by G. A. Buttrick. 4 vols. Nashville, 1962
Int	*Interpretation*
ISBE	*International Standard Bible Encyclopedia,* ed. G. W. Bromiley. Grand Rapids, 1979
JETS	*Journal of the Evangelical Theological Society*
JGES	*Journal of the Grace Evangelical Society*
JNTS	*Journal of New Testament Studies*
JTS	*Journal of Theological Studies*

LCC	Library of Christian Classics
LW	Luther's Works. Edited by Jaroslav Pelikan, H. T. Lehmann, et al. 56 vols. Philadelphia, 1955–1975.
NAC	New American Commentary
NCBC	New Century Bible Commentary
NCE	*New Catholic Encyclopedia,* 2nd ed. Edited by Bernard L. Marthaler. Washington 2003
NIBD	*The New Interpreter's Bible Dictionary.* Edited by Katharine Doob Sakenfeld, Samuel E. Balentine, and Brian K. Blount. 5 vols. Nashville, 2006
NICNT	New International Commentary on the New Testament
NICOT	New International Commentary on the Old Testament
NIDNTT	*New International Dictionary of New Testament Theology.* Edited by C. Brown. 4 vols. Grand Rapids, 1975–1985
NIGTC	New International Greek Testament Commentary
NPNF [1]	*Nicene and Post-Nicene Fathers,* First Series
NPNF [2]	*Nicene and Post-Nicene Fathers,* Second Series
NTC	New Testament Commentary
NTS	*New Testament Studies*
OTL	Old Testament Library
PNTC	Pillar New Testament Commentary
RevExp	*Review and Expositor*
RR	*Research Review*
SBJT	*The Southern Baptist Journal of Theology*
SE	*Studia evangelica*
SJT	*Scottish Journal of Theology*
SP	Sacra Pagina
TDNT	*Theological Dictionary of the New Testament.* Edited by G. Kittel and G. Friedrich. Translated by G. W. Bromiley. 10 vols. Grand Rapids, 1964–1976
TJ	*Trinity Journal*
TNTC	Tyndale New Testament Commentaries
TOTC	Tyndale Old Testament Commentaries
TRE	*Theologische Realenzyklopädie*
TWOT	*Theological Wordbook of the Old Testament.* Edited by R. L. Harris, G. L. Archer Jr. 2 vols. Chicago, 1980
WA	Weimar edition of Luther's Works
WBC	Word Biblical Commentary
WDTT	*Westminster Dictionary of Theological Terms*
WML	Works of Martin Luther. 6 vols. Philadelphia, 1915–1932
WTJ	*Westminster Theological Journal*

SECTION 1

THE DOCTRINE OF REVELATION

CHAPTER 1

Prolegomena: Introduction to the Task of Theology

Gregory Alan Thornbury

What Is Truth? The Inseparability of the Pursuit of Truth from the Theological Task

The words from the lips of Pontius Pilate compose the question that has perplexed the human mind throughout time: "What is truth?" It is the singularly most pressing interrogative from the time of Thales to the present. The spirit of the query is seen in Pilate's tone; it is at the same time inquisitive and dismissive. Pilate saw life in purely pragmatic terms. As a skeptic he viewed talk about truth and God as niceties in a world filled with brutal political realities. Armchair philosopher Pilate may have been, but one thing was certain: he was not an intellectually or morally neutral person. He handed over the Son of God to be crucified despite Jesus' innocence, despite his own wife's warning not to touch the "righteous man" who disturbed her in her nightmares and in the face of the Lord's kind invitation to enter the truth by listening to his voice (John 18:33–38; Matt. 27:19).

As Augustine noted, Pilate refused even to bother with Jesus' answer to his question.[1] The pursuit of truth cannot be separated from the task of theology. Like Pilate, all human beings must be confronted with the truth claims of the Lord Jesus Christ.

All claims to truth rely on presuppositions about what is fundamentally real. If a person regards a particular aspect of reality as necessary, then he has given it the status of being ultimate; and if something is ultimately necessary, it arguably has attained a divine status. Inevitably, *something* is going to function in a person's worldview with the imprimatur of religious

---

[1] Augustine, *Homilies on the Gospel of John, Homilies on the First Epistle of John and Soliloquies* 115.5, *NPNF*[1].

authority. Philosopher Roy Clouser refers to this phenomenon as "The Myth of Religious Neutrality."[2] Put differently, this means that every discussion of truth will wind up being a debate about some kind of theology, however tacit, hidden, or under-acknowledged. Human beings were created for worship, and many of them serve cognitive idols.

Christian theology advances the bold assertion that truth, goodness, and beauty cannot be known apart from God, their author. More pointedly, it challenges the notion that God can be known apart from the revelation of Jesus Christ. Pascal contended for precisely this point by stating that it is impossible to know the creature apart from the Creator:

> Not only is it through Jesus Christ alone that we know God, but it is only through Jesus Christ that we know ourselves. We know life and death only through Jesus Christ. Without Jesus Christ we do not know what our life, nor our death, nor God, nor ourselves really are.
>
> In the same way without the Scriptures, which have Jesus Christ as their sole object, we know nothing and see only darkness and confusion in the nature of God and in nature itself.[3]

Such claims are, of course, scandalous to the natural mind. It is an affront to human pride to suggest that man exists in a relationship of radical dependence upon the divine order. It is out of step with philosophical self-confidence to confess with theologian Carl F. H. Henry that "all merely human affirmations about God curl into a question mark."[4] If pure philosophy and natural law could lead us to transcendental verities, then God would not have to reveal himself to us. Unfortunately, even the best human minds have failed in their attempts to imagine something more godlike than the God of Abraham, Isaac, Jacob, and Jesus Christ. The Greek and Roman pantheon of gods proved powerful but petty, simultaneously superhuman and yet altogether too human. The same phenomenon holds true for the dizzying array of Hindu deities.

When the prurient novelist D. H. Lawrence attempted to construct an extrabiblical account of the life of Jesus, his project miserably failed to deliver even a scrap of convincing dialogue from its principle subject.[5] It is impossible to peer into the true divinity without recourse to God's

---

[2] Roy Clouser, *The Myth of Religious Neutrality: An Essay on the Hidden Role of Religious Belief in Theories* (Notre Dame: University of Notre Dame Press, 1991). Clouser's work is a helpful single volume summation of the prominent ideas in the work of the modern Dutch philosopher Herman Dooyeweerd.

[3] Blaise Pascal, *Pensées,* trans. Honor Levi (New York: Oxford University Press, 1995), 10.

[4] Carl F. H. Henry, *God Revelation and Authority,* vol. 2 (Dallas: Word, 1976), 8.

[5] D. H. Lawrence, *The Man Who Died* (New York: Ecco Press; reprint, 1995). Readers should be forewarned that this book is blasphemous and is not recommended in any way by the author.

own self-revelation. More broadly, it is dubious to argue for the unity and reality of truth *apart from* the eternal, transcendent, self-disclosing God of the Bible.

The Irrepressibility of Truth

In the early days and hours after September 11, everyone in America, or so it seemed, was affixed to a nearby radio or television. People from Flagstaff to Kalamazoo hung upon every word from the news anchors to get the latest update, to hear the horrible numbers, and to deal with their grief. But the one person who the country needed to hear from the most was their commander in chief. When the president appeared in the Cabinet Room at the White House to address the nation, a hush fell across the land. "Today our nation saw evil, the very worst of human nature," George W. Bush explained, promising to bring justice to "these evildoers."

As dark and horrible as that day was, one thing became crystal clear after September 11: good and evil were back. Now on one level, of course, good and evil never went away. What I mean is that after so many years of the idea of absolute truth being assaulted by the secular left, seemingly no one could deny any longer that there was a clear difference between right and wrong. Terrorist attacks on thousands of innocents were obviously and undeniably evil. The operative phrase here, however, is *seemingly no one.*

Only days after the attack on the American mainland, Reuters News agency announced that their reporters would not refer to the nineteen hijackers as "terrorists" because the term was judgmental and not appropriately objective. Evidently, according to Reuters, good and evil and absolute truth do not exist in their understanding of journalism.

Another even more blatant example of this denial of truth came only weeks after September 11 when Stanley Fish, the former dean of the School of Humanities at the University of Illinois, Chicago, stated in an op-ed piece in *The New York Times* that we cannot make an absolute moral judgment against the Al Qaeda members who murdered thousands of innocent civilians, nor should we call the assailants "terrorists." "We have not seen the face of evil," Fish intoned, but rather merely "the face of an enemy who comes at us with a full roster of grievances, goals, and strategies."[6] In other words, he is arguing that since no objective standard can be found for morality, one is prohibited from asserting that certain actions are either wrong or right. From Professor Fish's comments we can only assume that, in his view, all grievances are created equal, and yet none are endowed with any certain, inalienable claim to being right.

---

[6] Stanley Fish, "Condemnation without Absolutes," *New York Times,* 15 October 2001, Section A, 19, col. 2.

This pernicious position is known as relativism. Such a prejudice against the concept of objective truth arises from a deep and fundamental cultural presupposition against the possibility of moral certitude, against the notion of a body of truths that stay the same despite the vicissitudes of human society. Professor Fish's sortie into revisionist history, however, in fact turned out to be nothing more than a flight from reality. After September 11, the American public knew that the fundamental questions of our time are irrepressibly moral, undeniably related to making distinctions between good and evil. But clarity is needed. As political commentator George Will eloquently stated, "People cannot defend what they cannot define."[7]

A Working Definition of Truth and Why Truth Depends on God

So what is the definition of *truth?* Truth is that which corresponds with reality; it is the opposite of falsehood. Now the question that arises, of course, is "from where does truth come?" The answer is that truth comes from God. It is a mirror of his being. The notion of truth is an inherently religious idea. Only an eternal, transcendent sovereign could create everything in such a way as to make the universe knowable, personal, and understandable. Only such a being would be in a position to be the explanatory principle itself as well as the principal *explainer* of everything that exists. The attempt to find an ultimate hermeneutical device *other than* the living God of Abraham, Isaac, Jacob, and Jesus Christ results in continual frustration and failure. Perhaps the following visual depiction from Reformed

Figure A

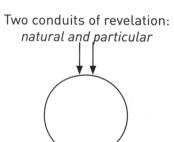

Two conduits of revelation: *natural and particular*

God's Knowledge: Independent, Complete, No Mystery

Human Knowledge: Dependent, Incomplete, Full of Mystery

[7] George Will, "So We Fight," *Washington Post,* 11 September 2002 [online]; available at: http://www.townhall.com/columnists/georgewill/gw20020911.shtml; accessed 15 October 2004.

thinker Richard Pratt (but modified by the author) will help explain the foregoing statement.[8]

Only the God of biblical proportions and depiction could create, maintain, and disclose the nature of everything that exists. God's omniscience entails the truth that he does not learn nor does he rely on any information that he himself did not create and sustain. God is never confused on any issue, nor is his mind boggled by any dilemma that similarly confronts his creatures. As Hebrews 1:3 discloses, God "holds together" every aspect of reality. Conversely, human beings have a very limited and incomplete view of knowledge. They are utterly dependent upon various tools for discovery whether those devices are empirical, rational, intuitional, or revelational—but the fact remains that all of these tools of discovery are gifts from God.

In generation after generation, the human race seeks to uncover knowledge, theorize about it, systematize it, and apply it. Ours is an epistemology of receipt. People receive wisdom from tradition, the discovery of norms already present in the universe, as well as direct verbal rational communication from God. The enormity and diversity of the universe—both metaphysical and physical—humbles any person who truly thinks through the issue. By its very nature, therefore, human knowledge finds itself full of questions, mysteries, and antinomies. This does not mean that truth cannot be obtained or that certainty cannot be acquired.

To the contrary, however, human beings must place themselves in a position to know such things, and the hard fact is that only the self-disclosing God of the biblical type can provide such resources through both an orderly creation and direct verbal conceptual communication. As a result of the human relationship of dependency upon God, anything approaching what might be considered certainty would have to come from an omniscient being.

Given that the scenario introduced in figure A on page 5 is the case, a string of theologians working in the Dutch Reformed tradition (notably Abraham Kuyper, Cornelius Van Til, and Herman Dooyeweerd) concluded from this fundamental starting point that no alternative theory can explain the universe apart from a transcendental referent who is ultimately necessary, namely, the God of Christian Scripture. Thinkers following this trajectory assert that one can take any known fact or logical principle and

---

[8] This illustration is employed by Richard Pratt in his elementary textbook on apologetics, *Every Thought Captive*. In a single image it sums up the central insight of the thought of Cornelius Van Til, the longtime Westminster Seminary professor who held that only Christian theism could adequately explain the existence of true propositions. I have modified Pratt's figure to include two arrows instead of one, thus allowing for both the possibility of the spheres of common grace (some call it general revelation) and special revelation (the Bible) to be conduits between divine and human knowledge. For Pratt's particular employment of this device, see *Every Thought Captive* (Phillipsburg, NJ: Presbyterian and Reformed Publishing Company, 1979), 24–25.

demonstrate that the idea cannot be proved without first presupposing the existence of God.[9]

This approach, known as the *transcendental argument,* vies for the impossibility of the proposition that God does not exist. As Van Til has written, one cannot have true propositions (in which something is objectively predicated of a subject) or even "get under way" unless the Christian view of reality is first presupposed.[10] Otherwise, a number of absurdities ensue.

Consider an example from the world of science. Oxford University zoologist Richard Dawkins is a committed naturalist. He believes that nothing exists save the physical properties and laws that govern the universe. In his worldview there is no God. Dawkins, however, has a problem: the universe that he studies as a scientist shows every indication that it has been put together by an intelligent designer. But Dawkins cannot admit this conclusion as it would disestablish his presupposition of naturalism. As such he penned the provocatively titled *Blind Watchmaker* in which he stated, "Biology is the study of complicated things that give the appearance of having been designed with a purpose."[11] Stated differently, Dawkins claims that the universe is not the plan of a personal Creator but the result of an impersonal and indifferent natural law that operates in axiomatic and predictable rational and scientific patterns. It is important to notice that he concludes this *in spite of what seems obviously to be the case—that an intelligent designer* did *create the universe.* How would the transcendental approach to truth work in this instance?

First of all, let us suppose that Dawkins in theory could be right. Unfortunately for the Oxford scholar there is no mechanism by which he could know whether his claim is true since his epistemology is one based on his assertion of independence (i.e., he claims to know this on the strength of his own personal apprehension of the facts). His knowledge of the universe is by definition finite, yet he claims for his own proposition of naturalism a

---

[9] This insight is a development of an idea from Immanuel Kant.

[10] The citation provided here appears in Cornelius Van Til, *Toward a Reformed Apologetics* (Philadelphia: privately printed, 1972); cited in Greg Bahnsen, *Van Til's Apologetic* (Phillipsburg, NJ: Presbyterian and Reformed, 1998), 22. Bahnsen's work contains a thorough discussion of the philosophical appeal of the transcendental argument. In all candor the author finds Bahnsen's explanation of the issues more elucidating than Van Til's own. See Bahnsen, particularly pp. 499–529. The author is also aware of the controversial nature of Van Til's presuppositional method in apologetics. The debate has often been acrimonious, especially between followers of Gordon Clark and those of Van Til regarding the role of reason in epistemology. The philosophical approaches are definitely distinct, but it is unclear if there is a way to resolve the matter as to which approach is the clearly superior biblical alternative. *Theologically speaking,* the argument between the two sides may be at an impasse. Despite the employment of the transcendental argument in this chapter, the author does not purport to be uncritically Van Tilian.

[11] Richard Dawkins, *The Blind Watchmaker* (New York: W.W. Norton & Company, 1986), 1.

rather resolute *certainty*. And yet his admission of the blind watchmaker exhibits a perplexing *uncertainty* about the problem that the universe *appears to be designed*.[12] Surely, an ambivalence arises in his thinking at this point.

Second, and further, the Christian also would like to hear from Dawkins on what grounds he knows there are predictable "laws" of biology in a purely naturalistic universe explicitly without a Creator. The naturalist/atheistic evolutionist says that the only thing that exists is energy and matter. As the naturalist and astronomer Carl Sagan began his best seller *Cosmos*, "The cosmos is all there is, all there ever was, and all there ever will be."[13] Now if that is true—that nothing exists outside of the physical properties of the cosmos—then one must eliminate anything in his worldview that defies a materialistic definition. But this is a *huge* problem for the naturalist. Why? Because he believes in scientific *laws*. But what is a law? Is it material or physical in nature? No. Therefore, the materialist faces a huge dilemma of how to account for the emergence of immaterial properties from material properties.

Whose epistemology is superior? The Christian's or Dawkins's/Sagan's? Perhaps someone may say that the two perspectives have simply reached an impasse between presuppositions. This may in fact be the case. Nevertheless, the Christian theist still contends that his position is privileged because his epistemology is based on a theory of dependence on an omnipotent, omniscient, omnipresent, and personal transcendent God. Surely if such a God exists, he is in the position to communicate universal knowledge to his creatures. Any other approach relies on an assertion of human independence clearly less satisfactory to the Christian knowledge claim.

A person who claims to come to the truth independently accepts the insuperable burden of coordinating massive amounts of data in order to reach anything approaching confidence, let alone certainty. This he clearly cannot do with his own extremely limited resources. Without the God portrayed in the Bible, all kinds of troubling questions arise for the nonbeliever. For example, let us analyze for a moment the basic belief that the universe arose in a naturalistic way. In that worldview the cosmos is mechanical and inert. How, then, can being arise from nonbeing in such a place? The personal from the nonpersonal? Order from disorder? A world of cause and effect without an ultimate cause? Such phenomena exist only in the type of world that God created.

The following interchange provides an example of the transcendental argument applied to a debate that occurred at the University of California

---

[12] Again the use of the terms *certainty* and *uncertainty* are being used in a way similar to Van Til and Pratt, *Every Thought Captive*.

[13] Carl Sagan, *Cosmos* (New York: Ballantine Books, 1985), 1.

(Irvine) in 1985 between theologian Greg Bahnsen and Gordon Stein, a prominent atheist and editor of *Free Inquiry* magazine. Stein prepared to critique the classical evidentiary proofs for the existence of God on the strength of the laws of logic and a naturalist/materialist understanding of the cosmos. Bahnsen baffled the skeptic by arguing from the transcendental position by challenging Stein to prove his reliance on logic given his acceptance of materialism. Consider the following exchange:

Bahnsen: Are all questions answered in the very same way?

Stein: No they are not. They are answered by the use of certain methods, though, that are the same: reason, logic, and presenting evidence as facts. . . .

Bahnsen: Do you believe there are laws of logic then?

Stein: Absolutely.

Bahnsen: Are they universal?

Stein: They are agreed upon by human beings. They aren't laws that exist out in nature. They are . . .

Bahnsen: Are they simply conventions then?

Stein: They are conventions, but they are conventions that are self-verifying.

Bahnsen: Are they sociological laws, or laws of thought?

Stein: They are laws of thought which are interpreted by men; and promulgated by men.

Bahnsen: Are they material in nature?

Stein: How can a law be material?

Bahnsen: That's a question I'm going to ask you!

Cross-examination: Dr. Stein questions Dr. Bahnsen

Stein: Dr. Bahnsen, would you call God material or immaterial?

Bahnsen: Immaterial.

Stein: What is something that is immaterial?

Bahnsen: Something not extended in space.

Stein: Can you give me an example of anything other than God that's immaterial?

Bahnsen: Laws of logic.

[Audience laughter][14]

---

[14] Needless to say, Bahnsen easily won the debate. The exchange, which came to be known as "The Great Debate," won Bahnsen a well-deserved reputation as a formidable debater. G. A. Wells, noted skeptic at Boston University who denied that Jesus of Nazareth was a historical figure, reportedly cancelled a debate with Bahnsen at the last minute, ostensibly for this reason. The audio of the debate is available through the Covenant Media Foundation at http://www.cmfnow.com/subcatmfgprod.asp?0=207&1=234&2=–1; accessed November 10, 2004. A transcript of the

Bahnsen demonstrated the central insight of transcendental thinking: any true predication ultimately relies upon presupposing a world that only God could have made.[15] Introducing pagans to the message of the Christian God remains not only the evangelistic but also the epistemological imperative of the church. What happens, however, when men are not in an ideal position either historically, culturally, or spiritually to receive such information? Left to their own senses and intuitions, their conclusions fail to result in a comprehensive worldview. In lieu of God, philosophers inexorably are drawn to some aspect of reality that they think explains the whole. If, as philosopher Roy Clouser proposes, "a religious belief is any belief in something or other as divine; and also if, 'Divine' means having the status of not depending on anything else"; then it follows that even supposedly pagan and secular philosophies are deeply religious in nature.[16]

A Case Study in the Religious Character of Ancient Philosophy

For centuries philosophers have attempted to ground their epistemologies in some realm of ultimacy. In the pre-Socratic period (roughly 585–399 BC), the Milesian philosophers sought to find a unitary principle as a foundation for their respective cosmologies. Perhaps more importantly, they sought to do this without an explicitly religious reference to the gods. Instead, they searched for a completely empirical or scientific explanation for how things worked and came to be. For this reason, these thinkers from the Ionian coast of Asia Minor came to be known as the "physicists" (coming from the Greek word *phusis* which can be translated "natural stuff"). Thales, an astronomer from the 6th century BC, concluded that water must be the principal "stuff" of the universe. According to Aristotle, he got "the notion perhaps from seeing that the nutriment of all things is moist."[17]

For Anaximander, Thales' student, the reduction of the ultimate explanation of all things to water failed to explain the diversity and plurality of life. Immediately, he sought a more sophisticated explanation that was

---

debate can be found at: http://www.popchapel.com/Resources/Bahnsen/GreatDebate/; accessed 10 November 2004.

[15] Van Til adamantly defended the notion that to know one proposition truly is to know everything exhaustively. This statement obviously means that "knowledge" in this highly qualified sense is reserved only for those who presuppose the Christian worldview. For reasons the author will outline later in the chapter, this extension of transcendental thinking may in fact be an overstatement.

[16] Clouser goes to great lengths to demonstrate that his definitions of religion and divine are the most satisfactory in light of the alternatives. His thesis persuasively illustrates that theorizing cannot be religiously neutral. See Clouser, *The Myth of Religious Neutrality*, 21–22. For the argument in its entirety, see chapter 2, "What Is Religion?"

[17] Aristotle, *Metaphysics* A3, 983b, trans. W. D. Ross; as cited in Forrest E. Baird and Walter Kaufmann, ed. *Ancient Philosophy*, 3rd ed. (Upper Saddle River, NJ: Prentice Hall, 2000), 49.

even more basic than the elements of air, fire, and water. He called this the *apeiron*—or the boundless or the infinite—an impersonal organizational principle or "cosmic soup out of which the four elements (and all of nature) separated."[18] Despite his desire to offer a scientific explanation, the *apeiron* certainly seemed to be a thinly veiled divine substitute. The third generation Milesian, Anaximenes, repaired to Thales' method, however, and suggested that air was the basic world principle. What tied all of these views together was the emphasis on the physical stuff of the universe as being necessary, self-sustaining, and *alive*—a principle known as *hylozoism.*

As primitive as the foregoing explanations may seem to modern readers, these pre-Socratic thinkers provide a case in point of the way in which theories about reality constantly are searching for an ultimate way to understanding the meaning of things. Yet without recourse to the knowledge of an eternal, personal, and transcendent God, such naturalistic theories fizzle out in frustration. Within one generation Anaximander rightly realized that Thales' water theory was inadequate. But his proposal of the *apeiron* failed to offer a satisfying alternative. Philosopher Gordon Clark once observed that "cultures in isolation" from contact with the Hebrew-Christian revelation never considered a theistic doctrine of creation *ex nihilo.* "Creation is an idea only found in Hebrew thought. . . . the point is simply that the pagans had never thought of such an idea."[19]

The rest of the pre-Socratic period witnessed a struggle over how to understand the universe without access to the God of the Bible. A second wave of philosophers posited more metaphysical explanations. Heraclitus of Ephesus described the cosmos as being in an ever-changing state of flux and conflict, and dubbed this process of change the *Logos*—an eternally burning fire that composed the basic element of all things. The Eleatic philosophers Parmenides and Zeno preferred to talk of a radical unity within the universe and emphasized, against Heraclitus, the constant, rational, unalterable, and never-changing oneness of being. But here again, the speculation ran aground. As Clark commented, "Succeeding generations have been wondering ever since how a simple One, devoid of any difference, could generate plurality."[20]

Following the Eleatics, pluralists such as Empedocles, Anaxagoras, and Democritus theorized that a varying number of substances, particles, or atoms explained the existence of everything without recourse to reason

---

[18] The image of cosmic soup was employed by Louis Markos in *Great Minds of the Intellectual Tradition,* Part One, excerpts read by the author, Chantilly, VA: 2000, compact disc.

[19] Gordon Clark, *Thales to Dewey: A History of Philosophy* (Boston: Houghton Mifflin Company, 1957), 15. Clark continues: "The logical point [of this observation] is to point that in any system of philosophy the axioms assumed and the method used determine the nature of the conclusions."

[20] Ibid., 29.

or some other metaphysical idea. This nascent pluralism eventually gave way to the genuine relativism espoused by the Sophists and their leading spokesman Protagoras, who coined the phrase "man is the measure of all things."[21] Since no objective truth can be found outside the individual, Protagoras surmised, then all that was left was the teaching of rhetoric to win others over to personal perspectives. Current-day relativism, therefore, is really nothing new, but a return to tired positions that have long since been discredited by more substantive philosophy.[22]

Of all of the pre-Socratic philosophers, the only ones honest enough to recognize what they were doing with their philosophy were the Pythagoreans. Pythagoras (famous for his theorem) and his followers held the position that "things are numbers," and therefore everything, even physical properties, could be boiled down to mathematical equations.[23] Accordingly, they argued, the numerical aspect thus held together all things in eternity and thus gave enlightenment and harmony to all of life. Mathematical relationships composed the "music of the spheres."[24] Pythagoras considered bringing one's life into balance by submitting to these relationships the path of salvation. In short, the Pythagoreans worshipped numbers, and they were transparent about their belief. "Like Plato after him," write philosophers John Baird and Walter Kaufmann, Pythagoras "believed that the study of mathematics could convert the soul from the world of the senses to the contemplation of the eternal."[25]

What makes the Pythagoreans so refreshing is that they did not pretend to have found a value-neutral path to understanding the universe. Their pagan interpretation of reality rightly saw that by emphasizing one aspect over the others as ultimately necessary, they were engaging in religious worship. In their case they deified numbers. By doing so, they hoped to in-

---

[21] Protagoras, "Refutatory Arguments," in Baird and Kaufmann, ed., *Ancient Philosophy*, 42.

[22] The relativism of the Sophists is decisively repudiated by Plato in the dialogues *Protagoras* and *Theaetetus*. In *Protagoras*, Socrates as interlocutor poses Protagoras with several dilemmas. If what the Sophist says is true, then why study with him? Socrates earlier in the dialogue tells young Hippocrates in this connection that if he had studied with his namesake, he would have become a physician and learned the science of medicine. What does one become when he studies relativism? A professional nobody since there is no truth to learn from him. Socrates also challenges Protagoras to defend why he would charge a fee for his services if there is no intrinsic value to his teaching. If all ideas are equally worthless, then there is no reason to pay Protagoras for this insight. If every man is his own truth, let him figure that out on his own. A classic refutation of relativism, the *Protagoras* is must reading for Christian philosophers and theologians. See *The Dialogues of Plato*, trans. B. Jowett, vol. 1 (New York: Macmillan Company, 1892; reprint, New York: Random House, 1937), 81ff.

[23] The view of the Pythagoreans, stripped of its intellectual honesty regarding their divine estimation of the mathematical aspect, has reappeared in modern philosophy under a secular guise. The systems of John Stuart Mill, Betrand Russell, and John Dewey all strive to reduce truth to a series of mathematic probabilities. See especially Clouser, *Myth of Religious Neutrality*, 111–27.

[24] Yes, the hymn "This Is My Father's World" borrows this line from the Pythagoreans!

[25] Baird and Kaufmann, *Ancient Philosophy*, 12.

herit eternal life. In sum, when it comes to theorizing about the way things are, it is impossible to escape the innate human drive to render worship. Unfortunately, the human mind by habit pays spiritual fealty to idols.

The end of the pre-Socratic period brought little resolution to even the most fundamental questions of epistemology. Was the universe a constantly evolving mass of entities like Heraclitus described, or a radical oneness as Parmenides proposed? Although Plato and Aristotle offered more sophisticated approaches to the nature of reality, neither of them constructed systems which gave any decisive insight into the problem. Plato stood in the tradition of Parmenides and Pythagoras and emphasized the presence of the world of forms that lay beyond this shadowy physical world. Aristotle resisted the notion that the real world lay beyond the one a person sees, but he returned to a variation of the physicists' understanding that the world is most importantly understood as material stuff. While Aristotle had a place for God as the unmoved mover, his theism exhibited a cold, distant quality. Neither God nor human beings seemed like real persons.[26]

The Absurdity of the Relativistic Thesis of Truth

The previous section highlighted the earliest attempts of philosophy to devise a theory of reality on purportedly neutral grounds. The result was an exchange of one kind of worship (the gods of the Greek pantheon) for another (the worship of water, air, numbers, or other kinds of "stuff"). In the second through fourth centuries, Christians began asserting that their theology actually did a better job explaining the insights of Plato than did Plato himself! Although we shall return to this theme later, history records that both the political and intellectual success of the Christian perspective, grounded in an objective reality, won the day in the Roman Empire. The medieval period conducted a massive experiment in the philosophical possibilities of a biblical worldview. But as Enlightenment skepticism arose (more on that later too), philosophers grew increasingly cynical about any one religious system being able to guide its inquirers to truth.

---

[26] Aristotle's God lacked the personal attributes of the God of Abraham, Isaac, Jacob, and Jesus Christ. For Aristotle, the theoretical, logical function is the primary aspect of reality, and according to Dooyeweerd, "From this he derived the thesis that the active intellect is immortal in contrast to man." See Herman Dooyeweerd, *In the Twilight of Western Thought* (Nutley, NJ: Craig Press, 1965), 13. Because of this feature in Aristotle's thought, the Aristotelian god is merely *part* of the laws of causality and motion, not the creator of them. This god is made subject to the principle of causality, even if he is the first cause. So cause and effect achieves a necessary and, by Aristotle's admission, an uncreated characteristic which God possesses and in which he merely participates. This approach also affected his view of the individuality of man, what makes persons distinct individuals. As Gordon Clark insightfully points out, "Aristotle's unfortunate answer is that the source of all individuality is matter. The form man is in all cases the same; hence only matter can distinguish Socrates from Crito." See Clark, *Thales to Dewey,* 143.

Consequently, some modern philosophers such as the nineteenth-century German philosopher Friedrich Nietzsche have claimed that there are no truths, just individual perspectives.[27] Other modernists following Nietzsche's lead have argued in their own manner that truth is constructed by resourceful human beings. William James, one of America's leading thinkers at the beginning of the twentieth century, likewise broke with nearly two millennia of Western philosophical thinking when he stated that "truth happens to an idea. It becomes true, and is made true by events."[28] In the same manner, Richard Rorty, widely regarded as one of the most important American philosophers of the past few decades, follows the pragmatist tradition espoused by William James and John Dewey.[29] Rorty subscribes to the view that objective truth does not exist. In *Philosophy and the Mirror of Nature* (1979), Rorty contended that there is no independent standard against which we can judge truth claims.[30] Truth is merely a complement one pays to a particularly useful idea.[31]

But the claim "there is no such thing as objective truth," for example, clearly contradicts itself. For as soon as one makes that statement, he has supposedly stated something that he thinks is the case in all times, in all places, and in all circumstances—and that itself is a claim to absolute truth. The claim "truth is relative," therefore, refutes itself. Further, as British philosopher Roger Scruton explains:

---

[27] See, for example, Friedrich Nietzsche, trans. Walter Kaufmann, *Beyond Good and Evil* (New York: Random House, 1966).

[28] William James, *Pragmatism, William James: Writings 1902–1910*, ed. Bruce Kuklick (New York: Literary Classics of the United States, 1987), 1322ff.

[29] Rorty shares Stanley Fish's view of good and evil. Rorty contends that no morally significant difference distinguishes human beings and animals, because neither have a given "nature." If this is true, then society obviously loses the ability to pass judgment on wickedness. In the place of condemnation, the philosopher opines, we should simply try to restore "bad people's" sense of potential or self-esteem. These individuals are merely deprived, not depraved. A "bad" person, in Rorty's view, is someone who does something that the majority does not like. Some might simply regard Rorty's comments as ridiculous, but those who dismiss his arguments do so at their peril. His views are influential and widespread in many centers of higher education and political thinking in both the United States and Europe. See, for example, Richard Rorty, "Human Rights, Rationality, and Sentimentality," in *Hatred, Bigotry, and Prejudice: Definitions, Causes & Solutions,* ed. Robert M. Baird and Stuart E. Rosenbaum (Amherst, NY: Prometheus Books, 1999), 265–66, 269–70, 273.

[30] Richard Rorty, *Philosophy and the Mirror of Nature* (Princeton: Princeton University Press, 1979). Rorty argues that philosophy is not the pursuit of truth or answers to ultimate questions but an amalgam of shared ideas that seem to amount to a workable intellectual, societal, or scientific project. In the wake of the eclipse of philosophy as a truth-seeking enterprise, the role of the philosopher becomes that of a message bearer who keeps a conversation going among disciplines that do not typically talk to one another while simultaneously keeping any one perspective from claiming ultimate explanatory power.

[31] This leads Rorty to assert that "truth is what is good in the way of belief." See *Consequences and Pragmatism* (Minneapolis: University of Minneapolis Press, 1982).

You need only ask yourself whether what Nietzsche says is true, to realise how paradoxical it is. If it is true, then it is false!—an instance of the so-called "liar" paradox. Likewise, the French philosopher Michel Foucault repeatedly argues as though the truth of an epoch has no authority outside the power-structure that endorses it. There is no trans-historical truth about the human condition. But . . . we should ask ourselves whether that last statement is true: for if it is, it is false. . . . A writer who says there are no truths, or that all truth is "merely relative," is asking you not to believe him. So don't.[32]

In summary, relativism is fallacious for two important reasons. First of all, as we have just demonstrated, the relativistic worldview is self-defeating and incoherent. It wants its central claim to be privileged at the exclusion of all others. This is obviously not possible as this would undermine the idea of relativism.

The second reason relativism fails is that it does not meet the test of practical experience. Right and wrong are not the contrivances of men. They are dictates of God. In the hours and days after September 11, 2001, for example, a remarkable phenomenon occurred. In the secular city of New York, people who were normally indifferent or skeptical about religion flocked to churches and public meetings of prayer. Someone even hung a banner on the George Washington bridge that read, "God Bless America." Not only did the citizens of that great city know that truth exists; they also, at least for a moment in time, remembered the source of truth. The deepest instincts of human beings inform them that truth comes from a transcendent referent. It is beyond us, independent from us, and not sustained by us.

For the reasons explained above, therefore, atheism as a philosophical position then faces a serious crisis of credibility. If there is no God to judge the wicked for their deeds at the end of time, then in what meaningful sense were the crimes of Hitler, Idi Amin, and Osama bin Laden blameworthy? For this reason Fyodor Dostoyevsky suggested in the *Brothers Karamazov:* "If there is no immortality, then all things are permitted."[33] It is not enough to say that truth is some mere consensus about cultural facts that men find convenient to obey. Human beings long for some final arbiter to set the record straight. The only philosophical and theological option that possesses the resources to do so is the Christian God.

---

[32] Roger Scruton, *Modern Philosophy: An Introduction and Survey* (New York: Penguin Books, 1994), 6.

[33] Fyodor Dostoyevsky, *The Brothers Karamazov,* trans. C. Garnett (New York: Signet Classics, 1957), bk. II, chap. 6; bk. V, chap. 4; bk. XI, chap. 8.

What Does the Bible Say?

The Existence of God and the Human Mind

As the introductory material to this chapter has established, there cannot be an eternal, transcendent, and all-powerful God who does not exist. The Scriptures begin with the express presupposition that God exists: "In the beginning, God" (Gen. 1:1).[34] No elaborate proofs are mounted in support of the existence of the deity save the implicit argument of the impossibility of the contrary. This does not mean that rational proofs and evidence for the existence of God are not available. They are everywhere. Nor is the difficulty in the lack of human capacity to receive truth about God or the proper way to relate to him. Man was created in the image of God at the creation, and in that state possessed a "true knowledge" of God (Col. 3:10 NASB).

Further, the book of Ecclesiastes proclaims that in the beginning, "God made man upright" (Eccles. 7:29). Contrary to the views of some, the image of God was not obliterated in the fall. Although defaced, the image of God still remains in all human beings, according to Genesis 9:6 and James 3:9. Man is morally capable of receiving the knowledge of God.

The problem of unbelief instead resides in the human heart. It is not that man *cannot* receive the truth about how he should respond to God but that in his natural state he does not *want* to receive the truth about the God of the Bible. Paul said in 1 Corinthians 2:14 that "the natural person does not accept the things of the Spirit of God, for they are folly to him, and he is not able to understand them because they are spiritually discerned." As the apostle explains elsewhere in Romans, there is ample evidence to convince any objective seeker that a supreme wisdom and power govern the universe. But he hastens to add that even though this is the case, men "by their unrighteousness suppress the truth" (Rom. 1:18). Consequently, "they became futile in their thinking, and their foolish hearts were darkened. Claiming to be wise, they became fools" (vv. 21–22). In other words, the knowledge that men do possess all comes to nothing apart from the grace of God.

What is more, God is not interested in his creatures' mere intellectual assent. He desires personal faith, trust, and love from those whom he has made. University of Loyola-Chicago philosopher Paul Moser distinguishes between thin theism ("the belief that it is epistemologically rational, at least for some people, to believe that God exists"), and "robust theism" (that a *filial* knowledge is what God requires):

---

[34] Unless otherwise noted, all Scripture citations in this chapter are from the English Standard Version (ESV).

The chief human deficiency regarding God is not in our explanatory or intellectual abilities but is rather in our moral orientation regarding authority, or lordship, over our lives. So, desiring genuine reconciliation, the true God would not settle for thin theism but would promote *cognitively robust theism,* the view that we epistemically should lovingly *believe in,* or trust, God as *the Lord of our lives.*[35]

This conviction means that apologetics must always have evangelism as its ultimate goal. As the Apostle Paul demonstrated at Mars Hill, it is not enough for people to possess a vague commitment to the unknown god; they need a personal relationship with God in Jesus Christ. Christian philosophers delight in pointing out that when the apostle arrived in Athens he went to the marketplace and then made his way to the Areopagus (or Mars Hill), the philosophers' *agora* where he demonstrated his mastery of Greek philosophy by citing passages from Stoic philosophy. Commentators on this historical high watermark for Christian cultural engagement emphasize that Paul established intellectual credibility with his audience.

But Paul was not concerned with such things; he knew that the Athenian elites were as much destined for hell without Jesus as anyone else. For this reason he quickly moved to the doctrine of the resurrection of the body from the dead, one of the most objectionable and disgusting notions imaginable to the Greek philosophical mind at the time (Acts 17:31–32). Despite his rigorous intellectual preparation that enabled him to gain a hearing from the Athenian philosophers, Paul showed his willingness to preach the "foolishness of the gospel" over what seemed to be "rational" to the secular mind at the time. He believed that only through divine disclosure could one fully come to a life of wisdom and knowledge.

The Bible's Radical Claim to Knowledge

The Bible clearly points out that all truth and knowledge originate from God's revelation and Word to us. Proverbs 1:7 instructs its readers that "the fear of the Lord is the beginning of knowledge." Paul makes the matter even more explicit when he writes in Colossians that in Christ are hidden "all the treasures of wisdom and knowledge" (Col. 2:3). Notice that the Scripture does not simply say that spiritual or theological truths are known through Christ; the text plainly says *all knowledge or truth.*

The concept of God as a "supreme being," remarked the philosopher Immanuel Kant, "is an ideal without a flaw, a concept which completes and

---

[35] Paul Moser, "Cognitive Idolatry and Divine Hiding," in *Divine Hiddenness: New Essays,* ed. Daniel Howard Snyder and Paul K. Moser (Cambridge: Cambridge University Press), 125–26.

crowns *the whole of human knowledge.*"[36] One familiar with the writings of this German intellectual giant might be surprised to read this statement from such a trenchant critic of traditional religion. But even a skeptic like Kant had to admit the truth: only an eternal and transcendent Creator God can explain the richness and diversity of human knowledge. Without God the world ultimately cannot make sense.

The Bible makes a radical claim about the nature of reality. It asserts that apart from the acknowledgement of its divine origin, the universe remains an unsolvable puzzle. Solomon—an impressive philosopher in his own right—understood this fact. God must be feared if knowledge is to be obtained (Prov. 1:7). This reverent recognition of the Creator (note: "fear" in this passage does not equal *fright*) provides the necessary foundation for every sort of education (Eccles. 12:13; Ps. 2:11; Isa. 12:6).

Attentive readers will note that the "fear of the Lord" is not just the starting point for spiritual axioms. The proverb states that it is the beginning of *all* knowledge. The Hebrew word used for knowledge here covers the entire scope of human inquiry. Presupposing the God of the biblical type offers the only sensible way to begin uncovering the true and unified meaning of things; Paul explained why: "For by him [i.e. Christ] all things were created, in heaven and on earth, visible [e.g. planets, plants, animals, material things] and invisible [e.g. numbers, laws, aesthetic and economic principles]" (Col. 1:16). Reinforcing the point, he concluded that in Christ "are hidden *all* the treasures of wisdom and knowledge" (Col. 2:3, emphasis added).

"All" is an audacious word for the apostle to use and Solomon to imply. The claim, however, does not mean that pagans never get anything right. After all, Solomon admired the king of Tyre's expertise with architecture and construction (2 Chron. 2:3). Paul appreciated the writings of the Stoic philosopher/poets (Acts 17:28). Nonbelievers will continue to make singular advances in their individual modes of expertise, whether that be in mathematics, medicine, or other disciplines. But until they come to terms with the transcendent ruler, they will never understand the "uni" in the word *universe.*

Scripture repeatedly returns to the theme that knowledge is only possible because of, and through the work of, God in Christ. The prologue to the Gospel of John furthermore teaches the comprehensive nature of Christ's work as the agent of creation when it says, "Through him all things were made, and without him, nothing was made that has been made" (John 1:3, author's translation). The book of Hebrews likewise underscores this

---

[36] Immanuel Kant, *Critique of Pure Reason,* trans. Norman Kemp Smith (London: Macmillan, 1933), 531, cf. 493, 497, 538; italics in original; cited in Colin Gunton, *The One, the Three, and the Many* (New York: Cambridge University Press, 1993; reprint 1995), 23

teaching and asserts that the second person of the Trinity "upholds the universe by the word of his power" (Heb. 1:3). This indicates the ongoing, active work of God. No matter how sinful or rebellious human beings may become, they can never alter the fundamental ordering of the universe. At best, they can only "experiment against reality."[37]

Because the church possesses access to the knowledge of God, it has an obligation to encourage those who engage in the cutting-edge research that alleviates suffering in the world, whether the pain of disease, political turmoil, or economic disarray. But while cheering all genuine advances in learning, the believer should always challenge his secular counterparts to account for how the bits and pieces of knowledge the human race has acquired fit together.

Only the Bible provides a satisfactory "big picture" in its account of the creation of every aspect of existence, the fall into sin and disorder, and the redemption through Jesus Christ. Critics of Christianity sometimes say that God's people are anti-intellectual. Quite to the contrary, the church is the only earthly institution equipped to pose the toughest question of all: how does one explain the beautiful but baffling complexity of the cosmos without reference to God—the "idea without a flaw"? The answer to that question must be as bold as the Bible's claim about knowledge itself.

The Nature of the Created Order Makes Knowledge Possible

Psalm 19 underscores the truth that all of the created order, and therefore all of knowledge, points back toward the Creator. The familiar phrase "the heavens declare the glory of God" is followed immediately by the notion that every aspect of the universe "reveals" this particular "knowledge." "There is no speech," reads verse 3, "nor are there words, whose voice is not heard." In other words, there is no independent domain or aspect in the universe that does not attest to the work of God. Reality cannot be explained apart from the transcendent and omnipotent Sovereign. The created order is not an intellectually neutral means of apprehending the fixity of things in the universe, but a radically dependent method that demonstrates the necessity of the God of the Bible. Such natural revelation remains precisely that—revelation. Rather than giving rise to pride in the powers of the human mind, natural revelation profoundly humbles the knower and calls forth faith in God.

Because the universe was created by God for his own glory and for the good of humanity, a concomitant truth becomes clear. God *wants* truth to be known, and truth *can* be known. Jesus told his disciples that, by entering into

---

[37] A phrase employed by Roger Kimball, *Experiments against Reality* (Chicago: Ivan R. Dee, 2000).

the kingdom of God, "you will know the truth, and the truth will set you free" (John 8:32). This notion that freedom accompanies the discovery of truth is what has made Christianity the singularly most powerful worldview in the history of the world. The oft-quoted Augustinian phrase "all truth is God's truth" has generated a spirit of inquiry and exploration in human hearts that has produced many of the greatest literary, artistic, and scientific achievements known to man. The church, therefore, has stood as the defender and chief advocate of this tradition. In the wake of the horrors of World War II, the great physicist Albert Einstein came to appreciate this fact. He wrote:

> Being a lover of freedom, when the [Nazi] revolution came, I looked to the universities to defend it, knowing that they had always boasted of their devotion to the cause of truth; but no, the universities were immediately silenced. Then I looked to the great editors of the newspapers, whose flaming editorials in days gone by had proclaimed their love of freedom; but they, like the universities, were silenced in a few short weeks. . . .
>
> Only the Church stood squarely across the path of Hitler's Campaign for suppressing truth. I never had any special interest in the Church before, but now I feel a great affection and admiration for it because the Church alone has had the courage and persistence to stand for intellectual and moral freedom. I am forced to confess that what I once despised I now praise unreservedly.[38]

Loving God with the Mind

The Christian intellectual tradition flows from the central imperative to believers from the Lord Jesus to "love the Lord your God with all your heart, and with all your soul, and with all your mind" (Matt. 22:37). Echoing the dictum of Deuteronomy 6:6, Jesus made a point to include the word *mind* in the list. The Hebrew worldview employed the word *heart* as the all-encompassing term for the totality of the human person. Because the Greek tradition separated the ideas of mind and heart, the Lord insisted on making the point that his followers are called upon to give offerings of spiritual and *intellectual* devotion in service to the kingdom of God. As C. S. Lewis so memorably put it, "Christ wants the heart of a child, but a grown up's head."[39]

Because God is the author of all things, both visible and invisible, human beings possess the assurance that the universe is not a random or in-

---

[38] Albert Einstein, as cited in Arthur C. Cochrane, *The Church's Confession Under Hitler* (Philadelphia: Westminster Press, 1962), 40.
[39] C. S. Lewis, *Mere Christianity* (New York: Macmillan, 1943; rev. ed., 1952), 75.

explicable place to live. Reality is fixed by God. But in order to access that reservoir of truth, the human being must place himself in a position of humility. Truth is a gift; it is discovered, but most importantly, it is *received*. Due to the effects of the fall, however, the reception of that knowledge becomes problematic. For the unbeliever certain domains of knowledge, especially those pertaining to spiritual things, are incredibly difficult to acquire. Paul taught that even if the "natural person" can conceive of the truth from God, he cannot finally "accept" them. The things of God "are folly to him," Paul writes, "and he is not able to understand them because they are spiritually discerned" (1 Cor. 2:14).

In contrast to this, the believer holds the interpretive key to understanding the world; he has a relationship with God. For him the acquisition of knowledge is a recovery effort from that which was lost as a result of the fall. The Christian must maintain a constant vigilance and discipline to seek out the truth wherever it can be found, for the glory of God. For this reason Paul exhorted the Christians in Corinth to develop a military mindset about the discovery and defense of truth. The apostle counseled, "We destroy arguments and every lofty opinion raised against the knowledge of God, and take every thought captive to obey Christ" (2 Cor. 10:5). The maxim of "every thought captive" thus must become the watchword of every committed disciple of Jesus Christ.

What Has the Church Believed?

The task of discussing what the great minds in church history have thought about the methodological issues of theology is, in one sense, anachronistic. Systematic theology in the sense in which the term is currently used did not really develop until the modern era and the work of Friedrich Schleiermacher. Although most theologians throughout the centuries did not explicitly lay out their presuppositions in an up-front and orderly way, they did have presuppositions. From the time of the early church fathers forward, philosophical systems and ground rules have always been deeply embedded in the work being done.

Worldview assumptions are always at work in an individual or culture's thought. The Christian theologian, therefore, must be ever diligent to analyze such presuppositions to see if they conform with the Bible's own claims about reality. A good way to begin such a self-critical way of thinking is to look at some representative examples throughout the history of theology to see how philosophical and cultural presuppositions operate in a given theologian's worldview.

The Early Church Fathers: A Tug of War between Philosophy and Theology

Christian philosopher Colin Brown explains that the early church possessed a "love-hate" relationship with secular philosophy.[40] This meant that the estimation of discussing philosophical issues necessary for approaching the task of philosophy varied from thinker to thinker. Among the second-century apologists and church fathers, some were converted to Christianity because they viewed the way of Jesus Christ to be the most complete and satisfying explanation of reality, a perfect continuation of the truths they had already obtained through their study of philosophy. For this reason, after his conversion, Justin Martyr (100–165) "still wore the pallium, the philosopher's cloak, proclaiming that the Christian faith was the 'only reliable and profitable philosophy.'"[41]

Justin claimed that his acceptance of Christianity resulted from a long and sometimes arduous rational search. Throughout his *Apology,* Justin gives a litany of historical, mythical, and philosophical preludes that inevitably culminated in the life and work of Jesus Christ. In a mysterious commentary on the *Timaeus,* Justin argued that Plato understood, in some prefigurative way, both the doctrines of creation and the cross.[42] For this and other reasons, he contended that "Socrates and Heraclitus, and men like them" were enlightened by a true knowledge of Christ before his earthly incarnation.[43] Clement of Alexandria (150–215) built upon Justin's notion of the compatibility of pagan philosophy and Christian truth. In his *Stromata* (*Miscellanies*), Clement extrapolated Christian themes extensively from the backdrop of his pre-conversion training in Middle Platonist thought.[44]

Athenagoras, another second-century giant, also provides an example of a pagan thinker turned Christian philosopher. He belonged to the elite circle of philosophers from which his name is derived. The Athenian *agora* (referring to the "philosophers' society") comprised the cadre of intellectuals to whom Paul preached at the Areopagus in Acts 17. The early centuries of church history preached that Christianity was indeed an intellectual *tour de force.* A small but impressive number of philosophers converted to Christianity and soon turned their mental powers to the defense of the Christian faith. Athenagoras was a well-rounded thinker steeped in Greco-Roman literature and well versed in the various schools of philosophy. As

---

[40] Colin Brown, *Philosophy and the Christian Faith* (Downers Grove, IL: InterVarsity Press, 1968), 13.

[41] Ibid., 13.

[42] Justin Martyr, *First Apology* 59,60.

[43] Ibid., 46.

[44] Clement of Alexandria, *Stromata;* see also E. F. Osborn, "Clement of Alexandria," *The Encyclopedia of Philosophy* (New York: Macmillan, 1967), 122–23.

Athenagoras's translator B. P. Pratten observed regarding this conversion, "In Athenagoras . . . we discover a remote result of St. Paul's speech on Mars Hill. The apostle had cast his bread upon the water of Ilissus and Cephisus to find it after many days."[45] In many ways Athenagoras represents the best example of the early philosopher-turned-Christian. His defense of the doctrine of the resurrection from the dead illustrates how sophisticated philosophical argumentation can be faithfully wedded to Christian truth.[46]

Origen (184–254), another Alexandrian, studied Clement's work and took his master's method to an entirely new level. Origen was a formidable scholar versed both in Middle Platonism and the Scriptures, but the results of his attempt to integrate philosophy and theology have caused controversy for centuries. Although he was publicly critical of the contributions of Plato and others (given that he believed the Bible is the only source of divine revelation), his ideas are an elaborate allegorical synthesis of pagan and Christian conceptions. This led Origen in his work *On First Principles,* for example, to teach that the material world was created by God as a consequence from a fall that took place in heaven when the spiritual beings there fell away from the love of God. Origen developed his theory from a similar concept employed by Philo of Alexandria. Building upon the thesis, Origen speculated that the one soul that had not abandoned the love of God was "chosen to be united with the divine Logos," who became the incarnate Lord Jesus Christ.[47]

Philosophical speculation such as this prompted the apologist Tertullian to offer his famous query, "What does Jerusalem have to do with Athens? What concord is there between the Academy and the Church? What between heretics and Christians?" or to paraphrase, "What does pagan philosophy have to do with biblical faith?" Tertullian's answer was simple and direct: absolutely nothing.[48] In rejecting the contributions of secular philosophy, was he right to dissuade future theologians from appropriating the contributions of secular thinkers? In Tertullian's defense, we have to say that his warning, even if it is not fully heeded, is an appropriate caution that keeps the theologian on his guard and constantly wary of idolatrous forms of thinking that can corrupt biblical thinking.

Still there is no need to go to the opposite extreme and dismiss all of the teachings of the Greek philosophers. The early church fathers, through the creedal formulas of Nicea, Constantinople, and Chalcedon, employed philosophical concepts (e.g., the language of *hypostases,* "substances").

---

[45] B. P. Pratten, "Introductory Note to the Writings of Athenagoras," *ANF* 2:125.

[46] Athenagoras, *On the Resurrection of the Dead.*

[47] See Henry Chadwick's discussion of Origen's doctrines in *The Early Church* (Middlesex, England: Penguin Books, 1967; reprint 1975), 100–14.

[48] Tertullian, *Prescription against Heresies* 7.

Anglican scholar Gerald Bray has pointed out that Christian scholars (with the notable exception of Origen) maintained a fierce spirit of intellectual independence throughout their work. And even though Origen took his Platonism too far, theologically speaking, his mistake lay not in reading and learning from philosophy, but by reading the Bible allegorically to the exclusion of its natural or literal sense. Certainly by the third century, Bray continues, Christian thought actually seemed to hold considerable influence *over* Neoplatonism. As a dynamic cognitive framework, Christianity affected both the academy and the common culture.

Further, Bray rightly notes that when, through mystic pseudo-Dionysius, Neoplatonism actually did "invade the Church, its effect was to stifle dogmatics, not to encourage confessional statements of an unbiblical character. Yet even pseudo-Dionysius bears witness in his own way to the triumph of the gospel. Neoplatonism survived the only way it could—by being clothed in the garb of an alien religion."[49] Christianity's success as a comprehensive world and life view triumphed on the intellectual field of battle. It became the ultimate philosophy.

Augustine and the Birth of the Medieval Synthesis

Even though Christian scholars were winning the war of ideas by the turn of the fourth century, the faith still suffered under imperial ban and tremendous persecution. Believers experienced intense but sporadic persecution at the hands of the Roman Empire, with a final protracted period of severe oppression during the great persecution during the reign of Diocletian in 303. That all came to an end in 313 with the Edict of Milan in which the emperor Constantine stopped the persecution by giving Christianity an official legal status and eventually making it the privileged religion of the Roman world. From that point forward, Christianity had to make its way in a world that gave it favor, not contempt. In this environment philosophy was combined with theology not only to preserve orthodoxy but in order to preserve the unity of the state and the rule of law, as was evidenced by the use of technical language of *ousia* ("being, essence") and *hypostases* to defend and explain the divine nature of the Son at the Council of Nicea.[50]

The church enjoyed its privilege of political beneficence from the state for nearly a century. Pagan thinkers, however, were also tolerated and

---

[49] Gerald Bray, *Creeds, Councils, and Christ: Did the Early Christians Misrepresent Jesus?* 2nd ed. (Ross-shire, Great Britain: Mentor, 1997), 90. The foregoing summary of Bray's analysis of Origen and others can be found on pp. 78ff.

[50] For an excellent discussion of these terms in light of both their philosophical and theological meaning, see Diogenes Allen, *Philosophy for Understanding Theology* (Atlanta: John Knox Press, 1985), 96–106.

not persecuted during this time as an extension of the new era of tolerance ushered in by Constantine under the banner of Christianity. When the "barbarians" from the East stormed the gates of Rome in the fifth century, the great empire fell, and the non-Christian critics were waiting in the wings to mount their attack. Ignoring more obvious reasons for the collapse (e.g., economic, military, and moral corruption), some leading citizens argued vociferously that Christianity was to blame. Since Constantine pronounced Christianity the state religion, they contended, the government had been weakened by the virtues Jesus taught such as love for one's enemy and meekness of spirit. These values, the detractors contested, moved Rome away from the austere, severe, and stoic mind-set which once made the empire great.

Responding to these charges, Augustine of Hippo stepped into the fray by writing *The City of God.* Writing toward the end of his lifetime of ministry, the bishop from northern Africa retorted that Rome's problem was not that it had taken Christianity too seriously but that it had not taken Christianity seriously enough. Augustine explained that two cities mark the reality in which we live. The city of man (pagans) is marked by a love of selfishness while the city of God (the people of God) finds its polestar in the love of God. The former is bound for destruction and judgment; the latter, the beatific blessing of God. Augustine accomplished with his massive tome nothing less than a comprehensive philosophy of history that initiated the seminal pattern for how Christianity should interact with culture throughout the Western tradition. The *City of God* introduced many of the animating ideals that inspire Western civilization, including the following:

1. *The city of man is not the city of God.* This dictum argues, contra competing utopian notions, that due to the fall heaven can never be fully realized here on earth. Further, Christians are pilgrims and strangers while they are residents on earth, and their final destination is heaven.

2. *Christians are to be characterized by good citizenship.* "Caesar looks for his own likeness, give it to him," Augustine observed. He understood that the Scriptures recognize the distinction between church and state. Believers are to give Caesar his due with excellence in service because we realize that his image is a dim reminder or representation of God. Further, Christians are allowed even to be devoted to the state when it extols and honors virtue. Throughout his work Augustine asserted that knowledge results in the demand for charity or care.

3. *The city of man is marked by the dangerous attribute of* "cupiditas" (greed, vanity, earthly desire). Augustine famously noted that even the emperor is a "robber king"—a pirate but only on a grander scale. It was this

notion that led to the English (especially American) notion of the limitations of powers in government.[51]

4. *Evil is a reality that is chosen freely by men.* Augustine cautioned perpetual vigilance with respect to "the darkness that attends the affairs of human society."[52] We should never be naïve enough to believe that any leader or group of rulers, no matter how wise, are free from making terrible errors in judgment.

5. *The traditional family is the basic building block of the polis (city).* Good homes, in other words, make good societies. In this connection, the people of God have an important role to play through modeling the principle of *koinonia.* Christians are to model in community for the watching world what the city of God is supposed to look like.

6. *Christians should be the first people to recognize the virtue of tolerance.* Augustine seemed to understand the principle that paved the way for religious liberty. Pluralism—if defined as the factual recognition that not all persons' worldviews are the same—can be embraced by the church and can encourage evangelism. Pluralism is dangerous, however, if it is taken to mean "relativism"—the understanding that no ultimate standard of truth exists. Rather, Christianity rises above the chaos of earthly politics and philosophies and unites the diversity of human cultures and races through the power of the gospel of Jesus Christ.[53]

It is little wonder, then, that scholars consider Augustine's contribution almost single-handedly to have given birth to the medieval period, with its complex synthesis of pagan philosophical and literary sources with biblical exegesis and theological reflection. As Yale historian Jaroslav Pelikan writes, the theology of Nicea was transmitted to the Latin Middle Ages with Augustine's "special stamp upon it."[54] It is clear that Augustine, like the other church fathers before him, thought carefully about prolegomena—the preliminary categories that allow disciplined theological thinking to begin. Karl Jaspers, the twentieth-century German thinker, paid the bishop of Hippo one of the highest compliments a theologian could receive from a secular counterpart when he remarked that "Augustine thinks in questions."[55]

---

[51] On this subject, for example, see Augustine *The City of God* 5.24, trans. Marcus Dods (New York: Random House, 1950), 178; and on the subject of "robber kings," see Augustine, *The City of God,* trans. Henry Bettenson (New York: Penguin, 1972), 139.

[52] Augustine, *The City of God* 19.6, trans. Henry Bettenson.

[53] I am particularly indebted in the summaries of 4, 5 and 6 above to the account given by Jean Bethke Elshtain in *Augustine and the Limits of Politics* (South Bend, IN: University of Notre Dame Press, 1995), 19–47. On the subject of how Christianity succeeds where other religions fail in its ability to be multiracial and multiethnic without sacrificing any of its central truth claims, see Lamin Sanneh, *Whose Religion Is Christianity?* (Grand Rapids: Wm. B. Eerdmans Publishing Co., 2003).

[54] Jarolsav Pelikan, *Christianity and Classical Culture* (New Haven: Yale University Press, 1993), 6.

[55] Karl Jaspers, *Plato and Augustine* (New York: Harcourt, Brace & World, 1962), 75.

Augustine's greatest contribution to theological method came in the form of the maxim which he claimed governed his thought—*crede ut intelligas* ("I believe in order to understand"). He developed his epistemology via an undeniably creative synthesis of biblical reflection and the Neoplatonism of Plotinus. Reason, however, was not independent, and thus even the Platonists could not find what they were looking for apart from Christian revelation. Despite pagan philosophical influences, according to the standard explanation, biblical categories come out on top. They discipline philosophy and thereby establish theology as the "queen of the disciplines."

Augustine, of course, has his share of detractors. A growing cadre of progressive theologians have taken upon themselves the task of reevaluating Augustine's legacy in the West. The late British theologian Colin Gunton, for example, located the origin of many modern cultural problems in what he considered Augustine's overly monistic conception of reality that stemmed from his intellectual dependence on Plato.[56] This idea has surfaced in a different form elsewhere, in the critiques by the so-called "openness of God" theologians such as John Sanders, who claim that Augustine's use of Greek philosophical categories prompted him to construct an unbiblical view of the sovereignty of God, including the fact that God knows the future.[57]

Although Gunton's arguments appear to have more merit than those of the open theists, his critique of Augustinian theological method is overstated. Theologian Bradley Green has carefully shown that Augustine is not guilty of the most serious charges laid against him by Gunton and others.[58] In a paper presented at the Evangelical Philosophical Society, Nicholas Wolterstorff likewise dismissed the notion that Augustine's biblical reflections had been fatally corrupted by Greek philosophical ideas.[59]

Thomas Aquinas and the Road to the Reformation

Downstream from Augustine in the thirteenth century stands the formidable Aquinas, the "last creative commentator on Aristotle's philosophy"

---

[56] Colin Gunton, *The One, the Three, and the Many*.

[57] John Sanders, "Historical Considerations," in Clark Pinnock, et. al., *The Openness of God* (Downers Grove, IL: InterVarsity, 1994), see especially pp. 80ff.

[58] Bradley G. Green, "Colin Gunton and the Failure of Augustine: An Exposition and Analysis of the Theology of Colin Gunton in Light of Augustine's *De Trinitate*" (Ph.D. Diss., Baylor University, 2000). For a concise version of Green's thesis, see "Augustine and the Trinity in Contemporary Theology" (paper presented at the Southeast Regional Meeting of the Evangelical Theological Society, 10–11 March 2000 [online]; available through EBSCOHOST via the Theological Research Exchange Network).

[59] Nicholas Wolterstorff, "Parallel Session: Evangelical Philosophical Society" (Danvers, MA: Evangelical Theological Society, 19 November 1999), presentation read by the author, cassette; available at: http://www.actsconferenceproducts.com/Merchant/EV0199B.pdf.

since the discovery of the latter's written corpus in the ninth century.[60] Although he admitted his great indebtedness to the author of *The City of God,* Thomas charted his own course. Following the method of the analogy of being *(analogia entis),* he argued that everything in the universe is linked together in one great chain of being. Every particular possesses a *telos,* a purpose or goal that connects it to the whole of creation. By way of cause and effect, he thought, one could answer ultimate questions. Most famously, he composed the *teleological* argument for the existence of God, in which he posited that a person could prove from an analysis of the purposes of particular things in the human beings' field of experience the existence of an ultimate design for the universe.

Thomas's view, quite unlike Augustine's, drew a sharp distinction between philosophy and theology, with the resulting effect, as one reviewer has explained it, of two distinct upward-leading ladders separated by an intervening platform.[61] Philosophy (via natural law and reason) leads us to such truths as the existence of God, the oneness of God, the existence of moral law, and the immortality of the soul. Theology (i.e., faith or revelation) must extend the reach of reason if we are to preach the presence of the Christian God of the Scriptures.

Further, Thomas exhibited great optimism about the powers of human reason apart from the direct influence of divine revelation. The issue relates to the *extent* or *radicality* of the fall in Thomas's theology. If one undertakes the matter on these grounds, then it is clear from Thomas's writings (most notably the *Summa Theologica)* that although he allowed that the intellect is fallen, his position essentially was that it is not *radically* fallen. "For it is evident that the intellect can know by natural knowledge," Thomas contends, "some things above itself, as it manifestly does in the natural knowledge of God."[62]

According to Thomas, theology—as distinct from philosophy—reveals to us those matters which can only be known by faith (e.g., the Trinity, the incarnation). This sentiment pervades Thomas's work: faith that begins to answer metaphysical questions at the point of pure reason encounters slow going. As such, in book 1 of *Summa Contra Gentiles,* Thomas leaves the impression that it is *possible* for the unaided human mind to make steady progress in the knowledge of God apart from faith. But one gains such knowledge only through arduous contemplation and study—a condition which, on Thomas's account, eliminates most human beings. Add to that obstacle "a third disadvantage . . . that, owing to the infirmity of our judg-

---

[60] Jeremy Adams, *Great Minds of the Western Intellectual Tradition, Vol. II,* excerpts read by the author (The Teaching Company, 2000), compact disc.

[61] Philosopher Ronald Nash helpfully employed this image.

[62] Ibid., 143.

ment and the perturbing force of imagination, there is some admixture of error in most of the investigations of human reason." Thomas concludes, "Wholesome therefore is the arrangement of divine clemency, whereby things even that reason can investigate are commanded to be held on faith, so that all might easily be partakers of the knowledge of God, and that without doubt and error."

In sum, Thomas held that although it is *possible* to obtain knowledge of the divinity purely through rational devices, it is not *likely*. Consequently, it is suitable for persons to believe on the basis of faith.[63] Despite his high estimation of faith, Thomas maintained a categorical possibility for reason as a source of authority alongside revelation.

During the High Middle Ages, scholastic theology, as epitomized by Thomas, achieved an intellectual and cultural hegemony that served as the glue which held Christendom together.[64] At the center of this worldview lay the philosophy of Aristotle, as interpreted by Thomas, with its inherently teleological structure. This teleology gave the universe, and particularly human beings, a sense of place and interpretive scheme for understanding the world, a great chain of being into which everything fit. This epistemology was known as the *via antiqua* (old path), referring to Aristotelian reason and scholasticism. Under its pedagogical gaze Christendom reached a certain intellectual zenith.

Thomism, however, experienced a philosophical disruption when the scholastic theologian William of Occam began questioning the medieval philosophical synthesis and suggested a different course subsequently dubbed the *Via Moderna* or nominalism. Occam dissented from Thomism and basically claimed that Thomas had actually gotten Aristotle wrong. One need not, Occam allowed, divine some inherent teleological structure to the physical world in order to understand it. Rather, one could go to the particular things themselves and learn how that thing, in fact, worked.

As a result, early modern thinkers like Francis Bacon, influenced by Occam, eventually said that if you wanted to understand what made a frog tick, you need not figure out where the frog fit in a universal scale of perfection—where the frog fit in the great chain of being—and conclude that you had answered the most important questions. No, to understand the frog and its systems, you *dissect the frog*. The world is made up of particulars, Occam observed, and particulars alone. Contrary to Thomas's interpretation, Occam claimed that *he* rightly understood Aristotle. Modern commentators

---

[63] Thomas Aquinas, *Summa Contra Gentiles* in Daniel Kolak, ed., *The Philosophy Source: Classic Masterworks on CD-ROM* [CD-Rom database]: Wadsworth Publishing Co., 2001.

[64] Some of the following material pertaining to the medieval synthesis and the rise of Reformation epistemology appeared initially in Gregory Alan Thornbury, "Carl F. H. Henry as Heir of Reformation Epistemology," in *SBJT* vol. 8, no. 4 (Winter 2004).

largely agree on this point. As Bernard Löhse concludes, "Occam has often been charged with epistemological skepticism. But he merely applied the Aristotelian scientific principle more critically than other thinkers."[65]

Further, Occam taught, if you want to understand the universe, you need not guess at some mysterious teleology behind things that is somehow simply given and necessary. Rather, things are the way they are simply because God has willed them to be that way, a truth which has come to be known as *voluntarism*. Due to this truth the universe can be studied and understood on its own merits without constantly giving reference to all of the complexities of Aristotelian physics.

Hence, Occam developed his law of parsimony, most commonly referred to as the "razor," which states that entities should not be multiplied beyond necessity. Occam's razor effectively made modern scientific inquiry as we know it possible and precipitated huge advances in our understanding of the natural world. Jacques Barzun gives one example of Occam's razor applied. He states:

> William of Occam's principle of economy, that the best explanation is the one that calls for the least number of assumptions, was an argument against Ptolemy, in addition to the awkward facts. It impelled Copernicus to revise—not destroy—the system, by supposing the sun to be the center instead of the Earth. He was thereby able to reduce the epicycles from 84 to 30.[66]

Occam's thought effectively caused a split within medieval scholarship and precipitated a new school of philosophy which emphasized the freedom of the will of God in creation more than its predecessors. In other words, the nominalists/voluntarists said that the universe exists in its present form simply because God wills it to be that way, in accordance with God's own nature. And it was *this* idea which attracted a young Augustinian monk named Martin Luther and, perhaps in a more indirect way, a French humanist named John Calvin.

How do we know what the world is all about? We must go to the will of God. And how do we know the will of God? By reading Aristotle? The church fathers? Thomas Aquinas? To the contrary, God reveals his will to those whom he wills, and he does this most preeminently in his Word. Only by the grace of God do we understand the full truth about ourselves and about the world. In the spirit of Paul's words to the Corinthians, the Christian worldview seems like foolishness to the worldly wise and nonsense to religionists (1 Cor. 1:18–25). As Luther declaimed in his own inimitable way at the

---

[65] Bernard Löhse, *Martin Luther's Theology* (Minneapolis: Fortress Press, 1999), 18.

[66] Jacques Barzun, *From Dawn to Decadence* (New York: Harper Collins Publishers, 2000), 192.

Heidelberg Disputation, "One cannot philosophize well unless he is a fool, that is, a Christian." And, "He who wishes to philosophize by using Aristotle without danger to his soul must first become thoroughly foolish in Christ."[67]

For his part, Calvin headed off the notion that a study of the particulars could be an end in and of itself. Understanding arose from what he termed the *duplex cognitio Dei,* or "twofold knowledge of God." Calvin scholar Richard Muller describes the teaching as

> a distinction emphasized by Calvin in the final edition (1559) of the *Institutes,* and carried over into Reformed orthodoxy as a barrier to the inclusion of natural theology in the orthodox system of doctrine, according to which the general, nonsaving knowledge of God as Creator and as the wrathful Judge of sin, accessible to pagan and Christian alike, is distinguished from special, saving knowledge of God the Redeemer.[68]

According to Calvin, the creation should be studied in consonance with what is revealed in Scripture if we want to understand the world in which we live. For as Calvin commented, "However fitting it may be for man seriously to turn his eyes to contemplate God's works, since he has been placed in this most glorious theater to be a spectator of them, it is fitting that he prick up his ears to the Word, the better to profit."[69] Calvin also elsewhere deprecated the notion that Christianity could make sense apart from a central epistemological axiom rooted in divine revelation. In the *Institutes of the Christian Religion,* the Genevan Refomer wrote that the greatest insights of the philosophers cannot begin to approach the episte-mological power of the Scriptures. He surmised that the "human writings" of the philosophers, "however artfully polished," are not

> capable of affecting us at all comparably. Read Demosthenes or Cicero; read Plato, Aristotle, and other of that tribe. They will, I admit, allure you, delight you, move you, enrapture you in wonder-ful measure. But betake yourself from them to this sacred reading. Then, in spite of yourself, so deeply will it affect you, so penetrate your heart, so fix itself in your very marrow, that, compared with its deep impression, such vigor as the orators and philosophers have will nearly vanish. Consequently, it is easy to see that the Sacred

---

[67] Martin Luther, *Luther's Basic Theological Writings,* ed. Timothy F. Lull (Minneapolis: Fortress, 1989), 32.

[68] Richard Muller, *Dictionary of Latin and Greek Theological Terms,* s.v. "duplex cognitio Dei" (Grand Rapids: Baker Books, 1985), 97.

[69] John Calvin, *Institutes of the Christian Religion,* ed. John T. McNeill; trans. Ford Lewis Battles (Philadelphia: Westminster, 1960), 1.6.2.

Scriptures, which so far surpass all gifts and graces of human endeavor, breathe something Divine.[70]

Understandably, Thomists expressed displeasure at the new configuration of the post-Reformation philosophical landscape and have been understandably complaining about it ever since. Unfortunately for Occam and the Reformers, their critics have only increased in number in recent years. In addition to his Thomist and Roman Catholic detractors, Occam and the residue of voluntarism in the Reformation draw the fire and ire of evangelical philosophers and those who have inspired recent evangelical philosophy. The list includes many admirable writers, including, variously, Richard Weaver, Arthur Holmes, A. J. Conyers, Craig Gay, Daryl Hart, and certainly many other Roman Catholic thinkers.[71] All of these point to Occam and the Reformers as the either witting or unwitting fountainhead for all of the subsequent problems of modern (and now postmodern) philosophy.

As Richard Weaver breathlessly (and peremptorily) concludes in *Ideas Have Consequences:*

> "It was William of Occam who propounded the fateful doctrine of nominalism, which denies that universals have a real existence. . . . The practical result of nominalist philosophy is to banish the reality which is perceived by the intellect and to posit as reality that which is perceived by the senses."[72]

By focusing on the particulars apart from the traditional medieval synthesis, Occam, or so Weaver and others charge, precipitated an unhelpful empirical turn in philosophy which gave birth to the subjective turn in philosophy with whose bitter fruit we are still dealing today. Further, these authors intimate that because the Protestant Reformers broadly followed the *Via Moderna* (i.e., nominalism as opposed to the old medieval realism), they are unwitting accomplices in the demise of the West. If only the poor Reformers would have known better, perhaps we may have never gotten to Nietzsche.

Prolific Thomist Ralph McInerny condemns the Reformation to the philosophical ash heap of history with the following observation: "It is not just a well-turned phrase that modern philosophy is the Reformation car-

---

[70] Ibid., 1.8.1.

[71] See for example, William A. Dembski, *Intelligent Design* (Downer's Grove, IL: InterVarsity, 1999), 110ff; Craig Gay, *The Way of the Modern World* (Grand Rapids: Eerdmans, 1998), 65ff, 237–70; Arthur Holmes, *Fact, Value, and God* (Grand Rapids: Eerdmans, 1997), 68ff.; and Daryl Hart, *The Lost Soul of American Protestantism* (Lanham, MD: Rowman and Littlefield, 2003).

[72] Richard M. Weaver, *Ideas Have Consequences* (Chicago: University of Chicago Press, 1948), 3.

ried on by other means. Most of the major figures are Protestant or apostate or both. Luther's attack on reason and his Manichean split between nature and grace poisoned the well of thinking."[73]

There is, no doubt, some explanatory power to this analysis. Clearly *something* went wrong in the modern period. Modernity gave way to modernism. But to suggest that the blame and bane of modernism as we now know it is to be laid at the feet of an unwitting group of Reformers is nothing short of ludicrous. The notion seriously lacks perspective and two-dimensionalizes intellectual history. Although it lies beyond the purview of the present chapter to offer a thoroughgoing response to these charges, three observations serve to begin the task.

First, Occam himself did not deny the existence of universals quite in the way he is often taken to have done. Rather, as far as this author can deduce, Occam feared positing universals in a way similar to Platonism, universal ideas which superceded even God. In other words, Occam wanted the biblical God who creates *ex nihilo,* not the Demiurge-like craftsman Plato suggests in *Timaeus.*[74] This is why, for instance, Occam claimed to be the true heir of Aristotle. Occam did not deny the objectivity of truth; he simply cautioned against adding a fourth or possibly more transcendental(s) or hypostasis(es) than the one God in three persons. To do that would be to commit heresy. As philosopher Ernest A. Moody stated:

> Insofar as Ockham is called a nominalist, his doctrine is not to be construed as a rejection of *any* ontological determination of meaning and truth, but rather as an extreme economy of ontological commitment in which abstract or intentional extralinguistic entities are systematically eliminated by logical analysis[75] (emphasis added).

A second reply to the charges against Occam and the Reformation includes the fact that Luther and Calvin were hardly faithful or slavish followers of nominalism as it developed throughout the remainder of the scholastic period. Luther's *Disputation against Scholastic Theology,* for example, is replete with references to his significant and sizable disagreements with Occam and Gabriel Biel, Occam's most famous disciple.[76]

---

[73] Ralph McInerny, *A Student's Guide to Philosophy* (Wilmington, DE: ISI Books, 1999), 25.

[74] Plato's cosmology and theology are contained in his dialogue, *Timaeus,* available in *The Dialogues of Plato,* vol. 2, trans. B. Jowett (New York: Random House, 1937), 3–70.

[75] Ernest A. Moody, "William of Ockham," in *The Encyclopedia of Philosophy,* vol. 8, ed. Paul Edwards (New York: The Macmillan Company and The Free Press, 1967; reprint, 1972), 307. The notion of eternal, uncreated metaphysical entities that exist alongside God himself is an irreducibly Aristotelian notion that has worried philosophers such as Herman Dooyeweerd that idolatries are created in metaphysical schemes of the Thomistic type.

[76] For example, Thesis 56 reads, "It is not true that God can accept man without his justifying grace. This is in opposition to Ockham." Cf. Luther, *Basic Theological Writings,* 17.

Specifically, Luther and Calvin chafed at the Pelagianism of the writings of the Scholastics in general and Occam in particular. Still the Reformers certainly appreciated Occam's work insofar as it emphasized the sovereignty of God over his creation.

Stated differently the Reformers focused on the concept of "voluntarism" (i.e., the creative power of God's will) as an appropriate critique of the medieval synthesis over and against "nominalism," a philosophy which certainly did take an unexpected, modern turn. The truth of voluntarism points humanity to our absolute dependence upon divine revelation for true understanding about both God and the created order. The world as we know it is so because God, who never changes, declares it to be so.

In his brilliant introduction to Luther's *Bondage of the Will*, J. I. Packer beautifully sums up the ethos of the epistemology of the Reformation.

> [Luther's] unflagging polemic against the abuse of reason has often been construed as an assault on the very idea of rational coherence in theology, whereas in fact it is aimed only at the ideal of rational autonomy and self sufficiency in theology—the ideal of philosophers and scholastic theologians, to find out and know God by the use of their own unaided reason. It was in her capacity as the prompter and agent of natural theology that "Mistress Reason" was in Luther's eyes, the Devil's whore; for natural theology is, he held, blasphemous in principle, and bankrupt in practice. It is blasphemous in principle, because it seeks to snatch from God a knowledge of himself which is not his gift, but man's achievement—a triumph of human brain power; thus it would feed man's pride, and exalt him above his Creator, as one who could know God at pleasure, whether or not God willed to be known by him. Thus natural theology appears as one more attempt on man's part to implement the programme which he espoused in his original sin—to deny his creaturehood, and deify himself, and deal with God henceforth on an independent footing. But natural theology is bankrupt in practice, for it never brings devotees of God; instead it leaves them stranded in a quaking morass of insubstantial speculation. Natural theology leads men away from the Divine Christ, and from Scripture, the cradle in which he lies, and from the *theologia crucis,* the gospel doctrine which Christ sets forth. But it is only through Christ that God wills to be known and gives saving knowledge of himself.[77]

---

[77] J. I. Packer, "Historical and Theological Introduction," in Martin Luther, *The Bondage of the Will,* trans. J. I. Packer and O. R. Johnston (Grand Rapids: Fleming H. Revell, 1957), 45–46.

A third point in response to the criticism of the Reformation as the hinge upon which modernism pivoted is that Renaissance humanism and late medieval Scholasticism contributed as much if not more to the rise of modernity as did the Reformation, and it did so largely with Rome's blessing and supervision. History is not so easily compartmentalized. The results of the collective efforts of humanism, the Reformation, and the Counter-Reformation helped to give rise to modern science as we know it today. The change was inevitable. Fourteenth- and fifteenth-century intellects realized increasingly that certain crucial elements of Aristotelianism could not be rehabilitated. Craig Gay, at least a partial supporter of the theory that "the Reformation opened up a modernistic Pandora's box," nonetheless qualifies his discussion of the matter with the following candid observation:

> It is important to stress . . . that, quite apart from the actual impossibility of turning the clock back, the attempt to repristinate the medieval social order would not be a very good idea. . . . In the first place Aristotelian science is simply not believable any more. Even more significantly, attempting to revitalize Aristotelian teleology by way of Aquinas would not really solve the problem of human individuality and creativity. Whatever the Aristotelian "god" is, it is not personal, and the Aristotelian system does not permit any real space for human freedom and creativity. Indeed, even modern scientific nominalism allows more latitude for personal agency than medieval (Aristotelian) science did.[78]

The Enlightenment, the Rise of Skepticism, and the Influence of Immanuel Kant

Despite the best intentions of leaders on both the Roman Catholic and Protestant side, the fortunes of traditional Christianity began to change rapidly by the beginning of the eighteenth century. The church had once enjoyed considerable social influence among both civil leaders and the common people, its voice in public life dignified and powerful. As the modern period wore on, however, the church increasingly found itself marginalized on the periphery of culture-shaping discourse. Once upon a time, people at least understood the great verities of Christian teaching, and either believed them or denied them. Theology mattered. Today secularism dominates the

---

[78] Gay, *The Way of the Modern World*, 278–79. The context for Gay's comments here relate to a theology of personhood. His consideration of the *imago dei* includes an ontological definition of person, which this author found compelling.

culture of the West.[79] Why? A two-word reply suffices for an answer: the Enlightenment.[80]

Enlightenment philosophers asserted human reason and potential over the biblical doctrine that man was a fallen sinner in need of divine corrective. Unrestrained by holy command, or so it was thought, man could improve and thus glorify himself. "The philosophers," wrote historian Peter Gay, "were modern pagans."[81] Voltaire (1694–1778), the French dramatist who parodied religion, sounded the battle cry of his time, "*Écrasez l'infâme*"—crush religious superstition. To Voltaire, the biblical account of man and his destiny must be discarded on the trash heap of history, destroyed before the altar of human reason.

Perhaps the greatest illustration of such Enlightenment arrogance came during the French Revolution. In 1789, after the storming of the Bastille, the revolutionaries turned their anger toward another long-standing institution: the church. Churches throughout France were completely shut down, only to be reopened some twenty days later as "Temples of Reason." Years later, during the so-called "Festival of Reason," "a prostitute, dressed in red, climbed onto Notre Dame Cathedral's high altar, where she was solemnly enthroned 'goddess of reason' in a building now consecrated to her worship."[82]

The declining fortunes of the Christian perspective in the modern period are often lamented but seldom understood. Two popular views on the demise of religion in cultural life have been offered. The *first*, advanced by those happy with the change, argues that science effectively replaced traditional religious belief. Bertrand Russell, the infamous atheist of the early twentieth century, asserted that "science . . . has forced its way step by step against the Christian religion, against the churches. . . . Science can help us get over this craven fear in which mankind has lived for so many

---

[79] Numerous excellent accounts of the rise of secularism are available. One perceptive and straightforward account can be found in George Weigel's *The Cube and the Cathedral: Europe, America, and Politics Without God* (New York: Basic Books, 2005). One of the most prophetic voices in this regard was the Catholic historian Christopher Dawson, who spent a great deal of his scholarly output on the subject of "how to preserve the spiritual inheritance of Europe, and restore a common purpose to Western civilization" in the post-World War II context. Dawson theorized that only by recovering the moral energy provided by its Christian background could Europe survive. His analyses seem more perceptive now than when he was alive. See Dawson's *Understanding Europe* (New York: Sheed & Ward, 1953), 131ff. The author is indebted to the excellent introductory summary of Dawson's contribution in Araceli Duque, "The Vision of Christopher Dawson" [online]; available at: http://www.catholiceducation.org/articles/history/world/wh0087.html.

[80] Most scholars date the Enlightenment as being the period beginning with the signing of the Peace of Westphalia in 1648 (thus bringing a close to the Thirty Years' War) and the publication of Immanuel Kant's *Critique of Pure Reason* in 1781.

[81] Peter Gay, *The Enlightenment: The Rise of Modern Paganism* (New York: Vintage, 1966), 8.

[82] Mark T. Coppenger and Greg Gilbert, "The Cult of Unreason," *Kairos Journal* [online]; available at: http://www.kairosjournal.org/document.aspx?DocumentID=278&QuadrantID=2.

generations."[83] Alexander Pope once summarized this scientific optimism in a proposed epitaph for Sir Isaac Newton: "Nature and Nature's laws lay hid in night: God said, Let Newton be! And all was Light."

The *second* view advocated by those friendly to historic Christianity argues that Western culture fell victim to a departure from a biblical understanding of the universe as a place of divinely ordered purpose. Warning church leaders to be neither intimidated nor impressed with modern man's attempts at rebellion, Carl Henry concluded that man's idolatrous state has not changed over the centuries. The scientific revolution could not and did not eradicate sin in the heart.

Henry wrote:

> We need therefore to abandon the notion that modern science and its discoveries are the major obstacles to a living faith in the God of revelation and redemption. In earlier prescientific times, men negotiated their spiritual revolt just as vigorously and did so without invoking science and technology as a pretext. . . . The modern crisis of truth and word is not something historically or culturally unique.[84]

Henry understood the real message of the Enlightenment. Man has not changed. He is simply in rebellion against God. At base, Enlightenment thinkers despised the idea of *revelation,* the fact that God has disclosed his will to men verbally through the Bible. By abandoning the commands of God, modern philosophers fancied themselves emancipated men. A key passage from Immanuel Kant makes the point. Answering the question, "What is Enlightenment?" Kant replied:

> Enlightenment is man's release from self-incurred tutelage. Tutelage is man's inability to make use of his understanding without direction from another. Self-incurred is the tutelage when its cause lies not in the lack of reason but in the lack of resolution and courage to use it without direction from another. *Sapere aude!* "Have courage to use your own reason!"—that is the motto of enlightenment.[85]

Kant stated the issue plainly: "enlightened" men such as himself disallow any directives from "outside" themselves. Philosophically, the Prussian thinker was trying to chart a middle course between Descartes' rationalism (which essentially claimed that all truth could be acquired

---

[83] Betrand Russell, *Why I Am Not a Christian* (New York: Allen & Unwin, 1957), 22.

[84] Carl F. H. Henry, *God Who Speaks and Shows: Preliminary Considerations,* in *God, Revelation, and Authority,* vol. 1 (1976; reprint, Wheaton, IL: Crossway, 1999), 21.

[85] Immanuel Kant, *Foundations of the Metaphysics of Morals and What Is Enlightenment?* trans. Lewis White Beck (Indianapolis: Bobbs-Merrill, 1959), 85.

through access to pure reason and not the empirical senses), and David Hume's empiricist skepticism which attacked truth claims of every sort whether they be based upon analogy or other forms of traditional epistemological justifications. Kant explained that Hume's writings had wakened him from his "dogmatic slumbers," but he considered Hume's brand of skepticism too radical.

Kant argued in *The Critique of Pure Reason* that human beings are not in a position to know *absolute* truth. The grounding for Kant's position came in his qualification for how knowledge is acquired. He explained that a person can know only things as they appear to him, not the things-in-themselves (*Ding an sich*). Kant referred to this development in thought as the "Copernican Revolution" in epistemology. It signaled a "shift to the subject" that divided the universe into two realms—the noumenal and the phenomenal world.

The phenomenal world is composed of the things human beings experience in everyday life—what we can see, taste, touch, hear, and quantify. Working with the materials of the phenomenal world, reliable predictions can be made in the disciplines of science and mathematics because they deal with matters that are observable, repeatable, and common to our everyday experience.

The noumenal world, however, is a completely different matter; it deals in the realm of metaphysics and seeks to answer questions about God, the soul, freedom versus determinism, good versus evil, and the like. Reason alone, Kant contended, could not give us reliable answers in the realm of metaphysics. With respect to this world of mind and spirit, we do not have access to objective answers, but are left only with speculative theorizing.[86] As Kant said in his own words:

> I maintain that all attempts of reason to establish a theology by the aid of speculation are fruitless, that the principles of reason as applied to nature do not conduct us to any theological truths, and consequently, that a rational theology can have no existence, unless it is founded upon the laws of morality.[87]

---

[86] Few secondary renderings of his work can parallel the brilliant summary found in Frederick Copelston, S.J., *A History of Philosophy* (New York: Image Books, Doubleday, 1964), 6:180–439. Copelston's multivolume history of philosophy is an indispensable resource for the theological student. Also highly recommended is Roger Scruton's introduction, *Kant* (New York: Oxford University Press, 1982). Although Kant's *magnum opus* is daunting even in the English translation, see Immanuel Kant, *Critique of Pure Reason,* trans. J. M. D. Meiklejohn (Amherst, NY: Prometheus Books, 1990).

[87] Immanuel Kant, *Prolegomena to Any Future Metaphysics,* trans. Paul Carus (Chicago: Open Court Publishing Co., 1902), 51.

Liberalism, Neoorthodoxy, and the Continuing Impact of Kantianism

What does all of this philosophical background have to do with the history of theology in the modern period? The answer is: virtually everything. Kant's influence on the development of modern theology can scarcely be overestimated. As Klaus Bockmuehl observed, the implications of Kant's legacy for theological method is that "the wall that separates this world and the beyond is impenetrable. No intervention of the beyond into this world, such as God's revelation in history, can take place. No Messiah can ever come, on principle."[88] This ground-shaking philosophical development resulted in a string of modern theologians engaged in what evangelical theologian R. Albert Mohler has called a series of "rescue attempts."

In other words, the nineteenth and twentieth centuries witnessed various projects which tried to carve out a place for theology in the post-Kantian world. Despite the different approaches that have been devised, the outcome of all of them have been to sequester the faith into a pietistic, private, and existentialistic enterprise.

The first major thinker to attempt theology in light of Kantian developments was Friedrich Schleiermacher, known as the "father of modern theology." Forged in the rationalistic environs of the University at Halle, Schleiermacher began to doubt the central doctrines of the orthodox Christian faith. He wrote to his godly father in 1787 that he had lost his faith, repudiated the divinity of Christ, the vicarious atonement of Christ, and the doctrine of eternal punishment for the wicked.[89] Schleiermacher returned to the bearings of his Moravian background through his reading of Kant, who had himself come from a German pietistic family. After meeting with the great philosopher of Königsberg in May 1791, he seemed to see a way to reclaim his Christianity without embracing traditional orthodoxy. Putting aside the historic claims of the gospel, he privatized his theology by referring to faith not as an apprehension of divinely revealed truths but rather as a "feeling of absolute dependence" upon God.[90]

Schleiermacher's method, an approach eminently fit for the age of Romanticism, marked the beginning of future developments in liberal theology. Men such as Albrecht Ritschl, Horace Bushnell, and Adolf Von Harnack carried forward the agenda of making theology less about

---

[88] Klaus Bockmuehl, *The Unreal God of Modern Theology* (Colorado Springs, CO: Helmers and Howard, 1988), 10. This volume provides an exceptional review of the theologies of Karl Barth and Rudolf Bultmann.

[89] Friedrich Schleiermacher, *The Life of Friedrich Schleiermacher, as Unfolded in His Autobiography and Letters,* vol. 1, trans. Frederica Rowan (London: Smith, Elder, and Co., 1860), 46.

[90] For an expanded consideration of Schleiermacher's theological method, see Gregory A. Thornbury, "A Revelation of the Inward: Schleiermacher's Theology and the Hermeneutics of Interiority," in *SBJT,* 3 (Spring 1999) 1:4–26.

historical fact and confident doctrinal assertions and more about socioethi-cal concerns subject to ever-shifting theological paradigms.[91]

The effects of the Kantian shift reverberated throughout the Christian world. In the arena of biblical studies, for example, the quest for the his-torical Jesus essentially became an enterprise in trying to discover what could be known about Jesus of Nazareth from secular historiographical inquiry and apart from revelation. The Kantian divide reared its head when Hermann Reimarus and Gotthold Lessing introduced a radical distinction between the "Christ of faith" and the "Jesus of history" by arguing that what the apostles believed about Jesus and what Jesus claimed about him-self were almost entirely different.

Following in the wake of that experiment, David Strauss opined in his *Life of Jesus Critically Examined* that the claims made about Jesus in the New Testament Gospels were mythological in nature and not historical.[92] Only when Albert Schweitzer revealed the presuppositional biases of these "first quest" writers as "liberalism . . . in historical garb" did the move-ment begin to lose ground.[93] For Rudolf Bultmann, however, the pursuit of the historical Jesus was pointless anyway. For him Jesus was a theological figure, and in a Kantian worldview the historical concerns were a waste of time. Therefore, Bultmann devoted his energies to drawing an existentialist portrait of Jesus that "demythologized" the Gospel narratives.[94]

The liberal trajectory in modern theology convulsed in the mid-twen-tieth century with the rise of Neoorthodoxy and the so-called "Barthian revolt."[95] Trained at elite German universities and taught by the promi-nent Adolf Von Harnack at the University of Berlin, Karl Barth realized the bankruptcy of traditional liberal thought early in his ministry when he found that he could not preach its dogmas from the pulpit of his church in the Swiss village of Safenwil during World War I. He discovered a differ-

---

91 Three classic resources that cover the developments during this period are G. C. Berkouwer, *A Half Century of Theology* (Grand Rapids: Wm. B. Eerdmans Publishing Co., 1977); H. R. Mackintosh, *Types of Modern Theology* (London: Nisbet and Co., 1937); Martin E. Marty and Dean Peerman, *A Handbook of Christian Theologians* (Cleveland, OH: World Publishing Co., 1965).

92 For a summary of these developments, see J. P. Moreland and Michael Wilkins, eds., *Jesus Under Fire* (Grand Rapids: Zondervan, 1996); Craig Blomberg, *The Historical Reliability of the Gospels* (Downers Grove, IL: InterVarsity Press, 1987); and for an antidote to the more recent offerings of the infamous Jesus Seminar, which has returned to the early approach of Strauss and Reimarus, see N. T. Wright, *Jesus and the Victory of God* (Minneapolis, Minn.: Augsburg Fortress Publishers, 1997).

93 "There is nothing more negative than the result of the critical study of the Life of Jesus," observed Schweitzer. "He is a figure designed by rationalism, endowed with life by liberalism, and clothed by modern theology in historical garb." Albert Schweitzer, *The Quest for the Historical Jesus*, 2nd ed. (London: A & C Black, 1936), 396.

94 Rudolf Bultmann, *Jesus and the Word*, trans. Louise Pettibone Smith and Erminie Huntress (New York: Scribners, 1934).

95 Gary Dorrien, *The Barthian Revolt in Modern Theology: Theology without Weapons* (Louisville, KY: Westminster/John Knox Press, 2000).

ent power in exposition when he simply taught directly from the text of Scripture. The experience prompted him to write two seminal works that indicated the new trajectory of his theology. The first was a commentary on Romans which, when published in 1919, "fell like a bomb on the playground of the theologians," according to Catholic writer Karl Adam.[96] The second piece, an essay entitled "The Strange New World in the Bible," dealt a massive blow to the anthropocentric approach to religion advocated by Schleiermacher and those who followed his pattern. "It is not right human thoughts about God which form the content of the Bible, but the right divine thoughts about men," Barth wrote. "The Bible tells us not how we should talk about God but what he says to us; not how we find the way to him but how he has sought and found the way to us."[97]

Barth's repudiation of traditional liberal categories and the Enlightenment program of a higher-critical "scientific theology" baffled his former mentor. After some correspondence on the differences between them, Von Harnack confessed that Barth's new understanding of revelation "is wholly incomprehensible to me."[98]

Although Barth's version of Neoorthodoxy certainly resembled the theology of the Reformers more than did the theology of the previous generation, his epistemology still bore all the hallmarks of a Kantian holdover. "If I have a system," he said, "it is limited to a recognition of what Kierkegaard called the 'infinite qualitative distinction' between time and eternity, and to my regarding this as possessing negative as well as positive significance: 'God is in heaven, and thou art on earth.'"[99] Although Barth's reference is given to the Danish philosopher, the similarity of this approach to Kant's noumenal-phenomenal distinction is unmistakable.

This feature in his epistemology generated two features essential to Barth's methodology: the chasm between faith and reason, and the fallibility of the text of the Bible. First, for the Swiss theologian, faith did not share any common ground with unbelief; God is "wholly other," and the natural man cannot understand the world of the supernatural—even if he saw a miracle.[100] In a famous response to fellow Neo-Orthodox

---

[96] As cited in Clifford Green, "Introduction: Karl Barth's Theological Existence," in *Karl Barth: Theologian of Freedom*, ed. Clifford Green, The Making of Modern Theology: Nineteenth and Twentieth Century Texts (Minneapolis: Fortress, 1991), 16.

[97] Karl Barth, "The Strange New World within the Bible," in *The Word of God and the Word of Man*, trans. Douglas Horton (New York: Harper & Brothers Publishers, 1956), 43.

[98] Adolf Von Harnack, "Open Letter to Professor Karl Barth," in *Adolf Von Harnack: Selected Writings*, ed. Martin Rumscheidt (London: Collins Liturgical Publications, 1989), 91.

[99] Karl Barth, *Epistle to the Romans*, trans. Edwyn Hoskyns (London: Oxford University Press, 1993), 10ff; also as cited in Green, "Introduction: Karl Barth's Theological Existence," in *Karl Barth*, 17.

[100] See, for example, *Epistle to the Romans*, 120ff.; and Karl Barth, *Church Dogmatics*, 3/1, ed. G. W. Bromiley and T. F. Torrance (Edinburgh: T & T Clark, 1958), 78ff.

theologian Emil Brunner, Barth replied *Nein!* to any suggestion that natural theology or traditional apologetics should be a part of the witness of theology to the world.[101]

Second, Barth eschewed the notion of propositional revelation—the notion that God speaks in intelligent sentences and paragraphs that human beings can reliably understand and state in doctrinal formulas.[102] For him revelation is an occasional in-breaking of the divine into history, and therefore he argued that the Bible is only a "witness to divine revelation" that possesses a "distinctiveness from revelation, insofar as it is only a *human* work about it" (emphasis added).[103] As J. I. Packer summarizes the matter, Barth regarded revelation "as a breaking forth of something that Scripture 'intends,' rather than as a systematic and integrated application to us of what Scripture actually says."[104]

Although a more expansive discussion of the implications of the doctrine of revelation is due later in this volume, the point to be made here pertains to Barth's presuppositions and theological method. He denied the inerrancy of the Bible because it is a categorical impossibility for someone operating out of a quasi-Kantian system. Inerrancy, for Barth and others like him, is an attempt to bring the metaphysical world into the natural world, the noumenal into the phenomenal. And this Barth could not bring himself to do.

Despite the fact that Barth admirably protested liberalism in a way that promised the potential of renewing the task of preaching and a theology done for the church, the product of his method was oddly similar to the earlier pietistic liberalism only without the rationalist apologetic. He offered fideism to the church—a warmhearted affirmation of the faith to those already inside the believing community but potentially blunting the prophetic witness of the people of God in culture. The Bible does not contain a "thus saith the Lord" but rather holds out the *possibility* that God may have a word for both the church and the unconverted.

But here too, the candid reviewer must accuse Barth of cheating. Although his *epistemology* does not methodologically allow for the concept of propositional revelation or truth, his *Church Dogmatics* (an unfinished work of thirteen hefty volumes) is curiously *full* of axiomatic theological and, dare we say, *propositional* assertions about all sorts of

---

[101] Karl Barth and Emil Brunner, *Natural Theology,* trans. Peter Frankel (London: The Centenary Press, 1946).

[102] The memorable phrase "intelligent sentences and paragraphs" was a phrase often employed by Carl F. H. Henry, the most able exponent of the doctrine of propositional revelation in the twentieth century.

[103] Barth, *Church Dogmatics,* 1/2:19, 463.

[104] J. I. Packer, "The Adequacy of Human Language," in *Inerrancy,* ed. Norman Geisler (Grand Rapids: Zondervan Publishing House, 1980), 205.

things. To his credit, Barth's life in certain ways also seemed to betray his governing pietistic and fideistic methodology.[105] With great courage, he opposed the theological claims of the Third Reich by authoring the Barmen Declaration.[106] Surely Barth would not have denied the assertion that "The Holocaust was evil" is a reliable report from the mind of God translated into language to which Hitler and the Nazi regime would be held accountable. But he denied the possibility of extending that trust and grace to Scripture and the interpretation of the Word of God to the realm of systematic theology.

---

[105] For example, Barth certainly adhered to the literality of the resurrection of Jesus from the dead: "The concrete content of the memory of the forty days is: Christ is risen, He is risen indeed! To be exegetically accurate we must understand by this 'indeed' corporeally risen; and thus, if we are not to make so bold as to substitute for the apostolic witness another one altogether, there cannot be any talk of striking out the empty grave" (Karl Barth, *Credo* [New York: Scribner's, 1962], 100). But even as Barth affirmed the bodily resurrection, he opposed the idea of discussing it as a matter of interest to apologetics. Famously in this regard, Carl Henry encountered Barth's epistemological stubbornness on the issue during the latter's trip to America. The story is best told by Henry himself:

> When Karl Barth came to America for a few lectures at University of Chicago Divinity School and Princeton Theological Seminary, George Washington University made a belated effort to bring him to the nation's capital. Barth was weary, but volunteered for an hour's question-answer dialogue. The university invited 200 religious leaders to a luncheon honoring Barth at which guests were invited to stand, identify themselves and pose a question. A Jesuit Scholar from either Catholic university or Georgetown voiced the first question. Aware that the initial queries often set the mood for all subsequent discussion, I asked the next question. Identifying myself as "Carl Henry, editor of *Christianity Today*," I continued: "The question, Dr. Barth, concerns the historical factuality of the resurrection of Jesus." I pointed to the press table and noted the presence of leading reporters representing United Press, Religious News Service, *Washington Post, Washington Star,* and other media. If these journalists had their present duties in the time of Jesus, I asked, was the resurrection of such a nature that covering some aspect of it would have fallen under their area of responsibility? "Was it news," I asked, "in the sense that the man on the street understands news?"
> Barth became angry. Pointing at me, and recalling my identification, he asked: "Did you say Christianity *Today* or Christianity *Yesterday?*" The audience—largely nonevangelical professors and clergy—roared with delight. When countered unexpectedly in this way, one often reaches for a Scripture verse. So I replied, assuredly out of biblical context, "*Yesterday, today, and forever.*" When further laughter subsided, Barth took up the challenge: "And what of the virgin birth?" he asked. "Would the photographers come and take pictures of it?" he asked. Jesus, he continued, appeared only to believers and not to the world. Barth correlated the reality of the resurrection only with personal faith (Carl Henry, *Confessions of a Theologian* [Waco, TX: Word Publishing Co., 1986], 210–11).

It is important to add to this story that Henry and Barth later met and had a friendly interaction. Henry recounted that "whenever I conversed with Karl Barth I had the clear sense that, however flawed was Barth's dialectical theology, I was in the presence of a believer in the gospel" (ibid., 243). Henry contrasted such interactions with those he had with Rudolf Bultmann.

[106] "The Barmen Declaration," cited in Arthur C. Cochrane, *The Church's Confession under Hitler* (Philadelphia: Westminster Press, 1962), 240–41. See also: http://www.creeds.net/reformed/barmen.htm. An account of Barth's personal activities in engaging culture with a public theology is recounted in Frank Jehle, *Ever against the Stream: The Politics of Karl Barth, 1906–1968* (Grand Rapids: Wm. B. Eerdmans Publishing Co., 2002).

Consequently, Barth opened the floodgates for a variety of liberation, protest, and special interest theologies throughout the balance of the twentieth century and into the present. If the groundwork for theology is a private or even communal matter, nothing in principle prevents the proliferation of theological agendas that bear little resemblance to the historic Christian faith.

Some might question the wisdom of giving over a considerable portion of a chapter on prolegomena for the twenty-first century to the discussion of a theologian who died in 1968. But the reality is that much of contemporary religious thought, and increasingly the evangelicals, is still reacting to the implications of Barth's attempt to reform theology in the modern world. The fascination with Barth continues to grow in evangelical circles as evidenced by the attempt to reclaim him as an evangelical at the Wheaton Theology Conference in 2001 and through thinkers such as Donald Bloesch, Trevor Hart, and via the current interest in the so-called postliberalism of Hans Frei and George Lindbeck, which is ostensibly an American extension of Neoorthodoxy.[107] Some so-called "postconservative" evangelical thinkers have claimed that theologians such as Carl F. H. Henry and Millard Erickson are modernists and rationalists. They say that such evangelicals need to be wary of modern philosophical entanglements in constructing theological proposals. But it is unclear whether these critics *themselves* steer clear of those influences that would commit them to some sort of lingering program of Enlightenment epistemology, Kantian, existentialist, or otherwise.[108]

Clearly, evangelicals must continue to be open to what can be learned about growing theological trends by keeping abreast of developments in the

---

[107] See, for example, Bruce L. McCormack, "The Being of Holy Scripture in Becoming: Karl Barth in Coversation with American Evangelical Criticism" (paper presented at the Tenth Annual Wheaton Theology Conference, 5 April 2001); Tim Perry, "Is Karl Barth the Bad Guy after All? Karl Barth's Doctrine of Scripture Reassessed" (paper presented at the Tenth Annual Wheaton Theology Conference, 5 April 2001); Donald Bloesch, *A Theology of Word and Spirit* (Downers Grove, IL: InterVarsity, 1992); Trevor Hart, *Regarding Karl Barth* (Downers Grove, IL: InterVarsity, 1999); and even a monograph attempting to portray Karl Barth as a model of cultural engagement has been attempted by Paul Louis Metzger in *The Word of Christ and the World of Culture* (Grand Rapids: Eerdmans, 2003). The consideration of postliberalism/evangelical dialogue got underway in earnest with the publication of Timothy Phillips and Dennis Okholm, ed., *The Nature of Confession: Evangelicals and Postliberals in Conversation* (Downers Grove, IL: InterVarsity, 1996).

[108] This statement is made a bit tongue-in-cheek given the penchant of some postconservative evangelicals to charge their conservative counterparts with being too highly indebted to Enlightenment philosophical schemes of different kinds. I would like to highlight, in the interest of fairness, the fact that all theological programs come with their respective epistemological *caveat emptors*, postliberal, postconservative, postmodern, and neobarthian experiments included. For the kind of critique to which I refer above, see Stanley J. Grenz and John Franke, *Beyond Foundationalism* (Louisville, KY: Westminster/John Knox, 2001), 13–15. At the time of this writing, the most recent attempt at a postmodern evangelical prolegomena is John Franke, *The Character of Theology: A Postconservative Evangelical Approach* (Grand Rapids: Baker, 2005). See especially pp. 88 ff.

field (such as the works by important figures such as Wolfhart Pannenberg and Robert W. Jenson) while maintaining a certain reserve and circumspection about adopting new models that corrode confidence in the self-revealing God of the Bible.[109]

Current Evangelical Projects in Prolegomena—Baptist and Southern Baptist Contributions

The twentieth century marked the appearance of some landmark achievements from traditionalist Reformed, Evangelical, and Baptist scholars. For the first time the matter of theological prolegomena was being taken seriously as a specific discipline for consideration. The century began with a work of remarkable depth and erudition in Herman Bavinck's *Gereformeerde Dogmatiek,* with the fourth and final edition appearing in 1928. Abraham Kuyper's successor at the Free University of Amsterdam, Bavinck continued the brilliant tradition begun by his mentor with a theological prolegomena that offered careful definitions, a thorough treatment of historical theology with respect to method, and an informed critique of Kantianism.[110]

With the rise of the neoevangelical movement in the mid-twentieth century, Protestant theology received a much-needed intellectual boost. Figures such as Carl F. H. Henry (discussed throughout this chapter) and Edward John Carnell contributed serious works on the philosophy of religion. Trained in philosophy under Gordon Clark at Wheaton College, Henry and Carnell gave the founding faculty of Fuller Theological Seminary its initial verve and demonstrated confidence in the ability of biblical theism to present itself as a rational alternative to the modern mind.

Carnell's written output was prodigious and three volumes in particular—*A Philosophy of the Christian Religion, Christian Commitment,* and *The Case for Orthodox Theology*—sought to demonstrate the superiority of Christian religion among the panoply of other worldview options.[111] Carnell memorably defined orthodoxy as "that branch of Christendom which limits the ground of religious authority to the Bible."[112] A simple and

---

[109] Recent forays into theological prolegomena include Robert W. Jenson, *Systematic Theology,* vol. 1: The Triune God (Oxford: Oxford University Press, 1997); and most notably, Wolfhart Pannenberg, *Systematic Theology,* vol. 1 (Grand Rapids: Eerdmans, 1988).

[110] English readers are now able to appreciate his *magnum opus* with the publication of Herman Bavinck, *Reformed Dogmatics,* ed. John Bolt, trans. John Vriend (4 vols.; Grand Rapids: Baker, 2003—). Three volumes have already appeared: *Prolegomena* (2003), *God and Creation* (2004), and *Sin and Salvation in Christ* (2006).

[111] Edward John Carnell, *A Philosophy of the Christian Religion* (Grand Rapids: Eerdmans, 1952); *Christian Commitment: An Apologetic* (New York: Macmillan, 1957); *The Case for Orthodox Theology* (Philadelphia: Westminster, 1959).

[112] Carnell, *Case for Orthodoxy,* 13.

profound statement, Carnell's concise definition summed up the spirit and mood of the burgeoning neoevangelical movement.

Henry, the founding editor of *Christianity Today* and hailed by *Time* magazine as "the leading theologian in evangelicalism," emerged as the movement's preeminent thinker and intellectual spokesperson. As Paul R. House affirmed, Henry's "vision was comprehensive in that it considered the proposed evangelical worldview as the hope of the world, not just the way to reform straying American denominations affected negatively by modernism."[113] Defining "the Christian Revelation-Claim" Henry wrote:

> In a sense, all knowledge may be viewed as revelational, since meaning is not imposed upon things by the human knower alone, but rather is made possible because mankind and the universe are the work of a rational Deity, who fashioned an intelligible creation. Human knowledge is not a source of knowledge to be contrasted with revelation, but is a means of comprehending revelation. . . . Thus God, by his immanence, sustains the human knower, even in his moral and cognitive revolt, and without that divine preservation, ironically enough, man could not even rebel against God, for he would not exist. Augustine, early in the Christian centuries, detected what was implied in this conviction that human reason is not the creator of its own object; neither the external world of sensation nor the internal world of ideas is rooted in subjectivistic factors alone.[114]

Thus, according to Henry, God circumscribes and determines what can be known. Nonetheless, the world remains knowable because God himself is an intelligent deity. Contrary to the trajectory of rationalism, no autonomous standard for reason can be offered since reason itself loses meaning apart from the divine character. Since the divine discloses himself as person, revelation is personal in nature and can therefore speak to all of humanity. Consequently, revelation both coheres and corresponds to reality because God is one. It is not a truism to say therefore that divine revelation is communication which we can trust. Thus, as Henry declares, "*Only* the fact that the one sovereign God, the Creator and Lord of all, stands at the center of divine disclosure, guarantees a unified divine revelation."[115]

Certainly the most programmatic exposition of Henry's Reformation-inspired epistemology comes from the panoramic *God, Revelation and*

---

[113] Paul R. House, "Remaking the Modern Mind: Revisiting Carl Henry's Theological Vision," in *SBJT* 8 (Winter 2004) 14:5.

[114] Carl F. H. Henry, *The Drift of Western Thought* (Grand Rapids: Eerdmans, 1951), 104.

[115] Carl F. H. Henry, *God, Revelation and Authority,* vol. 2: *God Who Speaks and Shows* (Waco, TX: Word Books, 1976), 9.

Authority, Henry's six-volume magnum opus which is often alluded to but seldom read with patience. The fifteen theses spell out in brief what Henry delivers in detail throughout volumes 2 and 3 of *GRA*. In thesis 5 in particular, Henry outlines his epistemology's defining characteristic:

> 5. Not only the occurrence of divine revelation, but also its very nature, content, and variety are exclusively of God's determination.
>
> God determines not only the *if* and *why* of divine disclosure, but also the *when, where, what, how, and who.* If there is to be a general revelation—a revelation universally given in nature, in history, and in the reason and conscience of every man—then that is God's decision. If there is to be a special or particular revelation, that, too, is God's decision and his alone. Only because God so wills it is there a cosmic-anthropological revelation. It is solely because of divine determination, Paul reminds us, that "that which may be known of God is manifest . . . for God hath shewed it. . . . For the invisible things of him from the creation of the world are clearly seen, being understood by the things that are made, even his eternal power and Godhead" (Rom. 1:19–20 KJV). It is solely by God's own determination that he reveals himself universally in the history of the nations and in the ordinary course of human events. He is nowhere without a witness (Acts 14:17) and is everywhere active either in grace or judgment.[116]

For Henry, there was no neutral, antiseptic path to knowledge. Knowledge, properly defined in the way Henry defined it, is permitted, made accessible, and circumscribed by God himself. Henry affirmed that all knowledge owes its origin to God who speaks and shows. Henry's doctrine of creation is not, therefore, deficient on the grounds that it does not appropriate natural theology. He affirmed the fact that God speaks in and through creation, but he rightly reminded his readers that general revelation remains precisely that—revelation. And yet for this very reason, Christians have a genuine and meaningful point of contact with the nonbelieving world simply because we all benefit whether we know it or not from God's self-disclosure whether in creation or most preeminently in his written Word.

If anything this principle explains simply Henry's long-standing gripe with the epistemology of Karl Barth. When Barth argued that the *imago dei* was obliterated in the fall, Henry repeatedly retorted that Barth summarily closed down the conduit through which God speaks to human beings. Recent attempts to rehabilitate Barth's legacy on this point in particular, and on revelation in general, have not yet explained to anyone still appreciative

---

[116] Ibid., 9–10.

of Henry's withering critique of neoorthodoxy how Barth's acceptance of Kant's radical phenomenal-noumenal distinction can produce a worldview which simultaneously engages and yet challenges the prevailing secular culture.[117] In sum, as British evangelical theologian Peter Hicks concurs:

> Henry's central thesis is that *God reveals and speaks.* There is no reason why we should limit God to one form of revelation (through either a person or a book, through either encounter or concept). God reveals and speaks in a number of ways, in his creation, in general revelation, and supremely in Christ, the incarnate Word. But, additionally and foundationally, he is able to formulate and communicate truth in an epistemic word, in which he articulates truth verbally through "intelligible disclosure"; and this, in sovereign grace, he has chosen to do.[118]

Three other twentieth-century contributions in the realm of theological prolegomena deserve special attention. The 1980s saw the arrival of Gordon Lewis and Bruce Demarest's *Integrative Theology,* a substantive three-volume work that sought to locate theological questions in their broader philosophical, cultural, and historical context. Both professors at Denver Seminary, Lewis and Demarest's *Integrative Theology* was one of the first attempts to include apologetics as part of the overall theological task. It began with a serious discussion that analyzed "theology's challenging task" to be a matter of "knowing ultimate reality" that took both logic and biblical fidelity seriously.

Millard J. Erickson's work stands as another significant evangelical approach that tackled tough philosophical issues as part of the theological enterprise. Throughout his career Erickson demonstrated an understanding that systematic theology ultimately rested on claims to authority, as evidenced by one of his early written forays, *The New Evangelical Theology.*[119] But it was his massive *Christian Theology,* first published as a three-volume set (1983–1985), and then in an updated second edition in 1998, that set the standard for evangelical theologies to be written in the future. In his second edition, Erickson committed a full 174 pages to prolegomena and surveyed some of the most important contemporary issues in the field, including matters related to the philosophy of language and theology's relationship to postmodernism.[120]

---

[117] See Stanley Hauerwas, *With the Grain of the Universe* (Grand Rapids: Brazos Press, 2001).

[118] Peter Hicks, *Evangelicals and Truth* (Leicester, England: Apollos, 1998), 89–90.

[119] Millard J. Erickson, *The New Evangelical Theology* (Westwood, NJ: Fleming Revell and Co., 1968).

[120] Millard J. Erickson, *Christian Theology,* 2nd ed. (Grand Rapids: Baker, 1998); see especially 135–74.

Erickson understands and takes seriously the way in which Ludwig Wittgenstein's philosophy of language changed the terms of philosophical debate in the twentieth century. He also explores John Searle's Speech-Act theory hypothesis as a possible ally in reaffirming divine command theory as a pattern of religious authority. Erickson is also a figure whose contribution has grown more significant and detailed after his retirement from full-time teaching and administration. His *Truth or Consequences: The Promises and Perils of Postmodernism* is the most rigorous and fair-minded analysis of postmodernism by an evangelical scholar to date.[121] History will doubtless regard Erickson as Carl Henry's most notable successor in the turn-of-the-century period.

Third, and finally, was the theology of Stanley J. Grenz, a prolific author whose life was tragically cut short in 2005. Grenz, a one-time student of Gordon Lewis at Denver Seminary, gained a reputation for being one of the most promising thinkers with the release of books like *Reason for Hope: The Systematic Theology of Wolfhart Pannenberg,* and his *20th Century Theology,* cowritten with Roger Olson.[122] With the release of *Revisioning Evangelical Theology,* however, Grenz signaled a shift in emphasis in his thought. He argued that evangelicalism's distinctiveness lay not in a particular epistemology or truth claims (as Carnell, Henry, Lewis, Erickson, and others have asserted), but in a shared spirituality that takes place in local, believing communities.[123] He called for a return to Pietism in the face of a postmodern culture that increasingly eschewed rational arguments in favor of personal and social relationships and constructs.

Perhaps the most notable change from traditional evangelical epistemologies was Grenz's surprising decision to remove divine revelation from its traditional position in Protestant theology as the foundation for religious authority and consign it as a subcategory of the doctrine of the Holy Spirit in his systematic theology entitled *Theology for the Community of God.*[124] The emphasis of communal piety and spirituality remained the persistent theme throughout his other works, and Grenz argued that his approach was a matter of "renewing the center" of the evangelical tradition.[125] In

---

[121] Millard J. Erickson, *Truth or Consequences: The Promises and Perils of Postmodernism* (Downers Grove, IL: InterVarsity, 2001). Erickson's summaries of the writings of Jacques Derrida, Michel Foucault, Richard Rorty, and Stanley Fish are impeccably steeped in the primary sources.

[122] Stanley J. Grenz, *Reason for Hope: The Systematic Theology of Wolfhart Pannenberg* (New York: Oxford University Press, 1990); Stanley J. Grenz and Roger E. Olson, *20th Century Theology: God & the World in a Transitional Age* (Downers Grove, IL: InterVarsity, 1992).

[123] Stanley J. Grenz, *Revisioning Evangelical Theology: A Fresh Agenda for the 21st Century,* (Downers Grove, IL: InterVarsity, 1993), 22–35.

[124] Stanley J. Grenz, *Theology for the Community of God* (Nashville: Broadman & Holman, 1994), 494ff.

[125] Stanley J. Grenz, *Renewing the Center: Evangelical Theology in a Post-Theological Era* (Grand Rapids: Baker, 2000).

response, R. Albert Mohler parried that, in his estimation, Grenz's project seemed like "a center without a circumference," with no clearly set or evident doctrinal boundaries.[126]

It is worthwhile to note that the (largely) twentieth-century examples given (Carnell, Henry, Lewis/Demarest, Erickson, Grenz) come from the Baptist tradition. This certainly should not be taken to imply, however, that outstanding work in the area of theological prolegomena has not emerged from other denominational traditions. To the contrary, some of the finest writing in this area has been produced in the last few years by Richard Lints, David Wells, Richard Muller, and Kevin Vanhoozer.[127]

While the representative examples in this section are selective to be certain, it is a remarkable achievement for Baptists historically to have so many prominent representatives in the list. Historically, in their earliest phase, Baptists did not contribute in a significant way to the discussion of the philosophical groundwork necessary for doing theology. By the nineteenth century, however, that picture began to change as Baptists became more educated and more widely read. Unfortunately, however, they often seemed to fall in line with whatever philosophical trends were current at the time. For early mid-nineteenth-century American theologians, this meant adherence to the Scottish common-sense philosophy.[128] The present author has chronicled elsewhere how the penchant for following *en vogue* modern epistemologies created an unstable environment in the Northern Baptist tradition in the intergenerationally connected thought of Francis Wayland, Ezekiel Gilman Robinson, Augustus Hopkins Strong, and Walter Rauschenbusch.[129]

Among Southern Baptists the phenomenon of philosophical followership also was more subtly evident among the prominent writing theologians of the period such as J. L. Dagg, James Petigru Boyce, and E. Y. Mullins. For their part, however, Dagg and Boyce largely avoided philo-

---

[126] R. Albert Mohler, "Reformist Evangelicalism: A Center without a Circumference," in *A Confessing Theology for Postmodern Times,* ed. Micahel S. Horton (Wheaton, IL: Crossway, 2000), 131ff.

[127] Perhaps the best single volume contribution in the area of theological prolegomena in recent years has come from Richard Lints, *The Fabric of Theology* (Grand Rapids: Eerdmans, 1993); David Wells explored the topic *via negativa* in *No Place for Truth: Or Whatever Happened to Evangelical Theology?* (Grand Rapids: Eerdmans, 1993); Richard Muller has painstakingly connected the subject historically to the Reformation with *Post-Reformation Reformed Dogmatics,* vol. 1, 2nd ed., *Prolegomena to Theology* (Grand Rapids: Baker, 2003); Kevin Vanhoozer has contributed several volumes that deal with the subject of theological hermeneutics and is currently the most significant writer on the subject. See *Is There a Meaning in This Text?* (Grand Rapids: Zondervan, 1998) and *First Theology: God, Scripture, Hermeneutics* (Downers Grove, IL: InterVarsity, 2002).

[128] For a look at the way in which common sense philosophy held sway over the American mind during this period, see Mark Noll, *America's God* (New York: Oxford University Press, 2002), 96–113.

[129] Gregory Alan Thornbury, "The Legacy of Natural Theology in the Northern Baptist Theological Tradition, 1827–1918" (Ph.D. diss., The Southern Baptist Theological Seminary, 2001).

sophical speculation in their work and failed to include any substantive approach to prolegomena with the exception of routine definitions of theology as a "science."[130]

Among Southern Baptist contributions to theological method, E. Y. Mullins by far stands out as the most important.[131] To his credit Mullins rightly sensed the need for a focus on a religion of the heart. "It requires little discernment to see," Mullins wrote in opening pages of *The Christian Religion in Its Doctrinal Expression,*

> that systematic theologies which are chiefly concerned with the logical or philosophical relations between truths in a unified order, may easily overlook vital interests of the spiritual life. The Scriptures rarely present truth in this way. They never present it apart from the vital needs of the soul.[132]

Regrettably, however, some of the sources Mullins chose for inspiration, notably Friedrich Schleiermacher and Borden Parker Bowne's personalism, prompted Mullins to shift his emphasis away from the historic truth claims of divine revelation and toward the subjective response of the human being toward God.[133] This feature of Mullins's thought lent an unpredictable character to his theology that has invited both liberals and conservatives to claim him as a fellow traveler.[134]

The balance of the twentieth century failed to produce much of interest for Southern Baptists in the area of theological method. The tradition increasingly favored a bibliographic approach to theological explanation. Authors such as Dale Moody and Eric Rust both released volumes in 1981 and seemed to prefer historical commentary with passing allusions to their own presuppositions. Rust employed a history of religions approach to philosophy of religion, and Moody evidently compiled his notes from years of classroom teaching.[135] James Leo Garrett's impressive *Systematic*

---

[130] J. L. Dagg, *Manual of Theology* (Harrisonburg, VA: Gano Books, reprint, 1990; originally published in 1857); James P. Boyce, *Abstract of Systematic Theology* (Hanford, CA: den Dulk Christian Foundation, reprint, n.d.; originally published 1887).

[131] W. T. Conner deserves honorable mention in this regard and dealt with the question in an introductory way in *Revelation and God* (Nashville, TN: Broadman Press, 1936), 35–54. He exhibited a similar interest in personalism and discusses distinctions between *a priori* and *a posteriori* knowledge (although Connor himself does not employ the latter term).

[132] E. Y. Mullins, *The Christian Religion in Its Doctrinal Expression* (Nashville, TN: The Sunday School Board of the Southern Baptist Convention, 1917), 5.

[133] R. Albert Mohler, "Introduction," in *E. Y. Mullins: The Axioms of Religion,* ed. Timothy and Denise George (Nashville: Broadman & Holman, 1997), 9ff.

[134] Russell D. Moore and Gregory Alan Thornbury, "The Mystery of Mullins in Contemporary Southern Baptist Historiography," in *SBJT* 3 (Winter 1999) 4:44–57.

[135] Eric Rust, *Religion, Revelation, and Reason* (Macon, GA: Mercer University Press, 1981); and Dale Moody, *The Word of Truth* (Grand Rapids: Eerdmans, 1981).

Theology continued the bibliographic approach but with a historical precision that sets it apart from similar efforts of the kind. Although Garrett's prolegomena is brief, it offers an encyclopedic presentation of various denominational approaches to theological method.[136]

How Does It All Fit Together?

Prolegomena: Theology Defined

Every theological system should begin with a prolegomena, a word that comes from the Greek, meaning "what needs to be said before one begins." A prolegomena outlines the methodological considerations, or presuppositions in play, that guide the theologian's work. In other words, it states the definitions and ground rules for discussion "up front" so that the reader can know what to expect.

Defining "theology" is, of course, that first order of business. Some theologians define theology merely etymologically. Since the word *theology* is composed of the two Greek words *theos* (God) and *logos* (study of), certain thinkers choose to go no further.[137] Uncertain of the ability of human beings to apprehend eternal truths, modern theologians tend to offer modest definitions of the discipline. Gustav Aulén, for example, claimed that "systematic theology has as its object the study of the Christian faith."[138] Brian Hebblethwaite, pursuing a minimalist approach, defines theology simply as "rational thought or talk about God."[139] Other philosophers and theologians are not in the mood to go even that far. Increasingly, theology has come to be seen as a "problem," a puzzle about how people talk about God. Ludwig Wittgenstein therefore referred to theology as "the grammar of faith."[140] Likewise, in a skeptical query, Dorothee Sölle asks:

> There is such a thing as mineralogy, because minerals exist and scientists can become knowledgeable and expert about them.

---

[136] James Leo Garrett, *Systematic Theology*, vol. 1 (Grand Rapids: Eerdmans, 1990).

[137] So, for example, Fisher Humphreys proceeds with the definition that theology is merely "thinking about God." See Fisher Humphreys, *Thinking about God* (New Orleans, LA: Insight Press, 1974), 7.

[138] Gustav Aulén, *The Faith of the Christian Church,* trans. Eric H. Wahlstrom and G. Everett Arden (Philadelphia: The Muhlenberg Press, 1948).

[139] Brian Hebblethwaite, *The Problem of Theology* (Cambridge: Cambridge University Press, 1980), 1.

[140] Wittgenstein made this suggestion in his 1953 posthumously published work *Philosophical Investigations,* trans. G. E. M. Anscombe, 3rd ed. (Oxford: Blackwell, 2002). The comment inspired in part the New Yale School of Theology, which views theology primarily as a discussion about the contours of biblical narrative, not propositional content from the mind of God. A key work in this connection that employed the phrase was Paul Holmer's *The Grammar of Faith* (San Francisco: Harper and Row, 1978).

Theology, too, is an –ology, derived from the words *theos* (God) and *logos* (teaching). But can there be any Logos, any systematic and rational clarification, of God? If theology were simply a "theory about God, analogous to ossology (the theory of bones), then it would be an insult to God, blasphemy. The object of theology can only be the relationship between God and human beings: in other words, reflection on the experiences that have compelled human beings to talk about something like "God."[141]

There is no need for such reticence and confusion. Christians serve a generous God who is capable of explaining himself to human beings in a way that they can understand. The key question for a person to ask when beginning to approach the task of theology is: what kind of character does the God we are studying possess? In light of the answer to this question, it is legitimate to seek the reply to the question, what might we expect of such a God in terms of his communications with us? To answer this question, the theologian has no choice but to repair to the only resource available to him: divine revelation. Revelation is a disclosure of God's reality and *therefore stands apart as the fundamental epistemological axiom of Christianity.*[142]

Carl F. H. Henry described this divine activity in terms of God forfeiting his own personal privacy in order to make himself known to his creatures.[143] If one thinks about the idea for a moment, it is an unparalleled concept in beauty. God opens up his eternal and transcendent mystery and invites the world to know him personally. This incredible act should not be taken for granted but rather should be cause for the Christian to fall down on his face and worship.

God is a personal deity who desires to have fellowship with those whom he has made. When God reveals himself, therefore, he is showing us intimate details about his being and nature.

It is not by accident, therefore, that the word for truth in Greek is *aletheia,* which etymologically means "without veil." Thus when Jesus told his disciples in John 14:6, "I am the way, and the *truth,* and the life," he meant, "I am God without veil—the unhidden God, available and accessible to anyone who would find me." As both fully God and fully human,

---

[141] Dorothee Sölle, *Thinking about God: An Introduction to Theology,* trans. John Bowden (Philadelphia: Trinity Press International, 1990), 1.

[142] Although the doctrine of revelation will be covered more exhaustively in subsequent chapters, it is imperative to raise the impossibility of the knowledge of God without raising divine revelation as the central epistemological confession of any evangelical theology.

[143] Henry's full definition is: "Revelation is a divinely initiated activity, God's free communication by which he alone turns his personal privacy into a deliberate disclosure of his reality." See Henry, *God, Revelation and Authority,* 2:8.

Jesus was, in every way, the Word of God. The entirety of Scripture as a divine revelation of the person and work of Jesus Christ characterizes the grandeur of evangelical confessional theology.

Theology, therefore, is the study of God organized in an orderly manner that seeks to portray accurately the divine reality in the light of revelation. This appears to be a good place to begin. Christianity cannot be understood apart from its genuine uniqueness in an intellectual marketplace cluttered by thousands of gods. As Princeton Seminary theologian B. B. Warfield asserted: "Christianity is the one revealed religion. That is to say, while the tenets of other religions are the by-product of human thought, the doctrines of Christianity are communications from God. Christianity thus stands fundamentally in contrast with all other religions."[144]

Because theology works with a revealed body of material, a good definition of theology is "the attempt to explain God's self disclosure in a consistently faithful manner." Henry offers an expanded definition along the same lines: "The proper task of theology is to exposit and elucidate the content of Scripture in an orderly way, and by presenting its teaching as an orderly whole to commend and reinforce the worship and service of God."[145] Because God spoke to his people throughout biblical history in intelligible sentences and paragraphs, it makes sense that the narrative of Scripture can be coordinated in a fashion that holds together as a system of thought. Herein, and herein alone, resides the promise for any attempt at "systematic theology."

The Branches of Theology

If theology is to be organized in an orderly manner, based on the self-disclosure of God, then the discipline can be broken down into discrete topics for investigation and inquiry. The traditional Protestant ordering of theology appears in the following "branches" organically tied to the overall system:

- Prolegomena
- Revelation (Bibliology)
- Theology Proper (Doctrine of God; Theology)
- Creation and Providence
- Angelology
- Doctrine of Humanity (Anthropology)
- Sin (Hamartiology)
- Person and Work of Jesus Christ (Christology)

---

[144] B. B. Warfield, *Selected Shorter Writings,* ed. John E. Meeter (Phillipsburg, NJ: Presbyterian and Reformed; reprint, 2001), 1:23.

[145] Carl F. H. Henry, *Gods of This Age or God of the Ages?* ed. R. Albert Mohler (Nashville: Broadman & Holman, 1994), 245.

- Doctrine of Salvation and Atonement (Soteriology)
- Doctrine of the Church (Ecclesiology)
- Doctrine of Last Things (Eschatology)

The Promise and Limits of Theology

Systematic theology, as the intellectual support mechanism of the Christian truth claim, therefore, becomes a project of explaining precisely *how* God's sovereignty applies in every domain of knowledge. The way to do this is to move in a coherent fashion throughout the text of Scripture and distill the doctrine therein in propositionally coherent language.[146] After all, Christians are foremost in advocating that an object can truly predicate a subject. The affirmation "Jesus is God" is a propositional statement about an ontological reality, not merely a way of talking about Jesus of Nazareth. While the theologian realizes that the deity of Christ is far more important an assertion than one's position toward the precise ordering of end-time events, he must nevertheless strive for accuracy to the best of his ability by using good biblical hermeneutics, consulting his betters in the history of the church, engaging logically sound judgment, and to a lesser extent, squaring his reflections with the experiences of God's people living in the world.[147]

One of the greatest lies of modernism was that it is possible to overcome all previous interpretation and engage in a completely critical and objective theological method. But this is an illusion. As Hans-Georg Gadamer wrote, "The fundamental prejudice of the Enlightenment is the prejudice against prejudice itself, which denies tradition its power."[148] Theology, as such, emerges as a conservative or *conserving* activity; the theologian strives to preserve from the past the deposit of truth that has served the church so well throughout the ages. The goal in theological endeavors remains not *novelty* in theology but an ongoing *faithfulness* to the "faith that was once for all delivered to the saints" (Jude 3). Attempts at "creative theology" must therefore be met with extreme caution until a thoroughgoing biblical examination of the approach can take place.

While theology must be disciplined in this way for it to be useful as a system of thought, the theologian must also realize that his conclusions are not co-extensive with the divine mind. Drawing upon the tradition of the early church

---

[146] Those who chafe at the suggestion that theology must be placed within propositional language must come up with a meaningful alternative. Approaches to theological discourse that deny the possibility of positive descriptions of God still must contend for their doctrines through the vessel of rational linguistic systems of representation.

[147] An excellent introduction to the task of biblical hermeneutics can be found in Grant Osborne, *The Hermeneutical Spiral* (Downers Grove, IL: InterVarsity, 1991, rev. 2007).

[148] Hans-Georg Gadamer, *Truth and Method,* 2nd rev. ed., trans. Joel Weinsheimer and Donald Marshall (New York: Crossroad, 1989), 259.

fathers, the Dutch thinker Herman Bavinck surmised that "the theory of God's incomprehensibility and of the unknowability of his being also became the point of departure and the basic idea of Christian theology."[149] In other words, the pagan religions of the rest of the world constructed deities that were thinly veiled superimpositions of human thoughts and ideals. The gods could be controlled because their words and actions emanated from the human imagination. Early philosophers like Plato saw through the construct and concluded that the gods were not essential to understanding the nature of reality. In contrast, the Christian theologian realizes the limits of what theology can accomplish.

Again, as Carl F. H. Henry so memorably put it:

> Divine revelation does not completely erase God's mystery, inasmuch as God the Revealer transcends his own revelation. The revelation given to man is not exhaustive of God. The God of revelation transcends his creation, transcends his activity, transcends his own disclosure. . . . In striking contrast to the Greek notion of prophecy, the Bible disavows any divine spark in man, any potentiality in man for divinization that qualifies him permanently to be a means of divine revelation.[150]

The theologian must also come to grips with the fact that his interpretation takes place within a culturally and historically located moment. Contrary to the theory of John Locke, man is not a *tabula rasa* (a blank slate) when he enters the world, nor is the theologian when he approaches the task of theological inquiry. He carries with him the urgencies of his own context and the challenges that need to be answered in that particular hour. By staying informed of the tradition while simultaneously remaining open to new light breaking forth from the Word of God, he will learn to construct a comprehensive Christian worldview.

The Importance of Worldviews and Presuppositions to the Task of Theology

The term *worldview* has been around for a long time. First employed by Kant, the concept of worldview (from the German word *Weltanschauung*)

---

[149] Citing passages from Barnabas, Justin Martyr, Irenaeus, Clement of Alexandria, Origen, Athanasius, Eusebius, Augustine, and John of Damascus, Bavinck remarks, "God's revelation in creation and redemption fails to reveal him adequately. He cannot fully impart himself to creatures, inasmuch as in that case the latter must needs be God. . . . There is no name that makes known unto us his being. No concept fully embraces him. No description does justice to him. That which is hidden behind the curtain of revelation is entirely unknowable. We cannot approach by means of our thought, imagination, or language." See *The Doctrine of God* (Grand Rapids: Eerdmans, 1951), 21.

[150] Henry, *God, Revelation and Authority,* 2:9.

took on new significance for Christians with the publication of James Orr's *The Christian View of God and the World.*[151] But only recently have Christians taken an interest in worldview studies as an essential task in the mandate to become serious Christian thinkers. In 2002, philosopher David K. Naugle published an exhaustive historical treatment of the emergence of the word *worldview/Weltanschauung* and its employment within various disciplines. For the purposes of this discussion, two senses of the word *worldview* are needed. The first refers to a philosophical system, a network of ideas that affects how one cognitively apprehends the world about him and, in so doing, lives his life by those dicta. The second sense recognizes that a worldview is a product of a culture, an amalgam of the beliefs of a given people in a particular time and place.

Sense 1: Worldview as Cognitive Apparatus

Although numerous good definitions of *worldview* might be offered, the Baptist philosopher Ronald Nash's concise wording is: "A worldview . . . is a conceptual scheme by which we consciously or unconsciously judge or interpret reality."[152] Notice the total scope indicated by the language. Our worldview acts upon both our conscious and unconscious impressions about everything around us. If you have ever met someone who had a blind spot (anything from body odor to an annoying personal habit), you know that we human beings are not always aware of our own weaknesses. Our blind spots extend to our beliefs about reality. And since we are incapable of proceeding on our own wisdom, or even the collective wisdom of a community (with corporate blind spots), we must rely upon an objective truth teller. This truth teller is God, the Creator of reality. Only a self-existent, eternal, and omnipotent God can steady one's rudder in the sea of competing worldviews.

Most social conflicts, wars, and even political struggles occur most fundamentally at the level of worldview presuppositions. Presuppositions are background beliefs. They form and frame worldview discussions even when they are not clearly stated; they serve as basic beliefs by which we govern everyday life. As Cornelius Van Til wrote, presuppositions are a "reference point" that serve as "the conditions which make experience intelligible."[153] The validity of a worldview is directly related to the validity of one's presuppositions.

---

[151] Orr wrote: "Christianity is neither a scientific system, nor a philosophy, yet it has a world-view of its own, to which it stands committed, alike by its fundamental postulate of a personal, holy, self-revealing God, and by its content as a religion of Redemption—which, therefore, brings it into comparison with other worldviews. As thus binding together the natural and moral worlds in their highest unity, through reference to their ultimate principle, God, it involves a *Weltanschauung.*" James Orr, *The Christian View of God and the World,* 3rd ed. (Edinburgh: Andrew Elliot, 1897), 9.

[152] Ronald Nash, *Worldviews in Conflict* (Grand Rapids: Zondervan, 1992), 16.

[153] Cornelius Van Til, *A Christian Theory of Knowledge* (Philadelphia: Presbyterian and Reformed, 1969), 18.

One of the primary goals in worldview evaluation, therefore, is to uncover a person's presuppositions. Keen cultural analysts examine the worldview-ish nature of all moral, political, and philosophical debates.

In 1991 University of Virginia sociologist James Davison Hunter stirred the academic community to recognize this fact with the publication of *Culture Wars: The Struggle to Define America.*[154] In the wake of the 2000 United States presidential election, the phrase "Red America, Blue America" came to describe the nation's ideological divide based on the electoral map. With red states being conservative regarding moral values in general and the blue trending toward more liberal positions, some analysts wondered whether a common cultural consensus still existed.[155] Whatever one makes of this political landscape, the dictum of Plato has never been more true: we become what we contemplate.

In broad terms the Christian worldview as a hermeneutic (interpretive) device examines data by placing events in the following theological categories: creation, fall, redemption, and restoration. In other words, whenever we encounter an idea, we ask whether the issue relates variously to how God created the world, how human beings through sin have corrupted the world, or how the world through the work of Jesus Christ is in the process of being redeemed and restored. *Creation* encompasses not only the natural world but all human cultural activity (e.g., art, economics, journalism, science). *The fall* affects *everything* in the created order. The redemption of Jesus Christ possesses power to overturn all the effects of the Fall.

According to writer Albert Wolters, the key to Christian worldview thinking is to discern between structure and direction in the created order and the subsequent effects of the postfall system.[156]

"Structure denotes the essence of a creaturely thing, the kind of creature it is by virtue of God's creational law."[157] *Direction* refers to a sinful deviation in the creature or modality from this divine design or from the renewed conformity that is available to the created order through the person of Jesus Christ, the new creation. This insight goes far in helping the Christian engage the world he lives and works in on a day-to-day basis.

Developing a Christian worldview is important for the Christian because it tempers the way we interact with and assess the fallen world in which we live. Some Christians fall into the trap of being "shocked" about

---

[154] James Davison Hunter, *Culture Wars: The Struggle to Define America* (New York: Basic, 1991).

[155] Columnist David Brooks, for one, thought so. See "A Polarized America," in *The Hedgehog Review,* 6 (Fall 2004) 1:14–23; and "One Nation, Slightly Divisible" in *The Atlantic Monthly* (October 2001) [online]; available at: http://www.theatlantic.com/issues/2001/12/brooks.htm.

[156] Albert M. Wolters, *Creation Regained: Biblical Basics for a Reformational Worldview* (Grand Rapids, MI: Eerdmans, 1985).

[157] Ibid., 72–73

beliefs which secular persons express on a given issue. For example, numerous Christians exhibited stunned disbelief when it became widely reported a number of years ago that Princeton University ethicist Peter Singer wrote that a healthy chimpanzee is of higher moral value than a severely retarded human infant.[158]

While the believer may be saddened or even outraged that a person teaching such nonsense holds an endowed chair in ethics at one of America's most prestigious universities, he must not be *shocked.* When encountering such news, the Christian worldview thinker would immediately realize that Peter Singer operates from philosophical utilitarianism. Founded by British thinkers Jeremy Bentham and John Stuart Mill, utilitarianism can be summed up by the oft-quoted dictum, "the end justifies the means." In other words, anything is permissible as long as persons or communities achieve their desired outcomes in a manner that benefits those concerned. According to Bentham and Mill, a person should try to achieve the maximum amount of happiness for the greatest number of people.[159] If one seriously holds this view, one cannot believe in a traditional view of God or morality, and in Singer's case one cannot arbitrarily discriminate between humans and animals.

A person's worldview is a roadmap to his soul: it shows where he will begin and where he will end up. The theologian must become skilled in worldview analysis so that he can prepare the church to respond intelligently and *rapidly* to the great crises confronting God's people today. Sadly, the church and the ministers who shepherd her have developed an ignominious track record of failure with regard to this responsibility in the recent past. The rise of moral relativism and a host of other social ills seemed to catch Christian churches off guard throughout the closing decades of the twentieth century. Christians remain largely unprepared to encounter the problem in the twenty-first century too. Examples could be multiplied on end if one thinks of the slow evangelical response to issues as varied as racism, abortion, euthanasia, homosexuality, and judicial tyranny. Today churches appear largely unprepared or perhaps even unwilling to counter attempts to redefine traditional marriage, clone human beings, or genetically alter the human species.[160]

---

[158] Singer infamously made this argument in his landmark book *Animal Liberation,* 2nd ed. (New York: New York Review of Books/Random House, 1990).

[159] One definitive discussion of the merits of utilitarian theory is available in J. J. C. Smart and Bernard Williams, *Utilitarianism: For and Against* (Cambridge: Cambridge University Press, 1973).

[160] The failure of evangelicals to develop a fully orbed public theology has received an excellent treatment in Russell D. Moore, *The Kingdom of Christ: The New Evangelical Perspective* (Wheaton, IL: Crossway, 2004).

The words of Francis Schaeffer seem more prophetic now than when they were first written in 1968:

> It was indeed unfortunate that our Christian "thinkers" in the time before the shift [toward relativism] took place and the chasm was fixed, did not teach and preach with a clear grasp of presuppositions. Had they done this, they would not have been taken by surprise and they could have helped young people to face their difficulties. The really foolish thing is that even now, years after the shift is complete, many Christians still do not know what is happening. And this is because they are still not being taught the importance of thinking in terms of presuppositions, especially concerning truth.
>
> The flood-waters of secular thought and liberal theology overwhelmed the Church because the leaders did not understand the importance of combating a false set of presuppositions. They largely fought the battle on the wrong ground and so, instead of being ahead in both defense and communication, they lagged woefully behind. This was a real weakness which it is hard, even today, to rectify among evangelicals.[161]

Sense 2: Worldview as Cultural Construct

A worldview is not a mere amalgam of facts collected by an individual. Worldviews are products of cultures. Johann Herder, the eighteenth-century German philosopher, defined culture as "the life-blood of a people, the flow of moral energy that holds a society intact." Cultures display the moral desires and attitudes of a collective "we" in an "ocean of they."[162] Consequently, and contrary to the popular view of modern social science theory, cultures do not produce religions, but rather it is the other way around: religion produces culture, a phenomenon that emanates from the deeply religious instincts of man. As Henry Van Til has rightly put it: "Since man is a moral being, his culture cannot be a-moral. Because man is a religious being, his culture too, must be religiously oriented. There is no pure culture, in the sense of being neutral religiously, or without positive or negative value ethically."[163]

This proves to be a valuable insight for the theologian, for it helps him to understand that not only individuals but entire nations and people groups

---

[161] Francis Schaeffer, *The Complete Works of Francis Schaeffer,* vol. 1, book 1, *The God Who Is There* (Wheaton, IL: Crossway, 1982), 7.

[162] Johann Herder; quoted in Roger Scruton, *An Intelligent Person's Guide to Modern Culture* (South Bend, IN: St. Augustine's Press), 3.

[163] Henry Van Til, *The Calvinistic Concept of Culture* (Grand Rapids: Baker, 1959; reprint, 2001), 27.

possess an agenda when it comes to the matter of what religious principles they hold. Earlier, we defined religion as the belief in something or other as divine.[164] If moral neutrality does not exist in the societal realm, then it follows that one cannot be a relativist when it comes to the matter of culture. Contrary to the theories of multiculturalists such as anthropologist Margaret Mead, it is entirely appropriate to make informed value judgments on how a given society thinks and behaves.[165] Either a culture is generally moving away from God's intended purposes for it or toward divine expectations—an extension of the culturative task that began in the garden of Eden. If this is the case, then *culture* may be defined as "any and all human effort and labor expended on the cosmos, to unearth its treasures and its riches and bring them into the service of man for the enrichment of human existence unto the glory of God."[166] Culture, on this view, is achieved when human creative activity matches God's purposes for it. Unfortunately, human beings excel at finding creative ways of substituting other agendas for God's own.

Every Christian knows what it is like to share the good news of Jesus Christ with someone only to learn that the person with whom he is speaking has basic disagreements with him. In his attempts to reach a lost world with the gospel, the Christian must realize that he faces not only someone with a wrong set of presuppositions but also a worldview that is deeply embedded in a culture. Such ways of thinking act like filters in a person's mind. Words, ideas, and arguments wash over the unbeliever's mind, get misinterpreted, misread, and misplaced. Such a state of affairs makes evangelistic dialogue more difficult.

Sociologist Peter Berger constructed a helpful theory that explains how worldviews take shape. He explains that societies inevitably search for explanations that make sense out of life; a theologian would say that this is the religious impulse of humanity working itself out. A society's answers to its ultimate questions unfold in three steps through a dialectical process, according to Berger, and result in what he calls a "plausibility structure"—a seemingly likely scenario about how the world works. Society is a "human product" that develops in the following cycle:

---

[164] See reference to Clouser on page 3.

[165] Mead gained notoriety for her 1928 book *Coming of Age in Samoa* which argued that such things as gender differences, marriage, and understandings of right and wrong vary radically from culture to culture and are not intuitive to human nature. In sum, she accepted *en toto* the philosophy of Jean-Jacques Rousseau and his theory of the "noble savage." No one perspective, therefore, can be privileged above others. Mead's work was later discredited for improperly interpreting the sociological data based on her philosophical commitment to Rousseau's utopianism. For a critical evaluation of Mead's work, see Derek Freeman, *Margaret Mead and Samoa: The Making and Unmaking of an Anthropological Myth* (Cambridge, MA: Harvard University Press, 1983).

[166] Henry Van Til, *Calvinistic Concept of Culture*, 29–30.

Externalization: "The ongoing outpouring of human being into the world, both in the physical and mental activity of men."

Objectivation: The product, resulting in "a reality that confronts its original producers as a facticity."

Internalization: Man *becomes* a product of society.

In the first step human beings theorize philosophically, they build cities, and they produce great works of art in an attempt to explain the universe around them. They *externalize* their rough outline of philosophy in tangible ways. Whether in literature or architecture, there exists an increasing amount of cultural product that serves as a visible reminder about "the way things are." As this deposit grows larger and larger, and as creative philosophy is done less and less, the amalgam takes on a life of its own; it becomes *objectified.* Once this occurs the average man is no longer lord and master over his own fate. Having unwittingly *internalized* so many of the basic beliefs that the culture has provided for him, man thus becomes a *product* of the society himself. Simply put, the creature comes to serve the created.

Probably without any collusion from Berger, this idea seems to be one of the most compelling ideas behind much of modern science fiction. Whether it is "Hal" the computer in *2001: A Space Odyssey* or the virtual world depicted in films such as *The Matrix,* the fear instilled is real: what if what we believe to be true is actually false; what if the cultural forces we have unleashed now lie beyond our control? Berger sums up his theory thus:

> Society, then, is a product of man, rooted in the phenomenon of externalization, which in turn is grounded in the very biological constitution of man. . . . The humanly produced world becomes something "out there." It consists of objects, both material and non-material, that are capable of resisting the desires of their producer. Although all culture originates and is rooted in the subjective consciousness of human beings, once formed it cannot be reabsorbed into consciousness at will. It stands outside the subjectivity of the individual as, indeed, a world. In other words, the humanly produced world attains the character of objective reality.[167]

Once the consciousness of a society has become "objectified," it has become a "plausibility structure"—a device for interpreting reality. After a plausibility structure has taken shape, cultures become increasingly resistant to alternative interpretations of knowledge—even if such a theory

---

[167] Peter Berger, *The Sacred Canopy* (New York: Anchor Books/Doubleday, 1967), 8–9. The other important work that details Berger's sociology of religion is Peter Berger and Thomas Luckmann, *The Social Construction of Reality* (New York: Anchor Books/Doubleday, 1967).

offers a better interpretation of available evidence. In place of the pursuit of truth, the goal becomes socialization and control. People are forced to fit into a certain *gestalt,* a frozen form that serves to legitimate the socially objectivated "knowledge" that serves to explain and justify the social order's understanding of "the world." Stated differently, anyone "in the know" realizes that worldviews possess the power to control the thoughts and behaviors of average citizens.

Once a "plausibility structure" is in place, its tentacles reach into nearly every aspect of life. Disentangling persons from an anti-real worldview requires the skill of something approaching the intellectual equivalent of neurosurgery.

The theologian, of course, has a different term in his vocabulary to describe Berger's concept of "plausibility structures." The word is *idolatry.* The most pernicious gods of the human heart are not made of wood, stone, or precious metal. They are *ideas* which purport to have an independent and unaccountable status from the very God who makes thought possible. In conclusion, worldview preparation emerges as a crucial skill in apologetic encounters. One must carefully determine which intellectual idols are loose in a person's philosophical system, expose them, and, speaking the truth in love, show his neighbor how to bring that area of thought into greater conformity with the lordship of Christ (2 Cor. 10:5).

Building a Theological System

With the appropriate analysis of worldview formation in place, the theologian's task becomes a process of the construction of a network of theological positions. Millard Erickson offers an organized approach in which one moves from exegesis to biblical theology to systematic theology.[168] Erickson expands upon this progression by delineating a ten-step method. These steps are:

1. *Collection of the Biblical Materials* (involving the gathering of relevant Bible passages)
2. *Unification of the Biblical Materials* (What themes emerge from the Scriptures?)
3. *Analysis of the Meaning of Biblical Teachings* (What do these passages really mean?)
4. *Examination of Historical Treatments* (What has been the collective wisdom of the church on the issue throughout history?)

---

[168] Erickson, *Systematic Theology,* 70.

5. *Consultation of Other Cultural Perspectives* (What might we have missed due to our context that others might have seen?)
6. *Identification of the Essence of the Doctrine* ("distinguish the permanent, unvarying content of the doctrine from the cultural vehicle in which it is expressed")
7. *Illumination of Extrabiblical Sources* (What insights can general revelation or other disciplines offer to theology?)
8. *Contemporary Expression of the Doctrine* ("clothe the timeless truth in an appropriate form")
9. *Development of a Central Interpretive Motif* (Is there a particular theme that elucidates the theological project as a whole?)
10. *Stratification of the Topics* (Arrange "the topics on the basis of their relative importance.")[169]

How Does Theological Prolegomena Impact the Church Today?

In his 1975 missive, *Blessed Rage for Order,* University of Chicago theologian David Tracy opined that the historic understanding of the theologian as a guardian of a faith community's tradition was no longer an intellectually viable option. The modern theologian, Tracy continued, must pledge his allegiance to "that community of scientific inquiry" that demands a critical reconstruction of his church's tradition on the basis of a host of modern presuppositions.[170] Now some thirty years later, it is Tracy's understanding of the task of theology that appears to be outdated. At no other time in recent memory has the interest in tradition, biblical exegesis, and community-focused approaches in theology been more vibrant. Leading scholars whose roots come from, or are at least sympathetic to, evangelicalism or traditionalist Roman Catholicism, hold prominent positions in the academy.[171] Evangelical colleges and universities continue to grow in prestige and evangelical seminaries increasingly account for a disproportionate amount of the theological student population in North America.[172] Denominationally, liberal churches are experiencing an "exodus" of their laity who are moving to more conservative denominations.[173] In

[169] Ibid., 70–83.

[170] David Tracy, *Blessed Rage for Order* (Minneapolis: The Seabury Press, 1975), 6ff.

[171] A partial list includes Nicholas Wolterstorff, N. T. Wright, Robert P. George, Jean Bethke Elshtain, Oliver O'Donovan, et al.

[172] "Despite wealth, liberal seminaries losing students," *Presbyterian Layman Online*; available at: http://www.layman.org/layman/news/news-around-church/despite-wealth-liberal-seminaries.htm. The divide has grown wider in the years that have elapsed since the writing of this article.

[173] Dave Shiflett, *Exodus: Why Americans Are Fleeing Liberal Churches for Conservative Christianity* (New York: Sentinel, 2005).

the midst of this apparent renewal, there is a sense that theology, once again, should be written with church and congregational life in mind.

Even as the evangelical moment appears to be at a zenith, new debates about the future of evangelicalism divide representatives into partisan camps. These debates are epistemological in nature. Specifically, they center around how the church should respond to postmodernity, both at a methodological and a practical level. What specifically is meant by the term *postmodern*? Sociologist Zygmunt Bauman described modernity as being a process of melting old traditions and institutions and recasting them into new solid forms conducive to the spirit of the modern age (e.g., opening at "Temple of Reason" at the cathedral at Notre Dame). Bauman thus describes postmodernity as "liquid modernity." He explains his metaphor by explaining that our culture today is "an individualized, privatized version of modernity, with the burden of pattern-weaving and the responsibility for failure falling primarily on the individual's shoulders."

Even accepted "modern" patterns of thinking, Bauman continues, have now arrived at their "turn to be liquefied":

> They are now malleable to an extent unexperienced by, and unimaginable for, past generations; but like all fluids they do not keep their shape for long. Shaping them is easier than keeping them in shape. Solids are cast once and for all. Keeping fluids in shape requires a lot of attention, constant vigilance, and perpetual effort—and even then the success is anything but a foregone conclusion.[174]

Postmodernity, then, gives rise to an environment where eclecticism, tension, and even outright contradictions are embraced. As journalist David Brooks memorably explained, ours is an age of "Bourgeois Bohemians," or "Bobos":

> Marx once wrote that the bourgeois takes all that is sacred and makes it profane. The Bobos take everything that is profane and make it sacred. We have taken something that might have been grubby and materialistic and turned it into something elevated. We take the quintessential bourgeois activity, shopping, and turn it into quintessential bohemian activities: art, philosophy, social action. Bobos have the Midas touch in reverse. Everything we handle turns into soul.[175]

---

[174] Zygmunt Bauman, *Liquid Modernity* (Cambridge, England: Polity Press, 2000).
[175] David Brooks, *BOBOS in Paradise: The New Upper Class and How They Got There* (New York: Simon and Schuster, 2001), 102.

Although amusing, Brooks's analysis touches on something much more serious. People in America especially are spiritually hungry. The fact that they seek to feed their hunger in trivial ways does not mean that they cannot (and would not) turn to something of more substance. How does a pastor minister to people whose lives pivot on the trivial and the profound—all within the space of a minute? The current question before church leaders revolves around how best to preach the truth of the gospel to a generation that seems simultaneously to be confused by, and yet oddly drawn to, spiritual things.

Two responses view the postmodern situation from opposite sides of the spectrum. The first camp, often linked with the so-called "Emerging Church" movement, argues that evangelicals must embrace postmodernity, not excoriate it. University of Denver philosopher Carl Raschke, arguing for this position, believes that postmodernism is a style of critique that engenders faith, not an amoral metaphysic, as many commentators have claimed. Raschke refuses to defend the radical diversity (chaos?) of perspectives and claims that parade under the postmodern banner, but he does claim that "the postmodern revolution in philosophy . . . has tendered an environment where the Christian gospel can at last be disentangled from the centuries-long, modernist gnarl of scientism, rationalism, secularism, humanism, and skepticism."[176] Raschke thinks that such a cultural context provides an opportunity in which persons will be open to supernatural categories, personal conversion, and a radical return to biblical faith.

A number of other popular writers similarly see the possibilities of engaging the postmodern moment. The best known (and most significant) of them is Brian McLaren, author of two influential books in the Emerging Church movement—*A New Kind of Christian* and *A Generous Orthodoxy*.[177] McLaren's contributions are variously hilarious, outrageous, insightful, and maddening. But insofar as his writings relate to the theme of this chapter, it seems that McLaren despairs at the notion that theology can provide meaningful solutions to perennial philosophical and cultural questions. The postmodern subtitle of McLaren's book itself makes the point:

> Why I am a missional + evangelical + post/protestant + liberal/conservative + mystical poetic + biblical + charismatic/contemplative + fundamentalist / Calvinist + Anabaptist/anglican + methodist

---

[176] Carl Raschke, *The Next Reformation: Why Evangelicals Must Embrace Postmodernity* (Grand Rapids: Baker, 2004), 20–21.

[177] Brian McLaren, *A New Kind of Christian* (San Francisco: Jossey-Bass, 2001); and *A Generous Orthodoxy* (El Cajon, CA: Grand Rapids: Zondervan, 2004).

+ catholic + green + incarnational + depressed-yet-hopeful + emergent + unfinished Christian.[178]

Apparently, in McLaren's view, traditional theological analysis and patient exegesis are powerless to synthesize or referee various ecclesial traditions or to ever provide an "either/or" answer when a "both/and" will do. When defining evangelicalism, he explains, "I mean something beyond a belief system or doctrinal array or even a practice. I mean an attitude."[179] Whatever one thinks of the prospects of postmodern cultural engagement to bring people the good news of Jesus, one thing seems to be clear. According to the author of *A Generous Orthodoxy,* systematic theology as traditionally understood will not be a helpful tool in accomplishing that goal.

Even more provocative than McLaren's eclecticism on the prospects for theological method are the views of another prominent pastor in the Emerging Church movement, Rob Bell. Bell illustrates the task of theology as a "trampoline" to help propel ourselves closer to God. He writes in *Velvet Elvis: Repainting the Christian Faith*:

> When we jump, we begin to see the need for springs. The springs help make sense of the deeper realities that drive how we live every day. The springs aren't God. The springs aren't Jesus. The springs are statements and beliefs about our faith that help give words to the depth that we are experiencing in our jumping. I would call these the doctrines of the Christian faith.
>
> They aren't the point.
>
> They help us understand the point, but they are a means and not an end. We take them seriously, and at the same time we keep them in proper perspective. . . .
>
> Our words aren't absolutes. Only God is absolute, and God has no intention of sharing this absoluteness with anything, especially words people have come up with to talk about Him. This is something people have struggled with since the beginning: how to talk about God when God is bigger than our words, our brains, our worldviews, and our imaginations. . . .
>
> This truth about God is why study and discussion and doctrines are so necessary. They help us put words to realities beyond words. They give us insight and understanding into the experience of God

---

[178] D. A. Carson gives a playful rejoinder that McLaren's book "is an attractive + manipulative + funny + sad + informed + ignorant + winsome + outrageous + penetrating + resoundingly false + stimulating + silly book." *Becoming Conversant with the Emerging Church* (Grand Rapids: Zondervan, 2005), 162. Carson's review of the Emerging Church movement is balanced, gracious, and insightful.

[179] McLaren, *Generous Orthodoxy,* 117–18.

we're having. Which is why the springs only work when they serve the greater cause: us finding our lives in God. If they ever become the point, something has gone seriously wrong. Doctrine is a wonderful servant and a horrible master.[180]

Bell is admittedly a popularizer of these issues and does not claim to dispatch complex issues about theological hermeneutics here in an exhaustive way. Certainly his words serve as a helpful reminder that the task of theology itself can become a form of idolatry in which the theologian worships his dogmatic formulation and not the God he serves. But there also may be a danger that Bell's casual, friendly, and post-hip manner of addressing holy things runs the risk of trivializing the goal he wants to reach—a personal, holy adoration of God.

When we confess in the Apostles' Creed that Jesus Christ our Lord was the only begotten Son of God, conceived by the Holy Spirit, and born of the virgin Mary, we are not bouncing on a trampoline (an unfortunate image). We are bowing low to worship holy mysteries while confessing our confidence in historical verities that resulted in our salvation. And when we utter the propositional statement, "Human beings are created in the image of God, and therefore life is sacred and worthy of protection," we are not verbalizing merely human words struggling for authenticity. We are saying something that is near to the heart of God because the Almighty has told us so in his Word.

Consequently, the church should work to replace abortion by adoption and stop the genocide in places like Darfur and the Sudan. Most assuredly, the greatest danger in deprecating the value of theological propositions and assertions is a diminution of the prophetic voice of the church to the culture. Dorothy Sayers has put it best:

> It is worse than useless for Christians to talk about the importance of Christian morality, unless they are prepared to take their stand upon the fundamentals of Christian theology. It is a lie to say that dogma does not matter; it matters enormously. It is fatal to let people suppose that Christianity is only a mode of feeling; it is virtually necessary to insist that it is first and foremost a rational explanation of the universe. It is hopeless to offer Christianity as a vaguely idealistic aspiration of a simple and consoling kind; it is, on the contrary, a hard, tough, exacting, and complex doctrine, steeped in a drastic and uncompromising realism.[181]

---

[180] Rob Bell, *Velvet Elvis: Repainting the Christian Faith* (Grand Rapids: Zondervan, 2005), 22–23, 25.
[181] Dorothy Sayers, *Creed or Chaos?* (London: Matheun, 1947), 28.

Immense challenges face the evangelical church in the twenty-first century regarding how best to reach a postmodern generation of people with the good news. More than ever, ministers of the Word of God must keep up with the philosophical and cultural currents that hold sway over the minds of those whom they seek to serve. Once regarded as the province of intellectuals, the study of epistemology has become a necessary tool for apologetics and well-rounded evangelism in an increasingly sophisticated Western world. As Os Guinness has written:

> Indeed, what we face today is the need for a "third mission to the West," or in the words of the new Pope Benedict XVI, "the re-evangelization of the West." For those who know God and the power of the gospel, history is never deterministic, no odds are so overwhelming that it's ever all over, and no door is truly closed unless God has closed it.
>
> Winning back the West will not be the work of five minutes, five months, or five years. It may take a hundred years, for the hardest spheres of our society such as the universities are not going to be won without immense toil and perseverance. And our motive must not be to win back the West for the West's sake (or for the sake of America or Europe, or even for democracy or civilization), but to win back the West for Christ's sake—out of faithfulness to the Great Commission. In other words, our concern is the West, not because it is in any way superior and worth saving—we could easily argue the opposite—but because the West is our Jerusalem and our Judea, from which we must join hands with others around the world and reach out to bring the gospel also to Samaria and the uttermost parts of the earth.[182]

Even as this new vision for evangelism appears, the hard work of theological prolegomena in the Christian academy must go on in order to support the effort. Old paradigms should be challenged if they are not faithful to the Bible's radical claim to knowledge. Vigorous debate and theological conversation must mark the hour. New proposals that challenge secularism deserve ongoing reflection. The "radical orthodoxy" movement, which challenges the notion that any "secular" or autonomous realm of thought exists, comes to mind.[183] The situation calls for careful analysis of traditional evangelical approaches to see if there are legitimate ways to extend

---

[182] Os Guinness, "Third Mission to the West," in *Kairos Journal* [online]; available at: http://www.kairosjournal.org/InsightDetail.aspx?InsightID=45.

[183] James K. A. Smith, *Radical Orthodoxy* (Grand Rapids, MI: Baker, 2004).

their contributions with added philosophical and hermeneutical balance. Kevin Vanhoozer's recent work is a leading voice in this connection.[184]

But those who offer a warning about what might be lost in theological reformulation in the postmodern age need to be heard as well. Millard Erickson cautions, "History shows . . . that a theology that blends too fully with its culture tends to prosper and decline with its culture, an appropriate exhortation for those who wish to replace modernism in evangelicalism with a postmodern *Zeitgeist*."[185] Similarly, in his plenary address at the 2004 annual meeting of the Evangelical Theological Society, R. Albert Mohler offered a needed word of challenge to those assembled about the temptation to scale back the evangelical presentation of truth, rather than expanding upon it:

> Contemporary culture presents us with a challenge, but in essence it is the same challenge that has confronted the church all along. We still stand where Paul stood in Acts 17. We have to give the same answer he gave. If we as evangelicals are not committed to a theological method with a robust understanding of truth, there is a great and imminent danger that Christ will not in fact be glorified, the Bible will not be obeyed, the gospel will not be preached, and the Kingdom will not be extended. Let us therefore be determined to be a people who will say more, but who will never say less.[186]

The task of staying committed to the truth of the Bible over and against the philosophies of men requires constant vigilance. God's people cannot afford to pursue such an undertaking without a firm commitment to life together in community, a willingness to submit to spiritual authority, and the courage to maintain a prophetic voice in culture. Mental agility without a personal relationship with the triune God will doubtless terminate in grave error or, even worse, apostasy. By drinking deeply from the wells of our fathers before us, the living church of Jesus Christ will press forward with all humility and confidence in the God who speaks, shows, stands, and stays.

---

[184] Kevin Vanhoozer, "Lost in Interpretation? Truth, Scripture, and Hermeneutics," in JETS 48 (March 2005) 1:89–114.

[185] Erickson continues: "It is obvious that none of us is completely objective in his or her thinking. We are all affected by the conditioning of our historical situation in culture. Rather than simply acknowledging this fact, however, [a new vision] for theology will seek self-understanding, together with taking steps to counter those conditioning influences." See Millard Erickson, "Evangelicalism and the Spirit of Our Age," interview by Crossway, *Crossway's Book Report* 3, no. 1 (Spring 2005): 6. Erickson expands on these ideas in "On Flying in Theological Fog," in Millard Erickson, Paul Kjoss Helseth, and Justin Taylor, eds., *Reclaiming the Center: Confronting Evangelical Accomodation in Postmodern Times* (Wheaton, IL: Crossway, 2004), 323–50.

[186] R. Albert Mohler, "What Is Truth? Truth and Contemporary Culture," in *JETS* 48 (March 2005) 1:75.

CHAPTER 2

Natural Revelation

Russell D. Moore

W hat did a young Jesus of Nazareth see when he gazed at the moon in the Galilean skies above him? This was, after all, the same moon that once prompted the psalmist to ponder the promised reign of the son of man (Ps. 8:3–6).[1] This moon was an ancient witness to God's faithfulness to his messianic promise to seat one of David's offspring on the Israelite throne forever (Ps. 89:36–37; 72:5–8). The rhythms of this moon in ordering times and seasons reflect the *Logos* that set it in motion (Gen. 1:16–18; Ps. 104:19; John 1:3). In truth this moon pointed to the young man from Nazareth himself—by whom and for whom it was created (Col. 1:16). And yet this same moon had for centuries served as an object of idolatry for rebellious humanity. The patriarch Abraham followed Yahweh from Ur, a region renowned for the worship of the moon gods. The Israelites were warned against joining their Canaanite neighbors in the worship of the moon (Deut. 4:19; 17:3; 2 Kings 23:5).[2] The righteous Job noted the human temptation to forsake the Creator Yahweh for the worship of "the moon moving in splendor" across the sky (Job 31:26–27).

But how can the same night sky evoke both worship and idolatry, both awe and superstition? The dilemma is magnified when one considers that the moon is only one example of a tension found throughout Scripture—nature is the revelation of God, and this revelation is always subverted by fallen humanity. This strikes against one of the most widely debated facets of Christian theology—what theologians call "general revelation" or "natural revelation." General revelation is the self-disclosure of God to all rational beings, a revelation that comes through the natural creation and through the makeup of the human creature. Natural theology is the attempt to build a theological structure on the basis of general revelation apart from God's witness in the Scriptures and in Jesus Christ.

---

[1] Unless otherwise noted, all Scripture citations in this chapter are from the English Standard Version (ESV).

[2] For a discussion of the moon cult in Ur and the rest of ancient Sumerian civilization, see Mark E. Cohen, "The Sun, the Moon, and the City of Ur," in *Religion and Politics in the Ancient Near East,* ed. Adele Berlin (Bethesda, MD: University Press of Maryland, 1996), 7–20.

71

'general' vs.
'special'

Biblical scholar C. John Collins contrasts general and special revelation by explaining that "general revelation comes to all people everywhere (hence it is 'general'), while special revelation is what God has specially revealed of himself in his covenant, made to his chosen people (Israel and the church)."[3] The challenge in constructing a thoroughgoing evangelical theology of general revelation lies in maintaining this biblical tension between the reality and the limits of general revelation, between the clarity of God's disclosure and the distortion of it by fallen humanity.

What Does the Bible Say?

That the Bible is necessary to define and explain general revelation highlights the tension between the universality of God's revelation and the universality of human rebellion against it. While no one passage expounds a full-blown theology of general revelation, both Old and New Testaments affirm that God has disclosed himself everywhere to all human beings. The special revelation of Scripture brings into focus the varieties and extent of this general revelation.

General Revelation in the Old Testament

Genesis 1–3

The Hebrew Scriptures begin with a narrative that is as far from a "natural theology" as one can imagine. Indeed it serves to correct the natural theologies of the pagan cultures—superstitions about nature that would be a perpetual pull for the people of God to idolatry (Exod. 20:4). Genesis reveals that nature is not self-created or divine but is the result of the creative activity of Yahweh, the God of Israel. The concept of God as universal Creator is foundational to the canonical vision of general revelation. Walther Eichrodt argues:

> It is true that the Babylonian priests also saw an important manifestation of the power of God in the fact that the Creator formed the cosmos in a purposeful order, and set its life in fixed paths; and Egyptian hymns too testify that this derivation of the world-order from a mighty creative will was part of an international priestly wisdom. A loving absorption in the marvelous organism of Nature, and in its witness to the power of its divine Creator, forms a link between the religion of Israel and the knowledge of God to be found in the higher religions of paganism. But this conception could only come

---

[3] C. John Collins, *Science and Faith: Friends or Foes?* (Wheaton, IL: Crossway, 2003), 181–82.

to full development where it was combined with the recognition that God was a transcendent Being, beside whom no force of Nature could pretend to divine status, and who, moreover, was himself in no danger of degenerating into a kind of vivifying cosmic energy. Only so could the unqualified dependence of the world on God—to the point of conceiving Creation as *ex nihilo*—be safeguarded.[4]

While the claim to "knowledge of God" in the "higher" religions of Israel's neighbors does not stand up to the exclusive claims of the text, Eichrodt is correct that the kind of general revelation affirmed in the rest of the Old and New Testaments could not be possible with a pantheistic, panentheistic, or animistic God concept.

Moreover, the Genesis cosmology does not simply unveil the origins of the universe but explains something of the creative purpose behind such natural phenomena as day and night (1:18), the changing of the seasons (1:14), human sexuality and gender roles (2:24), and the distinction between humanity and the rest of the creation (1:26–28). Genesis does not, however, simply explain nature. It identifies aspects of the cosmic order that are not "natural" at all but are indications that something has gone terribly awry in the fabric of creation. Death (2:16; 3:19), alienation (3:7–9), and the frustration of the human mandates of procreation and creativity (3:15–19) are not part of the rhythms of "nature" but are instead aspects of an ancient curse on the creation and its human rulers.

Job 38–41

In this ancient text a suffering God fearer hears the revelation of God in nature analyzed by Yahweh himself, speaking from a whirlwind in response to Job's complaints. In this narrative, the cosmos is said not only to speak of the provision and artisanship of the Creator, but it also indicates his transcendence, holiness, and freedom. This passage is all the more significant given the faulty "natural theologies" offered by Job's counselors to explain the ways of Yahweh with his creation in the preceding chapters. God points to the intricate design of the universe—in terms of the atmosphere, the seas, and animal life—as revelations of his sovereignty, wisdom, and goodness. In this passage God is revealed not only in the natural order but also in humanity itself. "Who has put wisdom in the inward parts or given understanding to the mind?" Yahweh asks in Job 38:36.

Significantly, what is *not* known is revelatory, as well as that which is clearly perceived in the creation. The mysteriousness of the universe speaks to the otherness of the Creator. "What is the way to the place where the light

---

4 Walther Eichrodt, *Theology of the Old Testament,* vol. 1, trans. J. A. Baker (Philadelphia: Westminster, 1961), 413.

is distributed," Yahweh taunts. "Or where the east wind is scattered upon the earth?" (Job 38:24). The implied answer is no, demonstrating the dependence of Job—and all creation—on the Creator God. Similarly, the relative power-lessness of humanity over the natural order reveals the finitude of humanity alongside the might of the Creator. God recounts for Job a dizzying array of natural phenomena and creatures over which Job has no control and contrasts this with the normative patterns of nature that reveal the provision of God.

Job's response recognizes not only the wisdom and power of Yahweh but also that Job himself is "of small account" before the God who creates and sustains such a universe (Job 40:4–5). His response to this revelation is not the theological speculation of his interlocutors or his own previous boastful contentiousness but is instead repentant silence and trustful depen-dence on his Creator (Job 40:15–41:34). The sovereignty and goodness of God in the natural order are tied, therefore, to his sovereignty and goodness in the moral order, a truth to which the righteous Job submits in faith.[5]

Nature Psalms

Perhaps the clearest proclamation of general revelation in the Hebrew Scripture is found in Psalm 19 where David extols the goodness of Yahweh in revealing himself both to all creation in the natural order (19:1–6) and to Israel in the Torah of Moses (19:7–14).[6] The psalmist does not merely point to the existence of the creation as an indication of a first cause but instead proclaims that the skies above reveal both the glory (19:1) and the vast creativity (19:2) of the Creator. This revelation in nature is said to be rational and propositional as it "reveals knowledge" (19:2). Indeed, the cre-ation discloses enough knowledge about nature's God that the natural order is analogous to human speech (19:2).

This revelation is not limited to the covenant community but is as uni-versal as the universe itself.[7] There is no place where the "voice" of cre-

---

[5] "Job can no more pronounce judgment in the moral realm (40:10–14) than he could control the natural realm, the subject of the previous speech. He must, therefore, be content to leave his life and its issues with God. He dare not provoke God any more than he would provoke Behemoth (40:15–24) or Leviathan (chap. 41), denizens of land and sea." William J. Dumbrell, *The Faith of Israel: A Theological Survey of the Old Testament,* 2nd ed. (Grand Rapids: Baker, 2002), 358–59.

[6] Some have seen significance in the psalmist's use of the creational title *Elohim* in the refer-ence to general revelation in the first section of this psalm in contrast to his use of the revealed covenantal title *Yahweh* in reference to special revelation in the latter section. See, for instance, Gordon R. Lewis and Bruce Demarest, *Integrative Theology,* vol. 1 (Grand Rapids: Zondervan, 1987), 68; and H. Leo Eddleman, "Word Pictures of the Word: An Exposition of Psalm 19," *RevExp* 49 (1952): 415.

[7] Paul House connects the "general revelation" theme of Psalm 19:1–6 with the special revela-tion theme of the rest of the psalm by showing that "God's word complements nature as a means of teaching monotheism and its meaning with the context of Yahweh's work with Israel. Creation points to the Creator; then the revealed word gives specific substance to the nature of the Creator." Paul R. House, *Old Testament Theology* (Downers Grove: InterVarsity, 1998), 410.

ation is mute (19:3–4), even at the outermost edges of the creation (19:4).[8]
This revelation is not found simply in the intricacy of the creation design but
also in the patterns of the cosmic order. The regularity of the rising and setting sun proclaims the creational sovereignty and universal reign of Yahweh
(19:4–6).[9] The poetry of this psalm is unique in ancient Near Eastern literature precisely because this cosmic revelation is rooted in Israelite creational
monotheism. Peter Craigie has noted that in pagan hymns to nature "nature
itself is deified; the gods are praised in nature" while in Psalm 19 "nature is
personified, not deified, and personified nature raises the chorus of praise to
the only Creator and only deity, the one true God."[10]

Like Psalm 19, Psalm 8 considers the self-disclosure of God in the starry
expanse above (8:1–3).[11] Here David again leads the Israelite community
to extol the "glory" of God seen in the "handiwork" of the creation, even
speaking of the majestic firmament as the work of the "fingers" of Yahweh
(8:3). It is not simply the design of the cosmos, however, that evokes such
wonder in the psalmist. The vastness of the universe—seen especially in
the canopy of the night sky—prompts David to marvel at the smallness of
human beings (8:3–4). Indeed, here a contemplation of the general revelation of God in nature propels the psalmist back to the special revelation of
Genesis and the rest of the Torah. It would not seem in the face of the sheer
immensity of the universe that the Creator would be "mindful" of relatively
tiny organisms such as human beings. And yet Yahweh, whose glory is seen
in the creation, has granted such glory to human beings. The Creator God,
who exercises lordship over his handiwork, grants to humanity "dominion"
over "the works of his hands," even putting all things under the feet of his
human vice-regents (8:6–8).

As the writer of Hebrews will argue centuries later in consideration of
this passage, this truth is not obvious in the creation itself since "we do not
yet see everything in subjection to him" (Heb. 2:8). Instead, the covenant

---

[8] Millard J. Erickson correctly observes that verse 3 is the most hermeneutically difficult section
of this passage, a difficulty on which several historic disputes over the nature of general revelation
have hung. Millard J. Erickson, *Christian Theology,* 2nd ed. (Grand Rapids: Baker, 1998), 192–93.
Contrary to the Barthian denial of general revelation, this text does not teach that the heavenly bodies do not communicate but rather that they do so inaudibly yet universally.

[9] As with Genesis 1–2, some scholars see in Psalm 19 a polemic against the pagan nations' worship
of the astral bodies. See J. Clinton McCann Jr., "The Book of Psalms: Introduction, Commentary,
and Reflections," in NIBD 4:751–52.

[10] Peter C. Craigie, *Psalms 1–50,* WBC (Waco: Word, 1983), 181.

[11] Bruce Demarest argues that "nature psalms" such as Psalms 8, 92, and 104 should not be categorized under a consideration of general revelation since they "represent songs from the perspective of
faith." Bruce A. Demarest, *General Revelation: Historical Views and Contemporary Issues* (Grand
Rapids: Zondervan, 1982), 237. This seems, however, to posit an unbiblical segregation between
general and special revelation. Psalm 19, after all, is also written "from the perspective of faith."
These psalms illuminate what is revealed in general revelation with what is revealed in the covenant
oracles of God. This is precisely what is happening elsewhere, as seen, for instance, in the Pauline
discussion of general revelation in Romans 1 and 2.

community understands the uniqueness of man in the cosmos on the basis of the biblical revelation about the creation of humanity in Adam and the new creation of humanity in Christ (Heb. 2:9).

The Psalms also point to the creation as revelatory of the covenant faithfulness and benevolent purposes of God. Psalm 104, for instance, points to the intimidating enormity of the atmosphere and geography of the earth system as a signal of the "greatness" of Yahweh (104:1–9). The creativity and power of God is also seen in the magnitude and diversity of the creatures of the earth (104:24–26). But the passage simultaneously identifies the patterns and rhythms of the creation as revelatory of the goodness and provision of the Creator. This cosmic rhythm is seen in the cycles of rain and sunlight necessary for the sustenance and nourishment of creatures (104:14–15, 27–28), the regularity of the days and seasons (104:19–20), the nesting cycles of wildlife (104:17–18), and the mysterious interplay between predator and prey (104:20–22).

Here the psalmist identifies a theme articulated repeatedly by Yahweh in the oracles of Israel, as the general revelation in nature is illuminated by the special revelation of God through the prophets. The stability and predictability of the natural order is illustrative of the covenant faithfulness and unchangeable purposes of God. The vastness of the cosmos, for instance, indicates the infinity of his "steadfast love" for his people (Ps. 103:11). The permanence of the moon, stars, and sun throughout the generations indicates the permanence of God's commitment to his covenant promises (Pss. 72:5; 89:36).

The Prophetic Writings

Like the psalmist the prophets affirm that the stability of God's "covenant" with the cycle of days and seasons indicates the stability of his covenant promises to vindicate his people and establish his kingdom. This is especially evident in the prophecies of Jeremiah to an Israelite nation under siege, a nation for whom all empirical evidence seemed to suggest that God had revoked his ancient covenants with Abraham and David. Through Jeremiah, Yahweh confirms the certainty of the promise of a new covenant by reminding Israel that it is he "who gives the sun for light by day and the fixed order of the moon and the stars for light by night, who stirs up the sea so that its waves roar" (Jer. 31:35). With this being the case, Yahweh declares, "If this fixed order departs from before me . . . then shall the offspring of Israel cease from being a nation before me forever" (Jer. 31:36).

But, of course, observation of nature reveals the stability of this order from generation to generation. "If I can break my covenant with the day and my covenant with the night, so that day and night will not come at their appointed time, then also my covenant with David my servant may be broken, so that he shall not have a son to reign on his throne" (Jer. 33:20). Perhaps it is significant that, in the New Testament, the godforsakenness of the curse-bearing Davidic son at his crucifixion is marked with a day shrouded in darkness (Matt. 27:45–46), and with the instability of an earth quaking beneath the feet of the Israelites (Matt. 27:51). After this seeming covenantal abandonment, however, the gospels note the transition from evening to morning (Matt. 27:57,62), the "fixed order" of darkness giving way to dawn (Matt. 28:1) even as the covenant promises to David are kept in the resurrection of Jesus (Acts 2:29–33; Rom. 1:2–4).

According to prophets such as Jeremiah, the people of Israel should know not only the faithfulness of God through the natural order, but they should also recognize his sovereign power to keep such promises. Hearkening back to the Abrahamic covenant's imagery of a nation as numerous as the stars of the sky (Gen. 15:5), Jeremiah directed the nation to the immensity of the created order as a signal of the power of their covenant God (Jer. 33:22). "If the heavens above can be measured, and the foundations of the earth below can be explored, then I will cast off all the offspring of Israel for all that they have done," Yahweh says to the people of Israel (Jer. 31:37). Observation of the natural order, it is presupposed, will reveal that humans indeed cannot quantify such a vast universe.

The prophets also disclosed something of God's general revelation in human nature. In their polemics against idolatry, for instance, both Jeremiah and Isaiah appealed to the rationality of their hearers (Isa. 44:9–20; Jer. 10:1–16).[12] Isaiah ridiculed the workman who plants a tree, cuts it down, kindles a fire, and then with the same lumber "makes a god and worships it" (Isa. 44:15). As Collins observes, "Isaiah appeals to the common sense of his hearers, not to special revelation."[13] Nonetheless, Isaiah highlighted the suppression of this "common sense" seen in the race toward idolatry. In terms as stark as those of the Apostle Paul in Romans 3, Isaiah described the folly of idolatry:

> No one considers, nor is there knowledge or discernment to say, "Half of it I burned in the fire; I also baked bread on its coals; I roasted meat and have eaten. And shall I make the rest of it an abomination? Shall I fall down before a block of wood?" He feeds on ashes; a deluded heart has led him astray, and he cannot deliver himself or say, "Is there not a lie in my right hand?" (Isa. 44:18–20).

---

12 Isaiah, speaking through the Spirit, is not the only one to have made this charge against man-made idols. Classical writers such as Horace, completely apart from special revelation, made similar taunts. "Once I was a trunk of a fig tree, a useless piece of wood, when a carpenter, uncertain whether to make a bench or a Priapus, preferred that I should be a god; and so I became a god." Edward J. Young, *The Book of Isaiah* (Grand Rapids: Eerdmans, 1972), 3:177–78.

13 Collins, *Science and Faith,* 187.

Human beings *ought* to know that idolatry is folly, but they deny the truth because they are in moral revolt against it.

One might not immediately think of plowing and planting as forms of general revelation, but Isaiah indicates that the insights of agriculture are drawn from the structures of cosmic order, placed in the fabric of the universe by the Creator. "Does he who plows for sowing plow continually? Does he continually open and harrow his ground?" Isaiah asks. "When he has leveled its surface, does he not scatter dill, sow cumin, and put in wheat in rows and barley in its proper place, and emmer as the border?" (Isa. 28:24–25). This knowledge does not come from autonomous human reason but from divine revelation. "For he is rightly instructed; his God teaches him" (Isa. 28:26).

This revelation furthermore is a gracious disclosure of God, which communicates truth about the deity's wisdom and goodness: "This also comes from the LORD of hosts; he is wonderful in counsel and excellent in wisdom" (Isa. 28:29). Alec Motyer explains the force of this prophecy: "What appears as a discovery (the proper season and conditions for sowing, farm management, rotation of crops, etc.) is actually the Creator opening his book of creation and revealing his truth—but revealing himself also, for can the God who teaches purpose be less than purposeful himself?"[14] The tilling of the ground should impress on the human mind the cause-and-effect laws the Creator has ingrained into his cosmos. As natural law theorist J. Budziszewski reflects on this passage, God "teaches" the farmer because agriculture depends on human beings observing the design of nature and submitting to its inbuilt disciplines through trial and error:

> One can imagine a universe in which this sort of thing could not happen. Nature might have been so designed that the patterns of cause and effect were too elusive for human observation and too subtle and complex to be learned by trial and error. Or nature might have been designed without any cause and effect whatsoever. In such a world, neither method of instruction would work. But we have been placed in a different kind of world, a world which does have causal patterns, in which causes are an index to purposes, and in which the patterns and causality and purpose most important to human life are at just the right scale for us to learn them. Experience assists wisdom because the universe has been designed to make it so.[15]

---

[14] J. Alec Motyer, *The Prophecy of Isaiah: An Introduction and Commentary* (Downers Grove: InterVarsity, 1993), 235–36.

[15] J. Budziszewski, *What We Can't Not Know: A Guide* (Dallas: Spence, 2003), 229.

Proverbs

Nowhere is the revelatory value of the cause-and-effect rules within the creation order more emphasized than in the wisdom literature of the Proverbs. As in Isaiah, this "wisdom" is not defined as intelligence or cunning but rather as understanding the patterns and principles God has built into his creation. Thus, Proverbs identifies features in the natural order that are "exceedingly wise," namely ants, rock badgers, locusts, and lizards (Prov. 30:24–28), all of which function according to a creation design. As Tremper Longman observes, these animals are not "intelligent" necessarily, but they "know how to navigate life well."[16] For the Proverbs, this means that there is embedded in the creation order a "way of wisdom" to which human beings are called to conform (Prov. 4:11).[17] The Proverbs root this wisdom not in common sense but in the "wisdom of God" found in the order of the cosmos—a wisdom present in the architecture of the universe from the very beginning (Prov. 3:19; 8:20–36).[18] This order can be perceived in the created order—and indeed it is senseless "folly" not to recognize it (Prov. 9:13).[19]

Thus, the Proverbs counsel humans to seek wisdom not in creation-denying asceticism or mind-clouding mysticism but by perceiving the "way of wisdom" in the mundane patterns of creation—such as the foresight and organization of the ant or the cause-and-effect principles of agriculture (Prov. 24:30–31). The Proverbs do not assume that human beings readily apprehend this "way of wisdom"—though it is obvious. Instead, the Proverbs speak of the deception of "the way of the wicked" which is "like deep darkness" (Prov. 4:19). Indeed, the Proverbs warn that the "way that seems right to a man" leads not to wisdom but to death (Prov. 16:25). And where there is

---

16 Tremper Longman, *How to Read Proverbs* (Downers Grove: InterVarsity, 2002), 15.

17 "Wisdom thus consisted in knowing that at the bottom of things an order is at work, silently and often in a scarcely noticeable way, making for a balance of events." Gerhard von Rad, *Old Testament Theology,* vol. 1, trans. D. M. G. Stalker (San Francisco: Harper Collins, 1962), 428.

18 This is not to say that "Lady Wisdom" in the Proverbs is a feminine expression of God. Instead, the figure represented here is a personification of the wisdom inherent in the creation of God—contrasted with another personification, "Lady Folly." Misinterpretations of this literary device have led to dangerous doctrinal deviations from orthodox Christianity—as seen from the early Arian constructs of the preincarnate Christ as "made" at the beginning of creation (Prov. 8:22) to the contemporary "Sophia" goddess movements of feminist theology. As Duane Garrett rightly observes, the wisdom portrayed here is an attribute of creation, not directly the second person of the Trinity. Duane Garrett, *Proverbs, Ecclesiastes, Song of Songs,* NAC (Nashville: Broadman & Holman, 1993), 112–13. This does not mean that this wisdom, however, is not ultimately derivative of and patterned after the eternal wisdom of God, the *Logos.*

19 Walter Brueggemann rightly observes that in Old Testament wisdom literature "Yahweh is the hidden guarantor of an order that makes life in the world possible." In proverbs and other wisdom sayings, Israel "marvels at, ponders, sings about, and counts on that good order without which life would not be possible." Walter Brueggemann, *Theology of the Old Testament: Testimony, Dispute, Advocacy* (Minneapolis: Fortress, 1997), 336.

no prophetic revelation, "the people cast off restraint" (Prov. 29:18). Instead, the "beginning of wisdom" is the fear of Yahweh (Prov. 9:10).[20]

General Revelation in the New Testament

The Gospels

The most debated passage from the New Testament Gospels concerning general revelation has been the prologue to John. Here the apostle identifies the incarnate Christ with the preexistent *Logos* through which God created and continually sustains all creation and all creatures (John 1:1–4). Although the "light" of the *Logos* is specifically identified in John with special revelation (John 3:19–20; 8:12; 9:5), in the prologue this *Logos* is said somehow to "enlighten every man" (John 1:9 NASB).[21] A sizable amount of scholarly attention has gone to the Johannine appropriation of the term *Logos* from the Greek philosophical traditions, especially the Stoic concept of *Logos* as the rational ordering principle of the cosmos. And yet John's use of *Logos*—a personal being who takes on a human nature—breaks with the *Logos* metaphysics of hellenic thought at crucial points and evokes instead the creative "Word" and "Wisdom" motifs of the Old Testament.[22]

The teachings of Jesus contain no systematic exposition of general revelation, but the Gospels do assume some form of universal revelation, however fragmentary or distorted. Jesus of Nazareth is, of course, himself special revelation (John 1:18; Heb. 1:2–3). And yet it is significant that, when addressing the crowds in parables and analogies, Jesus asks: "What do you think?" (Matt. 21:28). In continuity with the Old Testament Scriptures, the teachings of Jesus draw upon the patterns of the creation order to reveal something about the character and purposes of God.

Like the psalmist, Jesus points to the beauty and order of the creation to illuminate the fatherly providence of God and to reveal proper human response to such truth (Matt. 6:24–35). He finds in the affection and provision of a human father for his children—and in a human shepherd for his

---

[20] As Paul House observes, this theme in Proverbs reinforces the wisdom literature's insistence that "human beings are incapable of becoming wise without divine revelation." House, *Old Testament Theology*, 450.

[21] Translators have long disagreed on whether to translate John 1:9 with the phrase "coming into the world" modifying every man or the light itself. The KJV, NKJV, NIV, and HCSB opt for the former while the NASB, RSV, ESV, and NRSV opt for the latter. This lexical decision has implications for a theology of the *Logos* in terms of general revelation. For some scholars the verse indicates not the "inner illumination" of general revelation but the proclamation of Christ in the gospel. For this view see D. A. Carson, *The Gospel According to John*, PNTC (Grand Rapids: Eerdmans, 1991), 123–24.

[22] This case is argued compellingly, linking John's prologue with Proverbs, the Psalms, and the Wisdom of Solomon in Larry W. Hurtado, *Lord Jesus Christ: Devotion to Jesus in Earliest Christianity* (Grand Rapids: Eerdmans, 2003), 365–68. For a discussion of the marked difference between Stoic and Johannine conceptions of the *Logos,* see Carl F. H. Henry, *God, Revelation and Authority,* vol. 3, *God Who Speaks and Shows, Fifteen Theses, Part Two* (Waco: Word, 1979), 186–91.

lost sheep—a revelation of the affection and provision of the Father God for his people (Matt. 7:9–11; 18:10–14). Jesus appeals to the innate human sense of justice and fairness to affirm the justice and impartiality of a righteous God (Luke 18:1–7). Like the Proverbs, Jesus uses agriculture analogically to teach patterns of sowing and reaping, present both in the inanimate creation and in human moral relationships (Luke 6:43–45).[23]

Acts 14:8–18

In this narrative Luke recounts the preaching of Paul and Barnabas in the Gentile city of Lystra. After the apostle healed a crippled man, the crowds swarmed around the Christians, thinking Barnabas to be the pagan god Zeus and Paul to be Hermes. In his speech against this conduct, Paul maintained both the general revelation of God to all humanity and human suppression of this revelation. Paul reasoned with the crowds about the vanity of worshipping beings who are "of like nature with you" (Acts 14:15a). He contrasted the "vain things" they sought to worship with a "living God, who made the heaven and the earth and the sea and all that is in them" (Acts 14:15b).

These Gentiles were not without knowledge of this God, Paul contended, since God "did not leave himself without witness" among them. This revelation is defined as the benevolent provision of God in nature, "giving you rains from heaven and fruitful seasons, satisfying your hearts with food and gladness" (Acts 14:17). These occurrences in nature, the apostle proclaimed, should have led the nations to recognize the reality and the benevolence of the one Creator God (Acts 14:15–17). This revelation does not translate into a "natural theology" constructed by the pagan nations, much less a means of salvation. Even with this witness God "allowed all the nations to walk in their own ways" (Acts 14:16).

This suppression of the truth is seen throughout this narrative. The people of Lystra are steeped in the idolatrous worship of false deities, even after the apostolic preaching (special revelation) points them to the ongoing witness of God to them (general revelation). Luke concludes the narrative with a note of sadness: "Even with these words they scarcely restrained the people from offering sacrifice to them" (Acts 14:18).

Acts 17:16–34

Most of the apostolic preaching directly recorded in the New Testament is targeted to Jews and Gentile God fearers—both groups that were anchored in the Old Testament special revelation. Here, however, the Apostle

---

[23] The apostolic teaching continues this analogical connection throughout the New Testament. Paul employs the truth of sowing and reaping to teach the church at Galatia the inevitability of consequences for moral decisions (Gal. 6:7–8). To the church at Corinth, Paul draws from the principles of farming and animal husbandry to inform his discussion of the resurrection body and the degrees of glory in the new creation (1 Cor. 15:35–49). James likewise builds on both farming and animal husbandry to teach the relationship between nature and conduct (James 3:3–12) and the necessity of patience (James 5:7–8).

Paul announces the gospel to an assembly of Athenian philosophers—specifically identified by Luke as Stoic and Epicurean thinkers. Both philosophies were related at least tangentially to the Greek polytheism that so "provoked" Paul from the architecture of the city's temples (17:16). They were otherwise different—with Stoicism holding to a rationalistic pantheism and Epicureanism to quasi-naturalistic materialism.[24] Summoned before the Areopagus, Paul engaged both groups with his "new teaching" of Jesus and the resurrection (17:18). Here Paul begins his remarks with a reference to the "unknown god" inscribed on an Athenian altar, declaring that he would proclaim to them "what you worship in ignorance" (17:23 NASB).

In his speech Paul appealed to several points he believed the Athenians *already* knew—or ought to know. They should know, he said, that the divine could not be limited to human temples or human workmanship (17:23–25,29). They should know that human beings are dependent on God for existence—and not the other way around (17:25–29). They should realize that a Creator of humanity would seek to be acknowledged and found by his creatures (17:27–28). In the course of the argument, the apostle quoted from pagan poets familiar to the Athenians who make these precise points.[25] The Areopagus discourse makes clear that Paul believed all human beings could not help but cognitively apprehend at least some content about God on the basis of general revelation. Gordon Lewis and Bruce Demarest summarize these universally revealed propositions as the following:

1.) God is the invisible Creator and Sovereign of the universe (v. 24); 2.) God is self-sufficient and dependent on the creature for nothing (v. 25a); 3.) God is the source of life and everything humans value as good (v. 25b); 4.) God is an intelligent Being, for he has established the times and bounds of man's habitation on the earth (v. 26); 5.) God is immanent in the world (v. 27); and 6.), amplifying the idea advanced in verse 25b, God is the very ground of human existence (v. 28).[26]

Nonetheless, the central theme of Paul's discourse was not so much what the Athenians *knew* as what they *denied*. The altar to the "unknown

---

[24] For an analysis and comparison of ancient Hellenic Stoicism and Epicureanism, see A. A. Long, *Hellenistic Philosophy: Stoics, Epicureans, Skeptics,* 2nd ed. (Berkeley: University of California Press, 1986), 14–74, 107–209.

[25] John Polhill argues that only one Greek poet is cited here, with "in him we live and move and have our being" coming not from a direct quotation but from a traditional Greek triadic formula. Others identify the first citation with Epimenides of Crete in reference to Zeus. Most scholars identify the second citation with the Stoic thinker Aratus, also in reference to Zeus. John B. Polhill, *Acts,* NAC (Nashville: Broadman & Holman, 1992), 375–76.

[26] Gordon R. Lewis and Bruce A. Demarest, *Integrative Theology,* vol. 1 (Grand Rapids: Zondervan, 1987), 69.

God" did not constitute, for Paul, an acknowledgment of Yahweh. Instead, the altar rightly acknowledged *ignorance* of God—an ignorance he would correct with special revelation, the apostolic preaching of the gospel.[27] The apostle attacked key facets of Hellenic thought—the multiplicity of gods, their representation by images, their dwelling in temples, Greek racial superiority, and the distance of the gods from humanity.[28] Paul's affirmation that God's immanence is so that his creatures might "feel their way toward him and find him" (17:27) is not a note of optimism but an indictment of Athenian paganism. As James Dunn comments, the assertion highlights both "that this Creator God has not created a hunger for God within humankind only to see it unsatisfied"—a hunger evidenced by Athenian religiosity and the hopelessness of the Athenian's "uncertain reaching out in the dark," a futility evidenced by a city filled with idols.[29]

Indeed, far from "building a bridge" of common understanding with the Athenians, Paul's speech is fully consonant with the pessimistic view of the human knowledge of God systematically expounded in Romans 1–3. The Athenians knew God, but they rebelled against him, turning to idols instead (Rom. 1:21–23). While they ought to reverence the Creator—to "feel their way toward him"—they instead are "ignorant" of this unknown Creator, their "foolish hearts" are "darkened" (Rom. 1:21). The Athenians knew better than to worship their idols, and thus they were responsible for an insurgency against their Creator. "In both texts there is an affirmation of natural revelation but not of anything that amounts to an adequate natural theology as a response to that revelation," observes Ben Witherington, comparing Acts 17 with Romans 1. "This is why in Acts 17:23 Paul insists he must proclaim the truth about this God's nature and activities to his audience. Without such proclamation they would not really know it."[30]

Moreover, Paul did not preach to the Athenians from the "text" of general revelation. The dialogue began, after all, when the philosophers were intrigued by Paul's proclamation of "Jesus and the resurrection" (Acts 17:18). It is difficult to think of revelation more "special" than that, and, indeed, more contrary to human wisdom—as seen in the incredulous reaction

---

[27] F. F. Bruce, *Commentary on the Book of Acts,* NICNT (Grand Rapids: Eerdmans, 1954), 356.

[28] F. F. Bruce points out the relevance of Paul's insistence that God had created all peoples from "one man" and had determined their "bounds and habitations." This was hardly "common ground" but a challenge to the Greek pride in being "autochthonous—sprung from the soil of their native Attica." As Bruce notes, Paul's preaching "removed all imagined justification for the belief that Greeks were innately superior to barbarians." Ibid., 357–58.

[29] James D. G. Dunn, *The Acts of the Apostles* (Valley Forge: Trinity Press International, 1996), 233–34.

[30] Ben Witherington III, *The Acts of the Apostles: A Socio-Rhetorical Commentary* (Grand Rapids: Eerdmans, 1998), 523.

of most of the Areopagus intellectuals to it (Acts 17:32–33). Moreover, Paul's proclamation throughout is suffused with biblical revelation drawn directly from the Old Testament Scriptures. Grounding his speech in creational monotheism, he ridiculed the folly of idolatry and cultic images in ways strikingly similar to those of Jeremiah or Isaiah. He spoke of the inability of temples to house the Almighty, just as Solomon did at the dedication of the Israelite temple (1 Kings 8:27). He affirmed the unity of the race in Adam. Like Moses centuries before, he cited the biblical tension between the transcendence and immanence of God (Deut. 30:14), rejected on both sides by pagan philosophies.

Paul set all of this in the context of the apostolic gospel—the onset of the last days with the sacrificial death and vindicating resurrection of Jesus of Nazareth (Acts 17:30–31). He further declared the coming eschatological judgment of the dead through the resurrected Messiah of Israel. Nothing could be more alien to Epicurean and Stoic thought, both of which sought to combat the fear of death, a worldview summed up in Epicurus's maxim that fear of death is nonsensical since "when death is, we are not, and when we are, death is not."[31] The Pauline presentation of a resurrection judgment is likewise at odds with the insistence of Stoicism represented, for instance, in the later writings of Stoic philosopher-king Marcus Aurelius:

> Don't look down on death, but welcome it. It too is one of the things required by nature. Like youth and old age. Like growth and maturity. Like a new set of teeth, a beard, the first gray hair. Like sex and pregnancy and childbirth. Like all the other physical changes at each stage of life, our dissolution is no different. So this is how a thoughtful person should await death: not with indifference, not with impatience, not with disdain, but simply viewing it as one of those things that happen to us. Now you anticipate the child's emergence from its mother's womb; that's how you should await the hour when your soul will emerge from its compartment.[32]

The declaration of Christ, resurrection, and judgment was also alien to the Areopagus because it affirmed the essential goodness of created matter, including the human body.[33] But the specifically Christian message of revealed doctrines of Christology, soteriology, and eschatology are not simply tacked on to the end of Paul's "general revelation" commentary.

---

[31] Cited from Epicurus's *Letter to Menoeceus* in Ronald H. Nash, *Life's Ultimate Questions: An Introduction to Philosophy* (Grand Rapids: Zondervan, 1999), 45.

[32] Marcus Aurelius, *Meditations,* trans. Gregory Hays (New York: Modern Library, 2003), 118.

[33] Marcus Aurelius, for instance, would represent well Stoic thought on the human person by quoting Epictetus on man as a "little wisp of soul carrying a corpse." *Meditations,* 46.

Instead, this is precisely the case he is making—from start (Acts 17:18) to finish (Acts 17:30–31), at Athens and to the ends of the earth.[34]

Romans 1–3

As mentioned above, the Pauline example of a "point of contact" with the pagans at the Areopagus cannot be abstracted from the apostle's systematic exposition on general revelation delivered to the church at Rome, arguably the most crucial text on the subject in the entire canon. In this letter the apostle persuaded the Christian community at Rome to unify the divided Jew-Gentile church in support of his missionary thrust to the outermost edges of the empire and beyond.[35] Moreover, Paul demonstrated in this letter how the salvation of the world through the unified Jew-Gentile body of Christ fits in the logic of history.[36] In the introductory chapters of the epistle, Paul lays out in stark detail the justice of God in the condemnation of both Jews and Gentiles, a predicament that can only be reversed through the triumph of Christ. In explaining the depths of human sin against the Creator, Paul appeals specifically to a doctrine of universally apprehended general revelation and to a doctrine of universally rejected general revelation. Both facets of this argument are seen especially in the apostle's point-by-point argument of why the Gentiles, separated from the Torah of Moses, were held accountable for the law.[37]

The apostle appealed first to the revelation of God in nature. All people, he asserted, have knowledge of God, which is "clearly perceived, ever since the creation of the world, in the things that have been made" (Rom. 1:20). This revelation has a specific content, namely that God exists, he is Creator, he is powerful, he is righteous, and he is to be worshipped as God. This revelation is not only possible to discern in the creation order; it is actually "perceived" by all persons—who can actually be said to have "known" God (Rom. 1:21). As Thomas Schreiner points out:

---

[34] John Polhill insightfully notes the similarities between the Areopagus discourse and Paul's preaching in Thessalonica, described in 1 Thessalonians 1:9–10: "Turning from idols to a living God, the return of the Son from heaven, the resurrection, the wrath to come. This is almost a summary of the appeal in Acts 17:29–31." Polhill, *Acts,* 377.

[35] Thomas R. Schreiner, *Romans,* BECNT (Grand Rapids: Baker, 1998), 19–23. With this in mind, Leon Morris contends that the Roman correspondence set forth Paul's gospel so that the church at Rome would know the message they would be supporting in Paul's Spanish mission. Leon Morris, *The Epistle to the Romans,* PNTC (Grand Rapids: Eerdmans, 1988), 17.

[36] Paul Achtemeier, *Romans,* Interpretation Commentary Series (Atlanta: John Knox, 1985), 7–18.

[37] Mark Seifrid argues that Paul's contention in Romans 1 is not yet with the whole world but with yet unspecified persons involved in idolatry. To say otherwise is reading Romans 3 into Romans 1, when the "discussion has not yet progressed so far." Mark A. Seifrid, "Natural Revelation and the Purpose of the Law in Romans," *Tyndale Bulletin* 49 (1998): 116. However one sees the argument being unveiled, Romans 1 is indeed building to the universal indictment in Romans 3, and it seems Paul is making clearly universal claims as early as Romans 1. As Douglas Moo notes, the flow of the argument "makes any limitation impossible. Those who perceive the attributes of God in creation must be the same as those who suppress the truth in unrighteousness and are therefore liable to the wrath of God. Paul makes clear that this includes all people (see 3:9, 19–20)." Douglas J. Moo, *The Epistle to the Romans,* NICNT (Grand Rapids: Eerdmans, 1996), 105.

Thomas Schreiner

Paul is not suggesting that philosophical arguments for the existence of God are needed. On the contrary, he maintains that all people know that God exists and that he is powerful. The truth of God's existence and power may be suppressed (Rom. 1:18), and yet it is still present in *all* human beings. Nor does the text intimate that people come to belief in God's existence and power through a long chain of reasoning. Paul reflects on the experience of *all human beings,* not on the ability of a few gifted philosophers. The belief in God's existence and power is stitched into human beings in such a way that all people inevitably conclude that there is a God when they perceive the created order.[38]

This point is important for the Pauline argument and indeed for the Pauline understanding of the whole mission to the Gentiles. It is not just that persons *ought* to know God through his general revelation. It is instead that they *do* know God through this revelation, and they despise him anyway.

The apostle further contends that general revelation is present not just in the natural creation, but it is found also in the nature of the human creatures themselves. He speaks of those who distort the order of human sexuality as acting "contrary to nature" (Rom. 1:26–27). It would seem here, as Paul argues elsewhere, that human design makes clear the purposes and boundaries of human sexuality and gender identity (1 Cor. 11:13–15). Paul also affirms that God's design is present in a universal religious consciousness within all persons—both Jew and Gentile. Just as Paul recognized the "religious" nature of the Athenians, as evident in their pagan altars, he argues that the Gentiles universally worship—although they distort that religious consciousness since they "exchanged the truth about God for a lie and worshiped and served the creature rather than the Creator" (Rom. 1:25). Instead of the proper response to God, worshipful thanksgiving, the darkened hearts of rebellious humans "exchanged the glory of the immortal God for images resembling mortal man and birds and animals and reptiles" (Rom. 1:23).

Moreover, Paul argues, human beings do not just know that God is to be worshipped, but they also share universally a moral consciousness of the content of his law. This is demonstrated, he argues, in the fact that Gentiles—quite apart from special revelation—sometimes "do by nature

---

[38] Thomas R. Schreiner, *Paul, Apostle of God's Glory in Christ: A Pauline Theology* (Downers Grove: InterVarsity, 2001), 104. This is contra the natural theology interpretation of this text found especially in the Roman Catholic Communion. See, for instance, Joseph A. Fitzmyer, *Romans,* AB (New York: Doubleday, 1993), 269–82. There are, however, Catholic voices seeking to ameliorate the robust natural theology interpretations of this text found in the Thomistic tradition and in Vatican I. See, for instance, David M. Coffey, "Natural Knowledge of God: Reflections on Romans 1:18–32," *Theological Studies* 31 (1970): 674–91.

things required by the law" (Rom. 2:14 NIV). The fact that they have a moral conscience also reveals that God has placed within them a law "written on their hearts" (Rom. 2:15).[39] The conscience does not simply reveal the content of God's decree about human conduct, but it also reveals the consequences of disobedience, serving as a kind of precursor to the judgment seat of Christ. The human conscience "bears witness, and their conflicting thoughts accuse or even excuse them on that day when, according to my gospel, God judges the secrets of men by Christ Jesus" (Rom. 2:15b–16).

As John Murray explains, "Accusation and excusation, whether of ourselves or others, are activities which evidence moral consciousness and therefore point to our indestructible moral nature, the only rationale of which is the work of the law of God in the heart."[40] Through the revelation of conscience, all human beings both know the content of God's decree and know that the judgment against the violation of this decree is death (Rom. 1:32). Again this is for Paul foundational for the mission to the Gentiles since, as Ernst Käsemann notes, it asserts that "the Gentile, like the Jew, can understand the proclamation of the last judgment and the criteria which will apply in it."[41]

The response to this knowledge of God is not humans "feel[ing] their way toward him" (Acts 17:27), but precisely, in every instance, the polar opposite. Human beings reject the Creator they perceive in the creation for the creation itself (Rom. 1:23,25). They prefer the foolishness of their alienated minds to the wisdom declared in the natural order (Rom. 1:21–22). They run from the law written on the heart toward the irrationality of evil—even as they know this will bring judgment upon them (Rom. 1:28–32). Human beings are "without excuse" before the tribunal of God (Rom. 1:20; 2:15–16). Even in the face of universal revelation, all human beings "suppress the truth in unrighteousness" (Rom. 1:18 NASB). The problem is not cognitive ignorance of God but moral revulsion toward him.

Thus, Paul's argument climaxes in his indictment of all of humanity before God since "no one understands; no one seeks for God" (Rom. 3:11). This universal revelation of God's righteousness—to Israel and to the Gentile nations apart from the law—means that all human beings, Jew

---

[39] Herman Ridderbos distinguishes the Pauline understanding of a "natural" knowledge of the law from Stoic philosophy, which also ties moral rationality to the order of the cosmos. The distinction comes in Paul's concept of a personal lawgiver, transcendent over the "nature" of the universe. The law given to the Gentiles on the heart is, at its root, qualitatively the same as that revealed to Israel through special revelation. Herman Ridderbos, *Paul: An Outline of His Theology,* trans. John Richard DeWitt (Grand Rapids: Eerdmans, 1975), 106.

[40] John Murray, *The Epistle to the Romans,* NICNT (Grand Rapids: Eerdmans, 1959), 75–76.

[41] Ernst Käsemann, *Commentary on Romans,* trans. Geoffrey W. Bromiley (Grand Rapids: Eerdmans, 1980), 68.

and Gentile, are responsible for the law of God, "so that every mouth may be stopped, and the whole world may be held accountable to God" (Rom. 3:19). This common revelation, common law, and common condemnation is tied to the gospel announcement of a common redemption, Jesus' propitiation of the just wrath of God, "so that he might be the just and the justifier of the one who has faith in Jesus" (Rom. 3:26). And this common redemption is received, by both Jews and Gentiles, through faith in Jesus as Messiah (Rom. 3:27–30).

What Has the Church Believed?

General revelation has emerged as a focal point of controversy throughout the history of the church. The controversy rarely revolved around the same points of contention, however, but ricocheted back and forth around multiple areas of dispute. Thus, in constructing a theology of general revelation, Christianity has been forced to relate general revelation to questions of the authority of Scripture, the depravity of fallen humanity, the apologetic use of theistic "proofs," and the insights of pagan philosophy, world religions, archetypal mythology, and human experience. The following sketch is by no means exhaustive of these debates but traces how questions about general revelation have persisted in every era of Christian thought.

General Revelation in Patristic Theology

From the dusk of the apostolic age to the dawn of the medieval era, the most contentious debates in Christian theology were drawn from special revelation—especially trinitarian and Christological questions. And yet general revelation was an ongoing point of contention from the earliest fathers to Augustine. As Thomas Oden has demonstrated, there was a patristic consensus on general revelation, which echoed the insistence of Romans 1–2 of a universal revelation in the cosmos and human nature—along with a corresponding affirmation of human suppression of this revelation.[42] Most often general revelation was engaged in terms of orthodox Christian response to heretical movements within the church, the insights of Hellenic philosophy, or the religions of the Greco-Roman world.

Irenaeus of Lyons

Patristic thought on general revelation is seen in the early church's response to the Gnostic and Marcionite heresies, both of which severed

---

[42] Thomas C. Oden, "Without Excuse: Classic Christian Exegesis of General Revelation," *JETS* 41 (1998): 55–68.

God from the material creation and denied that he could be known from the cosmic order or from the constitution of human beings.[43] Against this, Irenaeus of Lyons offered an early defense of the Pauline idea that God is revealed everywhere both by "means of the world" and "the formation of man," both of which provide propositional content about the creatorship and lordship of God.[44] "For even the creation reveals Him who formed it, and the very work made suggests Him who made it, and the world manifests Him who ordered it," Irenaeus contended against the Gnostics. "The Universal Church, moreover, through the whole world has received this tradition from the apostles."[45] For Irenaeus, special revelation builds on the truths of general revelation but does not contradict them.[46]

Thus, Israel and the church know something of God "by the prophets of God, while the very heathen learned it from creation itself."[47] For Irenaeus, there is universal suppression of the truth of general revelation, but this should not be surprising given human rejection of special revelation.[48] Irenaeus was one of many in the early church who sought to reconcile the exclusive truth claims of Christianity with what seemed to be truth and wisdom in non-Christian thought, especially ancient Greek philosophy. For Irenaeus, some truth could be found in non-Christian thought, but it was a partial and clouded grasp of the wisdom God had woven into the fabric of creation. He found it an indictment on the church that what Plato could discern through general revelation—namely that the one God "is both just and good, has power over all, and himself performs judgment"—was denied by professing Christians such as Marcion.[49]

Justin Martyr

A Palestinian who converted to Christianity after a long pilgrimage through Pythagorean, Platonic, and Stoic philosophies, Justin sought to engage non-Christian philosophical reflection from the vantage point of God's general revelation. Justin did believe that some philosophers had

---

[43] Indeed both denied God as Creator at all. Gnosticism saw the material creation as the renegade activity of a cosmic Demiurge. Marcion specifically identified this Demiurge with Yahweh of the Old Testament, whom he deemed to be wicked and foreign to the God of Jesus Christ. Both Gnosticism and Marcionism held to the polar opposite of any concept of general revelation, revelation came only to the "enlightened." Gnosticism further taught that redemption was an escape from creation, including escape from such aspects of human nature as male/female duality.

[44] Irenaeus, *Against Heresies* 4.6.6.

[45] Ibid., 2.9.1.

[46] Charles K. Robinson, "St. Irenaeus on General Revelation as Preparation for Special Revelation," *Duke Divinity School Review* 43 (1978): 169–80.

[47] Irenaeus, *Against Heresies* 2.9.1.

[48] Irenaeus argues that God's revelation in nature and in humanity "do indeed address all men in the same manner, but all do not in the same way believe them. But by the law and the prophets did the Word preach both himself and the Father alike to all; and all people heard him alike, but all did not alike believe." Ibid., 4.6.6.

[49] Ibid., 3.25.5.

access to genuine wisdom, but he denied that they grasped such truth through autonomous human reason. Many of the pagan thinkers, he contended, knew truth that was a remnant from special revelation from the Hebrew Scriptures. Thus, for instance, Plato knew that the universe had a beginning because he was familiar with the Mosaic writings.[50]

But Justin and those after him also saw the wisdom in non-Christian philosophy emerging from the *Logos,* the seminal structure of order present in human rationality. The pagans were able to "see realities darkly through the sowing of the implanted word that was in them."[51] Like the Apostle John's use of the *Logos,* the *Logos* concepts in Justin and other early Christians were diametrically opposed to the concept in Stoic thought and other forms of Greek philosophy. It was often less a capitulation to Greek philosophy than a challenge to it.[52] If all truth is from the *Logos* of God, then, "Whatever things were rightly said among all men are the property of us Christians."[53] This did not mean, however, a wholesale adoption of Greek philosophical thought. Justin and his fellow apologists were highly critical of the self-contradictory nature of pagan philosophy, with Plato and others "having chosen to abide in harmony not even with their own opinions."[54]

Origen of Alexandria

Some have attributed to the Patristic era a hellenic hyperspirituality, influenced by Platonic and neoplatonist thought, that sought to distance the Creator from the material creation as a vehicle of revelation. This is certainly true of some Patristic thinkers, most notably Origen of Alexandria, who viewed the material cosmos as the "afterbirth" of the creation of those things most real—rationality and the immaterial spirit.[55] The Platonic bent of Origen—including an emphasis on the incomprehensibility of God—shaded his view of general revelation but did not utterly obliterate it. He affirmed a universal revelation of God in nature, although he set this forth in decidedly Platonic terms. The idolatry of Romans 1, for Origen, meant

---

[50] Justin Martyr, *Hortatory Address to the Greeks* 33. Citing a reference in Plato to the Greek gods riding winged chariots in heaven, Justin asks, providing chapter and verse from the Old Testament: "From what other source, if not from Moses and the prophets, did he learn this and so write?" Ibid., 31.

[51] Justin Martyr, *Second Apology,* 13.

[52] Justin's *Logos* philosophy was more consistent with Genesis, Proverbs, and John than with Stoic writings. For compelling arguments for Justin's biblical rather than philosophical basis for his *Logos* teaching, see M. J. Edwards, "Justin's Logos and the Word of God," *Journal of Early Christian Studies* 3 (1995): 261–80; and L. W. Barnard, "The Logos Theology of St. Justin Martyr," *Downside Review* 89 (1971): 132–41.

[53] Justin Martyr, *Second Apology* 13.

[54] Justin Martyr, *Hortatory Address to the Greeks* 7.

[55] For this critique of Origen, see Terence L. Nichols, *The Sacred Cosmos: Christian Faith and the Challenge of Naturalism* (Grand Rapids: Brazos, 2003), 29–30. Nichols contrasts the tradition of Origen with the nature-affirming theology of Celtic Christianity.

refusing to see in the creation the invisible forms to which they point.[56] Nonetheless, the Greek patristic tradition influenced by Origen affirmed a universal self-disclosure of God in the natural and human orders, an affirmation that would lead to theological explorations of the revelatory meaning of nature, especially in the writings of the Cappadocian fathers.[57] The Cappadocian theology also explored such questions as the universal human longing for religious transcendence as an aspect of general revelation.[58]

Athanasius of Alexandria

General revelation was also a subtext in the Christological controversies leading to Nicea. Athanasius of Alexandria argued that the universal human rejection of general revelation proves the necessity of the incarnation of the *Logos* since humans refuse to see the handiwork of God in nature.[59] Because human beings turned from the Creator to the material creation that proclaimed Him, the creative *Logos* takes on the stuff of material creation—a human nature—to restore the rebels to the Father's household.[60]

Like Justin, Athanasius maintained a critical acceptance of some truth in non-Christian philosophy. Athanasius condemned the "philosopher's noisy talk" about issues such as virtue and immortality while at the same time drawing categories from Hellenic philosophy to explain that the biblical ideas of the Trinity and the divine-human unity of Christ were not nonsensical.[61] Athanasius was less optimistic about the truth claims of non-Christian religions. He seemed to attribute ontological being to some pagan deities, including the Greek pantheon of gods, but he identified them as demons "who

---

[56] Origen specifically identifies the cult of the sun, moon, and the stars as illustrative of this suppression of general revelation. Origen, *Commentary on the Epistle to the Romans, Books 1–5,* trans. Thomas P. Scheck in *The Fathers of the Church: A New Translation,* vol. 103, ed. Thomas P. Halton, et al. (Washington DC: Catholic University of America Press, 2001), 87–97.

[57] For an analysis of the theological discussions within the Eastern Church about nature and the human constitution, see D. S. Wallace-Hadrill, *The Greek Patristic View of Nature* (New York: Barnes and Noble, 1968).

[58] See, for instance, Gregory of Nazianzus's discussion of the fact that "every rational nature longs for God and for the First Cause, but is unable to grasp him." Gregory Nazianzen, *Second Theological Oration,* 13.

[59] Athanasius writes: "You cannot put straight in others what is warped in yourself. Perhaps you will say, then, that creation was enough to teach men about the Father. But if that had been so, such great evils would never have occurred. Creation was there all the time, but it did not prevent men from wallowing in error. Once more, then, it was the Word of God, who sees all that is in man and moves all things in creation, who alone could meet the needs of the situation. It was his part and his alone, whose ordering of the universe reveals the Father, to renew the same teaching. But how was he to do it? By the same means as before, perhaps you will say, that is, through the works of creation. But this was proven insufficient. Men had neglected to consider the heavens before, and now they were looking in the opposite direction." Athanasius, *On the Incarnation,* trans. anonymous (1946; reprint, Crestwood: St. Vladimir's Seminary Press, 2003), 42.

[60] Ibid., 43–44.

[61] Ibid., 85.

used to deceive men's minds by taking up their abode in springs or rivers or trees or stones and imposing upon simple people by their frauds."[62]

Augustine of Hippo

Augustine developed a theology of general revelation while combating heresy, most specifically the Manichean dualism and Neoplatonic mysticism he once embraced. In his defense of Christian orthodoxy, Augustine notes how his previous understanding of creation made him "ridiculous" in light of what God clearly revealed in nature. He was, he confessed, "led to the absurd trivialities of believing that a fig weeps when it is picked, and that the fig tree its mother sheds milky tears."[63] In his revolt against the Creator, "I in my pathetic state believed that more mercy should be shown to the fruits of the earth than to human beings for whose sake the fruits came to be."[64] Augustine did not believe that God had been hidden from him, but was instead everywhere revealed in the natural order.[65] The problem was Augustine's own depravity, which searched not for God but for the "lovely created things" he had made. "The lovely things kept me far from you, though if they did not have their existence in you, they had no existence at all," he prayed.[66]

Against Neoplatonism Augustine affirmed the revelatory value of the material cosmos and, citing Romans 1, declared that all people everywhere have access to its witness about God.

> For, though the voices of the prophets were silent, the world itself, by its well-ordered changes and movements, and by the fair appearance of all visible things, bears a testimony of its own, both that it has been created and also that it could not have been created save by God whose greatness and beauty are unutterable and invisible.[67]

The same is seen, he argued, in the contemplation of the human soul.[68] Those, whether in paganism or in heretical Christian movements, who denied such things as creation *ex nihilo* did so not from simple ignorance but

---

[62] Ibid., 84.

[63] Augustine, *Confessions,* trans. Henry Chadwick (New York: Oxford University Press, 1991), 49.

[64] Ibid., 49.

[65] In language reminiscent of the nature psalms, Augustine exclaimed: "That you are to be praised is shown by dragons on earth, and all deeps, fire, hail, snow, ice, the hurricane and tempest, which perform your word—mountains and all hills, fruitful trees and all cedars, beasts and all cattle, reptiles and winged birds; kings of the earth and all peoples, princes and all judges of the earth, young men and maidens, old men with younger; let them praise your name. Moreover, let these from the heavens praise you; let all your angels praise you in the height, our God all your powers, sun and moon, all stars and light, the heaven of heavens and the waters that are above the heavens: let them praise your name." Ibid., 125.

[66] Ibid., 201.

[67] Augustine, *The City of God* 11:4, trans. Marcus Dods (New York: Modern Library, 1993), 348.

[68] Ibid., 348–49.

from rebellion against a revealed truth. In his sermons to his North African church, Augustine appealed to his hearers to think about the crops growing, fish leaping in the sea, and the stars above them—all things they cannot help but notice. "So why wouldn't it occur to you to cast an investigative eye about for the Creator who did all this?" he asked.[69]

Answering the hypothetical objections of those who claim they cannot see the Creator in the creation, Augustine appealed to Romans 1 and located the reason for such blindness: "Pride ran riot."[70] As Richard Dougherty points out, Augustine's conception of the natural law of Romans 2:14–15 was somewhat unique, given the fact that he denied that Paul was speaking of general revelation at all, but instead of evangelized Gentiles who are restored to their natural state of peace with God not by the Mosaic law but by the gospel of Christ.[71]

Like several of his predecessors, Augustine's discussions of the relationship between general revelation and pagan philosophy invariably turned to Plato, whose work shaped in various ways Augustine's own.[72] Noting similarities between Platonic and biblical conceptions of God, Augustine admitted that, when he compared Plato's view of divine immutability to the Exodus account of God's self-revelation as "I Am Who I Am," he was inclined "almost to assent" to the view that Plato was familiar with some of the biblical writings.[73] Instead, however, Augustine pointed to the general revelation in nature referred to in Romans 1:20.[74] Augustine did not see the polytheistic religions in the Roman Empire around him as a manifestation, however darkened, of general revelation. Like Athanasius, Augustine did not rule out the existence of the pagan gods but argued that they were demonic beings that disguised themselves as gods or ghosts in order to deceive the people of the world.[75]

General Revelation in Medieval and Reformation Theology

The debates of the Patristic era laid a foundation for further discussion in the medieval and Reformation periods, when the discussion turned to

---

[69] Augustine of Hippo, *Sermons to the People: Advent, Christmas, New Year's Epiphany,* trans. William Griffin (New York: Doubleday, 2002), 144.

[70] Ibid., 145.

[71] Richard J. Dougherty, "Natural Law," in *Augustine through the Ages: An Encyclopedia,* ed. Allan D. Fitzgerald (Grand Rapids: Eerdmans, 1999), 583–84.

[72] Augustine observed that Plato "is justly preferred to all the other philosophers of the Gentiles" and that among the followers of Socrates, "Plato was the one who shone with a glory which far excelled that of the others, and who not unjustly eclipsed them all." Augustine, *City of God,* trans. Marcus Dods, in *A Select Library of Nicene and Post-Nicene Fathers of the Christian Church,* ed. Philip Schaff (reprint, Edinburgh: T & T Clark, 1988), 146–47.

[73] Ibid., 152.

[74] Ibid.

[75] Ibid., 141.

how general revelation could be used in the task of theology. During the medieval era Catholic thought produced the flowering of natural theology as an inference from the biblical teachings on universal revelation. The Reformation and the movements that sprang from it turned largely to a more chastened understanding of the limits of general revelation.

Medieval Catholic Thought

Deeply affected by Augustinian thought on the attributes of God, Anselm of Canterbury planted the seeds of Catholic natural theology with an apologetic stance that assumed that human beings could discover through reason the necessary existence of a deity. Thomas Aquinas's modified Aristotelian philosophy led him to develop a view of faith and reason that moved toward a full-orbed natural theology. His metaphysics was, in the words of one Catholic philosopher, "a climax in the history of natural theology."[76] As Demarest observes, Thomas "broke with the Platonic-Augustinian intuitive approach and promoted the Aristotelian method that seeks knowledge of ultimate Reality on the basis of a purely empirical analysis of natural phenomena."[77] This view of knowledge was indeed a departure from Augustine, who believed that humans perceive general revelation in the cosmos through the foundational presence of an intuitive apprehension of God rooted in the *imago Dei,* to a more definitively empirical apprehension of general revelation.[78]

Thomas's natural theology was most easily seen in his "proofs" for the existence of God, or the "five ways" which he believed could be discovered through human reason, apart from divine revelation: (1) motion in the universe points to an initial "Unmoved Mover"; (2) existence points to a first cause; (3) contingency points to a Necessary Being; (4) degrees of beauty, truth, and goodness point to a universal standard of perfection; (5) the design in the natural order points to a Designer.[79] Thomistic natural theology held that certain truths about God (his existence and attributes) could be known through reason alone, thus building a bridge to the truths about God that could only be known through revealed theology (the gospel of Christ, for instance). All of this was built on a view of epistemology that believed even fallen humanity could still perceive and make use of the evidences for God built in the created order.

As philosopher Eugene Rogers observes, Thomistic epistemic "optimism" about the human condition was far different from the later

[76] Etienne Gilson, *God and Philosophy,* 2nd ed. (New Haven: Yale University Press, 2002), 67.

[77] Demarest, *General Revelation,* 41–42.

[78] This is not to say that Thomas was an empiricist by any strict definition of that term. See Richard A. Muller, "The Limits of General Revelation," *Reformed Journal* (July 1983), 30.

[79] Thomas Aquinas, *Summa Theologica,* trans. anonymous (New York: Benziger Brothers, 1947), 13–14.

Enlightenment optimism about human reason, but it nonetheless posits a natural knowledge of God, built upon innate structures of knowing and mediated through the cosmic order, accessible to all rational persons.[80] A Thomistic vision of natural theology shaped the medieval Catholic scholasticism and led to a formal adoption of this basic framework of general revelation at the First Vatican Council in the nineteenth century.[81] Thomas also articulated a view of natural law that would prove influential in the medieval era and beyond. Drawing on the "law written on the heart" in Romans 2, Thomas argued that "a certain order is to be found in those things that are apprehended universally."[82] For Thomas—and certainly for Thomistic thinkers after him—a common structure of universally recognized moral norms could be identified and used to govern certain aspects of human behavior, apart from revelation such as the Decalogue.[83]

Martin Luther

Medieval scholastic thought on general revelation took a blow from the protests of magisterial Reformers such as Martin Luther and John Calvin. Luther, for instance, anathematized Thomism in his 1517 disputation against scholastic theology by stating that "the whole of Aristotle is to theology as darkness is to light."[84] Throughout his life, Luther maintained a general revelation in creation and the human conscience.[85] But for Luther the problem with much of the speculative theology of the Reformation-era church was a failure to understand that the same texts that teach such a general revelation also teach the failure of depraved humanity to acknowledge God.[86] "The

[80] Eugene F. Rogers, *Thomas Aquinas and Karl Bath: Sacred Doctrine and the Natural Knowledge of God* (Notre Dame: University of Notre Dame Press, 1995), 141–44.

[81] For an analysis of the impact of Thomistic natural theology on Vatican I Roman Catholicism, see G. C. Berkouwer, *General Revelation: Studies in Dogmatics* (Grand Rapids: Eerdmans, 1955), 61–83. This is not to say that Thomistic or scholastic views of general revelation were monolithic in Catholic thought. Blaise Pascal, for instance, would later articulate a much less optimistic account of human cognition of the revelation of God in nature and conscience. Pascal found it "noteworthy" that no biblical figure ever attempted to "prove" the existence of God from nature. Blaise Pascal, *Pensées,* trans. A. J. Krailsheimer (New York: Penguin, 1966), 179.

[82] Thomas, *Summa Theologica,* 1009.

[83] For an examination of the path that natural law discussion took in medieval thought from Thomas onward, see Russell Hittinger, "Natural Law," in *The Blackwell Encyclopedia of Modern Christian Thought,* ed. Alister E. McGrath (Oxford: Blackwell, 1993), 398–402.

[84] Martin Luther, "Disputation against Scholastic Theology," in *Martin Luther's Basic Theological Writings,* ed. Timothy F. Lull (Minneapolis: Fortress, 1989), 16.

[85] See, for instance, Luther's clear teaching on both universal revelation in the creation and in the law written on the heart, along with his equally clear teaching on the suppression of that knowledge. Martin Luther, *Lectures on Romans,* trans. Wilhelm Pauck (Philadelphia: Westminster, 1961), 20–36, 50–54.

[86] "God gives us sun and moon and stars, fire and water, air and earth, all creatures, body and soul, all manner of maintenance, fruits, grain, corn, wine, whatever is good for the preservation and comfort of this temporal life. . . . Yet what gets he thereby? Truly, nothing, but that he is wickedly blasphemed. . . . Such a godly child is the world; woe be to it." Martin Luther, *The Table Talk of Martin Luther,* trans. Thomas S. Kepler, ed. William Hazlitt (Grand Rapids: Baker, 1995), 47–48.

person does not deserve to be called a theologian who looks upon the things of God as though they were clearly perceptible in those things which have happened," he wrote in the 1518 Heidelberg Disputation, citing Romans 1:20.[87]

Luther also attenuated the natural law emphases of the medieval thinkers, accenting the usefulness of the law "written on the heart" in the "civil righteousness" of sociopolitical governance but not in the realm of salvation or the Christian life, which is dependent upon divine revelation.[88] Luther found this suppression of general revelation in non-Christian world religions, which he believed were a twisted parody of the true worship of God, thus proving "the devil is ever God's ape."[89]

John Calvin

The Genevan Reformer articulated a more systematic vision of general revelation, one that would set the pace for Reformed thought for centuries. He spoke of nature as a "theater" of the glory of God, manifesting not just his presence but also his orderly providence, his creative wisdom, and his measureless omnipotence.[90] Calvin also articulated a theology of *sensus divinitas,* an immediate intuition of God rooted in the *Logos,* which manifests itself in a universal religious consciousness.[91] This intuitive knowledge of God was, for Calvin, "beyond controversy" and is evidenced by the fact that no people group in history have been without religion.[92] For him, therefore, cognitive atheism, in the strictest sense, is impossible.[93]

Calvin also saw in the human conscience a witness of the justice of God and the certainty of coming judgment.[94] The quest for order among humans—seen in social, political, artistic, scientific, and familial structures—is a "seed" of the law written on the hearts and thus distinguished humanity from the animals.[95] "For, while men dispute among themselves about individual sections of the law," he wrote, "they agree on the general conception of equity."[96] As Susan Schreiner notes, Calvin did not "develop a 'theology of natural law' but, rather, used the principle of natural law as an extension of his doctrine of providence to explain the survival of civilization."[97]

---

[87] Martin Luther, "Heidelberg Disputation," in *Martin Luther's Basic Theological Writings,* ed. Timothy F. Lull (Minneapolis: Fortress, 1989), 43.

[88] John T. McNeill, "Natural Law in the Thought of Luther," *Church History* 10 (1941): 211–27.

[89] Luther, *Table Talk of Martin Luther,* 42.

[90] John Calvin, *Institutes of the Christian Religion,* 1.14.20–22.

[91] For a discussion of the *sensus divinitas* in Calvin, see Demarest, *General Revelation,* 52.

[92] Calvin, *Institutes,* 1.3.1.

[93] Ibid., 1.3.3.

[94] Ibid., 1.15.1,4.

[95] Ibid., 1.11.12–17.

[96] Ibid., 1.11.14.

[97] Susan E. Schreiner, *The Theater of His Glory: Nature and the Natural Order in the Thought of John Calvin* (Grand Rapids: Baker, 1995), 94–95. Schreiner explains that natural law in Calvin explained God's "restraint" of the "chaotic forces" within fallen human nature.

This is because general revelation, far from the roots of a natural theology, was for Calvin "like a traveler passing through a field at night who in a momentary lightning flash sees far and wide, but the sight vanishes so swiftly that he is plunged again into the darkness of the night."[98] Response to the *sensus divinitas* and to the revelation of God in nature leads, inevitably, all humans without exception—and Calvin here even includes Plato—to devise "a fictitious and a new god, or rather a phantom."[99] Even human conscience is subsumed in the deception of human depravity. "The purpose of natural law, therefore, is to render man inexcusable," since humans never listen to the dictates of justice in conscience but purposefully rebel against them.[100] Thus, distinguishing his view from a Stoic conception of natural law, Calvin writes that the witness of conscience lies "in repose in man, bottled up as it were," which "watches and observes all his secrets so that nothing may be buried in darkness."[101]

Post-Reformation Protestantism

Calvin's affirmation of the universal apprehension of general revelation and the universal suppression of it continued in Reformed theology in the centuries after the Reformation. Reformed scholasticism built on Calvin, wrestling internally with whether there could be such a thing as a Reformed natural theology.[102] The Westminster Confession of Faith (1643–46), in its opening sentence, reflected the Reformed consensus on both the reality and limits of general revelation: "Although the light of nature, and the works of creation and providence do so far manifest the goodness, wisdom, and power of God, as to leave men unexcusable; yet are they not sufficient to give that knowledge of God, and of his will, which is necessary unto salvation."[103]

This trajectory continued through the Puritan stream of English Calvinism, which seemed at times to emphasize the suppression more than the universality of general revelation, and on through the Princeton and southern Presbyterian traditions of American Calvinism.[104] Jonathan Edwards, the pinnacle of American Puritan theology, combined a scientist's eye for the intricacies of the natural order with a metaphysician's

---

[98] Calvin, *Institutes*, 2.11.18.

[99] John Calvin, *Calvin's Commentaries*, vol. 19: *Commentaries on the Epistle of Paul the Apostle to the Romans,* trans. John Owen (reprint, Grand Rapids: Baker, 1999), 74.

[100] Calvin, *Institutes*, 2.11.22.

[101] Ibid., 1.14.20–22.

[102] Richard A. Muller, *Post-Reformation Reformed Dogmatics: The Rise and Development of Reformed Orthodoxy, ca. 1520 to ca. 1725,* vol. 1, *Prolegomena to Theology,* 2nd ed. (Grand Rapids: Baker, 2003), 270–310.

[103] Westminster Confession of Faith 1.1.

[104] This is well represented in John Owen, *Biblical Theology,* trans. Stephen P. Westcott (Morgan: Soli Deo Gloria, 1994), 20–168. Owen's work, written in 1661, contrasted the "natural theology of the first man" with the "loss of natural theology" in the fall.

inquiry into the meaning of God's order in nature, humanity, and the workings of history. Like Calvin, he combined a Pauline emphasis on both general revelation and human depravity, especially when contrasting revealed Christianity with world religions.[105] As Edwards put it: "What instance can be mentioned, from any history, of any one nation under the sun, that emerged from atheism or idolatry, into the knowledge or adoration of the one true God, without the assistance of revelation?"[106]

In the nineteenth and twentieth centuries, the Dutch Reformed stream of Calvinism, led by theologians Abraham Kuyper and Herman Bavinck, refined the Calvinist view of general revelation. On the one hand, the Dutch Reformed theologians linked general revelation to common grace, demonstrating the handiwork of God in human art, science, and culture.[107] On the other, the Kuyperian neo-Calvinists articulated a stark antithesis between the knowledge of regenerate and unregenerate humanity, thus highlighting the absolute necessity of special revelation for sinful humans to understand general revelation.[108] The Dutch Reformed tradition maintained the pessimism of the Calvin/Westminster/Puritan traditions toward general revelation in relation to the world religions or personal soteriology. Bavinck, for instance, rejected an evolutionary model of the origin of world religions in favor of a recognition that universal religious consciousness is an aspect of general revelation. But he argued that the sacred writings of the pagan religions, by their very existence, demonstrate that "natural religion cannot be found anywhere, nor can it exist."[109]

General Revelation in Modern Theology

The modern era in theology has been consumed with debates over general revelation, with theologians seesawing between ambitious proposals for natural theology and outright denials that general revelation exists at all. Both the left and right wings of Christian theology took up the task

---

[105] This is contrary to the contention that Edwards's view of general revelation was an incipient inclusivism found in Gerald McDermott, *Jonathan Edwards Confronts the Gods* (New York: Oxford University Press, 2000). For compelling historical repudiations of the McDermott thesis, see Greg D. Gilbert, "The Nations Will Worship: Jonathan Edwards and the Salvation of the Heathen," *TJ* 23 (2002): 53–76; and John J. Bombaro, "Historical Peculiarity, History, and Edwards's Evangelistic Appeal to Self-Love," *WTJ* 66 (2004): 121–58.

[106] Jonathan Edwards, "Miscellaneous Observations," *The Works of Jonathan Edwards*, vol. 2 (Edinburgh: Banner of Truth, 1974), 476.

[107] See, for instance, Abraham Kuyper, "Common Grace," in *Abraham Kuyper: A Centennial Reader*, ed. James D. Bratt (Grand Rapids: Eerdmans, 1998), 165–204.

[108] Abraham Kuyper, *Lectures on Calvinism* (Grand Rapids: Eerdmans, 1931).

[109] Herman Bavinck, *Reformed Dogmatics*, vol. 1, *Prolegomena*, trans. John Vriend, ed. John Bolt (Grand Rapids: Baker, 2003), 313. Bavinck explains that general revelation is insufficient precisely because it does not reveal Christ or the mercy of God but simply his existence and wrath toward sin.

of interpreting general revelation, especially in relation to epistemology, anthropology, and soteriology.

Natural Theology

In 1802, Anglican theologian William Paley culminated a growing list of Protestant thinkers arguing for a robust natural theology, based on the argument from design. Just as one could infer the existence of a watchmaker from a finely crafted watch, so one could infer the existence of a Designer from the intricate beauty and order of the creation.[110] Natural theology faltered when critics argued, among other things, that the project failed to account for the cruelty, suffering, and chaos in nature.[111]

The assumptions of natural theology were challenged by philosophers such as David Hume and Immanuel Kant and, later, by naturalists such as Charles Darwin.[112] Moreover, as Terence Nichols observes, eighteenth- and nineteenth-century natural theology was often more compatible with Deism than with orthodox Christianity. When Darwin emerged in the mid-nineteenth century with a credible explanation for apparent design in nature, "the whole edifice of physico-theology based on design collapsed in decades."[113]

Protestant Liberalism

The Enlightenment challenges to Christianity reshaped Protestant theology in the nineteenth and early twentieth centuries, as Christian thinkers such as Friedrich Schleiermacher, Albrecht Ritschl, and Adolf Von Harnack sought to "rescue" Christianity from the acids of modernity and from the "cosmic pessimism" that made natural theology seem so untenable.[114] Foremost among these liberal Protestant theologians stood Schleiermacher, who recast Christian doctrines of authority and revelation in the wake of Kant, Enlightenment rationalism, and Victorian romanticism. Schleiermacher grounded knowledge of God not in an abstract natural theology—and certainly not in the verbal revelation of Scripture—but in the

---

[110] William S. Paley, *Natural Theology: Evidences for the Existence and Attributes of the Deity, Collected from the Appearances of Nature* (reprint, Indianapolis: Bobbs-Merrill, 1963).

[111] This was a primary thrust of Hume's argument. Biophysicist Cornelius Hunter posits that Charles Darwin's theory of natural selection sought to provide a "theodicy" in response to this fatal flaw in the natural theology argument, distancing God from the violence and disorder in nature. Cornelius G. Hunter, *Darwin's God: Evolution and the Problem of Evil* (Grand Rapids: Brazos, 2001).

[112] For a survey of responses to nineteenth-century natural theology, see William A. Dembski, *The Design Revolution: Answering the Toughest Questions about Intelligent Design* (Downers Grove: InterVarsity, 2004), 66–69.

[113] Nichols, *Sacred Cosmos*, 44–45.

[114] Paul Tillich, *Complete History of Christian Thought*, (New York: Harper and Row, 1969), 54. Tillich blamed this "cosmic pessimism" not just on philosophical trends but on events such as the eighteenth-century Lisbon earthquake, which made teleological arguments from nature seem anachronistic.

God-consciousness of humanity, namely the human intuition of "absolute dependence" on the divine.[115]
  Schleiermacher's project had wide-ranging implications for a Christian theology of general revelation since he identified a universally accessible revelation of the deity, though not located in the rational observation of the cosmos or anthropology but instead in human experience.[116] Schleiermacher's concept of "piety" or "feeling" differed from natural theology projects before him because it insisted that God "cannot be experienced in the external, rational world, but only in the internal, emotional world."[117] It also differed markedly from Calvin's notion of a *sensus Divinitas* since, among other reasons, Schleiermacher believed humanity not only could construct a workable theology from this non-cognitive God consciousness but that doctrinal formulations themselves were simply reflections on this experience. Moreover, he held that the world religions could be legitimate manifestations of this experience of the divine, although Christianity was the highest expression of it.[118] As Demarest and Lewis note, Schleiermacher's existential notion of general revelation directly impacted twentieth-century liberal theology, especially in the theologies of Paul Tillich and Karl Rahner.[119]

Neoorthodoxy

  In the twentieth century general revelation was at the center of a theological firestorm, first and primarily between German theologians Emil Brunner and Karl Barth. Brunner rejected a Thomistic understanding of natural theology, but he did assert the reality of general revelation, grounded in God's providential care for his creation. Brunner believed that all humans retained a rationality rooted in the *imago Dei,* though this image was twisted by sin. General revelation then provides a "point of contact" with fallen humanity in Brunner's understanding, a truth that is borne out by human responsibility as a sinner.[120] After all, he reasoned, "only a being that can be addressed is responsible, for it alone can make decisions."[121] Indeed, Brunner argued

---

[115] Friedrich Schleiermacher, *The Christian Faith,* ed. H. R. Mackintosh and J. S. Stewart (Edinburgh: T & T Clark, 1989), 131–41.

[116] Friedrich Schleiermacher, *On Religion: Speeches to its Cultured Despisers,* trans. John Oman (New York: Harper and Row, 1958), 26–118.

[117] Clinton Curle, "The Schleiermacher Redemption: Subjective Experience as a Starting Point for Evangelical Theology," *Didaskalia* 9 (1998): 20–21.

[118] Ibid., 210–65.

[119] Demarest and Lewis, *Integrative Theology,* vol. 1, 63–64.

[120] One scholar explains the difference between Brunner and Barth by noting that Brunner "accepts a natural theology for Christians, but not for non-Christians" while Barth "rejects natural theology for both Christians and non-Christians." Richard Alan Young, "The Knowledge of God in Romans 1:18–23: Exegetical and Theological Reflections," *JETS* 43 (2000): 702.

[121] Emil Brunner, "Nature and Grace," in Karl Barth, and Emil Brunner *Natural Theology,* trans. Peter Fraenkel (rep., Eugene, OR: Wipf and Stock, 2002), 31.

special revelation presupposes general revelation—that human beings can be addressed intelligibly with words.[122]

Barth responded to Brunner's theology of general revelation with a resounding "No!" He argued that in any attempt at a natural theology, only "the theology and the church of the antichrist can profit from it."[123] Barth believed he had seen just such an "antichrist" theology in the "German Christian" movement of churchmen in collaboration with the nation's fascist regime. Instead, Barth articulated in his response to Brunner and in his *Church Dogmatics* a view of revelation that located all of God's disclosure of himself to humanity in Jesus Christ.[124] This Christomonism led Barth to deny, for instance, that Psalm 19 teaches a universal revelation in nature or that Romans 1 teaches that fallen humans can "reason" from the visible things to the invisible.[125] Barth saw any attempt at a "point of contact" with fallen humanity, whether in Roman Catholic expressions of Thomism or in Protestant liberal constructions of divine immanence, as a dangerous repudiation of the gospel; any attempt at revelation in the natural order was a dangerous repudiation of the uniqueness of Christ as God's word to the creation.[126]

Contemporary Theologies

After Barth, the focus of debate over general revelation took on various forms within Christian theology. Wolfhart Pannenberg built on Christian understandings of history as an aspect of general revelation to place all truth—including the acts of God in creation and redemption—within the rubric of universally accessible history.[127] There is for Pannenberg, therefore, no distinction between "general" and "special" revelation since all acts of God in creation and providence—including such events as the resurrection of Jesus—are "public."[128] Rahner applied

---

[122] Ibid., 40–41.

[123] Karl Barth, "No!" in Karl Barth and Emil Brunner, *Natural Theology,* trans. Peter Fraenkel (rep., Eugene, OR: Wipf and Stock, 2002), 128.

[124] Karl Barth, *Church Dogmatics,* vol. 2, *The Doctrine of God, Part I,* trans. T. H. L. Parker, et al., ed. G. W. Bromiley and T. F. Torrance (Edinburgh: T & T Clark, 1957), 63–254.

[125] Karl Barth, *Epistle to the Romans,* trans. Edwyn C. Hoskyns (New York: Oxford University Press, 1933), 42–54.

[126] Some have sought, unsuccessfully, to bridge the divide between Thomas Aquinas and Barth on general revelation. See Eugene F. Rogers Jr., "Thomas and Barth in Convergence on Romans 1?" *Modern Theology* 12 (1996): 57–84.

[127] Wolfhart Pannenberg, et al., *Revelation as History,* trans. David Granskow (New York: Macmillan, 1968).

[128] This means then "this history is the history of religions. On the world historical stage conflicting truth claims, which are at their core religious and are ultimately attempts to express the unity of the world are struggling for supremacy. The religious orientation that best illumines the experience of all reality will in the end prevail and thereby demonstrate its truth value." Stanley J. Grenz and Roger E. Olson, *20th Century Theology: God and the World in a Transitional Age* (Downers Grove: InterVarsity, 1992), 192.

general revelation to soteriology, arguing for the presence of "anony-mous Christians" among the unevangelized and within the world religions who know God but are not aware of Jesus or the gospel.[129] The Rahner thesis was modified and accepted by the Vatican II Council of the Roman Catholic Church in the 1960s.[130]

General revelation also played a role in the emergence of various liberation theologies in the 1960s and beyond. Gustavo Gutierrez constructed his theology of liberation around a universally accessible understanding of the scope of human history, albeit through the grid of a Hegelian-Marxist understanding of history. Gutierrez and others were a prototype for later theologies of liberation, which also sought to build on what could be defined as "general revelation." For instance, feminist theologians often reflected theologically on the common experience of women's embodiment. Process theologians worked to construct a doctrine of God and providence from the "book of nature," defined as Darwinian evolutionary understandings of progress and change. Pluralist theologians, such as John Hick, offered a "natural theology" of revelation and salvation based on the common human experience of the world religions as vehicles of divine truth.

Evangelical Theology

In postwar American evangelical theology, general revelation was most closely related to the question of apologetics and evangelism. From the very beginning of the contemporary evangelical movement, classical apologists have sought to reclaim a modified Thomistic understanding of general revelation as a point of "common ground" with unbelievers, often employing both the classical theistic "proofs" along with historical evidences for the resurrection of Jesus and the reliability of the New Testament documents.[131]

Reformed apologist and theologian Cornelius Van Til, among others, challenged such common ground by appealing to the universal suppression of general revelation by unbelievers, revealed by Paul in Romans 1.[132] Evangelical philosopher Gordon Clark shared with Van Til a presuppositionalist distrust of natural theology and classical apologetics, but he developed a view of the *Logos* concept of John to argue that the image of God carries with it a rationality based on logical consistency. Others, such as Donald Bloesch,

---

[129] Karl Rahner, *Theological Investigations,* vol. 9, *Writings of 1965–67,* trans. Graham Harrison (London: Darton, Longman and Todd, 1972), 145–64.

[130] Austin Flannery, ed., *Vatican Council II: The Conciliar and Post-Conciliar Documents* (Northport, NY: Costello, 1975), 738–65.

[131] See, for instance, Norman L. Geisler, *Thomas Aquinas: An Evangelical Appraisal* (Grand Rapids: Baker, 1991) and R. C. Sproul, John Gerstner, and Arthur Lindsley, *Classical Apologetics: A Rational Defense of the Christian Faith and a Critique of Presuppositional Apologetics* (Grand Rapids: Zondervan, 1984).

[132] Cornelius Van Til, *The Defense of the Faith* (Phillipsburg: Presbyterian and Reformed, 1967).

sought to import Karl Barth's rejection of general revelation and natural theology into evangelical theological method.[133]

Perhaps the most significant evangelical thinker on the issue of general revelation has been Carl F. H. Henry, the preeminent theologian of twentieth-century evangelicalism. Henry built on Clark's view of the *Logos* as the universal source of human rationality and as the explanatory principle of the cosmos. He also strongly affirmed general revelation, a revelation with real cognitive content. But at the same time he emphasized that human guilt universally revolts against this truth. "God's universal disclosure in nature, history, and to the human mind and conscience is not in dispute," Henry wrote. "What is rejected rather is the expectation that fallen man will translate general revelation into a natural theology that builds a secure bridge to special revelation; in that event special revelation has significance only as a crown that caps natural theology elaborated by man in sin."[134]

Henry dismissed the possibility not only of an optimistic use of natural theology but also that of natural law. Again, while holding to general revelation universally present in the conscience and human rationality, he rejected, because of human depravity, the understanding of natural law as "a body of ethical imperatives supposedly inherent in human beings and discovered by human reason."[135]

Since Henry, evangelical theology has faced a variety of challenges related to general revelation. Some evangelicals, seeking to build co-belligerent political and social relationships with Roman Catholics against the nihilism of postmodern Western civilization, have sought to reclaim a modest vision of natural law. The Intelligent Design movement attempts to recuperate some aspects of the theistic proof, especially the argument from design, in order to argue for the existence of the deity on scientific grounds. At the same time the left wing of evangelical theology has adapted general revelation arguments in order to appeal to some possibility of salvation for those who have never heard the gospel of Christ. Evangelical Christians have struggled for nearly a century to understand how to relate theology with disciplines such as psychology, and whether secular psychology can itself be identified as "general revelation."

Baptist Theology

From the very beginning of the Baptist movement, Baptist churches have held both to the reality of general revelation and to the impossibility of such revelation leading fallen humans to a salvific knowledge of God.

---

[133] Donald Bloesch, *A Theology of Word and Spirit: Authority and Method in Theology* (Downers Grove: InterVarsity, 1992), 34–66, 143–83.

[134] Carl F. H. Henry, *God, Revelation, and Authority,* vol. 2, *God Who Speaks and Shows, Fifteen Theses, Part One* (Waco: Word, 1976), 117.

[135] Carl F. H. Henry, "Natural Law and a Nihilistic Culture," *First Things* (January 1995): 54.

The 1689 London Baptist Confession of Faith, repeated in America in the Philadelphia (1742) and Charleston (1774) confessions, set forth that "the light of nature, and the works of creation and providence do so far manifest the goodness, wisdom, and power of God, as to leave men inexcusable; yet they are not sufficient to give that knowledge of God and his will which is necessary unto salvation." The early English Baptist theologians likewise held to this confessional consensus on general revelation, with such widely divergent theologians as John Gill and Andrew Fuller both interpreting Scripture to teach universal general revelation and universal human rejection of such revelation.

Fuller used general revelation as a foundation for evangelism from the Scriptures, especially in his understanding of the human conscience. "Every man, whatever he may pretend, feels himself to be a sinner, and to need forgiveness," he wrote. "Ignorant and idolatrous as the Philippian jailer had been all his life, yet, when death looked him in the face, he trembled and cried for mercy."[136] Fuller appealed to unbelievers to notice the fear of death and their sense of longing for something beyond nature as indicators that they "in your nature are united mortality and immortality; the dust of the ground and the breath of the Almighty."[137]

Among nineteenth-century Southern Baptists, theologian John L. Dagg also found a universal longing for eternity to be an aspect of general revelation. To this, he added moral and religious feelings such as maternal affection for children.[138] For Dagg, the law of sowing and reaping, sinful actions bringing consequences, also was a part of general revelation. "Things are so arranged by the Creator and Ruler of the world, that some actions tend to promote, and others to destroy, the happiness of the individual and of society," Dagg argued. "By observing the tendency of actions, we may learn what to do and what to avoid."[139] But Dagg also argued that a confessional Baptist view of depravity rendered such revelation insufficient for redemption or obedience. "Conscience is God speaking within us, but, because of man's apostasy from God, it often delivers false oracles," he asserted.[140]

James P. Boyce likewise affirmed the reality of general revelation, setting it in the context of a high view of human reason and the validity of the theistic proofs, all part of the common sense realism inherited from his Princeton background.[141]

---

[136] Andrew Fuller, "The Great Question Answered," in *The Complete Works of the Rev. Andrew Fuller,* vol. 1 (Philadelphia: American Baptist Publication Society, 1845), 541.

[137] Ibid.

[138] John L. Dagg, *A Manual of Theology* (Charleston: Southern Baptist Publication Society, 1858), 19.

[139] Ibid., 20.

[140] Ibid.

[141] James P. Boyce, *Abstract of Systematic Theology* (Charleston: Southern Baptist Publication Society, 1887), 1–53.

In the twentieth century, Northern Baptist theologian A. H. Strong applied a doctrine of general revelation to contemporary debates over the relationship of science to Scripture. Because God inspired both "books" of revelation, the believer is able to "interpret the one by the other."[142] While Strong maintained that Scripture, as the record of God's revelation to previous generations, was more reliable than ongoing scientific inquiry, his optimistic view of general revelation paved the way for the acceptance of Darwinian understandings of evolutionary thought among Northern Baptists. Strong also articulated a doctrine of Spirit illumination, not only of the biblical record, but of the interpretation of nature as well.

Among twentieth-century Southern Baptist theologians, none was more prominent than E. Y. Mullins. Mullins dismissed a natural theology approach to the theistic proofs, precisely because they do not prove the Christian God, only a generic deity. But he affirmed general revelation, not only in nature and humanity in general, but in psychology of religion, "truth" found in other world religions, and human experience with the divine.[143] Mullins's disciple, W. T. Conner, articulated a similar view of general revelation—emphasizing human religious consciousness, human ideas of infinity and perfection, and the relative values of truth, beauty, and goodness as aspects of general revelation.[144] Like Mullins, Conner saw world religions as being partly revelatory and preparatory for their "fulfillment" in Christ. Thus, he affirmed Islam as a "broken light" of general revelation, which "lifted" an idolatrous Arabian peninsula to a "higher plane" via monotheism.[145]

In the later twentieth century, Baptist theologians took such developments even further. Dale Moody, a student of European neoorthodoxy, rejected a Barthian denial of general revelation and instead developed a theology of general revelation that allowed for a salvific appropriation of general revelation for the unevangelized. Moreover, Moody saw certain streams of ancient and modern philosophy—including existentialism and process philosophy—as aspects of general revelation. Moody classified scientific discovery in the category of general revelation—including Darwinian evolutionary theories and even historical-critical biblical scholarship.[146] Likewise, Baptist theologians such as Molly T. Marshall and

---

[142] A. H. Strong, *Systematic Theology* (Philadelphia: Judson, 1907), 27.

[143] E. Y. Mullins, *The Christian Religion in Its Doctrinal Expression* (Nashville: Sunday School Board of the Southern Baptist Convention, 1917), 38–48.

[144] W. T. Conner, *Revelation and God: An Introduction to Christian Doctrine* (Nashville: Broadman, 1936), 57–69.

[145] Ibid., 73–74.

[146] Dale Moody, *The Word of Truth* (Grand Rapids: Eerdmans, 1981), 63–77.

William Hendricks used general revelation concepts to advance pluralistic theologies of world religions as vehicles of God's saving purposes.[147]

How Does It All Fit Together?

The act of asking what the Bible says about general revelation indicates human dependence on special revelation to bring into focus general revelation. Scripture nowhere treats general revelation as the "natural" insight of autonomous human beings. Indeed, the Apostle Paul affirms that truths about God are available to all human beings but precisely "because God has shown it to them" (Rom. 1:19). In this sense general revelation is no different from any other self-disclosure of God. "Had God insisted on remaining incommunicado we would know nothing whatever about Him," theologian Carl F. H. Henry rightly asserts. "Revelation occurs on God's R-Day as an act of transcendent disclosure. It pulses with the surprise of foreign invasion, and opens before us like the suddenly parted Red Sea waters."[148] Like special revelation, general revelation communicates truths—truths for which human beings must give account. Like special revelation, general revelation is intended to unveil the purposes of God for his creation and its human rulers.

The Reality of General Revelation

While some in the history of the church have sought to minimize or even deny the existence of a general revelation, an authentically biblical theology must acknowledge the presence of the voice of God to all humanity everywhere. Specifically, the Scriptures seem to identify general revelation as found within: (1) the order and design of the natural creation and, (2) the nature and identity of human creatures.

General Revelation and the Natural Creation

The prophets and apostles make clear that the universe is not silent. It points to the reality and identity of its Creator. The Scriptures assume that it is self-evident that the intricacies of nature are not self-existent or accidental but spring from the design of a cosmic architect (Job 38–41). There is nothing philosophically abstract or coldly rationalistic about the biblical theology of revelation in the natural order. Indeed, the Scriptures present God's self-disclosure in the cosmos in terms of worship, mystery, and awe. The Apostle Paul implies that general revelation embedded in the creation

---

[147] Molly T. Marshall, *No Salvation Outside the Church? A Critical Inquiry* (Lewiston: Edwin Mellen, 1993); William L. Hendricks, "Revelation," in *A Baptist's Theology,* ed. R. Wayne Stacy (Macon, GA: Smyth and Helwys, 1999), 14–16.

[148] Henry, *God, Revelation and Authority,* 2:18, 20.

is intended to elicit thanksgiving, adoration, and confessions of dependence from human beings. Indeed, for Paul it is a scandal when humans refuse such worship in the face of such a revelation (Rom. 1:21, 28).

The worship-directed intent of general revelation makes it unsurprising that the most detailed references to general revelation in the Old Testament come in the worship songs of Israel (esp. Pss. 8; 19:1–6). Thus, the psalmist does not simply expound on what can be seen of Yahweh in creation; he sings of it. In these psalms the expanse of the sky—especially the star-filled panorama of the night—is said to communicate the glory and creativity of Israel's God (Pss. 19:1–2; 8:1). For the psalmist the vastness of the cosmos should evoke both human wonder at the artisanship of the Creator (Ps. 8:3) and humility at human smallness within such a creation (Ps. 8:5). For the psalmist the creation does not simply stir emotion but communicates objective content about God—analogous to speech (Ps. 19:2).[149]

Moreover, this revelation—unlike the prophetic oracles—is not limited to the covenant people of God but is as universal as the universe itself (Ps. 19:3–4). According to Paul, the cosmos specifically reveals the Creator—especially in terms of his lordship and sovereignty over the creation: "For his invisible attributes, namely, his eternal power and divine nature, have been clearly perceived, ever since the creation of the world, in the things that have been made" (Rom. 1:20). As biblical scholar David Coffey notes, Paul identifies at least three propositional truths found in the created order: "God's eternity, to be known from the permanence of the universe; his omnipotence, to be known from its greatness; and his deity, or transcendence, to be known from the fact that he was the Creator and therefore other than all that he has made."[150] This communication about God is so clear that all human beings are said to "know God," even those who are steeped in idolatry (Rom. 1:21).

The creation reveals not just the existence and power of the Creator but also his goodness, mercy, and care for the universe. Thus the psalms lead the covenant community in the worship of Yahweh not only by reciting the historical manifestations of his might on Israel's behalf (such as the Exodus in Ps. 114) but also by pointing to the activity of Yahweh in what modern persons would call "nature" or "the environment." The roaring of the seas, the tumult of the storms, and the immensity of the mountains point to the greatness of Israel's covenant God (Ps. 104:1–9).

The order built into the cosmos—in the rhythm of seasons, the cycles of rain and sunlight, the instincts of nesting wildlife, the interplay between

---

[149] As Craigie points out, the "speech" of the firmament would seem in this psalm to have a "twofold thrust: it is addressed to God as praise, yet it is also addressed to mankind as a revealer of 'knowledge.'" Peter C. Craigie, *Psalm 1–50*, WBC (Waco: Word, 1983), 180.

[150] Coffey, "Natural Knowledge of God," 675.

predator and prey, and the diversity and grandeur of wildlife—reveals the wisdom of a Designer who personally intervenes for the good of his creatures (Ps. 104:10–30). In his announcement of the invasion of the messianic kingdom into history, Jesus pointed to the beauty and order of the creation to unveil the goodness and provision of God—along with the appropriate human response to such revelation (Matt. 6:24–35). Likewise, in his preaching to Gentiles at Lystra, the Apostle Paul maintained that God has fixed a "witness" to all people through the cosmic order—an order that includes the provisions of rain, seasons, and harvest. These occurrences in nature, the apostle proclaimed, should have led the nations to recognize the reality and the benevolence of the one Creator God (Acts 14:15–17).

General Revelation and Human Creatures

General revelation is found not only in the inanimate creation but also in the identity and experience of human beings created in the image of God. Perhaps the most explicit aspect of this revelation is found in the human moral consciousness, a conscience that testifies to the content and the rightness of the law of the Creator. The conscience thus is an act of God's grace. Although human beings seek to define "good" and "evil" apart from the authoritative Word of God, God nonetheless planted within all children of Adam a witness to his standards of good and evil. The fact that fallen humans acknowledge any standards of morality indicates that there is a transcendent code of law, somewhere above mere social constructs. Moreover, as Paul points out, this conscience points beyond itself to a day of reckoning. When humans make moral choices—or make immoral choices using moral arguments—they are tacitly acknowledging that they know of a day in which God will judge all the secrets of the heart (Rom. 2:16).

Beyond the conscience, however, general revelation testifies to the uniqueness of man. The human knows himself to be distinctive from nature, a regent in exile as it were. Regardless of how often fallen humans seek to classify themselves as merely biological, they know on the basis of their common rationality, morality, and search for meaning that this is not the case. In this, humans image a Father God who exists above and beyond his creation—which is a sharp distinction from other ancient Near Eastern religions. As Nichols notes, the polytheistic gods of the Gentile nations "tended to be personifications of natural powers."[151] This distinction from nature is seen perhaps most clearly in the universal religious consciousness of human beings (Acts 17:22, 28). All humans sense a disruption with the natural order, a frustration that comes to fruition in the cry of the regenerate heart for the consummation of all things in the new creation (Rom. 8:18–

---

[151] Nichols, *Sacred Cosmos*, 24.

23). All human beings are cognizant of this disruption between themselves and the natural order, a realization that leads to the universal fear of death, even among those who claim to believe in nothing beyond the grave other than cessation of consciousness (Heb. 2:15).

The Purpose of General Revelation

The ultimate purpose of all revelation is Christ Jesus. General revelation is not to be abstracted from Christology. Wisdom and power are closely related in biblical descriptions of God's activities in creation and providence (Isa. 10:13). In the New Testament the "word" of God which forms the universe at the beginning and likewise the "wisdom" of God through which he designed it are revealed as the personal *Logos* of God, who is incarnate as Jesus of Nazareth. Through him, the Apostles John and Paul reveal, the creation was initiated, executed, and is now held together (John 1:1–10; Col. 1:16–17). This means that God's power and wisdom—which are perceived by all in the creation—are not impersonal forces but Jesus Christ, "the power of God and the wisdom of God" (1 Cor. 1:24).

It is no accident, therefore, that the Scriptures tie the knowledge of God found in his cosmic revelation to God's creation purposes to rule the universe through his human vice-regents. Through the same wisdom God created the universe that "kings reign and rulers decree what is just" (Prov. 8:15). This wisdom culminates in Jesus of Nazareth, who bears the messianic Spirit of wisdom (Isa. 11:2; Luke 2:40; 4:17–21), through which he rules over Israel (Isa. 11:3–5). Jesus, then, as the incarnate Wisdom of God is the one through whom God reestablishes his reign over the universe he reveals to have been created through his wisdom. Jesus is not simply the fulfillment of the Mosaic Torah but also the embodiment of the wisdom of God seen in the revelation of the created order itself.[152]

With the New Testament's Christological prism in mind, it makes sense that Psalm 8 moves from the contemplation of the firmament to wonder at Yahweh's placing all things "under the feet" of humanity, a dominion that includes government of the natural order and the animal kingdom (Ps. 8:3–8). This psalm points back to the Genesis mandate to Adam to "subdue the earth" (Gen. 1:28–30); a stewardship that manifested itself in, among other things, Adam's naming the animals under his rule (Gen. 2:19–20). Biblical wisdom then includes not just "common sense" decision-making but also a consideration of the wisdom through which God designed the natural order to exercise dominion stewardship over the creation.

---

[152] For a discussion of the implications of such a concept of Jesus as the fulfillment of wisdom, see N. T. Wright, *The Epistles of Paul to the Colossians and to Philemon: An Introduction and Commentary* (Grand Rapids: Eerdmans, 1986), 66–73.

Thus, wisdom is not identified with the intelligence of philosophers or scholars but with the ways of God seen in his creation—including the mundane rhythms of creatures such as ants, rock badgers, locusts, and lizards (Prov. 30:24–28). Solomon's wisdom was not simply an admirable attribute but "the wisdom of God" (1 Kings 3:28), which was necessary for Solomon to govern the people of God with justice (1 Kings 3:9). With the enemies of God "under the soles of his feet" (1 Kings 5:3), Solomon drew all peoples to himself that they might marvel at this (1 Kings 4:34). It is significant that Solomon's Spirit-anointed wisdom is seen not only in his geopolitical decisions but also in proverbs drawn from a wide knowledge of the natural order, including plant and animal life (1 Kings 4:28–33). Thus, the Proverbs counsel humans to look, for instance, to the ant to discern the wisdom of foresight, organization, and labor (Prov. 6:6–9) or to the cause-and-effect principles of agriculture (Prov. 24:30–31) to spur humans to the creative wisdom through which they image their Creator.

The Limits of General Revelation

Just as we should not minimize the biblical doctrine of general revelation, neither should we overemphasize it. The Scriptures maintain that general revelation points to the mystery of the universe, but it does not disclose the meaning of creation—a meaning unveiled in Christ (Eph. 1:10). Thus, even from the beginning, God's word was needed to interpret general revelation. From observation, after all, the tree of the knowledge of good and evil appeared to be "good for food" and "a delight to the eyes" (Gen. 3:6). The voice of God, however, supplemented this "scientific" discovery with the warning that eating of the tree would result in death.

Humans can know from general revelation that the sexes are complementary and that gender boundaries must not be transgressed (Rom. 1:27; 1 Cor. 11:14). But only through the Scripture's revelation of the mystery of Christ can we know that these gender distinctions were created to point to the one-flesh union of Christ and his church (Eph. 5:31–32). Even here a natural theology or natural law theory is woefully inadequate. Observation of the natural order alone might well establish polygamy or some other form of institutionalized male promiscuity. Only the direct and Christocentric vehicle of Holy Scripture reveals to us that the creation order "from the beginning" establishes monogamous, lifelong marriage between one male and one female (Mark 10:6–9).

Moreover, we must remember that humanity's perception of general revelation is clouded by human depravity. As Paul says, the conscience, the religious consciousness, and even the perception of nature are distorted by the human's idolatrous drive to self-worship (Rom. 1:25).

Thus, as Jesus teaches, human beings do not sin because they reject the truth; they instead reject the truth because they are in bondage to sin (John 3:19; 8:34). This is the reason the appeal to general revelation in, for instance, Acts 14:18 came to nothing: "Even with these words they scarcely restrained the people from offering sacrifice to them." The people are not pagans because they are ignorant; they are ignorant because they are pagans.

The limitations of general revelation, then, result in the necessity of God's address of the human race through the special revelation of Christ and the prophetic-apostolic Scripture. Moreover, these limitations result in the priority of Scripture over any claim to general revelation. This priority results in the Protestant Reformation principle of *sola Scriptura*. This principle does not evaporate insights from general revelation. But it maintains that special revelation provides the sole, final authority for all human thought. As Graeme Goldsworthy put it, the principle of "Scripture alone" means that there is "no external epistemic authority by which to test Scripture's truth claims."[153] General revelation without special revelation is the despair of Solomon's search for meaning in Ecclesiastes. The proper Christian focus is the wise one's confession that "the fear of the LORD is the beginning of wisdom" (Prov. 9:10). What Solomon ultimately concluded is that knowledge of oneself and of the universe starts with a submission to the lordship of God and his anointed, not the other way around.

How Does This Doctrine Impact the Church Today?

General revelation does not exist for its own sake. It exists in order to advance God's redemptive purposes toward the establishment of the kingdom of Christ. Wisdom regarding general revelation, therefore, will have immediate consequences for the church's present kingdom activity.

General Revelation and the Great Commission

An accurate vision of general revelation transforms the missiological life and apologetic focus of the church. This vision must include both the reality and the limits of general revelation to prevent the church from absorbing errors significant enough to wreck the Great Commission enterprise itself.

---

[153] Graeme Goldsworthy, "Evangelicalism and Biblical Theology," in *The Futures of Evangelicalism: Issues and Prospects,* ed. Craig Bartholomew, Robin Perry, and Andrew West (Grand Rapids: Kregel, 2003), 141.

This is especially true when it comes to the questions of the necessity of the proclamation of Christ to the entire world. Religious pluralists argue that God has revealed himself in general revelation through at least some of the world's non-Christian religions. For evidence pluralists point to similarities between Christianity and other religions when it comes to, for instance, similar narratives of creation and the flood, and often similar conceptions of deity or salvation. This establishes nothing, however, for those who believe that all human beings bear an intuitive knowledge of God they are seeking to suppress. If the events of primeval humanity happened in history, as we believe they did, we should not be surprised that remnants of these narratives exist in fragmented form in other religious systems.

Moreover, if God has placed a longing for a virgin-born, dying and rising Rescuer in the hearts of all humanity, we should not be surprised if this archetypal longing is perverted into idolatrous paganisms by a humanity that simultaneously yearns for redemption and is running far from it. As N. T. Wright puts it, "The Christian claim always was that the Jewish story in general, and the Christian climax to it in particular, was the truth, the reality, of which paganism was the parody."[154]

Even for conservative evangelicals, the danger of pluralism raises its head when, for instance, missionaries are tempted to refer to God as "Allah" when evangelizing or to proclaim the "gospel" from passages about Jesus in the Qur'an. Do we really believe the Bible is not sufficient to expose sin and to reveal the glory of Christ to all unbelievers, even those who are Muslims? The Qur'an is not the product of the Holy Spirit, or even the product of godly humans. It is, at best, the forgery of a false prophet and, at worst, the dictation of a demon. Some would say that *Allah* is simply the Arabic word for God. And yet, it is much more. Allah specifically references the God of Islam, when used without qualification in a Muslim context. *Baal,* of course, means "master"; but for Elijah to refer, without qualification, to God as Baal at Mount Carmel would have been a grievous error.

Among evangelicals, the danger of inclusivism—with its misunderstanding of general revelation—is even more pronounced. Inclusivists argue that there is a possibility that those who respond positively to general revelation may be redeemed, even if they never hear the explicit proclamation of Christ and earnestly trust him.[155] Many Christians are troubled by the thought of a man on a deserted island who has never heard the gospel.

---

154 N. T. Wright, *Who Was Jesus?* (Grand Rapids: Eerdmans, 1992), 84.

155 John Sanders, *No Other Name: An Investigation into the Destiny of the Unevangelized* (Grand Rapids: Eerdmans, 1992); Clark H. Pinnock, *A Wideness in God's Mercy: The Finality of Jesus Christ in a World of Religions* (Grand Rapids: Zondervan, 1992); and Amos Yong, *Beyond the Impasse: Toward a Pneumatological Theology of Religions* (Grand Rapids: Baker, 2003).

What if he recognizes God in the beauty and order of creation, realizes sin on the basis of his conscience, and throws himself on the mercy of his unknown Creator for forgiveness? Even some conservative evangelical theologians have left this open as a possibility, though they caution that we do not know how often, if ever, this happens.[156]

The question itself, however, misses the point. It is akin to asking whether we should seek to evangelize our neighbor if he has never sinned and has perfectly obeyed the law of God. Well, no, but we know from the authority of Scripture that no such person exists anywhere (Rom. 3:23). No one responds positively to general revelation but instead rebels against it as part of an ancient conspiracy begun in the midst of Eden. No one comes to Christ apart from the convicting work of the Holy Spirit, and the Holy Spirit convicts only through the explicit proclamation of Jesus (Rom. 10:17; John 16:13–14).

General revelation informs our Great Commission activities when we understand that the universality of God's witness in the conscience means that *all* humans grapple with sin, guilt, and fear of death and judgment. We are able to speak in moral categories and judicial categories precisely because we know that God has implanted these categories in the internal makeup of all humans. We also know that all human beings share a common longing for meaning and indeed for worship. There is therefore no such thing as cognitive atheists—only sinners in deep denial of what they know to be true. This means that apologetics cannot be merely intellectual. We must engage non-Christians at the level of their flight from reality. We must portray for them the truth of Christianity but demonstrate also how their own worldviews cannot possibly account for the ways in which they live. Why does a Darwinist, who believes that everything can be explained by natural selection, celebrate the love he has for his wife of fifty years? Why does a moral relativist become morally indignant when her best friend has sex with her husband?

This likewise means that our apologetic appeals must value above any other authority the claims of Scripture, the "spectacles" through which we view general revelation. The Intelligent Design movement admirably seeks to engage nonbelieving scientists with evidence for a designer. But Intelligent Design should be careful that it does not veer down a path that, essentially, proves too much. Without Scripture to explain to us that the data of nature is skewed by a creation in bondage by the curse, we are unable adequately to evaluate signs of intelligence. We do not want to ignore the issue and suffer the fate of William Paley and the early natural

---

156 Millard J. Erickson, *How Shall They Be Saved? The Destiny of Those Who Do Not Hear of Jesus* (Grand Rapids: Baker, 1996), 143–58.

theologians, who celebrated a romantic notion of the "harmony of nature" as pointing to the goodness of God. Yes, it is easy to say that a formation of geese in the skyline declares the order of the Creator. But what does the bulge of a struggling pig in the midsection of a python tell us about the Designer? Instead, we must provide a "counter-story" to the Darwinist creation myth, a narrative that can be found only when we interpret nature through Scripture and not the other way around.[157]

General Revelation and Spiritual Formation

General revelation serves as a foundation upon which the special revelation of the Scripture is built. Human beings have the capacity to recognize in Scripture statements that are logically consistent and coherent. We have the inbuilt longing for communion with God, a longing that is awakened by the word of truth through the power of the Spirit. We are able to see patterns of Christian truth that are consistent with our everyday experiences and emotions as creatures. Thus, a central goal of general revelation, indeed all divine disclosure, is to provide the foundation for worship.

Terms such as "general revelation" tend to empty the concept of one of its most central components in Scripture—awe-filled wonder, even fear-filled trembling, at this disclosure of God. In Scripture this revelation is not simply a sentimental reflection on the goodness of God in the beauty of nature. Instead, general revelation is to elicit the kind of elation experienced by the psalmist but also the kind of terror experienced by Job. In the narrative of Job, Yahweh himself points to the creation revelation to silence the complaints of his creature (Job 38–41) before a terrifying Creator God whose voice is heard even in the whirlwind itself.

Pastors and church leaders, then, would do well to point to general revelation—as informed by special revelation—to prompt Christians to worship their covenant God. Photographs of distant galaxies from the Hubble telescope, for instance, could be projected onto a screen during a worship service as the pastor preaches from Psalm 19 about the beauty and order of creation.

Our understanding of general revelation also informs how we disciple and care for the psyches of those in our congregations. For almost a century, Christians have sought to "integrate" the claims of secular psychological thought with the Scriptures. Often these integrationists have argued that doing so takes seriously the data of the "Book of Nature"

---

[157] For a helpful treatment of science and religion that maintains the epistemic priority of Scripture, see John Byl, *God and Cosmos: A Christian View of Time, Space, and the Universe* (Edinburgh: Banner of Truth, 2001).

found in contemporary psychological observations. The theology of general revelation at the heart of the integrationist experiment, however, claims far more for general revelation and does so often at a strikingly simplistic level.

First of all, even many secularist intellectuals now find dubious many of the claims to objective "science" at the foundation of much of twentieth- and twenty-first-century therapeutic thought. Neil Postman, for instance, notes that "scarcely anyone believes today that Freud was doing science, any more than educated people believe that Marx was doing science, or Max Weber or Lewis Mumford or Bruno Bettelheim or Carl Jung or Margaret Mead or Arnold Toynbee."[158] This is nowhere more easily seen than the current debates between health insurance companies and the psychological establishment as to whether psychotherapeutic practices are actually "science" at all. If the psychotherapeutic guild itself cannot decide whether its discipline is science or something else, then why should evangelical Christians simply accept its claims as "general revelation"?

Moreover, the most popular "Christian counseling" models have not taken seriously the effects of the Adamic fall on the human race and its intellectual projects. While the Scripture is indeed insistent on a universal revelation of God to humanity, it is equally insistent that this revelation is universally suppressed (Rom. 1:18), jettisoned in favor of idolatry (Rom. 1:21–25). This suppression is seen in the inherently religious foundation of contemporary psychotherapeutic ideologies. It is no accident, after all, that Sigmund Freud devoted significant research to "debunking" the Mosaic claims to monotheism.[159] It is no mere coincidence that Carl Jung centered so much of his research on a transcendent alternative to orthodox Christianity.[160] It is no mere coincidence that contemporary "sociobiology" seeks to "explain" the human quest for God in terms of evolutionary naturalism.[161]

Our churches need pastors and leaders who understand depravity and the fall to the degree that they are able to see the ways in which fallen human self-interest often masquerades as objective "science"—especially when this "science" seeks to explain and prescribe a cure for the fallen condition of humanity.

---

[158] Neil Postman, *Technopoly: The Surrender of Culture to Technology* (New York: Random House, 1992), 153.

[159] Sigmund Freud, *Moses and Monotheism,* trans. Katherine Jones (New York: Random House, 1939).

[160] See, for instance, Murray Stein, ed., *Encountering Jung: On Christianity* (Princeton: Princeton University Press, 1999).

[161] See, for instance, Pascal Boyer, *Religion Explained: The Evolutionary Origins of Religious Thought* (New York: Basic, 2001).

General Revelation and the Cultural Mandate

General revelation has fueled, from the beginning of history, the efforts of man to subdue the cosmos. A thorough understanding of general revelation can enable Christians to engage with the larger world, knowing that even unbelievers can have correct observations about reality, although these observations are translated through the grid of an antirevelational framework. A Christian can undergo open-heart surgery without worrying that the surgeon is an atheist. The regularity of God's creation order means that even atheists can learn how the human body functions or how to harness electricity or how to breed dogs. We can also appreciate the art and music of those who do not know Christ, praising God for the talents he has given them and even noting the insights they have into the common human condition, even as we acknowledge that they cannot understand how this data has been impacted by the fall and redemption in Christ.

The beauty and order of God's creation mandates that human beings—especially those who are being conformed into the image of Christ—value what God values, and image his creativity in art, music, and science. This means that churches should equip those gifted in all areas to pursue excellence, order, symmetry, and beauty—even when these disciplines are not explicitly ecclesial or "Christian." A Christian filmmaker may choose to explore the meaning of love or the heartbreak of familial discord without simply creating a parable with an evangelistic invitation at the end. Such a work of beauty and truth can honor God by acknowledging the goodness of his creation and the pain of the curse of Adam. A Christian teenager gifted in science should be encouraged by his congregation to explore God's truth in nature with the same vigor that we encourage a teenage boy called to missions or a teenage girl called to women's ministry.

Moreover, a theology of general revelation means that we can work with others of goodwill on matters of social or political justice, even if they do not share our Christian faith. Christians may, at times, on the basis of common grace and general revelation join forces with, say, a feminist group to oppose pornography or to seek to outlaw sex slavery in the third world. Natural law theorists would argue that we should base such social and political action on universal, shared canons of morality, present in the human conscience. Since unbelievers reject the Scripture, they contend, we cannot point to what the Bible says but should point instead to general revelation. The problem is that unbelievers also reject the authority of general revelation; indeed they are in revolt against it. Christians would do better to unveil the revelational underpinnings of their social and political commitments and show how these underpinnings are consistent with what unbelievers already know about reality.

Conclusion

When Jesus looked into the night sky, he saw a moon that testified of the beauty, order, and faithfulness of his Father, the covenant Lord of creation. Sadly, those around him in Galilee may have seen the throne of the moon god or simply a freak natural phenomenon. Such has been true always and continues to this day. A Christian theology of general revelation recognizes both that God has spoken in his creation and in his creatures and that this revelation is suppressed and distorted by sinners. The task of the church is to call out and equip disciples who can see the moon and the stars—and indeed all reality—as Jesus did and does.

CHAPTER 3

Special Revelation

David S. Dockery and David P. Nelson

A rchbishop William Temple, in a famous essay on revelation, exclaimed, "The dominant problem of contemporary religious thought is the problem of revelation. Is there such a thing at all? If there is, what is its mode and form? Is it discoverable in all existing things or only in some? If in some, then in which, and by what principle are these selected as its vehicle? Where is it found or believed to be found? What is its authority?"[1]

The answers to these questions, which were posed in the 1930s, represent the myriad of voices that constitute modern theology. The radically different ways people understand revelation is sometimes confusing. The issues raised by Archbishop Temple are still striking issues today. We cannot address each question raised by Temple in this chapter, but we can address the major issue of how God makes himself known to his creation. In this chapter we will focus on God's self-revelation, that is, his manifestation of himself and his will.

What Does the Bible Say?

All knowledge of God comes by way of revelation. The knowledge of God is revealed knowledge since it is God who gives it. He bridges the gap between himself and his creatures and discloses himself and his will to them. God is the source of knowledge about himself, his ways, and his truth. By God alone can God be known. The knowledge of God is revealed by his self-disclosure.[2]

The word *revelation* means an uncovering, a removal of the veil, a disclosure of what was previously unknown. More specifically, revelation is God's manifestation of himself to humankind in such a way that men and women can know and have fellowship with him. An example of revelation

---

[1] William Temple, *Revelation,* ed. John Baille and Hugh Martin (New York: Macmillan, 1937), 83; see also David F. Wells, "Word World: Biblical Authority and the Quandary of Modernity" in *Evangelical Affirmations,* ed. Kenneth Kantzer and Carl F. H. Henry (Grand Rapids: Zondervan, 1990).

[2] See Millard J. Erickson, *Christian Theology* (Grand Rapids: Baker, 1983), 153–98. Erickson's direction is followed throughout this discussion on revelation.

is found in the biblical narrative in which Simon Peter declared that Jesus is the Christ, the Son of God (Matt. 16:16). Jesus responded to this declaration, "Blessed are you, Simon son of Jonah, for this was not revealed to you by man, but by my Father in heaven" (Matt. 16:17).[3] That Jesus is the Son of God could be known only through revelation. The veil was removed; the gap in the disciples' knowledge was bridged. God, the Father, revealed himself to the disciples, and they perceived the knowledge of Jesus, his Son. The knowledge of Jesus' sonship was not attained by human discovery, nor could it have been; it came from God alone.

What is needed to understand God's self-disclosure fully is his special revelation, which provides the viewpoint through which we can fully understand and appreciate God's self-disclosure. Divine truth exists outside special revelation; but it is consistent with and supplemental to, not a substitute for, special revelation. General revelation is consistent with special revelation yet distinct from it.

In contrast to God's general revelation, which is available to all people, God's special revelation is available to specific people at specific times in specific places. This revelation is available now only by consultation of sacred Scripture.[4] Special revelation is particular in its manifestation. God reveals himself to his people. These people of God are the children of Abraham whether by natural (Gen. 12:1–3) or spiritual descent (Gal. 3:16–29). Does this statement mean God confines knowledge of himself to a particular people? Not necessarily, because God's general revelation has been given to all, though perverted and rejected by the universal wickedness of humankind. He now chooses to whom and through whom he will make himself known. As with Abraham, God said, "All peoples on earth will be blessed through you" (Gen. 12:3). This is God's purpose in manifesting himself in a particular manner to his people—that they will be a channel of blessing to others.

Special revelation is also progressive. In the witness of biblical history is found a developing manifestation of God, his will, and his truth in the Old and New Testaments. The development is not contradictory in any fashion. It is complementary and supplementary to what has been previously revealed. We should think of the progress not from untruth to truth but from a lesser to a fuller revelation (Heb. 1:1–3). The revelation of the law in the Old Testament is not superseded by the gospel but is fulfilled in it. The latter fulfills the former. Thus we can say that God's particular revelation has been unfolded to us throughout redemptive history, ultimately being consummated in the person and work of Jesus Christ (John 1:1–18).

---

[3] Unless otherwise noted, all Scripture citations in this chapter are from the New International Version (NIV).

[4] See Erickson, *Christian Theology*, 175–98.

In recognition of the human predicament, God chose from the beginning to disclose himself in a direct way. God has entered this world throughout the course of history. He has made himself known to us within time and space. God has acted and spoken to redeem the human race from its own self-imposed evil. Through miracles, the exodus, and ultimately Jesus Christ, God has revealed himself in history. Special revelation includes not only those acts in history but also the prophetic-apostolic interpretation of those events, meaning that revelation occurs in deeds and words.[5]

Special revelation is primarily redemptive and personal.[6] God reveals himself personally as "I AM" (Exod. 3:14). He talked with Moses face-to-face as with a friend (Exod. 33:11). Like his appearance to Samuel (1 Sam. 3:21), his many personal encounters continued in the covenant and throughout the Old Testament.

The ultimate point of God's personal revelation is found in Jesus Christ. In him the Word became flesh (John 1:1,14,18; 14:9). God was decisively confronting people in Jesus Christ. The good tidings that the holy and merciful God promises salvation as a divine gift to people who cannot save themselves has been fulfilled in the gift of his Son. The redemptive revelation of God is that the incarnate Word (Jesus Christ) has borne the sins of fallen humanity, has died in their place, and has been raised to ensure justification. This is the fixed center of special revelation.[7]

Likewise, God's self-disclosure is propositional in that it made known truths about God to his people.[8] This assertion has been rejected by much modern theology, but it certainly seems plausible that knowledge about someone precedes intimate knowledge of them. The primary purpose of revelation is not necessarily to enlarge the scope of one's knowledge about God. Yet the purpose of knowledge about God is coming to know God. We can thus affirm that special revelation has three stages.

First is God's redemptive work in history, which ultimately centers in the work of the Lord Jesus Christ during the time of his incarnation. The second is the written source of God's revelation, the Bible. In Holy Scripture God has provided interpretative records of what he has done for the redemption of men and women. For instance, it is not enough to know that Jesus Christ died. What is necessary is the interpretation of that event: Jesus Christ died for our sins. The third stage is the work of the Holy Spirit

---

[5] See Bernard Ramm, *Special Revelation and the Word of God* (Grand Rapids: Eerdmans, 1961).

[6] Examples of those who think revelation is only relational or personal are Karl Barth, William Temple, John Baillie, Emil Brunner, and William Hordern. See the discussion in James Leo Garrett, *Systematic Theology*, vol. 1 (Grand Rapids: Eerdmans, 1990), 101.

[7] See *Baptist Faith and Message 2000*, article 1.

[8] The most significant defense of propositional revelation is Carl F. H. Henry, *God, Revelation and Authority*, 6 vols. (Waco: Word, 1976–83). Henry presents fifteen theses contending that revelation is rational and conveyed in intelligible ideas and meaningful words.

in the lives of individuals and in the corporate life of the church. The Spirit applies God's revelation to the minds and hearts of his people by helping them interpret and understand God's written Word (this is sometimes called illumination). As a result, men and women receive Jesus Christ as Lord and Savior and are enabled to follow him faithfully in a believing, covenant community.

The content of special revelation is primarily God himself. In revelation the veil is removed, the gap is bridged so that God makes himself known in his self-manifestation. Mystery remains in God's self-revelation (Eph. 3:2–13). God does not fully reveal himself to any person. No person could fully understand; and beyond that, the full manifestation of God would result in the death of the recipient (Exod. 33:20). However, God reveals himself to persons to the degree they can receive it.

Not only is the mystery of God himself unveiled, at least in part, but God's truth is also revealed. Special revelation is the declaration of truth about God, his character, and his actions in relationship with his creation. His self-disclosure is intelligible and meaningful, communicating divine truth for the mind and heart. The purpose of God's gracious manifestation is well stated by the Apostle Paul: "He made known to us the mystery of his will according to his good pleasure, which he purposed in Christ, to be put into effect when the times will have reached their fulfillment—to bring all things in heaven and on earth together under one head, even Christ" (Eph. 1:9–10).

The proper setting of special revelation is Christian faith. God makes himself known to those who receive his revelation in faith. Faith is the instrument by which we receive God's revelation. When faith is present, the things of God become manifest (Heb. 11:1–6). Faith is the glad recognition of truth, the reception of God's revelation without reservation or hesitation (Rom. 10:17). God is pleased to reveal himself and his majestic Word to people of faith. Thus we can conclude that God reveals himself both personally and propositionally. While there is tension between these two means of revelation, there is no contradiction. Revelation is both knowledge about God and knowledge of God. It is knowledge about God that leads us to know God in a personal and salvific way.[9]

Revelation and Scripture

The Bible claims to record divine communication. The creation account in Genesis 1 portrays a God who creates by speaking. The Scriptures

---

[9] See the insightful contribution in E. J. Carnell, *The Case for Orthodox Theology* (Philadelphia: Westminster, 1959), 173; also Ronald Nash, *The Word of God and the Mind of Man* (Grand Rapids: Zondervan, 1983).

portray a God who reveals, instructs, and guides by speaking. God speaks to various individuals in the Scriptures, and he speaks to his people through his prophets and apostles. Thus God's people have long considered the Bible the "word of the Lord" that is distinct from any other "word."

In Christianity the Bible is of crucial importance, for it is through the Bible that the Spirit witnesses to individuals of God's grace and the need for a response of faith. In the Bible we learn of God's redemption of sinners through Christ Jesus. Our response of faith to God's words and acts, recorded and interpreted by the prophets and the apostles, calls for us to embrace with humble teachableness, without finding fault, whatever is taught in Holy Scripture.

It is not enough to say that God has revealed himself only in words or only in acts.[10] We must say that this revelation has come to us in both words and acts and has been divinely interpreted through the writings of Holy Scripture for us.

God has initiated the revelation of himself to men and women. This revelation is understandable to humans, making it possible to know God and to grow in relationship with him.[11] God's self-manifestation provides information about himself for the purpose of leading men and women into his presence. For believers today the Bible is the source of God's revelation. Indeed we can go so far as to say the Bible is a written revelation of God's nature and his will for fallen humankind.

While we can identify Scripture as a mode of special revelation, along with God's words and acts, it must be acknowledged that Scripture and revelation are not identical. There was special revelation that was not preserved for us in the Bible (John 21:25). On the other hand, not all of what is in the Bible is necessarily special revelation in a direct sense. Some portions of the material found in the Bible were simply matters of public knowledge, such as the list of genealogies. These most likely were matters of public domain, which could have been recorded by the biblical writers without God's having to reveal them specially. Yet the Bible, while not identical at every point with special revelation, must be affirmed as God's written Word for his people and as revelation.[12]

In the written Word we can identify God; know and understand something about him, his will, and his work; and point others to him. Special

[10] G. Ernest Wright, *God Who Acts: Biblical Theology as Recital* (London: SCM, 1952) has argued that God only reveals himself in acts or events. Gordon H. Clark has come close to seeing revelation totally in the form of words and propositions; see *God's Hammer: The Bible and Its Critics* (Jefferson: Trinity Foundation, 1982). Both extremes need to be avoided.

[11] See Donald G. Bloesch, *Holy Scripture: Revelation, Inspiration, and Interpretation* (Downers Grove, IL: InterVarsity, 1994), 49–56.

[12] See Erickson, *Christian Theology,* 196–98; idem., "Revelation," in *Foundations for Biblical Interpretation* (Nashville: Broadman & Holman, 1994), 13–15.

revelation is not generally speculative. The Bible primarily speaks on matters of cosmology and history when these issues touch the nature of faith. God has manifested himself incarnationally through human language, human thought, and human action as ultimately demonstrated in the incarnation of Jesus Christ himself. Since the person and work of Jesus Christ are the fixed center of special revelation, we will move to a discussion of Jesus Christ and the Bible.

Jesus Christ and the Bible

The Bible presents a message about God and his purposes. It describes the creation of the universe, including the direct creation of men and women in a paradise on earth. The Bible describes the call of Abraham, the giving of the law, the establishment of the kingdom, the division of the kingdom, and the captivity and restoration of Israel. Scripture sees humankind as fallen from a sinless condition and separated from God. The promise of a coming Messiah who will redeem men and women and reign as King appears throughout the Old Testament.

The message of Holy Scripture proclaims that believers are restored to favor with God through the sacrifice of Christ. His sacrifice puts an end to the Old Testament sacrificial system in which the blood of animals represented the handling of the sin problem. The New Testament reveals the Christ who brought salvation and describes how these prophecies about him were minutely fulfilled. This unifying message ties the biblical library together. The Old Testament promises were fulfilled in the person of Jesus Christ, "the son of Abraham" and "the son of David" (Matt. 1:1).[13] As Augustine said more than fifteen hundred years ago, "The New is in the Old contained; the Old is in the New explained." This overarching unity centers in Jesus Christ, who is the primary subject and key to interpretation of Holy Scripture.[14]

Jesus Christ is the central figure of divine revelation and the focus of the Christian faith.[15] The Bible is our primary source of information about Jesus. Yet the Bible's testimony is amply supported by the impact of Jesus Christ on the world of the first century. We will briefly examine how Jesus as the central figure of divine revelation viewed Holy Scripture. We will look both at Scripture's view of Jesus and at Jesus' authentication of Scripture. We will also give attention to the significance of Jesus as both divine and human as a model for the divine-human aspect of Scripture.

---

[13] See R. T. France, *Jesus and the Old Testament* (Downers Grove: InterVarsity, 1971).

[14] See John W. Wenham, *Christ and the Bible* (Downers Grove: InterVarsity, 1972).

[15] See H. D. McDonald, *Jesus—Human and Divine: An Introduction to Christology* (Grand Rapids: Zondervan, 1968); also Carl F. H. Henry, *The Identity of Jesus of Nazareth* (Nashville: Broadman & Holman, 1992).

Jesus Christ as the Promised Messiah[16]

Jesus was born in Bethlehem of Judea, a few miles south of Jerusalem. He was born a Jew. He would be the apex of God's revelation to humanity. In different ways and at various times God had spoken to his people through his prophets (Heb. 1:1). The purposes of God had been made known through a series of covenants (Gen. 12; 2 Sam. 7; Jer. 31). In these covenants God's intent for establishing his kingdom and for redeeming humankind is progressively expressed. God's purposes were to be accomplished through a descendant of David. The people of God in the Old Testament looked forward expectantly to the coming of the promised King, their Messiah. In Jesus Christ these covenant promises found their ultimate fulfillment.

The Old Testament includes two different lines of teaching about the promised one, sometimes distinct and other times commingled. One line claims that the Messiah would be a Redeemer who would restore humankind to a right relationship with God. This theme is best developed around the idea of a Suffering Servant Messiah in Isaiah 52:13–53:12. Here the Messiah is pictured as one who would become an offering for the sins of men and women.

Another line of Old Testament teaching describes the Messiah as a coming King destined to restore Israel to its rightful place as God's people on earth. The promises portray the restoration as a time of peace and righteousness, as seen, for example, in Psalm 2 and Isaiah 9:6–7. Aspects of each purpose can be seen in the covenant promises and the prophetic pictures, though the details of the completion of these teachings remained somewhat unclear.[17]

The New Testament, however, interprets the Old Testament and announces that the promised Messiah had come in Jesus of Nazareth. Through his ministry, teachings, sacrificial death, and resurrection, Jesus fulfilled the messianic promises, accomplished the messianic mission, and provided for the salvation of the lost world. The New Testament also declares that Jesus will come again and reign as King, bringing peace and joy and righteousness.

In identifying Jesus as the Messiah, the New Testament authors affirm an essential unity between the Old Testament and the New Testament. The New Testament, which is rooted in the Old Testament, interprets and amplifies the Old Testament. The life and work of Jesus, therefore, were grounded in the Old Testament, which Jesus acknowledged to be

---

[16] This theme is addressed more fully in this volume in the chapter on the Person of Christ.

[17] See John Rogerson, et al., *The Study and Use of the Bible* (Grand Rapids: Eerdmans, 1988).

the Word of God (Matt. 5:17–18; John 10:35; 17:17), and on which he based his life.[18]

Jesus Christ and the Old Testament

Jesus was responsible for teaching his followers that his life and ministry fulfilled the Old Testament Scriptures. Jesus showed how the Scriptures of the Hebrew Bible spoke of a figure to come and his understanding that he was that figure. For example in John 5:39, Jesus said, "You diligently study the Scriptures because you think that by them you possess eternal life. These are the Scriptures that testify about me." In John 5:46 Jesus said, "If you believed Moses, you would believe me, for he wrote about me." Also on the Emmaus road with his disciples following the resurrection, Jesus said: "'How foolish you are, and how slow of heart to believe all that the prophets have spoken! Did not the Christ have to suffer these things and then enter his glory?' And beginning with Moses and all the Prophets, he explained to them what was said in all the Scriptures concerning himself" (Luke 24:25–27).

The method that Jesus used to interpret the Old Testament was entirely Christological.[19] We can see this in places like the temptation narratives (Matt. 4:1–11; Luke 4:1–13), in which we find Jesus' own estimation of his status and calling, where his answers were taken from Deuteronomy 6–8. In this passage Moses, following the forty years of wandering in the wilderness, exhorted Israel to wholehearted obedience and continued faith in God's provision for them. It was a time of hunger and testing, preparatory to a special task, in which God disciplined his nation Israel to teach it to worship only the true God (Deut. 8:5). Israel often failed to carry out the mission and call of God. Jesus, at the end of forty days, accepted afresh his messianic mission and his status as the Son of God. His belief in his forthcoming resurrection seemed to be motivated both by the promises of Israel's resurrection and by seeing the account of Jonah as a picture of his own resurrection (Jon. 1:17; Matt. 12:40). He observed that his own experience was prefigured in the psalms of vindication and suffering. These psalms were used both by individual Israelites and by corporate Israel (Pss. 22; 41–43; 118; Matt. 21:42; 23:39; 26:38; 27:46).[20]

In these and other pictures in the Old Testament, Jesus saw prophecies of himself and his work. The result was that Jesus was rejected by the majority of Jews, but those receiving him are given the right to become children of God (John 1:12). The history of Israel had reached its decisive

---

[18] See C. K. Barrett, "The Old Testament in the New," *CHB* (Cambridge: University Press, 1970), 1:377–411.

[19] See David S. Dockery, *Christian Scripture* (Nashville: Broadman & Holman, 1995), 97–172.

[20] See France, *Jesus and the Old Testament.*

point in the coming of Jesus Christ. The whole of the Old Testament was summed up in him. He embodied in himself the redemptive destiny of Israel. That status and destiny are to be fulfilled in the community of those who belong to him.[21]

Because Jesus is the fulfillment of God's purposes for Israel, words originally spoken of the nation could be rightly applied to him. Jesus is the key to understanding the Old Testament because everything points to himself. The New Testament writers, following the pattern of Jesus, interpreted the Old Testament as a whole and in its parts as a witness to Christ. It is not surprising that in providing different pictures of Jesus' life, the biblical writers saw that at almost every point he had fulfilled the Old Testament.[22] This realization provides the key to the way Jesus understood and used the Old Testament. It provides the framework and groundwork for Jesus' authentication of the New Testament. It also provides the hermeneutical keys for the Christian community in its interpretation of Holy Scripture.

Jesus Christ and the New Testament

In the Gospels we learn that Jesus understood his own life in light of the Scriptures. We learn, too, that he accepted the full authority and divine authorship of the Old Testament and that he claimed truth for his own teaching. We know that the New Testament was written after Jesus' life on earth. What then was his relationship to the New Testament?

During his ministry on earth Jesus trained disciples. Among these, twelve were given special attention and a special commission (Mark 3:14). It is impossible to speak with certainty about the methods Christ used to teach his disciples. Probably, however, Jesus instructed his followers by methods similar to those used by the rabbis of his day. Fifteen times in the Gospels he is called rabbi. At other times he is referred to as teacher (rabbi and teacher are vitally related ideas). The rabbis thought of themselves as bearers of truth or of the true tradition. It was their task to pass on truth to approved disciples, who memorized their teachings. The disciples of Jesus must have committed themselves to intensive instruction. After they received special commissioning, they gave themselves to the Word of God and to preaching. The church followed the example of the disciples by continuing steadfastly in the apostles' (disciples') teaching (Acts 2:42; 6:2).

Before and after his resurrection Jesus indicated that his disciples would have authority to teach and build his church in his name (Matt. 16:16–20;

---

[21] Matthew Black, "The Christological Use of the Old Testament in the New," *NTS* 18 (1971): 1–14.

[22] See E. Earle Ellis, "How the New Testament Uses the Old," in *New Testament Interpretation,* ed. I. Howard Marshall (Grand Rapids: Eerdmans, 1975), 199–219.

28:18–20). As the Father had sent Jesus, Jesus sent the apostles (John 20:21). In Jesus' name, repentance and forgiveness were to be proclaimed (Luke 24:47). All of these things were fulfilled in the early church because Jesus gave the Holy Spirit to the apostles. The Spirit brought events to their remembrance and led them into all truth (John 14–17). In this way the Spirit of God led the apostles in ministry and mission. The apostles' words were confirmed by Jesus through the inspiration of the Spirit. Paul's commissioning to preaching and teaching was different from that of the other apostles, but Jesus' affirmation of Paul's work was quite similar (Acts 9). Therefore, there is good reason to believe that Jesus authenticated the work of the apostles in their work of writing Scripture. Following Wenham, we seem justified in saying:

> To Christ, His own teaching and the teaching of His Spirit-taught apostles were true, authoritative, inspired. To Him, what He and they said under the direction of the Spirit, God said. To Him, the God of the New Testament was the living God; and in principle the teaching of the New Testament was the teaching of the living God.[23]

Over the past two hundred years much debate in scholarly circles has wrestled over the question of Jesus Christ. These discussions have led to the "quest for the historical Jesus," "the new quest for the historical Jesus," Christologies "from below," Christologies "from above," and now the so-called Jesus Seminar, which raises questions about the entire New Testament.[24] This is not the place to evaluate the relationship between the Jesus of history and the picture presented of him in the New Testament. But it seems clear to us that Jesus created the church; the church did not create Jesus. So the words of Jesus were not created by the church; the words of Jesus became the foundation and cornerstone for the church and its writings.[25]

Jesus Christ the God-Man

We have seen that God has revealed himself in acts and deeds, as well as in words. These words include the interpretation of the acts and deeds and make up the prophetic-apostolic witness. The prophetic-apostolic witness is for us today the source of God's divine revelation. Thus when we read the Bible we are not just reading a human interpretation of God's work in history, but we are reading a divinely inspired, divine interpretation of

---

[23] Wenham, *Christ and the Bible*, 123.
[24] See David F. Wells, *The Person of Christ* (Westchester, IL: Crossway, 1984).
[25] Barrett, "Old Testament in the New," 405.

God's own works. The central figure in God's revelation and the ultimate revelation himself is Jesus Christ (Heb. 1:1–2).

We have seen that the Old Testament looked forward to Jesus' coming. Jesus understood his life and ministry in light of the Old Testament. He lived in light of the truthfulness and authority of the Old Testament. Jesus Christ, the Son of God incarnate, who claimed divine authority for all that he did and taught, not only affirmed the absolute authority of the Old Testament but also unreservedly submitted to it. His reading of the Old Testament was shaped by his own messianic mission. At the heart of Jesus' biblical interpretation was a Christocentric perspective. Jesus thus became the direct and primary source for the church's understanding of the Old Testament.

Jesus stamped his authority on the Holy Scriptures by his submission to them and also by his commissioning of the apostolic witness. Jesus discipled and commissioned his followers to pass on his teaching. The Spirit of God was given to enable them to carry out this task. The result was Spirit-directed writings that focused on the life, ministry, death, resurrection, and exaltation of Christ. The New Testament equally affirms the deity and humanity of Jesus. This picture of the living Word serves as a model for rightly viewing the written Word. Our next section will develop a Christological model for understanding Holy Scripture as a divine-human book.

The Divine-Human Authorship of Inspired Scripture

The Bible is a book written by numerous authors over a period of hundreds of years, and yet at the same time it is the Word of God. The variety of views that will be surveyed in this chapter will attempt to do justice to the mystery of Scripture's divine inspiration and still maintain its human authorship. Clark Pinnock, who surveyed various approaches to this subject, acknowledged: "The prime theological issue which became evident in our survey of options on biblical authority is the need to maintain with equal force both the humanity and divinity of the Word of Scripture."[26] The precise relationship between divine revelation and the human writings that comprise the canonical Scripture has been and continues to be a subject of contention.[27]

Scripture cannot rightly be understood unless we take into consideration that it has dual-sided authorship. It is not enough to affirm that the Bible

---

[26] Clark Pinnock, "Three Views of the Bible in Contemporary Theology," in *Biblical Authority,* ed. Jack B. Rogers (Waco: Word, 1977), 71; also see J. I. Packer, "Encountering Present-Day Views of Scripture" in *The Foundation of Biblical Authority,* ed. James M. Boice (Grand Rapids: Zondervan, 1978).

[27] Cf. Donald G. Bloesch, *Essentials of Evangelical Theology* (San Francisco: Harper & Row, 1978–1979), 1:51–56.

is a human witness to divine revelation because the Bible is also God's witness to himself. An affirmation that Scripture is partly the Word of God and partly the word of humans is inadequate. What must be affirmed is that the Bible is entirely and completely the Word of God and the words of the human authors (Acts 4:25). It is the Word of God written in the words of men.

It is not entirely appropriate to make a direct correspondence between Scripture and Jesus Christ, but nevertheless there is an observable analogy.[28] However, just as the conception of Jesus came by the miraculous overshadowing of the Holy Spirit (Luke 1:35), so Scripture is the product of the Spirit's inspiration (2 Tim. 3:16). Likewise, as Jesus took on human form through a human mother, so the Bible has come to us in human language through human authors. The result is that Jesus is the living Word of God, the God-man, and the Bible is the written Word of God, the divine-human Scripture.

An affirmation that Scripture is completely the Word of God and the words of humans also points to its dual-sided nature. Because it is the Word of the infinite, all-knowing, eternal God, it speaks eternal truth that is applicable to readers of all time, beyond the original recipients. Yet, at the same time, it is the word from godly men to specific communities addressing problems and situations within certain contexts and cultures.

Some have contended that the Bible is primarily, if not entirely, a human product of an illumined religious consciousness.[29] Such a view maintains the possibility that the Bible could lead its readers to divine truth though it would deny that the Bible is a revelation of divine truth. By comparison with the heretical views in the early Christological statements, we could classify this position as ebionitic, a view that emphasizes the humanity while losing sight of the essential deity.[30] On the other hand, the divine aspect of Scripture has been emphasized so prominently by some that the human element is only an outward appearance of the divine. Such an approach denies the Bible's genuine humanity as well as its historicity. Again, parallel to the

---

[28] We recognize that diverse conclusions have been drawn from the analogy between the divine and human in Jesus and in Scripture by scholars with differing theological positions. It is not absolutely clear whether the analogy can be applied to the human authors through whom God was active in the composition of Scripture or to the actual result of inspiration. The doctrine of the incarnation does account for the true activity of God in the human dimension, thus allowing for at least the possibility that God could work in human beings to communicate his Word in human words. More important to the theology of Scripture than the analogy described above is Jesus Christ's own view of Scripture.

[29] Gene M. Tucker and Douglas A. Knight, eds., *Humanizing America's Iconic Book* (Chico, CA: Scholars, 1982); also see Edward Farley and Peter C. Hodgson, "Scripture and Tradition," in *Christian Theology: An Introduction to Its Traditions and Tasks,* ed. Peter C. Hodgson and Robert H. King (Philadelphia: Fortress, 1982).

[30] See Bloesch, *Evangelical Theology,* 1:134.

unorthodox views of the person of Christ, the latter view has tendencies toward a docetic view of Scripture.[31]

We can see the importance of affirming a balanced view of Scripture. But how does the Christian community maintain such a balance? How can it be affirmed that Scripture is the inspired Word of God when it is a collection of books by human authors? Can the words of the Bible be identified with the Word of God? Is some of the Bible God's Word? Or can this be affirmed for all of the Bible? How is it possible that the Bible can simultaneously be the Word of God and a human composition? It is to these questions that the next section is addressed.

The Divine Authorship of Inspired Scripture

In the history of the church, the divine character of Scripture has been the great presupposition for the whole of Christian preaching and theology. This is readily apparent in the way the New Testament speaks about the Old Testament. That which appears in the Old Testament is cited in the New Testament with formulas like "God says" and "the Holy Spirit says" (Acts 4:24–25; 13:47; 2 Cor. 6:16). Scripture and God are so closely joined together in the minds of the New Testament authors that they naturally could speak of Scripture doing what it records God as doing (Rom. 9:17; Gal. 3:8). The introductory phrase "It is [stands] written" (*gegraptai*) is also used of New Testament writings (John 20:31). The New Testament concept of faith is in accord with the divine character of the apostolic word (Rom. 1:5; 10:3; 16:26). The reference to the divine character of the apostolic word in its written and oral form deserves unconditional faith and obedience.

Because of the apostolic word's divine origin and content, Scripture can be described as "certain" (2 Pet. 1:19), "trustworthy" (1 Tim. 1:15; 2 Tim. 2:11; Titus 3:8), "confirmed" (Heb. 2:3), and "eternal" (1 Pet. 1:24,25). As a result, those who build their lives on Scripture will not be disappointed (Rom. 9:33; 1 Pet. 2:6). The Word was written for instruction and encouragement (Rom. 15:4), to lead to saving faith (2 Tim. 3:15), to guide people toward godliness (2 Tim. 3:16b), and to equip believers for good works (2 Tim. 3:17).

The purpose of Scripture is to place men and women in a right standing before God and to enable believers to seek God's glory in all of life's

---

[31] Ibid., 134–35; see also the discussion of the docetic view of Scripture in John Gerstner, "The Church's Doctrine of Biblical Inspiration," in *The Foundation of Biblical Authority*, ed. James Montgomery Boice (Grand Rapids: Zondervan, 1978), 12; Klaas Runia and Karl Barth, *Doctrine of Holy Scripture* (Grand Rapids: Eerdmans, 1962); James Tunstead Burtchaell, *Catholic Theories of Biblical Inspiration Since 1810: A Review and Critique* (London: Cambridge University Press, 1969), 290–91.

activities and efforts. But Scripture is not concerned solely with a person's religious needs. On the contrary, the divine character, origin, and content of Scripture teaches us to understand everything *sub specie Dei*—"humanity, the world, nature, history, their origin and their destination, their past and their future."[32] The Bible is not only a book of conversion but also a book of creation and history. It is a book of redemptive history, and it is this perspective that best represents and defines the divine character of Scripture.

We must recognize that central to Scripture is the unifying history of God's redeeming words and acts, of which the advent and work of Jesus Christ are the ultimate focus. Jesus Christ is the center to which everything in Scripture is united and bound together—the beginning and the end, creation and redemption, humanity, the world, the fall, history, and the future.[33] If this overriding unity is ignored, Scripture is denatured and can lose its "theological-Christological definition" and become "abstracted from the peculiar nature and content of Scripture."[34]

As we have noted, we cannot construct dualistic operations of Scripture that emphasize only its religious or pietistic sense.[35] This could lead to distinguishing between what is and what is not inspired Scripture, what is and what is not from God. We must resist relating divine inspiration merely to content and not to form, to the Bible's purpose and not to its essence, or to its thoughts and not to its words. The entirety of Scripture is divinely inspired and is God's light upon our path and God's lamp for our feet. We now turn our attention to the Bible's witness to itself and the nature of inspiration.

The Bible's Witness to Itself

In addition to those passages mentioned in the previous section, there are many other verses that address the divine aspect of Scripture (Pss. 19:7–11; 119; Matt. 5:17–18; Luke 24:25–27; John 10:34–35; Heb. 1:1–2; 2 Pet. 3:16), but the primary witness of the Bible to its own inspiration is found in 2 Timothy 3:16–17 and 2 Peter 1:19–21.

---

[32] Herman Ridderbos, *Studies in Scripture and Its Authority* (St. Catherines, Ontario: Paideia, 1978), 24. To say that we understand everything *sub specie Dei* is to say that we understand everything "under the aspect of God." That is, we view everything in light of the reality of God and all that this reality entails.

[33] See D. L. Baker, *Two Testaments: One Bible* (1976; Grand Rapids: Baker, rev. 1993).

[34] Ridderbos, *Studies in Scripture*, 25.

[35] See James E. White, *What Is Truth?* (Nashville: Broadman, 1994); Anthony Thiselton, "Truth," *NIDNTT*; Roger Nicole, "The Biblical Concept of Truth," in *Scripture and Truth*, ed. D. A. Carson and John D. Woodbridge (Grand Rapids: Baker, 1983), 287–98. For a different perspective, see Frank Stagg, "What Is Truth?" in *Science, Faith and Revelation*, ed. Robert E. Patterson (Nashville: Broadman, 1979), 239–60. There are hints of this dualism in E. Y. Mullins, *The Christian Religion in Its Doctrinal Expression* (Philadelphia: Judson, 1917), although his purpose was to affirm the religious and soteriological nature and purpose of Scripture.

Second Timothy 3:16–17 says, "All Scripture is God-breathed and is useful for teaching, rebuking, correcting and training in righteousness, so that the man of God may be thoroughly equipped for every good work."[36]

The term "inspiration," a translation of *theopneustos,* has a long heritage in the theological literature, and it is always used with further explanation and disclaimers. This is because *theopneustos* means "God-breathed."[37] In contemporary usage the term *inspiration* suggests the idea of "breathing into." Some take this to be generally synonymous with illumination or human genius. But the New Testament emphasis is that God "breathed out" what the sacred writers communicated in the biblical writings. A preferable term might be "spiration," rather than inspiration in order to emphasize the divine source and initiative rather than human genius or creativity. "In short, the Bible's life-breath as a literary deposit is divine."[38] Recognizing the shortcomings in the term *inspiration,* we shall continue to use the word, primarily because of its long-term standing in theological literature. The point that must be emphasized when using this term is that it points to God as the source of Scripture, a point that cannot be stated too strongly.

It has been suggested that 2 Timothy 3:16 does not refer to all of Scripture because of the possible translation, "Every Scripture inspired of God is also useful."[39] What is at issue is the meaning of the Greek term *pas,* which may be translated "all" or "every." I. Howard Marshall notes

---

[36] See Wayne A. Grudem, "Scripture's Self-Attestation and the Problem of Formulating a Doctrine of Scripture," in *Scripture and Truth,* ed. D. A. Carson and John D. Woodbridge (Grand Rapids: Baker, 1983), 19–59; also James M. Grier, "The Self-Witness of the Bible," *GTJ* 1 (1979): 71–76; Edwin A. Blum, "The Apostle's View of Scripture," in *Inerrancy,* ed. Norman L. Geisler (Grand Rapids: Zondervan, 1979), 39–53. The approach of self-attestation is sometimes rejected on the grounds of circular reasoning. But the dilemma involved in this approach is apparent: either the Bible has its starting point upon itself or upon some other foundation, in which case it would be guilty of inconsistency. We can allow for additional testimony, but surely the Scripture's own claim must be given prior consideration. As with all points of theology, a consistent method would call for a theological statement in Scripture about itself to be considered prior to an examination of the phenomena in Scripture. Yet Dewey M. Beegle (*Scripture, Tradition and Infallibility* [Grand Rapids: Eerdmans, 1973], 175–97) seeks to develop a theology of inspiration based upon the phenomena of Scripture. His approach and conclusions differ from those in this book.

[37] See Carl F. H. Henry, "The Authority & Inspiration of the Bible," *EBC,* ed. F. E. Gaebelein, 12 vols. (Grand Rapids: Zondervan, 1979), 1:13.

[38] Ibid. Cf. J. N. D. Kelly, *A Commentary on the Pastoral Epistles* (New York: Harper & Row, 1963), 203; also see B. B. Warfield, "The Biblical Idea of Inspiration," in *The Inspiration and Authority of the Bible,* ed. Samuel G. Craig (Philadelphia: Presbyterian & Reformed, 1967), 132–33.

[39] For an example of this approach, see especially Martin Dibelius and Hans Conzelmann, *The Pastoral Epistles,* trans. Philip Buttolph and Adela Yarbro (Philadelphia: Fortress, 1962), 120. However, such a translation is highly unlikely because it makes the *kai* ("also") quite awkward. It is doubtful that the apostle would affirm that Scripture has a second characteristic ("also") before describing its initial characteristic. The passage evidences a predicate construction and calls for the more straightforward translation: "The whole of Scripture is inspired . . ." (e.g. KJV, NASB, NIV). Cf. C. F. D. Moule, *An Idiom Book of New Testament Greek* (Cambridge: Cambridge University Press, 1953), 95. Also Gottlob Schrenk, *graphē* in *TDNT,* 1:759, who comments, "This obviously means every passage of Scripture." The extent of inspiration is discussed adequately by Erickson,

that this suggestion can be confidently rejected since no New Testament author would have conceived of the possibility of a book being classified as Scripture and yet not being inspired by God.[40] We realize that some disagree with Marshall and affirm a limited inspiration for the so-called salvific parts and thus prefer to read *pas* as "every," understanding the verse to mean "every writing that is God-breathed is inspired." The problem with this approach is its difficulty in distinguishing the salvific parts from the nonsalvific. Thus, one cannot tell precisely what parts of the Bible are inspired. George Knight demonstrates that *pas* is best understood as "all" in the context of 2 Timothy 3:16.[41] There are fifty occurrences of *graphē* in the New Testament, all of which refer to holy Scripture.[42] Undoubtedly *graphē* refers to the Old Testament.

Furthermore, it is not too much to affirm that the construction used in verse 16 has a broader meaning that allows for the inclusion of the New Testament writings, as well. The anarthrous construction, *pas graphē* ("all Scripture"), can have a characteristic idea, so that the phrase can mean "all that have characteristics of canonical Scripture."[43] In addition, it needs to be observed that *graphē* includes references to New Testament writings in 1 Timothy 5:18 and 2 Peter 3:18.

Second Peter 1:19–21 says:

> And we have something more sure, the prophetic word, to which you will do well to pay attention as to a lamp shining in a dark place, until the day dawns and the morning star rises in your hearts, knowing this first of all, that no prophecy of Scripture comes from someone's own interpretation. For no prophecy was ever produced by the will of man, but men spoke from God as they were carried along by the Holy Spirit (ESV).

In this text the Apostle Peter suggests the confidence with which the reader may approach the Bible, since it is a word "more sure." In this

---

Christian Theology, 210–12. Herman Ridderbos (*Studies in Scripture,* 27) says that "the predicative significance of *theopneustos* is not in my opinion disputable."

[40] I. Howard Marshall, *Biblical Inspiration* (Grand Rapids: Eerdmans, 1982), 25.

[41] George Knight III, *The Pastoral Epistles,* NIGTC (Grand Rapids: Eerdmans, 1992), 445.

[42] Ibid.

[43] It is highly probable that the author is not making a distinction in his mind between the LXX and the MT in making this assertion. See Homer A. Kent Jr. *The Pastoral Epistles* (Chicago: Moody, 1982), 281; also see Nigel Turner, *A Grammar of New Testament Greek,* vol. 3, *Syntax* (Edinburgh: T & T Clark, 1963), 199. Though Turner's comments are ambiguous, it seems best to take *pas* in an inclusive manner. We could then translate as, "Everything that takes on the character of Scripture," and thus the entire canon, even the New Testament, is included by inference. Yet we must note that the Old Testament is what is primarily in view as the term *graphē* indicates. Note the reference to the Holy Scriptures in verse 15.

context Peter makes a striking statement since he compares his own experience at the transfiguration of Jesus with the Scriptures. Peter saw with his own eyes the revelation of God in Christ, yet he knew that other believers would not have such an immediate experience with Christ, so he pointed them to the Scriptures, which are God's interpretation (not a private interpretation of man as in vv. 20–21) of the matters recorded. Why are these words "more sure"? Because, while they are in fact words "spoken" by men, they are truly words "from God." Peter's explanation about how human words may actually be from God is that these men were "carried along by the Holy Spirit" (v. 21).

From these texts we draw the following conclusions about the nature of Scripture. First, Scripture is verbally inspired. That is, all the *words* (*graphē,* i.e., "writings") of the Bible are inspired. Second, the Scriptures are completely inspired. That is, *all* (*pas*) the words are inspired. Third, the Scriptures are divinely inspired. That is, *God* inspired all the words of Scripture (i.e., the words are *theopneustos*). Taken together, these truths form the concept of plenary-verbal inspiration. That is, all the words of the Bible are inspired by God. Fourth, we affirm that not only the text of the Bible, but the human authors were inspired by the Holy Spirit. That is, while they are truly human words, the words of the Scriptures, inspired by God, are truly the words of the divine author. Again, Scripture is the Word of God written in the words of man.

What Has the Church Believed?

Patristic Period

The evidence of Christian acceptance of the inspiration and authority of the Scriptures is early and widespread. Justin Martyr held that the human authors of Scripture were moved by the "Divine Word"[44] and described inspiration in terms of the Holy Spirit as a musician playing upon the soul of the inspired human author.[45] While some such statements might be construed to diminish the role of the human authors, Irenaeus recognized both divine and human authorship[46] and, due to divine inspiration concluded that the Scriptures are perfect: "Being most properly assured that

---

[44] Justin Martyr, *First Apology* 36.
[45] Justin Martyr, *Address to the Greeks,* 8. A similar musical analogy is made by Athenagoras in *A Plea for the Christians* 9, where he speaks of the "prophets, who, lifted in ecstasy above the natural operations of their minds by the impulses of the Divine Spirit, uttered the things with which they were inspired, the Spirit making use of them as a flute-player breathes into a flute."
[46] Irenaeus, *Against Heresies* 4.9.

the Scriptures are indeed perfect, since they were spoken by the Word of God and His Spirit."[47]

(Augustine) insisted upon acceptance of the inspiration and authority of the Bible and linked Scripture's perfection to its trustworthiness.[48] For Augustine, if a book was accepted in the canon, then one should accept it as true and trustworthy: "But in consequence of the distinctive peculiarity of the sacred writings, we are bound to receive as true whatever the canon shows to have been said by even one prophet, or apostle, or evangelist. Otherwise, not a single page will be left for the guidance of human fallibility."[49]

Augustine considered it unacceptable to admit error or imperfection with respect to the Bible:

> For if you once admit into such a high sanctuary of authority one false statement as made in the way of duty, there will not be left a single sentence of those books which, if appearing to any one difficult in practice or hard to believe, may not by the same fatal rule be explained away, as a statement in which, intentionally, and under a sense of duty, the author declared what was not true.[50]

Augustine affirmed that the Bible reported events truthfully, including miraculous events,[51] and he also affirmed the continuity of the Old and New Testaments within the single Christian canon.[52] Augustine's affirmations about Scripture's perfection are not due to naivety regarding critical questions about the text. Augustine was aware of such issues but reasoned that the Scriptures were divinely inspired and, therefore, without error.[53]

Medieval Period

Such was the respect for Scripture in the medieval period that (Jaroslav Pelikan) says of the time, "The authority of Scripture was supreme over that

---

[47] Ibid., 2.28.2.

[48] See A. D. R. Polman, *The Word of God According to St. Augustine,* trans. A. J. Pomeraus (Grand Rapids: Eerdmans, 1961).

[49] Augustine, *Reply to Faustus the Manichean* 11.5.

[50] Augustine, *Letters* 28.3. See also *Letters* 40.5.

[51] See, e.g., his statement about Jonah in *Letters* 102.33: "Let him, therefore, who proposes to inquire why the Prophet Jonah was three days in the capacious belly of a sea monster, begin by dismissing doubts as to the fact itself; for this did actually occur; and did not occur in vain."

[52] Augustine, *Sermons on New Testament Lessons* 32.8: "We must fear, lest the divine precepts should be contrary to one another. But no: let us understand that there is the most perfect agreement in them, let us not follow the conceits of certain vain ones, who in their error think that the two Testaments in the Old and New Books are contrary to each other."

[53] Among such references see *Commentary on Romans* 111.7 and *Letters* 82:3. Typical of Augustine's view of these issues is his statement in *Reply to Faustus* 11.5: "If we are perplexed by an apparent contradiction in Scripture, it is not allowable to say, The author of this book is mistaken; but either the manuscript is faulty, or the translation is wrong, or you have not understood."

of reason; it was supreme over other authorities as well."[54] Aquinas, in the early pages of the *Summa Theologica,* affirmed the infallibility and authority of Scripture when he took up the question of whether sacred doctrine was a matter of argument. Thomas concluded that sacred doctrine "does not argue in proof of its principles," but from its "principles" it may prove something else.[55] Aquinas demonstrated his belief that sacred Scripture, which is divine revelation, is such a "principle" and it is "infallible truth."[56] Thomas made a clear distinction between the authority of the Scripture and the authority of the "doctors of the Church." The authority of the canonical Scriptures serves as "incontrovertible proof" for sacred doctrine while the authority of the fathers is merely "probable." This is because Scripture is divine revelation and the works of the fathers are not.[57]

A central question raised during this period was the relationship of the authority of Scripture and the authority of the church. A conception grew that an authoritative "tradition" formed through church fathers and ecumenical councils was guided by the Holy Spirit in the same manner as Scripture.[58] This conception of the relation of Scripture and tradition became a central concern for the Reformers.

Reformation Period

Martin Luther affirmed that "the Bible is God's Word written—presented in letters, as Christ is the eternal Word presented in human nature."[59] Because it truly is the Word of God, the Bible is to be heard and loved by God's people.[60] Since this is so, reasoned Luther, "we must remain content with them and cling to them as the perfectly clear, certain, sure words of God, which can never deceive us or allow us to err."[61] While Luther respected the church fathers, they were not granted the same authority as the Bible because the Bible is perfect and the fathers were not: "But everyone,

---

[54] Jaroslav Pelikan, *The Christian Tradition: A History of the Development of Doctrine,* vol. 3, *The Growth of Medieval Theology (600–1300)* (Chicago: University of Chicago Press, 1978), 122. He illustrates the point: "It was said of Anselm, for example, that he reposed such trust in Scripture that everything in it was unquestionably true for him and he made it his supreme goal to conform his faith and thought to the authority of Scripture." Ibid., 121.

[55] Aquinas, *Summa Theologica* 1.1.8. Thomas made his point from Titus 1:9, where the overseer must hold to the "trustworthy message" and rebuke those who contradict sound doctrine.

[56] The gist of his position is that first principles, in any "science," cannot be argued but must be accepted. Sacred Scripture is such a first principle. He then said that our faith rests on infallible truth (*infallibli veritati*). Sacred Scripture is, therefore, infallible truth.

[57] *ST,* 1.1.8. He quoted Augustine to this effect.

[58] Jaroslav Pelikan, *The Christian Tradition: A History of the Development of Doctrine,* vol. 2, *The Spirit of Eastern Christendom (600–1700)* (Chicago: University of Chicago Press, 1978), 287ff.

[59] WA, 48:31.4. Translated from the German.

[60] LW, 2:97.

[61] LW, 37:308.

indeed, knows that at times they [the fathers] have erred, as men will; therefore, I am ready to trust them only when they give me evidence for their
opinions from Scripture, which has never erred."[62]

John Calvin likewise affirmed the inspiration, authority, and perfection of the Scriptures. The Scriptures are God's Word because they are
spoken to man by God himself[63] and, because they are from God, they
are "the certain and unerring rule."[64] Calvin affirmed that believers can
observe the veracity of Scripture and that in the Bible the Christian can
see the majesty of God and should be moved to obedience, but this is not
true of the unbeliever:

> But even if one clears God's Sacred Word from man's evil speak-
> ing, he will not at once imprint upon their hearts that certainty which
> piety requires. Since for unbelieving men religion seems to stand
> by opinion alone, they, in order not to believe anything foolishly
> or lightly, both wish and demand rational proof that Moses and the
> prophets spoke divinely. But I reply: the testimony of the Spirit is
> more excellent than all reason. For as God alone is a witness of him-
> self in his Word, so also the Word will not find acceptance in men's
> hearts before it is sealed by the inward testimony of the Spirit.[65]

Modern Period

In the modern period there arose divergent opinions about the inspiration, authority, and perfection of Scripture. John Wesley affirmed that
"the Scripture therefore of the *Old and New Testament* is a most solid and
precious system of divine truth. Every part thereof is worthy of God; and
all together are one entire body, wherein is no defect, no excess."[66] His affirmation of the inerrancy of the Bible is clear: "If there be any mistakes in
the Bible, there may well be a thousand. If there be one falsehood in that
book, it did not come from the God of truth."[67]

But the influence of Enlightenment thought, including Cartesian methodological doubt, Humean skepticism, and the rise of deism, created a milieu
in which questions were raised about both the nature of Scripture and its
authority, and whether, in the case of the deists, God could even reveal

---

[62] LW, 32.11.

[63] See Calvin, *Institutes,* 1.7.1–4.

[64] Calvin, *Commentary on the Book of Psalms,* 5.11.

[65] Calvin, *Institutes,* 1.7.4. See similar statements in 1.71. and 1.7.5.

[66] Robert W. Burtner and Robert E. Chiles, ed., *John Wesley's Theology: A Collection from His Works* (Nashville: Abingdon, 1982), 18.

[67] *Works of John Wesley,* 23.25.

himself as the Bible claimed. In such an environment some theologians began to question the traditional orthodox doctrine of Scripture.

For Friedrich Schleiermacher, Christian faith begins with human experience, a "feeling of dependence," and is rooted in this religious experience. Therefore, "the authority of Holy Scripture cannot be the foundation of faith in Christ; rather must the latter be presupposed before a peculiar authority can be granted to Holy Scriptures."[68] The locus of authority has now moved from God and the word he has spoken to man and his subjective religious experience. To Schleiermacher the Bible possesses no unique character,[69] and is essentially a human book:

> On the contrary, faith might arise in the same way though no more survived than testimonies of which it had to be admitted that, in addition to Christ's essential witness to Himself and the original preaching of His disciples, they also contained much in detail that had been misinterpreted, or inaccurately grasped, or set in a wrong light owing to confusions of memory.[70]

Such notions of the Bible became less common with the rise of post-Enlightenment antisupernaturalism, typified by the nineteenth-century German biblical scholar David Strauss. To Strauss the miracles of the Bible were myths, inventions, for example, of the imaginative disciples of Jesus:

> The more the disciples became convinced of this necessity, the more they made themselves believe that Jesus must have performed miracles. . . . And so in their enthusiastic fancy without intending to deceive, they began to adorn the simple picture of Christ with a rich garland of miraculous tales, especially applying to him all the characteristics of the Messiah . . . till at length the real history was entirely covered, and in fact, destroyed by the "parasitic plants."[71]

Karl Barth led the revolt against classical theological liberalism beginning in the early twentieth century. Central to Barth's theology is a radical emphasis on the transcendence of God and a return to a conception of dogmatics that takes seriously the Bible as a source for theology. While Barth did attempt to recover the authority of the Bible in the church and theology, he did not recover a fully orthodox understanding of the nature and inspiration of Scripture. With respect to its nature, Barth distinguished the Bible from revelation itself: "Therefore when we have to do with the Bible, we

---

[68] Friedrich Schleiermacher, *Christian Faith*, S128:1.
[69] Ibid., S128.2.
[70] Ibid..
[71] David F. E. Strauss, *Life of Jesus*, 3:383.

have to do primarily with this means, with these words, with the witness which as such is not itself revelation, but only—and this is the limitation— the witness to it."[72] The Word of God is perfectly revealed in Jesus Christ; the Scriptures are witness, however imperfect, to the perfect revelation of the God-man. It is the church's responsibility to preach the Scriptures; and, Barth contends, as they are preached, the Holy Spirit works such that the Bible becomes the Word of God to the people.[73]

For Barth, then, the locus of inspiration is shifted. Instead of an inspired biblical text penned by authors under the inspiration of the Holy Spirit, Barth located divine inspiration in the event of preaching, particularly in the context of the church, at which point God's people experience a divine-human encounter. Barth's influence on modern and contemporary theology is enormous, and his views of revelation and Scripture have become popular even among some evangelicals.[74]

The modern period brought significant shifts from the orthodox conception of the Scriptures as the divinely inspired, authoritative Word of God. Theological liberalism largely reduced the Bible to a disparate set of human religious testimonies that bear no particular authority for faith and practice. Even the turn away from liberalism, led by Barth, did not adequately return to a biblical view of Scripture.

Critiques of an evangelical doctrine of revelation and Scripture like the one affirmed in this text suggest that the doctrines of verbal-plenary inspiration and inerrancy, in particular, are actually modern inventions. Ernest Sandeen, in *Roots of Fundamentalism,* argued that the doctrines of inspiration and inerrancy held by the Princeton theologians A. A. Hodge and B. B. Warfield were innovations since there was no well-defined doctrine of biblical authority in America prior to the late nineteenth century.[75] Jack Rogers and Donald McKim assert that the doctrine of inerrancy is a relatively new development and that the current debate surrounding the issue is based, in part, on a misunderstanding about the use of the term *infallibility*.[76] That is

---

[72] Karl Barth, *Church Dogmatics,* 1/2:463. Barth was willing to refer to the Bible as the Word of God, but he did so with an important qualification: "We know what we say when we call the Bible the Word of God only when we recognize its divine perfection in spite of its human imperfection." Because the Bible is a form of human witness and is not revelation, Barth insisted that the human authors of Scripture had "capacity for errors." *Church Dogmatics,* 1/2:508.

[73] See *Church Dogmatics,* 1/2:203–79, 473–537, 743–58.

[74] E.g., Bloesch, *Holy Scripture;* Brian McLaren, *A Generous Orthodoxy* (Grand Rapids: Zondervan, 2004). Interestingly, when one compares Barth with some evangelicals the more thoroughly scriptural engagement is often found in Barth.

[75] Ernest Sandeen, *The Roots of Fundamentalism: British and American Millenarianism, 1800–1930* (Grand Rapids: Baker, 1970).

[76] Jack Rogers and Donald McKim, *The Authority and Interpretation of the Bible: An Historical Approach* (San Francisco: Harper & Row, 1979). For responses to the Rogers-McKim proposal, see Robert Godrey, "Biblical Authority in the Sixteenth and Seventeenth Centuries: A Question of Transition" in D. A. Carson and John Woodbridge, eds., *Scripture and Truth,* 225–50, and also

to say, Rogers and McKim acknowledge that the term *infallible* has been commonly used to refer to the Scripture, but they deny that it is synonymous with the contemporary use of inerrancy.

To such assertions Donald Bloesch states:

> Contrary to what is commonly believed in liberal and neoorthodox circles, there is a long tradition in the church that represents the teaching of Scripture as being without error. References to the Scriptures as *inerrabilis* are to be found in Augustine, Aquinas, and Duns Scotus. The adjective *infallibilis* was applied to Scripture by John Wycliffe and Jean de Gerson. Luther and Calvin described the Bible as being infallible and without error.[77]

Baptist Theologians

Baptists have long been considered a "people of the Book." Various Baptist confessions demonstrate the way in which the Bible is viewed as the Word of God and is, therefore, authoritative for the faith and practice of every believer and church.[78] Baptist luminaries such as John Bunyan, William Carey, John L. Dagg, J. P. Boyce, and Charles Spurgeon were well known for their views of the complete trustworthiness and authority of the Bible as the divine Word of God.

This is not to say that there have never been dissenting views about the Scriptures among Baptists. Some Baptists have expressed views of the Bible consistent with the tenets of Enlightenment rationalism and higher criticism and less in keeping with the views of historic Baptists.[79] In words drawn from the New Hampshire Confession (ca. 1833), the Baptist Faith and Message affirms that the Bible "is a perfect treasure of divine instruction. It has God for its author, salvation for its end, and truth, without any mixture of error, for its matter" and that it is "the supreme standard by which all human conduct, creeds, and religious opinions should be tried." The Baptist Faith and Message 2000 affirms that the Bible "is God's revela-

---

John Woodbridge, *Biblical Authority: A Critique of the Rogers/McKim Proposal* (Grand Rapids: Zondervan, 1982).

[77] Bloesch, *Holy Scripture,* 34. Avery Dulles notes that something like this evangelical view of Scripture has been the dominant view throughout the history of Christianity. See Avery Dulles, *Models of Revelation* (New York: Orbis, 1983), 36.

[78] See, e.g., the Anabaptist Discipline of the Church (1527), the London Confession (1646), the Philadelphia Confession (1742), the New Hampshire Confession of Faith (ca. 1833), and the versions of the Baptist Faith and Message (1925, 1963, 2000), all of which rely heavily on Scripture citations to demonstrate the veracity of the confessional statements.

[79] See, e.g., the story of Crawford Toy in Bush and Nettles, *Baptists and the Bible,* 227–42. For views related to the more recent Southern Baptist Convention controversy, see *Proceedings of the Conference on Biblical Inerrancy* (Nashville: Broadman, 1987).

tion of himself to man" and that "all Scripture is a testimony to Christ, who is Himself the focus of divine revelation."

How Does It All Fit Together?

The Inclusiveness of Inspiration

Second Timothy 3:16 focuses primarily on the product of inspiration, while it includes the secondary aspects of purpose and process. What is being asserted is the activity of God throughout the entire process, so that the completed, final product ultimately comes from him. It is a mistake, however, to think of inspiration only in terms of the time when the Spirit moves the human author to write. The biblical concept of inspiration allows for the activity in special ways within the process without requiring that we understand all of the Spirit's working in one and the same way. Just as in the processes of creation and preservation of the universe, God providentially intervened in special ways for specific purposes; so too we can say that, alongside and within this superintending action of the Spirit to inspire human writings in the biblical books, we can posit a special work of the Spirit in bringing God's revelation to the apostles and prophets.[80]

God's Spirit is involved both in revealing specific messages to the prophets (Jer. 1:1–9) and in guiding the authors of the historical sections in their research (Luke 1:1–4). It is not outside the view of inspiration, then, to include the literary processes that take place on the human level behind Scripture. Summarizing the inclusiveness of inspiration, we can say that it encompasses

> the collection of information from witnesses, the use of written sources, the writing of and editing of such information, the composition of spontaneous letters, the committing to writing of prophetic messages, the collecting of the various documents together, and so on. At the same time, however, on the divine level we can assert that the Spirit, who moved on the face of the waters at creation (Gen. 1:2), was active in the whole process, so that the Bible can be regarded as both the words of men and the Word of God.[81]

Concursive Inspiration

This approach to inspiration attempts to take seriously the human factors in the composition of the Bible. Theologians have described the activity of

---

[80] Marshall, *Biblical Inspiration,* 43.
[81] Ibid., 42.

the Spirit with the activities of the human writers through which the Bible was written as a concursive work. While this perspective of inspiration is consistent with a plenary view of inspiration, it avoids any hint that God mechanically dictated the words of Scripture to the human authors so that they had no real part in the Scripture's composition.[82] Our approach to inspiration attempts to take seriously the circumstances of the human authors.

This concursive approach allows for a viewpoint that gladly confesses that God's purpose is accomplished through the writer, but the emphasis of the Spirit's work is on the product of inspiration (the inscripturated Word). We again can assert that inspiration extends to the choice of words based upon a comprehensive encompassing approach.[83]

This is accomplished by the Spirit's leading the human author in points of research, reflection, and subsequent writing or editing. It is possible that revelation and inspiration take place simultaneously at certain points in Scripture, such as the Ten Commandments and, perhaps, apocalyptic works like Daniel and Revelation.[84]

The Scope of Inspiration

It might be contended that we have contradicted ourselves by allowing for such direct inspiration at certain points or by asserting that inspiration extends even to the very words of Scripture while simultaneously allowing for the genuine human authorship. We think not, however. We believe the answer is found in the spiritual characteristics of the biblical writers. These men of God had known God, learned from him, and walked with him in

---

[82] Even though John R. Rice, *Our God-Breathed Book* (Murfreesboro, TN: Sword of the Lord, 1969), 192–287, accepted the term *dictation,* he denied the idea of mechanical dictation. Some have wrongly characterized inerrantists as advocates of mechanical dictation (e.g., Dale Moody, *The Word of Truth* [Grand Rapids: Eerdmans, 1981], 46–47), but this is not the case. Rice is perhaps one of the few fundamentalists who used the term *dictation,* but he denied mechanical dictation (see p. 287); see especially the discussion of the fundamentalist approach to Scripture in Donald K. McKim, *What Christians Believe about the Bible* (Nashville: Nelson, 1985), 56–57. Even Harold Lindsell (in *The Battle for the Bible* [Grand Rapids: Zondervan, 1976], 33) claimed he did not know any scholar who believes in biblical inerrancy who holds that the Scriptures were received by dictation. Many wrongly attribute the dictation approach to John Calvin. Calvin used the word *dictation* in *The Second Epistle of Paul to the Corinthians and the Epistles to Timothy, Titus, and Philemon,* trans. T. A. Small and ed. D. W. Torrance and T. F. Torrance (Grand Rapids: Eerdmans, 1964), 329–31. While he obviously employed the term *dictation,* numerous Calvin scholars, such as John Gerstner, W. Robert Godfrey, Kenneth Kantzer, and J. I. Packer, have shown that Calvin did not have a developed concept of mechanical dictation. His view of inspiration could be characterized as a "plenary" approach; see J. I. Packer, "Calvin's View of Scripture," in *God's Inerrant Word,* ed. J. W. Montgomery (Minneapolis: Bethany, 1974), 102–4.

[83] Bloesch, *Holy Scripture,* 117–30.

[84] It is possible that at these points, and perhaps at others where the prophet confesses "Thus says the Lord," that dictation may be possible, though not probable. The Ten Commandments quite likely can be considered dictation material, but we cannot know for sure about this or other portions of Scripture.

their spiritual pilgrimage for many years. God had prepared them through their familial, social, educational, and spiritual backgrounds for the task of inscripturating his word. The experiences of Moses, David, Jeremiah, Paul, Luke, John, and Peter differ; yet throughout their lives God was working to prepare and shape them, even their own vocabulary, to pen the Scriptures. Beyond this we dare not say much regarding the how of inspiration except to affirm God's providential oversight in the entire process of inspiration.[85] We think it quite plausible to suggest that just as revelation came in various ways (Heb. 1:1–2), so the process of inspiration differed with each author.

The ability to detect marks of inspiration may differ within passages and genres, but the quality and nature of inspiration is the same throughout. God is the source of Scripture, and his purposes are accomplished efficaciously.[86] This means that the Sermon on the Mount or the epistle to the Romans may be more readily recognized as inspired Scripture than the books of Esther or Chronicles. They are of equal inspiration but not of equal importance. Yet this is due in part to the subject matter. The inspiration in such historical passages assures the general characteristic of reliability that is brought to these records. Even if inspiration differs and is somehow less recognizable to the reader in some places, the entire Bible (*pas graphē,* that is, "all canonical Scripture") can be characterized as inspired (*theopneustos*).

The previous section, which focused on the Bible's teaching about itself, provides for us a framework in which to operate. Now, our focus must shift to the vantage point of the phenomena of Scripture, that is, to its humanness and historicity.[87]

The Human Authorship of Inspired Scripture

The biblical writers employed the linguistic resources available to them as they wrote to specific people with particular needs at specific times. The human authors were not lifted out of their culture or removed from their contexts. They were not autonomous but functioning members in

[85] Erickson, *Christian Theology,* 215–20; also see B. B. Warfield's classic work, *The Inspiration and Authority of the Bible* (Philadelphia: Presbyterian & Reformed, reprint 1948), 155–56.

[86] See Clark Pinnock, *Scripture Principle* (San Francisco: Harper and Row, 1984), 1–82. This is not to affirm that some parts are more inspired than others but that characteristics of inspiration are evidenced differently between Luke's Gospel, Proverbs, the Apocalypse, and the Ten Commandments. The biblical writers themselves either acknowledge or give indication of such differences.

[87] For a full treatment of the human dimension, see Pinnock, *Scripture Principle,* 106–29; Gordon R. Lewis, "The Human Authorship of Inspired Scripture," in *Inerrancy and Hermeneutic,* (Grand Rapids: Zondervan, 1986), 229–64. If we take the human situation seriously, it demands that we study Scripture not only theologically and devotionally but also grammatically, historically, contextually, and critically. See David S. Dockery, et al., eds., *Foundations for Biblical Interpretation* (Nashville: Broadman & Holman, 1994) and David A. Black and David S. Dockery, *New Testament Criticism and Interpretation* (Grand Rapids: Zondervan, 1991).

communities of faith, aware of God's presence and leadership in their lives. Whether they were fully aware that they were writing inspired Scripture, they did demonstrate a God-consciousness.[88] Obviously, the writers were not unbiased historical observers; they were people of faith. Thus, the concursive action of the Holy Spirit and human authorship are informed by the spiritual commitments of the writers.

Image of God and Cultural-Temporal Distance

The biblical writers were limited to their own contexts, yet they shared similarities that spanned time and place. The primary similarity was one the writers shared with all human beings since all men and women have been created in God's image (Gen. 1:26–27) and as a result share certain common characteristics.[89] As theologians since the time of Augustine have observed, human beings created in the image of God can have memories of the past, considerations of the present, and expectations of the future. To the extent that these potential capacities are employed, persons—contrary to objects—are neither temporally nor culturally bound. The writers are certainly time related, but not necessarily time bound.

Moses and Paul, among others, demonstrated cross-cultural influences and experiences. The writers were certainly not entirely culturally or behaviorally conditioned. Even though they were obviously influenced by the time and culture in which they wrote, it can be observed that the writers freely rejected some concepts of their culture and freely endorsed others.[90]

Eugene Nida has observed that humans created in God's image can develop the ability to think and communicate in linguistic symbols. Because of this, communication is a possibility among the diverse linguistic cultures of the world for three reasons: (1) The processes of human reasoning are essentially the same, irrespective of cultural diversity. (2) All people have a common range of experience. (3) All peoples possess the capacity for at least some adjustment of the symbolic "grids" of others.[91]

We do not want to press these assertions beyond their limits. Nevertheless, it can be granted that a revelation written through a human author in a particular language (Hebrew, Aramaic, or Greek) can be intelligible to those who know other languages. God can communicate with humanity, those who have been created in his image. Likewise, humans can communicate with other humans cross-culturally and cross-temporally. By maintaining these observations about humanity, we can affirm

---

[88] Erickson, *Christian Theology,* 204–6.
[89] See Anthony A. Hoekema, *Created in God's Image* (Grand Rapids: Eerdmans, 1986).
[90] Lewis, "Human Authorship," 244–46.
[91] Eugene Nida, *Message and Mission* (New York: Harper, 1960), 90.

the genuine humanness of Scripture without denying that God can speak through a divine-human Scripture.

D. E. Nineham draws attention to the cultural and temporal distance that exists between the biblical writers and our world and has concluded that the Bible is basically unusable today.[92] Because of the commonality discussed above, however, we disagree with Nineham and affirm that God's revelation can be communicated through human authors who lived two thousand years ago in various cultures. The biblical text is, indeed, the words of human authors in temporal-cultural context, but that does not limit the plausibility that God's eternal revelation can be communicated through their writings through contemporary men and women. We fully recognize the humanness and historicity of the biblical text but simultaneously acknowledge that God's Word can be communicated through this situation. The fact that the biblical authors were men of faith informed the issue of concursive inspiration; in the same way recognition that every person bears the image of God has implications for the possibility of communication across cultures and ages.

Unity and Variety in the Biblical Message

The emphasis upon human authorship in contemporary theological literature reveals the diversity of beliefs and theologies among biblical writers.[93] The concept of overall unity, characteristic of evangelical theology, merges from a full-orbed concept of biblical inspiration. As we observed, the overriding themes of redemptive history and the Bible's inspiration form the basis for recognizing the theological unity in the Bible. Yet this theological unity must be carefully examined in light of the genuine variety brought about by the unique theological emphases of the different authors and the diverse human and historical situations in the writings. It is readily obvious that the Bible is composed of different types of literature. Likewise, the forms in which the teaching is expressed is influenced by the literary genre. Each genre (whether legal, prophetic, poetic, gospel, epistolary, historical, or apocalyptic) has distinctive characteristics. It is from the

---

[92] See D. E. Nineham, *The Use and Abuse of the Bible* (London: SCM, 1976), who has presented useful insights regarding cultural and temporal distance. Yet his work is basically negative in its approach although he does not deny entirely the possibility that God can speak through the Bible. We agree with Pinnock (*Scripture Principle,* 110) that "we must resist a misuse of cultural relatedness as a cloak to evade what the Scriptures really want to teach. . . . God's Word comes to us in human language, it is true, and there are features in it incidental to its teaching purposes. But 'in all things necessary' that the Bible wishes to teach us it is true and coherent and possesses the wisdom of God" (p. 115).

[93] See Robert Sloan, "Canonical Theology of the New Testament," in *Foundations for Biblical Interpretation,* 565–94.

varied collection of writings that the basic prophetic-apocalyptic message is discovered.

Not only is there a variety of genres, but there is often variety within a particular genre. For instance, the different theological emphases among the synoptic writers demonstrate the variety even within the genre of gospel. Matthew's kingdom theology differs from Mark's servant theology, and they are each different from Luke's emphasis upon Jesus as Savior of the world. Yet the central unity of Jesus Christ and the developing history of redemption cannot be ignored.[94]

Beyond this matter is the possibility of theological development within the Old and New Testaments and even within the individual authors themselves.[95] Donald Guthrie's succinct comments on this difficult issue are extremely appropriate:

> The idea of progressive revelation is familiar in Old Testament interpretation and, also in the area of the relation of the Old Testament to the New Testament. . . . With Christ, the Old Testament ritual symbol became obsolete, as the epistle to the Hebrews makes clear. . . . One obvious area where this is undeniable (development in the New Testament) is the difference between the gospels and the rest of the New Testament. Before the death and resurrection of Christ, the revelation given to the disciples was limited. In the nature of the case, Jesus could not give a full explanation of his own death to his disciples until they had grasped the fact of it. But after the resurrection, the apostolic preachers were guided into an understanding of it, although again not in any stereotyped way, but with rich variety.[96]

We can see that the differences between the writers themselves and the development (progressive revelation) occurring within the Old and New Testaments and even some of the writers themselves (e.g., Isaiah, Paul) point to the genuine humanness of the biblical text. There is diversity, or variety in the sense of variations, within the expression of the central message of the gospel. The basis of unity is located in the oneness of the gospel. Therefore, diversity works within the parameters of the gospel and the overall redemptive canonical message.[97]

---

[94] Craig L. Blomberg, "The Diversity of Literary Genres in the New Testament," in *New Testament Criticism and Interpretation,* 507–32; also Robert H. Stein, *Playing by the Rules* (Grand Rapids: Baker, 1994).

[95] See Richard N. Longenecker, "On the Concept of Development in Pauline Thought," in *Perspectives in Evangelical Theology,* ed. Kenneth Kantzer and Stanley N. Gundry (Grand Rapids: Baker, 1979), 195–200.

[96] Donald Guthrie, *New Testament Theology* (Downers Grove: InterVarsity, 1981), 51.

[97] Ibid., 59.

Diversity does not imply contradiction. The different writers, with their own emphases, vary their expression according to their unique purposes and settings. However, within this very real and rich variety that evidences the humanness of Scripture, there is a genuine unity that is the result of the divine superintending work of inspiration.

Improper Deductions

Sometimes people reach improper conclusions from the data that has been presented related to the human authorship of Scripture. Five common, yet improper, deductions are often reached about the human authorship of Scripture. Let us briefly examine these issues.

1. The Phenomena of Scripture

The Bible generally represents things as they appear (phenomena). For example, the Bible refers to a sunrise when, in fact, we all know that the earth rotates on its axis; the sun does not rise. Yet the weather report tells us what time we can expect tomorrow's sunrise. Why do we speak this way? Because we are describing things as they appear. We call this "phenomenological" language. It is no mistake or error in Scripture when the biblical writers do the same. The Bible is a book of events and communication from common, everyday people. It is not a technical treatise of weather or other areas of science. The great Baptist theologian A. H. Strong asked, "Would it be preferable, in the Old Testament, if we should read: 'When the revolution of the earth upon its axis caused the rays of the solar luminary to impinge horizontally upon the retina, Isaac went out to meditate' (Gen. 24:63)?"[98]

It is illogical to assume that the Bible contains errors because the human authors reported things in a phenomenal manner. If the Bible taught that things appear one way but they did not appear that way, we would probably agree that that could be considered an error. If the Bible taught that things are one way but they were not that way, that too could be considered an error. But for the Bible to teach that things appear one way when they actually are another way is hardly an error. It reflects the genuine humanness of Scripture, for the authors are reporting things as they actually appear, just as we continue to do today.

2. The Accomodation of Scripture

John Calvin used expressions like "God must speak baby-talk for humans to understand his Word." He meant that God accommodated himself to the level and culture of the Bible's original recipients. It is true that the

---

[98] A. H. Strong, *Systematic Theology* (Philadelphia: American Baptist Publication Society, 1907), 223.

Bible represents God as accommodating himself to human language. But this recognition does not lead to the conclusion that accommodation to human language must involve accommodation to human error and, thus, the further conclusion that the Bible contains or teaches error. An example concerns the biblical phrase "God repents." Some say that this must be an error since God is unchangeable. The Bible presents God as changing his actions to be consistent with his overall will or purpose, because his will or purpose does not change. The Bible pictures God as repenting because that is how it appears to the human authors. This does not suggest contradiction or error in Scripture when it is rightly understood as accommodation to human language.

3. The Salvation Emphasis

Special revelation is primarily redemptive. Second Timothy 3:15 says that the Holy Scriptures make us wise for salvation. Obviously, the salvation message is the focal point of Scripture. But it does not follow that because the Bible emphasizes one thing, it errs in less crucial or less important matters. For example, it is not proper to conclude that because the Bible emphasizes salvation, it can be trusted on that matter, but that since it does not emphasize history, it may err in historical details. What the Bible says about history and other similar matters serves to support the truthful redemptive message of the Bible. When the Bible reports matters as history, they are intended to be understood as historical—though not necessarily with the kind of precisions expected of modern historiography. We should, however, expect and even require a precision that is in keeping with the standards of the time when the text was written.

4. Textual Criticism

Textual criticism is the science of determining the truest reading of a biblical passage by comparing one historical text with another historical text. Often textual critics decide that a certain verse or group of verses is not a faithful reading—that is, they doubt that it was a part of the oldest manuscripts and of the autographs. Examples of these kinds of passages include John 7:53–8:11; Mark 16:9–20; Romans 8:1; 1 John 5:7; and Matthew 6:13. Because scholars examine a text and decide that it does not belong to the original text of the Bible, some conclude that the Bible has errors. Questioning the ending of Mark's Gospel or the concluding doxology to the Lord's Prayer does not imply that the Gospel writers are in error. Textual criticism points us to the truthfulness of the genuine or authentic text. Such great scholars as A. T. Robertson affirmed that textual criticism is a necessary exercise in order to determine what is the original inerrant text.

What must be maintained is a distinction between the inspiration of the text (pertaining to the autographs) and the transmission of the text (pertaining to the copies of the autographs). We should also note that textual criticism has resulted in the recovery of the autographs to an extremely high degree of reliability and accuracy.[99]

5. Sinful Humanity

We have seen that the Bible was written by men. Even though these men were faithful believers, they were not sinless. Yet it does not follow that since God inspired these humans to write Scripture, he would be incapable of keeping them free of human error in their writing. We know that King David was an adulterer, but we cannot infer that the Psalms, therefore, contain error. The same applies for the Apostle Paul, who described his own struggle with sin in Romans 7:14–25. The same could be said for the rest of the biblical authors. God's Spirit could certainly keep these writings free from human error and the witness of the Bible is that he did (Matt. 5:17–18).

These common misconceptions or objections are really improper deductions or conclusions that develop from an imbalanced view of Scripture. We cannot in any way ignore the human authorship of Scripture. But neither can we emphasize only the humanness of Scripture and ignore its divine inspiration. A proper understanding of the Bible demands a balanced view of the divine-human authorship. The Bible as a divine-human book is indeed special. But this means that it must be treated as equal to, and yet more than, an ordinary book. We must study the Bible through the use of literary and critical methodologies. To deny that kind of study would treat the Bible as less than human, less than historical, and less than literature. The Bible is a literary work that is both human and historical yet simultaneously the Word of God. We will now turn our attention to the inspiration and dependability of Scripture, including various explanations of the divine-human authorship of Scripture.

Explanations of Inspiration

We would not naively maintain that the Bible fell from heaven on a parachute, inscribed with a particular heavenly language that uniquely suited it as an instrument for divine revelation. Nor would we claim that the Bible was dictated directly and immediately by God without reference to any local context, situation, or perspective. The presence of a multiplicity of historical, contextual, linguistic, and cultural factors must be maintained and accounted for.[100]

---

[99] See J. Ed Komoszewski, M. James Sawyer, and David D. Wallace, *Reinventing Jesus* (Grand Rapids: Kregel, 2006), 93–117

[100] R. C. Sproul, "Controversy at Culture Gap," *Eternity* 27 (May 1975): 13.

Many views attempting to account for the divine-human character of Scripture have arisen in recent years.[101] A brief survey of these attempts will prove helpful for our discussion. Many of the contemporary theories are attempts to deal seriously with the two-sided character of the Scripture and also to explain how a book penned two thousand years ago should be understood in a post-Enlightenment era.

The Enlightenment era was a watershed in the history of Western civilization. It was then that the Christian consensus was broken by a radical, secular spirit. The Enlightenment philosophies emphasized the primacy of nature, a high view of reason and a low view of sin, an antisupernatural bias, and encouraged revolt against the traditional understanding of authority. This philosophy was foundational for much of the liberal theology that dominated nineteenth-century European and early twentieth-century American thought. It was initiated by Friedrich Schleiermacher's *On Religion: Speeches to Its Cultured Despisers* at the turn of the nineteenth century. The modern assaults upon classic formulations of scriptural inspiration and authority can be traced to attacks upon the Bible initiated during the early period of the Enlightenment.

The positive element that has resulted from the questions raised by modern and postmodern scholars has been a more careful consideration of the human authorship and historical context of Scripture. In the following survey we will see that the dictation view has basically ignored modernity, the illumination view has surrendered to modernity, and in assorted ways, the encounter, dynamic, and plenary views have attempted to respond to the modern mind-set and still maintain the church's confession that the Bible is the Word of God. We face new challenges in a postmodern world, but many of the issues remain the same.

Dictation View

The dictation theory places the emphasis upon God's actual dictation of his Word to the human writers. The theory is developed from certain prophetic passages, primarily found in the Old Testament prophets, where the Spirit is pictured as telling the human writer what to communicate. What is a proper assessment of particular aspects of Scripture ("thus says the Lord") is applied to the whole Bible. This approach fails to consider seriously the distinctive styles of the different authors or the particular contexts to which they were addressed.

---

[101] See J. I. Packer, "Encountering Present-Day Views of Scripture," in *Foundations of Biblical Authority,* ed. James M. Boice (Grand Rapids: Zondervan, 1978); Robert K. Johnston, ed., *The Use of the Bible in Theology: Evangelical Options* (Atlanta: John Knox, 1985); McKim, *What Christians Believe about the Bible*; D. A. Carson, "Recent Developments in the Doctrine of Scripture," in *Hermeneutics, Authority, and Canon,* ed. D. A. Carson and John Woodbridge (Grand Rapids: Zondervan, 1986), 10–48.

While it is true that the prophets claimed to hear God addressing them before they proclaimed his Word, this is not always parallel with the way the other writers depict themselves. For example, Luke tells his readers that other people before him had attempted to write the story of Jesus and that he consulted their works and did additional research before compiling his Gospel (see Luke 1:1–4). Thus, it can be seen that the dictation theory cannot account for all aspects of Scripture. The dictation approach is without doubt confessed (perhaps unconsciously) by numerous faithful believers. Because of this, it is often assumed that advocates of a plenary view of inspiration hold to the dictation view. However, adherents of the plenary view take great pains to dissociate themselves from the dictation position. It is right to judge the dictation theory as docetic and, therefore, less than orthodox.

Illumination View

This view maintains little more than some kind of recognition of the Spirit's working within the human authors to raise their religious insight. This approach claims that the human authors were enabled to express themselves with eloquent language to produce a certain emotional response from the readers or hearers. In this view inspiration is the illumination of the authors beyond their normal abilities to express themselves creatively as men of human genius. Inspiration is limited when understood in this manner, not only in relation to the nature of inspiration but also as to the extent of inspiration.

The illumination view emphasizes the freedom and creativity of the human author but fails to account for the Spirit's guidance of the writers in the communication of divine truth; there is only a mere increase in sensitivity regarding spiritual matters. This view of inspiration can be characterized by the Ebionite error we noted earlier and is a failure as far as accounting for the divine character of Scripture.[102] Nevertheless, it needs to be observed that this view is more akin to the English term *inspiring* than the biblical concepts of a God-breathed Scripture (*theopneustos*). Fortunately, there are better options than these first two extreme positions, neither of which accounts for the two-sided character of Scripture.

Encounter View

A more complex approach developed by Karl Barth can be classified as an encounter view of inspiration.[103] This view states that in regard to

---

[102] See L. H. DeWolf, *A Theology of the Living Church* (New York: Harper & Brothers, 1960), 48–75.

[103] In some ways Karl Barth shares this view with Emil Brunner, Reinhold Niebuhr, and, to a much lesser extent, Rudolf Bultmann. We focus on Barth because he was not only the first but also in many ways the greatest and most brilliant of neoorthodox theologians. J. I. Packer ("Present-Day Views") comments that Barth is likely to have more long-term influence than other theologians of

its composition, the Bible differs little from other books. Yet the Bible is unique because of the Spirit's ability to use it as a means of revelation to specific individuals or communities. Through the ongoing work of inspiration, the Bible becomes revelation. The Bible is not the Word of God but becomes the Word of God in existential encounter. The Bible is correlated as a witness to God's original act of revelation.

Inspiration brings the Bible to the contemporary human situation as a source of God's revelation. Barth seeks to take seriously the human authorship of Scripture and the Bible as the Word of God. He attempts to avoid a concept of inspiration that in some way confines the Holy Spirit in the Bible. It is a misunderstanding on his part, however, to assume that those who hold that the Bible was Spirit inspired in its original composition ignore the Spirit's illumination of the text, thereby bringing it to life for present-day readers. Barth's emphasis on ongoing inspiration seems to ignore inspiration at the time of the Bible's composition.

Barth, however, seeks to make it possible for God's Word to be encountered through Scripture. In evaluating Barth's contention, Marshall states that "it is doubtful whether Barth's view does justice to that very character of the Bible as inspired Scripture which makes it possible for the Spirit to continue to witness through its words to the Word of God which it embodies."[104] The encounter view is inadequate in accounting for the human and divine aspects of inscripturation. In comparison to the illumination theory, it has many strengths, yet it does not fully explain why we should trust the text as Barth himself did. Barth preached the errancy of the text; however, as Clark Pinnock has observed, he "treated it with reverence and practiced its inerrancy."[105] However, Colin Brown's note is an appropriate concluding evaluation: "It is impossible to maintain high doctrines of revelation and inspiration without at the same time being willing to defend in detail the veracity and historicity of the biblical writings."[106]

Dynamic View

This broadly held approach endeavors to be a *via media,* in contradistinction to the liberal and fundamentalist camps, and seeks to em-

---

this type, both because neoorthodoxy appears at its strongest intellectually and noblest spiritually in the writings of Barth and because his weaknesses, however great, are comparatively less than the corresponding defects of others on the same trail. It should, however, be realized that Barth stands at the extreme right of the neoorthodox spectrum. See also Colin Brown, *Karl Barth and the Christian Message* (London: InterVarsity, 1967), 99–140; Karl Barth, *Church Dogmatics,* trans. G. W. Bromiley and T. F. Torrance (Edinburgh: T & T Clark, 1956), 1/1:51–335; see Dale Moody, *The Word of Truth* (Grand Rapids: Eerdmans, 1981); and Morris Ashcraft, *Christian Faith and Beliefs* (Nashville: Broadman, 1984).

[104] Marshall, *Biblical Inspiration,* 36.

[105] Pinnock, "Three Views of the Bible," in *Biblical Authority,* 37.

[106] Brown, *Karl Barth and the Christian Message,* 146.

phasize a combination of divine and human elements in the process of inspiration. A. H. Strong and E. Y. Mullins are Baptist representatives of this view, while Donald Bloesch represents more contemporary evangelical approaches to the dynamic viewpoint.[107] Also, contemporary advocates with nuanced approaches include G. C. Berkouwer (1975), Paul J. Achtemeier (1980), and William J. Abraham (1981).[108]

In many ways this approach originated as a reaction to the dictation theory. It sees the work of the Spirit in directing the writer to the concepts he should have and then allowing great freedom for the human author to express these ideas in his own style, through his own personality, in a way consistent with and characteristic of his own situation and context.

More contemporary approaches have expanded the view beyond the human author to see the place of the community in Scripture's composition. The complexity of this position sees the Bible arising out of several traditions that confess what God has done within the situation of the community, recognizing the respondents or authors who take up the traditions and reformulate them in specific situations. Inspiration is then generally limited to God's initiating impulse, and thus the emphasis of inspiration falls not upon the product—Scripture itself—but upon the purpose and process.

The dynamic view's strength is its attempt to maintain the two-sided character of Scripture. Its emphasis upon the creativity of the human author and his community is commendable. Inspiration, however, refers to the entire process, not just the momentary event of initiation. In some ways, similar to Barth's view, inspiration and illumination are conflated and confused. The theory properly emphasizes the relation of inspiration to ideas and concepts, but it fails to account for the relationship between ideas and words. In emphasizing the process of inspiration, it does not place the emphasis where Scripture itself places it—on the product of inspiration.

The real shortcoming of this approach, with its various nuances, is its imbalanced emphasis upon God's initiating impulse rather than his superintending work over the entire process and product. Finally, it must be seen that in this approach the emphasis is more upon the biblical writers (who, granted, are referred to in 2 Pet. 1:19–21) than upon the writings (which are referred to in 2 Tim. 3:16).

Verbal/Plenary View

The last theory we shall examine is that which is put forward in this book as the most acceptable model of inspiration based on the Scripture's

---

[107] See Strong, *Systematic Theology,* 211; also Bloesch, *Holy Scripture*; also see W. T. Conner, *Revelation and God* (Nashville: Broadman, 1936); and W. T. Conner, *Christian Doctrine* (Nashville: Broadman, 1937).

[108] See Paul J. Achtemeier, *The Inspiration of Scripture* (Philadelphia: Westminster, 1980); Abraham, *The Divine Inspiration of Holy Scripture*; Berkouwer, *Holy Scripture*.

own testimony and consensus within the history of the church. This approach is careful to see the Spirit's influence both upon the writers and, primarily, upon the writings. It also seeks to view inspiration as extending to all (thus, the adjective "plenary") portions of Holy Scripture, even beyond the direction of thoughts to the selection of words (thus, the adjective "verbal"). We readily admit and recognize the element of mystery involved in this process, a mystery that does not fully explain the how of inspiration.[109] The verbal/plenary view seeks to do justice to the human factors in the Bible's composition and avoids any attempt to suggest that the entire books of the Bible were dictated. We believe that this model for understanding biblical inspiration best accounts for the design and character of Scripture and the human circumstances of the Bible's composition.

Our approach to the doctrine of inspiration might appear circular; but it is a viable, not a viscous, circle. We have explored the Bible's message to affirm its own inspiration and divine character. The verbal/plenary model of inspiration accounts best for the Bible's own claim and affirms a balance of the divine-human authorship of Scripture.

The Bible's inspiration preserves divine revelation for God's people. We acknowledge Scripture's literary diversity and affirm that it is more than a historical accident or decorative device. This recognition of literary diversity brings a healthy realization of the divine-human authorship of the Bible. Inspiration is thus concursive, verbal and plenary, meaning that all Scripture is inspired. We affirm verbal inspiration, meaning that the Spirit's work influences even the choice of words by the human authors, while remaining cognizant of contemporary linguistic theory that suggests that meaning is located at the sentence level and beyond. The corollary of inspiration is its truthfulness and authority. It is to this issue that we now turn our attention.

The Truthfulness of Scripture

Building on a verbal/plenary model of inspiration we must ask, "In what sense can we confess that Scripture, which evidences genuine human authorship written in a time-related context, is normative?" Or must we conclude that Scripture is wholly descriptive and the student of Scripture is little more than a historian or an antique keeper who displays the exhibits in the best possible way? We think such a descriptive approach is unacceptable and lacks all the dynamic of the experience of the biblical authors and their communities of faith.[110]

---

[109] See David S. Dockery, *The Doctrine of the Bible* (Nashville: Convention, 1991); Carl F. H. Henry, "Authority and Inspiration," in *Expositor's Bible Commentary,* ed. Frank E. Gaebelein (Grand Rapids: Zondervan, 1979), 1:13–35; idem., *God, Revelation and Authority,* vol. 4; and Erickson, *Christian Theology,* 199–220.

[110] Donald Guthrie, *New Testament Theology* (Downers Grove: InterVarsity, 1981), 953–82.

Perhaps we should rephrase the question. Does any Bible student accept a descriptive approach completely? Is not the real issue to what extent is the Bible normative for the contemporary church? Even Rudolf Bultmann, while maintaining that first-century cultural patterns cannot be considered normative, nevertheless sought to reinterpret these patterns for the contemporary church.[111]

The Scripture as Normative

Although the cultural background and environment have radically changed since the biblical writings were penned, the human condition has not changed. It is to the human condition, men and women created in the image of God, yet fallen, that the unity of the biblical message speaks in a normative manner. We can maintain this confession for the following reasons: (1) The Scriptures are the result of divine inspiration. (2) They proclaim the saving acts of God. (3) They are historically proximate to the saving acts of God. (4) They are based on the prophetic-apostolic authority.[112]

Even with cultural advancements and scientific progress, the need of men and women for a right standing and a right relationship with God remains unchanged. The reason is that even the advancing wisdom and knowledge of the world cannot help humanity in the ultimate aspects of life (1 Cor. 1–4). The basic problem of how sinful humans are to approach a holy God and how these persons are to live in relationship to the life-giving Spirit of God is the same for all ages.

It is our belief, therefore, that divinely inspired teaching concerning God and matters relating to God and His creation are normative for the contemporary church. When such matters are proclaimed and confessed in the twenty-first century, however, mere repetition of early Christian beliefs may not be sufficient; a contextualized application that awakens modern readers to an awareness that the Bible speaks in relevant ways to contemporary issues in church and society is also necessary.[113] When Scripture is approached from this perspective, it will be necessary to determine underlying principles for all portions of Scripture that address the contemporary situation, even if the direct teaching of Scripture is somehow limited by cultural-temporal factors (1 Cor. 16:20; Eph. 6:5; 1 Tim. 5:23). Believers

---

[111] See Rudolf Bultmann, *New Testament Theology* (New York: Scribners, 1955).

[112] See R. P. C. Hanson, *The Bible as a Norm of Faith* (Durham, U. K.: University of Durham Press, 1963), 7; idem., *Tradition in the Early Church* (London: SCM, 1962), 213–24; H. E. W. Turner, *The Pattern of Christian Truth* (London: Maybrays, 1954); and Edward J. Carnell, *The Case for Orthodox Theology* (Philadelphia: Fortress, 1959).

[113] John Jefferson Davis, "Contextualization and the Nature of Theology," in *The Necessity of Systematic Theology,* ed. John Jefferson Davis (Grand Rapids: Baker, 1980), 169–85; Pinnock, *Scripture Principle,* 210–21; David Hesselgrave, "Contextualization and Revelation Epistemology," in *Inerrancy and Hermeneutics,* ed. Earl D. Radmacher and Robert D. Preus (Grand Rapids: Zondervan, 1986), 693–764.

will recognize that this is the case because of the two-sided character of Scripture. Because it is authored by humans in specific contexts, certain teachings may be contextually limited; but because Scripture is divinely inspired, the underlying principles are normative and applicable for the church in every age.

When approaching the Bible, recognizing its authoritative and normative character, we can discover truth[114] and its ramifications for the answers to life's ultimate questions as well as guidelines and principles for godly living as we move forward in the twenty-first century world.[115]

The Scripture as Truthful (Inerrancy)

Having affirmed the possibility of a normative Scripture, we must probe further and ask if we can also confess the complete truthfulness and reliability of Scripture. This issue must be addressed because of the ongoing misunderstanding in contemporary discussions about the Bible and because the doctrine of inerrancy is the corollary and result of our affirmations of the verbal/plenary view of inspiration. While the term *inerrancy* continues to be a red-flag word among many and subject to misunderstanding among others, it remains, when properly defined, a helpful and informative theological term to describe the results of inspiration.

These misunderstandings have resulted from false associations with a literalistic hermeneutic and dictation theories of inspiration. Additional problems have developed from careless statements on the part of advocates who have been overzealous in their defense of the doctrine (some even denying the use of textual criticism) or who have concentrated unduly upon issues of preciseness and "errors" when the focus should instead be placed on the issues of truthfulness and reliability. Others have attempted to prove that inerrancy is a direct teaching of Scripture instead of acknowledging that it is the proper implication of inspiration. Still others have attempted to defend the issue from a slippery slope standpoint and have unintentionally moved the primary focus of the issue away from theological concerns to historical concerns (this is not to say the historical concerns are unimportant).

One additional matter that we should consider is related to the importance of inerrancy. This teaching is important primarily for theological and epistemological reasons, and shifting the argument to the secondary realm of soteriological concerns has only confused the issue. Individual salvation is not dependent upon one's confession of inerrancy, but consistent theological method and instruction needs the base of inerrancy in order to

---

[114] Anthony C. Thiselton, "Truth," *DNTT*, ed. Colin Brown (Grand Rapids: Zondervan, 1979), 3:874–902.

[115] Anthony C. Thiselton, *The Two Horizons* (Grand Rapids: Eerdmans, 1980), 432–38.

continue to maintain an orthodox confession in salvific matters. Thus we see that inerrancy, as a corollary of inspiration, is a foundational issue upon which other theological building blocks are laid.

With these warnings behind us and an awareness of the complexity of the issue, let us suggest a definition of inerrancy. Inerrancy means that "when all the facts are known, the Bible (in its original writings) properly interpreted in light of the culture and communication means that had developed by the time of its composition will be shown to be completely true (and therefore not false) in all that it affirms, to the degree of precision intended by the author, in all matters relating to God and his creation."[116]

No doubt some will say that with the carefulness of this definition, which attempts to recognize the complexity of the issues, it is futile to carry on further discussion. But hopefully the exact opposite is true! We trust that the careful manner in which the definition is stated will help many who have misunderstood the doctrine to come to grips with what inerrancy is and what it is not. The definition seeks to be faithful to the phenomena of Scripture as well as theological affirmations in Scripture about the veracity of God. It will be helpful at this point to offer some brief comments about our definition.

1. "When all the facts are known." The statement begins from the vantage point of faith, recognizing that we may not have all the data necessary on this side of the eschaton to bear on the Bible. It is also likely that our sinful, finite minds may misinterpret some facts and information that we do have. Thus, we should exercise caution with things we might not understand until all the facts are known.

2. "The Bible (in its original writings)." Inerrancy applies to all aspects of the Bible as originally written. A claim to complete or full inerrancy is limited to the original words of the biblical text. A reference to these original writings is not restricted to some lost codex but is an affirmation relating to the original words that were written by the prophetic-apostolic messengers. Thus, our confession of inerrancy and inspiration applies to translations to the degree that they represent accurately the original words. It is our belief that we can express great confidence in our present translations. Therefore,

---

[116] Similar careful statements on the subject can be found in Erickson, *Christian Theology,* 221–40. Paul D. Feinberg has written several informative and helpful articles; e.g. "The Meaning of Inerrancy," in *Inerrancy,* ed. Norman L. Geisler (Grand Rapids: Zondervan, 1979), 267–304; "Bible, Inerrancy and Infallibility of," *EDT,* 141–45. Two extremely significant volumes are D. A. Carson and John D. Woodbridge, eds., *Scripture and Truth*; and Roger Nicole and J. Ramsey Michaels, eds., *Inerrancy and Common Sense* (Grand Rapids: Baker, 1992). Also see Louis Igou Hodges, "New Dimensions in Scripture" in *New Dimensions in Evangelical Theology,* ed. David Dockery (Downers Grove: InterVarsity, 1998), 209–34; Robert L. Saucy, *Scripture: Its Power, Authority and Relevance* (Nashville: Word, 2001); and Basil Manly Jr., *The Bible Doctrine of Inspiration* (New York: A. C. Armstrong and Sons, 1888). One should also consult "The Chicago Statement on Inerrancy" affirmed in 1978 by a significant number of respected evangelical scholars.

the qualifying statement regarding the original writings is not intended as an apologetic sidestep but is a theological appeal to the providential oversight and the veracity of God in his superintending work of inspiration.[117] Such a statement is never intended to remove trust from our present-day translations (whether KJV, NKJV, NIV, NASB, NRSV, ESV, HCSB, etc.) but to ensure and confirm faith in these translations because they rest upon a sure foundation.

   3. "Properly interpreted." The definition recognizes that statements concerning the nature of the biblical text cannot be separated completely from hermeneutical issues. While these issues must be distinguished, they cannot be separated.[118] Before falsehood can be recognized, it is necessary to know if a text has been interpreted properly. The author's intention must be recognized, and matters of precision and accuracy must be judged in light of the culture and means of communication that had developed by the time of the text's composition. The text, as a guideline, should be interpreted normally, grammatically, historically, contextually, and theologically. The context, background, genre, and purpose of the writing must be considered in interpretational matters.

   4. "Is completely true (and therefore not false)." An important aspect of the definition is the evaluation of whether the Bible is inerrant in terms of truthfulness and falseness rather than in terms of error or lack of error. This moves the discussion away from grammatical mistakes or lack of precision in reports. Inerrancy, on the other hand, must not be associated with strict tests of precision in which careless harmonization attempts to bring about a precision uncommon and alien to the text itself.[119] On the other hand, we cannot shift the emphasis to such general and meaningless definitions as willful deceit for inerrancy and infallibility.[120] The issue is

---

[117] See Greg L. Bahnsen, "The Inerrancy of the Autographa," in *Inerrancy and Hermeneutic*, 172–89. The issue of the autographa is one of the most misunderstood aspects of the doctrine of inerrancy.

[118] This is one of the real strengths of Clark Pinnock's work, *Scripture Principle*, 197–202. Pinnock's earlier work, *Biblical Revelation* (Chicago: Moody, 1971), is, in our opinion, a more consistent explanation of the doctrine of Scripture, but his discussion of the relationship of inspiration to interpretation in the latter work is an important contribution. See also E. Radmacher and R. Preus, eds., *Inerrancy and Hermeneutic*; Carson and Woodbridge, eds., *Hermeneutics, Authority, and Canon*.

[119] It seems to us that the kind of undue concern for excessive harmonization, as exhibited in Harold Lindsell, *Battle for the Bible* (Grand Rapids: Zondervan, 1976), 174–76, is more confusing than helpful in demonstrating the full truthfulness of the Bible. Even though Lindsell does not include precision or preciseness as an aspect of his definition of inerrancy, he nevertheless confuses the issue with his focus on excessive harmonization. A more constructive approach to the matter of harmonization can be found in Craig L. Blomberg, "The Limits of Harmonization," in *Hermeneutics, Authority, and Canon*.

[120] Rogers and McKim, *Authority and Interpretation*, 3, while not affirming inerrancy but acknowledging infallibility, nevertheless define their confession about the nature of Scripture in terms of a lack of willful deception. This is hardly an acceptable definition, for it says nothing about the

and always has been truthfulness. Some have inferred from this that inerrancy is an improper term to describe Scripture. But inerrancy, like inspiration, has become imbedded in the theological literature, and it is best to emphasize careful definitions rather than to attempt to change terms, especially in the midst of the ongoing controversy over the nature and meaning of Scripture.

5. "*In all areas.*" The definition states that inerrancy is not limited merely to "religious" matters, thus creating, or at least providing the framework for, an improper dualism. We affirm that inerrancy applies to all areas of knowledge, since all truth is God's truth. Yet issues of history and science must be evaluated in light of the communication means at the time of inscripturation. Modern canons of science and historiography and their concern for exactness are not proper standards for first-century (and earlier) authors. These matters must be analyzed in light of the author's intended level of precision, which most likely should be seen in terms of phenomenological observation.[121]

In light of this brief commentary on our definition, we can maintain that inerrancy primarily points to theological and epistemological matters. In providing a statement about an inerrant Bible, we must be careful with "slippery-slope" theories or avoid them altogether, though it is important to recognize that missions, evangelism, and zeal for ethical application of Scripture have declined where a high view of Scripture has likewise declined! Yet we know that God can, and certainly does, overrule departures from orthodoxy, as church history bears testimony.

We must avoid unnecessary associations with a literalistic, stilted hermeneutic, but we do not care to dissociate the issue from hermeneutics. It must be recognized that inerrancy is not a direct teaching in Scripture (though Matt. 5:18 and John 10:35; 17:17 may point in that direction) but is a direct implication and important corollary of the direct teaching about Scripture's inspiration, which can be described as plenary, verbal, and concursive.

We must seek a view of inerrancy that is consistent with the divine-human nature of Scripture. This means that the phenomena must be accounted for and Scripture's witness to itself and its divine character must

essence of Scripture but is only a general statement about Scripture's intent. The same misunderstanding is advanced by Russell Dilday, *The Doctrine of Biblical Authority* (Nashville: Convention Press, 1982). The weaknesses of the definition and the historiography behind this approach are ably discussed in John D. Woodbridge, *Biblical Authority* (Grand Rapids: Zondervan, 1983) and Richard Muller, *The Study of Theology: From Biblical Interpretation to Contemporary Formulation* (Grand Rapids: Zondervan, 1991).

121 For further discussion and clarification of this matter, see David S. Dockery, "The Inerrancy and Authority of Scripture: Affirmation and Clarifications," *Theological Educator* 37 (1988): 15–36; and Dockery, *Christian Scripture*, 61–75.

be satisfied. Such an approach is not primarily dependent upon a correspondence view of truth although many of the affirmations of Scripture can be verified. Most, if not all, of the theological and ethical statements in Scripture lie outside the realm of current verification, and thus a coherence view of truth is more encompassing and applicable for all of Scripture. We can work from a correspondence view of truth only in light of eschatological realities. Realizing these issues, we can gladly confess that the Bible is a dependable, truthful, trustworthy, faithful, and thus inerrant and infallible Word of God to humanity.[122]

Nevertheless, the term *inerrancy* may not go far enough. The Bible, like other forms of human communication, is certainly more than true assertions. Communication involves emotions, aesthetic and affective abilities, and the will, in addition to propositional statements. Certainly praise is more than a proposition. While a psalm may include a declaration of God's faithfulness, it is true even if it is not principally a proposition. The same can be said for ethical commands. So although we affirm the inerrancy of the Bible, the idea of total trustworthiness better describes the whole of the Bible and its uniqueness. It is important for us to say more than just propositions are true; in fact all aspects of Holy Scripture are totally reliable.

While truth is more than propositional, this certainly does not imply that it is less than propositional. Biblical truth is not just some mystical encounter or vague experience that we have as a result of reading Scripture. The fact that truth is more than doctrine should never be used to imply that doctrine is not necessary or important. Truth would be unknowable and incommunicable without the doctrinal framework and propositional grounding that we find in Holy Scripture.

Thus we can affirm the Bible's total truthfulness, its coherence, and its perspicuity (its clarity, made possible by the witness of the Holy Spirit). The Bible focuses on Christ, is applicable for the church, and is affirmed to us by the testimony of the Holy Spirit in our hearts. Without these presuppositions we cannot move forward in understanding how the Bible should be rightly interpreted or applied to our lives.

We can summarize this portion of our discussion by saying that the Bible has a two-sided divine-human character. Equally, we have observed that the Bible testifies to its own divine nature and inspiration. Divine inspiration should be understood primarily as referring to the final product (the written text) although we desire to avoid a conflict between the inspiration of the human authors of the text and the written text itself. But it is our conclusion that a view of inspiration limited to the human authors alone is insufficient.

---

[122] John Jefferson Davis, *Theology Primer* (Grand Rapids: Baker, 1981), 20–21.

While focusing on the product of inspiration—the inscripturated text—we do not want to ignore the purpose and process of inspiration. The purpose of inspiration is ultimately for salvific purposes, which in its full understanding includes teaching, reproof, correction, and training in righteousness, so that believers can be equipped for service and good works (2 Tim. 3:16–17). The process of inspiration is inclusive in the training and preparation of the authors, their research, and their use of witnesses. As a result we can posit that the Bible is simultaneously the Word of God and the words of men.

Having surveyed several approaches to the issue of inspiration, we noted that inspiration does not mean that God dictated all of Scripture, for this fails to account for the human activity. Neither can it be affirmed that the Bible is merely a human book whose authors, due to special spiritual sensitivity, produced inspiring works of literature. Not only must inspiration recognize the human authorship and the divine character of Scripture; it must not divorce God's deeds from his words. Neither must we create dichotomies between thoughts and words, processes and product, writers and written word, God's initiating impulse and his complete superintending work. A comprehensive, verbal/plenary view of inspiration is essential.

This understanding of biblical inspiration applies to all of canonical Scripture (including the process, the purpose, and ultimately the product) and asserts that by the concursive action of God the Scriptures are, in their entirety, both the work of the Spirit and the work of human authors. Such a view of inspiration is not only plausible but necessarily important for affirmations of truth. We believe that a plenary, verbal, inclusive view of inspiration alone does justice to the theological teachings and the phenomena within the text.

We examined these conclusions in light of the human authorship of the Bible. We recognized that a concursive view of inspiration accounted for the style, personality, background, and context of the human authors. We noted the possibility of confessing a concursive view because the human authors were not autonomous but were men of faith, functioning in communities of faith with an awareness of God's direction in their lives. Consistent with our view of the genuine humanness of the biblical text is the need to notice the cultural-temporal factors involved in this issue. But recognition that the writers were bearers of the image of God opens up the possibility of qualifying historical and cultural distance. This is due to the belief that they, along with their readers and hearers, had memories of the past, consideration of the present, and expectations of the future. This allows for the possibility of cross-cultural and cross-temporal communication. The reality of human authorship is evidenced by the variety of emphases in Scripture, the different writing styles, and the development within the Testaments and the writers themselves. It is our conclusion that this variety is complementary and not contradictory. The variety of Scripture has a genuine unity that is not forced upon the text but is present and evident as a result of divine inspiration.

We have already noted the plausibility of maintaining the normative character of Scripture while simultaneously affirming the historical situation of the human authors and the time-relatedness of the text. Because of the basic needs shared by men and women of all ages and races in all times and cultures, the central message of Scripture can speak in a normative and authoritative way. Beyond this we acknowledged that Scripture speaks not only to pietistic and religious needs but to the truth of and about God and to the ramifications affecting all matters related to life and godliness. We believe that such a normative Scripture can be described as inerrant when inerrancy is carefully defined to avoid overstatement or improper association with a dictation view of inspiration. We believe, therefore, that it is important, even epistemologically necessary, that the church carefully articulates a statement concerning Scripture that maintains with equal force both the humanity and deity of the Bible. Thus we can have confidence in the Bible as a trustworthy and authoritative guide. Now let us turn our attention to the issue of biblical authority.

The Authority of Scripture

The ultimate concern in a discussion of Christian Scripture is its authority. We confess the authority of the Bible and its rightful role in commanding obedience for the people of God. We recognize that the Bible is authoritative for contemporary cultural issues, as well as for ethics and decision making.

A view of the Bible that affirms its divine inspiration and total truthfulness is of little value if it is not accompanied by an enthusiastic commitment to the Bible's complete and absolute authority. An approach to the subject of biblical authority must begin with God himself, for in God all authority is ultimately located. God is his own authority. There is nothing outside him on which his authority is established. When God made his promise to Abraham, he pledged his own name because there was nothing or no one greater by whom he could swear (Heb. 6:13). God's authority is the authority of who and what God is. As we learned in earlier chapters, who God is has been made known in his self-manifestation since God can be known only in his own self-revelation. The key to God's authority is his revelation. In this manner, revelation and authority are seen as two sides of the same reality. God thus declares his authority through his revelation, and he alone is the ultimate source of authority for all other lesser authorities.

Christians are called to live lives of love toward others. Scripture in no way *denies* the right or ability of a congregation to care for the physical needs of non-Christians in their area. Neither does Scripture *require* the local congregation to alleviate the physical needs of non-Christians in our community. Rather, congregations have a call to preach, display, model, and express the good news of Jesus Christ. And in obedience to *that* call Christian congregations have both the liberty and responsibility to prudently take such initiatives in our community.

The Sufficiency and Clarity of Scripture

Corollary to the orthodox doctrine of inspiration are the doctrines of the sufficiency of Scripture and the perspicuity or clarity of Scripture. The doctrine of sufficiency entails the affirmation that Scripture is itself sufficient for doctrine and life (2 Tim 3:16-17) inasmuch as the Scriptures are learned with the illuminating assistance of the Holy Spirit (John 14:26; 16:13; 1 Cor 1:6ff.) and life is lived by the empowerment of the Holy Spirit (2 Pet. 1:3). That is, the believer is not lacking adequate revelation since the inspired Bible itself provides all the revelation necessary for knowing and living as God intends. The doctrine of sufficiency does not indicate that scriptural revelation is exhaustive, or that it contains all knowledge about the subjects taught therein, but the Bible is sufficient such that further revelation is not necessary beyond the scope of Scripture for faithfully living the Christian life. Since Scripture is sufficient, there is no warrant to add to or take away from the Word of God we know as the Bible (Prov. 30:5-6).

The doctrine of the clarity of Scripture entails the affirmation that Scripture is written in such a way that it may be understood by those who, with the aid of the Holy Spirit, read or hear the biblical text. Martin Luther identified two categories that frame our understanding of the clarity of Scripture. *External* clarity refers to the linguistic or grammatical clarity of Scripture. Because this clarity exists outside of the individual, it is a quality of the text itself; therefore that which we do not clearly see must be due to "our own linguistic and grammatical ignorance."[123] *Internal* clarity refers to "the knowledge of the heart."[124] In this sense, Scripture is only clear to those who believe the gospel. The work of the Spirit is necessary to illuminate darkened minds and blinded eyes, enabling them to understand (1 Cor. 2:14; cf. 2 Cor 4:3-4).

The doctrine of clarity does not indicate that the Scriptures are without passages difficult to understand, that the Bible is *easily* accessible, or that it is equally accessible to all readers. The doctrine does indicate, however, that the content of Scripture is clear—that content centers on Jesus Christ.

---

[123] Martin Luther, *The Bondage of the Will*, WA, 606–09.
[124] Ibid.

The doctrine also indicates that the Scriptures may be understood by the average reader and that knowledge of the Scriptures is not limited only to those who have, for example, specialized training.[125]

The Canon of Scripture

What do we mean by the term *canon*? Canon (from the Greek *kanōn*) means a standard by which something is measured. Designating a carpenter's rule, the word was possibly borrowed from a Hebrew term (*qaneh*) referring to a measuring reed six cubits long. Thus, we refer to Scripture as canonical, meaning that it serves as a rule, a measure, or a standard for God's people.[126]

We must not think that the church determined or defined the books in the church's canon. In reality the church did not create the canon but received the canon that God created for his people. The church recognized the canonical books as spiritually superlative writings by which all other books were measured and found to be of secondary value in general church use. The church then did not decide which books belonged in the canon but only affirmed those books that God had inspired.[127]

The Old Testament Canon

Most of the Old Testament canon, especially the Law and Prophets, was established long before the time of Christ. The details of the process by which the Old Testament writings were recognized as authoritative and distinguished from other Jewish works remain largely unknown. Later, Judiasm believed that the Word of God came in twenty-four books. The Talmudic treatise Baba Bathra (ca. AD 200) contains a list of books that is virtually the same as our present canon. Books are listed in tripartite form: the five books of Moses, eight books of the Prophets, and eleven Writings.

It is likely that Jesus and the apostles shared this view of the Old Testament (Luke 24:44). The implications of Jesus' words in Matthew 23:35 (see also Luke 11:51) are most informative. He spoke of "all the righteous blood that has been shed on earth, from the blood of righteous Abel to the blood of Zechariah son of Berekiah." Abel was obviously the first righteous person to suffer at the hands of the wicked, but why include Zechariah?

---

[125] We assume, for example, that when Jesus states, "You have heard . . ." (e.g., Matt. 5:21,27,33) that he actually means what he says, that those who hear the Word of God are able to understand it. His rebuke of those who do have the Scriptures, but who do not understand them is an indication of their hardness of heart, not lack of clarity in the divine revelation. Furthermore, the prophets and apostles assume that the Scriptures will be read, heard, and understood by the people of God.

[126] See David Dunbar, "The Biblical Canon," in *Hermeneutics, Authority and Canon*, 299–360.

[127] Linda Belleville, "Canon of the New Testament," in *Foundations for Biblical Interpretation*, 375–76.

Zechariah, son of Jehoiada (2 Chron. 24:20–22), is not chronologically the Old Testament's last martyr. He is mentioned because, probably, by the time of Jesus, Chronicles was recognized as the last book in the Hebrew Bible.[128]

Josephus, the Jewish historian (ca. AD 37–100), followed the tripartite grouping but included only twenty-two books. The reason is that he included only nine Writings, since Judges-Ruth was considered one book, as was Jeremiah-Lamentations. The Dead Sea Scrolls indicate that the Qumran covenant community had commentaries on most Old Testament books. These commentaries point to the high regard the convenanters had for the Scriptures. These writings make clear a marked difference between the canonical Scriptures and the numerous other books in the Qumran library.[129]

Much debate surrounds the details of the recognition of the Old Testament canon. Tradition has it that Ezra was primarily responsible for collecting the material into a recognized canon. Critical scholars challenge this tradition since they date several Old Testament books after Ezra. They instead point to a council of Jewish elders held at Jamnia (ca. AD 90) as the important time for establishing the Old Testament canon. But the supposed role of the council of Jamnia has been severely attacked by recent scholarship, as have other crucial assumptions of the nonevangelical reconstruction. R. T. Beckwith contends that the closing of the Old Testament canon was settled by the time of Judas Maccabaeus, around 165 BC. It is probable that the Old Testament canon was settled by the time of Jesus. In the absence of enough evidence on the origin of the Old Testament canon, it is impossible to be certain.[130] As men of the old were moved by the Spirit to write the holy books (2 Pet. 1:21), God providentially led his people to preserve, recognize, and treasure these writings.

The New Testament Canon

The New Testament writings functioned authoritatively from their beginning; yet, as with the Old Testament, their collection and distinction from other literature of the time was a gradual process spanning several centuries.

Authority was inherent in Jesus' commission to the apostles (Matt. 28:18), but it was not accepted without question by all (1 Cor. 9:1–3). Not all books written by apostles were included in the canon (1 Cor. 5:9; Col. 4:16). But by the late second century, Irenaeus considered apostolicity the fundamental test of canonical authenticity. Nonapostolic authors, like

---

[128] Paul House, "Canon of the Old Testament," in *Foundations for Biblical Interpretation,* 143–55. For an alternative interpretation see Craig Blomberg, *Matthew,* NAC (Nashville: Broadman & Holman, 1992), 349.

[129] House, 151–52.

[130] See R. T. Beckwith, *The Old Testament Canon of the New Testament Church and Its Background in Early Judaism* (Grand Rapids: Eerdmans, 1985).

Mark, Luke, and James, were considered to have equal authority because of their association and sanction by the apostles.[131]

When the apostolic writings were initially gathered is not known for sure. By the time of the writing of 2 Peter, several letters of Paul were known (2 Pet. 3:16). Letters were expensive to produce. Certainly letters from apostles would have been welcome blessings for the young churches during a time when no official New Testament existed. The churches' leadership was provided by the Spirit's ministry through gifted people (Eph. 4:11–16). The apostles' letters were to be read in the struggling churches during their worship meetings (Col. 4:16). They would have been received as valuable directives. The letters of Paul were widely circulated and read by the beginning of the second century (see 1 Clement 47:1–3).[132]

Tradition has held that the decisive period in the history of the New Testament canon was AD 140–200, during which time the basic form of the canon developed.[133] The reason for the canon's fixture came largely as a result of the church's need to counter the heresies of Marcionism and Montanism. The New Testament canon, in the majority, was accepted by growing consensus around the end of the second century.

The general acceptance and use in the first two centuries AD of all twenty-seven New Testament books was followed in the third and fourth centuries by a period of intense debate regarding the "apostles" portion of the canon as well as some of the commonly valued writings like the Apocalypse of Peter and the Shepherd of Hermas. Yet it was these debates that led to an increasingly more precise definition of what constituted a "canonical" writing and to a clearer determination of the limits of the canon. The Muratorian Canon (ca. AD 200) is of considerable value in understanding the kinds of distinctions that were increasingly employed by those wrestling with the issue of canon in the early church. A distinction was made between those books that were authorized for public reading, such as Jude, 2 John, 3 John, and those recommended only for private devotional edification such as the Shepherd of Hermas.

The Muratorian fragment is viewed as the earliest datable list in the history of the New Testament canon. The text is in Latin and most likely was translated from Greek. The list includes four Gospels, Acts, Pauline letters, 1 Peter, 1 John, and the book of Revelation. As mentioned above, it distinguished between which books should and which books should not be

---

[131] F. F. Bruce, *The Canon of Scripture* (Downers Grove: InterVarsity, 1988), 117–33.

[132] See Bruce M. Metzger, *The Canon of the New Testament: Its Origin, Development and Significance* (Oxford: Clarendon, 1987).

[133] Ralph P. Martin, "Muratorian Canon," *New International Dictionary of the Christian Church*, ed. J. D. Douglas (Grand Rapids: Zondervan, 1978), 684–85.

used in public church worship. Hippolytus of Rome (ca. AD 236) has been widely suggested as the author of this list, but this cannot be proven.

By the fourth century, Eusebius, the early church historian, delineated several categories of books: (1) accepted, (2) disputed, (3) rejected, and (4) heretical. The accepted books contain most of our present New Testament books. The disputed books contain James, Jude, 2 Peter, and 2 and 3 John. Revelation was accepted by some and rejected by others. Among the spurious books are the Epistle of Barnabas, the Shepherd of Hermas, the Acts of Paul, the Apocalypse of Peter, the Teachings of the Apostles, and the Gospel of the Hebrews. The category of disputed included books put forward under the name of the apostles including the Gospels of Peter, Thomas, and Mathias, and the Acts of Peter, Andrew, and John.[134]

Eusebius also included a list of heretical books which he considered to be out of harmony with the orthodox teachings of the apostles. Eusebius exhorted his readers not to refer to these writings since they were impious and "beyond the pale."[135]

Growing consensus and use of the term *canon* became solidified by the fourth century. From the common notion of a rule of faith, the term was used from the second century. It was easy to see how in the fourth century the term *rule* or *canon* came to be applied to a list of books whose content was viewed as inspired and authoritative for all matters of faith and practice. Athanasius, bishop of Alexandria (ca. AD 353), who stated that the Shepherd of Hermas did not belong to the canon, was the first church father to employ the word in this technical sense while the Synod of Laodicea (ca. AD 363) was the first church council to employ the term to distinguish canonical writings from noncanonical writings. The term *canon* had become a widely accepted reference by the end of the fourth century.

The emergence of a churchwide consensus was primarily the result of a series of councils that tackled the question of canon in the context of wider discussions related to the Trinity and Christology. As the church attempted to define orthodoxy and to protect books of the church in order to transmit the faith from one generation to the next, it was natural for the church leaders to seek a consensus regarding the orthodox writings that would provide the foundation for the church's belief. It is important to say again that these councils did not create the canon, but they merely acknowledged those inspired writings that were already recognized by the churches.[136]

The first list of canonical books that contains the twenty-seven books currently accepted appears in Bishop Athanasius's festal letter of AD 367.

---

[134] See Eusebius, *The History of the Church from Christ to Constantine*, trans. G. A. Williamson (Minneapolis: Augsburg, 1965), 6.25.
[135] Ibid., 3.25.
[136] Belleville, "New Testament," 392–94.

The order, however, is different. The first church council to list all twenty-seven books of the New Testament was the Council of Carthage in AD 397. The selection of the canonical books stabilized after each book proved its worth by generally passing the criteria or tests of canonicity. The consensus was more widespread in the West than in the East, where the limits of the New Testament canon remained elusive.

We have referred to these tests, but now we need to pursue this issue in more detail. It is somewhat debated as to how the tests were employed and which ones were used at which time and in what places. But following the work of F. F. Bruce, we will suggest five general questions that helped the church recognize what was already true: that these twenty-seven books are inspired and authoritative.[137]

Neither the church councils nor the application of these tests made any book authoritative or authentic. The book was inspired, authoritative, and therefore genuine when it was written. The councils recognized and verified certain books as the written Word of God, and eventually those so recognized were collected in what we call the Bible. The tests involved the following issues:

1. Was the book authored or sanctioned by an apostle or a prophet?
2. Was the book widely circulated?
3. Was the book Christologically centered?
4. Was the book orthodox, that is, faithful to the teachings of the apostles?
5. Did the book give internal evidence of its unique character as inspired and authoritative?

The bottom line for each of these questions was the relationship of inspiration to canonicity. The books were included in the canon because they were believed to be inspired.[138] Likewise, the books were known to be inspired because they were in the canon. How far was this the case in the early church? Ellen Flesseman-Van Leer claims that "apostolicity was the principal token of canonicity for the West, inspiration for the East; not indeed in a mutually exclusive way, since in the West apostolicity to a certain extent includes inspiration, while in the East apostolicity was an attendant feature of inspiration."[139]

Only one of the New Testament writers expressively based the authority of his writings on the prophetic inspiration. The book of Revelation is called

---

[137] See Bruce, "Canon," 255–69.
[138] See Richard B. Gaffin, "New Testament as Canon," in *Inerrancy and Hermeneutic,* 165–83.
[139] Ellen Flesseman-VanLeer, "Prinzipien der Sammlung und Ausscheidung bei der Bildung des Kanons," *Zeitschrift für Theologie und Kirche* 61 (1964): 415–16.

"this book of prophecy" (Rev. 22:19). John implied that his words were inspired by the same spirit of prophecy that spoke to the prophets of earlier ages; thus, he stands in succession to them (Rev. 22:9). Likewise, he claims "the testimony of Jesus is the spirit of prophecy" (Rev. 19:10). The readers of the book are expected to hear what the "Spirit says to the churches" (Rev. 2:7). While these passages are unique to the last book of the Bible, it is a clear indication that at the beginning of the Christian era, the inspiration of the prophetic oracles of the Old Testament was believed to extend to the New Testament Scriptures as well, at least in part if not in whole. While the New Testament writers were not always aware of inspiration as in the case of the writing of the Apocalypse, most of the New Testament writers believed they wrote with the "mind of Christ" (1 Cor. 2:16).

Some have suggested that inspiration was not a criterion of canonicity but a corollary of canonicity. Krister Stendahl has observed that "it was until the red ribbon of the self-evident had been tied around the twenty-seven books of the New Testament that 'inspiration' could serve theologians as an answer to the question: Why are these books different from all other books?"[140]

Consensus related to the canon was important for two primary reasons. First, it was imperative for the church officials in times of persecution to distinguish between those books that might be handed over to the church's opponents and those which must be preserved. The bottom line was that the church needed to know which books were worth dying for if indeed one's life were put on the line.[141] Second, canonicity enabled the theologians of the church to distinguish those books that might be used for settling doctrinal questions from those which were generally helpful for edifying and private reading. Only those books that carried apostolic authority or sanction were to be appealed to for the establishment of the truths to be believed and passed on to other generations.[142]

The early church displayed surprising unanimity about which books belonged to the inspired collection. Although it is true that a few books such as Jude, 2 Peter, and Revelation were the subjects of considerable debate, no book whose authenticity was doubted by a large number of churches was later accepted. The persecution of the church helped distinguish the canonical books from other helpful writings as the people were forced to decide what books should be protected during times of oppression.

---

[140] K. Stendahl, "The Apocalypse of John and the Epistles of Paul in the Muratorian Fragment," in *Current Issues in New Testament Interpretation,* ed. W. Klassen and G. F. Snyder (New York: Harper, 1962), 243.

[141] We are dependent here on William R. Farmer and Denis M. Farkasfalvy, *The Formation of the New Testament Canon* (New York: Paulist, 1983).

[142] See Bloesch, *Holy Scripture,* 141–60; also James Leo Garrett Jr., *Systematic Theology* (Grand Rapids: Eerdmans, 1990).

The Contemporary Debate

"Most points of the history of the canon are now so fully clarified that one can almost speak of a *communis opinion*," wrote Wilhelm Schneemelcher in his introduction to the long-awaited 1959 revision of Edgar Hennecke's *Neu Testamentliche Apokryphem.*[143] Likewise, H. von Campenhausen's monumental volume, *The Formation of the Christian Bible,* echoed this confidence, as did contributions by such outstanding and confessionally diverse scholars as F. F. Bruce, Wainwright, and Käsemann.[144] Yet Schneemelcher, in 1980, reopened the question of canon, observing that its history is still seen through a glass darkly.[145] In agreement, we find Albert Sundberg's revision of F. W. Beare's work, suggesting a demise of the previous consensus.[146] "What was the older consensus theory?" "What are the new suggestions?" are the matters that concern us at this stage.

Formerly, as we have described above, it was held that the decisive period in the history of the New Testament canon was AD 140–200, during which time the basic form of the canon developed. The New Testament canon was basically accepted by the end of the second century. Sundberg, on the other hand, has argued that the development of the canon should be seen as consisting of three stages: (1) the rise of the Christian writings to the status of Scripture; (2) the conscious collection of Christian writings into closed subcollection; and (3) the formation and standardization of New Testament lists, canonization proper. It is basically the third point of his suggestion that issues in a potential revision. He posits that the Muratorian Canon should be dated much later, perhaps as late as the fourth century with Eusebius.

Two major studies in more recent years, however, question the validity of Sundberg's thesis and point us to the previously described consensus. David Dunbar and Bruce Metzger have written major works that counter the revisionist authors. Dunbar maintains that

---

[143] Wilhelm Schneemelcher, "General Introduction" to *New Testament Apocrypha,* by Edgar Hennecke, trans. and ed. R. M. Wilson (Philadelphia: Westminster, 1963), 29. The consensus of this time is underscored by the discussions in the standard works of J. N. D. Kelly, *Early Christian Doctrine* (New York: Harper & Row, 1960), 52–60; and F. W. Beare, "Canon of the New Testament," *IDB* (Nashville: Abingdon, 1962), 334–58.

[144] See H. von Campenhausen, *The Formation of the Christian Bible,* trans. J. A. Baker (Philadelphia: Fortress, 1973); Bruce, *Canon;* Geoffrey Wainwright, "New Testament as Canon," *SJT* 28 (1975): 551–71; Ernst Käsemann, ed., *Das Neue Testament als Kanon* (Gottingen: Vandenhoeck & Ruprecht, 1970), 9.

[145] Wilhelm Schneemelcher, "Bibel I/II: Die entstehung des Kanons des Neuen Testaments und der Christlichen Bibel," *TRE* I, ed. Gerhard Krause and Gerhard Müller (Berlin: deGruyter, 1980), which develops prior concerns of Hans Lietzmann, *Kleine Schriften II: Stu dien zum Neue Testament, Texte und Untersuchungen* 68, ed. Kurt Aland (Berlin: Akademie-Verlag, 1958).

[146] See Albert Sundburg, *The Old Testament of the Early Church* (Cambridge: Harvard, 1964); idem., "Toward a Revised History of the New Testament Canon," *SE* 4 (1968): 452–61; idem., "Canon Muratori: A Fourth Century List," *HTR* 66 (1973): 1–41; idem., "The Bible Canon and the Christian Doctrine of Inspiration," *Int* 29 (1975): 352–71.

the revisionist authors simultaneously underestimate the stability of the canon as it has been held by the church during the last fifteen centuries and overestimated the creativity of the Reformation. That was marked indeed by a Protestant rejection of the Old Testament Apocrypha, but no change at all in the New Testament canon.[147]

Thus, while giving due consideration to Sundberg, we contend that the traditional thesis is a helpful foundation on which to base our understanding of the canon.

At every point in the transmission, translation, preservation, and canonicity of the Bible, we see God's providential hand at work. The testimony of the church witnesses to this providential guidance and cannot readily be dismissed. The sixty-six books that we have are the Word of God written, inspired, and authoritative. The canon of Scripture is authenticated by the testimony of the Holy Spirit, who inspired the writings, to the individual Christian and to the community as a whole.

When we read our present translations, we can read with the assurance that they faithfully represent the original sources. Also, we believe that they include neither more nor less than the writings God purposed to include in the canonical Scriptures. Since God has nowhere provided a table of contents for the Bible, how do we know that new books should not be added? While this is a complex question, we believe that the canon is closed and includes the inspired books that should be accepted as authoritative. This affirmation is based on the recognition that the church of the second, third, and fourth centuries was much closer to the time of the apostles and thus in a better position to recognize and preserve the written prophetic-apostolic materials. To consider expanding the canon simultaneously underestimates the stability of the canon as it has been held by the church during the past sixteen centuries and overestimates the creativity of the post-Reformation period.

Our belief in a closed canon also grows from a confidence that God in his providence not only inspired the authors of Scripture to write those things he wanted to communicate to his people but also superintended their collection and preservation.

How Does This Doctrine Impact the Church Today?

Men and women are creatures of the self-revealing, eternal God. Since he has created humankind, life's meaning is found in dependence on and relationship with him. God exercises authority over his creation; and God's people respond to his authority in obedience and worship, as well as in

---

147 Dunbar, "Biblical Canon," 299.

confession and repentance. God's authority is communicated in the church and its tradition, in human reason, in conscience and experience, in nature and history, in Christ and the Bible.

God reveals himself in all of the ways mentioned above, yet the Bible is the primary means of God's authoritative self-disclosure for people today. The Bible pictures Jesus' authority in terms of acting for God the Father. Jesus exercises all the rightful authority of God. He forgives sin (Mark 2:5–8), casts out demons (Mark 1:27), teaches with authority (Matt. 5:21–48; 7:28–29), and raises the dead (Luke 7:11–17; John 11:38–44). As the obedient Son of God, he follows the Word of God revealed in the Scriptures and acknowledges and appeals to the Scripture's authority (Matt. 4:1–11; John 10:33–36). Jesus' death and resurrection provided victory over sin, evil, and death (Col. 2:15; 1 John 3:8). All authority in heaven and on earth has been given to him (Matt. 28:18–20).

Jesus' authority is exercised over the church (Eph. 1:20–23) and is uniquely expressed through his personal ambassadors, the apostles (Mark 3:14; John 17:18; Acts 1:8; 2 Cor. 5:20; Gal. 1:1–2:9). In this way the apostles served as the foundation of the church (Eph. 2:20–3:5). In fulfillment of Christ's promises (John 14:26; 16:13), the apostles' authority has been placed permanently in their writings. Thus, the Spirit of God has inspired the prophetic-apostolic writings, and the Scriptures become the recognized authority that communicates God's truth, which is to be taught, believed, and obeyed. The Bible, then, is the Book of God's truth. Because the Bible is completely truthful, it must be wholly trustworthy in its affirmations. Because it is truthful and trustworthy, it is our final authority in all things that pertain to life and godliness.[148]

The Bible is to be seen as the ultimate standard of authority for God's people. The Bible derives its authority from the self-revealing and self-authenticating God. The Bible's authority can and does communicate across cultural, geographical, and temporal differences between the biblical world and our setting. Scripture is authoritative as it is rightly and faithfully interpreted in its historical setting. The Holy Spirit illumines our minds and hearts to understand the biblical message. Likewise, the Spirit leads us to recognize the authority of Scripture and to respond and obey its message today.[149]

The Bible calls for an obedience to the authority of God revealed in his Word, not in reaction to authority nor in an authoritarian sense but from a true freedom that belongs to the children of God. We must avoid a concept of freedom that loses a sense of "oughtness" and responsibility. At the same time we must avoid a swing toward authoritarianism, where our commit-

---

[148] See Bernard Ramm, *The Pattern of Authority* (Grand Rapids: Eerdmans, 1957).
[149] Garrett, *Systematic Theology,* 1:181–82.

ment to Scripture's authority is misplaced in a church leader or in a societal or cultural trend.

Many people confuse a desire to obey Scripture's authority with a personal insecurity that calls for a leader to tell them constantly what to do or think. More troubling is that some leaders encourage this confusion by commingling a commitment to biblical authority with a type of authority associated with certain positions of church leadership. What is needed more than ever is a clear-cut distinction between human and divine authority so that the authority of the Bible is not undercut or lost through a false equation with human structures.[150]

We demonstrate our concern for biblical authority not only by careful biblical interpretation but also by repentance and prayer. A commitment to the complete truthfulness and trustworthiness (or inerrancy) of Scripture is important because it is the foundation that establishes the full extent of Scripture's authority.[151]

Living with a Holy Spirit-prompted desire to respond to the message and authority of the Bible brings reproof and correction (2 Tim. 3:16), which results in contrition, discipleship, and enablement for worship and service (2 Tim. 3:17). It results in training in righteousness that bears on Christian business people and the integrity of their practice. It bears on Christians, who must speak to matters of injustice in society and in the church. Biblical authority addresses families and their commitments to one another. It tells preachers and teachers to handle carefully the Word of God (see 2 Tim. 2:15). The authority of the Bible calls on us to recognize God's desire for unity (through variety) in the church (Eph. 4:1–16; John 17; 1 Cor. 12) and the need to love one another (John 13:34–35), even when we disagree over the interpretation of Scripture itself.

Thus, we need a renewed commitment to biblical authority that enables us to relate to one another in love and humility, bringing about true fellowship and community and resulting in not only right doctrine but also right practice before a watching, unbelieving world. We need a renewed commitment to biblical authority that will transform our performance-oriented church meetings into authentic worship, that will turn our church programs into service that is pleasing to God. The Holy Spirit, through the Scriptures, illuminates our appreciation of grace and motivates us toward faithful evangelism, discipleship, social engagement, and worldwide missions.[152]

---

[150] See John R. W. Stott, *Decisive Issues Facing Christians Today* (Old Tappan, NJ: Revell, 1990).

[151] Helpful insights on the relationship of truthfulness and authority can be found in Kenneth S. Kantzer, ed., *Applying the Scriptures* (Grand Rapids: Zondervan, 1987); also see Kantzer, "Problems Inerrancy Doesn't Solve," *CT*, 31:3 (February 1987), 15.

[152] See Geoffrey W. Bromiley, "Authority," *ISBE*, ed. G. W. Bromiley, 4 vols. (Grand Rapids: Eerdmans, 1979), 1:346–71.

We confess that God has revealed himself to us. His revelation has been preserved for us in Holy Scripture by the Holy Spirit's work of inspiration. We confess our belief in the divine inspiration, total truthfulness, and supreme authority of the Bible. Even beyond this affirmation, with willing spirits and open minds and hearts, we must dedicate ourselves anew to the authority of Holy Scripture, assured that we can place our complete confidence in God's truthful and reliable Word.[153]

---

[153] D. A. Carson, "Recent Developments in the Doctrine of Scripture," in *Hermeneutics, Authority, and Canon,* 46–48; also see Philip E. Satterthwaite and David F. Wright, eds., *A Pathway into Holy Scripture* (Grand Rapids: Eerdmans, 1994).

SECTION 2

THE DOCTRINE OF GOD

CHAPTER 4

The Nature of God: Being, Attributes, and Acts

Timothy George

He who says, I believe in God, says more than he can justify,
more than he knows, more even than he senses or suspects;
he says that God's reality is more real than his own life,
that God is nearer than hands and feet, that he is the most sublime,
but also the most common, that he is a God "in heaven above and
on earth below," the furthest away and the closest at hand,
the unattainable One, who was already nearby us before we were born.

—*Gerardus Van der Leeuw*[1]

J ames Petigru Boyce was a theological educator, institution builder, and denominational statesman; but his first love was to teach theology to the ministerial students who flocked to his classes in Louisville. One of those students, David M. Ramsay, recalled the following incident about "Jim Peter," as the students fondly called Boyce.

> One Sunday at the seminary dinner, a bunch of students came in from church saying:
> "We heard the greatest sermon of our lives today."
> "Who preached it?"
> "Jim Peter."
> "What was his text?"
> "God."
> "What was his theme?"
> "God."
> "What were the divisions of the discourse?"
> "God."
> That was the man.[2]

[1] *Dogmatische Brieven* (Amsterdam: H. J. Paris, 1933), 43.
[2] David M. Ramsay, "Boyce and Broadus, Founders of the Southern Baptist Theological Seminary." Unpublished manuscript on file in the Boyce Centennial Library of The Southern Baptist Theological

Boyce defined *theology* as "the science which treats of God," and the first sixteen chapters of his *Abstract of Systematic Theology* deal with the being, attributes, and decrees of God. But what did Boyce mean by God? He meant by God what historic mainstream Baptists, and indeed all orthodox Christians, have always meant by God. One classic summary of this belief is from chapter 2 of the Philadelphia Confession of Faith (1742), known in England as the Second London Confession (1677/1689). Echoing the language of the Westminster Confession of Faith (1646), this classic Baptist document declares that

1. The Lord our God is but one only living and true God; whose subsistence is in and of himself, infinite in being and perfection, whose essence cannot be comprehended by any but himself; a most pure Spirit, invisible, without body, parts, or passions, who only hath immortality, dwelling in the light which no man can approach unto, who is immutable, immense, eternal, incomprehensible, Almighty, everyway infinite, most holy, most wise, most free, most absolute, working all things according to the counsel of his own immutable and most righteous will for his own glory, most loving, gracious, mercy, long-suffering, abundant in goodness and truth, forgiving iniquity, transgression and sin, the rewarder of them that diligently seek him, and withal most just, and terrible in his judgments, hating all sin, and who will by no means clear the guilty.

2. God, having all glory, goodness, blessedness, in and of himself, is alone in and unto himself all-sufficient, not standing in need of any creature which he hath made, nor deriving any glory from them, but only manifesting his own glory in, by, unto, and upon them; he is the alone fountain of all being, of whom, through whom, and to whom are all things, and he hath most sovereign dominion over all creatures, to do by them, for them, or upon them, whatsoever himself pleaseth; in his sight all things are open and manifest, his knowledge is infinite, infallible, and independent upon the creature, so as nothing is to him contingent, or uncertain; he is most holy in all his counsels, in all his works, and in all his commands; to him is due from angels and men, whatsoever worship, service, or obedience, as creatures they owe unto the Creator, and whatever he is further pleased to require of them.[3]

Seminary, Louisville, Kentucky. See also Ramsay's, "James Petigru Boyce—God's Gentleman," *Review and Expositor* 21 (1924): 129–45.

[3] Timothy and Denise George, eds., *Baptist Confessions, Covenants, and Catechisms* (Nashville: Broadman & Holman, 1996), 59–60. This is the most comprehensive statement about God in any Baptist confession, but other classic documents from the Baptist tradition echo the same sentiments, albeit more succinctly. Thus the New Hampshire Confession (1833) declares "that there is one, and

We shall return to some of these statements about God in the following pages, but at the outset it is important to make two preliminary comments. (First,) note that the anecdote about Boyce referred not to a lecture he gave but rather to a sermon he preached. The doctrine of God has immediate and practical implications for how we worship, what we preach, the content of our prayer life, and the way we live and act in the world. In his *Marrow of Sacred Divinity,* the first theology textbook used at Harvard College, the Puritan William Ames defined *theology* as "the knowledge of how to live in the presence of God." In this sense theology cannot be left to the theologians; it is a necessary spiritual discipline for every believer. This is true of every topic covered in this book, but it applies especially to the doctrine of God, for how we perceive the ultimate author and principal subject of the Bible will affect everything else we believe and teach.

Another caveat up front: when Boyce said "God"—and he represents believing theologians through the centuries in this sense—he did so confidently, reverently, and joyfully, though not easily, lightly, or casually. "Blessed assurance" is not cheap insurance, and genuine knowledge of God is not without struggle and doubt. However, in much contemporary theology today, the note of God's grandeur, greatness, and glory that so fills the Bible is noticeably missing. Such theology suffers from a doxological deficit. It cannot sing with the psalmist, "I will exalt you, my God the King; I will praise your name for ever and ever" (Ps. 145:1),[4] nor shout with the heavenly saints, "Hallelujah! For our Lord God Almighty reigns. Let us rejoice and be glad and give him glory!" (Rev. 19:6–7). Theology has lost its joy and become a dour enterprise of idea-shuffling and puzzle-scrabbling. The title of a book published by Gordon D. Kaufman in the 1970s summarizes this mood: *God the Problem.*

In these brief pages we cannot explore the complicated history that has led contemporary theology to its present impasse. Postmodernism (or better, ultramodernism) does present a radical challenge to the Christian faith, one that we can ill afford to ignore. But we are concerned here with a more basic enterprise: To discover what we can learn about the reality of God from "the infallible standard of religious truth," as John L. Dagg referred to

only one, living and true God, whose name is JEHOVAH, the Maker and Supreme Ruler of heaven and earth; inexpressibly glorious in holiness; worthy of all possible honor, confidence, and love; revealed under the personal and relative distinctions of the Father, the Son, and the Holy Spirit; equal in every divine perfection, and executing distinct but harmonious offices in the great work of redemption." Ibid., 131–32.

[4] Unless otherwise noted, all Scripture citations in this chapter are from the New International Version (NIV).

the Bible.[5] If it seems to some critics that we are just repeating the wisdom of the past, we appeal to C. H. Spurgeon's reply to the charge that he was a mere echo of the Puritans: "I would rather be the echo of truth than the voice of falsehood."[6] In setting forth the doctrine of God as found in the Bible, then, we are not trying to accommodate this teaching to contemporary sensibilities. Unlike Schleiermacher, we offer no "speeches on religion to its cultured despisers." The God of the Bible will prove unpalatable to many for three reasons especially:

1. The Bible nowhere attempts to prove or argue for the existence of God.

The Bible announces its awesome theme in four opening words: "In the beginning God." The Bible assumes that "God is there and he is not silent" (Francis Schaeffer). Though the identity of God is fiercely contested in the history of Israel, especially in the struggle with idolatry, the reality of God is never disputed, apologized for, or made the object of dispassionate inquiry. At one point the Bible does introduce us to a theoretical atheist, but such a person is promptly labeled a "fool," and even this dote has sense enough to keep his mouth shut! (Ps. 14:1). The Bible is much more concerned about those who may believe all the right things about God but whose pride and preoccupations crowd out any "room for God" in their daily lives (Ps. 10:4).

2. God's middle name is Jealous.

Perhaps it would be better to say that God's other name is Jealous, for this is what the Lord declared to the children of Israel: "Do not worship any other god, for the LORD, whose name is Jealous, is a jealous God" (Exod. 34:14). The God of the Bible will brook no rivals. The children of Israel may have "no other gods" (Exod. 20:3). "Apart from me there is no God," says the Lord (Isa. 44:6). This is an imperious claim, and it does not go down well in a world of radical pluralism and religious relativism. It is also an affront to theologians imbued with an overwhelming sense of human self-importance. The God of the Bible, Kaufman declares, is an "ego-agent par excellence" and must be rejected in the name of human freedom and autonomy.[7]

[5] John L. Dagg, *Manual of Theology* (Charleston, SC: Southern Baptist Publication Society, 1858), 14.

[6] Quoted, "Charles Haddon Spurgeon," in Timothy George and David S. Dockery, eds., *Theologians of the Baptist Tradition* (Nashville: Broadman & Holman, 2001), 118.

[7] Gordon D. Kaufman, "Reconstructing the Concept of God: De-reifying the Anthropomorphisms," in *The Making and Remaking of Christian Doctrine*, ed. Sarah Coakley and David A. Pailin (Oxford: Clarendon Press 1993), 104.

3. The God of the Bible requires accountability from all.

Immanuel Kant taught that "God," like "world," and "soul," was an ordering concept, a mental construct devised and used by human beings to make sense of the universe and to undergird moral order in society. It was not a huge step from Kant to Feuerbach (and later Freud) who held that "God" was the projection of human longings, the sum of human wishes and desires, a mythic ideal with no reality external to human consciousness. Such a God can hold no one accountable, for he/she/it is entirely at the disposal of its finite creator. How different the God of the Bible who is described as "a consuming fire" (Deut. 4:24), the living God into whose hands to fall is "a dreadful thing" (Heb. 10:31). This God cannot be relegated to the safety of the seminar room or scrutinized like a butterfly under a microscope. The God of the Bible is the God with whom we have to do in life and death, in time and eternity, the God to whom we must all give an account and whom no one can escape. Every human being, Calvin says, has *negotium cum deo,* "business with God."[8]

What Does the Bible Say?

One of the most important things the Bible says about God is that there is much about him that we do not know, and will never be able to know, for God is infinite; and we are not (and never will be). God dwells in "unapproachable light" (1 Tim. 6:16); his greatness "no one can fathom" (Ps. 145:3); his knowledge is too wonderful for us, too lofty for us to attain (Ps. 139:6). "To whom, then, will you compare God? What image will you compare him to?" Isaiah asks (Isa. 40:18). The answer is: to no one and no thing, for God is incomparably great, absolutely sovereign over, and radically other than, everything that exists outside of himself. This means that God is irreducible to the world's categories. He is explicable only in himself; his judgments are unsearchable and his paths beyond tracing out (Rom. 11:33).

On that note we could end this chapter and say nothing else. In fact, the way of silence is one of three responses made to the ineffable mystery of God in the history of theology. It is the way of the Christian apophatic tradition and mystical theology. Meister Eckhart represents this approach

---

[8] Throughout book 1 of the *Institutes,* Calvin shows that deep within every person God has fixed an awareness of himself. Calvin called this awareness "the seed of religion," "the sense of divinity," and "the worm of conscience." Such general knowledge of God does not lead to salvation apart from God's revelation in Jesus Christ, but it is sufficient, as Paul teaches in Romans 1–3, to leave human beings "without excuse" and thus morally accountable before God. See Timothy George, *Theology of the Reformers* (Nashville: Broadman & Holman, 1988), 189–92.

when he declares, "God is nameless because no one can say anything or understand anything about him."[9]

Another response is to begin with God's visible effects in the world and to argue from these, *a posteriori,* to God as first cause, final force, unmoved mover, and great designer of all that is. This is the way of natural theology so prominent in Roman Catholic thought and also in much Protestant evidentialist apologetics. There are severe limitations to this approach both because of creaturely finitude and human fallenness. This is not to say that we can learn nothing at all about God from his general revelation in the cosmos and in the human conscience. Indeed, Paul teaches in Romans 1–3 that God has revealed himself to some extent in every human culture and that this innate knowledge of God is sufficient to leave human beings without excuse for their disobedience.

But, at its best, knowledge of God discerned from the world by unaided reason is always partial, inadequate, and incomplete. After surveying the awesome power of God in nature, Job declares: "And these are but the outer fringe of his works; how faint the whisper we hear of him! Who then can understand the thunder of his power?" (Job 26:14).

While we must reject the tradition of natural theology, we can affirm a proper theology of nature. Spurgeon put it like this:

> The old saying is "go from Nature up to Nature's God." But it is hard work going up hill. The best thing is to go from Nature's God down to Nature; and, if you once get to Nature's God and believe him and love him, it is surprising how easy it is to hear music in the waves, and songs in the wild whisperings of the winds, and to see God everywhere.[10]

---

[9] Edmund Colledge and Bernard McGinn, eds., *Meister Eckhart: The Essential Sermons, Commentaries, Treatises and Defense* (New York: Paulist Press, 1981), 206. Not all Christian mystics have been as radical as Eckhart, who was posthumously condemned as a heretic in 1329. Most Protestants however have been suspicious of mystical theology unless it is clearly rooted in the revelation of God in Holy Scripture. For a more positive appraisal of mystical thought and its connection to classic spiritual and theological traditions, see Mark A. McIntosh, *Mystical Theology* (Oxford: Blackwell, 1998). Among Baptist theologians, no one offered a more positive appraisal of religious experience as a formative element in theological construction than E. Y. Mullins. Yet Mullins offered the following critique of mysticism: "It severs religion from ethics and the practical life of man because it gives no definite view of God and his requirements. . . . The vagueness and indefiniteness of its conception of God impresses upon it a pantheistic stamp. It cannot avoid the evils of pantheism." See *The Christian Religion in Its Doctrinal Expression* (Valley Forge: Judson Press, 1917), 14.

[10] C. H. Spurgeon, *Autobiography* (London: Passmore and Alabaster, 1899-1900), 1:66. Compare also Luther's comment: "If you begin your study of God by trying to determine how he rules the world, how he burned Sodom and Gomorrah with infernal fire, whether he has elected this person or that, and thus begin with the works of the High Majesty, then you will presently break your neck and be hurled from heaven, suffering a fall like Lucifer's. For such procedure amounts to be getting on top and building the roof before you have laid the foundation. Therefore, letting God do

How then may God be known? Only in the self-revelation of his words and deeds about which we learn assuredly in the Bible which not only contains the word of God in some symbolic sense but actually *is* the Word of God, the Word of God written, just as surely as Jesus Christ is the Word of God living. Thus in the rest of this section we shall review some of the major biblical themes on the nature and reality of God beginning with the core scriptural unfolding of his triune identity as the Father, the Son, and the Holy Spirit.

God the Holy Trinity

> I bind unto myself the name,
> the strong name of the Trinity,
> by invocation of the same,
> the three in one, and one in three.
> Of whom all nature has creation
> eternal Father, Spirit, Word,
> Praise to the Lord of my salvation;
> salvation is of Christ the Lord.
>
> —*St. Patrick*[11]

The one, eternal, and living God of the Bible, the only real God there is, is the God who has forever known himself, and who in the history of salvation has revealed himself to us, as the Father, the Son, and the Holy Spirit. To deny this truth is to lapse into heresy. Yet it is not at all obvious that a biblical account of the doctrine of God should begin with the Trinity. Scholastic theology of the Middle Ages set forth a different pattern which has been followed by many Protestant theologians including many Baptists (Gill, Dagg, Boyce, Strong, Mullins, Conner, Garrett, Erickson). This traditional pattern calls for dealing first with the essence and attributes of God (*de uno deo*) and only later with the divine persons within the Godhead (*de trino deo*).

During the Reformation Calvin at first followed the traditional pattern; but, when confronted with the antitrinitarian ideas of Servetus, Socinus, and other radical reformers, he relocated the doctrine of the Trinity, treating it, along with Scripture, in the context of the doctrine of the knowledge of

---

whatever he is doing, you must begin at the bottom and say: I do not want to know God until I have first known this Man; for so read the passages of Scripture: 'I am the way, the truth, and the life'; again: 'No man cometh unto the Father, but by me' (John 14:6)." Quoted, A. H. Strong, *Systematic Theology* (Philadelphia: Judson, 1907), 247.

[11] Attr. to St. Patrick, "St. Patrick's Hymn," trans. Cecil F. Alexander, in *Moravian Book of Worship* (Bethlehem, PA: Interprovincial Board of Publications and Communications, 1995), 237.

God in book 1 of the *Institutes*. Calvin's arrangement was followed by Karl Barth in his *Church Dogmatics* (I/2), and this move led to a renaissance in trinitarian theology in recent years.

Though followed by many orthodox theologians, there is a subtle danger in the former pattern. The danger is that it can lead to a low-grade unitarianism that reduces the doctrine of the Trinity to an afterthought. If we begin by treating the essence and attributes of God in the abstract and then come along and say, "Oh, yes, this God is also a triune reality," the latter affirmation can easily become a secondary or even dispensable element in one's theological system. The logic of this way of thinking is well illustrated by Schleiermacher's *The Christian Faith,* a massive systematic theology which devotes only a few paragraphs to the Trinity at the very end! We shall look at the biblical basis for the doctrine of the Trinity here, then review briefly some of the dogmatic struggles related to this teaching in the historical section, and finally consider God's attributes, understood as the perfections of the one undivided Trinity, in the systematic section of the chapter.

There is one further distinction we should introduce before turning to some key biblical texts. The *economic* Trinity refers to God's works *ad extra,* that is, what God has done outside himself in creation and redemption while the *immanent* Trinity denotes God's relations *ad intra,* that is, his eternal intratrinitarian communion as the Father, the Son, and the Holy Spirit. The immanent Trinity is also called the "ontological" Trinity. While this distinction is helpful in some respects, we should remember the axiom of Karl Rahner that the economic Trinity is the same as the immanent Trinity. This simply means that the God who freely chose to create the universe and to send his Son to redeem the world is none other than the God who eternally shares his three-personal life of love and holiness from all eternity.

The doctrine of the Trinity is the necessary theological framework for understanding the biblical account of Jesus as the true story of God—and if what the Bible says about Jesus is anything other than that, we have no gospel. Jesus was sent by Israel's God to be the Messiah, and the doctrine of the Trinity was already foreshadowed in significant ways in the Old Testament. If someone should accuse us of "reading Christian dogma back into the Hebrew Scriptures," we think we have good biblical warrant for doing so. Jesus clearly understood his own mission to be the fulfillment of God's promises to Israel in the past: "And beginning with Moses and all the Prophets, he explained to them what was said in all the Scriptures concerning himself" (Luke 24:27). Jesus did not misunderstand the Old Testament Scriptures, and neither did Peter when he wrote:

Concerning this salvation, the prophets, who spoke of the grace that was to come to you, searched intently and with the greatest care, trying to find out the time and circumstances to which the Spirit of Christ in them was pointing when he predicted the sufferings of Christ and the glories that would follow" (1 Pet. 1:10–11).

At the same time we should proceed with due caution, not looking for a three-leaf clover in every Old Testament verse![12]

It is nonetheless significant that the Bible opens on a triadic note. "In the beginning God created . . . and the Spirit of God was hovering over the waters . . . and God said 'Let there be light'" (emphasis added). In the New Testament, Jesus Christ, God's eternal Son, is identified as the Logos, the Word of God through whom God made all that is (John 1:1–3; Col. 1:15–17). Early Christian exegetes found traces of the Trinity in many other Old Testament references including Isaiah 48:16, where the Messiah, speaking in an anticipatory way, declares: "And now the Sovereign LORD has sent me, with his Spirit" (emphasis added). Likewise, the seraphic acclamation of the thrice-holy character of God in Isaiah 6:2–3 (also quoted in Rev. 4:8) was also seen as an adumbration of the New Testament disclosure of God as the Father, the Son, and the Holy Spirit: "Holy, holy, holy, is the LORD of hosts: the whole earth is full of his glory" (KJV). Even the plural form of God's name, Elohim, sometimes coupled with a singular verb, while not a proof of the Trinity as such, does "point indirectly to some mysterious plurality in the intra-subjectivity of God."[13]

On the basis of the analogy of faith we can rightly interpret these Old Testament texts in light of the full revelation of God at the coming of Christ, just as the early church did, but we should emphasize that

---

12 Thomas C. Oden has brought together principal Old Testament references interpreted by the early church fathers as *vestigia trinitatis*. Some of their interpretations are more convincing than others, but, as Oden remarks, their effort to identify an implicit triune teaching in the Old Testament Scriptures "deserves to be taken seriously." See Oden, *The Living God* (San Francisco: Harper & Row, 1987), 188–94. Among Baptist theologians, A. H. Strong is distinctive in placing the New Testament evidence for the Trinity prior to that from the Old Testament. He explains: "This tripersonality of the Godhead is exclusively a truth of revelation. It is clearly, though not formally, made known in the New Testament, and intimations of it may be found in the Old." *Systematic Theology,* 304. On the perils of trinitarian proof-texting, note these wise comments by Fisher Humphreys: "The Bible speaks of the fact of the God of Israel and the Father of Jesus Christ; it speaks of the fact of Jesus of Nazareth; it speaks of the fact of the Spirit who came to the church at Pentecost. The doctrine of the Trinity is a statement about the reality of the God who called Israel, who was incarnate as Jesus, and who now lives in Christians as the Spirit. So the data for the doctrine of the Trinity are not scattered texts; the data are the facts mentioned above, to which the texts refer." *Thinking about God* (New Orleans: Insight Press, 1974), 221.

13 Oden, *Living God,* 193. See also the classic study of George A. F. Knight, *A Biblical Approach to the Doctrine of the Trinity* (Edinburgh: Oliver and Boyd, 1953). Among Baptist theologians, John Gill, a distinguished Hebraist, dealt extensively with this issue. See his *Body of Doctrinal Divinity,* (1815; repr., Baptist Standard Bearer, 2000), 130–71.

these trinitarian vestiges are approximate and incomplete. The incident of the three heavenly visitors who appeared to Abraham under the oaks of Mamre in Genesis 18:1–15 is a case in point. Clearly, this is no direct vision of God for, as the Bible makes clear elsewhere, no one can see God and live (Exod. 33:20; John 1:18). But the three visitors do reveal something of the mysterious depths of the biblical God who cannot be reduced to a unipersonal entity, albeit they do so in a partial and fragmentary way.

Thus the Bible says, "The LORD appeared to Abraham," but when he looked up, he "saw three men." The three visitors also speak in a single, unitary voice. As Ambrose commented on this passage, Abraham "saw Three and worshiped One."[14] In Eastern iconography the appearance of the three visitors to Abraham is used as a symbolic representation of the Trinity in the Old Testament, often accompanied by the question, "Is anything too hard for the LORD?" (Gen. 18:14).

If the doctrine of the Trinity is budding in the Old Testament, it bursts into full flower in the New. Here, self-differentiation in God, seen proleptically in the history of Israel, is presented with unmistakable clarity through the incarnation. As John Chrysostom put it, the New Testament teaches that the Father is God, the Son is God, the Spirit is God, and that God is One.[15] The triune nature of the one God is evident at the baptism of Jesus. There, the voice of the Father from heaven identified the one being baptized by John in the Jordan as his beloved Son, while the Spirit of God descended like a dove, attesting the unique sonship of Christ and inaugurating his public ministry (Matt. 3:13–17)이 3½ 맛 등장.

The doctrine of the Trinity is not a speculative construct developed by the early church and read back into the New Testament but, as Arthur W. Wainwright contended, a teaching that is grounded in the "worship experience and thought of first-century Christianity."[16] Baptism was the central rite of initiation for believers in Jesus and, according to the Great Commission in Matthew 28:19–20, this act was to be done in the *one* name of the three divine persons—the Father, the Son, and the Holy Spirit. There is no historical or textual basis for regarding this instruction as something "invented" by the early church and placed on the lips of Jesus by a later redactor. Jesus himself is the originator of the triune baptismal formula, and Matthew places it at the end of his Gospel as a climactic summary of Jesus' entire ministry and mission.

---

[14] Ambrose, *Of the Holy Spirit* II, Intro 4, *NPNF* [2], 10:115.

[15] John Chrysostom, *Homily 7 on II Cor.*, *NPNF* [1], 12:319.

[16] Arthur W. Wainwright, *The Trinity in the New Testament*, (London: SPCK, 1962), vii. "It would be misleading to say that trinitarian theology is entirely post-biblical." The problem of the Trinity "did not first occur when later generations of thinkers reflected on the scriptures." Ibid., 265.

The three divine persons are named in many other New Testament passages as well, including Paul's apostolic benediction in 2 Corinthians 13:14: "The grace of the Lord Jesus Christ, and the love of God, and the fellowship of the Holy Spirit be with you all." The Trinity is not "explained" in the New Testament, but it is everywhere assumed as the basis for Christian life, liturgy, and ethics. The threefold formula appears in many different contexts (Rom. 15:30; 1 Cor. 12:4–6; Eph. 3:14–19; 2:18; 4:3–6; Titus 3:4–6; 1 Pet. 1:2; Jude 20–21).

Gerald Bray has argued that the "mature" doctrine of the Trinity that came to full expression in the classic creeds of the fourth century was a necessary implication of Christian conversion in the first. Bray argues that the key text in this development is Galatians 4:6, "Because you are sons, God sent the Spirit of his Son into our hearts, the Spirit who calls out, '*Abba,* Father.'" Just as the Father sent his Son into the world (Gal. 4:4), so too he sent his Spirit—who is the Spirit of the Son no less than the Spirit of the Father—into our hearts, and it is the Spirit who places the believer "in Christ," and who cries out to the Father on behalf of the believer that word of familial intimacy that Jesus himself used when addressing God—*Abba.* Elsewhere Paul declares that it is the Spirit who makes us "heirs with Christ," confirming this new relationship in our hearts, and enabling us also to "cry out, *Abba,* Father" (Rom. 8:15–17).[17]

Had the Gospel of John never been written, there is sufficient evidence in the rest of the New Testament to confirm the biblical basis of the doctrine of the Trinity. However, it is in the Fourth Gospel that we find "the supreme biblical pattern of trinitarian thought."[18]

> The Fourth Evangelist goes further than any other New Testament writer in stressing the fact that Jesus is God, and that the Spirit is a person whose functions are not wholly identical with those of Father and Son. Moreover, John works out more fully than any other New

---

[17] See Gerald L. Bray, "The Trinity and Galatians 4:1–6," in *God the Holy Trinity: Essays on Faith and Christian Life,* ed. Timothy George (Grand Rapids: Baker Academic, 2006). Robert W. Jenson also develops this theme in his discussion of "the soteriological necessity of trinitarian logic." Commenting on Romans 8:11, "If the Spirit of him who raised Jesus from the dead dwells in you, he who raised Christ Jesus from the dead will give life to your mortal bodies also through his Spirit which dwells in you" (RSV), Jenson explains: "The subject phrase displays in the uttermost conceptual compression the precise structure we have called 'the trinitarian logic': the Spirit is '*of* him *who* raised *Jesus*' and from the prepositional structure of this phrase, Paul then develops a rhetoric and argument which sweeps justification and the work of Christ and prayer and eschatology and ethics and predestination into one coherent understanding." Robert W. Jenson, *The Triune Identity* (Philadelphia: Fortress, 1982), 44.

[18] Wainwright, *The Trinity in the New Testament,* 260.

Testament writer the relationship between Father and Son. All these matters lay the foundation of trinitarian theology.[19]

Among the Johannine passages where Father, Son, and Holy Spirit are mentioned together are 1:33–34; 14:16,26; 16:15; 20:21–23 (cf. also 1 John 4:2; 4:13–16).

In sum, while the word *trinitas* is not found anywhere in the Bible, the Scriptures from first to last are thoroughly trinitarian. What was foreshadowed in the Old Testament became explicit in the New with the historical reality of God "manifested in the flesh" (1 Tim. 3:16 NKJV). While the Gospel of John takes center stage in the unfolding of the triune teaching, this doctrine is assumed, suggested, and explicated in various ways throughout the New Testament. Further, through the act of believing in Jesus, being baptized in God's triune name, communing with the one whose death, resurrection, and coming again is visibly proclaimed in the Lord's Supper, through their prayers, hymns, and, not least, through their witness to the apostolic faith unto death, the early Christians came more and more to love, praise, and adore the one eternal God—the Father who had sent his Spirit-conceived Son to die on the cross for their sins, the very Father who had also sent the Spirit of his risen Son into their hearts, giving them a new life fit for eternity.

We shall come back to the doctrine of the Trinity in the historical section of this chapter, but first we need to see how the one triune God made

---

[19] Ibid., 264. It must be said that the doctrine of the Trinity has not been a major theme in the work of most Baptist theologians. The orthodox trinitarian teaching is invariably assumed, duly noted, but usually given less attention than issues related to soteriology and ecclesiology. This is evident in the sparse references to the Trinity in William H. Brackney's *Genetic History of Baptist Thought* (Macon: Mercer University Press, 2004). In the eighteenth century many General Baptists in England lapsed into unitarianism, and this provoked a stout defense of orthodox trinitarian doctrine on the part of Particular Baptist theologians, most notably John Gill, *A Body of Doctrinal Divinity*, 1:27–31. Caleb Evans, an evangelical Calvinist who became principal of the Bristol Academy in 1781, also defended the Trinity in a much-publicized debate with Unitarians. For other Baptist treatments of the doctrine of the Trinity, see: Dagg, *Manual of Theology*, 55–56; Boyce, *Abstract of Systematic Theology*, 125–35; Mullins, *Christian Religion*, 205–13; Moody, *Word of Truth*, 115–26; Garrett, *Systematic Theology*, 1:262–88; Henry, *God, Revelation and Authority*, 5:165–213; Grenz, *Theology for the Community of God*, 68–99; Wayne Grudem, *Systematic Theology* (Grand Rapids: Zondervan, 1994), 226–61; Humphreys, *Thinking about God*, 219–24; Erickson, *Christian Theology*, 346–67; Strong, *Systematic Theology*, 304–52. See also S. J. Mikolaski, "The Triune God," in *Fundamentals of the Faith*, ed. C. F. H. Henry (Grand Rapids: Zondervan, 1969), 59–76; and Erickson, *God in Three Persons: A Contemporary Understanding of the Trinity* (Grand Rapids: Baker Book House, 1995). See also the earlier essay by James W. McClendon, "Some Reflections on the Future of Trinitarianism," *Review and Expositor* (Spring 1966) and Curtis W. Freeman, "God in Three Persons: Baptist Unitarianism and the Trinity," in *Perspectives in Religious Studies* (Fall 2006). Frank Stagg, whose *New Testament Theology* (Nashville: Broadman, 1962) influenced several generations of Southern Baptists, seemed to deny the tripersonality of God, though he denied being a modalist. See Robert Sloan's analysis of Stagg's views in George and Dockery, *Theologians of the Baptist Traditions* 274–75.

(handwritten Korean note: (사건의)모든 개념을 자신이)

himself known to his people throughout the history of salvation. Given the brevity of space, we can only identify some of the major themes of the doctrine of God unfolded in the biblical drama.

He Who Is: Pentateuchal Prelude

> God of gods, we sound his praises,
> highest heaven its homage brings;
> earth and all creation raises
> glory to the King of kings:
> holy, holy, holy, name him,
> Lord of all his hosts proclaim him:
> To the everlasting Father
> Every tongue and triumph sings.
>
> *Timothy Dudley-Smith*[20]

The whole Bible is a single, unified text with theological coherence, and in it the one supreme and true God, the God who exists in the entirety of his being as the Father, the Son, and the Holy Spirit, reveals himself to his people in personal self-disclosure. The initial five books of the Bible, Genesis through Deuteronomy, are the foundational texts for understanding God's self-revelation throughout the Scriptures. In the Pentateuch God's nature and character are revealed through the names by which he gives himself to be known. The God of the Bible is the God who names himself! Before looking at some of these names, it is important to see how in the act of naming himself, the God of Israel is distinguished both from the deity of philosophical speculation and from the gods of polytheistic religion.[21]

The Old Testament is filled with anthropomorphic images and analogies for God, each of which describes some aspect of God's majesty and power, as well as how he relates to his people. For example, God is referred

---

[20] Timothy Dudley-Smith, "God of Gods, We Sound His Praises," *Trinity Hymnal* (Atlanta: Great Commission Publications, 1998), 23.

[21] Paul R. House has emphasized the importance of a holistic canonical approach to the doctrine of God. "Just as it is quite difficult to build a complete doctrine of the Trinity or of the Son of God on the Old Testament alone, so it is exceedingly hard to construct an adequate doctrine of God founded solely on New Testament passages. Without question the New Testament confesses monotheism, the fact that the Lord is the Creator, the notion that God is creating a holy people and that the Lord is sovereign and timeless. Many of the reasons for these confessions, however, are assumed from the Old Testament, not proven by extensive analysis. Those who do not know the Old Testament canon are therefore more vulnerable to unbiblical definitions of God than those who do. Only serious attention to the Old Testament's theoretical, historical and experientially based statements about the Lord can render a full and certain theology. Anything less rests on a foundation weaker than the one the New Testament writers themselves considered safe." Paul R. House, *Old Testament Theology* (Downers Grove: InterVarsity, 1998), 547.

to as a shepherd (Ps. 23:1), as a physician (Exod. 15:26), a bridegroom (Isa. 61:10), a father (Deut. 32:6), and even a mother (Isa. 66:13)—though God is never directly addressed as "Mother"—as a friend (Exod. 33:11), a husband (Isa. 54:5; Jer. 3:14), as a prosecuting attorney (Jer. 2:9), and so on. In addition, the Bible also describes God's activities in terms of human body parts: a face (Exod. 33:20), eyes (Ps. 11:4), ears (Ps. 55:1), a nose (Deut. 33:10), a mouth (Deut. 8:3), hands (Num. 11:23), and a heart (Gen. 6:6). He is said to be capable of smelling, tasting, hearing, laughing, sitting down, walking. Further, God is also compared to various animals including the lion (Isa. 31:4), the eagle (Deut. 32:11), the lamb (Isa. 53:7), as well as inanimate objects such as a rock (Deut. 32:4), a tower (Prov. 18:10), a shield (Ps. 84:11), and a shadow (Ps. 91:1).

It would be a great mistake, however, to assume that God is to be equated with any of these creaturely realities, for to do so would be to lapse into idolatry. God is *like* a rock in some ways—he is sturdy, steadfast, no light-weight pebble that can be blown about in a windy storm—but it would be ludicrous to ask whether God is a sedimentary rock or an igneous rock! Herman Bavinck reminds us that "God is not named on the basis of that which is present in creatures, but creatures are named on the basis of that which exists in God."[22] Throughout the Bible God accommodates himself to our limited capacity as finite and fallen creatures by revealing himself to us in human words—for those are the only kinds of words that we have. Carl Henry used the word *stoops* to describe this self-condescension of God.[23]

The fact that God has a name means that he is intrinsically personal and can never be equated with the utterly transcendent god of Deism and Neoplatonism nor with the utterly immanent god of pantheism and Buddhism. Nor is he the impotent, ever-shifting, completely contingent god of process theology, the god Heraclitus long ago described as "day-night, winter-summer, war-peace, satiety-hunger—he changes his fire mixed with spices named for the scent of each."[24] All of these views present ultimate reality as a *that,* but in the Bible God is not "that thou art" but rather "he who is."

The Pentateuch displays a portrait of the deity whose awesome power and holy character are manifested in divine appellations. As Thomas Oden put it, "God has left a trail of language behind a stormy path of historical activities."[25] In the opening books of the Bible, we are confronted not with

---

[22] Herman Bavinck, *The Doctrine of God* (Grand Rapids: Baker, 1951), 134.

[23] Henry, *God, Revelation and Authority,* 5:17–19.

[24] Heraclitus, Fragments 53, 64, 32, 67. Quoted in L. E. Goodman, *God of Abraham* (Oxford: Oxford University Press, 1996), 6.

[25] Oden, *Living God,* 3.

"the awful Unnamable of this universe," as Thomas Carlyle described an ultimately anonymous deity, but rather with the true and living God who allows himself to be known and named. Loyalty to the name of God is at the heart of biblical faith, as can be seen from hundreds of references to "the name of God" and "the name of the LORD" throughout the Bible, including the following: "You shall not take the *name* of the LORD your God in vain" (Exod. 20:7 NKJV; emphasis added); "O LORD, our Lord, how majestic is your name in all the earth!" (Ps. 8:1); "Glorify the LORD with me; let us exalt his name together" (Ps. 34:3); "And everyone who calls on the name of the LORD will be saved" (Joel 2:32; Rom. 10:13); "The LORD will be king over the whole earth. On that day there will be one LORD, and his name the only name" (Zech. 14:9); "Our Father in heaven, hallowed be your name" (Matt. 6:9). What theologians call the *attributes* of God, which we shall consider in the systematic section of this chapter, are best understood as an extrapolation of the names of God.

Among the names of God revealed in the Pentateuch are the following:

Elohim

This is the plural form of *El* and *eloah,* which are also divine titles in the Pentateuch. This is the first name of God we encounter in the Bible (Gen. 1:1; also Gen. 1:26, "Let us make man in our image"), and it occurs 225 times in the Pentateuch. God is not only the Creator but also the one who blesses what he has made (Gen. 1:22,28; 2:3). But Elohim also judges (Gen. 31:53), curses (Deut. 27:15–26), and punishes (Gen. 19:29). This same word, *elohim,* is sometimes used to describe pagan deities (Pss. 96:5; 97:7); but when referring to the true and living God, it is accompanied by a singular verb or adjective. As Carl Henry explains, "In the Bible, Elohim is uniquely the one God who concentrates in himself the being and powers of all the gods, comprehending the totality of deity in himself."[26]

El

This is the generic semitic name for God and can be translated "the strong and mighty one." *El* corresponds to *theos* in Greek, *deus* in Latin, and *allah* in Arabic. *El* rarely occurs alone (but see Num. 12:13; Deut. 3:24; 32:18) but is usually found in combination with an explanatory adjective or in a genitive construction, thus Bethel, "the house of God" (Gen. 12:7–8). Another combination occurs in Melchizedek's blessing of Abraham in Genesis 14:19–20, "Blessed be Abram by God Most High [*El elyon*], Creator of heaven and earth. And blessed be God Most High, who delivered your enemies into your hand." It was this word in its vocative form, that Jesus uttered on the cross: "Eli, Eli . . . my God, my God" (Matt. 27:46 KJV).

---

[26] Henry, *God, Revelation and Authority,* 2:185.

El Shaddai

This name is sometimes translated "God Almighty" but is better rendered "God the All-Sufficient." The New Testament translates this term by *pantokratōr,* "The All-Powerful" (2 Cor. 6:18; Rev. 1:8; 4:8). El Shaddai is the God who nourishes and sustains what he has made, the God whose infinite and unfailing power displays itself not in brute force but in providential design.

El Roy

This name comes from the lips of Hagar. "She gave this name to the LORD who spoke to her: 'You are the God who sees me,' for she said, 'I have now seen the One who sees me'" (Gen. 16:13). El Roy is the God who sees all, whose "eyes . . . run to and fro throughout the whole earth," the God from whom nothing can be hidden.

El Olam

This name means "the everlasting God" and was first used with reference to the loyalty oath made between Abraham and Abimelech. "Abraham planted a tamarisk tree in Beersheba, and there called on the name of the LORD, the Everlasting God" (Gen. 21:33 NKJV).

Yahweh

Yahweh is the most common designation of God in the Bible, occurring some six thousand times, in contrast to Elohim which is found 2,590 times.[27] It is found many times in the book of Genesis, often in combination with Elohim, including the account of creation: "When the LORD God made the earth and the heavens" (Gen. 2:4).[28] Yahweh is God's personal proper name, and it is different from all of the other names for God in the Bible in one important respect: Elohim and all of its cognates can be used generically to refer to pagan deities and false gods, as we have seen, but this is never the case with Yahweh. So special was this name to the Jews that following the Babylonian captivity, they would not pronounce it orally but simply wrote the four Hebrew consonants YHWH, called the Tetragrammaton, literally, the "four-hyphen letter" word. Whenever the rabbis came across this sacred name in the text, they

---

[27] Erich Sauer, *The Dawn of World Redemption: A Survey of Historical Revelation in the Old Testament* (Grand Rapids: Eerdmans, 1952), 187.

[28] It is not necessary to review here the documentary theory of the Pentateuch for which, on the basis of Exodus 6:2–3, some scholars posit multiple sources for the text corresponding to the various names of God. J. A. Motyer, following Sigmund Mowinckel, argues that this controverted text teaches that what was withheld from the earlier patriarchs was not the name Yahweh itself but rather its significance. Motyer proposes this translation: "And God spoke to Moses, and said to him, I am Yahweh. And I showed myself to Abraham, to Isaac, and to Jacob in the character of El Shaddai, but in the character expressed by my name Yahweh I did not make myself known to them." See J. A. Motyer, *The Revelation of the Divine Name* (London: Tyndale, 1959), 12. See also the discussion in Henry, *God, Revelation and Authority,* 2:195–209.

substituted another word, _Adonai,_ which was translated in the Septuagint and the New Testament as _kurios._ The translators of the KJV rendered this as "the LORD," using all capitals.

Yah

The name Yahweh occurs in a shortened form, Yah (Exod. 15:2; 17:16), and in various combinations: Yehosua, "Yahweh is salvation" (Josh. 1:1); Yokebed, "Yahweh is glory" (Num. 26:59); "Yahweh will provide" (Gen. 22:14); "Yahweh my banner" (Exod. 17:15–16); "Yahweh our righteousness" (Jer. 23:6; 33:16).

What does the name Yahweh mean? We only learn the answer to this question by paying attention to God's encounter with Moses at the burning bush. There, on the backside of the desert, Moses first saw something—something highly unusual, indeed unique: a bush ablaze with a perpetual flame, a bush that did not burn up. Next Moses heard something—a voice calling out from within the bush, "Moses! Moses!" The voice commanded Moses to remove his shoes and then identified himself as "the God of Abraham, the God of Isaac and the God of Jacob." At God's command, Moses removed his shoes and also hid his face, for he was afraid. Moses had entered a realm of high voltage, and this tells us something important about the nature of the God who is about to reveal his personal name. He is not a God to be trifled with, nor approached in a casual, flippant manner, nor sidled up to as one might fraternize with a chum at a football game. For this God is holy, and holiness demands a response of reverence, awe, and reverential wonder. In response to God's announcement that he was sending Moses to deliver the children of Israel from slavery in Egypt, Moses asked two questions. First, "Who am I, that I should go to Pharaoh?" God never answered this question directly, for it was ultimately irrelevant to the mission Moses had been given. Instead, God made a promise, "I will be with you." In response to the second question, "Who shall I say sent me, what is his name?"

> God said to Moses, "I AM WHO I AM. This is what you are to say to the Israelites: 'I AM has sent me to you.'" God also said to Moses, "Say to the Israelites, 'The LORD, the God of your fathers—the God of Abraham, the God of Isaac and the God of Jacob—has sent me to you.' This is my name forever, the name by which I am to be remembered from generation to generation." (Exod. 3:14–15).

Yahweh is a form of the Hebrew word "to be": _haywah._ It may also be translated, "I will be who I will be," or, as Brevard Childs renders it, "I am there, wherever it may be—I am really there."[29] The God who spoke to Moses from the burning bush is none other than the God of creation, the God of the patriarchs, the God of the promises, the one who was, who is, and who will forever be. Shortly after his conversion, Augustine reflected on the reality of the God whom Moses met on the far side of the desert—He Who Is—in the form of an extended prayer to the Lord:

> Oh God, from whom to be turned is to fall;
> To whom to be turned is to rise;
> From whom to depart is to die;
> To whom to return is to revive;
> In whom to dwell is to live.
> Whom no man loses unless he be deceived,
> Whom no man seeks unless he has been admonished,
> Whom no man finds unless he has been cleansed.
> Whom to abandon is to perish,
> To reach out to whom is to love,
> To see whom is true possession.[30]

God Who Acts: The Lord of History

> Thou wast their rock, their fortress, and their might;
> Thou, Lord, their Captain in the well-fought fight;
> Thou in the darkness drear, their one true light.
> Alleluia, alleluia!
>
> —W. W. How[31]

The God of the Bible who names himself I AM THAT I AM is the most real reality in the universe, the effulgence of being, the source and end of all that is. However, there is a danger in talking this way about God. The danger is that, unless we are careful, we begin to think of God as a metaphysical principle, as Aristotle's Unmoved Mover or Hegel's World-Spirit. But the Bible will not let us get away with that for, from first to last, it presents the eternal God not as a distant deity, aloof and inert, but rather as a God who gives himself to be known in the most intimate ways, the God who *acts* decisively in the history of the world and in the lives of his people. When Moses was given the Ten Commandments at Mount Sinai, the Lord

---

[29] Brevard Childs, *Exodus: A Commentary* (London: SCM, 1974), 46.

[30] Augustine, *Soliloquies* 1.3.

[31] William W. How, "For All the Saints," *Trinity Hymnal* (Atlanta: Great Commission Publications, 1998), 358.

said: "I am making a covenant with you. Before all your people I will do wonders never before done in any nation in all the world. The people you live among will see how awesome is the work that I, the LORD, will do for you" (Exod. 34:10). The exodus was the greatest of God's acts in Israel's history; it signaled their coming to be as a discrete nation in covenant with the God who made heaven and earth. Later the Lord would instruct the children of Israel:

> Ask now about the former days, long before your time, from the day God created man on the earth; ask from one end of the heavens to the other. Has anything so great as this ever happened, or has anything like it ever been heard of? Has any other people heard the voice of God speaking out of fire, as you have, and lived? Has any god ever tried to take for himself one nation out of another nation, by testings, by miraculous signs and wonders, by war, by a mighty hand and an outstretched arm, or by great and awesome deeds, like all the things the LORD your God did for you in Egypt before your very eyes?
>
> You were shown these things so that you might know that the LORD is God; beside him there is no other (Deut. 4:32–35).

Again and again, Yahweh demonstrates himself to be the LORD of history. Thus, from the standpoint of the Bible there is no cleavage between God's being and God's action. God is made known by what he does: "The LORD works righteousness and justice for all the oppressed. He made known his ways to Moses, his deeds to the people of Israel" (Ps. 103:6–7). God is the "Transcendental Interferer," as C. S. Lewis aptly put it, and he is constantly interfering everywhere, all over the place, in all kinds of ways. The Bible presents the Lord of history as:

1. The Living God in Contrast to Dead Idols

God is incomparably alive, and his life is not contingent on anything or anyone else. This is what is meant by God's *aseity* (from the Latin: *a se,* from the self). God does not have a birthday! His life is self-generated and eternal. He is the "ancient of days." The phrase "as the LORD lives" is found forty-three times in the Bible while God's own words, "as I live," is repeated twenty-three times. In 1 Samuel 17:26, David asked concerning Goliath: "Who is this uncircumcised Philistine that he should defy the armies of the *living God*?" (emphasis added). The psalmist yearns to worship God in the temple: "My heart and my flesh cry out for the living God" (Ps. 84:2). When the children of Israel are about to cross the Jordan, Joshua said to them, "Come here and listen to the words of the LORD your God. This is how you will know that the *living God* is among you and that he will certainly drive out before you the Canaanites, Hittites, Hivites, Perizzites, Girgashites, Amorites and Jebusites" (Josh. 3:9–10, emphasis added).

The aliveness of the true God stands in sharp contrast to the inanimate idols of the surrounding nations. There is a progressive disparagement of idols in the Old Testaments as such worthless deities are mocked and derided. In Psalms 115 and 135, such gods are depicted as man-made puppets: "They have mouths, but cannot speak, eyes, but they cannot see; they have ears, but cannot hear, nor is there breath in their mouths. Those who make them will be like them, and so will all who trust in them" (Ps. 135:16–18). In Isaiah 44, those who make idols are described as "nothing . . . ignorant . . . put to shame . . . deluded," misled (Isa. 44:9). In Jeremiah 10 the derision deepens into irony as the idols are depicted as "a scarecrow in a melon patch," senseless, foolish artifacts "dressed in blue and purple—all made by skilled workers," lifeless nothings all dressed up with nowhere to go! Such idols are no substitute for "the true God . . . the *living God* . . . the eternal King . . . he who is the Portion of Jacob is not like these, for he is the Maker of all things, including Israel, the tribe of his inheritance—the LORD Almighty is his name" (Jer. 10:5,9–10,16, emphasis added).

For all this, idolatry remained a persistent temptation to the children of Israel. Their words to Aaron were echoed again and again: "Up! Make us a god that will walk before us" (Exod. 32:1, author's translation). The temptation to manufacture gods of our own devising is with us still, as the closing words of 1 John remind us: "Dear children, keep yourselves from idols" (1 John 5:21).

2. The\Acting\God in Contrast to Blind Fate

(a) *God acts in the history of Israel.* God is first identified as the "LORD of hosts" in 1 Samuel 1:3 (KJV), but the theme of God as warrior is pervasive throughout the Pentateuch and the books of history. As the children of Israel prepared to enter the promised land, Moses, who could not cross the Jordan with them, reminded them that "the LORD your God himself will cross over ahead of you. He will destroy these nations before you, and you will take possession of their land. . . . Do not be afraid or terrified because of them, for the LORD your God goes with you; he will never leave you nor forsake you" (Deut. 31:3,6).

This theme carries over to the book of Joshua, where God's deliverance of his people in the Jordan is compared to the earlier victory at the Exodus.

> For the LORD your God dried up the Jordan before you until you had crossed over. The LORD your God did to the Jordan just what he had done to the Red Sea when he dried it up before us until we had crossed over. He did this so that all the peoples of the earth might

know that the hand of the LORD is powerful and so that you might always fear the LORD your God (Josh. 4:23–24; see also Josh. 8:7; 10:19,25; 21:44; 23:3,5,9–10).

The victory, and thus the glory, belongs always to God. The dynamic power and reality of God is in marked contrast to the false gods such as Dagon, the Philistine deity, who falls, decapitated and smashed to pieces, before the ark of the Lord (1 Sam. 4–6).

(b) *God acts among the other nations.* While God has a unique covenant relationship with Israel, he is also active in the affairs of other nations. God holds the kings of the earth in derision and mocks their pretentions (Ps. 2). Moab was his wash basin and Edom his footstool (Ps. 60:8). God controls events not only in Israel but among all peoples. He controls the movements of the Nile as well as the Jordan; he not only brought Israel up from Egypt but also the Philistines from Caphtor and the Arameans from Kir (Amos 9:5,7). Beyond the forces of democracy, tyranny, and *Realpolitik,* beyond all secondary causation, it is the God of heaven who "changes times and seasons; he sets up kings and deposes them" (Dan. 2:21).

(c) *God acts in nature.* The Bible describes both the ordinary events in the course of nature, and the extraordinary and even miraculous happenings that occur from time to time, as the result of God's governing providence. This is the theme of the Song of Deborah in Judges 5:

> Hear this, you kings! Listen, you rulers!
> I will sing to the LORD, I will sing;
> I will make music to the LORD, the God of Israel.
> O LORD, when you went out from Seir,
> when you marched from the land of Edom,
> the earth shook, the heavens poured,
> the clouds poured down water.
> The mountains quaked before the LORD, the One of Sinai,
> before the LORD, the God of Israel. . . .
> From the heavens the stars fought,
> from their courses they fought against Sisera.
> The river Kishon swept them away,
> the age-old river, the river Kishon.
> March on, my soul; be strong! (Judg. 5:3–5,20–21).

3. The Sovereign God in Contrast to Feeble Creatures

The God of creation, the God of history and nature, is sovereign in all of his doings. In a series of devastating rapid-fire questions, God reminded Job of this great truth as he spoke to him out of the storm: "Where were you when I laid the earth's foundation?" he asked. "Have you ever given orders to the morning, or shown the dawn its place? . . . Can you bind the beautiful Pleiades? Can you loose the cords of Orion? Can you bring forth the constellations in their seasons or lead out the Bear with his cubs?" Job responded to this awesome display of God's sovereign majesty in repentance and confession: "I know that you can do all things; no plan of yours can be thwarted. . . . Surely I spoke of things I did not understand, things too wonderful for me to know" (Job 38:4,12, 31–32; 42:1,3).

One Who Inhabits Praises: Worship His Majesty

> O worship the King, all glorious above,
> O gratefully sing his pow'r and his love;
> Our shield and Defender, the Ancient of Days
> Pavilioned in splendor and girded with praise.

—Robert Grant [32]

The God of the Bible has revealed himself through words and actions in the past, and these require a response from God's people in the present. But how are we to respond to such a God? This question is not absent from the Bible itself. After extolling the greatness, glory, and majesty of God, after giving thanks and praise to his glorious name in the presence of the children of Israel, David asked, "But who am I, and who are my people, that we should be able to give as generously as this? Everything comes from you, and we have given you only what comes from your hand." Then David prayed, "O LORD, God of our fathers Abraham, Isaac and Israel, keep this desire [to worship God with joy] in the hearts of your people forever, and keep their hearts loyal to you" (1 Chron. 29:14,18). At the heart of the Bible are the Psalms, the prayer book of the church. The Psalms are first of all a gift of the living God to his people. When we join our prayers with the saints of old, heaven listens, and the God of the universe indwells these prayers and praises.

James Luther Mays has pointed out that the Psalms contain more direct statements about God than any other book in the two testaments of the Christian canon.[33] The works, names, and attributes of God fill nearly every

[32] Robert Grant, "O Worship the King," *Trinity Hymnal* (Atlanta: Great Commission Publications, 1998), 2.

[33] James Luther Mays, "The God Who Reigns," in *The Forgotten God: Perspectives in Biblical Theology,* ed. A. A. Doss and F. J. Matera (Louisville: Westminster/John Knox Press, 2002), 29–30.

page of the Psalms. The Lord is rock, refuge, fortress, strength and shield, shepherd, light, judge. He is God in Zion, God our Savior, the holy one of Israel, our dwelling place in all generations, the one who remembers his love and faithfulness, the mighty justice-loving king, the maker of heaven and earth, the one who is faithful to all his promises and loving toward all he has made. The Psalms are a God-intoxicated book. Truly, "Great is the LORD and most worthy of praise" (Ps. 145:3).

As the Psalms come to a climactic crescendo at the end, all of creation is summoned to praise the Lord—mountains and hills, lightning and hail, young men and maidens, old men and children, sun, moon, sea creatures of the deep, birds and grasshoppers, pear trees and mighty cedars—each has a section in the heavenly choir and when the psalmist, all out of breath, gets to the end, he exclaims: "Let everything that has breath praise the LORD" (Ps. 150:6).

The Psalms nowhere back away from the general Old Testament portrayal of God as sovereign king and Lord of all. If anything, this theme is intensified as God is portrayed as the one who smashes enemies and establishes righteousness: "Great is the LORD in Zion; he is exalted over all the nations. Let them praise your great and awesome name—he is holy. The King is mighty" (Ps. 99:2–4). Or, again, "I know that the LORD is great, that our Lord is greater than all gods. The LORD does whatever pleases him, in the heavens and on the earth, in the seas and all their depths" (Ps. 135:5–6).

But the Psalms also reveal another side of God's character, which is no less a mark of his greatness and sovereignty, that is, his loving compassion and tenderness. The Lord can be trusted (Ps. 25:2); he is an ever-present help in trouble (Ps. 46:1); he hears our voice when we cry out in distress (Ps. 55:17); he turns our darkness into light (Ps. 18:28); he is the shepherd who leads his people like a flock even through the valley of the shadow of death (Pss. 23:1–4; 77:20); he is compassionate and gracious, slow to anger, abounding in love; as a father, he pities his children; and his covenant faithfulness is from everlasting to everlasting (Ps. 103). How do we respond to such a God of forgiveness and tender mercies? We can do no better than to say with David: "One thing I ask of the LORD, this is what I seek: that I may dwell in the house of the LORD all the days of my life, to gaze upon the beauty of the LORD and to seek him in his temple" (Ps. 27:4).

Doubtless it is this feature of the Psalms that has made them such a rich treasury of prayer and devotion for the people of God through the centuries. On this theme see William Lee Holladay, *The Psalms through 3,000 Years: Prayer Book of a Cloud of Witnesses* (Minneapolis: Fortress, 1993). As a homiletical and devotional introduction to the Psalms, C. H. Spurgeon's *The Treasury of David*, originally published in seven volumes (1869–1885), remains unsurpassed.

One Who Keeps His Word: Prophecy and Covenant

> God has spoken by his prophets,
> Spoken his unchanging word;
> Each from age to age proclaiming
> God the one, the righteous Lord;
> In the world's despair and turmoil
> One firm anchor holding fast,
> God is on his throne eternal,
> He alone the first and last.

> *—G. W. Briggs* [34]

Theology is speech *about* God; revelation is the speech *of* God. Self-expression is constitutive of God's very being, as we can see from the name the Bible gives to the eternal Son: *Logos.* In the Bible God communicates his word and his will to his people through human messengers he has chosen and raised up for this purpose. These are the prophets, *nabi* (in the singular), a word found 315 times in the Old Testament. Among the prophets were Abel (Luke 11:51), Enoch (Jude 14), Noah (Heb. 11:7), Abraham (Gen. 20:7), and especially Moses (Num. 12:1–8). Jesus Christ himself is the Prophet par excellence, as well as being the ultimate Priest and King.

Biblical prophets had both a vertical and a horizontal mission. They were called to speak God's word to his people. "Surely the sovereign LORD does nothing without revealing his plan to his servants the prophets" (Amos 3:7). Amos, through whom this word was given, made clear that he did not belong to the "professional prophets" of his day but was called directly by God himself (Amos 7:12–15). But there were also false prophets, soothsayers, sorcerers, diviners of all kinds, fakers who pretended to speak for God but only proclaimed what their listeners wanted to hear. Some of the Bible's strongest condemnations are reserved for such pretenders (Deut. 13:1–5; Ezek. 13:10–15; Jer. 23:19; Zech. 13:1–6).

Through the prophets, God reveals himself to be the true and trustworthy Lord of the covenant. God's word (*dabar*) "came" to the prophets, not as mere verbiage, empty sounds, but rather as an effective, dynamic reality. God delivers his word through the prophets, but he himself "watches over" the message "to see that my word is fulfilled" (Jer. 1:12). Again, through Ezekiel, God says: "But I the LORD will speak what I will, and it shall be fulfilled without delay. For in your days, you rebellious house, I will fulfill whatever I say, declares the Sovereign LORD" (Ezek. 12:25). God's word

---

[34] George W. Briggs, "God Has Spoken by the Prophets," in *Worship and Rejoice* (Carol Stream, IL: Hope, 2001), 667.

does not come back empty-handed; it always accomplishes what the Lord has intended for it to do (Isa. 55:10–11).

The prophets were preachers of God's word, but there was also a horizontal dimension to their vocation. For they were called to warn, exhort, comfort, and teach the often wayward and rebellious people of God, ever calling them to repentance and renewal.

> The themes of the prophets' message embraced the whole spectrum of God's revelation through word and deed, but focused on four spheres of life: the religious-ethical, the socio-economical, the political (both internal and external), and the eschatological. In all these spheres, the prophets both proclaimed God's judgment and announced his salvation.[35]

Again and again the prophets called the children of Israel back to the covenant, reminding them of God's holiness and his demand for undivided loyalty from his people. While the prophets all recognized the God-given character of temple worship, they also warned that such religion is worthless unless it comes from a contrite heart and issues in a changed life. The prophets would not allow theology or worship to be divorced from ethics, as Jeremiah's famous "temple sermon" shows clearly:

> Do not trust in deceptive words and say, "This is the temple of the LORD, the temple of the LORD, the temple of the LORD!" . . . You are trusting in deceptive words that are worthless. Will you steal and murder, commit adultery and perjury, burn incense to Baal and follow other gods you have not known, and then come and stand before me in this house, which bears my Name, and say, "We are safe"—safe to do all these detestable things? . . . I will thrust you from my presence, just as I did all your brothers, the people of Ephraim (7:4,8–10,15).

God's judgment is a major theme in the prophets, but so is his unfailing love, his mercy and compassion. Patrick D. Miller has shown that God's wrath and judgment serve a larger purpose: the establishment of God's justice, and the renewing and reshaping of his people in the way of holiness.[36] God is "slow to anger." God is not to be trifled with, for his judgment is real. But so is his compassion and mercy. He is a God who abounds in steadfast love, as he himself reminded his reluctant Prophet Jonah (Jon.

---

[35] P. A. Verhoef, "Prophecy," in *The New International Dictionary of Old Testament Theology and Exegesis,* ed. Willem A. van Gemeren (Carlisle, U. K.: Paternoster Press, 1997), 4:1076.

[36] Patrick D. Miller, "'Slow to Anger': The God of the Prophets" in *The Forgotten God,* 39–55.

4:2). Jeremiah, too, knew this message: "Return, faithless Israel, says the LORD. I will not look on you in anger, for I am merciful, says the LORD; I will not be angry forever" (Jer. 3:12 NRSV). These words find their ultimate fulfillment in the coming of the Messiah, whose advent the prophets foretold, the Servant of the Lord—rejected and despised, smitten, pierced, afflicted and crushed for our iniquities—the promised one whose punishment has brought us peace and by whose wounds we are healed (Isa. 53).

Immanuel: Behold Your God!

> Meekness and majesty, manhood and deity
> In perfect harmony—the man who is God:
> Lord of Eternity, dwells in humanity,
> Kneels in humility, and washes our feet.
>
> —*Graham Kendrick*[37]

Some years ago Nils A. Dahl wrote that God may be the "neglected factor in New Testament theology."[38] Destructive biblical criticism, exemplified in the work of the Jesus Seminar, eviscerates the gospel narratives of all theological power and leaves us, at best, with a Jesus made in our own image—political agitator, cynic sage, new age guru, and the like. The words of weeping Mary in John 20:13 are appropriate: "They have taken my Lord away, . . . and I don't know where they have put him." But, in fact, Jesus of the gospels cannot be confined to the straitjacket of such pseudo-scholarly speculation. He bursts through those Scriptures today just as he rose bodily from the grave that first Easter morning.

What do the Gospels tell us about God?[39] It is customary to distinguish sharply the portrait of Jesus in the three Synoptic Gospels from that in John, usually to the detriment of the historical trustworthiness of the latter. While each Gospel writer has a distinct vantage point and develops his own unique theology addressed to a specific community, all four Gospels have one divine-human subject: Jesus the Messiah who is called the Son of God in each (Matt. 16:16; Mark 1:1; Luke 3:22; John 1:34; 20:31).

---

[37] Graham Kendrick, "Meekness and Majesty" in *Worship and Rejoice*, 97.

[38] Nils A. Dahl, "The Neglected Factor in New Testament Theology," *Reflection*, 73.1:5.

[39] While I cannot follow him in every respect, it is to the credit of N. T. Wright that he has placed the question of God on the agenda of New Testament theology. See his *The New Testament and the People of God*, vol. 1: *Christian Origins and the Question of God* (Minneapolis: Fortress, 1992). See also the important studies of Richard Bauckham, *God Crucified: Monotheism and Christology in the New Testament* (Grand Rapids: Eerdmans, 1998), and Marianne Meye Thompson, *The God of the Gospel of John* (Grand Rapids: Eerdmans, 2001).

All four Gospels present Jesus as truly human and fully divine, though the way in which they do this varies. For example, in the synoptic tradition, the oneness of Jesus with the Father is seen most clearly in what he does. Jesus does and says things that can only be attributable to the God of Israel: he forgives sins unilaterally (Mark 2:1–12), so that those around ask, "Why does this fellow talk like that? He's blaspheming! Who can forgive sins but God alone?" (v. 7). He teaches with imperious authority, surpassing that of Moses and the prophets—"But I say unto you . . ." (Matt. 5:22,28,32,34,39,44 KJV). He performs exorcisms "by the finger of God" as a sign that God's reign is present (Luke 11:14–20). He eats freely with sinners (Luke 15:1–2), anticipating the messianic banquet when "many will come from the east and the west, and will take their places at the feast with Abraham, Isaac and Jacob in the kingdom of heaven" (Matt. 8:11).

On the other hand, in the Gospel of John, Jesus' oneness with the Father is explicitly stated (John 10:30). In John, too, Jesus exercises divine prerogatives, including the power to give life (John 5:25–26; 10:28–29), to authorize work on the Sabbath (John 5:16–18), to send the Holy Spirit (John 14:15–18), and to make known to the disciples the Father's love for them (John 17:25–26). In John, when Jesus' enemies pick up stones to hurl against him, they do so, they say, not because of his miracles but "because you, a mere man, claim to be God" (John 10:33). Yet, as Marianne Meye Thompson rightly says:

> Jesus is not the Son because he exercises these divine functions; rather, he exercises them because he is the Son. Out of and by virtue of his relationship to the Father, the Son gives life to the world, makes the Father known, carries out the Father's will in the world, and so on. The activity and character of the Father are embodied in and through the Son.[40]

The God whom we encounter in the Jesus of the Gospels is none other than the God of Israel, the great I AM, the one—and only one—who could say, "Before Abraham was born, I am!" (John 8:58). He is, as Matthew quoting Isaiah proclaimed, Immanuel—"God with us" (Matt. 1:23).

Unlike Marcion in the second century, the New Testament does not present Jesus as the emissary of an "alien God" but as the Son and Word of the God of Israel; the God of Abraham, Isaac, and Jacob; the God of the prophets. Jesus himself quotes the *Shema* (Mark 12:29) and refers to his own work as the work of "the one who alone is God," "the only true God" (John 5:44 NRSV; 17:3). Matthew, more than any other Gospel writer, presents Jesus as the fulfillment of the law and the prophets, and his Gospel is

---

[40] Thompson, *God of the Gospel of John,* 232.

replete with expressions like this: "Then what was said through the Prophet Jeremiah was fulfilled" (Matt. 2:17); "This was to fulfill what was spoken through the Prophet Isaiah" (Matt. 8:17); "So was fulfilled what was spoken through the prophet" (Matt. 13:35); and "This has all taken place that the writings of the prophets might be fulfilled" (Matt. 26:56).

This point can hardly be emphasized too much, and yet it has been emphasized too much in recent New Testament scholarship which so ultra-contextualizes Jesus as the product of second temple Judaism that his radical newness and his uniqueness tend to be obscured.[41] Christianity cannot be understood apart from the revelation of the God of the Old Testament, but the Christian faith is not merely a Jesus sect within Judaism. Jesus is the new wine that bursts through the new wineskins giving us a deeper, richer understanding of God that both encompasses the earlier revelation and at the same time relativizes it in light of his own words and deeds as Immanuel. This is why the Jews in Paul's day found the gospel of Christ a scandal, and the Greeks saw it as foolishness (1 Cor. 1:18–25). Here are seven ways the biblical understanding of God is radically enriched through the Jesus we meet in the Gospels.

1. Abba.

The Old Testament refers to God as "Father" about a dozen times (see Isa. 64:8–9; Jer. 31:9; Deut. 32:6), and there are also references to God as Father in the literature of second temple Judaism.[42] Jesus refers to God as Father in all of the Gospels but especially in John where this title is used 110 times. However, in Mark (14:36), believed by many to be the first Gospel, we find the Aramaic word *abba* which Jesus uses in praying to his Father. As Joachim Jeremias has shown, this was a term of familial intimacy (and it can still be heard on the streets of the Middle East today) and points to Jesus' unique sonship.[43] Even more remarkable is the fact that this word, *abba,* becomes a part of the prayer life of the earliest church (see Rom. 8:15; Gal. 4:6), signifying Jesus' salvific role in opening up the heart of the Father to all believers.

2. Trinity

As we have seen, the triune nature of God is foreshadowed in the Old Testament, but only with the advent of the Messiah is it announced, as at the baptism of Jesus (Matt. 3:16–17). John pulls back the curtain and gives

---

[41] Paul F. M. Zahl, *The First Christian* (Grand Rapids: Eerdmans, 2003) clearly makes this point.

[42] See Marianne Meye Thompson, *The Promise of the Father: Jesus and God in the New Testament* (Louisville: Westminster/John Knox, 2000).

[43] Joachim Jeremias, *The Prayers of Jesus* (London: SCM, 1967). See also James Barr, "*Abba* Isn't Daddy," *Journal of Theological Studies* 39 (1988): 28–47, and J. A. Fitzmyer, "*Abba* and Jesus' Relation to God," in *À cause de l'Evangile,* ed. R. Gantoy (Paris: Cerf, 1985), 16–38.

us the most profound insight we have in the Bible into the inner-trinitarian life of God (John 1:1–18; 5:26; 17:1–5).

3. Spirit

The Spirit of God is present throughout the Old Testament from the first verses of Genesis onward, but this aspect of God's revealed nature is significantly deepened in the Gospels. The Son bestows the Spirit's life-giving power in the new birth (John 3:1–16). Jesus prays for the Father to send the Counselor or Paraclete (John 14:16,26; 15:26; 16:7). The Holy Spirit is associated with the Father and the Son in Jesus' baptismal commission (Matt. 28:19–20). In these and other ways developed more fully in the writings of Paul, the Holy Spirit is seen as a distinct personal reality within the divine Godhead. The presence of the Spirit in Jesus' own ministry is a sign that "the kingdom of God has come upon you" (Matt. 12:28).

4. Incarnation

In Jesus Christ "the Word was made flesh, and dwelt among us" (John 1:14 KJV). This is not only a key Christological affirmation but also a crucial statement about God. The Prophet Ezekiel witnessed the departure of God's shekinah glory from the temple (Ezek. 10:1–22) at the time of Israel's exile. John announced that in the person of the Palestinian peasant named Jesus, God's glory had returned. He claimed to have seen this glory, "the glory of the One and Only, who came from the Father, full of grace and truth" (John 1:14). Now God's glory is no longer localized in a building but is rather embodied in a person. "Meekness and majesty, manhood and deity in perfect harmony—the man who is God." In response, the early church sang: "Great is the mystery of godliness" (1 Tim. 3:16 KJV).

5. Way, Truth, Life

The mission of Jesus was not for his own sake, but for others. The God of Israel now gives himself to be known to all the world through his Son who is the way, the truth, and the life. Jesus is both the redeemer and the revealer, and he alone is able to be both: "All things have been committed to me by my Father. No one knows the Son except the Father, and no one knows the Father except the Son and those to whom the Son chooses to reveal him" (Matt. 11:27).

6. Savior of the World

The Gospels announce that God's salvation has come from Israel and is first preached to Israel, but that it extends beyond Israel to the farthest reaches of the earth. Jesus declared that his own work required that the good news of the kingdom of God be preached "to the other towns also" (Luke 4:43). Through Jonah and other prophets the universal scope of God's saving work had been known before, but in Jesus God's reach is extended to all, for "the Son of Man came to seek and to save what was lost" (Luke 19:10).

7. *Inaugurator of the End Times*

Jesus' message was imbued with apocalyptic—God's inbreaking presence in his life and work. But he also indicated that there was more to come. The end times have been inaugurated with Jesus' life, death, and resurrection, and so we are living now in the "last days," but Jesus also promised to come again "in clouds with great power and glory" (Mark 13:26), and so his followers live in "the blessed hope" of his return (Titus 2:13).

God of the Gospel: Pauline Patterns

Church of God, elect and glorious,
Holy nation, chosen race;
Called as God's own special people,
Royal priests and heirs of grace:
Know the purpose of your calling,
Show to all his mighty deeds;
Tell of love which knows no limits,
Grace which meets all human needs.

—James E. Seddon[44]

The word "God" (*theos*) occurs 153 times in Romans and hundreds of times in Paul's other writings.[45] Paul does not develop a systematic theology about God, but he everywhere presupposes the reality of God. His own apostolic vocation is "by the will of God" (1 Cor. 1:1). In Galatians he makes this more explicit: "Paul, an apostle—sent not from men nor by man, but by Jesus Christ and God the Father, who raised him from the dead" (Gal. 1:1). Who is God for Paul? He is incomparably great beyond all human imagining or comprehension—"God, the blessed and only Ruler, the King of kings and Lord of lords, who alone is immortal and who lives in unapproachable light, whom no one has seen or can see. To him be honor and might forever" (1 Tim. 6:15–16).

This God, Paul says, is invisible as well as eternal (1 Tim. 1:17; Rom. 16:26); he is righteous and holy (Eph. 4:24). He is the Savior (1 Tim.

---

[44] James E. Seddon, "Church of God, Elect and Glorious," in *Worship and Rejoice*, 402.

[45] See James D. G. Dunn, *The Theology of Paul the Apostle* (Grand Rapids: Eerdmans, 1998), 27–50. Paul's doctrine of God is also treated in J. Christiaan Beker, *Paul the Apostle: The Triumph of God in Life and Thought* (Philadelphia: Fortress, 1980); Thomas R. Schreiner, *Paul: Apostle of God's Glory in Christ* (Downers Grove: InterVarsity, 2001); Frank Thielman, *Theology of the New Testament: A Canonical and Synthetic Approach* (Grand Rapids: Zondervan, 2005).

2:3; Titus 2:10,13; 3:4); he is the Father of glory (Eph. 1:17); and he is the Father of mercies (2 Cor. 1:3). Everything legitimate and worthy that can be said about human fatherhood derives from the fatherhood of God (Eph. 3:14–15). True righteousness comes from this God and from nowhere else (Rom. 10:3; 2 Cor. 5:21). He is the God of peace (Rom. 15:33) and the God of all comfort (2 Cor. 1:3).[46] Paul's view of God is based on the Old Testament Scriptures which he knew thoroughly before he was converted to Christ. However, Paul's whole life, including his theology, was turned upside down when, as he put it, "God, who set me apart from birth and called me by his grace, was pleased to reveal his Son in me" (Gal. 1:15–16). Following that decisive encounter, Paul became, as Thomas Schreiner puts it, the "apostle of God's glory in Christ." His doctrine of God can be characterized as Christological monotheism, and the goal of his life and mission was to make known "the light of the knowledge of the glory of God in the face of Christ" (2 Cor. 4:6). Paul extols the glorious God of the gospel. This calling and this task are reflected in these five distinctive emphases:

1. God Is Creator

God stands over against the world and everything in it, which he made through his almighty creative power. This was the burden of Paul's famous sermon in Athens: "The God who made the world and everything in it is the Lord of heaven and earth and does not live in temples built by hands" (Acts 17:24). Unlike Plato's demiurge, who "creates" the world by reshaping primordial preexistent matter, the God of the Bible truly creates *ex nihilo*, "out of nothing"—he "calls things that are not as though they were" (Rom. 4:17). As Paul emphasized to the Colossians, God has created all things by Jesus Christ and for him as well (Col. 1:15–17). The Gnostic disparagement of matter was already at work in the early church, and Paul opposed it by emphasizing the goodness of creation: the bodies of believers are temples of the Holy Spirit (1 Cor. 6:14–16); all that God has created should be received with thanksgiving and used in a proper way (1 Tim. 4:3–5); sexual relations in marriage are part of God's design and should not be disparaged (1 Cor. 7:1–6).

2. God Is True and Living

First Thessalonians 1 gives us a picture of evangelism in the early church. Paul reminded those believers that their salvation was based on God's love and election manifested in "our gospel" which came to them through Spirit-anointed preaching as the Lord's message "rang out" like the sound of a trumpet throughout the region where they lived. Then he described their conversion to Christ as a turning "to God from idols to serve the living and true

---

[46] These and many other references to God in the Pauline corpus, along with an extensive bibliography, are found in D. Guthrie and R. P. Martin, "God," in *DPL*, 354–69.

God, and to wait for his Son from heaven" (1 Thess. 1:9–10). The lifeless idols could have been the deities of the mystery religions or the Greek household gods or the cult of the emperor, which was popular in Thessalonica (Acts 17:7). To serve the true and living God meant to say Lord Christ, not Lord Caesar, even though this was a costly decision. Paul encouraged these believers to "give thanks in all circumstances," even in their sufferings, "for this is God's will for you in Christ Jesus" (1 Thess. 5:18).

3. *God Is Holy*

The God of the gospel is the God who justifies sinners by faith alone through the atoning death of his Son on the cross. Apart from God's acquittal in the imputation of Christ's righteousness to guilty sinners, there is no escape from the righteous wrath of God. Paul's soteriology, which is often taken to be the center of his theology, presupposes the holiness of God as does Paul's call for those who are in Christ "to live a holy life" through the power of the Holy Spirit (1 Thess. 4:7–8).

4. *God Is Triune*

Paul does not hesitate to refer to the risen Christ as God (Rom. 9:5), and he presents the Holy Spirit as the divine personal agent of salvation, intercession, and sanctification. Paul's apostolic benediction in 2 Corinthians 13:14 brings together all three divine persons, just as Jesus did in the Great Commission: "May the grace of the Lord Jesus Christ, and the love of God, and the fellowship of the Holy Spirit be with you all."

5. *God Is Worthy of Praise*

Paul shows no interest in theological speculation, and he refers to ministers of Christ as "those entrusted with the secret things of God." Elsewhere he can speak of "the deep things of God" which only the Spirit searches and knows (1 Cor. 4:1; 2:10–11). This means that theology must give way to doxology just as preaching must yield to prayer and praise. In fact, Paul frequently breaks into doxology in his writings, as we can see from the many hymns, confessions of faith, and exhortations to praise embedded in his letters (Phil. 2:5–11; 2 Cor. 9:15). Among all of these, none surpasses the doxology which concludes Paul's treatment of election and predestination in Romans 9–11:

> Oh, the depth of the riches of the wisdom and knowledge of God!
> How unsearchable his judgments, and his paths beyond tracing out!
> "Who has known the mind of the Lord?
> Or who has been his counselor?"
> "Who has ever given to God, that God should repay him?"
> For from him and through him and to him are all things.
> To him be the glory forever! Amen (Rom. 11:33–36).

Alpha and Omega: Our God Reigns

> The King shall come when morning dawns
> And light and beauty brings:
> Hail, Christ the Lord!
> Your people pray,
> Come quickly, King of kings.'
>
> —*Ancient Greek Hymn*[47]

The book of Revelation is not only the last book in the Bible, but it also sums up and completes the doctrine of God developed in the first sixty-five. God speaks directly only twice in Revelation, and he says the same thing both times. First, near the beginning, in 1:8, we read: "'I am the Alpha and the Omega,' says the Lord God [*kurios ho theos,* the Greek translation of Yahweh Elohim] 'who is, and who was, and who is to come, the Almighty.'" Once more, near the end, this divine predicate is repeated: "He said to me: 'It is done. I am the Alpha and the Omega, the Beginning and the End'" (21:6). Just as these two letters stand at the origin and conclusion of the alphabet, so too does the Lord God reveal himself as the source of all that is and the terminus of all that can be.

Throughout Revelation God is depicted as Father (1:6; 2:27; 3:21), the thrice-holy one (4:8), the Creator of all things (4:11), Savior, or the one to whom salvation belongs (7:10), the one who sits on the throne (5:1), the one who reigns over the nations (11:17), just, true, and righteous (15:3–4), a God of glory and power (15:8), a God of fury and wrath (14:10; 16:1), a God who avenges the blood of his servants (19:2). Above all, he is the God who is eminently and eternally worthy of worship (14:7; 15:3–4).

John's vision is not only about revelation but also restoration. In older dogmatics textbooks, eschatology was referred to as *de novissimus,* "concerning the newest things." Here, in the finale of salvation history, we read about the new temple (21:1–22:5), the new covenant (21:3–4), the new Israel (21:14), and the new Jerusalem (21:2). Faithful believers are also promised a new name (2:17; 3:12). Indeed, God's work of restoration and renewal is all-encompassing: "I am making everything new!" (21:5). Revelation reminds us that there can be no authentic doctrine of God without eschatology, and apocalyptic eschatology at that. It is a shame that the book of Revelation is regarded by many as a bizarre science fiction fantasy. To think this way is to miss the great crescendo of biblical revelation: the

---

[47] Ancient Greek hymn, tr. John Brownlie, "The King Shall Come," *The Worshiping Church: A Hymnal* (Carol Stream, IL: Hope Publishing Co., 1990), 277.

triumph of God over sin, suffering, and the devil. Revelation is the answer to the question of Habakkuk: "How long, O LORD?" (Hab. 1:2).

Christianity without apocalyptic is reduced to a code of behavior or a set of maxims about the way the world is in its present disarray and chaos—a kind of therapeutic Confucianism. But Revelation makes clear that the God of the Bible is not only the maker of all that is but also the designer of what will be. He is the one who not only is, and was, but who is also "the one who is coming": "I am that I am" is also "I will be who I will be."

The book of Revelation is also a bridge between the doctrine of God in the Bible and its development in the history of the church. Throughout Revelation Jesus, the slain Lamb who occupies the heavenly throne, is associated and identified with God in the most intimate ways. He is the Son of God (Rev. 2:18). He too has the same divine title as God—the Alpha and the Omega, the First and the Last, the Beginning and the End (22:13). He is at the center of the throne and "salvation belongs to our God . . . and to the Lamb" (7:10). Above all, Jesus is seen as worthy of worship and, as Richard Bauckham has noted, this "raised the relationship of Christology to monotheism in its acutest form."[48] Indeed, it was the worship of Jesus Christ and the realization that salvation came only through him, which set the early church on the road to Nicene theology.

What Has the Church Believed?

The Nature of God: Patristic Reflections

One of the most common charges leveled against Christians in the early church was that they were atheists. They did not worship the gods of Rome and Greece, nor did they follow the mystery religions of the East. Indeed, they claimed to worship the one true God of Israel, the Creator of all that is, the one whom Jesus called "Father," by whose power he had been raised from the dead.

As we have seen, a trinitarian understanding of God is present already in the New Testament and surfaces again in the writings of the apostolic fathers in the early second century. In writing to the Corinthian church, Clement of Rome used trinitarian language: "Have we not one God and one Christ and one Spirit of grace, the Spirit that has been poured out on us?"[49] Ignatius of Antioch, writing to the Magnesians, exhorted them to act "by

---

[48] Richard Bauckham, "Worship of Jesus in Apocalyptic Christianity," *New Testament Studies 27* (1981): 335. See also Richard Bauckham, *The Theology of the Book of Revelation* (Cambridge: Cambridge University Press, 1993) and the magisterial commentary of G. K. Beale, *The Book of Revelation* (Grand Rapids: Eerdmans, 1999).

[49] I Clement, 46.

faith and by love, in the Son and Father and in the Spirit."[50] And, in a some-what clumsy metaphor, he used trinitarian language to describe the church, referring to its members as "stones of a temple, prepared for a building of God the Father hoisted up through the crane of Jesus Christ which is the cross, and using for a rope the Holy Spirit."[51]

The exact relation of Jesus Christ, the divine Logos, to the eternal Father, continued to be explored by Justin Martyr, Athenagoras, Clement of Alexandria, and other apologists of the second century. The triune nature of God was expressed in the "rule of faith," one form of which we know today as the Apostles' Creed. This statement was frequently recited at baptism as an essential summary of the biblical faith. In other words, in declaring their faith in God as the Father, the Son, and the Holy Spirit, the early Christians were not doing "constructive" theology but were simply declaring their faith in the God of Israel, who had raised Jesus from the dead, the God who by his Spirit was present in their midst. Irenaeus of Lyon gives this summary of the early Christian belief about God:

> God the Father, not made, not material, invisible; one God, the creator of all things—this is the first point of our faith. The second point is this: the Word of God, Son of God, Christ Jesus our Lord, who is manifested to the prophets according to . . . the Father's dispensation; through whom all things were made; who also, at the end of the age, to complete and gather up all things, was made man among men, visible and tangible, in order to abolish death and show forth life and produce perfect reconciliation between God and man. And the third point is: the Holy Spirit, through whom the prophets prophesied . . . who at the end of the age was poured out in a new way upon mankind in all the earth, renewing man to God.[52]

A major challenge to this understanding of God arose within the church when Marcion, a brilliant thinker, denied that the Father of Jesus was identical with the God of the Old Testament. Jesus was the emissary of an "alien" God, Marcion said, a God who had nothing to do with the messy business of creation, procreation—the world of mud, mosquitoes, diapers, and dung. Like the Gnostics, Marcion disparaged all things material and corporeal. He also encouraged the church to excise the entire Old Testament, and much of the New, from its canon, keeping only an expurgated version of Luke and Paul. Marcion advocated a form of radical dualism, splitting apart creation and redemption. One of the most important decisions made

---

[50] Ignatius, *Magnesians* 13.
[51] Ignatius, *Ephesians* 9.
[52] Irenaeus, *Demonstration of the Apostolic Preaching* 6.

in the entire history of theology was the rejection of Marcion's heresy. By saying no to Marcion, the church affirmed the basic continuity of the Old and New Testaments and the coinherence of creation and redemption. Christians would continue to struggle with the meaning of suffering and evil in the good world that God had made. But, after Marcion, they were bound to the lordship and ultimate victory of God over all that is.

One of those who opposed Marcion's views was Tertullian, the first major theologian to write in Latin, and it was he who coined the term *trinitas.* Writing against a certain Praxeas, Tertullian argued that there was both a threeness and a oneness within the divine being of God. In his exegesis of certain biblical texts, notably Psalm 110:1 and Isaiah 53:1, Tertullian observed: "So in these texts the distinctness of the three is plainly set out, for there is the Spirit who makes the statement, the Father to whom he addresses it, and the Son who is the subject of it."[53] At the same time, Tertullian said, we do not worship three gods, for each of the divine persons is "of one substance" (*una substantia*). Tertullian provided a useful vocabulary for clearly distinguishing the three and the one without relapsing into tritheism, and this became an important factor in the development of the Nicene doctrine of God.

In seeking to understand the relationship of Jesus Christ to the Father who had sent him, the early church faced two Christological dangers. These dangers did, in fact, precipitate a crisis in the doctrine of the Trinity. The first was modalism. This is a view that says the Trinity is three different modes or masks that God wears at different times in salvation history. In the Old Testament he appeared as the Father, in the New Testament as the Son, and now, in the age of the church, we experience God as the Holy Spirit. Not only does this view contradict the witness of Scripture (for example, Jesus prayed to the Father while on earth), it also eliminates the possibility of relationship within the Godhead. How could the Father "send" the Son if there is no distinction between them?

If modalism eliminates self-distinction within God, then subordinationism (the opposite danger) undercuts the unity of God. Here the Son and the Spirit are agents of the Father, but they do not share in his essential oneness. The most extreme form of subordinationism was taught by Arius, who claimed that the Son/Logos was a creature made by God— an exalted creature to be sure, perhaps the greatest creature of all but a creature nonetheless. The teaching of Arius brought about the Council of Nicea in AD 325.

Athanasius served as the bishop of Alexandria in Egypt. Arius was a presbyter (priest or elder) in his church. The conflict between the two

---

[53] Tertulllian, *Adversus Praxeas* 11.

became so intense that all the bishops in the Christian world were summoned to a gathering at Nicea in 325 to resolve this dispute. There they formulated a creed, which, with a few subsequent changes, Christian churches
all over the world still recite. On the crucial point of contention between
Arius and Athanasius, the Nicene Creed said this:

> We believe in one Lord Jesus Christ,
> the only begotten Son of God,
> begotten of his Father before all worlds,
> God of God, Light of Light,
> very God of very God,
> begotten, not made,
> being of one substance with the Father.[54]

This definition flew in the face of Arius's understanding of God. To say
that the Son was *homoousios*—of the same substance as the Father—was
to introduce plurality and division into the Godhead. It was to be guilty of
what was later described in Islam as *shirk,* that is, "associating" with God
something that is not God. But why is this? Because God's innermost being
or essence, according to Arius, cannot be shared, or even communicated,
with anyone else. "We know," Arius said, "there is one God, alone unbegotten, alone eternal, alone without beginning, alone true, alone immortal."[55]

To this way of thinking, God is the Alone with the Alone. He is utterly
transcendent, self-sufficient, and all-powerful in every way. He guards his
divinity jealously in the same way that Silas Marner guarded his gold in
George Eliot's famous novel. Silas Marner was a miser who kept a chest
full of gold coins under his bed. Every night before he went to sleep, he
would take out his gold coins, count them, stroke them, and admire them.
Then he would put them back under his bed and go to sleep. He never
spent any of his coins because they were *his.* They were not to be shared
with anyone else. Arius believed in a "Silas Marner" kind of God—a God
wealthy beyond measure, a God so self-contained in his absoluteness that
the thought of having to share his innermost reality, his "essence," with
anyone else, even with a "son," was anathema to him.

One of the prime arguments against Arius's view was that it left the
church with a Christ who was not worthy to be worshipped. If Jesus were
less than fully divine, it would be idolatrous to worship him. The Lord has

---

54 The Nicene Creed (traditional wording).
55 Cited in Arthur C. McGill, *Suffering a Test of Theological Method* (Philadelphia: Westminster,
1982), 70. I owe my interpretation of Arius and his role in the trinitarian controversy to McGill,
one of my former teachers at Harvard Divinity School. His untimely death left the world bereft of
a brilliant theologian. See also the important study by Bernard Lonergan, *The Way to Nicea: The
Dialectical Development of Trinitarian Theology* (Philadelphia: Westminster, 1976).

clearly said, "You shall have no other gods before me" (Exod. 20:3). This is precisely the point made by Muslims as well—that nothing other than God can be worshipped—and they would be entirely right in pressing this point against Christians if indeed Jesus were less than fully divine.

Athanasius made the further point that if Jesus was not *homoousios* with the Father, then he could not be the Savior of the world. Arius had ridiculed the idea that God could "beget" a son. Everyone knows that God is above all carnal procreation and does not reproduce sexually, just as the Qur'ran also declares, "God is one, the eternal God. He begot none, nor was he begotten. None is equal to him" (112:1–4).

Athanasius (and the theologians in the Nicene tradition who followed him) sought to explain the "begottenness" of the Son in a way that avoided both the sterility of Arius's Silas Marner-like God as well as the crass literalism derived from Greek mythology. The Nicene formula had described the Son as both the *same* in substance with the Father, and yet in some way also *distinct from* the Father: He was God *of (from)* God, Light *of (from)* Light, very God *of (from)* very God. The challenge was how to explain this from-ness without violating the same-ness, which they did by declaring that the Son was begotten—but not in the way that human fathers beget or generate their earthly children. No, the Son of the heavenly Father was begotten *from all eternity.* He did not "come to be" at a point in time. In fact, there never was a time when he was not. But from eternity the Father and the Son have always existed in "a relationship of total and mutual self-giving."[56]

Clearly this kind of eternal begetting would not be possible if the Father was selfish with his glory, his power, and his majesty. On the contrary, however, he is unspeakably generous. He gives all of these to the Son in an eternal interchange of holy love. Neither is the Son "self-seeking" (1 Cor. 13:5) but returns all that he has received to the glory of the Father, with the Holy Spirit as the bond of unity between the two. The mystery of God's unity is thus a unity *of love.* When we peer into the heart of God, we find not solitary absoluteness—the Alone with the Alone—but the mystery of eternal love and relationship, a begetting without a beginning and an indwelling without an ending.

---

[56] McGill, *Suffering,* 76. The technical term for the mutual indwelling or circumincession of the three divine persons in one another is *perichōresis.* This term was used by John of Damascus to describe the dynamic interchange and complementarity among the persons of the Godhead. Karl Barth says of this eternal relationality among the Father, the Son, and the Holy Spirit: "The divine modes of being mutually condition and permeate one another so completely that one is always in the other two"; *Church Dogmatics* 1/1:370. This theme is also a major motif in the theology of Jürgen Moltmann, though he construes it in a way that is not fully compatible with the historic orthodox doctrine. See his *The Trinity and the Kingdom* (San Francisco: Harper & Row, 1981), especially 174–78.

The Existence of God: Medieval Arguments

When we turn to the Middle Ages, we enter another world of theological discourse often characterized as "Scholasticism" because it developed in the monastic schools (*scholae*) and universities of the time. The Reformers of the sixteenth century reacted against the scholastic teaching of their day, and modern theologians have dismissed the medieval view of God as static and irrelevant, but it is important to recognize the intrinsic connection between theological inquiry and spiritual formation inherent in the scholastic enterprise. For example, Anselm begins his *Proslogion* with a call to meditation and prayer:

> Come now, little man, turn aside for a while from your daily employment, escape for a moment from the tumult of your thoughts. Put aside your weighty cares, let your burdensome distractions wait, free yourself awhile for God and rest awhile in him. Enter the inner chamber of your soul, shut out everything except God and that which can help you in seeking him, and when you have shut the door, seek him. Now, my whole heart, say to God, "I seek your face, Lord, it is your face I seek."[57]

Medieval theology inherited the trinitarian consensus of the early church and simply reformulated it in scholastic terminology. The rationalist impulse of this process sometimes led to heresy, as when Roscellinus applied the rules of dialectic to the Trinity and ended up with tritheism![58] However, this period is best remembered for developing a series of arguments for the existence of God. In the Middle Ages these arguments took three basic forms:

1. The Ontological Argument

In its classic form this argument was first put forward by Anselm, who sought to prove the existence of God from the definition of God. God is "that than which nothing greater can be conceived." His basic point was this: the idea of God implies the existence of God. If God only existed in the mind, but not in reality, then one could imagine a God who did exist in reality, and such a God would be greater than the one who did not. The ontological argument continues to fascinate philosophers of religion, but its validity depends on whether existence can be thought of as a predicate.

---

[57] *The Prayers and Meditations of Anselm,* trans. Benedicta Ward (Harmondsworth, England: Penguin Books, 1973), 239.
[58] On the views of Roscellinus, see Jaroslav Pelikan, *The Growth of Medieval Theology* (Chicago: University of Chicago Press, 1978), 277–84.

우주론[handwritten annotation]

2. The Cosmological Argument

ontological argument의 개념[handwritten annotation]

Unlike the ontological argument which seeks to show God's existence from the idea or definition of God, the cosmological argument begins with what can be seen and known about God in the created order. The classic statement of this argument is that of Thomas Aquinas, who set forth his famous "five ways," based on his observation of five features in the world of nature: (1) motion, (2) cause and effect, (3) necessary being, (4) degrees of perfection, and (5) purpose.

The cosmological argument fit well into the Aristotelian worldview which Thomas sought to adapt to his theology. By beginning with the observable world and arguing back to God as prime mover, first cause, perfect standard, etc., one need not appeal to the data of biblical revelation. However, Thomas knew that such an approach had its limits. On the basis of God's general revelation alone, we can know *that* God is, but not *who* God is; for this God's special revelation in Scripture and in Jesus Christ is required. Only there can we learn about God as the Father, the Son, and the Holy Spirit; only there do we learn about the incarnation, the atonement, and the way of salvation.

3. The Teleological Argument

목적론적 증명[handwritten annotation]

The Greek word *telos* means "goal or purpose," and this argument corresponds to the last of Thomas's five ways. This is sometimes called the argument from design since it teaches that the hand of an intelligent designer can be seen in the nature and purpose of everything that exists.

Thomas's arguments for the existence of God fall within the context of his general philosophy of being. Based on his interpretation of God's self-revelation to Moses in Exodus 3:14 as "he who is," Thomas can say that God is "nothing else than . . . the pure act of existing." Everything in all of reality, from the highest angel to the lowest demon, is linked by analogy to God in a "great chain of being." Thomas was later canonized as a saint and, still later, in 1879, his teaching was declared permanently valid for the Roman Catholic Church. But in the later Middle Ages, his views were much debated and some of them condemned.

John Duns Scotus brought a different emphasis to the doctrine of God. His focus was not so much God's *being* as God's *will*. His primary concern was to protect the freedom of God and to ground God's actions in his eternal decision or will. He thus emphasized the omnipotence of God, his independence of secondary causes, his governing providence over all creation, and his divine decree of predestination. Scotus's ideas were taken much further by William of Ockham, who emphasized God's absolute power to act in unprecedented ways that even contradicted his revealed will, and this led to an even greater disparity between what could be known of God on

바르트대답[handwritten annotation]   사역, 구속, 속죄함[handwritten annotation]

the basis of reason and "the increasingly mysterious truths of revelation."[59] Though the Reformers of the sixteenth century were well aware of these developments, they modified or broke with scholastic methods in "an attempt to restore human knowledge of God to its biblical setting in the history of God's acts of redemption and revelation."[60]

The Character of God: Reformation Retrieval

The doctrine of God in the Reformation was shaped by several factors: (1) the nominalist theology of the late Middle Ages which, in the tradition of Ockham, continued to undermine confidence in the Thomistic synthesis of the preceding centuries; (2) a pervasive quest for a sense of divine immediacy evident in new patterns of spirituality and the mystical theology of Meister Eckhart, Johannes Tauler, and others; (3) and, above all, the Renaissance revival of learning and literature which culminated in the rediscovery of both patristic writings and the Bible itself. Even before the indulgence controversy, the first stirrings of the Reformation began in a dispute over the theological curriculum of the University of Wittenberg when Luther and others sought to "throw out Aristotle" and do theology on the basis of biblical exegesis. Invariably, this move had important implications for the doctrine of God.

Luther and Calvin discovered in the Bible a God who was very different from the *summum bonum* of classical and scholastic thought. For this reason, they showed no interest in the traditional arguments for the existence of God. The God of the Bible, Luther said, is the God who is "clothed in his promises," the three-in-one God who reveals himself to us in Jesus Christ who is at once the center and Lord of the Scriptures.[61] God gives himself to be known only through Jesus Christ; revelation is not an add-on or supplement to what we can learn about God from reason alone. Jesus Christ is "the mirror, the means, and the way" to all true knowledge of God, and whoever seeks some other way is a thief and robber.[62]

Indeed, Luther could say that "to seek God outside Jesus is the Devil"![63] Where do we see the glory of God in the face of Christ? For Luther the answer was the cross. *Crux probat omnia*—the cross proved everything! The cross is not only an event that happened in history—though it was also surely that for Luther—the cross is an index to the heart of God. It tests all our ideas, philosophies, and assumptions about God. The cross reveals to us the love of God, and this is the basis of the gospel we proclaim:

---

59 Christopher B. Kaiser, *The Doctrine of God* (London: Marshall, Morgan and Scott, 1982), 94.

60 Ibid. See also Alister E. McGrath, *Reformation Thought* (Oxford: Blackwell, 1988).

61 LW 25:151. See George, *Theology of the Reformers,* 79–86.

62 WA, 40 (1), 602.

63 WA, 40 (3), 337.

The incarnation and passion of Christ therefore are set forth for our contemplation, in order above all that we may behold and know the love of God toward us. So John 3 says: "God so loved the world," etc. Here God pours out not sun and moon, nor heaven and earth, but his own heart and his dearest Son, and even suffers him to shed his blood and die the most shameful of all deaths for us. Shameful, wicked, ungrateful people. How can we here say anything else but that God is nothing but an abyss of eternal love. We have received from God naught but love and favor, for Christ has pledged and given us his righteousness and everything that he has, has poured out upon us all his treasures, which no man can measure and no angel can understand or fathom, for God is a glowing furnace of love, reaching even from the earth to the heavens.[64]

For all of the Reformers, there was no such thing as a disinterested or so-called objective knowledge of God apart from one's personal relationship with God. At every moment of human existence, from conception to death, and unto all eternity, every single person has *negotium cum deo*, "business with God" (Calvin). The first question of the Heidelberg Catechism expresses the confidence every believer can have in the fatherly goodness and care of the God we know in Jesus Christ:

Question: What is your only comfort in life and death?
Answer: That I, with body and soul, both in life and in death, am not my own, but belong to my faithful savior Jesus Christ, who with his precious blood has fully satisfied for all my sins, and redeemed me from all the power of the devil; and so preserves me that without the will of my Father in heaven, not a hair can fall from my head; yea, that all things must work together for my salvation. Wherefore, by his Holy Spirit, he also assures me of eternal life, and makes me heartily willing and ready henceforth to live unto him.[65]

Luther, Zwingli, and Calvin were all radical Augustinians who emphasized God's sovereign election and predestination, though they did so in different ways. In his great debate with Erasmus, Luther emphasized the impotence of the human will in relation to its ultimate direction. "The human will is like a beast of burden. If God rides it, it wills and goes as God wills; if Satan rides it, it wills and goes as Satan wills. Nor can it choose

---

[64] WA 426; WML II, 420 (cf. WA 36, 424). Quoted in Philip S. Watson, *Let God Be God* (Philadelphia: Muhlenberg Press, 1949), 133. See also Marc Lienhbard, *Luther: Witness to Jesus Christ* (Minneapolis: Augsburg Press, 1982), 359–70.
[65] Philip Schaff, *The Creeds of Christendom* (Grand Rapids: Baker, 1996), 3:307–8.

its rider, nor betake itself to him it would prefer. But it is the riders who contend for the possession."[66] Luther's greatest spiritual concern was the legalism and works-righteousness of medieval Catholicism and this led him to emphasize God's sovereign grace as the basis of justification by faith alone. Zwingli, on the other hand, was moved more by the fear of idolatry, so he emphasized God's immutable will and his transcendence over all creaturely forms.

Calvin's doctrine of God brings together the concerns of both Luther and Zwingli. More than the latter, he eschewed all abstract knowledge of God, focusing, like Luther, on God's self-revelation in Jesus Christ and the Bible. It is foolish to speculate about the essence of God, Calvin said, since God is so incomprehensible that "his majesty is hidden." But in Jesus Christ we can see God manifested in the flesh, though this recognition too only comes with the gift of faith. There is an inchoate knowledge of God given both in the cosmos and in the human conscience, but this knowledge is sufficient only to render human beings inexcusable before the bar of divine justice.

The human mind is a "factory of idols," and we can only know the true and living God when he chooses to reveal himself to us in his Son through his Word by his Spirit:

> Though indeed God alone is sufficient witness to himself in his word, nevertheless that word will obtain no credence in the heart of man if it is not sealed by the interior witness of the Spirit . . . wherefore it is necessary that the same Spirit who spoke with the mouth of the prophets must enter into our own hearts and touch them to the quick, in order to persuade them that the prophets have faithfully set forth that which was commanded them from on high.[67]

At first Calvin sought to defend the doctrine of the Trinity by using biblical words. However, when challenged by the antitrinitarians of his day, he resorted to the classical language of the creeds. Like the early fathers, Calvin found it necessary to use extrabiblical terminology precisely in order to be faithful to the message of the Bible. This same procedure would be followed by later Baptist theologians and confessions as well.[68] Calvin put it like this:

---

[66] E. Gordon Rupp and Philip S. Watson, *Luther and Erasmus: Freewill and Salvation* (Westminster: John Knox, 1978), 140. Luther's image of the two riders is meant to refute Erasmus's faulty definition of free choice. "Hence it follows that free choice without the grace of God is not free at all, but immutably the captive and slave of evil, since it cannot itself turn to good" (ibid., 141). On this classic exchange between Luther and Erasmus, see Harry J. McSorley, *Luther: Right or Wrong?* (New York: Newman Press, 1969).

[67] Calvin, *Institutes* 1.7.4.

[68] Perhaps the most explicit example of this in Baptist confessional literature is An Orthodox Creed (1679), first set forth by a group of General Baptists from the Midlands counties of England and bearing this subtitle: "A Protestant Confession of Faith, Being an Essay to Unite and Confirm All

True it is, that we must take from the scriptures the rules for our thinking as much as for our words, and refer to it both all the cogitations in our minds and all the words of our mouth. But who is to prevent us from expounding in clearer words those things that are obscurely shown in the scriptures, if that is done without too much license and upon good occasion?[69]

In the tradition of Augustine, Calvin emphasized the unity of the divine essence but in such a way as to allow for a genuine distinction though not a division among the three persons of the Trinity: "To the Father, the commencement of every action and the source and origin of all things are attributed; to the Son, the wisdom, the counsel and the order in which all things are disposed; to the Holy Spirit, the virtue and efficacy of all action."[70] At the heart of Calvin's strong trinitarian theology was his concern for the deity of both the Son and the Holy Spirit. No one less than God could procure our reconciliation to the Father through the atonement, and no one less than God could release us from sin and give us eternal life.

The Problem of God: Modern Perplexities

The centuries following the Reformation were marked by several orthodox movements of spiritual vitality, including Puritanism, Pietism, and the Great Awakening. However, a profound scientific and cultural transformation was also underway, culminating in the Enlightenment, an intellectual movement that exalted reason, downplayed revelation, and opened the way to a radically revised doctrine of God.

Among the forerunners of the Enlightenment were the English Deists such as John Toland and Matthew Tindal, who promoted a "natural" religion in which there was no place for mysteries, miracles, or the personal God of the Bible. The Deists emphasized God's transcendence at the expense of his immanence: God was a totally remote Creator, the great mechanic who had made the world and then left it to run on its own steam. Calvin had already warned against such a God whom he mockingly called *deus otiosus*,

---

True Protestants in the Fundamental Articles of the Christian Religion." As the title suggests, this confession of faith sought to "emphasize those doctrines held by all true Christians including the attributes of God, the Holy Trinity, the person and work of Jesus Christ, creation, providence, etc." Article 38 incorporates the Apostles', Nicene, and Athanasian creeds and declares that all three ought thoroughly to be received, and believed. "For we believe, that they may be proved, by most undoubted authority of Holy Scripture and are necessary to be understood of all Christians." See Timothy and Denise George, eds., *Baptist Confessions, Covenants and Catechisms*, 120–24. See also Steve Harmon, "Baptist Confessions of Faith and the Patristic Tradition," *Perspectives in Religious Studies* 29 (Winter 2002), 349–58.

[69] Calvin, *Institutes*, 1.3.3.
[70] Ibid., 1.13.18.

a "lazy deity" who idly observed the world from a distant watchtower, an absentee landlord kind of God who seldom if ever got mixed up with real human problems and concerns. Deism was not a sustainable religion, but it did pave the way for even more radical revisionists.

Both Immanuel Kant and Georg Hegel considered themselves Christians, but their philosophical writings left little room for the historic biblical view of God. For Kant "God" was an ordering concept which, like "world" and "soul," the human mind constructed and used as a matrix or mental grid in order to understand the reality that confronted human consciousness. Though Kant affirmed both the immortality of the soul and "the moral law within," the Kantian God was a product of the human mind, a self-made commodity, not the eternal, living, acting God of the Bible. It was a short step from Kant to Feuerbach and Freud, both of whom believed God to be nothing more than the projection of human wishes and desires onto a mythical deity construed as a heavenly Father.

Hegel, whose influence on modern theology rivals that of Kant, went to the opposite extreme from the Deists: he emphasized divine immanence to the exclusion of transcendence, though, in the end, Hegel's God, which he called Absolute Spirit, is no less impersonal. For Hegel, everything exists in God, and God is the World-Spirit that actualizes itself in the historical process.

Friedrich Schleiermacher is "the father of liberal theology." His task was to reinterpret Christian doctrine by accommodating it to the worldview of its "cultured despisers." He did this by associating religion with the faculty of feeling, notably, "the feeling of absolute dependence." God-consciousness is a part of self-consciousness; the doctrine of God is thus presented as an aspect of human religiosity—"God-feelings put into words," as J. I. Packer summed up this view.[71] Schleiermacher's influence on subsequent theology is enormous, even among some evangelicals, who find his appeal to subjective experience compatible with pietist aspirations. Schleiermacher's relegation of the doctrine of the Trinity to the final few lines of his systematic theology fits well with those who want a religion without revelation and pious emotions without doctrines of the faith. But at this point we would do well to heed the words of William Temple: "If your conception of God is radically false, then the more devout you are, the worse it will be for you. You are opening your soul to be molded by something base. You had much better be an atheist."[72]

The trajectory of liberal theology has not gone unchallenged over the past century. While we cannot pursue that story here, we should mention

---

[71] J. I. Packer, *The Lion Handbook of Christian Belief* (London: Lion Publishing Company, 1982),148.
[72] Ibid., 150.

the names of two theologians who rise above many others in setting forth a vigorous account of the doctrine of God based on the teaching of the Scriptures and in dialogue with the orthodox theological tradition. Karl Barth broke with the liberal theology in which he had been trained to emphasize the sovereignty of God and the sole mediatorship of Jesus Christ. Barth also placed the Trinity front and center in his *Church Dogmatics,* and this has led to a renaissance in trinitarian theology in recent decades. While evangelicals can appreciate many features of Barth's theological work, it must be asked whether his hesitant doctrine of biblical revelation is sufficient to bear the full weight of the orthodox doctrine of God he sets forth at great length.

Among Baptist and other evangelical theologians only Carl F. H. Henry can be compared to Karl Barth. His six-volume *God, Revelation and Authority* presents a compelling account of the doctrine of God in the context of an extensive theological epistemology. Henry takes as his starting point the *Deus dixit!* "God has spoken!" of the Reformers, and he elaborates a doctrine of God congruent with the historic faith of the church— transcendent, trinitarian, Bible based, and filled with hope for the victory of God over all human and supernatural foes. One weakness in Henry's theology is his relative neglect of the doctrine of the church, and this has made his work less useful in the postmodern context.[73] Both Barth and Henry, though, remain significant guideposts on the landscape of recent theology.

How Does It All Fit Together?

What is God like? In one sense the answer to this question is the message of the Bible in its entirety. The Bible, unlike this present volume, is not a textbook in systematic theology. It is the true and faithful account of what God has said and done in creating and redeeming the world through Jesus Christ. But when we stand back and ask how the Bible, in all of its diversity, fits together as a coherent whole, we engage in a systematic task. When theologians ask, "What is God like?" they talk about the divine attributes.

God's attributes are also referred to as his perfections, properties, virtues, and predicates. The attributes characterize God's nature and character.

---

[73] See the essay by Russell D. Moore, "God, Revelation, and Community: Ecclesiology and Baptist Identity in the Thought of Carl F. H. Henry," *SBJT* 8 (2004): 26–43. Although Henry was critical of Barth's doctrine of Scripture and carried on a running dialogue with him throughout his writings, it is interesting to note Henry's impression of his personal meeting with Barth: "Whenever I conversed with Karl Barth I had the clear sense that, however flawed was Barth's dialectical theology, I was in the presence of a believer in the Gospel. Bultmann, by contrast, had demythologized the Gospel, and seemed to lack the joy and buoyancy of Christian faith." Carl F. H. Henry, *Confessions of a Theologian* (Waco: Word, 1986), 243–44.

We should never think of the divine attributes as somehow extraneous to God's being and essence. No, God's attributes are his being itself as facing us and shown to us in biblical revelation. The attributes of God are too numerous to list; but they include infinity, incomprehensibility, immutability, omnipresence, omniscience, omnipotence, simplicity, eternity, spirituality, holiness, truth, wisdom, goodness, love, righteousness, unity, immensity, fidelity, mercy, self-sufficiency, indivisibility, immeasurability, personality, congruence, glory, blessedness, and freedom. Before we look at several of these attributes in more depth, we must consider some objections to speaking about God in this way at all.

One objection is this: since incomprehensibility is one of God's attributes, how can we say anything about him at all? Isn't it the height of arrogance for mere mortals to speak of the infinite one in human words? Doesn't the Bible itself say that God dwells in "unapproachable light," and that he is beyond compare (1 Tim. 6:16; Isa. 40:25)? Clearly, the God of the Bible is immeasurably rich and infinitely greater than all our efforts to describe him, and his ways are indeed "past finding out" (Rom. 11:33 KJV).

But the idea that we can know nothing at all about God, while masquerading as humility, is really a form of pride. For if God has truly revealed his character to us in his Word, who are we to spurn that revelation? Who are we to sit like judges, clothed in the robes of false humility, and deny what God has deigned to show to us of his infinite glory and grace? The God who dwells in inaccessible light is "exegeted" or made known by the Son who comes from the bosom of the Father (John 1:18; Matt. 11:27). The God of the Bible is not a black hole in space or a silent sheet of ice such as Ezekiel saw in his vision (Ezek. 1:22). God is the inexhaustible source of all that is, an ever-replenishing fountain of reality, goodness, and love.

Still, it is true that the divine attributes have sometimes been discussed in ways that obscure rather than illuminate the biblical doctrine of God. It is not helpful to begin with an extensive discussion of the attributes of God and then present his triune nature as an afterthought. In this chapter we started with the biblical revelation of God as the Father, the Son, and the Holy Spirit. For it is this God, and not another, to whom all of the attributes belong.

Another traditional way of treating the attributes in systematic theology is to distinguish them according to a threefold pattern. The *via negationis*, or negative way, abstracts from human beings all of those qualities that are true of us but do not apply to God and thus arrives at certain divine attributes in this way. (Thus, humans are changeable, but God is immutable; humans are finite, but God is infinite; human beings are born and die, but God is unoriginate and immortal, and so on.)

The second way, the *via eminentiae,* or the way of heightening, begins with some positive quality in human life and extrapolates from that to the highest degree of perfection in God. Thus, we know some things, but God is omniscient; we can do certain things, but God is almighty; we can love in various ways, but God *is* love, and so on.

The third way, the *via causalitatis,* the way of causation, begins with some incident of cause and effect that we observe in the external world and, like the cosmological argument, moves by inference from such an occurrence to an attribute in God such as unmoved mover, self-originating cause, and the like.

This threefold schema for discerning the divine attributes was first introduced into Christian theology by Pseudo-Dionysius the Areopagite, a Greek mystical thinker of the sixth century. He in turn derived this idea from Platonic philosophy. All three ways have this in common: they begin with the finite and attempt to reach upward toward the infinite. However, the method of biblical revelation begins at the other end of the spectrum: from God downwards, not from man upwards. We have warrant to speak about the divine attributes because God has revealed himself to be like this in his Word, not because we have projected such traits onto God from our broken, inadequate human standpoint.

W. T. Conner defined God's attributes as "those qualities or characteristics of the divine being, by virtue of which he is distinguished from all created beings and without which he would not be worthy of the worship and service of man."[74] We turn now to look briefly at six of God's attributes, the first three belonging to his absolute or immanent perfections, those traits which inhere to God's nature independently of his connection with the universe; then we shall turn to three of God's transitive or relational attributes which display his sovereign glory and majesty over the world he has created.

Holiness

Holiness so defines the character of God that it can be said to include all of the other divine moral perfections as well. As Thomas Oden explains:

---

[74] W. T. Conner, *Revelation and God* (Nashville: Broadman, 1936), 214. James Leo Garrett wisely warns against the tendency to privilege one set of the divine attributes over others. "One should avoid emphasizing one attribute or group of attributes so as to downplay, minimize, or deny another attribute or group of attributes. Late medieval popular theology, if not the writings of the best theologians, so totally identify the *justitia Dei* with punishment so that it could not be connected with salvation. Nels F. S. Ferré's absolutizing of *agapē* seemingly led him to embrace eschatological universalism. Every attribute may not deserve the same emphasis as every other, but a responsible correlation of divine attributes is a mark of good Christian theology." James Leo Garrett, *Systematic Theology,* 1:206–7. For a comprehensive review of the divine attributes from both biblical and philosophical perspectives, see John S. Feinberg, *No One Like Him* (Wheaton: Crossway, 2001).

The moral quality that best points to God's incomparably good character, as one incomparable in power, is holiness. For holiness (*godesh*) implies that every excellence fitting to the Supreme Being is found in God without blemish or limit. It also implies that all other divine excellences (goodness, justice, mercy, truth, and grace) are unified and made mutually harmonious in infinite degree in God.[75]

God emerges in Scripture as "the Holy One of Israel" (Isa. 41:16), the one who is "glorious in holiness" (Exod. 15:11 KJV), the God whose way is holy (Ps. 77:13), the one whose unblemished moral purity and covenant fidelity evokes the highest praise human beings can offer: "I will praise you with the harp for your faithfulness, O my God; I will sing praises to you with the lyre, O Holy One of Israel" (Ps. 71:22).

Like all of the divine attributes, holiness is a quality shared by all three persons of the one God. Jesus referred to God as "Holy Father" in his high priestly prayer (John 17:11), and he taught his disciples to attribute holiness to the Father in the Lord's Prayer, "Hallowed be thy name" (Matt. 6:9 KJV). The holiness of the incarnate Son was announced to Mary by the angel Gabriel: "The Holy Spirit will come upon you, and the power of the Most High will overshadow you; therefore the child to be born will be holy; he will be called Son of God" (Luke 1:35 NRSV). Some of Jesus' contemporaries merely thought of him as the carpenter's son, but the demons, with more insight than some contemporary theologians, recognized him as "the Holy One of God" (Mark 1:24). The sanctity of the Holy Spirit is recognized in the fact that he regenerates, purifies, enlightens, guides, and fills believers, sealing them and making them "saints." The Holy Spirit can also be called the Spirit of holiness. Jesus, Paul writes, was "declared to be the Son of God with power, according to the spirit of holiness, by the resurrection from the dead" (Rom. 1:4 KJV).

We cannot grasp the holiness of God without at the same time recognizing our own unworthiness and sinfulness before such a God. The primal experience of God's holiness in the Bible is depicted in Isaiah's vision of the Lord in the temple. He saw the Lord, high and lofty, surrounded by

---

[75] Oden, *The Living God,* 99. Dagg makes this point as well: "Goodness, truth and justice are moral attributes of God. Holiness is not an attribute distinct from these; but a name which includes them all in view of their opposition to contrary qualities. It implies the perfection of the assemblage; the absence of everything in it contrary to either of the properties included." *Manual of Theology,* 86. A. H. Strong takes a somewhat different view: "Holiness is not a complex term designating the aggregate of the divine perfections. On the other hand, the notion of holiness is, both in Scripture and in Christian experience, perfectly simple, and perfectly distinct from that of the other attributes." Positively, he defines holiness as God's self-affirming purity, an attribute of the divine nature by which God eternally wills and maintains his own moral excellence. Strong rightly says that this attribute can be understood only in the light of the doctrine of the Trinity since the object of God's willing in eternity past can be nothing outside of himself. Strong, *Systematic Theology,* 268–75.

six-winged seraphs who, in antiphonal refrain, declared: "Holy, holy, holy is the LORD of hosts; the whole earth is full of his glory." Immediately, Isaiah shrank from the presence of such an indescribably pure and set-apart God and exclaimed, "Woe is me! I am lost, for I am a man of unclean lips, and I live among a people of unclean lips" (Isa. 6:1,5 NRSV). In all genuine spiritual experience, these two are inseparably linked: a high sense of God's majesty and holiness, and the apprehension of radical depravity and human sin. The holiness of God is an aspect of his transcendence; it is an antidote to all idolatry because it means that God can never be equated with anything finite and fallen. As the Lord said through Hosea, "For I am God and not man, the Holy One in your midst" (Hos. 11:9 RSV).

Holiness in this absolute sense belongs only to God, since only God is untouched by evil: "Thou only art holy" (Rev.15:4 KJV). Yet in the Bible, in both the Old and New Testaments, God commands his people to be holy as well: "As he who called you is holy, be holy yourselves in all your conduct; for it is written, 'You shall be holy, for I am holy'" (1 Pet. 1:15 NRSV; cf. Lev. 11:44). Christians are those who are called to be *hagioi*—the saints—and the Lord intends for every believer to manifest the fruit of the Spirit—love, joy, peace, patience, kindness, generosity, faithfulness, gentleness, and self-control—in all that we do. Again, Paul says that we are to be renewed in our minds and clothed with a new identity in Christ because we have been "created according to the likeness of God in true righteousness and holiness" (Eph. 4:24 NRSV). Perhaps one reason our preaching about the love of God has such little resonance in the world today is that there is such meager evidence of the holiness of God in our walk and ways.

The holiness of God manifests itself in his righteousness as well as his mercy. God's wrath against sin (for "God is a consuming fire," Heb. 12:29) can only be understood in light of his impeccable holiness. The cross is the place where God's righteousness and mercy embrace, where the holy one of Israel was made to become sin on behalf of and instead of lost sinners. This is the basis of our reconciliation with God and also of our concern to maintain standards of justice and equity in society. We affirm the goodness of creation, the sanctity of human life, and the integrity of marriage not out of humanistic concerns but because we are accountable to a holy God who calls us to seek justice, love mercy, and work for peace in the world that this great God has made and will one day judge.

Love

The love of God should never be abstracted from his holiness because they belong inseparably together. Some theologians have claimed that the statement "God is love" is "the foundational ontological statement we can declare concerning the divine essence" (Grenz).[76] But this is misleading, for that love which constitutes the eternal being of God is always informed by, and never exercised apart from, God's character as the one who is always just, righteous, and holy. Dale Moody rightly describes the coinherence of these two primal attributes of God.

> As holiness is the starting point, so love is the high point in the biblical unfolding of the nature of God. One is the outer court and the other is the inner sanctuary in the theological temple of God. As the properties of holiness are the branches in the menorah of monotheism, so the properties of love are the beams that give light and warmth to what could be a barren theology of being.[77]

To fail to make this connection leads to a seriously distorted, one-sided view of God. To emphasize the love of God at the expense of his holiness leads to theological liberalism and process theism, just as an undue emphasis on God's holiness and transcendence ends up in the philosophical paganism of Aristotle or the unapproachable God of Deism.

Whenever we speak of the love of God, we usually mean God's love *for us.* Indeed, this is the great theme of the Bible: "When Israel was a child, then I loved him, and called my son out of Egypt" (Hos. 11:1 KJV); "This is love: not that we loved God, but that he loved us" (1 John 4:10). This is gloriously true, but when we speak of holy love as the primal attribute of God's very being, we are speaking of something antecedent to God's love for us in the history of salvation, antecedent even to the creation of the universe. When the New Testament declares absolutely that "God is love" (1 John 4:16), it refers to the fact that from all eternity the God of the Bible has known himself as a sweet society of three divine persons—the Father, the Son, and the Holy Spirit—freely united in the reciprocity of their uncoerced love for one another. This Johannine saying is not just describing a quality or action of God but the essence and nature of God as love. In other words, had God chosen never to create the world or human beings within it, he would not suffer a deficiency of love. In his very essence and from all eternity, he was the Father who loves the Son and the Son who loves the Father, each sharing fully in the communion and reciprocity of this love in the union each shares with the Holy Spirit. Each person of the Trinity ever seeks the joy, glory, and blessedness of the other two. Admittedly, the Bible only gives us a glimpse of what this inner-trinitarian divine life of eternal

---

[76] Stanley J. Grenz, *Theology for the Community of God* (Nashville: Broadman & Holman, 1994), 93.

[77] Dale Moody, *The Word of Truth*, 104.

love must have been like, but Jesus himself clearly refers to it when he speaks to the Father of "my glory, which you have given me because you loved me before the foundation of the world" (John 17:24 NRSV).

In his eternal sovereignty and aseity, God was under no obligation to share or communicate his love with anyone else. But the awesome message of the Bible is that God has chosen to do precisely this. The Hebrew term *aheb* is used more than two hundred times in the Old Testament to describe God's love for human beings, especially his covenant love for his elect people. The meaning of God's love is expressed in the multiple properties attributed to God in Exodus 34:6, a confessional hymn that was no doubt chanted and sung again and again when the children of Israel gathered to worship: "Yahweh, the Lord, a God compassionate and gracious, long-suffering, ever constant and true, maintaining constancy to thousands, forgiving iniquity, rebellion, and sin, and not sweeping the guilty clean away."

God's covenant love for his people echoes throughout the Psalms and the prophets. God's unconditional and never-failing love is illustrated in the example of the Prophet Hosea, who refused to forsake his wayward and adulterous wife Gomer but went after her, calling and wooing her back into the sacred marriage relationship. So it is with God's overcoming grace and love for his people:

> How can I give you up, O Ephraim! How can I hand you over, O Israel! How can I make you like Admah! How can I treat you like Zeboiim! My heart recoils within me, my compassion grows warm and tender. . . . I will heal their faithlessness; I will love them freely, for my anger has turned from them (Hos. 11:8; 14:4 RSV).

The Hebrew *chesed*, often translated "lovingkindness," expresses the depth and durability of God's unfailing compassion and mercy toward his people. This is the loyal love of God fully revealed in the face of Jesus Christ. The early Christians sang about the faithfulness of the God who could not deny himself: "If we have died with him, we shall also live with him; if we endure, we shall also reign with him; if we deny him, he will also deny us; if we are faithless, he remains faithful" (2 Tim. 2:11–13 RSV).

The place where God's holiness and love are most completely revealed is the cross. The New Testament describes God's love as the motive force that propels Jesus to Calvary. Various theories of the atonement have exalted God's love revealed at the cross to the exclusion of the doctrine of penal substitution. But such a one-sided interpretation misrepresents the meaning of atonement. James Denney was right on target when he affirmed that "if the propitiatory death of Jesus is eliminated from the love of God, it might be unfair to say that the love of God is robbed of all meaning, but it is certainly robbed of all its apostolic meaning."[78]

At the same time we must never fall into the trap of thinking that God loves us because Jesus died for us. According to the Bible, the exact opposite is the case: Jesus died for us because God loves us. And that same love has now been shed abroad in our hearts by the Holy Spirit who teaches us that Christ died for us while we were yet sinners, and that is God's own proof of his love toward us (Rom. 5:8).

Just as the holiness of God is to be reflected in the sanctification of his people, so too is the love of God to be demonstrated in the attitudes, demeanor, and relationships of all those whose lives have been transformed by divine grace. Jesus was clear about this: "By this shall all men know that ye are my disciples, if ye have love one to another" (John 13:35 KJV). As Francis Schaeffer once observed, in this verse Jesus gives the world the right to decide whether those who bear his name truly belong to him based upon their observable love for one another. Elsewhere the New Testament puts this even more bluntly: if someone says he loves God, but acts in hateful, unloving ways toward his brothers and sisters, that person is a liar (1 John 2:9–11). Schaeffer referred to such observable love as the "untried apologetic" the world is waiting to see demonstrated within the church. Such love is the mark of genuine Christianity.[79]

Eternity

Both God's holiness and his love imply his eternity. For God would be less than perfect if either of these divine attributes had come into being at a certain point within God's own divine life. To say that God is "the Maker of heaven and earth" is to claim that God antedates everything that exists outside of himself. "Before the mountains were born or you brought forth the earth and the world, from everlasting to everlasting you are God" (Ps. 90:2). Another way of defining God's eternity is to say that it refers to his infinity with respect to time. The Bible says that the number of God's years is "unsearchable" (Job 36:26 NRSV). God is the one "who lives forever" (Isa.

---

[78] James Denney, *The Atonement and the Modern Mind,* (London: Hodder & Stoughton, 1911), 58.

[79] See Timothy George and John Woodbridge, *The Mark of Jesus: Loving in a Way the World Can See* (Chicago: Moody, 2005). Although God does not "need" human beings in order to "be" the love that is constitutive of his divine essence from all eternity, it is nonetheless true that God delights in the love of his people. As Wayne Grudem writes, "It is one of the most amazing facts in all Scripture that just as God's love involves his giving of himself to make us happy, so we can in return give of ourselves and actually bring joy to God's heart. Isaiah presents God's people, 'as the bridegroom rejoices over the bride, so *shall your God rejoice over you*' (Isaiah 62:5 RSV), and Zephaniah tells God's people, 'the LORD, your God, is in your midst . . . he will rejoice over you with gladness, he will renew you in his love; he will exult over you with loud singing as on a day of festival' (Zeph. 3:17–18 RSV)." *Systematic Theology,* 199.

57:15). He is therefore utterly distinct from everything that exists outside of himself; he is before and after, above and beneath, incomparable to all creaturely realities including the heavens and the earth.

As the psalmist says, "They will perish, but thou remainest, and they all will become old as a garment, and as a mantel thou wilt roll them up; as a garment they will also be changed. But thou art the same, and thy years will not come to an end" (Ps. 102:26 as quoted in Heb. 1:11-12 NASB). "Before Abraham was," Jesus said, "I AM" (John 8:58 NKJV). The eternity of the Son was a major concern in the development of the orthodox doctrine of the Trinity in the early church. What Athanasius and the other Nicene theologians said about the *Logos* is no less true of the Father and the Holy Spirit: before he was, there was not.

In books 10 and 11 of the *Confessions,* Augustine takes up the mystery of time and eternity. He deals at length with a question often asked by children, but a question which is not childish at all: What was God doing before he made the world? There was a stock answer to this question (which Calvin repeated a thousand years after Augustine): "He was busy creating hell for overly curious people like you!" Augustine was aware of this joke, but he knew that it was not a sufficient reply to the serious intent behind the question, and so he gave a different answer. This is what he said: It makes sense to ask what God was doing before he made the world if, and only if, both God and the world are separate items within the same temporal continuum. But they are not. God's years, unlike ours, do not come and go. They are succeeded by no yesterday, and they give way to no tomorrow. "It is not *in* time that you precede all times, O Lord. You precede all past times in the sublimity of an ever-present reality. You have made all times and are before all times."[80]

So what was this eternal God doing before he made the world? On Augustine's reading there was no such "before." There was no "then" then. Eternity is the dimension of God's own life. It has no beginning and no end, no parameters or margins or boundaries outside of God himself. On the other hand, time was willed and created by God as a reality distinct from himself. In his treatment of the world, Augustine again proves to be original in his thinking. He says that time and the world were not only created by God but that they were created together. They were cocreated, for time is coextensive with the world. This is how Augustine puts it: God created the world not *in* time but *with* time. What this means is that time is not some primordial container in which certain events happen. Time is not a receptacle; it is a relationship.

---

[80] Augustine, *Confessions* 11.13.6. See the excellent commentary by R. J. O'Connell, *St. Augustine's Confessions: The Odyssey of Soul* (New York: Fordham University Press, 1989), 135–44.

Significantly, Augustine's remarkable intuition of the coextensiveness of time and the world, of time and space, anticipated by some fifteen hundred years the modern theory of relativity as developed by Einstein and others. Augustine arrived at this insight not by studying the world scientifically but by reflecting on the basic datum of the Christian faith: the doctrine of God as informed by the incarnation of Jesus Christ.[81]

Writing about one hundred years after the time of Augustine, Boethius defined eternity as "a perfect possession altogether of an endless life."[82] Such a definition, of course, applies to no one other than God. It has the advantage of transcending the purely negative connotations of nontemporality: eternity is not simply the negation of time with reference to God, but the arena of his full, majestic, unimaginably rich and overflowing life as the Father, the Son, and the Holy Spirit. We should keep this in mind when we think about another aspect of God's eternity: his immutability. God's changelessness does not mean that he is a static being, incapable of being affected by anything outside of himself, a deity locked forever in the prison of his own aseity. Such a concept might describe Aristotle's Unmoved Mover, but it falls far short of the God of biblical revelation, the God who is actively involved with the world he has made and who entered directly into that world as a squirming baby in a messy manger.

God's immutability refers instead to his constancy and faithfulness. "I am the LORD, I change not; therefore ye sons of Jacob are not consumed" (Mal. 3:6 KJV); "Every good endowment and every perfect gift is from above, coming down from the Father of lights with whom there is no variation or shadow due to change" (James 1:17 RSV). The God of the Bible is not only the Creator of time but also the Lord of time. Unlike human beings who are creatures of a day, God is the one whose steadfast love endures forever, whose faithfulness is to all generations: "The LORD reigns; he is robed in majesty; the LORD is robed, he is girded with strength. Yea, the world is established; it shall never be moved; thy throne is established from of old; thou art from everlasting" (Ps. 93:1–2 RSV).

Shall we say that God is impassible as well as immutable? Impassability is frequently equated with impassivity. When it is so construed, it is clearly contrary to the biblical portrayal of God. When the early church fathers spoke of God's *apatheia* (often translated "impassability"), what they had in mind was God's constancy, reliability, and his complete sovereignty over everything that exists outside of himself. Because God is the supreme Lord of time and eternity, nothing can catch him by surprise. He cannot "suffer" anything that he does not anticipate, foreknow, and choose to un-

---

[81] See Thomas F. Torrance, *Space, Time and Incarnation* (New York: Oxford University Press, 1969), 55.
[82] Boethius, *On the Consolation of Philosophy* 5:6.

dergo. This is why the psalmist can speak of the Lord whose "plans shall stand forever, and whose counsel endures for all generations" (Ps. 33:11 author's translation).

But God's reliability and immutability do not mean that he is incapable of responsive, empathetic love and compassion or that he is a static God lacking all passion and emotion. Thus Cyril of Alexandria's famous paradoxical statement about God, "He suffered impassibly," is an accurate summation of the atonement because "God was in Christ, reconciling the world unto himself" (2 Cor. 5:19 KJV). We should not say more than Scripture does at this point, but neither should we say anything less. Augustine's language is helpful here because it respects the mystery of God's sovereignty on the one hand and the fact of his interactivity with the finitude and fragility of the created realm on the other.

> You, my God, are supreme, utmost in goodness, mightiest and all powerful, most merciful and most just. . . . You are unchangeable and yet you change all things. You are never new, never old, and yet all things have new life from you. You're ever active, yet always at rest. You gather all things to yourself, though you suffer no need. You support, you fill, and you protect all things. You create them, nourish them, and bring them to perfection. You seek to make them your own, though you lack for nothing. You love your creatures, but with a gentle love. You treasure them, but without apprehension. You can be angry and yet serene. Your works are varied, but your purpose is one and the same. . . . You are my God, my life, my holy delight, but is this enough to say of you? Can any man say enough when he speaks of you? Yet woe betide those who are silent about you! For even those who are most gifted with speech cannot find words to describe you (*Confessions*, 1.4).

Comprehensive in Knowledge

God's omniscience—his comprehensive knowledge of all that was, is, and ever shall be—is a corollary of his eternity. The Bible teaches that God searches all hearts and knows everyone's ways. His eyes run to and fro throughout the earth missing nothing that goes on, even those things that are done in secret, hidden from the public glare. Everything is open and laid bare to his eyes, even those things which are yet to come into existence through the free actions of his creatures. As the psalmist put it: "Thy eyes beheld my unformed substance; in thy book were written, every one of them, the days that were formed for me, when as yet there was none of them" (Ps. 139:16 RSV). Jesus was not speaking in hyperbole when he declared that the very hairs of our head are numbered (Matt. 10:30). The Bible clearly teaches that God knows not only the present and the past but also all that will happen in the future. Micah's prediction of the place of the Messiah's birth was not a lucky guess! God revealed the name of the pagan king Cyrus and knew what he would do before he did it (Isa. 44:28). That Jesus would be born of a virgin was predicted by the Prophet Isaiah (Isa. 7:14), just as his sacrificial death on the cross was also foreknown and foreordained by God (1 Pet. 1:20; Acts 2:23).

The omniscient God of the Bible is the one who declares the end from the beginning and who knows before they ever happen all things that will surely come to pass. God's foreknowledge is revealed to us not as an item of divine curiosity but in connection with God's providential governance of the world and the fulfillment of his promises. "My purpose will be established, and I will accomplish all my good pleasure" (Isa. 46:10 author's translation).

In recent years the biblical teaching about God's comprehensive knowledge of the future has been challenged by several evangelical theologians who advocate what is called "the open view of God." Such thinkers are not pure process theologians, for they agree with the historic Christian tradition that God created the world out of nothing. They also say that God has exhaustive knowledge of all that has happened in the past and of everything that is going on now, including the motives and intentions of every human being. What God cannot know completely, they say, is the future, and this for two reasons. First, the future is not "there" to be known until it happens, not even for God; and second, if God could know the future acts of his creatures, that would destroy the libertarian free will with which he has endowed them and thus absolve them of all moral responsibility for their acts.

The open view of God is often set forth as a Christian response to the problem of evil. On their own grounds, though, it is hard to see how the seminiscient deity of the open theists helps much with this issue. If God has comprehensive knowledge of everything past and present, and if he has the capacity to intervene in the course of human affairs, then why doesn't he come to the rescue as soon as he sees things have gotten out of hand? Maybe he couldn't know for sure back in 1933 that Hitler would freely decide to carry out the Holocaust, but when it was well underway a decade later, why didn't he use his omnipotent resources to bring it to a halt? Did he "allow" it to go on just to preserve Hitler's libertarian free will? Such a God has just as much to account for as the old-fashioned deity dismissed by the process model. Open theism grants God too much power to get him off the theodicy hook but not enough power to support a plausible doctrine of providence.

On the other hand, the God of the Bible is presented throughout the Scriptures of both the Old and New Testaments as the Creator of time as well as space and Lord of the future no less than the past. Jesus predicted not only the death of Peter but also the precise mode of his martyrdom (John 21:18–19). We need not accept the false dichotomy of semi-process theism: either the static, loveless, uninvolved God of Aristotelian philosophy or a God of limited knowledge and power who may sympathize with us in the face of evil but is ultimately impotent to deliver us from it. Divine sovereignty and significant human freedom are not competitive exclusives. It is not as though God and human beings were locked together in a finite room with a limited supply of oxygen—the more God breathes with his big lungs, the less air there is for his human creatures. God is not in the suffocating business. We need not bring him down to size in order to lift up the true humanity of men and women made in his image. God's goodness is not threatened by his greatness. God's grace and glory coalesce.[83]

Omnipresence

Just as God's omniscience refers to his sovereignty over time, so the attribute of omnipresence denotes that, as the eternal Creator of all that is, God is not bounded by space. This does not mean, of course, that God fills every inch of the universe like an invisible cosmic glue poured into a vacuum. God is a spiritual being, and his presence cannot be explained in

---

[83] Some of the material in this paragraph was published in Timothy George, "What God Knows," *First Things* (June/July 2003), 7–9. Baptist scholars have been at the forefront of the intra-evangelical debate on open theism. Clark Pinnock, a Canadian Baptist theologian, is the principal author of *The Openness of God: A Biblical Challenge to the Traditional Understanding of God* (Downers Grove: InterVarsity, 1994). See also his essay, "God Limits His Knowledge," in *Predestination and Free Will: Four Views of Divine Sovereignty and Human Freedom*, ed. D. Basinger and R. Basinger (Downers Grove: InterVarsity, 1986). Gregory A. Boyd, a Baptist pastor, has also contributed much to this debate. See especially his *God of the Possible: A Biblical Introduction to the Open View of God* (Grand Rapids: Baker, 2000) and his *Trinity and Process: A Critical Evaluation and Reconstruction of Hartshorne's Di-Polar Theism Towards a Trinitarian Metaphysics* (New York: Peter Lang, 1992). Prominent on the other side of the debate are the writings of Baptist pastor John Piper. See especially his essay, "Why the Glory of God Is at Stake in the 'Foreknowledge' Debate," *Modern Reformation* 8 (September/October 1999): 39–43, and "Grounds for Dismay: The Error and Injury of Open Theism" in *Beyond the Bounds: Open Theism and the Undermining of Biblical Christianity*, ed. John Piper, Justin Taylor, and Paul Kjoss Helseth (Wheaton: Crossway, 2003), 371–83. Baptist theologian Bruce A. Ware has also been a major advocate for the historic Christian view of God's omniscience. See his *God's Lesser Glory: The Diminished God of Open Theism* (Wheaton: Crossway, 2001). See also Timothy George, "A Transcendence-Starved Deity," *Christianity Today* 39 (9 January 1995): 33–34. The 2000 Baptist Faith and Message addresses this issue in its article on God: "God is infinite in holiness and all other perfections. God is all powerful and all knowing; and his perfect knowledge extends to all things, past, present, and future including the future decisions of his free creatures."

terms of material structures or the laws of physics. The doctrine of God's immanence throughout the created order means, as Thomas Aquinas put it succinctly, that "he is in all things as giving them being, power, and operation."[84] God is not a boundless bulk filling all space, but by his divine agency he is available in the fullness of his power to sustain, order, govern, and guide everything that is, wherever it is.

The concept of God's omnipresence is expressed in the beautiful poetry of Psalm 139:

> Whither shall I go from thy Spirit?
> Or whither shall I flee from thy presence?
> If I ascend to heaven, thou art there!
> If I make my bed in Sheol, thou art there!
> If I take the wings of the morning
> And dwell in the uttermost parts of the sea,
> Even there thy hand shall lead me,
> And thy right hand shall hold me (Ps. 139:7–10 RSV).

Though God is present everywhere throughout the universe, he cannot be contained in any one part of it. Solomon recognized that even the beautiful temple he had erected for the worship of God, a place where God's presence dwelt in a unique way in the Holy of Holies, was not to be understood as a structure that could box God in. "But will God indeed dwell on the earth? Behold, heaven and the highest heaven cannot contain thee; how much less this house which I have built!" (1 Kings 8:27 RSV). One of the great temptations in all religious cultures is to localize God, to so contextualize God within a specific place, time, or idiom that he becomes captive to the whim and desires of those who conceive of him in these limited ways. Again and again, the prophets of the Old Testament challenge such theological provincialism. In Jeremiah 23:23–24 we read, "Am I a God who is only near," declares the Lord, "and not a God who is far away? Can a man hide himself in secret places where I cannot see him?" declares the Lord. "Do I not fill the heavens and the earth?" declares the Lord (HCSB).

The doctrine of God's omnipresence is one of the most comforting truths in all the Bible. It reminds us that we can never outrun the power and providence of our great Lord. Jesus promised his disciples that wherever two or three of them came together in his name, he would be present among them. God is equidistant to his people wherever they are; he hears their prayers and receives their worship whether it is offered in giant cathedrals or tiny country churches, in the great urban centers of Europe and North

---

[84] Aquinas, *Summa Theologica* 1. 7. 2.

America, in the steamy jungles near the equator, or at the frigid isolation of the North Pole. Every place is full of his glory.[85]

Almightiness

J. I. Packer defines omnipotence as God's "power to do everything that in his rational and moral perfection (i.e., his wisdom and goodness) God wills to do."[86] We know that God cannot tell a lie. He cannot commit a sin or violate his holy character in any way. He cannot fail to keep his promises. He cannot commit suicide. It is silly to imagine that he can make a square circle because such an idea is nonsensical.

Divine omnipotence is one of the most basic affirmations made about God in the Bible. After confronting God's awesome power and glory throughout the created realm, Job says, "I know that thou canst do all things, and that no purpose of thine can be thwarted" (Job 42:2 RSV). Isaiah refers to God as "the Mighty One of Israel" (Isa. 1:24). God's power is so vast that it is beyond all explanation. As the psalmist says, "Who can speak of the mighty deeds of the Lord, or can show forth all his praise?" (Ps. 106:2 author's translation). In giving the Great Commission to his disciples, the risen Christ claimed for himself nothing less than the full, almighty power of God: "All power is given unto me in heaven and in earth" (Matt. 28:18 KJV). Paul says the same thing about Jesus Christ, the one God has raised from the dead and exalted in heaven "far above all rule and authority and power and dominion, and above every name that is named, not only in this age but also in that which is to come" (Eph. 1:21 RSV).

The theme of God's almightiness is closely related to two other issues frequently discussed by theologians, the problem of evil and the reality of divine providence. If God is truly all-powerful, why does he allow suffering and evil in the world? Doesn't the presence of such tragic elements in human life call into question the character of God as a loving Creator who

---

[85] Dagg aptly describes the spiritual implications of the doctrine of divine omnipresence: "A man who sincerely believes the omnipresence of God cannot be indifferent to religion. To realize that the moral governor of the universe is ever near, in all his holiness and power, and as much present as if he were nowhere else, must awaken solicitude. When a sense of guilt oppresses, the presence of such a companion becomes intolerable. The guilty man strives to flee from the presence of God, as Jonah did; but the doctrine of God's omnipresence teaches him that the attempt is unavailing. The power of conscience tormenting the guilty man, wherever he goes, is terrible; but the presence of the God against whom he has sinned, and whose wrath he dreads, is still more terrible. To the soul, reconciled to God, the doctrine is full of consolation. In every place, in every condition, to have with us an almighty Friend, a kind Father, is a source of unspeakable comfort and joy. We need not fear, that we pass through fire or flood, if God be with us. Even in the valley of the shadow of death, we may fear no evil. In every circumstance and trial, it conduces to holiness, to know that God is present." Dagg, *Manual of Theology*, 62–63.

[86] J. I. Packer, *Concise Theology* (Wheaton: Tyndale, 1993), 36. Cf. Boyce, *Abstract of Systematic Theology*, 82–85.

wisely governs and guides all events? Both Deism and process theology, from different perspectives, try to sidestep this dilemma. Deism emphasizes God's transcendence and power at the expense of his compassion and personal involvement in the lives of his creatures. On the other hand, process theology strongly emphasizes God's love and empathy toward all who suffer "the slings and arrows of outrageous fortune," but the limited God of process is unable to do anything about the suffering and pain.

To see how Baptist Christians have affirmed the almightiness of God in the face of such challenges, let's look at two classic definitions from the Baptist heritage. The first comes from a seventeenth-century confession of faith called The Orthodox Creed, published by General Baptists in England in 1679:

> The Almighty God that created all things and gave them their being by his infinite power and wisdom, doth sustain and uphold and move, direct, dispose, and govern all creatures and things from the greatest to the least, according to the counsel of his own goodwill and pleasure, for his own glory and his creature's good.[87]

The second definition comes from the first confessional statement published by Southern Baptists after the founding of the Southern Baptist Convention in 1845. We call this the Abstract of Principles: "God from eternity, decrees or permits all things that come to pass, and perpetually upholds, directs and governs all creatures and events; yet so as not in any wise to be the author or approver of sin nor to destroy the free will and responsibility of intelligent creatures."[88]

Both of these statements show that Baptists with both Arminian and Calvinist leanings have strongly affirmed the omnipotence and providence of God. We can summarize the general thrust of these two statements in three affirmations:

1. Nothing Exists Except in Some Relationship to God

As we have seen, the Bible teaches that God made the world "out of nothing" (ex nihilo). God didn't make the world out of some kind of primordial matter, matter that already existed. Plato depicted him doing this in the Timaeus: an artisan shaping the world out of a kind of cosmic modeling clay. This is not the biblical view of creation. No, God spoke, and things that did not previously exist came into being. Every molecule or atom in the universe owes its origin to the sovereign Lord of time and eternity. Twenty-four elders in heaven acknowledge this truth when they sing: "You

---

[87] Timothy and Denise George, eds., *Baptist Confessions, Covenants, and Catechisms*, 101–2.
[88] Robert A. Baker, *A Baptist Source Book* (Nashville: Broadman, 1966), 138.

are worthy, our Lord and God, to receive glory and honor and power, for you created all things, and by your will they existed and were created" (Rev. 4:11 NRSV).

2. Nothing Happens Apart from God's Purposeful Activity

When the Abstract of Principles declares that God "decrees or permits all things that come to pass," it simply echoes the clear teaching of the Bible. The Psalms are filled with affirmations of God's comprehensive power and providence: "The LORD has established his throne in heaven, and his kingdom rules over all" (Ps. 103:19). And again,

> I know that the LORD is great,
> that our Lord is greater than all gods.
> The LORD does whatever pleases him,
> in the heavens and on the earth,
> in the seas and all their depths.
> He makes clouds rise from the ends of the earth;
> he sends lightning with the rain and brings out the wind from his
> storehouses (Ps. 135:5–7).

To us it might seem that things happen by chance, at random. "Oh, that was an accident," we say. But there are no accidents with God. Even events like rolling dice or flipping coins are ordered by him, as Proverbs 16:33 makes clear: "The lot is cast into the lap, but its every decision is from the LORD." This is why Paul can state so boldly that God "works *all things* according to the counsel of His will" (Eph. 1:11 NKJV, emphasis added).

3. Nothing Can Thwart God's Gracious Design in Christ

God's almightiness is not an abstract metaphysical principle but, as we have seen, a divine attribute claimed by the incarnate Christ during his earthly ministry. Jesus Christ continually upholds the universe by the power of his word (see Heb. 1:3). He is the one under whose feet God has put all things in subjection (Heb. 2:8). Amid all the ambiguities of history, he is guiding the world and everything within it toward its divinely appointed end, so that ultimately "Jesus Christ is Lord" will be on the lips of every sentient being from heaven down to hell (cf. Phil. 2:11).

Such a theology is true to the Bible, but it does not "solve" the problem of evil if by "solve" we mean explaining all the causes and answering all the objections posed by the presence of suffering and evil in the world. The Bible spends little time answering the whys and wherefores of life. Rather, it tells us that "the secret things belong to the LORD our God, but the things revealed belong to us and to our children forever" (Deut. 29:29).

What we can know for sure is that the God who used the innocent, shameful, despicable suffering of his own Son to reconcile the world unto himself is able to take the shards and broken fragments of our own lives and piece them together into a mosaic of beauty and wonder. The God who neither slumbers nor sleeps will see us through the darkest night and bring us safe at last to that blessed place where we will need neither lamp nor light of sun. God himself will be our radiance. What a great comfort! What a great God of majesty and wonder, worthy of worship and praise, as Isaac Watts knew when he wrote this hymn:

> Tell of his wondrous faithfulness,
> And sound his power abroad;
> Sing the sweet promise of his grace,
> And the performing God.
> Engraved as in eternal brass,
> The mighty promise shines,
> Nor can the powers of darkness rase
> Those everlasting lines.
> His very word of grace is strong
> As that which built the skies;
> The voice that rolls the stars along
> Speaks all the promises.[89]

How Does This Doctrine Impact the Church Today?

More than anything else in the life of the church today, we need a fresh emphasis on the priority and absolute authority of the living God, the real God with whom we have to do in life and death, in judgment and grace. A new understanding and a fresh encounter with the full-sized God of the Bible is a necessary prerequisite for genuine revival among the people of God.

For too long we have heard the old canard, "Missions unites; doctrine divides." Without the doctrine of God and all that flows from it, there is no missions worth doing. All of our frenetic activism, our chest-thumping and nose-counting will prove vacuous apart from the anointing of the Holy Spirit and the reclamation of a sound, God-centered theology. Some ninety years ago, George W. McDaniels, a leading pastor and later president of the Southern Baptist Convention, lamented the growing apathy about theology which he could discern in his day. "In other decades Baptists were better indoctrinated than they are today. The environment in which they live,

---

[89] Isaac Watts, "The Triune God."

sometimes inimical to them was conducive to the mastery of their principles. Of later years, a tendency to depreciate doctrinal discussion is easily discernable, and young converts particularly are not rooted and grounded in the faith. Modern nonchalance acts as if it made little difference what one believes."[90] What McDaniels detected as a trend in 1919 has become a floodtide in our own generation.

It is possible, of course, to study much about God and yet never personally know God. To attempt to study the doctrine of God apart from humility, reverence, and fervent prayer is to make a farce of the holy things of God. Anyone who would attempt such a treacherous undertaking should be reminded of the warning of Scripture: "It is a fearful thing to fall into the hands of the living God" (Heb. 10:31 NRSV).

But when approached in the right way, the doctrine of God can and should transform every area of church life.

Preaching

Preachers are heralds, and the message they proclaim is about the great King who has commissioned them to go forth in his name to spread the good news of his love and grace. God-centered preaching is difficult, but it is necessary if God's flock is to grow into spiritual maturity. Much contemporary preaching is all application with little if any foundation. Our people need to hear again about the God of creation and redemption, the God of holiness and love, the God of grandeur, majesty and omnipotence who, in his supreme sovereignty, did not disdain the virgin's womb and the ruddy cross.

Worship

Too much discussion in recent years has focused on the "worship wars" as we have rehearsed various arguments about musical styles, furniture arrangements, degrees of formality, and the like. What is often missing is a centering focus on the object of our worship: the living God. God-focused worship will not be entertainment prone. Whatever the style of music and the level of formality, there will be time for reflection and wonder, for repentance and confession, as well as for exuberant praise and joyous fellowship. Worship that pleases God is worship that glorifies God, that extols the greatness of his name and that celebrates his presence and victory.

Evangelism

Several years ago a little book was published with the title, *God the Evangelist*.[91] Its point was simple: in all of our evangelistic activities, our witnessing, church planting, and communicating of the gospel, we must

---

[90] George W. McDaniels, *The People Called Baptists* (Nashville: The Sunday School Board of the SBC, 1919), 8.

[91] David F. Wells, *God the Evangelist: How the Holy Spirit Works to Bring Men and Women to Faith* (Grand Rapids: Eerdsmans, 1987).

never forget that it is God who saves, the Holy Spirit who convicts, and that our own ministry of reconciliation is always in service to the divine evangelist. The God of the Bible is an evangelistic, missionary God. He sends forth his people into all the world with a message of salvation and with a promise—that his Word will not return empty but that it will accomplish what God has intended.

Prayer

God invites us to bring our requests and concerns, however small, into his presence in prayer. But we need to recover the pattern of prayer exemplified by the New Testament church. Acts 4:23–31 records one such prayer meeting. These early Christians began by extolling the sovereignty of God in creation and salvation history. They remembered the life and ministry of Jesus. They acknowledged God's eternal purpose in sending Christ into the world and the work of redemption he had accomplished on the cross. They recalled his miracles, and they besought the Lord to come to their aid, "Now, Lord . . . stretch out your hand." Such a God-honoring prayer had a practical result: "They were all filled with the Holy Spirit and spoke the word of God boldly."

Christian Witness and Public Life

There is both a propositional and an incarnational dimension to the life and mission of the church. Our calling as Christians requires us to speak out on matters of public life, especially where injustice prevails and the sanctity of life is under attack. But let us never forget that we care about such things because God cares about them. We do not speak as a political lobby or as a special-interest group but rather as emissaries of the King of kings and Lord of lords. Such wisdom will keep us from making an idol out of any political order, and it will also save us from despair when the tides of the times are not encouraging.

On January 7, 1855, a young Baptist pastor, barely twenty years old at the time, began his morning sermon at New Park Street Chapel in London by extolling the reality and character of the Lord God. Until his death in 1892, Charles Haddon Spurgeon never ceased to make God the theme of his preaching and his ministry. A century and a half later his words still ring true. Today as never before we need a fresh vision of this God, the God whom Isaiah saw high and lifted up in the temple, the God whose "unsearchable riches" Paul coursed the Roman Empire to proclaim, the God whom Jesus taught us to call Father, the glorious tripersonal God whom Spurgeon loved and found such a source of comfort in the midst of "the swelling billows" and "winds of trial." Here are some of Spurgeon's words from that sermon:

It has been said by someone that "the proper study of mankind is man." I will not oppose the idea, but I believe it is equally true that the proper study of God's elect is God; the proper study of a Christian is the Godhead. The highest science, the loftiest speculation, the mightiest philosophy, which can ever engage the attention of a child of God, is the name, the nature, the person, the work, the doings, and the existence of the great God whom he calls Father.

There is something exceedingly improving to the mind in a contemplation of the Divinity. It is a subject so vast, that all our thoughts are lost in its immensity; so deep, that our pride is drowned in its infinity. Other subjects we can compass and grapple with; in them we feel a kind of self-content, and go our way with the thought, "Behold I am wise." But when we come to this master science, finding that our plumbline cannot sound its depth, and that our eagle eye cannot see its height, we turn away with the thought that vain man would be wise, but he is like a wild ass's colt; and with solemn exclamation, "I am but of yesterday, and know nothing." No subject of contemplation will tend more to humble the mind, than thoughts of God. . . .

But while the subject *humbles* the mind, it also expands it. He who often thinks of God, will have a larger mind than the man who simply plods around this narrow globe. . . . The most excellent study for expanding the soul, is the science of Christ, and Him crucified, and the knowledge of the Godhead in the glorious Trinity. Nothing will so enlarge the intellect, nothing so magnify the whole soul of man, as a devout, earnest, continued investigation of the great subject of the Deity.

And, whilst humbling and expanding, this subject is eminently *consolatory*. Oh, there is, in contemplating Christ, a balm for every wound; in musing on the Father, there is a quietus for every grief; and in the influence of the Holy Ghost, there is a balsam for every sore. Would you lose your sorrow? Would you drown your cares? Then go, plunge yourself in the Godhead's deepest sea; be lost in his immensity; and you shall come forth as from a couch of rest, refreshed and invigorated. I know nothing which can so comfort the soul; so calm the swelling billows of sorrow and grief; so speak peace to the winds of trial, as a devout musing upon the subject of the Godhead. It is to that subject that I invite you this morning.[92]

---

[92] Quoted in J. I. Packer, *Knowing God* (Downers Grove: InterVarsity, 1973), 17–18.

CHAPTER 5

The Work of God: Creation and Providence

David P. Nelson

In the beginning, God created the heavens and the earth.

—Genesis 1:1

We believe in God the Father Almighty, Maker of Heaven and Earth.

—Nicaeno-Constantinopolitan Creed

He upholds the universe by the word of his power.

—Hebrews 1:3

Creation

The doctrine of creation is introduced in the first verse of the Bible, *"In the beginning, God created the heavens and the earth"* (Gen. 1:1).[1] This statement offers a simple, conclusive answer to questions universally asked by humans: Why does something exist rather than nothing? How does what exists exist? Where do we come from?

Various answers to these kinds of questions have been offered throughout the ages. Some answers are theistic. They indicate that creation exists because a divine being or beings caused it to exist. For example, Plato writes in *Timaeus* that this world was created by a "Framer," who used various preexisting elements to fashion the physical world.[2]

Others, like Plotinus, offer an emanationist answer to questions about creation. His is still a theistic position in that a divine being is involved, but the world is not created *by* God; rather it emanates *from* God. In this view,

---

[1] Unless otherwise noted, all Scripture citations in this chapter are from the English Standard Version (ESV).
[2] Plato, *Timaeus* 27c–34b.

along with its pantheistic relatives,[3] the distinction between Creator and creation is blurred.

Some offer materialistic or naturalistic answers to the questions of creation. That is, the universe exists without the work of divinity or a "creator." Instead, matter eternally exists, or it came into existence by purely natural means.

The Christian doctrine of creation is theistic, but it specifically attributes the work of creation to the God of the Bible. The Christian doctrine of creation is the free act of the triune God to create the entire universe from nothing, as well as every creature for his own purposes and glory.

What Does the Bible Say?

The Bible is full of references to the topic of creation. The entirety of Scripture is framed with the doctrine of creation beginning with Genesis 1 and ending with the description of the new heaven and new earth, God's re-creation, in Revelation 21–22. The following discussion traces the doctrine through some of the most important references in the Bible from its beginning in the opening section of the Bible.

Genesis

Gen. 1:1–2:4의 주제들

① that God created
② how   "
③ what   "
④ why   "

The opening chapters of the Bible offer an important account of the creation of the world and its inhabitants. Four particular lines of thought are developed in Genesis 1:1–2:4: (1) *that* God created; (2) *how* God created; (3) *what* God created; and (4) *why* God created. This account summarizes the reality that God by his word created a good world for his own purpose and blessing.

That God Created

The narrative structure of Genesis 1:1–2:4 emphasizes the reality that God, the God of the Bible, created all that exists. Genesis 1:1 assumes the existence of God and asserts that he created the world. Genesis 2:1–3 serves as an inclusio with 1:1[4] and emphasizes that this God is the Creator,

---

[3] Such views are found among the Gnostics, in the medieval theologian John Scotus Erigena and among philosophers like Baruch Spinoza and G. W. F. Hegel.

[4] See Kenneth A. Mathews, *Genesis 1–11:26,* NAC (Nashville: Broadman & Holman, 1996), 114 and Gordon Wenham, *Genesis 1–15,* WBC (Waco: Word, 1987), 5. Matthews notes, "The key terms of 1:1—*bārā'* ("created"), *'ĕlōhîm* ("God") and *haššāmayim wĕ'ēt hā'āreṣ* —are repeated, but in reverse order."

while Genesis 2:4 restates the creation formula and transitions[5] to the special creation of man, formerly introduced in 1:26–27, and recounted in the remainder of Genesis 2.

The assertion in the Genesis text that God is the sole Creator of the world (the heavens and the earth) stands against all forms of idolatry. Jeremiah 10:11 employs the language of Genesis 1:1 to indicate the futility of idolatry: "Thus shall you say to them: 'The gods who did not make the heavens and the earth shall perish from the earth and from under the heavens.'" This is spoken in the context of the affirmation that "the LORD is the true God" (Jer. 10:10), and that "it is he who made the earth by his power, who established the world by his wisdom, and by his understanding stretched out the heavens" (Jer. 10:12).

How God Created

The testimony of Genesis is remarkably simple with respect to how God created the world. The repeated refrain of Genesis 1, "and God said," indicates that God created by speaking the world into existence. In its simplicity this recurring statement reminds the reader of the immense power of the Creator.

What God Created

God by his word created a world, and it is a world identified as good by God himself. It is a good world in that it is ordered and purposeful. Order in the world is seen in several ways. On day one (Gen. 1:3–5) God establishes the distinction between day and night. On days two (vv. 6–8) and three (vv. 9–13) God creates boundaries for the waters, making way for the production of vegetation, plants, and trees.

Such ordering is also seen on day four (vv. 14–18). Here the Bible explains how the lights in the heavens are to function. They are to govern time with respect to days and seasons and to give light in the heavens and upon the earth. These verses not only indicate further ordering of the light created on day one but also serve as an antipagan polemic.[6] The sun and moon, the "greater" and "lesser" lights, are not divine; they are created and ordered by God. They do not rule the earth; rather they function at God's command and for the benefit of the earth.[7]

---

[5] Genesis 2:4 reemphasizes the statement of 1:1 with a chiastic structure:
A *the heavens and the earth*
  B *when they were created*
  B¹ *when the LORD God made*
A¹ *the heavens and the earth*

[6] See Mathews, *Genesis 1–11:26*, 154–55.

[7] Often the significance of these verses is overlooked due to the fascination with the question of the relationship between the creation of light on the first day (v. 3) and the reference to the lights in vv. 14ff. The description of divine activity on the fourth day may describe the completion of the "lights" that originated on the first day. See C. F. Keil and F. Delitzsch, *Commentary on the Old*

Day five (vv. 20–23) demonstrates order in the creation as the creatures are made "according to their kinds" (v. 21). Similar order is seen in day six (vv. 24–31) as there is a distinction in the order of creatures between living creatures and the man, the one kind of creature created in the image of God (vv. 26–27).

The world that God created is ordered, and it is a world created with purpose. That purpose is in one sense described by the opening line of Genesis itself. The phrase "in the beginning" causes the reader not only to think about the beginning of creation, but it also causes one to reflect on the concept of an end. From the very beginning of the Bible, one is drawn to think eschatologically and to contemplate God's goal for His creation.

Purpose in creation is also indicated by the repeated description of the creation by God as "good." At the conclusion of the sixth day God looks at everything he has created and declares that it is "very good" (1:31). It is good in the sense that it fulfills God's purpose in creation. That is, "everything is perfect in its kind, so that every creature might reach the goal appointed by the Creator, and accomplish the purpose of its existence."[8]

Why God Created

The answer to the question, Why did God create? is partially answered in the purposive nature of God's creation. God created people in his image to respond faithfully to him. He created a good land, one ordered with boundaries, in which people could dwell and live obedient lives of worship. Further, Genesis 1 indicates that God created man and woman in his image so he could bless them (1:22,28). The sad forfeiture of such a blessed life is seen in the following chapters of Genesis. Interestingly, in Jeremiah 4, when God anguishes over the desolation of his people due to their rebellion, he employs once again the language of the creation account of Genesis 1: "I looked on the earth, and behold, it was without form and void; and to the heavens, and they had no light" (Jer. 4:23). But it is God's desire to bless, and for his people to bless others (Gen. 12:1–3), a truth central to understanding the divine purpose laid out from Genesis to Revelation.

Testament (Peabody: Hendrikson, 1996), 1:35–37. Calvin held that day 4 is a description of assignment for the "lights" that were previously created on the first day. See John Calvin, *Commentaries on the Book of Genesis*, trans. John King (Grand Rapids: Baker, 2003), 83. John Sailhamer suggests, on the basis of the syntax of verse 14, that the text may be translated, "Let the lights in the expanse be for separating" instead of "Let there be lights in the expanse of the heavens." If the creation of "the heavens and the earth" includes all the universe, including the sun, moon, and stars, then verse 14 may simply describe God's assignment of order and purpose to the "lights." See John Sailhamer, *Genesis*, EBC (Grand Rapids: Zondervan, 1990), 33–34. If this is the case, then the emphasis of the text is not on what was created but rather upon how God has ordered a significant part of his creation.

8 Keil and Delitzsch, *Commentary on the Old Testament*, 41–42.

Isaiah

The doctrine of creation is recurrent in the text of Isaiah. It is often employed to explain the nature of God's provision and providential care of his people. Since God created them, he will preserve and care for them. God's promise of power and provision is offered with the affirmation that "the LORD is the everlasting God, the Creator of the ends of the earth" (Isa. 40:28). The promise of the divine Servant in Isaiah 42 begins with the assurance that it is the Lord "who created the heavens" (42:5) who sends the messianic servant.

On some occasions the promise of redemption is associated with the assurance of the Creator God (43:1,15; 44:24; 46:4). God's people should not fear because the God who created them will redeem them (Isa. 43:1; 46:4). Also, God, as he promises salvation in Isaiah 43 and exhorts the people to "fear not" (43:5), reminds his people that they were created for his glory (43:7).

Isaiah provides an interesting comparison between faithfulness to the Creator God and human idolatry. Man makes idols (2:8,20; 17:8; 31:7), but God made the world. The Creator has the ability to save, but idols have no such ability (Isa. 45:20; 57:13). In 17:7–8 the Bible states that the remnant of God's people will no longer "look to" the idols made with their own hands, but rather "in that day man will look to his Maker, and his eyes will look on the Holy One of Israel."

Psalms

Like the book of Isaiah, the Psalms emphasize the continuity of the doctrines of creation and providence. God's continual care for his people and his world is proclaimed on the basis that God created the world. In Psalm 74 Asaph is confident that God will defend the congregation (74:1–3), keep his covenant (74:20), and defend his own cause (74:22) against the enemy. His confidence in God as Redeemer is rooted in the reality that God is the Creator (74:16–17). Psalm 89, likewise, expresses confidence in the greatness and steadfast love of the Lord (89:1,14). The God who possesses the heavens and the earth (89:11), the Creator (89:12), will be faithful to send the Messiah (89:1–4).[9]

Further, God's protection of his people is related to his creative work: The Lord who made heaven and earth is our help (Pss. 121:2; 124:8). There is no more thorough instance of the connection between God's work as Creator of the world and his work as sustainer of the world than Psalm 104 "The poet sings the God-ordained present condition of the world with

---

[9] The text does not use the term *Messiah;* it speaks of David's offspring. Verses 3–4 call to mind the messianic promise of 2 Samuel 7.

respect to the creative beginnings recorded in Gen. 1:1–2:3; and closes with the wish that evil may be expelled from this good creation, which so thoroughly and fully reveals God's power, and wisdom, and goodness."[10]

God the Creator is the sovereign Lord in the Psalms. His lordship over man's worship is exhibited in Psalm 24. The earth is possessed by the Lord (24:1) because He created it (24:2). In this context significant questions are posed: "Who shall ascend the hill of the LORD? And who shall stand in his holy place?" (v. 3). The standards by which acceptable worship is established (24:4), along with the call for the worshipper to be prepared for the Messiah's entrance (24:7–10), are predicated upon God's sovereignty over his world. The distinction between God and man, and thus God's lordship over man, are considered in Psalm 90: "Before the mountains were brought forth, or ever you had formed the earth and the world, from everlasting to everlasting you are God" (90:2). God is eternal, but man is not (90:3–11). Because God is sovereign, the psalmist can pray, "Teach us to number our days that we may get a heart of wisdom" (90:12) and rightly appeal to God to satisfy him (90:14–15) and establish his work (90:17).

A recurrent theme in the Psalms is the call to worship God because he created the world. Psalm 33 indicates that since God made the world (33:6–7), all the earth should fear him (33:8–9). Psalm 96:5 rejects idolatry on the basis that "the LORD made the heavens." Psalm 115 affirms that glory is reserved for God, not for man, and reminds the worshipper that blessing comes from the Lord "who made heaven and earth" (115:15). Psalm 146 also calls for praise to the Lord and recounts that blessing comes to the worshipper from the God who helps and in whom there is hope (146:5), the same God "who made heaven and earth, the sea, and all that is in them" (146:6). Psalm 148:5–6 calls for praise from all of creation since he is the Creator: "Let them praise the name of the LORD! For he commanded and they were created. And he established them forever and ever; he gave a decree, and it shall not pass away."

Job

The poetry of Job 38–41 recounts the Lord's answer to Job out of the whirlwind. The subject matter of the Lord's reply begins with the theme of creation. God instructed Job about the distinction between Job and the Almighty by posing questions about creation: "Where were you when I laid

---

[10] Keil and Delitzsch, *Commentary on the Old Testament*, 5:652. For a schematic overview of the correspondence between Psalm 104 and Genesis 1, see Derek Kidner, *Psalms 73–150*, TOTC (Downers Grove: InterVarsity, 1975), 368. The significance of this psalm for the doctrine of providence will be discussed later in this chapter.

the foundation of the earth? . . . Who determined its measurements—surely you know!" (38:4–5). God instructed Job about the amazing diversity and majesty of his creation (Job 38–39) as he led him to contemplate knowledge of God in a manner that he had heretofore not realized. Two animals in particular, the "Behemoth" and the "Leviathan," are discussed in some detail in Job 40–41, showing God's great ability and amazing design in creation, demonstrating that Job must understand the sovereignty and wisdom of God in all the affairs of the world, especially in the face of human suffering, and fear God always.

John's Gospel

The opening verses of John's Gospel, reminiscent of the opening of Genesis ("In the beginning"), assert that the eternal Word, the *logos,* created all things that exist: "All things were made through him, and without him was not any thing made that was made" (1:3). The themes of light and life (1:4–5) also call to mind the creation account of Genesis.

Acts

In Acts 4:23–30 the believers in Jerusalem pray for boldness amid persecution. Their confidence that God will work powerfully through them is rooted in their belief that their God is the "Sovereign Lord, who made the heaven and the earth and the sea and everything in them" (4:24). On two occasions Luke records that Paul employed the doctrine of creation when proclaiming the gospel. In Acts 14:15 Paul urged his audience at Lystra to turn to the living God "who made the heaven and the earth and the sea and all that is in them." In Acts 17 Paul's gospel proclamation begins with the fact that God "made the world and everything in it" and that he is "Lord of heaven and earth" (17:24).

Paul's Epistles

Paul argued in Romans 4:17 that God, who demonstrated his power by making Abraham the father of many nations, "gives life to the dead" and also "calls into existence the things that do not exist." God's ability to save and to bring offspring and a nation from the aged body of Abraham is affirmed in the context of the reality that God created the world.[11] A doxological reflection on the existence of all things from God concludes

---

[11] Some commentators doubt that this text refers to creation. For example, see Douglas Moo, *The Epistle to the Romans,* NICNT (Grand Rapids: Eerdmans, 1996), 282, who concludes, "somewhat hesitantly and reluctantly, that the clause cannot refer to God's creative power as such, whether general or spiritual." I do not find such arguments persuasive.

Paul's expression of wonder at God's election of Israel in Romans 11:36. In Colossians 1:16 Paul affirmed the agency of the Son in creating "all things," both in the seen and unseen realm. Paul refuted the false teaching of the ascetics in the Ephesian church by noting the goodness and sacredness of God's creation in 1 Timothy 4:4–5.

Hebrews

The introduction to Hebrews affirms that God created the world through the Son (1:2). The rest into which believers enter in Christ is described in comparison with the Sabbath rest of God after creation (4:3b–4). Hebrews 11:3 indicates that the belief that God created the world is a fundamental expression of faith.[12] Belief that God created the universe and acknowledgement of the Creator is foundational for Christian faith, as Calvin states: "But it is by faith alone that we know that it was God who created the world."[13]

Revelation

The initial reference to creation in the Apocalypse is found in 3:14. Three names are attributed to Christ in this verse: "the Amen, the faithful and true witness, the beginning of God's creation." The third title, "beginning of creation," employs language similar to John 1:1 and Colossians 1:18 with the use of *archē* in which creation is attributed to the agency of Christ. The use of the first name "Amen" in conjunction with the name "beginning of creation," which echoes the language of Isaiah 65:16–17, refers to the new heavens and new earth.[14] The fulfillment of the prophecy of the new heavens and the new earth (Isa. 65:17; 66:22) is recorded in Revelation 21.

The song of the twenty-four elders in Revelation 4:11 ascribes worth to the Lord because he created all things and all things exist because of God's will. The angel with the little scroll in chapter 10 swears by the Creator God (10:6). The angel who proclaims the eternal gospel in chapter 14 calls for worship of the God "who made heaven and earth, the sea and the springs of water" (14:7). After recording the creation of the new heaven and new earth in Revelation 21, the final chapter of the Bible recapitulates

---

12 Karl Barth comments on this verse: "This recital (11³) of faith in God the Creator is obviously introduced by the writer as an illustration of the faith which, having its source and perfection in Jesus Christ, was tested by the ancients and has now to be tested by Christians. Whoever rightly and patiently, and therefore with certainty, believes in the fulfillment of the promise which was given in faith, believes that the world is created by God's Word." Karl Barth, *Church Dogmatics*, III.1:4.

13 John Calvin, *Hebrews*, trans. John Owen (Grand Rapids: Baker, 1999), 264.

14 In Isaiah 65:16 the Lord is "the God of truth"(אָמֵן אֱלֹהֵי) and in Isaiah 65:17 the creation of the new heavens and new earth are in view. In Revelation 3:14 Christ is first called ὁ ἀμήν and then the "beginning of creation." See Grant Osborne, *Revelation*, BECNT (Grand Rapids: Baker, 2002), 203–4.

the Genesis narrative with the description of the tree of life and the river in the New Jerusalem.[15]

What Has the Church Believed?

Patristic

In surveying the important work of the early Christian theologians, it is helpful to understand the context in which they composed their theology. The church fathers were, of course, familiar with the cosmology[16] of the Hebrew Bible, that the one true God created the heavens and the earth.

Two other ancient cosmologies were prevalent in the patristic context. First, a naturalistic cosmology existed in one stream of Greek thinking, associated with some of the presocratic philosophers and later with Aristotle. Aristotle believed the world, and matter, to be eternal.

Second, the Platonic tradition was influential during the Patristic period. For Plato, the physical world is a secondary reality to the "ideal" world. The physical world is made of earth, air, fire, and water; and the Framer uses these elements to fashion the world. While the physical world is created by the Framer, the universe itself is eternal, and creation of the physical world is accomplished with preexisting materials.

The dualism of the Platonic tradition retains the idea that matter is associated with evil while nonmatter is good. Plotinus, for example, had such a dualistic conception of the world and believed that the physical world is an emanation from the divine and that it exists eternally. As well, Gnosticism is another form of dualism. The church fathers found themselves not only struggling to defend the biblical doctrine of creation against such beliefs but sometimes also struggling with the intrusion of such thinking into their theology.

Theophilus of Antioch made two contributions to the doctrine of creation. First, he believed the days of Genesis 1 were literal twenty-four hour days.[17] Second, he articulated the doctrine of creation *ex nihilo*[18] against the views of ancient philosophers, who variously held that creation occurred without divine agency, that the world is eternal, or that a god crafted the world out of preexistent material. Theophilus insisted that God was uncreated and that he created the world from nothing.[19]

Irenaeus wrote *Against Heresies* in response to the Gnostic heretics. Against the Gnostic conception that the material world is the product of

---

[15] The association with the garden of Eden is noted in Sailhamer, *Genesis,* 42.

[16] A "cosmology" is an articulation of one's belief about the nature of what exists.

[17] Theophilus, *To Autolycus* 2.11.

[18] *Ex nihilo* means "out of nothing."

[19] Theophilus, *To Autolycus* 1.4; 2.10; 2.13.

emanation from various aeons, Irenaeus stated, following the teaching of Psalm 33:6, "The rule of truth which we hold, is, that there is one God Almighty, who made all things by His Word, and fashioned and formed, out of that which had no existence, all things that exist."[20]

Irenaeus affirmed the doctrine of creation *ex nihilo*.[21] He rejected any blurring of the distinction between the Creator and creation, rejected the Gnostic rejection of the goodness of the material world, and rejected the notion that creation was a necessary action of God. For Irenaeus, these Gnostic deviations indicated ingratitude toward the Creator and therefore led to idolatry.[22] Further, such rejection of the biblical truth about the material creation undermined the Christian doctrine of redemption. If human redemption depends upon the work of Christ on the cross, where his *body* was truly crucified, then Gnostic denials of the good nature of the material, along with occurrences of docetic Christologies, denied the possibility of salvation.[23]

Origen presented a mixed picture with respect to the doctrine of creation. On the one hand he affirmed that "God is one, who created and set in order all things, and who, when nothing existed, caused the universe to be."[24] This is consistent with the biblical teaching and the orthodox theological tradition.

On the other hand, Origen introduced a problem in his doctrine of creation when he insisted that "at no time whatever was God not Creator, nor Benefactor, nor Providence."[25] In so doing Origen admitted necessity into the doctrine of creation. That is, since God is Creator eternally, creation is necessary to God's being. Irenaeus had already rejected this idea, and it stands against the orthodox position that God created the world freely, not out of necessity.

Athanasius made his contribution to the development of the doctrine of creation in the context of the fourth-century Christological controversies. For Athanasius the doctrine of creation and the doctrine of Christ are interrelated. He began his treatise *On the Incarnation of the Word* by discussing the doctrine of creation and argued that "the renewal of creation has been the work of the self-same Word that made it at the beginning. For it will

---

[20] Irenaeus, *Against Heresies* 1.22.1.

[21] Ibid., 2.10.1–4.

[22] Ibid., 1.22.1. He compares the "pernicious doctrines" of the Gnostics to the pagans of Romans 1.

[23] Irenaeus discusses this matter throughout *Against Heresies*. His emphasis on the relationship of the doctrine of creation to the incarnation and redemption is seen in 5.18.3: "For the Creator of the world is truly the Word of God: and this is our Lord, who in the last times was made man, existing in this world . . . and therefore He came to His own in a visible manner, and was made flesh, and hung upon the tree, that he might sum up all things in Himself." See also Gerhard May, *Creation Ex Nihilo: The Doctrine of "Creation out of Nothing" in Early Christian Thought,* trans. A. S. Worrall (Edinburg: T. & T. Clark, 1994), 164–65.

[24] Origen, *On First Principles* 1.Preface.4.

[25] Ibid., 1.4.3.

appear not inconsonant for the Father to have wrought its salvation in Him by whose means He made it."[26]

In proceeding in this way Athanasius indicated that the doctrine of creation is corollary to a proper Christology. In *To Serapion* Athanasius argued for the divinity of the Son, noting that since it is God who created the world, and since the Bible says also that Christ created the world, then Christ is indeed God.[27]

Athanasius affirmed the *ex nihilo* doctrine. Having dismissed the various naturalistic and platonic views of creation, he said "that out of nothing, and without its having any previous existence, God made the universe to exist through His word."[28]

Finally, there is an important soteriological thrust to the doctrine of creation for Athanasius, which is related directly to God's free act of creation *ex nihilo*: "For God has not only made us out of nothing; but he gave us freely, by the Grace of the Word, a life in correspondence with God."[29] However, man chose to rebel against God, so God "called forth the lovingkindness of the Word . . . and for our salvation He dealt so lovingly as to appear and be born even into a human body."[30] In Athanasius we have affirmations of God's free act of creation, of creation *ex nihilo,* and a Christocentric doctrine of creation.

The *Hexaemeron* of Basil of Caeserea is a series of nine homilies on the six days of creation in Genesis 1. He argued firmly against the doctrine of an eternal world.[31] He also affirmed creation *ex nihilo,* since "if matter is uncreated, it has a claim to the same honours as God, since it must be of equal rank with Him."[32]

Christopher Kaiser notes that Basil's contribution to the doctrine of creation is important in that he rejected the view that the heavens are somehow a perfect or spiritual part of creation, while the earth is imperfect or physical.[33] This view of the "ontological homogeneity of creation," as Colin Gunton put it, erased the notion of a dualism of the heavens and the earth, and affirmed "a very different duality" between God and the world.[34]

---

[26] Athanasius, *On the Incarnation of the Word* 1.4.

[27] Athanasius, *To Serapion* 2.2–4.

[28] Athanasius, *On the Incarnation* 3.1.

[29] Ibid., 5.1.

[30] Ibid., 4:2–3.

[31] Basil, *Hexaemeron* 1. Christopher Kaiser notes Basil's particular criticism of Aristotle in Kaiser's *Creational Theology and the History of Physical Science: The Creationist Tradition from Basil to Bohr,* Studies in the History of Christian Thought, ed. Heiko A. Oberman (New York: Brill, 1997), 18.

[32] Ibid., 2.2.

[33] Christopher Kaiser, *Creational Theology,* 30–31.

[34] Colin E. Gunton, *The Triune Creator: A Historical and Systematic Study,* New Studies in Constructive Theology (Grand Rapids: Eerdmans, 1998), 71–72.

Kaiser sees in Basil's *Hexamaeron* some important cosmological components that indicate an orderly universe, which provides the foundation for the worldview that gives rise to modern science.[35]

Augustine made several contributions to the development of the doctrine of creation, some positive and some negative. On the negative side his exegesis of the creation account is highly allegorical and laden with the influence of Platonic thought.[36] Further, while he rejected the radical dualism associated, for example, with Manichaeism, there is an abiding discomfort with the material world that remains in Augustine's thought. As Gunton notes, for Augustine "it seems that if everything is very good, some things are definitely less 'very good' than others."[37] This runs counter to the contribution made earlier by Basil. Augustine also held that creation happened in a simultaneous event. The six "days" represent God's plan, laid out before the reader, which was brought to pass in the simultaneous creation event.[38]

Augustine also offered positive contributions to the doctrine of creation. First, he clearly affirmed and more fully developed the *ex nihilo* doctrine.[39] Second, he emphasized the trinitarian nature of the creation.[40] Third, Augustine saw a certain order and beauty in God's creation.[41]

Medieval

Anselm of Canterbury affirmed the doctrine of creation *ex nihilo*[42] and emphasized that God created through the Word,[43] and that the triune God is

---

[35] See especially chapter 1 of Kaiser, *Creational Theology.*

[36] See Augustine, *The Literal Meaning of Genesis,* trans. John Hammond Taylor, ed. Johannes Quasten et al. (New York: Newman, 1982), 41-42. One does not, however, find all that Augustine has to say about the doctrine of creation in his commentaries on Genesis. The doctrine is treated throughout his works. See, e.g., *City of God, Confessions, On Genesis, Against the Manichees,* and *On Faith and Symbol.*

[37] Gunton, *Triune Creator,* 78.

[38] Augustine, *Literal Meaning of Genesis* 5.23.44–46. The "days" of Genesis 1 refer to the knowledge the angels possess about God's plan of creation. Hilary argues likewise. Moses teaches that there is a certain order to creation reflected in the text of Genesis 1, "yet the creation of the heaven and earth and other elements is not separated by the slightest interval in God's working since their preparation had been completed in like infinity of eternity in the counsel of God." Hilary, *On the Trinity* 12.40, *NPNF*[2], 9:228.

[39] See *Against the Manichees* 1.55–57, *Confessions* 5, 7 (esp. 7.5.7), and *On Faith* 2.2.

[40] Rowan Williams, "Creation," in *Augustine Through the Ages: An Encyclopedia,* gen. ed. Allan D. Fitzgerald (Grand Rapids: Eerdmans, 1999), 254. He notes the following citations: *Confessions* 11.9; *Against the Manichees* 1.2; *Literal Interpretation* 1.4.9, 1.5.10–11, 1.6.12, 1.7.13. See also, *Enchiridion* 10.

[41] Williams, "Creation," 252.

[42] Anselm, *Monologion* 7–12; 28–29.

[43] Ibid., 12; 29–42. In chapter 12 he says that the supreme essence created everything *per suam intimam locutionem,* through its inner locution or "verbalization," as Simon Harrison translates it. See *Anselm of Canterbury: The Major Works,* ed. Brian Davies and G. R. Evans (Oxford: Oxford University Press, 1998). Later, in chapter 29, Anselm states that all things are created through "the

the one Creator.[44] He stated that creation owed the Creator a debt of love,[45] that man was created righteous so that he may enjoy blessed happiness as he rejoices in God,[46] and that the Creator redeemed the human race in the incarnation in order to overcome what had been ruined in the special workmanship of his creation—humanity.[47]

Peter Lombard resisted the Platonic tendencies of some church fathers, arguing that God, who created *ex nihilo,* is the single cause of creation.[48] He was hesitant to divide the work of creation among the persons of the Trinity, stating instead that creation was a work common to the divine nature.[49] Rejecting Augustine's idea that creation occurred in a simultaneous event, Lombard understood the days of Genesis 1 to be twenty-four-hour days.[50]

Thomas Aquinas also affirmed the *ex nihilo* doctrine.[51] While acknowledging that the Father is Creator, that all things are made through the Son, and that the Spirit is life-giver, Thomas, like Lombard, emphasized the common work of God in creation.[52] Aquinas entertained the possibility that the world is eternal but concluded, on the basis of John 17:5, that "nothing apart from God has been from all eternity." That the world began is an article of faith taught by Scripture (Heb. 11:1) and professed in the creeds. Moses also spoke of the beginning of the world. "That the world has not always existed cannot be demonstratively proved but is held by faith alone."[53]

Reformation

Martin Luther insisted that Genesis 1 "is written in the simplest language; yet it contains matters of the utmost importance that are difficult

---

supreme nature's verbalization." This "locution" or "verbalization" is not, Anselm says in chapter 30, many words but only one Word (*Non igitur constat pluribus verbis; sed est unum Verbum, per quod facta sunt omnia*). This Word is the Son begotten from the Father (37–42).

[44] Ibid., 57.

[45] Ibid., 68.

[46] Anselm, *Cur Deus Homo* 2.1.

[47] Ibid., 1.4.

[48] Marcia L. Colish, *Peter Lombard* (New York: E. J. Brill, 1994), 1:337. See *Setentiae in IV libris distinctae,* 2.d.1.c.1.2.

[49] Ibid.

[50] Ibid., 340–41.

[51] Thomas Aquinas, *Summa Theologica* 1a.45.1. Here he cites Genesis 1:1 and a gloss on the text attributed to Anselm of Laon.

[52] Ibid., 1a.45.6. He states that creation is "common to the whole Trinity."

[53] Ibid., 1a.46.1. He goes on to say, "We make the same stand here as with regard to the mystery of the Trinity." Brian Davies says that Aquinas is simply saying that we cannot prove that the world had a beginning, but we hold that it did by faith. Brian Davies, *Aquinas* (New York: Continuum, 2002), 74.

to understand."[54] He believed that the world is not more than six thousand years old though he was well aware of the competing view present in the Aristotelian tradition. He noted that the Bible does require the belief that the world has a beginning, but beyond this "there is hardly anything about which there is common agreement among all theologians."[55] Still, Luther contended that the basic message of Genesis is clear: "Everything that is, was created by God."[56]

Luther was critical of allegorical readings of Genesis, like that of Augustine, since Moses' purpose was to teach us about the real world and real creatures, not an allegorical world with allegorical creatures. For example, when Moses referred to evening and day, he meant literal twenty-four-hour days.[57]

Creation is a trinitarian work. Christ and the Spirit are involved in creation, and this is why the term *elohim* is employed in the Genesis narrative.[58] Luther also understood the creation account to display a certain anthropocentric emphasis since man is the special object of creation, since the ascription of goodness in Genesis 1 is associated with the earth and its provisions for humanity[59] and since blessing in Genesis 1 is associated with living creatures.[60]

John Calvin stated that "God by the power of his Word and Spirit created heaven and earth out of nothing."[61] God's creation is a "glorious theater" of which man is a spectator.[62] Calvin, like Luther understood the limitations of humans to understand the verities of creation. Yet God has spoken about these truths in the Bible, and the veracity of the report of creation by Moses in Genesis is demonstrated by the accuracy of biblical prophecy.[63] God speaks in the Bible about creation in order to avert idolatry among his people.[64] God creates through the Word, who is Christ.[65] Calvin

---

[54] Martin Luther, *Lectures on Genesis Chapters 1–5*, LW 1, trans. George V. Schick (St. Louis: Concordia, 1958), 3.

[55] Ibid., 4.

[56] Ibid., 7.

[57] Ibid., 5, 69.

[58] Ibid., 12. That Christ is involved as an agent of creation is seen in the fact that God brought the world into existence by his Word, which is reflected also in Psalm 33:6 and Colossians 1:16. The "spirit" in Genesis 1:2 is the Holy Spirit (see *Lectures on Genesis,* 9).

[59] Ibid., 35.

[60] Ibid., 53.

[61] Calvin, *Institutes,* 1.14.20.

[62] Ibid., 1.5.8. Though, Calvin argues, due to wickedness "scarcely one man in a hundred is a true spectator of it." Such references to creation as a "theater" recur in the *Institutes.* See 1.6.2, 1.14.20, and 2.6.1, where creation is a "beautiful theater" that should occasion "pious meditation."

[63] John Calvin, *Commentaries on the First Book of Moses Called Genesis,* trans. John King (Grand Rapids: Baker, 2003), 58–59. These accounts were written, Calvin states, in order to prevent corruption by men.

[64] Calvin, *Institutes,* 1.14.1.

[65] Ibid., 1.13.7.

also understood the Genesis account to bear a certain anthropocentrism, in that God has created the world for our good and salvation, and we should, therefore, be thankful to him.[66]

One sees in Calvin an awareness of the limitations of knowledge one must admit when taking up the doctrine of creation. It is here, both in his Genesis commentary and in the *Institutes,* that Calvin used the analogy of the spectacles. The Scriptures make plain to us what we otherwise would not see, just as spectacles enable us to overcome deficient vision.[67] In drawing this analogy, Calvin warned Christians to remain humble about their knowledge of creation and to avoid the error of speculation. In this Calvin showed at once an awareness of scientific advances in the Renaissance milieu, as well as limitations in scientific knowledge,[68] and insisted that Moses wrote Genesis in a popular manner as opposed to the more technical style of astronomy.[69]

Modern

The modern period is marked by the rise of the modern scientific method and the Copernican Revolution. Not only was the geocentric theory of the universe replaced with the heliocentric theory, but a mechanistic view of the universe became ensconced in the modern mind. Alongside the emerging mechanistic view of the world there arose certain questions about knowledge of the physical world due to the severe skepticism of Hume and Kantian conceptions of perception. An idealism emerged from the thought of Immanuel Kant which presented a bifurcation between the phenomemal and noumenal realms.[70] This bifurcation becomes the assumption of the modern period. In this case a doctrine or theology of creation becomes almost impossible to sustain since those matters that we raised at the beginning of this chapter—matters related to the physical world—are no longer matters that may be properly discussed in theological terms.

The doctrine of evolution was propounded by Charles Darwin in the mid-nineteenth century and centered on a theory of natural selection.[71] Darwin's theory, as well as the modern philosophical trends noted above, along with the rise of Deism and then the development of higher criticism in biblical studies, created an environment in which the orthodox doctrine

---

[66] Ibid., 1.14.22.

[67] See *Genesis,* 62 and *Institutes,* 1.14.1.

[68] Calvin, *Genesis,* 85–86. Here Calvin demonstrates the ignorance of his time about whether the moon produces its own light or whether it "borrows" its light from the sun.

[69] Ibid., 86–87.

[70] Gunton, *Triune Creator,* 130–34.

[71] See Darwin's *The Origin of the Species* (1859) and *The Descent of Man* (1871).

of creation was severely questioned. The revelation of the Bible and the claims of orthodoxy are now submitted to the criticism of human reason, a reason that assumes naturalistic explanations of the world. Liberal biblical scholars and theologians found in Darwin's theory a useful paradigm from which finally to discard the old orthodoxy.

Friedrich Schleiermacher took up the doctrine of creation under his description of religious self-consciousness. He did not maintain any kind of distinction between the doctrines of creation and preservation. He believed discussions about creation itself belonged "to the period of mythology," since the creation account of Moses along with the rest of the Pentateuch was "from primitive and prehistoric times."[72] Both preservation and creation are attributed to God, but the doctrine of creation is absorbed into the doctrine of preservation.[73] This is consistent with Schleiermacher's theological agenda since it is the doctrine of preservation and not the doctrine of creation that, as he sees it, most naturally arises out of human religious consciousness. On this basis Schleiermacher also asserted, "Since the doctrine of the Trinity is neither presupposed in every Christian religious experience nor contained in it, these definitions do not belong to the present discussion."[74]

In a move unsympathetic to modernism, Karl Barth understood the doctrine of creation to be an article of faith, not a matter of natural theology or scientific inquiry. This is the clear teaching of Scripture (Heb. 11:3) and is affirmed in the Christian creed.[75] The world is reality distinct from its Creator, the triune God.[76] Barth is not hesitant to critique modernist views of creation,[77] arguing that if God is not Creator of all, then he cannot be "Lord and Ruler of this history."[78] With the church fathers, Barth understood that God the Creator is also God the deliverer.[79]

---

[72] Friedrich Schleiermacher, *The Christian Faith,* trans. H. R. MacKintosh and J. S. Stewart (Edinburgh: T & T Clark, 1989), S 36.2.

[73] Ibid., S 38.1.

[74] Ibid., S 37.1.

[75] Karl Barth, *Church Dogmatics,* 3/1:3–4.

[76] Ibid., 5–13. See also the Christological focus of his doctrine of creation in *CD,* III/1, 29–31 and 51–56. On the role of the Holy Spirit, see pp. 57–59. Further, one should note the connection of creation and covenant in Barth's theology. See *CD,* III/1 94–329.

[77] This aspect of Barth's formulation of creation doctrine is occasionally overlooked because of his sometimes difficult discussions about history and "saga." Two things should be noted. First, Barth does consider the creation account to be genuine history: "What we read in Gen. 1 and 2 are genuine histories of creation" (*CD,* 3/1:89). For Barth, however, the divine action of creation cannot be understood on the basis of modern historicist criteria (*CD,* 3/1:76–94). Second, Barth's explanations of "saga" occur in a context in which he is rejecting the historicism of nineteenth-century liberalism and the notion of "myth" found both in ancient texts, like the *Enuma Elish* and among his contemporaries, like Rudolph Bultmann.

[78] Ibid., 45. Here Barth has F. C. Baur and Immanuel Kant in his sights.

[79] Ibid.

Wolfhart Pannenberg understands creation to be a free act of the triune God.[80] The reality of the free creation by the Word distinguishes the work of the God of the Bible "from analogous cosmogonic ideas in ancient Near Eastern cultures." The doctrine of creation *ex nihilo* emerges from this affirmation.[81] Pannenberg understands the theory of evolution to be useful in Christian theology in that it offers an explanation of the continuous creative activity of God. In fact, Christian opposition to "Darwinism was a momentous mistake."[82] Pannenberg also argues that the best theodicy is developed from a doctrine of creation properly connected to the doctrines of redemption and eschatology.[83]

Baptist Theologians

John Gill stated that creation "is the production of things out of nothing," which is an article of faith based on divine revelation (Rom. 4:17; Heb. 11:3).[84] The world is not yet six thousand years old.[85] It is the triune God who created the world,[86] and he did so for himself and his own glory.[87] Andrew Fuller, in his "Discourses" to the Baptist church at Kettering, affirmed that the triune God created the heavens and the earth.[88] Moses offers no argument for the existence of God; the Creator's being is "taken for granted."[89] While we are not told all that we might wish to know about creation, what we are told in Genesis is true. James Pendleton said that creation is the execution of God's eternal purposes and is *ex nihilo*.[90] Such an affirmation is an article of faith (Heb. 11:3). God created the world for his own pleasure and glory. For Pendleton the doctrine of creation must not be separated from the doctrine of Christ, the cross, and redemption.[91]

As James Boyce understood it, all theories of creation may be reduced to four: materialism, emanationism, dualism, and creationism. Theology is to evaluate these theories and explain that creation was made by God out of noth-

---

[80] Wolfhart Pannenberg, *Systematic Theology,* vol. 2, trans. Geoffrey Bromily (Grand Rapids: Eerdmans, 1994), 1, 20–35.

[81] Ibid., 13.

[82] Ibid., 119. He recognizes "the hypothetical character of the theory of evolution." But he worries that such opposition creates problems for the relationship of science and theology.

[83] Ibid., 165.

[84] John Gill, *A Body of Divinity* (Grand Rapids: Sovereign Grace, 1971), 256–57, 259.

[85] Ibid., 259.

[86] Ibid., 260.

[87] Ibid., 261.

[88] Andrew Fuller, "Expository Discourses," in *The Complete Works of Andrew Fuller* (Boston: Lincoln, Edmands & Co., 1833), 1:725.

[89] Ibid.

[90] James M. Pendleton, *Christian Doctrines: A Compendium of Theology* (Valley Forge: Judson, 2000), 115.

[91] Ibid., 125.

ing.[92] Boyce discussed the Genesis account with an awareness of the claims of modern science. He concluded that the term *day* in the Genesis narrative does not necessarily mean a twenty-four-hour period.[93] He also suggested that there may have been other men before Adam.[94] The Bible's use of phenomenal language to speak of scientific truths makes it a timeless document. Still, Boyce recognized that Moses had insight from God about the creation that human authors could not know themselves.[95] Whatever the challenges of modern science, Boyce was confident that the scriptural account can be reconciled with science and questionable matters in the Scripture can always be given reasonable explanation. Further, any who would deny the doctrine of inspiration of the Scripture on such a basis must themselves explain the way in which biblical teaching is consonant with scientific discoveries.[96]

Augustus Hopkins Strong stated, "By creation we mean the free act of the triune God by which in the beginning for his own glory he made, without the use of preexisting materials, the whole visible and invisible universe."[97] Strong articulated the doctrine while rejecting any form of dualism, emanation, or theories of eternal creation. God's purpose in creation is found in his own pleasure and glory.[98] While science may observe some things about the world, we are dependent on Scripture to know the truth about creation.[99]

Writing in the midst of the modernist milieu, Strong advanced the "pictorial-summary interpretation" of Genesis, which to him conveyed an accurate portrayal of the events of creation "in pregnant language, so that it could expand to all the ascertained results of subsequent physical research." In this way, Strong believed that the Genesis account had the "power to adapt itself to every advance in human knowledge."[100]

E. Y. Mullins, like Boyce and Strong, worked amid the pressures of modernism. He rejected the notion that the doctrine of creation rests on the conclusions of physical science. Instead, the doctrine is rooted in the new creation wrought by the redemptive work of Christ. This, for Mullins, is based on our religious experience rooted in our dependence on God. In this

92 James Pettigru Boyce, *Abstract of Systematic Theology* (Escondido: Dulk Christian Foundation, n.d.), 166. The phrase "create from nothing" is not in the Bible, "but the fact itself is taught expressly in Heb. 11:3." See 170.
93 Ibid., 171–72.
94 Ibid., 172–73.
95 Ibid., 173. For example, that light appears before the sun and moon in Genesis 1.
96 Ibid., 174.
97 Augustus H. Strong, *Systematic Theology* (Philadelphia: Judson, 1907), 371.
98 Ibid., 397.
99 Ibid., 374. He says here, "Scripture supplements science, and renders its explanation of the universe complete."
100 Ibid., 393–94. Among the possible ways of reading Genesis, Strong thinks the best involves the adoption of theistic evolution. See 395–96.

way creation is purposive.[101] Mullins also rejected various views opposed to the orthodox doctrine of creation such as materialism, dualism, emanation, and eternal creation.[102] Mullins affirmed that creation is the free act of God and that God's purpose in creation is to share life and blessing with created beings,[103] and he opposed the doctrine of evolution as he did "every form of infidelity and unbelief."[104]

Tensions created by modernist influences continued among Baptist theologians in the twentieth century. A controversy erupted in the Southern Baptist Convention in the 1960s directly related to the interpretation of Genesis. In 1961 Ralph Elliot published *The Message of Genesis*[105] in which he rejected Mosaic authorship and accepted higher critical assumptions about the biblical text. The controversy that ensued led to the appointment of a committee by the SBC which produced the 1963 Baptist Faith and Message. The Convention affirmed the orthodox reading of Genesis and the doctrine of creation.

Then, in 1969, Broadman Press published volume 1 of *The Broadman Bible Commentary* which included a commentary on Genesis by G. Henton Davies, in which Davies also subscribed to higher critical methods and assumptions. The outcry among Southern Baptists was such that a revised edition of the commentary was issued in 1973 in which the Genesis commentary was written by a new author.

How Does It All Fit Together?

Trinity
Lordship
Worldview
Salvation
Eschatology
Doxology

Creation and the Trinity

That God created the heavens and earth is the assumption of the Bible, as we have seen. The God who created this world is the God revealed in the Bible as Father, Son, and Holy Spirit. The agency of Christ, the eternal

---

[101] E. Y. Mullins, *The Christian Religion in Its Doctrinal Expression* (Valley Forge: Judson, 1917), 251–52.

[102] Ibid., 253–54.

[103] Ibid., 252–53.

[104] E. Y. Mullins, correspondence to Billy Sunday, 1 February 1927, in "Evolution, Legislation, and Separation: Correspondence between Billy Sunday and E. Y. Mullins" in *SBJT* 3 (Winter 1999): 88. This correspondence reveals that while Mullins opposed evolution, he also opposed legislative attempts to battle evolutionary teaching since it violated important principles of the separation of church and state and religious liberty. Mullins was implicated as a proponent of evolution during the Scopes trial in 1925 by Shailer Matthews. Mullins emphatically denied that he believed in any form of evolutionary theory and refused to help either Matthews (who supported Scopes) or William Jennings Bryan, who asked Mullins for a deposition. See William E. Ellis, *A Man of Books and a Man of the People: E. Y. Mullins and the Crisis of Moderate Southern Baptist Leadership* (Macon, GA: Mercer, 1985), 195. See also Shailer Matthews, *New Faith for Old: An Autobiography* (New York: Macmillan, 1936), 228–29.

[105] Ralph H. Elliot, *The Message of Genesis* (Nashville: Broadman, 1961).

Logos, the Son of God, in creation is clear (John 1:3; 1 Cor. 8:6; Col. 1:16; Heb. 1:2). The role of the Spirit as life-giver in creation is witnessed first in Genesis 1:2,[106] and also in Psalm 33:6 and Psalm 104:30.

The trinitarian nature of creation is affirmed in the Christological emphasis made by a number of the church fathers, in the articulation of the doctrine among some of the medieval theologians and also among the Reformers. The significance of the trinitarian understanding of creation is that such a view roots the doctrine itself in the work of the triune God who revealed himself to man in the Scriptures.[107] It is not just any god who created the world; it is the God who is Father, Son, and Holy Spirit.

Creation and Lordship

The relationship of creation and lordship is significant for several reasons. First, the rulership of God in and over his creation is prominent in the Bible (Isa. 37:16; Jer. 27:5; Amos 4:12–13; Jon. 1:9) and is critical to the development of the doctrine of providence. That God possesses the power and sovereignty to govern the world is repeatedly tied to the doctrine of creation.

Second, the doctrine of creation *ex nihilo* reflects the biblical distinction between the Creator and creation that is crucial to God's claim upon our lives for worship and obedience (Rom. 1). The *ex nihilo* doctrine may be implied in Genesis 1:1, though the doctrine is seen more clearly in Hebrews 11:3 and Romans 4:17. Additionally, Colossians 1:16 indicates that "all things" were created by the Son and John 1:3 states that there was nothing of the "all things" that was made without the *Logos*. Significant here is that the *ex nihilo* doctrine affirms a clear God-world distinction. The *ex nihilo* doctrine has important implications for Christology in that the God-world distinction applies directly to the Christ, the eternal Word (John 1:3; Col. 1:15–17).[108]

Third, the nature of God's wisdom and knowledge is related to the doctrine of creation (Ps. 104:24; Prov. 3:19). That God knows all things and that he is wise and can offer wise counsel is associated with his ability to create the world (Job 38). So God's lordship is expressed in his perfect wisdom and omniscience.

Fourth, as we saw previously (e.g., in the Psalms), the doctrine of creation is often used as a polemic against idolatry (see also Jer. 10:12; 51:15). Since idolatry is fundamentally opposed to lordship, the doctrine of creation serves as a prompt to appropriate worship among God's people.

---

106 See Keil and Delitzsch, *Commentary on the Old Testament,* 30.

107 On the broader significance of this, see Colin Gunton, *The Triune Creator.*

108 For example, Arian claims about the Son as firstborn creature (Col. 1:15) fail to understand the term προτότοκος in the context of vv. 16–17, which clearly refer to the Son (v. 13) as the Creator.

Creation and Worldview

The doctrine of creation establishes a particular worldview rooted in God's sovereignty over his creation. A worldview is simply the way in which one views the world; it is "the comprehensive framework of one's basic beliefs about things."[109] God's Word provides the proper way of thinking about God and his world; the Bible provides the framework for our basic beliefs about things. So, for example, Genesis 1–3 informs us that God made the world, and that he made the world by his Word for particular purposes. In Job 38 God answers questions about the nature of life in this world by reminding Job that God created the world and governs it wisely. This biblical worldview stands in contrast to other worldviews such as philosophical naturalism, the prevailing worldview in the Western world today, which denies not only the biblical account of creation by the divine Creator but also the existence of the Creator. The following are features of the biblical worldview that are associated with the doctrine of creation.

(1) The world God created is good (Gen. 1:31; 1 Tim. 4:4); it is ordered and purposeful. God created the world for his own pleasure and glory (Pss. 8:1; 19:1–2; Rev. 4:11). The God who created this world is a personal, powerful God who created man in his image and for his glory. (2) The doctrine of creation, while it demands a theocentric worldview, also has a certain geocentric and anthropocentric thrust. God created this particular world in which he made the special creature called man (Pss. 8; 115:16; Zech. 12:1). God will redeem the world (Rom. 8:19–23) and man so that he may enjoy fellowship with him forever. (3) Thinking about one's worldview in this manner helps us to develop a biblical worldview, one that is not rooted in a particular culture but a worldview that is rooted in biblical doctrine itself, such that life in this world is lived under the lordship of God and his Word (Isa. 66:1–2; cf. Acts 7:49–50).

Creation and Salvation

Repeatedly the Scriptures associate the doctrine of creation with the doctrine of salvation. The God who has the power to create also has the power to save (e.g., Isa. 43:1; 46:4; Col. 1:16). The preaching of the resurrection of Christ in Paul's gospel witness in Acts 17 is predicated on the truth of God's power to create (Acts 17:24–27).

We have seen how this connection is drawn among the church fathers (e.g., Irenaeus, Athanasius), particularly with respect to the humanity of Jesus and his propitiatory sacrifice (Heb. 2:17). In 2 Corinthians the Apostle Paul uses the metaphor of "new creation" (2 Cor. 5:17) to explain the doc-

---

[109] Albert M. Wolters, *Creation Regained: Biblical Basics for a Reformational Worldview* (Grand Rapids: Eerdmans, 1985), 2.

[handwritten: 은혜로,전기가]

trine of reconciliation in Christ. The culmination of God's redemptive plan is articulated in creation terms with the establishment of the new heavens and new earth in the eschaton (Rev. 21; Isa. 65:17; 66:22).

Creation and Eschatology

As noted previously, the opening sentence of the Bible causes us to think eschatologically (Gen. 1:1), to think of God's purpose for all of creation. The same eschatological thinking is evident in Isaiah 65:17 and 66:22, which look forward to the new heavens and new earth recorded in Revelation 21. In 2 Peter 3:11–13 such eschatological anticipation of the new heavens and new earth is associated with readiness for the "day of God" and the final judgment.

Creation and Doxology

[handwritten: 우상숭배를 정죄하고 거꾸로 Worship과 creation을 어떻게서하]

The Bible relates the doctrine of creation and the worship of God by first condemning idolatry and then promoting worship of the Creator God. The reality of God as Creator is employed as a warning against idolatry. Man is not to worship the creation made by God (Gen. 1:16; Rom. 1:25), nor is he to worship idols crafted by human hands (Exod. 20:3–5; Lev. 19:4; Isa. 2:8; 17:8; Hab. 2:18; Ps. 96:5; 1 Cor. 10:14). Instead, it is the rejection of idols that is definitive of genuine worship of God (1 Thess. 1:9; 1 John 5:21). The fitting response to the Creator is doxology, a theme seen, for example, in the Psalter (Pss. 33:6–7; 96:5; 115:15; 148) and the Apocalypse (Rev. 4:11).

How Does This Doctrine Impact the Church Today?

The doctrine of creation has many implications for life in God's world today. The following section considers some of these implications. First, we will explore a few issues related to the doctrine of creation in the context of life in modern culture. Second, we will explore some issues related to the doctrine as it relates specifically to life in the church.

[handwritten: ✓ Dignity of Human life ✓ Respect for other life and 환경도 ✓ Theology and Science]

The Doctrine of Creation and Life in Modern Culture

Dignity of Human Life

The doctrine of creation, rightly understood, leads to a deep appreciation for the value of all human life since all humans are created in the image of God (Gen. 1:26–27; 9:6). Since human life is highly valuable, murder must be rejected by any culture. This demands the rejection of practices like abortion and euthanasia which devalue the most vulnerable lives within society. As well, such appreciation for human dignity demands the rejection of hatred of one's fellow man (Matt. 5:21–24,43–48) and the glad acceptance of responsibility for "the least of these" (Matt. 25:34–40; James 1:15–17).

Marriage is another issue located at the intersection of the doctrine of creation and human dignity. When asked if it is lawful to divorce, Jesus answered by upholding the concept of the indissoluble union of a man and woman under God (Matt. 19:5–6). The rationale Jesus offered for this position was rooted in the doctrine of creation: "Have you not read that he who created them from the beginning made them male and female" (Matt. 19:4). In this way Jesus based his teaching on divorce and the sanctity of marriage on God's purpose in creation and also affirmed that marriage is, by definition, the union of a man and woman.[110]

Respect for Other Life and the Environment

Along with appreciation for human life, man should recognize the value of the rest of God's good creation. Animals, though clearly distinct from humans, are themselves cared for by God (Ps. 104:10–30) and also by man according to divine instruction (Exod. 20:10; Deut. 22:6; Prov. 12:10; 27:23).[111] Further, man should duly appreciate the rest of God's good creation itself. God gives man stewardship over creation (Gen. 1:26,28) and Christ's redemptive work will one day have a liberating effect on the good world God made (Rom. 8:20–21), culminating in the establishment of the new heavens and new earth (Rev. 21:1). Since God has given the natural resources of his world for the benefit of mankind, our concern for the well-being of humanity under the lordship of Christ ought to stimulate Christians to think and act wisely about our stewardship of God's creation.

Theology and Science

The relationship between theology and science is an often discussed and sometimes passionately debated matter. One finds various views of the relationship between the two. Some understand the two disciplines to be complementary and friendly laborers in understanding this world[112] while

---

[110] Thus, attempts to redefine marriage in terms of homosexual union are contrary to the teaching of Jesus in the Scriptures.

[111] One must take care, however, not to overlook the clear distinction between man and animals in Scripture. Man, not animals, is made in the image of God (Gen. 1:26–27). The animals are given to man for his consumption (Gen. 9:2–3). Further, the divine instructions for man's care of the animals are themselves given, in part, for the direct benefit of mankind (1 Cor. 9:9–10).

[112] For helpful insights on this point, see the following: J. P. Moreland, *Christianity and the Nature of Science* (Grand Rapids: Baker, 1989); Harry L. Poe and Jimmy H. Davis, *Science and Faith: An Evangelical Dialogue* (Nashville: Broadman & Holman, 2000). For a more succinct treatment of these matters, see J. P. Moreland and William Lane Craig, *Philosophical Foundations for a Christian Worldview* (Downers Grove: InterVarsity, 2003), chaps. 15–17.

others understand them in the context of conflict or warfare.[113] One should resist modernist temptations to submit theology to science, in which case science is afforded a sovereignty with respect to questions of origins that rightfully belongs to the Creator.[114] The Bible, as the Word of the God who created the heavens and the earth, speaks truthfully about God's world. It does not, of course, tell us everything about this world. Christianity itself, with its understanding of an ordered, purposeful cosmos provides the basis for inquiry into the nature of the world.[115] In this way both theology and science offer genuine insight into the reality of the universe. The Bible offers knowledge perfectly given by the Creator about his good creation while science offers knowledge given by humans about that same creation.

Recent developments in various fields contribute in a substantial way to our understanding of the proper relationship of theology and science. The rise of a newer discipline in the twentieth century, the philosophy of science, has shed light on some important issues related to the nature of scientific method and claims made on that basis, and has challenged the rise of "scientism" and the assumptions of philosophical naturalism.[116] Some scientists have begun to scrutinize theories associated with evolutionary naturalism, thus offering a needed challenge to "scientism" and also proceeding with work needed to sustain legitimate scientific inquiry. The work of those in the Intelligent Design movement is notable in this respect.[117]

One other important consideration when thinking of the relationship of theology and science is that we must not fall prey to the temptation to read the Bible through the lenses of science. Whether based on more liberal

---

[113] See the nineteenth-century works by John William Draper, *History of the Conflict between Religion and Science* (1874) and Andrew Dickson White, *A History of the Warfare of Science with Theology* (1896). The instance of Galileo is an interesting example of this question during the Renaissance period and one that is too often misunderstood. For a brief explanation, see Nancy R. Pearcy and Charles B. Thaxton, *The Soul of Science: Christian Faith and Natural Philosopy* (Wheaton: Crossway, 1994), 38–40.

[114] For example, those who espouse theistic evolution. This is not to say that the "hard" sciences cannot offer insights into such matters. It is simply to say that science should not be confused with any sort of "scientism" which pretends to speak authoritatively about matters with more confidence than it should or in ways that unduly extend beyond the bounds of scientific inquiry.

[115] Thus, Christians ought to be at the forefront of scientific inquiry about the universe.

[116] For an introductory discussion see Moreland and Craig, *Philosophical Foundations,* chaps. 15–16. For an example of this kind of work directly related to the underlying philosophical assumptions of Darwinian theory, see Phillip E. Johnson, *Reason in the Balance: The Case against Naturalism in Science, Law & Education* (Downers Grove: InterVarsity, 1995). An excellent introductory guide to these issues is Johnson's *Defeating Darwinism by Opening Minds* (Downers Grove: InterVarsity, 1997); see also two works by biophysicist Cornelius G. Hunter: *Darwin's God: Evolution and the Problem of Evil* (Grand Rapids: Brazos, 2001) and *Darwin's Proof: The Triumph of Religion over Science* (Grand Rapids: Brazos, 2003).

[117] See, for example, Michael J. Behe, *Darwin's Black Box: The Biochemical Challenge to Evolution* (New York: Touchstone, 1996). For an introduction to Intelligent Design, see Jimmy H. Davis and Harry L. Poe, *Designer Universe: Intelligent Design and the Existence of God* (Nashville: Broadman & Holman, 2002).

assumptions or more "fundamentalist" assumptions about origins, one must not bring such assumptions to the reading of the text of Scripture. One way in which this error occurs is that apologetics is sometimes confused with hermeneutics. That is, it is one thing to employ arguments based on scientific inquiry in order to demonstrate the reasonableness of Scripture to the skeptic. It is another thing to employ certain scientific theories as paradigms from which to read the Scriptures.[118] Attempts to read off the doctrine of creation from scientific theories and discoveries and to read the Scriptures through such theories and discoveries betray a misunderstanding of the doctrine of creation as an article of faith (Heb. 11:3).

The Doctrine of Creation and Life in God's Church

Authority in the Church

Articulating, as we have, the doctrine of creation from the basis of Scripture assumes a certain authority of the Bible consistent with the Reformation *sola scriptura* principle. Acceptance of the doctrine that God created and that he created by speaking the world into existence is based on the givenness of the Bible as the authoritative Word of God. Therefore, denial of the doctrine of creation expresses a denial of God's lordship over knowledge and our lives. To reject the reality that "the universe was created by the word of God" (Heb. 11:3) is to cast doubt on the authority of Scripture.[119] Further, the authority of Christ as head (that is, authority) of the church (Col. 1:18) is predicated on Christ's preeminence, established on the basis of his agency as Creator of all things (Col. 1:15–17). We see, then, that the doctrine of creation has important implications for the authority of Scripture with respect to epistemology and for the authority of Christ with respect to ecclesiology.

Sanctification and the Christian Life

The connection between creation and salvation noted previously has important implications for Christian discipleship. In Ephesians Paul notes that

---

[118] One example of this regards the question of the age of the earth. Some assume an old earth and thus read Scripture from that perspective. Others assume a young earth and read the Bible from that perspective. We think the clear reading of Genesis 1 includes an interpretation of the term *day*, described as the period marked off by evening and morning, as a twenty-four-hour period of time. Even if that is so, the question of the age of the earth cannot be settled from the text of the Bible. Further, subscription to a twenty-four-hour interpretation of "day" and a "young earth" theory are not themselves tenets of Christian orthodoxy. Arguments about this issue rage and unfortunately often do so while obscuring the most important teachings of the biblical text on the doctrine of creation.

[119] One should note the manner in which the doctrine of creation (that God made the world and everything in it) is proclaimed along with the doctrine of the resurrection. Both are articles of faith that are held on the authority of the Bible. Denials of the biblical doctrine of creation are really nothing more than the "arguments" and "lofty opinions" that are the strongholds described in 2 Corinthians 10:4–6 that raise themselves up against the knowledge of God.

those saved by grace through faith are God's "workmanship, created in Christ Jesus for good works" (Eph. 2:10).[120] From Israel and the Gentiles God has, in his reconciliatory work, created a redeemed people (Eph. 2:15), which is part of the fulfillment of "all things" by the Creator God (Eph. 3:9). The believer is to "put on the new self" precisely because he has been "created after the likeness of God in true righteousness and holiness" (Eph. 4:24). The God who created the world is the same God who creates redeemed people for good works and the same God who creates a sanctified people to accomplish those good works.[121]

The relation of the doctrines of creation and eschatology in Scripture (e.g., 2 Pet. 3:11–13) serves both to warn and encourage the church about holiness, godliness, and readiness as we who worship the Creator "are waiting for the new heavens and a new earth in which righteousness dwells" (2 Pet. 3:13).

Comfort and Encouragement in Pastoral Ministry

The doctrine of creation also has important implications for pastoral ministry. In Isaiah 40 the assurance of comfort offered to God's people is based on the reality that the Creator, the everlasting God (Isa. 40:28) who is omnipotent ("He does not faint or grow weary") and omniscient ("his understanding is unsearchable") will empower the weary (Isa. 40:30–31). Repeatedly the Bible connects the doctrine of creation to the doctrine of providence, as God who is sovereign, faithful, and powerful cares for his world and his people. Therefore, a fitting response to those who face the difficulties of life in a fallen world is the encouragement for them to "entrust their souls to a faithful Creator while doing good" (1 Pet. 4:19).

Providence

As we have seen, the doctrine of creation leads directly to the doctrine of providence. The Creator of the heavens and the earth is also the one who works continuously to provide for his world. God's world is "held together" (Col. 1:17) by the Son, and the entire universe is sustained by the triune Creator's "word of . . . power" (Heb. 1:3).

In one sense the term *providence* indicates simply that God "provides" for his creation. In another sense the term indicates that God "foresees" or "foreknows." The concept of providence is present in Genesis 22 when Isaac inquires of his father about the burnt offering. Abraham assures Isaac

---

[120] The verb κτίζω is used in Ephesians 2:10, 15; 3:9; 4:24. The term is used exclusively for creation by God in the New Testament.

[121] That he who began this "good work" (Phil. 1:6) in us will bring it to completion in Christ draws together nicely the soteriological and eschatological implications of the doctrine of creation for the Christian life.

that "God will provide for himself the lamb" (Gen. 22:8). The Hebrew verb *raah* is translated "provide" and literally means "to see." The Vulgate translates the phrase אֱלֹהִים יִרְאֶה־לּוֹ, as *Deus providebit* ("God will provide") also indicating the notion that Elohim "sees" Abraham's need. The LXX translators render *raah* with ὁράω also meaning "to see." The idea is that Elohim (22:8), Yahweh (22:14), is the God who sees and who will "see to it." The God who sees the needs in his creation is the God who will exercise his power wisely to provide for his creation.

Before surveying the biblical teaching on providence, we will employ the definition of the doctrine offered by Thomas Oden as a summary statement to guide our exploration of the doctrine of providence. Oden states: "Three affirmations summarize the Christian teaching of providence: God is preserving the creation in being. God is cooperating to enable creatures to act. God is guiding all creatures, inorganic and organic, animal and rational creation, toward a purposeful end that exceeds the understanding of those being provided for."[122] With this working definition we: (1) recognize God's work in preserving and governing his creation, and doing so while in some way cooperating with his creatures, (2) recognize that God is accomplishing the purposes for which he created his world; and (3) admit that our understanding of God's providence is limited and that at times we are unable to explain adequately all that we might wish to explain about the doctrine.

When considering the doctrine of providence one must be careful to avoid a few errors. First, one should reject Deistic notions that eliminate the doctrine of providence altogether. Deism is a view that assents to the idea of a Creator but, due to a mechanistic view of the universe, has no room for a God who is involved with the ongoing affairs of the world. Second, one will want to avoid formulations of the doctrine of God that limit God's ability to preserve and govern the world in the ways that the Bible so clearly describes. Contemporary examples of this problem are process theism and open theism.[123] Third, one ought to be wary of the subtle doctrine of "practical" Deism evident among some Christians. The practical Deist, while affirming the orthodox doctrine of providence, lives as though God is not actually involved in the affairs of daily life. A biblical formulation of the doctrine of providence should help to overcome these aberrations. Since the doctrine of providence is so prevalent in the Scriptures, we may only survey the biblical teaching.

---

[122] Thomas Oden, *The Living God: Systematic Theology* (Peabody: Prince, 1998), 1:272–73.

[123] That these versions of theism do so for different reasons is true. Both, nonetheless, articulate unbiblical doctrines of providence. Process theism does so by positing a God who is limited in his power and who, therefore, cannot preserve and sustain the world as the Bible describes. Open theism does so by denying that God has the foreknowledge necessary to care for the world in the manner described by the Bible.

What Does the Bible Say?

The Law

The creation narrative in Genesis 1 provides the first statement about God's providence when God states that he has given plants for food for both humans and animals (Gen. 1:29–30). God provides for fallen man by sustaining human life in general (Gen. 3:20; Eve is "the mother of all living") and providing clothing for the couple soon to be thrust from the garden into the curse-bearing world east of Eden (Gen. 3:21).

God's preservation of life throughout the story of man's rebellion is prominent in the book of Genesis and throughout the Pentateuch. God preserves the lives of Noah, his family, and the animals through the flood (Gen. 6–8). God exercises his providential care continually in both the making and keeping of the covenant with Abraham (Gen. 12:1–3; cf. Gen. 15 and 17).

Further evidence of God's providence within the context of the covenant is seen in the divine provision for Jacob's family through the events of Joseph's life (Gen. 37–50). The Joseph narrative offers a fine portrait of the biblical doctrine of providence. God provides for "the sons of Israel" (Gen. 42:5) through the Egyptians under the wise leadership of Joseph, himself a son of Jacob. This occurs after Joseph's cruel treatment at the hands of his own brothers years earlier (Gen. 37) and through various episodes in Joseph's life. When Jacob's sons appear before their brother in need of assistance, Joseph is able to say, "And now do not be distressed or angry with yourselves because you sold me here, for God sent me before you to preserve life" (Gen. 45:5). Later Joseph comments to his brothers, "As for you, you meant evil against me, but God meant it for good, to bring it about that many people should be kept alive, as they are today" (Gen. 50:20). Joseph then encourages his brothers, telling them, "I will provide for you and your little ones" (Gen. 50:21).

In this story we see God working to preserve his chosen people Israel, to provide generally for the well-being of other peoples, and we see God's providential care exercised in concurrence with the actions of those with evil motives (Joseph's brothers) and pure motives (Joseph).

The providence of God is seen consistently throughout the remainder of the Torah as God provides a leader, Moses, to deliver Israel from bondage to Egypt (Exod. 1–15) as the Lord provides sustenance for his people in the wilderness (Exod. 15–16), and as he grants Israel continued military success against their enemies (Exod. 17:8–13). God's provision is seen also in the giving of the law at Sinai (Exod. 20) and the establishment of codes for worship in the tabernacle and codes for civil conduct recorded in Exodus, Leviticus, Numbers, and Deuteronomy. The concluding chapters of the

Pentateuch rehearse the theme of divine providence, as Moses reminds the people of God's care and provision for them in the wilderness (Deut. 32:10–12) and God's salvation of his people from their enemies (Deut. 33:29). Because of God's providence his people are considered blessed among all the peoples of the earth (Deut. 32:29–30).

The Prophets

The themes of God's providence found in the Pentateuch continue in the prophets. In Joshua 1 God encourages the new leader of Israel, Joshua, to "be strong and courageous" (vv. 6–7,9) since he will be with him and all the people and will never leave them (vv. 5,9). In this text God announces his intention to fulfill his covenant promises by giving to his people the land, but he also reiterates his expectation that they will obey by keeping "all the law" given them through Moses (v. 7–8). Throughout the book of Joshua, the Lord is credited with bringing victory to Israel over the enemy during the conquest of the land of promise.

In 1 and 2 Samuel one sees the establishment of the Davidic lineage, in spite of the rebellious reign of Saul, and God's continuing preservation of David's life against enemies from within and without Israel. This is all in keeping with God's larger kingdom purposes: "He shall build a house for my name, and I will establish the throne of his kingdom forever" (2 Sam. 7:13). This throne and kingdom that will be established forever (2 Sam. 7:16) is, of course, to be fulfilled in Jesus Christ. These promises of throne and kingdom are recounted in prophetic books like Isaiah[124] and Jeremiah, where God sovereignly accomplishes his purposes in spite of the rebellion of his own people. It is made plain that God employs even the pagan enemies to accomplish these purposes in his people Israel.[125]

The Writings

The Psalms continually emphasize God's providential care for his creation, a point seen earlier in the doctrine of creation. In Psalm 33 we are called to praise the Lord (vv. 1–3) because he is faithful and righteous (vv. 4–5), because he is the Creator (vv. 6–9), and because he providentially oversees all of the affairs of man (vv. 10–22). This oversight extends to "all the children of man" (vv. 13–17) as well as to those who worship the Lord (vv. 18–22). Psalm 104 is a notable example of the doctrine of providence.

---

[124] See the comments on providence in Isaiah in the section on the doctrine of creation.
[125] Thus in Habakkuk, for example, the Lord uses Babylon to punish Judah, all the while affirming that the Lord will save his people.

The psalmist recounts God's work as Creator and then recalls his work as sustainer and provider, as shown in the following chart:

The Doctrine of Providence in Psalm 104					
Providential work of God	Governance of nature	Preservation of land and plants	Preservation of animals	Preservation of man	Governance of man
Verse(s)	9–10, 19–20, 22–26, 31–32	13,16	11,14,17–18, 21, 27–30	14–15	35

The book of Job is another classic text from which to explore the doctrine of providence.[126] One sees here the relationship of divine sovereignty to the power given and exercised by Satan (Job 1–2). God permits Satan to test Job (1:12), yet the Lord restricts the ways Satan may do so. God holds in his hand the life of every single creature (12:10) as well as the existence of nations and peoples (12:23–25).

The text of Job records the various opinions of Job's friends about why suffering has entered Job's life. In the end Job and the reader learn that God is sovereign and that the Lord exercises his power wisely to providentially bring about his good purposes, which include not only the restoration of Job's health and fortune (42:10–17), but particularly Job's depth of understanding of and relation with the Lord (42:1–6).

Various Proverbs offer insight into the doctrine of providence. In Proverbs 3:5–6 we learn that the person who trusts God will receive assistance from the Lord. Proverbs 16:1 teaches that whatever the musings of the human mind, right answers to questions ultimately come from the Lord.[127] A man may make certain plans, Proverbs 16:9 instructs, but it is Yahweh who establishes man's steps.[128] Finally, according to Proverbs 16:33, the outcomes of "chance" events are in reality the decision of the Lord, who providentially governs his world.

The book of Lamentations offers a description of providence that takes up some of the most difficult subjects in the doctrine. In particular, the book explains calamity, human suffering, and evil in direct relation to the sovereign acts of God. Calamity is attributed to divine causation (1:13–15; 3:1–17), as is death (2:20–22; 3:43–45). God does not comfort Jerusalem

---

[126] Thomas Aquinas says that "the whole intention of this book is aimed at showing how human affairs are ruled by divine providence." Thomas Aquinas, *A Literal Exposition on Job*, trans. Anthony Damico (Atlanta: Scholars Press, 1989), 71.

[127] See Keil and Delitzsch, *Commentary on the Old Testament*, 6:241.

[128] See also Proverbs 20:24.

(1:17), and he withdraws his hand of protection from his people in the face of the enemy (2:3). He enlists Jerusalem's foes against her (1:17) to bring divine judgment (Lam. 2) and give "full vent to his wrath" (4:11).

At the same time Jerusalem's filthiness is attributed to human causation (1:8), directly because of her sin. God "does not willingly afflict or grieve the children of men" (3:33). In the end the prophet is confident that God who "summoned . . . terrors" (2:22) will also hear prayers and take up the cause of Jerusalem once again (3:41,55–66). In recognizing both the divine and human agency involved in the terrible suffering around him, the author can confess, "The LORD is in the right, for I have rebelled against his word" (1:18), and admit that sinners have no right to complain about divine punishment (3:39). Lamentations reminds the reader that the God who providentially rules his world is a loyal, faithful God (3:22–23), faithful both to bless and to punish, and is the Lord in whom one may have ultimate confidence (3:24–26).

The Gospels

All of the Gospel writers understand their proclamation of the good news of Jesus Christ to be an announcement of the continuing work of God in his world. Matthew and Luke provide genealogies relating the birth of the Christ to God's plan for redemption through his people Israel. Matthew records the angelic announcement that the son born to the virgin Mary will be called Jesus, "for he will save his people from their sins" (Matt. 1:21), a fulfillment of the prophecy in Isaiah 7:14. Luke reports that Simeon, who was "waiting for the consolation of Israel" (Luke 2:25), the one called "the Lord's Christ" (Luke 2:26), held the baby Jesus in his arms in the temple and announced that he had seen God's salvation (Luke 2:29–32). Mark understands "the gospel of Jesus Christ" (Mark 1:1) to be concerned with the accomplishment of God's prophetic promises (Mark 1:2–3) and the coming of the Lord's kingdom (Mark 1:15). John's Gospel informs us that the Word, through whom God's world is created, is also the one through whom life is given (John 1:5), who saves people from sin (John 1:29), and who brings the coming kingdom of God (John 3:3).

The themes of God's providential care in sending the Savior and fulfilling his kingdom promises fill the pages of the Gospels and are demonstrated in various ways. First, by performing miracles Jesus demonstrates divine care, power, and purpose within the context of the divine kingdom. Second, Jesus' teachings relate God's desire and ability to bring to fulfillment his plan for salvation and, as well, continually to care for all of his creation (e.g., Matt. 5:45; 6:25–34). Third, the cross and resurrection of Christ serve as the ultimate expression of God's providential care, power, and purpose in his world. Themes prominent in the Torah, such as deliverance from slavery, sustenance amid trials and life's journeys, and victory over opposing forces, are recapitulated in the gospels with Christ's crucifixion and resurrection, with God's enduring provision for his church,[129] and the eternal life that results for those ransomed by the Son (Matt. 20:28; Mark 10:45).

The Acts

The themes just recounted in the Gospel narratives occur also in Luke's book of Acts. God's ongoing kingdom work is reported with the coming of the Holy Spirit at Pentecost and his work to establish the church (Acts 2), to advance and authenticate the gospel message (Acts 2,8,10), and to empower the church in its kingdom mission (Acts 1:8).

Paul notes God's providential oversight of the world in his witness to the people of Lystra (14:17), where God is seen to provide not only rain and "fruitful seasons" but also food and gladness for humans. Paul's sermon in the Areopagus includes a reminder to the pagan listeners that their very being is owed to their existence as "God's offspring" (17:28–29). Just as he providentially sustains the existence of every person, so he will require an account of "all people everywhere" (17:30) as he exercises his role as judge of his world (17:31).

Two passages in Acts serve as key texts for understanding the relationship of divine sovereignty and human freedom in the doctrine of providence. In his sermon at Pentecost Peter affirms that Jesus was "delivered up according to the definite plan and foreknowledge of God" and that his listeners "crucified and killed" Jesus by "the hands of lawless men" (2:23; cf. 4:10). Later the Jerusalem believers express a similar affirmation of the concurrence of divine sovereignty and human freedom when they state in a prayer that "both Herod and Pontius Pilate, along with the Gentiles and the people of Israel" did what God intended, "to do whatever your hand and your plan had predestined to take place" (4:27–28). That divine sovereignty and human freedom are affirmed in these statements is indisputable. How one explains the relationship between the two is a matter of ongoing dispute, one which we will take up later.

The Epistles

The continued existence of God's world and his creatures is a providential work of God (Rom. 11:36; Col. 1:17; Heb. 1:3). The fulfillment of God's salvific purposes in his world are in view in the epistles as well (Rom. 1:1–4; Eph. 1:3–14; Heb. 1:1–3; 1 Pet. 1:3–12). The Greek term *oikonomia* is employed by the Apostle Paul to refer to God's administration of his divine plan (Eph. 1:10; 3:9; 1 Tim. 1:4). Further, Paul encourages Christians with the counsel "that for those who love God all things

---

[129] See the prayer of Jesus in John 17.

work together for good, for those who are called according to his purpose" (Rom. 8:28) and that God gives comfort to those in affliction (2 Cor. 1:3–7). God also provides for the sanctification of believers through his providential care as an act of his grace (Titus 2:11–14) and by the work of the Holy Spirit (Rom. 8; Gal. 5:16–25). Even amid suffering believers can be confident that God is working out his purposes for them to live obedient and holy lives (1 Pet. 1:13–21) and may be certain that God will bring to completion his work of salvation in their lives (Eph. 1:13–14; Phil. 1:6) since "those who are called, beloved in God the Father" are "kept for Jesus Christ" (Jude 1).

The Revelation

The final fulfillment of God's promises, the final defeat of God's enemies (19:11–21; 20:7–15), and the final establishment of his kingdom are recorded in the Revelation given to John. In Exodus 19:6 God expressed his plan for his covenant people to be to him "a kingdom of priests and a holy nation." That privilege was forfeited by that generation due to their rebellion, but God accomplished his kingdom purposes through his Son, the Lamb of God. This worthy Lamb makes people "from every tribe and language and people and nation" a "kingdom and priests to our God" (Rev. 5:9–10; cf. 1:6; 1 Pet. 2:9).

Throughout the Revelation God's providential work to accomplish all this is seen as God exercises his power to fulfill his purposes to deliver and preserve his people (e.g., 11:17–18; 22:1–5), as Jesus sends the angel to testify of these things to come (1:1–3; 22:16), and as the Spirit of God intercedes with the church, Christ's bride (22:17), for the second advent of Christ (22:6–21). In Revelation the Lord is seen as the Almighty God (1:8; 4:8; 11:17; 15:3; 16:7; 19:6, 15; 21:22) who rules over all the earth.[130] He is "the Alpha and the Omega" (1:8), "the living one" (1:18) who establishes the new heaven and new earth, and the new Jerusalem (chap. 21) where he sustains eternal life for his creatures (22:1–5) who worship him forever (22:3).

What Has the Church Believed?

Patristic

The *Epistle to Diognetus*, a second- or early third-century explanation of Christianity, teaches that the Creator of the universe is also the one who

---

[130] Interestingly, the term *almighty* (παντοκράτωρ) is unique to Revelation in the New Testament, except for 2 Corinthians 6:18, which is an Old Testament quote.

orders and sustains all of creation.[131] The Creator also provides by sending his "beloved Child" to reveal the divine plan.[132] The justification of sinners by the Son of God is referred to as "the sweet exchange" and "the incomprehensible work of God," and this providential work of God should evoke trust among God's people.[133] The power and provision of God are also evident amid the Christian martyrs since the martyrs' refusal to deny Christ in the face of wild beasts and the increase of the church subsequent to their death is surely a demonstration of the power and presence of God.[134]

In the *Epistle to Diognetus* the discussion of God's continued work in his creation is referred with the term *oikonomia*, a term that refers to the administration of a plan. The term *oikonomia* is employed early in the development of the Christian doctrine of providence: "It was this flexible word, so widely adaptable to so many applications, that the early church teachers chose to express a major segment of Christian doctrine, later called the doctrine of providence."[135]

The Creator is the preserver or sustainer of all of creation and "He provides excellently" since he is good.[136] He exercises care over all things and all creatures.[137] God is also the governor of his world: "He willed that all things should be and they were. He wills the universe to be framed, and it is framed, and all that He wills comes to pass."[138] The author of the *Epistle to Diognetus* noted that God has appointed Christians to live as aliens among the world, and believers must not decline this divine assignment.[139] Irenaeus said that God's providential rule over all things ensures the just punishment of the wicked and the deliverance of the saved.[140]

---

[131] *Epistle to Diognetus* 7.2, in *The Apostolic Fathers,* ed. and rev. Michael W. Holmes (Grand Rapids: Baker, 1999).

[132] Ibid., 8.9–11.

[133] Ibid., 9.

[134] Ibid., 7.

[135] Oden, *Living God,* 273. See Oden, *Living God,* 273–74, for a discussion of how numerous church fathers employ the term (or the Lat. *dispensatio*) in this way, e.g., Justin, Irenaeus, Origen, Basil, Gregory of Nazianzus, Gregory of Nyssa, Augustine, and John of Damascus. Commonly understood to refer to God's "economy" of salvation, the term is also employed more generally to speak of God's providential care for his world. I am indebted to Oden for the material on the Patristic period. For a more extensive discussion of the use of οἰκονομία with reference to God's "providential ordering" in the fathers, see G. L. Prestige, *God in Patristic Thought* (London: SPCK, 1956), 57–67.

[136] John of Damascus, *On the Orthodox Faith* 2.29, NPNF², 9:41–42. See also Gregory of Nyssa, *The Great Catechism* 5, NPNF² 5:478.

[137] Irenaeus, *Against Heresies* 3.25.

[138] John of Damascus, *Orthodox Faith* 2.29. See also Athanasius, *Against the Heathen* 38. Athanasius employs the illustration of a lyre to explain God's rule. Were one to hear a lyre at a distance, one would not assume that the strings play themselves, or that there is more than one player, but rather that there is one musician.

[139] *Diognetus* 6.10.

[140] Irenaeus, *Against Heresies* 3.25.

Augustine noted that when God "rests" in Genesis 2:3, he does so only with respect to the work of creation but not with respect to providence: "[T]he universe will pass away in the twinkling of an eye if God withdraws His ruling hand."[141]

While God does govern his world, this does not negate genuine human volition. Augustine maintained that human will is not destroyed by divine necessity and that, for example, when a man sins it is the man himself who wills to sin.[142] Tertullian argued that the fall of man and subsequent evil that exists in the world are not attributable to God but result from the exercise of human choice that is contrary to God's law.[143]

This concurrent or cooperative effort of man with the providential God is seen throughout the patristic tradition.[144] Justin held together the doctrine of God's providence and human freedom.[145] Augustine insisted that God's promise to care for our daily needs is doubtless true but that we are not exempt from the exercise of our own ability to gain provision for daily life.[146] John of Damascus understood that God's providential care is sometimes according to God's good will and sometimes according to God's permission. For the Damascene, "[T]he ways of God's providence are many, and they cannot be explained in words nor conceived by the mind."[147]

Medieval

Anselm stated that "only an unreasonable mind can doubt that all created things flourish and persist in their existence as long as they do, because they are sustained by what gave them existence in the first place."[148] God the Creator is, therefore, God the sustainer. Aquinas, citing Hebrews 11:3, concluded that God's creatures are all sustained by the Lord himself.[149] God is the primary cause of preservation in the world, yet "there are some created beings that are preservers of others" in the sense of secondary causation.[150] To deny the doctrine of divine providence is "especially harmful to the hu-

---

[141] Augustine, *Literal Meaning of Genesis* 4.12.
[142] Augustine, *The City of God* 5.10.
[143] Tertullian, *Against Marcion* 2.5–10.
[144] Oden, *Living God,* 283–86.
[145] Justin Martyr, *First Apology* 44.
[146] Augustine, *Of the Work of Monks, NPNF*[1], 520–21.
[147] John of Damascus, *Orthodox Faith* 29. On the matter of divine and human agency, he says that the good that man does has its antecedent in God's "good will and pleasure," while evil works have no antecedent in God and are his concession to our free will.
[148] Anselm, *Monologion* 13.
[149] Aquinas, *Summa Theologica* 1a.104.1.
[150] Ibid., 1a.104, 2. For a brief explanation of the way in which Thomas understands primary and secondary causation, see Brian Davies, *Aquinas,* Outstanding Christian Thinkers (New York: Continuum, 2002), 77–78.

man race, for if divine providence is taken away, no reverence for or fear of God based on truth will remain among men."[151]

The triune God, said Anselm, is not only the sustainer of his world but is the superlatively powerful master and the superlatively wise controller of things, a truth that should evoke worship among God's creatures.[152] For Aquinas, God is the governor of his world, which is a result of his goodness.[153] Since there is only one God and he is Lord, the world is ruled by this one.[154] Evil is present in the world God governs, and it is understood as the absence of good.[155] God is not the author of evil, however, since evil is caused by defect and there is no defect in God.[156]

Reformation

The Reformers understood the doctrine of providence to be essentially tied to belief in the doctrine of creation. Luther, in his *Small Catechism*, commented on the first article of the creed by affirming that God the Father Almighty, who made heaven and earth, also preserved his life, including his body and soul, his intellect and senses, and all the necessities of life. God's providence included protection from danger and preservation from evil, and included his provision of mercy and grace. The fitting response to God's providence is "to thank, praise, serve, and obey him."[157]

Calvin insisted that to deny the doctrine of providence is to misunderstand what it means to say that God is Creator. He declared:

> But faith ought to penetrate more deeply, namely, having found him Creator of all, forthwith to conclude he is also everlasting Governor and Preserver—not only in that he drives the celestial frame as well as its several parts by a universal motion, but also in that he sustains, nourishes, and cares for, everything he has made, even to the least sparrow.[158]

---

151 Aquinas, *Exposition on Job* 68.

152 Anselm, *Monologion* 80.

153 Aquinas, *Summa Theologica* 1a. 103.1.

154 Ibid., 1a. 103, 3. Aquinas cites 1 Corinthians 8:6. He notes that a "lord" is one who rules (*gubernatio*) over his subjects and argues that the name "God" (*divinitatis*) "denotes some sort of providence. For this reason the almighty power of God somehow includes his knowledge and providence over all things; he would not have the power to do all that he willed with regard to creatures, unless he had knowledge about them and providence over them." See *Summa Theologica* 2a2ae. 1.8.

155 Ibid., 1a.48.1.

156 Ibid., 1a. 49.3. He employs the example of a man limping: "All the motion in the act of limping comes from a person's vitality, but not the ungainliness which comes from the crooked leg. Like all that [is] real and active in a bad action comes from God as its cause, yet the defect there arises from a deficient secondary cause."

157 Martin Luther, *Small Catechism* 2.1, in *The Creeds of Christendom*, ed. Philip Schaff (Grand Rapids: Baker, 1996), 3:77–78.

158 Calvin, *Institutes*, 1.16.1.

There is, therefore, no such thing as "fortune" or "chance" since God is the governor of all things, especially men, but including natural occurrences.[159] Events may seem "fortuitous" to us, however, since we cannot understand the ways in which God has ordained everything.[160] While evildoers are themselves subject to God's rule, nevertheless evil is done by deliberate rebellion against God's will and, therefore, man is culpable for his sin.[161] Calvin disliked the notion that God merely permits certain actions in creaturely agents, stating that those who resort to "bare permission" on God's part to explain things "babble and talk absurdly."[162]

Modern

In the modern period the doctrine of providence has found severe critics. In the seventeenth and eighteenth centuries John Toland and Matthew Tindal promoted Deism, the belief that while God created the world, he does not exercise any ongoing control over it. Deistic notions continue throughout the modern period. In contemporary theology two "risky" forms of providence that propose critiques of the orthodox doctrine of providence are process theism and open theism.

Process theists like John B. Cobb Jr. and David Ray Griffin contend that "the Biblical record is quite ambivalent on the question of whether God is in complete control of the world."[163] They conclude that God "cannot know the future, and God does not wholly control the world. Any divine creative influence must be persuasive, not coercive."[164] God, in fact, is not able to exercise control over the affairs of the world: "God cannot control the finite occasion's self-actualization. Accordingly, the divine creative activity involves risk. The obvious point is that God is not in control of the events of the world, the occurrence of genuine evil is not incompatible with God's beneficence toward all his creatures."[165]

Open theists propose yet another modernist revision to the orthodox doctrine of providence.[166] With process theists they share a risky view of

---

[159] Ibid., 1.16.4–7.

[160] Ibid., 1.16.9.

[161] Ibid., 1.17.5.

[162] Ibid., 1.18.1.

[163] John B. Cobb Jr. and David Ray Griffin, *Process Theology: An Introductory Exposition* (Philadelphia: Westminster, 1976), 52.

[164] Ibid., 53. The motivating factor for this position is the assertion that God's creative activity in the world is rooted in God's identity as "creative love." To suggest that God is in control of the world is antithetical to such love and is considered "coercive."

[165] Ibid., 53.

[166] See, for example, John Sanders, *The God Who Risks: A Theology of Providence* (Downers Grove: InterVarsity, 1998). For a treatment of one particular issue related to providence from an open theist perspective, see Gregory A. Boyd, *Is God to Blame? Beyond Pat Answers to the Problem of Evil* (Downers Grove: InterVarsity, 2003).

providence that includes a denial of the classical formulations of omni-science.[167] Open theists differ from process theists in that they affirm God's omnipotence. That is, God is able to exercise his power but will not do so in violation of human freedom. Open theists perceive this to be a more bibli-cal way of conceiving of providence and one that offers better prospects for issues like the problem of evil.

Baptist Theologians

Such is the pervasiveness of the doctrine of providence in the Scriptures that "should we take from the Bible all that it says of providence, the vol-ume would be greatly lessened and would, in truth, become another book," stated James Pendleton.[168] This is indicative of the manner in which the bib-lical doctrine of providence is received among many Baptist theologians. Boyce disapproved of attempts to distinguish between general providence and special providence. While it is true that God does act with "minute care" to direct certain affairs, Boyce insisted there is no "careless provi-dence about all things else."[169]

A. H. Strong contributed a useful fourfold description of God's providence:

> (a) Preventative,—God by his providence prevents sin which would otherwise be committed. . . . (b) Permissive,—God permits men to cherish and to manifest the evil dispositions of their hearts. . . . (c) Directive,—God directs the evil acts of men to ends unfore-seen and unintended by the agents. . . . (d) Determinative,—God determines the bounds reached by the evil passions of his creatures, and the measures of their effects.[170]

How Does It All Fit Together?

We have seen how the Bible teaches God's providential care and gover-nance of all of his creation. We have surveyed some of the major contours of the understanding of the doctrine in the history of the church. Now we will discuss some of the central teachings and critical questions associated with the doctrine of providence. As we saw in the history of theology, the doctrine of providence has generally been understood under the headings

---

167 They deny that God can properly possess knowledge of the future actions of free creatures. In so doing they deny traditional formulations of exhaustive foreknowledge and simple foreknowledge.
168 Pendleton, *Christian Doctrine,* 128.
169 Boyce, *Abstract of Systematic Theology,* 227.
170 Strong, *Systematic Theology,* 423–25.

of Preservation, Concurrence, and Government,[171] categories that are helpful when describing the biblical teaching about providence. We begin, then,
with these three important concepts.

Three Important Concepts

Preservation

The Bible often describes God's preservation and care for all of his
creation. The universe is sustained continually by the Lord who created it
(Neh. 9:6; Col. 1:17; Heb. 1:3). God cares for the good earth that he created (Pss. 65:9–13; 135:6–7) and preserves life among both plants (Pss.
104:13,16; 147:8; Matt. 6:28,30) and animals (Isa. 18:5–6; Pss. 104:11,14,
27–30; 147:9). He preserves all of humanity by generally sustaining human
life (Job 34:14–15; Acts 17:28), by his continual awareness of the human
condition (Ps. 139), and through his provision of basic necessities and satisfaction in life (Ps. 104:14–15; Acts 14:17). Special care is promised for
God's people, not least of which is God's assurance that he will preserve
man by salvation to eternal life. God's preservation of his people extends
to deliverance from enemies (Pss. 138:7; 143:11) as well as for the basic
needs in life (Matt. 6:25–34). The assurance of such provision is based not
only upon God's power to provide but upon his intimate knowledge of his
people (Ps. 1:6; Matt. 10:26–33; 1 Cor. 8:3).

Concurrence

By concurrence we mean that both God and his creatures work together to accomplish God's sovereign purposes in his world. Already in
the creation account in Genesis, one observes divine agency working together with creation to accomplish the Lord's work (Gen. 1:11–12). This
cooperation between God and creatures to accomplish his purposes occurs
at various levels. Psalm 104 provides examples of the ways in which the
natural processes of God's world, which is preserved and governed by him,
are used to provide for the sustenance of plants, animals, and humans (see
chart on p. 283).

Psalm 127 indicates that general activities in life are accomplished both
by divine and human agency: "Unless the Lord builds the house, those who
build it labor in vain. Unless the Lord watches over the city, the watchman
stays awake in vain" (v. 1). The basic activities of awakening, sleeping,
eating, and working, along with the maintenance of the family, are works
which involve divine and human cooperation.

---

[171] There are, of course, different ways of expressing these categories. One may say that God
"sustains" or "conserves" to speak of divine preservation. Thomas Oden says that God *upholds*
(preservation), *cooperates* (concurrence), and *guides* (governance) to speak of the way in which the
classical Christian exegetes speak of the doctrine. Oden, *Living God,* 270–71.

The consequences and judgment of sin are often portrayed with respect to both divine and human agency. We examined this in some detail in the book of Lamentations. Other texts speak similarly of divine and human concurrence in this matter (1 Kings 9:9; 2 Chron. 9:13; Ezra 9:13; Neh. 13:18).

The work of both evil spirits and evildoers is also viewed as concurrently a divine and creaturely activity. Certain texts indicate that God sends evil spirits to accomplish his purposes (1 Sam. 16:15,23; 18:10). Second Samuel 24:1 and 1 Chronicles 21:1 taken together offer the insight that while Satan performs his evil activity to accomplish his purpose, God sovereignly acts to order demonic activity to accomplish divine purposes. Such concurrence is evident in the book of Job as well. In Genesis 50:20–21 the Scriptures record that the evil actions of humans are employed by God to accomplish divine purposes. In the same way the dispersion of the Jerusalem church (Acts 8:1) by evil persecutors (Acts 4–7) resulted in the accomplishment of God's kingdom purpose (Acts 1:8) for the gospel to be carried abroad (Acts 8:4). In this case the concurrent work of human evildoers and the God of providence results in the accomplishment of God's gospel plan (Eph. 1:10; 1 Tim. 1:4).

Perhaps the epitome of the theme of concurrence with respect to God's economy, specifically his "economy of salvation" is recorded in Acts 2:23 (cf. Acts 4:10) and Acts 4:27–28, where the crucifixion of Jesus Christ is attributed to the agency of humans and to the plan and hand of God (Acts 2:23; 4:28). Clearly what men meant for evil God meant for good. This cooperative effort in God's work of salvation extends to the doctrine of sanctification as well (Phil. 2:12–13).

God's providential care for his church is often cast in terms of concurrence. It is God, through the Holy Spirit, who gives spiritual gifts to believers and empowers the saints to use them (1 Cor. 12:11), yet it is also true that believers are to exercise the gifts given them (1 Cor. 12–14; cf. Rom. 12:6). The ministry of prayer provides another example of such cooperative effort. In Acts 12 the church earnestly prayed for the release of Peter (Acts 12:5), and it was God who released him from prison (Acts 12:6–7,17). In 2 Corinthians 1:9–11 Paul was confident about God's deliverance, and he encouraged the Corinthian believers to help him through prayer since the blessing of God's deliverance is "granted us through the prayers of many." In James 5 the reader learns that the prayers of godly believers are effective but only insofar as God works as the church prays (James 5:15,18; cf. 1 Kings 18:41–46).

Governance

While God has so ordered his creation that he accomplishes his plan along with creaturely cooperation, we must not lose sight of the central biblical theme of God's governance or rule over the universe. This doctrine, the doctrine of sovereignty, is critical for understanding the doctrine of providence and for answering various questions that arise in light of the Bible's teaching of God's providence.

The Bible portrays God as Lord, King, and Ruler (Pss. 2; 29:10; 24; 1 Tim. 1:17; 6:15; Rev. 19:6). The terms Lord and King refer to God's sovereignty and signify that Yahweh is master of the world he made. As King, he is ruler of the kingdom he established (Isa. 9:7; Zech. 14:9; Matt. 6:10; 1 Cor. 15:24; Rev. 12:10). God exercises rule of the heavenly objects in the cosmos (Gen. 1:14–19; Ps. 104:19). He also commands the elements of nature to do his bidding (Gen. 7:4; 8:2; Job 26:8; 38:22; Pss. 107:25; 147:16; 148:4–5,8; Matt. 5:45; 8:27; Luke 8:24). The natural rhythm of nature, daily and seasonal change, is under the Lord's control (Gen. 1; Ps. 104:19–20). The occurrence of miracles, instances of God's special intervention in the affairs of his world, is also an example of his rule over his creation.

While human kings and nations possess certain power, they themselves are under the dominion of the Lord who is King (Deut. 32:8; Pss. 33:10–11; 47:2,7,9; 96:10; Prov. 21:1). Creaturely actions in general are governed by God's rule (1 Sam. 2:6–7; Ps. 31:14–15; Prov. 16:9). Sinful actions do not occur apart from God's governance (see above, under "Concurrence"; Acts 14:16; 17:30; Rom. 1:24,28). We have seen earlier the way in which God governs evil by way of judgment (Gen. 7:11), but the Bible also informs us that God governs man's rebellion by restraining evil (Matt. 24:22; 2 Thess. 2:6; 2 Pet. 2:9). God ultimately subjects and judges Satan and his demons, along with all those not redeemed by Christ (Rev. 20:7–15). God exercises control over death and Satan through the work of the cross where he also sovereignly provides for redemption for those who are in Christ (1 Cor. 15:54–57; Col. 2:13–15; Rev. 21).

God called Abram and chose to create a people for his own purposes from him (Gen. 12:1–3). God's electing providence is also at work in the redemption of sinners (Eph. 1:4–5). While awaiting the final establishment of the Lord's kingdom, the church exists under the headship of Christ (Col. 1:18; Eph. 5:23) and is sovereignly guided and empowered by the Holy Spirit (1 Cor. 12).

The following chart exhibits how these three concepts in the doctrine of providence are evident in one *sedes doctrinae* (seat of doctrine) that we have examined—Psalm 104:

Preservation, Concurrence, and Governance in Psalm 104	
Preservation	Land/Plants (vv. 13,16). Animals (vv. 11,14,17–18, 21, 27–30). Man (vv. 14–15).
Concurrence	Waters flow to provide for animals (vv. 10–11,13). Grass and other plants grow to feed animals and man (vv. 14–15). Trees watered by God provide nesting place for birds (vv. 16–17). Mountains and rocks provide habitable environment for animals (v. 18). The lion, which seeks its prey, seeks it from God (v. 21). Men and animals exist according to the rhythm of nature established by God (vv. 22–23). God gives food to the animals; the animals "gather up" the food (v. 28).
Governance	God sets and maintains the boundaries of the seas (v. 9). God causes waters to flow from springs, and he satisfies the earth with waters (vv. 10,13). God maintains the rhythm of seasons and days (vv. 19–20; 22–23). God continually governs the earth for his own glory (vv. 31–33). Man finds his just end under the providential rule of God (v. 35).

Providence and the Question of Divine Sovereignty and Human Freedom

A perennial question in Christian theology revolves around the relationship between divine sovereignty and human freedom. That the Scriptures affirm both divine sovereignty and human freedom is obvious. A few matters in this relationship, however, give rise to certain tensions.

First, one must determine the nature and extent of God's sovereignty. We have seen that God's sovereignty, his lordship, is absolute. He is the Lord (Ps. 115:3; Dan. 4:35); he exercises his lordship always and will ever be the Lord (Phil. 2:11; Rev. 1:8; 19:16). One should be careful, however, not to confuse divine sovereignty with divine omnipotence. The Bible does indeed affirm both doctrines; God is the Lord of heaven and earth, the ruler of all creation; and his power is complete and unlimited. While true, the fact of God's sovereignty does not logically entail the exercise of his power in such a way as to always limit or eliminate genuine human freedom.

Second, one must determine the nature and extent of human freedom. The Bible teaches that God created a world with genuine human freedom. Repeatedly the acts of humans are referred to in the Bible as genuinely free acts. Texts like Deuteronomy 30:15 reflect that God's call to obedience involves something other than the mere appearance of freedom. Man exercises genuine freedom in that he has the ability to make real choices, in particular, real moral choices. We are, as Wayne Grudem states, free to "make *willing* choices, choices that have *real effects.*"[172] These facts seem hardly in dispute. What is disputed is the manner in which one explains the tensions resident in the affirmation of the reality of divine sovereignty and genuine human freedom.

Third, one must consider possible explanations for understanding the relationship of divine sovereignty and human freedom since the doctrine of providence teaches that God, in his works of preservation and governance, does determine things in his world and, at the same time, the biblical account speaks of human freedom in God's world.

Incompatibilists argue that genuine human freedom is incompatible with any kind of determinism. As Moreland and Craig describe it:

> Real freedom requires a type of control over one's action—and, more importantly, over one's will—such that, given a choice to do A (raise one's hand and vote) or B (leave the room), nothing determines that either choice is made. Rather, the agent himself must simply exercise his own *causal powers* and will to do one alternative, say A (or have the power to refrain from willing to do something).[173]

The incompatibilist holds that determination from outside the free agent himself is incompatible with genuine human freedom. The freedom in mind here is often called "libertarian freedom" because, on this account of human freedom, humans have the "power of contrary choice." That is, one has the ability to do A or B, or perhaps to make other choices, in a given situation. For the incompatibilist this account of freedom is necessary if freedom is genuine and not merely apparent freedom.[174]

The compatibilist believes that genuine freedom is compatible with certain kinds of determinism.[175] As Feinberg put it, such

> genuine free human action is compatible with causal conditions that decisively incline the will without constraining it. . . . Compatibilists contend that there are free actions and that those actions, though causally determined, are free because they are done in accord with the agent's wishes.[176]

---

172 Wayne Grudem, *Systematic Theology* (Grand Rapids: Zondervan, 1994), 331.

173 Moreland and Craig, *Philosophical Foundations,* 270.

174 For helpful discussions of this position, its relation to indeterminism, and the view of libertarian free will, see John S. Feinberg, *No Other Name: The Doctrine of God* (Wheaton: Crossway, 2001), 626–31. For a comparison with compatibilist views, see Moreland and Craig, *Philosophical Foundations,* 269–82. For a helpful discussion of "varieties of libertarianism," see Thomas Flint, *Divine Providence: The Molinist Account* (Ithaca: Cornell University Press, 1998), 31–34.

175 On "hard" and "soft" determinism, see Feinberg, *No Other Name,* 635–39.

176 Ibid., 637. Feinberg is here describing what he terms "soft determinism" as opposed to "hard determinism."

The freedom in mind here is often called "volitional freedom" because the human agent is truly choosing to do what he wills to do; he is exercising his volition.[177]

There are at least a few things to keep in mind when attempting to think through this difficult issue. First, one must be clear about the nature of human freedom. The term *libertarian* may give those unfamiliar with the technical and more philosophical aspects of the discussion an impression of human freedom that is more consistent with Enlightenment human autonomy than with the biblical account of human freedom. While man does possess freedom, to suggest that "genuine" human freedom is necessarily incompatible with genuine sovereignty is to ignore a significant portion of the Scriptures.

Second, it sometimes appears that discussions of divine sovereignty and human freedom are defined by one's understanding of soteriological matters. That is, one adopts a position of either libertarian or volitional freedom with respect to the matrix of doctrines that constitute the doctrine of salvation[178] and then assumes that this particular view of human freedom must extend to the general discussion of providence. In so doing one may find himself equating his exercise of choice in soteriological matters with the exercise of a choice about something like, for example, the color of shoes one might wear today. We are not convinced that this is necessary. Even if one assumes the exercise of freedom in the volitional sense with respect to salvation, it is not necessarily the case that one assumes a "determinist" stance with respect to all manner of human actions.

Third, we should exercise humility in our treatment of this issue since it is apparent that sincere, thoughtful Christians who are committed to the authority of Scripture have for centuries disagreed about these matters. One might even consider that there may be alternative accounts of the divine sovereignty/human freedom issue that have more explanatory power. Such a recent example in Christian theology is the retrieval of the Molinist or

---

[177] Explanations of the compatibilist position vary with respect to the extent they attempt to explain the relationship of divine sovereignty to human freedom. J. I. Packer, understands this matter as an example of antinomy, that is, "an *apparent* incompatibility between two apparent truths." Guarding against equally dangerous exclusive concerns with either divine sovereignty or with human freedom, Packer wants to keep together what the Bible keeps together since both divine sovereignty and human freedom are biblical truths. Quoting C. H. Spurgeon, who was once asked if he could reconcile these two truths to each other, Packer noted that the great preacher replied, "I wouldn't try. I never reconcile friends." Packer's approach is to affirm the biblical teaching without offering much in the way of speculation as to *how* divine sovereignty and human freedom exist together. See J. I. Packer, *Evangelism & the Sovereignty of God* (Downers Grove: InterVarsity, 1961), 18, 61–62. Other compatibilist accounts attempt to offer more in the way of explanation. See, e.g., Feinberg, *No Other Name*; Paul Helm, *The Providence of God* (Downers Grove: InterVarsity, 1994).

[178] For example, election, providence, a particular view of divine foreknowledge (i.e., simple or exhaustive).

"middle knowledge" position by various theologians and philosophers. It is interesting that people from varying soteriological positions are finding some common ground within the middle knowledge position.[179] While there is value in our attempts to offer good explanations for the relationship of divine sovereignty and human freedom as revealed in Scripture, it is also well to remember that we must not err by speculating too much about such matters (Job 42:3; Ps. 147:5; Isa. 55:8–9; Rom. 9:20; 11:33), and especially in a way that minimizes either biblical doctrine.

How Does This Doctrine Impact the Church Today?

The doctrine of providence bears on many issues in the life of the church, including the most basic issues of life. We now take up three different issues to see the implications of the doctrine of providence for the lives of Christians beginning with two specific subjects (providence and evil and providence and prayer) and one general subject (providence and Christian discipleship).

Providence and the Problem of Evil

That evil is present in the world is typically not disputed.[180] We live in a world where evil is present. Evil is a reality with which humans must live. Since the reality of evil is sometimes seen as the prime defeater of Christian theism, it is necessary to examine the issue. Further, the reality of evil presents some important questions for those who subscribe to the doctrine of divine providence described in this text, not the least of which are important pastoral issues.

A Problem?

The traditional statement of what is known as the "problem of evil" is provided by David Hume in his *Dialogues Concerning Natural Religion*: "Is [God] willing to prevent evil, but not able? Then is he impotent? Is he able, but not willing? Then is he malevolent. Is He both able and willing?

---

[179] So, for example, Thomas Flint argues the middle knowledge position from a libertarian stance, and Terrance Tiessen does so from a volitional account of human freedom. See Thomas Flint, *Divine Providence* or, for a shorter treatment, Flint's "Two Accounts of Providence" in *Divine and Human Action: Essays in the Metaphysics of Theism*, ed. Thomas V. Morris (Ithaca: Cornell University Press, 1998); Terrance Tiessen, *Providence and Prayer: How Does God Work in the World?* (Downers Grove: InterVarsity, 2000); and Bruce Ware, *God's Greater Glory: The Exalted God of Scripture and the Christian Faith* (Wheaton, IL: Crossway, 2004).

[180] Granted, there are those who deny the reality of evil, a position sometimes termed illusionism. Such a position appears in some pantheistic systems, for example, in Christian Science, associated with Mary Baker Eddy. The notion that evil and the pain and suffering associated with it are illusory is difficult to sustain. What appears to be illusory is not evil but illusionism itself.

Whence then is evil?"[181] The perceived problem is this: the presence of evil in the world suggests that Christian claims about God's nature with respect to his power and goodness must fail at one point or another. That is, the claim that God is both omnipotent and omnibenevolent *and* that he made a world in which evil exists is not true.

We will see that there is not a "problem" for Christianity in the sense that Hume's critique suggests. The presence of evil, however, does sur-face certain problems or questions to which Christians should offer biblical answers.

Some Important Distinctions

To adequately answer the questions raised by the existence of evil, one must make at least two important sets of distinctions. First, it is necessary to distinguish natural evil from moral evil. Natural evil is that which "does not involve human willing and acting, but is merely an aspect of nature that seems to work against human welfare."[182] This includes natural disasters, such as earthquakes, hurricanes, and tornadoes that cause suffering among God's creatures. It may also include various diseases or human disorders, such as retardation or insanity.[183] Moral evil is that which is the direct result of human volition. This includes all manner of injustice and behavior performed by humans that results in human suffering. When formulating answers to the questions raised by evil, we will do well to consider the distinction between natural evil and moral evil.

Second, it is necessary to distinguish between religious/experiential questions and theological/philosophical questions that arise due to the presence of evil. Some questions about evil are primarily religious questions. That is, they are questions of human existence and are born of one's experience with evil, pain, and suffering. Such questions arise when one encounters evil, such as when a crime is committed by one human against another. These kinds of questions are personal and emotional and are born out of the very real pain and suffering associated with evil. Other questions about evil are primarily theological or philosophical. That is, they are rooted in one's intellectual reflection about evil, pain, and suffering. Hume's questions about evil are a case in point. The religious/existential and theological/philosophical questions may certainly be related. Yet when questions are raised about evil in relation to the nature of God and his providential care of his world, the adequacy of the answers given sometimes hinges on one's understanding of the distinct question posed.

---

[181] David Hume, *Dialogues Concerning Natural Religion,* part X in *Writings on Religion,* ed. Antony Flew (Chicago: Open Court, 1996), 261.

[182] Millard Erickson, *Christian Theology,* 2nd ed. (Grand Rapids: Baker, 1998), 437.

[183] For a discussion of various natural evils, see John Feinberg, *The Many Faces of Evil: Theological Systems and the Problems of Evil,* rev. ed. (Wheaton: Crossway, 2004), 191–94.

The couple who asks why their young child was run over by a drunk driver and the skeptic who inquires about the logical consistency of Christianity's claims of God's power and goodness in a world in which evil is present may require different kinds of answers.

Some Important Biblical Themes

To adequately offer answers to the various questions that arise due to the reality of evil, one should recognize some important biblical themes that, taken together, help us to form adequate responses.[184]

1. *The theme of a particular world.* The Bible teaches that God created a good world that is ordered and purposeful. He populated this world with various creatures, all for his glory. It is a feature of this particular world that certain creatures possess volition that might be used for either good or evil. It was not God's desire that man possess knowledge of evil (Gen. 2:17), but God in his wisdom did create a good world with such a possibility. And he did so with comprehensive foreknowledge of the actions of the creatures he created.

2. *The theme of creaturely rebellion.* Among the creatures that possess volition whom God created, Lucifer, along with other angels,[185] and Adam and Eve exercised their freedom and rebelled against God. The entrance of sin into the good creation affected not only the relationship of these beings to God[186] but also brought deleterious effects upon all of creation (Rom. 8:20). Thus, moral evil is present in the world due to actions of fallen creatures, both angelic and human; and natural evil is present in the world due to the corruption of creation. The reality of such evil does not defeat the doctrines of divine omnipotence or divine benevolence. Rather, the presence of evil is consistent with the kind of world created by the omnipotent, omnibenevolent God of the Bible.

3. *The themes of divine justice and discipline.* God is holy and just, and he will surely judge sin. The Bible explains that the evil deeds of men are met with divine justice (e.g., the flood of Gen. 6–8). So evil may be present in the world due to human rebellion that demands divine punishment. The Bible also describes instances of evil that occur within the context of divine discipline. We observed in the book of Lamentations that God's just expression of wrath against his people involves the evil deeds of men. In this instance God exercises his wrath *because* of the evil deeds of Judah

---

[184] I am indebted to my colleague and former professor, Russ Bush, for these insights, which he gained from his former professor John Newport. See L. Russ Bush, *A Handbook for Christian Philosophy* (Grand Rapids: Zondervan, 1991), 175–87, and John P. Newport, *Life's Ultimate Questions* (Dallas: Word, 1989), 229–35.

[185] See page 308, "Origin and Fall" in Peter Schemm's chapter, "The Agents of God: Angels."

[186] Satan is, due to his rebellion, the "adversary" of God. Adam through his sin reaps for all humanity corruption and death (Gen. 2:17; 3:19), and man, because of his sin, is universally the enemy of God (Rom. 5:10).

and *by* the evil deeds of the Babylonians. Yet in no way is evil ascribed to God himself. Rather, evil occurs due to the lack of goodness in both the people of God and their enemies, while God remains benevolent in his just discipline of his people.

4. *The theme of spiritual maturity.* Sometimes evil leads to human suffering that is fruitful in the life of believers for purposes of building character and maturity. The Apostle Paul was harassed by a satanic "thorn" (2 Cor. 12:7). Paul's relief was not found in the removal of the thorn; rather it was found in God's gracious use of the thorn to produce godly contentment and strength (2 Cor. 12:10). Job, a man considered righteous by God (Job 1:1), endured tremendous suffering due, with divine permission, to the evil work of Satan. At the conclusion of the book of Job, after being confronted by God himself, Job recognized that the greatest answer to evil is not an answer to the question of "why," but rather it is found in the answer to the question of "who." That is, the answer to evil is best found in the knowledge of God himself, who creates and sustains.

5. *The themes of redemption and eschatology.* The Bible records instances where evil is used by God for his redemptive purposes. The Joseph narrative in Genesis is such an example. The evil actions of Joseph's brothers (Gen. 37) and of Potiphar's wife (Gen. 39) toward Joseph resulted in the placement of Joseph in a position from which he could aid his family and fulfill his role in God's greater redemptive purposes through the people of Israel. So, what men meant for evil, God meant for good, "to bring it about that many people should be kept alive" (Gen. 50:20). This resulted in the providential care of Jacob's family through the concurrence of certain evil human actions, certain righteous human actions, and the divine ordering of all these affairs for God's good purposes, both in that particular situation and in the broader sweep of God's redemptive plan. The ultimate conclusion of God's redemptive purposes involves God's final triumph over evil through the deliverance of the saints and their gathering for the marriage supper of the Lamb (Rev. 19), the final defeat of Satan and all who reject the Lord (Rev. 20), and the fulfillment of the prophecy of the new heaven and new earth (Isa. 65–66; Rev. 21–22) in which God's people enjoy eternal blessing.

6. *The theme of mystery.* These biblical themes help us to answer questions raised by the presence of both moral and natural evil, and they apply in various ways to religious/emotional and theological/philosophical queries. Yet there remain some things we may not understand completely about the presence of evil in God's world or the ways in which God providentially orders the world's affairs (Isa. 55:8–9). Although Christians have compelling answers to the intellectual challenges presented by theological/

philosophical questions regarding evil,[187] at the level of religious/emotional questions we do not always find the answers we seek. As Bush notes, "All of these solutions found in the Bible are legitimate approaches to the problem of evil. Each principle has a specific application, but none of them claims to be the total or final answer. There is always an element of mystery."[188]

The Crucial Answer to the Problem of Evil

One other element in the discussion of providence and the problem of evil must not be overlooked. We refer to this as the "crucial" answer to the problem of evil because it is the "crux" of the matter. The English term *crucial* derives from the Latin *crux,* which means "cross." In the end the cross of Christ serves as the ultimate divine answer to the problem of evil. The crucifixion of Jesus Christ is man's ultimate act of evil. At the cross sinful men took the life of the innocent Son of God (Acts 2:23). At the same time the crucifixion of Jesus Christ is God's ultimate act of benevolence and power. There the Father gave up his Son (John 3:16; 2 Cor. 5:21) and the righteous Son, in the perfect expression of genuine human freedom (Mark 10:45), gave up his life (Rom. 5:8; 2 Cor. 5:21) so that mankind could be reconciled to God. Evil is indeed present in God's world, but it will not prevail. The doctrine of divine providence teaches that God himself answers the problems associated with evil by demonstrating his willingness and power to overcome evil with good.

Providence and Prayer

The ministry of prayer profits much from a biblical understanding of the relationship of providence and prayer. Prayer is a human work but not one done effectively without divine concurrence. In James's epistle we learn that effective prayer involves communication from a human and one of a particular kind. He is a man of faith (James 1:5–8), he is righteous (James 5:16), and he is fervent in his praying (James 5:17–18). At the same time we recognize that God works to answer prayer. James 1:5 states this explicitly. In James 5 there is reference to the narrative of Elijah found in 1 Kings 17–18. In 1 Kings 18:1 the Lord told Elijah that he would send rain, and the rain fell after the persistent prayer of the prophet (1 Kings 18:41–45).

God enables us to pray effectively through the work of the Holy Spirit (Eph. 6:18), which is corollary to the work of God's Word, the sword of the Spirit, in our lives (Eph. 6:17). Further, the Holy Spirit assists us when

---

[187] For a brief survey of some of the important logical answers to such problems, see Moreland and Craig, *Philosophical Foundations,* 537–50, and Feinberg, *Many Faces,* 33–206.

[188] Bush, *Handbook,* 185.

we do not know what we ought to pray (Rom. 8:26–27), and Jesus himself intercedes on our behalf (Rom. 8:34; Heb. 7:25). In this, God works not only in a concurrent fashion as we obediently participate in the ministry of prayer, but the Father also works to preserve and govern through the intercessory ministry of the Son and the Holy Spirit.

Providence and Christian Discipleship

We have examined how the doctrine of providence impacts the church with respect to two specific issues—the problem of evil and the ministry of prayer. Yet the doctrine of providence has implications for all of the Christian life and is critical to one's faithfulness as a Christian disciple. Consider how the doctrine of providence leads Christians to avoid certain things and accept others.

What to Avoid

The doctrine of providence, rightly understood, leads Christians to avoid unbiblical thinking and the actions that follow such beliefs. For example, if God really controls the affairs of the world and providentially sustains life, then Christians should not subscribe to the tenets of astrology, such as the reading of horoscopes, that attribute control of the world to impersonal forces or false gods.

The doctrine of providence also stands against the concept of "chance" or "luck" as a causal agent in the world. For the Christian, then, to wish someone "good luck" is inconsistent with the biblical view that God providentially governs the affairs of the world. Christians would do well, then, to pray for one another and with one another rather than offer meaningless verbal gestures.

The doctrine of providence subverts the practical Deism mentioned toward the beginning of this discussion of providence. We may, more than we think, live as practical Deists when we find ourselves mistakenly overlooking the continual providential work of God in all of human affairs. Thus, when we see a medical recovery that is miraculous, we attribute it to a divine work. But when we awaken in the morning, we give little thought to the reality that the Lord who does not slumber or sleep (Ps. 121:4) has kept us through the night, or we fail to recognize the numerous ways in which he protects us, guides us, and oversees us (Ps. 139). Recognition of the reality of God's providence ought to evoke deep devotion and glad praise.

What to Accept

The doctrine of providence should cause us to live as Christian disciples in at least a few concrete ways. First, the doctrine should help us to live with confidence and contentment since we are surely "kept by Christ"

(Jude 1 NIV). Second, the doctrine should lead us to enjoy peace and rest, even in the midst of difficult circumstances. Finally, the doctrine of providence should guide us to live a life of surrender to the purposes of God for the praise of his name. All this follows from the truth, expressed in the Bible, that God created the world and that he continues to sustain and govern his world, and does so from beginning to end.

CHAPTER 6

The Agents of God: Angels

Peter R. Schemm, Jr.

"Angels are bright still, though the brightest fell."

—Shakespeare, *Macbeth* 4:3

"No one who bows before the authority of the Word of God
can doubt the existence of angels."

—Louis Berkhof, *Systematic Theology,* 143

T he greatest of Christian thinkers have consistently recognized that angels and demons are far more than a divine embellishment designed
to make the Bible interesting. Angels are actual beings whose existence
affects human life. Augustine's classic *The City of God* explains the origin, history, and destiny of two cities and the angelic servants that attend
to them—the earthly city under the power of the devil and his minions
and the heavenly city ruled by God and his host. John Bunyan's work
The Pilgrim's Progress features Apollyon as the most formidable foe that
Christian encountered. By deception and force, Apollyon tries to turn
Christian back to the City of Destruction from which he has come. C. S.
Lewis's *The Screwtape Letters* details the correspondence between the af-
fectionate Uncle Screwtape and another demon, his nephew Wormwood,
whose strategy is marked by a consistent yet subtle undermining of the
faith of the believer to whom he is assigned. For each of these authors, a
spiritual battle rages "in the heavenly places" (Eph. 6:12)[1]—an ongoing
cosmic conflict of the most intense magnitude.
   Some people may be surprised to learn that the doctrine of angels is
directly and significantly related to most of the major doctrines treated

---

[1] Unless otherwise noted, all Scripture citations in this chapter are from the New King James
Version (NKJV).

in Christian theology. Consider the doctrines of *creation* and *providence*. Angels are created beings who administer, in part, God's providence.[2] Angelology relates to the doctrine of *revelation* in at least two ways. Positively, angels are messengers of God's personal revelation. Since God is both transcendent and personal, it makes sense that he chooses holy messengers to communicate truth on his behalf. Negatively, the fallen angel Lucifer is the father of lies (John 8:44). He casts doubt on the revealed Word of God, both living and written.

Regarding the doctrine of *man,* angels and humans share some common features as to their nature and purpose. They are both finite beings, endowed with intelligence and made to glorify God. They differ, however, in many ways. For example, angelic beings do not exist in permanent physical bodies. As to the doctrine of *salvation,* angels are permitted only to look into the things of redemption (1 Pet. 1:12). They do not personally experience salvation. Fundamental to the doctrine of salvation is the work of Christ on the cross or the doctrine of *atonement.* The doctrine of angels converges here with great intensity as the biblical writers speak in terms of the cross as a victory over the one who has the power of death, namely Satan. At Calvary, Jesus Christ triumphed over the principalities and powers of darkness, bringing resurrection victory for all who trust him.

What Does the Bible Say?

Good Angels

Biblical Terminology

In the Old Testament. The term most frequently used to designate angels in biblical Hebrew is *malak.* It is used of human messengers (Hag. 1:13) but predominantly refers to heavenly messengers (Gen. 28:12; Pss. 78:49; 91:11; Zech. 2:3). In either case, *malak* speaks of those who bring a message or act on behalf of another. For example, in Psalm 103:20, "Bless the LORD, O you his angels, you mighty ones who do his word, obeying the voice of his word!" (ESV). Other Old Testament terms used for angelic beings are: cherub (Gen. 3:24; Exod. 25:18–20), holy ones (Ps. 89:7; Job 15:15 ESV), heavenly host (1 Kings 22:19), watcher (Dan. 4:13,17,23), sons of God (Job 1:6; 2:1), and seraphim (Isa. 6:2–3).[3]

---

[2] A. H. Strong introduces his theology of angels by identifying them as "ministers of divine providence . . . some of whom positively serve God's purpose by holiness and voluntary execution of his will, some negatively, by giving examples to the universe of defeated and punished rebellion, and by illustrating God's distinguishing grace in man's salvation." Augustus Hopkins Strong, *Systematic Theology* (Valley Forge, PA: Judson, 1907), 443.

[3] For a helpful treatment of the Hebrew terms and their frequency of use, see James Leo Garrett, *Systematic Theology* (Grand Rapids: Eerdmans, 1990), 1:356–59.

[*In the New Testament.*]The word *angelos* is the corresponding Greek term used of one sent bearing a message. It is translated as either "angel" or "messenger." Of 175 occurrences in the New Testament, it refers to men only six times.[4] The rest of the occurrences speak of supernatural messengers. Often there are qualifiers that make the abode or allegiance of the messengers clear. For example, they are "angels of heaven" (Matt. 24:36; cf. Mark 12:25) or "holy angels" (Luke 9:26; Rev. 14:10). Other New Testament terms used for angelic beings are: spirits (Heb. 1:14), thrones (Col. 1:16), dominions (Col. 1:16; cf. Eph. 1:21), principalities (Rom. 8:38; Col. 1:16; cf. Eph. 1:21), powers (Col. 1:16; cf. Eph. 3:10), and living creatures (Rev. 4:6–9).

[*Individual angels.*] *Michael, Gabriel.* Only two good angels are identified by proper names in Scripture.[5] Michael is referred to as the "great prince" in Daniel (12:1; cf. 10:13,21), the "archangel" in Jude 9, and the one who has charge over a host of angels who prevail in battle over Satan in the Apocalypse (Rev. 12:7–9). The angel Gabriel is found in Daniel where he is the heavenly messenger sent to interpret Daniel's vision of the end times (Dan. 8:16; 9:21) and in Luke where he delivers the message of an answered prayer to Zechariah celebrating the birth of John (Luke 1:19; cf. 1:13). He also brings the message of the Savior's birth to Mary in the city of Nazareth (Luke 1:26).

Origin

Created by Christ. The biblical doctrine of creation is built on the simple fact that only God exists before the act of creation. Angels have not always existed. The psalmist speaks of them as created beings, "Praise him, all his angels; praise him, all his hosts. . . . Let them praise the name of the LORD! For he commanded and they were created" (Ps. 148:2,5 ESV). More specifically, John 1:1–3 says that the Word created "all things." Among the "all things" of Christ's creation are all things that were created whether in heaven or on earth, "visible and invisible, whether thrones or dominions or principalities or powers"—thrones, dominions, etc., includes the entire angelic world (Col. 1:16).

Created before day 1. Scripture does not state explicitly when the angels were created. However, it is understood that by day six they were created since Genesis 2:1 reads, "Thus the heavens and the earth, and all the host of them, were finished" (cf. Gen. 1:31; Exod. 20:11). All of creation, including the angels, was in place by the end of the sixth day, and it was very good. More significantly, Genesis 1:1 is best understood as referring to the

---

[4] Hans Bietenhard, *NIDNTT,* s.v. "Angels," 1:102.

[5] We have not included "Lucifer" here since he is now a fallen angel. See section on "Evil Angels" below.

entire universe, including angels.[6] This would put their creation before day 1. Job says that "the morning stars sang together and all the sons of God shouted for joy" in celebration of God's creation of the earth (Job 38:6–7). The "morning stars" and the "sons of God" had to be present in order to celebrate this creative act. There is no indication that angels continue to be created. Apparently they were all created at the same time.

Nature

In substance, personal spirits. There are several reasons for thinking that angels are personal beings. They express emotions (Job 38:7), render worship (Ps. 148:2), engage humans in conversation (Luke 1:13–17), and make moral choices, whether as holy or fallen creatures (Matt. 25:31; John 8:44). Angels are also spiritual beings. They do not normally appear in bodily form. Hebrews 1:14 reads, "Are they not all ministering spirits (*pneumata*) sent forth to minister for those who will inherit salvation?" Jesus taught that angels neither marry (Matt. 22:30) nor die (Luke 20:36). The Apostle Paul called the angelic world "invisible" (Col. 1:16). Though angels do not have physical bodies, they occasionally reveal themselves in bodily form (Gen. 18–19; Matt. 28:5; Heb. 13:2).

In appearance, often glorious. One of the defining characteristics of good angels is that they often appear with the brightness of God's glory. For example, Luke writes that an angel of the Lord stood before the shepherds of Bethlehem and "the glory of the Lord shone around them, and they were greatly afraid" (Luke 2:9; cf. 9:26). The psalmist speaks of the angels of God as "flames of fire" (Ps. 104:4; Heb. 1:7). In his apocalyptic vision John describes an angel who made the earth "bright with his glory" (Rev. 18:1 ESV; cf. Rev. 10:1; 15:6). Angels appearing in brightness manifest the glorious brilliance of the holy God from whose presence they have been sent (cf. Luke 1:19; Isa. 6:1–7).

In intellect, wise but not omniscient. To have the wisdom of an angel is to be very wise (2 Sam. 14:20). They were involved in the giving of the law (Gal. 3:19) and were sent by God to interpret visions (Dan. 8:16). The Lord Jesus implied that angels have great, although limited, wisdom. Speaking of his own future return, Jesus said, "But of that day and hour no one knows, not even the angels of heaven" (Matt. 24:36). Another limitation is seen in that angels evidently increase in knowledge by observing the unfolding mystery of salvation history (Eph. 3:8–11).

In power, strong but not omnipotent. Angels are "mighty" ambassadors of God who use their strength and authority for God's purposes (Ps. 103:20; Matt. 28:2; Acts 5:19; 12:7; Rev. 10:1; cf. Rev. 8–10). The titles of authority given to some of them indicate suprahuman power (Col.

---

[6] See John H. Sailhamer, *Genesis*, EBC (Grand Rapids: Zondervan, 1990), 20.

1:16; Eph. 6:12). Peter states directly that angels "are greater in power and might" than humans (2 Pet. 2:11). When the Son of Man comes in his glory to judge the nations, he will be accompanied by his holy angels (Matt. 25:31–32), who will assist in the administration of his judgment (2 Thess. 1:7–8). Limitations of their power are seen through their struggles in spiritual warfare (Job 1:12; 2:6; Dan. 10:13; Jude 9; Rev. 12:7).

In presence, many places but not omnipresent. It is impossible to explain the details of how spiritual beings function in the earthly realm of time and space.[7] Clearly though, they are unable to be in more than one place at one time. They move from one place to another, and sometimes this involves delays (Job 1:7; Dan. 9:21; 10:10–14; Luke 1:26). As in wisdom and power, their limited presence is consistent with the fact that angels are finite, created beings.

In status, more glorious than man. Psalm 8 suggests that angels have a more glorious status in the created order than man.[8] Here there is a clear contrast between what might be termed "heavenly glory" and "earthly glory"—both being manifestations of God's glory. Speaking of the difference between angels and man, the psalmist says of God, "Yet you have made him [man] a little lower than the heavenly beings and crowned him with glory and honor" (Ps. 8:5 ESV). The passage is not clear as to exactly how man is "lower" than the angels. It is clear, however, that man is the superior earthly creature since he is "crowned" with "glory and honor" and has dominion over all other earthly creatures (8:6–8). Perhaps the holy angels are more glorious than man in that they bear a more immediate and brilliant display of their Creator's glory. Whatever their status, Paul asserts that saints will one day judge angels (1 Cor. 6:3). These angels may be evil angels judged by Christ and his saints (2 Pet. 2:4; Jude 6), or they may be holy angels who are subject to the future earthly reign of Christ in which believers participate simply by virtue of being in Christ.

Number and Organization

They are many. Scripture speaks of multitudes of angels, so many that they are "innumerable" (Heb. 12:22; cf. Matt. 26:53). At the giving of the law at Sinai, the Lord is said to have come from "ten thousands" of his holy ones (Deut. 33:2). The psalmist says, "The chariots of God are twenty thousand, even thousands of thousands" (Ps. 68:17). One purpose for such a vast host of angelic beings is to offer ceaseless praise and glory to the Lamb, as is evident in John's vision:

---

[7] On the way angels function in space and time, see Norman L. Geisler, *Systematic Theology* (Minneapolis: Bethany House, 2003), 2:484–85.

[8] For the possibility of rendering *elohim* as "heavenly beings," see Willem A. VanGemeren, *Psalms,* EBC (Grand Rapids: Zondervan, 1991), 113. Cf. James Montgomery Boice, *Psalms* (Grand Rapids: Baker, 1994), 1:70–71.

Then I looked, and I heard the voice of many angels around the throne, the living creatures, and the elders; and the number of them was ten thousand times ten thousand, and thousands of thousands, saying with a loud voice: "Worthy is the Lamb who was slain to receive power and riches and wisdom, and strength and honor and glory and blessing!" (Rev. 5:11–12).

They are ordered. The Bible indicates that angels are an ordered company. First, Michael is referred to as an "archangel" in Jude 9. The title conveys some degree of authority and leadership over other holy angels. Michael exercises his authority as he leads a host of angels into battle against the great dragon, Satan, when war breaks out in heaven (Rev. 12:7). Second, Michael is identified as "one of the chief princes" (Dan. 10:13). If he is "one," there must be others. Presumably there are a number of archangels since there are myriads of angels. It may be an archangel other than Michael whose voice announces the Lord's glorious return from heaven (1 Thess. 4:16). Finally, there may be an indication of order and ranking among the angels implicit in these terms: thrones, dominions, principalities, and powers (Col. 1:16). Exactly how each of these terms differ in explaining the angelic order is not clear.[9]

Ministry

To God. The primary ministry of the holy angels is directed to God. There are several ways in which the Bible shows this. First, by nature the holy angels are "ministering spirits" created by God (Heb. 1:14; cf. Ps. 148:2,5). That they minister to God is clearly evidence of being created by God.[10] Accordingly, they are sent forth from God "to minister for those who will inherit salvation" (Heb. 1:14). The same God who initiates the salvation of man sends forth angels to minister to that end. Thus not only are angels sent forth as ministers of God but also as ministers unto God—salvation is from him and to him.

Second, the angels directly glorify God with praise and adoration. The psalmist exclaimed, "Praise the LORD! Praise the LORD from the heavens; praise Him in the heights! Praise Him, all His angels; praise Him, all His hosts!" (Ps. 148:1–2; cf. Job 38:7; Isa. 6:3; Ps. 103:20; Rev. 5:11). Third,

[9] A word of caution is in order here. Lewis Sperry Chafer seems to overstate the unique aspects of each of these words when he says: "Since the Bible does not indulge in useless tautology, it may be believed that there is a specific meaning to each of these denominations (designations). . . . The term *thrones* refers to those who sit upon them, *dominions* to those who rule, *principalities* to those who govern, *powers* to those who exercise supremacy, and *authorities* to those invested with imperial responsibility. Though there is seeming similarity in these denominations, it may be assumed that representation is made by these titles to incomprehensible dignity and varying degrees of rank." Lewis Sperry Chafer, *Systematic Theology* (Dallas: Dallas Seminary, 1947), 2:16–17.
[10] So Calvin, *Institutes,* 1.14.4.

the holy angels direct worship to God alone. This is a crucial point of theology given misguided views of angels that often promote angel worship. One of John's visions in Revelation was that of an angel flying in heaven saying with a loud voice, "Fear God and give glory to Him, for the hour of His judgment has come; and worship Him who made heaven and earth" (Rev. 14:6–7). Even more explicit is the correction John received after falling at the feet of the angel who revealed the new Jerusalem to him: "Then he said to me, 'See that you do not do that. For I am your fellow servant, and of your brethren the prophets, and of those who keep the words of this book. Worship God'" (Rev. 22:9; cf. Exod. 22:20).

Finally, the primary ministry of the holy angels is seen in their obedience to the will of God. All that they do is in accordance with his purposes (Ps. 103:20). Some specific examples of this ministry are:

- Giving the law (Gal. 3:19; cf. Deut. 33:2; Ps. 68:17; Acts 7:38)
- Delivering messages (Dan. 9:20–27; Luke 1:11–20; Acts 8:26)
- Caring for believers (1 Kings 19:5–7; Ps. 91:11)
- Patrolling the earth (Zech. 1:10–11)
- Administering wrath (2 Chron. 32:21; Acts 12:23; Rev. 16:1)
- Announcing Christ (Luke 1:26–38; John 20:12; 1 Thess. 4:16)
- Assisting Christ (Matt. 4:11; 26:53; 28:2–7; Luke 22:43)[11]

Ultimately each of these ministries for God is *unto* God. By nature they are servants of God, by praise and adoration they glorify God, by directing man to worship him alone they extol God, and by carrying out his will in specific ways they minister unto God.

To man. The ministry of the holy angels concerning man can be divided into two main categories: expressions of God's favor and expressions of God's judgment. The favor of God's protection may be seen as early as the garden of Eden, where God set cherubim to guard the way to the tree of life and to keep man from another dreadful, sinful act of defiance (Gen. 3:22–24). Lot and his family were protected by two angels, who led them out of Sodom (Gen. 19:1,15–17). The psalmist spoke of protection afforded by angels: "He shall give His angels charge over you, to keep you in all your ways" (Ps. 91:11; cf. Matt. 18:10).

Another expression of God's favor that sometimes comes through the ministry of angels is divine revelation. Though it is not typically thought of in terms of "favor," the giving of the law was nevertheless an act of favor in which the angels shared (Gal. 3:19; cf. Deut. 33:2). It is through the revealed law of God that the godly person is blessed and sinners are made

---

[11] A brief survey of how the angels were involved in the life of Christ is found in the third part of this chapter.

aware of their disobedience (Ps. 1:1–2; Rom. 7:7). The angel Gabriel revealed to Mary that she had found favor with God. She would soon be the mother of Jesus, the Savior (Luke 1:30–32).

Angels express the favor of God in salvation when they join with God in rejoicing over the conversion of even one sinner. In the words of Jesus, "Likewise, I say to you, there is joy in the presence of the angels of God over one sinner who repents" (Luke 15:10; cf. 15:7). This passage is often spoken of as if the angels are the only ones in heaven rejoicing. More accurately, the angels are here rejoicing with God over the repentance of one sinner.[12] All of heaven celebrates together when one sinner turns to Christ for salvation.

Angels also minister to humans by expressing God's judgment. Throughout Scripture angels administer the wrath of God toward man through plagues, wars, and various judgments (1 Chron. 21:12; 2 Chron. 32:21; Rev. 16:1–21). King Herod experienced the immediate judgment of God at the hand of an angel because he harassed the Jerusalem church and denied God the glory due his name: "Then immediately an angel of the Lord struck him, because he did not give glory to God. And he was eaten by worms and died" (Acts 12:23).

In the future there will be several points at which angels are actively involved in administering the judgment of God on man. The Lord's return will be announced with the voice of an archangel (1 Thess. 4:16), and he will be accompanied by "His mighty angels, in flaming fire taking vengeance on those who do not know God, and on those who do not obey the gospel of our Lord Jesus Christ" (2 Thess. 1:7–8). In the harvest at the end of the age, the Son of Man will send out his angels to separate the wheat from the tares in everlasting judgment (Matt. 13:36–43; cf. Rev. 16:1–21). Finally, as a result of God's perfect judgment, the New Jerusalem is protected by angels who stand at each of the twelve gates apparently as God's sentinels who guarantee that nothing unclean or defiled ever enters the city (Rev. 21:12).

Destiny

No biblical texts suggest that the holy angels will one day lapse or fall into sin. Rather, the passages treated above indicate that they are destined to continue in God's service throughout all eternity. Additionally, some of the passages where angels are actively involved in administering the judgment of God show that there are good angels who remain faithful until the end (cf. Rev. 5:8–14). Paul affirmed this idea when he spoke of the "elect angels" (1 Tim. 5:21), a term that clearly indicates a sense of permanency as well as goodness. This confirmation in holiness apparently took place at a time of testing when Lucifer and those who followed him (e.g., demons)

---

[12] See Darrell L. Bock, *Luke,* BECNT (Grand Rapids: Baker, 1996), 1304.

fell. Both good angels and demons are permanently sealed in their moral status before God.

Excursus 1: The Angel of the Lord

The phrase "the Angel of the Lord," as found in the Old Testament, refers to a mysterious messenger of God properly identified as the preincarnate Word, the second person of the Trinity. He appears in a temporary bodily form that anticipates his permanent incarnation—"a prelude to the mystery which was afterwards exhibited when God was manifested in the flesh."[13] He is called "the angel of the Lord" not because he is a created being like all other angels but because of his unique status as the divine messenger or Word of God. Other theories about the nature of the Angel of the Lord seem inadequate in light of the divine nature of his ministry and his direct identification as God.[14]

The phrase occurs throughout the Old Testament: in the Law, the Prophets, and the Writings. It appears more than once in the following chapters: Genesis 16,22; Numbers 22; Judges 2;6;13; 2 Kings 1; 1 Chronicles 21; Psalm 35; Zechariah 1; 3. In the Old Testament, "The angel of the Lord" should be understood as synonymous with "the angel of God" (Gen. 21:17; 31:11; Exod. 14:19) and the "Commander of the army (host) of the LORD" (Josh. 5:14). Additionally, some believe he is referred to as "the Angel who has redeemed me" (Gen. 48:16), "My Presence" (Exod. 33:14), and "the Angel of His Presence" (Isa. 63:9).[15]

The ministry of the Angel of the Lord derives from and accords with his divine nature. For example, he appeared to Hagar in the wilderness instructing her to return to Sarai and promising her that he would multiply her descendants exceedingly. The statement made by the angel, "I will surely multiply your offspring" (Gen. 16:10 ESV), the reference to "the LORD who spoke to her" (16:13 ESV), and Hagar's response, "You are the God who sees" (16:13), make it clear that this was no ordinary angel. Hagar understood that the angel promised to do for her what was peculiar to God alone—which is precisely why she identified him as "God."

In the land of Moriah, Abraham prepared to obey God by sacrificing his son Isaac when he had an encounter similar to Hagar's. The Angel of the Lord called out to him from heaven saying, "Now I know that you

---

[13] John Calvin, *Commentaries on the Book of Joshua,* trans. Henry Beveridge (Grand Rapids: Baker, 2003), 88.

[14] Garrett identifies four major theories as to the identity of "the Angel of the LORD," the first of which is the view affirmed here: (1) Logos theory (the preincarnate Christ), (2) angelic theory (a created spiritual being who acts as Yahweh's ambassador), (3) interpolation theory (the "angel of" phrase was redacted or inserted into the text as a literary device to soften the anthropomorphic language used of Yahweh), and (4) instrumental theory (a visible or audible instrument of divine manifestation and communication; Yahweh himself, not a distinct angel). The third view noted by Garrett is problematic for evangelical interpreters of Scripture. Though we see the first view as the best option, evangelical scholars also hold to the second and fourth view. See Garrett, *Systematic Theology,* 359–61.

[15] Cf. ibid., 359; Robert P. Lightner, "Angels, Satan, and Demons," in *Understanding Christian Theology,* ed. Charles R. Swindoll and Roy B. Zuck (Nashville: Thomas Nelson, 2003), 567.

fear God, since you have not withheld your son, your only son, from Me" (Gen. 22:12). Abraham understood that God was speaking to him and providing for him and so he named the place "the LORD will provide" (22:14). The Angel of the Lord called to him a second time saying, "By Myself I have sworn, says the LORD . . . In your seed all the nations of the earth shall be blessed, because you have obeyed My voice" (22:16–18). The call of the Angel of the Lord in verse 15 and the words of the Lord in verses 16–18 are best understood as coming from the same person—another direct identification as God. Thus God tested Abraham (22:1), provided the necessary substitute sacrifice (22:14), and promised to bless all the nations through Abraham's seed (22:18).

A final example of the ministry of the Angel of the Lord that confirms his divine nature is found in the life of Jacob. When "the Angel of God" spoke to Jacob in a dream, he instructed Jacob to return to his birthplace saying, "I am the God of Bethel, where you anointed the pillar and where you made a vow to Me" (Gen. 31:13). Note that the Angel of God is also the God of Bethel. Jacob met the Angel again at the Jabbok River when he wrestled until daybreak with a "man" who, as "God," blessed him (32:22–32). Here Jacob saw God "face to face" (32:30). The Prophet Hosea confirmed that the "man" Jacob met that night was "the Angel" and that he was also "God" (Hos. 12:3–4).

To conclude, there are several reasons to believe that the preincarnate Christ is the Angel of the Lord.[16] First, Jesus Christ is the eternal Son of God and the eternal Word of God (John 1:1–18; Heb. 1:1–4). This is the classic Christian expression of Jesus' preincarnate state.[17] His existence prior to the incarnation and his subsequent incarnation correspond perfectly with the manifestation of divinity in "bodily form" that sometimes characterizes the appearance of the Angel of the Lord.

Second, the Angel of the Lord is called God. We have seen that the Angel of the Lord is directly identified as God in the encounters of Hagar, Abraham, and Jacob. Additionally, the apparent interchangeability of "God" and "the Angel" used by Jacob in Genesis 48:15–16 clearly ascribes deity to the Angel.

Third, though identified as God, the Angel of the Lord is also distinct from God. For example, Zechariah 1:12 has the Angel of the Lord addressing the Lord directly saying "O LORD of hosts, how long will You have mercy on Jerusalem?" (cf. 3:1–2). The Angel, then, is distinct from Yahweh. In Genesis 21:17, the Angel of God (Elohim) spoke to Hagar on behalf of God (Elohim) who heard the voice of Ishmael crying from under a bush in the wilderness of Beer-sheba. Again, the Angel was distinct from Elohim. Thus there is a clear distinction between the Angel of the Lord and God himself. Given the identification of the Angel as a divine being, it is best to understand the distinction between the Angel

---

[16] We are following Robert Lightner's four main points here, though they are sometimes worded and supported differently as they relate to our treatment. Lightner, "Angels, Satan and Demons," 570–71.

[17] See Thomas C. Oden, *The Word of Life*, Systematic Theology, vol. 2 (Peabody, MA: Prince, 1998), 57–74.

and Yahweh or Elohim, in these cases, as a trinitarian distinction between the Father and the Son.[18]

Fourth, understanding the Angel of the Lord as the preincarnate Christ is the explanation that fits best with the doctrine of the Trinity. It is no mere coincidence that Christ is the only member of the Godhead who is ever manifested in permanent visible form—the incarnation—and that the Angel does not appear again in Scripture after the incarnation.[19] As the eternal Logos or Word of God it is most fitting that he is identified as this divine messenger. Additionally there is an obvious parallel between the ministries of the angel who is sent on behalf of the Lord in the Old Testament and the Son sent on behalf of the Father in the New Testament. Both the Angel and Jesus Christ ministered through revelation, deliverance, protection, intercession, confirmation of God's covenant, and judgment.[20] Therefore we believe that the Old Testament appearances of the Angel of the Lord are rightly called Christophanies, appearances of Christ.

Evil Angels

Biblical Terminology

[In the Old Testament.] The Hebrew verb *satan* means to oppose or to act as an adversary or accuser. In noun form, *satan* is used of human adversaries, as in the Philistine commanders fearing that David would be their "adversary" in battle (1 Sam. 29:4b; cf. 2 Sam. 19:22b; Ps. 109:6), and of a suprahuman being who opposes God and his people. As a fallen angel, Satan accused Job before God (Job 1:6–12; 2:1–7), Joshua before the Angel of the Lord (Zech. 3:1–2), and stood against Israel, inciting David to take a census of Israel (1 Chron. 21:1). The *helel* of Isaiah 14:12 (lit. "shining one") is translated "morning star" (NIV) or "Day Star" (ESV) or "Lucifer" (NKJV) and is rightly understood by many as a reference to Satan. Ezekiel 28:14 may also be a reference to Satan as an "anointed guardian cherub."[21]

---

[18] This is not to say that Yahweh or Elohim is always identified as the Father. It is to say, however, that given the distinctions in these specific texts, such a trinitarian reading is in order.

[19] There is one New Testament use of the phrase "the angel of the Lord" (Matt. 1:24). The repeated occurrence of "an angel of the Lord" in Matthew 1–2 refers to an angel, not "the Angel of the Lord" in the technical sense as in the Hebrew Scriptures. Matthew 1:24 is the single occurrence with the definite article in the entire New Testament—including the other three occurrences in Matthew's prologue (1:20; 2:13,19). The other occurrences are all missing the definite article. We take Matthew 1:24, then, to be a reference to 1:20—the angel already mentioned, not "the Angel of the Lord" in the technical sense.

[20] So C. Fred Dickason, *Angels, Elect and Evil* (Chicago: Moody, 1975), 81–82. The categories listed here are selected from Dickason's larger list which identifies nine distinct parallels in ministry.

[21] Contra Garrett, *Systematic Theology*, 1:373–74. Though hotly debated, we believe a typological understanding of both Isaiah 14 and Ezekiel 28 is warranted. The language of both texts transcends the earthly rulers being described and points to an evil spiritual power working in and through these rulers.

The children of Israel sinned by worshipping "demons" who were false gods (Deut. 32:16–17; cf. Lev. 17:7) and by sacrificing their children to "demons" in pagan idol worship (Ps. 106:35–37).

⌜*In the New Testament.*⌝The two most common designations for Satan are *diabolos,* "devil" (meaning slanderer or accuser) occurring thirty-seven times, and *Satanas* "Satan" (meaning adversary or opponent) occurring thirty-six times.[22] Jesus identified Satan as *Beelzeboul,* "Baal (lord) of flies," and thus "the ruler of the demons" (Matt. 12:22–32; Mark 3:22–30; Luke 11:14–23). Other New Testament terms used for Satan are: tempter (Matt. 4:3; 1 Thess. 3:5), enemy (Matt. 13:39), father of lies, murderer (John 8:44), Belial (2 Cor. 6:15), prince of the power of the air (Eph. 2:2), adversary (1 Pet. 5:8), wicked one (1 John 2:13; 3:12), great dragon, ancient serpent, deceiver (Rev. 12:9). "Demons" (*daimonia*) and evil "spirits" (*pneumata*) are subordinate to Satan and are his angels or messengers (Matt. 12:24; 25:41; Acts 19:12–16).

Origin and Fall

Not all of the angels that were created by God remained good angels. Sometime between Genesis 1:31 (everything was "very good") and 3:1–5 (the temptation), Satan rebelled against God and was cast out of heaven, bringing many evil angels under the same judgment (Isa. 14:12–15; Ezek. 28:11–19; Matt. 25:41; Luke 10:18). Some of them were bound until the final day of judgment (2 Pet. 2:4; Jude 6). Some are presently bound but will be released during the end times (Rev. 9:14). Others actively oppose God and work evil continually in the world (Eph. 6:11–12). Why some evil angels are bound and others are free to oppose God we are not told in Scripture. There is no indication in Scripture that evil angels can be redeemed from their fallen condition.[23]

Nature

Like their good counterparts, evil angels are intelligent personal spirits. As spirits, they do not normally appear in bodily form (Matt. 8:16; Acts 19:12; Eph. 6:12; Col. 1:16). That they are intelligent beings is clear

---

[22] Bietenhard, *NIDNTT,* s.v. "Satan," 3:469.

[23] Apparently, angels were initially endowed with the ability to choose good or evil and did so during a period of probation. The choice made determined their eternal destiny. A. H. Strong's understanding of "a period of probation" is fairly typical. He believes that: (1) all angels were created holy (Gen. 1:31); thus the beginning of their moral character was perfectly good (Jude 6); (2) like other free creatures (men), angels had a probationary period during which obedience or disobedience determined their future destiny (1 Tim. 5:21; cf. 1 Pet. 1:1, 2); (3) some angels preserved their integrity (Ps. 89:7; Mark 8:38); (4) some angels fell from their state of innocence (John 8:44; 2 Pet. 2:4; Jude 6); (5) the good angels were confirmed as good, and the evil angels were confirmed as evil (Matt. 6:10; 18:10; John 8:44; 1 John 5:18–19). He says, "From these Scriptural statements we infer that all free creatures pass through a period of probation; that probation does not necessarily involve a fall; that there is possible a sinless development of moral creatures." Strong, *Systematic Theology,* 450.

from their understanding of who Jesus is (Mark 1:34) and from their corruption of good doctrine (1 Tim. 4:1; cf. James 2:19). Limitations of their intelligence are seen in their foolish allegiance to Satan as well as the fact that they are finite, created beings. Satan and demons have supernatural strength used for destructive purposes, but they are not omnipotent (Mark 5:1–20; Acts 19:13–16; 1 Pet. 5:8; Rev. 9:1–11). Limitations of their power are seen through their struggles in spiritual warfare as well as in their ultimate defeat (Eph. 6:12; cf. Gen. 3:15; Rev. 20:1–10).

Appearance

There is one New Testament passage that is particularly instructive regarding the appearance of Satan and demons. Justifying his ministry, the Apostle Paul explained to the Corinthian church that there were some who claimed to be apostles when, in reality, they were false apostles. They were ministers of deception like the one who incited them: "And no wonder, for even Satan disguises himself as an angel of light" (2 Cor. 11:14 ESV). Scripture speaks often of deception as a hallmark of the devil's work. But here the point is that Satan transforms (*metaschēmatizō*) his appearance—a counterfeit of the glory of the Lord displayed by the good angels—in order to be attractive.

As one example, Paul may have in mind Genesis 3 and the disguise of the serpent who "enlightened" Eve.[24] He "disguises" himself (ESV, NAS) or "masquerades" (NIV) as an angel of light, but he is emphatically not an angel of light. He is the ruler of this present darkness (Eph. 6:12). If Satan disguises himself as an angel of light, it is fitting to expect that his angels do the same.

Organization

The clearest biblical evidence for Satan as the head of the demons is found in the New Testament. Jesus confirmed Satan's identity as "the prince of demons" when he made clear that he cast out demons by the Spirit of God and not by Beelzebub (Matt. 12:22–32). When Jesus spoke of "the ruler" or "the prince of this world," he clearly had Satan in mind (John 12:31; 14:30; 16:11). All evil angels are the devil's angels under his malicious command. Jesus said that the eternal fire of hell has been prepared for "the devil and his angels" (Matt. 25:41). There is no reason to think that the Apostle Paul had anyone other than Satan in mind when he referred to "the prince of the power of the air" (Eph. 2:2) and "the god of this age" (2 Cor. 4:4).

John's vision in Revelation confirms Satan's prominent role as the head of the demons (Rev. 20:1–10). Though the evil angels are spoken of as principalities, powers, and rulers in the plural form (Eph. 6:12;

---

[24] Colin G. Kruse, *2 Corinthians,* TNTC (Grand Rapids: Eerdmans, 1987), 190.

cf. Rom. 8:38; Col. 1:16), it is best not to speculate about the organization of the evil angels.[25]

Ministry

The self-serving ministry of Satan and demons is thoroughly and completely corrupted by sin. Satan was the originator of sin. Through his deception of Adam and Eve, sin entered the world (Gen. 3:1–6; cf. Rom. 5:12–21; 2 Cor. 11:3). In the words of Jesus, "He was a murderer from the beginning" (John 8:44). Whoever continually practices sin is of the devil because "the devil has sinned from the beginning" (1 John 3:8). The "beginning," in both of John's uses, refers not to the technical beginning of the creation of the universe (Gen. 1:1) but to that period when the devil introduced sin into the world through his own rebellion.[26] Thus all Satanic and demonic activity is not only inseparable from sin but also is the basis for the work of tempting others to sin.

The way Satan works is seen in his various names. As Satan, he opposes God (Matt. 16:23). As the devil, he slanders and accuses believers (Rev. 12:10). As the tempter, he lures people to commit sin (1 Thess. 3:5; cf. Matt. 4:3). Scripture speaks of many other ways Satan and/or his demons work:

- Inciting false worship (Lev. 17:7; Deut. 32:17)
- Inflicting physical suffering (Job 2:1–10; 2 Cor. 12:7)
- Enslaving in sin (John 8:34,44; Acts 26:18)
- Lying (John 8:44)
- Scheming evil (2 Cor. 2:11; 2 Tim. 2:26)
- Blinding unbelievers (2 Cor. 4:4)
- Disguising evil (2 Cor. 11:14)
- Opposing the progress of saints (Eph. 6:10–20)
- Hindering godly ministry (1 Thess. 2:18)
- Spreading of false doctrine (1 Tim. 4:1)
- Seeking to destroy (1 Pet. 5:8)
- Inspiring false teachers (1 John 4:1–4)
- Inciting persecution (Rev. 2:10)
- Deceiving the whole world (Rev. 12:9)

In short, Satan and his angels are forever opposed to God, his Word, and his work throughout all of the created order. It is for this reason that the Son of God appeared to "destroy the works of the devil" (1 John 3:8).

Destiny

Though there has been intense warring between good and evil—between God and Satan—from before the garden of Eden until today, the

---

[25] See n. 8 above for the same concern regarding the good angels.
[26] Daniel L. Akin, *1, 2, 3 John*, NAC (Nashville: Broadman & Holman, 2001), 146.

Bible nowhere indicates that this is an eternal conflict. That is, there is not an eternal dualism of good and evil taught in Scripture. The decisive victory over Satan, demons, and all evil was secured by Christ in the crucifixion and resurrection. At the cross, "He disarmed the rulers and authorities and put them to open shame, by triumphing over them" (Col. 2:15 ESV). In the resurrection he conquered sin and death and was empowered to one day put "an end to all rule and all authority and power" (1 Cor. 15:24).

Appropriately, the destiny of Satan and his demons is vividly portrayed in the last book of the Bible. Revelation 12 describes Michael and the holy angels opposing Satan and the evil angels in a heavenly war. Satan and his angels are cast down to earth, where they make war with believers, those who have the testimony of Jesus Christ (Rev. 12:17). Satan is then bound for one thousand years in the bottomless pit. During this time, known as the millennial kingdom, believers live and reign with Christ (Rev. 20:1–4). After this period Satan is loosed again for a little while in an attempt to deceive the nations (Rev. 20:7–8). His final demise comes as he is cast into the lake of fire to be tormented day and night, forever and ever (20:10). According to Jesus, this will also be the destiny of Satan's angels (Matt. 25:41).

Excursus 2: "Sons of God" (Gen. 6)

When man began to multiply on the face of the land and daughters were born to them, the sons of God saw that the daughters of man were attractive. And they took as their wives any they chose. Then the LORD said, "My Spirit shall not abide in man forever, for he is flesh: his days shall be 120 years." The Nephilim were on the earth in those days, and also afterward, when the sons of God came in to the daughters of man and they bore children to them. These were the mighty men who were of old, the men of renown (Gen. 6:1–4 ESV).

Throughout the history of interpretation, exegetes and theologians have questioned the identity of the "sons of God" (*bene ha'elohim*) found in Genesis 6:1–4.[27] A brief survey of differing views affords an opportunity to avoid fanciful exegesis about angels and serves as a cogent reminder of the importance of interpreting Scripture in its context. The three major views of the "sons of God," using the categories of C. F. Keil, are: (1) sons of princes, (2) angels, and (3) Sethites (godly men).[28] It is argued here that the third view offers the most natural reading of the passage in its context.

---

[27] One of the most well-balanced and thorough treatments of the question is found in Kenneth A. Mathews, *Genesis 1–11:26*, NAC (Nashville: Broadman & Holman, 1996), 320–39.

[28] C. F. Keil and F. Delitzsch, *The Pentateuch,* vol. 1, Commentary on the Old Testament, trans. James Martin (Peabody: Hendrickson, 1996 reprint), 81.

Sons of Princes

Here "sons of God" means "sons of princes" or "sons of lords." Royal men married women of a lower social status, taking many wives into their harems. The divine title is said to be a Near Eastern way of referring to nobles and kings. This view is based on ancient Jewish interpretations found, for example, in Targum Onkelos and Midrash Rabbah.[29] A modified approach has "sons of God" as "divine" kings.[30] They were divinely appointed rulers who were supposed to act justly but instead exalted themselves as divine. Thus, as Meredith Kline argues, "By reason of the polygamy and tyranny practiced by [this] dynasty . . . in the name of divine-royal prerogative and justice, the earth became corrupt before God and filled with violence (vv. 5–7,11–13) and so hasted to destruction."[31] In short, the "sons of God" ruled the earth corruptly, according to the cursed line of Cain. Bruce Waltke is cautious about this view but, nevertheless, suggests that a variation of it—divinely appointed kings who have been "demon possessed"—can be defended grammatically since human beings are called "sons of God" in 2 Samuel 7:14, Psalm 2:7, and Psalm 82:6.[32]

One weakness of this view is that while the Old Testament and other ancient Near Eastern texts attest to divinely appointed kings, there is no evidence that groups of kings were identified in that way.[33] A more significant problem for this view is the absence of "kingly" language in the immediate context of Genesis 1–6.[34] Keil's assessment of this view is that "[it] may be dismissed at once as not warranted by the usages of the language, and as altogether unscriptural."[35] This assertion may be too strong, but the view is not without problems.

Angels

Here the "sons of God" are fallen "angels" who committed yet another egregious sin by engaging in sexual relations with mortal women, "the daughters of man" (Gen. 6:2). Their union is said to have produced a strange progeny called the *Nephilim* (6:4). This view is based primarily

---

[29] See Sailhamer, *Genesis,* 76; Wayne A. Grudem, *1 Peter,* TNTC (Grand Rapids: Eerdmans, 1988), 212.

[30] Meredith G. Kline, "Divine Kingship and Genesis 6:1–4," *WTJ* 24 (1962): 187–204.

[31] Ibid., 196.

[32] Bruce K. Waltke with Cathi J. Fredricks, *Genesis* (Grand Rapids: Zondervan, 2001), 116, n. 19; Cf. Allen P. Ross, *Genesis,* in The Bible Knowledge Commentary, eds. John F. Walvoord and Roy B. Zuck (Wheaton: Victor, 1985).

[33] So Victor P. Hamilton, *The Book of Genesis, Chapters 1–17,* NICOT (Grand Rapids: Eerdmans, 1990), 264.

[34] The most compelling reason for adopting this view, it seems, is the biblical theme of divinely appointed kingship which anticipates *the* divinely appointed King, the Lord's Anointed, as in Psalm 2 (cf. 2 Sam. 7:14; Pss. 24; 82; 110). However, nothing in the immediate context of Genesis suggests such an interpretation. As to Kline's development of "Kingship from Adam to Abraham," it is established mainly on the theological concept of "dominion" and "rule" which he interprets as "kingly dominion." However, the language of "king" or "kings" is nowhere present in Genesis 1–6, making his proposal a bit forced. See Kline, "Divine Kingship," 199–204.

[35] Keil and Delitzsch, *Pentateuch,* 81.

on three plausible grounds: (1) the possibility that "sons of God" means "angelic beings" here, as it does clearly in Job 1:6; 2:1; 38:7 (cf. Ps. 29:1); (2) the possibility that the *Nephilim* are the result of a perverse union between demons and women; and (3) the possibility that 2 Peter 2:4–6 (cf. 1 Pet. 3:19–20) and Jude 6–7 are allusions to Genesis 6:1–4 and thus New Testament descriptions of the specific sin of these fallen angels and of the certain judgment that followed.

Regarding the first possibility, "sons of God" can mean "angels." It is not, however, "to angels only that the term 'sons of Elohim,' or 'sons of Elim,' is applied."[36] The Israelites are also identified as God's "sons" (Deut. 32:5), the "sons of the living God" (Hos. 1:10), and "the son" whom Elohim has strengthened for himself (Ps. 80:17). Thus, whether the "sons of God" are celestial or terrestrial must be determined from the context and the substance of the passage itself (see the argument for Sethites below).[37]

As to the second possibility, the text gives no indication of a "genetic connection between the *Nephilim* and the marriages concerned."[38] In fact, the sense of the passage is quite the opposite. The *Nephilim* cannot be the progeny of an illicit union between demons and women since these "men of renown" are said to be already present "on the earth in those days" (Gen. 6:4).[39] It is more likely that the "men of renown" are the ten great men just mentioned in Genesis 5.[40] Additionally, though this interpretation is perhaps the oldest, it has not been widely held because it appears to contradict the words of Jesus: "For in the resurrection they neither marry nor are given in marriage, but are like angels of God in heaven" (Matt. 22:30; cf. Luke 20:34–36).[41] Finally, there is no positive evidence anywhere in Scripture that angels or demons are capable of engaging in sexual relations.[42]

As to the third possibility, there are several militating factors. First, there is no clear textual link (i.e., canonically textual) between Genesis 6:1–4 and 2 Peter 2:4. To be sure, Peter referred to a specific event. But there is no compelling reason to identify the event in question with the early chapters of Genesis. The two immediate references to Genesis in 2 Peter 2:5 (the flood, Gen. 6–8) and 2:6 (Sodom and Gomorrah, Gen. 19) do not demand that 2:4 also refers to Genesis. It may simply be the case that Peter is identifying three distinct Old Testament examples of sin and judgment to make his point that the Lord will execute judgment on the wicked and save the righteous (2 Pet. 4:9).[43] Second Peter 2:4, then, is simply a reference to the rebellion of a host of wicked angels

[36] Ibid.

[37] Ibid., 83.

[38] John Murray, *Principles of Conduct* (Grand Rapids: Eerdmans, 1991 reprint), 247.

[39] Sailhamer, *Genesis*, 78–79.

[40] Cf. ibid., 77.

[41] Ibid., 76.

[42] For several additional reasons to question the angels view, see Paige Patterson, *A Pilgrim Priesthood* (Nashville: Thomas Nelson, 1982), 137–39.

[43] Grudem, *1 Peter*, 214.

who, unlike Satan and many other wicked angels, are already bound and awaiting the judgment of the end times.[44]

Second, this same line of argument when applied to Jude 6 is even less compelling.[45] Third, the argument that 2 Peter 2:4 (cf. 1 Pet. 3:19–20) and Jude 6 are allusions to Genesis 6:1–4 is heavily influenced by extrabiblical literature—evidence that should not be afforded the interpretive weight it often is.[46]

Sethites (Godly Men)

Here the "sons of God" are the godly Sethites and the "daughters of man" are the ungodly Cainites.[47] The immediate context of Genesis 6 attests to this view. The purpose of the genealogies of the two preceding chapters is to trace the development of mankind through two fundamentally different lines headed by Cain (Gen. 4) and Seth (Gen. 5).[48] The sin, then, is the intermarriage of the godly with the ungodly, believers with unbelievers. John Calvin aptly stated, "It was, therefore, base ingratitude in the posterity of Seth, to mingle themselves with the children of Cain."[49] The wickedness on the earth was so pervasive that God determined to destroy man as an act of judgment (Gen. 6:3,5–7). But Noah found grace in the eyes of the Lord (Gen. 6:8).

There are a number of important textual clues that further support this view. First, there is an undeniable contrast between the ungodly (e.g., Cain's anger, murder, deception, and departure from the presence of the Lord; 4:5,8–9,14,16) and the godly (e.g., the naming of Seth, the godly influence of Seth and his sons, and the account of Enoch who walked with God; 4:25–26; 5:6–7,22–24). This contrast demonstrates the willingness of mankind to depart from the repeated blessings of

---

[44] Interestingly, the judgment demonstrated in Genesis 6:13 (cf. "man" in 6:3,7) is on all "flesh"—it is not intended for celestial beings but rather terrestrial beings. The fact that other terrestrial creatures (innocent bystanders, as it were) suffer the judgment intended for man here does not undercut the value of this interpretation; cf. Hamilton, *Genesis*, 262–63.

[45] Grudem writes: "Jude 6 is even less persuasive. It mentions angelic sin and judgment on angels, but does not specify the sin except for a general statement that angels 'did not keep their own position' (a probable reference to rebellion against God's authority). And there is no connection with the time of the flood but rather the following sequence:

v. 5 exodus from Egypt; judgment on unbelievers (Ex. 14; Nu. 14)

v. 6 sin of angels; judgment

v. 7 Sodom and Gomorrah; judgment (Gen. 19).

No chronological connection is implied; Jude, like Peter, simply selects three noteworthy examples of judgment from the Old Testament. In neither text is there an implication of angelic sin at the time of the flood, or of angelic sin with human women." Grudem, *1 Peter*, 214.

[46] For a detailed argument of this type, see Richard Bauckham's explanation of Jude's dependence on "the earliest extant account" of the fall of these angels (and subsequently Peter's "clear dependence" on Jude) found in 1 Enoch 6–19. Richard J. Bauckham, *Jude, 2 Peter*, WBC (Waco: Word, 1983), 51, 246.

[47] It is unnecessary to insist that "daughters of man" refers exclusively to Cainite women—though whoever they are, they are clearly ungodly women. See Mathews, *Genesis*, 330.

[48] Keil and Delitzsch, *Pentateuch*, 80–81.

[49] John Calvin, *Commentaries on the First Book of Moses Called Genesis*, trans. John King (Grand Rapids: Baker, 2003), 238.

God—before and after the fall (Gen. 1:26–31; 2:18–25; 3:20–24; 4:25–26; 5:1–3). Thus the declaration of Genesis 6:5, "The LORD saw that the wickedness of man was great in the earth, and that every intention of the thoughts of his heart was only evil continually."

Second, the antithesis "sons of God" and "daughters of man" is a literary device that brings to mind the godly union of Adam and Eve, setting in high relief the sin of an ungodly union chosen by the Sethites. The antithesis simply alludes to the first union between man and woman—one that was very good and without shame (Gen. 1:31; 2:25). The designations "sons of God" and "daughters of man" are in keeping with the original creation of the man and the woman.[50] In other words, "though the description of the creation of man and woman in chapter 1 is clear that both have been created in God's image, chapters 2 and 3 specify that the man was created by the breath of God and that the woman was created from the 'side' of the man."[51] Thus the designations "sons of God" and "daughters of man" denote origin. The significance of the antithesis, then, is that it recalls the goodness of the God-ordained first union between Adam and Eve as contrasted to the God-forbidden union of the righteous and the unrighteous.

Third, the act of choosing for themselves wives among the "daughters of man" was a prideful act of disobedience. The sin of the "sons of God" is described in language that is clearly reminiscent of Eve's sin.[52] She "saw" that the fruit was "good" (Heb., *tob*) and "took" it (Gen. 3:6). Likewise, they "saw" the daughters of man who were "good" (Heb., *tob*) and "took" them. The great tragedy is that the "sons of God" replaced God's exercise of "the knowledge of good and evil" (Gen. 2:9,17) with their own exercise of that knowledge—"and the sons of God saw that they were good" (Gen. 6:2).[53]

To sum up, through ungodly unions the Sethites departed from the blessing of God that had been recently restored through Seth, the righteous offspring of Adam (4:25–5:32; cf. Gen. 1:26–28). This fits well the larger context of Genesis 1–11 in which there is a constant tension between the progress of God's blessing on mankind and threats to that blessing.[54]

What Has the Church Believed?

Christians have expressed belief in the existence of angels from the earliest days of the church in Jerusalem (Acts 12:1–17). They inherited this belief according to the Hebrew Scriptures. This is not to say that the church has come to a uniform consensus regarding the nature and purpose of angels. As Millard Erickson puts it, this doctrine has seen times of "preoccupation"

---

[50] Sailhamer, *Genesis*, 78.
[51] Ibid.
[52] Matthews, *Genesis 1–11:26*, 331.
[53] Sailhamer, *Genesis*, 78.
[54] Matthews, *Genesis 1–11:26*, 320.

and wild "speculation" on the one hand and been rejected as a "relic" of a prescientific way of thinking on the other hand.[55] Both of these extremes are evident in the following survey of representative theologians.

The Apologists and the Patristic Period

The second-century apologists Justin Martyr (ca. 100–165) and Athenagoras (ca. 177) affirmed the existence of angels but ascribed to them a status worthy of worship. Questioning their deviation from Scripture, Karl Barth explained that both Justin and Athenagoras believed that the angels were "a subject of Christian confession, reverence and worship together with the triune God."[56] Athenagoras is said to be the more suspect of the two apologists in ascribing divine status to the angels. But it is doubtful that this is in fact what Justin and Athenagoras were saying about angels. Perhaps these apologists were simply confessing the existence of angels in the context of the triune God who providentially orders all things, including the appointment of angels.[57]

Origen's (ca. 185–254) work, *De principiis* (*First Principles*), is recognized as one of the first systematic approaches to Christian theology. Here his treatment of angels is straightforward, though it becomes more complex in relation to his Christology.[58] Origen found in Scripture a variety of names (Heb. 1:14; Eph. 1:21) for the offices and orders of a host of angelic creatures.[59] The following points summarize his thoughts on angels. First, angels are rational and incorporeal. Though they are incorporeal, they nevertheless *were* created. Scripture makes clear that all things were made by God through Christ (John 1:1–3).[60] Second, God wisely assigned angels to particular offices, under the charge of archangels, based on their zealous service before the world was formed (e.g., Gabriel's assignment over the conduct of wars).[61]

Third, these free rational creatures had the ability to choose either good or evil. Even Satan was capable of choosing good: "There was once a time when he was good, when he walked in the paradise of God between the

---

[55] Millard J. Erickson, *Christian Theology,* 2nd ed. (Grand Rapids: Baker, 1998), 459.

[56] Karl Barth, *Church Dogmatics,* ed. G. W. Bromiley and T. F. Torrance (Edinburgh: T. & T. Clark, 1960), 3/3:381.

[57] Ibid., 380–81. We certainly appreciate Barth's rejection of a speculative angelology in favor of Scripture. However, the passages cited are not as convincing as Barth suggests. Cf. Justin, *First Apology* 6; *Dialogue with Trypho* 128; and Athenagoras, *Legatio pro Christianus* 10, 24.

[58] For a thorough treatment of Origen's reference to Christ as "angel," see Joseph W. Trigg, "The Angel of Great Counsel: Christ and the Angelic Hierarchy in Origen's Theology," *Journal of Theological Studies* 42 (April 1991): 35–51.

[59] Origen, *First Principles* 1.5.1.

[60] Ibid., 1.7.1.

[61] Ibid., 1.8.1.

Cherubim . . . [before he] fell away from a virtuous course, and turned to evil with all the powers of his mind."[62] Finally, it was "the opposing powers" or even "the devil himself" who contended with man, prompting him to disobey God.[63] Not all sinful desires can be attributed to the devil since Paul speaks of the "flesh" lusting against the Spirit (Gal. 5:17) and temptation as that which is "common" to all men (1 Cor. 10:13). But often temptation is incited by the opposing powers of wickedness.[64]

Augustine of Hippo (354–430) had much to say about angels.[65] This survey is limited to Augustine's discussion in *De civitate Dei* (*The City of God*) and is organized under four categories: the origin of angels, the nature of angels, worship and angels, and the evil angels.

First, according to Augustine, when Scripture speaks of the creation of the world in the Genesis account, it does not clearly indicate *that* the angels were created or *when* they were created.[66] But they must have been created before day six since God rested from his works of creation on day seven. Further, their creation was before day four since they offered praise when the stars in the heavens were made (Job 38:7). If they are to be included in the six-day account, they are referred to in the text as the "light" that God created at his spoken word (Gen. 1:3). It is possible, however, that they were created before the heavens and the earth (Gen. 1:1).[67]

Second, as to their nature, the holy angels are beings of light who were created to live in wisdom and blessedness.[68] They are immortal, though not eternal—once they are created, they exist forever. They are rational creatures who choose either "the craftiness of vanity" or "the certainty of truth."[69] The result of that choice is citizenship in either the earthly city under the rule of the devil or the heavenly city under the rule of God.

Third, the holy angels worship and serve God alone and direct man to do the same. The angels understand that worship (Gk. *latreia*, Lat. *servitus*) "is due exclusively to God who is the true God."[70] Any immortal being endowed with virtue would want man to be subject to the God from whom this endowment of virtue came. Since the angels truly worship God, they could never wish to be worshipped in place of him: "He

---

62 Ibid., 1.8.3.

63 Ibid., 3.2.1.

64 Ibid., 3.2.3–7.

65 Some of the passages where he most thoroughly discusses angels are *The City of God* 10–12, where he explains their origin and nature, and *The Trinity* 2–3, where he treats their role in theophanies. See Frederick Van Fleteren, "Angels," in *Augustine through the Ages: An Encyclopedia,* ed. Allan D. Fitzgerald (Grand Rapids: Eerdmans, 1999), 20.

66 Augustine, *The City of God* 11.9.

67 Ibid., 11.32.

68 Ibid., 11.11.

69 Ibid., 12.1.

70 Ibid., 10.1.

who sacrifices to any god, except to the LORD only, he shall be utterly destroyed" (Exod. 22:20).[71]

Fourth, Augustine explained the origin of the evil angels in the context of the two cities.[72] The heavenly and earthly cities were formed when the angels took opposing sides. All angels were initially created as beings of light. Some angels, however, turned from God and failed to remain faithful. By their own choice and their own perverseness, the evil angels fell in pride and disobedience.[73] Lucifer was the first angel to sin (Isa. 14:12). It is not that the devil did not understand the truth. Rather, he did not abide in the truth (John 8:44). The devil is the king of demons, the prince of Babylon, the prince of this world, and the ruler of darkness. Because of their sinful rebellion, eternal fire has been prepared for the devil and his angels (Matt. 25:41).[74]

The Medieval and the Reformation Period

It is typically noted that the major influence on angelology during the medieval period was the mystical and speculative theologian who wrote probably during the fifth or sixth century under the pseudonym of Dionysius the Areopagite.[75] Later theologians of the medieval period understood this Dionysius to be the Dionysius of Acts 17:34, thus the title "Areopagite." The work attributed to Dionysius, *De caelesti hierarchia* (*The Celestial Hierarchy*), took on a sense of apostolic authority and had great influence on what has been called the "angelic spirituality" of the period.[76] Dionysius organized the angels into three triads that formed nine orders or choirs.[77] The first triad (seraphim, cherubim, thrones) is closest to God; the second triad (dominions, powers, authorities) and third triad (principalities, archangels, angels) each share less directly in the Godhead than the preceding triad. Each of the nine orders represent an attribute of God which they convey to all who are below (or beyond) them in the hierarchy.

The purpose of the angelic orders, then, is to bring man to the greatest possible likeness of God. The hierarchy is God's ordained way of perfecting man, bringing him into conformity to the holy image of God.[78] Though

---

[71] Ibid., 10.3, cf. 10.1.

[72] Ibid., 11.1.

[73] Ibid., 11.11, 13.

[74] See Frederick Van Fleteren, "Devil," in *Augustine through the Ages*, 268.

[75] See Steven Chase, trans., *Angelic Spirituality: Medieval Perspectives on the Ways of Angels* (Mahwah, NJ: Paulist, 2002), xix.

[76] Ibid., 159. So influential was *The Celestial Hierarchy* that John Scotus Eriugena, Hugh of St. Victor, and Thomas Gallus all wrote commentaries on the work.

[77] Pseudo-Dionysius, *The Celestial Hierarchy* 6.

[78] Ibid., 3, 10.

scholars vary in their assessment of his use of Platonic thought, it is clear that Dionysius was largely influenced by the Neoplatonism of his day.

If Dionysius was the major influence on angelology for the early medieval period, then Thomas Aquinas (1225–1274) was the high point of speculative angelology. For this reason theologians and historians have named him the "Angelic Doctor." Aquinas's treatise on angels is spoken of as "probably the most brilliant piece of speculation on the subject produced by a western theologian."[79] Aquinas was aware of the speculative nature of his work, which included a critical assessment of those who preceded him, particularly Augustine and Dionysius.

However, it would be wrong to say that Aquinas was not biblical. He began with the biblical data even if he was given to saying much more than Scripture does about the nature of angels. Aquinas's angelology is found primarily in the *Summa Theologica* (*Sum of Theology*), where he covered the nature of "Angels" (Ia. 50–64) in seventy-two specific questions under fifteen major headings; he addressed the activity of angels in "The World Order" (Ia. 110–14) in twenty-five specific questions under five major headings.

For example, under the heading of "The Angelic Nature," Aquinas made these points. First, angels are spirits or incorporeal beings (Ps. 104:4). God's good creation would not be complete apart from other incorporeal and intellectual beings made in his likeness.[80] Second, it is perfectly reasonable to believe that the number of angels is enormous, exceeding all material things combined. Since God creates in a way that manifests his own perfection and since angels are more perfect creatures, it follows that God in the abundant exercise of his creative power has created an abundance of them.[81] Third, angels have an immortal nature. Since they are pure intellectual beings, there is no material element in them that would otherwise eventually perish.[82]

Under the headings of "Sin in the Angels" and "The Devil's Punishment" Aquinas explained the fall of the angelic host. According to Job 4:18, God found "wickedness" in some of his angels. Aquinas explained in his reply, "Any creature endowed with intelligence, whether angel or not, can act wrongly; and if any be found impeccable, this is a gift of grace, it cannot be due to the creature's nature alone."[83] It belongs to the angelic nature to turn toward God in love. However, to turn toward God as the source of

---

[79] Kenelm Foster, "Angelology in the Church and in St. Thomas," in Appendix 1 of *Summa Theologica* (New York: Blackfriars, McGraw Hill 1968), 303.

[80] Aquinas, *Summa Theologica* 50.1.

[81] Ibid., 50.3.

[82] Ibid., 50.5.

[83] Ibid., 63.1.

supernatural happiness is a result of grace—a grace which can be sinfully rejected. Indeed, the devil rejected the gift of grace when he aspired to be like God. In this pursuit he tried to obtain ultimate bliss "by the force of his own nature alone, rejecting the supernatural bliss which depends on the grace of God."[84]

In his fall the dragon drew down with him a third of the angels (Rev. 12:4). Satan caused the other angels to fall by prompting them in disobedience.[85] Their judgment will come in the eternal fire prepared for the devil and his angels (Matt. 25:41). They will be punished with pain and grief for all eternity.[86]

Martin Luther (1483–1546) and John Calvin (1509–1564), two of the most significant figures of the Reformation period, purposefully did not follow the speculative approach to angelology that characterized the medieval period. Luther suggested two reasons Moses did not record the account of the creation of angels: "First, because he wrote only about the creation of visible things and, second, because he didn't wish to give occasion for speculation."[87] God was wise in leaving many things unwritten, according to Luther, for otherwise we would eventually belittle what we have and would try to pry into what is beyond us.

Luther defined an angel as a "spiritual creature, a personal being without a body, appointed for the service of the divine church."[88] Good angels are our best friends. They guide our affairs in this life—including fighting evil angels on our behalf—as well as assisting in the life to come. "Therefore, we should learn that our best and most loyal friends are invisible."[89]

Evil angels, on the other hand, are our bitter enemies. It is certain that the angels fell and that as a result of that fall the devil is now an evil angel—but exactly *how* this happened is not known. However, "it is very probable that they fell by pride, because they despised the Word, or the Son of God, and wanted to exalt themselves above Him."[90] The devil's best strategy is to draw people away from the Word or to attack the Word, opposing it with all his might. He is the instigator of false teaching and every attack against the gospel. Referring to Matthew 4:6, Luther said, "The devil, too, can quote Scripture and deceive men with it. . . . He does not quote it completely but

---

[84] Ibid., 63.3.

[85] Ibid., 63.8.

[86] Ibid., 64.3.

[87] Martin Luther, *Table Talk,* trans. Theodore G. Tappert, LW 54:44.

[88] Martin Luther, quoted in *What Luther Says: An Anthology,* trans. Ewald M. Plass (St. Louis: Concordia Publishing House, 1959), 23; cf. *Table Talk* (W-T) in the Weimar edition of Luther's works, 5, no. 6229. Plass's translation is followed by the reference to the original German.

[89] Ibid., 23–24.

[90] Ibid., 391. Interestingly, Luther does not read Isaiah 14:12 as a description of Satan's fall. See LW 16:140.

only so much of it as serves his purpose."[91] In a word, the devil is always crooked. Like a serpent, that animal which he inhabited when he deceived Eve (Gen. 3:1–6), he is always "crooked, curved, and tortuous; it is not straight unless it is dead. So the devil is never straight."[92]

Perhaps Luther's angelology will best be remembered in the context of the God who reigns sovereign over the devil, expressed so vividly in the first and third stanzas of "A Mighty Fortress Is Our God":

> A mighty fortress is our God, A bulwark never failing;
> Our helper He, amid the flood Of mortal ills prevailing:
> For still our ancient foe Doth seek to work us woe;
> His craft and pow'r are great, And, armed with cruel hate, On earth is not his equal.

> And tho' this world, with devils filled, Should threaten to undo us,
> We will not fear, for God hath willed His truth to triumph thro' us:
> The Prince of Darkness grim, We tremble not for him;
> His rage we can endure, For lo, his doom is sure, One little word shall fell him.[93]

John Calvin's opposition to a speculative angelology is clearly stated in the *Institutes of the Christian Religion*. After explaining the necessity of the doctrine in light of a brief historical survey, he concluded that the doctrine must be carefully treated in order "that our readers may not, by speculating more deeply than is expedient, wander away from the simplicity of faith."[94] Calvin's warning had the work of Dionysius in mind. He did not deny that many matters are skillfully discussed in *The Celestial Hierarchy* but upon further examination found it to be "for the most part nothing but talk."[95] He went on, "The theologian's task is not to divert the ears with chatter, but to strengthen consciences by teaching things true, sure, and profitable."[96] Calvin set out, then, to say what Scripture says about the angels and nothing more.

According to Calvin, Scripture teaches that angels are celestial spirits who serve God by carrying out all that he has decreed (Ps. 103:20–21). They are called "hosts" (Luke 2:13) because, like soldiers guarding a prince, they "adorn his majesty and render it conspicuous."[97] Because God

---

[91] Ibid., 396.

[92] Ibid., 394; W-T 1, no. 1146.

[93] Martin Luther, "A Mighty Fortress Is Our God," trans. Frederick H. Hedge, as quoted in *The Baptist Hymnal*, ed. Wesley L. Forbis (Nashville: Convention, 1991). Cf. LW, 53:283. Here the hymn is titled in English "Our God He Is a Castle Strong."

[94] Calvin, *Institutes*, 1.14.3.

[95] Ibid., 1.14.4.

[96] Ibid.

[97] Ibid., 1.14.5.

exercises his authority through them, they are sometimes referred to as
principalities, powers, and dominions (1 Cor. 15:24; Eph. 1:21; Col. 1:16).
The Bible also teaches us that angels are dispensers of God's beneficence
on our behalf (Pss. 34:7; 90:11–12).[98] Since the splendor of God's majesty shines in them, it would be easy to adore them. Scripture, however,
expressly forbids this (Rev. 19:10; 22:8–9). As God did not make angels
his ministers in order to share his glory with them, "so he does not promise
us his help through their ministry in order that we should divide our trust
between them and him."[99]

The Modern Period

In contrast to the "unadorned" biblical emphasis of the Reformers, the
modern period is characterized by a "rejection of angelology."[100] Friedrich
Schleiermacher (1768–1834) epitomizes the dilemma of the modern theologian trying to articulate the faith in a scientific age. For Schleiermacher,
though angels appear throughout Scripture, there is no justification for including them in the province of Christian dogmatics because "nowhere is
anything taught respecting them."[101] By this Schleiermacher means that Jesus
and the apostles did not teach anything *new* concerning angels, demons, and
the devil. They simply accommodated their teachings to the popular belief
of the day. Even more significantly, the doctrine has no bearing at all on "the
plan of salvation" since one need not believe in the devil as a condition of
faith in God or Christ.[102] Schleiermacher allowed a qualified belief in angels
as long as that belief had no influence on one's conduct.[103]

Rudolf Bultmann (1884–1976) is characteristic of recent theologically liberal trends that abandon the miraculous nature of Scripture and
the supernatural world of angels and demons it describes. Bultmann is
known for his demythologizing hermeneutic by which he had hoped to
rescue the essential message of the Bible on behalf of modern man. Since
all modern men know better than to believe in the ancient "myth" of
the three-story universe of the Bible (e.g., heaven, earth, and hell), one
must demythologize the message in order to retain the deeper meaning
of Scripture.[104] The idea that God created a world that is now ruled by
the devil and his army and that they are the cause of sin and evil can no

---

[98] Ibid., 1.14.6.
[99] Ibid., 1.14.12.
[100] Stanley J. Grenz, *Theology for the Community of God* (Grand Rapids: Eerdmans, 2000), 216.
[101] Friedrich Schleiermacher, *The Christian Faith,* ed. H. R. MacKintosh and J. S. Stewart
(Edinburgh: T. & T. Clark, 1989), S 42.2.
[102] Ibid., S 45.
[103] Ibid., S 43.
[104] Rudolf Bultmann, *Jesus Christ and Mythology* (New York: Charles Scribner's Sons, 1958),
14–18.

longer be believed. In Bultmann's words, "It is impossible to use electric light and the wireless and to avail ourselves of modern medical and surgical discoveries, and at the same time to believe in the New Testament world of spirits and miracles."[105] One may still choose to believe this, but to ask others of our day to do so would be *sacrificium intellectus* (sacrifice of the intellect).

Karl Barth (1886–1968), on the other hand, wanted to explain the doctrine of angels in its proper place in Christian theology and rejected that a *sacrificium intellectus* is required. He purposed to avoid the theological caprice of the ancients and the doubtful skepticism of the moderns. He wanted to steer between Scylla (Dionysius) and Charybdis (Bultmann), "between the far too interesting mythology of the ancients and the far too uninteresting 'demytholigisation' of most of the moderns."[106] For Barth the only way to avoid such errors is to adhere strictly to the "Scripture-principle" of the Reformation.[107] The Bible alone should govern what is said and what is not said about angels: "All that is required is a firm resolve that the Bible should be allowed both to speak for itself in this matter, i.e., in the course of its message . . . and also to be very impressively, and in its own way very eloquently, silent."[108]

Angelology, then, according to Barth, ought to be set in its proper place theologically. That place is an "essentially marginal" place.[109] Angels are not independent, autonomous creatures who have a central place in Scripture. Rather, they are dependent creatures who ought never to be worshipped (Rom. 8:39; cf. Col. 1:15; Rev. 22:8–9). Thus, it is no surprise that Scripture speaks of angels only in relation to God and man, not independently. Angelology must also remember the incomprehensible nature of heavenly beings and therefore exercise great caution when speaking of their nature in relation to Scripture.[110] What one can know is that they are God's *entourage* who are in heaven and come from heaven in his service. Barth was keen to use the word *entourage* because it captured well the place of angels in God's service. He said, "It is their existence and nature to observe the will of God and stand at his disposal. . . . They follow the Word of God as riders on white horses. . . . Their only *raison d'etre* as heavenly beings is to render this service."[111]

---

105 Rudolf Bultmann, "New Testament and Mythology," in *Kerygma and Myth,* ed. Hans Werner Bartsch (New York: Harper & Row, 1961), 5.

106 Barth, *Church Dogmatics,* 3/3:369.

107 Ibid., 402–4. Barth is clearly following Calvin here. See Ibid., 370, 373.

108 Ibid., 410.

109 Ibid., 371.

110 Ibid., 450.

111 Ibid., 451–52.

According to Barth, Hebrews 1:14 may be seen as the *locus classicus* for the biblical view of angels. They are "ministering spirits sent out to serve, for the sake of those who are to inherit salvation" (Heb. 1:14 RSV). The main point here is not that they are spirits (*pneumata*) but that as such they are distinctively "ministering" spirits who are "sent" to serve on behalf of Christ. It is a significant exegetical error "to show far too lively an interest" in the nature of angelic "spirits" as Aquinas did.[112] Though angels exist as individuals, as the names Gabriel and Michael clearly indicate, they are the mighty ones "who do his word" (Ps. 103:20). Therefore, it is best to avoid thinking of them individually apart from God and his will. The name "Michael" (meaning "Who is like God?") even challenges us along these lines. Psalm 89:6 is particularly instructive here: "Who among the heavenly beings is like the LORD?" (ESV). Thus what is said of Michael, as to his name, can and must be said of all angels.[113] There is none like God.[114]

The last quarter of the twentieth century is marked by an extreme interest among evangelicals in angels and demons—in particular, the idea of "spiritual warfare."[115] The proliferation of literature on angels and demons ranges from the popular to the technical. Some of the popular notables are Merrill F. Unger, *Demons in the World Today* (1971); Billy Graham, *Angels: God's Secret Agents* (1975); Frank Peretti, *This Present Darkness* (1986); and Neil T. Anderson, *The Bondage Breaker* (1990). Works that are more theological in their approach, whether commendable or not, are Walter Wink's trilogy, *Naming the Powers* (1984), *Unmasking the Powers* (1986), and *Engaging the Powers* (1992); Duane A. Garrett, *Angels and the New Spirituality* (1995); Clinton E. Arnold, *3 Crucial Questions about Spiritual Warfare* (1997); Gregory A. Boyd, *God at War: The Bible and Spiritual Conflict* (1997); Robert P. Lightner, *Angels, Satan and Demons* (1998); and Stephen F. Noll, *Angels of Light, Powers of Darkness* (1998). Alongside this renewed interest among Christians, there is the current fascination with the new age movement and other forms of occultism and spirituality that are seen in society in general.

---

[112] Ibid., 453.

[113] Ibid., 456.

[114] We have intentionally omitted Barth's treatment of Satan and demons for two reasons. First, space does not permit. Second, it affords the opportunity to say that Barth would prefer that it be left out of this "theological" treatment. Of course, this is not to say that Barth does not see Satan as a real and formidable foe. Regarding theological formation, a brief glance is all that he allows: "The very thing which the demons are waiting for, especially in theology, is that we should find them dreadfully interesting and give them our serious and perhaps systematic attention" (ibid., 519, 522).

[115] Some of the more popular practices among those engaging in "spiritual warfare" are discussed in the fourth part of this chapter under the heading "Binding the Straw Man," pp. 332-36.

Baptist Theologians and the Doctrine of Angelology

Theologian	Source	Notes
Boyce, J. P.	James Petigru Boyce, *Abstract of Systematic Theology* (Escondido: den Dulk Christian Found., originally published, 1887), 174–89.	Content not to speculate beyond Scripture as to "the nature" of angels. Holy angels are "deeply interested" in the economy of redemption. Rejects the "theory" of guardian angels for individuals and nations.
Erickson, Millard	Millard J. Erickson, *Christian Theology*, 2nd ed. (Grand Rapids: Baker, 1998), 457–75.	Solid biblical explanation of angels and demons, introduced by a brief but helpful historical survey of the doctrine. Responsible treatment of "demon possession."
Fuller, Andrew	Andrew Fuller, *The Complete Works of Andrew Fuller* (Boston: Lincoln, Edmands, & Co., 1833), 2:155–57.	Brief comments on select aspects of angelology. Insightful treatment of 1 Peter 1:12 and *parakuptō*—things that angels desire to "look into."
Garrett, James	James Leo Garrett, *Systematic Theology* (Grand Rapids: Eerdmans, 1990), 1:356–88.	Thorough treatment of angelology and demonology. Excellent source material. Surveys four major theories as to the identity of the Angel of the Lord.
Grenz, Stanley	Stanley J. Grenz, *Theology for the Community of God* (Grand Rapids: Eerdmans, 2000), 213–42.	Treats angeology under the heading "Our Spiritual Co-creatures" in the doctrine of anthropology. Relates angelology most fully to "structures of human existence," based on the Pauline concept of "powers" (Col. 2:20). Also evaluates "The Demonic and Superstition."
Henry, Carl F. H.	Carl F. H. Henry, *God, Revelation and Authority* (Wheaton: Crossway, 1999), 6: 229–50.	Suggests that the scientific preoccupation of the modern era accounts for a disinterest in scholarly theological studies on angelology. Helpful overview and treatment of many aspects of the doctrine. Questions whether Isaiah 14 and Ezekiel 28 refer to the fall of Satan.
Moody, Dale	Dale Moody, *The Word of Truth* (Grand Rapids: Eerdmans, 1981), 165–69.	Suggests that the Angel of the Lord is the personal presence of the Lord. Explains the contrasting angeologies of Barth and Rahner, suggesting there is value in both approaches. Helpful survey and source material on medieval angelology.

Theologian	Source	Notes
Mullins, E. Y.	Edgar Young Mullins, *The Christian Religion in Its Doctrinal Expression* (Nashville: Sunday School Board, 1917), 276–80.	Denies biblical support for the belief in guardian angels and the practice of praying to angels. The Angel of the Lord should be understood as closely related to Jehovah, but it is saying too much to identify him as the second person of the Trinity.
Spurgeon, Charles	Charles Haddon Spurgeon, *Spurgeon's Expository Encyclopedia* (Grand Rapids: Baker, 1988), 1:243–65; 14:59–78.	Sermons on angels: "Mahanaim, or Hosts of Angels" (Gen. 32:1–2) and "Angelic Protection in Appointed Ways" (Ps. 91:11). Sermons on Satan: "Blinded by Satan" (2 Cor. 4:4) and "An Antidote to Satan's Devices" (Gen. 3:1).
Strong, A. H.	Augustus Hopkins Strong, *Systematic Theology* (Valley Forge: Judson, 1993), 443–64.	The doctrine comes under "The Works of God" because angels are "ministers of divine providence." Affirms a period of "probation" for angels regarding their moral nature. Offers several cogent replies to modern objections to the doctrine.

How Does It All Fit Together?

What the Bible teaches about angels ought not be missed by focusing only on the specific messages they deliver. Since angels are divine messengers, one might expect the entire biblical account of angels to send one clear message itself. The Bible reveals that these messengers are sent at strategic times and particular places to deliver the central message of salvation. Angels are an integral part of the story of God's unfolding plan to redeem man, even though they do not personally experience redemption. From paradise to paradise, the holy angels tell the story of the gospel.

Paradise (Creation)

In order to understand God's creation of all things, including the host of the angels, the first sentence of the Bible must be properly understood. "In the beginning God created the heavens and the earth" (Gen. 1:1) refers to the universe in totality. Every single created thing in the universe owes its origin and existence to God. The importance of this idea is seen consistently in the work of later biblical writers (e.g., Ps. 33:6; Isa. 44:24;

John 1:1–3; Heb. 11:3).[116] Thus, the angels were created by God, according to Genesis 1:1. Though they are not in view throughout the rest of the Genesis creation account, they are included in the first verse. Perhaps their conspicuous absence in Genesis 1:2–2:25 is a way of exalting man as the highest of all earthly created beings (Gen. 1:26; cf. Ps. 8). Adam and Eve were the ones for whom the earthly paradise was created, not the angels.

In the book of Job, the angels celebrate the creation of the material universe. God said to Job, "Where were you when I laid the foundations of the earth? Tell Me, if you have understanding. Who determined its measurements? Surely you know! . . . Or who laid its cornerstone, when the morning stars sang together and all the sons of God shouted for joy?" (Job 38:4–8). This angelic jubilation recognized God's glorious creation. And there seems to be no reason to limit this joy of the angels to amazement at the measurements of the earth. The scope of God's questions to Job entails more than what is mentioned in verses 4–6 alone. We may rightly assume that the angels not only rejoiced at these particular observations of creation but over all of creation. At this point biblically, we have no reason to believe that any angels have fallen. Thus *all* of the angels ever created join in this celebration of *all* of God's good creation.

Paradise Lost (Fall)

Sometime between the final act of creation by God (Gen. 1:31) and the moment of temptation by Satan (Gen. 3:1), the fall of the evil angels must have occurred. Satan, as the leading conspirator, was expelled from the paradise of heaven (Isa. 14:12–21; Luke 10:18; cf. Rev. 12:9). The serpent, not yet cursed to move on his belly, was a winsome yet deceptive manifestation of Satan. The serpent, then, became an evil intruder into man's earthly paradise created by God (Gen. 3:1). He was malevolent and crafty, "With subtle guise, the adversary speaks as a winsome angelic theologian."[117] He twisted the words of God to bring Adam and Eve under his rule. Through Satan evil entered the garden of Eden and paradise was lost. In the end, however, the seed of Eve will crush the serpent's head (Gen. 3:15).

After judgment was communicated to Adam and Eve, the Lord graciously clothed them both with tunics of skin (Gen. 3:21). In his next gracious act toward man, God appointed a number of angels as guardians of Eden. He drove man out of Eden lest he make another fatal mistake and eat of the tree of life in his now-fallen condition. Presumably there was great danger in combining eternity with sinful rebellion (Gen. 3:22). "So He drove out the man; and he placed cherubim at the east of the garden of

---

[116] Sailhamer, *Genesis,* 20.
[117] Waltke, *Genesis,* 90–91.

Eden, and a flaming sword which turned every way, to guard the way to the tree of life" (Gen. 3:24). These angels guarded the way to the tree of life because good angels are guardians of God's grace and mercy. Their presence was a constant reminder to Adam of God's grace since they did not bear the flaming sword in vain. The cherubim who guarded the entrance to Eden anticipate God's unfolding plan of redemption through the covenant at Sinai and the Torah.[118]

As the tree of life was guarded by the cherubim, so the ark of the covenant—that which contains the promise for blessing and life—was guarded by the cherubim who covered the mercy seat (Exod. 25:22). Ironically, the anointed cherub of Ezekiel 28:14, Satan, was a guardian of God's holy mountain before he sinned and was cast out of the mountain of God (Ezek. 28:16).

Paradise Regained (Redemption)

Angels, says the writer of Hebrews, are "ministering spirits sent forth to minister for those who will inherit salvation" (Heb. 1:14). The "cherubim of glory overshadowing the mercy seat" were physical representations of living ministering spirits (Heb. 9:5). They testified of the importance of the blood of the covenant from the first day of atonement under Aaron's ministry until the veil of the temple was torn from top to bottom (Heb. 9:19–22). In other words, the saving atonement on behalf of which angels minister is that which Jesus Christ accomplished with his own blood, having entered the Most Holy Place once for all to obtain eternal redemption (Heb. 9:12).

It is no coincidence that angels appear strategically in the narratives of all four gospels. They appear at four crucial events in the life of Jesus: incarnation, temptation, passion, and resurrection. As to the incarnation, the angel Gabriel appeared to Zacharias in the temple by the altar of incense to announce the miraculous birth of John the Baptist, whose ministry prepared the way for Jesus (Luke 1:11–25; cf. Matt. 3:3). The miraculous conception and birth of John anticipated the miraculous nature of the conception and birth of Jesus which was also announced by Gabriel (Luke 1:26–38). Gabriel even instructed Mary as to the name of her son: "you . . . shall call His name Jesus" (Luke 1:31). He is named Jesus because he will "save his people from their sins" (Matt. 1:21; cf. Luke 1:47,77).

At his temptation Jesus was led by the Spirit into the wilderness to be tempted by the devil (Matt. 4:1–11). One of the appeals the devil made to Jesus was to demonstrate his power as the Son of God by calling on God's angels to assist him. From the pinnacle of the temple, the tempter said, "If You are the Son of God, throw Yourself down. For it is written: 'He shall

---

[118] Sailhamer, *Genesis*, 59.

give His angels charge over you,' and, 'In their hands they shall bear you up, lest you dash your foot against a stone'" (Matt. 4:6). Jesus rejected this temptation, as with the other two temptations (Matt. 4:3,9), on the basis of the Word of God—"It is written." The devil left Jesus after these three temptations. Interestingly, without any indication that Jesus called on them, "angels came and ministered to Him" (Matt. 4:11).

As to his passion, an angel appeared to Jesus in the garden of Gethsemane in order to strengthen him. His prayer to the Father was so earnest and his agony so intense that his sweat became as drops of blood falling to the ground (Luke 22:43–44). Affirming his desire to do the will of his Father, Jesus said to Peter, "Put your sword back into its place. . . . Do you think that I cannot appeal to my Father, and he will at once send me more than twelve legions of angels?" (Matt. 26:52–53 ESV). Jesus needed no earthly assistance to save him from death. From this point on until the resurrection, angels are curiously absent from the gospel narratives. It is as if the angels could go no further in assisting the Son. He had to go alone into the holy place—"by a new and living way which He consecrated for us, through the veil, that is, His flesh" (Heb. 10:20).

As to his resurrection, two angels verbally proclaimed the gospel in a miraculous validation of the death, burial, and resurrection of Jesus. Mary Magdalene, Joanna, Mary the mother of James, and several other women came to the tomb on Sunday morning to find that the stone had been rolled away. At the tomb they saw two men in shining garments saying, "Why do you seek the living among the dead?" (Luke 24:5; cf. Matt. 28:1–8; John 20:12). The angels reminded the women of the words of Jesus himself: "The Son of Man must be delivered into the hands of sinful men, and be crucified, and the third day rise again" (Luke 24:7). The gospel of Christ is the message of the angels.

Paradise Forever (Consummation)

The consummation of this age and the beginning of the eternal state are described by the Apostle John in Revelation. Throughout this apocalyptic book, the angels not only repeat the glorious refrain of the gospel but also administrate God's judgment as the final acts of redemptive history unfold. In the fourth chapter the four living creatures are angelic beings much like the cherubim and seraphim of Isaiah 6 and Ezekiel 1 and 10. They exalt God around his throne with voices saying, "Holy, holy, holy, Lord God Almighty, who was and is and is to come!" (4:8). They also join with the twenty-four elders singing about redemption in the fifth chapter. Of the slain Lamb they say, "Worthy are you to take the scroll and to open its seals, for you were slain, and by your blood you ransomed people for God from every tribe and language and people and nation" (5:9 ESV). These angelic beings rejoice in the songs of redemption on behalf of others even though they have not been personally redeemed by the Lamb's atoning sacrifice.

The "great tribulation" (Rev. 7:14; cf. 6:17; Matt. 24:21), that period of time that marks the end of this age and in which God administers his wrath on those who have not obeyed the gospel, is the subject of most of the remaining chapters of Revelation (6:1–19:21). Angels assist God during this period at almost every turn. For example, as the first four seals of God's judgment are opened by the Lamb, the living creatures announce the entrance of the four horsemen saying, "Come!" (6:1–8). When the seventh seal is opened, seven angels stand before God with seven trumpets ready to sound (8:2). The sounding of each of the first six trumpets announces another unprecedented natural disaster of the tribulation period. The seventh angel's trumpet, however, introduces loud voices saying, "The kingdoms of this world have become the kingdoms of our Lord and of His Christ, and He shall reign forever and ever!" (11:15).

The angels continue to deliver the message of salvation even through the final three chapters of the Bible, which mark the consummation of the age and the beginning of eternal paradise (20–22). The literal one-thousand-year reign of Christ with his saints on the earth is inaugurated by an angel coming down from heaven and binding Satan in a bottomless pit (20:1–3). The power by which this angel exercises authority over Satan is no doubt the Lord God's omnipotence (19:6). John's vision of a new heaven and a new earth, including the New Jerusalem, is attended by a loud voice, which in all likelihood is the voice of another mighty angel (21:3; cf. 5:2; 7:2; 14:7). The angel says, "Behold, the dwelling place of God is with man. He will dwell with them, and they will be his people, and God himself will be with them as their God" (21:3 ESV).

Another angel escorts John to a high mountain to show him the beauty of this eternal city radiating with the glory of God and the Lamb who are at its center (21:9–11,22–23). This same angel then shows John the river of the water of life that flows from the throne of God and of the Lamb (22:1). On both sides of the river, which apparently meanders throughout the city, there stands the tree of life (22:2). The river and the tree are an unmistakable allusion to the garden of Eden. Paradise is now forever.

How Does This Doctrine Impact the Church Today?

Perhaps there is no area of doctrine in the church today more readily abused and less biblically understood than that which is practiced in the name of "spiritual warfare." Thus, the last component of our angelology may help in correcting some unwarranted abuses from a pastoral perspective. Three categories assist this process. First, the church needs clear teaching to understand rightly what is to be rejected as specious angelology. Second, biblical answers must be offered to challenging questions. Third, biblical teaching on spiritual warfare ought to be accepted and practiced.

Casting Down Strongholds: Rejecting Specious Angelology

Reject False Ways of Thinking

Believers are empowered by God to wage war against the fortresses or strongholds of the intellect: "casting down arguments and every high thing that exalts itself against the knowledge of God, bringing every thought into captivity to the obedience of Christ" (2 Cor. 10:5). False ways of thinking, whether directly or indirectly inspired by deceiving spirits (1 Tim. 4:1), are to be rejected. Believers battle with sophistries, ideologies, and every other idea that opposes the knowledge of God. Interestingly, Paul's metaphor in this passage does not picture a wrestling match with demons but rather a battlefield in the mind.[119] Those who develop an angelology that understands spiritual warfare as believers wrestling with demons have already given the enemy more ground than necessary. In order to be victorious, the battle must be rightly understood.

Reject the Worship of Angels

The most obvious example of that which must be rejected is the worship of angels. This is forbidden by the good angels as well as those who write about them in Scripture (Rev. 22:9; cf. Col. 2:18). For example, in Colossians Paul forbids angel worship because it defrauds both God and man. Not only does it defraud God of worship due only to Christ (Col. 2:8), but it is also the result of one who is "vainly puffed up by his fleshly mind" (Col. 2:18). Here Paul warns the church not to delight in or even pursue what some think they have discovered by entering into the heavenly realm of angelic visions. As N. T. Wright puts it, "All they have discovered in their vaunted mystical experiences is a set of imaginary fantasies."[120] Good angels would never tolerate such worship.

Reject New Age Angelphilia

Most Christians see clearly the problem with worshipping angels when it is put in terms of "worship." What they seem to be less aware of, however, is the undermining influence that the new age movement has had on

---

[119] See Philip E. Hughes, *Paul's Second Epistle to the Corinthians,* NICNT (Grand Rapids: Eerdmans, 1962), 350–53.
[120] N. T. Wright, *Colossians and Philemon,* TNTC (Grand Rapids: Eerdmans, 1986), 123.

Christians, particularly with regard to angels. It is not the intention here to document the influence of the new age movement on the church but rather to encourage the rejection of what Duane Garrett accurately terms new age "angelphilia." He coined the term *angelphile* (lover of angels) to describe someone who has "an extreme interest in or devotion to angels" in the context of the new spirituality.[121]

This movement is eclectic in its sources of religious authority, drawing on ancient and modern works with little concern for the credibility of such sources. According to Garrett, "they freely cite the Bible, . . . the Kabbalah, the Koran, the Book of Mormon, and other writings on angels."[122] Additionally, angelphiles are ever seeking new revelations from angels and measure spirituality by encounters with angels. The Bible knows nothing of such devotion to angels (Gal. 1:8–9). These beliefs and practices are "deleterious for the soul" and must be rejected without further question.[123]

Binding the Straw Man: Biblical Answers to Frequent Questions

The biblical idea that one should be content with divine revelation on difficult theological questions also applies to spiritual warfare. That is, Bible students ought to answer with biblical and theological precision in these matters as well as all others. Because of the potential deception concerning this subject matter, one ought to be even more careful to "bind the straw man" of false doctrine. Here are some brief answers to several of the most frequently asked questions concerning angels and spiritual warfare.

Do We Have Individual Guardian Angels?[124]   No!

The question is not, does God use angels to protect his people? Scripture contains several clear examples of such protection (2 Kings 6:17; Ps. 91:11–12; Matt. 26:53; Luke 16:22). The question is, does God assign one angel to one person for life (either to all people or only believers)? Two biblical texts are often cited in support of such a claim—Matthew 18:10 and Acts 12:15. In Matthew 18:10, Jesus said this about little children: "I tell you that in heaven their angels always see the face of my Father who

---

121 Duane A. Garrett, *Angels and the New Spirituality* (Nashville: Broadman & Holman, 1995), 9.

122 Ibid., 132.

123 Ibid., 153. D. Garrett sketches six salient dangers of new age angelphilia—dangers that apply to anyone who has a love for angels. They are: (1) new age angelphiles promote a "new source of revelation"; (2) this new religion is actually nothing more than a repackaged "old paganism"; (3) angelphiles often distort biblical ideas and terms such as "grace" and "love" by dressing their false teachings in biblical garb; (4) angelphiles revise morality, treating guilt as merely "illusory"; (5) angelphiles attempt to create reality through the process of "imagining" angelic encounters; (6) angelphiles are "dismissive" of the evil nature of Satan and demons. See ibid., 153–60.

124 For a brief historical survey of the view that all persons have an individual guardian angel assigned to them from birth (as well as the dangers of such a view), see ibid.,119–22.

is in heaven" (ESV). The phrase "their angels" is not, however, a reference to individual guardian angels. Jesus speaks here of angels in a collective sense, not an individual sense. Additionally, the children of this passage are young believers who are an example to all believers. Jesus is simply saying that there are angels in heaven, in the very presence of God, ready to act on behalf of those who believe.[125]

Acts 12:15 does not support the idea of individual guardian angels either. Some suggest that the disciples heard Peter's voice at the door and kept saying, "It is his angel!" because they were influenced by Jewish superstition that affirmed the idea of guardian angels. In this case Luke may have had the superstition in mind but was not corroborating it.[126] Or it may be that the word *angel* is to be understood as Peter's "spirit"—a sort of heavenly counterpart who sounded and looked like Peter.[127] Either way, Acts 12:15 does not give textual evidence for the idea of individual guardian angels.

Are We to Engage Territorial Spirits? No!

Is there a biblical basis, either by instruction or by positive example, for engaging territorial spirits in order to bind the power of demons in preparation for the proclamation of the gospel in a particular city? In other words, does the Bible encourage "strategic level spiritual warfare"?[128] There are at least two compelling reasons for answering no and thus avoiding such practices. First, there is little if any biblical evidence for it. The only Old Testament passage that comes close to the idea of a "territorial" spirit is Daniel 10, where the "prince of the kingdom of Persia" is identified (Dan. 10:13). Even here, though, Daniel does not bind or cast out the Persian prince by his prayer.[129] In the New Testament no explicit teaching exhorts believers to engage territorial spirits in spiritual warfare.

Second, the biblical pattern for preaching the gospel in a new city is clear. When Jesus or the apostles preached the gospel to unbelievers, they did not focus on local demonic spirits hindering those who would believe, though in a few instances they certainly cast out demonic spirits (Mark 5:1–20; Acts 16:16–18). As Wayne Grudem has noted, the usual pattern

---

[125] Cf. D. A. Carson, *Matthew*, EBC (Grand Rapids: Zondervan, 1984), 400–1.

[126] I. Howard Marshall, *Acts*, TNTC (Grand Rapids: Eerdmans, 1980), 210.

[127] Carson, *Matthew*, 401.

[128] For a sympathetic description of "strategic level spiritual warfare," see Clinton E. Arnold, *Three Crucial Questions about Spiritual Warfare* (Grand Rapids: Baker, 1997), 146–50. For an excellent critique, see Chuck Lawless, "Spiritual Warfare and Missions," *SBJT* 9:4 (Winter 2005): 34–48.

[129] Ibid., 155. Arnold's references to "biblical" foundations for "territorial" spirits (Deut. 32:8, 17; Pss. 82; 96:5; 106:37–38; Isa. 24:21) are sketchy at best. Additionally, though the "gods of the nations" are really demons masquerading as gods (Deut. 32:17), there is no reason to argue that they are localized territorial demons uniquely present in Canaanite worship. See ibid., 151–53.

is marked by an emphasis on the proclamation of the gospel (Matt. 9:35; Rom. 1:15–16; 1 Cor. 1:17–2:5; Col. 1:5–6).[130] Grudem says:

> In marked contrast to the practice of those who today empha-size "strategic level spiritual warfare," in no instance does anyone in the New Testament (1) *summon a "territorial spirit"* upon entering an area to preach the gospel . . . or (2) *demand information from demons about a local demonic hierarchy,* (3) *say that we should believe or teach information derived from demons,* or (4) teach by word or example that certain *"demonic strongholds" over a city have to be broken* before the gospel can be proclaimed with effec-tiveness. Rather, Christians just preach the gospel, and it comes with power to change lives![131]

Is Prayer-Walking a Biblical Strategy? No but positive.

If by "prayer-walking" it is meant that believers ought to pray before, during, and after personal evangelistic encounters or as they minister in a particular place, then who would dare argue with such a practice? Presumably Christians have done this from the time of Jesus until now. If, on the other hand, it is meant that one must be "on site" to pray with more "insight," as Steve Hawthorne and Graham Kendrick claim,[132] then there is certainly reason for caution. They advocate that being on site affords a more powerful prayer opportunity than is otherwise possible. Certainly prayers for the conversion of a particular people group may be informed by a heightened sense of awareness by being on location. And perhaps that increased awareness in earnest prayer would end up having an eternal impact. But that is altogether different from making powerful prayer con-tingent on a particular geographical location. What we are rejecting is "on site" prayer as the required means for effecting powerful prayer.

A number of problems attend this approach to spiritual warfare. First, it makes too much of the geographical location of the person praying. God is everywhere present, and his response is not dependent on our geographical location. Second, it does not recognize that the "sounds, sights and smells" of a community are often misleading[133]—particularly when assessed in re-lation to the spiritual realm. Third, it depends on "revealed" insights by the "Spirit" which will inevitably distract from or directly usurp the authority

---

[130] Wayne Grudem, *Systematic Theology* (Grand Rapids: Zondervan, 1994), 420.
[131] Ibid., 421. Emphasis his.
[132] Steve Hawthorne and Graham Kendrick, *Prayer-Walking: Praying On-Site with Insight* (Lake Mary, FL: Charisma House, 1993). Hawthorne and Kendrick's approach is typical of those who advocate prayer-walking strategies.
[133] Ibid., 16.

of the already revealed Word of the Spirit.[134] Fourth, it is rooted in an understanding of "territorial spirits" that is simply not biblical (see above).[135] Fifth, it wrongly assumes that the primary problem among lost peoples is the oppression of "territorial spirits" rather than the hardness and unbelief of the human heart. Thus the verbal proclamation of the gospel takes second place to a flawed view of prayer.[136] Sixth, and most importantly, it is not taught or modeled in Scripture. In its present form, it is best described as an attempt to wage spiritual war "according to the flesh" (2 Cor. 10:3).

Do All Believers Have Authority to Rebuke or Cast out Demons?[137] No!

The question is not, did Jesus and the apostles have authority over demons? Clearly they did (Matt. 12:27; Luke 9:1–5). The seventy that Jesus sent out returned and said, "Lord, even the demons are subject to us in Your name" (Luke 10:17). Their success came through a unique empowerment by Christ and the Spirit (not yet given in the sense of Acts 1:8; 2:1) and the preaching of the kingdom of God. The question for all believers, then, is this: what biblical evidence exists for demon deliverance as a permanent ministry of the church?

The best answer is that there is no compelling biblical evidence for affirming such a ministry as "normative" for believers. While all believers have a sense of "authority" by virtue of identification with Christ (Eph. 1:21; Col. 2:10), and even though Christ's authority is what guarantees victory in spiritual warfare, it does not follow that every believer is thus commissioned to a ministry of demon deliverance. After all, there is scant biblical evidence about the ministry of casting out demons in the New Testament church.[138] Furthermore, it is significant that the apostolic era was a special period of miraculous activity for the purpose of inaugurating and authenticating the gospel.[139] It is not surprising that Matthew's final word to the church, now known as the Great Commission (Matt. 28:18–20), quoted

---

134 Ibid., 20.

135 According to Hawthorne and Kendrick, once prayer-walkers enter a particular area, ensconced evil powers sense that spiritual trespassing has occurred. They claim that "walking embellishes spoken petitions with an undeniable body language that can be read in the heavenlies." Ibid., 18.

136 On the place of prayer in spiritual warfare, see below: "Stand Firm (Eph. 6:10–20)," pp. 338–40.

137 One of the most helpful and sane treatments on spiritual warfare published in the last decade is the work of David Powlison, *Power Encounters: Reclaiming Spiritual Warfare* (Grand Rapids: Baker, 1995). We are following Powlison in using the term "demon deliverance" to refer to ministries whose goal is to deliver Christians of evil spirits. Ibid., 27, 32–34.

138 So Robert Saucy, "An Open but Cautious View," in *Are Miraculous Gifts for Today?* ed. Wayne A. Grudem (Grand Rapids: Zondervan, 1996), 135. Additionally, the argument that Paul cast out demons as part of his ministry in Acts 16:16–18 and 19:11–12 seems to miss the point that he is uniquely exercising apostolic authority for the purpose of authenticating the power of the gospel.

139 And yet, even during this period, the Apostle Paul's example of calling on the Lord three times in order that a "messenger of Satan" might depart from him (2 Cor. 12:7) runs counter to the demon-deliverance movement. Paul was not only content with such suffering; he took pleasure in

Jesus' instruction to make disciples by preaching the gospel and teaching his commandments apart from any mention of demon deliverance. Neither is there instruction in the New Testament epistles that would lead one to assume such a ministry as a normative pattern and practice for the church.[140]

Standing Firm: Following Biblical Teaching on Spiritual Warfare

How then does a believer prepare for this battle known as spiritual warfare? What is his role in the engagement? Three biblical themes help to answer these sorts of questions about spiritual warfare. First, believers must recognize that they live in enemy-occupied territory. Second, believers ought to have a watchful respect for Satan and his evil hosts. Third, the battle must be fought according to the rules of engagement. There are specific instructions given in Scripture in order to teach believers how to wage war.

Enemy-occupied Territory

Understanding that Satan is presently the ruler of this world is necessary in order to grasp the cosmic scope of spiritual warfare. As C. S. Lewis put it, believers live in "enemy-occupied territory—that is what this world is."[141] Satan's rule is not limited to particular places here and there on the earth. He is the "prince of the power of the air" (Eph. 2:2) and "the ruler of this world" (John 16:11). As long as believers live in this *kosmos,* they will be engaged in spiritual warfare. Yet victory through the redemptive work of Christ is cosmic in scope as well. Jesus confronts demonic powers in his earthly ministry in anticipation of his crucifixion which ultimately casts out the ruler of this age (John 12:31). All of creation groans as it eagerly awaits liberation from the bondage of its corruption (Rom. 8:19–23). At his second advent Christ will establish his millennial kingdom on the earth; and, following its conclusion, the ruler of this world will be finally judged and tormented forever (Rev. 20:1–10; cf. John 14:30; 16:11; Eph. 6:12).

Watchful Respect for the Enemy

Having a watchful respect for Satan begins with recognizing him as a formidable foe—neither underestimating nor overestimating him. Far from portraying Satan as one whom believers should initiate war with, Scripture

---

suffering because the grace of Christ was sufficient—"for My [God's] strength is made perfect in weakness" (2 Cor. 12:9).

[140] This is not to say, however, that demons are not active in the world today such that there might be an occasion where demonic deliverance is necessary. We are not here articulating a "cessationist" view. We would characterize our view as "cautious but open"—not the typical designation "open but cautious."

[141] C. S. Lewis, *Mere Christianity* (New York: Macmillan, 1952), 51.

emphasizes a cautious respect. When the Lord Jesus taught that he cast out demons "by the Spirit of God" and that in doing so he was exercising authority over Satan (Matt. 12:28), he was not authorizing his followers to do the same. Rather, he was teaching that he had come to bind Satan in demonstration of the power of the kingdom of God. Because Satan is a formidable foe, "a strong man," the Lord Jesus is the one who must exercise authority over him. Even when Jesus called his disciples and "gave them power and authority over all demons" (Luke 9:1), their power was clearly tied to the preaching of the kingdom of God. That is, apart from the power and authority of Jesus expressed through the proclamation of the gospel, they had no spiritual authority.

There is a similar line of thought in Jude which shows how it is that Michael the archangel contended with the devil over the body of Moses. Michael "did not presume to pronounce a blasphemous judgment, but said, 'The Lord rebuke you'" (Jude 9 ESV). If the mighty archangel Michael understands that this battle is the Lord's, how much more should believers respect evil celestial powers?

The Apostle Paul also encouraged a watchful respect for the enemy when he appealed to forgiveness as the proper response to an erring brother in Corinth. He said, "Anyone whom you forgive, I also forgive. What I have forgiven . . . has been for your sake in the presence of Christ, so that we would not be outwitted by Satan; for we are not ignorant of his designs" (2 Cor. 2:10–11 ESV). Paul instructed forgiveness in order to avoid being tricked by Satan's evil schemes. The plural form of "designs" serves to heighten the sinister connotation that attends his work.[142] His designs are purposeful and well thought out, even if in the most menacing ways. Believers, then, ought to have a watchful respect for the enemy in order to avoid the consequences that follow his deception.

Rules for Engagement

The epistles of Peter, James, and Paul each contain clear teaching on how believers are to engage in spiritual warfare. It is instructive that today's popular approaches to spiritual warfare—whether engaging territorial spirits, binding demons, or prayer walking—are curiously absent from the divinely inspired exhortations of the apostles. At least four key phrases combine to form a biblical response to Satan and demons: be vigilant, give no place, resist the devil, stand firm.

1. *Be vigilant* (*1 Pet. 5:8*). Peter admonished believers to "be sober" and to "be vigilant" because their adversary is on the prowl "like a roaring lion, seeking whom he may devour" (5:8). The instruction is given in the form of a command because of the potential danger that must be

---

142 Hughes, *Paul's Second Epistle to the Corinthians*, 72.

avoided. Here "sobriety" suggests a keen awareness of the person and work of Satan.[143] "Be vigilant" means to be spiritually alert. It is sometimes translated "be watchful" (ESV). Grudem notes, "The opposite of this sober watchfulness is a kind of spiritual drowsiness in which one sees and responds to situations no differently than unbelievers, and God's perspective on each event is seldom if ever considered."[144] In spiritual warfare it is the Christian's responsibility to be alert to the calculated, cunning approach of the devil. This type of spiritual alertness enables believers to "resist the devil" in faith (5:9).

2. *Give no place* (*Eph. 4:27; cf. 2 Cor. 2:11*). When Paul commanded the saints in Ephesus to "give [no] place to the devil," he was not referring to a physical place (Eph. 4:27). Rather, he was warning them not to allow their anger to turn into a sinful and "wrathful" anger that the devil would likely use as an opportunity to bring division in the body (Eph. 4:25–26)—an opportunity he would otherwise not have. Apparently, the devil works havoc among personal relationships by fostering pride and hatred and evil thoughts. It is indeed a spiritual battle to ensure that Satan is given no chances to corrupt an individual's spiritual life or the welfare of the fellowship of the saints.[145]

3. *Resist the devil* (*James 4:7; cf. 1 Pet. 5:9*). The command to "resist the devil" is the fundamental idea behind all spiritual warfare (James 4:7). This idea is seen in each of the four key texts treated in this section.[146] What makes James's contribution unique is *how* one resists. James said, "Therefore, submit to God. Resist the devil and he will flee from you. Draw near to God and He will draw near to you" (James 4:7–8a). In short, the ability to resist the devil depends on humility before God. This is why James cited Proverbs 3:34, "God resists the proud, but gives grace to the humble," in the preceding verse and why he concluded the paragraph with "humble yourselves" (4:10). Humility, which Satan did not exercise and so was cast out of God's heavenly presence, is the key to victory in spiritual warfare. When we submit to God, we are not only empowered to resist the devil; but also we are, by virtue of allegiance, actually resisting him. James promises that though the devil wants to separate us from God, repentance allows us to "draw near to God" (4:8).[147] God's gracious response is to draw near to us. Significantly, we are nowhere instructed in the New Testament to take the offensive against the devil.

---

[143] Paige Patterson, *A Pilgrim Priesthood* (Nashville: Thomas Nelson, 1982), 187.

[144] Grudem, *1 Peter*, 196.

[145] Francis Foulkes, *Ephesians*, rev. ed., TNTC (Grand Rapids: Eerdmans, 1989), 141.

[146] On the striking similarity between James 4:6–10 and 1 Peter 5:5–9, see Douglas J. Moo, *James*, TNTC (Grand Rapids: Eerdmans, 1985), 147.

[147] Ibid., 148.

4. Stand firm (Eph. 6:10–20). The most vivid passage on spiritual warfare in the New Testament falls into three sections, each of which is worthy of our consideration.[148] First, verses 10–13 emphasize the need for putting on "the whole armor of God" in order to "be strong" and "to stand against" the enemy in battle. Since the language of "standing" occurs four times in one form or another throughout the paragraph (6:11,13–14), it is easily seen as the main idea of the entire paragraph. As H. C. G. Moule has it, "the present picture is not of a march, or of an assault, but of the holding of the fortress of the soul and of the Church for the heavenly King."[149]

The word translated "wrestle" (KJV, ESV) is better rendered "struggle" (NAS) or "battle."[150] There is nothing in the text to indicate that Paul shifts to the athletic metaphor of wrestling in mid-argument. This affords yet another opportunity to caution the reader that the image of Christians entering into a spiritual wrestling match with demons is simply foreign to the New Testament. In spiritual warfare, believers stand in resistance "against principalities, against powers, [and] against the rulers of the darkness of this age" (6:12); and they are empowered to do so by God's strength (6:10).

Second, verses 14–17 detail the armor of God and in so doing describe exactly what equips a believer to withstand the enemy's attack. The armor of God metaphor is probably not a result of Paul being chained to a Roman soldier, inspired by God to see such an analogy for spiritual warfare.[151] Rather, Paul's sustained imagery draws on the prophecy of Isaiah, "which describes the armour of Yahweh and his Messiah (11:4–5; 59:17; cf. 49:2; 52:7)."[152] As the Lord of Hosts fights with his own armor to vindicate his people, so believers are to don the armor of God as testimony to their identification with Him.[153] "Be strong in the Lord and in the strength of his might" (6:10 ESV).

To stand, having put on each piece of the armor—truth, righteousness, the gospel of peace, faith, salvation, and the word of God—is to stand completely unassailable before the enemy in Christ. The "whole armor of God" (6:11) then speaks of the absolute protection guaranteed by being "in Him" (cf. 1:4,6–7,11,13; 2:6; 3:12). In a word, the armor of God is about *identification* with Christ. Thus, to "put on" the armor speaks of both the victory believers *already* have in Christ's triumph over all principalities and powers (Eph. 1:21) and the divine enablement needed to stand against principalities and powers (6:12)—living in truth, righteousness, faith, etc.—in a world of darkness and evil where the final victory has *not yet* been realized.

---

[148] See Andrew T. Lincoln, *Ephesians,* WBC (Dallas: Word, 1990), 430.

[149] H. C. G. Moule, *Commentary on Ephesians* (Cambridge, 1884); cited in Foulkes, *Ephesians,* 178.

[150] Lincoln, *Ephesians,* 444.

[151] Cf. John F. MacArthur, *Ephesians* (Chicago: Moody, 1986), 338.

[152] Peter T. O'Brien, *The Letter to the Ephesians,* PNTC (Grand Rapids: Eerdmans, 1999), 457.

[153] Ibid., 463.

Third, verses 18–20 focus on the importance of prayer and watchfulness in spiritual warfare. Prayer is afforded a prominent place in battling the powers of darkness.[154] Presumably, it is impossible to stand against the enemy apart from vigilance in prayer. Prayer is not simply another weapon in the arsenal of the armor of God, nor is it identified with one weapon in particular.[155] Instead, it is seen here as the ongoing duty of the alert soldier. Paul's exhortation is grounded in the "watch and pray" language of Jesus, who taught his disciples to be vigilant in the face of temptation (Mark 14:38) and in view of his imminent return (Luke 21:34–36).[156]

Thus, alertness in prayer here does not speak of concentration in prayer as opposed to lazy praying. Prayer is the means by which believers sustain their opposition to the evil and darkness of this age. It is well to point out the importance of the phrase "in the Spirit" (Eph. 6:18). Prayer is to be offered to God the Father through the Son by the Spirit (Eph. 1:16–17; 2:18; 3:14; 5:20). Prayer is not the means by which believers engage Satan and demons in spiritual warfare; it is the means by which believers call on God for divine assistance in order to persevere and stand strong in Christ so that the gospel will continue to prevail not only for them but also for others who have not yet believed (Eph. 6:19–20).

Conclusion

In the final part of this chapter, we have tried to show the relevance of the doctrine of angels and demons for the church today. We have suggested that Christians reject patently false ways of thinking about angels, that they allow the Bible to inform with more precision than ever their answers to popular questions about "spiritual warfare," and that they wisely follow four biblical rules for engaging the enemy: be vigilant, give no place, resist the devil, and stand firm. Three verses from George Duffield's *Stand Up, Stand Up for Jesus* offer a fitting conclusion to the chapter in light of the final exhortation to "stand firm":

> Stand up, stand up for Jesus, Ye soldiers of the cross;
> Lift high His royal banner, It must not suffer loss:
> From vict'ry unto vict'ry, His army shall He lead,
> Till ev'ry foe is vanquished, And Christ is Lord indeed.

---

[154] Its prominence is seen in verse 18 in the repetition of the words *prayer* and *supplication,* both used twice, as well as the word *all,* which occurs four times. Believers are to pray at *all* times, with *all* prayer and supplication, with *all* perseverance, making supplication for *all* the saints.

[155] O'Brien, *Ephesians,* 483.

[156] Ibid., 485.

Stand up, stand up for Jesus, The trumpet call obey;
Forth to the mighty conflict, In this His glorious day:
Ye who are men, now serve Him, Against unnumbered foes;
Let courage rise with danger, And strength to strength oppose.

Stand up, stand up for Jesus, Stand in His strength alone;
The arm of flesh will fail you, Ye dare not trust your own:
Put on the gospel armor, Each piece put on with pray'r;
Where duty calls, or danger, Be never wanting there.[157]

---

[157] George Duffield Jr., "Stand Up, Stand Up for Jesus," in *The Baptist Hymnal,* ed. Wesley L. Forbis (Nashville: Convention, 1991).

SECTION 3

THE DOCTRINE OF HUMANITY

CHAPTER 7

Human Nature

John S. Hammett

In this chapter we consider a subject of perpetual interest to humans: themselves. Most people at one time or another pause to consider the enigma of human nature. Humans are capable of great acts of love, can create majestic works of art, and can even enter into a relationship with an infinite God; yet they are equally capable of horrific evil and cruelty and share many features in common with other animals. In the end, despite all their efforts to resist it, they die, and most are quickly forgotten. Scripture compares us to a mist "that appears for a little while and then vanishes" (James 4:14).[1] No wonder the psalmist marvels in amazement that God is mindful of us (Ps. 8:3–4).

The English poet Alexander Pope, in his "Essay on Man," saw our proper field of study as humans to be our own strange nature.

> Know then thyself, presume not God to scan;
> The proper study of mankind is Man.
> Placed on this isthmus of a middle state,
> Being darkly wise and rudely great;
> With too much knowledge for the Sceptic side,
> With too much weakness for the Stoic's pride,
> He hangs between; in doubt to act, or rest;
> In doubt to deem himself a God, or Beast . . .
> Sole judge of truth, in endless Error hurled:
> The glory, jest and riddle of the world![2]

Yet despite this paradoxical nature of humans and their relative unimportance in comparison with the vastness of space and time and the glories of almighty God, this field of study is essential for Christians for at least four reasons.

---

[1] Unless otherwise noted, all Scripture citations in this chapter are from the New International Version (NIV).

[2] Alexander Pope, "Essay on Man, Epistle II," from *The Complete Poetical Works of Alexander Pope,* ed. H. W. Boynton, found on http://www.theotherpages.org/poems/pope-i.html, accessed on 4/24/2006.

Human nature study가 피요한이 이유 ① *하나님이 인간을 가까이 때문*

First, humans are worthy of consideration because <u>God is supremely</u> *God's involve-worthy of attention*, and God has chosen to involve himself with humans. *ment w/ humanity* In fact, God has so thoroughly involved himself with humanity that <u>John Calvin insisted that knowledge of God and knowledge of man must pro-ceed hand in hand.</u> The first sentence of Calvin's classic work, *Institutes of the Christian Religion,* links the two: "Nearly all the wisdom we possess, that is to say, true and sound wisdom, consists of two parts: the knowledge *biblical teaching* of God and of ourselves. But, while joined by many bonds, which one pre- *on humanity* cedes and brings forth the other is not easy to discern."[3] *하나님과* ② *인간의 본질에 대한 말씀을 주셨기*

Second, the study of humanity is a worthwhile pursuit because <u>God 때문</u> has given revelation concerning humanity in Scripture.</u> Biblical teaching on humanity, like all biblical teaching, is "useful for teaching, rebuking, correcting and training in righteousness" and is part of that which equips *the Nature of* us "for every good work" (2 Tim. 3:16–17). The proper response to God's *Xian ministry* revelation is grateful study and faithful application.[3] *하나님께 대한 사랑을 하나님 백성이 이루는*

Third, the study of humanity is especially <u>important</u> for those who seek *통하여 것이기* to serve Christ because one way we express <u>our love for Christ is in loving 때문</u> and serving others.</u> But how can we serve others in a manner acceptable to God if we do not understand what he intends for humans to be? The study of humanity is imperative for Christian ministers, for it is humans to whom we minister. ④ *자녀로써 act하기 때문   the demands of Xian discipleship*

Finally, we engage in the study of humanity as <u>an act of discipleship.</u> We have only one brief life of service on this earth to offer to God. How can we offer it to God as an acceptable expression of our worship and devotion if we do not know what God desires a human life to be? Only he can pronounce the "well done, good and faithful servant" (Matt. 25:21) that we long to hear.

Thus, <u>God's involvement with humanity</u>, <u>biblical teaching on humanity,</u> the nature of <u>Christian ministry</u>, and the <u>demands of Christian discipleship</u> commend to us the study of the doctrine of humanity.

What Does the Bible Say?

We may begin this section by summarizing biblical teaching under six headings, all of which are introduced to us in <u>Genesis 1–3</u> and elaborated on elsewhere in Scripture.

Figure 1: Summary of Biblical Teaching on Humanity

<u>We are created</u> beings.

---

[3] Calvin, *Institutes,* 1.1.1.

> We are created in the image of God.
> We are created male and female.
> We are created to work.
> We are created for community.
> We are not today as we were created; we are fallen.

Of these six, only the first five will be considered here; the sixth belongs properly to the doctrine of sin, which is treated in the next chapter.

We Are Created Beings

The Fact of Creation

The first and focal point of biblical teaching concerning the creation of humans is the fact of divine creation. This fact is emphasized in a number of ways. First, the whole creation account in Genesis 1 is deliberately structured to reach its apex in the creation of humans. This is seen in the change from the repeated phrase "Let there be" for the other elements of creation, to the special phrase "Let us make" for the creation of humans. This act of creation is clearly special. It is even more obviously special when we realize the enormous amount of selectivity involved in the creation account. We are given nothing on the creation of angels, only passing reference to the stars, which we know today form galaxies extending for millions of light-years, and the thousands of species of animals are mentioned in large groups. The creation of humans was the feature the author of Genesis selected for special emphasis.

Next, references to God's creation of humans are pervasive throughout Scripture. The terms used in Genesis 1:26–27 are the most prominent ones. The term for "make" in verse 26 (*asah*) is common and is used hundreds of times in the Old Testament for all types of making. God is described fifteen times as the one who made humans, perhaps the most familiar being Psalm 100:3: "Know that the LORD is God. It is he who made us, and we are his." The noun form of *asah* is used to call God "Maker" of humans nine times, as when Job is questioned, "Can a man be more pure than his Maker?" (Job 4:17). The second term, "create" (*bara*), is a special word, used only for divine making. In Genesis 1, it is used once in verse 1 to refer to all of creation, but it is used three times in verse 27, emphasizing God's involvement in the origin of humanity.

Altogether, *bara* is used for the creation of humans in the Old Testament at least twelve times (Gen. 1:27; 5:1–2; 6:7; Deut. 4:32; Ps. 89:47; Eccles. 12:1; Isa. 43:7; 45:12; Mal. 2:10). Beyond these two terms, there are words used less frequently, such as those in Psalm 139:13–15, where the psalmist sees God as the one who "knit me together in my mother's womb."

New Testament teaching echoes much the same themes, citing the foundational text of Genesis 1:27 in Matthew 19:4 and Mark 10:6 and paraphrasing Genesis 1:26 in James 3:9. God is called Creator (1 Pet. 4:19) and the one who made all things (Eph. 3:9; Col. 1:16; Rev. 4:11; 10:6), which would include humans. Paul sees God's creation of humans as common ground he shares with the philosophers of Athens and from which he can start to tell them the gospel message about Jesus (Acts 17:24–28).

Scripture thus seems to focus on the fact that we are creatures, made by a Creator. The questions of most interest in recent times (how and when God created) are not as clearly addressed. We will seek to give a biblical response to those questions in later sections of this chapter, but it is always wise to keep the main thing the main thing. For anthropology, the main thing is the fact of creation.

The Human Constitution

The second feature of biblical teaching on the creation of humanity which calls for attention is the variety of elements or capacities with which humans are endowed. Terms like *body, soul, spirit, heart,* and others are found hundreds of times throughout Scripture and raise the issue of the human constitution. However, discussing these terms is a troublesome task for a number of reasons.

First, the Bible does not use these terms (*soul* and *spirit,* especially) in any consistent way. Rather, there is often a good degree of overlap between terms. There is also something of a changing perspective from the Old Testament to the New Testament as a Greek perspective begins to modify a largely Hebraic understanding. Also, there has been turmoil in contemporary discussions concerning these terms (especially the issue of the soul) as well as traditional debates over the trichotomist versus dichotomist views of human nature and traducian versus creationist positions on the origin of the soul.[4] Responding to these difficult questions begins with an understanding of the biblical terms.

Figure 2 gives what is the central or most distinctive meaning of these terms, but any single definition is artificial, for the Bible uses these and other terms somewhat interchangeably and with a variety of meanings. Moreover, as more and more theologians are concluding, the Bible uses most of these words to refer to humans in their totality, but from different points of view, and approaches humans more functionally than ontologically. Nevertheless, these definitions do highlight some theologically significant aspects of human nature.

---

[4] See pp. 346–52, 384–88 for definitions of these terms.

Figure 2: Key Terms for Biblical Anthropology

English	Hebrew	Greek	Theological Significance
body	*basar*	*soma*	the physical form
flesh	—	*sarx*	the capacity for weakness, sin, and rebellion
soul	*nephesh*	*psuchē*	the seat of life or being; the person
spirit	*ruach*	*pneuma*	the capacity for a relationship with God
heart	*leb*	*kardia*	the whole person at the deepest level of existence
mind	*bina*	*nous*	faculty of under-standing, discern-ment and judgment
conscience	—	*suneidēsis*	(fallible) moral guide

Body, Flesh. Perhaps no other term needs more biblical clarification, for one result of Christianity being born in a Greek context has been an unwitting adoption of a Greek, rather than a biblical, view of the body. The ideal of many Greek philosophers was to flee the body, for they thought of the body as the prison of the soul. What was nonmaterial was good and pure; what was material was inherently corrupt and impure. But this is emphatically not the Bible's view of the body. The dominant view of the body in Scripture is not that it is evil but rather a normal and necessary part of a human being. Several scholars have noted that there is no Hebrew word for body as something separate from the soul or spirit. The closest equivalent we find is *basar,* but it is almost always translated *flesh,* either human flesh (169 times) or the flesh of animals (104 times). When used to refer to humans, it most often has in view the whole person, though looking at that person's external aspect. But a word for the body as something separated from the nonmaterial aspect of human nature is missing, for the normal Hebrew conception of a person assumed the physical form as necessary.

Occasionally, *basar* denotes humans in their frailty or corruptibility, such as in Isaiah 40:6, where flesh is compared to grass that withers or flowers that fall. But flesh is not seen as something inherently evil or as something existing in opposition to the spirit or soul. Indeed, Psalm 145:21 speaks of "all *basar*" as giving praise to God's name forever. Edmund

Jacob says, "Israelite anthropology is monistic,"[5] though perhaps a better description would be functionally holistic.

Even in the New Testament, while body and spirit are at times distinguished (Matt. 10:28), they are not opposed. As in the Old Testament, the body can even be used to refer to the whole human person (Rom. 12:1), for human existence is a bodily existence, and human nature is an embodied nature. The culprit for the negative view of the body in Christian thought is mostly Greek philosophy, but can also be traced to a misunderstanding of the second New Testament word that refers to body or flesh, *sarx,* especially as Paul sometimes uses it. Most of the time in the New Testament, *sarx* is roughly equivalent to *basar,* referring to human flesh (Luke 24:39), or to humans in their external, physical aspect. In this sense John 1:14 teaches that Jesus shared this essential aspect of human existence. Both the Old Testament authors and Jesus recognized that human flesh was weak and could not be trusted (Jer. 17:5; Isa. 40:6; Matt. 26:41), but there is no idea that human flesh is inherently sinful.

Sometimes Paul uses *sarx* in a fairly neutral way to refer to human ancestry (Rom. 1:3; 9:3,5) or to physical human flesh (1 Cor. 6:16) or as another way to speak of a person (1 Cor. 1:29). But one important sense of *sarx* in Paul's writings goes further. About thirty-five times Paul uses *sarx* in a distinctive way to refer to the human capacity for sin, weakness, and rebellion (see Rom. 7:18; 8:5–13; Gal. 5:17). It is the opposing capacity to human spirit and is in conflict with the work of God's Spirit in his people. As the human spirit is the capacity to open one's life to the influence of God, so the flesh is the capacity to hear and respond to temptation. The spirit leads life in one direction; the flesh, in the opposite direction.

We should note that Paul's use of *sarx* in this sense does not mean sin is especially associated with the body. Many of the works of the flesh in Galatians 5:19–21 are sins of the mind or heart, and sometimes translating *sarx* as "flesh" has caused us to associate the body with sin. For this reason the NIV translation of "sinful nature" seems preferable. Some oppose that translation because they think it portrays Christians as schizophrenic, with two natures. But *sarx* refers to a capacity, not an ontological nature, and it seems undeniable that Christians do possess conflicting capacities.

In theory the sinful nature has already been crucified in those who belong to Christ (Gal. 5:24). In practice we find that the struggle continues. But the struggle in the Christian life is not between the body and the soul, or our physical flesh and the spirit, but between the spirit and the sinful nature. The body itself is most often seen in the Old Testament and New

---

5 Edmund Jacob, "*psuchē, ktl,*" in TDNT, 9:623.

Testament as a necessary aspect of humanity and is often used to refer to the human person as a whole.

Soul. Evangelicals like to talk of soul winning and saving souls, and the Bible does occasionally use the word *soul* for the form in which humans exist after death or that aspect of our nature whose fellowship with Christ continues even after the death of the body (Matt. 10:28; 1 Pet. 1:9; Rev. 6:9), but that is not the dominant idea behind the biblical words *nephesh* and *psuchē*.

H. Wheeler Robinson, in his helpful study *The Christian Doctrine of Man,* gives three central meanings for the word *nephesh* in the Old Testament.[6] The most frequent sense is the soul as the seat of life (according to Robinson, 282 times out of a total of 754 occurrences of *nephesh*). Thus, when Adam received the breath of life from God, he became a living soul. But likewise, in Genesis 1:20, the animals in the water are called living souls. This does not mean we need to evangelize fish but that the normal meaning of *soul* is the seat of life, that which makes a body—animal or human—a living being. Taking the life (or "lifeblood") of a man or animal in Genesis 9:4–5 is taking its *nephesh,* for, as Leviticus 17:11 says, the *nephesh* of an animal is in its blood. To shed blood is to pour out life. In 1 Kings 19:10, Elijah was hiding from those who were seeking his life (*nephesh*). In all, *nephesh* is translated as "life" 102 times in the KJV translation of the Old Testament, and it means the seat of life many other times when it is translated as "soul."

A second and closely related major usage (223 times, according to Robinson), is *nephesh* as subject or agent of life. In such cases the best translation is often a personal pronoun (such as "I" for *nephesh* in Ezekiel 4:14; this seems to be the usage as well in the well-known verse, Ezek. 18:4). Edmund Jacob says that *nephesh* "is the usual term for a man's total nature"[7] and so a personal pronoun is an appropriate translation. The third sense of *nephesh* Robinson calls a psychical sense, involving an emotional manifestation of life, often similar to the ideas associated with spirit or heart (see Ps. 19:7; Prov. 2:10).

The corresponding New Testament word, *psuchē* also often means simply life and is translated as "life" forty-one times in the KJV (compared to fifty-seven times as "soul") and even more often in more modern versions. Occasionally, the NIV even translates *psuchē* as simply a general reference to a person or persons ("you" in James 1:21; "themselves" in 1 Pet. 4:19), and often that is the clear meaning (Acts 27:37; cf. Acts 2:41; 1 Pet. 3:20).

---

6 H. Wheeler Robinson, *The Christian Doctrine of Man,* 3rd ed. (Edinburgh: T. & T. Clark, 1958), 16.
7 Jacob, "*psuchē,*" 620.

Nephesh and *psuchē* are also used in slightly different ways, some of which can be derived from the central sense of life. For example, in Psalm 107:9, it is "souls" that are hungry and thirsty, desiring that which is necessary for life. Other desires are also referred to as being in the soul, both evil desires (Gen. 34:3; his "heart") and godly desires (Pss. 42:1; 63:1). In these last cases the meaning of soul is virtually equal to "heart" and is often so translated (Ps. 10:3; Eph. 6:6; Col. 3:23), referring to the center of life and especially the seat of emotions, even the emotions of God. It is God's soul that hates (Ps. 11:5; Isa. 1:14) and loves (Jer. 12:7), and Jesus' soul that is sorrowful in the garden of Gethsemane (Matt. 26:38). Infrequently, *psuchē* is spoken of as the object of God's saving work (James 1:21; Heb. 10:39; 1 Pet. 1:9) or the locus of the spiritual life (Matt. 11:29; Acts 14:22; Heb. 13:17; 1 Pet. 2:11; 2:25). Thus, there is a narrow basis for speaking of "lost" and "saved" souls, though there would be little change of meaning in these verses if *psuchē* were translated as "life" or as a general reference to persons.

Finally, there is some overlap with "spirit." Some examples are Luke 1:46–47, where the two are used in parallel, and Revelation 6:9 and Hebrews 12:23, where both are used to refer to those who have died. But *nephesh* and *psuchē* more often overlap with the concept of heart and the dominant and distinctive meaning is that of life.

Spirit. The words for *spirit, ruach* and *pneuma,* are used in five senses in Scripture. In the physical sense these words can denote wind or breath (Exod. 14:21; John 3:8). In a psychological sense they can refer to an attitude or disposition (Ps. 51:10; Isa. 61:3). The divine sense of spirit is the Holy Spirit. The angelic sense is used for good spirits and unclean spirits (demons). Our major concern is with the anthropological sense, the human spirit.

As we mentioned above, *spirit* can sometimes be used almost interchangeably with *soul* (Ps. 31:5; Eccles. 12:7; Luke 1:46–47; Heb. 12:23) and at times overlaps with the idea of heart (Isa. 57:15, where spirit and heart are used in parallel), but the dominant use is slightly different from either soul or heart. W. D. Stacey states the difference in these terms:

> When reference is made to man in his relation to God, *ruach* is the term most likely to be used . . . but when reference is made to man in relation to other men, or man living the common life of men, then *nephesh* is most likely, if a psychical term is required. In both cases, the whole man was involved.[8]

---

[8] W. D. Stacey, *The Pauline View of Man* (London: Macmillan, 1956), 90.

게념 죽아은 in OT = 표가ᄆ in NT

What is true of *ruach* in the Old Testament is even more true of *pneuma* in the New Testament. James Dunn says *pneuma* denotes that

> man in so far as he belongs to the spiritual realm and interacts with the spiritual realm. . . . Thus, the spirit of man is that aspect of man through which God most immediately encounters him . . . that dimension of the whole man wherein and whereby he is most immediately open and responsive to God . . . that area of human awareness most sensitive to matters of the spiritual realm.[9]

Spirit refers to the human capacity for a relationship with God and the means by which that relationship is established. Usage is especially noteworthy in Paul's writings, particularly in Romans 8, but is found as well in the Gospels (Matt. 5:3; Mark 2:8; 14:38; Luke 1:47; John 11:33; 13:21) and less frequently in other parts of the New Testament (Heb. 4:12; 1 Pet. 3:4).

This does not mean that spirit is a separated compartment of the human being. Rather, it is a capacity that indwells the total person and only human persons. *Soul* may be used of the life principle or vitality in both animals and people; certainly both humans and other animals have bodies. But only human beings have spirit, the capacity for relationship with God. This would seem to indicate that spirit is related to that which distinguishes humans from all other creatures—that is, being created in God's image.

Heart. The heart (*leb, kardia*) in Scripture is the seat of personality, the central focus of one's life, who one really is (see 1 Sam. 16:7; Prov. 4:23; Matt. 12:34; 1 Pet. 3:4, where heart is translated "inner self"). *Heart* is the most important and most frequent term the Bible uses in reference to any aspect or capacity of humans (more than 900 times).

At various times the heart is spoken of as the center of thinking (1 Kings 3:9,12; Luke 2:19), feeling (Isa. 35:4; John 14:1), and especially volition. In Deuteronomy 6:5, we are commanded to love God with our hearts, the heart being responsible to obey. With the heart we choose to trust Christ (Rom. 10:10). The heart purposes to give (2 Cor. 9:7). Josiah is praised because his heart was responsive to God's word (2 Chron. 34:27), but the heart of the wicked is perverse and proud (Ps. 101:4–5). Robinson says *heart* is used 166 times for emotional states, 204 times for intellectual activities, and 195 times for volition. Even more frequent is heart as the personality or character as a whole (257 times, including 1 Sam. 16:7).[10]

Obviously there is a lot of overlap between heart and mind, soul, will, spirit, and even conscience (Rom. 2:15), but the central idea is that the

---

[9] J. D. G. Dunn, "Spirit, Holy Spirit," *NIDNTT*, 3:693–94.
[10] Robinson, *Christian Doctrine of Man*, 22.

heart is that which directs the course of one's life. Thus, it is crucial for the heart to be sensitive to the voice of the Lord, and not to become hardened (Ps. 95:8–10), for obedience begins in the heart. The heart can be the seat of sin (Gen. 6:5; Jer. 17:9) as well as the seat of faith (Prov. 3:5). The statement of Anthony Hoekema is a good summary of the importance of heart in Scripture: "*Kardia* stands for the whole person in his or her inner essence. In the heart man's basic attitude toward God is determined, whether of faith or unbelief, obedience or rebellion."[11]

At the same time we may note a slight difference of emphasis between Paul, on the one hand, and the rest of the New Testament and all of the Old Testament. Paul at times uses "mind" (*nous*) or "conscience" (*suneidēsis*) where the Old Testament and other New Testament writers normally use "heart." Thus we need to look at these terms as well.

Mind. The Hebrew word *bina* is used for understanding and can have a mental component (Dan. 1:20) but is more often seen in terms of a spiritual disposition and thus is linked with wisdom, which is a moral quality more than a mental achievement. What matters is not just knowledge but one's attitude and use of that knowledge. Thus, "fear of the LORD" is parallel to "knowledge of the Holy One" in Proverbs 9:10. And while we may value and use the mind's ability to understand, we are not to "lean upon" or fully trust our own understanding (see Prov. 3:5).

Moreover, the Hebrew view of the unity of human personality often leads the Bible to refer to the heart as the organ of thinking as well as of volition and emotion. Thus, when Lamentations 3:21 speaks of calling something to mind, the word used is *leb*. Conversely, when Mark wants to communicate all Moses meant by loving God with all the heart (Deut. 6:4–5, quoted in Mark 12:30), he adds "with all your mind." To communicate what Moses meant by "heart" to a Greek-influenced audience, Mark adds "mind."

The Old Testament's fluid use of words also includes *sometimes nephesh* as a word that can indicate mind. First Chronicles 28:9 uses *nephesh* for *mind*, that which devises "thoughts." Even *ruach* can be used for mental processes (Ezek. 11:5). But the most common synonym is heart (*leb*). It is clear, therefore, that *bina* is not the only Hebrew word for the Greek idea of mind.

The major New Testament term for *mind* is *nous*. It is predominantly a Pauline term (21 of 24 occurrences). As in the Old Testament, here too the idea of mental acquisition of facts is not the central issue. Mind is a faculty of judgment; it exercises discernment and disposes one toward faithful

---

[11] Anthony Hoekema, *Created in God's Image* (Grand Rapids: Eerdmans and Carlisle, UK: Paternoster, 1986), 215.

obedience. There is a mental component to it, as when Christ opened the minds of the disciples to understand the Scriptures (Luke 24:45), but the mind is also the faculty that seeks to serve and obey God (Rom. 7:23,25). It has been damaged by sin (sometimes called the "noetic effects" of sin) and so now needs renewal in the process of sanctification (Rom. 12:2; Eph. 4:23). Such renewal leads not only to increased knowledge but also to better judgment, as in approving what God's will is (Rom. 12:2) and putting on a whole new self (Eph. 4:24). Conversely, ignorance is not primarily a lack of facts but a hardened heart (Eph. 4:17–18) that turns away from true knowledge (Rom. 1:28).

Yet, when all is said and done, the mind takes a surprisingly minor role in the biblical portrayal of human nature. There is much more concern for developing the type of heart that the Bible sees as the instrument of godly thinking and understanding.

Conscience. There is no specific Hebrew word for *conscience*. The idea of sorrow or pain over sin is covered by the word *heart*. So when David confesses his sin, he asks for a clean heart (Ps. 51:10). In the New Testament, conscience is seen as a moral guide, useful as a check from moving into a wrong path, but far from infallible. First Corinthians 8:7–12 discusses the brother whose conscience is weak because he is ignorant of certain truths. Yet Paul's main point is not that the older brother should enlighten the weaker brother but that he should bear with his brother's weakness rather than causing him to sin against his conscience.

Conscience is therefore a useful guide and should not be sinned against, for it can become "seared" (1 Tim. 4:2) and "corrupted" (Titus 1:15). Thus, it too needs to be renewed and cleansed in salvation and sanctification (Heb. 9:14; 10:22). Indeed, one of the blessings of salvation in Christ is the cleansing from sin and guilt that could not be dealt with by the blood of bulls and goats. This is good news indeed for those hampered in their Christian walk by an oversensitive or overactive conscience still accusing them of guilt. God regards his children as cleansed. Still, the assurance of that cleansing does not always come just with proper teaching. Another source of assurance is seeing God change our hearts and give us a basis for believing we are his (see 1 John 3:19–20, where *heart* is virtually equivalent to *conscience*). Such objective markers can be used to deal with doubts and lurking fears.

The practical importance of all this is that ministry must address the whole range of human needs if it is to minister to the whole person. God has constituted us as beings who exist as a unity but a complex unity that includes physical, psychological, spiritual, mental, and emotional faculties.

We Are Created in the Image of God

The most important fact one can state about any human being is that he or she is created in the image of God *(imago dei)*. Many elements of our created nature are shared with animals, but only humanity was created with special deliberation ("Let us make" rather than "Let there be") and with a special design.

The image of God is important in a variety of ways. Historically, it has been an important and much-discussed issue, with major directions in the history of theology being affected by one's interpretation of it. One might easily (and correctly) argue that it was central in the Reformation and remains crucial today as the indispensable background for the doctrine of salvation. Theologically, it is not only important in itself but also leads us into discussions of the effects of the fall and regeneration. Practically, the image of God is the basis for human dignity. A correct understanding of it is the basis for truly Christian human relationships.

Surprisingly, only a handful of texts explicitly teach the creation of humanity in the image of God: Genesis 1:26–27; 5:1–2; 9:6–7 in the Old Testament and 1 Corinthians 11:7 and James 3:9–10 in the New Testament. Of these, Genesis 1:26–27 is clearly the key text. It is the focal point of the entire creation account in Genesis 1. It is the only account that has both key terms *(image* and *likeness)*, and it has the term "image" three times, as if to emphasize the centrality and importance of this point.

The two Old Testament terms, *demuth* (likeness) and *tselem* (image), are not helpful in providing a definition. *Demuth* is used twenty-six times in the Old Testament, sixteen in describing the visions of Ezekiel, and is only used of humanity in Genesis 1:26 and 5:1. The particular emphasis of the word seems to be on a visible likeness, as in the likenesses Ezekiel saw. *Tselem* is used a bit more frequently, thirty-three times, with more than half (seventeen) coming from Daniel 2–3, referring to the golden image of Nebuchadnezzar. It is the dominant term in Genesis 1, being used three times, as if to underscore its importance. It is also the term history has used for this doctrine. It is most often found in contexts of idolatry (though neither of these terms is used in the prohibition of idols in the second commandment), suggesting that the making of images is prohibited not only because no image can adequately represent God but also because God himself has already made the only authorized image—human beings.

For the sake of completeness, we may consider the New Testament terms that are the counterparts of *demuth* and *tselem*. The most common Greek word for *likeness, homoiōma,* is not used for humanity in the New Testment; a related and almost synonymous word, *homoiōsis,* is used once for the creation of humans in James 3:9 and is the word used to translate *demuth* in Genesis 1:26 in the Greek version of the Old Testament. The idea in both of these Greek terms is simply that of some similarity or correspondence. A more exact correspondence in nature is indicated by *charaktēr,* which is used for Christ in Hebrews 1:3, but never of human correspondence to God. The more common Greek term is *eikōn,* the counterpart of *tselem.* It too can be used of idolatrous images, as that of the beast in Revelation (similar to that of Nebuchadnezzar in Daniel), but is found in a positive way in several theologically important verses. Only one refers to our present possession of the image of God, 1 Corinthians 11:7, but five refer in some way or other to the restoration or eschatological completion of the image of God in believers (Rom. 8:29; 1 Cor. 15:49; 2 Cor. 3:18; Col. 3:10; the same meaning is found in Eph. 4:22–24 without the *eikōn* terminology).

In addition to the rather general clues to the meaning of our creation in the image of God found in the terms and context of Genesis 1:26–27, one distinctive insight is found in the New Testament. We mentioned above a number of verses that speak of the restoration of the image of God as an ongoing process in the Christian life (2 Cor. 3:18; Col. 3:10; and cf. Eph. 4:24) and still others that look to a full eschatological conformity to the image of Christ (Rom. 8:29; 1 Cor. 15:49). These verses seem to point to an answer to one often-debated question in the history of the interpretation of this teaching. Is the image of God lost in the fall? These verses that speak of the renewal or restoration of the image would seem to imply that the image of God was damaged at the fall but not destroyed. It was defaced, not erased. This implication is confirmed by the fact that all the texts that speak of humans being the image bearers of God, aside from Genesis 1:26–27, are postfall texts.

Despite the paucity of biblical teaching on the image of God, we may draw five biblical parameters. These parameters do not answer all the questions we have concerning the image of God, but they give us guidelines by which we may evaluate suggested interpretations of the image of God.

1. *Creation in the image of God is affirmed for all persons.* Genesis 1:27 specifically says "male and female," and the words used in the other texts in Genesis and in James 3:9 (*adam* and *anthrōpos*) are both universal words for all humans. Genesis 9:6 and James 3:9 seem to require a generic understanding of humans—all ages, all races, all sexes, and all statuses in life. To be human means to be an image bearer of God. This will have implications for our later discussion of what the image of God in humans is. It must be something that all humans possess.

2. *Creation in the image of God involves being like God in some unspecified way.* As we saw above, the words used for *image and likeness* (*tselem* and *demuth* in Genesis; *homoiōsis* in James, but more often *eikōn* in the New Testament) are not very specific, and Scripture does little to define them explicitly.

human uniqueness and dignity의 기반

3. *Creation in the image of God is the basis for human uniqueness and dignity (Gen. 9:6; James 3:9–10).* Genesis 9:6 sees murder as so heinous a crime that by it one forfeits his own life. Thus to kill a human or even curse one is an affront to and an attack upon God.   타락 후에도 인간

4. *Even after the fall, humans are spoken of as being in the image of God (Gen. 9:6; James 3:9), so the image is not completely lost in the fall.* However, it does seem that the image was damaged in the fall, for there are verses that speak of the restoration of the divine image or conformity to the image of Christ as an ongoing process in the Christian life (2 Cor. 3:18; Eph. 4:23–24; Col. 3:10). Humans today still bear God's image, even if in a distorted and fallen way.   창조뿐만 영상이미로 동말종적 맞게에 인성되는가

5. *Moreover, since Christ is the perfect image of God (Heb. 1:3) and the* 이기준함. *result of this process of restoration is being fully like Christ (Rom. 8:29; 1 Cor. 15:49; 1 John 3:1–2), we may speak of the image of God as being not only our created design but also our eschatological destiny.* If this is so, then image restoration may be related to the process we call sanctification, which is concluded with the event of glorification.

But these parameters are all that Scripture clearly affirms. Thus, in interpreting what the image of God is, we will follow these biblical clues and seek to stay within the biblical parameters. But beyond that, we have to discern where Scripture is pointing and what ideas seem to make the best sense of all the data we have or what approach best ties all of Scripture together.

We Are Created Male and Female

This is one of the major battlefields in theology today, with widely varying positions and controversy even within evangelical ranks. We begin with a preliminary semantic issue. Many today distinguish between sexuality, 의미상의 which they take in a narrow sense to refer only to the physical, biological manifestations of maleness and femaleness, and gender, which is used in a broader sense to refer to learned, culturally varying ideas we associate with male and female. This seems to assume that there are no real differences beyond the obvious physical, biological ones.

Others believe much more is involved, arguing that being male or female involves one's being in a far more profound way than just physically. Stanley Grenz believes that being male or female involves living with fundamentally different "modes of orientation."[12] A male relates to

---

[12] Stanley Grenz, *Sexual Ethics* (Dallas: Word, 1990), 8. Grenz draws upon the work of a number of social scientists and cites the work of J. Richard Udry, *The Social Context of Marriage* (Philadelphia: J. B. Lippincott, 1966), 37. Udry mentions "differing modes of orientation" as one of numerous possible ways of describing male-female differences. We believe Grenz is more accurate in seeing it as a fundamental difference of males and females.

and interacts with himself, others, and the world out of one orientation; a female, out of a differing orientation. The nature, extent, and source of the differences involved in these differing orientations are topics of considerable controversy in contemporary Western society and have been the source of innumerable studies by social scientists. Our concern here, however, is biblical teaching. The fact that God created two sexes would seem to imply some differentiation; we will see if Scripture indicates what some of those differences may be in some key texts.

At the same time we do not want to overemphasize the differences. Men and women are far more alike than they are different. They are both image bearers of God. Furthermore, Scripture addresses us far more often as humans, or believers, than as men and women. Males and females share a common calling (to Christlikeness); we may fulfill it differently, however, because of our differences.

The most heated debate concerning maleness and femaleness in evangelical churches has to do with what roles are appropriate for each sex. Egalitarians highlight biblical teaching on the equality of men and women and see a differentiation of roles based on sex as a violation of that equality. Complementarians affirm the equality of men and women, but they do not see equality of nature, worth, or dignity as incompatible with differing, complementary roles.[13] Limitations of space preclude a full discussion of all the claims and counterclaims from both sides of the debate here. Rather, we will attempt to summarize biblical teaching under four headings. These summaries reflect a complementarian position because that seems, *prima facie*, to be the most natural reading of the key biblical texts.

In fact, a recent egalitarian virtually concedes that complementarians have a better exegetical case. John Stackhouse says, "In truth, it is abundantly clear that there are hierarchies in the church and the home in the pages of the NT. The complementarians are simply right about that."[14] He examines the attempts of egalitarians to deal with the key texts and concludes: "Resorting to finely argued revisionist technical scholarship . . . seems to miss the patriarchal forest of the entire Bible for particular textual trees," adding that the complementarian readings can be avoided "only by

---

[13] The literature produced by the complementarian/egalitarian debate is enormous. The key work on the complementarian side is John Piper and Wayne Grudem, eds., *Recovering Biblical Manhood & Womanhood: A Response to Evangelical Feminism* (Wheaton: Crossway, 1991); among those arguing the egalitarian view are Gilbert Bilezikian, *Beyond Sex Roles: A Guide for the Study of Female Roles in the Bible* (Grand Rapids: Baker, 1985), Aída Besançon Spencer, *Beyond the Curse: Women Called to Ministry* (Nashville: Thomas Nelson, 1985), and Mary Stewart van Leeuwen, *Gender and Grace* (Downers Grove: InterVarsity, 1990).

[14] John G. Stackhouse Jr., *Finally Feminist: A Pragmatic Christian Understanding of Gender* (Grand Rapids: Baker, 2005), 50.

considerable exegetical heavy lifting."[15] The attempt of Stackhouse and other egalitarians will be considered later; our task at this stage is to present what we understand as the straightforward teaching of Scripture.

The Equality of Male and Female

The first key teaching of Scripture is that males and females share many things in common. Both are created in God's image (Gen. 1:27), and the so-called "cultural mandate" of Genesis 1:28 is addressed to "them." Indeed, the procreative aspect of that mandate requires both male and female participation. In the New Testament both males and females are found in the company of Christ's disciples (Luke 8:1–3); both receive the outpoured Holy Spirit (Acts 2:17–18); both are given spiritual gifts and are called to use them (1 Cor. 12:7); both enter Christ's body on the same basis and share in the oneness of that body (Gal. 3:28).

The usual term for this teaching is the *equality* of male and female, and that term is certainly appropriate, in many ways. However, it is interesting that Scripture nowhere uses the word *equal* of men and women. Even the text most often seen as central to the egalitarian position, Galatians 3:28, points to unity in Christ's body, rather than equality. Of course, the mere absence of a word is not determinative. The word *Trinity* is nowhere in the Bible, but the doctrine clearly is. As to equality, it is an appropriate term to describe the fact that men and women share equal value, dignity, and responsibility before God. However, in Western culture equality has also been an important political term, signifying equal rights; and rights are a dubious category in biblical thought.

Scott Bartchy notes that in the Greco-Roman world *egalitarianism* was a term used mainly in the political realm to refer to things like "equal access to vote, positions of public leadership, and the ownership of property;" the New Testament church is not portrayed as "an egalitarian community in the political sense, but a well-functioning family in the kinship sense."[16] It is this author's conviction that a crucial factor in the egalitarian-complementarian debate is the appropriate way to define equality. Equality seems to exist side by side in Scripture with differing roles, a position that to egalitarians violates equality. Those differing roles form the next two key points of biblical teaching on male and female.

Male and Female Roles in the Home

Male and female have differing roles within the home and male and female relationships. This difference is hinted at in Genesis 2:18–25, an

---

[15] Ibid., 52, n. 13.

[16] Scott Bartchy, "Divine Power, Community Formation, and Leadership in Acts," in *Community Formation in the Early Church and Today,* ed. Richard Longenecker (Peabody, MA: Hendrickson, 2002), 97–98.

important text for understanding God's intention for male and female, because it and Genesis 1 are the only prefall references to the male and female roles. Adam is specifically said to be in need of "a helper suitable for him"; Eve is created to meet that need. These are best understood as created, nonreversible roles. Adam is not created to be "a helper suitable for Eve," and 1 Corinthians 11:9 extends that difference from Adam and Eve to man and woman in general.

God's creation of Eve as a helper suitable to or corresponding to Adam implies a differentiation of role, which places man in the role of initiator or leader, and the female in the role of supporting, assisting, and adapting to his need. This difference cannot be taken to indicate an inferiority in Eve, for the word for "helper" is most often used for God in the Old Testament. Nevertheless, there does seem to be a different role. A parent helping a child with homework may take a subordinate role, one of adapting to the child's need; but the parent is clearly not inferior to the child. There is no claim that Eve is inferior to Adam or that a subordinate role implies inequality. Rather, there is simply the claim that, in designating Eve as the helper fit for Adam, God is giving woman a role that is not given to man, and that this role, within the marriage, is one of assistance and support.

This hint is substantiated by New Testament teaching on marriage in Ephesians 5:22–33; Colossians 3:18–19; Titus 2:4–5; and 1 Peter 3:1–7. These texts articulate the role of wives as involving submission to their husbands. Submission is not the only command addressed to wives in the New Testament, but it is the most often repeated command addressed to wives (*hupotassō* is found in all four key passages) and is by far the most controversial. Several comments are in order about this word.

First, it is impossible to remove legitimately all associations of authority from the word. It means literally "to place or appoint or ordain under." One who submits follows the leadership of another; he accepts the authority of another in a particular sphere. It does not imply the inferiority of the person submitting, but it does have to do with voluntarily accepting the authority of another. There have been numerous extended debates over whether the Greek term "head" (*kephalē*) implies authority,[17] but that question is secondary, for the command to submit stands either way.

Second, we must recognize that submission is not the duty of wives alone but is part of the Christian lifestyle. It is worth noting that the verb submit is applied to Jesus' relationship with his earthly parents (Luke

---

[17] The position that *kephalē* means "source," rather than "authority," has been argued by Catherine Kroeger in her article on "Head" in *DPL,* ed. Gerald Hawthorne, Ralph Martin, and Daniel Reid (Downers Grove and Leicester: InterVarsity, 1993), 375–77, but her work has been submitted to a devastating critique by Wayne Grudem, "The Meaning of *Kephalē* ('Head'): An Evaluation of New Evidence, Real and Alleged," *JETS* 44, no. 1 (March 2001): 25–65.

2:51), the relationship of citizens to the governing authorities (Rom. 13:1; 1 Pet. 2:13), the relationship of the Son to the Father in the eschaton (1 Cor. 15:28), that of church members to church leaders (Heb. 13:17), younger men to older men (1 Pet. 5:5), believers to one another (Eph. 5:21) and all of us to God (Heb. 12:9; James 4:7).

Third, there is no indication in Ephesians 5:22–33 that this command is limited to the particular time or culture to which Paul was speaking or is in any way a result of the fall. In Colossians submission is seen as "fitting in the Lord," and it could perhaps be argued that submission is no longer fitting. In Titus it is part of a larger lifestyle that prevents any from maligning the word of God, and some may contend that calling for wives to submit today would *cause* some to malign the word of God. In 1 Peter submission is related to moving unbelieving husbands to consider the Lord and thus would not be applicable to Christians who marry other Christians. Such arguments might perhaps be made to limit the applicability of Colossians 3, Titus 2, and 1 Peter 3; it is doubtful they could be made persuasively, but they could be made. But this would not be so in the case of Ephesians 5, for there submission is based on and patterned after the church's submission to Christ as her head, which would seem to be true in all cultures and at all times.

Fourth, the extent of submission is considerable. First Peter associates submission with obedience (3:6), and Ephesians 5 calls for submission "in everything." Despite these strong claims we may understand a couple of assumed limitations. First, God always retains first allegiance. Peter and John placed their submission to government under their submission to God's authority; and thus when the government's command contradicted God's command, they disobeyed the government. Similarly, no Christian wife should ever feel compelled by Scripture to disobey other Scripture; no wife should submit to her husband's leadership in following ungodly ways or doing ungodly things. This would also cover the issue of abuse. When a husband is abusing a wife, he is doing an ungodly thing. She is not called upon to condone, cooperate with, or submit to ungodliness; for God's authority must always remain paramount. Finally, there is nothing here about all women submitting to all men. This is about husbands and wives.

These passages also address the role of husbands. They are called to love their wives, not to be harsh with them, to be considerate and treat them with respect (Eph. 5:25–33; Col. 3:19; 1 Pet. 3:7). Perhaps the most striking aspect of the charge to husbands is what is missing. There is no command to demand submission from a wife or even a hint that submission is a right a husband may expect, demand, or even request. His command, rather, is in a different direction. It is to love his wife in a self-giving, self-sacrificing way which seeks the good and blessing of the wife above the husband's pleasure. His charge from God specifically excludes a domineering attitude that may come easy to men in the light of Genesis 3:16. The charge commands a thoughtful and respectful attitude toward one's wife, recognizing that her physical weakness makes her vulnerable to abuse and oppression, as has happened in countless cases down through history. First Peter 3 warns that a failure in this area of life can hinder one's spiritual life as well. If the Bible gives husbands a crown in marriage, it is a crown of thorns, for it calls for giving up rights and accepting responsibilities.

Beyond these matters it is remarkable how much of the marriage relationship is left undefined. While many see being the primary breadwinner as part of a husband's role in marriage, it may be better to conclude that this is more a cultural assumption with a weak exegetical base. The reference to the cursing of the ground in relationship to the man in Genesis 3 is suggestive but by no means conclusive. Headship may imply a husband's responsibility to see to it that the family is provided for but not that the husband must necessarily be the only one that provides.

Likewise, Titus 2:5 says a young wife should be "busy at home" (literally "a home worker"), but it does not say she should only be busy at home. And the example of Proverbs 31 is that of a wife who carried household responsibilities but also found time for outside interests. There appears to be no scriptural bar to a Christlike husband accepting more than a usual share of household responsibilities in cases where a wife wanted to complete her education or pursue a career, though both would want to consider the impact of this decision on family life and the wife's ability to fulfill her primary responsibility at home. But Scripture, it would seem, leaves room for individual decisions and arrangements in carrying out these broad assignments. And in any case, for every believer, male or female, married or single, the most important role is to be a child of God and an obedient servant, using one's gifts and life to bless and serve others. That is the role or calling given to all.

Some complementarians think that the order established by God in marriage should also be an argument for a similar order within the church. Thus, just as women cannot be husbands or fathers in the family, so they cannot (or at least should not) be elders or pastors within the larger family, the church. While this view has a good deal of merit, we are not left to such an inferential argument. There are a number of texts that bear directly on the question of male-female roles within the church.

Male and Female Roles in the Church

There is at least one role in the church that is limited to men. Several texts bear on this point, among them 1 Corinthians 11:2–16; 14:34–35; 1 Timothy 3:1–13; and Titus 1:6–9. However, discussions on this point usually focus on 1 Timothy 2:11–15. While there are interpretive difficulties, especially with verse 15, the rest of the passage seems fairly straightforward, though it is not easy to follow all of Paul's reasoning.[18]

The passage begins with a call to let women learn, a somewhat revolutionary idea in some parts of the Mediterranean world of that time. But, Paul continues, women should not teach or exercise authority over a man. But how does this text relate to roles in the church? It seems clear from elsewhere in Scripture that this is not a blanket prohibition. For example, believers are commanded to teach and admonish one another (Col. 3:16), and Paul gives instructions concerning the praying and prophesying of women (1 Cor. 11:2–16). Context seems to indicate that the type of teaching and authority Paul has in mind is that of an elder, for the qualifications for that office is the topic Paul turns to in 1 Timothy 3, and the duties of an elder include authoritative teaching and leading. Thus, 1 Timothy 2:11–15 prohibits women from serving in the role of elder or pastor.

Beyond that, application of this verse is difficult, for it is difficult to match Paul's understanding of teaching and exercising authority to contemporary situations. Does a female teacher of youth violate it? How about a female associate pastor, choir director, or seminary professor? These are difficult questions, for which Scripture gives no explicit answer. Perhaps the best approach is to consider the popular perception of the position: is it seen as involving an authoritative position of teaching and leading men? This seems to be the approach some churches are taking with the office of deacon. Since they do not see it as an office involving teaching or the exercise of authority, they feel free to have women deacons, or deaconesses. The presence of qualifications for *gunaikos,* or women, in the midst of the qualifications for deacons (v. 11 in the midst of 1 Tim. 3:8–13), seems to point to deacons and their wives serving together as a team; but the evidence is too sparse and too evenly balanced to take a dogmatic position on this issue. What seems far clearer is the prohibition of women serving as pastors or elders in a church.

Male and Female Singleness

The fourth area of biblical teaching on maleness and femaleness to be considered here is biblical teaching on singleness, a topic often ignored, especially among Protestants. Yet this is an increasingly important topic. With people waiting longer to get married, or divorced and single again, singles are one of the fastest-growing segments of the American population; and according to one article, they are the most unchurched group in America.[19] What does Scripture say about singleness? The key elements may be summarized in three statements.

---

[18] See Andreas J. Köstenberger and Thomas R. Schreiner, eds., *Women in the Church: An Analysis and Application of 1 Timothy 2:9–15,* 2nd ed. (Grand Rapids: Baker, 2005).

[19] Margaret Feinberg, "A Singular Mission Field," *CT* (June 11, 2001): 33. See also several related articles on singleness in the same issue.

First, singleness is a commended state (1 Cor. 7:32–34). While married people are not to put their mates above God (see 1 Cor. 7:29), they are commanded to love their mates; and when children come along, they need to be loved and cared for. Singles do not have such responsibilities. Thus, they have freedom to serve in ways that married people cannot. Often, in this country especially, they have financial resources that can be used as well. Churches, especially Protestant churches, have been so concerned to honor marriage that they have not done a good job of communicating the positive view of singleness in the Bible. It was the lifestyle of Christ and Paul and that of thousands of Christian leaders and missionaries throughout history. Thus, Paul commends it and wishes that all could enjoy the freedom it allows for undivided devotion to Christ.

Second, singleness is not a commanded state (1 Cor. 7:7–9). It is spoken of as a gift, given to some, but not to all. The requirement of clerical celibacy developed slowly in the Roman Catholic Church, fueled by unbiblical attitudes toward sexuality itself and, within the monastic movement, by the perception that celibacy was a necessary part of obedience to Jesus' command to the rich young ruler (Matt. 19:21). For someone to follow the so-called "counsels of perfection," the threefold vow to poverty, celibacy, and obedience was seen as requisite. The elevation of celibacy "reached its apex with the imposition of celibacy in the twelfth century as a universal requirement for priests of the Latin rite."[20] But the requirement was routinely disregarded and has been almost impossible to enforce, in part because celibacy is a gift bestowed by God rather than a standard that can be imposed. Paul indicates that the apostles had wives (1 Cor. 9:5), and overseers were expected to have a wife and children (1 Tim. 3:2,4–5; Titus 1:6).

Third, singleness may come from a variety of sources. Matthew 19:11–12 indicates that some are single involuntarily. They are either born or become incapable of a marital sexual relationship. Others voluntarily choose singleness for the sake of the kingdom. An excellent contemporary example is John Stott. Though he loves children and has had several opportunities to pursue a marital relationship, he has never felt God's guidance to pursue such a relationship. Eventually he realized that the global ministry God called him to would be difficult, if not impossible, to accomplish if he had a wife and family.

Today many who are single do not see singleness as a long-term plan. Either they are not yet ready to settle down, or are not yet mature enough, or perhaps most often, have not found the right person. However, some keep looking forever for a perfect mate out of fearfulness, either fear of

---

[20] Richard P. McBrien, *Catholicism,* new ed. (New York: HarperSanFrancisco, 1994), 870.

making a mistake or fear of commitment. Both may be symptoms of a lack of understanding of what Christian marriage is. It is not so much a matter of finding the perfect person as it is being the right person. The Bible gives no indication that there is one right person for every other person. Rather, Paul writes that a widow is "free to marry anyone she wishes, but [her new husband] must belong to the Lord" (1 Cor. 7:39). Marriage, like everything else in the Christian life, is a matter of faith. It involves a trust in God's providence and a sacred commitment, one that should drive us to total dependence on Christ in this as in every area of life.

Some are not yet married because they are too selfish to give of themselves in the way marriage requires. On the part of men, sexual desire used to be a strong motivator to marriage, but the sexual revolution has led to a culture where sexual intercourse is common outside of marriage. But for Christians both selfishness and promiscuity are sins that call for repentance.

Finally, there are some in the difficult position that one might call "single not by choice." This phrase refers to those who deeply desire marriage, take seriously Paul's counsel that it is better to marry than to burn with passion (1 Cor. 7:8–9), and yet have no marital prospects on the horizon. Here, contentment in one's circumstances (Phil. 4:12–13; 2 Cor. 12:8–9) and trust in God's sovereignty are crucial. God's grace is sufficient for the challenge of living a single life. Despite what American culture seems to assume, the Bible indicates that sexual expression is not the highest good of life nor a necessity for full joy and humanity. Jesus is sufficient proof against that, as are missionaries like Lottie Moon and pastors like John Stott.

At the same time churches could do a better job of ministering to single people, accepting them as whole people, and providing singles groups, not just as a place to find a spouse but a place to serve as well. Pastors could check their sermon illustrations for applicability to the single and to the married and intentionally challenge singles to use their time to serve. For their part, singles need to use the advantages their singleness gives for undivided devotion (1 Cor. 7:32–35) but also be ready to face the pressures singleness involves (loneliness, sexual temptation) and develop support and accountability relationships.

Despite this lengthy treatment and the genuine importance of sexuality, we should not end this survey of what the Bible says about male and female without noting that while sexuality is a good gift from the great God (see the Song of Songs), it is not of ultimate importance. Jesus placed obeying the will of God over sexually distinct roles (Luke 11:27–28), and Isaiah said there are greater joys than having a spouse and family (Isa. 56:3–5). In a society crazed over sex and sexuality, this is a word that needs to be said clearly.

We Are Created to Work

For most people work is a major part of life. Indeed, for many it is the most important aspect of their lives. Yet churches rarely give their members teaching on how to integrate their vocational life as part of their Christian life. As a result, most Christians think about their work as a separate compartment, something outside their Christian life. But since we are all called to be full-time Christians, then our work must be part of our service to God. Fortunately, the Bible has much to say about work, and it gives us a strong basis for developing a theology of work. Here, as in many other areas, we need to consider work in terms of its relationship to four crucial focal points of biblical history: work as created and intended by God, work as distorted by the fall, work as part of the life of the redeemed, and work as it will be in the consummation. DtÐ21.82M3

Work as Created and Intended by God

The first important fact from Scripture we need to note about work is that it is a prefall institution. Thus, it is included within the description that all God had created was "very good" (Gen. 1:31). It is not a necessary evil but, as God intended, is part of our created nature and good. We may trace four implications from the brief but important teaching on work in Genesis 1–2.

1. *Work reflects something of the image of God in humanity.* The God of the Bible is a working God. Though he completed his work of creation and rested, he is still working today in providence and governance (John 5:17; 9:3–4). The creativity, energy, and authority we exert in working reflects something of God's character in us.

2. *Work begins with our responsibility to creation.* What exactly is our assignment in the realm of creation? It begins with the office of parenthood. The command to "be fruitful and multiply and fill the earth" is fairly straightforward and is a command. Those who are married should thus assume that part of the responsibility joined to the privileges of marriage (sexual oneness) is the office of parenthood. It is not the only reason, but it is at least part of the reason for sexual attraction, leading to sexual union, and it should normally be a part of the work of most people, apart from special callings, either to singleness or to being married without children (a calling that may be discerned through medical inability to have children or some other extraordinary sense of explicit divine direction).

A generation ago numerous books and speakers encouraged Christian couples to realize that sexual intimacy in marriage was "intended for pleasure."[21] Today the need may be to emphasize that sexual intimacy is not

---

[21] This phrase is from Ed Wheat and Gaye Wheat, *Intended for Pleasure* (Old Tappan, NJ: Fleming H. Revell, 1977), and is typical of the message in numerous similar works.

intended *just* for pleasure but also for procreation, as well as partnership and protection.

The second aspect of our work from these early texts in Genesis is the care of creation. Two sets of commands relate to what is sometimes called the "cultural mandate." The first is Genesis 1:26,28; the second is Genesis 2:15. The fuller and more definitive statement is in Genesis 1, where it is addressed to both man and woman (note the "them" in vv. 26 and 28). The context marks it as a foundational statement, giving an important command relating to God's purpose for humanity. The statement in Genesis 2 is addressed to the man alone, and it comes almost as an aside. The two statements together seem to give an early pattern of complementariness. Man and woman are equal; both are made in God's image; both are blessed and commanded to reproduce and exercise dominion over the earth. But they exercise that dominion in complementary roles. Adam is commanded to tend the garden; Eve is commanded to help Adam.

The word for "rule" or to "have dominion" (*radah*) appears in Genesis 1:26,28. It is a fairly strong word, found sometimes in contexts of harsh or ruthless ruling (Lev. 25:43,46; Ezek. 34:4) but also at times in contexts of a just and proper rule (1 Kings 4:24; Pss. 110:2; 49:14) and even, in one place, of foremen (1 Kings 5:16). Even stronger, strikingly so, is the word for "subdue" (*kabash*). It is used once to refer to attempted rape (Esther 7:8), occasionally for subjecting to slavery (Jer. 34:11,16), and most often in military contexts (2 Sam. 8:11), where land is often described as "subdued" (Num. 32:22; Josh. 18:1).

If Genesis 1 was all we had, there might be a basis for the often-made charge that Christianity led to the modern environmental problem. It has been claimed, most classically in an essay by Lynn White Jr. that the ultimate source of our environmental problem is "the Christian dogma of man's transcendence of, and rightful mastery over, nature."[22] Judged purely from the witness of history, White may have a point. Christianity was the mind-set of most of western Europe in which science and technology developed, and part of that mind-set was the desire to master nature. Moreover, Christians have not, for the most part, been enthusiastic in their support of the environmental movement, partly due to the pantheistic, nature-worshipping attitude of much of that movement. But there has been some change in attitudes among evangelical Christians since White's address in 1966, and more importantly, it can be argued cogently that the Christian dogma he cites as so damaging was never well founded exegetically.

---

[22] Lynn White Jr., "The Historical Roots of our Ecologic Crisis," *Science* 155 (1967): 1203–7, reprinted in *The Care of Creation,* ed. R. J. Berry (Leicester, England: InterVarsity, 2000), 31–42.

Alongside the strong, forceful words in Genesis 1 are the gentler words in Genesis 2: Adam is to "work" and "take care of" the garden. Both are common and general words. *Abad* in noun and verb form appears more than one thousand times in the Old Testament, most often used in the sense of serving (either God or idols) but occasionally in a more general sense of working or doing. The second word, *shamar,* also is common, appearing more than 450 times in the Old Testament. It is most commonly used in the sense of keeping, observing, and guarding the commands of God (Deut. 6:2; Ps. 119:9). According to the *Theological Wordbook of the Old Testament,* the basic idea behind the word is "to exercise great care over."[23] Such terms should lead us to an idea of care for creation, not exploitation of it.

Even apart from this specific exegetical base, there is a larger theological basis for stewardship as care rather than exploitation. It is the recognition that we are not the owners of earth (Ps. 24:1) and that the created order is meant to present something of the glory of God (Ps. 19:1–6). As such, the Christian's responsibility for creation should be that of a careful stewardship, seeking to exercise our rule in a manner that reflects God's ownership, not ours, and seeks to preserve creation as a reflection of God's glory.

3. *Work includes the development of culture.* Part of our dominion over creation includes using all of the gifts and endowments given to us, either physically in the environment or personally in human nature, to bless others and thus glorify God, who gave such gifts to be used. This imperative reflects the fact that culture is a natural part of our life as humans and that the only alternative to a Christian-influenced culture is a non-Christian-influenced culture. People are going to sing and write books and paint pictures and be involved in sports. As all these activities are part of being human, they are ways God should be glorified in our humanity.

4. *Work is part of God's will for humans.* The most important truth about work in these verses is that it is not an evil thing thrust upon us by the necessity of earning a living, but it is part of God's will for humanity. It is a gift of common grace, given to all humans, and is good for them. The goodness of work is implied by its presence before the fall, and is made explicit in later biblical revelation (especially the book of Ecclesiastes; see 2:24–25; 3:13,22; 5:18–20). Even nonbelievers can find a sense of satisfaction in their work and can contribute to the good of others through it.

For believers, however, work has the additional quality of being a "calling" or "vocation." Whatever we do as work, we should do in the belief that it is part of God's will for our lives (Col. 3:23–24). This applies not just

---

[23] John E. Hartley, *"shamar," TWOT,* 2:939.

to ministry positions but work that allows us to support ourselves and our families (which is certainly God's will) and even housework (for a clean home and clothes and well-cooked meals are a way of blessing others and, thus, glorifying God). Whether one is paid for the work done is entirely beside the point, theologically. We are given the ability to exert ourselves in varied ways that bless others and glorify God; to do such activities is work, in the biblical perspective.

Work as Distorted by the Fall

Immediately after the fall a curse is laid upon humanity that affects work (Gen. 3:16–19). The woman is affected in relationship to bearing children and in her relationship to her husband, while the man is affected in his toil and labor to produce food. This may reflect the differing spheres or roles for male and female, but it is suggestive more than explicit. Here and elsewhere we see two ways that the fall changes work into labor.

The first change is in encountering resistance, rather than cooperation, in fulfilling our mandate. We are called upon to multiply and fill the earth, but to do so requires enduring pain on the part of the woman. We are called to rule the earth and care for it as stewards, but only through "painful toil" (Gen. 3:17) will it produce food for us. This speaks of an objective change both in our own bodies and in the physical creation as a result of human sin. For now we experience work as, at best, a mixed blessing. We enjoy accomplishing something. We seem to sense that it is good to exert ourselves, to use the gifts of mind, body, and soul. The book of Ecclesiastes sees finding satisfaction in one's toil as one of the greatest blessings "under the sun" (see Eccles. 2:24–25; 3:13; 5:18). But most forms of work include some frustrating, difficult, and monotonous aspects as well. It is toil, as well as work, and does not provide ultimate meaning to life, as the book of Ecclesiastes also acknowledges (4:4–8).

The second change is that work, created to be a blessing, becomes an occasion of temptation. Three such areas of temptation are pointed out in Scripture. First is the temptation to injustice and oppression. James 5:4; Amos 2:7; 5:11–12; 8:4–7; and Isaiah 58:3,6–7 mention the need to preserve integrity, honesty, and fairness in all our business dealings. Some of God's harshest words of judgment are directed against people who sinned in their work situations.

Another temptation presented by work is the temptation to laziness. We are directed in Proverbs 6:6–11 to study the work habits of the ant and warned that if we do not live wisely, poverty will be the result. Believers are warned against idleness in 2 Thessalonians 3:6,11–12. More positively, Titus 3:14 directs believers to live with devotion and diligence so as not to lead "unproductive lives." Beyond the financial repercussions, laziness is an affront to God, for it involves misusing or underusing gifts given by him to be used in service to him and to others. It also involves opting out of the responsibility laid on us to be partners with God in ruling and caring for the world and in embracing the cultural imperative.

The third temptation associated with work in a fallen world is the temptation to idolatry. Gordon Dahl makes the point well in his book *Work, Play, and Worship in a Leisure Oriented Society.*[24] Americans tend to worship their work, work at their play, and play at their worship. For most people, work is their highest priority. We are tempted to worship our work for a variety of reasons. For those who are good at their work, it gives them a sense of competence and self-esteem, whereas they may feel more difficulty in fulfilling parental or marital responsibilities and use work as an excuse to avoid them. But for many the motive is simply materialism. Jesus called upon examples from the work world to illustrate the excuses people use for ignoring God's call (see Luke 14:18–19). Proverbs 23:4–5; 30:7–9 illustrate the folly and danger of seeking riches, as do many of Jesus' parables.

Still, an increasing number of people today are practical worshippers of their work. They want to devote themselves to something in a total way, to be totally committed. Lacking a belief in the true God, they substitute work, the corporation, or their career. Their commitment will not lead to the contentment, satisfaction, and ultimate meaning they are seeking; yet because there is a goodness to work, many continue to take this path, especially since it also dovetails with the affluence hard work often provides (at least in this country) and the growing tendency to tie personal identity to one's work. One of the purposes of the Sabbath was countering this temptation to worship work, which we will discuss in some detail in a later section of this chapter.

Work as Redeemed by Christ

Whatever changes redemption may have on our character, it does not change our calling to be workers. Rather, it clarifies the various reasons we work and restores it to its rightful position.

First, we work as a means to honor Christ. Paul wrote Ephesians 6:6–7 and Colossians 3:23–24 to slaves. If their service could be directed to Christ, then any honorable service can be rendered to him. Any job that blesses others in some way is a way to glorify God. But if there is a job that in no way enriches others but only destroys, denigrates, or injures others, or requires unethical behavior, it should not be a job performed by a Christian.

---

24 Gordon Dahl, *Work, Play, and Worship in a Leisure-Oriented Society* (Minneapolis: Augsburg, 1972).

Second, we work as a testimony to others (1 Tim. 5:13–16; Titus 2:3–6,9–10). If Christ is real, his reality in us should show especially at our place of work, both by excellence in doing our work and excellence in relationships with others.

Finally, we work in order to have something to share with others, as well as to provide for our own needs (Eph. 4:28; 2 Thess. 3:10–12; Titus 3:14). The New Testament simultaneously urges Christians to be generous and to work to have something to share with others, but it also takes a dim view of those who would use the generosity of Christians to indulge their own laziness. The assumption is that God's normal means of providing for people is through their own work but that in a fallen world there will also be occasions of genuine need (James 1:27; 2:14–17). For such occasions, generosity is a Christian virtue that should be evident among God's redeemed people, but generosity is impossible unless one works and has something to share.

Work as It Will Be in the Consummation

Scripture indicates that heaven will involve rest (Rev. 14:13), but it will not be an eternal day off, for it also says that in heaven God's servants will serve him (Rev. 22:3). Revelation 21:26 speaks of the glory and honor of the nations being brought into God's consummated kingdom. All aspects of human culture that are honorable will be brought in and continued. So painters will paint, builders will build, singers will sing—all with gratitude toward the giver of all good gifts. There is no indication that the cultural mandate is ended by the transition to the new heavens and the new earth. Our work in heaven will continue to honor him there as here.

We Are Created for Community

Since its inception, the United States has been one of the most individualistic cultures in the world. We have glorified the rugged self-reliant individual like Daniel Boone, who felt it was time to move on when he could see the smoke from another man's campfire. In Baptist life this ideal was seen most clearly in the theology of E. Y. Mullins, called by one "the theologian of individualism par excellence" and "probably the single most influential theologian in Southern Baptist history."[25] Such attitudes, however, are sharply at odds with the biblical portrayal of humans, which clearly shows humans as created for community, with God and with other humans.

Perhaps the first place this aspect of our created nature is seen is in our creation in God's image (Gen. 1:26–27). Though not made explicit in

---

[25] LeRoy Moore, "Crazy Quilt: Southern Baptist Patterns of the Church," *Foundations* 20 (1977): 20.

Scripture, some see significance in the fact that the first-person plural is used in the foundational statement in Genesis 1:26: "Let us make man in our image" (emphasis added). The plural foreshadows later biblical teaching on the nature of God as a triune being: Father, Son, and Spirit existing in perfect union, communion, and community. Thus, it may be argued that one aspect of being made in God's image is being made for community.

This interpretation of the image of God is strengthened by further statements in the early chapters of Genesis. After repeated statements of the goodness of creation, Genesis 2:18 notes one aspect of creation that was not good: "It is not good for the man to be alone." While this text is usually and properly associated with marriage, that is not its only significance. For example, it also reflects the incredible divine humility. It would be easy to object to the statement in Genesis 2:18 with the reply, "But the man is not alone. He has God!" But God created humans with a need that he does not meet in himself. He made us with a need for other humans. Clearly, the first context in which that need is met is in the family. Children need parents, and families are the first contexts for the development of community. But once sin entered the world, it began disrupting marriage, families, and community. The man blamed the woman (Gen. 3:12), and Cain killed Abel (Gen. 4:8) as sin began to spread. Eventually, the human community was divided by sex, race, and class.

Even more importantly, humans are cut off from communion with God. Rather than joyfully meeting with God, Adam and Eve hid from the God who was coming to meet with them (Gen. 3:8). Human sin so grieved God that he sent a flood (Gen. 6:5–7). But God did not give up on humanity. He chose one man, Abraham, and with him began to restore community, both with himself and with other humans. This is seen in the promise, "I will be your God and you will be my people." This promise is found in various forms throughout Scripture, from its initiation with Abraham (Gen. 17:7–8), to its continuation with Moses and the children of Israel (Exod. 19:5–6; 29:45–46; Lev. 26:12–13), to a further, future fulfillment in the new covenant (Jer. 31:33), to a final fulfillment in the new Jerusalem (Rev. 21:3). It is important to note the plurals in this promise: "their God . . . my people." God does not call isolated individuals to himself; he calls a people.

The theme of community is also central to the New Testament. Christ comes to accomplish reconciliation. The work of the cross restores our relationship with God (Eph. 2:16) but also creates a new community among humans—the church. In this new community the old divisions no longer divide: "There is neither Jew nor Greek, slave nor free, male nor female, for you are all one in Christ Jesus" (Gal. 3:28). Every image of the church is inherently plural: the church is God's people (not his isolated individuals); it is Christ's body (not separate members); it is the temple of the Spirit (not disconnected stones). Community is our created design, God's ongoing work, and our eschatological destiny.

As we noted earlier, this theme of community has been drastically underemphasized in the North American context, but that is changing. Virtually every discussion of postmodern culture identifies the importance of community. One of the common characteristics of churches identified with the diverse movement called the Emerging Church is an emphasis on community. Even an important element of successful megachurches is the cultivation of community through small groups. Today, those who want to hear great preaching can download from the Internet better sermons than they can hear at most local churches; they can download better music into their MP3 player than they can hear from most local choirs; if they want fellowship and community, however, where will they find it? One of the key callings of churches in the twenty-first century, both biblically and practically, is to provide and cultivate community.

What Has the Church Believed?

We turn now from biblical teaching to historical developments, and we do so for three reasons.

The first is simple humility. We are not the first people to read the Scriptures and seek to understand them. It would be the height of arrogance and a denial of the earlier work of the Holy Spirit to act as though we have nothing to learn from those who came before us. Moreover, a strong consensus in the interpretation of Scripture over the course of centuries is a strong argument for that interpretation. Church history is not inerrant, but a novel interpretation of Scripture never held by any significant portion of the church definitely has the burden of proof.

Second, we read history as a safeguard against being imprisoned by the spirit of our age. We read Scripture in today's historical context, which has its own blind spots and unquestioned assumptions. Reading the ideas of earlier Christians gives us another point of view from which we may be able to see and correct some of the errors of our day unless we foolishly assume that our era represents the apex of understanding and enlightenment.

Third, we study history because we do not read Scripture with minds that are blank slates. Rather, we are the inheritors of a theological tradition that shapes the questions we ask as well as the answers we receive. Studying that tradition enables us both to better understand the background to those questions and to better assess the validity of the answers we have received.

A full review of all the historical developments relating to the doctrine of humanity is impossible within the scope of this chapter. Rather, we will highlight the most important issues relating to each of the five key biblical teachings discussed in the first section of this chapter.

Our Nature as Created Beings in Historical Context

The affirmation of human beings as creatures, created by God, has been a staple of Christian thought throughout the centuries. It was assumed by Augustine in his famous saying, "Thou hast made us for Thyself, and our hearts are restless until they rest in Thee,"[26] and it is reflected in the argument for God's existence from the design evident in human nature and creation—an argument popular since the days of Thomas Aquinas. Indeed, some would claim that the Christian doctrine of God as Creator explains why science developed only in the Christian-influenced culture of western Europe and not in any other.[27] Yet a variety of claims set forth by scientists in the nineteenth century posed questions to the Christian view of humans as creatures created by God, culminating in the challenge posed by Darwinism and evolutionary thought.

It should be noted that evolution per se was not seen as a problem by many of the early respondents to Darwin. For example, Charles Hodge, perhaps the foremost American theologian of the nineteenth century, saw Darwinism as consisting of three ideas: evolution, natural selection, and the denial of design. What Hodge saw as objectionable in Darwin was the third item, the idea that natural selection must be seen in purely natural terms, thus ruling out any role for God in the process. David N. Livingstone says that for Hodge, "Darwinism was atheism *precisely* and *solely* because it was inimical to design."[28]

Here is Hodge's own assessment in his 1874 work *What Is Darwinism?* "It is . . . neither evolution nor natural selection which give Darwinism its peculiar character and importance. It is that Darwin rejects all teleology, or the doctrine of final causes."[29] This left open the possibility that if evolution and natural selection could be conceived in a way consistent with divine design, then they could be accepted within a Christian view of humans as created by God.

Such a view, called theistic evolution, in which God remains the designer and evolution merely the mechanism, was soon developed and em-

---

[26] Augustine, *Confessions* 1.1.
[27] See Rodney Stark, *For the Glory of God: How Monotheism Led to Reformations, Science, Witch-Hunts, and the End of Slavery* (Princeton and Oxford: Princeton University Press, 2003), 147ff.
[28] David N. Livingstone, *Darwin's Forgotten Defenders: The Encounter between Evangelical Theology and Evolutionary Thought* (Grand Rapids: Eerdmans and Edinburgh: Scottish Academic Press, 1987), 104. Emphasis in original.
[29] Charles Hodge, *What Is Darwinism?* (New York: Scribner's, 1874), 48.

braced by theologians as prominent as B. B. Warfield and A. H. Strong.[30] In fact, Livingstone sees an "openness to the new biology" as characteristic of "mainstream evangelicalism" prior to the 1920s,[31] when the fundamentalist-modernist controversy and the Scopes trial precipitated a strong antievolution movement, in which evolution was seen as inherently antisupernatural, ethically suspect, and inconsistent with Scripture.

Today both special creation and theistic evolution are widely held by Americans in general. A 1997 survey found 44 percent of those surveyed affirming the idea that God created humans in their present form within the last ten thousand years while 39 percent believed that humans have developed from less advanced forms of life over millions of years but that God has guided this process.[32] However, among scientists, only 5 percent believed in special creation, while 40 percent accepted theistic evolution.[33] This seems to parallel a wider acceptance of theistic evolution among evangelical scientists than among evangelical theologians or evangelical believers as a whole.

For example, scientist Howard Van Till, in presenting what he prefers to call "the fully gifted creation view," refers to evolution as "a concept that is judged by the vast majority of natural scientists to be a highly credible theory" and asserts that "those persons most knowledgeable about the data and its responsible interpretation are in remarkable agreement regarding the credibility of the general concept of biotic evolution."[34] But evangelical theologian Wayne Grudem offers six objections to theistic evolution, most centrally charging that "the driving force that brings about change and the development of new species in all evolutionary schemes is *randomness.* ... But the driving force in the development of new organisms according to Scripture is God's *intelligent design.*"[35] There are, however, still some

---

[30] For Warfield's strong support of theistic evolution, see the writings gathered in B. B. Warfield, *Evolution, Science, and Scripture: Selected Writings,* ed. Mark A. Noll and David N. Livingstone (Grand Rapids: Baker, 2000). Concerning Strong, Greg Thornbury says, "Strong's acceptance of theistic evolution remains the most well-known aspect of his theology." See Greg Thornbury, "Augustus Hopkins Strong," in *Theologians of the Baptist Tradition,* ed. Timothy George and David Dockery (Nashville: Broadman & Holman, 2001), 153.

[31] Livingstone, *Darwin's Forgotten Defenders,* 169.

[32] From a survey reported at http://www.religioustolerance.org/ev_publi.htm; accessed 18 July 2005.

[33] Ibid. Rodney Stark cites a survey of biologists listed in *American Men and Women of Science* in which 45 percent affirm theistic evolution. See Stark, *For the Glory of God,* 192.

[34] Howard J. Van Till, "The Fully Gifted Creation ('Theistic Evolution')," in *Three Views on Creation and Evolution,* ed. J. P. Moreland and John Mark Reynolds (Grand Rapids: Zondervan, 1999), 179, 183.

[35] Wayne Grudem, *Systematic Theology: An Introduction to Biblical Doctrine* (Leicester: InterVarsity and Grand Rapids: Zondervan, 1994), 276. Emphasis in original. Here Grudem seems to be echoing Hodge's criticism that Darwinism involves a denial of divine design; Hodge, however, did not object to evolution per se, as Grudem does.

evangelical theologians who see no theological problem with theistic evolution. J. I. Packer sees nothing in Scripture that "bears on the biological
theory of evolution one way or the other," and opts to follow the lead of
B. B. Warfield.[36] Thus, the nature of God's activity in the creation of humans remains a disputed question in the church today.

The Image of God in Historical Context

Interpretations of the meaning of the image of God in church history
have for the most part sought to resolve the riddle posed by biblical teaching that the image is both something that all humans and only humans
possess and yet is something that has been damaged in the fall and is now
being restored or renewed in Christ.

One attempt to solve the riddle involved separating the image of God
and the likeness of God. An important early formulator of this view was
Irenaeus.[37] He saw the image as consisting in reason and free will, both of
which remain intact and undamaged in humanity after the fall. The likeness, by contrast, is not something essential to humans as humans but what
medieval theology later came to call a *donum superadditum*, an added gift,
something in addition to essential humanity. Irenaeus associated this additional gift with the Spirit, which he said only believers have. More often,
however, this additional gift was seen as an original gift of righteousness,
which made Adam and Eve not just innocent but positively righteous, and
enabled them to have fellowship with God. This righteousness is what was
lost at the fall and is being restored in Christ.

Among the numerous problems with this view, two stand out. First, as
many students of Scripture have noted, the terms *image* and *likeness* are
used synonymously in Scripture. Second, the image, as well as the likeness, has been affected by the fall and is in need of restoration.

Thomas Aquinas maintained some aspects of the view of Irenaeus but
modified others. He affirmed that what was lost in the fall was not the image but a *donum superadditum*, which he did not identify with the likeness
but with an added gift of grace that enabled reason to rule the lower powers
in human nature. The image itself he saw as "man's natural aptitude for understanding and loving God, an aptitude which consists in the very nature
of the mind, which is common to all men."[38] This aptitude becomes active

---

[36] Packer's words and views are recounted by Mark Noll and David Livingstone, "Introduction," in
Warfield, *Evolution, Science, and Scripture,* 38–39.

[37] Irenaeus's view is developed in various parts of his work "Against Heresies." For an exposition of
Irenaeus, see David Cairns, *The Image of God in Man,* rev. ed. (London: Collins, 1973), 80–84.

[38] Thomas Aquinas, *Summa Theologiae: Latin Text and English Translation, Introductions, Notes,
Appendices, and Glossaries,* trans. Fathers of the English Dominican Province, vol. 13 (New York:
Blackfriars, McGraw-Hill, and London: Eyre & Spottiswoode, 1964), 61 (Q.93, art. 4).

in believers who do know and love God yet imperfectly. The image reaches its fullest sense in the blessed who know and love God perfectly.

This view improves on that of Irenaeus by not making a distinction between image and likeness, but it still suffers from two defects. Aquinas, like Irenaeus, underestimates the effects of the fall. We humans do not just lose something additional to our humanity; our humanity itself is affected. Second, while Aquinas did include the idea of loving God in his view of the image of God, he, like most of those in the early and medieval church, gave far too large a place to reason. For Aquinas, "the image of God is found only in the mind," and "the intellect is the most Godlike quality in man."[39]

One of the most influential Protestant formulations of the image of God was that given by Calvin, who said:

> The likeness of God extends to the whole excellence by which man's nature towers over all kinds of living creatures. . . . And although the primary seat of the divine image was in the mind or heart, or in the soul and its powers, yet there was no part of man, not even the body itself, in which some sparks did not glow.[40]

Calvin differed most from his Catholic predecessors by seeing the whole of human nature as affected by the fall. While Calvin used strong language, which has led some to think he believed the image was totally lost as a result of the fall, a careful reading shows that Calvin saw the image not as totally erased but hideously distorted and deformed. Humans retain their humanity, but every aspect or faculty in human nature, including the image, is corrupted (which is the meaning of the phrase "total depravity").

All these interpretations see the image of God in what Millard Erickson calls "substantive" terms; that is, the image of God is seen as some capacity, ability, or characteristic that only humans possess.[41] This has historically been the dominant view, but it has been challenged or supplemented by two other approaches.

Karl Barth has been one of a number of theologians who have emphasized the importance of relationships for understanding the image of God. Barth's point of departure was noticing in Genesis 1:27 that the affirmation of creation in God's image is immediately followed by the affirmation of our creation as male and female. He then compared human existence to that of the Trinity. Just as the members of the Trinity exist in relationship with one another, so humans image God by existing in relationship with one another, initially seen in our creation as male and female. It is this fact of

---

[39] Hoekema, *Created In God's Image,* 36.
[40] Calvin, *Institutes,* 1.15.3.
[41] Millard Erickson, *Christian Theology,* 2nd ed. (Grand Rapids: Baker, 1998), 520–21.

"the existence of the I and the Thou in confrontation" that is "constitutive for God, and then for man created by God."[42] Barth did not limit the image to the male-female relationship but extended it to include other human relationships, especially a relationship with God. What remains ambiguous in Barth is whether the image is some capacity for relationship, or the fact of relationship itself. Others incorporate this emphasis on relationship but clarify that the image itself includes those capacities that make relationships possible.

For example, Emil Brunner sees the formal aspect of the image of God as the responsibility humans have to respond to God in a love relationship, but the image includes elements such as freedom, reason, and conscience, which enable the relationship and belong to the image.[43] These two, along with G. C. Berkouwer, Erickson, Hoekema, and others, have highlighted the importance of including a relational element in our understanding of the *imago dei*.

2) Still another approach that has some historical roots but has become more prevalent in the past two hundred years is a functional approach. Most often the function associated with the image is that of dominion, drawing on the close association of the two in Genesis 1:26–28. James Leo Garrett identifies J. L. Dagg, Charles Hodge, E. Y. Mullins, and Hoekema as theologians who incorporate the functional idea as one element in their view of the image of God, and Gerhard von Rad, Sigmund Mowinckel, C. F. D. Moule, Leonard Verduin, and Frank Stagg among those who see the idea of dominion as central to their conceptions of the image of God.[44] Others include the idea of function in relationship to the image of God but in a different sense, such as Berkouwer, who virtually defines the image as the function of obedience to God,[45] and Hoekema, who includes the functions of worshipping God, loving others, and ruling over nature in his view of the image.[46]

While the dominant position historically has been to consider the image in substantive terms (i.e., as capacities, characteristics, or abilities only humans possess), increasingly attention has been given to relational and functional aspects, and a sizable number of theologians have opted for composite views (such as Dagg, Charles Hodge, A. H. Strong, E. Y. Mullins, H. C. Thiessen, H. Orton Wiley, and Anthony Hoekema).[47]

[42] Karl Barth, *Church Dogmatics,* ed. G. W. Bromiley and T. F. Torrance, trans. Harold Knight, G. W. Bromiley, J. K. S. Reid, R. H. Fuller (Edinburgh: T&T Clark, 1960), 3/2:203.

[43] Emil Brunner, *Man in Revolt,* trans. Olive Wyon (New York: Scribner's, 1939), 510.

[44] James Leo Garrett Jr., *Systematic Theology: Biblical, Historical, & Evangelical* (Grand Rapids: Eerdmans, 1990), 1:395–96, 401–2.

[45] G. C. Berkouwer, *Man: The Image of God,* trans. Dirk Jellema (Grand Rapids: Eerdmans, 1962), 99–100.

[46] Hoekema, *Created in God's Image,* 69.

[47] Garrett, *Systematic Theology,* 1:401-2.

Male and Female in Historical Context

The teaching of the church regarding male and female throughout most of church history has been tragically different from the biblical teaching presented in the first section of this chapter. Theologians as influential and important as Augustine and Aquinas have viewed women as the source of sin and even called women misbegotten men. Churches have treated women as second-class citizens and condoned their oppression at the hands of men.

In defense of Christianity, it can be said that in the past two hundred years the modern Christian missionary movement has done more to elevate women around the world than any other religion in the world. Wherever missionaries have planted the gospel, one consistent result has been a rise in the status of women. But the record sadly shows that for most of history, most men (Christian and non-Christian) have viewed women as inferior; and at most times and places, the church has offered little protest or help to women.

It is this historical reality that, at least in part, supplied the fuel for the feminist movement of the past fifty years. A variety of social forces in the West, such as the rise of modern technological society with its functional view of equality, the increasing education of women, and even the rising materialism of American society in which families feel they cannot survive on one income, have all contributed to setting the fuel on fire. With many of the important functions of the home lost, with women educated and encouraged to work outside the home, and with rising desires for material prosperity, women set out to achieve a new identity. As they did so, they began to recognize more and more past and present injustices and oppression, calling for change. While there are numerous issues and aims in the feminist movement, many of them fully justified, the major goal seems to be the complete functional equality of women and men, such that there are no roles or opportunities available only to men.[48]

Within churches there have been a variety of responses. Mainline and liberal churches have largely adopted egalitarian views, with most accepting or even requiring ordination of women to all forms of leadership. Among evangelicals, engagement with the feminist movement is seen by many to begin with Paul Jewett's 1975 work, *Man as Male and Female.* His was the first influential evangelical voice to call for the rejection of the traditional view of male headship and female submission. He saw the equality of male and female in the creation narrative, the attitude of Jesus toward women in the Gospels, and Paul's statement in Galatians 3:28 as

---

[48] For a substantive and thorough critique of feminism, see Mary Kassian, *The Feminist Mistake: The Radical Impact of Feminism on Church and Culture* (Wheaton: Crossway, 2005).

incompatible with female subordination. He said, "It is not the subordination of some women to some men, but the subordination of all women to all men, because they are women, that constitutes the indefensible thesis, indeed the unscriptural thesis."[49]

Where Jewett was more controversial and gained fewer followers in his dealing with the passages, especially in Paul, that appear to teach female subordination, he argued frankly that Paul was mistaken and did not follow through fully on the implications of statements such as Galatians 3:28, where he saw more clearly God's intention for males and females. Most evangelical egalitarians have followed Jewett in emphasizing texts that support the equality of men and women but have found other explanations that blunt the force of the difficult Pauline passages without accusing Paul of error, an explanation that weakens biblical authority in a way unacceptable to most evangelicals.

Evangelicals today are split between egalitarians, who accept the principle of total equality of roles, and complementarians, who see equality of nature and worth compatible with differing, complementary roles. Despite the gallons of scholarly ink spent on articles and books, there seems little movement toward a consensual position acceptable to both sides. Three basic disagreements seem to divide complementarians and egalitarians.

The first is different understandings of what equality involves. Egalitarians assume that equality requires that all roles open to men be open to women, while complementarians distinguish between ontological equality and functional equality. Perhaps neither side has done good work on deriving and defending their definition of equality from Scripture. One suspects that most of our ideas about equality include political overtones of equal rights, a category about which Scripture says little.

A second fundamental disagreement is that egalitarians think that the difficult Pauline passages are in tension with the overall thrust of Scripture. They reason, if God created men and women truly equal, why would he ordain that only men be given certain roles of leadership? The rationales of complementarians seem unpersuasive to them, amounting in the end to "because the Bible says so." But *why* does the Bible say so? The tension seems so strong to them that they conclude the problematic passages cannot mean what they superficially seem to mean. Here, complementarians could possibly advance the discussion by giving more attention to the "why" question.

Finally, egalitarians may be reacting excessively to past sins. When they hear of headship in the home, they think of oppressive, dictatorial leadership. When they hear of limiting certain church offices to males, they hear

---

[49] Paul Jewett, *Man as Male and Female* (Grand Rapids: Eerdmans, 1975), 131.

a denial of the giftedness and value of women as ministers. Both no doubt were often true in the past. But a position deserves to be evaluated by its best models, and the best contemporary formulations of complementarianism find a moderating position between past oppression and modern egalitarianism that involves servant leadership in homes, following the pattern of Christ, and full affirmation of the value and giftedness of women, with only a small fraction of possible ministries being restricted. The arguments of egalitarians sometimes seem directed against positions that may have been held by many fifty years ago, and may be held by a few today, but are not the consensus position of complementarians today.

Work in Historical Context

The positive attitude toward work reflected in Scripture is something of an exception in the ancient world. For most people in most times, work has been an unavoidable necessity for survival. However, in the Greco-Roman world, freedom from work became possible for those with slaves, allowing them to devote themselves to the duties of citizenship or the arts.

Even among Christians, the healthy attitude toward work seen in Scripture quickly waned. While there were many factors involved in the development of monasticism, at least one factor was the perception that work could be a hindrance to one's spiritual life. One of the earliest writers on monasticism, John Cassian, said, "Inhabitants of cities and villages and hamlets, men engaged in the ordinary and virtuous pursuits of life, sometimes see Jesus; but they cannot see him with the distinctness possible to those who climb up with him upon the mount of saintliness."[50]

Over the years a rationale developed for the distinct lifestyle seen in monasticism. The ordinary Christian was obligated to obey the *commands* of Christ, but there were others who chose to obey the *counsels* of Christ, the counsels of perfection, seen in Christ's words to the rich young ruler in Matthew 19:21. To be perfect one had to leave ordinary life behind. This pursuit of perfection was not required of all; but to those who chose to pursue it, vows of poverty, chastity, and obedience were involved.[51]

The Reformers uniformly denounced monasticism and the rationale given for it. Calvin shows an awareness of the argument of Aquinas but rejects the idea "that a more perfect rule of life can be devised than the common one committed by God to the whole church."[52] Luther, who had himself once taken monastic vows, renounced them as without any biblical

---

[50] John Cassian, "Conferences," in *Western Asceticism,* ed. Owen Chadwick, LCC (London: SCM, 1958), 236–37.

[51] Perhaps the classic formulation of this rationale was that given by Aquinas, *Summa Theologica,* 184.3.

[52] Calvin, *Institutes,* 4.13.12.

foundation and contrary to Christian freedom.[53] By abolishing any distinction between so-called states of perfection and imperfection, or higher and lower callings, Luther was also challenging the Catholic idea that life as a monk or nun was a special, holy calling. Not only did Luther argue for the priesthood of all believers; he also extended the idea of vocation beyond supposed spiritual work to all types of labor, thus helping to spark what has been called the Protestant work ethic.[54]

Leland Ryken highlights four major themes in the Reformers' teaching on work from which this ethic developed.[55] First is a generally positive attitude toward work and the virtuous nature of hard work. Coupled with this was, second, the affirmation that all legitimate work was a vocation, or calling from God. As such, all workers can offer their work as part of their service to God. This leads to the third theme, that the goal of work is to glorify God and benefit others.[56] Finally, the Reformers maintained a balance of work and rest. The later Puritans maintained the emphasis on rest through a strict keeping of the Sabbath.

While elements of the Protestant work ethic still survive today, especially in evangelical circles, the theological roots which sustain that ethic have increasingly been cut off. The motivation for hard work is to get wealthy and be able to retire early. The idea that work is good, a means of glorifying God and serving others, is one that needs recovery in contemporary Christian theology, teaching, and practice.

Community in Historical Context

There has been little theological reflection on community for most of church history. Whether in tribes, clans, or extended families, humans have normally existed in communities. Some have seen Martin Luther's stand against the combined forces of the Catholic Church and the Holy Roman

---

[53] See Martin Luther, "The Judgment of Martin Luther on Monastic Vows," in LW, 44:349. Altogether Luther offered five arguments against monastic vows: they were contrary to Scripture, conflict with faith, are contrary to Christian freedom, violate the first commandment, and are contrary to common sense.

[54] In commenting on Genesis 13:13, Luther referred to ordinary work as "worship of God . . . well pleasing to God" and "more desirable than all the works of monks and nuns." LW, 2:349.

[55] See Leland Ryken, *Redeeming the Time: Work and Leisure in Christian Perspective* (Portland: Multnomah, 1987), 101–9.

[56] This goal needs to be underscored because a widely read study by German sociologist Max Weber, *The Protestant Ethic and the Spirit of Capitalism,* trans. Talcott Parsons (New York: Scribner, 1932) argues that Protestants worked hard because they thought that success in business would assure them of being within the elect of God. The result of their hard work was the accumulation of capital; since they could not wastefully spend such capital, they invested it, sparking the economic development of capitalism in Protestant countries. While Weber's thesis is still often mentioned, it has few defenders today, in part because it so clearly misrepresents the teaching of Calvin, the other Reformers, and their Puritan descendants.

Empire at the Diet of Worms as one of the earliest indicators of the indi- *[handwritten Korean annotations]* vidualism that would become pervasive in modernity. But Luther himself clearly taught the communal nature of the church and the Christian life. Individualism is more properly rooted in Enlightenment thought, especially its political thought; and it developed more fully in the eighteenth and nineteenth centuries, particularly in North America.

The early church met primarily in homes and spread through homes where the quality of Christian community was evident and attractive. Michael Green, in his classic study *Evangelism in the Early Church,* says of early Christians, "Their community life, though far from perfect . . . was nevertheless sufficiently different and impressive to attract notice, to invite curiosity, and to inspire discipleship" even in the midst of a pagan culture.[57] Contemporary house church advocates like Wolfgang Simson think the conversion of Constantine and the transition from homes to church buildings were twin factors in the decline of Christian piety and the undermining of Christian fellowship and community in the post-Constantinian church.[58]

However, the effects of individualism on church life become clearer in the eighteenth century and thereafter. Paul Harrison, in his study of Baptist life, states:

> Pressed by the secular spirit of individualism current in the eighteenth and nineteenth centuries, and proud of their religious contribution to the movement, later Baptists slipped off their theological base and cooperated in the support of an ideology grounded in the spirit of individual voluntarism. In every decade since the beginning of the nineteenth century one can find in Baptist literature reaffirmations of the freedom and competency of the totally independent individual.[59]

With the collapse of modernity and the onset of postmodern life, there has been a healthy and helpful return to a longing for community, especially among those in the post-baby boom generations. However, the development of community still faces difficulties in American culture, such as consumerism, in which church members do not see themselves as parts

---

[57] Michael Green, *Evangelism in the Early Church* (Grand Rapids: Eerdmans, 1970), 274–75. For more on the importance of households in the early church, see 207–23.

[58] Simson says that in undergoing the transition from house churches to "cathedral" churches, the church experienced "the biggest single derailment in history." See Wolfgang Simson, *Houses That Change the World: Towards a Re-Incarnation of Church,* draft copy (Madras, India: Wolfgang Simson, 1998), 49.

[59] Paul M. Harrison, *Authority and Power in the Free Church Tradition* (Princeton: Princeton University Press, 1959), 21–22.

of a body, but simply fellow consumers, shopping for religious goods and services at the same outlet.[60]

Moreover, another difficulty, peculiar to church life, may be the imperative of growth, for it could be argued that as churches grow, fellowship becomes more problematic. For example, Ralph Neighbour argues for cell churches as the only way to ensure that all Christians experience community.[61] A proper Christian theology of community should address these difficulties and relate community to other Christian imperatives.

How Does It All Fit Together?

Thus far, we have derived from Scripture five major affirmations about humans and traced the understanding of these truths through history. We turn now from biblical investigation and historical consideration to theological formulation. We will consider each of the affirmations we saw as central to biblical teaching on humanity but now formulate them as answers to key questions about humanity that are important to this and every age.

Who Are We?

The first question that demands a theological formulation is that of human nature. Who are we? Or, in other words, what is a human being? *Humans are creatures, created by God as persons, with a complex constitution.* Three implications of this answer need to be unpacked.

We Are Creatures, Created by God

First, the idea that we are creatures, created by God, has been sharply challenged in the past 150 years by Darwinian evolution. That challenge has been answered in two ways. Some Christians have challenged the Darwinian paradigm on logical and scientific grounds, asserting that there are illegitimate leaps of logic, unexplained gaps in the data, and contradictory evidence that is ignored. They maintain that God acted directly in the creation of humans. Other Christians have found the evidence for evolution persuasive and have seen it as the mechanism which God used and guided to perform his creative will, though some in this camp allow for God's special intervention at various points, including the creation of humanity.[62]

---

[60] For an insightful study of this issue, see Bruce Shelley and Marshall Shelley, *Consumer Church: Can Evangelicals Win the World Without Losing Their Souls?* (Downers Grove: InterVarsity, 1992).

[61] Ralph Neighbour Jr., *Where Do We Go from Here? A Guidebook for the Cell Group Church* (Houston: Touch Publications, 1990), 112–13.

[62] These differing perspectives can be found in varying degrees by the ten contributors to *Three Views on Creation and Evolution,* ed. Moreland and Reynolds.

This second response to the Darwinian challenge, called theistic evolution, has been critiqued by some as being theologically inadequate because Scripture teaches God's purposefulness in creation, whereas evolution demands randomness. Which of these responses should be part of our formulation of the doctrine of God's creation of humanity?

The first response to the Darwinian challenge—that evolution is ill founded logically and scientifically—is one that few Christians have the competence to evaluate. Our approach, therefore, should be one of careful investigation carried out in an attitude of genuine humility. Certainly, Christians can and should read the arguments from both sides, but most will lack the means to evaluate independently the arguments in a fully competent manner. In one sense we are left with "dueling scientists." However, it should honestly be noted that the great majority of scientists support evolution, either naturalistic or theistic.[63] Some aspects of theistic evolution, admittedly, are unsettling and problematic both scientifically and theologically, but an assessment of the scientific arguments for and against it lies outside the scope of this chapter.

We Are Created by God as Persons

By the word *person,* we are emphasizing the distinctness of humans. Plants and animals can also be described as created by God, but only humans are created as persons. We will explore in more detail the distinctness of humans later; at this point we use the term *person* to emphasize the central fact that humans are "centrally related to, totally dependent on, and primarily responsible to God."[64] This duality of being created, yet persons, distinguishes the Christian view of humans from two major competing categories.

Figure 3: Contemporary Views of Human Nature

Free Views	The Christian View	Deterministic Views
Secular Humanism	Influenced yet	Reductive Physicalism
Existentialism	Responsible	Freudian Psychology Skinnerian Behaviorism Genetic Determinism

The views on the left side in figure 3 emphasize human freedom to the exclusion of any created design. They think humans can create their own essence and be whatever they want to be. They fail to reckon with the fact that we are created with a God-given nature that we ignore or suppress to our own

---

[63] Of scientists surveyed in a 1997 poll, only 5 percent affirmed the direct creation of humans by God, while 40 percent supported theistic evolution, and 55 percent naturalistic evolution. See the report of this survey on http://www.religioustolerance.org/ev_publi.htm, accessed 18 July 2005.
[64] Hoekema, *Created in God's Image,* 6.

destruction. For example, we are created with a conscience that restrains us from acting out all our desires. When we see someone who has totally suppressed conscience, we describe such a person as inhuman. We have limitations and a designed purpose, inherent in being created by God.

But we are asked to participate responsibly and voluntarily in God's purposes for us. That is what we mean by the term *person*. Other creatures fulfill God's purposes for them involuntarily. They have no choice. That is the common element in all views of human nature on the right. They deny all human responsibility, for to them human choice is an illusion, and thus human responsibility an impossibility. All our supposed choices are in fact just playing out a predetermined hand. They differ only in the source of the predetermination.

The Christian view can be characterized by two words: *influenced* and *responsible*. We acknowledge that a variety of factors impinge upon our lives, some by God's design. For example, God made families to shape children, and they do, for better or for worse. Those growing up in severely dysfunctional families face greater challenges; those growing up in healthier families have advantages. God knows and judges accordingly (Luke 12:48). But the influences we receive from our physical frame, our psychological makeup, our environmental conditioning, and our genetic inheritance, do not rise to the level of determinism, for God holds us responsible for how we play the hand we are dealt.

We Are Created with a Complex Constitution

There are three issues subsumed under this brief phrase. The first is the traditional Christian understanding of humans as embodied souls; that is, our complex constitution includes both a material aspect (which we call the body) and a nonmaterial aspect (which we call the soul but could equally call the spirit). This widely held idea has recently sustained two attacks. One is from materialists, or reductive physicalists, who assert that the body is all there is. This is reflected in what Francis Crick, codiscoverer of the structure of DNA, calls "the astonishing hypothesis," in his book by that title, a widely used guide to neurobiology. "The Astonishing Hypothesis is that 'You,' your joys and your sorrows, your memories and your ambitions, your sense of personal identity and free will, are in fact no more than the behavior of a vast assemblage of nerve cells and their associated molecules."[65] Of course, if his hypothesis is true, then his hypothesis itself is only the product of his nerve cells and their molecules, as is this author's evaluation of it, and neither have any claim to being true or false. In other words, his hypothesis is self-stultifying.

---

[65] Francis Crick, as excerpted in David P. Barash, *Ideas of Human Nature: From the Bhagavad Gita to Sociobiology* (Upper Saddle River, NJ: Prentice-Hall, 1998), 86.

A second version, somewhat related to it, has been developed recently by a number of Christians, including some at Fuller Theological Seminary, and is called nonreductive physicalism. It is like the first perspective in seeing our creation as involving only a material aspect, but it sees the complex functioning of the brain as giving rise to "soulish" capacities like morality and spirituality.[66] This view is trying to accommodate what some see as a tightening link between mind and brain that leaves little room for anything outside of the brain. However, it seems clear that the Bible uses the terms *soul* and *spirit* not just as capacities called into existence by the functioning of our brains, but as entities capable of existence apart from the brain, which this view denies.

The traditional view that we are composed of two "substances" (metaphysical substances, not physical) has been ably defended by J. P. Moreland and John Cooper.[67] Philosophically, Moreland points to the fact that our body experiences a total change of cells over seven years; if there is nothing beyond the body, what gives us enduring personal identity?[68] Issues like self-awareness, memory, and personal consciousness are also problematic for purely physicalist views, but the clearest support for substance dualism is the biblical doctrine of the intermediate state. It seems clear from Scripture (Luke 23:46; 2 Cor. 5:8; Phil. 1:21–24) that we continue to exist and enjoy being in the presence of the Lord after the death of the body, while we await the resurrection of the body. But if the physical is all there is, what exists in the intermediate time? We know what happens to the body at death, but Scripture describes the spirit or soul as still existing (Heb. 12:23; Rev. 6:9). This seems to require something like the position of substance dualism.

The usual criticism of the dualist view is that Scripture treats humans holistically, and it may be granted that there is a functional unity. Humans act and experience life holistically. However, that functional unity does not preclude an ontological dualism, and the intermediate state makes such a dualism necessary. God created us to be embodied souls. In the unnatural situation of death, soul and body are temporarily separated, but that unnatural situation will not endure. That is the importance of the doctrine of the resurrection of the body. It reminds us that we were created embodied souls, and that is how we will live forever one day.

---

[66] This is the perspective presented in Warren Brown, Nancey Murphy, and H. Newton Malony, eds., *Whatever Happened to the Soul? Scientific and Theological Portraits of Human Nature* (Minneapolis: Fortress, 1998).

[67] For Moreland, see J. P. Moreland and David Ciocchi, eds., *Christian Perspectives on Being Human* (Grand Rapids: Baker, 1993); for Cooper, see John W. Cooper, *Body, Soul and the Life Everlasting: Biblical Anthropology and the Monism-Dualism Debate* (Grand Rapids: Eerdmans, 1989).

[68] J. P. Moreland, "A Defense of a Substance Dualist View of the Soul," in *Christian Perspectives*, 70.

The second issue raised by our complex constitution is whether we are trichotomous or dichotomous. The trichotomous position sees human nature as composed of three distinct parts: body, soul, and spirit. The dichotomous view is usually expressed in terms of the duality of soul and body, but many recognize that soul and spirit are often used interchangeably in Scripture so the immaterial aspect could be called either the soul or the spirit. As argued above, the biblical words for body, soul, and spirit point to different aspects of the human constitution; the question here is, do they indicate distinct, separable parts of human nature? If so, are those parts three or two?

There are two major proof texts claimed to support trichotomy. Hebrews 4:12 is cited to prove a distinction between soul and spirit, but F. F. Bruce suggests that it would "be precarious to draw any conclusions from these words about our author's psychology." The words are used only to indicate "the whole mental nature of man," or "the inmost recesses of our spiritual being."[69] There are a number of ways that soul and spirit can be differentiated without the two being separate elements in humans. The second major proof text is 1 Thessalonians 5:23, in which Paul prays that the Thessalonians will be sanctified and that their "whole spirit, soul and body [will] be kept blameless at the coming of our Lord Jesus Christ." But to use this verse as a proof text for the trichotomous nature of humans either proves too much or not enough. If each word listed in a text of Scripture denotes a different part in human nature, trichotomy is not enough, for Mark 12:30 gives four elements, and three of them differ from those listed in 1 Thessalonians 5:23, so that would mean humans are composed of six parts: body, soul, spirit, mind, heart, and strength.

On the other hand, if these different words are just different ways to speak of the totality of a person from different aspects, and not necessarily separate elements, then it proves too little. Anthony Hoekema gives six areas in which soul and spirit are used virtually as synonyms, and it is difficult to answer his examples.[70] Few today hold to trichotomy, though it is affirmed by Watchman Nee, some dispensationalists, and is taught in the Scofield Reference Bible.

The arguments for dichotomy are stronger. While soul and spirit are used sometimes synonymously, there is a difference between either of them and the body. Humans are sometimes described as body and soul (Matt. 10:28) and sometimes as body and spirit (Eccles. 12:7; 1 Cor. 5:3). Strongest of all, if humans continue to exist after the death of the body, and Scripture teaches they do, there must be some nonmaterial aspect of human

[69] F. F. Bruce, *The Epistle to the Hebrews,* NICOT (Grand Rapids: Eerdmans, 1964), 82.

[70] Hoekema, *Created in God's Image,* 206–7.

nature that can exist in separation from the body. Thus, we are more than just a body; there is another element, whether one calls it soul or spirit.

A third issue raised by our complex constitution is the origin of the soul. To put it more precisely, is the nonmaterial aspect of humanity transmitted along with the body from parents to children, or is it created directly by God? Nothing of tremendous value theologically hangs on this question, and nothing in Scripture explicitly answers it, though it was historically important to Catholics because of its implications for the sinlessness of Jesus, and because it has some importance for us in keeping a consistent anthropology.

There are essentially three views on this question. First, the minority view, held in different ways by Origen and the Mormons, is that souls eternally preexist and join with the bodies at birth. This view has numerous theological problems and has been rightly rejected by orthodox Christians for centuries. The two more viable positions are called creationist (God directly creates each soul) and traducian (children receive all of their human nature, body and soul, from their parents at conception).

The creationist position is the majority view in church history. It is particularly favored by Catholics, in large part because it seems to safeguard the purity of the soul of Jesus from the taint of original sin. It is held for other reasons by a number of contemporary evangelicals. It has claimed biblical support from four texts: Genesis 2:7 (God's creation of Adam's soul), Ecclesiastes 12:7 (where at death, the spirit is said to return to God "who gave it"), Zechariah 12:1 (which says the Lord "forms the spirit of man within him"), and Hebrews 12:9 (which calls God "the Father of our spirits"). Traducianists object that the creationist view cannot explain how each soul, created perfect and pure by God, becomes infected with original sin.

Moreover, traducianists claim Genesis 2:21 (the creation of Eve from Adam), Hebrews 7:9–10 (where children are seen as existing in the loins of their fathers prior to birth), and Genesis 2:2 (which states that God began his rest from his creative work on the seventh day) as supporting their view. Creationists object to the traducian view on the grounds that the material (i.e., the body) cannot transmit the nonmaterial (i.e. the soul or spirit).

Berkouwer calls this an "apparently hopeless controversy."[71] Until the fifth century traducianism was the majority view, but the creationist position has been dominant since. More recently, the division has been between Catholics and most of those in the Reformed camp who favor the creationist view on the one side, and Lutherans and some Reformed who support the traducian view, on the other side. The fact of such division, coupled

---

[71] Berkouwer, *Man,* 307.

with the nondecisive nature of the scriptural support claimed by each side and the refusal of theologians as keen as Augustine to take either position, should alert us to the possibility that both sides may have it partly right and partly wrong. → אדם הראשון

Creationists are right to see God as the Creator of each soul, but they are wrong to limit God's creative work to the soul. God is the Creator of the whole person, whether he uses human parents as his instruments or not. The traducianist view is right to emphasize the unity of body and soul in human nature, and to see the organic nature of the human race, with our inheritance of a fallen nature from Adam. But they are wrong if they infer from this that God is uninvolved in the creation of every individual or that there is nothing in human nature beyond the body. On balance, the traducian view seems preferable, but the creationist position is neither heretical nor dangerous. The statements of both positions can be combined in a healthy synthesis.[72]

What Makes Us Special?

The second topic we want to formulate is that of the image of God. Earlier, we laid out some parameters that Scripture establishes and surveyed some historical interpretations, but now we want to argue for a particular understanding of the *imago dei*. We will frame this formulation by the question, what makes us special? That seems to be the emphasis in Genesis 1:26–27, the key text on this topic. In contrast to all the other creations of God, and listed last and introduced in a distinctive and deliberate way, the creation of humans is clearly marked off as special and signified as such by the thrice-repeated phrase, "the image of God."

We begin with a conclusion of what the image of God is, and then try to show how it fits the biblical data together. The image of God is *the capacity of human beings to have a relationship with God.* What is the basis for such a definition?

First, the idea, expressed by Calvin, Barth, Brunner, and others, that we cannot understand or define human beings apart from God is impressive. To try to understand humanity in the abstract, or apart from our creation by God, is futile. Moreover, the Bible is clear that God created us for a relationship with himself. These considerations move us toward the relational view, but the image should not be seen as a relationship itself. The substantive view is the majority view in history, and that is probably for a reason. So we side with the substantive view in seeing the image as some capacity within human nature and suspect it may involve reason, will, and some of the other capacities mentioned by Calvin, Grudem, and others.

→ p.373
Calvin

---

[72] For a fuller discussion of these and other issues involved in this question, see ibid., 279–309.

Still, the focal point of the substantive view is the capacity for relationship with God. This understanding incorporates aspects of other capacities as contributing to the image of God (reason, will, emotion, conscience) but not as necessarily involved in the image of God. This allows a reasonable position on the issue of children and the mentally retarded: all humans have the capacity for a relationship with God, for that is determined by God's power, not by our possession of a fully functioning reason. Moreover, this formulation is simple and gives a proper focus to the question of God's image in humanity.

This capacity is localized in the spiritual nature of humanity, to be specific, the human spirit. God establishes his relationship with us by means of his Spirit relating to the human spirit. Union with Christ is established through the Spirit indwelling our being and establishing communion between his Spirit and the human spirit (see Rom. 8:9–11,16). As mentioned above, the capacities of reason, will, and other capacities may be involved here, but not necessarily so. In particular, the idea of nonreductive physicalism—that brain activity is necessary for soulish (or spiritual) activity—is opposed. Only God knows what is absolutely necessary for a relationship with him; only God knows how he deals with the spirits of the retarded, children, those with Alzheimer's, and those with other disabilities.

We may affirm that each person has the capacity for a relationship with God because we believe God has the capacity to reach every human spirit. Normally that relationship is expressed through activities of life that involve the brain, but such activities may not be absolutely necessary. In the intermediate state it will not be so; there are some who claim to have had out-of-body experiences in this life (Paul, 2 Cor. 12:2–4), and the possibility that God can establish relationships with humans in exceptional ways in exceptional circumstances should be left open.

Under this interpretation, the image is damaged by the fall, but not destroyed. The immediate death referred to in Genesis 2:17 as the result of sin is spiritual death, or the death of the human spirit. In the fall it was the human spirit that died. Our bodies became mortal and destined to die, but spiritually we are dead all our lives, apart from the new birth. Thus, the image of God remains after the fall but as a latent capacity, requiring activation by the Spirit. Conversion is in fact a rebirth of the spirit, and sanctification is the growth and development of the spirit as it becomes increasingly conformed to the image of Christ, or, we may say, as that capacity for relationship reaches increasingly all that it was created for.

This interpretation fits together the fall, the effect of the fall on the image of God, and conversion and sanctification. It seems to fit all the biblical parameters and answers in the most profound way the question, what makes us special? It also establishes human uniqueness and distinctiveness securely. For example, if science found tomorrow that animals can in fact think and communicate exactly as we do, it would not militate against this view. It would not require us to think humans are no longer unique. What makes us special is our capacity for a unique type of relationship with God. Scripture in no way allows for that capacity in animals, nor could science ever establish the existence of such a capacity. Thus, this view safeguards the uniqueness of humanity against increasing claims of science that we are just clever animals and complicated machines.

Why Did God Create Us Male and Female?

Perhaps the most controversial aspect of the doctrine of humanity among evangelicals has been our creation as male and female. Countless books and articles have been written arguing the nuances of the key biblical texts, but egalitarian John Stackhouse makes a perceptive point when he says, "I am grateful for excellent technical biblical scholarship, but I have come to conclude that only a *theological* take on these matters will avail."[73] He grants that complementarians have the better case exegetically but remains egalitarian because he cannot see a theological rationale for the complementarian position. He challenges complementarians to complete the sentence, "It is better for church government to have only men and no women because . . ." with a rationale other than "because the Bible says so."[74] Stackhouse's question (why does God assign males and females differing roles?) leads us to a prior and even more fundamental theological question: why did God create us male and female?

The Bible nowhere explicitly asks or answers that question, so the theological task before us is to seek a framework within which the biblical teaching makes sense, one that gives a theological rationale for the specifics of biblical teaching. This question is also raised in an indirect way by those who define equality in a way that emphasizes the functional interchangeability of male and female and minimizes any differences between males and females. If male and female are equal (and interchangeable), why did God choose to create humans in two sexes? Answering this question will require us to fit biblical teaching together and will, in the end, provide a theological as well as an exegetical rationale for the complementarian position.

To Provide for the Propagation of Humanity

The first way we should answer this question is to say that creation as male and a female was the way God chose for the propagation of the species. It thus provides the basis for marriage and the family, which God

---

[73] Stackhouse, *Finally Feminist*, 52, n. 13. Emphasis in original.
[74] Ibid., 109–10.

ordained as the context for the giving and raising of children. No doubt God could have provided for the propagation of the species in another way; there are numerous examples of asexual reproduction in the animal world. But God has constructed humans in such a way that it takes a contribution from both a male and a female to produce another human life, and these contributions are not interchangeable. No male will ever carry, bear, or nurse a child; no woman will ever beget or father a child. These roles are complementary and definitely sex based. Yet no one seems to think we need a rationale for why males should always be the fathers and females always the mothers. Biology sets some hard barriers.

Not only does our sexuality allow for reproduction, but the hormones that accompany sexual maturity produce in us a strong sexual drive that attracts us toward the opposite sex and is meant to lead us where it led Adam and Eve—to a marital commitment. Adam's reaction to Eve and the interesting comment of Genesis 2:25 reflect the fact that sexual attraction was originally a pure thing. That God should make that which is necessary for the propagation of the species and the satisfaction of our sexual drive, also a way to symbolize and cement the union of a man and woman in marriage and provide pleasure, is a mark of his gracious character.

Theologians have spoken of the procreative and unitive functions of sexual relations within marriage. Official Catholic teaching has been for years that in every act of sexual intercourse, the possibility of conception must be present for it to be a valid part of a couple's life. Thus contraception is seen as "intrinsically evil."[75] But the unitive function justifies sexual relations even apart from the procreative function. At the same time the procreative purpose should not be permanently denied apart from some special circumstances. But it can be delayed by contraception for a time, as some times and circumstances seem more propitious for child-bearing and child-rearing than others. Thus, family planning is not rebelling against God or a lack of trust in God. To let things happen "naturally" in a fallen world would mean not taking aspirin when you're sick or not putting out fires caused by lightning. In this world what happens naturally is not always God's will (Matt. 6:10). Therefore, we may seek to intervene but in a spirit of submission, faithful to Scripture, and mindful that part of God's will for most couples is the office of parenthood. Some couples suffer the pain of infertility; some individuals never marry; but for most individuals one of God's purposes in sexual expression is children.

From this we may draw a number of implications. First, God wants humanity to continue. That is why we are commanded to multiply and somewhat driven to it by sexual desire. Second, God wants children who are

---

[75] *Catechism of the Catholic Church*, 2nd ed. (Vatican: Libreria Editrice Vaticana, 1997), § 2370.

raised by mothers and fathers (not primarily by a village or by two fathers or two mothers). Contemporary studies bear out the wisdom of God's plan, as we are finding the long-lasting effects of divorce on children. Third, heterosexuality is God's norm for sexual expression, and marriage is the ordained context. This rules out homosexual activity, adultery, bestiality, and all extramarital sexual activity. Those who are single or struggle with the sin of homosexuality must seek grace to live a chaste life, unless and until God leads them to a heterosexual marriage relationship. Heterosexuals must be faithful to their spouses. Despite the claims of many today, such a life is neither impossible nor unhealthy.

But while marriage and family are two of the reasons God made us male and female, they are not the only ones. The maleness and femaleness of singles is not wasted or irrelevant. This leads us to a second reason for our creation as male and female.

To Provide for Mutually Enriching Relationships

God made us male and female as a way of providing for us mutually enriching relationships. Genesis 2:18–25 tells us that even before the fall, man is incomplete apart from woman. Adam was made with a need that neither God nor another man could satisfy. First Corinthians 11:8–11, in commenting on Genesis 2, concludes that man and woman are not independent of each other "in the Lord." The point is that we need each other, and God made us to enrich each other.

The possibility of enriching one another comes from our differences. As was said earlier, being male or female involves living with differing "modes of orientation."[76] Men and women see themselves, the world, others, and even God with different eyes. By creating us with these differing orientations, God gives us the possibility of seeing the world in differing ways. This implies that many of the differences we are discovering between men and women are not the result of nurture, and neither are they a result of the fall. They are part of God's created intentions. God intended men and women to have different aptitudes, abilities, and perspectives. The differences are so pronounced that we sometimes refer to each other not as the *other* sex but as the *opposite* sex. But if we use these differences aright, we are not frustrated by them but rather are enabled to see the world from two different perspectives and thus know the world, ourselves, and others more fully.

The obstacle to this enrichment is the insistence, usually by men, that the male way of seeing things is the right way. We need to accept that two ways can be different without one being better or worse, superior or inferior. It may be that one reason for the drive to deny or minimize differences between males and females in contemporary culture is the tendency to see

---

[76] Grenz, *Sexual Ethics*, 8.

differences as involving superiority and inferiority rather than as a source of enrichment.

A Rationale for Roles

These first two answers to the question of why God created us male and female could be affirmed by both complementarians and egalitarians, though highlighting the importance of the differences between men and women fits more naturally within a complementarian view. But we have not yet given a rationale that applies specifically to the roles of men and women in the home and church. Why does God assign leadership roles to males and submissive roles to women? One answer that clearly no longer makes sense is to base the prohibition on differing abilities. Many women are clearly gifted in teaching and leading; many wives seem to have superior abilities to their husbands to be the heads of their families. They find submission difficult and frustrating. Why should they not serve in leadership roles in their families and churches? Three answers to this critical "why" question, which also relate, at least in part, to the larger question of why God made us male and female, should be considered.

First, for many believers, to answer the question, "Why should males be leaders and females submissive?" with the answer, "Because the Bible says so," is a sufficient rationale. They distrust their ability to understand all the reasons God may ordain things as he does, but they trust him and find satisfaction in humble obedience. Stackhouse argues that normally God's commandments make sense; that is, we can understand why they should be obeyed.[77]

But in fact, it can be argued that often there is no obvious rationale for God's commandments. There was no reason for Eve not to eat the fruit in the garden. The text indicates that it was ripe and desirable (Gen. 3:6); the only reason for not partaking was that God had said not to. Abram was told to leave his home without knowing the destination, with no reason as to why he had to leave (Gen. 12:1), and Jesus commands his followers to act in ways that seem to conflict with good sense, such as rejoicing when persecuted, turning the other cheek when slapped, and going the second mile when forced to go one (see Matt. 5:12,39–41). So obedience should not be conditioned on understanding the rationale for a command. Indeed, if we obey just because we see a good reason for doing so, are we acting in faith and obedience or mere human prudence?

Yet while a theological rationale is unnecessary, there is at least one strong possibility. It may be that males and females are given different roles because in doing so they reflect something of the nature of the triune God.

---

[77] Stackhouse, *Finally Feminist,* 109. He makes the same point several times elsewhere in this book, such as pp. 27 and 72.

To broaden the point, it may be that God made us male and female because it takes two sexes to reflect fully the glory of the Trinity.

Within the equality of the three persons of the Trinity, what is it that distinguishes the Father from the Son and the Spirit? They share the same nature, abilities, and attributes (much as males and females do). One suggestion for the distinction in the members of the Trinity was made by Augustine, who argued that the distinction is relational. The Father differs from the Son in that he is and has always been the Father, relating to the Son as a Father, leading, initiating, and directing the Son. The Son differs from the Father in that he has always been the Son, joyfully obeying and submitting to the Father. To complete the Trinity, the Spirit is identified with love, particularly the love that binds Father and Son together.[78] Some egalitarians have argued that the submission of the Son to the Father, which is clearly seen, particularly in the Gospel of John, was temporal and limited to his earthly ministry, but Augustine's argument assumes that the relational distinction is eternal, and 1 Corinthians 15:28 extends Christ's submission into the eschaton.[79]

Could it be that God desires the relationships of men and women, especially in Christian homes and churches, to reflect the relationship of Father and Son in the Trinity, with men reflecting the leadership of the Father, and women the submissiveness of the Son, and with self-giving love binding them together? This seems to be a viable rationale for the differing roles assigned to men and women.

There seems another, more obvious rationale for the differing roles within marriage. That rationale is God's desire that husbands and wives reflect the relationship of Christ and the church, a relationship that is not at all egalitarian (see Eph. 5:22–33). It is worth noting that in relationship to Christ, all of us, male and female, reflect the submissive role, just as in relationship to the rest of creation, all of us, male and female, reflect the leadership role (see Gen. 1:26,28, where man and woman are to "rule" over the creation). This relationship of male and female in marriage seems to lead to differing roles in the church, for it is difficult to see how a wife could simultaneously be in submission to her husband while he is in submission to her as his pastor (Heb. 13:17), though the prior rationale applies more clearly to roles in the church.

---

[78] For Augustine's relational distinction of Father and Son, see Augustine, *The Trinity,* trans. Stephen McKenna, in *The Fathers of the Church* (Washington, DC: Catholic University of America Press, 1963), 179–80 (5.5); for the Holy Spirit as love, see 491–96 (15.17).

[79] For opposing views on this topic, see Gilbert Bilezikian, "Hermeneutical Bungee-Jumping: Subordination in the Godhead," *JETS* 40, no. 1 (March 1997): 57–68 and Stephen D. Kovach and Peter R. Schemm, Jr., "A Defense of the Doctrine of the Eternal Subordination of the Son," *JETS* 42, no. 3 (September 1999): 461–76.

A final point is more of an observation than a rationale. Could it be that ③the submission of wives to their husbands is just another of a number of submission relationships that God gives us as training grounds for learning to submit to him? After all, younger men are commanded to submit to older men (1 Pet. 5:5); all church members, male and female, are commanded to submit to church leaders (Heb. 13:17), citizens to governmental officials (1 Pet. 2:13), children to parents (Luke 2:51), and Christians to one another (Eph. 5:21). Both males and females must learn the lesson of submission, for that is crucial to their eternal destiny (James 4:7). It seems that God has organized human life to give all of us relationships in which we learn the lesson of submission. Women simply have one more context in which to learn that lesson. Seen in this context, is the submission of women to men in the home and the church really that objectionable?

The Bible is clear that God did create us male and female and that he does ask us to fill differing roles in the home and church. No text explicitly addresses the question of why he created us in two sexes or why he assigns to us complementary roles. Nowhere in Scripture is there any indication that we will always see the rationale for God's commands, and indeed the first command of God was given with no rationale and indeed seemed contrary to reason (Gen. 3:6: the fruit looked good, pleasing, and desirable). C. S. Lewis argues that there should always be in Christian revelation "an element that unbelievers will call irrational and believers will call suprarational . . . something . . . opaque to our reason though not contrary to it." He concludes that if we abandon that "opaque element" and retain "only what can be justified by standards of prudence and convenience at the bar of enlightened common sense," we have exchanged Christian revelation for natural religion.[80] God's purposes in creating us male and female and giving us distinctive roles may be one of the suprarational, opaque areas, yet it is not contrary to reason, either.

What Is Our Calling?

We may approach the theological formulation of the doctrine of work by asking, what is our calling? To put the same question in the words of one of the most famous catechetical formulations (the first question of the Westminster Shorter Catechism), what is the chief end of man? The answer given by the cathechism is "to glorify God and enjoy him forever." That answer serves well for the question we are asking and opens up two key ideas in our formulation of work. First, we want to emphasize the God-glorifying

---

[80] C. S. Lewis, "Priestesses in the Church?" in *God in the Dock: Essays on Theology and Ethics*, ed. Walter Hooper (Grand Rapids: Eerdmans, 1970), 238.

aspect of work. Second, we want to put alongside work the Christian doctrine of rest or leisure, which is part of enjoying God forever.

The Purpose of Work: Glorifying God

Seeing the purpose or goal of work as the glory of God is an idea with many implications and serves to tie together numerous aspects of the doctrine of work. For example, work is an inherent part of being a creature made in God's image, for the overall purpose of our creation is to glorify God. As part of God's original creation, work is a good thing. It is good not just as a means to some other good; it is good to work. It is not an evil necessity from which we seek to escape. Even those who are wealthy enough or old enough to retire from a job should never retire from work, for we never retire from being humans made in the image of a God who himself is at work even to this day (John 5:17). We do acknowledge the fall and its negative effect on work. Especially in our industrial age, some work is mindless, monotonous, and tedious. But the goal is not to make the work week shorter, or to make work easier, or to escape work, but to make work better, more fulfilling, more fitting for humans to do.

A second implication of the purpose of work as glorifying God is that it includes benefiting our neighbors. God's glory is promoted when humans, made in God's image, are blessed. This will affect both the type of work we do and how we do it. Some jobs provide nothing that benefits anyone and thus cannot be done to the glory of God and thus should not be done, especially not by Christians. The social implications of what we do should be examined thoughtfully by believers. Furthermore, all jobs should be done in a way that reflects integrity and a genuine concern for others. That means doing our jobs to the best of our abilities, working honestly, and acting justly in our relationships with others. Thus, a Christian who is in a position of authority must balance concern for the welfare and profit of the company with the welfare of others working for him.

Third, seeing the goal of work as the glory of God and the good of others will enable us to value properly forms of work that do not bring monetary reward, such as homemaking, child-rearing, art, or volunteer labor. They are important, valuable, God-honoring forms of work. Even those who lose their jobs, and correspondingly often lose their sense of self-esteem and worth, need not be without work. There are countless ways to glorify God and serve others.

Fourth, if we see all legitimate work as glorifying God, blessing others, and fulfilling his will for our lives, we can avoid the sacred/secular or the lay/clergy dichotomies. Those in Christian ministry are not following a holier or higher calling, only a different calling. All Christians should believe they have a calling to do whatever they do. Thus, all Christians should be full-time Christians, serving Christ in all they do. Vocational workers devote full time to ministry because their gifts lend themselves to such ministries, but Paul saw nothing wrong with doing other work to support himself when that was necessary and then preaching full-time when that was possible (Acts 18:1–5). If other Christians or a church want to pay someone for using their gifts, it enables them to devote their full time and attention to vocational ministry. If not, they glorify God as they work in other contexts that enable them to pay their bills and use their gifts in Christian ministry as time and opportunities allow.

There are two errors to avoid here. Some think they cannot minister unless they receive a paycheck. But we minister because we are gifted, not because we are paid. Thus, all Christians should minister, volunteering to do what their gifts qualify them to do. But second, they should not think that their volunteer service is their only work that glorifies God. When they go to their paying job, they are still doing God's will. Both are legitimate ways of glorifying God.

Finally, seeing the goal of work as the glory of God can relieve us of the frantic push for affluence (see Prov. 23:4). Our paycheck is not the measure of our personal worth or the worth of our work. We do not need all the things we see around us to satisfy; we do need to do God-honoring work to be satisfied.

The Limited Nature of Work: The Christian Doctrine of Rest

Alongside our calling to glorify God is our calling to enjoy him forever. Work may be one way that we enjoy him but certainly not the only way. The Bible is clear that our work is not salvific, nor is it the most important aspect of our lives. It is only part of being Christlike. Alongside the command to work is the command to rest. Thus our theology of work must be linked to our theology of rest, or leisure.

The fourth commandment (Exod. 20:8–11; Deut. 5:12–15) is the most often-mentioned basis for a theology of rest or leisure. It points to God's example of resting on the seventh day and was a matter of great importance to the scribes and Pharisees of Jesus' day. The Gospels are replete with stories of Sabbath controversies, and it seems at times that Jesus went out of his way to heal on the Sabbath and challenge their misunderstanding of the purpose of the Sabbath command. In fact, the fourth commandment is the only one of the Ten Commandments that is not specifically reaffirmed in New Testament teaching. Jesus' claim to be Lord of the Sabbath and that the Sabbath was made for man (Mark 2:27–28) seems to have precipitated a change in attitude among early believers. Paul never condemned observance of the Sabbath but made it an item of Christian liberty (Rom. 14:5). Thus, it is not surprising that Christians have practiced the Sabbath in a variety of ways over the years. At least four major approaches have developed.[81]					*to keep Sabbath.*

①Seventh-Day believers, or Sabbatarians have sought to keep the literal Old Testament Sabbath, which is the seventh day. This is the position of Seventh-Day Adventists, and a small group of Seventh-Day Baptists. They point out that the command is not any one day in seven but the seventh day. That day is Saturday, not Sunday.

Perhaps the most common position in Christian history has been that which sees Sunday as the Christian Sabbath. By the time of John's Apocalypse, the first day of the week was called "the Lord's Day" (Rev. 1:10) and was the normal day for Christian worship virtually from Easter onward (John 20:19; Acts 20:7; 1 Cor. 16:2). From the time of Constantine, Sunday became by law a day of rest and worship. And with the work of Thomas Aquinas, the idea of Sunday as the Christian Sabbath became official doctrine, one which continued through the Reformation and beyond, despite the dissenting views of Luther and Calvin, who saw worship on Sunday as a convenience more than a command, and Sunday as theologically distinct from the Old Testament Sabbath.[82]

② In England the Puritans and Presbyterians went well beyond Calvin and earlier teaching in being especially rigorous about Sabbath observance so that in mid-seventeenth-century England it was against the law to engage in any type of recreation on Sunday, even going for a walk. This Puritan attitude entered the new world in New England and was reflected in the blue laws that governed what activities and businesses were allowed to open on Sunday. Such laws were on the books and observed until very recent times and are still observed to a degree in some parts of the South.

There has grown increasingly in recent times a third position that sees ③ the Sabbath commandment as part of the Jewish ceremonial law that applied to Israel but not to the church. While it is good to have a common day to gather with believers for corporate worship, advocates of this position do not see Sabbath recreational activity or work as inherently sinful, for the Sabbath commandment no longer applies either to activity on the seventh day or first day of the week.

---

[81] See the discussion of Sunday and the Sabbath in John S. Hammett, "The Lord's Day," in *An Exposition of the Baptist Faith and Mission,* ed. Doug Blount and Joseph Wooddell (Lanham, MD: Rowman & Littlefield, forthcoming). Further documentation is found in D. A. Carson, ed., *From Sabbath to Lord's Day: A Biblical, Historical, and Theological Investigation* (Grand Rapids: Zondervan, 1982).

[82] See the historical surveys by Richard Bauckham, "Sabbath and Sunday in the Medieval Church in the West," and "Sabbath and Sunday in the Protestant Tradition," both in *From Sabbath to Lord's Day,* 299–309, 311–41.

The view taken here sees the coming of Christ as marking a change in our relationship to the Old Testament law, a change summarized in the word *fulfillment* (Matt. 5:17). Christ fulfilled the Sabbath for us in providing rest for our souls (Matt. 11:28–30) and thus giving us a true Sabbath rest (Heb. 4:9–12). This explains why Paul left Sabbath observance as a matter of Christian liberty. This also seems to be the position to which Southern Baptists have moved in their 2000 version of the Baptist Faith and Message. The 1963 Baptist Faith and Message, while not calling Sunday the Christian Sabbath, does say that the Lord's Day is "a Christian institution for regular observance" that should be "employed in exercises of worship and spiritual devotion, both public and private, and by refraining from worldly amusements, and resting from secular employments, work of necessity and mercy only being excepted." But the 2000 version of the Baptist Faith and Message changed the wording about what activities Christians should refrain from doing, simply saying: "Activities on the Lord's Day should be commensurate with the Christian's conscience under the Lordship of Jesus Christ."

We agree that there is no theological basis for an absolute prohibition of certain activities, either on the seventh day (the Sabbath) or on Sunday. We fulfill the Sabbath rest through faith in Christ. At the same time there are some good reasons for a Christian observance of a modified Sabbath rest, not as a matter of obedience to a biblical mandate but as a helpful spiritual discipline. We will return to this point when we discuss practical applications of this doctrine.

Beyond the command to rest, biblical teaching includes a number of themes that allow us to suggest some aspects of a Christian view of leisure. First, work and leisure must be considered together. The essential goodness and God-givenness of work means that we must not dichotomize work as an evil necessity and leisure as where we find pleasure and self-fulfillment. To demand that leisure compensate us for working hard is to ask too much of it. Work when done for God's glory and the good of others has a measure of inherent reward. Leisure is not the reward we get for work; we do not earn it. Work and leisure are both gifts.

Because work also partakes of the fall, it also has some aspects of toil, and thus there is a need for rest or recreation. This term more properly reflects the Christian belief that the original creation is now fallen and needs attention. Since work involves toil and tires us, part of leisure is rest, which re-creates our bodies. Work can also tear down other parts of life, such as relationships with God and others, and appreciation for God's blessings. So in the Old Testament, provision was made for leisure times such as festivals and holidays, where families would naturally spend more time together and in worship, and thus would re-create those relationships. Leisure time also affords opportunities to do nonutilitarian activities, which remind us that work is not ultimate, that we live by grace, and allow us to re-create our appreciation for grace. Not just children, but adults are allowed to play.

All this parallels the re-creating work God does in us. He makes believers new creations in Christ (2 Cor. 5:17), and in the end he will make everything new (Rev. 21:5). Thus, recreation is related spiritually to the themes of justification, sanctification, and glorification. For the believer recreational activities should enhance our relationship with God and be occasions for thanks. This principle would rule out many activities that are commonly seen as leisure or recreation.[83]

Why Do We Need Others?

The Bible teaches and experience confirms that we are made for community. Yet all the manifestations of sin—anger, pride, self-centeredness, envy, greed—frustrate our attempts to build community. The theological motif that underlies the doctrine of community is that it must be a divine creation, not a human achievement. This is seen in three ways.

First is the promise running throughout the Bible, "I will be their God, and they will be my people." The order of these phrases is important. It is only as people come to God that they can come together in any lasting way. Thus the tabernacle, the place where God met with his people, was central physically to the Israelite camp (Num. 2:2,17). Later on, Jerusalem, the location of the temple, was the spiritual center of Jewish life. The psalmist, even in exile, called Jerusalem "my highest joy" (Ps. 137:6), and all Jewish males were to appear before God in Jerusalem three times a year (Deut. 16:16). Yet this centrality in location and expectation did not translate into centrality in heart and life. Rather than communion and community, God's presence in the midst of Israel brought down judgment upon them. The quest for community, both vertical and horizontal, was largely frustrated.

The second place where we see God working in a new way to create community is in Acts 2:42. On the day of Pentecost, God poured out on the church the gift of the Holy Spirit. This was a new level of experiencing God. In the Old Testament the Spirit had come upon individuals for a time but could also depart (1 Sam. 11:6; 16:14); in the Gospel, the Spirit had been with the disciples, but now he was in them (John 14:17). Almost immediately upon the Spirit's arrival, we find the word "fellowship" (koinonia) for the first time in the New Testament. It is not found in Matthew,

---

[83] For more on leisure, see the insightful comments of Ryken throughout *Redeeming the Time: A Christian Approach to Work and Leisure*.

κοινωνία는 act 2011 처음등장

Mark, Luke, John, or Acts 1. But when the Spirit arrives, he brings with him an experience of fellowship that is the expression of their community. It is seen in their common life (Acts 2:44–45; 4:32–35), a life that political systems (e.g., communism) have been unable to impose because such a common life can only flow from genuine community, which is the creation of God.

The coming of the Spirit signals a change in how God brought community to his people. Rather than a symbolic mediation of his presence through a temple made with hands, God now dwells within them, making their own bodies his temples (1 Cor. 6:19). Even more importantly, he brings believers together, building them into one holy temple (1 Cor. 3:16; 2 Cor. 6:16; Eph. 2:21). Their common possession of the Spirit produces the mortar of fellowship that binds them into a community, as living stones that together become a temple.

Yet community is still frustrated by human sin. So the third way that God works to create community is seen in Jesus, who is the bringer of reconciliation and the ultimate source of the church's unity and community. He brings reconciliation by his work on the cross, which both reconciles humans to God and breaks down the barriers between humans (Eph. 2:14–18). The church is the answer to the human quest for community, for there believers of all classes, races, and ages come together and find community in Christ. As the head of the body, he is the ground of their unity, the authority for their life together, and the goal toward which they all are growing. As long as they grow toward him, they will grow closer together and experience deeper community. But if they seek community on their own, they will degenerate into a social club, with the limited community people can create on their own.

As we noted earlier, community is one of the most obvious desires of postmodern people. Churches need to respond to this desire, but in so doing, they must beware of settling for common affinity groups, social clubs, and even human friendships. Good as these may be, they fall short of God's desire. He has always purposed first of all to be our God and bring us to experience communion and community with him, and then he calls us to be his people and experience the depth of community he makes possible in the church. Church growth specialists tell us that churches grow fastest when they attract people like those already in the church. That may well be true, but our calling is not to gather around a commonality of background, or perspective, or life situation but to find community in a common possession of Christ, a common experience of the indwelling Spirit, and a common calling to be God's people. God is at the heart of all true community.

How Does This Doctrine Impact the Church Today?

In the first sentence of the first textbook of theology used in the first Southern Baptist seminary, J. L. Dagg clearly states the purpose of all theological study:

> The study of religious truth ought to be undertaken and prosecuted from a sense of duty, and with a view to the improvement of the heart. When learned, it ought not to be laid on the shelf, as an object of speculation; but it should be deposited deep in the heart, where its sanctifying power ought to be felt. To study theology, for the purpose of gratifying curiosity, or preparing for a profession, is an abuse and profanation of what ought to be regarded as most holy. To learn things pertaining to God, merely for the sake of amusement, or secular advantage, or to gratify the mere love of knowledge, is to treat the Most High with contempt.[84]

In keeping with Dagg's charge, this chapter concludes by suggesting some of the ways this doctrine should improve the hearts and lives of those who study these truths. The examples given here will be simply illustrative, and far from exhaustive, but will suggest how the "sanctifying power" of God's design for humanity "ought to be felt" and reflected in our churches.

Creation and Human Accountability

The first application of the doctrine of humanity derives from the fact that we are created by God. That fact establishes universal human accountability to God. No one can say, "Let God go his way, and I'll go mine." No one can treat the issues of God's existence and will as unimportant matters, unworthy of concern. For creatures, the most urgent and important question of their existence is, Why am I here? Who is my Creator, and what is his will for my life? God, as Creator, has the perfect right to say to every creature he made, "What did you do with the life I gave you? Did you live it in ways I approve?"

This truth should affect the way we do evangelism, especially in our increasingly postmodern, post-Christian, biblically illiterate world. The gospel, it is believed, has no claim on an independent, autonomous human being. He lives for his own pleasures and purposes, unless he recognizes his accountability to a creator. We have found only one evangelistic tract that clearly emphasizes the importance of God as Creator in establishing

---

[84] John L. Dagg, *A Manual of Theology* (Charleston, SC: Southern Baptist Publication Society, 1857; reprint Harrisonburg, VA: Gano Books, 1982), 13.

human accountability to God.[85] Perhaps in the past our created nature and resulting accountability to God could be assumed as generally accepted, but that is certainly not the case today.

The fact of our creation by God is crucial; the means of divine creation is secondary. Those working to establish Intelligent Design as a legitimate scientific theory should be applauded. Christians most certainly should be encouraged to acquaint themselves with some of the amazing facts that point to design. However, few of us will have the expertise to evaluate and refute the claims of evolutionists. A wiser evangelistic strategy is to reframe the question in terms of "who" more than "how." In other words, granting the evolutionist, for the sake of argument, his claim that humanity began its evolutionary trek in a primeval pond, who made the pond? If the universe began with a big bang, who was the banger?

We are told that contemporary culture loves narratives, or stories. Perhaps the following story would do more to bring our secular friends to consider their accountability to a Creator than pages of scientific evidence:

> Imagine a family of mice who lived all their lives in a large piano. To them in the piano-world came the music of the instrument, filling all the dark spaces with sound and harmony. At first the mice were impressed by it. They drew comfort and wonder from the thought that there was Someone who made the music—though invisible to them—above, yet close to them. They loved to think of the Great Player whom they could not see.
>
> Then one day a daring mouse climbed up part of the piano and returned very thoughtful. He had found out how the music was made. Wires were the secret; tightly stretched wires of graduated lengths which trembled and vibrated. They must revise all their old beliefs; none but the most conservative could any longer believe in the Unseen Player.
>
> Later, another explorer carried the explanation further. Hammers were now the secret, numbers of hammers dancing and leaping on the wires. This was a more complicated theory, but it all went to show that they lived in a purely mechanical and mathematical world. The Unseen Player came to be thought of as a myth.
>
> But the pianist continued to play.[86]

This story illustrates the difference between knowing how and knowing who. It is the who behind creation that is primary in biblical teaching and

---

[85] The tract "2 Ways to Live," published by Matthias Media of Australia, makes this important emphasis.

[86] Reprinted from the *London Observer* in *Leadership* 4, no. 3 (Summer 1983): 95.

should be primary in our evangelistic presentation, for he is the one to whom we must all one day give an account.

Creation in God's Image and Human Dignity

Millions of people struggle with feelings of worthlessness, and Christians have been accused of compounding the difficulty by teaching that all are sinners. But in fact, the Christian worldview provides the only transcendent basis for human worth and dignity. For example, a small but growing number of animal rights activists are arguing the evil of specie-sism, the idea that one species is somehow better than another. What right, they say, do we have to act as if other species are here somehow for the benefit of *homo sapiens*? While we can agree with them that animals and all of God's creatures should be treated with care, because they are first of all *God's* creatures, we maintain that humans have a special place in cre-ation and that God has given animals to us for food (Gen. 9:3). Along with the special place of humans comes a special responsibility, one of them being to care for creation. More important is the human responsibility to relate to God.

In fact, the Christian teaching of human sinfulness is a reflection of human dignity. God treats humans as morally responsible creatures whose choices issue in eternal destinies. Dogs, cats, and other animals cannot be sinners, for they lack the dignity of moral conscience and responsibility. Yet in spite of their sinfulness, humans are to be treated with the dignity befitting image bearers of God. That dignity means that anyone who at-tacks the image of God forfeits his own life (Gen. 9:6). Even cursing God's image draws censure (James 3:9–10).

The challenge is to treat all humans with the dignity they deserve. Evangelical Christians have done well in championing the dignity of the unborn; they have not done as well in treating their enemies with the re-spect due to those who bear God's image. Islamic terrorists, abortion rights activists, those promoting the rights of homosexuals—even these persons are creatures made in God's image and deemed by God as worthy of re-spect in how we speak of them and how we treat them.

For those suffering from a sense of worthlessness, the knowledge that we are made in God's image is the ultimate antidote. But while it should fill us with a sense of dignity, it should also warn us of our awesome responsi-bility. C. S. Lewis offers these profound comments that summarize well the practical impact of our creation in the image of God:

> It is a serious thing . . . to remember that the dullest and most uninteresting person you talk to may one day be a creature which, if

you saw it now, you would be strongly tempted to worship, or else a horror and corruption such as you now meet, if at all, only in a nightmare. All day long we are, in some degree, helping each other to one or the other of these destinations. It is in the light of these overwhelming possibilities, it is with the awe and circumspection proper to them, that we should conduct all our dealings with one another, all friendships, all loves, all play, all politics. . . . It is immortals whom we joke with, marry, snub, and exploit—immortal horrors or everlasting splendors.[87]

The Challenge to Live Out the Beauty of Male and Female Under God's Design

The complementarian position championed in this chapter is sometimes accused of fostering oppressive marriages and stifling churches, where women are dominated and denied opportunities necessary for their growth and fulfillment. But the proof is in the pudding. The challenge before complementarians is to show forth the beauty of male-female relationships lived out in marriages and churches that embody biblical teaching.

The place where most people experience the deepest and most important male-female relationship is of course in marriage. Despite high rates of divorce, the increase in couples living together without marriage, homosexual unions, and many delaying marriage until later for the sake of their careers, the desire for marriage is remarkably persistent and the institution of marriage remarkably resilient. A recent survey found that "about 90 percent of baby boomer men and women either have married or will marry, a ratio that's well in line with historical averages," with commitment to marriage strong among Gen Xers as well.[88] That does not mean that all is well in marriages. The prevalence of divorce, domestic abuse, and simply dull marriages show otherwise. Sadly, Christians have not shown the difference Christ can make in a marriage, with the rates of divorce among Christians closely paralleling the rates of society as a whole.

If we are to commend our doctrine of male and female relationships, we must first of all live it out. This begins with church leadership. Is it not significant that one area in which both pastors and deacons must be examples to the flock is in marriage and family life (see the phrase "husband of but one wife" in 1 Tim. 3:2,12; Titus 1:6)? Beyond setting the example, pastors must also set the standard in teaching. If we believe husbands are to take the lead in their families, then we should emphasize the husband's responsibility to love his wife as Christ loved the church first, and then

---

[87] C. S. Lewis, *The Weight of Glory* (Grand Rapids: Eerdmans, 1966), 14–15.
[88] Daniel McGinn, "Marriage by the Numbers," *Newsweek* (5 June 2006): 43, 48.

add the wife's responsibility to be submissive. Pastors should also review church programs and emphases to assure that church activities do not harm and hinder family life but support and nourish it.

Finally, pastors can take with the utmost seriousness the responsibility of premarital counseling. Too many young people will enter marriage with no example of a healthy marriage, their own parents perhaps having divorced. Thorough counseling will be necessary to counteract the distorted ideas of marriage in our culture, and the provision of mentoring couples to support couples in their early years should be the goal of every church.

All too many marriages produce strife, conflict, and hatred rather than beauty, harmony, and love; all too many end in divorce. Our arguments for the preservation of traditional marriage in the face of this reality cannot be persuasive. But this situation presents an ideal opportunity for biblically founded, Christ-honoring marriage to shine like light in the midst of this culture's darkness.

In the area of church life, most men and women will not be pastors, so most will not be directly affected by a complementarian position regarding church leadership, yet even here there is room for improvement. Rather than focusing on the few roles that are limited, why not recognize, highlight, and honor the many ministries in which women in local churches serve? It is incumbent on men, especially complementarians, to check themselves for lingering male chauvinism. Do we really believe that women are gifted by God, that they can enrich our lives, and that we have much to learn from them? Visitors in our churches should have no doubt that women are respected and valued.

If the complementary view is to remain viable among Christians and to be commended to society at large, our biblical and theological arguments will need to be fleshed out in churches and homes where men and women live out and celebrate their distinctive roles in ways that produce joy, growth, and genuine human freedom. That is the challenge before us. ·

The Rhythm of Work and Rest

Work occupies the largest chunk of the waking hours of most Americans. Many find in their work their identity and meaning. Yet most also complain about their work and suffer stress, burnout, and fatigue from their jobs. Princeton sociologist Robert Wuthnow believes Americans have lost their grasp of "the moral dimension of work" and need to recover an ethic to guide their economic lives.[89] That moral dimension is provided in the biblical teaching of work as good and intended by God as a means of glorifying

---

[89] See Robert Wuthnow, *Poor Richard's Principle: Recovering the American Dream through the Moral Dimension of Work, Business, and Money* (Princeton: Princeton University Press, 1996).

him and serving others. What would be the impact if the doctrine of work presented in this chapter was taught and embraced in our churches?

First, Christians would become known as the best employees any employer could ask for. They would not be found complaining about their work, cutting corners, and trying to get by with the least. Rather, because they understand that their work is a means of glorifying God, they would be grateful for it and seek to do it in a way that would honor God. Moreover, they would not separate Sunday from the workweek; the same God they serve on Sunday at church they serve Monday through Friday on the job, for they see their job as a calling. Moreover, nonpaying forms of work would also be honored as ways to glorify God. Child raising, housework, and everyday chores are not just mundane necessities; as we serve others, we glorify God.

Perhaps the goodness and God-intendedness of work should also challenge our ideas of retirement. As our bodies deteriorate, we may need to retire from a particular job whose physical demands are beyond us. In recognition of the inevitable corruption of our bodies, preparation for retirement (pensions, long-term care insurance, etc.) is not contrary to a trust in God but is a wise imitation of the example of the ant (Prov. 6:6–8). However, as long as God gives health and strength, our bodies should be used in some way to serve others and glorify God. Most churches depend heavily on volunteer labor and should provide the contexts in which senior citizens can use their time and abilities to serve others. We may retire from a job but never from work, never from service to our Lord.

However, if we are to fully recover a biblical doctrine of work, it must include a theology of leisure as well. Americans as a whole have a strong tendency to workaholism. Workers in Germany on average work only 37 weeks per year; in Great Britain, the figure is 43.5. Even Japanese workers take on average five weeks of vacation a year. Americans are the workaholics of the world, putting in an average of 49.5 forty-hour workweeks per year.[90] While the New Testament gives no command regarding resting from certain activities on the Sabbath, or Sunday, there are good reasons for encouraging a Christian observance of a modified Sabbath rest, not as a matter of obedience but as a spiritual discipline to help us recover the rhythm of work and rest. Setting aside a day to abstain from our normal work can serve several valuable purposes.

First, there is still a need for physical rest, and perhaps even more so in our day than ever. Even children find their days packed with so many activities that relaxed family time is far too rare. Observing something of

---

[90] These figures are from a report issued by the International Labor Organization, reported in Steven Greenhouse, "U.S. clocks in as workhorse of the world," *Raleigh News & Observer,* 1 September 2001, 1.

a Sabbath safeguards us from getting too caught up by the business of the world. Of course, in the families of pastors, Sunday may not be possible as that day of rest. But still time should be set aside for rest of mind, body, and soul and recreation with loved ones.

Most importantly, some type of Sabbath observance can allow us to make concrete in life beliefs that we often confess only in theory. In not working, we confess that we live by grace and not by our work, that Christ is more important than work, that there are higher priorities than our work, that we trust more in Christ than in our ability to take care of ourselves, that our identity is not tied up in our work, and that we are not indispensable to our place of work or to the world. Actually disciplining ourselves to refrain from normal activities helps make these beliefs more than pious words. What activities any individual refrains from may vary from one individual to another. The point is to set some time apart to make real a genuinely Christian attitude toward work, one that subordinates it to more ultimately important things. If we emphasize this purpose of the Sabbath, we may help people benefit from the Sabbath without going through legalistic debates about what should and should not be allowed.

The Cultivation of Community in Churches

If it is true that the need for community is part of God's design in the creation of humans, then humans will seek ways to fulfill that need. People identify themselves with sports teams and find community with fellow fans; they join clubs where they can socialize with those who have similar interests; they hang out at places where they find a sense of camaraderie. This God-given desire is both an obvious commandment and a golden opportunity for churches. By their very nature, churches are called to be community. But human sinfulness, along with cultural obstacles such as individualism and the consumer culture, as well as religious obstacles such as churches so large that individuals fall between the cracks or ignorance of the biblical teaching on community, has left many churches sorely lacking in this area. What are some practical steps churches can take to cultivate community?

First, it is important to note the indispensable prerequisite of the gospel. Bruce Milne wisely says, "Only the truths of apostolic Christianity, embraced and whole heartedly adhered to, effectively break up the sinful isolation of the human heart and create the possibility of true relationship at depth with others."[91] This means that one way not to create community

---

[91] Bruce Milne, *We Belong Together: The Meaning of Fellowship* (Downers Grove: InterVarsity, 1978), 94.

is to focus on it to the exclusion of the teaching and preaching ministry of the church.

Concretely, churches need to thoughtfully create contexts in which community can grow. Worship services are by their nature vertical; the focus is on God (or should be!). Where in the church's life can a member develop relationships that produce community? Often, community develops when people work together. Choirs, mission teams, and ministry groups often develop a sense of community on the job. But most often community grows in small groups where people can share their lives. Bible study or Sunday school classes are the most common type of small group in most churches, but they must balance the assignment of teaching Scripture with the cultivation of fellowship. Home groups are becoming increasingly prominent and effective in cultivating community. The growing number of churches using new member classes is encouraging because they provide a natural small-group context to assimilate newcomers. The constant creation of small groups is the single most important concrete step a church can take in cultivating community among its members.[92]

However, some say that simply creating small groups within the church is not enough. Churches should be small groups. This is seen in the rise of cell churches, house churches, and most models within the Emerging Church movement. Ralph Neighbour believes true community is possible only in a cell church, a group no larger than fifteen.[93] Those in the house church movement believe Paul's description of the church assumes a small, family-like structure.[94] Most of those surveyed by Eddie Gibbs and Ryan Bolger in their research on the Emerging Church deliberately limit the size of their churches in order to preserve fellowship.[95]

Despite these claims, the New Testament does not mandate small churches only. The book of Acts records the explosive growth of the church in Jerusalem and reflects both large and small-group meetings (Acts 2:46). Thus the New Testament seems to allow for both megachurches and microchurches.[96] However, many megachurches have found small groups to be

---

[92] For more on this, see John S. Hammett, *Biblical Foundations for Baptist Churches: A Contemporary Ecclesiology* (Grand Rapids: Kregel, 2005), 232–38.

[93] Ralph Neighbour, *Where Do We Go from Here? A Guidebook for the Cell Group Church* (Houston, TX.: Touch Publications, 1990), 112–13.

[94] Robert and Julia Banks, *The Church Comes Home* (Peabody, MA: Hendrickson, 1998), 30–41.

[95] Eddie Gibbs and Ryan K. Bolger, *Emerging Churches: Creating Christian Community in Postmodern Cultures* (Grand Rapids: Baker, 2005). See especially their chapter on community, the longest chapter in the book (89–115).

[96] *Microchurch* is Leonard Sweet's term for house churches and similar small groups. See Leonard Sweet, *Faithquakes* (Nashville: Abingdon, 1994), 76. John N. Vaughan defines *megachurches* as those having two thousand or more in attendance at their weekly worship services. He has been among the most prolific writers on the topic and is a recognized authority. See John N. Vaughan, *Megachurches & America's Cities: How Churches Grow* (Grand Rapids: Baker, 1993), 41.

an essential part of their ministry. Bill Hybels tells of the transformation of Willow Creek from a church with small groups to a church of small groups, linking this change to the need to cultivate community: "We've set up all our leadership structures and goals to grow a fully functioning Acts 2 community, as opposed to just an evangelizing machine that doesn't drive the roots deep and do all the other things it's supposed to do."[97] According to the research of Scott Thumma, virtually all megachurches use a variety of small groups in their ministry, and 50 percent say small groups are "central to their strategy for Christian nurture and formation."[98]

The cultivation of community is a mandate given to all churches, whether large or small. The preaching and acceptance of the gospel is the necessary prerequisite. As the gospel progressively liberates believers from the sinful hindrances to community, the church must provide the contexts in which believers begin to share their lives. For most churches of even moderate size, small groups will be the likeliest context for the development of such community.

Conclusion

The doctrine of humanity is viewed with suspicion by some theologians. They are rightly concerned about the danger of theology becoming anthropocentric, and they see culture over the past two hundred years as unduly elevating humans and diminishing God. These are proper matters for concern. The fact that God is mindful of us should be a cause for wonder (Ps. 8:3–4); it should never be taken for granted. Yet we are "fearfully and wonderfully made" (Ps. 139:14), and that should be a cause for gratitude and study, rather than pride. Indeed, as we see the divine design in Scripture and realize how far short of it we fall, the only appropriate response is humility, confession, and repentance. Thus, a study of the doctrine of humanity, such as that presented in this chapter, rightly merits our consideration. It should produce gratitude and repentance. At the very least, it holds up the target of the divine design in the creation of humans and highlights the goal to which we should aspire.

---

[97] Bill Hybels, as quoted in Verla Gillmor, "Community Is Their Middle Name," *CT* 44, no. 11 (November 13, 2000): 50.
[98] Scott Thumma, "Megachurches Today: Summary of Data from the Faith Communities Today Project," available at http://www.hirr.hartsem.edu, accessed 15 October 2004.

CHAPTER 8

Human Sinfulness

R. Stanton Norman

In the film *The Village*, M. Night Shyamalan recounts the tale of a small, rural community situated in what appears to be nineteenth-century Pennsylvania. As the story unfolds, we slowly discover that the troupe of elders who lead the village all have been victimized or traumatized earlier in their lives by human evil in the "outside world." In an attempt to shield themselves from further suffering, the elders manufacture a reality (i.e., the village) they believe is insulated from the wickedness of their previous lives. They devise a fictitious story of horrible creatures who share an uneasy truce with the inhabitants of the village. As long as the villagers stay within certain prescribed boundaries, the creatures will not venture into the village. If the inhabitants stray beyond the borders, the creatures will invade and terrorize the townsfolk. Their ruse of horror is the means by which the unsuspecting residents (save for the elders) are kept from straying into the "other towns." The fearful tale achieves its intended purpose, and most of the villagers do not venture beyond the perimeter into the outside world.

The elders go to great lengths and make great personal sacrifices to perpetrate their myth. Their goal is to protect themselves and the other villagers from the brutalities of the outside world. Their extreme and fanciful efforts, however, fail to keep evil and tragedy away. Their utopian world is shattered by the intrusion of the wickedness that arises from human nature. Human sinfulness manages to invade their idyllic state. In images reminiscent of the biblical account of the fall, the serpent slithered into their "garden."

Among its many subtle themes, the movie *The Village* provides an astute commentary on two prevalent fallacies about human sinfulness. First, the elders of the village naively believed that they could create a simple, innocent society by shielding themselves from all external, corrupting influences. They mistakenly supposed that they could invent a reality free from human evil. This notion imbibes in many ways the modern, optimistic belief that humanity is essentially good and pure. As the film demonstrates, this is a flawed assumption. Even if it were possible to isolate themselves from all wicked people and environments, the villagers would still have to contend with the sinfulness within each of them.

Second, the film underscores the futility of humanity's epic struggle against sin. Despite their best efforts, the people depicted in the movie could not in their own strength and cleverness conquer the sinful nature of humanity. Shyamalan has rightly identified the classic struggle of human existence. Since the fall, no one has been able to elude the entanglements of their own sinfulness. No matter how enlightened we may be or how advanced our technological discoveries, we still find ourselves ravaged by hatred, lust, rage, and covetousness. We contend against the adversary of our ancestors: the sin that resides within each of us. We do not like to think of ourselves as helpless, yet the doctrine of sin reminds us that we are unable to extricate ourselves from the grip of our sinfulness.

These misunderstandings about the nature of sin may stem in part from the demise of meaningful and honest discourse on the subject. Although important and relevant, the topic of sin is not the most popular of issues. Modern attitudes about the subject consider it either unpleasant and inappropriate or irrelevant and passé. Recent years have witnessed a decline even in the use of the word. Several years ago, psychiatrist Karl Menninger wrote a book entitled *Whatever Became of Sin?*[1] In this work Menninger called attention to the fact that "sin" is an all-but-extinct term in the American vocabulary. He noted that simply removing the word *sin* from our collective vocabularies would not make it disappear. Menninger argued for an understanding of sin that included willful rebellion against the standards of God.

We should take this observation to heart. We deceive ourselves if we believe that we can either minimize or eliminate the reality of sin simply by ignoring it or changing its name. Redefinitions or misunderstandings about sin do not lessen our accountability. We should also admit that such evasive efforts are themselves manifestations of sin. We live in an age that strives to ease or eradicate moral and spiritual culpability; to confess our sinfulness will painfully confront us with our shortcomings and accentuate our guilt. Our unwillingness or failure to address sin truthfully will not, however, achieve our liberation from its insidious presence, power, and penalty. The rejection of the biblical doctrine of sin does not invalidate its reality or power. To disregard the reality of sin will eventuate in individual and societal destruction.

---

[1] Karl Menninger, *Whatever Became of Sin?* (New York: Hawthorn, 1973).

The Interrelationship of the Doctrine of Sin with Other Doctrines

As is the case with most of our beliefs, the doctrine of sin is interrelated with other theological tenets. For example, our view about the person and will of God will determine our understanding of sin. If God is a holy being who expects all human creatures to be as he is, then any deviation from his holy standard is sin, and the human condition is a matter of utmost seriousness. On the other hand, if God is imperfect or indulgent, a grandfatherly figure who may be unaware or indifferent about our activities, then the human condition is not a critical matter. In fact, such a god may himself be imperfect or sinful.[2]

The doctrine of humanity also intersects with our understanding of sin. If humans are creatures made in God's image, then they are made to reflect that image to God, others, and creation. People would be judged not in comparison with other people, but by their conformity to God's divine intentions and the manner in which they reflect his image. In addition, if humans are created as free, moral beings who are not determined by the forces of nature, then they are responsible for their actions and dispositions. Each individual would be culpable for any failure to measure up to God's standards. Any inability or unwillingness to achieve his intended purpose would be regarded as sin.[3]

Our doctrine of salvation is equally interrelated to our doctrine of sin. If human beings are essentially good and their spiritual, rational, emotional, and volitional capacities are whole and well, then any prospect of an infraction against God is unlikely. Any shortcomings they might experience would be due to intellectual limitations. Salvation in this scenario is overcoming ignorance by means of education. On the other hand, if human beings are sinfully corrupt as well as unable and unwilling to do what is right, then a radical transformation of their person is required. The more severe the problem of sin, the greater is the need for the supernatural, salvific intervention of God.[4]

Our belief about sin also determines in large measure our view of the nature and purpose of the ministry of the church. If human beings are essentially good and capable of accomplishing what God requires, then the mission of the church is to exhort persons to achieve what is already in their ability to do. Appeals to kindness, compassion, generosity, and charity would be sufficient to move people in the right direction. If human beings are sinful, then our message is to proclaim the good news of salvation

---

[2] Millard J. Erickson, *Christian Theology,* 2nd ed. (Grand Rapids: Baker, 1998), 580–81.

[3] Ibid., 581.

[4] Ibid.

that comes by faith in Jesus Christ. In this case, the ministry of the church would engage sinful humans with calls to repent of sin, place one's trust in Christ, and be born again.[5]

The doctrine of sin is therefore important because of its relationship to other doctrines in the Christian faith. As is the case with most of our theological beliefs, a biblical understanding of sin intersects with other doctrines. As we construct our belief about sin, we will also interact with the doctrines of God, humanity, salvation, and the church.

What Does the Bible Say About Sin?

The Bible uses numerous words to describe various aspects of sin. While some of these overlap in meaning with other concepts, others are unique and distinctive in their emphases. Some focus on the relational disruption between the individual and God or between the sinner and others. Other terms describe the corrupting and disintegrating impact of sin upon the sinner. Still other concepts describe the deficiencies or shortcomings of the sinner to the standards of God. Although the descriptions are many and diverse, two common themes tie them together: (1) sin never pleases God; and (2) sin always destroys the sinner.

Depravity/Corruption

① porneria (G): active
② kakos ("): inactive, passive + moral active

The Greek word *pornēria* can be translated as "depravity" or "corruption." The word suggests the active desire to harm; that is, "one who brings trouble to others."[6] Those guilty of *pornēria* are not simply content to perish in their own corruption; they also seek to draw others into destruction and destitution.[7] The word is also used to describe Satan as the "evil one" (Matt. 6:13; 13:19,38; John 17:15; 1 John 2:13–14; 5:18)[8] and designates demons as "evil spirits" (Luke 11:26; Acts 19:12).[9] *Ponēros* typically specifies moral evil.[10] Jesus in Matthew 7:11 states that "if you then, who are evil [*ponēroi*], know how to give good gifts to your children, how much more will your Father in heaven give good things to those who ask him!" (also Matt. 12:39; 15:19; Acts 17:5).

---

[5] Ibid.

[6] Richard C. Trench, *Synonyms of the New Testament* (London, 1854; repr. Grand Rapids: Baker, 1989), 330.

[7] Ibid.

[8] Unless otherwise noted, all Scripture citations in this chapter are from the New Revised Standard Version (NRSV).

[9] Armin Kretzer, *"ponēros," EDNT*, 3:135.

[10] Günther Harder, *"ponēros," TDNT*, 6:554.

The Greek word *kakos* is closely linked with *ponēria*. Although the adverbial form is sometimes used of physical blemish or disease (Mark 1:32), the word normally refers to moral badness. Paul admonished the Roman believers, "Do not repay anyone evil for evil" (Rom. 12:17). Again, the apostle noted in 1 Timothy 6:10 that "the love of money is a root of all kinds of evil." Other examples of the concept include Matthew 21:41; Mark 9:21; Acts 9:13; Romans 13:3–4,10; and 16:19. If *ponēria* describes the active intent to corrupt or destroy, then *kakos* describes evil as the lack of good that should be present. In Matthew 24:48, Jesus implied that the wicked servant is a person lacking in fidelity and diligence.[11] An individual is considered culpable and guilty for withholding or lacking what is expected or properly due.

Inattention : parakoe (G): bad hearing שבע

Parakoē can mean "disobedience," "inattention," or "disobedience to a voice." The word is found only three times in the New Testament (Rom. 5:19; 2 Cor. 10:6; Heb. 2:2). In Romans 5:19 (HCSB), Paul alludes to the disobedience that resulted from Adam's "disobedience to a voice": "For just as through one man's disobedience the many were made sinners, so also through the one man's obedience the many will be made righteous." In its strict sense *parakoē* is a failing to hear or an incorrect hearing; thus, *parakoē* always means "bad hearing" as a consequence of an unwillingness to hear.[12] The sense of guilt and disobedience that results from this failure/unwillingness to hear is contrasted with an obedience that results from a genuine hearing.[13]

Error : shogag (H): accidental mistakes שגג

The word *shōgag* and its cognates describe the straying of sheep (Ezek. 34:6) or the stumbling of a drunkard (Isa. 28:7). With regard to sin, the word *group* refers to the tendency to go astray, to make mistakes, or to commit error. The term can refer to accidental mistakes (Gen. 43:12). Some passages explicitly refer to the breaking of a commandment and the later discovery of that error (Lev. 4:2,22,27; Num. 15:22). Leviticus 22:14 describes the case of someone who mistakenly eats food exclusively reserved for consumption by priests. Although committed in error, a small fine was assessed, indicating that the offender should have exerted greater care. The Bible distinguishes between innocent and culpable error, as evidenced by the provision of cities of refuge for those who unwittingly killed someone (Num. 35:9–15). Outside

---

[11] Ibid., 330.
[12] Ibid., 258.
[13] Gerhard Kittel, "*parakoē*," *TDNT*, 1:223; Kretzer, "*paralambanō*," *EDNT*, 3:29.

the ritualistic passages, however, the references to erroneous conduct suggest moral culpability (1 Sam. 26:21; Job 6:24; Ps. 119:21,118; Prov. 5:23).

The error in question is the conduct in which the person chooses to go astray. An individual is responsible for knowing. Ignorance, or an unwillingness to know, is inexcusable. Such a person cannot plead, "I did not know." He should have known and chose rather not to know. The person is responsible for his ignorance as well as the error that resulted from it. A similar term, *tā'â,* carries similar connotations and can be translated literally as "wander." As was the case with *shāgag, tā'â* refers to error that is deliberate, not accidental (Pss. 95:10; 119:110; Prov. 21:16; Ezek. 48:11). A person sins because he does something for which, either by choice or neglect, he is responsible. No sin is altogether an accidental or innocent error.[14]

Guilt

asham (OT) · guilt, ritual in the תברנכל והמקדש
enochos (NT)

The most common word for guilt in the Old Testament is the word *'asham.* Almost all uses of this word are found in connection with the ritual of the tabernacle and the temple (Lev. 4:13,22,27; 5:2–3,5–6,17; Num. 5:6–8; Ezek. 22:4; 25:12). The term means "to do a wrong, to commit an offense, to inflict injury." *'Asham* is a sin that is perpetrated against another person. Restitution to the injured party is the means by which the guilt is alleviated. The primary idea is that all guilt is ultimately before God. The guilt and sin offerings made for such offenses are for intentional and unintentional sins (Lev. 4:13; 5:2–3). *'Asham* describes those sins that have been committed through error, negligence, or ignorance. Regardless of whether the individual knew that his offense was sinful, guilt is incurred and can only be alleviated by some means of atonement.[15]

The word in the New Testament rendered as guilt is *enochos.* In Matthew 5:21–22, Jesus uses the word to teach that whoever hates his brother is guilty of murder in the sight of God. Paul warns that whoever takes of the Lord's Supper in an unworthy manner is guilty of profaning the body and blood of Christ (1 Cor. 11:27). James 2:10 says that "whoever keeps the entire law, yet fails in one point, is guilty of [breaking it] all" (HCSB). In all contexts where *enochos* is used, the standard of justice is God. Sinners are guilty and liable to punishment when they abrogate the justice of God.[16]

---

[14] Charles R. Smith, *The Bible Doctrine of Sin and of the Way of God with Sinners* (London: Epworth, 1953), 18–19.

[15] Robert B. Girdleston, *Synonyms of the Old Testament,* 2nd. ed. (Grand Rapids: Eerdmans, 1953), 84–85.

[16] Erickson, *Christian Theology,* 595.

Godlessness : asebeō =βō (G) : Worship a? ozoz
active

The Greek word *asebeia* and its cognates can be translated as "impiety." "irreligion," or "godlessness." The verb *asebeia* is the negative of *sebomai* ("to worship" or "to reverence"), suggesting the contrary of worship or reverence of God.[17] Unregenerate persons are designated as "ungodly" (Rom. 4:5; 5:6). "Godlessness" is linked with unrighteousness in Romans 1:18. First Timothy 1:9 includes the "ungodly" with the lawless, rebellious, sinful, unholy, irreverent, and those who kill their fathers and mothers (also Titus 2:12). *Asebeia* refers to godless apostates in 2 Peter and Jude. The sin described by these terms is always directed toward God. Godlessness is an active irreverence toward God, an impious attitude that neglects the appropriate worship of God.[18]

Ignorance : agnoeo (G) : deliberate

The verb *agnoeō* and the noun *agnoēma* refer to ignorance. The words are built upon the verb *ginōskō,* meaning "to know," and are negated by the alpha privative. The English word *agnostic* is derived from these terms. Some uses of *agnoeō* refer to things done in ignorance which, in the sight of God, were innocent of guilt or were regarded as insignificant and inconsequential (Acts 17:30; Rom. 1:13; 2 Cor. 6:9; Gal. 1:22).

Other instances of *agnoeō* directly or indirectly signify culpable ignorance.[19] In Ephesians 4:18 Paul says that the Gentiles were "*darkened in their understanding,* excluded from the life of God, because of the ignorance that is in them and because of the hardness of their hearts" (emphasis added) (also Acts 3:17 HCSB). Peter's appeal to his readers to repent suggests a measure of responsibility for their sin (1 Pet. 1:14). The one use of the noun in Hebrews 9:7 refers to the annual visit of the high priest into the Holy of Holies. The high priest was to offer sacrifices to atone both for himself and "for the sins of the people committed in ignorance" (HCSB). *Agnoeō* was a deliberate, disobedient closing of the mind to the word of God (Acts 13:27; Rom. 10:3). The ignorance of what one ought to have known was considered sinful as well as any extenuating circumstances that resulted from the ignorance (1 Tim. 1:13; Heb. 5:2). Exposure to the written revelation of God brings greater responsibility. The more you know, the greater the accountability.[20]

---

[17] Peter Fiedler, "*asebeō,*" *EDNT,* 1:169.
[18] Walther Günther, "*sebomai,*" *DNTT,* 2:92.
[19] Walter Schmithals, "*agnoeō,*" *EDNT,* 1:21.
[20] Trench, *Synonyms of the New Testament,* 261.

Iniquity/Lack of Integrity

(handwritten note: (H) owel: iniquity)

The word '*ōwel* denotes a lack of integrity and can be translated as "iniquity." The word can mean "unjust" (Pss. 43:1; 82:2; Isa. 26:10; Zeph. 3:5), "unrighteous" (Deut. 25:16; Job 27:7; Ps. 71:4), "ungodly" (Job 16:11), "perverse" (Isa. 59:3) or "wicked" (Ps. 89:22). The majority of uses of the word, however, are "iniquity." The general sense of the term is a departure from what is right and true (Mal. 2:6).[21] This lack of integrity can mean failure to fulfill and maintain the just demands of the law of God (Lev. 19:15), or the discrepancy of an individual's past character with his or her present character; that is, a disunity within the individual.[22]

Lawless

(handwritten note: anomia (G))

The *anomia* word group can be translated as "lawlessness," "law-breaking," or "iniquity" (Rom. 6:19; 2 Cor. 6:14; Heb. 10:17; 1 John 3:4).[23] Jesus used the term to describe those who breached the universal law known to everyone (Matt. 7:23; 13:41; 23:28; 24:12).[24] The concept generally has lawbreakers in view, whether Jew or Gentile (2 Pet. 2:8; 1 Tim. 1:9).[25] *Anomos* can refer to a person without the law or to someone who has not received the law (e.g., 1 Cor. 9:21). For Paul the absence of explicit law does not, however, remove responsibility for obedience; even the Gentiles continually violate the law written upon their hearts (Rom. 2:12). "Where *anomia* is used, the concepts of law and judgment are present, and . . . the reference is not to Jewish Law, but to anything and everything that any man knows that God has commanded."[26] In 2 Thessalonians 2:8, *anomia* is applied to the greatest enemy of all law, the man of sin, the lawless one, the one John identifies as the antichrist (1 John 2:18; 4:3; 2 John 7). The law of God has been received and understood, yet the man of lawlessness intentionally acts contrary to this standard.

Lust

(handwritten note: epithymia (G) : 좋은사랑도 이용될수 있으나 신자들에게는 부정적으로 이용.)

The term *epithymia* can be translated as "desire," "longing," or "lust." The word can have positive connotations (Luke 22:15; Phil. 1:23; 1 Thess. 2:17).[27] The majority of instances in the New Testament, however, carry sinful implications (Matt. 5:28; Mark 4:19; Rom. 1:24; James 1:14–15).[28]

---

21 Girdleston, *Synonyms of the Old Testament,* 82.
22 Erickson, *Christian Theology,* 590.
23 Meinrad Limbeck, "*anomia,*" *EDNT,* 1:106.
24 Erickson, *Christian Theology,* 589.
25 W. Gutbrod, "*anomia,*" *TDNT,* 4:1085.
26 Smith, *Bible Doctrine of Sin,* 145.
27 Hans Hübner, "*epithymia,*" *EDNT,* 2:27.
28 Ibid.

Paul illustrated this negative use in Galatians 5:16 when he exhorted the believer to "walk by the Spirit and you will not carry out the desire of the flesh" (HCSB). Peter warned his readers to "abstain from fleshly desires that war against you" (1 Pet. 2:11 HCSB). The Apostle John described *epithymia* as "the lust of the flesh, the lust of the eyes, and the pride in one's lifestyle" (1 John 2:16 HCSB). *Epithymia* signifies a corrupt desire that strives after what is inappropriate or illicit. The term is broad enough to encompass the illicit desire, the activity to attain what is prohibited, and the illegitimate sense of self-gratification that arises from the pursuit. All are considered sinful in the eyes of God.[29]

Missing the Mark

The most common concept for sin in the Old Testament (approximately six hundred occurrences) is *chātā'*, which can be translated "a missing," "missing the right point," "missing the mark," or "deviating from the norm."[30] One of the most literal uses of the term is found in Judges 20:16. The text states that the tribe of Benjamin possessed seven hundred chosen men who were all left-handed. Each of these soldiers could "sling a stone at a hair, and not miss." Another example is Proverbs 19:2, which states that the one who is hasty "misses the way." The term can be variously translated as fault (Gen. 41:9; Exod. 5:16), trespass (1 Kings 8:31), harm (Lev. 5:16), blame (Gen. 43:9; 44:32), and offense (Gen. 20:9; 1 Kings 1:21; Eccles. 10:4; Isa. 29:21; Jer. 37:18).[31]

The verb *hamartanō* and the nouns *hamartia* and *hamartēma* (approximately three hundred occurrences in the New Testament) are closely related to the Hebrew *chātā'* word family.[32] In fact, *hamartia* and its cognates are the most commonly used words to translate the *chātā'* word group in the Septuagint.[33] The meaning of the *hamartia* word group is basically the same as the *chātā'*: "to miss, miss the mark, or to err."[34] *Hamartia* can denote either the act of sinning or the actual sin itself, while *hamartēma* (Mark 3:23; 4:12; Rom. 3:25; 1 Cor. 6:18) refers to the result or consequence of the sin.[35] When used in the Gospels, the term almost always occurs in a context that speaks of forgiveness or salvation (Matt. 1:21; John 1:29).

---

[29] Trench, *Synonyms of the New Testament*, 340–41.

[30] Girdleston, *Synonyms of the Old Testament*, 76–77; Smith, *The Bible Doctrine of Sin*, 16.

[31] Girdleston, *Synonyms of the Old Testament*, 77.

[32] Fiedler, "*hamartia*," *EDNT*, 1:66.

[33] Smith, *The Bible Doctrine of Sin*, 69.

[34] Gustav Stählin, "*hamartanō*," *TDNT*, 1:295.

[35] Trench, *Synonyms of the New Testament*, 257. Other references where the *hamartia* cognates can be found include Acts 2:38; Romans 5:12; 6:1; 1 Corinthians 15:3; 2 Corinthians 5:21; James 1:15; 1 Peter 2:22; 1 John 1:7, 2:2; and Revelation 1:5.

The general idea of *chātā'* and *hamartia* is that all wrongdoing is a failure, "missing the mark" which God intends for all persons to attain. Man, as made in the image of God, has implanted within him an innate sense to live as God directs. Every departure from this sense is a coming short of the purpose for which man was made, a missing of the mark. This failure to hit the mark is always a sin against God; that is, the sinner always fails to achieve the standard set or to hit the mark established by God.[36] The moral connotations of the concept stipulate that a person misses the right mark because he intentionally chooses to aim at a wrong mark; he misses the right path because he deliberately chooses to follow a wrong path.[37] We miss the mark and sin against God when, for example, we fail to love our brother, since loving our brother inevitably follows a true love for God.[38]

With regard to moral culpability, there is no question of an innocent mistake or a negative idea of failure. The terms suggest an active, deliberate missing of the right mark or way in order to choose intentionally a wrong mark or path. The sinner is responsible and accountable for the behavior that results in missing the mark, whether overtly intentional or not.[39]

Perversion 'āwa(H)

Perversion translates the Hebrew word *'āwâ,* which literally means "to bend," "to twist," "to be bent or bowed down." Isaiah 21:3 ("I am bowed down so that I cannot hear; I am dismayed so that I cannot see") is a literal example of the concept (also Ps. 38:6; Isa. 24:1; Lam. 3:9). Proverbs 12:8 connotes the idea of a twisted mind: "A man is commended according to his good sense, but one of twisted mind is despised" (ESV). The metaphorical meaning of the term is illustrated in Genesis 4:13, where Cain states, "My punishment is greater than I can bear." Hosea 5:5 and 14:1 suggest that *'āwâ* is that which "bends" or "twists" the condition or character of the sinner. The sinner thus becomes perverted (distorted or twisted) from God's original intention. Perversion is thus both the cause and result of sin.[40]

Rebellion pesha(H), mara(H): active, apeitheia (G)

The Hebrew words *pesha'* and *pāsha'* emphasize the rebellious aspect of sin. The most common translation of the terms is "transgress," and the basic idea is "to rebel." Although the cognates sometimes describe rebellion

---

[36] Günther, "hamartia," *DNTT,* 3:579; Walter Grundmann and Gustav Stählin, "hamartanō," *TDNT,* 1:289, 295.

[37] Smith, *The Bible Doctrine of Sin,* 17.

[38] Erickson, *Christian Theology,* 587.

[39] Fiedler, "hamartia," *EDNT,* 1:66.

[40] Girdleston, *Synonyms of the Old Testament,* 78.

against human kings (1 Kings 12:19; 2 Kings 3:5; Prov. 28:21), the concept normally refers to rebellion against God (e.g. Isa. 1:2). The terms can be translated as "sin" (Prov. 10:12,19; 28:13), "trespass" (Gen. 31:36; Exod. 22:9; 1 Sam. 25:28; Hos. 8:1), and "revolt" (2 Kings 8:20,22). Another Hebrew term, *mārâ* (1 Sam. 12:15; Isa. 1:20) and *mārad* (Josh. 22:16–29) also means "rebel." These words signify a revolt against or a refusal to submit to rightful authority. The idea is that sin involves the willful refusal of an individual to submit to the authority of God.[41] The word *sārar* means a stubbornness leading to rebellion (Deut. 21:18; Ps. 78:8).

The Hebrew people had an extensive vocabulary for the act and attitude of rebellion, an all-too-common sin. During the prophetic period, the temptation to rebel against the rule of God had become especially acute; thus, the prophets of God regularly denounced this sin.[42]

A term found in the New Testament translated as "rebellion" or "disobedience" is *apeitheia*. The word can be rendered as "unbelief," "lack of faith," or "disobedience." Although the term can describe disobedience to parents (Rom. 1:30; 2 Tim. 3:2), the more common use refers to disobedience to God. *Apeitheia* and its cognates can refer to the disobedience in "ancient times" of the Jews (Heb. 3:18; 4:6) or the Gentiles (Heb. 11:31; 1 Pet. 3:20). The Gentiles of Paul's day were disobedient to the law "written on their hearts" (Rom. 2:14–15). Paul also warned, "Let no one deceive you with empty arguments, for because of these things God's wrath is coming on the disobedient" (Eph. 5:6 HCSB). In the New Testament the disobedient are regarded as rebels (John 3:36; Acts 14:2; 19:9; Eph. 2:2; Heb. 4:6; 1 Pet. 2:8; 3:1; 4:17). The sinner knows that he should obey the demands of God and the claims of the gospel. Yet, when confronted by the gospel, many sinners who know that they should embrace the truth of God's message do not. These persons disobey and rebel against the good news of Christ.[43]

Transgression ① *abar* (H)
② *parabasis* (Gr)

The Hebrew word *'ābar* means "to cross over" or "to pass by." Although most instances of the term are literal, the word can refer to transgressing or exceeding the established limit of a command. In Numbers 14:41–42 the people of Israel wanted to go to the land that God had promised, but Moses said, "Why are you going against the LORD's command? . . . Don't go, because the LORD is not among you and you will be defeated by your enemies" (HCSB). The Israelites were not to transgress God's covenant

---

[41] Ibid., 81.
[42] Erickson, *Christian Theology,* 591.
[43] Smith, *The Bible Doctrine of Sin,* 148–49.

(Deut. 17:2) or his commandments (Deut. 26:13; see also Jer. 34:18; Dan. 9:11; Hosea 6:7; 8:1).[44]

The Greek word *parabasis* can be translated as "transgression" and is conceptually related to *'ābar*.[45] The verb appears in Matthew 15:2–3 in a context where the Pharisees and scribes attempted to confront Jesus: "'Why do Your disciples transgress the tradition of the elders? For they do not wash their hands when they eat bread.' He answered and said to them, 'Why do you also transgress the commandment of God because of your tradition?'" (NKJV). *Parabasis* may refer to the transgression of a specific commandment, such as the eating of the forbidden fruit by Adam and Eve (Rom. 5:14; 1 Tim. 2:14), or the word may have a wider reference to Jewish law in general (Rom. 2:23,25,27; Gal. 3:19; Heb. 2:2; 9:15).[46] Both in the Gospels and the writings of Paul, transgression of the law of God always provokes the wrath of God.[47]

Treachery   ① ma'al (H) ② paraptoma (G)

A sin closely associated with rebellion in the Old Testament is treachery. The word *mā'al* can be translated as "treachery," "infidelity," or "breach of trust."[48] The basic idea is the betrayal of the most intimate of relationships, such as marital unfaithfulness (Num. 5:12,27). The majority of references regard treachery as being against God (Josh. 7:1; 22:20). Leviticus 26:40 (HCSB) provides a clear example of treachery against God: "But if they will confess their sin and the sin of their fathers—their unfaithfulness that they practiced against Me, and how they acted with hostility toward Me . . ." (also Ezek. 14:13; 15:8). Persons guilty of this sin were often those in positions of authority, such as Uzziah (2 Chron. 26:18), Ahaz (2 Chron. 28:22), and Manasseh (2 Chron. 33:19). People who married wives outside the covenant community were also considered guilty of acting treacherously toward God (Ezra. 9:2,4; Neh. 13:27). Individuals who committed this sin were considered to have violated a certain trust invested in them. God regards the act of "breaking trust" as especially heinous.[49]

The Greek word *paraptōma* and its cognates mean "treachery," "rebellion," or "trespass" and is conceptually related to *ma'al*. Of the twenty-one occurrences of the word, eleven are used by the Apostle Paul; six times in Romans 5:15–20 (also Matt. 6:14; 2 Cor. 5:19; Gal. 6:1; Eph. 2:1; James

---

[44] Ibid., 145.

[45] Ibid.

[46] Michael Wolter, *"parabatēs," EDNT,* 3:14.

[47] Ibid.; Johannes Schneider, *"parabasis," TDNT,* 5:740.

[48] H. Wheeler Robinson, *The Christian Doctrine of Man,* 3rd ed. (Edinburgh: T & T Clark, 1926), 45.

[49] Girdleston, *Synonyms of the Old Testament,* 82.

5:16).[50] Although the word is semantically related to *hamartia,* categorical distinctions of meaning should not be pressed too hard.[51] At best, *paraptōma* may refer to a specific, sinful act whereas *hamartia* may emphasize more the controlling power of sin.[52] *Paraptōma* may be best understood as "falling where one should have stood upright." The concept describes the action of someone who falls away from what is expected or a violation or betrayal of a trust that has been given.[53] The falling activity communicates treachery, a violation (falling away) of what has been entrusted to the individual. "It is likely that, in the New Testament as in the LXX, the idea of a traitor's desertion is never wholly lost."[54]

Wickedness/Badness ① ra(H) ② rasha(H)

The Hebrew word *ra'* can be rendered as "evil," "wickedness," or "badness." The fundamental idea of the concept is "breaking up" or "ruin." The term connotes calamity (Ps. 141:5), distress (Neh. 2:17), adversity (1 Sam. 10:19; Ps. 94:13; Eccles. 7:14), grief (Neh. 2:10; Prov. 15:10; Eccles. 2:17; Jon. 4:6), affliction (Num. 11:11), misery (Eccles. 8:6), sorrow (Gen. 44:29; Neh. 2:2), trouble (Ps. 41:1), and wretchedness (Num. 11:15).

The word *ra'* is a generic concept describing anything that is harmful or malignant. The expression can refer to food that has gone bad or to an animal that is dangerous (Gen. 37:20; 2 Kings 4:41; Jer. 24:8).[55] With regard to sin, *ra'* refers to what is morally wrong and that which causes injury. The concept links together a deed with its consequences, both considered wicked or evil (Gen. 38:7; Deut. 4:25; Ps. 51:4). The ungodly person is one whose wickedness inflicts injury upon himself and also upon those associated with him. *Ra'* ruins what is good and pleasing to God.[56]

The word *rāsha'* typically is used in the moral sense of "wicked" and is found most frequently in Ezekiel, Psalms, and the wisdom literature. A related Arabic word means "to be loose" (of limb), and the root of *rāsha'* may mean "disjointed, ill regulated, abnormal, wicked."[57] Examples of the literal meaning can be found in Job 3:17 ("There the wicked cease from troubling, and there the weary are at rest") and Isaiah 57:20–21 ("But the wicked are like the tossing sea; for it cannot be quiet, and its waters toss up

---

[50] Wolter, "*paraptōma*," *EDNT,* 3:33.

[51] For example, Augustine described *paraptōma* as the negative omission of good contrasted with the positive doing of evil denoted by *hamartia.* Augustine, *Quaestiones ad Leviticum* 20.

[52] Wolter, "*paraptōma*," *EDNT,* 3:33.

[53] Trench, *Synonyms of the New Testament,* 260.

[54] Smith, *The Bible Doctrine of Sin,* 149.

[55] Ibid., 15.

[56] Girdleston, *Synonyms of the Old Testament,* 80.

[57] רָשַׁע, *BDB,* 957.

mire and dirt. There is no peace . . . for the wicked" ESV) The term refers to the activity, the tossing, and the confusion in which the wicked live, and the perpetual agitation that they cause to others.[58] The wicked create agitation and discomfort, chaos and confusion, for themselves and for those close to them.[59]

Unrighteousness adikia : Paul & Lukeon 在 強調

Although found in most of the books of the New Testament, the words *adikia, adikeō,* and *adikos* are used most often in the writings of Paul and Luke.[60] The terms are derived by applying the alpha privative to the Greek word *dikaios* ("righteous") and its cognates. The word group typically refers to unrighteousness. In classical Greek the concept suggests that which is "wrong, useless, not of a right nature" and signifies neglect of one's duties toward the Greek gods.[61] In the New Testament the word group typically occurs in contexts that discuss legal issues such as judgment, condemnation, vindication, or pardon. For example, in 1 Corinthians 6:9, Paul asks, "Do you not know that the unrighteous [*adikoi*] will not inherit the kingdom of God?" (ESV). Again, in Colossians 3:25, the apostle states, "For the wrongdoer [*adikōn*] will be paid back for whatever wrong has been done [*ēdikēsen*], and there is no partiality" (see also Matt. 5:45; Acts 24:15; Rom. 1:18; 2 Thess. 2:10; 1 Pet. 3:18).

The terms in the New Testament essentially describe any behavior contrary to the standard of righteousness. The concept can have immediate, contextual connotations for violations against stated or understood principles of divine law. The unrighteous behavior or disposition, however, is ultimately directed against God and his law.[62]

Significance of Key Biblical Terms

This brief survey, though not exhaustive, provides a broad cross-section of the nature, manifestations, and consequences of sin. The biblical descriptions teach us that sin is a powerful force that destroys the perpetrator. In no way does Scripture suggest that sin is ever advantageous to the sinner. Among its many attributes, sin creates death in the midst of life, evil in the midst of good, and corruption in the midst of purity. Without the gracious intervention of God, sinners are truly "dead men walking."

[58] Smith, *The Bible Doctrine of Sin,* 15–16.
[59] Erickson, *Christian Theology,* 594.
[60] Meinrad Limbeck, "*adikeō, adikia, adikos,*" *EDNT,* 1:31.
[61] Smith, *The Doctrine of Sin,* 144.
[62] Limbeck, "adikeō, adikia, adikos," *EDNT,* 1:31.

The Essential Nature of Sin

[handwritten annotations in Korean]

Although numerous terms describing sin are found in Scripture, theologians often try to determine if one sin is the "core essence" of all other sins. In other words, do all sins share one essential nature? If so, what is the essence of that nature? We will now investigate several concepts that various theologians have suggested for the essence of sin.

Disruption of Shalom

Cornelius Plantinga Jr. suggests that the essence of sin is the disruption of shalom. Plantinga understands *shalom* to mean more than the mere cessation of hostilities. *Shalom* is defined as

> *universal flourishing, wholeness, and delight*—a rich state of affairs in which natural needs are satisfied and natural gifts fruitfully employed, a state of affairs that inspires joyful wonder as its Creator and Savior opens doors and welcomes the creatures in whom he delights.[63]

Shalom is the created order existing and functioning perfectly as the Creator intended, a "webbing together" of God, humans, and all creation in justice, fulfillment, and delight. For Plantinga, shalom encompasses the constitution and internal relations of all entities, including the Trinity, the cosmic order, the human race, and all relational, social, and political entities and communities (including governments, families, friendships, churches, etc.).[64] All entities in this reality would exist and function with integrity and structured wholeness, and each entity would rightly relate and edify the other entities. All actions and responses to other entities would always be appropriate. Shalom is "the way things ought to be."[65]

Sin for Plantinga is any agential evil comprised of evil acts and dispositions for which some person (or group of persons) is to blame. Moral and spiritual evil are agential evil—that is, only persons can perpetrate evil. God is for shalom and therefore against sin. The essential nature of sin is therefore culpable shalom-breaking.[66]

---

[63] Cornelius Plantinga Jr., *Not the Way It's Supposed to Be: A Breviary of Sin* (Grand Rapids: Eerdmans, 1995), 10.

[64] Among all the entities listed by Plantinga, the holy Trinity is the only one that is always as it should be. The members of the Godhead always relate to one another and to the created order in perfect holiness. Because all of God's relationships are perfectly holy, he is not the author or a moral agent of sin. God never sins in disposition, power, or act.

[65] Ibid., 10.

[66] Ibid., 14.

Idolatry

Another suggestion for the essential nature of sin is idolatry. Idolatry is the worship of the creature or that which is created. In a sense idolatry is the attempt to define all of reality in finite terms.[67] Idolatrous worship can be directed to inanimate objects, living creatures, or human beings. In all cases the worship that rightfully should be directed to the Creator is misdirected or misplaced to someone or something else.[68] Created things supplant that which is exclusively reserved for God. Idolatry is a perverted faith because it is a commitment of devotion and adoration given to finite objects or beings. The quintessential expression of idolatry occurs when an individual idolizes himself or herself.[69]

The Old Testament contains numerous prohibitions against the practice of idolatry. From the incident at the Tower of Babel (Gen. 11:4–9) to the first commandment in the Decalogue (Exod. 20:3; Deut. 5:7), the worship of anything other than God was considered the most heinous of offenses. The prophets declared idol worship to be the epitome of folly (Ps. 115:4–8; Isa. 40:18–20; Jer. 10:1–5).

The New Testament likewise strongly condemns idolatry. As we noted in our survey of biblical terms, idolatry was understood as the negation of appropriate worship and reverence that belonged exclusively to the living God. Paul interpreted the practice of idol worship as a sign of the judgment of God (Rom. 1:22–25). Jesus himself affirmed that the most important commandment is, "And you shall love the Lord your God with all your heart and with all your soul and with all your mind and with all your strength" (Mark 12:30 ESV).

Trust in a false god is thus trust in the wrong god. "Choosing any finite object over God is wrong, no matter how selfless such an act might be."[70] Idolatry is the enthronement of the finite over the infinite, ascribing ultimate value to that which is temporal, transitory, and created. Supreme allegiance misplaced or misdirected to anything or anyone other than God is sin. Sin is thus a failure to let God be God. In our failure to acknowledge God as God, we displace him with someone or something else.[71]

Selfishness

Another possibility for the essential nature of sin is selfishness. A. H. Strong defines *selfishness* as the "choice of self as the supreme end which

---

[67] John Macquarrie, *Principles of Christian Theology* (New York: Scribner's, 1966), 238–39.
[68] James Leo Garrett Jr., *Systematic Theology: Biblical, Historical, and Evangelical* (Grand Rapids: Wm. B. Eerdmans, 1990), 1:530–31.
[69] Macquarrie, *Principles of Christian Theology*, 238–39; Reinhold Niebuhr, *The Nature and Destiny of Man* (London: Nisbet & Co., 1941), 1:150.
[70] Erickson, *Christian Theology*, 598.
[71] Ibid.

constitutes the antithesis of supreme love to God" and as "a fundamental and positive choice of preference of self instead of God, as the object of affection and the supreme end of being."[72] If love of God is the essence of all virtue, then the antithesis is the choice of self as the supreme end. Selfishness is more than merely an exaggerated self-love that is the opposite of compassion and benevolence toward others. Selfishness is the preference or exaltation of self against God. The preference of self over God accounts for "nearly and perhaps all sin."[73]

Selfishness expresses itself in many different forms. Sensual, inordinate appetites, such as avarice, ambition, vanity, pride, covetousness, etc. are regarded as selfishness. Selfishness can manifest itself as unbelief in or enmity with God. It can be understood as turning away from the truth and love of God. The selfish person sacrifices the claims of God and his law for his own gratification. Selfishness is loving self more than God; preferring one's own ideas as opposed to God's truth; doing one's own will rather than God's will. In this paradigm, idolatry, unbelief, rebellion, law-breaking, and pride are considered expressions of selfishness.[74]

Pride

Some theologians contend that pride is the essence of all sin. Medieval theologians classified pride as one of the "seven deadly sins" and considered it the opposite of humility. *Pride* may be defined as "the exaggerated valuing of one's self or too much love of the self."[75] As we can see in this definition, pride is closely related to the sin of selfishness. Some theologians regard pride as a form of rebellion and treat the topic under this category.[76]

Augustine considered pride the most basic sin and believed it to be the sin at the root of the fall of Adam in the garden of Eden. In his commentary on Psalm 19:15, Augustine states: "'And I shall be cleansed from this great offence.' What but pride? for there is none greater than apostasy from God, which is the beginning of the pride of man.' And he shall indeed be undefiled, who is free from this offence also."[77] Pride thus led to the apostasy of Adam in the garden of Eden. John Calvin favorably cited Augustine at this point when he stated:

---

[72] Augustus Hopkins Strong, *Systematic Theology* (Valley Forge: Judson, 1907), 567, 572.

[73] Alvah Hovey, *Manual of Christian Theology,* 2nd ed. (New York: Silver, Burdett and Co., 1900), 160–62.

[74] Strong, *Systematic Theology,* 568–70.

[75] Donald K. McKim, "Pride," *WDTT,* 220.

[76] Garrett, *Systematic Theology,* 458–59.

[77] Augustine, *On the Book of Psalms, Psalm 19.*

Hence it is not hard to deduce by what means Adam provoked God's wrath upon himself. Indeed, Augustine speaks rightly when he declares that pride was the beginning of all evils. For if ambition had not raised man higher than was meet and right, he could have remained in his original state.[78]

Reinhold Niebuhr contended that pride (*hubris*) is the major form of man's opposition to God.[79] Although noting that in "real life" distinctions are not so neat, Niebuhr attempted to distinguish three types of pride: pride of power, pride of knowledge, and pride of virtue. By pride of power

human ego assumes its self-sufficiency and self-mastery and imagines itself secure against all vicissitudes. It does not recognize the contingent and dependent character of its life and believes itself to be the author of its own existence, the judge of its own values, and the master of its own destiny.[80]

Another expression of the pride of power is prompted by human insecurity. "It is the sin of those, who knowing themselves to be insecure, seek sufficient power to guarantee their security, inevitably of course at the expense of other life."[81] The most common expression of this aspect of the pride of power is greed.

The pride of knowledge is an "intellectual pride" that "pretends to be more true than it is. It is finite knowledge, gained from a particular perspective; but it pretends to final and ultimate knowledge."[82] According to Niebuhr, a significant aspect of intellectual pride is the inability of the agent to recognize the same or similar limitations of perspective in himself which he has detected in others.

Finally, pride of virtue is a moral pride revealed in "self-righteous" judgments. The self-righteous individual condemns others because the judged person is unable to conform to the highly arbitrary standards of the self. "Since the self judges itself by its own standards it finds itself good. It judges others by its own standards and finds them evil. . . . Moral pride is the pretension of finite man that his highly conditioned virtue is the final righteousness and that his very relative moral standards are absolute."[83]

---

[78] John Calvin, *Institutes*, 2.1.4. Some confusion seems to exist in Calvin's thought at this point, for later he asserts that unfaithfulness is the heart of all sin. "Unfaithfulness, then, was the root of the Fall. But thereafter ambition and pride, together with ungratefulness, arose, because Adam by seeking more than was granted him shamefully spurned God's great bounty, which had been lavished upon him." Ibid.

[79] Niebuhr, *The Nature and Destiny of Man* (New York: Scribner's, 1951), 1:186-207.

[80] Ibid., 188.

[81] Ibid., 190.

[82] Ibid., 194.

[83] Ibid., 199.

Sensuality

Another suggestion for the essence of sin is that all sin arises from sensuous desire. This view regards sin as the tendency of a person's sensuous (or physical) nature to dominate and control a person's spiritual nature. In this theory the senses are the means by which temptation leads to the domination of the spiritual nature by the physical body: "The soul never shakes off the body."[84] The Apostle Paul's warnings against "living according to the flesh" are literal admonitions to restrain the physical, material part of human nature. According to this view, materiality is assumed to be inherently evil.[85]

Rebellion

Rebellion is another option for the essence of sin. All human beings, whether Jew or Gentile, are in contact with the truth and person of God. All people possess volition, which can be exercised either in obedience or disobedience. Failure to submit to the will of God is regarded as rebellion. Human disobedience is defiance of God. Rebellion can be directed against the revelation of God in creation, conscience, law, and ultimately the person of Jesus Christ.[86] Rebellion is against God and a declaration of "high treason" as traitor to God.

In addition to the biblical terms for rebellion already surveyed, the Bible contains numerous examples of and warnings against rebellion. The Israelites at Rephidim (also called Meribah; Exod. 17:1–7; Deut. 33:8) murmured against Moses and incited a rebellion against his leadership and ultimately the leadership of God. At the rebellion at Mount Sinai (Exod. 32:1–35), the children of Israel cajoled Aaron into making a golden calf, claiming that this was the "god" who liberated them from their Egyptian slavery. The Israelites who participated in this rebellion are described as a "stiff-necked" and "stubborn" people who committed a "great sin," thereby rebelling against the LORD (Deut. 9:6–21). Isaiah called upon the people to repent of their rebellion and return to the Lord (Isa. 1:20). The Apostle Peter warned his readers not to rebel as did those who lived during the time of Noah and fell under God's wrath in the flood (1 Pet. 3:20).

Rebellion has occasionally been equated with pride.[87] Pride is regarded as a rebellious spirit with a misplaced allegiance (in this case, rebellion against God in order to pledge allegiance to one's self). Pride is attempting to displace God with self or living as if there were only the self and no God. In this framework pride/rebellion is closely aligned with idolatry.

---

[84] Friedrich Schleiermacher, *The Christian Faith* (New York: Harper and Row, 1963), S 66.

[85] Erickson, *Christian Theology*, 596.

[86] W. T. Conner, *Christian Doctrine* (Nashville: Broadman Press, 1937), 131–32.

[87] Garrett, *Systematic Theology*, 529, connects the concept of pride with willful rebellion.

Unbelief

Unbelief as the essential nature of sin is not a common theme in the Old Testament. Certain negative uses of the Hebrew verb *'ēmūn* could be translated as "to not believe," "unbelieving," or "to be unsteadfast" (Num. 20:12; Deut. 1:32; 2 Kings 17:14; Ps. 78:22,32). The notion of "not believing" or "not trusting" is minimally developed in the Old Testament.[88]

The New Testament more explicitly develops sin as unbelief. The sin of unbelief is a major theme in the Gospel of John. "Those who do not believe are condemned already, because they have not believed in the name of the only Son of God" (John 3:18). Jesus equated unbelief with disobedience (John 12:48) and described unbelief as blindness (John 9:39). Unbelief and Disobedience are so intertwined that some theologians define *sin* as "unbelieving-disobedience" or "disobeying-in-unbelief."[89]

Unbelief in the New Testament is depicted in the most pointed terms: blasphemy against the Holy Spirit (Matt. 12:22–32); an evil, unbelieving heart (Heb. 3:12); deliberate sinning after the reception of the knowledge of truth (Heb. 10:26–29); and the "sin leading to death" (1 John 5:16 NKJV).[90] Unbelief includes the rejection of the general revelation of God within creation and conscience (Rom. 1:18–23; 2:14–15). The rejection of Jesus Christ as the Son of God, the revealer and Redeemer, is the quintessential denial of the light and truth of God. This "Christological-unbelief" could be directed at the works and miracles of Jesus (John 10:25–26; 10:38; 12:37,39) or at the person of Christ himself (John 8:45–46; 16:9).[91] Although the wrath of God is currently manifested against those who refuse to believe his general revelation (Rom. 1:18–19), the rejection of Jesus Christ as Lord and Savior compounds the condemnation of those entrenched in unbelief.

Assessment

Sin is multifaceted and complex. In light of this complexity, is it possible to identify the core essence of sin? After all, if the Bible uses such diverse terms to describe the nature of sin, is the effort to reduce sin to a single concept legitimate? The endeavor to construct a comprehensive definition of sin suggests that we attempt to identify the core essence of sin. In this regard, the process is valid and necessary. Toward that end some of the theories examined hold more promise than others.

Although sin assuredly includes selfishness, as an explanation for the essence of sin, the concept has significant shortcomings. Certain attitudes or

---

[88] Ibid., 460.
[89] Dallas M. Roark, *The Christian Faith* (Nashville: Broadman Press, 1969), 214–15.
[90] Garrett, *Systematic Theology*, 532.
[91] Ibid.

behaviors may not be characterized as selfish in the strictest sense of the term, yet they may still be sinful. Individuals can sin against God in that they love another person more than they love God (as opposed to loving self more than they love God). In addition, many people show selfless devotion to a false religion or to a secular ideology or philosophy. Some may even suffer or die for a cause that is opposed to God in which an immediate, personal preference is not readily apparent. We could argue, however, that loving another person, sacrificial devotion to an ideology, or dying for a cause meets their selfish needs and desires.[92] Such counterarguments would, however, define selfishness in such a conceptually vacuous way "that nothing could possibly count against the theory that selfishness is the essence of sin."[93]

Sensuality as the essence of sin is likewise lacking. The assumption that matter is inherently evil (thus the physical nature of humanity) is more akin to the teachings of Gnosticism than of the Bible. God is the Creator of both the physical and spiritual elements of human beings, and he declared his original creation of human beings to be "good" (Gen. 1:31). To contend that sensuality is the essential nature of sin is to implicate God as the author of sin. In addition, many sins (perhaps the worst sins) are not physical in nature. Paul's list of "works of the flesh" in Galatians 5:19–21 identifies sins that are physical in nature. Other listed sins are, however, more "spiritual" in nature: idolatry, hatred, strife, envy, ambition, etc. These "nonphysical" sins may in fact be the impetus behind sins that are physical in nature.[94]

Further, one would have to posit that rigid control of bodily appetites could control or quash one's sinful activity. Ascetic attempts have succeeded to some degree in controlling certain "physical sins," yet other sins less physical in nature may still be present (i.e., pride, hatred, jealousy, etc). Repression of the physical nature in one area may result in the manifestation of sin in other areas, such as impatience, lack of compassion or mercy, etc.[95] Finally, sensuality as the core sin rests upon a faulty understanding of Paul's use of the word *flesh*. Although it may on occasion refer to the physical or material part of a person, the term normally describes a principle or disposition that is antithetical to the person and will of God.[96]

Although rebellion is a common theme in the Bible, should we regard it as the essential nature of sin, or should we consider rebellion an outworking or external expression of another sin or sins? Rebellion appears to be the sinful outflow of other sin(s). Although a heinous sin, rebellion should not be identified as the essential nature of sin. The same criticism could be

---

[92] Erickson, *Christian Theology,* 598.

[93] Ibid.

[94] Ibid., 597.

[95] Strong, *Systematic Theology,* 562

[96] Erickson, *Christian Theology,* 596–97.

leveled against pride. Do all sins arise from pride, or is pride the expression of a deeper sin? What makes someone proud? As already noted, Calvin himself seemed unclear or inconsistent on this matter.

Unbelief is a common theme for sin in the New Testament. The concept is not, however, as well developed in the Old Testament. This lack of development in the Old Testament precludes understanding the essence of sin as unbelief.

Disruption of shalom as the essence of sin has several commendable features. Unlike some of the other theories (such as sensuality and selfishness), this perspective is more theocentric; sin is an affront to the person and plan of God. Further, this theory has implications for the created order. Human sin vandalizes the design and intention of God for all creation and is an affront to the architect and builder of all reality. In addition, this view emphasizes primarily what God is for (*shalom*) and secondarily what God is against (sin). Finally, this theory is capable of encompassing the other theories of covenant unfaithfulness, rebellion, sensuality, selfishness, and unbelief.

Two concerns, however, prohibit identifying this interpretation as the essence of sin. If the culpable disturbance of shalom is the essence of sin, is this disruption the *cause* or the *result* of all sin? This perspective seems to focus on the result of human sinfulness rather than on the core from which all other human sinfulness arises. In addition, this perspective concentrates mainly on sin's effects on creation. The essence of sin should primarily emphasize the offense against the person of God and secondarily the disruption of creation. The culpable disturbance of shalom reverses this important ordering.

Another concern with this perspective is the significant overlap that it shares with idolatry. There seems to be little distinction between the displacement of God and the disruption of shalom. I contend that anything disruptive to God's creation can be regarded as idolatrous; conversely, attempts to displace God from his rightful place disrupt his intention for creation. One could argue that the distinctions between these two positions are a matter of semantics more than of theology.

In light of the shortcomings of the other perspectives, idolatry is the best option for our understanding of the core essence of sin. The displacement of God can be regarded as the cause for all the other manifestations of sin. Rebellion, sensuality, selfishness, unbelief, and the disruption of shalom are the results of our sinful attempts to displace God. The notion that idolatry is the essence of all sin is further strengthened by the fact that the first commandment given by God in the Ten Commandments was that "you shall have no other gods before me" (Exod. 20:3). This commandment reveals the absolute importance God places upon our exclusive worship of him. Jesus reiterated the magnitude of this command when he said, "Love the Lord your God with all your heart, and with all your soul, and with all your mind. This is the greatest and first commandment" (Matt. 22:37–38). Idolatry is the antithesis to this commandment.

Having said this, by no means can we be absolutely definitive on this issue. Much about human sinfulness remains a mystery. For example, theologians have grappled for centuries without much success for an answer to the question, what caused Adam to sin? No truly definitive solution has satisfactorily settled the matter. These kinds of issues may never be resolved this side of the eschaton. Further, we should always guard against offering simple answers to complex questions, particularly when the Bible has such varied descriptions of the nature and manifestation of sin. Nevertheless, mindful of these concerns and qualifications, <u>idolatry seems to be the most biblical way to understand this issue. All human sinfulness ultimately arises from the failure to let God be God.</u>

What Has the Church Believed about Sin?

Christian theologians throughout the centuries have struggled with the meaning of the fall, the nature of sin, and original sin. Although the early church gave little attention to the systematic construction of the doctrine of sin, the apologists and early church fathers were not completely silent on the subject. Interest in the doctrine gained momentum, culminating in Augustine's development of original sin. The implications of the Augustinian synthesis were refined and modified during the medieval and Reformation periods. The modern period witnessed both restatements and redefinitions of the classical position.

The following survey will provide a historical overview of what the church has said on the doctrine of sin. Key developments and select theologians will be examined. Special attention is devoted to representative Baptist theologians.

Justin Martyr

<u>Justin Martyr</u> had no a systematically constructed doctrine of sin as evidenced in some of his beliefs about sin. He believed that the transgression of Adam placed the entire human race under the curse of sin. In a discussion of the role of the serpent in Genesis 3, Justin suggested that Adam's fall was connected in some way to the sinful condition of the entire human race: "The race of men, who from Adam's time have fallen under death and

the deceit of the serpent."[97] Justin could be saying that, by succumbing to the temptation of Satan, the sin of Adam is as a prototype for each person's sin. All people fall and die in the same way as Adam.[98] Adam thus brought death to all people and began the spread of evil through his bad example.

On the other hand, Justin also asserted that each person is responsible for his own sin. He rigorously contended for individual freedom and human responsibility.[99] In the same passage cited above, Justin noted that "each man sinned by his own fault." Justin may have meant that sin is the willful act of the individual. A corrupt nature is not transmitted from Adam to his descendants; rather, what Adam brought to all humanity was mortality. In spite of any connection with Adam, each person is still culpable for his own sin.

Justin's understanding of sin is also connected with his belief in demons. Like many of his contemporaries, he was attracted to the idea that demons were in some measure to blame for human sinfulness. Believed to be the offspring of the union between fallen angels and the daughters of men (Gen. 6:1–2), demonic creatures were thought to swarm everywhere, afflicting men's souls and bodies with vice and corruption. Justin believed that these malevolent beings are in some sense responsible for human sinfulness and for the presence of evil. He also believed that all people have been nurtured, raised, and taught wickedness and sinfulness through a fallen, sinful environment.[100]

Irenaeus

Irenaeus is commonly recognized as the first systematic theologian of the church. The doctrines of the fall and sin, as well as other theological tenets, find formal expression in his writings and teachings. His thought is a converging point for many extant beliefs about sin, and it provided fresh insights about the nature of sin and the fall.

Irenaeus regarded Adam as a moral, spiritual, and intellectual child. Prior to the fall, Adam was undeveloped and imperfect.[101] Original righteousness was not something Adam innately possessed but was a goal to be attained. Although God infused into Adam the breath of life, he did not bestow upon him the Spirit of adoption granted to Christians.[102] Adam was to

---

[97] Justin Martyr, *Selections from Justin Martyr's Dialogue with Trypho, A Jew,* ed. and trans. R. P. C. Hanson (London: Lutterworth, 1963), 50; J. N. D. Kelly, *Early Christian Doctrines,* rev. ed. (San Francisco: Harper & Row, 1978), 167.
[98] Kelly, *Early Christian Doctrines,* 167.
[99] Justin Martyr, *First Apology* 51.
[100] Kelly, *Early Christian Doctrines,* 167–68.
[101] Irenaeus, *Against Heresies* 4.38.1.
[102] Ibid., 5.12.2.

advance toward an ever closer semblance to the Creator through a process of submission and obedience.[103]

Adam's fall is attributed to his weakness and inexperience. The process of advancement was interrupted almost from the beginning. Because of his spiritual and moral immaturity, Adam was easy prey for the wiles of Satan and fell into his clutches. Although impacted by the fall, the divine image and likeness of God remained in a damaged form.[104]

For Irenaeus, the essence of Adam's sin was disobedience that carried grave consequences for the entire human race. Human sinfulness, mortality, and enslavement to sin find their source in Adam's sin: "For as by the disobedience of the one man who was originally molded from virgin soil, the many were made sinners and forfeited life."[105] Irenaeus believed that all people participated in Adam's deed and shared in his guilt: "By which things He clearly shows forth God Himself, whom indeed we had offended in the first Adam, when he did not perform His commandment. . . . For we were debtors to none other but to him whose commandment we had transgressed at the beginning."[106] Although believing that the human race sinned in Adam, Irenaeus did not develop a theological argument for the connection between Adam's guilt and the rest of humanity. He presupposed some solidarity or identity between the father of the human race and his descendants.[107]

Tertullian

Tertullian stands as the progenitor of the doctrine of original sin in the Latin theological tradition. His discussions on this topic establish a trajectory that would fix "once and for all the main lines along which speculation was to proceed to the Latin Churches."[108] Tertullian's view on original sin was shaped largely by his understanding of traducianism.[109] As W. G. T. Shedd notes: "Tertullian's Traducianism, which gradually became the received psychology of the Latin Church, paved the way for the doctrine of innate sin, in distinction from innate evil, and also for the theory of monergism in regeneration."[110]

---

103 Ibid., 4.38.3.
104 Ibid., 3.18.1; 5.21; Kelly, *Early Christian Doctrines,* 171.
105 Irenaeus, *Against Heresies* 3.18.7.
106 Ibid., 5.16.3.
107 Kelly, *Early Christian Doctrines,* 172.
108 F. R. Tennant, *The Source of the Doctrine of the Fall and Original Sin* (New York: Schocken, 1903), 329.
109 Traducianism is the belief that the human soul is propagated or transmitted from the parents to the child. Traducianism is contrasted with creationism, which is the belief that God directly and immediately creates each human soul at conception. See McKim, "Traducianism," *WDTT.* See above, pp. 387–91.
110 W. G. T. Shedd, *History of Christian Doctrine* (New York: Charles Scribner, 1863), 2:43–44.

Tertullian developed his view of traducianism from his notion that all existences have corporeality. All that exists has bodily existence; nothing lacks bodily existence but that which is nonexistent.[111] Corporeality extends both to the physical and to the spiritual elements of man. Tertullian concluded that, since the human soul truly exists, the soul is corporeal.[112] He contended that the origin of the soul is identical to the body. Like the body the soul is produced from the physical union of the parents. The soul does not enter the body after birth but is produced simultaneously with it.[113]

The corporeality and transmission of the soul explains Tertullian's inclusion of the human race within the sin of the first parents. Inasmuch as the soul, along with its spiritual characteristics, is inherited from the parents alone, the sin of Adam and its lingering corruption is also transmitted to his descendants. The propagation of the soul necessitated for Tertullian the propagation of sin.[114]

Every soul has its nature in Adam until it is born again in Christ. The unregenerate soul is unclean and sinful both in condition and in action.[115] Tertullian believed that the source of original sin could be traced to Satan, who entrapped man by breaking the commandment of God. On account of Adam's sin, the entire human race transmits the taint and culpability of Adamic guilt.[116] Original sin was a corrupting nature that did not completely obliterate the good of the soul, yet "that which is from God is rather obscured than extinguished."[117] Tertullian was a forerunner to the idea of inherited sin. He believed that this condition was propagated from one generation to the next.

Augustine

Although he used traditional and ecclesiological evidences to support his ideas, Augustine primarily developed his doctrine of original sin

---

[111] Tertullian, *Of the Soul* 7.

[112] Ibid.

[113] Ibid., 25. "How, then, is a living being conceived? Is the substance of both body and soul formed together at one and the same time? Or does one of them precede the other in natural formation? We indeed maintain that both are conceived, and formed, and perfected simultaneously, as well as born together; and that not a moment's interval occurs in their conception, so that a prior place can be assigned to them."

[114] Ibid., 41.

[115] Ibid., 40.

[116] Tertullian, *On the Testimony of the Soul,* Ante-Nicene Christian Library, vol. 11, eds. A. Roberts and J. Donaldson (Edinburgh: T & T Clark, 1869), 3; see also idem, *De Resurrectione Carnis,* trans. E. Evans (London: S.P.C.K., 1960), 34; idem, *De Paenitentia,* trans. W. P. Le Saint (Westminster: Newman, 1959), 5; idem, *De Spectaculis,* trans. T. R. Glover and M. Felix (Cambridge: Harvard University Press, 1977), 2.

[117] Tertullian, *De Anima* 41.

from the Bible. The principal text for Augustine's doctrine of original sin was Romans 5:12. Augustine relied on the Old Latin versions of the New Testament for the development of his understanding of the nature and transmission of original sin. These manuscripts mistranslated the phrase *in quo* to mean "in whom." "By the evil will of that one man [Adam] all sinned in him, since all were that one man, in whom, therefore, they individually derived original sin."[118]

Original sin resides within all human beings because all persons were descended physically and spiritually from Adam.[119] Augustine interpreted Paul to say in Romans 5:12 that all people were actually present in Adam and thereby shared in the actual commission and guilt of the original sin.[120] When Adam sinned, all people were "one in and with him," participating in the willful commission of the sin.[121]

> Inasmuch as all then sinned in Adam, when in his nature, by virtue of that innate power whereby he was able to produce them, they were all as yet the one Adam; but they are called another's, because as yet they were not living their own lives, but the life of the one man contained whatsoever was in his future posterity.[122]

No one prior to Augustine had so thoroughly depicted the sinful complicity of all humanity with Adam.[123] Based upon his interpretation of Psalm 51:10, Augustine regarded infants as guilty of original sin.[124] Because of their seminal unity in Adam, they were equally guilty by virtue of their presence and participation in Adam's deed. The Adamic guilt in infants is remitted through baptism.[125] Adamic sin also corrupts the *imago dei* in all persons. Despite the fall, humanity still retains a nobility of virtue that arises from God's likeness within man. Adam's rebellion did not destroy the *imago dei* in all persons, but his sin did injuriously scar human nature.[126] All persons therefore have need for healing from the devastating consequences wrought by sin.

---

[118] Augustine, *On Marriage and Concupiscence* 2.15; idem, *On Rebuke and Grace*; idem, *Against Two Letters of the Pelagians* 3.24.

[119] This view, called natural or seminal headship, states that all human beings were physically, or seminally, present in our ancestors (Adam and Eve). Because all persons were "present" in Adam, his action was not merely that of a single individual. Rather, his action involved the entire human race. Thus, when Adam sinned, "all sinned."

[120] Augustine, *On the Merits* 3.11.

[121] Augustine, *On Marriage and Concupiscence* 2.15.

[122] Augustine, *On the Merits* 3.14.

[123] Kelly, *Early Christian Doctrines,* 364.

[124] Augustine, *Retractions* 1.13.5.

[125] Augustine, *Against Julian* 6.49.

[126] Augustine, *City of God* 13.3.

Thomas Aquinas

Thomas Aquinas defined original sin as the privation of original righteousness.[127] He believed that God created Adam and Eve in a state of original righteousness. At the fall, this original righteousness was lost. Original sin resides in the soul of the person and is thus an integral part of the individual. The transmission of original sin occurs in the reproductive processes. "The semen by its own power transmits the human nature from parent to child, and with that nature, the stain that affects it."[128] All humans are guilty of Adamic sin since all persons derive their nature from a single, common individual.

For Aquinas, original sin had a devastating impact on Adam's descendants. With the fall the gift of life was lost, and man became subject to death. Death is the result of original sin and is passed down to every human being descended from him. In addition, original sin clouds human reason. After the fall, human beings were controlled by their passion or desires rather than their reason.[129]

The effects of original sin begin at birth. Infants must be baptized in order to remit Adamic guilt. Although baptism removes the guilt of original sin, the sin nature remains with the infant and is disseminated to that child's progeny. Should baptism be withheld from an infant, and if the child should die, then "original sin incurs everlasting punishment, since children who have died in original sin through not being baptized, will never see the kingdom of God."[130]

Aquinas did acknowledge the division of sins into two categories: venial and mortal sins. "Venial and mortal sins are infinitely different, for venial sin incurs punishment, whereas mortal sin incurs eternal punishment. . . . Therefore, venial and mortal sins are not even of the same genus, to say nothing of the same species."[131] Venial are of lesser importance than mortal sins and can hinder a person's access to or experience with God. Forgiveness of venial sins comes through prayer, fasting, and almsgiving. Mortal sins are willful, serious transgressions. Mortal sins include apostasy, murder, or adultery, and merit eternal punishment. Only the sacrament

---

127 Thomas Aquinas, *Summa Theologica,* trans. Fathers of the English Dominican Province (New York: Benziger Brothers, 1947), 956.

128 Ibid., 952–53.

129 Thomas Aquinas, *Compendium of Theology,* trans. Cyril Vollert (St. Louis: B. Herder, 1947), 205–9.

130 Thomas Aquinas, *Summa Theologica,* Latin text and English translation, vol. 25 (New York: McGraw Hill, 1964), 976.

131 Ibid., 41. Although affirming the "infinite difference" between venial and mortal sin "as regards turning away from God," Aquinas does see an interconnectedness between the two. "A given kind of sin can be either venial or mortal, e.g. the preliminaries to an act of adultery might be venial, and a thoughtless remark which is usually venial might be mortal," p. 45.

of penance (confession, priestly absolution, and restitution) can provide forgiveness for mortal sins.[132]

Ulrich Zwingli

Ulrich Zwingli defined *sin in a twofold way.* First, sin is a "disease" which we contract from the author of our race, in consequence of which we are given over to love of ourselves. . . . This defect is the disease native to us in consequence of which we shun things hard and burdensome and pursue things pleasant and agreeable."[133] This spiritual defect is transmitted from parent to child, much like a congenital disease in a family such as "stammering, blindness, or gout."[134] This disease, or depravity, is uncondemnable; human beings are neither guilty nor condemned for their depravity. Original sin is a pollution of human nature but not an actual, culpable transgression. Only actual sin brings guilt because "sin implies guilt, and guilt comes from a transgression or a trespass on the part of one who designedly perpetrates a deed."[135] Zwingli believed that original sin was "damning" in the sense that its nature and force inevitably led to sin. The children of Christians are exempt from this damnation; the blood of Christ is sufficient for the children of believers to overcome their damnation.[136]

Second, Zwingli understood sin as any action contrary to the law of God.[137] The sin of transgression is born from the sin that is disease.[138] The source of transgression is self-love, "from which flowed all evils which exist anywhere among mortals."[139] Zwingli understood original sin to be the spiritual defect inherited from Adam, and actual sins are those deeds which flow from the disposition.

Martin Luther

Impugning those theologians who denied original righteousness, Martin Luther believed that God conferred the gift of original righteousness to Adam and Eve. Adam's nature was "to love God, to believe God, to know God, etc. These things were just as natural for Adam as it is natural for the eyes to receive light." When Adam fell into sin, he lost his original

---

132 Ibid.

133 Ulrich Zwingli, *Commentary on True and False Religion,* ed. Samuel Macauley Jackson and Clarence Nevin Heller (Durham: Labyrinth, 1981), 138–39.

134 Ulrich Zwingli, *On Original Sin,* in *On Providence and Other Essays,* ed. for Samuel Macauley Jackson by William John Hinke (Durham: The Labyrinth, 1922), 4.

135 Ibid., 5.

136 Ibid., 3, 15.

137 Zwingli, *Commentary on True and False Religion,* 139.

138 Ibid., 139–40.

139 Zwingli, *On Original Sin,* 8.

righteousness. His "natural endowments" were no longer sound but corrupted through sin.[140]

As a result of the fall, the image of God was totally lost, and all of Adam's descendants now possess a corrupt nature. "By one sin Adam makes all those born of him guilty of this same sin . . . and gives them what he has, though it is quite foreign to them."[141] Luther posited that guilt, depravity, and condemnation are transmitted to all persons via procreation.

> This curse is called *peccatum originale,* hereditary sin or natural sin, which we received by nature from our parents in our mother's womb. . . . This means that by nature, as we are conceived and born, we bring sin with us into the world, and through sin comes God's wrath and death so that we are all lost and damned. And this hereditary sin is the true fountainhead whence spring and issue all the actual sins of men.[142]

The natural endowments of intellect, will, and emotions still remain but are severely corrupted in all people. Luther contended that the human race has become completely corrupted. All human beings are now inclined toward evil, are guilty before God, and are subject to the God's divine wrath.[143] Because of original sin, the sinner is "bent in on himself;" that is, the sinner is habitually seeking his own selfish ends. Greed, materialism, lust, anger, hatred, and all types of vices now fill the hearts of all men and women.[144] The sinner's nature is totally corrupted, and all sinners are spiritually enslaved to sin. No one is able to do good apart from divine grace. Those who "will maintain that man's free-will is able to do or work anything in spiritual cases be they ever so small, denies Christ."[145] The human will is hopelessly in bondage to sin. Human beings no longer exist in God's image but rather in the image of the devil.

Luther distinguished between two kinds of sin: original and actual. Original sin is that guilt which is inherited from Adam and merits condemnation. "Even if no actual sin is present, the tinder of original sin hinders the entrance into the kingdom of heaven."[146] Actual sins are those that the

---

[140] Martin Luther, *Luther's Works,* vol. 1, ed. Jaroslav Pelikan (St. Louis: Concordia, 1958), 165.

[141] Luther, *Luther's Works,* vol. 2 (Weimar: Hermann Boehlau, 1884), 45.

[142] Luther, *Luther's Works,* vol. 20 (Weimar: Hermann Boehlau, 1884), 337.

[143] Martin Luther, *What Luther Says: An Anthology,* vol. 3, comp. Ewald M. Plass (St. Louis: Concordia Publishing House, 1959), 1291.

[144] Ibid., 1296.

[145] Martin Luther, *A Compend of Luther's Theology,* ed. Hugh T. Kerr (Philadelphia: Westminster, 1966), 90.

[146] Martin Luther, *Luther's Works,* vol. 7 (Weimar: Hermann Boehlau, 1884), 344.

individual personally commits. Luther understood all actual sins as attempts for self-deification. By his sinful act, the first man sought to become God. Adam "was not satisfied to be a fine creature of God, created in the image of God; he did not want to remain man; he wanted to be God too and to know good and evil." All persons follow the first father in this regard. "Adam wanted to be God Himself, and God was to be of no account. All the children of Adam act in this way."[147] Actual sin is an expression of creaturely self-will that is contrary and hostile to the will of God.[148]

John Calvin

John Calvin believed that the garden of Eden was a place in which the obedience of Adam would be tested. Adam was to demonstrate his submission to the command of God by refraining from eating of the tree of the knowledge of good and evil.[149] Adam, however, failed the test and brought the curse, judgment, and disaster to himself and his posterity.

Calvin asserted that Adam's guilt passed down to his progeny. All persons thus receive guilt, a depraved nature, and a liability to punishment. "Therefore all of us, who have descended from impure seed, are born infected with the contagion of sin."[150] "Hence Adam, when he lost the gifts received, lost them not only for himself but for us all."[151] All persons participated in the original sin. Calvin viewed original sin as more than the absence of original righteousness. For Calvin, original sin is "a hereditary corruption and depravity of our nature, extending to all parts of the soul, which first makes us obnoxious to the wrath of God, and produces in us works which in Scripture are termed works of the flesh."[152]

Calvin defined *depravity* as a hereditary corruption of the person's total being. This depravity is total in that this corruption taints every part of the person. "The whole man is overwhelmed—as by a deluge—from head to foot, so that no part is immune from sin and all that proceeds from him is to be imputed to sin."[153] With regard to volition, Calvin believed that sin has impaired the human will. The human will is free in the mundane affairs of everyday life but is unable to respond favorably to God. The sinner's will is not compelled by external influences but is driven by the internal compulsions of the fallen nature.[154]

---

147 Luther, *Luther's Works,* vol. 28 (Weimar: Hermann Boehlau, 1884), 349.
148 Luther, *Luther's Works,* vol. 18 (Weimar: Hermann Boehlau, 1884), 712.
149 Calvin, *Institutes of the Christian Religion,* 2.1.4.
150 Ibid., 2.1.5.
151 Ibid., 2.1.7.
152 Ibid., 2.1.8.
153 Ibid., 2.1.9.
154 Ibid., 2.2.1–12.

Although the primary result of the fall is spiritual death, other aspects of human existence are also affected. The natural endowments of the sinner, such as intelligence, will, and emotions, are corrupted by sin. Spiritual endowments, such as faith, love of God, holiness, etc., are lost.[155]

Friedrich Schleiermacher

Friedrich Schleiermacher defined religion, or true piety, in terms of a consciousness of God, a feeling of absolute dependence. The heart of the experience of absolute dependence is the total givenness of our being. Givenness of being means that the human self is not the ground of its own being. Human existence is a gift that we neither create nor sustain. Human beings therefore do not embody the principle of existence in themselves. Rather, our finite existence points beyond ourselves to our absolute dependence on God.[156] The Christian religion is thus the experience of the total givenness of our being to God.

> The common element in all howsoever diverse expressions of piety, by which these are conjointly distinguished from all other feelings, or, in other words, the self-identical essence of piety, is this: the consciousness of being absolutely dependent, or which is the same thing, of being in relation to God.[157]

For Schleiermacher, sin arises in human experience (i.e., self-consciousness) as it relates to God and as it affects the created order. Sin can best be understood as the dominance of the flesh (the sensual self-consciousness) over the spirit (God-consciousness). "We have the consciousness of sin whenever the God-consciousness which forms part of an inner state, or is in some way added to it, determines our self-consciousness as pain; and therefore we conceive of sin as a positive antagonism of the flesh against the spirit."[158] Ideally, the flesh (the lower powers of the soul) should be directed by the individual's spirit (the God-consciousness). Sin inverts or disrupts this anthropological hierarchy, causing the individual to lose his or her consciousness of God.

Schleiermacher regarded sin as anything that interfered with the individual's consciousness of God. Sin is thus the experience of God accompanied by a sense of alienation or guilt; it is the stifling by the flesh of the human awareness of God struggling for expression. For Schleiermacher,

---

[155] Ibid., 2.1.9; 2.2.12.
[156] Friedrich Schleiermacher, *The Christian Faith*, 2nd ed., ed. H. R. Mackintosh and J. S. Stewart (Edinburgh: T & T Clark, 1928), S 3.
[157] Ibid., S 4.
[158] Ibid., S 66.

human fallenness is not a reference to the historical fall of Adam but rather to the universal warring of the flesh against the spirit.

Schleiermacher believed that an awareness of sin could arise only from a God-consciousness. The awaking of our God-consciousness arouses in the self a sense of a higher life that humans do not currently possess. The more acute the feeling of absolute dependence upon God, the more intense becomes our awareness of sin. Schleiermacher thus believed that sin could not be defined independently of grace, and grace could not be rightly understood independently of sin. He thus regarded sin "on the one hand as simply that which would not be unless redemption was to be; or on the other hand as that which, as it is to disappear, can disappear only through redemption."[159] The Christian could not possess a consciousness of sin without a consciousness of the power of redemption, and a consciousness of the power of redemption required a consciousness of God.

Although he had little regard for the concepts, Schleiermacher did use the terms "original sin" and "actual sin." Original sin is that state of sin that was received prior to any act upon the part of the individual and in which guilt was latent. Actual sins are sinful acts which were perpetrated by the individual and which revealed the presence of original sin, along with its latent guilt.[160] Original sin always issues in actual sin.

Schleiermacher understood original sin as "the sinfulness that is present in an individual prior to any action of his own, and has its ground outside his own being, [and] is in every case a complete incapacity for good, which can be removed only by the influence of Redemption."[161] Whereas the earlier theologians understood original sin in terms of biological transmission or in terms of imputed guilt, Schleiermacher interpreted the transmission of sin in terms of its social dimension and presence among people.[162] Original sin also refers to the corporate guilt of the human race. Sins are thus interrelated; an individual's sin ultimately impacts society, which in turn affects the individual.[163]

Walter Rauschenbusch

In his formulation of the social gospel, Walter Rauschenbusch rejected the traditional, historical understanding of the fall in the garden of Eden. The intent of the Genesis account was not to provide an actual history of the entry of sin into the world but was rather to explain the entry of death,

---

[159] Ibid., S 65.2
[160] Ibid., postscript to S 69.
[161] Ibid., S 70.
[162] Bernard Ramm, *Offense to Reason: The Theology of Sin* (San Francisco: Harper and Row, 1985), 130.
[163] Schleiermacher, *The Christian Faith*, S 71.

and evil.[164] So much weight had been placed upon Adamic sin and guilt by previous Christian theologians that contemporary developments for the problem of sin were greatly diminished, if not ignored. The focus of the social gospel is upon the present-day struggles and problems of sin.[165]

Although he rejected the historicity of the garden of Eden and the fall, Rauschenbusch affirmed original sin. He contended that moral evil was transmitted biologically. Believing that scientific evidence could corroborate the biological transmission of moral evil from parent to child, he asserted that "depravity of will and corruption of nature are transmitted wherever life itself is transmitted."[166] Despite this affirmation, Rauschenbusch placed greater emphasis upon the social transmission of evil. He believed the Augustinian conception of original sin denigrates free will and responsibility as well as individual and corporate sins. Rauschenbusch often referred to social sins with the concepts of the "kingdom of evil" (in contradistinction to the kingdom of God) and "collective guilt." He believed that sin inhered within societal structures and customs and was disseminated to the individual by social contexts. "A theology for the social gospel would have to say that original sin runs down the generations not only by biological propagation but also by social assimilation."[167]

Karl Barth

Karl Barth argued for an existential interpretation of the account of Adam and Eve in the garden. He contended that the events of Genesis are to be understood as saga, not history.[168] The fall of Adam describes the event that happens to all as each individual reenacts personally the events described in the garden. Adam is thus an existential symbol for every person and the fall a saga of the existential, sinful demise of all people.[169] Sin originated in the fall, but the precise details of sin's origin transcend human comprehension.

Barth repudiated the doctrine of original sin as hereditary corruption. Original sin is not a disease passed from one person to another but rather

---

[164] Walter Rauschenbusch, *A Theology for the Social Gospel* (1917; repr., Nashville: Abingdon, 1945), 5.

[165] Ibid., 43–44.

[166] Ibid., 58.

[167] Ibid., 61.

[168] Karl Barth, *Church Dogmatics,* trans. G. W. Bromiley (Edinburgh: T & T Clark, 1956), 4/1.508 describes the historicity of the fall in Genesis as follows: "We miss the unprecedented and incomparable thing which the Genesis passages tell us of the coming into being and existence of Adam if we try to read and understand it as history, relating it either favorably or unfavorably to scientific paleontology. . . . The saga as a form of historical narrative is a genre apart. . . . [It] is the form which, using intuition and imagination, has to take up historical narrative at the point where events are no longer susceptible as such of historical proof."

[169] Ibid.

is the radical, prideful departure of every person from the will of God.
In the development of his understanding of sin, Barth did not begin with
Adam but with Christ. As humanity is joined with Christ in redemption,
so also is humanity joined with Adam in condemnation. Jesus is the true
and original Adam; the Adam of Genesis is the negative side of the work
of Christ.[170] Because of the universal experience of the fall, God has
placed all persons under the sentence of sin and guilt. The moral condition of the sinner is depraved, with each person perverted and ruined
by sin and guilt.[171] The will of the sinner is in bondage, and the mind is
distorted by sin.   = Calvin, Luther

John L. Dagg
O.S. transmission

John Dagg asserted that "all men are by nature totally depraved."[172]
Because Adam was as the representative for the human race, his depraved
condition is transmitted to his progeny, assuring the depravity of all people.
Dagg believed that depravity was total. He did not believe, however, that
human conduct is as bad as it could be or that "amiable affections" no longer have a place in the human heart. Depravity means that "the love of God
is dethroned from the heart, and therefore the grand principle of morality is
wanting, and no true morality exists. A total absence of that by which the
actions should be controlled and directed, is total depravity."[173]

Prior to the fall, Adam had perfect love for God and for others. With
the fall, love of self replaced love of God. Dagg contended that this love of
self came to all of Adam's descendents via their natural, moral, and federal
unions with Adam.[174] He believed that the natural union of all humanity
with Adam resulted in the biological propagation of depravity from parent
to child. With regard to the moral union, all persons do commit sin actually
and willingly. The federal union is established in that "the first man, having
been placed under a covenant of works, violated it, and brought its penalty
on himself and his descendants."[175]

For Dagg, depravity is a "disease and debility" corrupting the image
of God in man.[176] Depravity has infected human conscience, action, and

[170] Ibid., 4/1.512, 516.

[171] Ibid., 3/4.43.

[172] John Leadley Dagg, *Manual of Theology* (1871; repr., Harrisonburg: Gano, 1982), 152.

[173] Ibid., 153.

[174] Mark Dever, "John L. Dagg," in *Theologians of the Baptist Tradition,* eds. Timothy George and
David S. Dockery (Nashville: Broadman & Holman, 2001), 57. Federal headship is the view that
Adam was appointed by God to act as the representative for the whole human race. Because of
Adam's fall into sin, the entire human race now experiences the consequences of his sinful act. God
has imputed both the guilt and consequences of Adam's sin to his posterity.

[175] Dagg, *Manual of Theology,* 144.

[176] Ibid., 152.

rational capacities. The human will is not lost in the fall, but the will has been affected by human sinfulness. Since a person's will always follows the person's nature (which is now sinful), depravity inevitably leads the person to sin. "No inclination to holiness exists in the carnal [unregenerate] heart; and no holy act can be performed or service to God rendered, until the heart is changed. This change, it is the office of the Holy Spirit to effect."[177]

James P. Boyce

James Petigru Boyce stated that the condition of Adam before the fall is not a state of mere innocence. Adam lived in a condition of original righteousness in which he possessed a love of holiness. In this state Adam was inclined toward goodness rather than evil.[178] Adam, however, disobeyed God, thereby causing the corruption of his holy nature and rendering him incapable of further acts of holiness. Because of God's just demands and the terms of the covenant, Adam's act of rebellion resulted in the loss of paradise and reception of punishment. Adam immediately experienced shame, fear, and denial.[179]

The devastating impact of Adam's sin was threefold: natural, spiritual, and eternal death. Spiritual death, which Adam experienced immediately, brought alienation from God as well as loss of God's favor and acceptance. Eternal death was the quality of death that resulted from Adam's sin. The spiritual death that came immediately upon Adam would result in eternal death apart from God's gracious, atoning intervention. Natural, or physical, death was also a consequence of the fall. The death of the soul eventuated in natural death. The effects of Adam's sin were devastating. His nature was corrupted, and he could not alleviate his corrupted, alienated existence. Even if he had the will to be delivered from his state, Adam did not possess the ability to extricate himself by his own acts.[180]

Boyce believed that Adamic guilt is transmitted in two ways. First, he argued that Adam was the "natural head" of the human race. Adam's corrupt nature is passed to his descendants through natural procreation. This inherited, corrupt nature is liable to punishment; thus, all persons are born guilty before God because of their corrupt nature. Second, Boyce advocated the theory that Adam is the "federal head" of the human race. While in the garden, God entered into a "covenant of works" with Adam and appointed him as the representative of the human race. When Adam violated

---

[177] Ibid., 277.
[178] James Petigru Boyce, *Abstract of Systematic Theology* (Philadelphia: American Baptist Publication Society, 1887; repr., Handford: den Dulk Christian Foundation, n.d.), 230.
[179] Ibid., 234–39.
[180] Ibid., 240–46.

the terms of the covenant of works, all humanity was affected. This covenant was designed to test Adam's confidence in the goodness and trustworthiness of God. Boyce declared that the test was not unduly demanding or trying. As such, any act of disobedience makes the sinful act that much more heinous.[181]

Boyce believed that both natural and federal headship are taught in Scripture. The effects of Adam's sin upon his progeny result from the dissemination of Adam's character to his progeny. He also asserted that the federal headship is necessary in order to provide for future salvation. Since Adam is the representative head of the human race in the fall, Christ can serve as the representative head in the salvation of humanity.[182]

E. Y. Mullins

E. Y. Mullins believed that, prior to the fall, Adam was perfect, sinless, free, and inclined toward righteousness.[183] Because he was created free, Adam had the capacity either to obey or to sin against God. The moral freedom that Adam possessed was one facet of being created in the image of God.[184] Adam's freedom did not necessitate that he would in fact sin.[185] Mullins, affirming the historicity of the garden and the fall, believed that Adam's sin revealed the nature of human choices and the nature of sin.

Mullins understood the fall to be progressive, occurring in several stages. Adam, as an intelligent and free moral being, was first confronted with two courses of action: obedience or sin. He then experienced internal and external conflicts. Internally, Adam craved the knowledge that would come to him by eating of the fruit of the tree of the knowledge of good and evil. Externally, he was enticed to choose evil by an outside agent, Satan. Finally, Adam yielded his will to the temptation and committed sin, thus experiencing shame and guilt.[186] The sin committed by Adam was "the perversion of the good: the desire for food, the craving for knowledge, and the love of the beautiful."[187]

With regard to the relationship of Adam's guilt to the rest of humanity, Mullins rejected federal headship. He contended that no clear, biblical evidence existed to support the notion that Adam functioned as the head of the human race or that a covenant of works existed between God and

---

[181] Ibid., 239.

[182] Ibid., 250–54.

[183] E. Y. Mullins, *The Christian Religion in Its Doctrinal Expression* (Philadelphia: Judson, 1917), 259.

[184] Ibid., 283.

[185] Ibid.

[186] Ibid.

[187] Ibid.

Adam. He also rejected the notion that "we [humanity] sinned because we were actually present in him [Adam] when he sinned."[188] Mullins rather understood the spread of Adamic guilt via natural headship. As a result of common origin, all persons inherit Adam's tendency to sin. "Adam was the natural head of the race. Our tendency to sin is derived from him. All men are affected by his act through the medium of natural propagation."[189] The tendency to sin is inherited from Adam and is imputed to all humanity by means of the solidarity that all persons share through their common, biological ancestry.

Mullins defined original sin as an inherited tendency to sin. The proclivity to sinfulness is received via biological transmission. People are not condemned because of the reception and presence of this sinful tendency. Individuals are rather condemned because of the actual commission of sin.[190] The reception of the tendency to sin renders it certain that the individual will commit sin. According to Mullins, this bias "always manifests itself in actual sin in every person who attains to a state of moral consciousness."[191] Mullins believed that the reception of the tendency is sin itself, although moral culpability did not occur until hereditary sin manifested itself in actual sin. Both hereditary sin and actual sin corrupt the individual, bringing guilt and condemnation.[192]

W. T. Conner

W. T. Conner believed that sin must be defined from a theocentric perspective. For Conner, "sin is against God. In a godless world the idea of sin would have no meaning. As men lose the consciousness of God, the sense of sin also goes out of their minds and hearts."[193] The nature of sin is both rebellion and unbelief or willful rebellion.[194] Unbelief is the active rejection of the moral and spiritual light, natural (or general) revelation, available to all persons.[195] Unbelief is manifested in volitional rebellion against God and could be directed against the person of God or against the law of God.[196] Knowledge and will are considered necessary elements for the incurrence of guilt.[197] The antitheses to knowledge and will are respectively unbelief and rebellion. Conner believed sin to be a cognitive act; persons

[188] Ibid., 293.
[189] Ibid.
[190] Ibid., 301–2.
[191] Ibid., 268.
[192] E. Y. Mullins, *Baptist Beliefs* (Louisville: Baptist World, 1912), 25.
[193] W. T. Conner, *The Gospel of Redemption* (Nashville: Broadman Press, 1945), 1.
[194] Ibid., 10, 17.
[195] Ibid., 12–13.
[196] Ibid., 18–19.
[197] Ibid., 10–11.

are not guilty of sin unless they are sentient beings capable of both knowledge and will.[198] Sin is the result of the culpable rejection of the knowledge of God manifested in willful rebellion. = Mullins ≠ Boyce

Conner rejected the federal headship theory of original sin, stating that "so far as individual responsibility and guilt are concerned, there can be no such responsibility and guilt for an act committed thousands of years before one was born and with which he had nothing to do."[199] He did assert, however, that the entire human race is affected by the evil effects of Adam's sin. "The doctrine of original sin means that . . . the race is an organic unity, and as an organic unity it was affected by the sin of the first man, the head of the race. Through the law of natural generation, the whole race has inherited the evil effects of that first transgression."[200] As a result of hereditary evil, "all men have been born on a lower moral and spiritual plane than they would have been if Adam had not sinned."[201]

Conner's view of human solidarity has implications for the social influences of sin. Not only is sin transmitted via hereditary processes, but sin is also "passed down by social influence."[202] He argued that God ordained ξει X societal institutions and orders. When the vision of God is manifested or revealed in or through these entities, a consciousness of sin is manifested or experienced. "As the vision of God is renewed in an individual or a society of people, he (or they) will be smitten with a sense of sin."[203] Sin was self-propagating and corrupted the whole human social order, penetrating "every phase of the life of man. . . . All human relations and all social institutions have been pervaded by the power of sin and the corruption produced by it."[204] The entirety of man's existence, individually and corporately as well as biologically and socially, is corrupted by the evil power of sin.

Dale Moody
* Ungodliness & Unrighteousness
guilty ≠ X   O.S transmission X   but inherited tendency oƖ⊼∂

Dale Moody employed two concepts that he believed best describe the nature of sin. He defined ungodliness as a broken relationship with God and unrighteousness as broken relationships between persons.[205] Each of these aspects is intended to emphasize the direction or focus of sin. Ungodliness is ignorance of God. This ignorance results from a rejection of the knowledge of God found in general revelation. The rejection of general revelation

198 Ibid., 11–13.
199 Ibid., 31.
200 Ibid.
201 Ibid.
202 Ibid.
203 Ibid.
204 Ibid.
205 Dale Moody, *The Word of Truth* (Grand Rapids: Eerdmans, 1981), 279.

leads to personal estrangement from God and is expressed in ignorance and idolatry. Unrighteousness is manifested either as the defilement of human flesh or the defilement of the human spirit. Sins of the human flesh defile the body while sins of the human spirit corrupt the mind.[206]

Moody rejected the Augustinian position on original sin and the imputation of Adamic guilt. He did, however, believe that tendencies toward sinful behavior are biologically inherited. These sinful tendencies eventuate in actual transgressions. "Transgression is personal, not inherited, yet transgression as imputed sin is conditioned by inherited sin."[207] Moody thus distinguished between sin as inherited tendencies and sin as imputed transgression, yet he did so without adequate clarification of these distinctions. Also without explanation or rationale, Moody asserted that sin is transmitted psychologically or socially.[208]

Moody understood the universality of sin both in individual and corporate terms. With regard to individual sin, Moody noted that much of the New Testament, especially the writings of Paul, clearly teach that all individuals commit actual sin. The Bible makes no references to the sin of Adam as the cause of each individual's sin.[209] Moody regarded corporate sin as the collective sins of the group. Corporate sin in no wise undermines personal responsibility for sin. "Corporate sin is universal, but each individual is responsible for his personal involvement in the consequences."[210]

Millard J. Erickson

Millard Erickson defines sin as "any lack of conformity, active or passive to the moral law."[211] Sin has the negative result of separation of the individual from God as well as with others. For Erickson, the essence of sin is an idolatrous displacement of God, a failure to "let God be God."[212] He contends that the Bible teaches that the sinfulness of man can be traced back to an historical Adam. Erickson opts for a natural headship theory for the transmission of sin; that is, all persons are biologically present in Adam. He states that "we were actually present within Adam, so that we all sinned in his act. There is no injustice, then, to our condemnation and death as a result of original sin."[213] Adam's sin "was not merely that of one isolated individual, but of the entire human race."[214] Further, the entirety of humanity (physical and

---

[206] Ibid., 276–78.
[207] Ibid., 290.
[208] Ibid., 291.
[209] Ibid., 280.
[210] Ibid., 283.
[211] Erickson, *Christian Theology*, 596.
[212] Ibid., 598.
[213] Ibid., 654.
[214] Ibid., 652.

spiritual; material and immaterial) is received immediately from our biological parents and ultimately from the first pair of humans. All humans inherit a corrupted nature and are responsible for this sinful nature.

Regarding original sin, Erickson suggests that a corrupted sin nature is received biologically and the guilt for that polluted nature is conditionally imputed. Human beings, while inheriting both a corrupted nature and guilt, first become guilty when they approve their corrupted nature.[215] Sin is transmitted via conditional imputation according to the level of responsibility and maturity of the individual. Infants begin life with a corrupted nature and the guilt associated with the actual sin of Adam (Adamic guilt). Children are not regarded as sinful and guilty. Individuals are not responsible for the guilt of their sin until they are able as sentient beings to "accept" or "approve" one's sin nature. Children who die in infancy have not attained an appropriate level of moral responsibility. These infants are not sufficiently able to approve their sin and are therefore not morally responsible.[216] They will be received into heaven.

Assessment

We can draw several conclusions based on the historical evidence. First, the Augustinian doctrine of original sin has exerted profound influence upon the theology of the church. Since his time, theologians have affirmed, rejected, or modified the Augustinian position. One cannot construct a Christian understanding of sin without engaging in some way Augustine's doctrine of original sin. Second, no consensus exists within Christianity on the effects of sin upon humanity. The diverse understandings of sin as presented in our brief historical overview demonstrate the disagreement among theologians on the precise definitions and interpretations on the nature and spread of sin.

Finally, theological and confessional traditions will have a significant influence upon the development of one's doctrine of sin. No one constructs a doctrine of sin independent from the influences of history. All of our perspectives on the doctrine of sin will in some manner be informed and shaped by the theological formulations of others.

// Today

How Does It All Fit Together?

Having examined biblical and historical teachings, we now turn our attention to a systematic construction of the doctrine of sin. The following

---

[215] Ibid., 656.
[216] Ibid.

section will attempt to define sin as well as its universal presence and corrupting influence. We will also examine the concept of original sin and its implications for the spiritual status of infants.

Definition of Sin

A biblical definition of sin can only be understood in relationship with God. Although having moral and social implications, sin is basically an affront against the person of God. King David clearly sinned against Bathsheba (adultery) and Uriah (murder). In his penitential confession, however, David confessed that his sin was foremost against God.

> Be gracious to me, God,
> according to Your faithful love;
> according to Your abundant compassion,
> blot out my rebellion.
> Wash away my guilt,
> and cleanse me from my sin.
> For I am conscious of my rebellion,
> and my sin is always before me.
> Against You—You alone—I have sinned
> and done this evil in Your sight.
>
> Psalm 51:1–4 HCSB

Our definition of sin must therefore be constructed in theological and personal categories. Efforts to define sin independent of God prove unintelligible and vacuous, as illustrated in the conclusion of the atheistic philosopher Bertrand Russell: "But although the sense of sin is easy to recognize and define, the *concept* of 'sin' is obscure, especially if we attempt to interpret it in nontheological terms."[217] The biblical descriptions of sin already surveyed assume the existence of God and are only coherent when interpreted in relation to God. Sinful acts and dispositions essentially disrupt our relationship with God. Our relational breach with God results in relational disruptions with others and disintegration of self. These disruptions and disintegrations are, however, derivative realities; what creates sin against others and self is ultimately sin against God.[218]

Sin can be defined as "any act or disposition that displeases God and deserves blame."[219] Sin is the commission of ungodly acts (thoughts, desires, emotions, words, deeds) and the omission or neglect of righteous acts. Sin

---

[217] Betrand Russell, *Human Society in Ethics and Politics* (New York: Mentor, 1962), 73.
[218] Geoffrey W. Bromily, "Sin," *ISBE*, vol. 4, rev. (Grand Rapids: Eerdmans, 1988).
[219] Plantinga, *Not the Way It's Supposed to Be*, 13.

is also a state of being; disposition refers to a corrupted human nature. "Displeasure" and "blame" emphasize that sin brings enmity between God and us, that sin causes God to react unfavorably toward us, and that we are accountable for this relational rupture. This understanding of sin is thus criteriological (describing how something qualifies as a sin) as well as ontological (the nature to effect sin).[220]

We can further distinguish between the concepts "sin" and "sins." "Sin" (sing.) refers to a sinful disposition or state. In Matthew 7:17 Jesus said that the nature of the tree affects the type of fruit produced by the tree. His point was that the inner disposition of the person determines the acts, deeds, or thoughts of the person. In a dispute with the Pharisees, Jesus taught that inner defilement was more detrimental than ceremonial defilement (Mark 7:18). John the Baptist alluded to the singularity of sin in his declaration, "Here is the Lamb of God who takes away the sin of the world!" (John 1:29). "Sins" (pl.) refers to sinful acts, deeds, habits, or omissions. The primary emphasis of the Old Testament is upon sins as deeds. The New Testament retains this emphasis, as evidenced in "vice lists" (Rom. 1:29–31; Gal. 5:19–21). "Sin" is thus interconnected with "sins": "sinful motives issue in sinful actions. Sinful actions, deeds, or omissions establish the pattern or habit that is the sinful state."[221]

Universality of Sin

Sin is not limited to a few isolated individuals or to a majority of people. Sin is universal. All people (with the exception of Jesus Christ) are sinners, and all people sin.

The Old Testament provides abundant testimony to the universality of sin. The first sin committed by human beings is recorded in Genesis 3:4–6; Adam and Eve both disobeyed God and ate the fruit from the forbidden tree. From that moment sin spread like a fast-growing cancer. Genesis 6:5 recounts a time upon the earth when the wickedness of man was so rampant that "every scheme his mind thought of was nothing but evil all the time" (HCSB). God regretted having created man and resolved "to put an end to all flesh, for the earth is filled with violence because of them" (Gen. 6:13 HCSB). In Genesis 8:21, God stated that "man's inclination is evil from his youth" (HCSB). In Psalm 143:2, David said that "no one alive is righteous in Your sight" (HCSB). Solomon noted in his prayer, "There is no one who does not sin" (1 Kings 8:46).

The New Testament also provides ample witness to the universal presence of sin. The Apostle Paul argued in Romans 1:18–3:20 that all people

---

[220] Ibid.
[221] Garrett, *Systematic Theology,* 464–65.

(Jews and Gentiles) are sinners and guilty before God. In his most definitive statement (Rom. 3:10–18), Paul used a catena of Old Testament citations to establish unequivocally that all are sinners (Pss. 14:1–3; 53:1–4;
5:9; 140:3, 10:7; 36:1; Isa. 59:7–8). The Apostle John likewise declared
that "if we say that we have not sinned, we make him a liar, and his word
is not in us" (1 John 1:10). The assumption of the New Testament is that
each person is a sinner.

> The universality of sin is taken as a matter of fact. On examina-
> tion, it will be found that every speech in Acts, even Stephen's, and
> every Epistle just assumes that men have all sinned. This is also the
> assumption of Jesus in the Synoptic Gospels. . . . Jesus deals with
> everyone on the assumption, "Here is a sinner."[222]

The Bible not only teaches but also illustrates the universality of sin. Old
Testament saints such as Noah, Abraham, Moses, Jacob, and David are presented not only as men of great faith but also as men who struggle with sin.
In the New Testament, men such as Peter, James, John, and Paul are shown
to have sinful shortcomings. The overwhelming truth of the Bible is that all
people, in all times and places, are subject to the presence, power, and penalty
of sin. "All have sinned and fall short of the glory of God" (Rom. 3:23).

Total Depravity

If all people are sinful, how sinful are they? How intense is the sin problem? Are human beings essentially good with a proclivity toward evil, or
is human nature sinfully corrupt? These questions turn our attention to the
concept of depravity.

Depravity refers to the sinfulness, corruption, or pollution of one's nature. Although most references refer primarily to sin as act or deed, the Old
Testament does speak of sin as a disposition or state of being. The Prophet
Jeremiah declared that "the heart is more deceitful than anything else and
desperately sick—who can understand it?" (17:9 HCSB). In the book of
Ezekiel, God promised: "I will give them one heart, and put a new spirit
within them; I will remove the heart of stone . . . and give them a heart of
flesh" (11:19).

Psalm 51:5 clearly describes a sinful, corrupt disposition: "Indeed, I
was guilty [when I] was born; I was sinful when my mother conceived me"
(HCSB). This psalmist does not mean that sexual intercourse, procreation,
or childbirth are inherently evil but rather that sinfulness is deeply rooted in
human existence and permeates all human life from generation to genera-

---

[222] Smith, *The Bible Doctrine of Sin*, 159–60.

tion. David prayed to be washed and cleansed (v. 2), purged and washed (v. 7), and asked God to create a clean heart and to renew a steadfast spirit within him (v. 10). The psalmist is not just a person who commits sin; he understands himself to be a sinful person in need of transformation.

The New Testament is more exact in its depiction of depravity as corrupted human nature. For Jesus, human action originates from human nature: "Either make the tree good and its fruit good, or make the tree bad and its fruit bad; for a tree is known by its fruit. . . . A good man produces good things from his storeroom of good, and an evil man produces evil things from his storeroom of evil" (Matt. 12:33, 35 HCSB). Paul equated the concept "flesh" with corrupted, human nature: "For I know that nothing good lives in me, that is, in my flesh" (Rom. 7:18 HCSB). He also alluded to sinful human nature in Ephesians 2:3: "We too all previously lived among them in our fleshly desires, carrying out the *inclinations of our flesh* and thoughts, and *by nature* we were children under wrath, as the others were also" (HCSB, emphasis added).

Most Christian theologians agree that depravity universally exists in all human beings, and most concur that actual sins emanate from this depravity. Disagreements arise, however, about the nature of this depravity. Some define depravity as a hereditary, sinful corruption of human nature that encompasses all aspects of the person.[223] Others understand depravity as an inevitability of sinning, a moral weakness and inherent tendency toward evil by which a person will certainly, although not necessarily, commit sin.[224]

From Genesis to Revelation, sin is presented as a universal deformity of human nature, placing all people in all times and places under the reign of death and the inescapable wrath of God (Rom. 3:9–20).[225] As already noted, Psalm 51:5 gives persuasive evidence that depravity is not only present at birth but also inherited. In Ephesians 2:3, the Apostle Paul declared that all unbelievers are "*by nature . . . children of wrath*" (emphasis added). The Greek word *physis*, translated here as "nature," refers to an inherited, or acquired condition.[226] This nature "signifies something inborn and original, as distinguished from that which is subsequently acquired. The text implies that . . . sin is a nature, in the sense of a congenital depravity of will."[227] Other descriptions of sinfulness in the New Testament depict the corruption, heartlessness, and wickedness of human nature (Rom. 1:18–32; 2 Tim. 3:2–5; Titus 1:15). Although depravity includes an inevitability to

---

[223] Calvin, *Institutes*, 2.1.8.

[224] Conner, *Gospel of Redemption*, 22.

[225] Timothy George, *Amazing Grace: God's Initiative—Our Response* (Nashville: LifeWay, 2000), 72.

[226] R. P. Meye, "Natural, nature," *ISBE*, rev., vol. 3 (Grand Rapids: Eerdmans, 1986), 497.

[227] Strong, *Systematic Theology*, 578.

sin, the biblical evidence suggests that depravity is an inherited corruption of human nature and constitutes us as sinners before God.[228]

"Total depravity" is the idea that all of human nature is corrupted by sin. Humankind was originally created to know, love, and serve God perfectly. Depravity is the contamination of these capacities. Our essential nature is corrupted; our relationships with God and others are disrupted. No capacity of our unregenerate nature is free from the pollution of sinful corruption.[229]

The doctrine of total depravity is often subject to misunderstanding, and some of its proponents have on occasion added to the confusion with exaggerated interpretations. The concept does not mean that the sinner is totally insensitive or indifferent to matters of conscience. Although the unregenerate suppress the truth of God because of their sin, they still retain some sense of right and wrong (Rom. 2:15). Total depravity does not mean that all human beings are equally sinful in every respect or sin to the greatest degree. Nor does total depravity mean the sinner is as sinful as he can possibly be. Unbelievers do not continuously do evil in the most wicked way possible. Because of common grace, unbelievers can perform acts of service that genuinely benefit others. Such acts are neither meritorious nor qualify the individual for salvation but are part of the providential working of God. Finally, total depravity does not mean that the sinner engages in any and every form of sin.[230]

Total depravity does convey two important truths about the extent of sin's contamination. Total depravity means that sinful corruption "taints" every dimension of human life. Sin cannot be located or relegated to one aspect of human existence, such as the body or the mind. Depravity has tainted all aspects of the sinner's existence: the physical body (Rom. 6:6,12; 7:24; 8:10,13), the mind or reason (Rom. 1:21; 2 Cor. 3:14–15; 4:4), the emotions (Rom. 1:26–27; Gal. 5:24; 2 Tim. 3:2–4), and the will (Rom. 6:17; 2 Tim. 2:25–26). Sinful corruption exists at the center of every person's being and infects the entirety of the person.

Total depravity also means "total inability"; that is, an individual cannot extricate himself from his sinful condition. A sinner cannot by his

---

228 Ibid.

229 Misunderstandings regarding the phrase "total depravity" abound in Christian theology. Efforts to clarify what is and what is not meant by the idiom have led some theologians to offer alternative designations for the concept "total depravity." For example, George, *Amazing Grace*, 72, suggests the phrase "radical depravity." Gordon R. Lewis and Bruce A. Demarest, *Integrative Theology,* (Grand Rapids: Zondervan, 1990), 2:211, use the phrase "holistic depravity." Wayne Grudem, *Systematic Theology* (Grand Rapids: Zondervan, 1994), 497, refrains completely from using the term. Although efforts to rectify misperceptions and characterizations are commendable, attempts at renaming have not been successful in theological discourse. Because of its longstanding use, we will retain the expression "total depravity" and make appropriate qualifications and clarifications when necessary.

230 Charles C. Ryrie, "Depravity, Total," *EDT,* 312.

own volition bring his life and character into conformity with the demands of God. The taint and power of sin is such that the individual cannot deliver himself from sin or justify himself in God's sight.[231] As sinners, we are powerless "to please God or come to him unless moved by [God's] grace."[232] "We are totally unable to do genuinely meritorious works sufficient to qualify for God's favor."[233]

Theories of Original Sin

If all people are sinners by nature, how do we account for the universal presence of depravity and sin among all people? It is one thing to assert that Adam fell into sin; it is another to maintain that his sin affects his progeny. What is the relationship between Adam's sin and the rest of humanity?

Nonimputation Theories

Theologians for centuries have grappled with the relationship between the sin of Adam and that of his descendents. Of the various theories propounded, several see little or no connection between the original sin and our sin. These theories stipulate that Adamic guilt is not imputed to the human race. Two of the more prominent theories are Pelagianism and Arminianism.

1. *Pelagianism.* Pelagianism is the belief that emphasizes a person's ability to approach and relate to God solely through human effort. The movement derives its name from the British moralist Pelagius, a popular teacher in Rome ca. AD 400. Although questions exist as to whether he was actually a monk, Pelagius was nevertheless a devout ascetic who clearly supported monastic ideals. While in Rome, Pelagius studied Augustine's anti-Manichean writings, particularly the monograph *On Freewill*. He came to oppose, among other things, the Augustinian understanding of original sin and infant baptism.

Pelagius took great exception to the prayer of Augustine reflected in his *Confessions*: "Give what you command, and command what you will." Pelagius interpreted this prayer as an invitation to license and laxity. He believed that God had given humanity all it needed to obey his commands perfectly.[234] A dispute inevitably ensued between Augustine and Pelagius. The views of Pelagius and his followers were eventually condemned at the Synod of Carthage (418) and the Council of Ephesus (431).[235]

---

[231] Strong, *Systematic Theology,* 640.

[232] Donald Bloesch, *Essentials of Evangelical Theology* (San Francisco: HarperCollins, 1978), 1:90.

[233] Erickson, *Christian Theology,* 648.

[234] Pelagius, "Letter to Demetrias," in *Theological Anthropology,* trans. and ed. J. Patout Burns (Philadelphia: Fortress Press, 1981), 42–43.

[235] John Ferguson, *Pelagius* (Cambridge: W. Heffer, 1956), 40.

Pelagius and his followers rejected the notion that man's will has any intrinsic bias toward evil. Each human soul is directly and specially created by God, free from any taint of guilt or corruption.[236] Original sin is not imputed to Adam's offspring; Adam's sin injured only himself. The impact of Adam's sin upon his posterity is simply a bad example.[237] Man has no congenital corruption. Infant baptism does not remit Adamic guilt but instead brings "spiritual illumination, adoption as children of God, citizenship of the heavenly Jerusalem, sanctification and membership of Christ with the inheritance in the Kingdom of heaven."[238]

Pelagius believed that a person could fulfill God's commands without sinning simply through human effort.[239] He insisted that the fall did not affect human free will.[240] Every newborn is innocent and able to obey God, just like Adam at his creation. Since no bias toward sin exists, any sinful inclinations that may arise are simply bad habits. Pelagius left no room for the regenerative action of God upon the sinner. He equated grace with human free will, the apprehension of God through reason, and the moral teachings of Moses or Jesus. In addition, he taught that an individual could grow in holiness toward God based upon human merit.[241] Salvation is therefore not from human sin, guilt, and condemnation but rather a process of preserving or maintaining our right standing with God.

2. *Arminianism.* Although named for Jacob Arminius, the Arminian tradition of theology finds its most systematic and popular expression in the writings of John Wesley. Arminian theology focuses on the effects of the fall upon the progeny of Adam and the mitigation of the consequences of the fall by prevenient grace.[242] John Wesley believed that God imputed Adam's sin, as well as the ensuing depravity, guilt, and condemnation, to all his descendants. He also affirmed that this corrupted nature is sinful and renders the person guilty before God. "The sin of Adam, without the sins which we afterward committed, brought us death."[243] Wesley understood that the sinful corruption infected the entirety of the individual.[244]

---

[236] Pelagius, "Letter to Demetrias," 41–42.

[237] G. F. Wiggers, *An Historical Presentation of Augustinism and Pelagianism,* trans. Ralph Emerson (Andover: Gould, Newman & Saxton, 1840), 83–88.

[238] Kelly, *Early Christian Doctrines,* 359.

[239] Pelagius, "Letter to Demetrias," 42.

[240] Ibid., 49.

[241] Christopher A. Hall, *Learning Theology with the Church Fathers* (Downers Grove: InterVarsity, 2002), 132–56.

[242] Although differing opinions exist within this theological tradition, I will summarize a moderate form of Arminianism.

[243] Robert W. Burtner and Robert E. Childs, *A Compend of Wesley's Theology* (Nashville: Abingdon, 1954), 114.

[244] Ibid., 120.

Wesley contended, however, that each person is responsible only for the deeds that the individual actually commits. Inherited guilt and its penalty are nullified by "preventing grace," so that each person is actually born into the world free from the judicial consequences of Adam's sin. The person is not considered "sinful" until the commission of actual sins. Prevenient grace therefore nullifies inherited depravity. The mind and will are freed from the influence of depravity and guilt, and each individual is enabled by his own volition to repent and exercise faith toward God. "There is no man that is in a state of mere nature; there is no man, unless he has quenched the Spirit, that is wholly void of the grace of God. No man living is entirely destitute of . . . preventing grace."[245] "Man is not now condemned for the depravity of his own nature, although that depravity is the essence of sin; its culpability, we maintain, was removed by the free gift of Christ."[246]

Infants theoretically inherit depravity, guilt, and punishment. Prevenient grace, however, removes these things so that no child of Adam is condemned eternally. "Where all were born sinful, they were also born in grace."[247] Each child at the time of moral accountability determines his own destiny by either a reception or rejection of the claims of Christ.

Imputation Theories

Other theories contend that all human beings are guilty of original sin. Adamic guilt is imputed in some way to all humanity. The major theories that teach the imputation of guilt are federal and natural (seminal) headship.

1. *Federal headship.* Federal headship asserts that God appointed Adam as the "federal head" of the entire human race. Each person inherits his physical nature from his parents, but the human soul is specially created by God for the individual and is united with the body at birth. We were not physically or spiritually present in our ancestor.

God entered into a "covenant of works" with Adam and appointed him to act in behalf of the entire human race. Adam was our representative, acting for us in the garden of Eden. Adam was "not only the natural, but also the federal head of his progeny."[248] The consequences of Adam's actions would be imputed to all his descendants: on the condition of his obedience,

---

[245] Ibid., 148.

[246] Wesley, as quoted in H. Orton Wiley, *Christian Theology* (Kansas City: Beacon Hill, 1958), 2:135.

[247] A. Elwood Sanner, "Total Depravity," *Beacon Dictionary of Theology,* ed. Richard S. Taylor (Kansas City: Beacon Hill, 1984), 525.

[248] Charles Hodge, *Systematic Theology* (New York, 1874; repr., Grand Rapids: Eerdmans, 1981), 2:117–22.

all human beings would have eternal life; on the condition of his disobedience, all humanity would receive corruption and death.[249]

Because Adam sinned, the consequences of his actions are passed to all his descendants.

> All members of the human race were represented by Adam in the time of testing in the Garden of Eden. As our representative, Adam sinned, and God counted us guilty as well as Adam. . . . God counted Adam's guilt as belonging to us, and since God is the ultimate judge of all things in the universe, and since his thoughts are always true, Adam's guilt does in fact belong to us. God rightly imputed Adam's guilt to us.[250]

John Calvin appears to support this position: "The contagion does not take its origin from the substance of the flesh or soul, but because it had been so ordained by God that the first man should at one and the same time have and lose, both for himself and for his descendants, the gifts that God had bestowed upon him."[251] Our historical survey earlier revealed that James Boyce believed that "federalism" was necessary to preserve the Adam-Christ parallelism.[252]

Adam's descendants are also born with a depraved nature, which always leads to sin. This depravity is the effect of the imputation, not the cause of it. From Adam "sin flows on as an impure stream to all the generations of men, polluting everyone and everything with which it comes in contact."[253] Infants are infected with original sin and in need of salvation through Jesus Christ. Some scholars who advocate federal headship suggest that those infants who are born into Christian families and die before they reach an age of accountability have the promise of salvation by virtue of their status in the covenant of grace. Those infants who are born into non-Christian families and die before they reach an age of accountability are likewise the

---

[249] John Murray, *The Imputation of Adam's Sin* (Grand Rapids: Eerdmans, 1959), 38, in his arguments for the representative (federal headship) view, notes that seminal union is somewhat assumed in the representative position. "The natural or seminal union between Adam and posterity is not in question; it is assumed." Murray argues, however, that natural headship does not adequately explain why the Bible teaches that only Adam's *first* sin is imputed to all humanity. Ibid., 38–39. "The sin is the one sin of Adam. If the relationship to Adam were simply that of seminal union, that of being in his loins, this would not provide any explanation why the sin imputed is the first sin alone. We were as much in his loins when he committed other sins and these other sins would be just as applicable to us as his first sin if the whole explanation of the imputation of his first sin resides in the fact that we were in his loins. Hence some additional factor is required to explain the restriction to the one sin of Adam."

[250] Grudem, *Systematic Theology,* 495.

[251] Calvin, *Institutes,* 2.1.7.

[252] Boyce, *Abstract of Systematic Theology,* 252–58.

[253] Louis Berkhof, *Systematic Theology* (Grand Rapids: Eerdmans, 1941), 221.

object of God's secret election.[254] In other words, all infants who die prior to moral culpability are elect.

2. *Natural Headship*. Another theory propounding the imputation of guilt is natural headship (also known as seminalism or realism). Natural headship advocates a tradución view of the origin of the soul. Physical and spiritual natures are transmitted biologically from parent to child. All of humanity was present in germinal form in our ancestors; the entire human race was seminally "in Adam."

Because all of humanity was present in Adam, his actions were also the actions of the entire human race. Augustine believed that Adam transmitted original sin via the processes of natural generation. Since the race as a whole was seminally in Adam when he sinned, each member received at birth the sin and guilt of Adam. "We all existed in that one man. . . . Although the specific form by which each of us was to live was not yet created and assigned, our nature was already present in the seed from which we were to spring."[255] Martin Luther asserted that guilt, depravity, and condemnation were transmitted to the human race through procreation. "The human seed, this mass from which I was formed, is totally corrupt with faults and sins. The material itself is faulty."[256] W. G. T. Shedd interpreted Romans 5:12 to refer to the sin of the common humanity in Adam as opposed to actual sins committed by individuals. "The individuals Adam and Eve were no more guilty of this first act . . . than their descendants are; and their descendants are as guilty as they."[257]

Affirming natural headship as "the most satisfactory of the theories for understanding original sin," A. H. Strong stated that "Adam's sin is imputed to us immediately . . . not as something foreign to us, but because it is ours—we and all other men having existed as one moral person or one moral whole, in him, and, as the result of that transgression, possessing a nature destitute of love to God and prone to evil."[258] Adam's actions were therefore not those of an isolated individual but of the entire human race. Since all were present in Adam, the imputation of depravity and guilt is the just result of our participation in his sin.[259]

[254] Lewis and Demarest, *Integrative Theology*, 194. See also Ronald H. Nash, "Restrictivism," in *What about Those Who Have Never Heard? Three Views on the Destiny of the Unevangelized*, ed. John Sanders (Downers Grove: InterVarsity, 1995), 118–20, who affirms the election of all infants.

[255] Augustine, *City of God* 13.14.

[256] Luther, *LW*, 12:348.

[257] W. G. T. Shedd, *Dogmatic Theology* (1888-94; repr., Grand Rapids: Zondervan, n.d.), 2:186.

[258] Strong, *Systematic Theology*, 622, 620.

[259] Erickson, *Christian Theology*, 651–52.

The Key Passage: Romans 5:12–19

Romans 5:12–19 is the principal text for a biblical understanding of original sin. Verse 12 serves as the key text: "Therefore, just as sin entered the world through one man, and death through sin, in this way death spread to all men, *because all sinned*" (HCSB, emphasis added). Whatever the meaning of "because all sinned," Paul stated that death originated in the human race because of the sin of Adam. In verse 15, Paul identified the cause of all death with the sin of Adam, "by the one man's trespass the many died" (HCSB). In verse 17, the apostle reiterated that "because of one man's trespass, death reigned through that one man" (ESV). The interpretative task is how to harmonize the fact that death came through the sin of Adam with the reality that all die "because all sinned."

As previously noted, Augustine used Old Latin versions of the Greek New Testament in his interpretation of verse 12. He mistakenly read "*eph hō*" as the Latin equivalent of "*in quo*," meaning "in whom." Augustine misinterpreted the phrase to read, "In this way death spread to all men, *in whom* all sinned." He erroneously assumed that that relative pronoun had a pronominal force, with "one man" serving as the antecedent. Augustine's mistranslation served as "biblical support" for his influential doctrine of original sin. Since his interpretation rested upon an inaccurate translation and interpretation, further investigation of the phrase *eph hō* is necessary.

Verse 12 states that death entered the world through the sin of Adam and comes to all people because all sinned. The entrance of death is a consequence of sin, and this death extends to each individual. Commentators agree that the phrase "in this way" compares the manner in which death entered the world (through sin) and the manner in which death spread to everyone (through sin). Sin (v. 12a) produces death (v. 12b); all die (v. 12c) because all sin (v. 12d). As death came into the world through sin, so also death spread to everyone "in this way" or "in the same way;" that is, by sinning.[260]

How is it that all people sinned? How does the sin of the one man, Adam, result in the sin of all people? Unlike Augustine, most commentators interpret *eph hō* in verse 12 as causal, in the sense of "for this reason" or "because" (see also 2 Cor. 5:4 and Phil. 3:12). The constantive aorist *hēmarton* signifies the particular historical event in which humanity sinned collectively in the original sin of Adam. Verse 12 states that universal death is the result of the universal sin. In verse 19, the aorist passive *kathistēmi* can also be rendered "became" ("through the disobedience of the one man the many *became* sinners"). Paul's statements in verse 15 ("the many died

---

260 Douglas J. Moo, *The Epistle to the Romans*, NICNT (Grand Rapids: Eerdmans, 1996), 320–21.

[aorist tense] by the trespass of the one man") and verse 17 ("by the trespass of the one man, death reigned through that one man") suggest that we experience death by virtue of the sin of Adam (cf. 1 Cor. 15:21–22). Adam's original sin brought condemnation for all (v. 16) because all sinned (v. 12). All of us sinned when Adam sinned because we were "in Adam." Romans 5:12–21 indicates that the original sin of Adam constitutes all persons as guilty sinners, subject to death and liable to eternal damnation.[261]

God's righteous judgment against all is due in part to the solidarity of the human race. The idea of corporate solidarity common in Paul's Jewish world (and rooted in the Old Testament) emphasizes that the actions of certain individuals have a "representative" character and are simultaneously regarded in some sense as the actions of other individuals (cf. Josh. 7). Paul may have had this concept in mind when elaborating upon the significance of both Adam and Christ within salvation history. For Paul, Adam was a historical as well as a corporate figure whose sin could be regarded at the same time as the sin of all his descendants.[262]

Is there a deeper relationship, however, between the sin of Adam and our sin? Can we press the point further by asking how Adam's original sin implicates us? The federal headship theory attempts to answer this question forensically, postulating the existence of a covenant of works between God and Adam. The major and most significant criticism against this perspective is that no explicit biblical evidence or teaching mentions the existence of such a covenant. Most adherents of Arminianism affirm natural headship but argue that effects of sin are eliminated by prevenient grace. People are judged only for their own actual sins. This position suffers the same criticism as the federal headship theory; namely, the Bible contains no explicit teachings regarding a "preventing grace" that diminishes sinful corruption in order to retain libertarian free will.

Pelagianism denies any connection between Adam's sin and the sin of all people other than by a bad example. Any relationship between Adam's sin and our sin is purely imitation. Adam's sin does not render it certain or even likely that we will sin. This interpretation suffers from numerous problems, not the least of which is that the Bible clearly makes the sin of Adam to be in some way the cause of our sin and condemnation. Pelagianism is also deficient because it discounts the Bible's teachings regarding the sinful corruption of all humans, disregards the need for salvation from human sin, and redefines the biblical teachings for grace and sin.

Natural headship best accounts for the relationship between Adam's sin and guilt and the universal presence of sin and guilt in all people. Realism

---

[261] Ibid., 324–28.
[262] Ibid., 327.

appeals to biblical passages where the actions of one person are reckoned as the actions of another because the latter was seminally present within the former (cf. Heb. 7:10). Our relationship to Adam is therefore "real" in the sense that we all are biologically descended from Adam and therefore "in Adam." Adam and Eve reproduced after their kind. The entirety of human nature, both physical and spiritual, is transmitted from our primal parents to the rest of the human race. "Granting the unity of the race and a traducian origin of the soul, each person receives from fallen parents, and they from theirs, back to Adam and Eve, an inherent tendency to sin."[263]

The entire human race was present in an undifferentiated form in the person of Adam. When Adam committed the original sin, all of us were involved with him. We are responsible for his sin. For this reason, all of Adam's descendents bear the guilt and condemnation of the original sin (Rom. 1:18–3:20). Adam's initial rejection of God corrupted his ability to believe and obey God. Adam's progeny has likewise received a corrupted nature with impaired abilities to know, love, and serve God. "There is no injustice, then, to our condemnation and death as a result of original sin."[264]

Original Sin and Infants

Natural headship raises the question of the status of children who die in infancy as well as all persons who never obtain moral consciousness or understanding with respect to their relationship to God and their sin. If original sin is transmitted from parent to child, then every person begins life with a corrupted nature as well as the consequent guilt and condemnation of sin. Should we conclude that, if an infant or child dies before having the ability to "receive the overflow of grace and the gift of righteousness" (Rom. 5:17 HCSB), he is lost and condemned to eternal death?

Certain passages in the Bible are often cited to support a concept popularly called the "age of accountability" or the "age of responsibility." In the pronouncement of God's judgment found in Numbers 14:29–31, people twenty years of age and older could not enter the promised land. Those younger than twenty would eventually enter because they did not "know right from wrong" (Deut. 1:39). In 2 Samuel 12:23, David declared that he would one day see his child that had died in infancy.[265] Although children might suffer the sinful consequences of their parents (even until the third

---

[263] Lewis and Demarest, *Integrative Theology*, 2:221.

[264] Erickson, *Christian Theology*, 654.

[265] One could interpret David's statement as saying that he would go to the state of death just as his son had. Grudem, *Systematic Theology*, 501, states that this interpretation does not fit the language of the passage. "David does not say, 'I shall go where he is,' but rather, 'I shall go to him.' This is the language of personal reunion, and it indicates David's expectation that he would one day see and be with his son."

and fourth generations [Exod. 20:5; 34:7]), their spiritual relationship to God is not determined by their parents. Ezekiel's teaching of personal accountability asserts that each individual is responsible for his own actions (Ezek. 18:20).

In addition, children enjoyed a special place in the teachings and ministry of Jesus. Jesus said that children exemplified the kind of humility that is greatest in his kingdom (Matt. 18:3–4; 19:14). No one should cause the downfall of a child (18:6–9), and no one should look down upon "these little ones" (18:10). Jesus also declared, "Let the little children come to me, . . . for it is to such as these that the kingdom of heaven belongs" (Matt. 19:14). Although these passages do not explicitly describe a definite age in which a child attains moral responsibility, they do suggest that infants and children are not typically regarded or described as sinful, condemned, and lost. In fact no passage in the Bible makes such an overt claim.

The ultimate issue regarding culpability is not the age of the individual; rather, the issue is whether the person is able to become a disciple of Jesus Christ as described in Scripture. Can this person repent of his own sin? Is this person competent enough to trust personally in Jesus Christ to save him from his sin? Is this person able to profess his own faith in believer's baptism? Is this person capable of receiving instruction and "observing all things" that Christ has commanded? We know experientially and intuitively that infants are incapable of making these types of decisions or participating in these kinds of activities.

How do we then account for the spiritual standing of infants before God? Since infants cannot repent and believe in order to receive the benefits of Christ's atonement, special provision must be made to negate the effects of the curse upon children who die in infancy. According to natural headship, infants do in fact inherit a depraved nature, and this nature is condemnable. Christ's salvific work is applied to these children through special application. The ground of their salvation is not different from ours, but the mode of application is. Based on the allusions of the previously identified passages of Scripture regarding children and on our understanding of the nature of conversion and discipleship, infants who die before attaining moral responsibility are not punished eternally for original sin. They are instead the objects of the good and merciful electing grace of God.

Is it possible to affirm both the concept of original sin as described herein and the notion that the atonement of Christ is applied to children who die as infants? Millard Erickson offers an approach that coherently synthesizes these two concepts. He notes that in Romans 5, the Apostle Paul develops a parallelism in which both Adam and Christ each have an influence on us (Adam's sin leads to death, Christ's act of righteousness leads to life). Some could press the parallelism to mean that if Adam's condemnation and guilt are imputed to all absent of any conscious choice on our part for his act, then Christ's righteousness and redemption are likewise imputed to all irrespective of a conscious choice on our part. Does this, however, necessarily follow? Is this the comparative parallelism Paul is making? Does Christ's death justify simply by virtue of his identification with humanity through the incarnation, independent of any conscious, personal acceptance by an individual of his work?[266]

The response most evangelicals give to these questions is, "No." The biblical evidence specifying two classes of human beings, the lost and the saved, is abundantly clear. Only a personal decision to accept the work of Christ makes his atonement efficacious. If this is the case, would not the imputation of guilt based on the action of Adam require some sort of conscious decision as well? Or, if there is no "unconscious faith," can there be "unconscious sin"? How do we explain the presence of original sin in infants and yet maintain that they are somehow not condemned?

As an advocate of natural headship, Erickson contends that all were involved in the original sin; thus, all receive a corrupt nature along with the attendant guilt and condemnation. With regard to guilt, however, Erickson believes that responsibility for guilt requires a conscious, voluntary decision on the part of the person, as is also the case with the imputation of Christ's righteousness. Until this occurs, the imputation of guilt is only conditional. Although guilty, culpability and condemnation are not attributed to the individual until that person attains moral responsibility. The person can therefore have the guilt of original sin without the culpability of guilt. If a child dies before he or she is capable of making genuine moral decisions, the child is innocent in God's sight. Spiritual death is not imputed to the child. According to Erickson, the atoning work of Christ provides for children who die in infancy the same type of future existence in the presence of the Lord as those persons who have attained moral responsibility and have had their sins forgiven as a result of accepting the offer of Christ's salvation.[267]

If this is the case, then what is the nature of the voluntary decision that would end childish innocence and constitute ratification of the first sin? One possible answer to this question is that there is no final imputation of the first sin until we consciously and with understanding commit a sin of our own. The commission of our first sin constitutes ratification of Adam's sin. At the moment of our first sin, the person becomes guilty of both of his own sin and the original sin.

---

[266] Erickson, *Christian Theology,* 655.
[267] Ibid., 656.

Although appealing, Erickson offers a more tenable option that better preserves the parallelism of accepting the work of Adam and the work of Christ. A person becomes responsible and guilty when the individual accepts or approves his corrupt nature. According to Erickson, there is a time in our moral development when we become aware of our personal tendency to sin. At that point we should "abhor the sinful nature that has been there all the time."[268] We ought to repent of this sinful propensity and, if there is an awareness of the gospel, seek God's forgiveness and cleansing. We ought minimally to detest and reject our sinful nature. When we acquiesce *=Agree* to the sinful nature, we place our tacit approval upon the corruption. In so *obey* doing, we embrace the sinful nature and thereby concur with the action in the garden of Eden. According to Erickson, "We become guilty of original sin without actually having to commit a sin of our own."[269]

Erickson's explanation of natural headship, original sin, and the state of children who die in infancy appears to make the most sense of all that Scripture says on these matters. Natural headship is the best explanation for the transmission and universality of original sin. All were involved in Adam's sin; therefore, all receive a corrupt nature and the accompanying guilt and condemnation. The individual is not culpable for the guilt of original sin until that person becomes conscious of the presence of the sinful *{el X}* nature. Upon this awareness the individual acquiesces and embraces the corrupt nature. All individuals who reach a moral awareness without exception embrace their sin nature. The concurrence of one's sinful nature becomes the point at which he is culpable and accountable for original sin.

Just as the imputation of Christ's work includes a conscious, voluntary reception on our part, so also does our moral responsibility for the imputation of Adam's sin include a conscious, voluntary reception. Children who die in infancy do possess the guilt of original sin, but they are regarded as innocent by God through the atoning work of Christ. Infants who die prior to attaining moral awareness will not suffer eternally but will instead enjoy the perfect and blissful presence of God for eternity. As R. Albert Mohler and Daniel L. Akin have astutely noted: "The accomplished work of Christ has removed the stain of original sin from those who die in infancy. Knowing neither good nor evil, these young children are incapable of committing sins in the body—are not yet moral agents—and die secure in the grace of our Lord Jesus Christ."[270]

---

[268] Ibid.
[269] Ibid.
[270] R. Albert Mohler and Daniel L. Akin, "The Salvation of the 'Little Ones': Do Infants Who Die Go to Heaven?" in *Fidelitas*, http://www.sbts.edu/mohler/ FidelitasRead.php?article=fidel036, accessed 05.24.05.

The Consequences of Sin

Scripture indicates that serious effects are attached to both our sinful condition and the actual sins we commit. Some results of sin are the natural consequences of certain sinful acts. Others are the penalty for sin directly ordained by God. Sin has an adverse effect on three different levels: the effect of sin on our relationship to God, the effect of sin on our relationship to others and the effect of sin on the sinner.[271]

The Effect of Sin on Our Relationship to God

The first and most serious effect of sin is in our relationship to God. In the account of the first sin, Adam and Eve's intimate fellowship and perfect knowledge of God were replaced by distrust, doubt, and fear. Their act of rebellion and disobedience made them enemies of God. In their attempt to hide from him, they sought to avoid God and the effects of their sin. In like manner sin alters our relationship with God. The effects of sin include wrath, enmity, guilt, punishment, death, and, in the case of Christians, chastisement or discipline (Heb. 12:5–13).

1. *Wrath.* Human sin brings the wrath of God upon the sinner. In the Old Testament, God declares his hatred of sinful Israel. In Hosea 9:15 (HCSB) God declares, "All their evil appears at Gilgal, for there I came to hate them. I will drive them from My house because of their evil, wicked actions. I will no longer love them; all their leaders are rebellious" (cf. Jer. 12:8). Other passages indicate that God hates either the wicked (Pss. 5:5; 11:5) or wickedness (Prov. 6:16–18; Zech. 8:17).

The Bible teaches that sin angers God. God was angry with Israel for making and worshipping the golden calf (Exod. 32:10–11). God's anger is depicted as consuming and burning (Judg. 2:14; Ps. 30:5; Jer. 10:24). The Bible also describes God's aversion to sin as wrath. The wrath of God frequently is connected with the last days (Luke 21:21). Paul reminded the Thessalonian believers that Jesus is the one who delivered them from the wrath to come (1 Thess. 1:10). The approaching wrath is a direct consequence of earthly sins (Col. 3:5–6). The full demonstration of God's holiness and aversion to sin will come in the final judgment of sin and Satan (Rev. 20:10–15). Wrath is not relegated only to the future; the wrath of God is also a present reality (John 3:36). Paul declared that God's wrath is now upon the ungodly (Rom. 1:18). Sinners are by nature "children of wrath" (Eph. 2:3).

Wrath is God's appropriate displeasure and resistance to human sin. God intensely hates all sin, meriting his anger and displeasure. God's dis-

---

[271] The outline for this section is adapted from Garrett, *Systematic Theology*, 510, who categorizes the consequences as sinners and God, sinners and their fellow human beings, and sinners and themselves, and Erickson, *Christian Theology*, 619, who discusses the consequences of sin as results affecting the relationship with God, effects on the sinner, and effects on the relationship to other humans.

approval toward sin is not arbitrary; rather, God's holiness ensures that he will always reject and despise sin. God's reaction to our sin is determined by his holy nature. God's anger should not be equated with being excessively emotional or uncontrollable. He exercises patience and longsuffering toward human sinfulness. The nature of God, however, demands that he respond with holy disapproval to that which is contrary to his very being.

Sin has a devastating effect on our relationship with God. When we sin, we move into a state of divine disfavor. We become the objects of his wrath. Although loving, God cannot tolerate sin and will always oppose it. On the one hand, the effect of God's wrath "is to show that man who rebels against his relation of creaturely dependence on God . . . becomes subject to degenerative processes."[272] On the other hand, God is actively revealing his righteousness (Rom. 1:17) and demonstrating his "divine indignation . . . to human impiety or transgression of divinely approved laws."[273] Sin is a departure from a life that experiences the favor and goodness of God and entrance into an existence that bears the brunt of his displeasure and disapproval.

(2. *Enmity*) A consequence of sin closely related to wrath is enmity. Upon "having their eyes opened," Adam and Eve sought to hide from God because of their disobedience (Gen. 3:7). As a result of their sin, God banished them from the garden (Gen. 3:22–24). Both of these passages indicate the alienating effects of sin. The parable of the prodigal son teaches that rebellion brings hostility and alienation (Luke 15:13). Our need for reconciliation to God suggests that we are estranged from him (Rom. 5:10). The mind-set of the flesh is "hostile to God" (Rom. 8:7). Paul declared that the Gentiles, before they came to Christ, were "alienated from the life of God" (Eph. 4:18).

Enmity results in alienation and hostility between the sinner and God. We were created to relate intimately with God, but our sin leads us to live as his enemies (James 4:4). We no longer seek or yearn for his presence; rather, we flee and hide from him. We live in fear of God and rebel against him. We express our hostility toward God in that we defy him. In the sense that he actively works to thwart our disobedience and rebellion, God can be said to be "hostile" to our intentions. Although we were created to live in harmonious dependence upon God, we contemptuously pursue paths that lead us away from the only one who can fulfill our deepest needs.

(3. *Guilt.*) Guilt has both subjective and objective dimensions. Subjectively, we may feel guilty about a particular situation or relationship. This consciousness of guilt, however, is not the best indicator of actual

---

[272] James D. G. Dunn, *Romans 1–8*, WBC (Dallas: Word, 1988), 55.
[273] Ibid., 54.

guilt. Sinners often go to great lengths to rationalize and explain sin. The worst sinner is actually the one who is conscious of no sins.[274] Conversely, one may feel guilty for a situation in which no sin has actually been committed. Guilt must be understood objectively in relation to God and only secondarily in relation to our consciousness of it.[275] Our primary concern is with objective guilt.

Guilt can be defined as "the objective state of having violated God's intention for man and thus being liable to punishment."[276] Guilt means that sinners are rightly subject to the wrath and judgment of God. Any and all sins constitute us as guilty before God. The basis of guilt is the holy character and will of God. "It is against the background of God's spotless character that the blackness of sin is to be seen."[277] We incur guilt by our actual and culpable commission of sins (Ezek. 18:20). "We are guilty only of that sin which we have originated or have had part in originating. Guilt is not, therefore, merely liability to punishment, without participation in the transgression for which the punishment is inflicted. . . . We are accounted guilty only for what we have done, either personally or in our first parents, and for what we are, in consequence of such doing."[278]

The Bible teaches that there are degrees of guilt. Guilt is not equal in all cases. In the Old Testament, a distinction is made between unintentional sin and sin with "a high hand"—defiant and deliberate transgression.[279] The priests atoned for the former; the latter were reviling to God and resulted in the removal of the individual from the covenant community (Num. 15:28–30). In the New Testament, Jesus differentiated between the judgment of a willingly disobedient servant and an ignorant one (Luke 12:41–48). In a similar vein, Jesus attached greater guilt to those towns that rejected the witness of his disciples than the cities of Sodom and Gomorrah (Matt. 10:15).[280] A base principle is clear: revelation brings responsibility. The more we know, the greater is our responsibility.

(4. Punishment) Liability to God's punishment is another consequence of sin. Punishment can be the direct or indirect consequence of sinful actions. Certain punishments are inherent within the sin itself. For example, cirrhosis of the liver may the consequence of an alcoholic lifestyle.

---

[274] Conner, *Gospel of Redemption,* 19. See also Strong, *Systematic Theology,* 647.

[275] Strong, *Systematic Theology,* 647.

[276] Erickson, *Christian Theology,* 623.

[277] Conner, *Christian Doctrine,* 21.

[278] Strong, *Systematic Theology,* 644.

[279] Philip J. Budd, *Numbers,* WBC (Dallas: Word, 1984), 174.

[280] Strong, *Systematic Theology,* 648–52, identifies four instances in which degrees of guilt are evident. First, sinners are guilty by virtue of possessing a sinful nature. However, guilt is increased by acts of personal transgression. Second, sins of knowledge involve more guilt than sins of ignorance. Third, sins of presumption merit more guilt than sins of infirmity. Fourth, greater guilt attaches to the sin of final obduracy than sins of incomplete obduracy.

Likewise, a promiscuous man may endure a lifetime of incurable sexually transmitted diseases. In both of these cases, the sinful behaviors and life-styles also produce the punishment for the sin. Cirrhosis of the liver and sexually transmitted diseases do not, however, account for the full extent of the penalty for sin. "The natural consequences of transgression, although they constitute a part of the penalty of sin, do not exhaust that penalty."[281]

Impugning God's character incites God to judgment and prompts the exercise of his wrath. Punishment extends beyond the natural consequences of the sin committed.

> Those who would confine all penalty to the reaction of natural laws are in danger of forgetting that God is not simply immanent in the universe, but is also transcendent, and that "to fall into the hands of the living God" (Heb. 10:31) is to fall into the hands, not simply of the law, but also of the Lawgiver.[282]

For the non-Christian, God's punishment is retributive and punitive.

Although saved from the penalty of sin, Christians do commit actual sin. God does punish, or chasten, his children. God's response to the sin of a believer is remedial and disciplinary in intention. "[God] does it for our benefit, so that we can share His holiness. No discipline seems enjoyable at the time, but painful. Later on, however, it yields the fruit of peace and righteousness to those who have been trained by it" (Heb. 12:10–11 HCSB). Although a painful consequence of sin, God's discipline of believers is a sign of their adoption and an encouragement toward sanctification.

(5. *Death.*) The Bible teaches that death is a result of sin. Adam and Eve were forbidden to eat from the tree of the knowledge of good and evil; their disobedience would result in certain death (Gen. 2:17). Paul explicitly connected sin with death: "For the wages of sin is death" (Rom. 6:23). In what sense does sin entail death? Theologians have classically identified three types of death that are the consequences of sin: physical, spiritual, and final (or eternal) death.

Physical Death. Most theologians believe that sin brings physical death.[283] Several Scriptures seem to support the contention that physical death is a result of sin. The judgment pronounced by God in Genesis 3 upon Adam and Eve entailed physical death (Gen. 3:19). Paul made a connection between physical death and sin (1 Cor. 15:55–56). Furthermore,

---

[281] Ibid., 652.
[282] Ibid.
[283] For example, Strong, 656–59; Erickson, *Christian Theology,* 629–31; and Wolfhart Pannenberg, *Systematic Theology,* trans. Geoffrey W. Bromiley (Edinburgh: T & T Clark, 1991), 2:274.

several passages state that Christ's physical death was a direct consequence of human sin (Rom. 4:25; 6:10; Gal. 3:13).

Spiritual Death. Aside from the physical death resulting from sin, the Bible describes the natural man as "dead" even while living. Adam and Eve were told to avoid eating from the tree of the knowledge of good and evil, for "on the day you eat from it, you will certainly die" (Gen. 2:17 HCSB). The immediate consequence of the sin of Adam and Eve was spiritual death, resulting in alienation from God. No longer did Adam and Eve enjoy the immediate presence of God; rather, they were banished from the garden of Eden. Paul reminded the Ephesians of their spiritually dead condition before their salvation in Christ:

> And you were dead in your trespasses and sins in which you previously walked according to this worldly age, according to the ruler of the atmospheric domain, the spirit now working in the disobedient. We too all previously lived among them in our fleshly desires, carrying out the inclinations of our flesh and thoughts, and by nature we were children under wrath, as the others were also (Eph. 2:1–3 HCSB).

In this passage spiritual death involves more than alienation from God. There is also a subjective element that involves an impaired sensitivity to spiritual realities and an inability to do good deeds with consistency or right intentions.[284]

Final Death. Final death (also called eternal death or second death) is "the extension and finalization of spiritual death."[285] The final death is the culmination of spiritual death in which the unbeliever is banished, both body and soul, into hell for eternity. At this time there will be an accurate correlation between the inner condition of the soul and the outer condition of the body.[286] The Apostle John spoke of the final judgment in Revelation 20. Following the resurrection of the righteous, the [spiritually] "dead" will be raised for judgment, along with death and hades. John wrote: "Death and Hades were thrown into the lake of fire. This is the second death, the lake of fire; and anyone whose name was not found written in the book of life was thrown into the lake of fire" (Rev. 20:14–15). The lake of fire is the consequence for those who experience physical death while also spiritually dead. Eternal death is the permanent abode deliberately chosen by the sinner while physically alive.

---

[284] Erickson, *Christian Theology*, 631.
[285] Ibid.
[286] Strong, *Systematic Theology*, 660.

The Effect of Sin on Our Relationship to Others.

Although primarily an offense against God, sin also has relational consequences. Sin has adverse consequences in our relationships with other persons. Among these horizontal consequences are alienation, disharmony, envy, and progressive corruption.

1. *Alienation.* The entrance of sin into the world alters human relationships radically. The fall disrupts our relationship to God and ruptures our relationship with one another. We were created on a human level to enjoy wholesome, enriching fellowship with other persons. Because of our sin, we are alienated from God and estranged from others. Jealousies and hatreds fragment our relationships. Instead of radiating God's image to other persons, sinfulness now darkens our mutual image-bearing.

> Those who have no more ultimate concern than themselves become estranged from others and tend toward the idolatry of narcissistic self-worship. To center our highest values on ourselves is sin. Made for God, the human self finds its security, peace, and hope in God and not in itself. Without that foundation, sin shatters the most fundamental relationships we have.[287]

2. *Disharmony.* Sin also creates disharmony in our relationships. In Galatians 5:19–21, Paul stated that disharmony is the result of sin. He contrasted the "works of the flesh" with the fruit of the Spirit, identified in verses 22–23. We immediately are struck by the disparity of the two lists: the fruit of the Spirit brings unity while the works of the flesh bring discord. The fruit of the Spirit leads to harmony and fellowship; the works of the flesh tear at the fabric of society and usher in disharmony.

3. *Envy.* Envy has been described as the "resentment of someone else's good, plus the itch to despoil her of it."[288] We may regard envy as one of the most basic and devastating forms of sin: "Envy is pure evil, as toxic and sickening to the envier as to everybody else."[289] The Bible offers numerous examples of envy's destructive nature. Cain was envious of Abel's offering and standing before God. Joseph's brothers envied the special favor he enjoyed with Jacob. Saul was envious of David's popularity among the Israelites. Pilate perceived that the chief priests had delivered up Jesus "because of envy" (Mark 15:10 HCSB). Regardless of envy's root, the consequences are always devastating to both the envier and the envied.

4. *Progressive Corruption.* The interconnectedness of humanity means that the sin of one individual often leads to more sins (by that person and

---

[287] Lewis and Demarest, *Integrative Theology,* 2:216–17.
[288] Plantinga, *Not the Way It's Supposed to Be,* 169.
[289] Ibid., 170.

others). This cyclical perpetuation creates a culture of sin that is progressively destructive and corrupt. Not only do we reap what we sow; we often resow what we reap. For example, "Abusive children who abuse *their* children sow what they have reaped."[290] Sin is like a polluted river that continually branches and rebranches, creating an entire system of contaminated water.[291]

The pattern of sin is difficult (but not impossible) to overcome. The corruption of society does not absolve personal responsibility for sin. Following the counsel of others, we must reject the notion that sinful behaviors are "merely conditioned responses to inherited cultural givens or unfortunate social situations."[292] People, not social structures or environments, yield to temptation.

The Effect of Sin on the Sinner

Sin has personal consequences in addition to those in relation to God and other persons. Sin has a disintegrating, damaging impact upon the person committing the sin. For the individual sinner, sin brings in bondage, self-centeredness, and delusion.

1. *Bondage.* Enslavement to sin is also a personal consequence of sin. Sin has a power to ensnare an individual in its web of chaos and destruction. Paul reminded the Roman believers that, prior to their conversion to Christ, they "used to be slaves of sin" (Rom. 6:17 HCSB). Jesus also spoke of the enslaving power of sin: "Everyone who commits sin is a slave to sin" (John 8:34). Only those liberated by the Son are truly free (John 8:36). Sin has an addicting effect, trapping the sinner in a vicious, perpetual cycle of sin, propelling the sinner from one sin to another. Cain murdered his brother Abel out of a jealous spirit and then lied to avoid admitting his sin to God (Gen. 4:9). Abraham found that masquerading his wife as his sister (Gen. 12:10–20) was so easy that he would repeat it (Gen. 20). After committing adultery with Bathsheba, David murdered her husband Uriah to keep his sin secret (2 Sam. 11:14–27).

2. *Self-Centeredness.* The essence of self-centeredness is "a turning in upon oneself."[293] We are self-seeking and self-serving, like the sons of Zebedee who wished to obtain the prime seats around Jesus' throne (Mark 10:35–37). The consequences of self-centeredness are deadly. According to James, selfishness breeds all kinds of evil: "For where envy and selfish ambition exist, there is disorder and every kind of evil" (James 3:16 HCSB). Erickson notes: "We call attention to ourselves, and to our good qualities and accomplishment, and minimize our shortcomings. We seek

---

[290] Ibid., 70.
[291] Ibid., 53.
[292] Lewis and Demarest, *Integrative Theology,* 2:231.
[293] Erickson, *Christian Theology,* 635.

special favors and opportunities in life, wanting an extra little edge that no one else has. We display a certain special alertness to our own wants and needs, while we ignore those of others."[294]

(3. *Delusion.*)An ironic twist of our sinful condition is a denial of that very sinfulness. At the heart of sin is "the persistent refusal to *tolerate* a sense of sin, to take responsibility for one's sin, to live with the sorrowful knowledge of it and to pursue the painful way of repentance."[295] Sinners are simultaneously aware of their sin and desperately trying to resist that awareness. Jeremiah wrote, "The heart is more deceitful than anything else and desperately sick—who can understand it?" (Jer. 17:9 HCSB). King David denounced the injustice of the rich man in Nathan's parable who took the poor man's one little ewe but did not see his own injustice in taking Uriah's life (2 Sam. 12:1–15). Jesus identified our propensity for self-deception when he asked: "Why do you look at the speck in your brother's eye but don't notice the log in your own eye?" (Matt. 7:3 HCSB). Paul also addressed the self-deceit that results from sin. The thinking of the unredeemed has become "senseless" and their heart has become "darkened." Delusion is the end result: "Claiming to be wise, they became fools" (Rom. 1:21–22).

How Does This Doctrine Impact the Church Today?

As has been demonstrated, all of human existence is impacted by sin. Despite the modern tendency to ignore or disregard sin, a study such as this is still much needed today. The following section will identify certain aspects of sin that impact the ministry of the church and our understanding of the Christian life.

The Immensity of the Sin Problem

We should never underestimate the enormity of our sinfulness. Our sin problem must be assessed with the utmost seriousness, understanding that eternal destinies are at stake. Sin must never be taken lightly.

The Bible presents a horrific picture of the devastation of sin. Sin is idolatry, rebellion, missing the mark, straying from the path, treachery, lust, ungodliness, and wickedness. Sin disregards, commits willful error, brings guilt, and lacks integrity. Sin lusts, perverts, and breaks the law. Sin is overstepping a boundary and a failure to reach it, a transgression and a shortcoming. Sin is like a beast "lurking at the door" (Gen. 4:7). Our

---

[294] Ibid.
[295] Plantinga, *Not the Way It's Supposed to Be,* 99.

depravity reaches to the totality of our being. Society in general and sinners in particular are not merely sick or morally weak; they are polluted and corrupted. The Bible says that the unregenerate live under the wrath and condemnation of God (Rom. 1:18–2:16).

Sin is the epitome of futility and folly. Sin promises a divinity that is no true divinity (Gen. 3:5). The freedom offered by sin is enslavement. The works of sin are real, but they are not true accomplishments. Sinful humanity is only a caricature of real humanity, a paradoxical existence. We are still God's image bearers, but the image is distorted and corrupted. We live, yet we are dead in sins and trespasses (Eph. 2:1). Instead of a perfect garden filled with abundance, sin brings a wasteland of thorns and deprivation (Gen. 3:17–18). We are destined for eternity, but the eternity that sin gives is death in life and life in death.

The magnitude of the sin problem must be considered against the backdrop of the incarnation of Jesus Christ. The severity and depth of sin is nowhere more fully revealed and its judgment nowhere more strongly depicted than in the crucifixion of Jesus Christ. The sinless one took upon himself the curse of sin in order to liberate us from it (Gal. 3:13). By taking our guilt upon himself, Christ destroyed sin in his own body (Rom. 8:3). Through the death of Jesus, sin is judged and destroyed, bringing true liberation from sin's penalty and power. By his resurrection Christ ensures the resurrection of believers from the grave to an eternal, righteous life in the presence of God. The gospel itself is a message that God is not indifferent or indulgent to sin. God will execute his judgment on sin or the sinner.

Although contemporary culture belittles the problem of sin and makes light of its devastating effects, the Bible underscores the plight of the lost and the need for the power of the gospel of Jesus Christ to save us from our sin. The magnitude of our sin problem is revealed when we contemplate the majesty and wonder of the gospel of Christ. The gospel is the revelation of the profound measures that God undertook to bring salvation from sin. To ignore or downplay the plight of fallen humanity is to belittle the sacrifice of the Son of God. "For the Christian church . . . to ignore, euphemize, or otherwise mute the lethal reality of sin is to cut the nerve of the gospel. For the sober truth is that without full disclosure on sin, the gospel of grace becomes impertinent, unnecessary, and finally uninteresting."[296] For those who have an overly optimistic opinion of the human condition, the concepts of sin and total depravity provide a realistic assessment of our sinful predicament and magnify the necessity of the salvation of God.

---

[296] Ibid., 199.

Human Nature Must Now Be Assessed in Light of the Fall and Its Effects

Numerous social, political, theological, and philosophical projects contend that sin did not originate with human beings or that humanity is not ultimately responsible for sin. Many have attempted to understand and explain sin independent from belief in an actual historical fall and the corruption of human nature. Unitarians assert that human beings are morally neutral. Human conduct is sinful when it acts contrary to accepted social customs or cultural mores. Thus sin is defined as antisocial behavior.[297] Corliss Lamont also contends that human nature is morally neutral, believing that propaganda and cultural conditioning result in selfish and violent impulses. According to Lamont, communal education will bring the transformation of antisocial passions, motives, ambitions, and habits.[298]

Karl Marx located human evil in the dialectical conflict of social classes. He believed that a socialist redistribution of resources and power would inevitably lead to utopia.[299] Jose Miranda identified the root of all human evil in the economic oppression of the poor by unjust social structures. Transformation of social structures would ultimately lead to real justice for all people, thereby eliminating human wickedness.[300]

A biblical understanding of sin mandates that we assess human nature in light of the fall and its effects. The disobedience of Adam and the judgment pronounced by God radically altered humanity. Opinions that regard human beings as morally neutral are at best naïve and superficial or at worst defective and delusional; all such assessments are unbiblical. Jesus assumed the sinfulness of all those with whom he came into contact, and he insisted that everyone who sins is a slave to sin (John 8:34). In a postfall world, sinfulness is part of the warp and woof of our existence. Sin is a corrupting presence in each human being. We are infected and enslaved by sin. Contemporary understandings of human nature must take into account humanity's fallenness and the inherited corruption that issue in sinfulness.

Sin Is Not God's Intention for Human Existence

Should we regard sin as "natural" or "unnatural" to human existence? On the one hand, since human sinfulness was not part of God's original creation, we should consider sin unnatural. The Bible clearly affirms that

---

[297] H. Shelton Smith, *Changing Conceptions of Original Sin* (New York: Scribner's, 1955), 76–78.
[298] Corliss Lamont, *The Philosophy of Humanism*, rev. ed. (New York: Frederick Ungar, 1982), 241–42.
[299] Karl Marx, *Capital and Manifesto of the Communist Party*, Great Books, vol. 50 (Chicago: Encyclopedia Britannica, 1952).
[300] Jose Miranda, *Marx and the Bible* (Maryknoll: Orbis, 1974), 181, 202.

man is the grandeur of creation. God created man in his image and endowed him with freedom for service and fellowship. Although distinct from God's being, man comes from the hand of God; he has God-given nobility. When God proclaimed that his creation was good, human beings were included in his pronouncement. God was perfectly pleased with his human creation. Adam was not simply the sinful result of God's best effort. Adam was untainted by evil and enjoyed perfect communion with God prior to the fall. Sin was and is an unnatural and unwelcome intruder into human existence.

On the other hand, although unnatural according to God's intention, sin is universally present. Man has squandered his God-given privileges and responsibilities by aspiring to be God. Man is not content to be finite; he futilely strives to be infinite. Man was created superior to the beast yet often descends to the level of animals in behavior. Sin corrupts us all in our personhood, our relationships, and our social structures. The universal presence of sin gives the impression that sin is intrinsic to our existence and world. We can say that sin is not unexpected in a postfall world.

Sin is contrary to the will of God, and its presence signifies an invasion of the highest order. Sin is a parasite, a cancer that needs removal. Although sin is universally present among all people, we must never define human nature in a way that makes sin appear normal or inherent to our existence. Sin is "not the way it should be." Wisdom dictates that we remain vigilant to the presence and power of sin as well as to its devastating impact upon human beings, both individually and corporately. The goal of our existence is to be "conformed to the image of His Son" (Rom. 8:29). The will of God is that our identities be transformed from sinner into saint, from disfavor and wrath to favor and blessing with God. We are only healed from our sinful corruption through the grace and mercy of God. Our existence was not constituted in sinfulness, and our destiny is not continuation in sin.

Humanity Is Helplessly Mired in Sin

Countless strategies have been developed and implemented in an effort to conquer human sinfulness. Education, social programs, psychological methods, genetic engineering, and other similar efforts have all failed in this quest. For example, communism was considered by many as the way to transform human sinfulness. The Cold War of eastern Europe in the mid-twentieth century supposedly provided a social laboratory to demonstrate that the right form of government could bring divergent ethnic groups and social classes together to live and work harmoniously for the common good. Yet, when the Berlin wall came down, the guns came out. Centuries-old antagonisms that allegedly had been eradicated by the communist revolution were lurking below the surface. The moment governmental and military constraints were removed, the animosities that had been kept in check by oppressive, authoritarian rule burst forth like torrents of water through a punctured dam. Although certain human strategies and structures can curb and control behavior, the human heart cannot be transformed by governmental coercion.

Only God can extricate us from the quagmire of our sin. The reality of our depravity should foster a desperate dependence for God to intervene graciously in the midst of our polluted existence. We cannot transform our own hearts, and we cannot do anything to save ourselves. Human effort cannot transform the human heart. Our depravity and sinfulness highlight the supreme necessity of God's merciful redemption to liberate us from our horrible plight. "It is only when we realize the enormity of our sin that we can appreciate the inexhaustible abundance of God's mercy and love."[301] Our corrupted condition graphically depicts our spiritual standing before God. Although each person retains the image of God, it is defaced and tainted by sin. Because of our sinful state, all sinners stand justly condemned before the bar of God's righteous judgment. This truth should remind us of our utter need for God and elicit our gratitude, humility, and worship.

The Church Must Have Ministries of Repentance and Reconciliation

The instrument through which God manifests his power to overcome sin is the church. The mission of the church is contained in Jesus' statement: "Go, therefore, and make disciples of all nations, baptizing them in the name of the Father and of the Son and of the Holy Spirit, teaching them to observe everything I have commanded you" (Matt. 28:19–20 HCSB). As part of the disciple-making process in which we observe everything that Christ has commanded, the church is to preach "repentance for forgiveness of sins . . . in His name to all the nations" (Luke 24:47 HSCB). The message of repentance is a declaration that all persons are to abandon and repudiate their sinfulness. The message of reconciliation is that God is ever ready to forgive and bring the repentant sinner into a relationship with himself.

Repentance and reconciliation lie at the heart of the mission of the church. For example, evangelism is the proclamation of the gospel with the goal of bringing the hearers into a right relationship with God. The gospel declares that God has atoned for human sin in the death and resurrection

---

[301] George, *Amazing Grace*, 75.

of Jesus Christ. Those who by faith receive the gift of Christ's sacrifice for the forgiveness of their sin are reconciled to God. The ordinances also declare repentance and reconciliation. Through baptism believers profess their death to self and sin as well as their union with God. In the Lord's Supper, believers drink of the cup of the new covenant, commemorating the blood of Jesus, "shed for many for the forgiveness of sins." Church discipline is the ongoing ministry of a local church in which the members are exhorted to repent of sin, to be reconciled to God and one another, and to grow in holiness.

Benevolent ministries (acts of mercy) are a declaration that God is able to reverse and heal the devastating consequences of sin. "Spiritual warfare" can be defined broadly to mean that the Spirit of God through the church engages and overcomes evil and human sinfulness in the world and in the lives of individuals. In a sense all aspects of the ministry of the church declare that God now "commands all people everywhere to repent" of their sin (Acts 17:30) and has committed "the message of reconciliation to us" (2 Cor. 5:19).

In light of the Great Commission, the church must always develop ministry strategies that target human sinfulness. People find freedom from their sinful enslavement as the Holy Spirit brings transformation through the gospel of Christ and the ministries of the church. Healing from the devastating effects of sin can occur in the context of the ministries of the church. Reconciliation of sinners to God and to others comes when the message of the gospel is embraced. Although strategies and methods may change, the message that Christ has conquered sin does not.

409 - 478

SECTION 4

THE DOCTRINE OF CHRIST

CHAPTER 9

The Person of Christ

Daniel L. Akin

What Does the Bible Say?

Christology is the study of the person and work of Jesus Christ. It examines who he is (his person) and what he does (his work). In the study of Christology, theologians talk about a starting point, where to begin. This is an important and much-contested issue. The early church followed what is called a "Christology from above" approach. They began with texts like John 1:1–18, Philippians 2:6–11, Colossians 1:15–20 and the church's proclamation that Jesus is Lord (Acts 2:36; 1 Cor. 12:3). A second approach called "Christology from below" begins with the earthly life of Jesus and starts the investigation of him from that perspective.[1] Both of these approaches are valuable for developing a full-orbed Christology. We do not have to opt for one or the other.

However, there is also a third approach that should be considered: "Christology from behind." Here we start with the Old Testament, looking to see what it has to say about the coming of a Jewish Messiah, a Savior. Whoever Jesus of Nazareth is, he did not appear in a vacuum. There was a historical context out of which he emerged. There were hopes and expectations, especially on the part of Jewish people, that God's kingdom would come in an eschatological in-break through a deliverer. A survey of the Old Testament's redemptive story line reveals a developing and comprehensive portrait.[2]

---

[1] Wolfhart Pannenberg popularized this approach in *Jesus—God and Man* (Philadelphia: Westminster, 1968).

[2] It is interesting to note that James P. Boyce begins his treatment of Christology in a similar manner. See his *Abstract of Systematic Theology* (Philadelphia, 1887; repr., Escondido, CA: den Dulk Christian Foundation, n.d.), 258–67. In contrast W. T. Conner began with a "Christology from below." He writes, "Throughout Christian history, many theologians have so emphasized the deity of Christ, and assumed such a chasm between God and man, that they have practically nullified the human life of Jesus. This is a fundamentally wrong procedure. We should begin with the facts of the life of Jesus as recorded in the New Testament. If we do, we should not argue toward a human life for Jesus; we will rather begin with that as a datum, and that will be our starting point rather than our stopping place." See his *Christian Doctrine* (Nashville: Broadman, 1937), 47–48.

The Old Testament's Messianic Story Line

(from behind → Gen. 3:15   2 Sam 7:1-2
Gen. 12:1-3 Psalms
Gen. 49:9-10 (2,16,22,110
Deut. 18:15   Isa. 7:14
Isa. 9:6-7
Isa 52, 53
Dan. 7:13, 14
Micah 5:2

① *Genesis 3:15*

The story of salvation begins in the garden of Eden. Adam and Eve disobeyed God and plunged all of creation into sin (Gen. 3; Rom. 8:19–23). God took the initiative to remedy the situation, and in Genesis 3:15 God gives us the first promise of redemption. Theologians refer to this as the *Protoevangelium*, the first gospel proclamation. God promises that a male offspring of the woman (Eve) will come and crush the serpent. Someone is coming who will conquer the evil one and restore to humanity what was forfeited when humans disobeyed God in the garden. This deliverer will come from the seed of woman.[3]

② *Genesis 12:1–3*

Out of sinful humanity God called a man and formed a nation through whom he would bless the earth and send his deliverer. God called a man named Abram. God chose a man who would give birth to a nation, the nation of Israel. By this man and through his descendents God would bless "all the peoples on earth." Abram, whose name was later changed to Abraham, meaning "father of many" (Gen. 17:5), would be the means by which God would bless the whole world.

③ *Genesis 49:9–10*

As he neared death, Jacob gathered his sons around him and gave what is in essence a "prophetic poem" (Gen. 49:2–27), telling them what would be their future. His words about his son Judah are of particular importance and begin to narrow the specific line by which God would bless the nations. The crucial portion of the text reads: "Judah is a young lion. . . . The scepter will not depart from Judah, or the staff from between his feet, until He whose right it is comes and the obedience of the peoples belongs to Him" (Gen. 49:9–10).[4]

The text points to the coming of a deliverer, a Messiah. Ross notes:

> This verse moves into the promise for the eschatological future, looking beyond the normal period of Israel's history to the dawn of the messianic age. The "scepter" was the symbol of kingship—it would be Judah's. The word is paralleled with "lawgiver's staff" to strengthen the idea that the theocratic administration would remain with Judah. . . . God had created humankind to "rule and have dominion" over the earth as his vice regent [Gen. 1:26–30]. And now,

---

[3] See the excellent comments on this text in Kenneth A. Mathews, *Genesis 1–11:26*, NAC (Nashville: Broadman & Holman, 1996), 245–48.

[4] Unless otherwise noted, all Scripture citations in this chapter are from the Holman Christian Standard Bible (HCSB).

as the plan to restore that blessed estate and purpose for his creation developed, God selected one family with a view to the restoration of rulership. The New Testament affirms that the anticipated King is Jesus the Messiah, the second Adam [Rom. 5:12–21], a son of David of the tribe of Judah.[5]

⊕ *Deuteronomy 18:15*

Moses led the Hebrews out of Egypt, divided the Red Sea, worked miracles, brought the Ten Commandments down from the mountain, and produced the Torah, the first five books of the Old Testament. Given all that he had done, the words of Deuteronomy 18:15 are important: "The LORD your God will raise up for you a prophet like me [Moses] from among your own brothers. You must listen to him."

From the greater context (18:15–22), it is clear that a series of prophets would be raised up by God to follow Moses. Yet he did say, "A prophet like me," and in Israel's history the nation began to anticipate a prophet whom they associated either with or as the Messiah. Thompson points out,

> In later times, particularly after the cessation of prophecy, an individual interpretation was given to this passage and 'the prophet who should come' became a figure associated with the Messianic age and sometimes identified with the Messiah himself (cf. John 1:21,45; 6:14; 7:40; Acts 3:20–22; 7:37, etc.).[6]

God's deliverer would be someone who would speak for God in an authoritative manner similar to the way that Moses had.

✆ *2 Samuel 7:1–29*

Here is the Lord's great promise to his servant King David. Verses 9–14 are especially significant as they delineate the specific promises God made to David in the Davidic covenant:

- "I will make a name for you like that of the greatest in the land" (7:9).
- "[I] will make a house (royal dynasty) for you" (7:11).
- "I will raise up after you your descendant, who will come from your body, and I will establish his kingdom [and] . . . the throne of his kingdom forever" (7:12–13).
- "I will be a Father to him, and he will be a son to Me" (7:14).
- "But My faithful love will never leave him" (7:15).

---

[5] Allen Ross, *Creation and Blessing* (Grand Rapids: Baker, 1988), 703–4.
[6] J. A. Thompson, *Deuteronomy,* TOTC (Downers Grove: InterVarsity, 1974), 212–13.

- "Your house and kingdom will endure before Me forever, and your throne will be established forever" (7:16).

God had been working in and through the nation of Israel since the time of Abraham. Now he committed himself to one of Abraham and Judah's descendents in order to fulfill his promises to Adam and Eve (Gen. 3:15), Abraham (Gen. 12:1–3), and Judah (Gen. 49:9–10). By means of an unconditional covenant (note the repeated "I will's"), God promised to establish an eternal Davidic dynasty. This is a classic example of a prophecy with a dual fulfillment, with both a near and a far focus. Immediately David's son Solomon is pictured as the one who would succeed his father in the Davidic monarchy. He is the one to build the temple, and God will punish him when he sins. The prophecy also has a distant fulfillment as 2 Samuel 7:16 clearly indicates when it speaks of a throne that will be established forever. This promise now becomes the focal point of messianic hope and expectation. A future descendent of David will come and reign as Israel's messianic King.

Encapsulating the promises made to Abraham and Judah, he will be a blessing to the whole earth and also a sovereign King. Bergen highlights what this entails:

> The Lord's words spoken here demonstrate him to be the promise-keeping God; having prophetically placed the scepter in Judah hundreds of years earlier (Gen. 49:10), he here secured its place within that tribe. . . . David is made the founder of the only royal family the Lord would ever sanction in perpetuity. . . . The covenant that the Lord established with the house of David became the nucleus around which the messages of hope proclaimed by Hebrew prophets of later generations were built (cf. Isa. 9:1–7; 11:1–16; 16:5; 55:3; Jer. 23:5–6; 30:8; 33:15–26; Ezek. 34:23–24; 37:24–25; Hos. 3:5; Amos 9:11; Zech. 12:7–8).[7]

The nation anticipates a deliverer who will be a king and a descendent of David. What the nation expects will be fulfilled in Jesus of Nazareth.

(b) *The Psalms*

The Psalms are some of the most fertile soil in all of Scripture to help us see the emerging portrait of God's coming deliverer. Psalms which are categorized as royal or messianic include Psalms 2; 16; 18; 20; 22; 45; 72; 89; and 110. The song of lament, Psalm 22, is so striking in its similarity to the crucifixion of Jesus that many Bible scholars have referred to it as the

---

[7] Robert D. Bergen, *1, 2 Samuel,* NAC (Nashville: Broadman & Holman, 1996), 336–37.

"crucifixion psalm." Psalm 16 is significant because of its promise of life beyond the grave and its ultimate fulfillment in the resurrection of Jesus (see Acts 2:25–31; 13:35–37).

Psalm 2. In this royal Psalm composed perhaps for the coronation of a Davidic king, he is called the Lord's "Anointed One (i.e. Messiah)": "You are My Son; today I have become Your Father" (v. 7). And again in verse 12, "Pay homage to the Son, or He will be angry, and you will perish in your rebellion."

This king (v. 6) is a Son who will rule not just Israel but the nations (2:8–9). All are called to pay homage to (submit to) him. Though Davidic kings in the past could have celebrated their coronation in this psalm, it looks beyond these kings to God's eschatological King, his Anointed One who will rule over David's house forever. VanGemeren notes this psalm is one of the most quoted in the New Testament:

> The first-century church applied the second psalm to the Messiah as an explanation of the crucifixion of Christ by the rulers (Herod and Pontius Pilate), the nations, and Israel (the priests, scribes and Pharisees). They had conspired together against the Messiah of God (Acts 4:25–28). Paul applied it to Jesus' ministry: his sonship, resurrection, and ascension to glory, which confirmed God's promises in Jesus as *the* Messiah (Acts 13:22–33).[8]

This psalm held hope for a greater day and a greater King that all the nations would recognize.

Psalm 16. This prayer song expresses confidence and trust in God both in life and in death. Verses 10–11 are crucial in their expression of hope beyond the grave: "For You will not abandon me to Sheol; You will not allow Your Faithful One to see the Pit. You reveal the path of life to me; in Your presence is abundant joy; in Your right hand are eternal pleasures."

This psalm of prayer is also a psalm of prophecy. It includes the provision of resurrection or deliverance from the grave for God's faithful one. Both Peter (Acts 2:25–28,31) and Paul (Acts 13:35–37) interpreted and applied this text Christologically.

Psalm 22. Spurgeon calls Psalm 22 "the Psalm of the Cross."[9] A psalm of lament, it is properly applied first to King David. However, the words of anguish of the godly sufferer in the psalm transcend any experience of David. There will be a righteous sufferer who will be forsaken by God (22:1–2). He will suffer spiritually as well as physically. He will experience spiritual separation (22:1–2), verbal scorn (22:6–8), personal solitude

---

8 Willem A. VanGemeren, *Psalms,* EBC (Grand Rapids: Zondervan, 1991), 65.
9 C. H. Spurgeon, *The Treasury of David* (Grand Rapids: Zondervan, 1979), 1:324.

(22:9–11), bodily suffering (22:12–16), and personal shame (22:17–18). Yet in spite of his great loss, God's servant rests in the confidence of God's deliverance (22:19–21). He is certain that God will allow him to again proclaim the Lord's name (22:22) even to the ends of the earth (22:27). Kidner says of Psalm 22:

> No Christian can read this without being vividly confronted with the crucifixion. It [Psalm 22] is not only a matter of prophecy minutely fulfilled [note in particular 22:1,6–9,14–18], but of the sufferer's humility—there is no plea for vengeance—and his vision of a world-wide ingathering of the Gentiles."[10]

Here is the prediction of God's righteous sufferer being crucified one thousand years in advance, and several hundred years before the Medes and the Persians would even invent this torturous and inhumane method of execution.[11]

Psalm 110. No psalm is more clearly messianic than this king-priest hymn, It bears the marks of a coronation psalm for the Davidic king, but the language transcends any ancient king of Israel. So exalted is the language that the Hebrew people viewed it messianically, even before the Christian era. House notes that "the whole text assumes divine authority and future (both immediate and long term) perspective. Not everything promised in Psalm 110 can unfold in David's lifetime, so his descendents must be included in some manner."[12] Two verses in particular stand out: "The LORD declared to my Lord: 'Sit at My right hand until I make Your enemies Your footstool'" (Ps. 110:1). "The LORD has sworn an oath and will not take it back: 'Forever, You are a priest like Melchizedek'" (Ps. 110:4).

Several important observations arise from these two verses. First, Yahweh (trans. LORD) gives to David's Lord authority over all his enemies in words that recall the glory and honor given to God's anointed in Psalm 2. Second, it makes this Davidic king a coregent with Yahweh (cf. Ps. 89:27). Third, because of the Lord's promise, this Davidic ruler will "extend Your mighty scepter from Zion" (110:2–3).[13] Fourth, this Davidic ruler will be a "king-priest" but one of a unique order. On rare occasions a king from Israel functioned temporarily as a priest (cf. 2 Sam. 6:13–17). More often they

---

[10] Derek Kidner, *Psalms 1–72*, TOTC (Downers Grove: InterVarsity, 1973), 105.

[11] Grant Osborne, "Crucifixion," *BEB*, ed. W. A. Elwell (Grand Rapids: Baker, 1988), 1:555.

[12] Paul House, *Old Testament Theology* (Downers Grove: InterVarsity, 1998), 419–20.

[13] In Psalm 110:6 we read, "He will judge the nations, heaping up corpses; He will crush leaders over the entire world." The word that is translated "leaders" can also mean "heads," which recalls Genesis 3:15, where the Lord had sworn to the serpent that the seed of the woman would crush his "head."

were rebuked and punished for usurping an assignment that was not theirs (Saul in 1 Sam. 13:8–15 and Uzziah in 2 Chron. 26:16–21).[14]

This king-priest is altogether different. The Lord invokes the oath whereby his priesthood is established. Further, he is to be a priest forever. Finally, his order is not that of Aaron but of the ancient and mysterious king-priest Melchizedek (Gen. 14:17–20). As House writes:

> This passage reaffirms not only the importance of the Davidic covenant but also its eternal nature and partially redefines it at the same time. . . . A Davidic King will emerge who will rule victoriously as both king and priest, who will defeat all enemies, who will endure forever. Higher privileges could hardly be imagined.[15]

(7) Isaiah 7:14

Isaiah is the most significant book among the prophets concerning the coming of Messiah, the Lord's deliverer. Texts like Isaiah 7:14; 9:6–7; 11:1–16; and the Servant Songs of 42:1–7; 49:1–6; 50:4–9; 52:13–53:12 are crucial to the developing picture which the Lord paints as redemptive history unfolds.[16]

Isaiah 7:14 is a prophecy to King Ahaz (735–715 BC) as he faced international threats. It is also another example of an Old Testament prophecy with a dual fulfillment, a near and a far aspect. Ahaz's rejection of the Lord (7:10–12) will bring judgment upon him and an apparent end to the Davidic dynasty (7:2). However, God will remain faithful to David. This is promised in the "Immanuel" prophecy (meaning "God with us") of 7:14. In some mysterious and sovereign act a divine-human Messiah will appear. If Ahaz will not ask for a sign (7:12), God will give him one anyway, one for him and all persons: "The virgin will conceive, have a son, and name him Immanuel" (7:14).

The word virgin is important. It is the Hebrew word almah. This word is more fluid and ambiguous than another Hebrew word, betulah, which always refers to a virgin. Almah means simply, "a young woman of marriageable age." While the word does not demand that the woman in view is a virgin, the idea would naturally be present in the Hebrew culture of the day.[17] However, it is the ambiguity of almah that allows for the near fulfillment in Isaiah's day and an eschatological fulfillment in another. Oswalt writes:

---

[14] House, Old Testament Theology, 420.

[15] Ibid.

[16] B. H. Carroll said, "Of the ancient prophets Isaiah was perhaps the most notable witness of the coming Messiah. An orderly combination of his many Messianic utterances amounts to more than a mere sketch." B. H. Carroll, Jesus the Christ (Nashville: Broadman, 1937), 23.

[17] John Oswalt, The Book of Isaiah, Chapters 1–39, NICOT (Grand Rapids: Eerdmans, 1986), 210.

The conclusion to which we are driven is that while the prophet [under divine inspiration] did not want to stress the virginity, neither did he wish to leave it aside. . . . Possibly, then, it is the dual focus of the oracle that explains the use of *álmâ* here. In the short term, the virgin conception does not seem to have had primary importance. Rather, the significance is that a child conceived at that moment would still be immature when the two threatening nations would have been destroyed (vv. 16,22).[18]

But there is something more. A child born in Ahaz's day, whether his own or one born to Isaiah, is not a sign of God's continuing presence. Oswalt adds,

> If a virgin overshadowed by God's Spirit should conceive and give birth, it would not only be a sign of God's presence with us. Better than that, it would be the reality of that experience. So Ahaz's sign must be rooted in its own time to have significance for that time, but it also must extend beyond that time and into a much more universal mode if its radical truth is to be any more than a vain hope.[19]

③ *Isaiah 9:6–7*

The passage is an extension of the "virgin conception/Immanuel prophecy" of Isaiah 7:14. Israel would be attacked and crushed in humiliating defeat in 722 BC by the Assyrians. And yet, in the midst of their despair and hopelessness, a word of hope arrives. The gloom, distress, humiliation, darkness, and death of 9:1–2 would be turned into the rejoicing, joy, light, liberation, and peace of 9:2–5. How? By the coming of the Messiah-King. E. J. Young nicely paraphrases the hope that springs out of the despair of their immediate circumstances:

> There is great rejoicing among God's people, because God has broken the yoke of burden and oppression, and the burden and oppression are removed because the weapons and garments of the warrior are destroyed, and the basic reason for these blessings is that a Child is born. In contrast to the mighty foe of Assyria and also to the Syro-Ephraimitic coalition, a Child brings deliverance to the people of God.[20]

---

[18] Ibid., 211.
[19] Ibid.
[20] E. J. Young, *The Book of Isaiah* (Grand Rapids: Eerdmans, 1965), 1:329.

This child is the same as the child of 7:14. There his birth was a sign; here it is the means of deliverance and salvation.[21]

Oswalt notes that Jewish writers in the medieval period (ca. AD 500–1500) attempted to counter the prevailing Christian interpretation that this was a reference to Jesus the Messiah by arguing that it was simply a royal hymn honoring the birth of Hezekiah. He goes on to show, however, that "this view flies in the face of the chronology of Hezekiah's birth, and even more seriously, it is evident from the language that no merely human king is being spoken of. This is clearly an eschatological figure, the Messiah."[22] This Davidic ruler is now described in terms that carry messianic hope to an entirely new level. "A child will be born" emphasizes his humanity. "A son will be given" emphasizes his deity. "The expected perfect king will be human and divine."[23] Government will rest on this child. He will be a king, a ruler, a sovereign lord.

Note also his titles: He will be called Wonderful Counselor, Mighty God, Eternal Father, Prince of Peace (Isa. 9:6).

He is a "wonder of a counselor." This divine deliverer is wondrous and unfathomable in his wisdom. With perfect insight and a heart of compassion he will guide, lead, and provide direction. "Mighty God" is striking. Such a bold declaration causes some to see it as "an example of popular hyperbole."[24] Such a reading is untrue to the plain meaning of the text. "Mighty God" (Heb. *el gibbor*) is always used in the Old Testament as a reference to God (Isa. 10:21; cf. also Deut. 10:21; Jer. 32:18).[25] This is a clear and direct affirmation of Messiah's deity. What that would mean was, no doubt, shrouded in mystery at the time of the prophecy, but there is no textual reason for shying away from what it says. "Eternal Father" is nearly as striking as "Mighty God." The Messiah's fatherhood is said to last forever. It is eternal. It will never end. The word *Father* is qualitative. It tells us something about the character of Messiah and his relationship to his people.[26] "Prince of Peace" reveals that he is a king who brings peace. "This one is a Prince, and he seeks the greatness of His kingdom and of Himself, not in war, as do ordinary rulers, but in peace."[27]

---

[21] Ibid.

[22] Oswalt, *The Book of Isaiah,* 245.

[23] Ibid.

[24] Young, *The Book of Isaiah,* 335.

[25] Oswalt, *The Book of Isaiah,* 247.

[26] Describing the character of Messiah as "fatherly" does not compromise trinitarian doctrine. The oneness of God as to his essence or essential being would demand that each person of the Godhead share and possess the same characteristics and qualities. Messiah is not God the Father, but he is fatherly in his love and care for his people.

[27] Young, *The Book of Isaiah,* 339.

Verse 7 of Isaiah is eschatological in focus. This King "will be the final king, the king to end all kings."[28] His government and peace will not end. He will reign as the messianic heir to David's throne (cf. 2 Sam. 7:12–16) forever. It is clear that Messiah will be a great King, a world Savior and a harbinger of peace.

Isaiah 52:13–53:12

This text introduces us to the Suffering Servant of the Lord. Kyle Yates, former Old Testament professor at Southern Seminary, says it is "the Mt. Everest of Old Testament prophecy." Engnell said that it "may without any exaggeration be called the most important text of the Old Testament."[29] According to Delitzsch, it is "the most central, the deepest, and the loftiest thing that the Old Testament prophecy, outstripping itself, has ever achieved. . . . It looks as if it had been written beneath the cross upon Golgotha."[30] The text is the fourth of the great Servant Songs of Isaiah, and it is climactic (cf. 42:1–7; 49:1–6; 50:4–9). The twin themes of exaltation and humiliation are woven into a beautiful tapestry.

Who is the Suffering Servant? Commentators may be grouped into three schools of interpretation. First, some understand the text *corporately*. The text speaks of either the nation or the remnant within the nation as the ideal Israel (cf. 49:3). This view developed in medieval Jewish thought but fails to account for the work accomplished by this servant. Israel could not atone for her own sins, much less the sins of the nations. Second, some view the servant as Isaiah himself, Hezekiah, Jeremiah, Zerubbabel, or Moses. Yet what is said of the servant scarcely fits the life or ministry of any of these. Third, some hold that the servant represents the coming Messiah, the royal Davidic King, the *ideal* Israelite who is totally committed to and consecrated for Yahweh's will and work. This servant embodies all that is good in Israel. The picture of the Servant of the Lord, of his mission to Israel and to the world, and of his substitutionary suffering, is prophecy of the future.

However, the New Testament reveals, as does the intertestamental period, that prior to the cross, Isaiah 53 was not uniformly interpreted or identified with the Messiah. Support for a suffering Messiah from the prophetic literature finds support in only two books: Isaiah and Zechariah. Indeed, the idea of a suffering Messiah was rejected outright by the followers of Jesus, as Peter's remarks in Mark 8:31–34 make abundantly clear. Yet the cross and resurrection functioned as an interpretative key which opened the eyes of the early church to the true identity of the Suffering Servant. Philip the

28 Oswalt, *The Book of Isaiah,* 248.
29 I. Engnell, "The 'Ebed Yahweh Songs and the Suffering Messiah in Deutero-Isaiah," *Bulletin of John Rylands Library* 31 (January 1948): 73.
30 C. F. Keil and F. Delitzsch, *Isaiah,* Commentary on the Old Testament, trans. James Martin (repr., Grand Rapids: Eerdmans, 1975), 303.

evangelist makes plain in Acts 8:35 that the Suffering Servant is Jesus, and Isaiah 53 is directly cited no less than seven times in the New Testament with more than forty allusions. Jesus (Mark 10:45) weds Isaiah's Suffering Servant to Daniel's son of man (Dan. 7:13–14) and thereby redefines for us who and what Messiah will be.

What did the Servant accomplish? He bore our griefs (53:4). He carried our sorrows (53:4). He was wounded for our transgressions (53:5). He was bruised for our iniquities (53:5). He was chastised for our peace (53:5). He healed us by his stripes (53:5). He bore our iniquities (53:6,11). He was oppressed and afflicted (53:7). He was slaughtered (53:7). He was cut off (53:8). He was stricken for our transgressions (53:8). He was bruised by the Lord (53:10). He was put to grief (53:10). His soul was made a sin offering (53:10). He poured out his soul to death (53:12). He was numbered with the transgressors (53:12). He bore the sin of many (53:12). He made intercession for the transgressors (53:12).[31]

Isaiah 53:6 is especially crucial. Ironside called this "the most wonderful text in the Bible."[32] "We all went astray like sheep." We are prone to get lost, ever unaware of the danger that is about us, oblivious to the consequences of wrong choices. "We all have turned to our own way." Each of us has chosen our way over God's way. "And the Lord has punished Him (caused to land, caused to fall) for the iniquity of us all." Beginning with verse 4 we are immersed in the language of sacrifice and atonement, of substitution and salvation.

Daniel Block joins these various themes together. He notes:

> The messianic hope is a single line that begins in broadest terms with God's promise of victory over the serpent through 'the seed of woman' (Gen. 3:15), then is narrowed successively to the seed of Abraham (Gen. 22:18), the tribe of Judah (Gen. 49:10), the stem of Jesse (Isa. 11:1), the house/dynasty of David (2 Sam. 7) and finally the suffering and slain servant of Yahweh (Isa. 53).[33]

Daniel 7:13–14

In this text the mysterious "son of man" is introduced against the backdrop of judgment against the empires of this world and the ultimate victory of God. This is the only overt reference in the Old Testament to Messiah as the Son of Man. That the Messiah is in view, however, is certainly the teaching of the text.

---

[31] Isaiah's use of the perfect tense should not go unnoticed. He clearly intends to emphasize the certainty of these events.

[32] H. A. Ironside, *Isaiah* (Neptune, N. J.: Loizeaux Brothers, 1952), 301.

[33] Personal notes shared with the author.

I continued watching in the night visions,
and I saw One like a son of man
coming with the clouds of heaven.
He approached the Ancient of Days
and was escorted before Him.
He was given authority to rule,
and glory, and a kingdom;
so that those of every people,
nation, and language
should serve Him.
His dominion is an everlasting dominion
that will not pass away,
and His kingdom is one
that will not be destroyed (Dan. 7:13–14).

The language of these verses is reminiscent of Genesis 1:28; 2 Samuel 7:12–16; Psalms 2; 8; and Isaiah 9:7. The one described as "like a son of man" has the appearance of a man, but he is much more than a mere mortal. He comes with the clouds, a signature of deity in the ancient world.[34] He is given rule over all things, coronated by the "Ancient of Days," God himself. He is to be served, and his kingdom is everlasting. This final eschatological ruler is not just a man; he is "the heavenly Sovereign incarnate."[35] That Daniel 7:13–14 speaks of Messiah is a view that dates back to early Jewish, and of course Christian, interpreters. Rabbinic interpreters and the Talmud (*Sanhedrin* 98a) saw the one described in these verses as God's Messiah.[36] That he would partake of characteristics and honor that are both human and divine would be something of a mystery to the initial Hebrew readers. In the coming of the Son, the veil is removed.

(11) *Micah 5:2*

A day of judgment is on Jerusalem's horizon (Mic. 5:1). However, a promised deliverer will appear from the tiny and insignificant town of Bethlehem. He is "to be ruler over Israel," and amazingly, "His origin is from antiquity, from eternity." There is, at least by implication, an indication that Messiah will be divine, that in some sense he is a preexistent person. He is born in Bethlehem, but he is also one who has existed from eternity.

There is no question that the Old Testament picture of Messiah is mysterious and complex. Step-by-step God reveals to us who the deliverer would be and what the deliverer would do. Kaiser is correct when he says, "The

---

[34] Stephen Miller, *Daniel*, NAC (Nashville: Broadman & Holman, 1994), 207.

[35] Gleason Archer, *Daniel*, EBC (Grand Rapids: Zondervan, 1985), 90.

[36] Miller, *Daniel*, 209.

OT writers did consciously and knowingly write and point to the Messiah as being a special son born in the line of David, with the special divine nature that belonged to God alone."[37]

This, then, is what was revealed. This is what we will discover in Jesus of Nazareth, a first-century Jew and God's Messiah-Son.

(handwritten note: From above →Jn 1:1–18; Phili. 2:5–11; Col. 1:15–23; Heb. 1:1–4)

The New Testament's Witness to Christology

Biblical Christology sees no distinction between the Jesus who actually lived, the Jesus as reported in the Gospels, the Lord Jesus Christ of the letters of the New Testament, and the Jesus Christ of the Christological creeds. The Jesus of history and the Christ of faith is one and the same. It is recognized that the New Testament witness to Christ is rich, but there are certain core beliefs that underlie and unite the wonderful diversity of the New Testament.

The witness of the New Testament is that God indeed became one of us in the person of Jesus Christ. The Old Testament promised that he would come, and the New Testament testifies that he came. The New Testament records a varied and complementary witness to the God who took on humanity, the Word who became flesh (John 1:14). A quintessential quartet stands out in what they teach concerning both the deity and humanity of Jesus. The texts are John 1:1–18; Philippians 2:5–11; Colossians 1:15–23 (2:9–10); and Hebrews 1:1–4. They provide for us what Pannenberg identified as a "Christology from above." Giving careful attention to each one is, in our judgment, a healthy and wise approach to Christology.

① *John 1:1–18: The God of Incarnation (The Prologue of John).*

Modern persons often have difficulty with the deity of Christ. People of the first century actually had more difficulty with his humanity. John's prologue (1:1–18), as well as other parts of his Gospel, addresses both. Jesus is identified as the *Logos* (revelation/communication) of God; the Life (creation/salvation) of God; and the Light (salvation/revelation) of God. The doctrine of the incarnation is clearly set forth, tying together his deity and humanity. The importance of John 1:14 can scarcely be overemphasized: "The Word became flesh and took up residence among us." In addition, John elsewhere emphasizes the Son's unique relationship to the Father and provides the most significant material in Scripture for the development of the doctrine of the Trinity. This is found in the upper room discourse of Jesus in John 14–17. Here a number of important themes are expressed: (1) the essential oneness of the Father and the Son (14:9–10); (2) the distinc-

---

[37] Walter Kaiser, *Toward Rediscovering the Old Testament* (Grand Rapids: Zondervan, 1987), 109. One should also consider the intriguing treatment of Messiah and the Old Testament by John Sailhamer, "The Messiah and the Hebrew Bible," *JETS* 44 (March 2001), 1:5–23.

tiveness of persons within the Godhead (14:16–18); and, (3) the functional subordination of the Son to the Father (14:24,31; 16:5,28).

Jesus: The Logos of God. Jesus is called the Word or *Logos* in John 1:1,14. *Logos* is a word with a rich and varied history. A number of potential sources for John's concept and usage have been proffered: (1) Palestinian Judaism—Wisdom is often personified, and this usage is found in some ancient Jewish writings outside the Bible. Here *Logos* is the wisdom or thought of God. (2) Greek Philosophy—*Logos* stood for reason, reflecting the Greek view that divinity cannot come into direct contact with evil, or inferior, matter. The Stoics saw *Logos* as both divine reason and reason distributed in the world (and therefore the mind). It is a creative force, the rational principle of order. (3) Hellenistic Judaism—Prominent for example in the writings of the Greek Alexandrian Jew and philosopher Philo (the term appears over 1,300 times), the Word is fully personified in relation to creation, being the means whereby God creates the world from great waste. Furthermore, it is the way in which God is known in the mind. However, the *Logos* (or "Word") is neither personal nor preexistent. (4) The Old Testament—Here the "Word of God" is seen as (a) the agent of creation (Gen. 1; Ps. 33:6ff; Prov. 8:22ff); (b) the agent of revelation (Gen. 12:1; 15:1; 22:11; Prov. 8; Isa. 9:8; Jer. 1:4; 20:8; Ezek. 33:7; Amos 3:1,8); (c) eternal (Ps. 119:89); (d) the agent of redemption (Ps. 107:20).[38]

Bruce notes, "The 'word of God' in the O.T. denotes God in action, especially in creation, revelation, and deliverance."[39] John uses *Logos* because of its capacity to communicate to multiple cultures, i.e., Jewish and hellenistic. He uses it for the purpose of missions and evangelism. The term itself was well-known, but John fills it with "new meaning." Philo's *Logos* was "reason" and an "it." John's *Logos* is "the Word" and a "he." Philo's *Logos* was a principle. John's *Logos* is a person. John's *Logos* is not only God's agent in creation; he is God. He is God's personal, visible (1:14) communication to man in revealing and redeeming power. The term *Logos* does not explain Jesus; Jesus explains and fills *Logos* with new meaning. Wisdom has become a person; divine reason, a man. The Greeks were correct in affirming that we could not reach the *Logos*. John informs us that the *Logos* came down and lived among us.

Walls notes, "It is not accidental that both the gospel and Christ who is its subject are called 'the word.' But the use of 'Logos' in the contemporary Hellenistic world made it a useful 'bridge word.'"[40] To the Greeks *Logos* is reason. To the Jews *Logos* is the word/wisdom. In John these

---

[38] Jim Parker, "The Incarnational Christology of John," *CTR* 3 (Fall 1988): 31–39; Andrew Walls, "Logos," *BDT* (Grand Rapids: Baker, 1960), 327–28.

[39] F. F. Bruce, *The Gospel of John* (Grand Rapids: Eerdmans, 1983), 29.

[40] Walls, "Logos," 328.

ideas find new meaning as they are embodied in a person, Jesus Christ. John's use of *Logos* is an example of cross-cultural communication of the gospel at its best.

Theological truths gleaned from the prologue. Although John 1:1 is verbally parallel to Genesis 1:1 and 1 John 1:1, the context of these beginnings is different. Genesis 1:1 speaks of the beginning of creation. First John 1:1 emphasizes the manifestation of God in Christ. In John 1:1, the Apostle John establishes the preexistence of the Word in eternity past. "In the beginning was the *Logos*." The *Logos* already "was" when the beginning took place. Furthermore, this *Logos* was "face-to-face with" God, indicating a distinction of persons within the Godhead, as well as an equality of persons. There was never a time when the *Logos* was not fully God. Indeed, he is affirmed as being coequal, coeternal, coexistent, and consubstantial with the Father.

Tenney gives support to this understanding when he writes:

> The three statements of v. 1 bring out . . . different aspects of the nature of the Word. The first speaks of His pre-existence. The second statement "The Word was with God," is an assertion of the Word's distinctiveness. The preposition *pros* [translated "with"] indicates both equality and distinction of identity. [A. T.] Robertson says, "The literal idea comes out well, "face to face with God"" (*RHG,* p. 623). This implies personality and coexistence with God. The third statement, "The Word was God is especially significant. This is a clear statement of deity."[41]

The Watchtower Society (Jehovah's Witnesses) has attempted to build a theology that denies the full deity and eternality of the Son, and the grammar of this verse is central to their argument. They argue that the last phrase of verse 1 should be translated "and the Word was a god." In translating the last phrase of verse 1 like this, the Jehovah's Witnesses actually accomplish what they wish to avoid. Following the plain sense of their interpretation, we now have two gods. There is the supreme God, the Father, and there is a lesser god, the Son. This is ditheism plain and simple. Furthermore, to say that the absence of the definite article "the" before the word "God" somehow teaches a denial of the full and undiminished deity of the Son is clearly incorrect. There are many places in the Gospel of John where the anarthrous *theos* (the word "God" appearing without a definite article "the" in front of it) is used (e.g., 1:6,12–13,18), and not once is there the slightest

---

[41] Merrill Tenney, *John,* EBC (Grand Rapids: Zondervan, 1981), 29. The A.T. Robertson quote is from *A Grammar of the Greek New Testament in the Light of Historical Research* (Nashville: Broadman Press, 1934), 623.

hint that the text is referring to just "a god." It is clear that John is strongly asserting, "The Word was God."

Tenney notes, "'The Word' was deity, one with God, rather than 'a god' or another being of the same class. . . . Unity of nature rather than similarity or likeness is implied. The external coexistence and unity of the Word with God is unmistakably asserted."[42]

This opening verse in a real sense serves as the basis for all that follows in John's Gospel and in another sense is the foundational pillar upon which the Christian faith rests. John goes on in verse 3 to affirm that not a single thing that exists came into being except through him. This truth is also affirmed in Colossians 1:16 and Hebrews 1:2. That he created all things logically and necessarily leads to the conclusion that he himself is not created. The importance of this theological proposition cannot be emphasized too strongly. Bruce writes:

> When heaven and earth were created, there was the Word of God, already existing in the closest association with God and partaking of the essence of God. No matter how far back we may try to push our imagination, we can never reach a point at which we could say of the Divine Word, as Arius did, "There once was when He was not."[43]

Join this with the fact that a Jew like the Apostle John would only know the God of Genesis 1–2 as the Creator, and you have further evidence of the full deity of Jesus, testified by one who was an eyewitness.

Perhaps some type of incipient Gnosticism, or better, Docetism, necessitates verse 14. Gnosticism, from the Greek word *gnosis* meaning "knowledge," teaches that salvation is by mystical knowledge and that the material world is inferior or evil. Docetism, meaning "to appear," says Christ was some type of phantom or mystical spirit who did not have a real, physical body. Both false teachings denied the genuineness of the incarnation whereby God took to himself humanity. Heresy is always our enemy, but on occasion it serves as an unwitting friend to sharpen our focus and refine our theological thinking. John insists that the Word is not only truly God; he has also become truly human. In this Gospel John records that our Lord was tired and thirsty (4:6–7); he wept (11:35); he was troubled in spirit (12:17; 13:21); and he bled and died (19:30). Without becoming less than God (cf. Phil. 2:5–11), the Son took upon himself complete humanity, apart from sin (2 Cor. 5:21; Heb. 4:15). John affirms, "He became flesh" (*sarx*, Gk.).

---

[42] Ibid., 28.
[43] Bruce, *The Gospel of John,* 31.

At his incarnation God did not become man; he became God-man. The words "dwelt among us" (*eskēnosen*, Gk.) can be understood to mean "pitched his tent" or "tabernacled among us." Just as the Hebrew *Shekinah* ("glory"), the bright cloud of God's glorious person settled upon the tabernacle (Exod. 24:16; 40:35), even so in Christ God's glorious person dwelt among men and they beheld, gazed upon, and examined his glory.[44] To be theologically precise, we can say there was a time when Jesus was not. However, there was never a time when the Son was not. At the incarnation the Son became Jesus; the second person of the triune God became the God-man. The one who was from all eternity in the most intimate and personal relationship with the Father "exegeted," declared, explained, and made known the Father (John 1:18).

> Light looked down and beheld darkness,
> thither will I go said light.
> Life looked down and beheld death,
> Thither will I go said Life.
> Love looked down and beheld despair,
> Thither will I go said love.
> So came Light and shone truth,
> So came Life and conquered death.
> So came Love and gave hope.
> "And the Word became flesh and dwelt among us."
> —Author Unknown

(2) Philippians 2:5–11: The God of Humiliation.

The "Christ hymns" of the New Testament provide insight into the theology and worship of the early church. Many students of the Bible believe that at least the following should be recognized as early confessional/worship hymns to Christ: Ephesians 2:14–16; Philippians 2:6–11; Colossians 1:15–20; 1 Timothy 3:16; Hebrews 1:1–3; 1 Peter 3:18–22 (and perhaps the prologue of the Gospel of John).

When we consider the date, context, and varied locations of these hymns, certain things stand out: (1) The hymns are confessional and liturgical (occurring in the context of worship) and reveal the kind of Christological affirmations made by the early church. (2) Because the hymns are earlier than their citation in the New Testament, they are more primitive than the New Testament as to their origin. (3) The hymns represent "Christological explosions" of worship and adoration in the early church. (4) The rich Christological content of the hymns teaches us that early in the history

---

[44] D. A. Carson, *The Gospel According to John* (Grand Rapids: Eerdmans, 1991), 126–28.

of the church, the believing community in praise, worship, and teaching had a high Christology. Already they viewed Jesus as God and man. There was simply insufficient time between the Christ-event and the composition of these hymns for embellishment, myth, and fanciful elaboration to take place as some modern critics assert.[45]

Philippians 2 stands out in its significance for constructing a biblical Christology. Hawthorne calls it "a Christological gem unparalleled in the New Testament."[46] This particular passage is especially noted for two important aspects of Christology: (1) The kenosis doctrine or "emptying of Christ," as God the Son became a man, and (2) the "hypostatic union" (the uniting of two natures in one person). Paul authored or possibly adapted an existing hymn. The primary intent is ethical, teaching us how to live out the "attitude of Christ" (v. 5) by following the example of Christ. However, theological and soteriological questions also may legitimately be answered from this text.[47]

The hymn should be arranged in its simplest and most basic form of two stanzas: (A) stanza 1, verses 6–8, Christ's humiliation; and (B) stanza 2, verses 9–11, Christ's exaltation. That the hymn has an ethical context is clear from 2:1–5. Here Paul urges the Philippians to "make your own attitude that of Christ Jesus." Verse 5 literally reads, "think you," and is a present imperative of command. This command is preceded by a call to: (1) unity (v. 2), (2) humility (v. 3), and (3) sensitivity (v. 4). Humility above all is identified as that character trait that exemplifies the mind of Christ. Thus, the hymn of 2:6–11 actually serves as an illustration of the mind of Christ, the mind that the believer should pursue and cultivate. Believers need to express genuine concern and compassion for one another, but this is not possible without adopting the same mind or attitude (disposition) which we discover in Christ. That Christ demonstrated such self-disregard, concern, and compassion is the theme of this hymn.

For Paul, like John, the starting point of the hymn is the preexistence of Christ. Both begin with a Christology "from above." Philippians 2:6 reads: "who, existing in the form of God." "Existing" emphasizes continued existence. Christ exists, and he forever has in the realm of eternity. He always is (cf. John 8:58). There never was a time when he was not. He is eternally existent. By definition this would mean he is God. The

---

[45] For an outstanding treatment of this and related issues, see Larry Hurtado, *Lord Jesus Christ: Devotions to Jesus in Earliest Christianity* (Grand Rapids: Eerdmans, 2003). Hurtado notes, "An exalted significance of Jesus appears astonishingly early in Christian circles. Well within the first couple of decades of the Christian movement . . . Jesus was treated as a recipient of religious devotion and was associated with God in striking ways. In fact . . . we probably have to posit a virtual explosion of devotion to Jesus toward the earlier part of this short period" (2).

[46] Gerald Hawthorne, *Philippians*, WBC (Waco: Word, 1983), 79.

[47] Ibid.

word translated "form" is *morphē* (Gk.). This word has been variously understood. Views include: (1) the essential nature and character of God; (2) the mode of being or way of being; (3) the image of God (a second Adam Christology, cf. Gen. 1:26–27); (4) the glory of God (viewed as a continuation of Johannine theology, cf. John 17:5). These perspectives are similar in meaning, and each highlights a truth about Jesus taught in the Bible.

An examination of *morphē* reveals that the word "refers to that form which truly and fully expresses the being which underlies it." Hence the idea "does not refer simply to external appearance but pictures the preexistent Christ as clothed in the garments of divine majesty and splendor."[48] The word itself can mean "form," "shape," "appearance," or "essence." Here *morphē* identifies Jesus with the essential nature and character of God. The idea is that of "outward display of an inner reality or substance." If this is correct, a combination of views number 1 and number 4 above is Paul's intended meaning. He affirms that Christ eternally exists in the nature, essence, essential being, and glory of God. *Morphē* (form) denotes Christ as possessing, or being the permanent unchangeable pattern of, deity.

But Christ "did not consider equality with God as something to be used for His own advantage" (Phil. 2:6b). This phrase looks back to the expression "existing in the form of God." Fiercely debated, it may mean that his equal status and privileges with God were not things that he violently sought to seize or believed he must forcibly retain. "Grasped" (HCSB marginal reading) is *harpagmos* (Gk.), and can mean (1) robbing (active sense) or (2) a prize gained through robbery (passive sense).[49] The idea seems to be that being coequal and coeternal with God by the very nature of his being, equality with God was not something Christ had to forcibly strive for (as if he did not possess it) or assert (as if he could lose it). Bruce notes in this context: "There is no question of Christ's trying to snatch or seize equality with God: that was already his because he always had the nature of God. Neither is there any question of his trying to retain it by force. The point is rather that he did not treat his equality with God as an excuse for self-assertion or self-aggrandizement; on the contrary, he treated it as an occasion for renouncing every advantage or privilege that might have accrued to him thereby, as an opportunity for self-impoverishment and unreserved self-sacrifice."[50]

There also may be a contrast here with the story of Adam: Christ enjoyed true equality with God but refused to derive any advantage from it in

---

[48] Peter O'Brien, *The Epistle to the Philippians* (Grand Rapids: Eerdmans, 1991), 207–11.

[49] Ibid., 212–16.

[50] F. F. Bruce, *Philippians* (San Francisco: Harper & Row, 1983), 45.

becoming man, whereas Adam, a man made in the image of God, snatched at a false and illusory equality. Christ achieved universal lordship through his renunciation, whereas Adam forfeited his lordship through his "snatching." If a Christ/Adam contrast is in Paul's mind, a comparison of the two is instructive:

Adam and Christ
Comparison and Contrast

Adam	Christ
1. He was made in the divine image.	1. He was and is the very essence of God.
2. He thought it a prize to be grasped to be as God.	2. He thought it not a prize to be grasped to be as God.
3. He aspired to a reputation.	3. He made himself of no reputation.
4. He spurned being God's servant.	4. He took upon himself the form (*morphē*) of a slave (*doulos*).
5. He sought to be in the very likeness of God.	5. He was made in the likeness of men.
6. He, being found in fashion as a man (of dust, now doomed), exalted himself and became disobedient unto death.	6. He being found in fashion as a man (Rom. 8:3), humbled himself and became obedient unto death.
7. He was condemned and disgraced.	7. He was highly exalted by God and given the name and position of Lord.

Christ therefore grasped not at sovereignty but service. Adam was humanity seeking deity. Christ was deity seeking humanity. Philippians 2:7–8 says, "He emptied Himself." The crucial word is *kenaō* (Gk.), meaning simply "to empty." The import of this word requires both a contextual and theological interpretation, or an ethical and metaphysical perspective. Exegetically, verses 7–8 express a clear and straightforward understanding of what it means that Christ "emptied himself": (1) He assumed the form (*morphē*, Gk.) of a servant (*doulos*, Gk.). (2) He took on the likeness (*homoiōma*, Gk.) and external form (*schēma*, Gk.) of a man. (3) He humbled himself (cf. vv. 2–4). (4) He became obedient to the point of death. (5) He died a cross-type of death (one of ultimate humiliation). These verses express the idea that there was an emptying by addition. The Son did not surrender his deity; he added humanity. Further, the type of humanity he added was not that of a sovereign but that of a servant. He received not a crown but a cross.

Bruce notes, "It was in the manner of His death, His death on the cross, that the rock bottom of humiliation was reached. . . . By the standards of the first century, no experience could be more loathsomely degrading than that."[51] However, we must maintain a nonnegotiable truth: Deity cannot cease to be deity, so any understanding of *kenaō* ("to empty") which would point in this direction must quickly be dismissed.

Nevertheless, a real and genuine emptying took place. John 17:5 is crucial at this point. In his high priestly prayer our Lord said, "Now, Father, glorify Me in Your presence with the glory I had with You before the world existed." Jesus did not surrender his deity, but he did surrender his glory. He became in a sense "God incognito." He laid aside willingly, in humble obedience to the Father (1) the praises of heaven, (2) the position of heaven, and (3) the prerogatives of heaven. The wedding of deity and humanity was permanent. The emptying, however, was only for the time of incarnation. Christ temporarily laid aside the free and voluntary exercise of the rights and privileges of deity. The emptying therefore involved self-limitation as well as ultimate humiliation. Christ partook of unglorified humanity. He voluntarily forfeited, for a time, the free use of his divine attributes, depending instead on his Father and the Holy Spirit.

God, however, did not leave the drama unresolved. Jesus in humiliation totally reversed the priorities and principles of this world system. His Father affirmed his pleasure in his Son in his exaltation. Verses 9–11 affirm a threefold exaltation of the Savior: (1) verse 9, an exalted position; (2) verse 10, an exalted adoration; and (3) verse 11, an exalted confession. Philippians 2:9–11 begins with "for" and notes the consequent action of God the Father in light of the Son's voluntary obedience and humiliation by death on a cross. "Highly exalted" means to exalt above and beyond, "to super-exalt." No doubt Paul had in mind here our Lord's resurrection, ascension, and present session in heaven.[52]

"Gave Him the name" may have reference to the name Yahweh, Lord, or Jesus. Merit lies in all three options. The bowing of adoration (Phil. 2:10) and the word of confession (v. 11) serve to emphasize the deity and universal lordship of the Son, a reality that glorifies the Father. Isaiah 45:23 is echoed in verse 10. In Isaiah, Yahweh is in view. In Philippians, it is Jesus. It is no accident that Jesus has ascribed to him that which is ascribed to the God of the Old Testament, for Jesus is God. All will bow (v. 10). Nothing in all of creation is outside of the lordship and authority of the Lord Jesus Christ. Bruce is again helpful as he notes:

> "Jesus (Christ) is Lord" is the quintessential Christian creed, and in that creed "Lord" is given the most august sense that it can bear. When Christians in later generations refused to say "Caesar is Lord,"

---

[51] Ibid., 47.
[52] The parallels of Philippians 2:6–11 to Isaiah 52:13–53:12 are too striking to be accidental.

they refused because they knew that this was no mere courtesy title that Caesar claimed: It was a title that implied his right to receive divine honors, and in this sense they give it to none but Jesus. To them there was "only one God, the Father, . . . and . . . only one Lord, Jesus Christ" (1 Cor. 8:6). . . . When divine honors are thus paid to the humiliated and exalted Jesus, the glory of God the Father is not diminished but enhanced. When the Son is honored, the Father is glorified; for none can bestow on the Son higher honors than the Father himself has bestowed.[53]

(3) *Colossians 1:15–23: The God of Creation.*

Colossians 1–2 also plays a significant role in the battles that the church has fought in the area of Christology. Here we find one of the strongest statements of the full deity of Jesus Christ in the whole of Scripture. Bruce notes concerning the Christ-hymn of 1:15–20: "This is one of the great Christological passages of the N.T., declaring as it does our Lord's divine essence, pre-existence, and creative agency."[54]

These verses constitute a Christ-hymn exalting the Son as the supreme Lord.[55] Verse 15 begins with the affirmation that Christ is the "image (*eikōn*) of the invisible God" (cf. 2 Cor. 4:4). Carroll and Mullins note, "The word 'is' declares a permanent and abiding truth. Christ is in his essential nature the image of God."[56] *Eikōn* is a word meaning "likeness," "representation," "image," "form," "manifestation" and "reflection." This is a relative term in which the degree of likeness must be inferred from the context. The word is used twenty-three times in the New Testament but only twice with reference to Jesus. Here and in 2 Corinthians 4:4, it is used of a precise and absolute correspondence. Jesus Christ is the perfect visible manifestation of the invisible God. He is the representation and manifestation of the God who is invisible. Calvin, commenting on this text, wrote:

> [Paul] calls Him the *image of the invisible God,* meaning by this, that it is in him alone that God, who is otherwise invisible, is manifested to us. . . . Christ is called the *image of God* on this ground—that He makes God in a manner visible to us. . . . We must, therefore, beware of seeking Him [God] elsewhere, for everything

---

[53] Bruce, *Philippians,* 50–51.

[54] E. K. Simpson and F. F. Bruce, *Commentary on the Epistles to the Ephesians and Colossians,* NICNT (Grand Rapids: Eerdmans, 1957), 192.

[55] See F. F. Bruce, *The Epistles to the Colossians, to Philemon, and to the Ephesians,* NICNT (Grand Rapids: Eerdmans, 1984), 56–57.

[56] B. H. Carroll and E. Y. Mullins, *Studies in Romans, Ephesians, and Colossians* (Nashville: Broadman, 1936), 298.

that would set itself off as a representation of God apart from Christ, will be an idol.[57]

Eikōn does not imply a weak imitation or a feeble copy of something here. It implies the outward manifestation and illumination of something's inner core and essence. The word involves the twin ideas of representation and manifestation. The idea of perfection, however, does not lie in the word itself but must be inferred from the context. Here *eikōn* means that Christ is essentially and absolutely the perfect expression and representation of God the Father. The "image of the invisible" gives the sense that Christ is the visible representation and manifestation of the invisible God to created beings. Christ is the image of God in the sense that the nature and being of God is perfectly revealed in him. Adam may have been created *in* God's image, but Christ *is* God's image.

Paul's point is simple. Christ is not simply a picture of what God is like; he is God himself. As Jesus himself said, "The one who has seen Me has seen the Father" (John 14:9), and "Before Abraham was, I am" (John 8:58; see Exod. 3:14). Colossians 1:15 is an explicit affirmation of Christ's divine essence. Paul is affirming Christ as Lord and God, both of the cosmos (his material creation) and the church (his spiritual creation).

1. Christ is Lord of creation (1:15–17). Christ is called the firstborn (*prototokos*), both a "kind" or genus word and a "time" word. It may be *either/or*, or *both/and*. Here it conveys the ideas of primacy, priority, and supremacy; of priority in time and supremacy in rank. The word in this verse has both a temporal and a positional sense. To understand this term, particularly as it is applied to Christ, one must rid his mind of the idea that Christ is somehow the first of a long succession of creatures. Christ is not a creature; he is the Creator himself. This term points to the preeminence and preexistence of Christ.

"Firstborn" originally had the idea of the first son of the family who inherited the rights of the family; its name, property, etc. In fact, in some cases, his primogeniture (i.e., his "firstborn-ness") made him uniquely eligible to be the king. Psalm 89:27 should be noted in this context, pointing to the Davidic Messiah's special position of honor.[58]

In Colossians 1:15b, Paul has in mind that Christ is God the Father's first (and only) Son. This is analogous to John's use of *monogenēs* ("only-

---

[57] John Calvin, *Commentary on the Epistle to the Colossians,* Calvin's Commentaries, trans. William Pringle (Grand Rapids: Baker, 1996), 149–50. John Owen adds, "Without Christ we would have known nothing truly about God for he would have been eternally invisible to us." See his *The Glory of Christ* (repr. Edinburgh: Banner of Truth Trust, 1994), 11.

[58] Bruce, *Philippians,* 59.

begotten") in John 1:14,18; 3:16.[59] The idea is not that Christ was ever somehow "born" to God but rather that in his relationship to the Father in the Trinity, he enjoys all of the rights and privileges that the Father bestows upon him. This includes the _right_ to oversee the creation of all things, a creation that was created by him, for him, and in him. He is creation's conception, continuance, and consummation.

In Colossians, "firstborn" obviously has the nuance of supremacy and preeminence from the expressions that follow in verses 16–17. Christ is the source-agent and preserver of creation and is worthy of all honor. It is Christ as sustainer ("by Him all things hold together") who makes the universe a cosmos instead of a chaos. A rare word in the New Testament, *prōtotokos* is used twice here because of its emphasis on the divine preeminence of Jesus as the Lord of his universal creation and his new creation, the church.

Paul's point is that Christ is the Creator. A Jew such as Paul could only conceive of God as Creator. Further, since Christ created "all things," he himself must be uncreated, or the statement is untrue. The New World Translation, the Bible of the Jehovah's Witnesses, recognizes that this is a problem for its theology, and thus it supplies the word "other" five times in verses 16–20. Their Bible reads, "By means of him all [other] things were created" (v. 16). Note that "other" is in brackets. This, of course, reveals the word is not a part of the original text. The Son is not God's greatest creation through whom all else came into existence. He is the Creator, and by him all that is came into existence.

2. Christ is the Lord of the church (1:18–20). Christ also is the head of the body (18a), the church. The church owes him exclusive allegiance, complete devotion, and total obedience. This type of commitment is reserved only for God and, thus, for Christ because he is God. Paul affirms Christ's deity from every direction.

Notice again the term "firstborn" (Gk. *prōtotokos*) in verse 18b: "He is the beginning, the firstborn from the dead." Beginning (Gk. *archō*) may mean (1) supremacy in rank, (2) precedence in time, or (3) creative initiative. All three ideas are true, though creative initiative seems to be the idea Paul intends to convey.[60] We saw that *prōtotokos*, "firstborn," has to do with reference to Christ's position as Creator of all things. It is a word denoting source and preeminence. Here it has to do with the fact that Jesus conquered death in his resurrection. He is sovereign even over death. His resurrection is his claim to be head of the church.

---

[59] *Monogenēs* has usually been understood to mean unique, one of a kind. However, there has arisen some debate over the best understanding of the term. For a discussion of the issue, see Daniel L. Akin, *1,2,3 John,* NAC (Nashville: Broadman & Holman, 2001), 179.

[60] Curtis Vaughn, *Colossians,* EBC (Grand Rapids: Zondervan, 1978), 183.

Christ has full rights over the church because he conquered the great enemy of his people—death. In so doing he proved himself to be God. Hence, verse 18c sums up the matter: Christ should "have first place in everything."

Verse 19 explains that in Christ we see the essence of God. "All His fullness" means that Christ lacks nothing of what it means to be God. He possesses all the attributes of God (e.g., saving grace, love, goodness, light, omniscience, etc.). The word *fullness* was probably a technical term in the vocabulary of the false teachers. Paul uses this word eight times in this letter. It has the sense of "undiluted," "unalloyed"; Christ is "pure deity," (i.e., the sum total of all the divine power and attributes). "Nothing of deity is lacking in Christ."[61]

The phrase "dwell in Him" means to be at home permanently, to reside. There was never a time when Christ did not possess deity; he is always God. It is in this context that we add the contribution of Colossians 2:9–10, since it expands and supplements Colossians 1:19. The verse reads, "For in Him the entire fullness of God's nature dwells bodily."

"In Him" is emphatic and exclusive. It recalls 1:19. "The entire fullness" emphasizes comprehensiveness and completeness. This reiterates that Christ is completely God: there is nothing about the nature and essence of God that Christ does not possess.

"In Him the entire fullness of God's nature dwells" means that Christ is in his essence God. Paul takes this expression of Christ's deity one step further than in 1:19 by linking it with Christ's incarnation in the word *bodily*. Paul's point here is that Christ is fully God and fully man. This verse is therefore one of the New Testament's strongest affirmations of both Christ's deity and Christ's humanity, as well as the fact that he is both fully God and fully man at the same time.

3. Christ is Lord of the Christian (1:21–23). Paul now applies the doctrine he has presented to the Colossian believers. First, in verses 20–22, he explains that Christ, the mediator, has been able to reconcile the Colossian Christians to God, despite their initial hostility and sin, by his blood. Second, Paul declares that Christ can be counted on to take the Colossians on to a complete spiritual transformation so that they will become people acceptable to the Father. Their responsibility is to continue on in faith as they originally heard it and believed it and not to fall away into syncretistic errors. Christ's preeminence is of the utmost importance to the personal lives and destiny of the Colossian believers.

Summary. The point to remember from Colossians 1–2 is that Christ is God. The key verses that show this are 1:15; 1:19; and 2:9. Christ is fully

---

61 Ibid., 185.

and completely God. Because of his resurrection, believers confessed the lordship of Jesus in terms of his victory over death and his vindication by God. This lordship was seen to extend to creation itself. Nothing exists outside the sovereign lordship of Christ.

④ *Hebrews 1:1–4: The God of Revelation.*

Hebrews is a finely crafted series of sermons. There is, however, an overriding theme which links its thirteen chapters together: Jesus is God's very best. The words *better* or *superior* or *best* occur nineteen times in the New Testament, thirteen of those in Hebrews. Here we discover that Jesus:

- is better than the angels (1:4),
- provides a better hope (7:19),
- provides a better covenant (7:22; 8:6),
- provides better promises (8:6),
- provides a better sacrifice (9:23),
- provides a better possession (10:34),
- provides a better land (11:16),
- provides a better resurrection (11:35), and
- provides a better blood testimony (12:24).

The author of Hebrews believes Jesus is the best that God could send, the best that God could give; and, therefore, in the coming of Christ, God speaks, he speaks clearly, and he speaks with finality. Hebrews 1:1–4 affirms in a single and superlative sentence several crucial truths.

1. The superior revelation of the Son (1:1–2). Francis Schaeffer reminds us, "The infinite personal God is there, but also He is not silent; that changes the whole world."[62] Indeed the Christian God is a talking God, one who has been talking continually to his people. God's revelation through his prophets was true but partial (1:1). At different times and in different ways, God spoke. "God spoke"; and because it was God speaking, it was true; and because it came in many portions and in many ways, it was partial, progressive, fragmented. What he gave the fathers and prophets was inerrant but incomplete. It was promise, not fulfillment.

In contrast, God's revelation through his Son is true and perfect (1:2). "Last days" speaks of the final age, the messianic age, where we have been since the cross. "Spoken" is the same word as in verse 1. The same God spoke in both, but now there is a difference in time and quality: (1) time: last days; (2) quality: His Son. "Son" emphasizes one whose nature and

---

[62] Francis Schaeffer, *He Is There and He Is Not Silent* in *The Complete Works of Francis Schaeffer* (Wheaton: Crossway, 1982), 1:276.

character are that of a Son (of God). The coming of the Son brought to completion and fulfillment all that the Old Testament predicted and promised concerning Messiah. God spoke in his Son. As Mullins notes, "In Jesus we have the true revelation of God."[63]

2. *The superior person of the Son (1:2–3)*. Jesus is the face of God. Jesus is the invisible God made visible (cf. John 1:14; Col. 1:15). When you look at Jesus, you are looking at God. Hebrews provides us with seven glorious affirmations of the Son.

(1) He is the divine inheritor (1:2). "Whom He has appointed heir of all things" looks to the future. Christ has supreme place in all of creation. The Father delights to honor the Son. All things belong to him.

(2) He is the divine Creator (1:2). "Through whom He made the universe" addresses again the Son's role in creation. All three members of the triune God are active in creation. The Father is the author, the Son is the administrator, and the Holy Spirit is the agent. Here attention is on the Son. Through him the Father made, literally, "the ages." It is the universe as sum total of all the various periods of time that is in view.[64]

(3) He is the divine revealer (1:3). "He is the radiance of His glory" reveals that the Son is the shining forth of brightness from within. He is the outshining of the glory of God. In Jesus, the Son, we see the true and authentic glory of God. As Jesus himself said in John 14:9, "The one who has seen Me has seen the Father." As the sunlight is to the sun, so the eternal Son is to the Father.[65]

(4) He is the divine character (1:3). "The exact expression of His nature" teaches that "the Son is the perfect representation of God's being."[66] "Exact expression" originally meant an instrument of engraving and then the mark stamped by that instrument. Jesus is the very stamp of God's nature, the precise impression or mark.[67] Whatever it is that constitutes God being God, the Son is all of that as well. If God is omnipotent, then the Son is omnipotent. If God is omnipresent, then the Son is omnipresent. If God is omniscient, then the Son is omniscient. If God is eternal, then the Son is eternal. If God is immutable (unchanging), then the Son is immutable. If God is holy, just, righteous, and love, then the Son is holy, just, righteous, and love. Jesus Christ, God's Son, alone reveals to us exactly what the Father is like.

---

[63] E. Y. Mullins, *Baptist Beliefs* (Louisville: Baptist World, 1912), 32.

[64] Leon Morris, *Hebrews*, BSC (Grand Rapids: Zondervan, 1983), 19.

[65] Simon Kistemaker, *Hebrews*, NTC (Grand Rapids: Baker, 1984), 29.

[66] Ibid., 30.

[67] Ibid.

(5) He is the divine Sustainer (1:3). "He sustains all things by His powerful word" looks to the present. "Sustains" (present tense) means "carries along." He created it, he maintains it, and he is carrying it toward its appointed goal. Nothing is excluded on either a global scale or a personal one.

(6) He is the divine Redeemer (1:3). He made "purification for sins." Jesus did what no forefather or prophet could do. He did what no apostle or angel could do. He did what only he could do: He took care of our sin. Purification is *katharismos* (Gk.). It means to "cleanse," "purge," "purify." Jesus cleansed us of sins (1:4); he made a satisfaction for sins (2:17); he puts away sins (8:12; 10:17); he bore our sins (9:28); he offered a sacrifice for sins for all times (10:12); he made an offering for sin (10:18), and he annulled sin by his sacrifice (9:26). "Look at sin how you will, the Son has dealt with it; He has defeated it."[68] The words "after making" means "provided," and here it affirms a once-for-all completed action in the past. The purpose for which he came was to make atonement by his blood. All of humanity had a heart problem, not a physical one but a spiritual one. We needed a spiritual catharsis, a divine cleansing. Jesus provided that for us.

(7) He is the divine Savior (1:3). "Sat down at the right hand of the Majesty on high" speaks of his exaltation in heaven following his perfect work of redemption. Hebrews 10:12 says, "But this man, after offering one sacrifice for sins forever, sat down at the right hand of God." The Lord has completed his work. Unlike any high priest under the old covenant, his work is finished. There was no chair in the Holy of Holies because the work was never finished. More sacrifices always needed to be made. Not so with the Son. He is at the right hand of God, the majesty on high. Sitting, he rests in the position of greatest honor because his work of atonement is over.

3. The superior worship of the Son (1:4). In the first century, as in the twenty-first, there was confusion about the proper place of angels. For the first of thirteen times, the author of Hebrews uses the word *better* or *higher* to put angelology in proper perspective. Angels are God's good creation, and they are mentioned 105 times in the Old Testament and 165 in the New Testament. They are ministering spirits for the saved (1:14). Jesus is the Son. They are servants. Jesus is sovereign (1:7). They are creatures. Jesus is the Creator. They are workers. Jesus is worshipped (1:6). They themselves worship him (Rev. 5:11–12).

Angels are called servants. Jesus is called Son. Angels continue to serve for God. Jesus is now seated at the right hand of God. "Name" connotes

---

[68] Morris, *Hebrews,* 20.

all that a person is in character and conduct. In all respects Jesus is better, better in his person (he is God) and better in his work (he dealt with sin once and for all), better in his position (at God's right hand), and better in adoration (he is worshipped).

[handwritten: From Below   Virgin birth   Miracles / Early years   Transfiguration / Baptism   Ascension / Temptation]

The Witness of the Gospels

Those who wish to understand the first century and the context out of which Christianity was born must examine the life of Jesus of Nazareth revealed in the Gospels. N. T. Wright notes, "The historian of the first century . . . cannot shrink from the question of Jesus."[69] Who Jesus was, what he said, and what he did must be carefully considered and studied.

In his brief life of approximately thirty-three years, a number of events stand out. They are not only historically important; they are also theologically significant. The New Testament provides for us testimony that comes from eyewitnesses or those closely associated with these witnesses. Luke, for example, though not an eyewitness himself, tells us that he carefully investigated these things (Luke 1:1–4).

Luke noted that many had sought to put down in writing the events of Jesus' life. Eyewitnesses had been the source of their information and in Luke's case, he had carefully investigated everything from the first so that there could be a "certainty" about what had been taught. A fair and honest examination of the Bible reveals eyewitness testimony that fits well into the historical world of the first century. Here we pursue a "Christology from below."

The Virgin Birth

Its importance. The virgin birth is critical to our understanding of Christology and the union of deity and humanity in Jesus. It teaches that God became man as the Holy Spirit and Mary participated in the event. That this actually happened demonstrates that there is no contradiction in the idea that God can take on human nature. God in his essence is certainly beyond human apprehension, and yet the incarnation/virgin birth demonstrates that he is not so transcendent as to be "wholly other" and, hence, utterly unknowable or incapable of contact with his creatures.

Furthermore, because the virgin birth is presented in Scripture and accepted by orthodoxy as a bona fide miracle, it becomes something of a "test case" of one's belief in supernaturalism. Those who deny the virgin birth deny God's supernatural act of incarnation. Moreover, a denial of the virgin birth is also a denial of the clear teaching of Scripture.

Attacks against the virgin birth began early in the second century when, in the Talmud, the story was told that Jesus was actually the illegitimate son

---

69 N. T. Wright, *Jesus and the Victory of God* (Minneapolis: Fortress, 1996), xiii.

of a Roman soldier by the name of Pandira. This story, concocted by Jewish persons, was used by the pagan philosopher Celsus to attack Christianity. The French Deist Voltaire propagated the same story. Influential scholars like Brunner, Bultmann, Tillich, Ferre, Baillie, and Pannenberg have all denied the virgin birth, though their reasons for doing so vary.

The biblical witness. Several key texts address the issue of the virgin birth:

- Isaiah 7:14ff. (cf. also 9:6–7; 11:1ff.)
- Matthew 1:18–25
- Luke 1:26–38
- Genesis 3:15 (a veiled reference to be sure)

Possible allusions may also include Romans 1:3; 5:12–21; Galatians 4:4; Philippians 2:6.

Matthew examined the birth from Joseph's perspective and provided a legal genealogy back to David beginning in 1:1–17. Luke looked at the event from Mary's perspective and provided a natural genealogy, also back to David, in 3:23–38. The accounts complement each other.

Both Gospel accounts further emphasize certain aspects of Joseph and Mary, which indicate their innocence, righteousness, purity, and devotion to God. Matthew teaches us that Joseph was in no way involved in the conception of Jesus (1:25). He did have normal marital relations with her after Jesus was born (1:25), and he was responsible for the naming of the child (1:25). All of this was a fulfillment of the prophecy of the virgin birth in Isaiah 7:14 (1:22–23). The name Immanuel ("God with us") is significant. The central point of the virgin conception is that it is a sign that God is going to act again in the midst of his people (cf. Isa. 7:14).

Luke, on the other hand, emphasized that Mary was a virgin (Matthew also taught this), and that the entire series of events was a surprise to her (1:29–30). Luke also emphasized the divine agency of the Holy Spirit. This point is again not ignored in Matthew but is given greater attention in Luke (1:35). Luke shows that the Holy Spirit was the divine agent in the virginal conception. The emphasis here is not on the method of virginal conception—though that is not completely out of view—but rather on the divine generation of the Messiah by means of the Spirit.

Luke also makes several important theological points: Luke 1:33 emphasizes Jesus' eternal reign in fulfillment of the Davidic covenant (cf. 2 Sam. 7:14ff). Verse 37 emphasizes the impossibility of the virgin birth apart from a divine miracle. Verses 43–44 emphasize the miracle of recognition by Elizabeth and John. Luke also draws attention to Jesus as the Son of God, which gives him both his identity and title.

In summary, the story of the virgin birth, or virgin conception, is prophesied in Isaiah 7:14 and described in the infancy narratives of Matthew 1:18–25 and Luke 1:26–38. Mark and John did not record it. The biblical record reveals that Jesus Christ was born without a human father, conceived by the Holy Spirit, and born of the virgin Mary. The virgin birth impacts our understanding of the incarnation. The incarnation teaches that God became man in the person of Jesus of Nazareth. The virgin birth emphasizes both the reality of Jesus' humanity and his divinity as God's Son.

Did the virgin birth really happen? Some scholars, especially those committed to an antisupernatural worldview, have dismissed the historical nature of the virgin birth. Disbelief in the virgin birth arises for others in what they see as the historical difficulties associated with the biblical accounts found in Matthew and Luke. Wolfhart Pannenburg denies the virgin birth because he contends that it conflicts with the preexistent divinity of Jesus. He says that "in its content, the legend of Jesus' virgin birth stands in an irreconcilable contradiction to the Christology of the incarnation of the preexistent Son of God found in [the writings of] Paul and John."[70] However, there is no reason to view the two doctrines as mutually exclusive; rather they are complementary.

Christ's preexistence relates to his divinity, whereas the virgin birth relates to his humanity. At a finite point in time, the second person of the Trinity assumed a human nature and was born as Jesus. Erickson correctly notes that there is "no reason why the preexistence [of God's Son] and the virgin birth should be in conflict if one believes that there was a genuine incarnation at the beginning of Jesus' earthly life."[71] For those who affirm the witness of the Bible, the virgin birth is "simply the means by which God brought about the incarnation of his Son."[72]

Others who reject the virgin birth claim that it is cast in a mythological and legendary framework. The idea of the Son of God assuming a human nature in the womb of a virgin too closely parallels ancient myths and legends. Stein contends that "probably the most frequent argument raised against the virginal conception is that too many other parallels exist in ancient literature to allow [one] to take the Christian account seriously."[73] According to this argument the story of the virgin birth arose out of Greek mythology and its many miraculous birth stories. However, a careful reading of the Gospel accounts reveals no Greek mythological origin. Luke's account of the virgin birth is the most Jewish part of his entire Gospel.[74]

[70] Wolfhart Pannenberg, *Jesus—God and Man* (Philadelphia: Westminster, 1977), 143.
[71] M. J. Erickson, *Christian Theology* (Grand Rapids: Baker, 1985), 753.
[72] R. H. Stein, *Jesus the Messiah* (Grand Rapids: Zondervan, 1996), 79.
[73] Ibid., 65.
[74] Ibid., 66.

Many are familiar with stories of how Zeus fathered Hercules, Perseus, and Alexander; and of Apollo's fatherhood to Ion, Asclepius, Pythagoras, Plato, and Augustus. However, when we examine these stories we discover that "all the alleged parallels turn out to be quite different from the New Testament accounts. <u>Almost all the pagan accounts involve a sexual encounter.</u>"[75] These myths "are nothing more than the stories about fornication between divine and human beings, which is something radically different from the biblical accounts of the virgin birth."[76] Jesus was not the result of sexual intercourse between God and Mary. Nothing in Scripture even remotely implies such an understanding.

In *The Myth of God Incarnate*, John Hick and his colleagues argue that the doctrine of Christ's preexistence and incarnation represent ancient myths that carry only religious meaning for its hearers. According to Hick:

> The stories (for example) of the six day creation of the world and the fall of Adam and Eve after their temptation by the serpent in the Garden of Eden are now seen as profound religious myths, illuminating our human situation, so the story of the Son of God coming down from heaven and being born as a baby will be seen as a mythological expression of the immense significance of our encounter with one in whose presence we have found ourselves to be at the same time in the presence of God.[77]

Therefore, it is asserted that while modern persons must abandon the incarnation (and the virgin birth) as a genuine reality, it can be retained as a religious claim. The virgin birth acts as a symbol of the truth that Jesus was special and that he was God's gift to humanity, without any necessary reference to the mechanism of his birth. For these scholars, "The very possibility of such a conception and birth is excluded as a logical consequence of the elimination of the supernatural from history [for] if miracles cannot happen, then by definition there cannot be a virginal conception."[78] However, in redemptive history, miracles accompany God as he acts in salvation history. Evangelicals affirm that God exists outside the world and intervenes periodically within the natural processes through miracles. Anyone who affirms the impossibility of the virgin birth is confessing his or her unbelief in the omnipotent God of the Bible. The virgin birth is no more miraculous than any of the other miracles in the Bible. If miracles are rejected, then nothing important to Christianity remains.

---

[75] Ibid., 65.

[76] Erickson, *Christian Theology*, 752.

[77] John Hick, ed., *The Myth of God Incarnate* (Philadelphia: Westminster, 1977), 184.

[78] Stein, *Jesus the Messiah*, 64.

Because of its significance, the teaching of Christ's virgin birth is "*in-dispensable* to a biblically based Christology and Soteriology. Although we can imagine other ways by which God could supernaturally have kept Jesus sinless, in historical actuality the sign of the virgin birth is a historical nonnegotiable."[79] If our beliefs are to be governed by Scripture, then we cannot deny this teaching.

The virgin birth should not be an obstacle to faith but rather a help. Jesus Christ did not enter the world like any other human. He came as God incarnate, conceived in the womb of a virgin by the power of the Holy Spirit. Jesus is a miraculous gift to humanity and the world. He "is a gift that comes ultimately from God, but comes through Mary in a way that allows one to say that Jesus' origins are both human and divine."[80] If one rejects the virgin birth, he receives the approval of some people in the modern academy. If one affirms the virgin birth, he receives the support of Scripture and almost two thousand years of church history.

② *The Early Years of Jesus*

The time from Jesus' early childhood to the beginning of his public ministry has been referred to as "the silent years." The only record we have of any specific event is the family trip to Jerusalem for the Passover when Jesus was about twelve. He was left behind for several days and was eventually found astonishing the teachers at the temple with his knowledge (Luke 2:41–50). Only one particular statement made by Jesus is given, but what he says is potentially significant. When asked by his mother why he had behaved in such a manner, causing his parents such anxiety (Luke 2:48), Jesus responded, "Didn't you know that I had to be in My Father's house?" (2:49). These are the first words of Jesus recorded in Scripture, and it raises the issue of Jesus' messianic consciousness. How and when did he know that he was God's Son? Evidence is scarce.

However, Jesus' response to his parents points to the fact that even at a young age the things of God were of supreme importance to him. He must be involved in the work of divine things and therefore what better place for him to be than the temple?[81] Still more important is his statement, "My Father's house." The first recorded words out of Jesus' mouth draw attention to the intimate relationship he enjoys with the Father. Bock says,

---

[79] Gordon Lewis and Bruce Demarest, *Integrative Theology* (Grand Rapids: Zondervan, 1990), 2:274.

[80] Ben Witherington III, "Birth of Jesus," *DJG*, ed. Joel B. Green, Scot McKnight and I. Howard Marshall (Downers Grove: InterVarsity, 1992), 72. Macleod notes, "There was no Jewish expectation that the Messiah would be born of a virgin (as there was that he would be the Son of David). The only motive for recording such a doctrine was that they believed it to be true." For his superb treatment of Christology, see Donald Macleod, *The Person of Christ* (Downers Grove: InterVarsity, 1998), 32.

[81] Darrell L. Bock, *Luke 1:1–9:50*, BECNT (Grand Rapids: Baker, 1994), 270.

"'My Father' suggests the mystery that is a part of Jesus' person. Jesus has a strong sense of identity with the Father and is committed to the mission God sent him to do."[82] Jesus, even at the early age of twelve, already demonstrated filial obedience to the Father. He is here to do his will. Whether all the details of his future are known is not revealed. What is clear, however, is that he already sees himself and knows himself to have an intimate and personal relationship with the Father, the kind only a Son would know.

The Baptism of Jesus

This event in the life of Jesus is recorded in all three of the Synoptic Gospels, and it is also alluded to in John (Matt. 3:13–17; Mark 1:9–11; Luke 3:21–22; John 1:31–34). Jesus came to John the Baptist, his cousin, who was baptizing in the Jordan River. John was hesitant to baptize Jesus. He realized Jesus' birth was more significant than his own, that Jesus' knowledge and understanding of Scripture surpassed his own, and that Jesus' life required no repentance or confession of sin. If anyone needed baptizing, it was John by Jesus (Matt. 3:13–14).[83] Jesus, however, admonished John that his baptizing Jesus would "fulfill all righteousness" (Matt. 3:15). John relented and baptized Jesus. The heavens opened, and the Spirit of God descended upon Jesus like a dove. Then a voice from heaven said, "This is My beloved Son. I take delight in Him!" (Matt. 3:17). Why was Jesus baptized? What does it mean that his baptism fulfilled all righteousness? Why did the Spirit descend upon him? What is the significance of the voice from heaven? Several crucial points of theological import can be drawn from this event.

First, Jesus' baptism is the inauguration of his public ministry. The twenty years of silence have come to an end. The boy in the temple is now a man about the age of thirty. God has prepared him for the mission for which he came and the time for that assignment to start had arrived. His baptism signified the commencement of his public ministry.

Second, his baptism identified him with sinful humanity. Jesus came to provide salvation for sinners. He would accomplish this by his perfect sacrifice when he died on the cross. At the beginning of his ministry, he declared his solidarity with sinners, not as a sinner himself, but as the one who came "to seek and to save the lost" (Luke 19:10).

Third, the baptism of Jesus was preeminently a public declaration of his submission to the will of the Father. Jesus is the Suffering Servant of the Lord (Isa. 42; 49; 50; 53).

But the Servant's first mark is obeying God: he "fulfills all righteousness" since he suffers and dies to accomplish redemption in

---

82 Ibid., 271.
83 D. A. Carson, *Matthew,* EBC (Grand Rapids: Zondervan, 1984), 107.

obedience to the will of God. By his baptism Jesus affirms his determination to do his assigned work ... at this point Jesus must demonstrate his willingness to take on his servant role, entailing his identification with the people.[84]

Fourth, the baptism of Christ was an occasion for a revelation of the triune God. The Son was immersed in the Jordan River, the Holy Spirit came down upon him, and the Father spoke from heaven. It is interesting to note that in Matthew's Gospel, Jesus' earthly ministry concludes with another revelation of the Trinity in the giving of the "Great Commission" (Matt. 28:18–20).

Fifth, the baptism of Jesus was an opportunity for God the Father to honor his Son. His voice from heaven gave assurance to his Son of his love and pleasure in him and what he was about to do.

Sixth, the baptism of Jesus was when the Spirit of God anointed or coronated him for his public ministry. While the Scriptures are abundantly clear in their witness to the full deity of Christ, they are equally clear in their witness to his full humanity. Again, during his incarnate state, the Son laid aside (temporarily) the free exercise of his divine attributes. He lived his life in obedience to the Father and in dependence on the Holy Spirit. The Spirit was upon him as he conducted his ministry and accomplished his work of redemption. As he began his Galilean ministry, he read in the synagogue from Isaiah 61:1–2, "The Spirit of the Lord is on Me" (Luke 4:18).

Seventh, Jesus' baptism defined and set the course for the type of Messiah he would be. Verse 17 is especially crucial. The Father's declaration is a combination of Psalm 2:7 and Isaiah 42:1. Psalm 2 is Davidic and messianic. Isaiah 42 is the first of the Servant Songs. In the declaration of the Father, the course of ministry for our Lord is set. He is indeed the Messiah, but his messiahship will be realized by suffering service. Carson puts it well, "At the very beginning of Jesus' public ministry, His Father presented him, in a veiled way, as at once Davidic Messiah, very Son of God, representative of the people, and the Suffering Servant."[85]

It is no accident then, that the same Spirit who had just anointed Jesus immediately "drove" (Mark 1:12) him into the wilderness to be tempted. His willingness to be this kind of Messiah, a Suffering Servant King, was immediately put to the test.

The Temptation of Jesus

This event is recorded in each of the Synoptic Gospels, with Matthew and Luke providing the most extensive accounts (Matt. 4:1–11; Mark 1:12–

---

[84] Ibid., 108.
[85] Ibid., 109.

13; Luke 4:1–13). This testing of Jesus (the Greek verb "tempted" can also be rendered "tested") was divinely intended. Note that it was the Spirit who led him into the wilderness. The background is Deuteronomy 8:1–5, from ‏לֹא תַנַּסוּ‎ which Jesus quoted in his first response to the devil (see v. 4). Our Lord was subjected to a similar test, as was Israel, and showed himself to be the true Israelite who lived "on every word that comes from the mouth of God."

There is also a clear comparison with Adam and Eve in the garden. Adam and Eve failed their test in a perfect environment and plunged the whole world into sin (Gen. 3). By contrast, Jesus was faithful in the barren wilderness and proved his qualification to become the Savior of the world. It is important that Jesus was tested /tempted like Israel and like us, so that he can be our "merciful and faithful high priest" (Heb. 2:17) and be "able to help those who are tested" (Heb. 2:18; see Heb. 4:15–16).

The baptism of Jesus and his temptations in the wilderness are intentionally connected. Jesus was declared by God the Father at the baptism to be his Son and to be the Messiah. However, it was a Servant-Messiah role that he would fulfill, a role that would involve suffering and death. Is he truly submissive to the Father's will for his life? Is he qualified to be this kind of Messiah?

The devil (Gk. *diabolos*) appears at the end of Luke 4:2. His sole purpose was to tempt Jesus to sin. The word *tempted* carries with it the idea of a solicitation to evil or sin. The devil engaged Jesus in three simple dialogues. Prior to the devil's appearance, Jesus had been fasting for forty days. His only sustenance would have been water (cf. Luke 4:2). He was hungry, and the tempter showed up to begin the contest, issuing the first of three challenges. The first two in Matthew are a direct attack upon the declaration from heaven in 3:17 regarding the sonship of Jesus.

In the three confrontations there are challenges by the devil to do certain things, which Jesus refused to do: turn stones to bread, jump from the wing of the temple, bow down and worship the devil. Jesus was steadfast in his devotion and submission to his Father's purpose and plan for his life. This man is qualified to be Israel's Messiah. He will be the King who obtains his kingdom by being the Suffering Servant of the Lord (Isa. 53).   *Akim's View*

Could Jesus have sinned in his incarnate state? The issue of "impeccability" (Lat. *non potuit peccare*, "not able to sin") or "peccability" (Lat. *potuit non peccare*, "able not to sin") of Christ has been debated by Christians for centuries. Two facts must be affirmed regardless of one's position: (1) Christ was genuinely tempted, and (2) he did not sin.

Those who hold to the peccability of Christ, that Christ could have sinned but did not sin, do so on the basis of texts like Hebrew 4:15: He "has been tested in every way as we are, yet without sin." If the temptation was real, then Christ had to be able to sin. Otherwise, the temptation was not really genuine. Charles Hodge is a good representative of this view. He states:

> If He was a true man He must have been capable of sinning. That He did not sin under the greatest provocation; that when He was reviled He blessed; when He suffered He threatened not; that He was dumb, as a sheep before its shearers, is held up to us as an example. Temptation implies the possibility of sin. If from the constitution of His person it was impossible for Christ to sin, then His temptation was unreal and without effect, and He cannot sympathize with His people.[86]

The strength of this view is that it honors the genuine humanity of Jesus, identifies our Lord with humans, and holds that just as our temptations are real, his temptations were real. The weakness of this view is that it does not sufficiently consider Christ in his person as God. God cannot sin. Christ's deity and humanity cannot be separated or divorced from each other. He is now and forevermore the God-man, a theanthropic person.

Those who hold to impeccability believe Christ's temptations by Satan were genuine but that it was impossible for Christ to sin. The purpose of the temptations was not to see if Christ could sin but to demonstrate that he could not sin. The temptations came at a particularly significant time: the beginning of Christ's public ministry. The temptations were designed to show the nation of Israel and the world the qualified Savior they had: the impeccable Son of God. It is interesting to note that it was not Satan who initiated the temptation but the Holy Spirit (Matt. 4:1; Mark 1:12). If Christ could have sinned, then it seems that the Holy Spirit enticed Christ to sin because it was the Spirit who led him into the wilderness. However, temptation to sin is something God does not do (James 1:13). Satan could *tempt* Jesus to sin. The Spirit would *test* him for the purpose of proving his character.

It is argued that Christ's peccability could relate only to his human nature; his divine nature is obviously impeccable. Although Christ has two natures, he is one person. If the two natures could be separated, then he could sin in his humanity. However, the human and divine natures cannot be separated in the person of Christ. Since the divine nature cannot sin, it is held that Christ could not have sinned. Christ is the God-man. If he were only a man, then he could have sinned, but God cannot sin. In the union of these two natures, the human nature submits to the divine nature (otherwise the finite is stronger

---

[86] Charles Hodge, *Systematic Theology* (New York, 1874; repr., Grand Rapids: Eerdmans, 1977), 2:457.

than the infinite). United in the one person of Christ are two natures: humanity and deity. Because Christ is also deity, he could not sin.

It is also said that in moral decisions, Christ could have only one will: to do the will of his Father. If Christ could have sinned, then his human will would have been stronger than the divine will.

Finally, Christ had complete authority over his humanity. For example, no one could take the life of Christ except he lay it down willingly (John 10:18). If Christ had authority over life and death, he certainly had authority over sin.[87]

In the end we must affirm the two propositions with which we began: (1) Jesus was genuinely tempted, and (2) Jesus did not sin. Scripture does not address directly the "could he have sinned" question, and we should rest content in what has been revealed to us. Second Corinthians 5:21 and Hebrews 4:15 make clear that Jesus was sinless. This is the nonnegotiable teaching of the Bible.

(5) The Miracles of Jesus

One of the evidences put forward by Scripture for the messiahship and deity of Jesus is his miraculous works. The Gospels record thirty-five separate miracles performed by Christ. Matthew mentions twenty; Mark, eighteen; Luke, twenty; and John built his Gospel around seven sign miracles. These, however, are not all of the miracles performed by Jesus. Matthew, for instance, alludes to several occasions when Jesus performed a number of miraculous works (4:23–24; 9:35; 10:1,8; 11:4–5,20–24; 12:15; 14:14,36; 15:30; 19:2; 21:14). Each Gospel writer selected from the large number of miracles performed by the Lord Jesus those which assisted his purpose.

Examine the Gospel of John. In the first eleven chapters, sometimes called "the book of signs," the apostle focuses on seven particular miracles performed by Jesus that witness to his deity and should cause us to put our faith in him in order that we "may have life in His name" (John 20:31). In fact, John 20:30 specifically tells us, "Jesus performed many other signs in the presence of His disciples that are not written in this book," and in John 21:25, using hyperbole, John says, "And there are also many other things that Jesus did, which, if they were written one by one, I suppose not even the world itself could contain the books that would be written." John's seven signs/miracles include:

- Jesus turns water into wine (2:1–11),
- Jesus heals a royal official's son (4:46–54),
- Jesus cures a paralyzed man (5:1–16),

[handwritten margin notes: G : 35 / Matt : 20 / Mark : 18 / Luke : 20 / John : 7 / → 이거 다 합하면 only.]

---

[87] William G. T. Shedd, *Dogmatic Theology* (New York, 1889; repr., Nashville: Nelson, 1980), 2:330–49.

- Jesus feeds five thousand men (6:1–15; the only miracle recorded in all four Gospels besides the resurrection),
- Jesus walks on water (6:16–21),
- Jesus heals a blind man (9:1–42), and
- Jesus raises Lazarus from the dead (11:1–57).

All of these are "signs" or witnesses to his deity and a confirmation of John 1:1,14,18.

6. The Transfiguration of Jesus.

The theological significance of the transfiguration is often neglected. The transfiguration is recorded in each of the Synoptic Gospels (Matt. 17:1–8; Mark 9:2–13; Luke 9:28–36). Peter also alludes to the event in his second letter (2 Pet. 1:16–18). Peter, James, and John accompanied Jesus up to a high mountain. While they were there, Moses and Elijah appeared, and our Lord was "transformed" (HCSB) or "transfigured" (NIV) before them. The Greek word translated "transformed" is *metamorphoō* and "suggests a change of inmost nature that may be outwardly visible or invisible."[88] In this case the change was most clearly outward. This outward manifestation of the inward reality of Christ allowed the disciples "to glimpse something of his preincarnate glory (John 1:14; 17:5; Phil. 2:6–7) and anticipate his coming exaltation (2 Pet. 1:16–18; Rev. 1:16)."[89]

The heavenly declaration of Matthew 17:5 is crucial to the whole dramatic scene. The language is reminiscent of Jesus' baptism (Matt. 3:13–17). God the Father again spoke and said, "This is My beloved Son. I take delight in Him. Listen to Him!" (Matt. 17:5). Moses and Elijah disappeared from the scene (Matt. 17:8) with only Jesus remaining.

What are we to glean from this in terms of Christological and theological significance? First, the disciples received a foretaste of Jesus' coming exaltation and kingdom. Second, it was a revelation of the glory and deity of the Son of God. For a brief moment the God who had walked among his disciples incognito allowed his deity to shine forth in its splendor and glory. Third, it was a confirmation of Peter's confession in Matthew 16:16, "You are the Messiah, the Son of the living God." Fourth, it was an encouragement in light of our Lord's prediction of his passion in Matthew 16:21. Fifth, it served as a motivation for the task to which the disciples had been called to follow Jesus. They must deny themselves, take up their cross, and follow him. The transfiguration said, "Look who you are following!" Sixth, it fulfilled Matthew 16:28,

---

[88] Carson, *Matthew*, 385.
[89] Ibid.

which says, "I assure you: There are some standing here who will not taste death until they see the Son of Man coming in His kingdom." The transfiguration gave them a vision of that kingdom. Seventh, it was a declaration of the Son's unique and definitive revelation of the Father. Eighth, it was a witness to the Son's superiority to and fulfillment of the Law (Moses) and the Prophets (Elijah). Ninth, it was a reaffirmation of the Father's love and delight in his Son. Tenth, it was a restatement that Jesus was the Messiah (Ps. 2) who would realize his kingdom as the Suffering Servant of the Lord (Isa. 42).

Carson is correct when he says:

> The narrative is clearly a major turning point in Jesus' self-disclosure . . . The contrast between what Jesus had just predicted would be his fate (16:21) and this glorious sight would one day prompt Jesus' disciples to marvel at the self-humiliation that brought him to the cross and to glimpse a little of the height to which he had been raised by his vindicating resurrection and ascension.[90]

(h) *The Ascension of Jesus*

The ascension of our Lord is recorded only in the two-volume work of Luke (Luke 24:50–53; Acts 1:9–11). It is a particular aspect of our Lord's ministry which is seldom mentioned in theologies.

It could be argued that there are five extraordinary events in the life and ministry of Jesus Christ. There is his incarnation, his crucifixion, his resurrection, his ascension, and his exaltation. The ascension of Jesus Christ is inseparably linked to all four of the others, especially his incarnation and exaltation. The Son came down in incarnation that he might in ascension return to heaven in exaltation.

Ephesians 4:10 says, "The One who descended is the same as the One who ascended far above all the heavens, that He might fill all things." First Peter 3:22 says, "Now that He has gone into heaven, He is at God's right hand, with angels, authorities, and powers subjected to Him." There is now glorified humanity in heaven, the God-man Jesus Christ.

Jesus ascended to heaven as our *Master.* Jesus sits at the right hand of the throne of God. There he resides as the Lord of this universe. In Acts 2:33,36, Peter says, "Since He has been exalted to the right hand of God . . . God has made this Jesus . . . both Lord and Messiah!"

Jesus ascended to heaven as our *forerunner* (Heb. 6:19–20). As our great forerunner, Jesus Christ has gone into the very Holy of Holies. Jesus Christ, our High Priest, ascended into the Holy of Holies in heaven. Hebrews

---

[90] Ibid., 384–85.

10:11–12 reminds us, "Now every priest stands day after day ministering and offering time after time the same sacrifices, which can never take away sins. But this man, after offering one sacrifice for sins forever, sat down at the right hand of God."

Jesus ascended as the *Victor.* Ephesians 4:8 says, "When He ascended on high, He took prisoners into captivity; He gave gifts to people."

In summation, what can we say about the significance of our Lord's ascension? (1) It ended the earthly ministry of Christ. It marked the end of the period of self-limitation during the days of his sojourn on earth. (2) It ended the period of his humiliation. His glory was no longer veiled following the ascension (John 17:5; Acts 9:3,5). Christ is now exalted and enthroned in heaven (Phil. 2:9–11). (3) It marks the first entrance of resurrected humanity into heaven and the beginning of a new work in heaven (Heb. 4:14–16; 6:20). A representative of the human race in a resurrected, glorified body is the Christian's intercessor (1 Tim. 2:5; Heb. 7:25). (4) It made the descent of the Holy Spirit possible (John 16:7). It was necessary for Christ to ascend to heaven in order that he could send the Holy Spirit.[91] (5) It is the necessary corollary of the resurrection. That is, it is the abiding proof that the resurrection of Jesus was more than a temporary resuscitation. To accept the bodily resurrection but deny the ascension, one must affirm either that Christ is still an inhabitant of earth or that he later died again.

(6) It conveyed to the disciples the realization that the appearances, which had occurred at intervals over a period of forty days, were at an end. Thus, it relieved their tension, put their minds at ease, so that, with the arrival of each new day, they did not wonder whether their Lord would reveal himself. (7) It suggested that Jesus was no longer to be perceived by physical sensation but by spiritual insight. (8) It provided the occasion for the commissioning for witness and the promise of the Spirit (Acts 1:1–8). (9) It provided for our Lord the occasion to bless his church with gifted men (Eph. 4:11). (10) It provided the occasion for the promise that he would come again (Acts 1:9–11). As *king,* Jesus is enthroned at God's right hand. As *priest,* he has atoned for sin and now prays for us. As *prophet,* he is the final spokesman for God. This is the clear and consistent witness of Scripture to the person of Christ.

---

[91] Carson (*The Gospel According to John,* 533–34) rightly notes that there is no metaphysical reason the Son and the Spirit cannot minister to God's people at the same time in the earthly realm. The point of Jesus' words is eschatological. "The many biblical promises that the Spirit will characterize the age of the kingdom of God (e.g. Is. 11:1–10; 32:14–18; 42:1–4; 44:1–5; Ezk. 11:17–20; 36:24–27; 37:1–14; Joel 2:28–32; cf. notes on Jn. 3:5; 7:37–39) breed anticipation. But this saving reign of God cannot be fully inaugurated until Jesus has died, risen from the dead, and been exalted to this Father's right hand, returned to the glory he enjoyed with the Father before the world began."

What Has the Church Believed?

The Witness of History to Jesus of Nazareth

The church has always believed certain basic tenets concerning the person and work of Jesus Christ. The first five hundred years of church history was a time when the church was especially active in wrestling with how to understand and comprehend the biblical witness to Jesus. Two issues in particular guided the conversation: the monotheism that Christianity inherited from Judaism and the fact that the New Testament clearly affirmed Jesus as God. How these competing truths could be reconciled was a significant challenge the church had to face.

The Road to the Christological Councils

1. Docetism

The church was forced to confront the issue of Christ's deity and its monotheistic faith early in its history. We find evidence of the struggle even in the New Testament. First John was written, in part, to confront a heresy known as Docetism. False teachers were harassing the Johannine communities. They did not confess Jesus of Nazareth as the Christ (1 John 2:22) and denied that the Son had come in the flesh (1 John 4:2–3; 2 John 7). It is likely these false teachers were influenced by early Gnosticism, a heretical movement that flourished in the second century. The Greek word *gnosis* means "knowledge." Though Gnosticism developed into many forms, two basic teachings were always present: (1) salvation comes by way of mystical knowledge and (2) matter is inferior or evil. In and around Ephesus, John battled the Docetists, as well as a man named Cerinthus.

Docetism comes from the Greek word *dokeō,* which means "to seem" or "to appear." Docetists denied the reality of Jesus' body as well as his sufferings and death. Jesus only appeared to have a body. Gnosticism taught there was a great distance that separated God and the material world. This distance was bridged by a strange host of intermediaries that were similar in some ways to angelic beings. One of these intermediaries, an inferior power called the "Demiurge," created the material world. The Demiurge is sometimes associated with the God of the Old Testament. Spirit and matter exist but are in serious antithesis to each other. The human problem is the fact that our spirit/soul is alienated and separated from God and trapped in an evil body. The true God, who had nothing to do with the creation of the material world, sent the Christ to rescue our souls. This Christ cannot be incarnate, however, for this would involve his taking to himself sinful and evil flesh (matter). Christ then only appeared to have a body (Docetism).

something John refutes in John 1:1,14,18 and 1 John 1:1–4, or the Christ temporarily adopted the man Jesus (Cerinthianism).

In this view "the Christ" came upon the man Jesus at his baptism (Matt. 3:13–17) but left him prior to his death on the cross (Matt. 27:46). John refutes this heresy in 1 John 5:6–8.[92] The church father Ignatius (died ca. 110) countered the Docetists in his letter to the Ephesians when he wrote:

> For there are some who maliciously and deceitfully are accustomed to carrying about the Name while doing other things unworthy of God. You must avoid them as wild beasts. For they are mad dogs that bite by stealth; you must be on your guard against them, for their bite is hard to heal. There is only one physician, who is both flesh and spirit, born and unborn, God in man, true life in death, both from Mary and from God, first subject to suffering and then beyond it, Jesus Christ our Lord.[93]

And again in his letter to the Trallians he charged:

> Be deaf, therefore, whenever anyone speaks to you apart from Jesus Christ, who was of the family of David, who was the son of Mary; who really was born, who both ate and drank; who really was persecuted under Pontius Pilate, who really was crucified and died . . . who, moreover, really was raised from the dead. . . . But if, as some atheists (that is, unbelievers) say, he suffered in appearance only (while they exist in appearance only!), why am I in chains? And why do I want to fight with wild beasts? If that is the case, I die for no reason; what is more, I am telling lies about the Lord.[94]

In similar fashion the church father Irenaeus (ca. 130–ca. 200) rejected the Cerinthians. In his polemic *Against Heresies (Refutation and Overthrow of the Gnosis Falsely So Called),* he exposed the error of the Gnostics, including those of Cerinthus:

> John, the disciple of the Lord, proclaimed this faith and wished by the proclamation of the gospel to destroy the error which had been planted among men by Cerinthus. . . . Now according to them neither was the Word made flesh, nor Christ, nor the Savior. . . . For they allege that the Word and Christ never came into this world, and that the Savior was neither incarnate nor suffered, but that he de-

---

[92] Akin, *1,2,3 John*, 29.

[93] Ignatius, *Ephesians* 7, *The Apostolic Fathers,* trans. J. B. Lightfoot and J. R. Harmer (London, 1889–90; repr., Grand Rapids: Baker, 1989), 88.

[94] Ignatius, *Trallians* 9.

scended as a dove upon that Jesus . . . and when he had proclaimed the unknown Father, ascended again.[95]

2. *Ebionism.* deity부정, incarnation부정

Ebionism was another early heresy that rejected the reality of the incarnation and the deity of Jesus. An offshoot of the Judaizers and committed to an ascetic lifestyle, they denied the essential deity of Jesus. Jesus was the prophet predicted by Moses in Deuteronomy 18:15, but he was not the preexistent Son of God. Jesus was made the Anointed One at his baptism, a form of adoptionism similar to Cerinthus, and he was chosen because of his perfect obedience to the law, something highly esteemed by the Ebionites.[96] Irenaeus also addressed this teaching and wrote, "Vain also are the Ebionites who do not accept in their souls by faith the union of God and man . . . not wishing to understand that the Holy Spirit came upon Mary, and the power of the Most High overshadowed her, and so what was born [of her] is holy and the Son of God Most High."[97]

3. *Adoptionism and Patripassionism.*

Debate and discussion concerning the person of Christ, his nature, and his relationship to the Father would continue into the second and third centuries, eventually leading to the four great Christological councils:

- Nicea (325) by Constantine. Arianism (Adoptionism, 영원부터 나신 분이) 부정 → Athanasius [Homoousia]
- Constantinople (381) by Theodosius. Arianism + Apollinarius (완전한 인성 없다 분이) 부정
- Ephesus (431) by ?. Nestorianism (two separate persons) 부정
- Chalcedon (451) by ?. Eutychianism (one modified nature) 부정

Prior to these four councils, Christological debate was constant. Origen (ca. 185–ca. 254) argued for the eternal generation of the Son but also for his essential subordination.[98] Essential subordination teaches that the Son is truly subordinate to the Father in his essence, being, and person. The dynamic Monarchianists or Adoptionists such as Theodotus of Byzantium and Paul of Samosata (c. AD 260) would continue to argue that God adopted Jesus as a unique and special man on whom his power would rest. This too was a denial of his full deity and eternality. This heresy would undergo some modification with men like Lucian and Arius, and it would provide the catalyst for the Nicene Council. Arianism, as we will see, is the forerunner of the modern cult of Jehovah's Witnesses.

---

[95] Irenaeus, *Against Heresies* 3.11.1, cited in Cyril Richardson, ed., *Early Church Fathers*, LCC (New York: Macmillan, 1970), 378–79.

[96] V. L. Walter, "Ebionites," *EDT*, ed. Walter Elwell (Grand Rapids: Baker, 2001), 362.

[97] Cited in Richardson, *Early Church Fathers*, 386.

[98] C. C. Kroeger, "Origen" *EDT*, 870.

There were, on the other hand, those who wanted to maintain radical monotheism and yet affirm the deity of Jesus Christ. They have come down to us in history by the designations of modalistic Monarchianism, Patripassionism, or Sabellianism (each of which is a variation of the same view). This false teaching affirms that the three persons of the deity are simply three ways (or "modes") in which the one God has revealed or manifested himself. Father, Son, and Holy Spirit are in a sense simply names. They do not constitute genuine and real distinctions. The Father is the Son is the Holy Spirit is the Father. It could be said that the Father was born at Bethlehem and crucified at Calvary (hence the term *Patripassionism* meaning "the suffering of the Father"), but at the time he was manifest as the Son and was called Jesus.

The church father Tertullian (ca. 155–220) wrote a major work against a prominent supporter of this view. In *Against Praxeas* he wrote:

> In various ways has the devil rivaled and resisted the truth. Sometimes his aim has been to destroy the truth by defending it. He maintains that there is only one Lord, the Almighty Creator of the world, in order that out of this *doctrine of the unity* may fabricate a heresy. He says that the Father himself came down into the Virgin, was Himself born of her, Himself suffered, indeed, was Himself Jesus Christ.[99]

Tertullian would also make another important contribution to the doctrines of theology proper (God) and Christology. He introduced the terms "*trinity*," "unity of *substance*," and "three *persons*," into the discussion of the relation of Father, Son, and Holy Spirit. He wrote that this heresy

> supposes itself to possess the pure truth, in thinking that one cannot believe in One Only God in any other way than by saying that the Father, the Son, and the Holy Ghost are the very self same Person. As if in this way also one were not All, in that All are of One, by unity (that is) of substance . . . , which distributes the Unity into a Trinity, placing in their order the three *Persons*—the Father, the Son, and the Holy Ghost.[100]

However, Tertullian did not work out the implications of these terms. That would come about in the first four councils of the church.

---

[99] Tertullian, *Against Praxeas* 3:597.
[100] Ibid., 3:598.

The Council of Nicea (AD 325)

The Roman emperor Constantine convened the Council of Nicea. His goal was to keep the empire unified, but a major theological dispute between Alexander, bishop of Alexandria (died 328), and one of his presbyters, Arius (ca. 250–336), put a significant obstacle in his way. Arius had adopted the theology of Paul of Samosata, called Adoptionism or Dynamic Monarchianism. In this view the man Jesus, having the Holy Spirit poured out on him at his baptism, became godlike. It emphasized the manhood of Jesus but did so at the expense of his deity. When Paul of Samosata thought of "the Word" being in Jesus, it only meant the impersonal power of God. Jesus was a mere man who was controlled by "the Word," the power of God. Arius, following his teacher Lucian, built on this perspective, and also viewed Jesus as less than fully God. Because there is only one true God who is eternal, immutable, and indivisible, the Christ must be of a different substance. God must have created Christ, a creature that had a beginning. Being created, his essence was substantially different from God's, yet he was created out of nothing. Thus the Arian party had two main points of contention going into the Council of Nicea: Jesus was not coeternal, and he was created from nothing.

These points were lamented as the cause of persecution by Arius himself in a letter he wrote to his friend Eusebius of Nicomedia.

> And before He [the Son] was begotten or created or defined or established, He was not. For He was not unbegotten. But we are persecuted because we say, "The Son has a beginning, but God is without beginning." . . . We are persecuted because we say, "He is from nothing." But we speak thus inasmuch as He is neither part of God nor from any substratum. On account of this we are persecuted.[101]

Arius was opposed not only by Alexander but also by Alexander's young protégé, the famous Athanasius (ca. 296–373). Athanasius is thought of as a key participant in the Nicean controversy although his significance really developed later, after Alexander died when he was appointed bishop of Alexandria.

The leaders of the church were brought together by Constantine in AD 325. Supporters of both Arius and Alexander were present. However, the largest group at the council was the "middle of the road" group whose main spokesman was the great church historian, Eusebius of Caesarea (ca. 265–339). Many in this group had orthodox instincts but little biblical

---

[101] "Arius's Letter to Eusebius of Nicomedia," in William G. Rusch, ed., *The Trinitarian Controversy, Sources of Early Christian Thought* (Philadelphia: Fortress, 1980), 30.

understanding of why they believed what they believed.[102] On May 20, the council began. There were approximately 318 bishops in attendance. Debate would center on the key term *homoousia*, which affirmed that the Son was fully divine and of the *same substance/essence* as the Father. In the end Alexander and his followers were successful, and the result of the first church council is what we know as the Nicene Creed.

The Nicene Creed

We believe in one God, the Father All Governing, Creator of all things visible and invisible;

And in one Lord Jesus Christ, the Son of God, begotten of the Father as only begotten, that is, from the essence of the Father, God from God, Light from Light, true God from true God, begotten not created, *of the same essence [homoousion]* as the Father, through whom all things came into being, both in heaven and earth; Who for us men and for our salvation came down and was incarnate, becoming human. He suffered and the third day he rose, and ascended into the heavens. And he will come to judge both the living and the dead. . . .

But, *those who say,* Once he was not, or he was not before his generation, or he came to be out of nothing, or who assert *that he, the Son of God, is of a different hypostasis or ousia,* or that he is a creature, or changeable, or mutable, *the Catholic and Apostolic Church anathematizes them.* [emphasis added]

The Nicene Council was crucial for establishing what the church believed the Bible taught concerning the person of Christ. Blaising provides a summary of what the Nicene Creed accomplished:

The theology expressed in the Nicene Creed is decisively anti-Arian. At the beginning the unity of God is affirmed. But the Son is said to be "true God from true God" . . . . It is positively asserted that he is "from the being (*ousia*) of the Father" and "of one substance (*homoousia*) with the Father." A list of Arian phrases, including "there was when he was not" and assertions that the Son is a creature or out of nothing, are expressly anathematized. Thus, an ontological [essential or real] rather than merely functional deity of the Son was upheld at Nicea."[103]

---

[102] Philip Schaff, *History of the Christian Church,* vol. 3, *Nicene and Post-Nicene Christianity* (1867; repr., Grand Rapids: Eerdmans, 1977), 628.

[103] Craig Blaising, "Nicea, Council of," *EDT,* 838.

The Council of Constantinople (AD 381)

This council was called by Emperor Theodosius. It put an end to Arianism, which had experienced several resurgences in the fifty years following Nicea. It essentially reaffirmed the decision of the Council of Nicea and completed the final version of the Nicene Creed. It also condemned the teachings of a man named Apollinarus (c. 310–390). While Arius erred by denying the deity of the Son, Apollinarus erred by overemphasizing it.

Apollinarus was a staunch defender of the Nicene doctrine and a former friend of Athanasius. He taught that while all other human beings are body, soul, and spirit coexisting in a union (trichotomy), in Christ there was only the human body and soul, the divine *Logos* having displaced the human spirit (*nous*). Christ is perfect God, but he lacked a complete humanity. Apollinarus held to a literal interpretation of John 1:14—Jesus took on a human body *alone,* not the human spirit. Jesus, then, did not have a human will, but only a divine will. Hence, Jesus had a human body and a divine spirit. Apollinarus's problem was that he allowed the divine to swallow the human, essentially denying the full humanity of Jesus Christ. It is not only our human bodies that need redemption but also our soul and spirit, our inner person. Christ had to be fully and truly man if he was to save all of us. As Gregory of Nazianzus argued, "For that which he has not assumed He has not healed; but that which is united to his Godhead is also saved."[104] Constantinople affirmed the full humanity of the Son.[105]

The Council of Ephesus (AD 431)

This council saw the condemnation of a man named Nestorius (d. 451). Some scholars believe that Nestorius himself was not a Nestorian. However, through unfortunate religious and political circumstances he was blamed and condemned nonetheless.

Nestorianism is the view that there are *two separate persons* in Christ, a human person and a divine person. Within a single body resides two

---

[104] Gregory the Theologian to Cledonius, *Against Apollinarus* 51.

[105] Prior to the sixth general council held at Constantinople (AD 681), a theory called Monophysitism asserted that Jesus had only one nature (his divine nature) and thus only one will (Monothelitism). The denial of Christ's human nature, however, is problematic for two reasons: First, it necessitates a denial of his full humanity—an assertion which contradicts Scripture. Second, a one-natured Christ would have "separated him so far from his people that he could not sympathize with them in their temptations." Charles Hodge, *Systematic Theology* (New York, 1874; repr., Grand Rapids: Eerdmans, 1977), 2:405. The Council of Constantinople, however, declared that the one person of Christ has both two distinct natures and two distinct wills. This view has been supported by the overwhelming majority of the church. Erickson summarizes well the accepted, orthodox position: "Christ's full humanity, then, required two natural wills, but not two natural wills contrary to each other. The human will was completely subject to the will of his divine nature." Millard Erickson, *The Word Became Flesh* (Grand Rapids: Baker, 1991), 75.

persons. This view was rejected because nowhere in Scripture do we see that the human nature of Christ acting as an independent person, deciding to do something contrary to the divine nature of Christ. Rather, we have a consistent picture of a *single* person always acting in wholeness and unity. The council insisted that Jesus was one person, although possessing both a human nature and a divine nature. Nestorianism was rejected.

The Council of Chalcedon (AD 451)

This is the final and climactic of the four great Christological councils. In many ways it solidified and established what the church believes the Bible teaches concerning the person of Christ. It incorporated the major components of the three previous councils. In a real sense its affirmations concerning Christ would not be attacked until the time of the Enlightenment when the rejection of supernaturalism called for a redefining of the person and work of Christ.

A man by the name of Eutyches (ca. 378–454), who was the head of a large monastery in Constantinople, was condemned, excommunicated, and deposed. He held a view called Monophysitism, meaning "one nature." Eutyches taught that the human nature of Christ was taken up and absorbed into the divine nature so that both natures were changed, and thus a new third kind of nature resulted. Jesus, according to this view, was a mixture of divine and human elements in which both were somewhat modified to form one new nature. The problem with this view is that it held that Christ is neither truly God nor truly man. If that is so, then he could not truly represent us as a human being, nor could he be true God and thus be able to pay our sin penalty and redeem us as our substitute. A total of 630 bishops gathered at the Council of Chalcedon. The following is the statement they formulated:

> Following, then, the holy fathers, we unite in teaching all men to confess the one and only Son, our Lord Jesus Christ. This self-same one is perfect both in deity and also in human-ness; this self-same one is also actually God and actually man, with a rational soul and a body. He is of the same reality [*homoousion*] as we are ourselves as far as his human-ness is concerned; thus like us in all respects, sin only excepted. Before time began he was begotten of the Father, in respect of his deity, and now in these "last days," for us and on behalf of our salvation, this selfsame one was born of Mary the virgin, who is God-bearer [*theotokos*] in respect of his human-ness.
>
> [We also teach] that we apprehend this one and only Christ-Son, Lord, only-begotten—in two natures; without confusing the two

natures, without transmuting one nature into the other, without dividing them into two separate categories, without contrasting them according to area or function. The distinctiveness of each nature is not nullified by the union. Instead, the "properties" of each nature are conserved and both natures concur in one "person" [*prosōpon*] and in one hypostasis. They are not divided or cut into two "persons" [*prosōpa*], but are together the one and only and only-begotten *Logos* of God, the Lord Jesus Christ. Thus have the prophets of old testified; thus the Lord Jesus Christ himself taught us; thus the Symbol of the Fathers has handed down to us.

The creed of Chalcedon sought to summarize and address every problem that had plagued the church with regard to the person of Christ. It argued against:

- *Docetism*: The Lord Jesus was perfect in his humanity and truly human, consubstantial with us according to his humanity and born of the virgin Mary.
- *Adoptionism*: It affirmed the eternality of the Logos, "begotten of the Father before the ages." He has always existed as the Son.
- *Modalism*: It distinguished the Son from the Father both by the titles of "Father" and "Son" and by the reference to the Father having begotten the Son before time began. The Father is not the Son.
- *Arianism*: It affirmed that the Lord Jesus was eternal and perfect in his deity, truly God.
- *Apollinarianism*: It confessed that the Lord Jesus Christ was "truly man of a reasonable soul [spirit] and body . . . consubstantial with us according to his humanity; in all things like unto us."
- *Nestorianism*: It affirmed Jesus' full deity and the truth of a real incarnation. It also spoke throughout of one and the same Son and one person and one subsistence, not parted or divided into two persons and whose natures are in union without division and without separation.
- *Eutychianism*: It confessed that in Christ there were two natures without confusion and without change, the property of each nature being preserved and concurring in the one person.

Chalcedon teaches that Christ is "one person with two natures," with the person being that of the Son of the triune God. The eternal Son of God took to himself a truly human nature, and Christ's divine and human natures remain distinct and retain their own properties. Yet they are permanently and inseparably united together in one person. In other words, Jesus Christ is fully God and fully man. Taking on a human nature did not involve mixing divine attributes with human or converting one nature to the other. The two natures are inseparably joined together in one person now and forever.

Nicene-Chalcedonian Christology affirms that in our Lord Jesus Christ we come face-to-face with God. We meet God, not subsumed under human flesh, not merely associated with it, not merely accompanying it, not merely shining through it, but in undiminished moral splendor, giving to humanity the moral completeness which has been missing since the time of the fall. The divine Word, then, was not united to a human nature that was antithetical to his own life, but rather the divine Word already possessed everything that was necessary to be human. The deity and humanity coincide, not because the human has grown into the divine but because the divine has taken the human into itself in an action in which the human reaches its fulfillment. In Christ we see all that Adam was intended to be but never was, all that we are not but which we will become through resurrection and glorification (1 John 3:1–3).

Christology in the Church Councils

The resolution of trinitarian relationships
and the hypostatic union of Christ

Error Against Deity	Church Position	Errors Against Humanity
Arius Christ is a created being.	**Nicea, 325** CHRIST IS ETERNAL AND TRULY GOD	
	Constantinople, 381 FULL HUMANITY OF CHRIST IS AFFIRMED	Apollinarus dominant Logos over the humanity
Nestorius Christ is two natures in a mechanical union.	**Ephesus, 431** UNITY OF CHRIST'S PER- SONALITY IS AFFIRMED	
	Chalcedon, 451 ORTHODOX CHRISTOLOGY ESTABLISHED: Two natures in one person	Eutyches divine nature swallows up the human nature

Modern Attacks on the Christ of the Bible

Christological thinking went basically unchallenged in the Middle Ages and through the Reformation period (sixteenth century). With the dawning of the Enlightenment and the age of reason, all of that changed. The Christ revealed in the Bible and the Christ confessed by the church for most of its history came under fierce assault as an antisupernatural bias came to the forefront. Attacks come from several directions, and yet virtually each attack is comprised of two common characteristics: (1) a denial of Christ's deity, and (2) a rejection of his work on the cross as the sufficient provision for salvation. With the advent of classical liberalism, redefinitions of the person and work of Christ came forth like a flood.

The Jesus of the Liberal Theologians

The Jesus of liberalism is an outgrowth of what has been called "the quest for the historical Jesus," a designation that caught on as a result of the landmark work by Albert Schweitzer: *The Quest for the Historical Jesus* (1906). Friedrich Schleiermacher (1768–1834) was the most influential theologian of the nineteenth century. He is rightly called the father of modern liberal theology. He helped launch the attacks on the Jesus of the Bible, offering an adoptionist understanding of Jesus that rejected his preexistence. Jesus was not the eternal Son of God become human, the *Logos* incarnate. For Schleiermacher, what distinguished Jesus from other humans was "the constant potency of his God-consciousness, which was a veritable existence of God in him."[106] Recommending belief in inspiration instead of incarnation, he presented Jesus as a God-filled man, a God-intoxicated man. This Jesus, who differed from us only in having been a better person than we are, is an inspiring example for us to follow. He is not the Savior in the biblical sense.

At a later date (ca. 1880–1920), the history-of-religions school would dominate. It argued that Christ's preexistence and incarnation were only myths intended to give him a stature equal to that of other heroic figures of his day. The doctrine of Jesus' preexistence resulted from the attempt to push his divine status earlier and earlier in his existence. A distinction was created between the Jesus of history (the man who actually lived) and the Christ of faith (the mythical Christ created in the minds of the early church). It is out of this boiling cauldron of Christological redefinition that the "quest for the historical Jesus" emerged.

The quest for the historical Jesus, with its post-Enlightenment skepticism, antisupernatural bias, and alleged use of a rigorous scientific methodology, began in earnest in the nineteenth century. Three phases of the modern quests can be identified.

The first quest. David Friedrich Strauss wrote *The Life of Jesus* in 1835–1836. In it he questioned the Gospel accounts as accurate historical

---

[106] Friedrich Schleiermacher, *The Christian Faith* (Philadelphia: Fortress, 1976), S 94. See also Schleiermacher's *The Life of Jesus,* trans. S. Maclean Gilmour (Minneapolis: Fortress Press, 1975). The Jesus later imagined by John Hick in the twentieth century is little different from that of Schleiermacher. Hick writes, "He was a man of God living in the unseen presence of God, and addressing God as *abba,* father. His spirit was open to God. . . . He was so powerfully God-conscious that his life vibrated, as it were, to the divine life." See Hick, ed., *The Myth of God Incarnate,* 172.

records of Jesus' words and deeds. This work shook the theological world. Joseph Ernest Renan came to similar conclusions and as a result lost his job at the University of Paris. The first quest for the historical Jesus—the Jesus behind the embellished Gospels—was off and running. The search moved forward until Albert Schweitzer halted its progress with his book. Schweitzer demonstrated that these questers ignored the eschatological and apocalyptic dimensions of Jesus' life, teachings, and actions, and that their Jesus looked suspiciously like they themselves. Schweitzer's Jesus was not God incarnate either, but he did effectively point out the shortcomings and flaws in the first quest.[107]

The second quest. A new quest was launched around 1950. In 1953 Ernst Käsemann suggested that even though the Gospel traditions reflected the perspectives of Jesus' followers, they could not be discounted as witnesses of authentic historical evidence.[108] The second so-called "new quest" was inaugurated. The Jesus of the "new questers" also was distorted, looking very much like an existentialist philosopher. This is not surprising since that worldview greatly influenced the presuppositions of the new quest's most influential scholars. But the new quest also experienced something of a setback in the early 1970s when existentialism waned. It did not completely vanish, but it did encounter new opposition.

The third quest. A period of reevaluation, methodological refinement, and new archaeological and manuscript evidence created a renewed sense that historians could get back to the historical Jesus, the Jesus behind the Gospels. Since the 1980s the number of scholars who have written major works on the historical Jesus has exploded. First, there are those looking for a Jewish Jesus in a first-century context. Second, there is the infamous "Jesus Seminar," a movement that is essentially an extension of the second questers. The third quest believes a portrait of Jesus that historically fits into first-century Judaism can be defended. They argue that there is reliable material in the Gospels that tells us about what Jesus did and taught. The Jesus Seminar argues that the portrait of Jesus in the Bible is mostly a theological creation of the early church. Thus in the midst of the activity of the two quests, we now possess multiple competing portraits of Jesus, portraits which picture him as a first-century Jew, a revolutionary, a Cynic-

---

[107] Albert Schweitzer, *The Quest of the Historical Jesus* (1910; repr., New York: Macmillan, 1964), 367–71.

[108] This was the view of his mentor Rudolf Bultmann, who sought to demythologize the New Testament, stripping it of anything supernatural. See his *Jesus Christ and Mythology* (London: SCM, 1960). One cannot help but appreciate the telling, if somewhat sarcastic, comment of Macleod: "Bultman appears to assume that the people of the first century were credulous to the point of universal stupidity" (*Person of Christ*, 111).

like sage, a reforming teacher of Judaism, a prophet, a restorer/reformer of Israel, and/or a messianic claimant.[109]

What should be our response to all this? There are a number of short-comings in the third quest's method and conclusions, especially those of the more radical wing.

1. Their antisupernatural worldview biases their evaluation of the biblical material before they even begin. They are not really open to where the data might lead because they have determined in advance where it must lead: to a purely human Jesus who cannot be God.

2. All the information we have on Jesus demands that he look like a first-century Jew who spent his life in Israel.

3. The object of Christian faith is the triune God revealed in history and the Old and New Testaments. Here we discover the promise of a Savior (Old Testament) and the coming of that Savior (New Testament). The flow of redemptive history is something all the questers fail to fully consider and appreciate.

4. The Jesus of history and the Christ of faith cannot be separated, for they are one and the same. Therefore, it is not surprising that each quest has failed at some point.

5. All evidence points in the direction that the high Christology of the church has its source in Jesus and that worship of Jesus as God was there from the beginning. Davis puts it this way:

> A convincing case can be made that much of the material in the Gospels that implies a high Christology can in some form be traced back to Jesus, and that he implicitly claimed the high status that the church attributed to him. Here is one telling fact about the earliest Christians: They practiced worship of Jesus. Early Christian prayers were addressed to Jesus, one preserved even in Aramaic ("Maranatha"), which attests to its earliness (1 Cor. 16:22; see also 2 Cor. 12:8; 1 Thess. 3:11–13; 2 Thess. 2:16–17; 3:5,16; Acts 1:24; 7:59–60). There were also doxologies addressed to Christ, or to Christ and the Father together (Rom. 16:27; cf. 2 Cor. 1:20; 2 Tim. 4:18; 2 Pet. 3:18; Rev. 1:5–6,13; cf. 7:10), and hymns of praise to Christ (Phil. 2:6–11; 1 Tim. 3:16; cf. Eph. 5:19; Col. 3:16). In Matthew's Gospel, after the resurrection, Jesus is worshiped (*proskynesis*) by Mary Magdalene and the other

---

[109] For an excellent survey of these various portraits, see B. Witherington III, *The Jesus Quest* (Downers Grove: InterVarsity, 1995).

Mary (28:9) and by the 11 disciples on the mountain (28:17).[110]

6. If Jesus was little more than a witty sage or cynic philosopher who spoke only in short pithy sayings or parables, why was he crucified? What threat was he either to the Jewish authorities or the Roman government? A sage or cynic philosopher would have challenged certain social and cultural conventions in his day, but this is hardly the kind of activity that gets one nailed to a cross.

7. The work of the Jesus Seminar, in particular, is not really new. It is simply a continuation of the antisupernatural approach of persons like Rudolf Bultmann who attempted (and failed) to get back to the historical Jesus by means of "demythologization." Strip away anything and everything that looks supernatural and see what is left. The result: such a Jesus could not have inspired worship, much less martyrdom, on the part of his followers.

8. The uncertainties of critical scholars and the varied portraits that they paint of Jesus should give us pause. If they are so fair and objective with the evidence, why is it that they cannot agree among themselves on who Jesus was? Is it perhaps that they are guilty of biases, prejudices, and agendas that cause them "to discover" a Jesus very much to their liking?

9. The Gospels were written from the standpoint of faith for the purpose of spreading the faith. This is honestly admitted in the biblical texts themselves, and it does not lessen their credibility but actually enhances it. James Edwards says:

> Modern scholarship has correctly shown that the Gospels are not strict biographies, but presentations of Jesus told from the standpoint of faith and for the purpose of furthering faith. The Gospels are part of the kerygma, the proclamation of the early church, which means that Jesus can be known only through the testimony of his followers. Liberal scholarship errs, however, in assuming that this testimony results in a distortion of the historical Jesus. Contrary to the assumption of discontinuity, the New Testament not infrequently testifies to the respect with which the Jesus tradition was held (1 Cor. 7:6,12,25). There is reason for confidence that the early

---

[110] Steven Davis, "Why the Historical Jesus Matters," in *Theology News and Notes* (June 1999).

church acted as custodian of the Jesus tradition rather than as corrupter of it.[111]

10. Numerous eyewitnesses were alive when the Gospels were written. They most certainly would have functioned as custodians and protectors of the testimony concerning Jesus.

Edwards rightfully concludes, "The most reasonable answer to the question why the Gospels present Jesus as they do is that this is essentially who Jesus was. The Gospels faithfully preserve the memory that He left on His followers, that He was divinely legitimated and empowered to be God's Son and Servant."[112] This is the Jesus of Scripture. This is the Jesus confessed by the believing church.[113]

How Does It All Fit Together?

Systematizing our understanding of the person of Jesus Christ is challenging but essential. There will always be an element of mystery, and this is as it should be. Yet there are some basic nonnegotiables that we can and must affirm if we are to be true to biblical revelation, and if we are to honor the witness of the church throughout her history. At least seven bedrock affirmations must be affirmed and defended. There is some overlap in these affirmations, but each highlights and emphasizes a particular aspect of Christology.

1. There is a true incarnation of the *Logos,* the second person of the triune God. The Son of God, being sent by the Father, actually and truly assumed the whole of human nature. The incarnation is not a subtraction of deity; it is an addition of sinless humanity. In this event the second person of the Trinity truly and genuinely invaded time and space, taking to himself real humanity. Any form of docetic theology must be firmly rejected and dismissed.

Further, it is the Father who sent the Son. A functional (not essential) subordination of the Son to the Father is clearly evident and gives us some understanding of the innerrelationship that exists within the Godhead. It also helps us understand that there is no inherent inferiority in submission in human relationships as well. Bauman is helpful when he writes:

---

[111] James Edwards, "Who Do Scholars Say That I Am?" *Christianity Today* (4 March 1996): 16.
[112] Ibid., 20.
[113] For a fine treatment of Christology as reflected in various modern theologies, see Erickson, *The Word Became Flesh,* 89–379.

If a theologian posits a subordination of order or of function
and not of essence or nature, he is orthodox. His view is one of
economic and not emphatic subordinationism. The emphatic is a
subordination of essence and not merely of external function. This
position is heretical because it posits a Godhead not only unequal
in office but also unequal in nature. In the orthodox, or economic,
Trinity, however, the Son occupies a secondary position not meta-
physically, but only voluntarily. . . . Such subordination is theologically acceptable.[114]

Dagg properly emphasizes the integrity of Christ's humanity in his theology when he notes:

The testimony of the inspired word on this point is very explicit.
Whatever else Jesus Christ may have been, he was certainly a man;
for so innumerable passages of Scripture declare . . . Adam is called
the first man, and Christ the second man. The humanity of the latter
is as real as that of the former."[115]

In this context we affirm that the humanity of Jesus was exactly like that
of Adam and Eve prior to the fall: it was a sinless humanity.[116] The human
nature which the Son took to himself had no taint of sin whatsoever. It is
for this reason that the truest and most genuine expression of humanity, and
what it means to be human, is made manifest in Jesus Christ.

2. There is a necessary distinction between the natures of Jesus Christ
and his person. He is a single person who possesses the totality of both the
divine and human natures. "Nature" constitutes the totality of powers and
qualities which constitute a being, while "person" is the self-conscious,
self-asserting, and acting subject. This distinction is embedded in Scripture,
particularly the New Testament, and it was hammered out in the four great
Christological councils. Jesus Christ is no schizophrenic. It is not true that
in Jesus there are two self-consciousnesses, but as Macleod notes, "There
are two levels of consciousness of the one self. There is a divine consciousness that he is the eternal Son of God, and there is a human consciousness
of the same fact. The two forms of consciousness remain distinct, united in
the one person, communicating through the Holy Spirit."[117]

---

[114] Michael E. Bauman, "Milton, Subordination, and the Two-Stage Logos," *WTJ* (Spring 1986):
174. Macleod, *The Person of Christ*, notes, "Some kind of functional subordination is clearly implied in the incarnation and the mission of the Son" (76).
[115] John L. Dagg, *Manual of Theology* (Charleston: Southern Baptist Publication Society, 1858),
179–80.
[116] Boyce, *Abstract of Systematic Theology*, also emphasized this point (276).
[117] Macleod, *The Person of Christ*, 193.

Mullins correctly asserts, "In Jesus Christ there was an alliance between God and man rather than God becoming man."[118] This is not to deny that "at one time the human, at another time the divine, aspect of his person is emphasized. But there is no evidence of disunion or contradiction manifested at any time."[119] The emphasis Mullins rightly recognizes is seen clearly, for example, in the normal and natural development of Jews from infancy to adult male. Carroll addresses this when he writes:

> And Jesus advanced in wisdom and stature. In other words, his humanity was not mere appearance. It was an actual humanity. . . . His mind and body as a child were susceptible of the same development as the minds and bodies of children of the present day, or of any period of the world's history. Very clearly and necessarily does the pure humanity of Jesus appear.[120]

Yet it was this human nature, possessing its full integrity, that is united to the divine nature, possessing its full integrity, wedded in the one person Jesus Christ. The result is a theanthropic person. As Garrett says, "The unity of the person of Jesus Christ means that there is no double personality or independent functioning of separate natures."[121]

3. The God-man is the result of the incarnation,[122] and the virgin birth is the means by which God chose to accomplish this. Jesus Christ is not a double being, a compound being, or some kind of hybrid being. He is the one person of our Lord Jesus Christ, complete in his deity and perfect in his humanity. John Owen summarizes this point well, "He is God and man in one person. In him are two distinct natures, the one eternal, infinite, immense, almighty, the form and essence of God; the other having a beginning in time, finite, limited, confined to a certain place, which is our nature."[123]

The connection between the virgin birth and the sinlessness of Jesus is often taken for granted within evangelical circles. One will often hear from a pulpit, "No virgin birth, no sinless life. No sinless life, no Savior." The

---

[118] E. Y. Mullins, *The Christian Religion in Its Doctrinal Expression* (Philadelphia: Judson, 1927), 178.

[119] Ibid., 176.

[120] Carroll, *Jesus the Christ,* 34.

[121] James Leo Garrett, *Systematic Theology* (Grand Rapids: Eerdmans, 1990), 1:624. Garrett adds, "Jesus is 'a very complex person' but not 'an amalgam of human and divine qualities merged into some sort of *tertium quid.*'"

[122] Dargan notes, "He was God-man. Never did a hyphen mean so much! It both joins and divides. There is distinction and yet unity." Edwin Charles Dargan, *The Doctrines of Our Faith* (Nashville: Sunday School Board of the Southern Baptist Convention, 1920), 63.

[123] Owen, *The Glory of Christ,* 28. Owen adds, "He became what he was not, but he did not cease to be what he always was (John 3:13)" (41).

latter affirmation is without question correct. However, one must proceed carefully on this issue and make a clear distinction between scriptural affirmation and theological deduction. Macleod accurately notes, "The New Testament never sets forth the miraculous conception as an explanation for his sinlessness. Nor would the elimination of the male factor in the conception of our Lord by itself explain his sinlessness."[124] Dagg sees the issue in a similar fashion: "Had it been his pleasure, Jesus Christ might have had a human father as well as a human mother; and have been, nevertheless, without sin; for with God all things are possible."[125]

Having said this, it is still the case that several observations can be made by theological reflection that would suggest strongly a legitimate connection between the virgin birth and the sinless life. First, Jesus is the only virgin-conceived person who lived a sinless life. Second, the activity of the Holy Spirit in the process of conception must not be overlooked or underappreciated. Third, the virgin conception "helps us understand how Christ can stand outside the guilt of Adam."[126] This is an especially important point. Fourth, a sinless humanity is scarcely conceivable, if not impossible, without divine intervention. As "the first man was holy because God made him so; the new man (the Christian) is holy because God makes him so; the last man is holy because God makes him so."[127] Therefore, we do affirm a legitimate and vital link between the virgin conception and the sinless life of Jesus.

4. In the incarnation there is no qualification or diminution of either Christ's deity or his humanity. Each nature retains its own integrity and genuineness. Whatever it is that constitutes God as God, the Son is this in all of its fullness (Col. 2:9–10). Further, whatever it is that constitutes man as man, Jesus of Nazareth is this in all of its fullness. Boyce notes, "He is as properly a human person, therefore as he would be if not divine, just as he is as properly a divine person as he would be if not a man."[128] From this we learn that sin is not needed for humans to be human. Again, it is in Jesus that we see humanity perfectly displayed as God intended. It is fallen and sinful humanity that lives on a subhuman plane, not Jesus.

The crucial importance of maintaining "two nature" Christology is well defended by B. B. Warfield. In fact he saw in the two-nature doctrine the essence of the Christian faith itself. Warfield writes:

> One of the most portentous symptoms of the decay of vital sympathy with historical Christianity which is observable in present-day

---

124 Macleod, *The Person of Christ,* 39.
125 Dagg, *Mauual of Theology,* 181.
126 Macleod, *The Person of Christ,* 41.
127 Ibid.
128 Boyce, *Abstract of Systematic Theology,* 286.

academic circles is the widespread tendency in recent Christological discussion to revolt from the doctrine of the Two Natures in the Person of Christ. The significance of this revolt becomes at once apparent, when we reflect that the doctrine of the Two Natures is one other way of stating the doctrine of the Incarnation; and the doctrine of the Incarnation is the hinge on which the Christian system turns. No Two Natures, no Incarnation; no Incarnation, no Christianity in any distinctive sense.[129]

In our judgment Warfield's concern is neither misplaced nor overstated. The doctrine of the "two natures" is essential to any expression of biblical and historical Christology. To comprise or jettison the doctrine can only result in a radical redefinition of Christianity itself.

5. <u>There is a genuine hypostatic union in which the divine nature and the human nature come together and are present in the one person Jesus Christ</u>. This union is real, supernatural, personal, inseparable, and permanent. The permanence of the union should be firmly maintained. There is today in heaven a God-man who is "at the right hand of the Majesty on high" (Heb. 1:3) and who "always lives to intercede for [us]" (Heb. 7:25). "The Son is exactly like the Father in all respects except that he is the Son."[130] Jesus is like every human in all respects except that he did not sin. That which is truly divine and truly human has been really united in the one Lord Jesus Christ.

Wells seeks to address the importance of the hypostatic union, and he addresses how the divine taking to himself the human is not inconceivable but actually reasonable. He writes: "The Christ whom we meet, in whom and because of whom we find forgiveness, is personally identical with the Galilean whom the Gospels describes. . . . Christ is not other than Jesus."[131] Wells then adds:

> Human nature as created is the echo of which the Creator is sound. He is original, and we are derivative . . . a perfect humanity, one unspoiled by sin, would not only coalesce naturally with the divine but would, in fact, find its perfection in the divine from which it was derived. . . . In Christ we see all that Adam was intended to be, but never was, all that we are not but which we will become through resurrection.[132]

6. <u>The whole of Christ's work, that is all that he does, is to be attributed to his person and not to one or the other nature exclusively</u>. As will become

129 Benjamin Breckinridge Warfield, *The Person and Work of Christ* (1950; repr., Philadelphia: Presbyterian and Reformed, 1970), 211.
130 Macleod, *The Person of Christ,* 129.
131 David Wells, *The Person of Christ* (Westchester: Crossway, 1984), 175.
132 Ibid., 178.

clear in our examination of the work of Christ, there is an ontological necessity to the incarnation. It is required that Christ be both God and man.
It was only as man that he could be a redeemer for humanity and only as a
sinless man that he could die in the place of another. It was only as God that
his life, ministry, and redeeming death could have infinite value and satisfy
the demands of God so as to deliver others from sin. We need a God-man.
The person of Jesus Christ is the God-man, the second person of the triune
God who took to himself a human nature for the work of redemption.[133]

In the incarnation the Son assumed a human nature in addition to his
eternal nature. Within the one person Jesus Christ, these two natures function with full integrity and interrelatedness. Jesus Christ is a theanthropic
person who possesses all the essential qualities of both the human and the
divine nature. Deity and humanity have been perfectly and permanently
joined together with the totality of Christ's work being attributed to his total person. As the God-man he performs and accomplishes all that he does.
Any attempt to separate the natures and ascribe certain actions or works to
one nature or the other is wrongheaded and must be refused, regardless of
how appealing it might be. Boyce points out, "So intimate is the union of
the one person with two distinct natures, that we cannot always separate
what Christ says of himself as God, from what is said of himself as man."[134]
We would remove the word "always" from Boyce and maintain both the
tension and mystery of this point of Christology.

7. Jesus Christ exists only by means of the incarnation. There is no
Jesus of Nazareth who possesses an independent life of his own. There was
a time when Jesus did not exist. There has *never* been a time when the Son
did not exist.[135] The man Jesus had his beginning when he was conceived
in the womb of the virgin Mary. Prior to this he had no existence. Mullins
points out, "He is not man from eternity past, as is true of his Godhead. He
became man at a particular point in time through the Incarnation."[136]

How Does This Doctrine Impact the Church Today?

And most certainly, the mystery of godliness is great: He was
manifested in the flesh, justified in the Spirit, seen by angels,

---

[133] Mullins, *The Christian Religion,* agrees with this assessment and states, "But now, having become man, he is the God-man to whom we look for salvation" (278).
[134] Boyce, *Abstract of Systematic Theology,* 288.
[135] These seven tenets also are briefly summarized in a similar manner in Bernard Ramm, *An
Evangelical Christology* (Nashville: Nelson, 1985), 9–10.
[136] Mullins, *The Christian Religion,* 278.

preached among the Gentiles, believed on in the world, taken up in glory (1 Tim. 3:16).

No person has ever impacted the world like Jesus of Nazareth. C. S. Lewis summarizes well the witness of Scripture to the impact Jesus made when he began his public ministry:

> Among these Jews there suddenly turns up a man who goes about talking as if he was God. He claims to forgive sins. He says he has always existed. He says he is coming to judge the world at the end of time. Now let us get this clear. Among Pantheists, like the Indians, anyone might say that he was a part of God, or one with God: there would be nothing very odd about it. But this man, since he was a Jew, could not mean that kind of God. God, in their language, meant the Being outside the world who had made it and was infinitely different from anything else. And when you have grasped that, you will see that what this man said was, quite simply, the most shocking thing that has ever been uttered by human lips.[137]

The self-claims of Jesus are a crucial component of our understanding of Christology. What Jesus believed about himself must be carefully weighed as we begin to construct a theology of his person and work. If he did believe and say what Scripture attributes to him, the impact is significant. Lewis is again helpful:

> I am trying here to prevent anyone saying the really foolish thing that people often say about him: "I'm ready to accept Jesus as a great moral teacher, but I don't accept his claim to be God." That is the one thing we must not say. A man who was merely a man and said the sort of things Jesus said would not be a great moral teacher. He would either be a lunatic—on a level with the man who says he is a poached egg—or else he would be the Devil of Hell. You must make your choice. Either this man was, and is, the Son of God; or else a madman or something worse. You can shut him up for a fool, you can spit at him and kill him as a demon; or you can fall at his feet and call him Lord and God. But let us not come with any patronizing nonsense about his being a great human teacher. He has not left that open to us. He did not intend to.[138]

---

[137] C. S. Lewis, *Mere Christianity* (New York: Macmillan, 1952), 54–55.
[138] Ibid., 55–56.

It is from this statement that we have the famous "trilemma" of Lewis concerning who Jesus is. He is Lord, liar, or lunatic. However, we would suggest a slight adjustment in light of modern developments in Christology. Actually there are four possible answers to the question, "Who is Jesus?" They are:

- **Liar**—He was not who he said he was, and he knew it.
- **Lunatic**—He was not who he thought he was and did not know it.
- **Legend**—He was not who others later imagined him to be.
- **Lord**—He was who he said he was; and his life, death, and resurrection prove it to be so.

If Jesus of Nazareth was not the Christ, the fulfillment of Old Testament promise and prophecy, the Son of God, and the Savior of the world and he knew it, He is a *liar* of the worst sort; and we should scorn him and ignore him. On the other hand, if he was not who he thought he was, given his tragically deluded self-understanding, we should pity him and dismiss him for a *lunatic*. It is rather difficult, however, on this position, to explain the remarkable teaching that flowed from his mouth. If he is simply a *legend,* something of a heroic make-believe character along the lines of the ancient Hercules or Santa Claus, we might admire the biblical stories for their wonderful charm, but we would certainly not view this person as the most significant individual to walk the earth, much less worship him. But if he is *Lord,* the Son of God, the Messiah, the risen and ascended and exalted King of kings, we are confronted with a completely different decision altogether.

Dale Moody says, "The belief that Jesus is the Christ, the one uniquely anointed by God for the fulfillment of his promise to Israel and through Israel to the world, is the central doctrine of the Christian faith."[139] Dagg, complementing this perspective, sees the claim of Christ's deity as the non-negotiable: "We must believe that the deity of Christ is an essential doctrine of Christianity. As there can be no religion without the existence of God; so there can be no Christian creed in which the doctrine of Christ's deity is not a fundamental article."[140]

Christology is the focal point and essence of Christianity. As we have seen, from Genesis to Revelation, Jesus is the Bible's great theme. Scripture provides an incomparable portrait of the Word who "became flesh and took up residence among us" (John 1:14). No doctrine has a more significant im-

---

[139] Dale Moody, *The Word of Truth* (Grand Rapids: Eerdmans, 1981), 366. Macleod adds, "The central feature of Christology is (and always has been) the worship of Jesus" (*Person of Christ,* 119).

[140] Dagg, *Manual of Theology,* 191.

pact on one's theology than the doctrine of Christ. What we believe about Jesus, who he is and what he did, will greatly shape the rest of our theology—what we believe about the Bible, God, humanity, the Holy Spirit, salvation, the church, and eschatology.

Exclusive and ultimate truth claims about Jesus Christ often do not receive a welcoming reception. However, the Bible must be the fundamental way to see Jesus. Jesus' coming was promised throughout the Old Testament, and his virgin birth is not mythology but took place in space and time.[141] Jesus is the God-man, complete in his deity and perfect in his humanity. As we now prepare to turn to his work in the next chapter, we confess that it is God's Son who came into this world to save sinners and that he is the only way to God, as Jesus declares himself (John 14:6). It was the God-man who died on a Roman cross outside the city of Jerusalem. Because he was the God-man, he could make a perfect sacrifice and atonement for the sins of the whole world (1 John 2:2).

On the Sunday following his crucifixion, God raised his Son from the dead. Jesus' resurrection is not fable or fiction but historical fact, establishing him as "the powerful Son of God" (Rom. 1:4). It establishes further, by tangible proof, Jesus' lordship over all things (Phil. 2:9–11; Col. 1:18). Forty days following his resurrection, Jesus ascended back to heaven as the God-man, where he was exalted at his Father's right hand (Acts 1:9–11; Heb. 1:3). Scripture promises that Jesus will come again to this earth as "KING OF KINGS AND LORD OF LORDS" (Rev. 19:16). This is the "blessed hope" for which Christians wait (Titus 2:13).[142] This event will bring history to a close. How then are we to respond?

John Knox said, "No one else holds or has held the place in the heart of the world which Jesus holds. Other gods have been devoutly worshipped; no other man has been so devoutly loved." Augustine described him simply as "beauty ever ancient, ever new."[143] Charles Spurgeon, the great British Baptist, understood well the preeminent position Jesus Christ must have when it comes to the mission and ministry of the church. When the Metropolitan Tabernacle opened in 1861, Spurgeon boldly stated, "I would propose that the subject of the ministry of this house, as long as

---

[141] Barth well states, "The Virgin Birth at the opening and the empty tomb at the close of Jesus' life bear witness that this life is in fact marked off from all the rest of human life, and marked off, in the first instance, not by our understanding or our interpretation, but by itself." Karl Barth, *Church Dogmatics,* (Edinburgh: T. & T. Clark, 1956), 1/2:182.

[142] Mullins provides his own summation and states: "We should keep in mind the aim in any effort to express in words the doctrine of Christ's Person. It is to unify our impression of Jesus as he stands forth in the New Testament and in Christian experience generally. This involves his preexistence, his deity, his sinlessness, his humanity with its humiliations and limitations of knowledge, his subordination, along with his equality with the Father." Mullins, *The Christian Religion,* 179.

[143] Augustine, *Confessions,* as quoted in Jaroslav Pelikan, *Jesus through the Centuries* (New Haven: Yale University Press, 1985), 1.

this platform shall stand, and as long as this house shall be frequented by worshippers, shall be the person of Jesus Christ."[144] Later, in his *Lectures to My Students,* he would add, "Of all I would wish to say this is the sum; my brethren, preach Christ, always and evermore. He is the whole gospel. His person, offices, and work must be our one great, all-comprehending theme."[145]

Paul reminded the Colossians, "Whatever you do, do it enthusiastically, as something done for the Lord, and not for men . . . you serve the Lord Christ" (Col. 3:23–24). Only one who is God should be Lord in our lives. Only one who is divine should have the right to have every knee bow and every tongue confess his lordship (Phil. 2:10–11). God the Father loves to exalt his Son and magnify his name, and so should we. For every believer, "living is Christ and dying is gain" (Phil. 1:21). To live for Christ is to "make your own attitude that of Christ Jesus" (Phil. 2:5). Every thought, every emotion, every word, every action, is to be taken "captive to the obedience of Christ" (2 Cor. 10:5). Only one who is God can rightly demand such allegiance. Only one who is God should be granted such allegiance. This worship and service Christians gladly give to the one whom they confess, as did Thomas, as "my Lord and my God!" (John 20:28).

---

[144] Susannah Spurgeon and J. W. Harrald, *C. H. Spurgeon's Autobiography* (London: Passmore & Alabaster, 1899), 3:1.

[145] C. H. Spurgeon, *Lectures to My Students* (Grand Rapids: Baker, 1987), 1:82–83.

CHAPTER 10

The Work of Christ

Paige Patterson

J esus Christ, the Son of God, was born to die. Unlike any other person who has ever lived, he came into this world for the expressed purpose of dying on the cross as the perfect sacrifice for the sins of the world (1 John 2:2; 4:10). First John 4:14 teaches us, "The Father has sent the Son as Savior of the world."[1] John Stott reminds us, "Evangelical Christians believe that in and through Christ crucified God substituted himself for us and bore our sins, dying in our place the death we deserved to die, in order that we might be restored to his favor and adopted into his family."[2]

Only hours before the passion of Jesus, the disciples sat with him at a Passover meal. Arriving at a poignant moment, Jesus took bread, broke and distributed that loaf, and said to his followers, "Take, eat; this is my body which is broken for you; do this in remembrance of me." He also took the cup and observed that it represented the new covenant in his blood (1 Cor. 11:24–25). Together with the initiatory act of baptism (commanded by Jesus in Matthew 28:18–20 and explained by Paul in Romans 6:1–6), these two ordinances served as the totality of ritual given by Christ to his church.

Emphasizing Spirit-inspired preaching, singing, and prayer, the worship of the earliest assemblies was relatively unencumbered with rite or ritual except for baptism and the Lord's Supper, which by their very existence provide a powerful declaration. In the work of Christ, only the atonement is memorialized. In the Lord's Supper the church is encouraged to remember the broken body and shed blood of Jesus in his passion. Baptism commemorates his burial and his triumphant resurrection on the third day. Both ordinances focus on the incarnation (body, shedding of blood, burial, resurrection) and on the Lord's work of atonement for the sins of humanity. The two together focus the attention of the believing community on the central facts of salvific history—Christ's incarnation, atonement, and resurrection.

---

[1] Unless otherwise noted, all Scripture citations in this chapter are from the Holman Christian Standard Bible (HCSB).

[2] John R. W. Stott, *The Cross of Christ* (Downers Grove: InterVarsity, 1986), 7.

What Does the Bible Say?

The Offices of Christ

The work of Christ has often been considered under the rubric of three offices: prophet, priest, and king. John Calvin summarized the matter in these words: "Therefore, in order that faith may find a firm basis for salvation in Christ, and thus rest in him, this principle must be laid down: the office enjoined upon Christ by the Father consists of three parts. For he was given to be prophet, king, and priest."[3]

While most evangelical commentators follow this structure, Millard Erickson notes that "office" does not always convey precisely what the interpreter may wish in the minds of contemporary audiences. He suggests, therefore, an evaluation based on function, viewing the work of Christ as revealing, ruling, and reconciling.[4] The point is well taken. The Scriptures do not speak of "offices" Christ holds. On the other hand, Jesus is called a prophet, a priest, and a king in Scripture; and those surely were "offices," for which, as Calvin notes, anointings with the holy oil were prescribed.[5] Hence, to employ the traditional and scriptural categories to describe the work of Christ is appropriate.   Patterson's Calvin?

Prophet

In his concluding address to the children of Israel, Moses promised a new day. In Deuteronomy 18:15–18, the lawgiver himself prophesied with these words:

> The LORD your God will raise up for you a prophet like me from among your own brothers. You must listen to him. This is what you requested from the LORD your God at Horeb on the day of the assembly when you said, "Let us not continue to hear the voice of the LORD our God or see this great fire any longer, so that we will not die!" Then the LORD said to me, "They have spoken well. I will raise up for them a prophet like you from among their brothers. I will put My words in his mouth, and he will tell them everything I command him."

Grudem notes that the New Testament documents do not abound with references to Jesus as a prophet. He further observes correctly the growing recognition among Jesus' followers and interpreters that he was much

---

[3] John Calvin, *Institutes of the Christian Religion,* LCC (Westminster: John Knox, 1960), 2.15.1.

[4] Millard Erickson, *Christian Theology* (Grand Rapids: Baker, 1985), 763.

[5] Calvin, *Institutes,* 2.15.2.

more than a prophet. Indeed he was the one of whom prophecy primarily spoke, which doubtlessly affirms this understanding.[6]

Nevertheless, there are references in the Gospels to Jesus as a prophet. More important, Peter in Acts identifies Jesus as the explicit and specific fulfillment of the Deuteronomic promises. Peter said, "The Lord your God will raise up for you a Prophet like me from among your brothers. You must listen to Him in everything He will say to you. And it will be that everyone who will not listen to that Prophet will be completely cut off from the people" (Acts 3:22–23).

Equally significant are the passages in which Jesus is presented as a revelation of God in word and deed. In Hebrews 1:1–2, the author notes that in the last days God, after speaking to his people at different times and in a diversity of ways through the prophets, has spoken through his Son. The prologue to John's Gospel presents Christ as the *Logos* of God (John 1:1,14). The context of the phrase "the word of God" as used of Christ is richer than human interpreters can fully unpack, but surely it means minimally that when Jesus spoke, God spoke and revealed himself.

Köstenberger writes concerning the *Logos:*

> The designation "Word"—used in a Christological sense only in the prologue (1:1,14)—conveys the notion of divine self-expression or speech (cf. Ps. 19:1–4). . . . As a comprehensive Christological designation, the expression 'the Word' encompasses Jesus' entire ministry, placing all of Jesus' works and words within the framework of both his eternal being and existence and God's self-revelation in salvation history.[7]

Other examples of this messianic self-understanding may be found in Jesus' synagogue sermon in Nazareth when, having read Isaiah 61:1–2, Luke reports in 4:21, "He began by saying to them, 'Today as you listen, this Scripture has been fulfilled.'" Again, when the Samaritan woman of John 4 was confronted with a dawning reality of the one whom she had engaged in conversation, she ventured the half-declaration, half-interrogative, "I know that Messiah is coming (who is called Christ). When He comes, He will explain everything to us" (John 4:25). The reply of Jesus evoked the aura and claim of a prophet when He declared, "I am He" (John 4:26).

What then is the significance of the claim that Jesus is a prophet? Does such a declaration call for red-letter editions of the Bible with the words of Jesus in red type, suggesting that they are somehow more the word of

---

[6] Wayne Grudem, *Systematic Theology: An Introduction to Biblical Doctrine* (Grand Rapids: Zondervan, 1994), 624–25.

[7] Andreas Köstenberger, *John,* BEC (Grand Rapids: Baker Academic, 2004), 25.

God than the words of Paul, John, or Moses? To the contrary, the church has always acknowledged that because of the inspiration of the Holy Spirit (the third person of the Trinity), beyond the specific words of Jesus, all the words of the Bible are just as surely the words of God (2 Tim. 3:16–17; 2 Pet. 1:20–21).

Jesus revealed God, however, not merely through his words but also through his deeds; and he did so in a way that no other prophet could ever have accomplished. This is important when assessing the claims of Muslims regarding the superiority of Mohammed. Jesus not only spoke for God; he spoke as God, revealing the character and purposes of God in the fullest sense. The prophet speaking is God (John 8:58).

For example, when the Bible declares that "God is love" (1 John 4:8), the tendency in contemporary society is to understand that love in a rather sentimental and emotional fashion. The deeds of Christ, however, demonstrate the nature of God's love as mercy, as severity, and as sacrifice, to name just three. In the Johannine pericope of the woman caught in adultery, the love of God is forgiving and merciful (John 7:53–8:11). In the narrative of the temple cleansing, Jesus defends his Father's house as a house of prayer, citing Psalm 69:9 to the effect that zeal for God's house had consumed him (John 2:17). Love for his Father as well as for the disadvantaged worshippers led him to a demonstration of severe love. The cross and the events associated with it provide an inestimable picture of sacrificial love. While Jesus spoke of love, his deeds were equally prophetic, revealing the true nature of such divine attributes as love, justice, judgment, and holiness.

In this sense then, Jesus is the ultimate Prophet. When he speaks in either word or action, God speaks. What he declares is unabridged truth. To an extent that transcends all previous or future prophets, his words and deeds transform lives and, ultimately, even the cosmos. Jesus is prophet.

King

The passion narrative in John's Gospel records the question put to Jesus by Pilate, "Are you the King of the Jews?" (18:33). The answer of Jesus included the declaration of a kingdom distinct from all mere worldly kingdoms (John 18:36), followed by a confession that he had been born for this very purpose—to be a king (18:37). In John 19:19, the evangelist records that Pilate followed his interrogation by affixing to the cross the epithet "Jesus the Nazarene, the King of the Jews." Whether Pilate was attempting to belittle Jesus or irritate the Jews, he inadvertently bore witness to the truth.

Two of the four definitive Christological passages in the New Testament include avowals of the kingship of Jesus the Christ. The author of Hebrews,

Heb.1 , Phil. 2

~~Hebrews 1~~

in the first chapter, cites Psalm 45:6–7 and then Psalm 110:1 in ascribing to the Son an eternal throne, a scepter of justice, and a footstool consisting of his enemies (vv. 4–14). The declaration of the fulfillment of Old Testament messianic prophecy with a declaration of the sovereignty of Christ is significant.

No message asserts the ultimate exaltation of Christ with greater clarity than the Christological declaration of Philippians 2:5–11. Having elaborated upon the humiliation of Christ at his atonement, Paul comes to his enthronement confessing that Jesus is Lord. Similarly, the Apocalypse abounds in references to the reign of Christ as King. John presents Jesus as the one who is alive forever and has the keys of death and the grave. So awesome is this appearance of Christ that John falls before him as though dead (Rev. 1:9–20). In the throne room vision of chapters 4 and 5, the Lamb who "sits on the throne" is worthy not only to open the seven-sealed scroll but also to receive honor and glory. In chapter 19, the triumphant, returning Christ has a name, "King of kings and Lord of lords" (Rev. 19:16).

Of this nomenclature, Gregory Beale observes:

> The name of Christ was "King of kings and Lord of lords," a title expressing the idea of "ultimate ruler over all kings." The name is taken from LXX of Dan. 4:37, where it is a title for God, and has already been applied to Christ in Rev. 17:14. Just as the Babylonian king was wrongly addressed by this title, so the king of latter-day Babylon (Rome) in John's day was similarly addressed. The title in Daniel 4 refers to God as the one who demonstrated his genuine divine sovereignty and revealed Nebuchadnezzar as an empty parody of the name by judging that beastly king of "Babylon the Great." And he exposes as false the divine claims of the emperor, the beast, and others like him.[8]

However, Erickson provides a cogent warning regarding the roles of Jesus as prophet and as king. When rehearsing Christ's role as prophet or revealer, the tendency is to think of this function of Jesus' ministry as belonging wholly to the past, whereas his ruling function is conceived as belonging to the future.[9] However, one of the words employed by New Testament writers for the return of Christ is *apokalypsis* or "unveiling." In other words, when Jesus returns, more will be revealed concerning the nature and purposes of God. For example, at that time, the saints of God will have understanding and knowledge not possible at the present (1 Cor. 13:12).

---

[8] G. K. Beale, *The Book of Revelation*, NIGTC (Grand Rapids: Eerdmans, 1999), 963–64.
[9] Erickson, *Christian Theology*, 766, 768.

By the same token, the reign of Christ does not begin with the second advent. His reign is already under way (Acts 2:32–36), though its full manifestation awaits his second advent. Satan may be the prince of this age (Eph. 2:2), but the one for whom all of creation was established (John 1:3) and who alone is able to sustain the cosmos (Col. 1:17) is Lord. In addition, Christ manifests his sovereignty with his headship over the church of God (Eph. 5:23). However, the revealing and ruling functions of Jesus are not complete until he reconciles all things (1 Cor. 15:20–28; Col. 1:20).

Priest

Consideration of the office of priest includes Jesus' preparation for entry into the Holy of Holies, his sacrifice offered in the Holy of Holies, and his intercessory session in behalf of the saints. In preparation for priesthood, a man had to be born into the tribe of Levi, anointed to serve in the priestly capacity, and give evidence of being without discernible blemish. The priesthood of Christ was Melchizedekian rather than Levitical (Heb. 6:20), and it began with a special birth (Matt. 1:18–25).

This has been addressed in the previous chapter, so it is appropriate here to affirm again that there is a connection between the virgin conception of Jesus and the fact that Jesus is presented as fully man and fully God. It appears that the virgin birth was the means whereby God circumvented the inheritance of a sin nature. Jesus is declared sinless in the New Testament documents (2 Cor. 5:21; Heb. 4:15; 1 Pet. 2:22), and Jesus himself asked if anyone could successfully lay a charge of sin against him (John 8:46). This condition of sinlessness is essential to his mediatorial work as priest on behalf of the human family. Having no sin of his own for which to atone, he was the Lamb of God, the sacrifice with neither spot nor blemish, the one able to make atonement for the sins of others (John 1:29). He experienced the reality of temptation (Luke 4:2; Heb. 2:18; 4:15) but without the devastating effects of acquiescence.

Just as the birth of Jesus was the result of a virgin conception rather than natural generation, so also the anointing of Jesus took a unique turn. At the baptism of Jesus, the Spirit of God descended upon him as a dove and a voice from heaven spoke saying, "This is My beloved Son, in whom I am well pleased" (Matt. 3:17 NKJV). Speculations about the reason for the baptism of Jesus include his official affirmation of and identification with the ministry of John the Baptist, his identification with the race he came to save, and the declaration through baptism of the kind of Messiah he came to be, namely a dying and resurrected Messiah. These are all reasonable and logical deductions, but the "why" question is not asked or answered in Scripture.

Without denying the truth of any of these ideas, one can affirm the witness of the Holy Spirit to the priesthood of Jesus based on this text (Matt. 3:13–17). Baptism is an initiating rite. Thus, the conclusion may be safely drawn that at the initiation of the ministry of Jesus, this incident in which the Holy Spirit descended, augmented by the Father's voice, is tantamount to the anointing of the Lord for the priestly ministry.

A miraculous birth, a remarkable anointing, a prophetic career of teaching verified by multiple signs, and a sinless life are preludes to the great work that Jesus envisioned for himself. In describing his purpose, Jesus said that he came "to seek and to save the lost" (Luke 19:10). Today he continues his high priestly work, interceding for us at God's right hand (Heb. 7:25). The events associated with the offices of Christ set the Christian faith at variance with all other religious expressions. Scripture's witness is that in the incarnation God's Son came into time and space. He came to serve as Prophet (revealer), Priest (mediator) and King (ruler). He can fill these offices because of who he is. No founder or leader of any other religion compares to this one.

The Atonement in Anticipation—the Old Testament

The Old Testament people of God were introduced to the economy of God through historical circumstances and incidents, through rich illustrative metaphors, through Levitical ritual, and through prophecy. The frequency with which an incident, a teaching, or a prophecy occurs in the Old Testament is sufficient to demonstrate that the concept of redemption, both corporate and individual, permeated the life of Israel. Some features appear dominant in such instruction: the absolute holiness and therefore unapproachableness of God, the hopelessness of life cut off from God, the loving-kindness of God's provision, and the consequence of his resulting approachableness vis-à-vis the offering of a sacrifice. It is instructive to consider several incidents that make no overt claims to the teaching of atonement but that have been understood by generations of believers as possessing didactic insights into God's redemptive plan.

In Genesis 3, the progenitors of the race violated the one prohibition that God gave them, giving rise to several ill-advised attempted human cover-ups. First, Adam and Eve attempted to hide from an omnipresent, omniscient God. Second, having become aware of their nakedness, they supplied fig leaves as a human solution. Finally, when confronted, the human ability to pass guilt along to other available parties presented itself. Having pronounced the judgment demanded by justice, verse 21 states that "the LORD God made clothing out of skins for Adam and his wife, and He clothed them."

The reticence of the scholarly community to see any allusion to sacrifice or atonement in this narrative is well-known. Refreshing is the reserved but accurate comment of Mathews:

> Here God bestows "garments of skin" upon the guilty in the garden. Although the text does not specify that animals were slain to provide these coverings, it is a fair implication and one that likely would be made in the Mosaic community, where animal sacrifice was pervasive. Since the garden narrative shares in tabernacle imagery, it is not surprising that allusion to animal sacrifice is found in the garden too. Through an oblique reference to animal sacrifice, the garden narrative paints a theological portrait familiar to the recipients of the Sinai revelation who honored the tabernacle as the meeting place with God. Sacrifice renewed and guaranteed that special union of God with his people (e.g., Day of Atonement, Lev. 16).[10]

To see this passage as instructional for later generations regarding sacrifice as the means of appearing appropriately before God assumes much. Yet the text is clear that the couple's respective personal efforts at covering were deemed inadequate, and an animal forfeited its life so God could clothe the man and the woman in his own way. Small wonder that Christian thinkers have viewed the incident as a foreshadowing of the cross through which the sacrifice of Christ enables the believer to be clothed in his righteousness (Rom. 13:14; 1 Cor. 1:30; 2 Cor. 5:21).

Even more striking is the story of Abraham's sacrifice of Isaac. In Genesis 22, Isaac asked Abraham about the absence of a lamb for the sacrifice since all else necessary was provided. Abraham's assurance that God himself would provide a lamb has a prophetic ring that transcends the contemporary event. On Moriah, the intended sacrifice of Isaac is circumvented by the intervention of God and the substitute of a hitherto unnoticed ram caught in the bushes. The themes of the father offering up his only son and the substitution of the ram for Isaac, who lived because the ram died in his place, were inevitably viewed in many Christian communities as precursors and definers of God's plan of redemption (John 8:56).

Different but nonetheless informative motifs occur in the story of Ruth and the enigmatic prophecy of Hosea. In Ruth, the concept of the "kinsman redeemer" resonates with the purpose of the incarnation when the word becomes flesh and the Lord "purchases" his church. Harris notes the significance of the *goel* used both in the famous declaration of Job (19:25) and in Ruth:

---

10 Kenneth A. Mathews, *Genesis 1–11:26,* NAC (Nashville: Broadman & Holman, 1996), 265.

The primary meaning of this root is to do the part of a kinsman and thus to redeem his kin from difficulty or danger. It is used with its derivatives 118 times. One difference between this root and the very similar root *pōdâ* "redeem," is that there is usually an emphasis in *gā'al* on the redemption being the privilege or duty of a near relative.[11]

In the case of Hosea, his unfaithful wife Gomer was to be auctioned away into slavery. Her new master, however, turned out to be Hosea, who in love purchased her from slavery, took her home, and even pledged afresh his commitment to her. While the immediate application of the text is doubtless to Israel, her impending exile, and a promise of return, Christians may be pardoned for noting the remarkable similarity of Hosea's redemptive act to the work of Christ.

If these incidents foreshadowed the atonement of Christ, much of the prescribed worship of Israel was far less subtle in its redemptive message. In Exodus 25–30, lessons from the tabernacle are impressed on Israelite minds. Rigid distinction between the holy and the profane and even between the holy place and the Holy of Holies is enforced in several ways. The consecration of priests in Exodus 29:1–21 required the priests to lay hands on the head of a sacrifice, transferring the guilt of the priest to the head of the innocent animal (Lev. 8:1–29). Further, the priest had to don special vestments to appear before God in the service of the tabernacle. The sprinkling of sacrificial blood on an ear, thumb, and big toe was a part of the priest's consecration.

The Levitical offerings generally required a sacrificial victim. Grain offerings and the like were acceptable, though generally as thanksgiving offerings. Otherwise, as the author of Hebrews notes, "Without the shedding of blood there is no forgiveness" (Heb. 9:22). The laws for the cleansing of lepers involved the death of one bird and the sprinkling of its blood on the bird that was released (Lev. 14:1–32). The celebration of the year of Jubilee witnessed the "redemption" even of property, which was returned to its original owners (Lev. 35:8–25).

However, the celebration of the Passover and the austere events associated with the Day of Atonement give insight into the work of Christ on the cross in the most explicit and perceptive ways. The initial Passover is recorded in Exodus 12:1–51. Instruction established Passover as the beginning of months for the Jews and required a yearling lamb or goat, which was to be without blemish and subject to a period of fourteen days of observation. Following this, the animal was to be slain, its blood sprinkled on

---

[11] R. Laird Harris, Gleason L. Archer Jr., and Bruce K. Waltke, eds., *TWOT* (Chicago: Moody, 1980), 1:144.

the door posts and lintel of each house, and the flesh roasted and consumed by the family, along with bitter herbs and unleavened bread. Additionally, even the apparel for the occasion was specified—sandals on feet, belt around waist, staff in hand. The meal was to be eaten in haste.

The primary significance of the Passover clearly related to the terminal plague, the passing of the "death angel" through the land of Egypt and the consequent demise of the firstborn of every family. The exception is stated.

> They must take some of the blood and put it on the two doorposts and the lintel of the houses in which they eat them. . . . I will pass through the land of Egypt on that night and strike every firstborn [male] in the land of Egypt, both man and beast. I am the LORD; I will execute judgments against all the gods of Egypt. The blood on the houses where you are staying will be a distinguishing mark for you; when I see the blood, I will pass over you. No plague will be among you to destroy [you] when I strike the land of Egypt (Exod. 12:7,12–13).

At the very least, the implication of substitution lies at the heart of this entire project. The innocent animal died instead of the firstborn in Jewish families. This act was associated with the death angel's notice concerning the blood (Lev. 17:11), which resulted in the "Passover" or the restraining of judgment on the firstborn. The death of a near perfect lamb or goat as a substitute to set free an otherwise doomed victim is the unavoidable lesson of the text. Its blood having been sprinkled, the animal is consumed by the Jewish family, thus, as it were, internalizing the life of the animal for their own sustenance in preparing the family for the hasty exodus from a land of slavery and into the freedom provided by God. The accoutrements of the meal are significant also, bitter herbs reminding the children of Israel of the bitterness of the sojourn in Egypt.

Jesus, in the inauguration of the eucharistic meal,[12] appears deliberately to invoke this imagery, as he did also on other occasions. He embraced the sacrificial imagery of Passover, seeing himself as the Lamb whose blood would avert judgment and whose flesh imbibed would provide life. This sacrifice results in the deliverance of the prisoner from the slavery of sin.

If anything, the Day of Atonement is even more poignant in its imagery.[13] Prescribed for Israel in Leviticus 16, this feast called for the Israelites

---

[12] The Lord's Supper is appropriately called a eucharistic meal in the sense that the Supper is, among other things, a thanksgiving (Gk. *eucharisteō*).

[13] Rooker notes the seriousness of this ritual when he says, "The word *peša',* translated 'rebellion' in the NIV, is the most grievous word for sin in the Old Testament. The term refers to sin in

to "afflict [their] souls" (Lev. 16:31 NKJV), an act of sorrow for sin against God (Lev. 16:24). On the specified day the people appeared before God. Two goats were presented to the high priest. Lots cast over these goats determined which would be the scapegoat and which would be the sacrificial goat. The high priest of Israel then placed his hands on the head of the scapegoat, confessing the sins of all the people over the head of the goat. This symbolic act depicted the transfer of the sins of the guilty to the innocent. The terminology *scapegoat* carries now the idea of an innocent party taking the fall for a guilty party. The scapegoat was led to the wilderness and released, symbolizing the taking away of the sins of the people.

While there is some dispute over terminology, Wenham is correct in his conclusion: "Whatever we understand by Azazel, there is little doubt about the total meaning of the ceremony. Whether Azazel means the mountain where the goat is destroyed, the sin which is given to destruction, or the evil angel who is given a bribe so that he does not become an accuser, it all comes back to the same basic idea: that sin is exterminated from Israel."[14]

Returning to the sacrificial goat, the high priest killed the animal, retrieving its blood in a basin. With this blood from the sacrificed innocent victim in his possession, the high priest—and only the high priest—entered the *kadosh kadoshim,* the Holy of Holies, on this one day a year and only with blood. The way was prepared by an incense offering and coals from the altar of sacrifice, the smoke and aroma of which provided a temporary covering for the ark of the covenant until the high priest sprinkled the blood of the sacrifice (Lev. 16:12–13). Next, the high priest sprinkled the blood of the sacrifice on the mercy seat (Lev. 16:15), which resided on the top of the ark of the covenant. Thus, the blood of the innocent goat was interposed between the just demands of the law of God as written on the tablets of the law contained in the ark of the covenant and the sinful priest representing himself and the people.

As is the case of the Passover, the implications were clear to the early church. In the event of the cross, Jesus the great High Priest entered into the Holy of Holies, God's presence, with his own blood and made atonement for the souls of men. He was both the scapegoat, carrying sin away, and the

---

its grossest manifestation. It indicates a breach of relationship between two parties and was probably borrowed from the diplomatic realm, where it indicated a covenant-treaty violation. The word thus indicates that a violation of the covenant has been perpetrated. This initial use of the word in Leviticus indicates that on the Day of Atonement not only were intentional sins atoned for but that the tabernacle was purified to allow God's presence to reside. The notion that atonement was to be made for purification is not introduced here for the first time. Purification resulting from atonement occurred in the context of the cleansing of the young mother in 12:8 and the person with a skin disease in 14:18–19. The unrestricted nature of forgiveness on this day indicates why the blood was to be carried so close to God's presence." Mark Rooker, *Leviticus,* NAC (Nashville: Broadman & Holman, 2000), 218–19.

[14] Gordon Wenham, *The Book of Leviticus,* NICOT (Grand Rapids: Eerdmans, 1979), 235.

sacrificial goat, alleviating the problem of human guilt by paying the price
for sin in his own body.

Two other passages merit special attention. The first of these is the remarkable Psalm 22, and the second is the Suffering Servant passage of
Isaiah 52:13–53:12. As previously noted, Psalm 22 is often identified as
the "crucifixion psalm." Not surprisingly, it is the subject of considerable
debate. Clearly, Jesus appropriated the language of the psalm while hang-
ing on the cross (Ps. 22:1= Matt. 27:46). Beyond this self-identification
with the sorrows of the psalmist, is there anything in the psalm that should
be accorded prophetic significance? Jewish, and many Christian, scholars
see the psalm as a song of David's agonies and perhaps of Israel's sorrows,
but certainly as containing nothing Christological.

Other Christian thinkers, however, consider the psalm to be a rather
startling piece of prophecy that provides a look at the mind of Jesus during
the hours on the cross. The possibility of a dual venue for understanding
the psalm gains credibility because of those involved in the crucifixion
whose behavior seems to be forecast in Psalm 22. Romans cast lots for
the clothing of Jesus (Ps. 22:18), and hostile Jews shouted that since Jesus
trusted in God, then God should rescue him (Ps. 22:8). Even if the translation of verse 16, "They pierced my hands and my feet," is dismissed or
denied its application to the passion narrative, enough is here to account
for the messianic significance assigned to the passage by many commentators. Therefore, one is not in error to discover in Psalm 22 something of
a poignancy of the ongoing physical and spiritual grief associated with
Christ's death.[15]

Even more compelling and precise is the Isaianic passage of the
Suffering Servant, which begins in 52:13, and encompasses the entire fifty-
third chapter.[16] The Suffering Servant grew up tenderly and unobtrusively
(Isa. 53:2). However, when his suffering was initiated, he was marred to
the extent that he was an astonishment even to kings, who presumably had
not seen such things before (52:14–15). He was pictured as being despised
and rejected of men and a man of sorrows who was acquainted with grief
(53:3). So much was this observation true that Isaiah found people who did
not esteem him highly and hid their faces from him.

Then, there follows a litany of expressions, which, taken together, provide one of the strongest statements to be found anywhere in the Scripture for
the substitutionary and vicarious nature of the atonement of this Suffering,

---

[15] See the helpful comments on the psalm by Derek Kidner, *Psalms 1–72*, TOTC (Downers Grove:
InterVarsity, 1973), 105–9.

[16] For a superb examination of the ways in which both Jewish and Christian sources have understood the Suffering Servant passage, see Bernd Janowski and Peter Stuhlmacher, eds., *The Suffering
Servant* (Grand Rapids: Eerdmans, 2004).

Servant. The plight of the Suffering Servant was said to be one in which he "bore our griefs" and "carried our sorrows" (53:4 NKJV). Further, he was "wounded for our transgressions" and "bruised for our iniquities." In fact, our peace appears to have derived from the chastisement of this Suffering Savior, and we are healed by his stripes (53:5). For the transgressions of Isaiah's people, he was stricken (53:8). He is the one who, by his knowledge and righteousness, justifies many because he "bears their iniquities" (53:11 NKJV) and "bore the sin of many" (53:12 NKJV).[17]

In the final analysis, it is difficult to discern how anyone reading these verses could arrive at any other conclusion but that the sinful people of Israel described by Isaiah have found themselves in a hopeless condition. Yet none other than the Suffering Servant has accepted the burden of their sin, and somehow his suffering has paved the way for their forgiveness and salvation. John D. W. Watts believes that the Suffering Servant is Zerubbabel, but even he acknowledges that the passage gives rise to the idea of substitutionary atonement. "The language has changed from political rebellion to the religious and moral sense of iniquity, and an understanding of substitutionary atonement is born. It had long existed in the sacrificial cult (Lev. 16), but in this verse it finds classical expression in a new sense."[18]

If this is not astonishing enough, Isaiah 53 also chronicles all of the suffering as somehow the deliberate act of God. In verse 4, the Suffering Servant is "smitten by God and afflicted" (NKJV). In verse 6, it is the Lord who has "laid on Him the iniquity of us all" (NKJV). More startling yet is the affirmation of verse 10, which declares, "It pleased the LORD to bruise Him" and "He has put Him to grief" (NKJV). Brevard Childs recognizes this unexpected turn in the text:

> Second, it was God's will and purpose that the servant was dealt this affliction. Not only did God allow it (the passive voice softens the theological tension), but God is understood as the active agent of his suffering: He was "smitten by God and afflicted" (v. 4): "Yahweh laid on him the guilt of us all" (v. 6). What occurred was not some unfortunate tragedy of human history but actually formed

---

[17] Explaining Isaiah's reference to the soul of the Suffering Servant as an offering for sin, E. J. Young notes, "This obligation is designated by the word *'asham,* which basically refers to an offense or trespass, and then to a trespass offering. In this passage the precise nature of the *'asham* is not primarily in view, but the word stands generically for expiatory sacrifice. The thought of the protasis is that the very life of the servant will be made an expiatory sacrifice. So in the New Testament Christ is said to be our Passover. The verb *śim* ("to place"), which in Job 17:3 is used of the giving of a pledge, further strengthens the idea that the sacrifice is expiatory." *The Book of Isaiah,* NICOT (Grand Rapids: Eerdmans, 1972), 3:355.

[18] John D. W. Watts, *Isaiah 34–66,* WBC (Waco: Word, 1987), 231.

the center of the divine plan for the redemption of his people and indeed of the world.[19]

Evangelicals typically voice their confidence in the aseity of God, the doctrine that God has everything that he needs within the Godhead and therefore, strictly speaking, has no need in the way that human beings have need. However, in the light of Isaiah 53, not to focus on an ontological necessity for justice, which makes up the divine character, would be irresponsible. Hence, in Isaiah 53, God's character expresses itself simultaneously in both forgiveness and just judgment. Since justice must be maintained, God is pleased to present the Suffering Servant as accepting the weight of the guilt of the sheep who have gone astray, thereby paying the full price for their iniquity and thus somehow satisfying the just demand of a holy God.

In light of Isaiah 53, the frequent critiques of the modern and postmodern periods which charge Anselm and the Reformers such as Calvin and Luther with excessive use of forensic metaphors seem destined to be dashed. Seven hundred and fifty years before Christ and a long time before the development of modern systems of jurisprudence, Isaiah championed just such a perspective. The metaphor of substitution is not only used but also pressed as an explanation for what is transpiring in the suffering of the servant. One can only conclude that Isaiah, while certainly not negating the significance of other metaphors to describe the atonement, has clearly focused on the metaphor of substitution and the acceptance of guilt by an innocent one in behalf of those who are clearly guilty as resulting in the resolution and the restoration of relationship with a holy God.

When the evidence of vicarious substitution in the Suffering Servant paragraphs of Isaiah is joined with the significant insights of other Old Testament passages, particularly the Passover and Day of Atonement rituals, one can arrive at no other conclusion than that vicarious substitution is a major emphasis. This evidence is buttressed by Leviticus 17:11 and the implication of the Old Testament regarding the shedding of blood and the life of an innocent victim poured out in behalf of one who is guilty. How could the Old Testament testimony to this end possibly be strengthened? One has now only to see if those same concepts are contained in and affirmed by the New Testament.

The New Testament and the Atonement

The story of Simeon and his approach to Mary and Joseph in the temple is one of the earliest hints at the developing doctrine of the atonement in the

---

[19] Brevard S. Childs, *Isaiah,* OTL (Louisville: Westminster John Knox, 2001), 415.

New Testament. The narrative of <u>Luke 2:25–34</u> reveals that after Simeon expressed his thanksgiving to God for seeing the salvation that God had prepared before all people, he spoke a chilling word to Mary, the mother of our Lord: "Indeed, this child is destined to cause the fall and rise of many in Israel and to be a sign that will be opposed[20]—and a sword will pierce your own soul—that the thoughts of many hearts may be revealed" (Luke. 2:34–35). These ominous words anticipate the agonizing experience for which the child was destined and which also would have the effect of profoundly wounding Mary. However, Simeon is clear not only in his language about salvation but also in his language about that which would transpire in the agonies of this child born to Mary and of his transforming effect on the lives of others. As such, Simeon anticipated the Pauline and Petrine theology that would later appear.

The crucifixion narratives found in the Gospels are exhibitions of human cruelty, rage, jealousy, and hatred. These narratives also focus clearly on human irresponsibility in the persons of Pilate, Herod, and many of the Jewish religious leaders. The stark physical agonies depicted in the Gospel narratives, which include the indignities of being spit upon and mocked; the agonies of being hit with a reed, crowned with thorns, having feet and hands pierced by nails, unquenchable thirst, and perhaps enduring even cruel asphyxiation are certainly wrenching themes to contemplate. Nevertheless, the more profound significance of what transpired on the cross is provided only in glimpses in the Gospel narratives and then analyzed more conclusively in the epistles that follow.

Even in the Gospel accounts of the crucifixion, however, there are insights that cannot be passed without comment. A case in point would be the crown of thorns pressed down upon the brow of Jesus. From the viewpoint of the Romans, this was a mere act of mockery, but the significance is not lost on the writer, who remembered that because of human sin in Genesis 3:17–18, Adam was told that the ground would bring forth thorns and thistles. Apparently, the Gospel writer saw the redemptive act of Christ affecting even the natural order of creation. This hint surfaces in <u>Matthew 19:28</u> where the word *palingenesia* or "regeneration" is used of a cosmic regeneration that awaits the eschaton but that is apparently guaranteed by the death of Christ on the cross.

This concept is later explicated by Paul in Romans 8:18–22, when the apostle notes that the whole creation

---

[20] Luke Timothy Johnson remarks, "The verb *antilegō* is used by Luke of those who 'resist' or 'oppose' (see 20:27; Acts 13:45; 28:19,22). The prophetic image here suggested, therefore, is this: Jesus is within the people a stone of stumbling, a sign to create opposition, and in response to him the people will be divided, some falling and some rising." *The Gospel of Luke,* SP (Collegeville, MN: Liturgical Press, 1991), 56.

eagerly waits with anticipation for God's sons to be revealed. For the creation was subjected to futility—not willingly, but because of Him who subjected it—in the hope that the creation itself will also be set free from the bondage of corruption into the glorious freedom of God's children. For we know that the whole creation has been groaning together with labor pains until now (vv. 20–22).

Additional indications of the substitutionary nature of the atonement are found in several of Jesus' sayings from the cross. Concerning those who crucified him, there is a prayer of intercession, "Father, forgive them, for they do not know what they do" (Luke 23:34 NKJV). Although there is no indication in the prayer itself about the conditions upon which such forgiveness could be predicated, seemingly the evangelist recorded the prayer at this particular stage and with a significance far greater than that same prayer on the lips of Stephen (Acts 7). Again, the conclusive assessment of Christ concerning what had taken place was wrung from his heart in the word *tetelestai* or "it is finished" (John 19:30). Apparently, the Gospel writer understood this exclamation to be a confident avowal that the cross itself had accomplished all that God intended and that, in effect, it paved the way for the reconciliation of man to God.

In addition to that, serious meaning is apparently assigned by the Gospel writers to the tearing of the veil of the temple at the time of Jesus' death (Matt. 27:50–51). No longer is the Holy of Holies to be understood as the place where God in some sense uniquely dwells in hiddenness and inaccessibility. Even as the veil of Christ's body was torn through his death on the cross, so the way was opened for all to come to God. As B. H. Carroll put the matter:

> Here it is evident that the veil which hid the holy of holies typified Christ's body. When his body died that veil was forever rent. Through this rent body he entered the heavenly holy of holies and there offered his own expiating blood an offering through the eternal Spirit, hence in [Hebrews] 12:22–24, the last glorious thing the Christian comes to is "the blood of sprinkling," not on his heart as applied by the Holy Spirit in regeneration, but that blood sprinkled on the mercy seat in the heavenly sanctuary.[21]

---

[21] B. H. Carroll, *An Interpretation of the English Bible* (Nashville: Broadman, 1947), 15:214. On the other hand, Craig Blomberg thinks that the curtain in view is the one that separated the court of Israel from the court of the Gentiles but allows for the alternative, acknowledging, "If the curtain protecting the Holy of Holies was in view, then Matthew's point could be the new access to God provided by Jesus' atoning death (as in Heb. 4:16)." Craig L. Blomberg, *Matthew,* NAC (Nashville: Broadman & Holman, 1992), 421.

Prior to the agonies associated with Golgotha, Jesus met with the disciples in a concluding Passover celebration. That Passover celebration, recorded in 1 Corinthians 11:17–34 as well as in the Gospels, is replete with atonement significance. Among the more important observations arising out of the Last Supper is the expression of Jesus as he broke the bread and distributed it to the disciples, "This is my body, which is given for you" *(hyper hymōn)*. *Hyper* is a Greek preposition frequently carrying a substitutionary significance. Here, its substitutionary intent is obvious. Anticipating his death on the cross, Jesus assured the disciples that what would be done through his body on the cross would be in their behalf.

In addition to this, as Jesus handed them the juice of the fruit of the vine, he spoke of this cup being a "new covenant" in his blood. The significance of the shedding of blood as referenced already in Leviticus 17:11 once again comes to the front, coupled together with the promise of Jeremiah that there would be in the last days a new covenant (Jer. 31:31–34). Jesus brought the two together and showed that the provision, which makes possible the new covenant, is the shedding of his blood on the cross.

Other avowals in the Gospel narratives include those of Matthew 20:28 and Mark 10:45. These texts appear to have a clear connection with the Suffering Servant text of Isaiah 53. Here Jesus spoke of his mission on earth as being that of giving his life as a ransom for many. Leaving aside the question of the recipient of the ransom, Jesus saw his sacrifice in Jerusalem to be a ransom paid in behalf of many who would be brought to God through that action.

In John 1:29, John the Baptist saw Jesus approaching and cried out "Behold! The Lamb of God who takes away the sin of the world!" (NKJV). The link in John's mind to the Passover and to the Day of Atonement is evident. In John 3:14–15 the Johannine interpretation of the basis of Jesus' witness to Nicodemus was tied to Numbers 21:9 and the lifting up of the bronze serpent in the wilderness. Those who looked upon this serpent were healed of the venomous bites of the Egyptian serpents. In the same fashion John declared that the Son of Man would be lifted up, and whosoever believed on him would not perish but have everlasting life. The vicarious nature of the atonement is paramount in John's thinking at this point.

In John 10:7–18, the Good Shepherd lays down his life for his sheep. In John 12:23–24 the grain of wheat has to die in order to produce much grain. In John 12:31–33, the Lord asserts that if he is "lifted up," he will "draw all men to himself," which is a reference to his death. These and many other references establish in the Gospels a rather compelling picture of a substitutionary and vicarious atonement on the part of Jesus the Christ.

Nowhere, however, is the explanation of the atonement more lucidly provided than in Paul's assessment of the work of Christ in the book of Romans and in the book of the atonement, namely, the book of Hebrews. The first eight chapters of Romans are devoted to anthropology and soteriology. In 1:18–3:20, Paul paints a vivid portrait of the human dilemma, concluding that all are "without excuse" (Rom. 1:20) and that "there is no one righteous, not even one; there is no one who understands, there is no one who seeks God" (Rom. 3:10–11). Furthermore, the condition described therein ends up being hopeless from a human perspective because "no flesh will be justified in His sight by the works of the law" (Rom. 3:20). As Käsemann colorfully states it, "Rebellion is seen as the signature of human reality before and apart from Christ."[22]

This desperate dilemma is ameliorated, however, by the fact that there is a "righteousness of God apart from the law" that is revealed, having been witnessed previously by both the law and the prophets. This is the righteousness of God that is available to the human family through Jesus Christ for all who believe (Rom. 3:22). While indeed all have sinned (Rom. 3:23), people may also be "justified freely by His grace through the redemption that is in Christ Jesus" (Rom. 3:24).[23] Such a redemption is provided upon the basis that Jesus was set forth by God "as a propitiation by means of His blood."

The word *propitiation* (Gk. *hilastērion*) has been the subject of heated debate in scholarly ranks. Multiple authors have insisted that it be rendered something other than "propitiation." The reasons for objecting to the translation "propitiation" range from the fact that contemporary audiences would find the word to be beyond their understanding to the fact that the concept of propitiation inevitably suggests that God possesses wrath toward sinners and that this wrath has to be assuaged by the pummeling of the Savior, a concept which many scholars find unacceptable to modern and postmodern aesthetic sensibilities. There is also the tendency to see in discussions of "the wrath of God" that which is totally incompatible with the New Testament avowals of God's love.

Other scholars, however, have demonstrated that the concept of propitiation has a New Testament nuance of its own that is quite different from

---

22 Ernst Käsemann, *Commentary on Romans* (Grand Rapids: Eerdmans, 1980), 42.

23 Commenting on the relationship of this righteousness, which comes through faith in Christ, Adolf Schlatter calls attention to the connecting preposition *dia* in Romans 3:22. "If, with *dikaiosynē,* he simply had in mind an attribute of the divine being, it could not be followed by *dia,* since a quality such as this would from the outset be the property of its substance and would not arise from the behavior of the individual. But because righteousness establishes a relationship in which justice is effective, there follows not an ambiguous conception, but a very obvious one, if *dia* after *dikaiosynē* introduces a reference indicating the individual's behavior that God establishes by his righteousness in order for the individual to be linked with God by that behavior." Adolf Schlatter, *Romans: The Righteousness of God* (Peabody: Hendrickson, 1995), 93–94.

pagan concepts of propitiation. They observe that the word occurs here in sequence following a considerable explanation of the wrath of God that "is revealed from heaven against all ungodliness and unrighteousness of men" (Rom. 1:18 NKJV).

John R. W. Stott eloquently addressed this issue of a decidedly New Testament understanding of God's wrath. Acknowledging error in crude concepts, Stott noted:

> Crude concepts of anger, sacrifice and propitiation are indeed to be rejected. They do not belong to the religion of the Old Testament, let alone of the New. This does not mean, however, that there is no biblical concept of these things at all. What is revealed to us in Scripture is a pure doctrine (from which all pagan vulgarities have been expunged) of God's holy wrath, his loving self-sacrifice in Christ and his initiative to avert his own anger. It is obvious that "wrath" and "propitiation" (the placating of wrath) go together. It is when the wrath is purged of unworthy ideas that the propitiation is thereby purged. The opposite is also true. It is those who cannot come to terms with any concept of the wrath of God who repudiate any concept of propitiation.[24]

That there is within the Godhead righteous indignation against sin and its consequences in the human family is a fact that cannot be deleted from either testament in the Bible. If the biblical witness itself is embraced, then one cannot avoid the concept of the wrath of God; consequently, "propitiation through His blood" becomes an understandable affirmation. Even more to the point is the insight of Romans 3:26, which is a continuation of the thought of Romans 3:25 that Jesus provided propitiation through his blood.[25] Verse 26 explains how this phenomenon works by saying that it demonstrates at the present time God's righteousness in that "He might be just and the justifier of the one who has faith in Jesus" (NKJV).

The importance of this declaration can scarcely be overestimated. According to Paul, what happens in the propitiatory sacrifice of Christ on the cross is a grand exhibition of God's righteousness in which whoever

---

[24] Stott, *Cross of Christ*, 169. See also "Excursus: Propitiation or Expiation: The Debate over *Hilaskomai*," in Daniel L. Akin, *1, 2, 3 John*, NAC (Nashville: Broadman & Holman, 2001), 253–65.

[25] For objections to *hilaskomai* being rendered "propitiation," see C. H. Dodd, "ΙΛΑΣΚΕΣΘΑΙ, Its Cognates, Derivatives, and Synonyms, in the Septuagint," in *JTS* 32 (July 1931): 352–60. For a rather definitive response, see Leon Morris, *The Apostolic Preaching of the Cross* (Grand Rapids: Eerdmans, 1965), 125–85. Joseph Fitzmyer also has trouble with the translation "propitiation," preferring instead what he calls a LXX translation of "mercy seat." Joseph A. Fitzmyer, *Romans*, AB (New York: Doubleday, 1993), 351–53.

comes to God by faith in Jesus is justified, and more importantly, he is justified justly.[26]

If God simply announces forgiveness of the sinner by fiat, then the problem of justice remains unaddressed; but since the wages of sin is death (Rom. 6:23), Jesus' death on the cross provided the just payment for sin, enabling God to be true to his own nature and yet still provide justification for the sinner. This justification in turn gives believers peace with God through the Lord Jesus Christ (Rom. 5:1). Paul further explains that "Christ died for (*hyper*) the ungodly" (Rom. 5:6 NKJV), making it possible for humans to be "justified by His blood," which results in the believer being "saved from wrath through Him" and "reconciled to God through the death of His Son" (Rom. 5:9–10 NKJV). Paul goes on to draw the analogy of death that came to the entire human family due to one man's offense, showing correspondingly that "through one Man's righteousness" the free gift came to all men, which results in "justification of life" (Rom. 5:18 NKJV).

As a result of the death of Jesus, those who are "in Christ Jesus" no longer fear condemnation since Christ has already paid the price for their sins on the cross (Rom. 8:1). Among other things this means that no one can ever bring a charge against God's elect because it is God who has justified them. No one can condemn them because Christ died and accepted that condemnation in their place on the cross; and, consequently, nothing can separate God's elect from the love of Christ (Rom. 8:31–39).

Those commentators with a modern or postmodern perspective who attempt to find a way around vicarious substitution as the principal motif for the cross of Christ must do so based on scattered references here or there. These references are largely disconnected from the remainder of the biblical narrative and ignore the great redemptive story line or metanarrative that runs from Genesis to Revelation. The Scriptures do say that the cross of Christ is an example of how to suffer righteously. While there is no question but that the moral example provided by Jesus is certainly compelling, the long theological dissertation of Paul in Romans 1–8 is, nevertheless, a sustained argument establishing the central and most critical features of the atonement of Christ as being vicarious and substitutionary in nature.

Hence, the idea of Christ paying a price demanded by the justice of God arises not out of the judiciary of the Middle Ages or from Roman times but directly out of the earliest understandings of the Hebrew people as

---

[26] D. A. Carson's assessment of the value of these verses is, "In short, Romans 3:25–26 makes a glorious contribution to Christian understanding of the 'internal' mechanism of the atonement. It explains the need for Christ's propitiating sacrifice in terms of the just requirements of God's holy character. This reading not only follows the exegesis carefully, but it brings the whole of the argument from Romans 1:18 on into gentle cohesion." D. A. Carson, "Atonement in Romans 3:21–26" in *The Glory of the Atonement*, ed. Charles E. Hill and Frank A. James III, (Downers Grove: InterVarsity, 2004), 138.

they grappled with the clear substitutionary and vicarious teaching of such events as Passover and the Day of Atonement. Further, what the Gospels proclaim in passing assertions, the Apostle Paul develops as the principal pillar in his own theology, explaining that the acceptance of the penalty of death enabled Jesus the righteous one to accept the guilt of sinful man while transferring to him Jesus' own righteousness.

The Book of the Atonement

If Romans 1–8 represents a theology of the atonement, then almost the entire book of Hebrews constitutes a book of the atonement. In fact, the work of Christ, as represented in the book of Hebrews, corresponds more closely to the book of Leviticus than any other book in the Bible. However, it also has intimate connections with large segments of the Old Testament, especially those passages in the Torah that describe the worship rituals and practices of the ancient Hebrew people. At the outset of the epistle, the author launches into one of the most important Christological passages in the Bible as he describes the way in which God has spoken in the last day through his Son. He focuses first on who Jesus is, and then he turns to the work of Christ, indicating two aspects, namely that he "purged" sins and that he has now "sat down on the right hand of the majesty on high" (1:3).[27]

These two expressions introduce the reader to major themes addressed in the book: (1) the act of God in Christ whereby the penalty, power, and presence of sin is ultimately defeated, and (2) the session of Christ at the right hand of the Father. The author begins chapter 2 with a discussion that links the incarnation of Christ and the death of Christ, seeing the latter as the purpose of the former. In Hebrews 2:9, Jesus is presented as having been made "a little lower than the angels" (NKJV), and the expressed purpose for that incarnation of the eternal God in such a state is that he might suffer death and later be crowned with glory and honor. This incarnation is accomplished that he "might taste death for everyone." The presence of the Greek preposition *hyper* once again suggests that his act of tasting death would be a substitutionary experience.

As will be seen later in this chapter, Gustaf Aulén propagates the idea that the atonement is primarily a victory over sin and the devil. Begging

---

[27] Calvin contrasts this purgation of sin with that afforded by the Levitical priesthood, ascribing to Christ a unique act based on who he is. "When he further says, *by himself,* there is to be understood here a contrast, that he had not been aided in this by the shadows of the Mosaic Law. He shows a clear difference between Christ and the Levitical priests; for they also were said to expiate sins, but they derived this power from another. In short, he intended to exclude all other means or helps by stating that the price and the power of purgation were found only in Christ." John Calvin, *Commentaries on the Epistle of Paul the Apostle to the Hebrews* (Grand Rapids: Baker, 1979), 36. Christ alone can ultimately effect the remedy for sin.

the question, he refers to this interpretation as the "classical view" of the atonement, and he is partly correct. Almost every early view of the atonement, however construed, had a significant emphasis on the triumph of Christ over evil and the devil. That theme is clearly enunciated in Hebrews 2:14, where Christ is said to be a partaker in flesh and blood so that "now since the children have flesh and blood in common, He also shared in these, so that through His death He might destroy the one holding the power of death—that is, the Devil."[28] Here, the author acknowledges the truth of what Paul affirms in Romans 6:23, that "the wages of sin is death." But Christ, who had no such claim on him because he had no sin, accepted that death in his own body, thus defeating the plan and the power of the devil and releasing those who would receive his death.

Hebrews 2:17 then emphasizes the necessity of this action as not merely an option, but rather that Jesus "had to be made like His brethren" (NKJV) so that he could be a merciful and faithful High Priest in things pertaining to God and therefore be able to "make propitiation for the sins of the people." The word *propitiation* discussed previously in Romans is once again *hilaskomoi*, but here it is the verb form rather than the noun as it appeared in Romans.[29] Summarizing these thoughts from chapter 2, Christ's incarnation is for the purpose of tasting of death for everyone. For him to be made like his brethren is necessary, and his death as High Priest makes both propitiation for the sins of the people and destroys the one who had the power of death, that is, the devil.

An objection might be raised that the devil's work apparently goes on now two thousand years after the death of Christ. But the objection fails on the simple ground that an injury, fatal in its consequence, may be inflicted

---

[28] Johannes Schneider picks up this theme and sees it as one of several motifs in Hebrews. Like Aulén, Schneider focuses on how the cross and resurrection together conquer the power of the devil. "Verses 14–17 answer the question, Why did Christ have to become a man and die? still more exactly. The first answer to this special question is: Christ had to suffer and die because only through His death was He able to overpower him who has power over death. Upon first glance this is a strange and contradictory statement which, however, will at once become meaningful when we consider the death of Christ together with His resurrection. The death of Christ is a unique death not only because it is the gracious act of God for the salvation of the world, but it is unique also because He who suffered this death did not remain in death. Through His resurrection Christ has demonstrated that death has no power over Him. He had to die, and yet He was not delivered up to the power of death." Johannes Schneider, *The Letter to the Hebrews* (Grand Rapids: Eerdmans, 1957), 21.

[29] Westcott is of the persuasion that it is not God who is propitiated but rather that which alienates. "The essential conception is that of altering that in the character of an object which necessarily excludes the action of the grace of God, so that God, being what He is, cannot (as we speak) look on it with favour. The 'propitiation' acts on that which alienates God and not on God whose love is unchanged throughout." Brook Foss Westcott, *The Epistle to the Hebrews* (New York: Macmillan, 1889; repr., Grand Rapids: Eerdmans, ca. 1960), 57. This seems difficult to embrace. Propitiating an inanimate object stretches logic and fails to do justice to the concept of God's wrath and the personal nature of sin.

on a person, and yet that person may survive for a while, even though there is no doubt about the outcome. In like manner, the bruising of the head of the serpent by the heel of the promised Messiah was a deadly wound from which Satan cannot recover and which will eventually vanquish him (Gen. 3:15; Rom. 16:20).

The theme of the priesthood of Christ is picked up again in chapters 7–10. Having discussed the Melchizedekian priesthood's superiority to the Aaronic priesthood, the author begins to explicate the necessity of this new priesthood. The first priesthood was a component of the Levitical covenant, but this new priesthood is founded in Jeremiah's promised new covenant (Jer. 31:31–34; Heb. 8:1–13). The differences in the old priesthood and the new priesthood are explained clearly in the latter verses of Hebrews 7. Levitical priests could not continue for long because of their own inevitable deaths, but Christ, our High Priest, continues forever with an unchangeable priesthood (vv. 23–24). By virtue of this unending priesthood, he is "able to save to the uttermost those who come to God through Him, since He always lives to make intercession for them" (v. 25 NKJV).

This ability is based on the fact that he is a high priest without sin. In fact, he is totally "separated from sinners" (v. 26). As a consequence, he has no need daily to offer up sacrifices as Levitical priests did, first for their own sins and then for the people's; but, rather, Jesus did this "once for all when He offered Himself" (v. 27). Here, the reader cannot help but be struck with the fact that the priests knew they could not absolve guilt and sin. The sacrificial offering was the best that could be done, and the sacrifice was not of the priest but of an innocent lamb. Now, in the new covenant, the high priest offers himself as a sacrifice for sin. This new way corresponds to Jeremiah's new covenant, which ultimately changes the worshipper internally and not just externally.

After discussing in Hebrews 8 why the old covenant was ineffective and needed to be altered by the coming of the new covenant, the author arrives at the discussion of chapter 9, which has in view primarily the Day of Atonement narratives found in Leviticus. The author affirms that Christ is a high priest who brings with him a more perfect tabernacle that is not made with hands (Heb. 9:11). Consequently, he enters into the Most Holy Place not with the blood of bulls and calves but with his own blood, once for all having obtained redemption. Here, two themes are set side by side. First, the Day of Atonement ritual in which after the scapegoat had been taken away, the priest laid his hand on the second goat; and while the goat was killed, the blood was caught and taken into the Holy of Holies and there sprinkled on the mercy seat. This act "obtained eternal redemption" (Heb. 9:12).

Redemption, as will be noted, is strongly related to the concept of ransom, and it indicates that the "purchase made" set the worshipper free. The author now recalls the entire Levitical system:

> For if the blood of goats and bulls and the ashes of a heifer sprinkling those who are defiled, sanctify for the purification of the flesh, how much more will the blood of the Messiah, who through the eternal Spirit offered Himself without blemish to God, cleanse our consciences from dead works to serve the living God? (Heb. 9:13–14).

F. F. Bruce says:

> But while it was necessary under the old covenant for the sacrificial blood first to be shed in the court and then to be brought into the holy of holies, no such division of our Lord's sacrifice into two phases is envisaged under the new covenant. When upon the cross He offered up His life to God as a sacrifice for His people's sin, He accomplished in reality what Aaron and his successors performed in type by the twofold act of slaying the victim and presenting its blood in the holy of holies.[30]

These words, in turn, focus the author's attention on the fact that Jesus is the mediator of the new covenant, and he is mediator by means of his death (Heb. 9:15). Wherever there is a testament, the testament has no validity or force until after the testator actually dies; but when he dies, then the terms of the testament are applied (Heb. 9:16–17). Jesus, as that testator, has appeared to put away sin by the sacrifice of himself; and while men must die and then face the judgment, Christ was "offered once to bear the sins of many" (Heb. 9:26–28).[31] The whole concept of "bearing sins" calls attention once again to the sacrifices offered in ancient Israel. The calf, the goat, and the sheep offered as sacrifices died because death is the penalty for sin. The sacrifice bore the guilt of the offerer, so Christ in the end of the ages has appeared to abolish sin through bearing the sins of many.

In chapter 10, the author of Hebrews returns to the theme of the incarnation as it relates to the atonement. Having stressed the fact that, in reality, the Old Testament sacrifices could never actually take away sin, the author cites Psalm 40:6–8 to the effect that a body was prepared for the Lord. The result of this incarnation is that "we have been sanctified through the offering of the body of Jesus Christ once and for all" (Heb. 10:10). The writer

---

[30] F. F. Bruce, *The Epistle to the Hebrews,* NICNT (Grand Rapids: Eerdmans, 1977), 201.

[31] Moffatt sees the necessity of forgiveness required and bestowed as understood in the terms of the Testament. James Moffatt, *A Critical and Exegetical Commentary on the Epistle to the Hebrews,* ICC (Edinburgh: T. & T. Clark, 1963), 127.

of Hebrews has made his case that all of the Levitical priesthood with its varying rites was simply a harbinger for the coming of Christ, who would fulfill all of those prophetic rites and rituals through his own incarnation and death on the cross. This incarnation and death would pay the debt for sin, release the captives, and set them free.

Summing up the work of Christ as set forth in the book of Hebrews, Morris cogently states:

> Christ has opened up the way to God by taking our sin out of the way. There are many ways in which he sees Christ to have done this. Christ made propitiation for our sins (2:17), offered a sacrifice for sins (10:12), did away with sin (9:26), bore sin (9:28). Because of what He has done there is no longer a sacrifice for sin (10:18). Sins have been forgiven (10:18), God remembers them no more (10:17). Christ's death is a ransom to set people free from sins (even those committed in Old Testament days, 9:15). By contrast, the older way could not deal with sin (10:1–2, 4, 6, 11). Clearly the writer sees the salvation Christ brought about as many-sided. Look at sin how you will, the Son has dealt with it.[32]

Various New Testament Avowals about the Atonement

That which is explicated at some length in Romans and Hebrews is discussed with some frequency throughout the rest of the New Testament. At no point is there a divergent perspective but rather complementary affirmations of the truths explained in greater detail in Romans 1–8 and in Hebrews. In Matthew 20:28 (also Mark 10:45), Jesus himself identifies his mission as "giving His life—a ransom for many." In John 1:29, John the Baptist observed the approach of Jesus, and using language that reflected the substitutionary rituals of the Levitical priesthood said, "Here is the Lamb of God, who takes away the sins of the world." In 2 Corinthians 5:15, Jesus is described as the one "who died for them" and rose again.

One of the most interesting assessments of the significance of the atonement is found in Galatians 3:10,13. Here, the Apostle Paul explained that all who attempt to satisfy God by their works are "under" the curse. All people are under this curse because, citing Deuteronomy 27:26, "Cursed is everyone who does not continue doing everything written in the book of the law." The author finds that no one, in fact, is justified by the law in the sight of God (Gal. 3:11). However, Christ has redeemed us from the curse of the law having "become a curse for us" (NKJV). The

---

[32] Leon Morris, *Hebrews*, BSC (Grand Rapids: Zondervan, 1983), 20.

explanation for this lies in Deuteronomy 21:23, where it is stated that "cursed is everyone who hangs on a tree" (NKJV). A passage in which Paul refers to Christ's crucifixion.

The three prepositions used in the passage are instructive. Men are "under" (*hypo*) the curse, but Christ has become a curse "for" (*hyper*) us, which makes it possible for us to be redeemed "from" (*ek*) the curse of the law. The gospel in this passage is found in three prepositions describing the believer's relationship first to the law and then to the redeeming sacrifice of Christ.[33] A different angle is presented by Paul in Galatians 4 when he mentions that redemption in Christ also enables the redeemed to be adopted as sons in the family of God.

Paul's letters to the Ephesians, Philippians, and Colossians contain similar references. In Ephesians 1:7, redemption is said to be by means of his blood which also provides the forgiveness of sin. The cross is the means of reconciliation of men to God, thus reestablishing our relationship to our Creator (Eph. 2:16). The same affirmation is repeated in Colossians 1:13–14. In the Pastoral Epistles, Paul suggests in 1 Timothy 2:5–6 that Jesus is the only mediator between God and man, and he is that mediator because he gave himself as a ransom for all. Peter makes use of the same language: One is not redeemed by that which is perishable but rather "with the precious blood of Christ, like that of a lamb without defect or blemish" (1 Pet. 1:19). Here, the purchase price is the blood of Christ, which is described as being "precious." The word is *timaō,* and it is often used to denote that which is rendered precious because the thing described is not common and, therefore, is valuable as a result of its sparsity. The blood of Jesus Christ is the only blood that could ultimately effect salvation.

Again, the concept of the lamb focuses on the Old Testament sacrificial system. In 1 Peter 2:24, Jesus is pictured as the one who bore the sins of all in his own body on the tree so that any who are in him have died to sins that they might live to righteousness. In 1 Peter 3:18, the author once again emphasizes the substitutionary nature of what Christ accomplished. He also suffered once for sins, the just for (*hyper*) the unjust that he might bring us to God. In 1 John 2:2 and 4:10, Jesus is said to be the propitiation for sins, even for the sins of the whole world.

These themes are also notable in the Apocalypse. In Revelation 1:4–6, Jesus is presented as the one who has "loved us and loosed us from our sins in His own blood."[34] The song of the heavenly elders in 5:9–10 chronicles

---

[33] See also Paige Patterson, "Reflections on the Atonement," *CTR* 3.2 (Spring 1989): 307–20, esp. 319–20.

[34] This passage is variously translated "washed us from our sins" or "loosed us from our sins." It is a classic case in point on the question of manuscript evidence. Some manuscripts read "washed us

the lyrics of the new song they sang, "You are worthy to take the scroll, and to open its seals; for You were slain, and have redeemed us to God by Your blood out of every tribe and tongue and people and nation, and have made us kings and priests to our God" (NKJV). Here, once again, the price of the redemption is the blood of Christ.

In Revelation 12:11, the conflict with Satan featured in the text finds Satan having come in fury to the inhabitants of the earth because he knows he has only a short time. The means by which he can be defeated is made plain: "They conquered Him by the blood of the Lamb and by the word of their testimony." Here, the blood of the Lamb is the source of power and strength to overcome the devil.

This survey of the biblical record serves to establish several features about the doctrine of the atonement based on the scriptural evidence. First, the work of Christ on the cross was not simply an unfortuitous development of history. It was the plan of God from eternity past since Jesus is "the Lamb slain from the foundation of the world" (Rev. 13:8 NKJV). Second, in order for the plan of God to take place, the incarnation of the eternal Word of God was a necessity. Third, in his incarnation as a man, Jesus had to live a life without sin. Though he was tempted in all points as every other human being, yet he was without sin (2 Cor. 5:21). Fourth, as the sinless Lamb of God, he was able to die a death in the place of men and women, who by virtue of their sin had brought condemnation on themselves.

Fifth, the death of Jesus constituted a ransom, purchasing the slave from the shackles of Satan and setting him free. Sixth, the death of Jesus on the cross was also a propitiation in that the wrath of God against sin was satisfied so that God could be both "just and the justifier of the one who has faith in Jesus" (Rom. 3:26 NKJV). Seventh, Christ's death on the cross was also a stunning and decisive defeat of Satan and evil in the world and the enthronement of righteousness forever. Eighth, in his death on the cross, Jesus also provided an example of how his followers are to live and respond to others in the present age. However, "neither good example nor moral influence ever gets men to God and to heaven. Sin and its penalty must be addressed. The primary significance of the atonement from which all other meanings draw their dynamic is that of penal substitution."[35]

---

from our sins," but the preponderance of the evidence favors "loosed us from our sins." How these divergent readings could have happened is apparent when you consider that the word for washed is *louō*, while the word for loosed is *luō*. They were very probably pronounced almost identically, so if the copier of the manuscript was responding to a reading, he might easily have chosen the wrong word. However, no theological harm is done, since neither reading is technically incorrect. Certainly, it is the blood of Christ that looses one from his sins, but it also washes him and cleanses him from his sins. It breaks the chain and removes the stain of sin.

[35] Patterson, "Reflections on the Atonement," 320.

What Has the Church Believed?

Jesus is "the Lamb slain from the foundation of the world" (Rev. 13:8 NKJV). For New Testament Christians, this grand metanarrative informs all of life and eternity. Understandably, Christian thinkers have expended incredible energy attempting to fathom the significance of an event that took place in Roman Palestine at a particular moment in history but having already existed in the heart and purpose of God forever. Early Christians also grasped something of the consequences associated with receiving or rejecting the benefits of the atonement. One should not expect to know the mind of God in its fullness (Rom. 11:34), and one should, therefore, find no surprise that the various theories attempting to account for the meaning of the atonement always leave one with the sensation of a mystery not fully comprehended.

Neither should it be thought strange that more than a few of the ideas about the atonement find support in the Bible. The value in revisiting many of these historical perspectives is first of all to be certain that one understands as many of the nuances of the work of Christ as possible. Second, one will probably discover that some views more than others get to the heart of the significance of the cross. The earliest atonement theology belongs to the texts of the Old and New Testaments which we have previously noted. How, then, has the church throughout its history sought to explain what Christ accomplished by virtue of his death and resurrection?

Irenaeus of Lyons (AD 130–202) set forth what is called the *recapitulation theory* of the atonement, whereby Jesus recapitulated in his incarnate state all stages of human life, including those aspects that relate to us as sinners. Irenaeus wrote, "He [Christ] summed up in Himself the long line of the human race, procuring for us salvation thus summarily, so that what we had lost in Adam, that is, the being in the image and likeness of God, that we should regain Christ Jesus."[36] In essence, Christ reversed the course for mankind upon which Adam had set humanity. And while Christ did reverse our course, he never became a sinner. Further, there is significantly more in the Bible than this theory notes.

Another of the earliest postapostolic views of the atonement is called the *ransom* or *ransom to Satan theory*. Advocates of this theory believe that on the cross a commercial transaction took place in which Jesus' death was the price paid to ransom the human race from its bondage to sin. This idea seems to be precisely what Scripture suggests in Matthew 20:28, which

---

[36] Irenaeus, *Against Heresies* 3.18, in *Documents of the Christian Church*, ed. Henry Bettenson (London: Oxford, 1963), 30. E. Ferguson, "Recapitulation," in Walter Elwell, *EDT,* 2nd ed. (Grand Rapids: Baker, 2001), 992.

cites Jesus himself as saying, "The Son of Man did not come to be served, but to serve, and to give His life—a ransom for many."

But, while the concept of ransom is not difficult, it begs the question of to whom the ransom was paid. Here agreement ends. Origen (AD 185–254), Gregory of Nyssa, Augustine, and Irenaeus thought that the ransom was paid to the devil, to Satan. For Gregory of Nyssa and Rufinus, the body of Jesus was the bait that concealed the hook of his deity. Gregory wrote:

> For since, as has been said before, it was not in the nature of the opposing power to come in contact with the undiluted presence of God, and to undergo His unclouded manifestation, therefore, in order to secure that the ransom in our behalf might be easily accepted by him who required it, the Deity was hidden under the veil of our nature, that so, as with ravenous fish, the hook of the Deity might be gulped down along with the bait of flesh, and thus, life being introduced into the house of death, and light shining in darkness, that which is diametrically opposed to light and life might vanish; for it is not in the nature of darkness to remain when light is present, or of death to exist when life is active.[37]

Rufinus of Aquileia (c. AD 400) reproduced Gregory's illustration and shows us how this view was understood:

> The purpose of the Incarnation . . . was that the virtue of the Son of God might be as it were a hook hidden beneath the form of human flesh . . . to lure on the prince of this age to a contest; that the Son might offer him his flesh as a bait and that then the divinity which lay beneath might catch him fast with its hook.[38]

This theory falters in that Satan is owed nothing by a holy, sovereign God. It is interesting to note that this would be the dominant understanding of the atonement for almost one thousand years, at least until the time of Anselm.

Cyprian (died AD 258) modifies the ransom to Satan theory, conjecturing that the ransom was paid to God since Satan clearly had no rightful claims on man. Jesus' suffering earned merit that was paid to God, the benefit of which is applied to those in Christ.[39]

How should we respond to Cyprian's model? As we noted, payment to the devil seems contradictory to the sovereignty of God as well as to God's

---

[37] Gregory of Nyssa, *The Great Catechism* 24.
[38] Rufinus, *Commentary on the Apostle's Creed* 14, in Bettenson, *Documents of the Christian Church,* 34–35.
[39] Robert Letham, *The Work of Christ* (Downers Grove: InterVarsity, 1993), 163.

prerogative to provide forgiveness on his own terms. Payment to God does appear to be less problematic; but there is no statement from Scripture to substantiate the view. Must there be a recipient for the ransom payment? Some conclude that to demand payment of a ransom does not necessarily demand a recipient for the payment. The metaphor need not be pushed to this point.

In *The Incarnation of the Word of God*, Athanasius (ca. AD 296–373) penned the most important single treatise on the life and work of Christ. L. W. Grensted says of Athanasius:

> No writer of the early Church has grasped so clearly the twofold condition, the necessity of the satisfaction of justice, and the necessity for a new nature in the sinner. This twofold condition could not be satisfied except by the Word as Creator. By coming in the flesh He could fulfill the law of death. And as the author of life He could give new life to perishing man.[40]

The linking of the person of Christ with the necessity of the atonement was the foremost concern of Athanasius. He avoided the problematic expressions of other Patristic authors while marshalling ideas that grasped as much as possible the significance of the biblical metaphors. Concerning the necessity of the incarnation, Athanasius wrote, "Because it was precisely in order to be able to die that He had taken a body, and to prevent the death would have been to impede the resurrection."[41]

Athanasius confirmed that the death of Jesus was an offering to the Father. He wrote:

> He surrendered His body to death instead of all, and offered it to the Father. This He did out of sheer love for us, so that in His death all might die, and the law of death thereby be abolished because, having fulfilled in His body that for which it was appointed, it was thereafter voided of its power for men.[42]

Not only was the Savior's offering to God, but also the atonement and resurrection together vanquished the corruption of sin:

> The Word perceived that corruption could not be got rid of otherwise than through death; yet He himself, as the Word, being immortal and the Father's Son, was such as could not die. For this

---

[40] L. W. Grensted, *A Short History of the Doctrine of the Atonement* (Eugene, OR: Wipf and Stock, 2001), 75.

[41] Athanasius, *The Incarnation of the Word of God* 21.

[42] Ibid., 34.

reason, therefore, He assumed a body capable of death, in order that it, through belonging to the Word Who is above all, might become in dying a sufficient exchange for all, and, itself remaining incorruptible through His indwelling, might thereafter put an end to corruption for all others as well, by the grace of the resurrection.[43]

Among the Patristic writers, Athanasius not only appears to be the most committed to biblical interpretation regarding the incarnation and atonement, but he also has more in common with Reformation understandings as we shall see.

Anselm of Canterbury (1033–1109) made two major contributions to theology. He provided specificity and development for the ontological argument for the existence of God. Even more important, Anselm fashioned the satisfaction theory of the atonement.[44] Both Augustine and Gregory of Nyssa had previously noted that something within the nature of God seemed to mandate the atonement. In his classic work *Cur Deus Homo,* Anselm developed the idea that heaven had been depleted of its full coterie of inhabitants in the fall of Satan and his entourage. The necessity of replacing these fallen angels with redeemed humans called for an atonement in which payment was provided to satisfy the wounded honor and majesty of God. On the one hand, only man, as the offender, could render this satisfaction. On the other hand, God alone can forgive sin. The dilemma is resolved by the incarnation of the Word of God. The incarnate Son, the God-man, satisfies this debt on the cross. Anselm wrote:

> For God will not do it, because he has no debt to pay; and man will not do it, because he cannot. Therefore, in order that the God-man may perform this, it is necessary that the same being should be perfect God and perfect man, in order to make this atonement [satisfaction]. For he cannot and ought not to do so, unless he be very God and very man.[45]

Boso, Anselm's interlocutor, pressed for an explanation as to why God could not simply forgive sin based on his compassion alone. To this Anselm replied:

---

[43] Ibid., 35.

[44] Grensted's estimate of Anselm ranks him as the most "revolutionary" thinker of his day. "Bold as were the speculations of Abelard, in reality the most revolutionary thinker of his day was Anselm, saint and loyal upholder of the authority of the Church. This fact was obscured for his contemporaries by his life of devoted suffering for the Papal cause, by his unquestioned sanctity, and by the supreme dialectical skill of his writings. Yet it has seldom been given to any writer to work such a change in the history of thought as that wrought by Anselm's short treatise, *Cur Deus Homo?*" (Grensted, *A Short History of the Doctrine of the Atonement,* 120).

[45] Anselm, *Cur Deus Homo,* in *St. Anselm,* trans. Sidney N. Deane (LaSalle: Open Court, 1968), 246.

To remit sin in this manner is nothing else than not to punish; and since it is not right to cancel sin without compensation or punishment; if it not be punished, then is it passed by undischarged. ... There is also another thing which follows if sin be passed by unpunished, viz., that with God there will be no difference between the guilty and the not guilty; and this is unbecoming to God.[46]

Anselm's argument that the majesty and honor of God were wounded by the rebellion of man means that in order for reconciliation to take place, God's majesty has to be satisfied. Since the penalty for sin is death, the death of Jesus satisfied the demands of God for recognition of his honor. These two theories, the ransom and the satisfaction, have in common a commercial and a forensic foundation. They also feature an objective view of the atonement in which God is affected by means of Christ's death on the cross. Of all the theories the satisfaction theory posits the most profound effect upon God.

Hugo Grotius (1583–1645), a Dutch jurist, found exactly this last feature objectionable in both ransom and satisfaction theories of the atonement. To maintain any theory that is ontologically mandated by the character of God seemed intolerable to Grotius. However, something of incredible consequence had to have gone awry for such an act as Christ's death to be necessary. Grotius propounded the *governmental theory*, which posited the death of Jesus as an offering to God, not to make possible forgiveness of sin but to restore moral order to the universe. Thus, God can freely forgive sin, and the cross restores a sense of moral rightness to the universe.

In 1931, the Swedish theologian Gustaf Aulén (1879–1977) penned an influential volume entitled *Christus Victor* in which he proposed a view that he calls the *classical view* of the atonement. Aulén argued that the cross was the ultimate expression of the cosmic conflict in which Christ conquered the forces of sin and Satan forever. He picked up on similar emphases in the writings of Irenaeus, Origen, Augustine, and others and found biblical basis for the view in Genesis 3:15; Colossians 2:15, Hebrews 2:14; and 1 John 3:8. Aulén introduced and defined the idea saying:

This type of view may be described provisionally as the "dramatic." Its central theme is the idea of the Atonement as a Divine conflict and victory; Christ—*Christus Victor*—fights against and triumphs over the evil powers of the world, the "tyrants" under which mankind is in bondage and suffering, and in Him God reconciles the world to Himself. Two points here require to be pressed with special emphasis: first, that this is a doctrine of Atonement in the

---

46 Anselm, "Cur Deus Homo?" in *St. Anselm's Basic Writings.* (LaSalle: Open Court, 1994), 217.

full and proper sense, and second, that this idea of the Atonement has a clear and distinct character of its own, quite different from the other two types.[47]

Luther (1483–1546) and Calvin (1509–1564), operating in the context of the Reformation, developed views that incorporated and sometimes expanded some of the views enumerated above. Conflating the classic view and the satisfaction model, Luther saw the death of Jesus as a substitute for human condemnation. Death is the just penalty attached inevitably to sin, and it is the death of Jesus which defeats Satan and evil. For Luther, the impossibility of securing salvation by human efforts rendered penal substitution inevitable, even though his own struggles against personal and ecclesiastical evil led him to expressions of the doctrine that echoed the classic view. Meditating on the passion of Christ led to this understanding.

classic + satisfaction

> They contemplate Christ's passion aright who view it with a terror-stricken heart and a despairing conscience. This terror must be felt as you witness the stern wrath and the unchanging earnestness with which God looks upon sin and sinners, so much so that he was unwilling to release sinners even for his only and dearest Son without his payment of the severest penalty for them. Thus he says in Isaiah 53 [:8], "I have chastised him for the transgressions of my people." If the dearest child is punished thus, what will be the fate of sinners? It must be an inexpressible and unbearable earnestness that forces such a great and infinite person to suffer and die to appease it. And if you seriously consider that it is God's very own Son, the eternal wisdom of the Father, who suffers, you will be terrified indeed. The more you think about it, the more intensely will you be frightened.[48]

Calvin's view, elucidated both in the *Institutes* and in his commentaries, emphasized both the sacrifice of Jesus and the *penal substitution* view of the atonement. In a vivid passage from the *Institutes,* he observed:

> On the other hand, suppose he learns, as Scripture teaches, that he was estranged from God through sin, is an heir of wrath, subject to the curse of eternal death, excluded from all hope of salvation, beyond every blessing of God, the slave of Satan, captive under the yoke of sin, destined finally for a dreadful destruction and already

---

[47] Gustaf Aulén, *Christus Victor* (London: Society for Promoting Christian Knowledge, 1945), 20.

[48] Martin Luther, *Devotional Writings I,* ed. Martin O. Dietrich, LW, American ed. (Philadelphia: Fortress, 1969), 8–9.

involved in it; and that at this point Christ interceded as his advocate, took upon himself and suffered the punishment that, from God's righteous judgment, threatened all sinners; that he purged with his blood those evils which had rendered sinners hateful to God; that by this expiation he made satisfaction and appeased God's wrath; that on this foundation rests the peace of God with men; that by this bond his benevolence is maintained toward them. Will the man not then be even more moved by all these things which so vividly portray the greatness of the calamity from which he has been rescued?

To sum up: since our hearts cannot, in God's mercy, either seize upon life ardently enough or accept it with the gratefulness we owe, unless our minds are first struck and overwhelmed by fear of God's wrath and by dread of eternal death, we are taught by Scripture to perceive that apart from Christ, God is, so to speak, hostile to us, and his hand is armed for our destruction; to embrace his benevolence and fatherly love in Christ alone.[49]

Calvin noted the necessity for a mediator who is both truly God and truly man. Citing John 3:16; Romans 5:8,25; and Philippians 2:7, he insisted that Christ's sacrificial death was a propitiation of the wrath of God. Understandably, the views of Calvin and Luther dominated Reformation thinking.

All of the perspectives discussed thus far have been typically styled *objective* views of the atonement. Either God himself or at least some cosmic circumstance is affected by the death of Jesus. In response to these kinds of views, *subjectivist* ideas also emerged, focusing primarily on the effects of the atonement on the individual sinner. Peter Abelard (1079–1142) noted that the barrier to fellowship with God and to salvation was in the

---

[49] Calvin, *Institutes*, 2.16.2. For an excellent defense of penal substitution, see J. I. Packer, *What Did the Cross Achieve? The Logic of Penal Substitution* (Leicester: Centaprint, 1974). Summarizing what Jesus accomplished on the cross, Packer makes nine cogent observations: (1) God . . . "condones nothing," but judges all sin as it deserves: which Scripture affirms, and my conscience confirms, to be right. (2) My sins merit ultimate penal suffering and rejection from God's presence (conscience also confirms this), and nothing I do can blot them out. (3) The penalty due to me for my sins, whatever it was, was paid for me by Jesus Christ, the Son of God, in his death on the cross. (4) Because this is so, I through faith in him am made "the righteousness of God in him," i.e., I am justified; pardon, acceptance, and sonship become mine. (5) Christ's death for me is my sole ground of hope before God. "If he fulfilled not justice, I must; if he underwent not wrath, I must to eternity." (6) My faith in Christ is God's own gift to me, given in virtue of Christ's death for me: i.e., the cross procured it. (7) Christ's death for me guarantees my preservation to glory. (8) Christ's death for me is the measure and pledge of the love of the Father and the Son to me. (9) Christ's death for me calls and constrains me to trust, to worship, to love, and to serve. One should also consult the superb treatment by Stott, *The Cross of Christ*.

estranged persons, their sinful pride and stubborn wills. Jesus' death so revealed God's love that this sacrificial act provided the inspiration for the revival of moral fortitude in man. God's love for us moves us to love him in return. Thus, the perspective is known as the *moral influence* view. Modern theologians such as Horace Bushnell (1802–1876)[50] and Hastings Rashdall (1858–1926)[51] developed the idea in a later context.

In fairness to Abelard, his view is not so simply dismissed as nothing more than a moral influence view of the atonement. For example, Abelard wrote:

> A most pressing problem obtrudes itself at this point, as to what that redemption of ours through the death of Christ may be, and in what way the apostle declares that we are justified by his blood—we who appear to be worthy of still greater punishment, seeing that we are the wicked servants who have committed the very things for which our innocent Lord was slain. And so it seems that we must first investigate why it was necessary for God to take human nature upon him so that he might redeem us by dying in the flesh; and from what person holding us captive, either justly or by fraud, he has redeemed us; and by what standard of justice he has liberated us from the dominion of that person who has given commands to which he willingly submitted in order to set us free.[52]

Or again Abelard said, "'In his blood.' This means by his death; and since this propitiation is set forth and established by God, not for all but only for those who believe, he adds, 'through faith'; for this reconciliation affects them only who have believed it and hoped for it."[53]

The *example theory* of the atonement is similar to the moral influence theory. Developed by Socinus (1552–1562), the theory differs, if at all, from the moral influence theory primarily because it begins with a robust confidence in the essential goodness of human nature. The death of Christ is so compelling as an example that it draws all men to act as Jesus acted in response to such open forgiveness of God. First Peter 2:21 is a major text marshaled in defense of this view: "For you were called to this, because Christ also suffered for you, leaving you an example, so that you should follow in His steps."

More recent discussions of the atonement tend to have more in common with the last two views. A smorgasbord of these include the perspectives of

---

[50] Horace Bushnell, *The Vicarious Sacrifice,* 2 vols. (1886; repr., New York: Scribner's, 1903).

[51] Hastings Rashdall, *The Idea of the Atonement in Christian Theology* (1919; repr., London: Macmillan, 1919).

[52] Eugene R. Fairweather, *A Scholastic Miscellany: Anselm to Ockham* (Philadelphia: Westminster, 1956), 280.

[53] Ibid., 279.

neoorthodoxy, which, though hardly monolithic, generally picture Christ's death on the cross as an act of solidarity with all human suffering. Elected in Christ, the real elect one, humankind triumphs with Christ. This or similar views are espoused by Karl Barth (1886–1968), Hendrikus Berkhof, and Vincent Taylor.[54]

Meanwhile, *liberation theology* has, in various hues, found easy identification with aspects of Barth's neoorthodox thinking. The death of Jesus as a first-century freedom fighter is important only as the part of his life that was lived to liberate all for social injustice. Advocates of such views are Jürgen Moltmann (*The Crucified God*), Leonardo Boff (*Jesus Christ Liberator*), and Jon Sobrino (*Christology at the Crossroads*). A feminist version of liberation theology sees Jesus as especially liberating women from patriarchal oppression, or in the more radical phase, raising concerns about the Father's child abuse of Jesus in the atonement.[55]

Postmodernism recognizes that different communities have their own metanarratives, which may be helpful to that one community, even true for that community, without necessarily being true for others. The atonement then functions this way for Christians but not for others. Meanwhile, advocates of open theism tend to see the atonement as opening the way to God for nearly everyone.[56] In the context of salvation, most open theists are inclusivists in their understanding of redemption.

How Does It All Fit Together?

Key Concepts in the Doctrine of the Atonement

While these have been mentioned previously in various ways, another way to examine the significance of the atonement of Christ is to bring together the key concepts under which the doctrine is unveiled in Scripture in a systematic analysis. The atonement of Christ is said to provide propitiation, redemption, reconciliation, forgiveness, and justification. In addition to these, some consideration must again be given to the concept of blood as it relates to the atonement and to covenant.

The first crucial concept is redemption. This English word, redemption, in the New Testament is a translation of *lytron, lytroō, antilytron,* and

---

[54] For Barth's refutation of Anselm, see Karl Barth, *Church Dogmatics,* (Edinburgh: T&T Clark, 1964), 2/1:92.

[55] Joanne Carlson Brown and Rebecca Parker, "For God So Loved the World," in *Christianity, Patriarchy and Abuse: A Feminist Critique* (New York: Pilgrim, 1989).

[56] For a view of salvation by an open theist, see Clark Pinnock, *A Wideness in God's Mercy: The Finality of Jesus Christ in a World of Religions* (Grand Rapids: Zondervan, 1992). Also note the dependence of Pinnock on Karl Rahner and Vatican II as demonstrated by Kenneth D. Keathley in "An Examination of the Influence of Vatican II on Clark Pinnock's 'Wider Hope' for the Unevangelized" (unpublished Ph.D. dissertation of Southeastern Baptist Theological Seminary, 2000).

apolytrōsis. In addition, the New Testament words *agorazō* and *exagorazō* are also employed. Every beginning student of Greek will recognize the simple verb *lyō,* which provides the genesis of the *lytron* word group. *Lyō* signifies in its most basic meaning "to loose." The word group occurs a number of times in the New Testament and is used in the Septuagint to translate three different Hebrew words, *goel, padah,* and *kopher.* The general concept (wherever it occurs) seems to involve the use of a payment to attain deliverance.

Agorazō, on the other hand, makes use of the verbal form of the Greek word for the market, *agora.* More often than not, the emphasis here also includes purchase, but when *exagorazō* is added, the emphasis is intensified slightly to suggest "buying out." The latter word was used with reference to the purchase of slaves, perhaps even looking toward the prospect of the granting of freedom to those enslaved. When both word systems are considered in regard to redemption, one may glean that salvation in Christ required that a payment be made. That payment, somehow in the divine economy, effects deliverance from sin in both its power and its penalty, and ultimately its very presence. Early debates about the recipient of the payment are probably not even germane to the biblical narrative. As noted previously, problems arise when any attempt is made to designate the recipient of the payment. Suffice it to say that the cross of Christ represents an enormous sacrifice, which in turn provides the currency necessary for the purchase of eternal life and forgiveness of sin for those who had previously been shackled by sin.

Agorazō appears prominently in the Apocalypse in Revelation 5:9; 14:3–4. *Exagorazō,* on the other hand, is one of the Apostle Paul's preferred terms, appearing in Galatians 3:13; 4:5; and Ephesians 5:16. *Lytroō* is used by Luke in 24:21 in his description of the disciples on the road to Emmaus when they expressed their confidence in Jesus as the one who would redeem Israel. The same word is used in Titus 2:14 to speak of Christ's sacrifice redeeming us from all iniquity, while Peter uses it in 1 Peter 1:18 to suggest that we were redeemed by the blood of Jesus Christ.

Paul's preference, however, is for the term *apolytrōsis,* which is used in Romans 3:24; 8:23; 1 Corinthians 1:30; Ephesians 1:7,14; 4:30, and Colossians 1:14, all in similar ways noted in the previous discussion. The author of Hebrews likewise makes use of the word in 9:15, but in 9:12 he uses just *lytrōsis* without the appended preposition. This brief survey should confirm the description of the significance of the words used.

Reconciliation is the translation of the Greek word *katallagē* and its verb forms *katallassō* and *apokatallassō.* The word reflects, as it is used in the doctrine of the atonement, a changed relationship to God. Though the word is less frequently used than words from the *lytron* family, *katallassō* is, nevertheless, of profound significance in the Bible and speaks readily to to-day's broken and factured world. Paul uses *apokatallassō* and *katallassō* on at least nine different occasions whereas he uses the noun form *katallagē* in at least three places. Some of the more prominent usages occur in Romans 5:10ff and 2 Corinthians 5:18–20. The strongest associations with the ac-tual atonement of Christ are found in Romans 5:10; Ephesians 2:16; and Colossians 1:20–21, where it is said that all are reconciled to God by means of Christ's death. A point made by other writers, which perhaps ought not to be pressed too far but apparently is true to the biblical text, is that the atonement seems to reconcile man to God while it propitiates God toward man. This observation suggests that the atonement has a dual effect—partly on the Father and partly on humanity.

Forgiveness is *aphesis* or *aphiēmi.* This concept is used broadly in the Scriptures, but at least some of its uses focus directly on the atonement and its purchase of forgiveness for sinners. Ephesians 1:7 and Colossians 1:14 provide significant association of a concept of forgiveness with the gra-cious atonement of Christ.

The concept of justification in its various nominal and verbal forms is probably the most frequently used terminology to describe the impact of the atonement. This includes *dikaios, dikaiosynē,* and *dikaioō.* Perhaps the most important passage relating justification to the atonement is the one already discussed in Romans 3:23–26, where Paul argues that the death of Christ on the cross made it possible for God to be both just and the justifier of those who trust in Christ. Specifically, Paul links the concept of righ-teousness with the idea of propitiation. This righteousness cannot come from the law but only through the death of Christ. This is the affirmation of Paul in Galatians 2:21. Forensic justification or right standing with God is the major emphasis of the word. The sinner's legal standing before God is changed by virtue of the atonement, bringing about justification; but also it appears that the New Testament knows the actual bestowal of Christ's righteousness as seen in Romans 13:14.

The word "propitiation," *hilaskomai* and *hilastērion,* occurs with rela-tive infrequency. Nevertheless, at each occurrence the word seems to be a term of considerable importance. First John 2:2 declares that Christ is the propitiation for our sins and not for ours only but also for the sins of the whole world, and 1 John 4:10 makes a similar statement. Infinitely, the most important of the verses where propitiation occurs is Romans 3:25, where propitiation takes place as a result of "faith in His blood." The author of Hebrews affirms that the merciful and faithful High Priest makes "pro-pitiation for the sins of the people" (Heb. 2:17).

The vigorous debate that has raged across the years about whether *hi-laskomai* should be translated as "propitiation" or "expiation" has been dealt with earlier in this chapter. However, at this point, it should be noted that the real distinction is not bound up in whether expiation is an appropriate translation for *hilaskomai*. *Expiation,* which focuses on the cancellation of the sin debt, is certainly a biblical concept and can be enthusiastically affirmed. Having affirmed it, however, one still must conclude that the word *hilaskomai* is inadequately translated as "expiation." Propitiation is the appropriate translation because there is more than simple cancellation of sin or its debt. Justice is necessary (Rom. 3:25–26); hence, the settled wrath of God against sin is important and must be considered. In order to deal with the justice of God and his wrath against sin, "propitiation" becomes the only translation that incorporates both concepts of cancellation and the satisfaction of the wrath of God.

Two final related issues to be considered are the nature of covenant and the question of whether the blood of sacrifices in the Old Testament and of Christ in the New Testament represent essentially life or death.[57] Regarding the word *covenant,* the difficulty arises from the fact that the Septuagint uses the Greek word *diathēkē,* which generally means "will," to translate the Hebrew word for covenant (*berith*). A covenant in the minds of most people involves a two-party agreement with both parties upholding certain facets of the covenant. If this is the way "covenant" should be interpreted in all cases, then, of course, the new covenant (*kainē diathēkē*) of the New Testament might be interpreted as a form of salvation partially earned by works: God would do his part on one hand, but then man would also have to do his part.

However, this understanding seems not to be the case universally, even in the Old Testament. For example, Abraham seems to be an observer in the covenant ritual recorded in Genesis 15:17. In order successfully to have a covenant, there must be the drawing up of terms, an oath to keep that covenant, and, in the Old Testament, the ritual slaughter of animals. In the New Testament, however, in 1 Corinthians 11:17–34 and Hebrews 8:7–13, the new covenant is something God commits himself to do in behalf of the objects of his love. The covenant is actuated by the death of the testator, in this case, the Lord Jesus. Specifically, the testator dies through the shedding of his blood.

The question is then raised concerning the significance of the blood. As already indicated, the key passage here is Leviticus 17:11, which specifies that "the life of the flesh is in the blood" (NKJV). However, does the word *dam* in the Old Testament or *haima* in the New Testament refer essentially to the life of an animal or a person as Westcott and Taylor both believe,

---

[57] For a recent examination of the significance of blood in the Old Testament, see William K. Elders, *Blood Ritual in the Hebrew Bible* (Baltimore: Johns Hopkins University, 2004).

suggesting therefore that sacrifice represents the offering up of life? Or does it stand for death, as Denny and Moffatt argue? In a sense, it seems unnecessary to decide between these.[58] Leviticus 17:11 affirms that the life is in the blood, and hence, certainly Jesus' shedding his blood on the cross is an offering up of his life. Still, the idea of offering life through the shedding of blood obviously speaks of death. This understanding is certainly Paul's in Romans 3:25; 5:9, and Ephesians 2:13. So the covenant established is something that is accomplished by God himself, even to the point of offering his own Son as a sacrifice for sin through the shedding of his blood.

Special Issues in the Atonement

Two remaining issues must be briefly discussed. The first concerns the extent of the atonement, and the second focuses on the relationship of the atonement to physical healing.

The Extent of the Atonement

Regarding the extent of the atonement, the question must be answered: Did Christ die only for the elect, hence, a limited atonement or particular redemption; or did he die for all people, hence, a universal or general atonement? Clearly, the benefits of the atonement are applicable only to those who trust Christ, and those who trust Christ are obviously the ones who are the elect, since no other would come. All evangelical theologians can affirm that Jesus died "sufficiently for all but efficiently for the elect." Furthermore, all evangelicals limit the atonement in some manner. Otherwise, one would, of necessity, be driven to universalism. Interestingly, uncertainty exists as to whether Calvin himself believed in particular redemption, though there is no question that classical Reformed doctrine embraces this idea.[59]

It should be pointed out that the Arminian view is not the only view that rejects particular redemption or limited atonement. Amyraldians, for example, should be viewed as part of the Reformed tradition though they embrace only four of the points of classic Calvinism, rejecting the doctrine of limited atonement.[60]

---

[58] Leon Morris, *The Apostolic Preaching of the Cross* (Grand Rapids: Eerdmans, 1965), 108. However, A. M. Stibbs notes the importance of the issue when he writes, "This is the more important because in this connection the word is used so often. As Vincent Taylor has pointed out, the 'blood' of Christ is mentioned in the writings of the New Testament nearly three times as often as the 'death' of Christ. The term 'blood' is, in fact, a chief method of reference to the sacrifice of Christ, particularly in contexts which define its efficacy." A. M. Stibbs, *The Meaning of the Word "Blood" in Scripture* (London: Tyndale, 1954), 3.

[59] For an examination of Calvin's view of the extent of the atonement, see Kevin Dixon Kennedy, *Union with Christ and the Extent of the Atonement in Calvin* (New York: Peter Lang, 2002).

[60] See B. A. Demarest, "Amyraldianism," in *EDT*, 41–42.

Among the texts cited as favoring a limited atonement or particular redemption are Matthew 1:21, where Jesus is said to have come to "save His people." John 10:11 speaks of the shepherd who "lays down His life for the sheep." A variation of that in John 15:13 says that an example of the greatest of all loves occurs when a person "lays down his life for his friends." Further, in the high priestly prayer of Jesus in John 17:9, Jesus seems specifically to pray not for the whole world but for those whom his Father had given him. Those who favor limited atonement argue that if Christ died for all people, then God somehow failed in the atonement, since clearly some are lost. In fact, if the lost perish, sin is said to be punished twice: in the death of Christ and in the death of the sinner. The only alternative for some is that if the atonement is universal, then so must salvation be universal. Thus, only the elect are objects of God's redemptive love and, therefore, of his sacrifice.

On the other hand, those favoring universal atonement cite John 1:29, which speaks of Jesus' taking away the sins of the world. John 3:16 would be characteristic of the "whoever" passages: God so loved the world and sent Jesus to die that "whoever believes in Him should not perish but have everlasting life" (NKJV). John 12:31–33 promises that Jesus will "draw all people to [Himself]," while Romans 5:12–21 insists that just as all died in Adam, so in one shall all be made alive. First John 2:1–2 (already cited) seems to speak definitively to the matter by juxtaposing the forgiveness of "our sins" on one hand with the sins of the whole world on the other. The writer of Hebrews also seems to endorse that theme, insisting that Jesus would "taste death for everyone" (Heb. 2:9). In 1 Timothy 4:10, Paul speaks of Jesus as the Savior of all but in a special way of those who believe. Second Peter 2:1 goes so far as to say that false prophets deny the Master who bought them, apparently affirming they had provision made for their sin in the atoning work of Christ.

The conclusion that one draws on this subject is based largely on the presuppositions that he brings to the text and on the decision about which texts will be the foundational indicators driving the interpretation of other texts which seem less supportive of one's position. Virtually all evangelical theologians on both sides would agree that there are some benefits from the cross that accrue to all the world, but this conclusion does not resolve the issue of the actual extent and intent of the atonement.

Acknowledging the enigma that remains, the tension that all exegetes experience when attempting to provide credible explanations for the electing providences of God and at the same moment to account for the pervasive assignment of human responsibility throughout the Scriptures ought to engender a level of humility not frequently found in such debates. The idea of an atonement limited only to the elect is a concept that belongs to a logical system including other elements, such as irresistible grace, which many find appealing. But irresistible grace is difficult to establish from the Scriptures, depending instead on the logic of the system. Effectual calling is a more biblical concept, but it should be maintained that God's calling of the elect to salvation does not infringe on the responsibility of sinners to repent and believe the gospel.

It is significant that the Abstract of Principles, written in 1859 as the confession for The Southern Baptist Theological Seminary, affirms man's "free will and responsibility" as "intelligent creatures."[61] But whenever that logic is applied beyond reasonable limits, conclusions like those of R. C. Sproul become inevitable: "God desired for man to fall into sin. . . . God created sin."[62]

Or, again:

> It was his desire to make his wrath known. He needed, then, something on which to be wrathful. He needed to have sinful crea-tures. He wanted to make his mercy known. He needed, then, some-thing that deserved wrath on which he could show mercy instead. All of this serves his eternal and ultimate desire, to glorify himself.
>
> If he is pleased, then he is glorified, even if we think it's not so great. We don't often think, for instance, of the glory God receives from the torment of souls in hell.[63]

How then is God in some sense not the author of evil and even sin? Sproul's view is extreme (he would argue that it is logically consistent and therefore necessary), and this position is difficult to reconcile with the teachings of Scripture concerning: (1) the love of God for all persons made in his image, and (2) the character of God described in the Bible and with the justice of God. The concept of double predestination, that God actively saves some people and actively damns others cannot be defended from the plain teachings of Scripture.

If God created some people only to damn them for the purpose of exhib-iting the glory of his wrath, then the doctrine of limited atonement, which denies that Jesus died for all people, is not only understandable but also logical. But is this the teaching of the Bible or the logic of a theologi-cal system taken too far? This discussion is about heaven and hell, about people made in the image of God spending an eternity of incredible agony,

---

[61] Article 4 on Providence. The extent of the atonement is not addressed in this confession, a con-fession recognized by all as Reformed in its orientation.

[62] R. C. Sproul, *Almighty over All: Understanding the Sovereignty of God* (Grand Rapids: Baker, 1999), 53.

[63] Ibid.

separated forever from God and from good. God is appropriately and gloriously wrathful against all destructive rebellion against him. But how could he justly create some people specifically for such damnation? Indeed, did he do this according to Scripture? Justice is a concept like love and truth, which derives its definition from the character of God.

Consequently, the following texts should function straightforwardly as radiant sunbeams revealing the heart of God:

... who wants everyone to be saved and to come to the knowledge of the truth (1 Tim. 2:4).

... who gave Himself—a ransom for all, a testimony at the proper time (1 Tim. 2:6).

In fact, we labor and strive for this, because we have put our hope in the living God, who is the Savior of everyone, especially of those who believe (1 Tim. 4:10).

But we do see Jesus—made lower than the angels for a short time so that by God's grace He might taste death for everyone—crowned with glory and honor because of the suffering of death (Heb. 2:9).

My little children, I am writing you these things so that you may not sin. But if anyone does sin, we have an advocate with the Father—Jesus Christ the righteous One. He Himself is the propitiation for our sins, and not only for ours, but also for those of the whole world (1 John 2:1–2).

The atonement of Christ is universal in scope but applicable only for those who receive him (John 1:10–12). It is universal or unlimited in its provision but limited in its application. It is sufficient for all but efficient only for those who believe, who are the elect of God.[64]

---

[64] The literature on the extent of the atonement is voluminous. For typical positions favoring particular redemption, see not only Sproul's volume mentioned earlier and others by Sproul including *Grace Unknown* (Grand Rapids: Baker, 1997) but also James R. White, *The Potters Freedom* (Amityville: Calvary, 2000) and Francis Turrettin, *The Atonement of Christ* (Grand Rapids: Baker, 1978). The view of many in the Reformed tradition is that the classic defense of particular redemption is that of John Owen, *The Death of Death in the Death of Christ* (1852; repr., Carlisle: Banner of Truth Trust, 1967). For views supporting a general atonement, see Laurance M. Vance, *The Other Side of Calvinism* (Pensacola: Vance, 1994), Norman F. Douty, *Did Christ Die Only for the Elect?* (Eugene: Wipf and Stock, 1998), and Robert Picirilli, *Grace, Faith, Free Will: Contrasting Views of Salvation: Calvinism and Arminianism* (Nashville: Randall House, 2002). Mediating views which attempt to span the divide are Luis De Molina, *On Divine Foreknowledge* (Ithaca: Cornell University Press, 1988) and William Lane Craig, *Divine Foreknowledge and Human*

Healing in the Atonement   No! проверь знатьмоб...

There also is the question of physical healing as a possible benefit of the atonement. Cessationists often believe that the sign gifts, such as healing and tongues, have ceased in the post-apostolic era. Others are convinced that because of Christ's death on the cross, physical healing of disease is at least a possibility. Advocates of this position cite 1 Peter 2:24: "He Himself bore our sins in His body on the tree, so that, having died to sins, we might live for righteousness; by His wounding you have been healed." This passage is a citation of Isaiah 53:5. A portion of the logic involved suggests that if sickness is a result of the fall, then why should the atonement not effect healing in the body?

Over against this perception, William Edward Biederwolf penned an influential volume responding to Aimee Semple McPherson's thesis that "at the whipping post He purchased your healing."[65] Biederwolf interpreted the 1 Peter 2:24 and Isaiah 53:5 verses as another way of expressing the spiritual benefits of the atonement. This volume remains one of the most extensive treatises ever written on the subject.

Actually, Scripture teaches that physical healing is a benefit of the atonement but not in the way some Charismatics have suggested. The flaw in the idea that the work of Christ on the cross produces the healing of sickness is the unavoidability of death (Heb. 9:27). All physical healing in the present is inevitably trumped by physical death. Evangelicals committed to the sovereignty of God do not question that God can heal, has healed, and continues to heal. But the healing present in the atonement is as permanent as regeneration itself. This irreversible healing is included in the final soteriological act of God, i.e., glorification. The hope of the glorification of the body is so certainly a part of the salvific enterprise that Paul even speaks of it as a past event along with foreknowledge, predestination, and justification (Rom. 8:29).

Death, consequently, has no numbing fear for believers (Rom. 8:34–39). The anticipated heavenly healing provides a condition according to Revelation 21:4 in which "He will wipe away every tear from their eyes. Death will exist no longer; grief, crying, and pain will exist no longer, because the previous things have passed away."

Prudence suggests then a view that includes the body in its resurrected/glorified state as a benefit of the death of Jesus. However, to promise physi-

---

Freedom (Leiden: E. J. Brill, 1991). The last two works attempt to resolve the mystery on the basis of "middle knowledge."

65 J. Rodman Williams, *Renewal Theology* (Grand Rapids: Zondervan, 1992), 2:256–57. Writing from a Charismatic perspective, Williams chronicles this view in writers and evangelists as diverse as Charles Parham, Aimee Semple McPherson, Oral Roberts, A. J. Gordon, and A. B. Simpson. William Edward Biederwolf, *Whipping Post Theology* (Grand Rapids: Eerdmans, 1934).

cal healing in the present corporeal state based on the atonement seems to have insufficient biblical support.

The Intercessory Work of Christ

The ascension of Christ is recorded in Acts 1:4–11. Jesus, having completed his prophetic teaching ministry, which included the working of miracles, and having purged the sins of all people through his death on the cross, and having been raised from the dead on the third day after his passion, now appeared with his disciples and commissioned them for the assignment at hand. Then, as they watched, Jesus ascended into heaven and was received into a cloud and out of their sight. Angels appearing to the astonished disciples explained that the disciples need not stand gazing into heaven anymore but could leave with the quiet assurance that this same Jesus who had been received into heaven would also come again in the same way that they had seen him ascend into heaven. The question naturally then arises about the location to which the risen Lord departed and the nature of the activity that he would then pursue awaiting the Father's decisive time of the consummation of all things.

Jesus said in John 14:1–6 that he would go away and that his departure would give rise not only to the coming of the Spirit but also to a season of preparation in heaven where he would "prepare a place" for the disciples. No precise information is provided about the nature of this preparatory mission, but the language chosen is sufficient to indicate vigorous activity on the part of the risen and ascended Lord.

On the other hand, Jesus is repeatedly pictured in the New Testament as "seated at the right hand of God" (Eph. 1:20; Col. 3:1; Heb. 1:3; 8:1; 10:12). The posture of sitting generally is indicative of either one who is at rest or else one who sits in judgment. In this case, the posture seems to reflect still a third idea. Jesus is at rest at the right hand of the Father as an indication of the completion of his work of atonement for the sins of mankind. Bernard Ramm observed:

> After Jesus' ascension into heaven, the New Testament affirms that he was seated at the right hand of the Father. This is called the session of Christ. It is a far richer concept than most theologies represent, for it becomes involved in both the framing and understanding of some important theological topics.[66]

---

[66] Bernard L. Ramm, *An Evangelical Christology: Ecumenic and Historic* (Nashville: Thomas Nelson, 1985), 99–100. Ramm adds,

The book of Hebrews sets out the intercessory ministry of Christ within the imagery of the tabernacle, priest, and sacrifices. One finds these materials in Exodus and Leviticus. (i) The Son of God became incarnate so that he could experientially know what it was like

The purpose of this session at the right hand of the Father specifically relates to intercession in behalf of those who have inherited salvation. This emphasis is the point of 1 John 2:1, where we have an advocate with the Father, and of Hebrews 7:25, where the author of Hebrews informs us that Jesus always lives to make intercession for us. In 1 John 2:1, the advocacy of Christ is related to the problem of human sin and guilt and gives assurance of the ongoing work of mercy as the Lord makes intercession in behalf of his followers before his heavenly Father. However, in the Hebrews passage, the act of intercession seems to be one of broader scope and doubtless includes the general providential intervention of God in behalf of the saints.

Concerning this session, Hodge focuses on the identification of Christ with his people:

> Christ presents Himself before God as our representative. His perfect manhood, his official character, and his finished work, plead for us before the throne of God. All that the Son of God as incarnate is, and all that He did on earth, He is, and did for us; so that God can regard us with all the favour which is due to Him. His presence, therefore, is a perpetual and prevailing intercession with God in behalf of his people, and secures for them all the benefits of his redemption.[67]

The doctrine of the session of the Son at the right hand of the Father is developed little beyond these references. Nevertheless, the doctrine provides a cause for solace and comfort in the presence of both human weakness and the general necessity for divine intervention in the lives of believers. In addition to that, there is associated with the doctrine of the session of the Son a parentheses of rest between the initial work of the incarnation and atonement of Christ and the concluding final epiphany when the consummation of all things is brought about and the Lord returns to the earth (Rev. 19:11–21).

The Resurrection

Christianity stands or falls with the bodily resurrection of Jesus. The whole of New Testament faith and teaching orbits about the confession and

---

to be a pilgrim in this world (Heb 2:14–16). (ii) He is first of all a Savior because he offered up himself for the salvation of his people (Heb 9:11–28). (iii) The place of his intercessory work is heaven itself, the true tabernacle (Heb 6:19–20; 8:1–2). (iv) The basis of his intercession is his experience of temptation and suffering (Heb 2:19; 4:14–16; 5:7–10). And the power of his priesthood is that he ever lives to make intercession (Heb 9:11–28).

67 Charles Hodge, *Systematic Theology* (1874; repr., Grand Rapids: Eerdmans, 1970), 2:592.

conviction that the crucified Jesus is the Son of God established and vindicated as such "by the resurrection from the dead according to the Spirit of holiness" (Rom. 1:4).

Resurrection Options

When one approaches the issue of the bodily resurrection of Jesus, those who affirm its truth readily acknowledge that they bear the burden of proof. After all, we are making the claim that Jesus did what no other person has ever done: He died, rose from the dead and remains alive until this day. In formulating an understanding of this doctrine, it is beneficial to note the naturalistic theories that dominated the nineteenth and early twentieth centuries. Following that, we will construct an apologetic—a defense—for the historic, bodily resurrection of Jesus.

The Swoon Theory. Jesus did not really die, according to this theory. He passed out or fainted as a result of the enormous physical punishment he suffered. Later he revived. In *The Passover Plot,* Hugh Schonfield says the whole thing was planned by Jesus with help from Joseph of Arimathea. Jesus was drugged while on the cross, which made it appear that he had died. Unfortunately, he was seriously injured and did actually die a short time later.[68]

The Spirit Theory. Jesus was not raised bodily, but he did return in a spirit form or as a spirit creature. This view is held by the Jehovah's Witnesses cult. They teach that Jesus was created by God as the archangel Michael and that while on earth he was only a man. Following his death on the cross, God restored him in a spiritual form only. In *Let God Be True,* the Watchtower asserts, "King Christ Jesus was put to death in the flesh and was resurrected an invisible spirit creature."[69]

The Hallucination Theory. This perspective was initially set forth by the German scholar David Strauss (1808–1874). The disciples, wanting desperately to believe Jesus was alive, simply imagined his resurrection.

The Vision Theory. The disciples had experiences which they interpreted or understood to be appearances of the risen Jesus. Jürgen Moltmann believes that the disciples saw visionary appearances of the risen Christ and that he communicated to them a call and mission.[70]

The Legend/Myth Theory. Over time the Jesus stories were embellished and exaggerated. This view is radically committed to an antisupernatural agenda, and it separates the Jesus of history (who he really was) from the Christ of faith (what the church later imagined him to be). The resurrection

---

[68] Hugh J. Schonfield, *The Passover Plot* (New York: Bantam, 1965), 112–65.

[69] *Let God Be True,* rev. ed. (Brooklyn: Watchtower Bible and Tract Society, 1982), 138.

[70] Jürgen Moltmann, *The Crucified God,* trans. R. A. Wilson and John Bowden (New York: Harper & Row, 1974), 167–68.

is something of a wonder story indicating the significance the mythical Jesus held for them.

The Stolen Body Theory. This is actually the earliest theory that attempts to explain away the bodily resurrection of Jesus. It goes back to Matthew 28:11–15, where it is recorded that the soldiers who guarded Jesus' tomb were bribed by the Jewish leaders to lie and say, "His disciples came during the night and stole Him while we were sleeping" (v. 13). Occasionally it is alleged that the body could also have been stolen by the (1) Jewish leaders, (2) the Romans, or even (3) Joseph of Arimathea. This theory was revived for a brief time by Deists in the eighteenth century, though it is held by virtually no one today.[71]

The Wrong Tomb Theory. Belief in the bodily resurrection of Jesus rests on a simple mistake: first the women and later the men went to the wrong tomb by accident. Kirsopp Lake first defended this theory in 1907.

The Lie-for-Profit Theory. The alleged resurrection of Jesus was a "religious hoax" perpetuated by Jesus' disciples. His death by crucifixion was a huge disappointment, but his followers saw a way to turn it into financial profit.

The Mistaken Identity Theory. Sometimes related to the wrong tomb theory, this view says the women mistook someone who they thought was Jesus. Support for this view is sometimes sought from John 20:11–18.

The Twin Theory. In a debate in 1995 with Christian apologist William Lane Craig, philosopher Robert Greg Cavin argued that Jesus had an identical twin brother. They were separated at birth and did not see each other again until the crucifixion. Following Jesus' death, his twin conjured up a messianic identity and mission for Jesus, stole his body (a new candidate for the stolen body theory!), and pretended to be the risen Jesus. Craig rightly notes that theories like Cavin's make great comedy and give evidence of an incredible imagination. They are, however, of no real value if one is serious about discovering what really happened on the first Easter morning.[72]

The Muslim Theory. Islam rejects the biblical witness concerning the crucifixion of Jesus. God instead provided a substitute for Jesus, perhaps even making the person look like Jesus. Surah 4:157 in *The Koran* says, "They declared: 'We have put to death the Messiah Jesus the son of Mary, the apostle of Allah.' They did not kill him, nor did they crucify him, but they thought they did."[73] Among Muslims there is no unanimity on who took the place of Jesus.

---

[71] William Lane Craig, *Reasonable Faith: Christian Truth and Apologetics,* rev. ed. (Wheaton: Crossway, 1994), 278.

[72] William Lane Craig and Robert Greg Cavin, "Dead or Alive? A Debate on the Resurrection of Jesus" (Anaheim: Simon Greenleaf University Press, 1995), audiotape.

[73] *The Koran,* trans. N. J. Dawood (New York: Penguin, 1956, rev. 1974), 382.

Contemporary Models for Explaining the Resurrection

Habermas points out that the naturalistic theories of the nineteenth century basically devoured one another so that they are seldom held today as they once were.[74] They were found to be flawed and wanting, and so scholars moved on, but where? Habermas believes we can summarize recent thinking on the bodily resurrection in terms of five models.

The first model is held by those who tend either to dismiss or at least seriously question the authenticity of the resurrection appearances. These persons tend to dismiss any literal claims that Jesus' tomb was empty or that he was actually seen by his followers. They conclude that the nature of the original eyewitnesses' experiences cannot be discovered. (Examples are Bultmann, Marxsen, Koester, Küng, Van Buren.)

The second model is characterized by those more interested in the nature of the disciples' experiences and who often accept a literal resurrection of Jesus. However, these scholars still insist that these experiences cannot be historically verified (examples: Karl Barth, Brunner, Bonhoeffer, Bornkamm, Rahner, Markus Barth [son of Karl Barth], Torrence).

The third model is characterized by persons who believe the resurrection is probable and who set forth an abstract reconstruction of the historical nature of the appearances. They often provide reasons the empty tomb is the best explanation for all of the data, and they seek "to ascertain at least a minimalist understanding of what really happened, including the providing of reasons for the acceptance of the appearances of Jesus and the empty tomb."[75] Jesus' appearances are usually viewed as spiritual in nature rather than a physical phenomenon (examples: Grass, Moltmann, Wilkens, Reginald H. Fuller, Jeremias, and O'Collins).

The fourth model believes available historical data is sufficient to demonstrate the probability that the tomb was empty and that Jesus was literally raised from the dead. Pannenberg, for example, thinks the historical facts support the likelihood of the empty tomb and the literal appearances of Jesus. However, Pannenberg favors appearances in terms of a spiritual body which appeared from heaven, was recognized as Jesus when he spoke and, at least in Paul's case, was accomplished by a phenomenon of light. Others in this camp include Hunter, Brown, Dunn, Goppelt, and Ramsey.

The fifth model is the historic, orthodox position. Scholars here agree that the evidence refutes the naturalistic theories. They further believe that the tomb in which Jesus was buried was found empty and that Jesus actually appeared to his followers. Scholars in this fifth model include

---

[74] Gary Habermas, *The Resurrection of Jesus: A Rational Inquiry* (Ann Arbor: University Microfilms, 1976), especially 114–71.

[75] Gary R. Habermas, "Jesus' Resurrection and Contemporary Criticism: An Apologetic," *CTR* 4.1 (Fall 1989): 167.

Craig, Ladd, Osborne, Daniel Fuller, Geisler, Wenham, Bruce, Green, Hoover, C. S. Lewis, McDowell, Montgomery, Moreland, Nash, and Habermas.[76]

An Apologetic for the Bodily Resurrection of Jesus

Why should anyone believe in the bodily resurrection of Jesus of Nazareth? Is not the claim itself incredible and unbelievable from the start? Actually one can marshal a strong case of compelling evidence that Christ did indeed rise from the dead. Such evidences include the following:

- The failure of naturalistic theories to explain the event.
- The birth of faith in the disciples and the radical change in their lives.
- The empty tomb and the discarded grave clothes.
- His appearance first to women.
- Change in the day of worship from the Sabbath to Sunday by Jews.
- Unlikely nature of mass hallucination.
- Numerous and varied resurrection appearances which lasted for forty days and then abruptly ended.
- The fifty-day interval between the resurrection and the proclamation of the gospel at Pentecost (Acts 2) in Jerusalem.
- The failure of the Jewish leaders and the Romans to disprove the message of the empty tomb.
- The unexpected nature of the bodily resurrection of Jesus.
- The conversion of two skeptics: James the half brother of Jesus and Saul of Tarsus.
- The moral character of the eyewitnesses.
- The early creedal witness of 1 Corinthians 15:3–7.
- The accepted character and claims of Jesus.
- Reliable eyewitness documents recording the events.

Taken in a cumulative fashion, the evidence is impressive that the tomb of Jesus was discovered to be empty, and his followers had real and genuine encounters with the resurrected Christ.[77]

Theological Significance

In one sense, to speak of the resurrection as a work of Christ appears inappropriate since the Bible seems to indicate that God the Father "raised Him from the dead" (Acts 13:30; Rom. 10:9; Gal. 1:1). However, it is also the case that Jesus said in John 10:18, "No one takes [My life] from Me,

---

[76] Ibid., 163–71.

[77] For a fuller development of these fifteen evidences, see Daniel L. Akin, *Discovering the Biblical Jesus* (Nashville: LifeWay, 2003), 105–14.

but I lay it down on My own. I have the right to lay it down, and I have the right to take it up again." It is appropriate to treat the doctrine of the resurrection in the context of eschatology, acknowledging Christ as the firstfruits of the resurrection which all who are in him will enjoy (1 Cor. 15:22). In the discussion of soteriology in Romans 4:25, Christ is said to have been raised for our justification. The point here is that the biblical writers propound a close connection between the vicarious substitutionary death of Christ on the cross and his resurrection as both being tied to the miracle of salvation.

The classic and definitive text on the resurrection is 1 Corinthians 15. It is both apologetical and theological in its treatment of this great doctrine. Both the death of Christ and his resurrection are a part of the definition of the gospel. In 1 Corinthians 15:1, Paul declares the gospel that had been preached to the people and in which they stand and by which they are saved. That gospel is that Christ died for (Gk. *hyper*) our sins, according to the Scriptures, he was buried, and on the third day, he was raised once again according to the Scriptures.[78] Paul then notes that the resurrection is a historical reality witnessed by numerous eyewitnesses (15:5–9). Paul points out he is passing on a tradition that he previously received (15:3). This creedal declaration was formed within a few years following the passion of Christ.

There then follows a laundry list of inevitabilities if there is no such thing as the resurrection of the dead (15:12–19). If there is no resurrection, then Christ himself cannot be risen (v. 13). Consequently, if Christ is not risen, then our preaching is vacuous, and our faith is empty (v. 14). Then, in turn, those who claim the resurrection become false witnesses (v. 15), resulting in the fact that all are still in their sins (v. 17). Not only this, but those who have died believing in Jesus have perished (v. 18); and since believers have hope only in this life, then they are of all men to be most pitied. Furthermore, there is no meaning in baptism for the dead if it were known that there is no resurrection (vv. 29–30).[79]

---

[78] Paul has in view the Old Testament Scriptures and texts like Genesis 22:1–19; Psalms 16:8–11; 22; Isaiah 52:13–53:12; Jonah 1:17; 2:10; Zechariah 12:10.

[79] The frequently debated verse 29, "Otherwise, what will they do who are baptized for the dead, if the dead do not rise at all? Why then are they baptized for the dead?" is a favorite verse of Mormonism that leads to surrogate baptisms by the hundreds of thousands. However, a key to the possible meaning of the verse has to do with the preposition *hyper* that is translated "for" in the verse "baptized for the dead." Whereas *hyper* usually carries the substitutionary sense, as has been noted repeatedly in this chapter, so here appearing with the ablative the sense of substitution is not lost but is to be understood in the sense of "with reference to" or "concerning." In 2 Corinthians 8:23, Paul uses the word this way when he speaks concerning (*hyper*) Titus. In 2 Thessalonians 2:1, the word is used the same way, "Concerning (*hyper*) the coming of the Lord." Hence the expression "baptism with reference to or concerning the dead" is possibly not so difficult as some interpreters have imagined. The logic of Paul's argument throughout the chapter is the necessity of the resurrection. Here he simply points out that baptism as though one

The resurrection itself is the crowning moment of the work of atonement provided by our Lord.[80] It is a trinitarian accomplishment with each person of the Godhead participating (Rom. 1:1–4). Even if we are forgiven of our sins, if there is no hope for the future, New Testament salvation would be incomplete at best and meaningless at worst. The resurrection of Christ is the completing event that provides not only for the cleansing of guilt but also for a guarantee that the believer shall live again. Barth was most certainly correct when he wrote:

> The mystery of the incarnation unfolds into the mystery of Good Friday and of Easter. And once more it is as it has been so often in this whole mystery of faith, that we must always see two things together, we must always understand one by the other . . . for there is no *theologia cruces* which does not have its complement in the *theologia gloriae*. Of course, there is no Easter without Good Friday, but equally certainly there is no Good Friday without Easter![81]

Consequently, all believers join Job in his confident avowal: "For I know that my Redeemer lives, and He shall stand at last on the earth; and, after my skin is destroyed, this I know, that in my flesh I shall see God, whom I shall see for myself, and my eyes shall behold and not another" (Job 19:25–27).

How Does This Doctrine Impact the Church Today?

In 1978, Fisher Humphreys, commenting on the views of John Calvin, noted a major problem with the way the church has for centuries understood and represented the work of Christ. "Men today do not ordinarily hold this view of God as simply willing right and wrong, and so they cannot believe that vicarious punishment is either meaningful or moral. No illustration can be given, so far as I can tell, which makes vicarious punishment morally credible to men today. . . . It always seems morally outrageous that any

---

were dead and raised up again from the watery grave is meaningless unless there is resurrection. Hence, the verse focuses on the meaning of baptism itself.

[80] Hans W. Frei remarks, "A further implication—which I do not develop in argument—is that the resurrection must, in the eyes of those who believe, be a factual occurrence of a wholly unique kind, the conceptual content of which is the climactic establishment of Jesus' identity. This means that the resurrection events are not, in the first place, reducible to an ontological status allowing us to call them peculiarly 'verbal' in contrast to 'objective' or 'factual' events (the position of Gerhard Ebeling)." Hans W. Frei, *The Identity of Jesus Christ* (Eugene: Wipf and Stock, 1997), 2.

[81] Karl Barth, *Dogmatics in Outline,* trans. G. T. Thomson (New York: Philosophical Library, 1949), 114.

judge would require a substitute. However noble the substitute's act might be, the judge's act seems despicable."[82]

Humphreys' position not only distances him from the views of twelfth-century theologian Anselm (1033–1109) and from the perspectives of the major Reformers but also anticipated the *zeitgeist* of the early twenty-first century. Diverse views of the atonement, of course, are not unique to the common era. The postmodern ethos, in anticipation of which Humphreys's observations were prescient, even if virtually abandoned by the philosophers of the academy, nevertheless enjoys vivacity in popular culture and in contemporary theology. The distaste of Enlightenment theologians for the "bloody theology" of the Reformers has given way to a general cultural disinfatuation with the forensic theology characteristic of the evangelical community of past years.

This same criticism of "Western models" for thinking about the atonement may be observed in authors like Joel B. Green and Mark W. Baker.[83] They extend the critique of such theories, calling into question the viability of traditional understandings for other cultures. Green and Baker understand that there is something about the death of Jesus that is equally riveting and repulsive to the postmodern mind. A portion of this ambivalence experienced by all Bible readers relates to the question of the identity of the one who died on a Roman cross nearly twenty centuries ago. If Jesus is in fact God incarnate, then his death at the hands of ungodly men takes on a significance which transcends the circumstances of an early first-century Roman capital execution.

The most creative contemporary approach to the effort to find meaning in the death of Christ is that of René Girard.[84] Girard's view establishes a sort of sociological meta-narrative to explain both the anthropological

---

[82] Fisher Humphreys, *The Death of Christ* (Nashville: Broadman, 1978), 61. Pannenberg, on the other hand, sees substitution as a common theme in human anthropology. Wolfhart Pannenberg, *Jesus—God and Man* (Philadelphia: Westminster, 1968), 258–59.

[83] Joel B. Green and Mark D. Baker, *Recovering the Scandal of the Cross* (Downers Grove: InterVarsity, 2000). Other recent works parroting those same themes include Anthony W. Bartlett, *Cross Purposes: The Violent Grammar of Christian Atonement* (Harrisburg: Trinity Press International, 2001); J. Denny Weaver, *The Nonviolent Atonement* (Grand Rapids: Eerdmans, 2001); and Darby Kathleen Ray, *Deceiving the Devil* (Cleveland: Pilgrim, 1998). In 1959, Theodore R. Clark wrote *Saved by His Life* (New York: Macmillan, 1959), which caused major upheaval at New Orleans Baptist Theological Seminary where he taught. Published by Macmillan, this volume came to conclusions similar to the more contemporary works mentioned above. For something of a sympathetic response and critique, see Hans Boersma, *Violence, Hospitality, and the Cross* (Grand Rapids: Baker Academic, 2004). Also of importance is the anthology edited by Charles E. Hill and Frank A. James, *The Glory of the Atonement* (Downers Grove: InterVarsity, 2004).

[84] Girard's books include *Violence and the Sacred* (Baltimore: Johns Hopkins University Press, 1977); *The Scapegoat* (Baltimore: Johns Hopkins University Press, 1986); *Things Hidden Since the Foundation of the World* (Stanford: Stanford University Press, 1987); and *I Saw Satan Fall like Lightning* (Maryknoll: Orbis, 2001).

dilemma that fostered Christ's death as well as the theological meaning of the event. Boersma charges that Girard's view of the atonement is "a variant of the moral-influence theory."[85] He further alleges that Girard's nonsacrificial reading of the gospel "leads to a deprecation of the Old Testament and the judicial categories of the atonement."[86]

For Girard, the only violence discernible in the crucifixion of Jesus is the violence of men. All of the social order is enveloped in violence engendered by competitiveness for those things that someone has viewed as desirable. In such a society, participants eventually tire of constant revenge and seek instead a scapegoat—someone who though in reality innocent, or at least guiltless in the immediate confrontation, can be saddled with the blame and in essence pay the price of peace through his own suffering. Thus, the violence of the cross unmasked the satanic violence of men, and through Jesus, the scapegoat brings forever to an end the necessity for sacrifice.[87]

Girard writes:

> Before Christ and the Bible the satanic accusation was always victorious by virtue of the violent contagion that imprisoned human beings within systems of myth and ritual. The Crucifixion reduces mythology to powerlessness by exposing violent contagion, which is so effective in the myths that it prevents communities from ever finding out the truth, namely, the innocence of their victims.
>
> This accusation temporarily relieves communities of their violence, but it turns back again and "stands against" the persecutors, for it subjects them to Satan, or in other words to principalities and powers with their deceitful gods and bloody sacrifices. Jesus, in showing his innocence in the Passion accounts, has "canceled" this accusation; he "set it aside." He nails the accusation to the Cross, which is to say that he reveals its falsity. Though ordinarily the accusation nails the victim to the cross, here by contrast the accusation itself is nailed and publicly exhibited and exposed as a lie. The cross enables the truth to triumph because the Gospels disclose the falseness of the accusation; they unmask Satan as an imposter. Or to say it in another way, they discredit once and for all the untruth of the principalities and powers in the wake of the Cross. The Cross of Christ restores all the victims of the single victim mechanism, whether it goes under the label of legal accusation, Satan, or principalities and powers.[88]

---

85 Boersma, *Violence, Hospitality, and the Cross*, 134.
86 Ibid., 136.
87 Girard, *The Scapegoat*, 200–2.
88 Girard, *I Saw Satan Fall like Lightning*, 138.

In a sense, all of these modern attempts to provide a rationale for the death of Jesus carve out little new ground. The medieval juxtaposition of objectivist theories like that of Anselm of Canterbury and subjectivist theories like that of Peter Abelard appear to provide an unchanging topography for theological discussion, even if the direction of the lighting changes the colors of the two perspectives to a lesser or greater degree.[89] No, such departures from the biblical and historical understanding of the atonement do not open a way forward but a theological retreat. They miss the ontological necessity of the work of Christ and the beauty and glory of what the Father accomplished in the death of his precious Son.

> In Gethsemane . . . Jesus cries to His Father for deliverance from the agony of making atonement. What kind of Father does it make of God if he insists that the Son endure the cross when there remained some other option available to the Father through which he could save men? If it be objected that this removes the atonement from being a free, loving act of God, we must reply that the necessity of a particular action in no way necessarily prevents the action from being free or loving. . . . The point remains that God will have difficulty avoiding the charge of being a "cosmic sadist" if he failed to exercise other options to save men, while choosing instead to allow his beloved Son to be crucified.[90]

John Stott agrees that the atoning sacrifice of Jesus was necessary, and that that necessity resides within the nature and character of God himself. The offense of sin demands satisfaction, atonement, and that demand is found within God himself:

> To say that he must "satisfy himself" means that he must be himself and act according to the perfection of his nature or "name." The necessity of "satisfaction" for God, therefore, is not found in anything outside himself but within himself, in his own immutable

---

[89] Anthony Thiselton called attention to Bultmann's objection to the mixing of sacrificial and juridical analogies, which are not tenable in the contemporary world in *The Two Horizons* (Grand Rapids: Eerdmans, 1980), 270. But to his credit, Bultmann does not deny that the New Testament teaches both but only that one has to sacrifice his intellect to believe it. "For modern man the mythological conception of the world, the conceptions of eschatology, of redeemer and of redemption, are over and done with. Is it possible to expect that we shall make a sacrifice of understanding, *sacrificium intellectus,* in order to accept what we cannot sincerely consider true—merely because such conceptions are suggested in the Bible?" R. Bultmann, *Theology of the New Testament* (New York: Scribner's, 1955), 2:295.

[90] Patterson, "Reflections on the Atonement," 314.

character. It is an inherent or intrinsic necessity. The law to which he must conform, which he must satisfy, is the law of his own being.[91]

Calvin adds: "It was also imperative that he who was to become our Redeemer be true God and true man. It was his task to swallow up death. Who but the Life could do this? It was his task to conquer sin. Who but very Righteousness could do this?"[92] The Son of God had to come. The Son of God had to die. God's holiness demanded satisfaction. God's love sent a Savior.

Conclusion

The person and work of Christ as prophet, king, and priest are certainly the anticipation of the Old Testament and the focus of the New Testament. Given the limitations of human comprehension, understandably, intense debate has surfaced on the issues of both his person and his work. Regarding specifically the work of Jesus on the cross, this chapter may conclude with the following affirmations.

First, the death of Jesus on the cross was a sacrificial act with multiple benefits of eternal consequence. Second, since God is God, nothing can be more important than his response to sinners, making propitiation the most important aspect of the atonement. Third, the cross of Christ also justifies the believer, making it possible for him to have access to God legally. Fourth, this access is more than merely forensic in nature. It is, in fact, actual reconciliation, a restoration of relationship. Fifth, Jesus did all of this by accepting the penalty of human sin, a penalty which man should have received. Hence, his death on the cross was a vicarious penal substitution.

Sixth, the cross was also a monumental defeat for Satan and all the forces of evil in that Christ conquered the powers of evil through his death and resurrection. Seventh, the death of Jesus also provides moral influence and an incredible example for Christians to follow, though such views have no salvific significance. Eighth, ultimately, the cross also guarantees glorification and, hence, the ultimate healing of the body. Through the passion of his Christ, the Father turns evil back on itself, thereby overcoming and defeating it decisively and climatically. It is perhaps that the best theodicy is discovered right here in the "cross work" of the Savior.

In 1853, Friedrich Wilhelm Krummacher, an evangelical pastor in Berlin, was chosen to become the *Hofprediger* (court preacher) of King Frederick IV and moved to Potsdam. The next year, he published *The*

---

[91] Stott, *The Cross of Christ,* 124.
[92] Calvin, *Institutes,* 1:466.

Suffering Servant, a work which went through several editions in German and was even more influential in the English-speaking world.[93]

Krummacher's sterling devotional work on the atonement concentrates on the week leading up to and including the crucifixion of the Lord. Krummacher divides that week into three stages corresponding to the temple itself. In the outer court Krummacher discusses such anticipatory events as the Passover meal, the washing of the disciples' feet, the Lord's Supper, and the revelation that one of the disciples would betray the Lord.

Moving to the Holy Place, Krummacher ushers his readers into Gethsemane, the palace of Annas, the chambers of the Sanhedrin, the praetorium, and the trial of scourging. Entering the Most Holy Place, the German preacher explicates the hours of Jesus on the cross. The impression left on the reader is that of the progressive movement from the general sanctity of these events in the environs of the temple into the presence of God and the mercy seat of God within the Holy of Holies. Krummacher says of Golgotha:

> Where are we now? We are standing on the summit of Mount Calvary—Golgotha—horrifying name—the appellation of the most momentous and awful spot upon the whole earth. Behold a naked and barren eminence, enriched only by the blood of criminals, and covered with the bones of executed rebels, incendiaries, poisoners, and other offscourings of the human race. An accursed spot, where love never rules, but where naked justice alone sits enthroned, with scales and sword, and from which every passer-by turns with abhorrence, a nocturnal rendezvous of jackals and hyenas.[94]

But while the cross and Golgotha comprise a tragic environment in one sense, Krummacher, the evangelist, also captured the pathos of ultimate victory in the cross.

> Ah see! His bleeding arms are extended wide; He stretches them out to every sinner. His hands point to the east and west; for He shall gather His children from the ends of the earth. The top of the cross is directed toward the sky; far above the world will its effects extend. Its foot is fixed in the earth; the cross becomes a wondrous tree, from which we reap the fruit of an eternal reconciliation. O, nothing more is requisite, than that God should grant us penitential

---

[93] See Mark David Walton, "The Christology of Friedrich Wilhelm Krummacher (1796–1868): A Theological Analysis of His Contribution to English Evangelical Literature" (unpublished Ph.D. dissertation, Southeastern Baptist Theological Seminary, 2002).

[94] F. W. Krummacher, *The Suffering Saviour* (Chicago: Moody, 1958), 327.

tears, and then, by means of the Holy Spirit, show us the Savior suffering on the cross. We then escape from all earthly care and sorrow, and rejoice in hope of the glory of God. For our justification in His sight, nothing more is requisite than that, in the consciousness of our utter helplessness, we lay hold on the horns of that altar which is sprinkled with the blood that "speaketh better things than that of Abel." And the Man of Sorrows displays to us the fullness of His treasures, and bestows upon us, in a super-abundant degree, the blessing of the patriarch Jacob on his son Joseph:—"The blessings of thy father have prevailed above the blessings of my progenitors unto the utmost bound of the everlasting hills."[95]

For theologians and biblical scholars, the cross of Christ remains a subject shrouded with the mystery of a holy and transcendent God. But for those same theologians and for the church at large, the cross remains the astonishing matrix of the atonement of Christ, about which we say with Paul, "But God forbid that I should boast except in the cross of our Lord Jesus Christ, by whom the world has been crucified to me, and I to the world" (Gal. 6:14).

---

[95] Ibid., 332.

SECTION 5

THE DOCTRINE OF THE HOLY SPIRIT

CHAPTER 11

The Person and Work of the Holy Spirit

Malcolm B. Yarnell III

> No believer, who has any just sense of his dependence on the
> Holy Spirit, for the divine life which he enjoys, and all its included
> blessings, can be indifferent towards the Agent by whom all this good
> is bestowed. He cannot willingly "grieve the Holy Spirit, by whom
> he is sealed to the day of redemption." He will seek to know, in all
> things, what is the mind of the Spirit; and, to him, the communion of
> the Holy Spirit will be the sweetest foretaste of heaven, that can be
> enjoyed on earth. And to him, therefore, the study of the Holy Spirit's
> character and office, will be a delight.
>
> —*John L. Dagg*

Pneumatology, the doctrine of the Holy Spirit, has caused discomfort for traditional Christians due to the sometimes unwelcome influence of charismatic and pentecostal Christians. Some churches have experienced intense controversy concerning Spirit baptism and the nature and purpose of spiritual gifts, especially speaking in tongues. This encourages some to neglect rather than study the Holy Spirit. This is unfortunate, for the Holy Spirit is a member of the Trinity and is thus worthy of worship. Moreover, the redemption and sanctification of Christians is made possible only by the Spirit. According to the earliest Southern Baptist systematic theologian, John Leadley Dagg, pneumatology should be "a delight."[1]

We begin our study by surveying the Old Testament and New Testament passages which consider the Spirit. The development of the doctrine in Christian history will then be reviewed. A systematic analysis of the doctrine follows. This chapter concludes with a discussion of the doctrine's relevance to modern Christianity.

---

[1] John L. Dagg, *A Manual of Theology* (Charleston, SC: Souther Baptist Publication Society, n.d.), 235.

What Does the Bible Say?

Gregory of Nazianzus, who helped define trinitarian orthodoxy, summarized the progressive revelation in Scripture of the doctrine of the Holy Spirit: "The Old Testament proclaimed the Father openly, and the Son more obscurely. The New manifested the Son, and suggested the Deity of the Spirit. Now the Spirit Himself dwells among us, and supplies us with a clearer demonstration of Himself."[2] Although early orthodox theologians detected doctrinal development within Scripture, they were just as adamant that the God who revealed himself progressively did not himself change. "Let no one therefore separate the Old from the New Testament; let no one say that the Spirit in the former is one, and in the latter another."[3] Before reviewing the Old and New Testament doctrines of the Spirit, linguistic concerns are considered.

Linguistic Concerns

The English noun "spirit" is used to translate the Hebrew Old Testament term *ruach,* the Greek Septuagint and New Testament term *pneuma,* and the Latin *spiritus,* along with their respective cognates. These words are onomatopoeic, indicative of the sound of air in motion. The Hebrew word *neshamah,* normally translated as "breath," may also be translated as "spirit." There are five general uses of the words translated as "spirit" in the Bible.[4] The fifth use is of primary concern, but the second is also important.

- The natural use: e.g., "wind."
- The human use indicating vitality or constituency: e.g., "breath" or "spirit," that part of the human which enables life and fellowship with God.
- The human use indicating attitude: e.g., "a spirit of distortion."
- The angelic use: e.g., "an evil spirit."
- The divine use: e.g., "the Spirit of God" or "the Holy Spirit." A related use is the divine attribute that God is a spirit.

---

[2] Gregory of Nazianzus, *On the Holy Spirit* 26.
[3] Cyril of Jerusalem, *Catechetical Lectures* 16.4.
[4] Sinclair B. Ferguson, *The Holy Spirit* (Downers Grove: InterVarsity, 1996), 16. Veli-Matti Kärkkäinen detects three uses of *ruach* and three uses of *pneuma.* James Leo Garrett Jr. discerned four uses of *ruach.* Kärkkäinen, *Pneumatology: The Holy Spirit in Ecumenical, International, and Contextual Perspective* (Grand Rapids: Baker, 2002), 26–29; Garrett, *Systematic Theology: Biblical, Historical, and Evangelical,* 2nd ed. (North Richland Hills: BIBAL Press, 2000–2001), 2:140. Cf. the various lists of uses in the Greek world, the Hebrew Bible, and Judaism delineated by Friedrich Baumgärtel, Werner Bieder, Hermann Kleinknecht, and Erik Sjöberg, "*Pneuma,*" in *TDNT,* ed. Gerhard Friedrich and Gerhard Kittel, trans. Geoffrey W. Bromiley (Grand Rapids: Eerdmans, 1968), 6:334–39, 359–72, 375–89.

The Old Testament

Gregory of Nazianzus said the Lord chose not to reveal the full doctrine of the Holy Spirit until the deity of the Father and then the deity of the Son were first revealed because humanity could not handle the sublime truth of the Trinity except through "advances and progress from glory to glory." Isidore of Pelasium believed Moses knew about the doctrine of the Trinity but concealed it for fear of polytheism. More recently, Benjamin B. Warfield argued that the full revelation of the Spirit in the Old Testament "could have wrought nothing but harm to the people of God."[5]

Warfield also sought to answer the question as to whether the Spirit of God was conceived in hypostatic (personal) terms in the Old Testament. He broke this important question into three subsidiary questions:

1. May the Christian properly see in the Spirit of God of the Old Testament the personal Holy Spirit of the New?
2. Are there any hints in the Old Testament anticipating and adumbrating the revelation of the hypostatic Spirit of the New?
3. Are these hints of such clearness as actually to reveal this doctrine, apart from the revelation of the New Testament?

To the first two questions, Warfield answered unequivocally in the positive. To the third question, he responded negatively.[6] For Christians, who interpret the Bible canonically or according to the principle of analogy, letting Scripture interpret Scripture, this answer is acceptable. The Spirit of God implicitly prepares us in the Old Testament for the explicit revelation of himself as a distinct person of the one God in the New Testament.

There are various ways by which a survey of the Old Testament doctrine of the Spirit, especially with regard to his work, might be conducted. Warfield speaks of the Spirit's threefold work in terms of "the cosmic," "the theocratic," and "the individual," revealing him to be "the immanent, inspiring, indwelling God." Heron discerns four contexts in which the divine *ruach* acts: creation, outstanding gifts, prophecy, and future hope. Ferguson organizes his review of the Old Testament doctrine according to the Spirit as "*creator Spiritus*," "governing presence," "*Spiritus recreator*," and inspiration. The contribution of Montague, although otherwise substantial, is marred by his naive appropriation of the historical-critical method.[7] Rather than employing a systematic or historical-critical

---

[5] Gregory of Nazianzus, *On the Holy Spirit* 26. Benjamin B. Warfield, "The Spirit of God in the Old Testament" (longer version), in *The Person and Work of the Holy Spirit*, ed. Michael Gaydosh (Amityville: Calvary 1997), 139–40.

[6] Warfield, "The Spirit of God in the Old Testament" (shorter version), in ibid., 115.

[7] Warfield, "The Spirit of God in the Old Testament" (longer version), in ibid., 123–37. Alasdair I. C. Heron, *The Holy Spirit: The Holy Spirit in the Bible, the History of Christian Thought, and*

method, this chapter follows the traditional exposition of Torah, Neviim, and Ketuvim used by Jesus Christ in Luke 24:44: "the Law of Moses and the Prophets and the Psalms."[8]

The Law of Moses

The first appearance of *ruach* occurs in Genesis 1:2 and is connected with God. Christians have traditionally interpreted *ruach elohim* here as "Spirit of God," but modern critics prefer "almighty wind." The modern objection is that Christians should not read the creation account hypostatically to discern the Trinity. However, the preceding and succeeding verses undoubtedly point to a divine movement, and later Old Testament passages identify the Spirit of God as an agent of creation. The Spirit of God acted concurrently with the Word of God to bring about creation at the direction and for the glory of God the Father. The Spirit of God dismisses the chaos as the Word of God brings order and purpose to creation.[9]

In Genesis, the Spirit of God also gives and sustains human life, communicating with mankind through his spirit. The Lord breathed "the breath of life" into the man he formed from dust (Gen. 2:7), and man's life was sustained as long as the Spirit abided with him (Gen. 6:3). Although the KJV translates the Hebrew verb here as "strive," it is more properly translated, "abide."[10] Indeed, "death" and the expiration of "the breath of life" are identical (Gen. 7:22). Movement from an inoperative to an operative psychological state is described as the reviving of the human spirit (Gen. 45:27). Pharaoh's spirit was troubled by a dream from the Lord (Gen. 41:8), and Joseph's ability to interpret the dream was recognized as due to his spirit's relation with God (Gen. 41:38).

In the remainder of the Pentateuch, the Spirit represents the sovereign presence of God while the human spirit proves malleable. Human spirits may be broken (Exod. 6:9), overcome by jealousy (Num. 5:14), show fidelity (Num. 14:24), or be obstinate (Deut. 2:30). Ancient Jewish commentators on the book of Exodus believed the divine Spirit was implicitly present with the people of God in the *shekinah* glory in the pillar of cloud and fire.

Recent Theology (Philadelphia: Westminster, 1983), 10–22. Ferguson, *Holy Spirit,* 18–27. George T. Montague, *Holy Spirit: Growth of a Biblical Tradition* (Peabody: Hendrickson, 1976), vii–viii, and part 1.

[8] Unless otherwise noted, all Scripture citations in this chapter are from the New American Standard Bible (NASB).

[9] Interestingly, G. Henton Davies, whose commentary was recalled by the Sunday School Board of the Southern Baptist Convention, allowed for the traditional translation as "a maximum of meaning." *The Broadman Bible Commentary,* ed. Clifton J. Allen (Nashville: Broadman 1969; reprint, London: Marshall, Morgan & Scott, 1970), 1:125. Clyde T. Francisco, who wrote the revised commentary, only allowed for its translation as "wind of God" or "mighty wind." *The Broadman Bible Commentary,* rev. ed., ed. Clifton J. Allen (Nashville: Broadman 1973), 1:122. Ferguson, *Holy Spirit,* 18–21. Montague, *Holy Spirit,* 67.

[10] Wayne E. Ward, *The Holy Spirit* (Nashville: Broadman 1987), 19–20.

In Deuteronomy 32:10–11, God hovers over his people in the wilderness, protecting and providing for them. The rare verb used here is identical with that describing the Spirit's activity in Genesis 1:2.[11]

The Spirit of God sovereignly grants gifts to various leaders. Among these gifts are craftsmanship, prophecy, and leadership. The Lord fills Bezalel "with the Spirit of God, in wisdom, in understanding and in knowledge and in all craftsmanship" (Exod. 35:31). "Skillful persons" are "endowed with the spirit of wisdom" for the task of adorning the tabernacle (Exod. 28:3; 31:1–11; 35:30–35). In Numbers 11:16–30, the Lord takes the Spirit "who is upon" Moses and lays him upon seventy elders. In response, the elders prophesy, including two elders who remain in the camp of the people. When Joshua objected to this irregularity, Moses declared, "Would that all the LORD's people were prophets, that the LORD would put His Spirit upon them!" This desire of Moses (Num. 11:29) becomes a prophecy of Joel (Joel 2:28–32) which is fulfilled at Pentecost (Acts 2:17–18).[12] Interestingly, the Spirit also comes upon a prophet not identified with God's people (Num. 24:2).

The seventy elders are given the Spirit so that they might share leadership or "bear the burden of the people" with Moses (Num. 11:17). When Moses commissions Joshua with authority, he places his hand upon the younger man so that the congregation will obey him. An earlier account implies the Spirit independently came upon Joshua (Num. 27:15–23) while a later account implies Joshua received a "spirit of wisdom" when Moses laid hands upon him (Deut. 34:9). The gift of the Spirit appears to have been sovereignly conveyed by God in conjunction with human activity. Bloesch notes that God freely used numerous means by which to "communicate his Spirit with humanity," including dreams, the laying on of hands, with water, by anointing with oil, and through the proclamation of the Word.[13]

The Prophets

The prophets are considered according to the former prophets in the historical books and the latter prophets whose writings we possess, the latter prophets being further divided between four major prophets (Isaiah, Jeremiah, Ezekiel, and Daniel) and twelve minor prophets. Among the prophets, *ruach*, the Spirit, is clearly related to *dabhar*, the Word, in the divine work of redemption. Effective, transforming communication requires the Spirit to work with both speakers and hearers of the Word.[14]

---

[11] George Foot Moore, "Intermediaries in Jewish Theology," *HTR* 15 (1922): 55–59. Ferguson, *The Holy Spirit,* 19–20.

[12] Ferguson, *The Holy Spirit,* 62–63.

[13] Donald G. Bloesch, *The Holy Spirit: Works and Gifts,* Christian Foundations (Downers Grove: InterVarsity, 2000), 69–73.

[14] Gary Smith, *The Prophets as Preachers* (Nashville: Broadman & Holman, 1994), 22–23.

Among the former prophets, the Spirit of God works upon three historical groups: Joshua and the judges, Saul and David, and Elijah and Elisha. The people of God lose their spirit when they face the Amorites (Josh. 5:1). The loss (and restoration) of human vitality permeates the cycle of sin, judgment, repentance, and deliverance that the early Israelites repeatedly experienced in the promised land (Judg. 3:7–10). Deliverance of the tribes of Israel occurs when the Spirit comes upon or stirs the judges. Othniel (Judg. 3:10), Gideon (Judg. 6:34), Jephthah (Judg. 11:29), and Samson (Judg. 13:25) are all compelled by the Spirit to lead the people of God, though one should not therefore identify all their actions as holy. In Judges 9:23, "God sent an evil spirit between Abimelech and the men of Shechem." Since God neither tempts nor is tempted by evil, this passage indicates that God is sovereign over evil and uses even rebellious spirits for his purposes. The evil spirit was apparently sent for the purpose of judgment.

The Spirit comes upon the kings of Israel at their anointing and to enable them to do God's will but departs from the disobedient. When Saul is anointed by Samuel, the Spirit comes upon him mightily: Saul is changed and begins to prophesy (1 Sam. 10:1–10). After Saul's disobedience at Gilgal, Samuel anoints David, and the Spirit comes upon David. Concurrently, the Spirit of Yahweh departs from Saul and "an evil spirit" is sent to terrorize the fallen king. David plays his harp to subdue the evil spirit sent to Saul, but Saul seeks to kill David (1 Sam. 16:12–23; 19:8–10). Subsequently, the Spirit comes upon Saul but only to prevent him from harming David (1 Sam. 19:1,14–23).

In the Elijah and Elisha narratives, we learn of the mobility of the Spirit, the relation of the Spirit to the Word, and the distinction between the Spirit of the Lord and a deceiving spirit. The Spirit may physically transport a prophet (1 Kings 18:12; 2 Kings 2:16), and the Spirit may transition from prophet to prophet (2 Kings 2:9,15). The Spirit of the Lord and the Word of the Lord are concurrently evident in the life of a single prophet (2 Kings 2:15; 3:12). However, the people have difficulty in discerning whether the spirit active in a prophet is the Spirit of the Lord or "a deceiving spirit" allowed to come forth by the Lord, until the test of time proves one true and the other false (1 Kings 22:19–28).

Among the latter or writing prophets, Isaiah and Ezekiel have the most detailed pneumatology. The Isaiah prophecies consider both past and future. Looking back, Isaiah recalls that the Spirit is sovereign (Isa. 40:13); that God creates and sustains the human spirit (Isa. 42:5; 57:15–16); that humans, by being gifted with spirit, are thereby distinguished from animals (Isa. 31:3); and that human spirits are subject to divine power and judgment (Isa. 19:14; 29:10). Isaiah also reminds Israel that the Spirit had dwelt in their midst, giving them rest, but they had grieved him with rebellion

(Isa. 63:10–14; cf. Deut. 32). Looking forward, Isaiah emphasizes the gift of the Spirit to the Messiah and the messianic community. In contradistinction with former kings, he would come and remain upon the messianic king, endowing him with multiple gifts for godly and wise rule (Isa. 11:1–3). With the Spirit upon him, this anointed one will proclaim good news and bring comfort to the afflicted people of God (Isa. 61:1–2).

In the Suffering Servant Songs (Isa. 42:1–7; 49:1–6; 50:4–9; 52:13–53:12), songs that relate the Messiah with the messianic people, it is declared that God uniquely gives the Spirit to the Messiah to dispense justice (Isa. 42:1). The messianic community will be composed of those who have been regenerated by the outpouring of the Spirit (Isa. 32:15), gathered by the Spirit (Isa. 34:16), and blessed by him (Isa. 44:3). Through their Redeemer, the messianic community is promised a covenant in which the Spirit will never leave them (Isa. 59:20–21).

In Ezekiel the Spirit interacts with the living beings (*cherubim*), the prophet, and the people of God, leaving Jerusalem but promising to return. The spirits of the four living beings, located within the wheels, depart Jerusalem with the Spirit and glory of God (Ezek. 1:20–21; 10:17–20). The Spirit moves the prophet and inspires him with the Word of the Lord. The Spirit, also identified as "the hand of the Lord," profoundly affects the spirit of the prophet, giving him visions and revealing God's glory (Ezek. 2:2–4,12–16; 3:24–27; 8:3–4; 11:1–5,24; 40:1–3). The false prophets could also claim to be inspired but by their own spirits (Ezek. 13:2–3). Although the people of God treated the name of the Lord profanely, God promises to regenerate them in order to vindicate the holiness of his name. They would receive "a new heart and a new spirit," being enabled to obey the Lord because his Spirit would dwell within them (Ezek. 36:22–32).

In the vision of the valley of dry bones, Ezekiel sees the Spirit of the Lord put "the breath" back into the dead people of Israel. The re-creation account of Ezekiel 37:1–14 thus recalls the creation account of Genesis 2:7. Although the Spirit of the Lord had departed from the temple, he will return with the divine glory, restoring the people of God (Ezek. 39:29; 43:4–5).

The correlation between the divine Spirit and the prophetic Word is also affirmed by other prophets (Mic. 3:8; Zech. 7:12; cf. Isa. 40:7–8). Those prophets who claim the Spirit but lack the Word are false (Jer. 5:13). Recalling the prayer of Moses in Numbers 11:29 for a universal prophetic ministry, Joel foresees a day when the Spirit would come upon all people, regardless of gender, age, or social status (Joel 2:28–29). Finally, among the Minor Prophets, the Spirit is identified with divine judgment on the one hand (Mic. 2:7) and covenant restoration and rebuilding of the temple on the other (Hag. 2:3–5; Zech. 4:6; Mal. 2:15).

The Psalms

By "the Psalms," Jesus means "the Writings," which included Psalms, wisdom literature, and Chronicles. In the Psalms, the work of the Holy Spirit centers on the believer's personal life and worship. According to David, the Spirit influenced his music. He credits the *ruach* of Yahweh with inspiring him to speak his *dabhar* (2 Sam. 23:1–2). Recalling creation, David says that the Spirit and the Word cooperated in creation (Ps. 33:6); that the Spirit is the sovereign provider of human life (Pss. 31:5; 104:30); and that when God hides his "face," the human spirit dies (Ps. 104:29). The Spirit has the divine attribute of omnipresence (Ps. 139:7) and guides the believer (Ps. 143:10). Looking forward to regeneration from an attitude of brokenness, David begs God not to withdraw his Spirit but to "renew" and sustain his spirit (Ps. 51:10–12,17). Psalm 51 contains one of three instances in which the later common title of "Holy Spirit" is used in the Old Testament (cf. Isa. 63:10–11).

In the Wisdom literature the books of Proverbs, Job, and Ecclesiastes continue the development of pneumatology. Most references to the spirit in Proverbs refer to the human spirit, which is open to and judged by God (Prov. 16:2; 20:27). The intertestamental wisdom literature identifies the personified "wisdom" of Proverbs (Prov. 1:20–33; 8:1–9:6) with the Spirit. This comes through most clearly in the Apocrypha, where wisdom is not only personified but divine (Wisdom of Solomon 1:6–7). Proverbs 8:22–31 might be understood, then, as a pre-Pentecost manifestation of the third person of the Trinity, who is with God before creation. Alternatively, in Christian tradition, the hypostatic wisdom of Proverbs has been connected with the second person of the Trinity. Proverbs 1:23 could support the alternative view since wisdom sends its spirit (cf. Wisdom of Solomon 7:22). It is better to exclude dogmatism on the matter as the personification of wisdom is primarily a teaching metaphor.[15]

In Job, *ruach* and *neshamah* may refer to men, angelic beings (Job 4:9–18), or God. The human spirit is intimately related to the divine Spirit (Job 27:3; 32:8). The Creator Spirit creates human life, sustains it, and may diminish it (Job 27:3; 33:4; 34:14–15; cf. Job 26:13). In Ecclesiastes, *ruach* as the natural wind presents a vivid image of the vain life (Ecc. 2:11,17; 4:4,6; 6:9). Judgment is evident when the breath of man departs from the body of dust (Eccl. 3:17–21). In Chronicles, God places his Spirit "upon" the prophets to proclaim his Word (2 Chron. 14:1; 24:20), but he "stirs up" the spirit of pagan kings to do his will (1 Chron. 5:26; 2 Chron. 36:22).

---

[15] Montague, *Holy Spirit*, 91–110; Heron, *Holy Spirit*, 34–38.

The Intertestamental Period

At Qumran, the two spirits of truth and falsehood rule mankind (1 QS 3:13–26). The spirit of God's counsel was believed to come upon those entering the community (1 QS 2:25–3:12). In the Apocrypha, the human spirit could be resuscitated or resurrected (2 Macc. 7:23; Jub. 33:11). The Septuagint translates *ruach* as *pneuma*; thus the Greek word conveys the Old Testament meanings previously assigned it. The rabbinic tradition made the phrase "Holy Spirit" commonplace and affirms the doctrine of the resurrection with a disembodied state beforehand. The Holy Spirit is universally seen as having worked in the past and in the future but has fallen silent in the present.[16]

The New Testament

While Old Testament appearances of the divine Spirit fuel scholarly debates, in the New Testament "the Holy Spirit really enters on the centre of the stage."[17] The more detailed New Testament accounts will be considered according to the Synoptic Gospels, the Acts, the writings of John, the letters of Paul, and the General Epistles.

The Synoptic Gospels

In the four centuries following the prophecies of Malachi, there was no measurable activity of the Spirit. But with the annunciation of the incarnation of the Son of God, there was a magnificent burst of spiritual activity: "The Spirit is said once again to be at work in the lives of human beings." The work of the Spirit in relation to the Son was not, however, limited to the incarnation: "From womb to tomb to throne, the Spirit was the constant companion of the Son." The Spirit was explicitly evident during the life of Jesus Christ, especially in his incarnation, baptism, ministry, and resurrection.[18]

There are five contemporary witnesses to the work of the Holy Spirit in the incarnation. First, in a trinitarian statement, Gabriel informs Mary that the Holy Spirit, "the power of the Most High," would "come upon her" and she would conceive "the holy child" who would be called "the Son of God" (Luke 1:35). Later an angel of the Lord informs Joseph that the child conceived in Mary was "of the Holy Spirit" (Matt. 1:18–20). Third, Mary's relative, Elizabeth, is "filled with the Holy Spirit" and given a message of encouragement for Mary (Luke 1:41–42). Then Zechariah, the husband of

---

16 Heron, *Holy Spirit*, 23–33. The rabbis also had no concept of regeneration by the Holy Spirit. Montague, *Holy Spirit*, 111–15.

17 Heron, *Holy Spirit*, 39.

18 Gerald F. Hawthorne, *The Presence and the Power: The Significance of the Holy Spirit in the Life and Ministry of Jesus* (Dallas: Word, 1991), 53. Ferguson, *Holy Spirit*, 37. Hawthorne identifies the Holy Spirit as active in the boyhood and youth of Jesus. Although undoubtedly true, his psychological analysis is speculative. *The Presence and the Power*, 97–111.

Elizabeth and father of John the Baptist,[19] is "filled with the Holy Spirit" and "prophesied" concerning the Messiah (Luke 1:67–79). Finally, the Holy Spirit comes "upon" Simeon and "reveals" a message to him. Simeon then "came in the Spirit into the temple," signaling that the Spirit who left the temple in the time of Ezekiel now returned with the Messiah (Luke 2:25–35).

At the baptism of Jesus, the Holy Spirit, in an unusual "bodily" manner, descends "like a dove" from heaven (Matt. 3:15; Mark 1:10; Luke 3:22). The emblem of the dove may allude to the Spirit's finding a holy place to rest.[20] In the Gospel of John, the messianic significance of this unique manifestation of the Spirit is explicit: "He upon whom you see the Spirit descending and remaining upon Him, this is the One who baptizes in the Holy Spirit" (John 1:33). Fulfilling Isaiah 11, this serves as an indication of the Messiah, upon whom the Spirit would come and not depart. It also means the Messiah not only receives the Spirit fully but gives the Spirit fully. As with the incarnation, the trinitarian nature of the baptism of Jesus is unmistakable: the Father speaks, the Spirit descends, and the Son is manifested.[21]

During the earthly ministry of Jesus, the Spirit was active in Jesus' roles as Second Adam, as victor over demonic spirits, as teacher, and as Suffering Servant. In the temptation in the wilderness, toward which the Spirit "drove out" Jesus and for which the Spirit "filled" him (Mark 1:12–13 and par.), the temptation of Eden is "rerun" and the Second Adam is victorious where the first Adam failed. At numerous points in his earthly ministry, Jesus "cast out demons by the Spirit of God," thus proving that "the kingdom of God has come upon you" (Matt. 12:28). The Holy Spirit anoints Jesus at the beginning of his public ministry, granting him power in teaching, fulfilling the messianic prophecy of Isaiah 61:1–2 concerning God's comforting Word (Luke 4:14–30). The prophecy of the Suffering Servant in Isaiah 42:1–3 is also fulfilled (Matt. 12:18–21). The Synoptic Gospels, especially Luke, emphasize "that Jesus' whole ministry is empowered by the Spirit."[22] Jesus is continually and abidingly "full" of the Holy Spirit (Luke 4:1–2; Acts 10:38).

---

[19] Although the birth of John the Baptist is miraculous, there is not even a hint that his conception is by the Holy Spirit. Rather, John is to be "filled" with the Spirit, has the "spirit and power of Elijah," and is "strong in spirit" (Luke 1:15–17, 80). John himself points to Jesus and the Holy Spirit who would come through him (Mark 1:8 and par.). John is the last and greatest of the prophets and was filled with the Spirit, yet he could not endow others with the Spirit. Cf. Ward, *Holy Spirit,* 57.

[20] Criswell discusses a number of emblems of the Holy Spirit: "a dove, a seal, oil, water, fire, wind, clothing, an earnest." An emblem is "a visible sign of an idea, suggesting the idea by common qualities or recognized associations," which in the case of the Spirit are "figurative representations of the work and ways of the Holy Spirit." W. A. Criswell, *The Holy Spirit in Today's World,* 2nd ed. (Grand Rapids: Zondervan, 1966), 69–74.

[21] The Father's allusions to Psalm 2:7 and Isaiah 42:1 should be taken in an official, not adoptionist, sense.

[22] Ferguson, *The Holy Spirit,* 48–49; Ward, *Holy Spirit,* 60–61. Cf. Matthew 10:1; 12:43–45; Mark 1:22–27; Luke 4:33–37; 6:18; 7:21; 8:1–2; 9:37–43; 10:20; 11:14–26; 22:3–4; 22:31–32. Heron, *Holy Spirit,* 41.

One of the most important teachings of Jesus concerns "blaspheming," or "speaking against," the Holy Spirit. The Pharisees accused Jesus of casting out demons, "by Beelzebul the ruler of the demons" (Matt. 12:24 and par.). Jesus responded that he cast out demons "by the Spirit of God" (Matt. 12:28; cf. "by the finger of God," Luke 11:20). He also warned the Pharisees that "blasphemy against the Spirit shall not be forgiven" (Matt. 12:31 and par.). Although some early commentators thought Christians could commit this sin, it is evident Jesus was speaking to the Pharisees, not to Christians. Blasphemy against the Holy Spirit concerns more his work than his person. Literally, it means "to attribute to demons the Holy Spirit's manifestation in Jesus' mission." This blasphemy is "the conscious, malicious, and wilful rejection and slandering, against evidence and conviction, of the testimony of the Holy Spirit respecting the grace of God in Christ, attributing it out of hatred and enmity to the prince of darkness."[23]

In the Synoptic Gospels, overt references to the Holy Spirit during the week of Christ's passion are absent. "The period of the passion is one in which the Spirit, so active in Jesus' ministry, is momentarily eclipsed by the powers of darkness." However, other New Testament texts show the Holy Spirit was with Christ in his atoning death (Heb. 9:14) and glorious resurrection (Rom. 1:4; 8:11; 1 Tim. 3:16; 1 Pet. 3:18). When Luke refers to Jesus committing his "spirit" to the Father and dying on the cross, this refers to his human spirit (Luke 23:46; cf. Luke 24:36–39). The divine Logos and the human spirit were distinct but never separated.[24]

The Acts

Among the synoptic writers, Luke gives far more attention to the divine Spirit. This is evident, for instance, in his recounting of the gift of the Spirit to believers. The Holy Spirit is promised to be given from the Father by Jesus to believers (Luke 11:13; 24:49; cf. Acts 1:4–5). Thus, the disciples will have power over the unclean spirits (Luke 10:20). In the book of Acts, Luke continues the discourse begun in his "first account," the Gospel, by showing how the church is spiritually empowered to witness to Christ. Luke's second account is called *praxeis apostolōn,* "Acts of the Apostles," by the early church, but it might well have been entitled, "Acts of the Holy Spirit." According to F. F. Bruce, "In all the book, there is nothing which is

---

[23] E. Earle Ellis, *The Gospel of Luke,* rev. ed., NCBC (Grand Rapids: Eerdmans, 1974), 176. Louis Berkhof, *Systematic Theology,* 4th ed. (Grand Rapids: Eerdmans, 1949), 253. R. T. France more simply defines it as "a hardening against God which is deliberate and irreversible." France, *The Gospel According to Matthew: An Introduction and Commentary,* TNTC (Grand Rapids: Eerdmans, 1985), 210–11.

[24] Montague, *Holy Spirit,* 267. Cf. Luke 22:3,31,43,53; 23:8–9. The Chalcedonian formula promulgated in 451 is helpful here in distinguishing, though not separating, the divine and human natures of Christ. Cf. R. C. H. Lenski, *The Interpretation of St. Luke's Gospel* (Minneapolis: Augsburg, 1946), 1153–54.

unrelated to the Holy Spirit."[25] In considering the work of the Spirit among the disciples of Jesus in the book of Acts, salvation and the Christian life are paramount.

The Spirit is the agent of salvation as seen in the Lukan concepts of regeneration, baptism with the Holy Spirit, the gift of the Spirit, and the meaning of Pentecost. The Holy Spirit regenerates men, whether Jew or Gentile, by cleansing their hearts by faith (Acts 15:8–11). Bloesch concluded that "the gift of the Spirit is not contingent on faith and obedience but is correlative with them."[26]

There are seven references to the phenomenon of baptism "with" or "in" the Holy Spirit in the New Testament, of which four are the parallel accounts of the Baptist's promise that Jesus would baptize with the Spirit (Matt. 3:11; Mark 1:8; Luke 3:16; John 1:33); one is a promise by Jesus, before he ascended, that he would soon baptize the church with the Holy Spirit (Acts 1:5); one is Peter's recounting that Jesus promised he would baptize with the Holy Spirit (Acts 11:15–17); and one is Paul's declaration that "by one Spirit we were all baptized into one body" (1 Cor. 12:13).

This phenomenon has been historically conceived in three ways, each of which is evident in various translations of the fullest account in Acts 11:17, where Peter identifies Spirit baptism as a gift received in conjunction with faith in Jesus as Lord. The Greek word, *pisteusasin*, (aorist active participle), has been translated as "when we believed" (RSV), "who believed" (NIV), and "after believing" (NASB). The first translation corroborates the Reformed and Regular Baptist view that baptism with the Holy Spirit was a unique occurrence for the church at Pentecost. The second translation corroborates modern evangelical and Southern Baptist view that baptism with the Holy Spirit is a unique occurrence for every Christian at the time of conversion. The third translation may corroborate the Pentecostal view that full baptism with the Holy Spirit occurs subsequent to conversion.[27]

---

25 Matthew adds that the Holy Spirit will guide the speech of Jesus' disciples (Matt. 10:20). F. F. Bruce, *The Acts of the Apostles: The Greek Text with Introduction and Commentary,* 2nd ed. (Grand Rapids: Eerdmans, 1952), 1, 30.

26 Cf. Acts 2:38–41; 10:44–48; 11:15–18. Bloesch notes that "the gift of the Spirit is not contingent on faith and obedience, but is correlative with them." *Holy Spirit,* 307–9.

27 "That as the baptism of the Holy Ghost was given for the confirmation of the gospel dispensation, it has effected its design; the sacred prophecy is fulfilled, and it has ceased." Moreover, "we have no right to call regeneration baptism." Circular Letter (1802) by T. B. Montanye, in *Minutes of the Philadelphia Baptist Association,* ed. A. D. Gillette (Philadelphia: American Baptist Publication Society, 1851), 376. There is no reference in either the Second London Confession (1689) or the works of John Gill to this doctrine. Frederick Dale Bruner, *A Theology of the Holy Spirit: The Pentecostal Experience and the New Testament Witness* (Grand Rapids: Eerdmans, 1970), 59–61. The older Pentecostal separation between regeneration or baptism "in" the Holy Spirit and a later, fuller baptism "by" the Holy Spirit cannot be maintained. J. Rodman Williams, *Renewal Theology: Systematic Theology from a Charismatic Perspective* (Grand Rapids: Zondervan, 1988–1992), 2:86–93, 198–200.

Following the outline provided by Jesus in Acts 1:8 as a key to the structure of Acts, it has been surmised that the baptism of the Holy Spirit occurred for the Jews at Jerusalem during Pentecost (Acts 2), later for the Samaritans (Acts 8) and for God-fearing Gentiles in Caesarea (Acts 10), and even later for full Gentiles in Ephesus (Acts 19).[28]

The "gift" of the Holy Spirit is related to baptism in the Holy Spirit and to conversion (Acts 11:17). This gift must be carefully distinguished from the gifts of the Spirit. "The gift of the Spirit is the Spirit Himself, bestowed by the exalted Lord under the Father's authority; the gifts of the Spirit are those spiritual faculties which the Spirit imparts."

The major contexts in Acts in which the Spirit is manifestly given have been variously understood. Some Christians construe these narrative passages in such a way as to support their belief in a multistage blessing of the Spirit, separating conversion from baptism in the Spirit. They argue from these narratives for various doctrines such as baptismal regeneration, the conveyance of the Spirit by sacramental confirmation, or the necessary accompaniment of Spirit-baptism by speaking in unknown tongues. However, these passages indicate "a splendid variety" in relation to water baptism, the laying on of hands, and speaking in tongues.[29] In Acts 2:37–42, the Spirit is apparently received at baptism, and hands are not laid upon the recipients, while tongues are not evident. In Acts 8:4–17, the Spirit is received after baptism, but hands are now laid, while tongues are again not evident. In Acts 10:44–48, the Spirit is received before baptism, and hands are not laid, but tongues are evident. There is no normative narrative concerning the gift of the Spirit in relation to water baptism, the laying on of hands, or speaking in tongues.

However, with each occurrence, the gospel was preached and believed, converts were baptized, converts received the Holy Spirit, and converts gave evidence of new life. Evangelicals should focus on commonalities in the narratives rather than variables. A related event is described in Acts 19:1–7. The "disciples" who previously "believed" and were "baptized" but had not received the Spirit were earlier followers of John the Baptist. Their subsequent baptism was Christian, and the Holy Spirit was now given

---

[28] Ward, *Holy Spirit*, 92. Abraham Kuyper perceived an original outpouring of the Spirit at Pentecost and supplementary outpourings thereafter, along similar lines to Ward's. Kuyper, *The Work of the Holy Spirit*, trans. Henri De Vries (1900; reprint, Chattanooga: AMG Publishers, 2001), 134–35. Ferguson discerned "three decisive points of advance" in Acts chapters 2, 8, and 10, while the occurrence in chapter 19 is atypical. It should be noted, that the group in Acts 19 is comprised of disciples of John the Baptist. Ferguson, *The Holy Spirit*, 83.

[29] F. F. Bruce, *The Book of the Acts* (Grand Rapids: Eerdmans, 1988), 71, cited in J. W. MacGorman, *Acts: The Gospel for All People*, Adult January Bible Study (Nashville: Convention Press, 1990), 16. Bloesch identifies such beliefs in the Catholic and Pentecostal traditions as "perilous" manifestations of either "formalism" or "spiritualism." Bloesch, *Holy Spirit*, 13–16, 52–55, 82–85, 189–207. MacGorman, *Acts*, 56–57.

to them as Christians. Discerning a temporal separation of Spirit-baptism from conversion is "terribly amiss" and "wholly unjustified."[30]

The central meaning of Pentecost is that the Spirit has come upon the church, empowering believers for the ministry of proclamation. The disciples longed for Jesus to return and establish his kingdom in its fullness, but Jesus reminded them they would remain on earth to serve as his witnesses (Acts 1:8). Conversion is not limited to the first disciples; conversion is the fruit of the disciples' worldwide task of evangelism empowered by the Spirit. The speaking in other languages evident at the Pentecost outpouring of the Spirit manifests that spiritual empowerment for witnessing. (There is speculation that the gift here was one of hearing, but the text is clear that they began to "speak" with other tongues [Acts 2:4].)

It has been argued that the Spirit gave utterance in other tongues as a symbolic reversal of the confusion of tongues at Babel (Gen. 10). Similarly, the rushing wind may recall the promise of new life in Ezekiel 36 and the flame of fire, the *shekinah* glory.[31] Whatever the symbolic meanings, Peter's sermon declares that this universal proclamation certainly fulfills the prophecy of Joel and by implication the prayer of Moses (Acts 2:16–21).

The Spirit is the agent of the Christian life as seen in Luke's language concerning the filling of the Spirit, guidance by the Spirit, and wonders and signs. The goal of these spiritual manifestations is for empowering the proclamation of the gospel of Jesus Christ. In numerous places, subsequent to their conversion, Christians are said to be "full of" or "filled with" the Holy Spirit (Acts 2:4; 4:8,31; 6:3–5; 7:55; 9:17; 11:24; 13:8–10,52). Such filling of the Spirit marks chosen Christian leaders and empowers proclamation and the performance of good deeds.[32] The Spirit guides the church to prophesy or witness to Christ (Acts 2:4,18; 4:8,31; 5:32; 7:55; 11:24; 13:8ff), to be comforted and filled with joy (Acts 9:31; 13:52), to be of one mind (Acts 15:22–28), to choose leaders (Acts 6:3; 20:28), to set apart and send missionaries (Acts 13:1–4), to witness in specific geographical areas (Acts 16:6–7), and to exercise judgment (Acts 5:1–11). For the overarching purpose of proclaiming the gospel, the Holy Spirit even guides Paul into situations of persecution (Acts 20:22–23; 21:3–4,10–11).

---

[30] Bloesch, *Holy Spirit,* 198, 311–12; Ferguson, *Holy Spirit,* 82–84. James D. G. Dunn, *Baptism in the Holy Spirit: A Re-examination of the New Testament Teaching on the Gift of the Spirit in Relation to Pentecostalism Today,* Studies in Biblical Theology (Naperville: Allenson, 1970), 4. Cf. Rom. 8:9.

[31] Craig S. Keener, *The Spirit in the Gospels and Acts: Divine Purity and Power* (Peabody: Hendrickson, 1997), 190–92; MacGorman, *Acts,* 16–17. George Smeaton, *The Doctrine of the Holy Spirit,* 2nd ed. (1889; reprint, Edinburgh: Banner of Truth, 1997), 54.

[32] Ward, *Holy Spirit,* 93–94.

Luke often speaks of *terata kai semeia* (wonders and signs).[33] References to such miracles in Acts may be divided into five groups: "ordinary" healings, restoration from death, healings brought about with the aid of physical objects, miracles of judgment, and miracles of liberation. In comparison to other biblical writers, Luke is not very critical of the miraculous. Whereas he appears to correlate miracles with faith, others question the connection. However, Luke never considers miracles for entertainment value; indeed, Simon Magus is denounced for seeking to acquire the Holy Spirit for apotropaic purposes (Acts 8:18–19). "In the Acts of Luke the miraculous is subordinated to the theological purpose of demonstrating the wonderful progress of the 'Word of God.'"[34]

The Writings of John

Some scholars downplay the pneumatology written in the Gospel, letters, and Apocalypse of John in order to focus on the letters of Paul. However, John has a rich pneumatology; indeed, his Gospel may be "the summit of New Testament pneumatology."[35] The writings of John consider the Holy Spirit according to his major roles as regenerator, helper, and witness.[36]

First, Jesus gives the Holy Spirit as regenerator so that believers are "born again." As noted previously, the Spirit's descent upon Jesus was unique in that he remained (John 1:29–34). Moreover, not only does Jesus receive the Spirit fully, Jesus is the one who gives the Spirit fully. He gives the Spirit "without measure" (John 3:34) through full immersion as in baptism (John 1:33) and proleptically in his breathing upon the disciples (John 20:22). Jesus himself gives the Spirit in order to create life (John 6:63–64). Like the wind, which "blows where it wishes," the Spirit sovereignly regen-

---

[33] *Terata* and *sēmeia* may be interchanged. Acts 2:43; 4:30; 5:12; 6:8; 14:3; 15:12. *Sēmeion* may be used on its own. Acts 4:16; 4:22; 8:6. *Dynameis* may substitute for *terata*. Acts 8:13.

[34] Acts 3:16; 5:14; 9:42; 13:12; 14:9; 19:18. Cf. Mark 8:11–12; 13:22; Matthew 12:38–39; John 2:23; 4:48; 20:29; 2 Corinthians 12:12; 13:3–4; 2 Thessalonians 2:9. James D. G. Dunn, *Jesus and the Spirit: A Study of the Religious and Charismatic Experience of Jesus and the First Christians as Reflected in the New Testament* (Philadelphia: Westminster, 1975), 163–68.

[35] Gordon Fee's massive pneumatology is singularly devoted to Paul, while James Dunn's important study devotes more than two hundred pages to Paul but only seven pages to "the Johannine alternative." Fee, *God's Empowering Presence: The Holy Spirit in the Letters of Paul* (Peabody: Hendrickson, 1994); Dunn, *Jesus and the Spirit,* 350–57. H. B. Swete's treatment is more balanced, devoting two chapters to John and three to Paul. Swete, *Holy Spirit in the New Testament: A Study of Primitive Christian Teaching* (London: Macmillan, 1910), 129–68, 169–253. Montague, *Holy Spirit,* 333.

[36] Cf. Yves Congar's outline: Jesus gives the Spirit, the promised Paraclete, and the Spirit in the disciples and in the time of the Church. Congar, *I Believe in the Holy Spirit,* trans. David Smith, 3 vols. (1983; repr., New York: Crossroad Herder, 2001), 1:49–59. James Dunn found four themes in John's treatment of the Spirit: the Spirit continues the presence of Jesus, the Spirit reveals Jesus, the Spirit enables worship, and the Spirit separates Christians from the flesh. Dunn, *Jesus and the Spirit,* 350–57.

erates believers (John 3:4–8). The motif of water or "rivers of living water" in the human spirit "springing up to eternal life" refer to regeneration by the Spirit (John 4:13–14; 7:37–39; cf. John 3:5).[37] Worship of and communion with God are possible only on the basis of the Spirit's regenerating work (John 4:21–24).

Second, Jesus instructs the disciples concerning the Spirit as *paraklētos*, which literally means "one called alongside" but has been translated as "comforter," "counselor," "advocate," and "helper." Johannes Behm says that "the history of the term in the whole sphere of known Greek and Hellenistic usage outside the New Testament yields the clear picture of a legal advisor," and that Wyclif's and Luther's translation of "comforter" should be summarily dismissed. But the Johannine use is broader than the merely legal, so the translation "helper," which retains the legal connotation, is preferred. Christ is our helper before the Father, while the Spirit is our helper in the world.[38]

In the five *paraclētos* sayings of Jesus found in John 14–16, the Spirit is related to the other persons of the Trinity on the one hand and to the world on the other. In relation to the Trinity, the Father gives and sends the Spirit (John 14:16,26), while the Spirit "proceeds" from the Father (John 15:26). The Spirit is *allon paraclētos,* another paraclete like—compare *allos,* "another of the same type," with *heteros,* "another of a different kind"—the Son (John 14:16), and is sent and given by the Son (John 14:16,26; 15:26; 16:7). He testifies about and glorifies the Son (John 15:26; 16:14). In relation to the world, he resides within believers, bringing fellowship with God the Father and the Son (John 14:16–17,20). As helper, the Spirit will teach, remind, testify, guide, speak, and disclose to the disciples things concerning the Son (John 14:26; 15:26; 16:13–14). The helper will also convict the world of sin, righteousness, and judgment (John 16:8–10).[39]

Third, in the Johannine writings, the Spirit fulfills the major role of a witness. While the baptism and the cross of Jesus testified to his lordship, the Spirit serves as witness in the church today (1 John 5:6).[40] He is the witness par excellence in inspiration, illumination, assurance, and evangelism. By inspiration is meant that the Holy Spirit witnesses through the apostle by revelation and by inspiring him in his writing (Rev. 1:10–11;

---

[37] Congar, *I Believe in the Holy Spirit,* 1:50. Craig Keener notes that the Gospel of John focused on the Spirit as purifier. The water motif is evident in such language as his being "poured out" or "welling up." The Spirit is "the agent of purification over against ritual" or merely sacramental waters. Keener, *Spirit in the Gospels and Acts,* 137, 150.

[38] Johannes Behm, *"Paraklētos,"* in *TDNT,* 5:803–4, 812–14. Cf. Swete, *Holy Spirit in the New Testament,* 149.

[39] John Aloisi, "The Paraclete's Ministry of Conviction: Another Look at John 16:8–11," *JETS* 47 (2004): 55–70; Congar, *I Believe in the Holy Spirit,* 1:54–56.

[40] Swete, *Holy Spirit in the New Testament,* 270–71; Smeaton, *Doctrine of the Holy Spirit,* 97–98.

4:2; 14:13). By illumination is meant that he witnesses to the churches by enlightening them (Rev. 2:7,11,29; 3:6,13,22). By assurance is meant that he witnesses to Christians concerning their salvation through enabling their obedience toward God, confession of Christ, and love toward one another (1 John 3:24; 4:2–3,12–13). His manifold witness to the churches allows John to describe him as the sevenfold Spirit (Rev. 1:4; 3:1; 4:5; 6:6).[41] By evangelism is meant that he witnesses to the world through the apostles and the churches (Rev. 22:6,17; John 20:21–23).

The giving of the Spirit in John 20 and the coming of the Spirit in Acts 2, distinct events separated by the ascension, are related, but there are various views as to how. Swete sees the Johannine giving in terms of potentiality and the Lukan giving in terms of actuality; Congar implies John relays the beginning of the gift and Acts the completion. Leon Morris speaks of the Johannine giving as "proleptic," while Carson speaks of a giving of the Spirit in "anticipation."[42] The giving of the Spirit in John 20 must be delayed since Jesus affirmed that he would not come unless Jesus departs (John 16:7). Whenever the church invites people to come to Christ, it is in conjunction with the Spirit who says, "Come" (Rev. 22:17).

The Letters of Paul

Paul refers to the Spirit some 145 times, and individual scholars have written numerous large volumes concerning Pauline pneumatology.[43] Due to space limitations, such a complete discussion of Paul's contributions to the doctrine of the Spirit is impossible here. Swete and Fee follow a chronological format in their discussions of Paul, while Dunn and Heron follow systematic formats.[44] We trace key systematic doctrines as Paul relates the Spirit to revelation, the Trinity, anthropology and hamartiology, Christ, soteriology, the Christian life and the church, and eschatology. Paul is more concerned about the human spirit than other writers but is supremely concerned for the divine Spirit's redemptive role. The Corinthian letters, especially 1 Corinthians 12–14 and 2 Corinthians 3, and the letter

---

[41] Swete takes *septiformis spiritus* as an indication of his manifold workings. Swete, *Holy Spirit in the New Testament*, 273. Smeaton discerns a reference to the seven gifts of Isaiah 11:2. Smeaton, *Doctrine of the Holy Spirit*, 99.

[42] D. A. Carson, *The Gospel According to John*, PNTC (Grand Rapids: Eerdmans, 1991), 649–56. Swete, *Holy Spirit in the New Testament*, 164–68. Congar, *I Believe in the Holy Spirit*, 1:53. Leon Morris, *The Gospel According to John*, rev. ed., NICNT (Grand Rapids: Eerdmans, 1995), 747–48.

[43] Fee, *God's Empowering Presence*, 14. Cf. Ward, *Holy Spirit*, 97. Fee, *Paul, the Spirit, and the People of God* (Peabody: Hendrickson, 1996). Dunn, *Baptism in the Holy Spirit*; idem, *Jesus and the Spirit*; idem, *The Christ and the Spirit: Pneumatology* (Grand Rapids: Eerdmans, 1998).

[44] Swete, *Holy Spirit in the New Testament*, 169–253; Fee, *God's Empowering Presence*, 39–795. Heron, *Holy Spirit*, 44–51; Dunn, *Jesus and the Spirit*, 95–134, 199–349. Cf. Fee, *God's Empowering Presence*, 796–915.

to the Romans, especially chapter 8, contain the largest amount of pneumatic material.[45]

With regard to the doctrine of revelation, Paul clearly considers the Spirit the agent of revelation. The Corinthians were saved not by human persuasion but by the "proof" or "demonstration" of the Spirit working powerfully (1 Cor. 2:4–5). God "revealed" the wisdom of Christ through the Spirit, who both knows God and knows man and thus can reveal divine things to man (1 Cor. 2:10–12). Contrasting the natural man with the spiritual man, Paul says the natural man cannot understand or accept spiritual truth. The spiritual man may appraise all things but may not himself be appraised because he has been "taught" by the Spirit and thus shares "the mind of Christ" with the church (1 Cor. 2:13–3:1). In defining the gospel in the preface to Romans, Paul says Jesus Christ was "designated" the Son of God according to the Spirit of holiness, who raised Jesus from the dead (1 Cor. 1:4). The law, which was revealed to Moses, though unable to justify, is nevertheless "of the Spirit" (1 Cor. 7:14). The mystery of Christ has been "revealed" to the apostles and prophets by the Spirit (Eph. 3:3–5). Christians should ascribe their "wisdom and understanding" to the Spirit (Col. 1:9). Second Timothy 3:16 teaches that the biblical revelation is the result of divine breathing. Here, *theopneustos,* although often translated as "inspired" or taken in a weaker sense, is more properly translated strongly as "God-breathed."[46]

With regard to the doctrine of the Trinity, Paul relates the Holy Spirit to the other persons in the one Godhead both essentially and economically. The Spirit, because he is God, knows the things of God in an intimate way (1 Cor. 2:10). To inherit the kingdom of the Father, one must be restored in the name of Christ and in the Spirit (1 Cor. 6:10b–11). Diverse spiritual gifts find their unity in the Spirit, the Son, and the Father (1 Cor. 12:4–6). The Father establishes us with Christ and gives us the Spirit (2 Cor. 1:21–22). Paul's trinitarian doxology affirms that Christian participation with God is of the Holy Spirit (2 Cor. 13:14). The book of Romans begins and ends with trinitarian statements: the gospel of the Father concerning his Son is declared by the Spirit (Rom. 1:1–6); and prayer to the Father is enabled by the Son and by the love of the Spirit (Rom. 15:30).

The letter to the Ephesians repeatedly proclaims the Spirit's trinitarian work: in the magnificent doxology that begins the letter we are blessed by the Father (Eph. 1:3–6), redeemed by the Son (Eph. 1:7–12), and sealed by the Spirit (Eph. 1:13–14); through Christ and in one Spirit, we have access to the Father (Eph. 2:17–18); the Father grants the indwelling of

---

45 Ibid., 82, 472.
46 Ibid., 508–10. Benjamin B. Warfield, *Revelation and Inspiration,* in *The Works of Benjamin B. Warfield* (New York: Oxford University Press, 1932), 1:280.

Christ through the power of the Spirit (Eph. 3:16–17).[47] Christian unity is maintained by the one Spirit, one Lord, and one Father (Eph. 4:3–6); worship is empowered by being filled with the Spirit, in the name of Jesus, and to the Father (Eph. 5:18–21); and the sword of the Spirit is the Word of God (Eph. 6:17). In his letter to Titus, Paul rejoices that the Father saves through regeneration by the Spirit who is given by Christ (Titus 3:4–6).

With regard to anthropology, Paul's employment of *pneuma* and its cognates can be difficult to translate, especially when he uses an anarthrous *pneuma,* It has been argued that when lacking an article, *pneuma* should be translated as "a spirit," often understood as a human spirit. However, with the genitive, the presence or absence of an article is controlled by whether the modified noun has an article. Moreover, the scriptural context is often determinative where the anarthrous *pneuma* occurs. Even when the human spirit is meant by Paul, "the Divine Spirit is at least in the background of the thought, for the spiritual conditions described are not attainable apart from Divine help."[48]

The spiritual man, *pneumatikos,* is distinguished from the natural man and the carnal man (1 Cor. 2:14; 3:1). The church and the individual Christian are the temple of the Spirit (1 Cor. 3:16; 6:19). Although Paul is absent from Corinth in body, he is present in spirit, and wishes them to discipline a sinful disciple so that man's spirit might be saved (1 Cor. 5:3–5). Virgins are to be holy in body and spirit (1 Cor. 7:34). The people of the flesh are juxtaposed to the people of the Spirit, who grants them life (Gal. 4:29; 6:8). With regard to hamartiology, it should be emphasized that the Spirit is referred to as "holy," separated from sin.

With regard to Christology, in addition to the trinitarian relations previously discussed, Paul sees the Spirit active in the work of Christ. Union with Christ is effected by means of the Spirit (1 Cor. 6:17), who indwells Christians concurrently with the Son (Rom. 8:9–10). There are two divine missions, of the Son who shares the rights of sonship through adoption and of the Spirit who empowers us to exercise those rights (Gal. 4:4–6). Christ was revealed in the flesh at the incarnation and "vindicated" by the Spirit in the resurrection (1 Tim. 3:16).[49] Paul closely relates the Spirit and the Son by using the titles "the Spirit of the Lord" (2 Cor. 3:17), "Spirit of Christ" (Rom. 8:9), "Spirit of Jesus Christ" (Phil. 1:19), and "Spirit of His

---

47 The entire Trinity is involved in filling. Cf. Eph. 1:23; 3:19; 4:10. In 5:18, *en* may be taken as an instrumental dative, "filled by the Spirit."

48 Swete, *Holy Spirit in the New Testament,* 398. Fee suggests the translation of "S/spirit" to approximate what "Paul's somewhat flexible language intends." Fee, *God's Empowering Presence,* 14–25.

49 Swete, *Holy Spirit in the New Testament,* 243–44.

Son" (Gal. 4:6). Paul even appears to equate Christ and the Spirit with such statements as "the last Adam became a life-giving spirit" (1 Cor. 15:45) and "the Lord is the Spirit" (2 Cor. 3:17).

Following the German liberal tradition, Dunn argues for a "Spirit Christology" which identifies the Spirit with Christ: "as the Spirit was the 'divinity' of Jesus, so Jesus became the personality of the Spirit." Although Dunn denied engaging in systematic theology, he nevertheless contended with trinitarian theology. Against Dunn, Fee effectively shows these passages must be understood soteriologically, not ontologically. Moreover, Paul identifies the Spirit separately by the name of Holy Spirit seventeen times, and as the Spirit of the Father some sixteen times, yet from a few occurrences, considered in isolation, Dunn developed an untenable supposition. Moreover, the genitive relation of the Spirit and Christ definitely implies distinction rather than identification.[50]

With regard to soteriology, Paul identifies the Spirit as the agent of the commencement, continuation, and completion of salvation. "The Spirit is preeminently 'the Spirit of life,' the 'life-giver,'" who makes "the whole application of redemption" to the believer. The Spirit's work in granting the entirety of salvation is perceptible in Romans 8:1–27, "unquestionably the high point of Paul's theology of the Spirit." The Spirit is the agent of the Father in commencing the Christian life by giving both faith (2 Cor. 4:13; cf. Eph. 2:8) and repentance (Gal. 5:17) to the believer. Not only does the Spirit give faith, believers "receive the promise of the Spirit through faith" (1 Thess. 4:8; Gal. 3:1–5,14). The Spirit indwells the Christian, thus bringing him into union with Jesus Christ (Rom. 8:9–11). "Every element in the classical *ordo salutis* is thus a further perspective on the one reality of the believer's union with Christ."[51] As a result of this union, the Spirit applies to believers the beginning soteriological graces of regeneration (Gal. 4:29; Titus 3:5) and justification (1 Cor. 6:11).

The grace of sanctification applied by the Spirit concerns both commencement and continuation of salvation (Rom. 8:13; 1 Cor. 6:11; 2 Thess. 2:13). Yet other graces concern the commencement, continuation, and consummation of salvation. The "Spirit of adoption" is received, continues to lead, and anticipates final redemption (Rom. 8:9,15–16,23). The Spirit as *arrabōn*, *aparchē*, and *sphragis* (discussed further below) is given at the commencement of the Christian life in order to complete it. Finally, the

---

[50] Dunn, *Jesus and the Spirit*, 325–36. Cf. Dunn, *The Theology of Paul the Apostle* (New York: T.&T. Clark, 1998), 260–64. Fee, *God's Empowering Presence*, 831–42.

[51] Dunn, *Theology of Paul*, 423, 429. Smeaton, *Doctrine of the Holy Spirit*, 66. Ferguson, *Holy Spirit*, 106.

Spirit is written indelibly upon the heart, finalizing the glorification begun at conversion (2 Cor. 3). With regard to the Christian life, Paul teaches that the Spirit is an experienced reality. "Long before the Spirit was a theme of doctrine, he was a fact in the experience of the community."[52] These experiences encompass the totality of life, including the emotional, intellectual, relational, and moral dimensions. Emotionally, the Spirit creates love in Christians (Rom. 5:5), enriches them (1 Cor. 15:7), gives them joy (1 Thess. 1:6), and brings conviction (1 Thess. 1:5). Intellectually, he illumines them with wisdom and understanding (1 Cor. 2:12–3:1; 2 Cor. 3:12–16; Col. 1:9). Relationally, he enables prayer to, communion with, and worship of God, setting the Christian free from the law of sin and death (Rom. 8:2,26–27; 2 Cor. 13:14; Eph. 5:13–21; Phil. 3:2; Col. 3:16). Morally, he sets the Christian mind on life and peace, engendering the fruit of the Spirit in his walk and enabling obedience (Rom. 7:6; 8:4–6; Gal. 5:22–25). He also sets the Christian against the flesh and its deeds, putting them to death (Rom. 8:4–6,13–14; Gal. 5:16–21).

With regard to the church, the Spirit breaks down the dividing barrier between Jew and Gentile, building them together "into a dwelling of God in the Spirit" (Eph. 2:17–22). He unites Christians with fellowship (Phil. 2:1–2) and endows the church with gifts, official and charismatic, for its edification and ministry (Eph. 4:7–13; 1 Cor. 12).

With regard to eschatology, the Spirit engenders and completes the Christian hope. He creates within Christians a desire for the consummation of their redemption (2 Cor. 5:2; Gal. 5:5). Paul employs three metaphors to describe the indwelling Spirit's role in preservation.[53] In a financial metaphor, the Spirit is *arrabōn*, the "pledge" or "first installment," given at the beginning of salvation as a reminder that spiritual transformation will be completed in the resurrection (2 Cor. 1:22; 5:4–5; Eph. 1:14). In an agricultural metaphor the Spirit is *aparchē*, the "firstfruits," assuring us that our salvation includes more (Rom. 8:23). And, in a legal metaphor, the Spirit is *sphragis*, the "seal" by which we are juridically marked as promised for God (Eph. 1:13; cf. 2 Cor. 1:22; Eph. 4:30). At the resurrection from the dead, the Spirit will transform the Christian's natural body into a spiritual body, which has both continuities and discontinuities with the body's former existence (Rom. 8:23; 1 Cor. 15:42–49). Throughout the New Testament, especially in Paul's letters, pneumatology influences the entire range of Christian doctrine.

---

[52] Albert Schweitzer, *"pneuma,"* in *TDNT*, 6:396.

[53] "The life which is characterized by the indwelling of the Spirit of God, which is a life in which God's law is established, is a life characterized by hope." C. E. B. Cranfield, *A Critical and Exegetical Commentary on the Epistle to the Romans*, rev. ed., ICC (New York: T.&T. Clark, 2001), 1:404. Ferguson, *Holy Spirit*, 177–82.

Christ
Eschatology
Church

Soteriology
Anthropology
Hamartology

Christian life
Revelation
Trinity

The Person and Work of the Holy Spirit 625

The General Epistles

Although Swete asserts that in Hebrews, "there is no theology of the Spirit," Marshall discovers parallels with Luke's treatment of the Spirit in Acts. The author of Hebrews says signs and wonders and miracles and gifts of the Holy Spirit confirm the message of the Lord to the apostles (Heb. 2:3–4). The implication is that certain gifts, as well as signs and wonders and miracles, may no longer be needed after the canon of the apostles' writings was set.[54] The author of Hebrews also affirms the inspiration of Scripture by the Spirit (Heb. 3:7; 9:8; 10:15) and that Christ offered himself to the Father through the "eternal" Spirit (Heb. 9:14). Hebrews 4:12 may be read as an affirmation of the trichotomous nature of man, but it is more likely an affirmation of the close correlation of soul and spirit (cf. 1 Thess. 5:23).

James employs *pneuma* only twice, but his reference to wisdom as the source of Christian life indicates the Spirit's working. In 2:26, he asserts that the human body dies without a spirit. James 4:5 is notoriously difficult to translate. If taken as a reference to the divine Spirit, the *pneuma* is either jealous for us or opposes envy in us. Bauckham discusses seven previous translations of the passage and discerns a reference to Numbers 11:29 and the apocryphal book of Eldad and Modad, which identifies envy over prophetic leadership as inappropriate.[55] Jude contrasts those who are "devoid of the Spirit" and follow natural instincts, with those who are "praying in the Holy Spirit" and remain in God.[56]

The Petrine Epistles teach that the Spirit is on the one hand, "the divine agent of sanctification," and on the other, "enabler of charismatic (or inspired) exegesis." Affirming the Trinity, Peter identifies sanctification as the work of the Spirit (1 Pet. 1:1–2). *Pneuma* is also used of human disposition (1 Pet. 3:4), of the divine presence with the persecuted (1 Pet. 4:12–14), and of Christ's descent to preach to the spirits in prison (1 Pet. 3:18). The church is a spiritual house and a holy priesthood that offers spiritual sacrifices (1 Pet. 2:5). The prophets were inspired by the Spirit, and preachers of the gospel are empowered by the Spirit (1 Pet. 1:11–12). Moreover, when the prophets spoke, they were moved by the Holy Spirit, not by their

---

[54] Swete, *Holy Spirit in the New Testament*, 248–49; I. Howard Marshall, *New Testament Theology: Many Witnesses, One Gospel* (Downers Grove: InterVarsity, 2004), 607. Martyn Lloyd-Jones, *God the Holy Spirit*, Great Doctrines of the Bible (Wheaton: Crossway, 1992), 269–71.

[55] Marshall, *New Testament Theology*, 637–38. Swete, *Holy Spirit in the New Testament*, 258; Ralph P. Martin, *James*, WBC (Waco: Word, 1988), 149–51. Bauckham, "The Spirit of God in Us Loathes Envy: James 4:5," in *The Holy Spirit and Christian Origins: Essays in Honor of James D. G. Dunn*, ed. Graham N. Stanton, Bruce W. Longenecker, and Stephen C. Barton (Grand Rapids: Eerdmans, 2004), 270–81.

[56] Marshall, *New Testament Theology*, 665.

own will. Similarly, interpretation of Scripture should not be arbitrary but directed by the Spirit (2 Pet. 1:20–21).[57]

What Has the Church Believed?

The Early Church

It has been argued that in early Christian pneumatology, two competing traditions developed. These have been dubbed the "major tradition" and "minor tradition." The major tradition was characterized by an emphasis on order. Clerical officeholders in the church were endowed with the Spirit and entrusted with the carriage of apostolic truth. The minor tradition was characterized by enthusiasm. In this tradition the desire for order was sublimated to the immediacy of prophecy. The minor tradition retreated into heretical movements while the major tradition became the persecutor. These categories should not, however, serve as the only, or even an indisputable, paradigm for early pneumatology. Congar believes "the increasing affirmation of the part played by the bishops did not in any way minimize the charismatic life of the Church."[58] We begin our review of early pneumatology with the subapostolic fathers.

The Earliest Fathers

The "apostolic fathers," more properly "sub-apostolic fathers," wrote during the first and second centuries, after the passing of the apostles. These writers addressed occasional, pastoral issues rather than doctrinal definitions, and their pneumatological language suffered from a lack of precision. Both Clement of Rome and Ignatius of Antioch believe their admonitions to the churches of Corinth and Philadelphia to submit to the clergy were directly inspired by the Spirit. Some sub-apostolic writers fail to differentiate between the second and third persons of the Trinity, even confusing the Spirit with the Son.[59] In perhaps the earliest trinitarian dox-

---

[57] Joel B. Green, "Faithful Witness in the Diaspora: The Holy Spirit and the Exiled People of God according to 1 Peter," in *Holy Spirit and Christian Origins,* 282–95. "This has surely some negative implications for the contemporary, postmodern view that readers are free to interpret texts as they please." Marshall, *New Testament Theology,* 672n. Cf. Richard J. Bauckham, *Jude, 2 Peter,* WBC (Waco: Word, 1983), 228–35.

[58] Alternatively, Eduard Schweizer identified three dangerous strands of pneumatology—the Gnostic-Substantial, the Ecstatic, and the Official. Schweizer, *"pneuma,"* in *TDNT,* 6:451. Stanley M. Burgess, *The Spirit and the Church: Antiquity* (Peabody: Hendrickson, 1984), 3–4. Cf. Hans von Campenhausen, *Ecclesiastical Authority and Spiritual Power in the Church of the First Three Centuries,* trans. J. A. Baker (London: A&C Black, 1969; reprint, Peabody: Hendrickson, 1997). Yves Congar, *I Believe in the Holy Spirit,* 1:65.

[59] "Apostolic Fathers" is first used in the seventeenth century, but Swete prefers the term "Sub-Apostolic." Swete's terminology avoids confusion with the apostles. Johannes Quasten, *Patrology* (1950; reprint, Allen: Christian Classics, 1995), 1:40–41; Henry Barclay Swete, *The Holy Spirit in the Ancient Church: A Study of Christian Teaching in the Age of the Fathers* (London: Macmillan, 1912), 9–31. Burgess, *Spirit and Church,* 16–17. Clement of Rome, *First Epistle to the Corinthians,*

ology, Polycarp, the bishop of Smyrna, explicitly worshipped the Trinity as he was martyred: "O Lord God Almighty, the Father . . . I bless Thee, I glorify Thee, along with the everlasting and heavenly Jesus Christ, Thy beloved Son, with whom, to Thee, and the Holy Ghost, be glory both now and to all coming ages. Amen."[60]

Pneumatological language received only minor clarification by the apologists of the second century. Although more theological than the sub-apostolic fathers, the apologists' primary contribution is in the arena of Christology. Manifesting the influence of Platonic philosophy, Justin Martyr subordinated both the Son and the Spirit, failing to differentiate between the role of the Son and the Spirit in the incarnation. Theophilus of Antioch was the first to use the term *triados* to describe the three-in-one Godhead. "In spite of incoherencies, however, the lineaments of a trinitarian doctrine are clearly discernible in the apologists. The Spirit was for them the Spirit of God."[61]

Heresy and Orthodoxy

Orthodox pneumatology was clarified only after the emergence of early heresies: Gnosticism, Montanism, Monarchianism, Manichaeism, and Marcionism. Drawing heavily on dualistic Platonism, Gnosticism located man in one of the inferior emanations from God and believed "pneumatic" men could escape the lower emanations through secret knowledge. Basilides of Alexandria believed the Holy Spirit was ontologically less than the Son. The Gnostic gospels describe the Holy Spirit as the divine "Mother" of Jesus and others. The Gnostics valued spiritual gifts and a number of early texts document the practice of glossolalia.[62] Another heresy, Montanism or "The New Prophecy," emphasized spiritual gifts, primarily prophecy. Montanists saw themselves as especially enlightened by the Spirit. Their founder, Montanus, believed he was the mouthpiece of the Spirit. Two prophetesses, Maximilla and Priscilla, left their husbands to join Montanus, and Maximilla claimed she was "word and spirit and power." Although its enthusiasm was eventually suppressed, Montanism "stood for a recognition of the active presence of the Paraclete in the body of Christ" and temporarily counted Tertullian as a follower.[63]

57; Ignatius, *Epistle to the Philadelphians* vii; Pseudo-Clement, *Second Epistle to the Corinthians* 14; *Pastor of Hermas* 3.5.6, 3.9.1.

[60] *Martyrdom of Polycarp* 14.

[61] Burgess, *Spirit & Church*, 28. Theophilus, *To Autolycus* 2.15, in *ANF*, 2:101. Burgess, following Marcus Dods in *ANF*, translates *triados* as "Trinity," but Kelly prefers the literal "triad." Burgess, *Spirit and Church*, 32; J. N. D. Kelly, *Early Christian Doctrines*, rev. ed. (San Francisco: Harper Collins, 1960), 102. James Leo Garrett Jr., carefully affirms Theophilus as the first to use the Greek term *trias* while Tertullian was the first to use the Latin *trinitas*. Garrett, *Systematic Theology*, 2nd ed., 1:315. Kelly, *Early Christian Doctrines*, 103.

[62] Bloesch, *The Holy Spirit: Works and Gifts* 86–87; Burgess, *Spirit and Church*, 35–44.

[63] Swete, *Holy Spirit in the Ancient Church*, 67–83; Burgess, *Spirit and Church*, 49–52; Bloesch, *Holy Spirit*, 88.

Monarchianism sought to preserve the unity of the Godhead and manifested itself in two forms. Dynamic Monarchians such as Paul of Samosata saw the Son and the Spirit as qualities of God, not distinct persons. Jesus was a mere man adopted as God's Son at his baptism, and the Spirit was grace indwelling the apostles. Modalistic Monarchians, such as Sabellius, saw God as a monad who operated behind distinct historical masks called Father, Son, and Spirit. Modalists affirmed "patripassianism," that the Father suffered on the cross, and denied the Spirit distinction within the Godhead. Tertullian said the modalist Praxeas "did a twofold service for the devil at Rome: he drove away prophecy and brought in heresy; he put to flight the Paraclete, and he crucified the Father."[64]

The fourth heresy, Manichaeism, drew from a number of philosophical and religious traditions to promote a strong dualism. Its founder, a Babylonian named Mani, claimed that he himself was the Holy Spirit.[65] Prior to his conversion, Augustine was a Manichaean. In contradistinction to these other heresies, and no doubt encouraged by his rejection of the Old Testament and dismembering of the New Testament, Marcion had no apparent doctrine of the Spirit yet claimed to be a prophet.[66]

The polemical writers of the late second century, while vigorously refuting heresies, developed orthodox pneumatology. Refuting the Gnostic denigration of creation, Irenaeus of Lyons asserted man was created in the likeness of God "by the hands of the Father, that is, by the Son and the Holy Spirit." Refuting their supposition of a secret knowledge available through Gnostic teachers, he elevated the visible church as the guardian of orthodoxy through its succession of bishops. The Spirit works through the church, "for where the Church is, there is the Spirit of God; and where the Spirit of God is, there is the Church, and every kind of grace; but the Spirit is truth." Irenaeus unflinchingly denied the self-gratifying works of the Gnostics and claimed spiritual gifts were active in the orthodox churches. Miracles, casting out demons, prophecy, healings, and raising the dead occurred in the church "to promote the welfare of other men, according to the gift which each one has received from Him."[67]

Tertullian of Carthage took up his pen against the Gnostics, Marcion, and the Monarchians. In *Against Praxeas*, he contributed the terminology of *trinitas, substantia,* and *personae,* affirming that the Trinity is "connected in the simple Unity" and that he "must everywhere hold one only substance in three coherent and inseparable" persons. These persons of Father, Son, and

[64] Tertullian, *Against Praxeas* 1. Burgess, *Spirit and Church,* 46–49; Kelly, *Early Christian Doctrines,* 115–23.

[65] Bloesch, *Holy Spirit,* 87–88.

[66] Burgess, *Spirit and Church,* 44–46. Cf., Tertullian, *Against Marcion.*

[67] Irenaeus, *Against Heresies* 2.32.3–4, 3.3.2–4, 3.24.1, 5.6.1.

Spirit were "distinct, but not separate." Tertullian used natural analogies to describe the inseparable nature of the Third Person within the Godhead:

> Now the Spirit indeed is the third from God and the Son; just as the fruit of the tree is third from the root, or as the stream out of the river is third from the fountain, or as the apex of the ray is third from the sun. Nothing, however, is alien from that original source whence it derives its own properties.

Like Irenaeus, Tertullian, in his Montanist phase, affirmed the continuance of spiritual gifts in the life of the church. He proved it with the occasion of "a sister whose lot it has been to be favoured with sundry gifts of revelation, which she experiences in the Spirit by ecstatic vision." However, unlike the bishop of Lyons, the lay theologian of Carthage did not want to confuse spirituality with office. "And accordingly 'the Church,' it is true, will forgive sins: but the Church of the Spirit, by means of a spiritual man; not the Church which consists of a number of bishops."[68]

Origen of Alexandria informed both heretical and orthodox theologians in later debates. Swete notes "an apparent inconsistency" in Origen's doctrine of the Spirit but believes he was suffering "from the lack of terms and definitions which besets theologians who are ahead of their age." The inconsistency came specifically in Origen's advocacy of an essential subordination of the Spirit at one point and of an essential equality elsewhere. In his commentary on John, Origen wrote that "the Holy Spirit was made by the Word." On the other hand, in his *De Principiis,* Origen affirmed that "there is no difference in the Trinity." All three persons of the Trinity are involved in the work of regeneration together. Perhaps the final position of Origen can be explained in a fragment which affirms a shared essence along with procession: "The Son and the Spirit are also in their degrees divine, possessing, though derivatively, all the characteristics of deity, distinct from the world of creatures."[69]

The Triumph of the Major Tradition

Hippolytus of Rome, in the early part of the third century, taught that the Spirit of God was active in the laity as well as in the clergy of the church. "For Hippolytus it is still the Holy Spirit with his abundant gifts who is the real creator of the life of the Church; but at the same time he lays great emphasis on the fact that it is the bishops who as successors of

---

[68] Tertullian, *Against Praxeas* 8, 11, 12; *On the Soul* 9; *On Modesty* 21.
[69] Congar, *I Believe in the Holy Spirit,* 3:21; Swete, *Holy Spirit in the Ancient Church,* 131–32. Origen, *Commentary on John* 2.10, cited in Swete, *Holy Spirit in the Ancient Church,* 127. Origen, *De Principiis* 11.3.7. Origen, *Fragments in Hebrews* 6.33, cited in Kelly, *Early Christian Doctrines,* 131.

the apostles have received the Spirit." Hippolytus left posterity the earliest extant rites of ordination, which call the Holy Spirit and his graces down on the ordinand. While the bishop prays publicly, the laity are encouraged to pray silently for the descent of the Spirit. The bishop is to receive "the Spirit of high-priesthood to have the power to forgive sins"; the presbyter is to receive "the Spirit of grace and counsel of the presbyterate"; and, the deacon is to receive "the holy Spirit of grace and caring and diligence." The connection between the Spirit and the ordained ministry is strengthened by subsequent reflection on such ecclesiastical practices.[70]

Scion of Roman nobility, Cyprian of Carthage died a martyr's death but not before penning major ecclesiological treatises and numerous letters that propelled the major tradition to ascendancy. Cyprian argued that outside the church there is no salvation. Moreover, "you ought to know that the bishop is in the Church, and the Church in the bishop; and if anyone be not with the bishop, that he is not in the Church." Salvation is thus dependent on unity with the clergy: "They are the Church who are a people united to the priest." Encouraging the development of Donatism, Cyprian confined the soteriological power in the administration of baptism to the legitimately ordained priest. "If one could baptize, he could also give the Holy Spirit. But if he cannot give the Holy Spirit, because he that is appointed without is not endowed with the Holy Spirit, he cannot baptize those who come."

For Cyprian, the sacraments were the Spirit's means of salvation and these means are available only in the church. Cyprian restricted the administration of the sacraments—including baptism, communion, ordination, and confession—to the properly ordained. Cyprian, in effect, legally reserved the Spirit for the hierarchical administration of the church. Burgess's "major tradition" thus established its hegemony.[71]

The Nicene Church

Arius and Athanasius

The struggles that eventually coalesced in a tightly defined orthodox doctrine of the Holy Spirit began in Alexandria with the controversial teachings of a presbyter named Arius. The actual beliefs of Arius, seen as "a kind of Antichrist among heretics," must be carefully discerned from the fragments available primarily through the writings of his enemies. Arius, drawing on the exegetical heritage of Origen and the philosophical legacy

---

[70] Burgess, *Spirit and Church,* 80–84; Von Campenhausen, *Ecclesiastical Authority and Spiritual Power,* 176; Hippolytus, *Apostolic Tradition,* 3,7,8, in *Ordination Rites of the Ancient Churches of East and West,* by Paul F. Bradshaw (New York: Pueblo, 1990), 107–9. John Chrysostom, *De Sacerdotio* 3,7,8, cited in Quasten, *Patrology,* 3:460–61.

[71] Cyprian, *On the Unity of the Church* 6. Cyprian, Epistle 68 (alt., 66). Cyprian, Epistle 69 (alt., 70); and cf. Epistle 73 (alt., 74). Burgess, *Spirit and Church,* 84–86.

of Neo-Platonism, emphasized the remoteness and self-subsistence of the Father, over against his Son and his Spirit. Arius said that "the substances [*ousiai*] of Father, Son and Holy Spirit are separate in nature, alienated and cut off from each other." Advocating a separate nature for the Spirit, Arius claimed he was created by the Logos.[72]

Both Arians and semi-Arians disputed the divinity of the Spirit. Athanasius wrote against an Arian group known as *tropici* due to their figurative hermeneutics. Macedonius, a deposed semi-Arian bishop of Constantinople, was influential upon the leading group of pneumatological heretics, the *pneumatomachi*, "Spirit-fighters." The Macedonians taught the consubstantiality of the Son but not the Spirit, prompting the orthodox to write in defense of the Spirit. Cyril of Jerusalem listed some six different heresies regarding the Holy Spirit before affirming the personhood of the Spirit. The emperor Constantine called a council at Nicea in 325 to address the Arian Christological controversy since it threatened the unity of the Roman religio-political system. This council adopted a confession that, after a tumultuous period, was accepted as encapsulating orthodox theology. The Nicene Creed, however, was primarily concerned with the relation between Father and Son as *homoousia*, "of the same substance," and indefinitely treated the Spirit.[73]

Athanasius, a major opponent of Arius at Nicea, was asked by Serapion of Thmuis nearly forty years later to address the divinity of the Spirit. The *Tropici* had challenged the consubstantiality of the Spirit with the Father and the Son. Athanasius replied that the Spirit "belongs to and is one with the Godhead which is in the Triad." Although he argued exegetically, his primary proof is found in the liturgy. The only way the Spirit can make men "partakers of the divine nature" is if the Spirit himself is divine. "If the Spirit makes men divine, His nature must undoubtedly be that of God." Although every member of the Trinity shares in redemption, each person has a separate role described as "from the Father through the Son in the Holy Spirit" (Eph. 2:18).[74] Athanasius did not inquire into the internal relations of the Godhead, although he was sure the Spirit is *homoousia* with the Father and the Son.

---

[72] Rowan Williams, *Arius: Heresy and Tradition,* rev. ed. (Grand Rapids: Eerdmans, 2002), 1, 131–48, 179–232.

[73] Quasten, *Patrology,* 3:57; *Oxford Dictionary of the Christian Church,* rev. 2nd ed. (Oxford: Oxford University Press, 1983), s.v., "Eunomius," "Eustathius," "Macedonius," and "Pneumatomachi"; Cyril of Jerusalem, *Catechetical Lectures* 16.6.10; Quasten, *Patrology,* 3:371–72; H. A. Drake, *Constantine and the Bishops: The Politics of Intolerance* (Baltimore: Johns Hopkins University, 2000), 250–57; *Decrees of the Ecumenical Councils,* ed. Norman P. Tanner (Washington, DC: Georgetown University Press, 1990), 1:5.

[74] Athanasius, *To Serapion* 1.21, in *Letters Concerning the Holy Spirit,* trans. C. R. B. Shapland (New York: Philosophical Library, 1951), 120. Swete, *Holy Spirit in the Ancient Church,* 214–18; Athanasius, *To Serapion* 1.27, in *Letters,* 132. E.g. Athanasius, *To Serapion* 1.14, in *Letters,* 94. Cf. Quasten, *Patrology,* 3:76–77.

The Cappadocians

Basil of Caesarea, the first Cappadocian, defended the divinity of the Spirit from a liturgical perspective. Basil had been attacked for using two doxologies, alternatively glorifying the Father "through the Son in the Holy Spirit" and "in fellowship with the Son together with the Spirit." The Macedonians objected, arguing from traditional language that the Holy Spirit is third in dignity and in nature, and that he was created by the Son. Basil defended his use of both doxologies and argued against the subordination and subnumeration of the Spirit for unity in the Godhead. He noted Scripture does not limit the use of the prepositions "from" to the Father, "through" to the Son, and "in" to the Spirit; rather, the Bible ascribes a variety of prepositions to each. In using various prepositions, the Scripture writers carefully distinguish the *hypostaseis* and do not subordinate the Son or the Spirit.

Moreover, Basil argued from the baptismal formula for the identification of Father, Son, and Holy Spirit. In a letter to his brother, Gregory of Nyssa, Basil clarified Greek terminology by distinguishing the one *ousia* from the three *hypostaseis*. He also accepted *prosōpon* as an acceptable synonym of *hypostasis*. Basil thus advanced orthodox pneumatology, although never explicitly identifying the Spirit as God.[75]

Following Basil, Gregory of Nyssa took up the battle with the Macedonians. He provided clarification concerning both the economic and essential aspects of the Trinity. As for the essential Trinity, Nyssa noted the Macedonians were arguing illogically that the Spirit was partially divine. But since God is perfect, he cannot be partial, so the Spirit is either fully divine or not divine at all. While the Spirit is third in order (*taxis*) to the Father and the Son, "in all other respects we acknowledge His inseparable union with them." This inseparable union yet distinction is pictured as a "revolving circle of the glory moving from Like to Like." The Spirit glorifies the Son who glorifies the Father, while the Father glorifies the Son who glorifies the Spirit. Moreover, the internal relations between the *hypostaseis* are grounded in the Father, who is the cause of Son and Spirit.

Nyssa clarified the economic Trinity by pointing to the common yet distinct working of the Trinity. Father, Son, and Holy Spirit work jointly, never apart. However, each has a peculiar role in the common work. For instance, it is the Spirit who sanctifies and gives life. In a closer description of the economic Trinity, Nyssa noted that the Spirit unites the redeemed into trinitarian life. He can do this because all three persons share equally

---

[75] Basil, *De Spiritu Sancto* 7; Congar, *I Believe in the Holy Spirit,* 3:31. Basil, Letters, 38.1. Cf., Letters, 214.4 in ibid., 254. Didymus "the Blind" of Alexandria repeatedly uses the phrase *mia ousia, treis hypostaseis,* but Basil's impact on the Council of Constantinople was more direct. Quasten, *Patrology,* 3:93–97, 228–29. Burgess, *Spirit and Church,* 138; Quasten, *Patrology,* 3:231–33.

in the divine attributes. However, Nyssa did not sever the economic from the essential Trinity, "the identity of operations indicating, rather, as we said, community of nature."[76]

The third Cappadocian, Gregory of Nazianzus, writing shortly after Basil's death before the Council of Constantinople of 381, was more than willing to call the Spirit "God." "Is the Spirit God? Most certainly. Well then, is He Consubstantial? Yes, if He is God." Because the Spirit is definitely God, Christians must worship him as God. Nazianzus also affirmed the "monarchy" of the Father in the order of the *hypostaseis*. He was not concerned about the different terminologies used by Basil and Athanasius; rather, what their thoughts meant to convey was most important. As we have seen, this one-time bishop of Constantinople posited a progression in God's revelation of himself and in the church's dogmatic development. Nazianzus also recognized human language is inadequate for comprehending the Trinity. Ultimately, we must return to the Bible for our theological language; therefore, in describing the interrelations of the "undivided" Trinity, we speak of the Father as "unbegotten," the Son as "begotten," and the Spirit as "proceeding."[77]

The pneumatological contributions of the Cappadocians are numerous and profound. Where Basil was instrumental in affirming the worship of the Spirit and the distinction of *mia ousia, treis hypostaseis,* "one essence, three persons," and Nyssa developed the order of the persons and the distinct yet common operations of the Trinity, Nazianzus clarified the internal relations of the Trinity. Congar summarizes the contributions made by Athanasius and the Cappadocian Fathers under four rubrics: "the distinction between substance and hypostasis"; "the monarchy of the Father"; "the distinction between the begetting of the Son and the *ekporeusis,* 'procession,' of the Spirit"; and "the relationship between the Spirit and the Word." This relationship between the second and third persons of the Trinity could be expressed in four possible ways; the Spirit "coming from the Father through the Son, or in the form of a resting of the Spirit in the Son, or by the fact that the Spirit expresses the Son and is the image of the Son, or, finally, at the level of the 'economy,' by the fact that the Spirit is communicated by the Son and makes

---

[76] Quasten, *Patrology,* 3:257–60; Gregory of Nyssa, *On the Holy Spirit,* in *NPNF*², 5:316–18, 320–24; Congar, *I Believe in the Holy Spirit,* 3:32; Swete, *Holy Spirit in the Ancient Church,* 250–51. Nyssa, *On the Holy Trinity,* in ibid., 329; Quasten, *Patrology,* 3:285–87.

[77] Writing *circa* 374, Epiphanius of Salamis is perhaps the earliest theologian to directly identify the Holy Spirit as "God." He also describes the Holy Spirit as "the bond of the Trinity" and affirms that the Spirit comes from both the Father and the Son, but he never unequivocally states that the Spirit "proceeds from the Son." Swete believes the creeds of Epiphanius were used at the Council of Constantinople. Epiphanius, *Ancoratus* 16 cited in Swete, *Holy Spirit in the Ancient Church,* 226–28. Gregory of Nazianzus, *Theological Orations* 5.9-14, 5.24, 5.26, 5.31; Quasten, *Patrology,* 3:249–51.

him known."[78] In light of later crises, it is important to note there was no definition of the Spirit proceeding from the Father and the Son.

Orthodox Pneumatology

The Council of Constantinople gathered at the behest of the empire in 381 and formalized Nicene pneumatology. At Nicea, the creed's third article, structurally following the articles on the Father and the Son, simply stated belief "in the Holy Spirit." At Constantinople, over fifty years later, the article was expanded to say, "And in the Holy Spirit, the Lord and Life-giver, Who proceeds from the Father, Who is worshipped and glorified together with the Father and the Son, Who spoke through the prophets." The creed was intentionally restricted to the scriptural language,[79] but the council endorsed the Cappadocian theology. The creed, the council wrote, "tells us how to believe, . . . believing also, of course, that the Father, the Son, and the Holy Spirit have a single Godhead and power and substance *(ousias),* a dignity deserving the same honour and a co-eternal sovereignty, in three most perfect hypostases *(hypostasesin),* or three perfect Persons *(prosōpois)."* Although it took centuries,[80] the Nicene faith as clarified by Constantinople eventually triumphed over its Arian and pneumatomachian opponents, defining orthodox pneumatology.

John of Damascus, writing in the early eighth century and drawing from an anonymous writer, completed the Nicene tradition by defining the intra-trinitarian hypostatic relations in terms of *perichōresis.* This doctrine clarifies the relationship of the persons and has been variously translated as circumincession, interpenetration, or mutual indwelling. It "points to the in-existence of the Persons within each other, the fact that they are present to each other, that they contain one another and that they manifest each other." According to John, "the subsistences dwell in one another, in no wise confused but cleaving together." The monarchy of the Father is affirmed along with the begetting of the Son and the procession of the Spirit from the Father. The distinction between begetting and proceeding is upheld although the exact difference is not defined.

As for the Spirit, he proceeds from the Father and not from the Son; however, the Spirit proceeds "from the Father through the Son." The Father is the only cause, but the Son is not excluded totally from the procession of the Spirit. The work of the Spirit is to perfect creation. John's *Exposition of the Orthodox Faith* became a standard textbook for Greek theologians and

---

[78] Congar, *I Believe in the Holy Spirit,* 3:40.

[79] *Decrees of the Ecumenical Councils,* 1:24, 28. "Lord," 2 Corinthians 3:18; "Life-giver," John 6:63; "Proceeds," John 15:26. Worship and glorification of the Spirit was argued from the baptismal formula, Matthew 28:19. Swete, *Holy Spirit in the Ancient Church,* 186–87.

[80] Even Eusebius of Caesarea, Constantine's most fervent episcopal supporter, was not totally committed to the Nicene language. Quasten, *Patrology,* 3:197–98, 341–42.

was translated into Latin. In the West he became known as *doctor Graecus,* "the Greek teacher," and is compared with Augustine, *praecipuus doctor Latinus,* "the special Latin teacher."[81]

Augustine of Hippo

The writings of Augustine, described as so voluminous no person could read them all, lay the foundation for the Latin tradition. The influence of Augustine on Western theology is evident in a number of areas but perhaps nowhere more than in his doctrine of the Holy Spirit, especially the double procession of the Spirit from the Father and the Son. Augustine may have read the double procession into Hilary of Poitiers and Ambrose of Milan, but the only earlier Latin theologian to conflate the procession was Marius Victorinus.[82]

Augustine first broached the doctrine of the Holy Spirit before the Council of Hippo in 393, affirming the Spirit as "consubstantial and co-eternal" with the Father and the Son. The analogies he drew upon to illustrate the Trinity are natural: the common water in a fountain, a river, and a lake, or the common tree with root, trunk, and branches. The Father is the begetter and the head of the Trinity, while the Son is begotten, "although absolutely and without difference equal." Augustine offered a biblically informed doctrine of the "special individuality" of the Spirit. The Spirit is "the Gift of God" and "the communion of the Father and the Son, and (so to speak) their Godhead." He is also "the love [*amor*] and charity [*caritas*] subsisting between these two, the one toward the other."

---

[81] John of Damascus, *Exposition of the Orthodox Faith* 1.8; 1.12, in *NPNF²,* 3:6–11, 13–15; Congar, *I Believe in the Holy Spirit,* 3:36–40. Michael Robson, "Saint Bonaventure," in *The Medieval Theologians: An Introduction to Theology in the Medieval Period,* ed. Gillian Rosemary Evans (Malden: Blackwell, 2001), 189.

[82] Peter Brown, *Augustine of Hippo: A Biography* (Los Angeles: University of California Press, 1967), 433; Garry Wills, *Saint Augustine* (New York: Viking, 1999), xii. Jaroslav Pelikan, *The Christian Tradition: A History of the Development of Doctrine* (Chicago: University of Chicago, 1971–1989), 3:21. Largely dependent on Eastern theologians, Hilary of Poitiers wrote a treatise on the Trinity before the doctrine of the Spirit was summarily defined at Constantinople. At one point he does appear to affirm a double procession of the Spirit, "proceeding, as He does, from Father and Son." However, Hilary more often speaks in terms of a single procession from the Father although the Son is involved in the sending and receiving of the Spirit. In a confession from his twelfth book, which Swete considered his last, the Holy Spirit is said to proceed "from" the Father and "through" the Son. Certain names for the Holy Spirit—"Gift" and "Bond of union"—probably impressed Augustine, who was familiar with Hilary's work. Hilary of Poitiers, *On the Trinity* 2.29–33, 12.55, in *NPNF²,* 9.60–61, 233; Swete, *Holy Spirit in the Ancient Church,* 301; Congar, *I Believe in the Holy Spirit,* 3:80. Victorinus says the Spirit is the "bond of the Father and the Son" in a way that apparently confused the persons. Swete, *Holy Spirit in the Ancient Church,* 307–8; Congar, *I Believe,* 1:77. Ambrose of Milan wrote the first Latin treatise devoted to the Holy Spirit. Ambrose refers to the procession of the Spirit from the Son, but he is concerned with the economic sending of the Spirit, not the eternal relation. For Ambrose, the saving presence and work of the Spirit cannot be separated from the Father and the Son. Augustine, *On Christian Teaching* 4.21, trans. R. P. H. Green (New York: Oxford University, 1997), 133. On Augustine's relation to Ambrose, see Brown, *Augustine,* 74–87. Ambrose of Milan, *Of the Holy Spirit* 1.10–11, 1.15, in *NPNF²,* 10:108–9, 113; Congar, *I Believe in the Holy Spirit,* 3:50.

To establish the truth that the Spirit is the love between the Father and the Son, he appealed to Scripture, primarily Romans 5:5. "For the love of God is shed abroad in our hearts by the Holy Spirit." Other passages cited reflect back on the work of the Spirit manifested in this Pauline text. The only noneconomic passage to which Augustine referred is 1 John 4:16. "For God is love." As to why the Holy Spirit is not explicitly mentioned by John, Augustine tautologically replied that this is "an application of the principle that, in general, the connection itself is not wont to be enumerated among the things which are connected together." In essence, love connects the Father and the Son, and since the connection is the Spirit, the Spirit is love.[83]

In *On Christian Teaching*, begun about 395, Augustine emphasized the unity, equality, and harmony of the three persons of the Godhead. "These three have the same eternal nature, the same unchangeableness, the same majesty, the same power." The distinctions within the Godhead are these: "In the Father there is unity, in the Son equality, and in the Holy Spirit a harmony of unity and equality. And the three are all one because of the Father, all equal because of the Son, and all in harmony because of the Holy Spirit." In a sermon he similarly identified the Spirit as "the common life [*communitas*]" of the Father and the Son. As the *communitas* of both, the Spirit is also God's gift to us, thus gathering us into communion.[84]

In his *Homilies on the Gospel of John*, written about 416, Augustine again broached the issue of the double procession. He bypassed the chance to address the issue when he considered John 15:26, the only literal reference to the Spirit's procession. While discussing the Paraclete passages, Augustine alluded repeatedly to Romans 5:5, "the love of the Spirit." Augustine perceived both a single and a double procession. "For the Son is born of the Father, and the Holy Spirit proceedeth from the Father; but the Father is neither born of, nor proceedeth from, another." After defining this procession as eternal in nature, he said, "The Holy Spirit proceedeth also from the Son." A number of exegetical proofs are brought forward to support the double procession: He is the "Spirit of" both Father and Son (Matt. 10:20; Rom. 8:9; Gal. 4:6); God as Father and Son have in common the name of "a Spirit" (John 4:24); the Son gave the disciples the Spirit by "breathing" on them (John 20:22); and, the "virtue" or "power" of the Holy Spirit came from the Son (Luke 1:34–35; 6:19; 8:46; 24:49). He then explains Christ's failure to mention the double procession in John 15:26 as the Son is "wont to attribute" everything that is His to the Father.

---

[83] There was as yet no "discussion full enough or careful enough" to understand the person of the Spirit. Augustine, *On Faith and the Creed* 9, in *NPNF*[1] 3:327–31. Romans 5:5 is again the critical referent. Augustine, *Homilies on the First Epistle of John* 7.12 in *NPNF*[1], 7:512.

[84] Augustine, *On Christian Teaching* 1.5.10. Sermon 214, cited in Swete, *Holy Spirit in the Ancient Church*, 327.

Augustine concluded by both qualifying the double procession and rejecting a procession through the Son: "But the Holy Spirit proceedeth not from the Father into the Son, and then proceedeth from the Son to the work of the creature's sanctification; but He proceedeth at the same time from both; although this the Father hath given unto the Son, that He should proceed from Him also, even as He proceedeth from Himself."[85]

It is commonplace that where the Greek fathers began with the interrelations of the persons of the Trinity and then discussed their consubstantiality, Augustine began with the unity of God and only then discussed the persons. This commonplace is supported by *De Trinitate*, Augustine's "work of greatest genius and originality," even in comparison to his *Confessions* and *De Civitate Dei*.[86] Augustine began with "the inseparable equality of one substance," although he recognized the Father, the Son, and the Holy Spirit must be differentiated: "The Holy Spirit is neither the Father nor the Son, but only the Spirit of the Father and of the Son, himself coequal to the Father and the Son, and belonging to the threefold unity."

Theologically, Augustine progressed from the oneness to the threeness of God. This same priority occurs in his analogies for the Trinity. Forgoing natural analogies, Augustine adopted a series of psychological triads. Eight psychological analogies of the Trinity are found in *De Trinitate* and six in *De Civitate Dei*. The most prominent psychological analogy is that of memory, understanding, and will. The third psychological component, the will, is synonymous with love. Although all three persons participate in memory, understanding, and will, it is the Father who is especially identified with memory, the Son with understanding, and the Spirit with the will. The Holy Spirit is also identified by Scripture as "the gift of God," and as "gift" the Holy Spirit is "a kind of inexpressible communion or fellowship of Father and Son."[87]

It is evident by his choice of scriptural references and his analogies that Augustine began with the economic manifestations of God in creation (the psychological analogies) and redemption (the soteriological sending of the Spirit), and interpreted God's essence through his manifestations. The Holy Spirit deserves "the title of creator" as much as the Father and the Son, and he is God's gift to us in salvation. These economic manifestations reinforce the fact that the Spirit is coequal and consubstantial with the Father and the Son, eternally proceeding from both. The Spirit himself is

---

[85] Augustine, *Homilies on the Gospel of John* 97-99, in *NPNF*[1], 7:362–84.

[86] Congar attributed this commonplace to T. de Régnon. Congar, *I Believe in the Holy Spirit,* 3:83. Augustine, *The Trinity,* trans. Edmund Hill (Brooklyn, NY: New City Press, 1991), 18.

[87] Congar, *I Believe in the Holy Spirit,* 3:89. Augustine, *The Trinity* 1.2.7, 5.3.12, 15.5.28, 15.6.43.

the bond of unity, charity, holiness, and friendship between Father and Son. The substance of God is indeed God's love, which is God's Spirit.[88]

In book 15 of *De Trinitate,* Augustine incorporated material from his previous writings, concluding this influential work with a careful definition of the Spirit's procession, from both the economic and essential standpoints. From the essential standpoint, the procession of the Spirit is similar to the generation of the Son, except the Spirit is not a son. Only God can give God; the Son gives the Spirit; therefore, the Spirit proceeds from the Son, too. There is an eternal distinction in the procession, in that the Spirit proceeds from the Father "principally," and from both "jointly," for the Father is alone "not from another," and the Spirit is given to the Son by the Father. Difference must be maintained between "generation" and "procession." The Holy Spirit is not generated by the Father and the Son, for that would be "the height of absurdity"; rather, the Holy Spirit "proceeds from them both."[89]

Augustine failed to bring his views of the saving work of the Holy Spirit into one place. However, he was concerned with the interior state of man in relation to God. When the Spirit indwells the believer, the Father and the Son are included. This indwelling occurs through the remission of sins in regeneration, which is the first gift from God. The gift of love which Christians have for God is shed abroad in our hearts by the Holy Spirit. Those who have rebelled against God are without repentance, and lifelong impenitence is itself the blasphemy against the Holy Spirit.[90] Augustine's greatest opponent, Pelagius, saw the Holy Spirit coming upon the Christian only on the basis of personal moral purity. Against Pelagian moralism, Augustine taught that original sin totally disables the Christian so that God must overcome human inability by grace.

East and West in the Midde Ages

The Filioque Controversy

Schism between East and West occurred over the question of the filioque after a long and complicated process. Cultural, linguistic, and politi-

---

[88] Augustine, *The Trinity* 5.3.14-16, 6.1.7.

[89] From the economic standpoint, Augustine considers the mission of the Holy Spirit. Christ both gave the Spirit and received the Spirit. Christ, as God, gave the Holy Spirit; but as man, he received the Holy Spirit. Christ gave the Spirit twice, "once on earth for love of neighbor, and again from heaven for love of God." Christ was twice anointed with the Spirit, at the incarnation invisibly and at his baptism visibly. At his baptism Christ was prefiguring the gift of the Holy Spirit to the church, which is his body. Augustine, *The Trinity* 15.5.27–37; 15.6.45–48.

[90] Phillip Cary, *Augustine's Invention of the Inner Self: The Legacy of a Christian Platonist* (New York: Oxford University Press, 2000); Augustine, *The Trinity* 1.3.19; Augustine, *Confessions* 13.31 in *NPNF*[1], 1:205; Augustine, Sermon 71, cited in Swete, *Holy Spirit in the Ancient Church,* 335.

cal factors contributed to the schism, but the primary doctrinal factors were the papal claims to superiority and the filioque.[91] Filioque, literally "and the Son," had been added by the Western church to the Nicene Creed (as revised by Constantinople) to redefine the procession of the Spirit from the Father to a procession from the Father *and* the Son. The controversy over the filioque revealed "a fundamental difference of approach to the problem of the mystery of the triune God." The East adamantly maintained a biblical literalism that said the Spirit proceeds from the Father alone although many countenanced procession from the Father *through* the Son.[92]

The double procession, inherited from Augustine, made its first creedal appearance in Spain, perhaps as early as the late fourth century, as a response to the Priscillianist heresy. At the Council of Toledo (Spain) in 589 and at the Synod of Hatfield (England) in 680, the double procession was evident. The Council of Gentilly (France) in 767 is the first place where the East objected to the filioque; subsequently, the new Holy Roman emperor, Charlemagne, pursued the issue with vigor. After hearing the filioque recited in a royal chapel at Aachen, some Latin monks returned to Jerusalem in 808 with the new practice, creating a stir. Upon learning of a doctrinal attack on these monks, Charlemagne appealed to Pope Leo III to pronounce in favor of the filioque. Leo affirmed the orthodoxy of double procession but refused to recite the addition in worship, even affixing two silver shields with the unaltered creed in Greek and Latin to the basilica in St. Peter's. The earliest evidence that the altered creed was pontifically approved was when Benedict VIII (1012–24) allowed it to be sung during the Eucharist.[93]

According to Jaroslav Pelikan, East and West employ diverse theological methodologies. Eastern theologians make a strong distinction between the economic sending of the Spirit and the essential procession of the Spirit. They agree that Christ sent the Spirit, but this is an economic work; only the Father has the Spirit ontologically proceeding from him. Eastern theologians argue from the distinct hypostases: if a characteristic belongs to two of the persons, then it must belong to all three and is thus not distinctive to a person. Western theologians argue from the common essence: the procession of the Spirit is from the Father and the Son because they possess the same substance. There is, moreover, disagreement about which person unites the Godhead. Eastern theologians believe the Father as monarch and source guarantees the unity of

---

[91] Timothy Ware, *The Orthodox Church,* new ed. (New York: Penguin, 1993), 43–49.

[92] Kelly, *Early Christian Creeds,* 3rd ed. (New York: Longman, 1983), 359–60.

[93] Bede, *Ecclesiastical History of the English People,* rev. ed., trans. Leo Sherley-Price (New York: Penguin, 1990), iv.xvii, 232–33; Kelly, *Early Christian Creeds,* 360–67; Eamon Duffy, *Saints and Sinners: A History of the Popes* (New Haven: Yale University Press, 1997), 77, 85–86.

the Godhead, while Western theologians believe the Holy Spirit as love and communion guarantees divine unity.[94]

A comparison between representative theologians in this debate is instructive. In the East, Photius, a late ninth-century patriarch of Constantinople, was embroiled in controversy with the papacy and with another claimant to Constantinople. He was deposed and condemned by the Fourth Council of Constantinople but was restored when Pope John VIII annulled that council's decisions. Photius died in fellowship with Rome but wrote extensively against the filioque. In a letter of 883, he based the single procession on three foundations: Jesus declared procession from the Father in John 15:26; the First Council of Constantinople and subsequent councils affirmed the single procession; and the church fathers who affirmed single procession far outnumbered those who affirmed double procession.

In *The Mystagogy of the Holy Spirit*, Photius formulated the doctrine of monopatrism, procession "from the Father alone." Photius believed a double procession endangered the monarchy of the Father by suggesting modalism. If the Spirit proceeds from the common nature, as the West taught, then he absurdly proceeds from himself. The procession of the person of the Spirit is from the person of the Father. When Scripture speaks of the "Spirit of Christ," it is not referring to procession but to the Spirit having anointed Christ. The position formulated by Photius became the standard in the East; however, he has been criticized for ignoring procession "through the Son."[95]

In the West, Anselm, archbishop of Canterbury in the late tenth century, defended the double procession. In his early *Monologion* (circa 1070), Anselm defined the Spirit as the "self-love" that "proceeds equally from the Father and the Son." "Love is nothing other than the supreme essence," and "Father, Son and Love are one supreme essence." In *On the Procession of the Holy Spirit,* he argued at length from the common faith shared with the Greeks and the common substance of the Godhead. Only after rational argumentation did he approach Scripture, and then he merely mimicked Augustine's exegesis. He defended Western theology by noting that where the Greeks worried double procession is from two sources, the Latin posi-

---

[94] In addition to the different theological methods, there is disagreement over theological authority. For the East, a persistent problem is the arbitrary alteration of the creed without conciliar approval; for the West, the concern is to maintain a statement that will deny adoptionism. The Eastern theologians are also concerned that the papacy is arrogating too much authority to itself, forgetting the collegial nature of the patriarchate. Moreover, the Eastern theologians did not appreciate the innovations introduced by Augustine and prefer the pneumatological explanations offered by the more numerous Eastern fathers and the councils. Pelikan, *The Christian Tradition*, 2:183–98; cf. Justo L. González, *A History of Christian Thought*, rev. ed. (Nashville: Abingdon, 1987), 2:127–30.

[95] *Decrees of the Ecumenical Councils*, 1:157–86; Stanley M. Burgess, *The Holy Spirit: Eastern Christian Traditions* (Peabody, MA: Hendrickson, 1989), 48–51; Congar, *I Believe in the Holy Spirit*, 3:57–60.

tion defined the double procession as from the single source that is common to Father and Son. He believed his "irrefutable logic" better preserved the trinitarian distinctions: "Of the three Persons, only the Father is one who is from no one, only the Son is one who is from one and from whom one is, only the Holy Spirit is one from whom no one is." Anselm's double procession characterizes the Latin tradition. Thomas Aquinas argued along similar lines, although he began with Scripture.[96]

The Spirit of Salvation

There are significant differences in the understanding of the Spirit's role in salvation between East and West.[97] In the East the writings of the fourteenth-century monk Gregory Palamas have approached the status of official dogma. Palamas developed the ancient Greek doctrine of salvation as *theōsis* or deification. Echoing Simeon the New Theologian, he says the highest point of the spiritual life is in perceiving the divine light. Such perception occurs when the Christian is given the deifying gift of the Holy Spirit. Palamas kept *theōsis* from encroaching on the Godhead by distinguishing the divine energies from the divine essence and Persons. The energies are described as the "light," "glory," "face," or "power" of God that manifest the activity of the Spirit. The Holy Spirit effects human participation in these outgoing energies of the divine persons.[98]

In the West soteriology follows two distinct but related Augustinian models, the psychological model and the model of mutual love. Both models understand the highest point of the spiritual life as the beatific vision

---

[96] *Monologion,* 49–70, in *Anselm of Canterbury: The Major Works,* ed. Brian Davies and G. R. Evans (New York: Oxford University Press, 1998), 60–76; Stanley M. Burgess, *The Holy Spirit: Medieval Roman Catholic and Reformation Traditions* (Peabody: Hendrickson, 1997), 29–35. *On the Procession of the Holy Spirit,* in *Anselm: Major Works,* 390–434; Congar, *I Believe in the Holy Spirit,* 3:96–102; Thomas Aquinas, *Summa Contra Gentiles* 4.24-25, trans. Charles J. O'Neill (1957; reprint, Notre Dame: University of Notre Dame Press, 1975), 133–43.

[97] A related pneumatological debate between East and West occurred over the *epiklēsis,* the calling down of the Spirit during the Eucharist. Latin theologians primarily focused on the words uttered by the priest as the agent of change in the elements of the Eucharist to a real presence. Greek theologians believed that the Holy Spirit, by invocation, changed the elements to a real presence of Christ in the Eucharist. The Eastern theologians were more concerned with the direct activity of the Holy Spirit while Western theologians were more concerned with human mediation. This difference in focus between Eastern pneumatocentrism and Western Christocentrism and ecclesiocentrism is evident in the contributions of Thomas Aquinas and Nicholas Cabasilas. Cabasilas emphasized the role of the Holy Spirit in giving grace through the mysteries, or sacraments. In comparison, Aquinas emphasized the giving of grace by the efficacious working of the sacraments, treating the sacraments in light of the incarnation and the clergy rather than the Spirit. Pelikan, *Christian Tradition,* 3:277–78; Congar, *I Believe in the Holy Spirit,* 3:228–49; Burgess, *Holy Spirit: Eastern,* 74–78; Aquinas, *Summa Contra Gentiles* 56-78; Aquinas, *Summa Theologica,* trans. Fathers of the English Dominican Province (1911; reprint, Westminster, MD: Christian Classics, 1981), IIIa and Supplement, vols. 4–5.

[98] Congar, *I Believe in the Holy Spirit,* 1:93–103, 3:61–67; Burgess, *The Holy Spirit: Eastern,* 6–9, 69–73.

of God, which is perfectly experienced only in glory but glimpsed here. According to the psychological model, the mind is created in the image of the trinitarian God through its memory, understanding, and will. The Holy Spirit brings the presence of the Trinity to "the rational creature" by making it a lover of God. Aquinas described this variously as, "by the Holy Spirit," we are mutually indwelt with God, established as friends of God, speak the mysteries, commonly possess the gifts, and are adopted, forgiven, renewed, and cleansed. The effects of coming to the "beatitude of divine enjoyment" are that we contemplate God, delight in him, fulfill his commands freely, and mortify the deeds of the flesh. Characteristically positive in his rationalism, Anselm concluded "that every rational soul that strives, as it ought, to love and desire supreme happiness will, at some point, behold and enjoy it."[99]

The second Western model emphasizes the Spirit's role as *vinculum caritatis,* the bond of love. William of St. Thierry, an early twelfth-century Cistercian, defined the Spirit as the unity of God and the love of man for God. "The Holy Spirit, the unity of the Father and the Son, is also the love between God and the human being, and their likeness." The love of humans for God literally is the Holy Spirit. Our ascent to God is in the Spirit, through the Son, to the Trinity. The Holy Spirit infuses himself into a human's love and draws that person to God.[100]

Where the advocates of the psychological model easily spoke of "self-love," Richard of St. Victor differed, because "for there to be charity, there must be a love that is directed towards the other." Richard conceived of "sovereign charity," perfect love within the Godhead, as requiring a plurality to augment the divine simplicity. Richard's idea of "person" is not of an isolated individual but of an individual in relationship with others. Internally, the Father is *gratuitus,* love that gives; the Son is love that gives and receives; the Spirit is *debitus,* love that purely receives. Externally, the Holy Spirit creates *debitus* in the human soul, a "self-transcending love."[101]

Bonaventure used both models but placed the psychological model at an earlier stage in the soul's journey to God. Since good is "self-diffusive . . . , the highest good must be most self-diffusive." The self-diffusion of God occurs primarily within the trinitarian processions and secondarily in creation. At the final stage of ecstasy in God, the Holy Spirit inflames our

---

[99] Congar, *I Believe in the Holy Spirit,* 3:96; Aquinas, *Summa Contra Gentiles* 4.21–22; Aidan Nichols, *Discovering Aquinas: An Introduction to His Life, Work, and Influence* (Grand Rapids: Eerdmans, 2002), 70–73; Anselm, *Monologion* 66–70 in *Major Works,* 72–76.

[100] William of St. Thierry, *Aenigma fidei* 4, cited in Emero Stiegman, "Bernard of Clairvaux, William of St. Thierry, the Victorines," in *Medieval Theologians,* 140–42.

[101] Congar, *I Believe in the Holy Spirit,* 3:103–08; Burgess, *Holy Spirit: Medieval and Reformation,* 63–69.

desire, enabling us to see God. The beatific vision is ultimately dependent not on human efforts but on the gift of God, the Holy Spirit.[102]

The Protestant Reformation

The Protestant Reformation must be considered in three major theological manifestations under Martin Luther, the Reformed theologians, and the Radical Reformers.

Martin Luther

Luther both received and modified the pneumatological legacy of the medieval church. He made a distinction between the person and the work of the Spirit. "So we distinguish the Holy Spirit as God in his divine nature and essence from the Holy Spirit as he is given to us." As for the person of the Spirit, Luther treated him as a distinct person within the Godhead who shares in the divine essence and proceeds from both Father and Son. Luther expressed no disagreement over who the Holy Spirit is. Luther's dissatisfaction with the medieval tradition was over how the Holy Spirit did his work and may be glimpsed in his vehemence that we do not know the essence of God by reason but by revelation from the Holy Spirit.[103]

As for the Spirit's work, Luther encapsulated it in the term *sanctification*. Although all three persons share in the major works of creation, redemption, and sanctification, each has a peculiar work. Creation is especially predicated of the Father; the acts of redemption in incarnation, death, and resurrection are peculiar to the Son; and the revelation and application of redemption to the human heart is the peculiar work of the Spirit. Luther understood this peculiar work through the paradigm of the Apostles' Creed. Because the Spirit is the Holy Spirit, he makes us holy. Sanctification occurs through the means of the church, i.e., the preaching of the gospel, which issues forth in forgiveness, resurrection, and eternal life. In preaching, he used the metaphor of a treasure. Christ made the treasure by accomplishing everything for our salvation. "But the treasure lies yet in one pile; it is not yet distributed nor invested." The office of the Holy Spirit is to "invest the treasure" by coming and teaching "our hearts to believe and say: I, too, am one of those who are to have this treasure."[104]

---

[102] Bonaventure, *The Soul's Journey into God* 3,6–7, in *Bonaventure*, Classics of Western Spirituality (Mahwah: Paulist, 1978), 79–86, 102–16.

[103] Hugh Thomson Kerr, *A Compend of Luther's Theology* (Philadelphia: Westminster, 1943), 38–41, 65–67; Paul Althaus, *The Theology of Martin Luther*, trans. Robert C. Schulz (Philadelphia: Fortress, 1966), 199–200. Luther's essential pneumatology is Christological. Bernhard Lohse, *Martin Luther's Theology: Its Historical and Systematic Development* (Minneapolis: Fortress, 1999), 232–34.

[104] Kerr, *Compend*, 40–42, 67–68; *The Large Catechism of Martin Luther*, trans. Robert H. Fischer (Philadelphia: Fortress, 1959), 59–64.

Although Lutheran scholars previously downplayed the significance of the Spirit's sanctifying work, Prenter concludes, "The concept of the Holy Spirit completely dominates Luther's theology." The Holy Spirit's work is to infuse love for God into the human heart. While adopting Augustine's form here, Luther provided a different content. Where the Augustinian tradition emphasized the Spirit's work of love as the imitation of Christ, Luther spoke of union with Christ. He understood the psychology of the Spirit's work in terms of *Anfechtungen,* "inner conflict." The Holy Spirit mortifies then vivifies us by conforming us to Christ's death and resurrection. His commentary on Romans 8:26 states, "It is the nature of God first to destroy and tear down whatever is in us before He gives us His good things."

It is only when we have reached the limit of our own efforts and become passive that the Spirit does the work that is impossible for us to do.

> Therefore, when everything is hopeless for us and all things begin to go against our prayers and desires, then those unutterable groans begin. And then "the Spirit helps us in our weakness." For unless the Spirit were helping, it would be impossible for us to bear this action of God by which He hears us and accomplishes what we pray for.

The Spirit as Paraclete is an advocate in that he speaks for us forensically when we cannot, and a comforter when we despair. "We need someone else to intervene for us."[105]

After his controversy with the spiritualists or *Schwärmer,* "enthusiasts," began in 1522, Luther clarified the relation of the Word and the Spirit in the soteriological process. The Schwärmer defined the *ordo salutis,* order of salvation, as beginning with mortification and ending with the Spirit. The authoritative Word of God was internal rather than external. Luther summarized their teaching thus: "You yourself must hear the voice of God and experience the work of God in you and feel how much your talents weigh. The Bible means nothing. It is Bible—Booble—Babel." Against grossly dividing Word from Spirit, Luther claimed it is always in and by the Word that the Spirit works. Althaus summarizes Luther's attitude: "Word and Spirit therefore not only belong together but constitute an indissoluble unity." Reversing the spiritualist emphasis on self-mortification, Luther placed the preaching of the Word and the coming of the Spirit prior to mortification, vivification, and good works. For Luther, anthropocentric spiritualism must

---

[105] Regin Prenter, *Spiritus Creator,* trans. John M. Jensen (Philadelphia: Muhlenberg, 1953), ix–xx, 12–27, 48–54; Luther, *Lectures on Romans,* ed. Hilton C. Oswald, LW, vol. 25 (Saint Louis: Concordia, 1972), 365–68.

give way before pneumatic biblicism. The Spirit uses Word and sacraments as instruments.[106]

Luther was also clear that the Spirit's work of sanctification, though certainly promised, is not completed in this lifetime. "We do not preach the doctrine that the Spirit's office is one of complete accomplishment, but rather that it is progressive; he operates continuously and increasingly." The Christian must still struggle with sin and "experience the terrors of death." "We must take heed we do not arrogantly and presumptuously boast possession of the Holy Spirit, as do certain proud fanatics." Perfectionism is not an option since "the pious Christian is still flesh and blood like other men." Luther's doctrine of the Christian as *simul justus et peccator,* "at once justified and sinful," is evident in his pneumatology. "Because we are encumbered with our flesh we are never without sin. . . . The Holy Spirit must continue to work in us through the Word, daily granting forgiveness until we attain to that life where there will be no more forgiveness."[107]

The Reformed Theologians

Where Luther defines the priority as Word and Spirit, Ulrich Zwingli reverses it to Spirit and Word. Zwingli, the early reformer of Zürich, appreciated Luther; but his pneumatology was influenced by an aggravated polemic for reform, a mild Platonic dualism between flesh and Spirit, and an emphasis on the sovereignty of the Spirit. Zwingli's pneumatology thus emphasizes the freedom of the Spirit. The Spirit is sovereign in salvation, giving faith to whom he will. Although the Spirit is "related to the word: the incarnate word, the written word, and the audible and visible word," the Spirit has priority. Word and sacrament require the presence of the Spirit for the conferral of grace, but the Spirit does not require Word and sacrament. "Moreover, a channel or vehicle is not necessary to the Spirit, for He Himself is the virtue and energy whereby all things are borne, and has no need of being borne."

This statement was prompted by the need to proclaim the freedom and sovereignty of the Spirit, especially in relation to the sacraments. Sacraments do not convey grace *ex opere operato*; rather, they are "a public testimony of that grace which is previously present." Zwingli never opposed Spirit and Word like Sebastian Franck, a spiritualist opponent. Rather, he reacted violently to the church hierarchy's attempts to monopolize the sacraments and the interpretation of the Word.[108]

---

[106] Luther, *Letter to the Princes of Saxony Concerning the Rebellious Spirit,* ed. Conrad Bergendoff, *LW,* vol. 40 (Philadelphia: Fortress, 1958), 50; Prenter, *Spiritus Creator,* 248–59; Lohse, *Luther's Theology,* 144–50; Leonard Verduin, *The Reformers and Their Stepchildren* (Grand Rapids: Eerdmans, 1964), 18; Althaus, *Theology of Luther,* 38.

[107] Kerr, *Compend,* 71–72; Luther, *Large Catechism,* 62.

[108] W. P. Stephens, *Zwingli: An Introduction to His Thought* (New York: Clarendon, 1992), 61–63; Zwingli, *A Short and Clear Exposition* (1531), in *The Latin Works of Huldreich Zwingli,* trans.

In *On the Certainty and Clarity of the Word of God,* Zwingli formulated the Reformed doctrine of the revelatory relation between Spirit and Word. The medieval church discouraged lay Bible reading, citing Scripture's complexities, even dangers, in the hands of the untrained. To refute this, Zwingli established that man is created by the Spirit for God. All things live by the Spirit's gift of life, but the spirit of man is created in the image of God for fellowship with God. Because of the fall, this relationship is broken and many lack the Spirit, being under divine judgment. The old *flesh* must be replaced by the *spirit* through the renewal of the divine image. The Word of God has the power to accomplish this renewal and possesses an accompanying clarity: on the one hand, "the Word of God brought its own enlightenment." On the other hand, the illumination of the Word of God belongs to the Holy Spirit: "not that this is due to man's own understanding, but to the light and Spirit of God, illuminating and inspiring the words in such a way that the light of the divine content is seen in his own light."

The Spirit, therefore, is encountered by the reader in the Word as he who inspired the prophets and illumines our reading. For a person truly to understand the Word, he must be drawn and taught by the Spirit. The person who thus receives the Word is regenerated by the Spirit. For Zwingli, the hermeneutical task follows a process: "Before I say anything or listen to the teaching of man, I will first consult the mind of the Spirit of God." Only after praying for the Spirit should one read the Word. Zwingli listed twelve ways to judge whether the Word is rightly interpreted. Echoing Luther, he concluded, "When you find that the fear of God begins to give you joy rather than sorrow, it is a sure working of the Word and Spirit of God. May God grant us that Spirit. Amen."[109]

John Calvin received major credit for developing the nuances of Protestant doctrine, but this second-generation reformer compiled rather than created Protestant pneumatology. Consider two significant aspects of the Spirit's work. First, Warfield refers to Calvin as "preeminently the theologian of the Holy Spirit" with regard to his doctrine of the testimony of the Spirit to Scripture. However, as noted, Zwingli fostered the Reformed doctrine of the Spirit's relation to the Word. Second, John Webster claims that, "of all the masters of the Reformation," Calvin is "the theologian of sanctification par excellence." However, as Prenter notes, Luther developed the significance of sanctification by the Holy Spirit prior to Calvin. Calvin did not formulate these important doctrines but brought them into a coherent system in his *Institutes of the Christian Religion.*

Samuel Macauley Jackson (New York: Putnam, 1912; Philadelphia: Heidelberg, 1922, 1929), 2:254–55; Zwingli, *An Account of the Faith* (1530), in *Latin Works of Zwingli,* 2:46–47.

[109] Zwingli, *Of the Clarity and Certainty of the Word of God* (1522), in *Zwingli and Bullinger,* ed. G. W. Bromiley, LCC (Philadelphia: Westminster, 1953), 59–95.

While Calvin did not originate Reformed pneumatology, the Holy Spirit certainly occupies, in Barth's words, "the central place" for Calvin. In book 1 of *Institutes,* Calvin discussed the testimony of the Holy Spirit to the trustworthiness of Scripture and the Spirit as God. In book 3, Calvin described the intimate working of the Holy Spirit in the salvation of the believer. In book 4, Calvin considered the external means used by the Spirit.[110]

Calvin began his discussion of the testimony of the Holy Spirit by refuting the Catholic interpretation of Augustine's statement that he would not "embrace the gospel as the certain truth of God unless constrained by the authority of the Church." Catholicism said this meant that faith was founded on the authority of the church, but Calvin noted Augustine only meant the church's consensus compels unbelievers to consider the gospel. The church's witness is preparatory and ineffective without the Spirit's internal witness. We come to a certain faith only by the Spirit who inspired the Word. "The same Spirit, therefore, who has spoken through the mouths of the prophets must penetrate into our hearts to persuade us that they faithfully proclaimed what had been divinely commanded." When Calvin says Scripture is "self-authenticated," he means "the certainty it deserves with us, it attains by the testimony of the Spirit."

Calvin did not deny the reasonableness and credibility of Scripture; however, reason cannot rise to faith, for "the only true faith is that which the Spirit of God seals in our hearts." Scripture is the objective side of our knowledge of God while *testimonium Spiritus sancti* is the subjective side. Rebuking the "fanatics who wrongly appeal to the Holy Spirit" and despise the reading of the Word, Calvin devoted a chapter to the "mutual bond" which joins together Word and Spirit. The Spirit does not give new revelations but seals our minds with the Word. "The Word is the instrument by which the Lord dispenses the illumination of his Spirit to believers."[111]

Following a trinitarian paradigm in the *Institutes,* Calvin treated the work of the Holy Spirit in book 3, "the way in which we receive the grace of Christ." Consideration of the subjective or experiential comes only with book 3, books 1 and 2 being more concerned with the objective operations of Father and Son. Book 3 addresses "the secret energy of the Spirit, by which we come to enjoy Christ and all his benefits," beginning with union with Christ, wherein "the Holy Spirit is the bond by which Christ

---

[110] Benjamin B. Warfield, *Calvin and Calvinism* (New York: Oxford University Press, 1932), 107; John Webster, *Holiness* (Grand Rapids: Eerdmans, 2003), 89; François Wendel, *Calvin: Origins and Development of His Religious Thought,* trans. Philip Mairet (New York: Harper and Row, 1963), 121; Karl Barth, *The Theology of the Reformed Confessions,* trans. Darrell L. Guder and Judith J. Guder (Lousville: Westminster John Knox, 2002), 121.

[111] John Calvin, *Institutes of the Christian Religion,* 1.7.3–5, 1.10.1–3, ed. John T. McNeill, trans. Ford Lewis Battles, LCC (Philadelphia: Westminster, 1960), 76–81, 93–96; Warfield, *Calvin and Calvinism,* 29–130; Wendel, *Calvin,* 156–57.

effectually unites us to himself." Among the titles ascribed to the Spirit are "Spirit of sanctification" and "Gift." As for the operations of the Spirit in human salvation, "faith is the principal work of the Holy Spirit" and "has no other source than the Spirit."

Combining Zwingli's emphasis on the Spirit's sovereignty with Luther's stress on the Spirit in soteriology, Calvin assigned hegemony to the Spirit over every aspect of salvation. "Consequently, he may be called the key that unlocks for us the treasures of the Kingdom of Heaven; and his illumination, the keenness of our insight." Salvation becomes a human possession only because the Spirit works entirely within and for the sinner from beginning to end. The Spirit causes our union with Christ and brings with himself every "benefit" or "gift" of our salvation: faith, sealing, repentance, forgiveness, perseverance, and so forth. As Calvin continues discussing the details of salvation, references to the work of the Spirit give way to descriptions of the psychological effects within, and the demands placed upon, the Christian. On the one hand, there is little doubt that, for Calvin, the Spirit begins, continues, and brings to completion Christian salvation. As Wendel notes, Calvin has a "constant preoccupation not to grant too much to man." On the other hand, salvation is "the hidden work of the Holy Spirit" within the Christian and may be misconstrued as to origin.[112]

The Radicals

G. H. Williams identifies two major groups within the Radical Reformation: Spiritualists and Anabaptists. The earliest exponent of spiritualism was Andreas Bodenstein von Carlstadt, a teacher at Wittenberg whose iconoclasm ended Luther's exile in the Wartburg castle in 1522. Carlstadt employed 2 Corinthians 3:6 to divide internal Spirit from external Word. "As far as I am concerned, I do not need the outward witness. I want to have the testimony of the Spirit within me." Williams identifies three types of Spiritualists: revolutionary, rational, and evangelical.

Thomas Müntzer, a revolutionary Spiritualist, said the Spirit came to help the believer overcome the experience of mortification. Once the Spirit comes, he reveals the deep things of God to the enlightened person through dreams and visions quite apart from the Bible. Sebastian Franck, a rational Spiritualist, also opposed letter and spirit. He believed the visible church of the apostles had fallen and that the spiritual church now exists invisibly and without sacraments or structure. Since everything must be done "in the Spirit and in truth," "the Church is today a purely spiritual

---

[112] Calvin, *Institutes*, 3.1.1–4, 3.2.7, 3.2.35–36, 3.3.19, 3.3.21, 3.6–10; Kevin Dixon Kennedy, *Union with Christ and the Extent of the Atonement in Calvin*, Studies in Biblical Literature (New York: Peter Lang, 2002), 98, 116–19; Wendel, *Calvin*, 233, 263; Burgess, *Holy Spirit: Medieval and Reformation*, 167–68.

thing . . . , all in the Spirit and no longer outward." Franck also affirmed the unitarianism of Michael Servetus, who dispensed with the distinct personhood of the Spirit.[113]

Evangelical Anabaptists came to oppose the Spiritualists because their focus on invisibility threatened to dissolve gathered congregations, and extrascriptural revelation encouraged violent revolution. Evangelical Anabaptists often speak of the Spirit, but "virtually all Anabaptist statements regarding the Holy Spirit are orthodox." For instance, Pilgram Marpeck maintained a concurrence between Spirit and Word: "Only by means of the Word of truth does the Holy Spirit generate faith, even in all truly believing hearts, no matter how foolish and contemptible they may often seem to man." Menno Simons believed the Spirit empowers the Christian to live a life of holiness. Menno was accused of perfectionism but denied it. He affirmed the orthodox doctrine of the Spirit as a distinct person and as God. He also described the procession of the Spirit "from the Father through the Son" in a fashion reminiscent of the Eastern tradition.[114]

The Modern Era

Scholastic Orthodoxy

After the passing of the first reformers, the Lutheran and Reformed branches of Protestantism experienced a "theological autumn" with scholastic orthodoxy. The role of the Holy Spirit was somewhat diminished as emphasis fell on the rational systematization of doctrine, the supernatural nature of Scripture, and an increasingly elaborate *ordo salutis.* Of two dominant systematic methods, the catechetical and the scholastic, the catechetical method gave the Holy Spirit separate treatment while the scholastic method mostly buried the Holy Spirit under other doctrines. Following the catechetical method, which necessarily treated the Spirit as a separate article of the Apostles' Creed, are Caspar Olevianus, Herman Witsius, and Zacharias Ursinus. Following the

---

113 George Huntston Williams, *The Radical Reformation,* 3rd ed., Sixteenth Century Essays and Studies (Kirksville: Sixteenth Century Journal, 1992), 1247–55; Müntzer, *Sermon Before the Princes* (1524), in *Spiritual and Anabaptist Writers,* ed. George H. Williams and Angel M. Mergal, LCC (Philadelphia: Westminster, 1957), 56–59; Burgess, *Holy Spirit: Medieval and Reformation,* 203–9; Franck, *Letter to John Campanus* (1531), in *Spiritual and Anabaptist Writers,* 149–50, 157–59.

114 *Anabaptism in Outline: Selected Primary Sources,* ed. Walter Klaassen, Classics of the Radical Reformation (Scottdale: Herald, 1981), 72; Williams, *Radical Reformation,* 715; Marpeck, *To Caspar Schwenckfeld* (1544), in *The Writings of Pilgram Marpeck,* trans. William Klassen and Walter Klaassen, Classics of the Radical Reformation (Scottdale: Herald, 1978), 370; Simons, *A Solemn Confession of the Triune God* (1550), in *The Complete Writings of Menno Simons, c.1496–1561,* trans. Leonard Verduin (Scottdale: Herald, 1956), 495–96; Simons, *Reply to Gellius Faber* (1554), in *Complete Writings,* 759–63; Burgess, *Holy Spirit: Medieval and Reformation,* 210–17.

scholastic method are William Ames, Francis Turretin, Thomas Watson, and much later, Charles Hodge. English Puritans often ruminate concerning their experience of the Holy Spirit. John Owen authored several works on the Holy Spirit, but Puritan systematic theologies generally reflected the scholastic method.

The scholastic method begins by proving the divine attribution of Scripture, emulating the form used by the Second Helvetic Confession, and then proceeds to discern the counsels of God in creation and redemption through a series of Aristotelean propositions drawn from Scripture as a textbook. Calvin had made the Spirit a prominent organizing principle in his system, and he relegated discussion of election to his third book, after prayer and concurrently with assurance. The Reformed scholastics disagreed, making election the dominant organizing principle and treating the Spirit under various doctrines, such as Scripture, God, and salvation. Human reasoning, although seeking to preserve divine sovereignty, subtly dominates. (The scholastic method was adopted by a number of early Baptist theologians, including John Gill, John L. Dagg, and James Petigru Boyce. Although Dagg employed the scholastic method, he unusually dedicated a separate section to the Holy Spirit.) In addition to the methodological subsuming of the Spirit by reason in the scholastic theological method, Karl Barth notes the psychological subsuming of the Spirit within the process of salvation, especially by the Westminster Confession.[115]

---

[115] Bernard Holm, "The Work of the Spirit: The Reformation to the Present," in *The Holy Spirit in the Life of the Church: From Biblical Times to the Present,* ed. Paul D. Opsahl (Minneapolis: Augsburg, 1978), 106; Justo L. Gonzalez, *A History of Christian Thought,* rev. ed. (Nashville: Abingdon, 1987), 3:261–65, 267–79. Representative pneumatologies employing the catechetical method: Caspar Olevianus, *A Firm Foundation: An Aid in Interpreting the Heidelberg Catechism* (1567), trans. Lyle D. Bierma (Grand Rapids: Baker, 1995), 90–95; Zacharias Ursinus, *Commentary on the Heidelberg Catechism* (1591), trans. G. W. Williard (1852; reprint, Phillipsburg: n.d.), 270–85; Herman Witsius, *Sacred Dissertations* (1681), trans. Donald Fraser (1823; reprint, Escondido, CA: Den Dulk, 1993), 2:303–45. Representative pneumatologies employing the scholastic method: William Ames, *The Marrow of Theology* (1629), trans. John Dykstra Eusden (Grand Rapids: Baker, 1997), 91, 94, 149, 186–88; Francis Turretin, *Institutes of Elenctic Theology* (1679–85), trans. George Musgrave Giger (Phillipsburg: Presbyterian and Reformed, 1992); 1:87–92, 302–10, 647–52; 2:501–5, 521–46, 602–6, 689, 692, 697–99; 3:353, 514–18; Thomas Watson, *A Body of Divinity* (1692; reprint, Carlisle, PA: Banner of Truth, 1958), 33–35, 45–50, 108–13, 133, 193, 209, 215–17, 220–21, 227–28, 238–39, 241, 250–51, 261–62, 267–68, 280–81; Charles Hodge, *Systematic Theology* (1873; reprint, Peabody: Hendrickson, 2001), 1:376–80, 477–78, 522–34; 2:639–41, 654–732; 3:29–36, 103–13, 185–87, 213–31. Thomas Watson's scholastic divinity is constructed on the Westminster Catechism, but the Westminster Catechism is itself a product of Puritan scholasticism. The seventeenth-century Puritan John Owen authored numerous works on the Holy Spirit. *The Works of John Owen,* ed. William H. Goold (reprint, Carlisle, PA: Banner of Truth, 1965), vols. 3, 4; Sinclair Ferguson, "John Owen and the Doctrine of the Holy Spirit," in *John Owen: The Man and His Theology,* ed. Robert W. Oliver (Phillipsburg: Presbyterian and Reformed, 2002), 101–29. Barth identifies a shift from the divine givenness of salvation through the Holy Spirit to a concern for personal assurance in salvation. Barth, *Theology of the Reformed Confessions,* 121–23, 135–47.

To discern the pneumatology of Protestant orthodoxy, one must turn to their discussions of Scripture, God, and salvation. When it comes to Scripture, the scholastics spoke of the inspiration of Scripture by God more than by the person of the Spirit. Calvin had advocated a simple theory of verbal inspiration, saying that the Scriptures were composed "under the Holy Spirit's dictation" and the human writers were the Spirit's "amanuenses." The scholastics developed the doctrine of verbal plenary inspiration and continued the Protestant doctrine of the illumination or testimony concerning Scripture. According to the Second Helvetic Confession, "instruction in true religion depends on the inward illumination of the Spirit." According to Francis Turretin, authentication of the Bible is due to "a threefold cause": the objective cause is the Bible's attesting to its divinity, the efficient cause is the Holy Spirit which induces belief, and the instrumental cause is the church through which we believe.

When it comes to the doctrine of God, the scholastic tradition continues Western orthodoxy. Scriptural and rational proofs are offered to affirm the Holy Spirit as a divine person, distinct from Father and Son, who proceeds from both Father and Son. When it comes to soteriology, the scholastic tradition usually teaches that the Spirit is responsible for all of the graces of salvation, from beginning to end. According to Watson, "every grace is a divine spark lighted in the soul by the Holy Ghost," and the Spirit is "the spring of all grace." Hodge agreed, saying, "A work of grace is a work of the Holy Spirit." Hodge defined seven types of grace: common, sufficient, efficacious, preventing, *gratia gratum faciens,* cooperating, and habitual. References to the sovereign work of the Spirit pepper the extended scholastic discussions of soteriology.[116]

Heterodox Responses

The scholastic tradition represents orthodox Protestantism, but there were numerous reactions in the seventeenth century. Among those opposing orthodoxy were Socinians, Arminians, Quakers, and Pietists. The Socinians followed the teachings of Faustus Socinus as embodied in the Racovian Catechism of 1605, which denies orthodox trinitarianism. The Arminians approve the theology advocated by Jacobus Arminius and the Remonstrants. Arminius opposed the strict Calvinism of the Dutch Reformed Church which emphasized divine predestination and downplayed human freedom. The soteriology of Arminius was anathematized by strict Calvinists at the Synod of Dort (1618–1619).

---

[116] Calvin, *Institutes,* 4.8.6, 4.8.9; González, *History of Christian Thought,* 3:262–63; Second Helvetic Confession (1566), in *The Creeds of Christendom with a History and Critical Notes,* 6th ed., ed. Philip Schaff (1931; reprint, Grand Rapids: Baker, 1993), 3:831–32; Turretin, *Institutes,* 1:63, 87. Watson, *Body of Divinity,* 113, 216; Hodge, *Systematic Theology,* 2:654–55.

In the writings of Arminius, the person of the Holy Spirit is treated in an orthodox manner, including double procession, his distinctiveness, and his deity. The work of the Holy Spirit, is, however, conceived differently. The Spirit can be resisted, for his grace only assists the sinner to salvation. Calvinists, such as Watson, believe the will must be overcome: "The Spirit with sweet violence conquers, or rather changes it." Arminius did not envision the Spirit overpowering but cooperating with the will. "All unregenerate persons have freedom of will, and a capability of resisting the Holy Spirit." The diminution of the Spirit's sovereignty may be seen in Arminius's *Letter on the Sin against the Holy Ghost.* Correlating ten passages which discuss sin against the Spirit, Arminius concluded that all sins against the Spirit are blasphemy against the Spirit.

Two types of persons commit this unforgivable sin, both of whom have been illumined by the Spirit: those who refuse to believe and those who have believed and then fall away. Arminianism sees the Holy Spirit working soteriologically in a wider group than the elect but at the expense of his sovereignty. Calvinists preserve the Spirit's sovereignty but narrow the effectual working of the Spirit to the elect. These contrasting emphases are evident in the assertion of the Arminian Remonstrants that the Spirit's grace is *auxilio,* assisting, and the response proffered by the Synod of Dort that the Spirit's regeneration is *efficacia,* effective.[117]

The Quakers of England, under George Fox, emphasized the internal, immediate working of the Holy Spirit. Fox knew spiritual truth before reading Scripture and expressed dismay when "Baptists and others" charged him with blind zeal since he only expressed what the Spirit said. William Barclay placed "divine inward revelations" by the Spirit above Scripture. "The Spirit is the first and principal Leader," while the Bible is "a secondary rule, subordinate to the Spirit." The Scriptures cannot be opposed to the inner light experienced by Christians, for they are "only a declaration of the fountain" and the fountain is the Spirit.

German Pietism developed in reaction to the "fleshly illusion of faith" and mere formalism seen in the orthodox clergy and laity. Extending the work of Johann Arndt, Philip Jacob Spener asserted that "godly faith does not exist without the Holy Spirit, nor can such faith continue when deliberate sins prevail." Spener encouraged Christians to seek moral perfection,

---

[117] Williams, *Radical Reformation,* 973–89, 1162–75; Holm, "Work of the Spirit," 108. R. David Rightmire, "Arminius, Jacobus," in *Biographical Dictionary of Christian Theologians,* ed. Patrick W. Carey and Joseph T. Lienhard (Peabody: Hendrickson, 2000), 30–31; Watson, *Body of Divinity,* 216–17; *The Works of James Arminius,* trans. James Nichols and William Nichols (1825–1875; reprint, Grand Rapids: Baker, 1986), 1:764; 2:20–22, 144–50, 395–403, 721, 731–54; *Articuli Arminiani sive Remonstrantia* (1610), arts. 4 and 5, in *Creeds of Christendom,* 547–48; *Canones Synodi Dordrechtanae* (1618–1619), heads 3 and 4 in articles 3, 4, and 11, in *Creeds of Christendom,* 564–65, 571–73, 588–90, 593–94.

although he recognized it is unattainable in this life, for sanctification by the Spirit can and is hindered by the human will. Spener ended his influential work with six methodological proposals to reform the church, and Pietism developed into an international conversionist movement but offered no major writings on the Holy Spirit.[118]

John Wesley and Perfectionism

The unique theology of John Wesley was influenced by Lockean empiricism, Arminian soteriology, Moravian piety, and the Anglican latitudinarian and high church movements. He was not a systematic writer but was eclectic and fluid, developing his theology with reference to an overarching concern for personal salvation resulting in holiness. Wesley preached little on the Trinity, even though it was under attack from several corners, preferring to focus on morality rather than theology. Turning empiricism in a religious direction, he taught that through the "spiritual senses," one may claim direct knowledge of God. Following Arminius, he sought a balance between human responsibility and divine grace. While affirming original sin, Wesley advanced the Arminian cause with his doctrine of "preventing" or "prevenient grace." Prevenient grace is a divine gift to all people that enables them to accept or reject the offer of salvation. Justification and sanctification are distinct, and sanctification necessarily follows justification. "The one [justification] implies what God does for us through His Son; the other, what he works in us by His Spirit."

Although Wesley defended justification by faith against detractors, he developed reservations, eventually adopting a position close to that of the Council of Trent, finding that works necessarily precede, follow, and complete salvation. Like Arminius, he limited the Spirit: "The Holy Spirit here represents himself as one who would be glad to spare sinners if he could."[119]

Wesley's overarching goal was to foster holiness in the Christian life. He sought assurance of his salvation by affirming salvation by faith alone through an instantaneous experience. This foundational event occurred for him at a meeting in Aldersgate Street in May 1538, where, he says, "I felt that I did trust in Christ, Christ alone for salvation." Although there are disagreements as to what exactly occurred in 1738, the experience of "assurance" was later identified by him as a distinct event subsequent to the

---

[118] George Fox, *A Journal* (1694), ed. Nigel Smith (New York: Penguin, 1998), 33, 440–41; *The Confession of the Society of Friends* (1675), in *Creeds of Christendom*, 3:790-91. Arndt, *True Christianity* (1606), trans. Peter Erb, Classics of Western Spirituality (New York: Paulist, 1979); Spener, *Pia Desideria* (1675), trans. Theodore G. Tappert (Minneapolis: Fortress, 1964), 64, 80, 85, 87–122; Bloesch, *Holy Spirit*, 119–25; Holm, "Work of the Spirit," 110–12.

[119] Henry D. Rack, *Reasonable Enthusiast: John Wesley and the Rise of Methodism*, 3rd ed. (London: Epworth, 2002), 24–42. Sermon 5, in *The Works of John Wesley*, 3rd ed. (1872–93), 400. Sermon 138, in *Works of John Wesley*, 7:487.

experience of justification. The subsequent experience of "assurance" verifies present salvation, not final perseverance, as that can be lost. Assurance comes through two sensible experiences of faith: observation of the fruit of the Spirit in one's life and the "Spirit witnessing with our spirit."

Assurance, however, is not the final goal; perfection is. Wesley fostered a doctrine that he called "Christian perfection" or "entire sanctification." In his *A Plain Account of Christian Perfection,* perfection delivers fully from sin, is received by mere faith in an instant, and can be received "now." Perfection, attainable in this life, is perceived on the one hand as an instantaneous second conversion and on the other as a continual process. After Wesley began teaching this doctrine, his followers experienced the second blessing in perfectionist revivals, but he never claimed to have reached it himself. When challenged by Calvinist opponents, he moderated his understanding of Christian perfection in this life, contrasting it with perfection in the next. Moreover, his conception of sin was severely limited to "a voluntary transgression of a known law which it is in our power to obey."[120]

Although some conclude Wesley was not a systematic theologian who effected major theological changes, it is clear that his "intellectually flawed" theology influenced later denominations. In the nineteenth century, while mainline Methodists largely followed Wesley's doctrine of progressive sanctification, Wesleyan Holiness denominations furthered his ideas of a second blessing. Charles Finney developed Wesley's Arminian evangelicalism into perfectionism, radicalizing Arminian soteriology in the process. According to Finney, justification is conditioned upon Christ's atonement, repentance, faith, present sanctification, and perseverance in faith and obedience. Baptism of the Holy Spirit, identified as instantaneous sanctification, is similarly conditional upon human effort. The role of the Holy Spirit is severely restricted to illumination.[121]

Radical perfectionists such as John Humphrey Noyes and the Oneida Community took Wesley's doctrines of second conversion and perfectionism into entire communism and eschatological promiscuity.[122] Reuben A. Torrey separated regeneration by the Holy Spirit from baptism with the Holy Spirit.

---

[120] *The Journal of John Wesley,* in *Works of John Wesley,* 1:98–104. Rack, *Reasonable Enthusiast,* 149–58. *A Plain Account of Christian Perfection,* in *Works of John Wesley,* 11:382–83. Sermon 40, in ibid., 6:1. Sermon 76, in ibid., 6:411–24; Rack, *Reasonable Enthusiast,* 397–400. Letter to Mrs. Pendarves (1731), cited in ibid., 399.

[121] Rack, *Reasonable Enthusiast,* 408–9. Cf. Thomas A. Langford, *Methodist Theology* (Peterborough: Epworth, 1998), 13–14, 67–71. Charles Finney, *Finney's Systematic Theology,* new expanded ed. (1878; reprint, Minneapolis: Bethany House, 1994), 363–69. John L. Gresham Jr., *Charles G. Finney's Doctrine of the Baptism of the Holy Spirit* (Peabody: Hendrickson, 1987), 58–63; Warfield, *Perfectionism,* in *Works of Benjamin B. Warfield,* 8:203.

[122] Warfield, *Perfectionism,* in *Works of Benjamin B. Warfield,* 8:219–333.

It is one thing to have the Holy Spirit dwell within us, perhaps dwelling within us way back in some hidden sanctuary of our being, back of definite consciousness, and something far different, something vastly more, to have the Holy Spirit take complete possession of the one whom he inhabits.[123]

Pentecostals, who have roots in the apocryphal rediscovery of the gift of tongues by Charles Parham in Topeka, Kansas, in 1901 and in the Azusa Street revivals in Los Angeles, California, in 1906, have equated the second blessing with baptism in the Holy Spirit as necessarily evidenced by speaking in unknown tongues. The later charismatic movement also attempted to recover the spiritual gifts, most spectacularly through "signs and wonders" and other "faith" ministries. "Charismatic" is used to classify a broad grouping of individuals and churches from many denominations, Protestant and Catholic, that has grown tremendously, especially in the developing world. Charismatics commonly seek after further blessing or a deepening of faith through practicing the primitive gifts.

A friendly critic says the real question for the charismatic movement is, are the gifts of the Spirit manifested in it really legitimate? Another friendly critic questions the movement's emphasis on the immediate as well as its construal of Scripture, superficial spirituality, and interiority. Some Southern Baptists, including foreign missionaries, have likewise rejoiced in the "fresh excitement" of the miraculous in spite of seminary training.[124]

Philosophers and Liberals

The Enlightenment of the eighteenth century was "a value-system rooted in rationality" inspired by the recovery of classical pagan learning. Many of this philosophical movement's proponents, including its continental rationalist and British empiricist wings, were anticlerical and antisupernatural in outlook. Others, such as Georg Hegel and Immanuel Kant, incorporated Christianity into their systems but profoundly altered theology. Those aspiring to reconcile Christianity with the new rationalistic temperament were accused of treachery for their efforts. The antitheistic French philosopher Voltaire believed theologians were wasting their lives. The transcendence of God was diminished in favor of his immanence, especially by the

---

[123] Reuben A. Torrey, *The Baptism with the Holy Spirit* (New York: Fleming Revell, 1895); idem, *The Person and Work of the Holy Spirit* (1910; reprint, New Kensington, PA: Whitaker House, 1996), 193. Cf. Richard Gilbertson, *The Baptism of the Holy Spirit: The Views of A. B. Simpson and His Contemporaries* (Camp Hill: Christian Publications, 1993).

[124] Robert M. Anderson, *Vision of the Disinherited: The Making of American Pentecostalism* (Peabody: Hendrickson, 1979), 47–97. Badcock, *Light of Truth and Fire of Love: A Theology of the Holy Spirit* (Grand Rapids: Eerdsmans, 1997), 137. Congar, *I Believe in the Holy Spirit*, 2:165–69. Erich Bridges, "Acts of God," *The Commission* (January–February 2003): 6–18.

Deists, who pictured God as having created the world and then leaving it to function according to natural law.[125] Although Enlightenment philosophers and theologians did not seek to address the Spirit in particular, their concerns for reasonable religion and divine immanence inevitably impacted pneumatology.

Hegel developed a philosophical view of *Geist,* "Spirit," whose immanence is so severe that it displays elements of pantheism. In a work first published in 1807, Hegel claimed that Spirit is the self-awareness of the essence of universality, the Absolute. As universal essence, Spirit opposes itself into individuality in the activity of human spirits, and through historical process comes to self-awareness. In *The Philosophy of Right* of 1821, the Spirit is said to develop itself through world history in the nations, modern Germany being the highest self-achievement of the Spirit. In *The Philosophy of History,* "the Kingdom of the Spirit" began with the Reformation "principle of free spirit" and realized itself in German Christianity. While Hegel related the Spirit to the world and history, his extreme immanence was problematic for orthodox Christians who sought to maintain a balance between immanence and transcendence.[126]

Hegel's immanent Spirit found parallels in the theological inventions of Friedrich Schleiermacher, "the father of theological liberalism," whose Pietism predisposed him against orthodoxy. In *On Religion: Speeches to Its Cultured Despisers* (1799), Schleiermacher pictured a religion of the "world spirit" that discovers itself in human spirits. "To join the different moments of humanity to one another and, from its succession, to divine the spirit in which the whole is directed, that is religion's highest concern." This process of self-discovery occurs when the human spirit is "intuiting itself." Schleiermacher defined intuition as "feeling," distinguished from "knowing" and "doing."[127] Although he mentioned Christ and the Spirit, they are merely aids to personal consciousness and freedom and have parallels in other religions. In the 1804 dialogue, *Christmas Eve,* he again

---

[125] Ernst Cassirer, *The Philosophy of the Enlightenment* (1932), cited in Dorinda Outram, *The Enlightenment* (New York: Cambridge University Press, 1995), 3; Peter Gay, *The Enlightenment: The Rise of Modern Paganism* (New York: Norton, 1966). "The Treason of the Clerks," in Gay, *Enlightenment,* 336–57; Voltaire, *Philosophical Dictionary* (1764), s.v., "Theologian," cited in Outram, *Enlightenment,* 31. Outram, *Enlightenment,* ch. 4.

[126] G. W. F. Hegel, *The Phenomenology of Spirit,* trans. A. V. Miller (New York: Oxford University Press, 1977), 438–47; idem, *The Philosophy of Right,* trans. T. M. Knox, Great Books of the Western World (Chicago: Encyclopaedia Britannica, 1952), 341–60; idem, *The Philosophy of History,* trans. J. Sibree (Chicago: Encyclopaedia Britannica, 1952), 315–17. Frederick Copleston, *A History of Philosophy* (New Jersey: Paulist, 1963), 7:159–247. Cf. Stanley J. Grenz, *Theology for the Community of God* (Grand Rapids: Eerdmans, 1994), 82–84.

[127] C. W. Christian, *Friedrich Schleiermacher,* Makers of the Modern Theological Mind (Waco: Word, 1979), 36–37, 51–56. Schleiermacher, *On Religion: Speeches to Its Cultured Despisers,* 2nd ed., trans. Richard Crouter (New York: Cambridge University Press, 1996), 43, 60, 75, 132.

defined man-in-himself as the "Earth-spirit" and the human individual as the place where the earth achieves self-awareness.[128]

Schleiermacher's theological method is man centered, experiential, and verified by the feeling of absolute dependence. God is thereby depersonalized while man becomes intensely personalized. This transformation of theology into anthropology is evident in his systematic theology where the "common spirit" of human nature, the nation, or the church displaces the trinitarian doctrine of the Holy Spirit. "What we wish to denote by the expression 'Holy Spirit' would be exactly the same thing as the racial consciousness." The doctrine of the Trinity, normally treated near the beginning of systematic theology, is thus treated as a secondary doctrine requiring reconstruction.[129]

On Schleiermacher's foundation, theological liberalism undermines many orthodox doctrines. Liberalism is difficult for many Christians to discern because it "makes use of traditional Christian terminology," although it is "a totally diverse type of religious belief" that is "un-Christian" because it has forsaken revelation for modern reason.[130] The Spirit becomes equated through immanence with humanity. "The Spirit is in us," says Paul Tillich, as he dismisses the objective character of orthodoxy. The orthodox doctrines of the Trinity are dismissed as pagan hellenistic constructs.

"The Christian religion on Greek soil entered the proscribed circle of the native religious philosophy and has remained there," asserts Adolf von Harnack. Reason negates the supernatural so the highest form of religion becomes ethics, a rationalist form of perfection. Jesus Christ is an example to follow that shows God is love and need not be feared. Albrecht Ritschl believed that sin is an illusion and that salvation is entirely dependent on a mere change in human attitude. Reason is elevated in authority, and higher criticism eats away at the foundations of scriptural authority.

According to a recent proponent of liberalism, the inspiration of an inerrant Bible by the Holy Spirit must now be considered simply "inadequate." The twentieth century witnesses efforts by some theologians to begin reclaiming an orthodox doctrine of the Holy Spirit, especially with Emil Brunner and Karl Barth. Brunner believes man can only experience Christ as a result of the work of the Holy Spirit. In a conscious rejection of

---

[128] Schleiermacher, *On Religion,* 191, 219–20, 232. Richard R. Niebuhr, *Schleiermacher on Christ and Religion: A New Introduction* (New York: Scribner, 1964), 64.

[129] Stanley J. Grenz and Roger E. Olson, *20th Century Theology: God and the World in a Transitional Age* (Downers Grove: InterVarsity, 1992), 43. Niebuhr, *Schleiermacher on Christ and Religion,* 16. Schleiermacher, *The Christian Faith,* 2nd ed., trans. H. R. Mackintosh and J. S. Stewart (Edinburgh: T&T Clark, 1928), §§ 121, 170–72.

[130] J. Gresham Machen, *Christianity & Liberalism* (Grand Rapids: Eerdmans, 1923), 2, 7.

Schleiermacher's method, Barth bases his systematic theology on a trinitarian foundation.[131] Orthodoxy is furthered in the systematic section.

How Does It All Fit Together?

As noted above, Dagg writes that "the study of the Holy Spirit's character and office, will be a source of delight."[132] By "character and office," Dagg distinguishes the Spirit's person from his work. The person of the Holy Spirit will be considered first. Second, the work of the Holy Spirit will be addressed. Finally, some errors concerning the Spirit will be explained.

The Person of the Holy Spirit

Following earlier Baptist theologians, who typically devoted space to such a discussion, the person of the Holy Spirit will be considered according to three major concerns: his deity, his distinction from the Father and the Son, and his personhood. Before explaining this threefold positive definition, however, three foundational notes about the Spirit and trinitarian relations are considered.

Foundational Notes

First, in considering God as Spirit, a distinction is maintained between spirituality as an attribute of God and the Holy Spirit as the third person of the Trinity. "In the name Spirit two things are included: First, His nature or essence, namely that he is a pure, spiritual, or immaterial substance; . . . [and second, the name is] characteristical of the third person in the Trinity." One of the attributes of God, an eternal characteristic of deity, is that God is spiritual. Dagg notes two classes of substance: mind and matter. Matter has extension, solidity, divisibility, figure, and color while mind is capable of perceiving, remembering, judging, and willing. "The term spirit is used to denote an immaterial and intelligent substance, or being; one which is without the peculiar properties of matter, and possesses properties analogous to those of the human mind. In this sense, God is a spirit." John Gill agrees: "God as essentially considered, is said to be a Spirit, i.e., a spiritual Substance." Since God is Spirit, all three persons in the Godhead are spirit, too. All three persons

---

[131] Paul Tillich, *Perspectives on 19th and 20th Century Protestant Theology* (New York: Harper & Row, 1967), 21. Cf. Grenz and Olson, *20th Century Theology*, 11–13. Adolf Harnack, *What Is Christianity?*, trans. Thomas Bailey Saunders (New York: Harper & Brothers, 1957), 228–37. Warfield, *Perfectionism*, in *Works of Benjamin B. Warfield*, 7:55–60. Daniel L. Migliore, *Faith Seeking Understanding: An Introduction to Christian Theology*, 2nd ed. (Grand Rapids: Eerdmans, 2004), 47–49. Holm, "The Work of the Spirit," in *Holy Spirit in the Life of the Church*, ed. Paul D. Opsahl, 120–23.

[132] Dagg, *Manual of Theology* (Charleston: Southern Baptist Publication Society, 1859), 235.

also have the common divine attribute of holiness. In this way we can say that all three persons are both holy and spirit. However, the third person of the Godhead alone is called "Holy Spirit." The term "Holy Spirit" refers "to a special person in the divine being distinct from the Father and the Son."[133]

The second foundational note concerns Karl Rahner's *Grundaxiom,* "foundational axiom," which states that the economic Trinity is the immanent Trinity and vice versa. Although Congar makes legitimate qualifications, it is nevertheless necessary to affirm that the economic Trinity reveals the essential Trinity. God acts in history as three persons because he is in eternity three persons. This axiom is a necessary corollary to the doctrine of inspiration by the Holy Spirit. It has been speculated that the number of persons in the Godhead may be greater than that which has been revealed. Rebuking such speculation, we note that because the Spirit is divine, the divine attribute of perfection protects his inspiration from misrepresenting himself.[134] In other words, Christians may discern who the Spirit is by recounting what the Spirit does.

The third foundational note concerns a paucity of treatment of the person of the Holy Spirit by evangelicals in the last century. For instance, the idea that the Holy Spirit is the love between the Father and the Son— an idea rooted in the exegetical work of Augustine and developed in the Western filioque—is not seriously treated by Baptist writers. Such neglect toward divine ontology is not a conscious rejection of Christian tradition, but it betrays a preoccupation with modern ideas concerning the work of the Spirit. Indeed, most twentieth-century Baptist writers on the Holy Spirit have focused, often exclusively, upon his work. Those Southern Baptist writers who have dealt with his person have done so only summarily while addressing contemporary concerns about the Spirit's work.[135]

---

[133] Owen, *Pneumatologia,* in *The Works of John Owen,* 3:54–55; Dagg, *Manual of Theology,* 56–57; John Gill, *The Doctrine of the Trinity Stated and Vindicated,* ch. 9; cf. Augustine, *The Trinity* 15.5.37; Herman Bavinck, *Reformed Dogmatics,* vol. 2, *God and Creation,* trans. John Vriend (Grand Rapids: Baker, 2004), 277.

[134] Karl Rahner, *The Trinity,* trans. Joseph Donceel (Tunbridge Wells: Burns & Oates, 1970), 22; idem, *Theological Investigations,* trans. Kevin Smith (Baltimore: Helicon, 1966), 4:77–102; Congar, *I Believe in the Holy Spirit,* 3:11–17; John G. Stackhouse Jr., *Evangelical Landscapes: Facing Critical Issues of the Day* (Grand Rapids: Baker, 2002), 168–69.

[135] Augustine, *The Trinity* 15.5. Cf. B. H. Carroll, *The Holy Spirit: Comprising a Discussion of the Paraclete, the Other Self of Jesus, and Other Phases of the Work of the Spirit of God* (Grand Rapids: Zondervan, 1939); Walter Thomas Conner, *The Work of the Holy Spirit: A Treatment of the Biblical Doctrine of the Divine Spirit* (Nashville: Broadman, 1949); Criswell, *The Holy Spirit in Today's World*; Billy Graham, *The Holy Spirit: Activating God's Power in Your Life* (Waco: Word Publishing, 1978); Kenneth S. Hemphill, *Spiritual Gifts: Empowering the New Testament Church* (Nashville: Broadman, 1988); Herschel H. Hobbs, *The Holy Spirit: Believer's Guide* (Nashville: Broadman, 1967); Landrum P. Leavell II, *The Doctrine of the Holy Spirit* (Nashville: Convention, 1983); Ramm, *The Witness of the Spirit*; William Thomas Rouse, *The Holy Spirit* (Nashville: Sunday School Board, 1935); Ward, *The Holy Spirit*; H. Wheeler Robinson, *The Christian Experience of the Holy Spirit* (London: Nisbet, 1947).

The Deity of the Holy Spirit

First among the major considerations on the person of the Holy Spirit is his deity. Almost nonchalantly, Dagg in the nineteenth century affirmed, "The Holy Spirit is God." But Dagg reflected two millennia of theological tradition in uttering this simple yet profound truth. In their disputes with Arianism, the Eastern fathers affirmed the Spirit's deity as a necessary corollary of salvation. According to Athanasius, the Spirit is *homoousios* with the Father and the Son because if the Spirit is not God, he cannot conform us to the Son and unite us to the Father. Nazianzus, without reservation, claimed the Holy Spirit is God. A later theologian connected the divine Spirit with human salvation: "There is no salvation or communion with God apart from the Holy Spirit. Only if the Holy Spirit is truly God can he impart to us the Father and the Son. He who gives us God himself must himself truly be God."[136]

Dagg provides seven biblical reasons we can affirm the Holy Spirit is God: First, he is equally included with the Father and the Son in the baptismal commission (Matt. 28:19–20). Second, he is equally offered prayer with the Father and the Son in the benediction (2 Cor. 13:14). Third, the temple of God is the temple of the Holy Spirit (1 Cor. 3:16). Fourth, sin against the Holy Spirit is sin against God (Acts 5:3–4). Fifth, Old Testament passages concerning Yahweh are applied to the Holy Spirit in the New Testament (cf. Exod. 17:7 with Heb. 3:9; Isa. 6:8 with Acts 28:25; Jer. 31:31–34 with Heb. 10:15–17). Sixth, the divine attributes of eternity, omnipresence, and omnipotence are applied to him. And seventh, the divine works of creation, providence, miracles, and resurrection are ascribed to the Spirit.[137]

Historically, orthodox theologians have refuted those who would reduce the Spirit from the status of being God himself to being merely a divine force or influence. William Thomas Rouse agrees: "It is a long way from that conception of the Holy Spirit which regards him as an influence in the world and that which conceives of him as very God; but that the latter is correct and in keeping with the Word of God, is very evident." Upon reviewing the scriptural and historical evidence, Barth concluded, "The Holy Spirit is no less and no other than God Himself, distinct from Him whom Jesus calls His Father, distinct also from Jesus Himself, yet no less than the Father, and no less than Jesus." The Spirit is "God Himself, altogether God."[138]

The Distinctiveness of the Holy Spirit

Gill taught that the Spirit is "a distinct Person, both from the Father and the Son." The language of three *hypostaseis* or *prosōpa* alongside the one

---

[136] Dagg, *Manual of Theology,* 238; Congar, *I Believe in the Holy Spirit,* 3:29–33; Bavinck, *Reformed Dogmatics,* 2:259.

[137] Dagg, *Manual of Theology,* 239–40.

[138] Rouse, *Holy Spirit,* 28; Barth, *Church Dogmatics,* I/1:459.

ousia was used by the Cappadocians to describe the relative distinctions within the Godhead. At first, there was some confusion concerning the terminology. Athanasius did not distinguish between *ousia* and *hypostasis*, and the literal translation of the Greek *hypostasis* was the Latin *substantia* rather than *personam*. The exact terminology was not as important as the affirmation of the truths of the immanent Trinity revealed in Scripture. One should be "looking, not so much at the terms used, as at the thoughts they were meant to convey." Dagg would agree. Although he knew the terms "Trinity" and "Person" were not used in Scripture, we are "at liberty to use" such terms out of convenience.[139]

Premier among the revealed truths about the immanent relation of the Holy Spirit is his eternal procession from the Father (John 15:26). Alongside John's witness is Paul's statement that the church has access "to" the Father "through" Christ "in" the Spirit (Eph. 2:18). The Eastern fathers took a literal approach to the biblical witness concerning the procession of the Spirit, construing it in terms that preserved the monarchy of the Father. As seen above, arguments between East and West over the procession of the Spirit from the Father "through the Son" (Eastern preference) or from the Father "and the Son" (Western preference) are perennial. Baptist theologians have demonstrated their Western roots by affirming the double procession. However, Dagg's language strikes an Eastern note with a "stream of mercy" that "flows" from the Father through the Son in the Holy Spirit. Like the orthodox theologians, Dagg affirms the functional subordination of the Spirit and the Son to the Father, while maintaining their essential equality.[140]

Gill lists five proofs that the Spirit is distinct from the Father and the Son: First, his procession is from them both. Second, his mission is from them both. Third, he is identified as "another Comforter." Fourth, he makes distinct appearances alongside both the Father and the Son. Finally, he is listed distinctly in the baptismal formula. Historically, the Spirit's distinction from the Father and the Son has been discussed in terms of subsistent relations or origination. Christians affirm that all three persons are uncreated and eternally subsist in the divine essence. The Father is ungenerate and unproceeding source. "Generation expresses the Son's distinct mode of subsisting in the divine essence." Procession or "spiration may also express the Spirit's distinct mode of subsisting therein."[141]

---

[139] Gill, *Body of Doctrinal Divinity*, 168; Gregory of Nazianzus, *Theological Orations* 5.24, in *NPNF*[2], 7:325; Dagg, *Manual of Theology*, 251–52.

[140] Ibid., 255–57, 333.

[141] Gill, *The Doctrine of the Trinity Stated and Vindicated*, ch. 9.

The Personhood of the Holy Spirit

Boyce lists several scriptural reasons the Spirit may be called a person. Premier among them are that the Holy Spirit displays personal characteristics in his actions and that personal pronouns are used to describe him. Conner offered a constituent definition of personality as including intelligence, moral discrimination, and purposiveness, each of which the Spirit displays. Calvin defined the divine persons as distinctions though not divisions within the Godhead. A "person" is "a subsistence in God's essence, which, while related to the others, is distinguished by an incommunicable quality. By the term 'subsistence' we would understand something different from 'essence.'" The eternal deity of the Spirit is evident in his divine work in creation and redemption and by "express testimonies" in Scripture. In the timelessness of the Trinity, there is yet an "order" among the persons. The Spirit essentially proceeds from Father and Son.[142]

More recently, Karl Barth and John Zizioulas taught that "person" in the Godhead should not be construed inappropriately. While in classical Latin, a *persona* was a mask used in a play, Christians do not understand the three *personae* in the Godhead in the modalistic manner of an actor in a play easily changing his character. Moreover, neither the classical understanding nor the Christian understanding regarding *personam* conveyed anything akin to modern individualism with its emphasis on independent psychological categories. The orthodox conception of the person of the Holy Spirit (or the Father or the Son) is of a subsistent relation within the Godhead. Against modern mechanistic misdefinitions of "person" and "personality," emphasis should be placed upon the relational aspects of personhood. Persons are defined by their relations to and identity with other persons. The relations of the divine persons must not be confused with nonbiblical definitions of human personhood. Conner agrees that the three distinctions in the Godhead may be called persons only "in a modified sense," and that emphasis should be placed on "the social" rather than "the individual" aspect of personality.[143] This relational emphasis is rooted in the Western teaching that the Spirit is *vinculum caritatis,* the bond of love, between the Father and the Son.

---

[142] James P. Boyce, *Abstract of Systematic Theology* (Louisville: C. T. Dearing, 1882), 131–32; Conner, *Work of the Holy Spirit,* 177–81; Calvin, *Institutes,* 1.13.6, 1.13.14–15, 1.13.18; Wendel, *Calvin,* 168; Warfield, *Calvin and Calvinism,* 224–37.

[143] Barth chose to use the terminology "modes (or ways) of being" but distanced himself from the heresy of modalism. *Church Dogmatics,* I/1:353–68. John Zizioulas, *Being as Communion: Studies in Personhood and Church* (Crestwood, NY: St. Vladimir's Seminary Press, 1985), 27–65; Conner, *Work of the Holy Spirit,* 182–84.

The Work of the Holy Spirit

The work of the Spirit is considered according to his roles as Creator, governor, revealer, companion of Christ, re-Creator, companion of the church, and witness and judge. Before addressing this sevenfold definition, two foundational notes concerning the work of the Spirit are considered.

Foundational Notes

The first foundational note concerns the way in which Baptist systematicians have intimately correlated the person of the Spirit with his work. Baptists place the Spirit alongside the other persons of the Trinity, at first by showing he was a party to the eternal covenant.[144] This represented a development away from the Reformed tradition, which emphasized the covenant was "between the Father and the Son, about the redemption of the elect." Although the Spirit was allowed to apply the grace of the covenant, some Reformed theologians did not explicitly make him a party to the covenant.[145] Gill pioneered the Baptist response in that, while agreeing with the Reformed that the covenant "was especially between the Father and the Son," the Holy Spirit was still "not a mere bystander, spectator, and witness." The Spirit is "a party concerned," having assented in the eternal counsel to carrying out the covenant.

Dagg rejected Reformed covenantal binitarianism in favor of covenantal trinitarianism: "The Holy Spirit concurs in this arrangement, and takes his part in the work, in harmony with the other persons of the Godhead." Boyce, apart from the language of covenant, furthers the trinitarian scheme, discerning concurrence between the "personal relations in the Trinity" and the "outward relations of the Trinity," even using the latter to structure his systematic theology. Mullins, Conner, and Garrett retain this close correlation between the Spirit's place within the essential Trinity (*ad intra*) and the external work of the economic Trinity (*ad extra*), either in statement or in outline. According to Conner, the two major works of

---

[144] The origins of the covenant tradition are disputed but have a basis in the works of William Tyndale, Heinrich Bullinger, and John Calvin. Leonard J. Trinterud, "The Origins of Puritanism," *Church History* 20 (1951): 37–57; Calvin, *Institutes,* 2.10.1, including the note in LCC, 20.428; Cornelis P. Venema, *Heinrich Bullinger and the Doctrine of Predestination: Author of "the Other Reformed Tradition"?* (Grand Rapids: Baker, 2002), 27–32.

[145] Confession of Faith Put Forth by the Elders and Brethren of Many Congregations of Christians (Baptized upon Profession of Their Faith) (London, 1677), vii.iii. This confession, also known as the Second London Confession, was a Particular Baptist work. John Gill, a Particular Baptist, was well aware of the binitarian covenant, having sponsored the printing of Witsius's standard work on the subject. Cf. *The Work of William Perkins,* ed. Ian Breward (Abingdon: Sutton Courtenay, 1970), 91; Herman Witsius, *The Economy of the Covenants between God and Man: Comprehending a Complete Body of Divinity* (1693), trans. William Crookshank (1822; reprint, Escondido, CA: Den Dulk, 1990), 1:v, 163–92; Turretin, *Institutes,* xii.ii.v–ix, 2:175–76; Hodge, *Systematic Theology,* 2:359–60.

creation and redemption "might thus come to be seen as grounded in the trinitarian relations in the Godhead."[146]

The second foundational note concerns the common yet distinct operations of the Father, the Son, and the Holy Spirit. There is a trinitarian unity in all the major divine works. Dagg writes that, as "the three divine Persons co-operate in man's salvation according to an eternal covenant," so the Trinity's "agreement and co-operation extend to all the works of God." Conner agrees: "The work of the Son is the work of the Father, and the work of the Spirit is the work of the Son. The work of one is the work of all, and each works in and through the others." However, "the divine Persons co-operate in different offices." Boyce teaches a subordination in office which arises from a subordination in personal relations. This subordination is "in no respect inconsistent with the perfect equality of the persons." Dagg concurs: "The fulness of the Godhead dwells in each of the divine Persons." In his reading of Scripture, Henry Wheeler Robinson contrasts "a line of intensive approach, always in the Spirit, always through Christ, always to the Father" (Eph. 2:18) with the three "equidistant" *hypostases* evident in the benediction (2 Cor. 13:14) and the baptismal formula (Matt. 28:19).[147]

Boyce believes that in each of the major works—creation, providence, and redemption—the source of the work is the Father, the mediator is the Son, and the operating agent is the Spirit. Carroll names the Spirit "the administrator" of the divine will. The Spirit's administration is rooted in the *oikonomia* of the Trinity. The Spirit perfects or brings to completion the work and will of the Godhead. Referring to the eternal counsels of the Trinity, Ambrose of Milan proclaimed that "the Spirit is the Arbiter of the Divine Counsel."[148] With this understanding that the Spirit participates in the entire divine work yet has a particular role in its application, we turn to his sevenfold administration of the divine will.

The Spirit as Creator

Hovering over creation in the beginning, the Spirit executed the divine will (Gen. 1:2–3). The Spirit and the Word were involved in creation to-

---

[146] Gill, *Body of Doctrinal Divinity*, 214, 244–46; Dagg, *Manual of Theology*, 255; Boyce, *Abstract of Systematic Theology*, 136–55, 156–66, 234–36; Mullins, *Christian Religion in Its Doctrinal Expression*, 359–65; Conner, *Work of the Holy Spirit*, 187; Garrett, *Systematic Theology*, 2:133–39. A trinitarian view of the covenant is also evident in Jonathan Edwards. Stephen R. Holmes, *God of Grace & God of Glory: An Account of the Theology of Jonathan Edwards* (Grand Rapids: Eerdmans, 2001), 134.

[147] Dagg, *Manual of Theology*, 253–55; Conner, *Work of the Holy Spirit*, 187; Boyce, *Abstract of Systematic Theology*, 154; Wheeler Robinson, *Christian Experience of the Holy Spirit*, 230–33.

[148] Boyce, *Abstract of Systematic Theology*, 157; Carroll, *Holy Spirit*, 20–21; Thomas C. Oden, *Life in the Spirit: Systematic Theology: Volume 3* (New York: HarperCollins, 1992), 32; Ambrose, *On the Holy Spirit* 2.21.

gether (Ps. 33:6). The Spirit's creative activity concerns both creation in general and man in particular. Generally, without the divine breath, the beauty of the skies would not exist (Job 26:13–14). Particularly, the breath of mankind is entirely dependent on the breath of God (Gen. 2:7; 6:3; Job 27:3; 33:4; 34:14; Ps. 104:29). Without the Spirit there is no life, human or otherwise. John 6:63 describes the Spirit as "the giver of life." The biblical symbol or "emblem" of the dove is often identified with the Spirit of God in his role as beginner of something new. "It is clear that the divine Spirit is not a creature, but takes part in the act of creation. The Father creates all things through the Word in the Spirit."[149]

The human spirit is utterly dependent upon the divine Spirit for its creation and sustenance. The human "spirit"—intimately related to "heart," "conscience," "mind," "image," and "soul"—is that aspect of man with which the divine Spirit communicates. "In other words, for man to receive spirit, man must be spirit in himself." Wheeler Robinson assumes "a real kinship between the human spirit and the divine." The spirit of man enables him to relate to God. Barth warns, however, that "the Holy Spirit is not identical with the human spirit"; rather, "He meets it." Arnold Come states, "As creature, man is 'over against' God, but as spirit he is created for relationship with God." Because of sin, man's spirit is perverted, and though the human spirit inherently "aspires" for God, the divine Spirit must graciously restore the human spirit for relationship with a holy God.[150] The Spirit thus both creates and re-creates (Ps. 104:30).

The Spirit as Governor

The Holy Spirit not only creates but also sustains and governs his creation. His government reflects his sovereignty and is displayed in providence. The biblical evidence for the Spirit's sovereignty is strong. First, there is the imagery of the Holy Spirit as the "finger of God," which signifies the "unity of power" in the Trinity. Second, there is the emblem of the Spirit as "wind." Jesus said the Spirit "blows where He wishes," signifying not only that he is invisible but also that he is beyond human control (John 3:8). Third, Paul said the Spirit is autonomous in his dispersion of gifts (1 Cor. 12:11). C. R. Vaughn has shown that the Spirit "gifts" both believers and unbelievers, both before and after the coming of Christ. "For the Holy Spirit is not subject to any foreign power or law, but is the Arbiter

---

[149] Criswell, *Holy Spirit in Today's World*, 69–70; Hawthorne, *The Presence and the Power*, 125–26; Kärkkäinen, *Pneumatology*, 25; Oden, *Life in the Spirit*, 44; Athanasius, *Letter to Serapion* 3.5, quoted by Denis Edwards, *Breath of Life: A Theology of the Creator Spirit* (Maryknoll: Orbis, 2004), 41.

[150] Arnold B. Come, *Human Spirit and Holy Spirit* (Philadelphia: Westminster, 1959), 73, 99; Robinson, *Christian Experience of the Holy Spirit*, 285; Heron, *Holy Spirit*, 120–30; Barth, *Dogmatics in Outline*, trans. G. T. Thomson (New York: Harper, 1959), 140; George S. Hendry, *The Holy Spirit in Christian Theology* (Philadelphia: Westminster, 1956), 96–117.

of His own freedom, dividing all things according to the decision of His own will, to each, as we read, severally as He wills."[151] The Spirit's sovereignty is displayed in all of his major works but especially in providence and salvation.

The Spirit as governor works in providence. As reviewed above, Hegel believes *Geist* is world history in process working through the dialectic of thesis, antithesis, and synthesis. Although Hegel confuses Creator and creation, his insight recalls the dynamic aspect of the Spirit's work, especially his involvement in history. Others discern a working of the Spirit in history without embracing Hegel's pantheism. Herbert Butterfield, a highly respected British historian, concluded after years of investigation into historiography that "in the workings of history there must be felt the movement of a living God." He called this pattern of working "Providence." Vaughn finds biblical and theological reasons for the Spirit's role in providence. Theologically, the general truth of the divine activity of providence must be particularly applied to the divine Spirit. Biblically, the Spirit's role is that of the restraint of evil in human community (2 Thess. 2:6–7).

> He exerts that grand restraining influence without which there can be no such things as home, society, government, civilization, or individual enjoyment anywhere among all the millions of the sinning human race. He restrains both the sinful acts and the natural tendencies of the acts within some tolerable bounds."

The Spirit is to be credited with giving virtues to unconverted men, rulers to stabilize society, general respect for law, even the arts and sciences. "There is no work or thought or achievement of humanity that can be called good, true or beautiful that is not premised by the Spirit's gift.[152]

The Spirit guides history to achieve the divine will at both the personal and universal levels. This truth is exemplified in Augustine of Hippo. In his *Confessions,* Augustine presented personal history as the outworking of divine providence prior to, during, and after his conversion. Augustine praised God because "you made us for yourself and our hearts find no peace until they rest in you." Through all of Augustine's circumstances, even in his misery, God patiently drew him into a personal relationship. In

---

[151] Ambrose, *Of the Holy Spirit* 3.31; Criswell, *Holy Spirit in Today's World,* 83–84; Oden, *Life in the Spirit,* 42; C. R. Vaughan, *The Gifts of the Holy Spirit: To Unbelievers and Believers* (1894; reprint, Carlisle, PA: Banner of Truth, 1994); Ambrose, *Of the Holy Spirit* 1.18.

[152] Grenz, *Theology for the Community of God,* 82–83; Oden, *Life in the Spirit,* 35–36; idem, *The Rebirth of Orthodoxy: Signs of New Life in Christianity* (San Francisco: HarperCollins, 2003), 47–48, 117–22; Herbert Butterfield, *Christianity and History* (New York: Scribner, 1950), 111; Vaughn, *Gifts of the Holy Spirit,* 26, 32–33.

The City of God, Augustine presented world history as the outworking of divine providence. History is "being shaped and guided by the indwelling Spirit of God even in the midst of natural disorders and human follies." Boyce agrees, distinguishing general providence from special providence. God governs all things yet without violating human free will or ascribing evil to God. "The universal Spirit [is] everywhere operating, though much of the mysterious and incomprehensible is therein involved."[153]

The Spirit as Revealer

The Holy Spirit superintends the entire process of revelation, "not only universally in the history of the cosmos and of the nations, but also redemptively." David Dockery defines *revelation* as "an uncovering, a removal of the veil, a disclosure of what was previously unknown." This revelation is both general and particular. First, the Spirit superintends general revelation. Since Christ is "the true Light which, coming into the world, enlightens every man" (John 1:9), Augustine developed a theory of illumination conceiving all knowledge as divine gift. Carl Henry focused on revelation as the self-disclosure of God. Since nobody knows the things of God except for the Spirit of God (1 Cor. 2:9–11), Henry concluded, "Human beings know only what God has chosen to reveal concerning the spiritual world." General revelation is limited to the discovery of divine existence and human culpability.[154]

Second, the Spirit superintends particular revelation. "Among the divine works of art produced by the Holy Spirit, the Sacred Scripture stands first." Henry outlined the Spirit's overarching superintendence of Scripture according to an epistemological system consisting of inspiration, inerrancy, infallibility, canonization, illumination, evangelism, and regeneration. Inspiration is "a supernatural influence upon divinely chosen prophets and apostles whereby the Spirit of God assures the truth and trustworthiness of their oral and written proclamation." Derived from inspiration, inerrancy resulted when "the Holy Spirit superintended the scriptural writers in communicating the biblical message in ways consistent with their differing personalities, literary styles and cultural background, while safeguarding them from error." Infallibility means the Spirit kept extant copies of the autographs reliable. Canonization occurred when "only those letters which the Spirit of God so intended were preserved in the canon" by the church.

---

[153] Augustine, *Confessions,* trans. R. S. Pine-Coffin (New York: Penguin, 1961), 1.1, 6.16, 8.12; Mary T. Clark, *Augustine* (New York: Continuum, 1994), 94–97; Boyce, *Abstract of Systematic Theology,* 223–29.

[154] Carl F. H. Henry, *God, Revelation and Authority,* 6 vols. (Waco: Word, 1976–1983; new ed., Wheaton: Crossway, 1999), 2:8, 11; David S. Dockery, *The Doctrine of the Bible* (Nashville: Convention, 1991), 12–13; Clark, *Augustine,* 18–23; Millard Erickson, *Christian Theology,* 2nd ed. (Grand Rapids: Baker, 1998), 198–99.

Following the Reformers, Henry says illumination occurs when the Spirit enables correct interpretation of Scripture. In evangelism, "Spirit-anointed couriers" proclaim the Word, which the Spirit uses "to reshape the mind and life in the image of Christ." In regeneration, "Bestower of Spiritual life, the Holy Spirit enables individuals to appropriate God's truth savingly and attests its power in their personal experience."[155]

The Spirit as Companion of Christ

While the ontological relationships within the Trinity have been discussed, the Spirit's economic relationship to the other persons must also receive attention. Robinson summarizes the relation of the Spirit to the Father in three brief sentences: "God gives Spirit. God has Spirit. God is Spirit."[156] The economic relation of the Spirit to the Father is that he gives of himself by giving the Spirit through the Son (John 14:16; 15:26), who in turn brings the believer through the Son back to the Father (Eph. 2:18). The Spirit searches the depths of the Father, revealing him to "the mind of Christ" in the church (1 Cor. 2:10–16).

The complex work of the Spirit in the human life of the Son is manifested in the Son's incarnation, baptism, ministry, death, resurrection, and exaltation. In incarnation,

> It was through the Holy Spirit that the Holy One was conceived. By that same act in the mystery of virgin conception, the humanity which the Son assumed in the womb of the Virgin Mary was sanctified. Thus the "thing" that was conceived in her was simultaneously fully human and fully holy.

The Holy Spirit descended upon Christ at his baptism, not to confer divinity or to make Christ holy but to commission him for messianic ministry. It has been claimed that the divine power evident in the ministry of Christ was not exercised by Christ as God but through the Holy Spirit. With reference to his death, Hebrews 9:14 says Christ "through the eternal Spirit offered Himself."

Some have equated "eternal Spirit" with Christ's divine nature, but Calvin concluded it refers to the Holy Spirit. Hobbs agrees: "Like the unblemished heifer, Christ, through the Holy Spirit, presented himself without spot before God as the once-for-all sacrifice." The Spirit's role in the resurrection of Christ became for Paul the hope of the Christian's personal

---

155 Kuyper, *Work of the Holy Spirit,* 61; Henry, *God, Revelation and Authority,* 4:129, 167, 234, 266, 408, 476, 479, 494. Malcolm Yarnell, "Whose Jesus? Which Revelation?" *Midwestern Journal of Theology* 1 (2003): 41–46.
156 Robinson, *Christian Experience of the Holy Spirit,* 226.

resurrection (Rom. 8:2; 1 Cor. 15:44–46).[157] Through resurrection, the Spirit vindicated and exalted Christ by declaring him to be the Son of God (Rom. 1:4; 1 Tim. 3:16).

The Son is the promised bearer and bestower of the Spirit. In the Old Testament the Spirit empowered only certain individuals and resided with the community only generally. The Spirit's presence was transitory and incomplete. He came upon Saul and departed from him (1 Sam. 16:14). David cried out for his retention (Ps. 51:11). Ezekiel saw the Spirit leaving the temple, signifying judgment upon Jerusalem (Ezek. 1:20–21, 10:17–20). "The partial, unsatisfying experience of his presence led God's people to direct their attention to the future."[158] The prophets said God's Spirit would be poured out upon the Anointed One (Isa. 11:1–3; 42:1; 61:1–2) and ultimately upon all the people (Joel 2:28–29). In the New Testament, Jesus is identified as the promised bearer of the Spirit (Luke 4:18–19). Furthermore, only Jesus Christ may bestow the Spirit "without measure" (John 3:34). When Christ gives the Spirit, it will be internal and regenerative (John 7:37–38).

However, Christ's bestowal of the Spirit upon the church must await his own glorification (John 7:39). Christ promised to send the Spirit to be an advocate and companion to his followers, guiding and comforting them (John 14:16–19; 16:12–15) and confronting the world (John 16:7–11). His promise to send the Spirit was fulfilled proleptically before his ascension (John 20:22) and actually during Pentecost (Acts 2:1).

The Son not only bestows the Spirit, but he regenerates and indwells through the Spirit and baptizes in the Spirit. It is the Spirit who now makes the Son present to and within the church.[159] There is a profound intertwining of Word and Spirit in the life of believers. The Spirit of God concurrently regenerates and indwells the people of God with the Word of God. As this relates to Old Testament saints, Jesus' words in John 14:17 are crucial. Prior to the descent of the Spirit (Acts 2), the Spirit of truth is merely with them. Later he will reside eternally in them (John 14:16).[160] Anyone

---

[157] Ferguson, "John Owen," 109–12; Hawthorne, *The Presence and the Power,* 132–34, 145–46; Kuyper, *Work of the Holy Spirit,* 102–19; Herschel H. Hobbs, *Hebrews: Challenges to Bold Discipleship* (1981; reprint, Fincastle: Scripture Truth, 2002), 90; Swete, *Holy Spirit in the New Testament,* 190–91, 194, 216–18.

[158] Grenz, *Theology for the Community of God,* 365.

[159] "On earth every day we have an advocate, not Jesus, but the other self of Jesus, the Holy Spirit." Carroll, *Holy Spirit,* 17.

[160] Six possible positions concerning regeneration of the old covenant remnant have been identified: (1) they were both regenerate and indwelt by the Spirit; (2) there was no fundamental change in them; (3) they were regenerate but not indwelt; (4) they were operated upon but not indwelt; (5) there is no way to explain the regenerating work of the Holy Spirit in the Old Testament; and, (6) the Holy Spirit had nothing to do with faithfulness among old covenant believers. We affirm a combination of the third and fourth position—old covenant believers were regenerate and operated upon

who does not have the Spirit does not have Christ (Rom. 8:9). Anyone who
has new life in Christ has it by the indwelling of the Spirit (Rom. 8:11).
Regeneration in Christ by the Spirit is intimately correlated with mutual
indwelling of the believer, the Spirit, and Christ.

Conversion to Christ and baptism in, with, or by the Holy Spirit is concurrent. Brand offers a sevenfold typology for the historical development
of different views of Spirit baptism: In Catholicism, the Spirit is given in
the sacraments of the church, originally in baptism and subsequently in
confirmation. Among some Puritans, a sealing by the Spirit subsequent to
salvation procured assurance of salvation. Wesley discovered a two-stage
process of salvation and perfection, the latter which he identified with
Spirit baptism. Keswick theologians believe the Spirit is received at salvation but deliverance from sin awaits subsequent baptism. Pentecostalism
developed two or more stages of salvation, with Spirit baptism necessarily evidenced by speaking in tongues. Charismatics, while questioning
Pentecostalism's various stages and the necessity of speaking in tongues,
emphasize both spiritual gifts and Spirit baptism. Finally, Augustinian
and Reformed scholars correlate Spirit baptism with conversion to Christ.
James Leo Garrett Jr. argues that baptism by the Holy Spirit is "synonymous with being born of the Spirit (John 3:5) or having received the
gift of the Spirit (Acts 2:38) or having the Spirit of Christ (Rom. 8:9b)."
Dunn concludes that separating conversion to Christ from Spirit baptism
is based in experience and tradition, not Scripture.[161] With this judgment
we strongly agree.

The Spirit as Re-Creator

Reformed theologian George Smeaton declares, "The application of
redemption is from first to last by the Holy Spirit." Following the Reformed
tradition, although sometimes willing to depart from its rigid formulations,
Baptists provide complex soteriologies, recognizing the Spirit's work in
salvation.[162] Since this book contains a separate chapter on salvation, this
discussion is limited to the Spirit's sovereignty in salvation, his work as
grace, and the debate over apostasy.

---

but not indwelt by the Spirit. See James Hamilton, "Were Old Covenant Believers Indwelt by the
Spirit?" *Themelios* 30 (2004): 12–22; see also idem., *God's Indwelling Presence: The Holy Spirit
in the Old and New Testaments*, NAC Studies in Bible & Theology (Nashville: B&H Academic,
2006), 9–24.

[161] Chad Brand, "The Holy Spirit and Spirit Baptism in Today's Church," in *Perspectives on Spirit
Baptism: Five Views*, ed. idem (Nashville: Broadman & Holman, 2004), 9–14; Garrett, *Systematic
Theology*, 2:182. "At the moment of regeneration He baptizes every believer into the Body of
Christ." *Baptist Faith & Message* (2000), art. ii.c; Dunn, *Baptism in the Holy Spirit*.

[162] Smeaton, *Doctrine of the Holy Spirit*, 202. Gill, *Body of Doctrinal Divinity*, 501–78; Dagg,
Manual of Theology, 258–304, 331–35; Boyce, *Abstract of Systematic Theology*, 367–436;
Mullins, *Christian Religion in Its Doctrinal Expression*, 359–438; Garrett, *Systematic Theology*,
2:241–497.

In the early fifth century, Pelagius downplayed the Spirit's sovereignty in salvation, elevating the role of humanity in the process. Pelagius began a debate with Augustine by criticizing the latter's prayer to God: "Give me the grace to do as you command, and command me to do what you will." Pelagius believed Adam was merely a bad example and taught the capacity of human free will to attain perfection. He encouraged elite Christians to achieve perfection through natural sanctity.

In opposition, Augustine believed that all humans inherited Adam's guilt and sin nature, that divine grace is required to overcome the will's propensity to sin, and that Christians continue to struggle with sin. In his commentary on Romans 8, Pelagius translated *spiritus* as human spirit as often as possible, making the human spirit the active agent in its relation with the divine Spirit. Drawing upon Romans 5:5; 1 Corinthians 4:7; and Philippians 2:13, Augustine declared the Spirit must shed love in the human heart for the will to desire God, for "a man's free-will, indeed, avails for nothing except to sin." Although Pelagius was more subtle than his followers, his teachings were condemned at the Council of Ephesus in 431.

With Augustine, Protestants emphasize the Spirit's sovereignty in salvation while retaining human free will. The crucial point concerns the initiatory role of God in salvation. "When man's own action, whatever its pretence or form, is made into a condition with regard to fellowship with God, then the Holy Spirit has been forgotten."[163]

The Spirit's work of salvation as a whole or in its various aspects is often referred to as "grace" or "graces." "A work of grace is the work of the Holy Spirit." These graces may be considered individually, or as various phases of a "unit," "one eternal, uninterrupted act, proceeding from the womb of eternity, unceasingly moving toward the consummation of the glory of the children of God." There is no uniform agreement concerning the phases of grace. The following demonstrates not a complete *ordo salutis* but simply the Spirit's initiation, continuance, and completion of salvation: "The grace of God first precedes, then prepares, and lastly performs."[164] The Spirit exercises both "awakening influence" and "convicting influence" among sinners. He calls all to salvation through the preaching of the Word.

---

[163] Augustine, *Confessions* 10.29. Pelagius, *To Demetrias* 11.1, in B. R. Rees, *Pelagius: Life and Letters* (Woodbridge: Boydell, 1998), 48–49; *Pelagius's Commentary on St Paul's Epistle to the Romans,* trans. Theodore de Bruyn (New York: Clarendon, 1993), 19–24, 107–12. Augustine, *On the Spirit and the Letter* 5. Rees, *Pelagius,* 7–13. Karl Barth, *The Holy Spirit and the Christian Life: The Theological Basis of Ethics,* trans. R. Birch Hoyle (Louisville: Westminster/John Knox, 1993), 20.

[164] Hodge, *Systematic Theology,* 2:654–55; Kuyper, *Work of the Holy Spirit,* 221. Garrett, *Systematic Theology,* 2:241–43, discusses various methodologies. Oden, *Life in the Spirit,* claims his is "the familiar sequence." Kuyper, *Work of the Holy Spirit,* 307, 311–14, offers different lists.

The Heidelberg Catechism assumes, without controversy, "we are re-generated by the Spirit of God." The Spirit establishes our subjective union with Christ. "The effectually called become adopted sons, and are trans-lated by the power of the Spirit into the family of God." The Holy Spirit, working with the wills of men, brings conversion, granting both active faith and active repentance.[165] "Saving faith is a persuasion, wrought by the Holy Spirit, that the Scripture is a true testimony concerning the salvation of souls, and that this salvation includes my soul." With the Father and the Son, the Holy Spirit has a role in justification, causing sinners "to appropri-ate it to themselves." Sanctification is a major grace, "whereby in a super-natural way He gradually divests from sin the inclinations and dispositions of the regenerate and clothes them with holiness." Glorification is also his work, when "by an act of omnipotent grace the soul will be reunited with its glorified body, and be placed in such heavenly glory as becomes the state of perfect felicity."[166] Salvation in its application is the gracious work of the Spirit.

The sovereignty of the Spirit in salvation has stirred controversy. Calvin equated references to apostasy and blasphemy against the Holy Spirit with reprobation. "The elect are also beyond the danger of finally falling away." The reference in Hebrews 6:4 to apostates who "have been made partakers of the Holy Spirit" concerns the Spirit's illumination of truth to unregen-erate men. Their minds experience only "some sparks of his light," but this "afterwards vanishes away." In contrast, Arminius distinguished two classes of apostasy: the unregenerate and those "who embrace Christ with a temporary faith." The followers of Arminius, the Remonstrants, limited the sovereignty of the Spirit in favor of human freedom, defining his grace as assisting and resistible. The Reformed Synod of Dort responded by reaf-firming the sovereignty of the Spirit in salvation and perseverance.[167]

The debate over perseverance and apostasy reappeared among Southern Baptists. Hobbs believed the author of Hebrews "was not speaking of losing one's regeneration, but of the danger involved in a state of arrested develop-ment in Christian growth by which his readers were in peril of falling short of their ultimate purpose in Christian service in God's world-mission."

[165] Vaughn, *Gifts of the Holy Spirit,* 41, 57; Erickson, *Christian Theology,* 942–43, 954; Kuyper, *Work of the Holy Spirit,* 352, 359, 367, 420; Heidelberg Catechism, viii; Smeaton, *Doctrine of the Holy Spirit,* 206.

[166] Kuyper, *Work of the Holy Spirit,* 313, 390, 421, 499.

[167] Calvin, *Institutes,* 3.2.11, 3.3.21–25; idem, *Commentaries on the Epistle of Paul the Apostle to the Hebrews,* trans. John Owen (reprint, Grand Rapids: Baker, 1996), 137–38; idem, *Commentary on a Harmony of the Evangelists, Matthew, Mark, and Luke,* trans. William Pringle (reprint, Grand Rapids: Baker, 1996), 2:74–76. Arminius, *The Sin against the Holy Ghost* (1599), in *Works of Arminius,* 2:742. *Articuli Arminiani sive Remonstrantia* (1610), 4–5, and *Canons Synodi Dordrechtanae* (1618–1619), 5.5–8, in *Creeds of Christendom,* 547–48, 571–72, 593–94.

Dale Moody disagreed, claiming "it is possible for believers who do not press on to maturity to commit apostasy." Moody said the Augustinian-Calvinist-Evangelical tradition triumphed over Scripture. But in 2000, the Southern Baptist Convention ratified perseverance *in toto.*[168]

The Spirit as Companion of the Church

John 14–16 is probably the most extensive teaching on the Holy Spirit in Scripture. Prior to his ascension, Jesus promised to send another *paraklētos,* a legal advocate, encourager, or companion (John 14:16). This other *paraklētos* helps (John 14:16), guides (John 14:26; 16:13), and empowers the church (John 15:26–27).

First, Christ promised the Spirit would help the church through abiding with and indwelling her. According to Carroll, "Jesus in the Spirit" is "present and with His Church forever." The Spirit helps the church by unifying Christians in the one body of Christ (Acts 15:22,25,28; Col. 1:7–8; Phil. 1:27, 2:1–2), by granting gifts for the common good, and by endowing Christians with virtue. Historically, there are various approaches to spiritual gifts.[169] Hemphill clarifies the biblical doctrine by not confining the issuance of gifts to the third person of the Trinity and by advocating the more common biblical term of *charismata,* "grace gifts." Employing Hemphill's suggested terminology reinforces the freedom of God while rebuking human pride. Hemphill also says the purpose of grace gifts is edification: "The gifts were given for the common good, and it is in the life of the body that the gifts can be used most effectively to minister to others."[170]

There is a definite priority among the gifts, including the elevation of prophecy and the demotion of tongues and their interpretation (1 Cor. 14). Elevating certain gifts does not, however, denigrate the spirituality of any Christian. All who confess Jesus as Lord are spiritual and integral to the body of Christ (1 Cor. 12:3,12–13).

---

[168] Hobbs, *Hebrews,* 59; *Baptist Faith & Message* (1925), xi; *Baptist Faith & Message* (1963), v; *Baptist Faith & Message* (2000), v. Moody subscribes to the Scripture affirmed by the confession. Dale Moody, *The Word of Truth: A Summary of Christian Doctrine Based on Biblical Revelation* (Grand Rapids: Eerdmans, 1981), 355, 358–65; idem, *Spirit of the Living God: What the Bible Says about the Spirit,* rev. ed. (Nashville: Broadman, 1968), 185–91.

[169] Carroll, *Holy Spirit,* 21. Historically, there are three major traditions concerning spiritual gifts. The medieval tradition elaborated upon the seven messianic gifts or virtues of Isaiah 11:2—fear, holiness, knowledge, might, counsel, understanding, and wisdom. Burgess, *Holy Spirit: Medieval and Reformation,* 8–9, 46–48, 73–75, 79–81; Aquinas, *Summa Theologica,* I–II, q. 68. art. 4; Bonaventure, *The Tree of Life,* and *The Life of Saint Francis,* in *Bonaventure,* 174–75, 205, 280–314; Michael Robson, "Saint Bonaventure," in *Medieval Theologians,* 194–96. The Reformed tradition stressed the soteriological gifts. Kuyper, *Work of the Holy Spirit,* 193–94; Vaughn, *Gifts of the Holy Spirit.* The Pentecostal movement of the early twentieth century interjected miraculous *charismata* into the modern discussion.

[170] Hemphill, *Spiritual Gifts,* 63, 93.

The diversity evident in the various gift lists suggests a certain fluidity which defies rigid classification (Rom. 12:6–8; 1 Cor. 12:8–10,28–30; Eph. 4:11; 1 Pet. 4:10–11). However, the listed gifts might be loosely classified as speaking (official), service, and sign (miraculous) gifts. Among the official gifts are apostles, prophets, evangelists, pastors, and teachers, and the related activities of prophecy, exhortation, ruling, and teaching. Among the service gifts are administration, giving, showing mercy, and helps. There are competing views as to whether the miraculous gifts—word of wisdom, word of knowledge, faith, healing, miracles, discerning of spirits, tongues, and interpretation of tongues[171]—and certain official gifts such as apostles and prophets are still active today.

The "cessationist" view argues the miraculous gifts were for confirming, authenticating, corroborating, or substantiating the apostolic message (Heb. 2:3b–4). Once this message was incorporated in the canon, miraculous gifts were no longer necessary. "The infant church, blessed with the gift of miracles, confirmed in its doctrine and practice by signs of approval from heaven, is now firmly founded and the need for the sign has ceased to exist. We have the Bible and that is enough."[172]

The Pentecostal view contends that all the gifts are intended for today and that tongues are a necessary sign for those baptized in the Spirit. The Charismatic view modifies the Pentecostal by disjoining tongues from Spirit baptism. The Third Wave view believes the Spirit empowers evangelism with signs, wonders, and miracles. Saucy, representing an "open but cautious" view, concludes, "Scripture nowhere explicitly teaches that some spiritual gifts were destined to cease with that age. . . . But neither does this text affirm the continuation of these gifts until the coming of Christ."[173]

The dependence of the Pentecostal, Charismatic, and Third Wave views upon personal experience and recent tradition, and the abusive practices of some modern "faith healers" and "health and wealth" preachers only strengthen the cessationist argument. However, Saucy presents a defensible

---

[171] If the gifts of word of wisdom, word of knowledge, and discerning of spirits are active today, they especially should be found among theologians.

[172] Criswell, *Holy Spirit in Today's World,* 185. Cf. Richard B. Gaffin Jr., "A Cessationist View," in *Are Miraculous Gifts for Today? Four Views,* ed. Wayne A. Grudem (Grand Rapids: Zondervan, 1996), 25–64; Paige Patterson, *The Troubled Triumphant Church: An Exposition of First Corinthians* (Dallas: Criswell Publications, 1983), 213–15, 225–26; J. Dwight Pentecost, *The Divine Comforter: The Person and Work of the Holy Spirit* (1963; reprint, Grand Rapids: Kregel, 1997), 166–67; Yarnell, "Expository Notes on 1 Corinthians," in *Helping Your Church Stay on Course: Studies in 1 Corinthians* (Nashville: LifeWay Church Resources, 2002), 57–59.

[173] Grudem, "Preface," in *Are Miraculous Gifts for Today?* 11–12; J. Rodman Williams, *Renewal Theology: Systematic Theology from a Charismatic Perspective,* 3 vols. (Grand Rapids: Zondervan, 1996), 2:209–36, 323–409. Robert L. Saucy, "An Open but Cautious View," in *Are Miraculous Gifts for Today?,* 123.

position by (1) putting the biblical burden of proof on the Charismatics/ Pentecostals; and, (2) not pressing Scripture beyond its clear affirmations.

Four gifts currently in dispute should be considered here:

1. Apostle. There are two meanings for the Greek term for messenger, *apostolos,* a general one and a restricted one. In general, all Christians are messengers sent to proclaim the gospel. In the restricted sense, an apostle is one who knew Christ in the flesh, saw him after his resurrection, and was directly commissioned by him. Such apostles lived only in the New Testament period.[174]

2. Prophet and Prophecy. Within the Reformation tradition some define the gift of prophecy as "forth telling" or proclaiming the gospel, distinguishing it from the completed office of the prophet, who practiced both "forth telling" and "fore telling." Modern prophecy would then be seen in many pulpits, would contain edification, exhortation, and consolation (1 Cor. 14:3), and would never contradict Scripture. Influenced by the charismatic movement, Grudem argues that prophecy continues in the church but believes modern prophets may err. His position has been criticized for misreading or having "overschematized" the biblical evidence. It could also be criticized theologically. Grudem provides no exegetical clue for distinguishing errant New Testament prophets from inspired prophets and apostles.[175]

3. Healing. Criswell protests against "the distressing doctrines" of today's professional faith healers since they presume upon God's power and cause people to doubt God's grace. Yet we should still turn to God and pray for healing.[176]

4. Tongues. The Pentecostal belief that Spirit baptism must be accompanied by speaking in tongues relies on a few descriptive passages and does not adequately account for the previously discussed diversity of the Spirit's work in Acts. Is speaking in tongues a valid spiritual gift? Strict cessationists deny its continuance. Whether or not this gift continues, 1 Corinthians 14 teaches that unknown tongues are a lesser gift, that public worship must be orderly, that speaking in tongues must be strictly limited and accompanied by interpretation, and that unintelligible speech is a sign of judgment.

---

[174] Criswell, *Holy Spirit in Today's World,* 163; Yarnell, "Expository Notes," 23.

[175] E. Earle Ellis, *Prophecy and Hermeneutic in Early Christianity: New Testament Essays* (Tübingen: Mohr, 1978), ch. 2; Criswell, *Holy Spirit in Today's World,* 165–67; Patterson, *Troubled Triumphant Church,* 214–15; Yarnell, "Expository Notes," 57, 64. Grudem, *The Gift of Prophecy in the New Testament and Today,* rev. ed. (Wheaton: Crossway, 2000), 40, 77–83. Saucy, "Open but Cautious," 127–29; Max Turner, *The Holy Spirit and Spiritual Gifts in the New Testament Church and Today,* rev. ed. (Peabody: Hendrickson, 1998), 214.

[176] Criswell, *Holy Spirit in Today's World,* 188–97; Saucy, "Open but Cautious," 129–31.

Some allow tongues for private prayer, but since spiritual gifts are for the common good, private practice is irrelevant in this discussion.[177]

The Spirit also helps the church by endowing all Christians with virtues encapsulated in the theological virtues and the fruit of the Spirit. What Aquinas later called "theological virtues"—faith, hope, and love—are extolled by Paul as having primacy over the spiritual gifts. The greatest virtue, which motivates the exercise of the grace gifts and outlasts them, is "the more excellent way" of unfailing and selfless love (1 Cor. 12:31; 13:13; 14:1). The fruit of the Spirit—love, joy, peace, patience, kindness, goodness, gentleness, faithfulness, and self-control—are endowed virtues that characterize Christian life (Gal. 5:22–23). The background of Paul's discussion of spiritual fruit is of "a struggle in our souls" between the flesh and life in the Spirit. The competing works of the flesh are set against the unity of the singular fruit of the Spirit. "The life that exhibits this fruit must be rooted in the Spirit, quickened by the Spirit, alive in the Spirit."

Criswell contrasted the nine gifts of the Spirit from 1 Corinthians 12:8–10 with the nine graces of the Spirit in Galatians 5:22–23: "The ninefold gifts of the Spirit are for power, service and ministry. The ninefold graces are for Christian character. . . . The nine gifts are distributed among the members of the congregation. . . . The nine graces are to be represented in every Christian." The fruit of the Spirit challenges Christian character since "no grace can enjoy perfect expression if it is not accompanied by every other member in the list."[178]

The second promise Christ made concerning the Holy Spirit was that he would guide the church. Roman Catholics regard the Holy Spirit as "the transcendent subject of tradition" and "the soul of the Church." Benedict XVI conceives tradition as "the living process whereby the Holy Spirit introduces us to the fullness of truth and teaches us how to understand what previously we could still not grasp." Although Protestants object to excessive correlation of Spirit and tradition, they too detect the Spirit's guidance of the church in the formulation of doctrine. Oden's three-volume systematic theology expounds upon "the consensual teaching of the Holy Spirit," especially according to the Patristic era, but with recognition that "the general consent of the laity" throughout history, including the contributions of the Reformation, is "the principle of legitimacy" that allows doctrine to be defined and heresy refuted. The major Southern Baptist proponent of his-

---

[177] Hemphill, *Spiritual Gifts,* 92–127; Patterson, *Troubled Triumphant Church,* 261–69; Yarnell, "Expository Notes," 64–67; Saucy, "Open but Cautious," 131–35.

[178] Aquinas, *Summa Theologica* I–II, q. 62; Criswell, *Holy Spirit in Today's World,* 227–42.

torical theology states flatly, "The task of the Holy Spirit as Revealer and Teacher is not to be ignored (see John 14:26; 16:13–15)."[179]

Although the Paraclete promises of John 14–16 were intended in the first place for the apostles, the secondary effects upon the church are profound. For instance, that the apostolic writings are considered Scripture and other writings are not is due to the guiding work of the Spirit upon the · historical church. While modern biblical scholars influenced by the historical-critical method may claim "history is silent as to how, when, and by whom [the canon] was brought about," the eyes of faith understand it was the Holy Spirit who brought the church to define the canon. Consensus was reached no later than the fourth century that the Old Testament and the twenty-seven books of the New Testament were inspired Scripture. Apocryphal books and heretical emendations of the canonical books were rejected and the New Testament books accepted on the basis of conformity to the *regula fidei,* "rule of faith," apostolic authorship, and consent by the various churches.[180] Christ promised the Spirit would "teach you all things, and bring to your remembrance all that I said to you." The Spirit accomplished this by providing the church with Scripture and today illuminates it for correct interpretation.

The development of true doctrine occurs when the Spirit enables the church to understand the truth contained within the Word he inspired, truth that at times has been suppressed by fallen man. The Reformers said the Spirit and the Word may not be separated. In book four of the *Institutes,* Calvin turned to "the external means or aids by which God invites us into the society of Christ and holds us therein." The primary means of grace is the preaching of the Word, and preaching is used instrumentally by the Spirit to bestow spiritual benefits. Calvin refused to divorce the means from the Spirit, who maintains his sovereignty. Likewise, Luther refused to separate Word from Spirit, for Scripture is the "bearer of the divine Spirit" who is "actually wrapped in the swaddling cloth of the human word."[181] Theology is utterly dependent upon concurrent submission to Word and Spirit. The biblical commentator without the Spirit is spiritually dead; the spiritual man without the Word is dangerously deluded.

---

[179] Congar, *The Meaning of Tradition,* trans. A. N. Woodrow (New York: Hawthorn, 1964), 51–58; Joseph Ratzinger, *Milestones: Memoirs 1927–1977,* trans. Erasmo Leiva-Merikakis (San Francisco: Ignatius, 1998), 59. Oden, "Postscript" and "Epilogue," in *Life in the Spirit,* 469–501; idem, *The Rebirth of Orthodoxy,* 117–26, 130–36. Garrett, *Systematic Theology,* 1:8.

[180] Bruce M. Metzger, *The New Testament: Its Background, Growth, and Content,* 3rd ed. (Nashville: Abingdon, 2003), 309–19.

[181] Calvin, *Institutes,* 4.1.6; P. Meinhold, *Luthers Sprachphilosophie* (Berlin: Lutherisches Verlagshaus, 1958), 56, quoted in Lohse, *Martin Luther's Theology,* 191.

(Third) Christ promised the Spirit would empower the church to bear witness to Christ. The Spirit witnesses both to divine judgment and mercy. We consider the Spirit as witness and judge in the final section on his work.

The Spirit as Witness and Judge

In the third Paraclete saying, Jesus connected the witness of the Spirit with the witness of his disciples (John 15:26–27). Immediately before his ascension, Christ clarified that the Spirit would come in order to empower their witness. They were to begin witnessing in Jerusalem, continue in Judea and Samaria, and proceed to the very ends of the earth (Acts 1:6–8). The Spirit appeared powerfully at Pentecost, and the church's witness bore much evangelistic fruit. All those filled with the Spirit boldly proclaimed the Word (Acts 4:31), and the Spirit prompted the church to set aside leaders for its missionary effort (Acts 13:1–5). In describing the Spirit as witness and judge, pneumatology embraces ecclesiology and eschatology. The Spirit constitutes the body of Christ, edifies it, and sends it into the world. "The Holy Spirit is the enlightening power of the living Lord Jesus Christ in which He confesses the community called by Him as His body, i.e., as His own earthly-historical form of existence, by entrusting to it the ministry of His prophetic Word." The church is the community called together by God and sent into the world to proclaim the Word in the power of the Spirit.[182]

In the final Paraclete sayings, Jesus explained the content of the Spirit's testimony: convincing man and glorifying Christ (John 16:5–15). On the one hand, the Spirit convinces man of sin, righteousness, and judgment. The Spirit demonstrates to human souls "that we are sinners; that we need a God-provided righteousness; that otherwise we must partake in the judgment of the prince of this world."[183] Sin is not believing in Jesus. Righteousness is found only in Christ vindicated before the Father. Judgment is proclaimed against "the ruler of this world." On the other hand, the Spirit glorifies Christ by disclosing to man the wonderful depths of the Trinity. The content of the Spirit's testimony may be summarized as judgment, in both its negative and positive aspects.

Few theologians regard the Spirit as judge, even when considering the biblical image of the Spirit as fire. The Spirit as fire has been interpreted by modern theologians as "power," "the one who kindles our hearts," or "cleansing agent." Others recognize the Spirit as judge but overlook his role in the negative, eternal side of judgment. Jürgen Moltmann considers

---

[182] Zizioulas, *Being as Communion*, 110–11, 140; Barth, *Church Dogmatics*, IV/2:614, 727, IV/3:681, 762–63; John Thompson, *The Holy Spirit in the Theology of Karl Barth* (Alison Park, PA: Pickwick, 1991), 99–104; George Hunsinger, *Disruptive Grace: Studies in the Theology of Karl Barth* (Grand Rapids: Eerdmans, 2000), 171.

[183] Warfield, "The Conviction of the Spirit," in *Person and Work of the Holy Spirit*, 21–22.

the negative side of the Spirit but primarily his role in restraining temporal evil. Dwight Pentecost affirms the Spirit as judge but primarily by helping the Christian battle flesh, the world, and Satan. However, Isaiah prophesied of "the spirit of judgment and the spirit of burning," and the "spirit of justice" who strengthens human judges but consumes sinful nations (Isa. 4:4–6; 28:6; 33:11). Montague claims these texts encompass eschatological salvation, the positive aspect of judgment.[184] If so, they also encompass the negative aspect of eschatological judgment, eternal condemnation. Old Testament imagery about fire accentuated the judicial wrath of God more than grace. In the New Testament, John the Baptist correlated the Spirit with fire (Matt. 3:11), and fire generally indicates eternal judgment (Matt. 3:12; Luke 12:49–50; 1 Cor. 3:13–15; Heb. 12:27–29). Fire "covers both aspects of the eschatological denouement, whether in hell on the one side or heaven on the other."[185] The Spirit executes the negative judgment of God both in time and at the end of time.

The Spirit also executes the positive judgment of God both in time and at the end of time. When the Spirit uses human instruments to proclaim the Word, he works within the sinner's heart to apply the graces of salvation. Many of these soteriological graces have legal connotations which elucidate the positive judicial work of the Spirit. The Spirit of adoption applies to man the legal declaration of filial relationship to God as Father. The Spirit of justification applies to man the legal declaration of the righteousness of Christ. The Spirit provides the pledge that guarantees the believer's final redemption. And the Spirit seals the believer, providing valid documentation that this coheir with Christ is to be raised from the dead and glorified. Basil of Caesarea believed the Spirit's role in judgment means the Spirit executes positive judgment by giving himself to the redeemed and negative judgment by withholding that gift.[186] The Spirit witnesses to and executes divine judgment, condemning or showing mercy, temporally and eschatologically.

Errors Concerning the Holy Spirit

Moral and theological errors propagated against the person and work of the Holy Spirit have biblical, historical, and recent manifestations. The

---

[184] Criswell, *Holy Spirit in Today's World,* 84–86; Clark H. Pinnock, *Flame of Love: A Theology of the Holy Spirit* (Downers Grove: InterVarsity, 1996), 14, 187; Ray Pritchard, *Names of the Holy Spirit* (Chicago: Moody, 1995), 111. Moltmann, *The Spirit of Life: A Universal Affirmation,* trans. Margaret Kohl (Minneapolis: Fortress, 2001), 123–42; Kärkkäinen, *Pneumatology,* 24. Pentecost, *Divine Comforter,* 193–232. Montague, *Holy Spirit,* 38–39.

[185] Friedrich Lang, "*pyr,*" in *TDNT,* 6:934–47.

[186] Malcolm Yarnell, "Christian Justification: A Reformation Baptist View," *Criswell Theological Review,* n.s., 2 (2005): 89; Garrett, *Systematic Theology,* 2:191–93; Basil of Caesarea, *De Spiritu Sancto* 15.

most fatal error manifested in the Bible is blasphemy against the Spirit, committed by unbelievers. It is literally the ascription of evil to him (Matt. 12:24–31). Such an attitude places the blasphemer outside the realm of forgiveness because it separates him from the only one who can apply forgiveness. Carroll defines it as a "sin of character," committed "against spiritual knowledge" out of malice and wilfully. He warns that "an unpardonable sin is one which from the moment of its committal is forever without a possible remedy." Zwingli concludes, "It is, therefore, the utmost blasphemy against God not to trust in Him. . . . It is, therefore, lack of faith alone, which we call infidelity or disbelief, that is never forgiven."

Blasphemy by unbelievers ought to be distinguished from grieving of the Spirit by believers. Christians may grieve the Spirit (Eph. 4:30) through deception, resistance, legalism, quenching, or the threat of apostasy (Acts 7:1–11,51; Gal. 3:2–3; Eph. 4:25–32; 1 Thess. 5:19; 1 Tim. 1:19). Simony, named for Simon Magus, is the attempt to secure authority over the Spirit for one's own ends (Acts 8:14–24). Simony is historically associated with "an inordinate desire to exchange spiritual for temporal goods."[187]

Other historical errors include nominalism, enthusiasm, Marcionism, Arianism, and tritheism. Nominalism, or modalism, says that Spirit is merely a name assigned to divine action and that he is not a person in the Godhead. Enthusiasts confine "the inner light" to oneself personally, rather than seeing revelation as commonly available in the Bible. Marcion believed the Spirit did not inspire the entire Bible, including the Old Testament and parts of the New Testament. Arianism ontologically subordinated the Spirit to the Son and the Father or denied the Spirit's distinctiveness.[188] Tritheism understands the three persons of the Trinity as three separate Gods.

Recent errors concerning the person of the Spirit include a trend in biblical studies called "Spirit Christology" and a trend in theological studies to address the Spirit in feminine terms. Spirit Christology rejects classical trinitarianism by beginning with the humanity of Christ (a Christology "from below") and then failing to distinguish between the risen Christ and the Spirit.[189] Dunn's beliefs in this regard were discussed in the section on Pauline pneumatology. In response, it is noted that the Holy Spirit's work focuses upon Christ, thus his person is not to be confused with Christ. The person of the Spirit has come in order to glorify the person of the Son

---

[187] Carroll, *Holy Spirit,* 106, 117–24. Oden's reclassification of this sin as pardonable seems to counter Jesus' teaching that it is unforgivable. Oden, *Life in the Spirit,* 21–23; Zwingli, *Commentary on True and False Religion* (1525), in *Latin Works of Zwingli,* 3:154. John Wyclif, *On Simony,* trans. Terrence A. McVeigh (New York: Fordham University Press, 1992), 30.

[188] Oden, *Life in the Spirit,* 29–31; Bloesch, *Holy Spirit,* 85.

[189] Harold D. Hunter, "Spirit Christology: Dilemma and Promise (1)," *Heythrop Journal* 24 (1983): 127–40; idem, "Spirit Christology: Dilemma and Promise (2)," *Heythrop Journal* 24 (1983): 266–77.

(John 16:13). Distinction must be maintained between the second and third persons of the Trinity.

Recently, some theologians have described the Holy Spirit in feminine terms because they believe patriarchal language leads to idolatry. They contend that the Spirit is female because some biblical words for the Spirit—*ruach* and *sophia*—are in the feminine gender, and feminine imagery is sometimes used to describe the character or actions of God. These feminists argue primarily, however, from nonbiblical literature, goddess analogies, and personal experience. Elizabeth Johnson, uncomfortable with describing only one person of the Trinity as feminine, describes all three persons as females. Liberal theologians, while allowing for feminine attributes in God and denying patriarchy, have opted for gender-neutral language. More conservative theologians, while decrying some forms of cultural patriarchy, argue that *ruach* is often used in a masculine sense and that masculine language in reference to God is analogical not univocal.

Since the masculine terminology is inspired, using feminine terminology distorts the biblical message and opens the church to the idolatry of goddess worship. The liberal attempt at gender-neutral language runs the risk of depersonalizing God. Moreover, those who mediate by trying to speak of God in both masculine and feminine terms create "a deity who is bisexual or androgynous rather than one who transcends the polarity of the sexes."[190] Humans, male and female, are made in the image of God and should refrain from casting God in their image. Scriptural language must not be changed by personal or social preferences.

How Does This Doctrine Impact the Church Today?

It is popular in modern American culture to misdefine "spirituality" as emotionalism, mysticism, elitism, and intimacy.[191] However, true spirituality is understood only with regard to the person and work of the Holy Spirit. Jesus said, "God is Spirit, and those who worship Him must worship in spirit and truth" (John 4:24). This passage does not indicate a vague and formless spirituality. The first reference to Spirit attests the divine nature,

---

[190] Elizabeth A. Johnson, *She Who Is: The Mystery of God in Feminist Theological Discourse* (New York: Crossroads, 1992), 44–57, 124–87. David S. Cunningham, *These Three Are One: The Practice of Trinitarian Theology* (Oxford: Blackwell, 1998), 46–50, 65–72; Shirley C. Guthrie, *Christian Doctrine,* rev. ed. (Louisville: Westminster/John Knox, 1994), 76; Daniel L. Migliore, *Faith Seeking Understanding: An Introduction to Christian Theology,* 2nd ed. (Grand Rapids: Eerdmans, 2004), 233–34. Donald G. Bloesch, *The Battle for the Trinity: The Debate over Inclusive God-Language* (Eugene: Wipf and Stock, 2001), 54; idem, *Holy Spirit,* 60–62; Oden, *Life in the Spirit,* 6–8.

[191] Eugene Peterson with Mark Galli, "Spirituality for All the Wrong Reasons," *Christianity Today* 49 (March 2005): 42.

while the second venerates the divine person. Jesus himself is "the truth" (John 14:6). Those who worship God the Father must worship him in and with the second and third persons of the Trinity. Without the Spirit, man may not approach the Son, through whom the Father is approached. To worship God is to worship the trinitarian God in his one essence and three persons. The Holy Spirit is both the subject of worship and the object of worship. The subjectivity of the Spirit draws attention to his divine work in worship; the objectivity of the Spirit draws attention to his divine person in worship.

The Holy Spirit as Subject of Worship

The Holy Spirit as the subject or agent of worship of God establishes the divine-human relationship that allows us to worship. The Spirit is that member of the Trinity who enables, administers, and perfects human prayer toward God. Apart from the Spirit we are incapable of properly engaging in prayer. "We . . . groan within ourselves. . . . In the same way the Spirit also helps our weakness; for we do not know how to pray as we should, but the Spirit Himself intercedes for us with groanings too deep for words . . . according to the will of God" (Rom. 8:23,26–27). Moreover, apart from the Spirit we are incapable of savingly confessing Jesus Christ as Lord. "No one can say, 'Jesus is Lord,' except by the Holy Spirit" (1 Cor. 12:3). The Holy Spirit establishes the relationship that allows the sinner to pray to God and confess Christ. In eternity, the three divine persons covenanted to save man through the incarnation, death, and resurrection of the Son by the Spirit's power. In time, the eternal God reaches out through the Son and in the Holy Spirit to bring man into a loving relationship with himself. "For through [Christ] we both have our access in one Spirit to the Father" (Eph. 2:18).

Eastern Orthodox and Roman Catholics speak of a "eucharistic epiclesis," the calling down of the Spirit upon the Lord's Supper to grace their offering and change the elements. Variant traditions of eucharistic epiclesis divide East from West, but both traditions lack explicit biblical support.[192] Evangelical Protestants focus upon proclaiming the Word. There is biblical precedent for calling upon the Spirit to regenerate hearers of the Word. In the premier Old Testament passage concerning regeneration, Ezekiel was commanded to speak to both the dead and the Spirit. "Again He said to me, 'Prophesy over these bones and say to them, "O dry bones, hear the word of the LORD."' . . . Then He said to me, 'Prophesy to the breath, son of man, and say to the breath, . . . "Come from the four winds, O breath, and breathe on the slain, that they may live"'" (Ezek. 37:4,9). The Spirit is

---

[192] Congar, *I Believe in the Holy Spirit,* 3:228–44.

called down by the proclaimer of the Word to bring new life to the hearers of the Word. The Spirit works inwardly the Word proclaimed outwardly by the preacher (Rev. 22:17).

The instrumentality of the Christian in proclaiming the Word and calling for the Spirit to quicken the hearers of the Word must be affirmed against both hyper-Calvinism and Pelagianism. Hyper-Calvinism denigrates the instrumentality of human beings by not offering the Word to sinners.[193] Pelagianism denigrates the instrumentality of human beings by not praying for the sovereign Spirit to regenerate sinners. Preachers necessarily and concurrently invite sinners to salvation through proclaiming the Word and invite the Spirit to quicken the hearers of the Word. Such a call on the Spirit to convert sinners should accompany and be accompanied by a call to sinners to repent and believe in Jesus Christ as personal Lord and Savior.

The Holy Spirit as *Object of Worship*

To say that the Holy Spirit is the object of worship is to recognize the full deity of the Spirit and to worship him. If the Spirit is God, and he is, then he must be worshipped together with the Father and the Son. An alternative translation of John 4:24 expresses this truth: "The Spirit is God and those who worship in Spirit and in Truth necessarily worship Him."

Similarly, in the blessing of 2 Corinthians 13:14, Paul substantially correlated the Holy Spirit with the Father and the Son. Paul's prayer to the triune God concluded with a triune blessing upon the gathered congregation: "The grace of the Lord Jesus Christ, and the love of God [the Father], and the fellowship of the Holy Spirit, be with all of you." To participate in the Holy Spirit is to know the love of the Father and the grace of the Son. God the Holy Spirit must be worshipped. All Christians should proclaim with the Niceno-Constantinopolitan Creed their belief "in the Holy Spirit, the Lord and life-giver, who proceeds from the Father, who is to be co-worshiped and co-glorified with the Father and the Son, who spoke through the prophets."

Carroll recognizes the Holy Spirit both as divine presence and as divine person. With Carroll, we affirm the subjectivity or presence of the Holy Spirit enabling worship. Only in the spirit and in the truth may human beings truly worship the Father. With Carroll, we affirm the objectivity or personhood of the Holy Spirit in worship. Since he too is God, the Spirit is worthy to receive worship and honor and glory and praise.

---

[193] Timothy George, "John Gill," in *Theologians of the Baptist Tradition*, ed. Timothy George and David S. Dockery (Nashville: Broadman & Holman, 2001), 24–29.

O blessed Spirit of God, the administrator of Jesus Christ, breathe on Thy church and let the inspiration of the Almighty enter it! Let us feel that Thou art a presence, a presence that can be known, a presence that will comfort, a presence that will protect, a presence that will shine on heaven and make it glitter like diamonds, a presence that will shine on death and make a portal of glory. So, Spirit of God, breathe on us![194]

---

[194] Carroll, *Holy Spirit,* 29.

Section 6

The Doctrine of Salvation

CHAPTER 12

The Work of God: Salvation

Kenneth Keathley

And this is the testimony: that God has given us eternal life,
and this life is in His Son (1 John 5:11).

Salvation is *the work of God* that *delivers us from sin and its penalty, restores us* to a right relationship with him, and *imparts to us eternal life*. God accomplished and is accomplishing this work through his Son, Jesus Christ. The Bible presents Christ as the Alpha and Omega, the first and last of our salvation, and as the author and finisher of our faith. He is Alpha of our salvation because he is the foundation of our election in eternity past. He is the Omega because he will be the basis of our justification in the day of judgment. From beginning to end, salvation is the work of God and is not found in any program, process, or prayer. Salvation is a person, Jesus Christ, and therefore, "he who has the Son has life" (1 John 5:12).[1]

The Bible emphasizes several aspects to salvation—justification, sanctification, and adoption, among others—but all fit under the general heading of "union with Christ." The New Testament presents salvation as the uniting of Christ with the believer and the believer in Christ (John 15:5; 2 Cor. 5:17; Gal. 2:20). At first, such language is strange to modern, Western ears, but getting a good grasp of the concept is the key to understanding what it means to be saved. Paul states that "in Adam all die, even so in Christ all shall be made alive" (1 Cor. 15:22). The apostle's point is that just as Adam, our representative, brought sin, judgment, and death upon us, so Jesus as our new representative brings us forgiveness, righteousness, and life.

Salvation is completely by grace because it has to be. Humanity is guilty of deliberately and freely choosing sin and as a result no longer has the inclination or ability to turn away from it. Scripture describes the human condition in drastic and graphic terms; it portrays us as "ungodly," as "sinners," and even as God's "enemies" (Rom. 5:6–10). We exist in a state of spiritual death, and though everyone can tell something is terribly wrong with humans individually and humanity collectively, we are too blind to

---

[1] Unless otherwise noted, all Scripture citations in this chapter are from the New King James Version (NKJV).

know what the problem is. Even if we could discern our true condition, there is nothing we can do about it. In short, we are lost. Yet it is while we are in such an inexcusable state that Christ dies for us. The good news of the gospel is that the Son of Man comes "to seek and to save that which was lost" (Luke 19:10).

Sin is rebellion against God, and as such it is totally irrational and destructive. God, because of his nature, and sin, because of its nature, cannot coexist indefinitely. God in his holiness will judge sin in its perverseness, so all who have committed sin are under his wrath. If there is any deliverance available from sin and its effects, then it is of the utmost importance that we who are sinful make the best of it. Not all who are morally responsible for sin have access to salvation; there is no redemption for Satan and his angels. However, humans, who were created in God's image, are those for whom Christ died. We have an eternal destiny, and for this reason the salvation of each person is a matter of great significance (Matt. 16:26).

What Does the Bible Say?

The Bible proclaims that Jesus Christ is salvation, and all who have a relationship with him (i.e., are united with him by faith) are saved. Union with Christ is the core truth of salvation that can be seen either as encompassing all of salvation or as the center to which all components of salvation are connected. Scripture presents the components of salvation from four different perspectives: eternal, historical, present, and eschatological.[2] *(experiential)*

Union with Christ: The Central Truth of Salvation

In Ephesians 1:3–14, Paul gives his great soliloquy on the scope and grandeur of salvation (all twelve verses comprise just one sentence in Greek!). He declares that "every spiritual blessing" (i.e., everything about salvation) God gives to us "in Christ" (v. 3), and he repeats this or a similar expression ("in him") no less than eleven times. These prepositional phrases are found throughout the New Testament, and they highlight the core principle of salvation: *union with Christ is not one phase or aspect of salvation; it is the whole of salvation in which all other aspects are subsets.* As John Murray states:

---

[2] Timothy George, *Amazing Grace: God's Initiative, Our Response* (Nashville: LifeWay, 2000), 19–23. George delineates "a continuum with four distinct but interrelated moments which derive both their unity and their uniqueness from God's free and sovereign grace." He lists the first moment as *metahistorical* rather than *eternal* and the third moment as *experiential* rather than *present*. See also A. H. Strong, *Systematic Theology* (Valley Forge: Judson, 1907), 793.

Union with Christ is really the central truth of the whole doctrine of salvation not only in its application but also in its once-for-all accomplishment in the finished work of Christ. Indeed the whole process of salvation has its origin in one phase of union with Christ and salvation has in view the realization of other phases of union with Christ.[3]

The importance of the prepositional phrase "in Christ" and other similar expressions can be seen, in part, by noting how many times the New Testament uses them. Of the biblical writers, John and Paul employ the expressions most often. Paul uses "in Christ" (38 times), "in Christ Jesus" (51 times), "in him" (21 times), "in the Lord" (44 times), and other similar expressions no less than 216 times.[4] Clearly, "in Christ" is not an empty phrase, a throw-away line, or a space-filler expression to the apostle. His repetition is not a mantra. Paul's repeated use of the term reveals that it is the central key to the apostle's doctrine of salvation and perhaps even his whole theology. However, since "in him," "in Christ," "in the Lord," and so forth, are so ubiquitous in his writings, we sometimes tend to gloss over them and miss their true importance. Besides, the expressions seem abstract and difficult to understand.

Along with Paul, John is the other apostle to make frequent use of the theme of union with Christ.[5] He uses the expression "in him" no less than twenty-six times (e.g., 1 John 2:5–6, 27–28). In addition, over sixty times

---

[3] John Murray, *Redemption Accomplished and Applied* (Grand Rapids: Eerdmans, 1955), 161. Murray continues, "Union with Christ is a very inclusive subject. It embraces the wide span of salvation from its ultimate source in the eternal election of God to its final fruition in the glorification of the elect. It is not simply a phase of the application of redemption; it underlies every aspect of redemption both in its accomplishment and in its application. . . . Union with Christ is the central truth of the whole doctrine of salvation" (165, 170). Murray may be one of the most adamant in his claim about the centrality of the "union with Christ" concept, but he is not alone. Both Erickson and Grudem concur. Erickson states, "In one sense, union with Christ is an inclusive term for the whole of salvation; the various other doctrines are simply subparts" (Millard Erickson, *Christian Theology*, 2nd ed. [Grand Rapids: Baker, 1998], 961). Cf. Wayne Grudem, *Systematic Theology* (Grand Rapids: Zondervan, 1994), 840. Besides Murray and Erickson, Garrett lists H. R. Mackintosh, Albert Schweitzer, Lewis Benedict Smedes, and James S. Stewart as additional theologians who see union with Christ either as the central core of salvation to which all other aspects are connected or as the summation of the components of redemption. See James Leo Garrett, *Systematic Theology*, vol. 2 (Grand Rapids: Eerdmans, 1995), 329–30. Perhaps the most influential proponent of the union with Christ position is John Calvin, who argued that "the Holy Spirit is the bond by which Christ effectually unites us to himself." (John Calvin, *Institutes of the Christian Religion* [1559; repr., Philadelphia: Westminster, 1960], 3.1.1). However, not all see union with Christ as the central core or the summation of soteriology. Garrett cites A. H. Strong, E. Y. Mullins, and W. T. Conner as representatives of those who hold union with Christ as merely one of several facets of salvation. See Garrett, *Systematic Theology*, 329–30.

[4] Mark Seifrid, "In Christ," in *DPHL*, Gerald F. Hawthorne and Ralph P. Martin, eds. (Downers Grove: InterVarsity, 1993), 433–36.

[5] Garrett, *Systematic Theology*, 333–34.

in his Gospel and his three epistles, John employs the concept of "abiding" in Christ (e.g., John 15:1–7).[6]

Grudem notes that *"every aspect* of God's relationship to believers is in some way connected to our relationship with Christ" and so he concludes that "the entire study of the application of redemption could be included in this subject."[7] A brief perusal of the New Testament demonstrates he is correct: *all the blessings of salvation are accomplished in Christ.* The Bible locates each of the four perspectives of salvation—eternal, historical, experiential, and eschatological—within him.

First, from the eternal perspective, *we were elected in Christ.* Paul states that God "chose us in Him before the foundation of the world" (Eph. 1:4). He also declares that God called us "according to his own purpose and grace which was given to us in Christ Jesus before time began" (2 Tim. 1:9). How could God call us before we ever existed? Paul supplies the answer: we were elected in Christ Jesus. God elected his own Son, who is our representative, and we find our election in him.

Second, from the historical perspective, *we were represented as united to Christ in his life, death, burial, and resurrection.* Paul states that God has accepted us "in the Beloved" by which "we have redemption through his blood" (Eph. 1:6–7). Jesus Christ lived in perfect obedience to the Father, and all who are united to him by faith are viewed by God also as "holy and without blame" (Eph. 1:4). Believers are considered by God to have died with Jesus (Col. 3:3–4) and to be buried with him (Rom. 6:2–4). Similarly, when Jesus rose from the dead, the Father viewed us as rising with him positionally (Rom. 6:5–8).

God declares that whatever our representative, the Lord Jesus Christ, has accomplished, those who trust in him have also achieved. His riches, righteousness, and merit belong to all who are in him (Rom. 8:17). Our union with Christ in his life, death, and resurrection provides the basis for our justification, sanctification, and glorification. From a historical perspective, our salvation is a finished feat, accomplished by Jesus of Nazareth nearly two thousand years ago.

The metaphor of the church as the body of Christ expresses the position that Christians enjoy in him (Eph. 5:25). According to Paul, Christ is the head of the church and is seated in heaven at the right hand of the Father (Eph. 1:20). And as far as God is concerned, every believer is positionally

---

[6] W. L. Kynes, "Abiding," in *DJG,* Joel Green and Scot McKnight, eds. (Downers Grove: InterVarsity, 1992), 2–3. However, some do not believe that the meaning of the concept of abiding in Christ is as broad as the meaning of the term "union with Christ." Radmacher understands the concept of abiding in Christ to be a subsequent act or process that occurs after salvation. He presents abiding as remaining in a state of fellowship with the Lord through continued obedience and confession of sin. See Earl D. Radmacher, *Salvation* (Nashville: Word, 2000), 212–18.

[7] Grudem, *Systematic Theology,* 840 (emphasis original).

already in heaven "in Christ Jesus" ("And God raised us up with Christ and seated us with him in the heavenly realms in Christ Jesus," Eph. 2:6 NIV). Third, from the present perspective, *we are united with Christ the moment we trust him for salvation, and we enjoy all the present benefits of salvation in him.* The apostle declares, "You also were included in Christ when you heard the word of truth, the gospel of your salvation. Having believed, you were marked in him with a seal, the promised Holy Spirit" (Eph. 1:13 NIV). God eternally foreknows all who will trust him, but until we place our faith in his Son we are unsaved and under the wrath of God (Eph. 2:1–3). Calvin stated, "We must understand that as long as Christ remains outside of us, and we are separated from him, all that he has suffered and done for the salvation of the human race remains useless and of no value to us. . . . It is true that we obtain this by faith."[8] It is only when we believe that simultaneously we are placed positionally in him and experientially Christ comes to dwell within us (Gal. 2:20).

Experiencing all of the current blessings of salvation comes about from our union with Christ. The Scriptures present us as regenerated in Christ ("If anyone is in Christ, he is a new creation," 2 Cor. 5:17; see Eph. 2:5, 10); as justified in Christ ("There is therefore now no condemnation to those who are in Christ Jesus," Rom. 8:1; "In Him we have . . . the forgiveness of sins," Eph. 1:7); as sanctified in Christ ("To those who are sanctified in Christ Jesus," 1 Cor. 1:2); and as adopted in Christ ("He predestined us to be adopted as his sons through Jesus Christ," Eph. 1:5 NIV).

Last, from the eschatological perspective, *all of the future benefits of salvation will be bestowed upon those who are united with Christ.* Believers who die are said to "die in the Lord" (Rev. 14:13) and to "sleep in Jesus" (1 Thess. 4:14). Paul promised that when the Lord returns "the dead in Christ will rise first" (1 Thess. 4:16). We will be resurrected in Christ ("For as in Adam all die, even so in Christ all shall be made alive," 1 Cor. 15:22) and with him we will be glorified (Rom. 8:17; 1 John 2:28; 3:2).

The Two Aspects of Union with Christ: *Positional and Experiential*

Perhaps one reason the doctrine of union with Christ sometimes does not get the emphasis it should in evangelical circles is that its specific meaning is so difficult to grasp. As Erickson points out, to modern readers the concept "is less than lucid."[9] Consider Paul's profound but paradoxical declaration: "I have been crucified with Christ; it is no longer I who live, but Christ lives in me; and the life which I now live in the flesh I live by

---

[8] Calvin, *Institutes*, 3.1.1.
[9] Erickson, *Christian Theology*, 962.

faith in the Son of God, who loved me and gave Himself for me" (Gal. 2:20). This verse makes clear that Paul considers union with Christ crucial to salvation and Christian living, but what exactly union with Christ *is*, is not obvious from the passage.

Some interpret the expression to refer to a vague, mystical experience that believers feel or undergo. Those who hold this view generally argues that a Christian experiences this mystical encounter only when he is perfectly surrendered to God. However, even though there is an experiential component to the concept, a careful examination of the biblical evidence reveals that the phrase primarily refers to our position in Christ. The subsequent life-changing power of our union with Christ is experienced when we trust by faith the reality of our position in him.

Alternative Views of Union with Christ

Two major alternative views of union with Christ compete with the positional/experiential perspective. The first position views union with Christ as *deification* and is generally associated with Eastern Orthodoxy. Union with Christ as *sacrament* is the second position and has the Roman Catholic Church as its primary proponent.

First, Eastern Orthodoxy understands union with Christ to be a mystical process that results in the deification of the believer. Orthodox teaching relies heavily on Peter's description of Christians as "partakers of the divine nature" (2 Pet. 1:4) and interprets the apostle to mean that union with Christ brings about our divinization through a development sometimes called *theosis*. Stavropoulos explains *theosis* accordingly: "In other words, we are each destined to become a god, to be like God himself, to be united with him. . . . It means the union of the human with the divine. That, in its essence, is the meaning of *theosis*."[10]

Understanding union with Christ as a process of deification naturally leads to mysticism.[11] The goal of such a mystical approach is to lose oneself in God and eventually be "fused with God."[12] Christians are to enter into the step-by-step process of deification through great effort, and though *theosis* is a gift from God, it is received "in conjunction with our own efforts."[13] Such mysticism often has pantheistic overtones and has more in common with a philosophy called neoplatonism than with the New

---

[10] Christoforos Stavropoulos, "Partakers of the Divine Nature," in *Eastern Orthodox Theology: A Contemporary Reader*, ed. Daniel B. Clendenin (Grand Rapids: Baker, 1995), 184.

[11] Schweitzer argues that Paul understood union with Christ entirely in mystical terms. See Albert Schweitzer, *Paul and His Interpreters: A Critical History* (New York: Macmillan, 1956).

[12] Bruce Demarest, *The Cross and Salvation* (Wheaton: Crossway, 1997), 315.

[13] Stavropoulos, "Partaker of the Divine Nature," 188.

Testament. In fact, the interpretation of union with Christ by some mystics is overtly pantheistic.[14]

A second interpretation of union with Christ is to understand the concept in sacramental terms. The sacramental approach views the Christian's union with the Lord as being accomplished in quite literal ways. According to Catholic doctrine, a person enters into Christ when he enters into the Catholic Church through the sacrament of baptism.[15] The Catholic Church is the visible body of Christ, and baptism provides a tangible, physical way to unite with him. In turn, Christ enters into the practicing Catholic whenever the parishioner ingests the Eucharist. The elements of the Lord's Supper are understood to be the literal body and blood of Christ, so Christ literally enters into the partaker of the Supper.[16] Not much is metaphorical about this approach. The Roman Catholic Church believes the sacraments provide concrete, literal union with Christ.

Two results follow immediately from the sacramental view of union with Christ. First, since the Roman Catholic Church is the repository of grace, which it dispenses through the sacraments, the hierarchy of the Roman Church becomes the doorkeeper of salvation. Throughout church history, the threat of excommunication is a weapon the papal authorities have wielded on numerous occasions. The second corollary is that salvation is viewed as a process that must be sustained, which leads naturally to an emphasis on the necessity of works for salvation.

The sacramental view of union with Christ highlights how soteriology and ecclesiology are often intertwined. For now it suffices to note, as Erickson points out, that the sacramental view of union with Christ contradicts the biblical teaching that the work of the cross has eliminated the need for human mediators (Heb. 9:23–10:25).[17] If the deification view of union with Christ over-spiritualizes the concept, then the sacramental view is overly literal.

"Union with Christ" is an all-encompassing phrase that presents the two aspects of salvation—the positional component and the experiential component—encapsulating all the benefits believers receive from Jesus Christ.[18]

---

[14] Demarest, *The Cross and Salvation,* 315; Erickson, *Christian Theology,* 963.

[15] Burkhard Neunheuser, "Baptism," in *Sacramentum Mundi: An Encyclopedia of Theology,* vol. 1, ed. Karl Rahner (New York: Herder and Herder, 1968), 139. Neunheuser states, "In baptism, then, the Church possesses something that is alive and operative . . . by uniting us with Christ's death and resurrection it enables us to hope for the great eschatological fulfillment in the future."

[16] Johannes Betz, "The Eucharist," in *Sacramentum Mundi: An Encyclopedia of Theology,* vol. 2, ed. Karl Rahner (New York: Herder and Herder, 1968), 262–63.

[17] Erickson, *Christian Theology,* 965.

[18] Grudem gives a similar definition: "Union with Christ is a phrase used to summarize several different relationships between believers and Christ, through which Christians receive every benefit of salvation. These relationships include the fact that we are in Christ, Christ is in us, we are like Christ, and we are with Christ" (Grudem, *Systematic Theology,* 840).

First, positionally God looks upon Jesus Christ as our representative, and all his accomplishments are considered by God to be our accomplishments, too. Second, experientially we begin to undergo the transforming benefits of our union with him when at conversion the Holy Spirit comes to dwell within us.

When Jesus lived his life of complete obedience to the will and commands of the Father, he acted on our behalf. Accordingly, as Jesus was accomplishing his lifelong walk of sinless perfection, God viewed us as being "in him" and therefore also walking in perfect righteousness. We were not somehow actually or literally inside Jesus during his earthly life, but rather God looked upon Christ as our substitute who represented us, and the righteousness of Christ's obedience is credited to us. As Paul states, "By one Man's obedience many will be made righteous" (Rom. 5:19).

The same positional reality holds true concerning his death, burial, and resurrection—God views us as being in him during the entire ordeal. Therefore, Christ's payment for sin and his victory over death are ours also.

The *positional* work that Christ accomplished for us provides the basis for the *experiential* work the Holy Spirit is now doing *in us.* The Holy Spirit subjectively applies to us what Christ objectively obtained for us. Because we are positionally in Christ, we are declared righteous; because experientially Christ is in us, we are being made righteous. By faith we accept our new standing in Christ, and taking this truth to heart liberates and transforms our lives.

Christ has sent to us his Spirit, and now the Holy Spirit indwells every believer from the moment of conversion. Christ, in the person of the Holy Spirit living within us, is the experiential component of our union with him. Our relationship with Christ is a spiritual rapport because the bond of our union is the Holy Spirit himself (Rom. 8:9–11; 1 Cor. 6:17, 19; 12:13; Eph. 1:13–14; 1 John 3:24; 4:13).[19] Since our experiential union with Christ is a spiritual union, this reality can be illustrated by tangible examples but not fully explained by them. Concrete analogies allude to the reality of the spiritual bond we have with him, but an allusion is not an exact explanation. Our spiritual union with Christ has, to an extent, a certain element of mystery (Eph. 5:32).[20]

---

[19] Calvin, *Institutes,* 3.1.1; Murray, *Redemption, Accomplished and Applied,* 166.

[20] Murray, *Redemption, Accomplished and Applied,* 166. When Murray contrasts our spiritual union with Christ with other examples of union, he is careful to point out that, though there are important similarities, there are even greater fundamental differences. Our union with Christ is not like the union within the Godhead (three persons in one God), or like the hypostatic union of Christ (two natures in one person), or even union of body and soul to constitute a human being. The spiritual union believers enjoy with Christ has to be understood in a different way.

Scriptural Analogies of Our Union with Christ

Even though we are not able to define specifically our experiential union with Christ, we are not holding to something completely vague or unintelligible. The Scriptures provide a wide range of analogies to help us understand our union with Christ. The Bible employs six different metaphors to illustrate the scope and nature of the relationship brought about by our salvation in Christ.[21]

First, remarkably, Jesus states that our union with him is analogous to the relationship that exists within the Godhead. In his priestly prayer he requested that "they all may be one, as You, Father, are in Me, and I in You; that they also may be one in Us. . . . I in them, and You in Me; that they may be made perfect in one" (John 17:21, 23). This, obviously, is the highest of comparisons, and it indicates that Christ is speaking metaphorically since believers are not ontologically united with the Trinity or to each other the way the persons within the Godhead are. But it demonstrates that Christ expects our union with him to be manifest by our unity with one another.

Second, the Scripture likens our union with Christ to the relationship of the stones of a building and the chief cornerstone (Eph. 2:19–22; 1 Pet. 2:4–5). As Murray points out, if the relationship within the Godhead is the highest level of comparisons, then this must be the lowest.[22] The symbolism highlights that Christ is the foundation of our salvation and that we are the temple of God in which the Holy Spirit resides.

A third but significant analogy is the contrast Paul makes between the relationship of Adam to the human race and the relationship of Jesus to the church (Rom. 5:12–19; 1 Cor. 15:19–49). On the one hand, humanity is joined with Adam in a "union of death."[23] On the other hand, believers enjoy a solidarity of life with Christ.

Fourth, Jesus likens our union with him to the union of a vine with its branches (John 15:1–17). Just as branches depend entirely on the vine for life and the ability to produce fruit, so believers are to depend completely upon him. Our Lord applies the metaphor thus: "For without Me you can do nothing" (v. 5).

Paul supplied the fifth and sixth analogies in his epistle to the Ephesians. There he likened the union of Christ with believers to the marriage of a husband and wife (Eph. 5:22–23) and to the organic connection of the head to the body (Eph. 4:15–16). These metaphors emphasize the intimacy and the essentiality of the relationship between Christ and his church. They illustrate that the concept of union with Christ is primarily positional, but

---

[21] Murray, *Redemption, Accomplished and Applied,* 167–68; Demarest, *The Cross and Salvation,* 327–29.

[22] Murray, *Redemption, Accomplished and Applied,* 168.

[23] Demarest, *The Cross and Salvation,* 328.

not only so. When a man and woman marry, they enter into a new legal and covenantal standing, but marriage is not just the acquisition of a contractual status. The couple has entered into a new relationship that will affect every area of their lives. Similarly, our new positional standing in Christ impacts us in a transforming experiential way.

Since our union with Christ is a mystery, the scriptural analogies provide similarities but not identical relationships. However, because Christ resides in us, we experience a real relationship that brings us into fellowship and communion with him and the entire Godhead. Jesus promises us that "if anyone loves Me, he will keep My word; and My Father will love him, and We will come to him and make Our home with him" (John 14:23). Our Lord pledged a similar relationship between us and the Holy Spirit (John 14:16–17). Our union with Christ brings about communion with God, which in turn produces holiness in us (1 John 2:5–6).

Tension between "Now" and "Not Yet"

As stated earlier, the Bible presents salvation from four perspectives: eternal, historical, present, and eschatological. First, God eternally purposed and planned our salvation before the world existed. Second, Jesus of Nazareth historically accomplished our salvation by offering his sinless life as a sacrifice upon the cross and rising from the dead. Third, we presently experience the benefits of salvation when we repent from our sins and respond in faith to the gospel message. And fourth, ultimately we will enjoy the completion of our salvation along with the transformation of all creation at the end of the age, the *eschaton,* when Christ returns.

All four moments of our salvation should be understood in the light of our union with him because each aspect is accomplished "in him." The first two moments—the eternal and the historical—accomplish the *objective* and the *positional* aspects of redemption. The last two moments—the present and eschatological—fulfill the *subjective* and *experiential* components of salvation. *Objective* refers to the redemptive act God has done for us; *subjective* refers to the transforming work God is doing in us. Objectively, Christ paid our sin debt (Rom. 3:25); subjectively, he empowers us to overcome sin (1 Cor. 10:13).

The difference between *positional* and *experiential* should be understood in similar terms. Positionally, the believer in Christ is viewed by God as righteous (Rom. 4:3–5); experientially, the same believer is being made righteous by Christ living in him (Col. 1:27).

The eternal and historical aspects of our salvation are already completed. But presently and eschatologically, our redemption is a work in progress. We who believe the gospel are now experiencing the beginning of salvation's benefits, but we will not know the full blessings until our resurrection. Objectively, salvation is a finished event. By faith we are redeemed, adopted, and justified in him. However, subjectively, we are experiencing our sanctification as an ongoing process that will not be completed until we see him face-to-face. Literally, the church experiences the "now—not yet" reality of living in between Christ's resurrection and his return, between Easter and the second coming.

The Bible presents the "now—not yet" experience of being between the beginning and completion of salvation as a tension that is often called *inaugurated eschatology.* When Scripture speaks of the work of Christ or the believer's position in him, salvation is presented as an objective, finished reality (Eph. 1:3). But when the Bible deals with the believer's daily walk and practical living, redemption is characterized as a subjective, ongoing work (Phil. 2:13). It is important to distinguish between these two conceptions. The believer now enjoys all the objective blessings of salvation, but he is yet to realize the full redemption—the glorification—of his body. This tension is lived out as a practical matter in the lifelong sanctifying walk of faith.

Sometimes, maybe even often, believers experience frustration and impatience because the walk is difficult or they are disappointed with their level of obedience and commitment. Yet every Christian confidently can know by faith that his sins are forgiven, victory over temptation is available, and the completion of his salvation is inevitable. We have the security of knowing God will complete the work that he has begun (Phil. 1:6), so we are to continue to work and serve with reverent fear (Phil. 2:12). The "now—not yet" reality of salvation can be summed up by the saying, "God calls us to become what he declares we already are."[24]

What Has the Church Believed?

The church has consistently believed that redemption is the free gift of God and is available entirely and only in Jesus Christ. However, at various times there has been intense debate over the conditions to receiving salvation. This controversy became the main issue of the Reformation, and we argue that the Reformers were right in affirming that redemption is received by grace alone through faith *alone.* The message of the gospel is that a person is saved when he places personal trust in Jesus Christ as Lord and Savior.

---

[24] This is just one of many profitable adages recited by my colleague, Dan Holcomb, at New Orleans Baptist Theological Seminary.

95 11th

The Patristic Era

In the first centuries after the apostolic period, the church was preoccupied with the Christological controversies. Therefore, the early fathers recognized that the debates about the nature of Christ were also disputes about the nature of salvation.[25] In his treatise *On the Incarnation,* Athanasius (296–373) pointed out that if Jesus Christ is not divine, then his death provides only an example of how the creature is supposed to obey the Creator, which means salvation is by works. But since the Savior is God incarnate, then his atoning death was the act of God satisfying himself—therefore salvation is by grace alone. In defending the deity of Christ, the early fathers such as Athanasius were particularly concerned to preserve the gracious nature of salvation.

No ecumenical council dealt with disputes concerning salvation until the fifth century, so the patristic era displays a remarkable lack of clarity or consensus on the subject. For example, the Western church began to understand the doctrine of justification in terms of merit. Since Latin was the language of the Western church, some of the misunderstandings may result from problems in translating the Greek New Testament word *dikaioō,* "to justify," to the Latin *meritum.*[26] The Greek term means "to consider one as righteous" while the Latin word means "to be worthy." This subtly shifts justification from being God's acquittal of the believing sinner to the sinner's transformation into a person worthy of God's esteem. Early Latin writers such as Tertullian began to teach that man can earn merit so as to make God his debtor and can satisfy his obligations to God through deeds of penance.[27]

Another problem concerning soteriology during this time was the rise of sacramentalism, the belief that one receives grace by partaking of the ordinances of baptism and the Lord's Supper. In early church teaching, baptism became associated with regeneration and the washing away of original sin, so this naturally led to the conclusion that one should be baptized as soon as possible—hence the rise of the practice of infant baptism. The Lord's Supper was seen as the means by which one receives the grace of the atonement, so the church soon understood itself to have literal possession of the saving power of Christ.

---

[25] See Harold O. J. Brown, *Heresies: The Image of Christ in the Mirror of Heresy and Orthodoxy from the Apostles to the Present* (Garden City: Doubleday, 1984), 150. Brown observes, "The spiritual contrast between these variant views and what we now call orthodoxy lay first of all in the goal which each sought to accomplish: the heretical positions had in common a desire *to understand the mystery of God*; the orthodox sought to *preserve the salvation* Christians find in Christ" (emphasis original).

[26] Alister McGrath, *Iustitia Dei: A History of the Christian Doctrine of Justification,* 2nd ed. (Cambridge: Cambridge University, 1998), 14–16.

[27] Ibid., 23.

However, the greatest threat to the gospel during the patristic era came at the end of the period in the form of a heresy called *Pelagianism*. Pelagius (ca. 354–420), a British monk, was concerned about the lax moral condition of the church and considered the writings of Augustine (354–430) on grace to be a major contributor to the problem.[28] Bromiley sums up Pelagius's teachings in three points: (1) if God expects moral perfection from humans, then it must be possible to live above sin; (2) humans have the natural ability both to choose righteousness and to live righteously; and (3) the impact of Adam's fall upon his offspring is simply one of providing a bad example.[29] With the debate between the respective followers of Pelagius and Augustine, the church's theological focus shifted from the person of Christ to the work of Christ.

In *The Spirit and the Letter*, Augustine responded to the Pelagian challenge by arguing that humanity inherits the corruption and guilt of Adam's sin. Due to Adam's fall, the intellectual, volitional, and moral faculties of all his descendants are depraved, the entire race is lost, and no one has the ability to save himself.[30]

Building on the doctrine of total depravity, Augustine reasoned that salvation is possible by grace alone with God acting as the sole agent. Even the repentance and faith necessary for receiving salvation are gifts from God. Why then did God not give saving faith to all? Augustine answered that God has predestined only a certain number to eternal life for reasons known only to him.

The councils of Carthage (418) and Orange (529) affirmed the Augustinian view and rejected Pelagianism; however, they also rejected some of the implications of Augustine's position on predestination, such as the doctrine of reprobation.[31] It is important to note that though Augustine understood salvation to be by grace, he did not believe faith is the only condition for receiving redemption. Rather, he viewed love as the primary requirement. In addition, he accepted the Latin interpretation of justification to mean "to make righteous", and taught the sacramental view of receiving grace. Combining these together ironically resulted in opening the door to

---

[28] Augustine's prayer in his *Confessions* particularly exercised Pelagius: "You command continence: give what you command, and then command whatever you will." Augustine, *The Confessions* 10.29.40 (397; repr., Hyde Park: New City, 1997), 263.

[29] Geoffrey Bromiley, *Historical Theology: An Introduction* (Edinburgh: T and T Clark, 1994), 117.

[30] Alister McGrath, *Historical Theology: An Introduction to the History of Christian Thought* (Oxford: Blackwell, 1998), 35.

[31] The Synod at Orange concluded, "We not only do not believe that any are foreordained to evil by the power of God, but even state with utter abhorrence that if there are those who want to believe so evil a thing, they are anathema." Second Council of Orange, "The Doctrinal Chapters of the Synod of Orange, 529," in *Creeds and Confessions of Faith in the Christian Tradition,* vol. I, ed. Jaroslav Pelikan and Valerie Hotchkiss (Yale University Press: New Haven, 2003), 692–97.

semi-Pelagianism (the belief that God and man cooperate in salvation) in the medieval church.[32]

The Medieval Era

During the medieval era Catholic theology solidified the view that the church is the repository of the saving merit of Christ and that one receives salvation by obediently receiving the sacraments of the church.[33] The sacraments were viewed as concrete, visible means by which inward grace is received, further sanctifying the practicing believer. The list of sacraments expand from the original two of baptism and the Eucharist (the Lord's Supper) to include confirmation (the bestowing of the status of full membership in the church), penance (acts of contrition to have one's sins absolved), extreme unction (last rites for one who is dying), orders (ordination of priests and ministers), and marriage (as symbol of Christ and the church), for a total of seven sacraments.[34]

In addition to sacramentalism, the medieval church embraced the practice of praying to the saints on behalf of the dead. Salvation was understood to be a lifelong progression of being made holy, and for many within the church the process was not finished by the time they died. Therefore, most parishioners expected to spend a time of unknown duration in purgatory where their remaining sins would be purged. The faithful would intercede with the saints, particularly Mary, for the deliverance of their departed loved ones. In 1439, the Council of Florence declared the doctrine of purgatory to be official church dogma when it decreed:

> Also, if truly penitent people die in the love of God before they have made satisfaction for acts and omissions by worthy fruits of repentance, their souls are cleansed after death by cleansing pains; and the suffrages of the living faithful avail them in giving relief from such pains, that is, sacrifices of masses, prayers, almsgiving, and other acts of devotion which have been customarily performed by some of the faithful for others of the faithful in accordance with the church's ordinances.[35]

---

[32] Bromiley, *Historical Theology,* 122.

[33] McGrath, *Historical Theology,* 120.

[34] Jeroslav Pelikan, *The Christian Tradition: A History of the Development of Doctrine,* vol. 3 (Chicago: University of Chicago, 1978), 209–10. Pelikan states that though "it is not clear where the notion of seven as the number of the sacraments began," by the middle of the twelfth century the number had received general acceptance.

[35] Council of Florence, "Decree of Union with the Greek Church, 1439," in *Creeds and Confessions of Faith in the Christian Tradition,* vol. 1, ed. Jaroslav Pelikan and Valerie Hotchkiss (New Haven: Yale University, 2003), 755.

By the late medieval period semi-Pelagian thinking dominated the church's understanding of the nature of salvation. The semi-Pelagianists did not believe a person had it within his own power to live in such a way as to save himself, but they did teach that one had the natural ability (or free will) to make the first move toward God and that one cooperated with God in salvation. The most prominent theologian of this time, Gabriel Biel (d. 1495), summed up the semi-Pelagian position when he stated, "God will not deny grace to those who do what lies within them."[36]

The Roman Catholic Church of the medieval era vigorously affirmed an entirely gracious salvation, but at the lay level and as a practical matter, the penitential system operated very much as a salvation by works. This became clear when in 1517 Pope Leo X sold exemptions from purgatory (called indulgences) in part to pay for the building of St. Peter's Basilica in Rome. Martin Luther (1483–1546), a German monk, challenged the legitimacy of the practice by nailing his famous Ninety-five Theses to the door of the Wittenburg church.

The Reformation

The Reformation came about with Martin Luther's rediscovery of the biblical doctrine of salvation by grace alone, and in this way the Reformation can also be described as the recovery of Augustine's doctrine of grace. However, the Reformers went beyond Augustine and further refined his teaching by emphasizing the biblical doctrine of justification by faith *alone*.

As a monk, Luther sensed that, despite his fastidious attempts at holiness, God still viewed him as a terrible sinner. The more rigorous his efforts, the greater were his feelings of failure. Deliverance came to Luther through his reading of Paul's declaration to the Romans, "For in it [the gospel] the righteousness of God is revealed from faith to faith; as it is written, 'The just shall live by faith'" (Rom. 1:17).[37] Luther previously understood "the righteousness of God" to be the standard by which he judges sinners, but Luther came to see God's righteousness as a gift God gives to sinners. God justifies the believing sinner by robing him with his own divine righteousness. Justification is not a status a person merits with God's help through great effort; rather it is a free gift God bestows on whoever will receive it by

---

36 McGrath, *Historical Theology,* 151.

37 Luther testified of his meditations on Romans 1:17, "There I began to understand that the righteousness of God is that by which the righteous lives by a gift of God, namely by faith. And this is the meaning: the righteousness of God is revealed by the gospel, namely, the passive righteousness with which merciful God justifies us by faith. . . . Here I felt that I was altogether born again and had entered paradise itself through open gates. There a totally other face of the entire Scripture showed itself to me." Martin Luther, "Preface to Latin Writings," in *LW,* 34.337.

faith. The doctrine of justification by faith liberated Luther from the burden of the church's penitential system and introduced him to the gracious God he so desperately had been seeking.

Luther's protest against the Roman Catholic practice of the sale of indulgences was the "tipping point" that set the Reformation in motion. He demonstrated the doctrinal error and the unethical simony of indulgences and other similar teachings by presenting the biblical case that salvation is the free gift of God and is to be received by faith. Luther accused the Roman Church of being guilty of the worst of sins: the church was supposed to bring people to God, but the church's teachings and practices had the opposite effect of setting up insurmountable barriers to heaven.[38]

As voluminously as Luther wrote, he left no systematic exposition of theology. This task was performed by John Calvin (1509–1564), the most influential theologian of the Reformation. Calvin's *Institutes of the Christian Religion* became the benchmark for many Protestants throughout northern Europe, and those who subscribe to the general outline of his soteriology are called Calvinists.

Perhaps Calvin's greatest contribution to our understanding of salvation is not his doctrine of predestination, even though in many circles this is considered to be the hallmark of Calvinism. Rather, Calvin was the first to distinguish clearly between justification and sanctification and to treat them as two distinct aspects of salvation.[39] Separating justification from sanctification clarifies how believers can be declared already righteous (justification) and yet simultaneously be made righteous (sanctification).

The Reformers—Luther, Calvin, and others—set in motion a revolution that literally changed the world. Their proclamation of the free gift of salvation knocked out the underpinnings of the merit-based system of the medieval Roman Church. The gift of the Reformation was nothing less than the recovery of the good news of the gospel.

The Counter Reformation and Post Reformation

The Roman Church responded to the challenge of the Reformation by calling an ecumenical council that met from 1545 to 1563 in the Italian city of Trent. Several earlier attempts had been made to reconcile the Catholic and Protestant factions, but by the time the Council of Trent met the breach was irreparable.[40] Though it enacted a number of moral reforms, the council firmly rejected the doctrine of justification by faith alone, anathematized

---

[38] See Martin Luther, "The Babylonian Captivity of the Church," in *LW,* 34.3–126.

[39] See Calvin, *Institutes,* 3.11.14; 3.14.9.

[40] See Anthony N. S. Lane, "Twofold Righteousness: A Key to the Doctrine of Justification? Reflections on Article 5 of the Regensburg Colloquy (1541)," in *Justification: What's at Stake in the Current Debates,* ed. Mark Husbands and Daniel Treier (Downers Grove: InterVarsity, 2004), 204–24.

all who held to such a view of justification, and reaffirmed the sacramental and penitential system as official church dogma. The decisions made by the Council of Trent determined the character and makeup of the Roman Catholic Church for the next four hundred years until the Second Vatican Council (1962–65).

Within Protestantism, the generation that followed after the original Reformers focused on systematizing the doctrines of the Reformation. Both Luther and Calvin wrote about predestination, but it was not the primary focus of their theological efforts.[41] However, Theodore Beza (1519–1605) replaced Calvin at the academy of Geneva, and through his influence the central doctrine of Reformed theology shifted from justification to predestination.[42]

Beza was the principle architect of a particularly extreme view of predestination called *supralapsarianism*, which argued that, logically speaking, even before God ordained the fall of Adam, he chose certain persons to eternal life and he predestined others to eternal damnation.[43] From this understanding of predestination, other conclusions are deduced, such as a belief that Christ died only for the elect and that God's offer of grace to the elect is irresistible.

James Arminius (1560–1609) studied under Beza in Geneva but never accepted Beza's doctrines of election and reprobation. Eventually Arminius also became a professor of theology at the University of Leiden in the Netherlands, where he taught a different view of predestination from the predominant Reformed position of the day.[44] Arminius died during the controversy surrounding his teachings, so his followers picked up his cause. They became known as the Remonstrants when they published a petition of protest called a "remonstrance."[45] The petition contained five points which contended that (1) God conditionally elects individuals according to their foreseen faith; (2) Christ died for the sins of the whole world; (3) no one has the power within himself to turn to God without the assistance of God's grace; (4) God's grace can be resisted; and (5) it is possible for a Christian to lose his salvation.

---

[41] See Martin Luther, *Bondage of the Will* (1525; repr., London: Camelot Press, 1957); and John Calvin, *Concerning the Eternal Predestination of God* (1552; repr., Louisville: Westminster John Knox, 1961).

[42] See Alister McGrath, "The Article by Which the Church Stands or Falls," *Evangelical Quarterly* 58 (1986): 208.

[43] We will discuss supralapsarianism further in the next section concerning the origin of salvation.

[44] See Roger Olson, *The Story of Christian Theology: Twenty Centuries of Tradition and Reform* (Downers Grove: Inter-Varsity, 1999).

[45] See The Remonstrants, "The Remonstrance, or The Arminian Articles, 1610" in *Creeds and Confessions of Faith in the Christian Tradition,* vol. 2, ed. Jaroslav Pelikan and Valerie Hotchkiss, (New Haven: Yale University, 2003), 549–50.

The Synod of Dort (1618–1619) rejected all five assertions of the Remonstrants and answered with its own five corresponding points.[46] The canons of Dort affirmed (1) total depravity—sinners are incapable in their own power of responding to the gospel; (2) unconditional election—God elects and reprobates according to his own inscrutable will; (3) limited atonement—Christ died only for the elect; (4) irresistible grace—the Holy Spirit works irresistibly in the hearts of the elect; and (5) perseverance of the saints—God gives sufficient grace to the elect for them to persevere until death. Of course, these are the famous five points of Calvinism, and the first letter of each point spells the acronym TULIP.

Since Dort, the debate over predestination generally has been framed as Calvinism versus Arminianism, typically with Calvinists putting the primary emphasis on divine sovereignty while Arminians emphasize human responsibility. However, discussing the doctrine of election under the headings of Calvinism and Arminianism can be an oversimplification.

First, there is a wide spectrum of views within each camp, and there is significant overlap of common points in the middle ground between the two positions. Second, it is important to remember that Arminianism arose from within Reformed theology as a protest against the more extreme views of predestination that ran the risk of fatalism. Rightly or wrongly, Arminius always considered himself a faithful disciple of Calvin. And third, the positions espoused by Calvin and Arminius have a long history that predates both men. Calvin continued the Augustinian tradition that began when Augustine opposed the Pelagian heresy of the fifth century. What is called Arminianism was nearly the universal view of the early church fathers and has always been the position of Greek Orthodoxy. The issues raised deserve more attention, which we will give in the section in this chapter on the origin of salvation.

The Church's Response to the Enlightenment

The Reformation and Counter Reformation periods ended with the church divided into Eastern Orthodox, Roman Catholic, and Protestant blocs. With the arrival of the Enlightenment and the subsequent modern era, the church fractured even more as Protestantism divided significantly further. Protestant churches separated into denominations over issues of church polity and differing beliefs about the doctrine of salvation. Methodist, Wesleyan, and Pentecostal churches embrace various aspects of Arminianism while Presbyterian and most Baptist churches affirm some form of Calvinism. However, the challenge of the Enlightenment transcends

---

[46] The Synod of Dort, "The Canons of the Synod of Dort, 1618–19," in *Creeds and Confessions of Faith in the Christian Tradition.*

denominational lines, and in the church's attempted response denominations divide internally into groups labeled as liberal and evangelical.[47] By and large, liberalism accepts the conclusions of the Enlightenment, while evangelicalism does not, which in turn affects how the respective group understands the doctrine of salvation.

The modern era began in the seventeenth century with the arrival of an intellectual movement its proponents call the Enlightenment.[48] As the label indicates, Enlightenment philosophers sought to move society and culture from the "dark ages" of the medieval period into the light of the age of reason. They argued that in the pursuit of knowledge the individual must start with himself and that a person can then arrive at truth through the use of reason alone. Progress in the natural sciences and historical studies encouraged the Enlightenment thinkers to embrace an antisupernatural bias that viewed religious belief as little more than superstition. They believed the quest for truth required complete freedom from all strictures such as church tradition or the authority of the Bible. Alexander Pope (1688–1744) summed up the attitude of the Enlightenment when he wrote:

> Know thyself then. Seek not God to scan.
> The proper study of mankind is man.[49]

The philosophers of the Enlightenment rejected the biblical doctrine of salvation because they did not believe humanity needs to be saved.

The approach of liberal theology to the Enlightenment was one of accommodation. Liberal theologians such as Friedrich Schleiermacher (1768–1834) and Albrecht Ritschl (1822–1889) reinterpreted Christian doctrines through the lens of modern skepticism and attempted to "peel away" what they viewed as layers of tradition and myth to ascertain the true message of Jesus of Nazareth. Adolf Von Harnack (1851–1930) determined that the essence of Jesus' teaching was the love of God and the brotherhood of man.[50] He and other like-minded theologians rejected the Chalcedonian understanding of the two natures of Christ in favor of a functional Christology. Christ is divine only in the sense that he was filled with the vision of God, and his death provides simply a moral example. Generally, liberal theologians embrace universalism and reinterpret salvation to be the transforma-

---

[47] When assigning such broad categories of liberal and evangelical, there is obvious oversimplification. For example, *neoorthodoxy* is a theological approach that consciously attempts to reject the philosophical presuppositions of the Enlightenment and does not fit well in either category.

[48] See Immanuel Kant, "What Is Enlightenment?" in *The Philosophy of Kant* (1784; repr., New York: Random House, 1949), 132.

[49] Quoted in Olson, *The Story of Christian Theology,* 540.

[50] See Justo L. Gonzalez, *A History of Christian Thought,* vol. 3, rev. ed. (Nashville: Abingdon, 1987), 380–81.

tion of society.[51] In developing a theology that conforms to the modern mind-set, liberalism loses the radical message of the gospel.

In contrast, evangelicalism responds to the challenge of the Enlightenment by reaffirming the biblical doctrines of sin, salvation through Jesus Christ, and the coming judgment of God. Evangelicalism focuses inwardly on the personal nature of salvation. While the Reformation rediscovered the biblical doctrine of justification by faith alone, it gave less attention to the other aspects of salvation. The evangelical revivals of the eighteenth and nineteenth centuries reemphasized the doctrines of regeneration and sanctification by proclaiming the necessity of the new birth and the call to holy living.

Evangelicalism does not ignore the social implications of the gospel (both the abolitionist and temperance movements were born of evangelical convictions), but the primary focus of its understanding of salvation is individualistic. In too many instances some factions of evangelicalism present the gospel as if a person can experience all aspects of redemption in complete isolation from the church and the community of faith, a notion alien to the New Testament. Despite this occasional shortcoming, evangelicalism attempts to proclaim faithfully the biblical message of salvation: God has planned and provided salvation through his Son, Jesus Christ, and all people are called to repentance from sin and faith in his finished work.

How Does It All Fit Together?

The good news of the gospel is that salvation "all fits together" in Jesus Christ. First we will look at the origin of our redemption. Salvation originates within God's sovereign choice of Jesus Christ to be the Savior of the world, and we are saved because of God's plan to redeem a people for himself. Second, the Holy Spirit communicates Christ's redemption by calling, equipping, and empowering the church for the task of proclaiming the good news to the rest of the world. Third, we will examine the conditions of salvation. God requires that sinners repent and believe in order to be saved. Just as humanity is responsible for its rebellion against God, so also are all people responsible for turning from their sin and for trusting the gracious offer of the gospel.

At the moment a person believes, he is also regenerated. The aspects, or components, of salvation—justification and sanctification—are the consideration of the fourth point under discussion. Justification is the act where God declares us to be righteous in Christ, while sanctification is the process by which God conforms us to the righteousness of Christ.

---

[51] See Olson, *The Story of Christian Theology,* 551.

All of these facets of salvation—redemption's origin, the ability to respond to the gospel call, the accomplishment of our justification and sanctification, and the bestowing of the benefits of salvation—are all "summed up" in Jesus Christ to the glory of God (1 Cor. 15:24–28; Eph. 1:10–12).

The Origin of Salvation

When discussing the doctrine of election, most Christians make a distinction between what God *permits* and what he *ordains,* and we are careful to say that God merely permitted creation's fall into sin, but he actively ordains the church's salvation.[52] The nuance between permission and ordination is difficult to keep in mind, but it is crucial when considering God's relationship to sin and salvation. God ordains the salvation of those who believe, but he allows the damnation of those who eternally reject the Savior.

The distinction between permission and ordination comes from our understanding of the difference between God and his creation. God, the sovereign Creator, created the world according to his plan and purpose. However, creation is not divine or a part of God; so by creating, God allowed something other than himself to exist. How God, with his infinite attributes, and creation, which is "not God," can simultaneously exist is not easy to comprehend. Since God is all-knowing, all-powerful, and present everywhere, it is hard to see how there is "room" for anything or anyone else.

Much more difficult to understand is how creation can have any type of freedom from God, yet the level of free choice God gives to his handiwork is remarkable. Lucifer freely rebelled, we freely joined him, and God allowed it. God is not the author of sin—he permitted the fall; he did not ordain or cause it. God sovereignly chose to allow a certain amount of freedom to his creation, and we call this decision *divine permission.* By contrast, God actively ordains salvation. Salvation is the deliberate outworking of God's plan to rescue that which he permitted to revolt.

Salvation originates with God. Paul declared, "He chose us in Him [Christ] before the foundation of the world," and that he "predestined us to adoption as sons by Jesus Christ to Himself, according to the good pleasure of His will" (Eph. 1:4–5). Contained within God's plan to create

---

[52] Most Calvinists and all Arminians recognize the concept of divine permission. See Gordon Lewis and Bruce Demarest, *Integrative Theology,* vol. 1 (Grand Rapids: Zondervan, 1987), 318–19; Bruce Ware, *God's Greater Glory: The Exalted God of Scripture and the Christian Faith* (Wheaton: Crossway, 2004), 102–30; and Thomas Oden, *The Transforming Power of Grace* (Nashville: Abingdon Press, 1993), 125–39. However, some Calvinists consider the differentiation between permission and ordination to be a distinction without a difference. Calvin is critical of the notion of divine permission. See John Calvin, *Concerning the Eternal Predestination of God,* 176; and *Institutes,* 1.16.8; 1.18.1.

was the decision to allow the world to rebel (or fall), and—more importantly—his decision also included the plan to save (or redeem) his creation. The salvation we enjoy in the Lord Jesus Christ is the fruition of God's glorious plan which he purposed before the world began. We are saved because God chose to save us in eternity past, and we call his choice of the redeemed *election*.

Election is the gracious decision of God by which he chooses certain ones to be the recipients of salvation. Whether God chooses the elect individually or as a group and whether he bases his choice on the foreseen faith of the elect are issues of intense debate. Also, some contend that election in the Bible refers only to service and not to salvation. Those who argue for understanding election only in corporate terms or only in relationship to service have some valid points, for when Scripture speaks of election it generally refers to God's choice of a group as a whole (i.e., Israel or the church, Deut. 7:7–8; Eph. 1:3–13) or to God's call to an individual for special service (i.e., Jeremiah or John the Baptist, Jer. 1:5; Luke 1:15–17). However, the Bible also teaches there is an election of individuals to salvation, and it is this type of election we are exploring.

The doctrine of election addresses the question of the ultimate cause of a person's choice to trust Jesus Christ as Lord and Savior. Every believer has the keen awareness that if God's Spirit had not first come to him, he never would have come to God. And all orthodox Christians, Calvinists and Arminians alike, understand God to be the origin and ultimate cause of salvation, but the question at hand is whether God is also the ultimate cause of our choice to receive (or reject) salvation.

All of the approaches to the doctrine of election (and they are many and varied) can be grouped under three headings: *unconditional, conditional,* and *concurrent.* Unconditional election understands God's choice of an individual to be the ultimate cause of that person's choice to believe; conditional election sees God's selection of a person to be based or conditioned on that person's foreseen faith; while concurrent election contends that somehow the arguments for the unconditional and conditional positions are both true. Some advocates of the concurrent election position appeal to God's timelessness, others base their arguments on his ability to know even hypothetical situations (this ability is called *middle knowledge*), while still others argue that, since the Bible clearly teaches concurrence but does not provide an explanation about how concurrence works, then the matter should simply be left as a mystery.

Most Christians accept that God's sovereignty and man's responsibility are simultaneously true even if they disagree about how to reconcile these biblical doctrines. In practice, particularly in evangelism, Christians operate with the twin truths in tension. We preach and witness with the fervent aim of persuading the lost to repent and believe. Concurrently, we recognize that salvation is a work of God, and we pray earnestly that he will turn many hearts to himself. In every area of life, believers conduct themselves with faith in God's sovereign control while also recognizing the human ability to choose (for example, even the strongest believer in predestination looks both ways when he crosses the street). However, this congruent tension is most acute in the area of salvation.

In brief, Calvinism contends that God's choice of individuals for salvation, or election, is unconditional (i.e., there is no consideration of any foreseen merit or faith on the part of the elect). Arminianism, by contrast, argues that God elects persons according to foreknowledge (i.e., he chooses persons according to their foreseen faith). Calvinists operate with the control beliefs of a strong view of God's sovereignty, the conviction that salvation is completely gracious, and that the effects of sin render all incapable of responding to the gospel. Arminians are guided by a high view of the holiness of God, the conviction that he is just in his dealings, and that we are responsible for our response to the gospel call because we *are* able to respond. The dispute between the two groups often has been bitter and divisive because both positions have strong arguments and because adhering to either viewpoint has substantial consequences for doctrine and practical ministry.

Unconditional Election

Calvinism argues that though God has not revealed why he chose one person and not another or how he arrived at his choices, he does have the sovereign right to make this judgment, and the purpose for his decision is to bring glory to himself. Calvinists freely acknowledge that their interpretation of the doctrines of election and of reprobation presents logical and moral problems, but they contend that Scripture and reason allow no other conclusion.

Indeed, the biblical case for unconditional election seems compelling. When Moses declared to Israel why God chose them out of all the nations of the earth, he explicitly excluded any type of merit or inherent value in Israel which would commend them to God. "The LORD did not set his affection on you and choose you because you were more numerous than other peoples, for you were the fewest of all peoples," Moses explained, "but it was because the LORD loved you . . . he . . . redeemed you from the land of slavery" (Deut. 7:7–8 NIV). In other words, God's choice of Israel was an expression of his sovereign love.

Similarly, the Apostle Paul claimed that just as God unconditionally chose the collective nation of Israel, so also God sovereignly selected him as an individual. He stated, "God, who set me apart from birth and called me by his grace, was pleased to reveal his Son in me so that I might preach him among the Gentiles" (Gal. 1:15–16 NIV). Note how Paul tied together his call to salvation and to service. Though the Bible focuses primarily on the corporate and vocational aspects of election (which therefore should be our primary emphases, too), that is not all it teaches. Scripture also teaches that God chooses individuals for salvation.[53]

Critics of the Calvinistic understanding of unconditional election point out three problems. First, Reformed theology bases its approach to the doctrine of unconditional election on the premise that God is the cause of all things.[54] Since God sovereignly ordains all things that come to pass, he is obviously the cause of our choice to believe, and in an ultimate sense he is the cause of the unbelief of those who reject Christ. But this starting assumption poses great moral problems for our understanding of the character of God. Since "all things" would include the fall, Calvinism's beginning premise appears to make God the author of sin.

Second, if God decrees (either actively or passively) the damnation of persons before they or the world they inhabit ever existed, then he does not love all humanity, nor does he desire the salvation of all persons. This seriously affects our understanding of the love of God and seems to be at variance with certain biblical texts (Ezek. 18:23; John 3:16; 1 Tim. 2:4; and 2 Pet. 3:9).

And third, human responsibility presents a particular problem. It is difficult to see how persons can be responsible for not responding to a gospel to which they were not able to respond. In addition, if Christ did not die for the non-elect, then the reprobate are accountable for rejecting a redemption that was never available to them in the first place. Calvinists affirm human responsibility, but by definition, to be responsible means that one is able to respond. The primary issue concerning human responsibility is not whether humans have free will but whether the Calvinist teaching does justice to God's character.

Within Calvinism the debate has been over whether God predestines persons prior to considering the fall or after taking the fall into account. In other words, did God elect and reject humans as humans, or did he look

---

[53] Even William Klein, who is a strong proponent of the corporate view of election, admits that Paul seems to be teaching individual election to salvation in Galatians 1:15–16. See William W. Klein, *The New Chosen People: A Corporate View of Election* (Grand Rapids: Zondervan, 1990), 195.

[54] The Westminster Confession states, "God from all eternity did, by the most wise and holy counsel of his own will, freely, and unchangeably ordain whatsoever comes to pass." The Westminster Assembly, "The Westminster Confession of Faith, 1610, 3.1" in *Creeds and Confessions of Faith in the Christian Tradition,* vol. 2, ed. Jaroslav Pelikan and Valerie Hotchkiss (New Haven: Yale University, 2003) 610. Those who disagree with the Westminster definition of providence would say that whatever God wills comes to pass, but not everything that comes to pass is God's will. This alternative view of providence makes room for the concept of God's permission, by which he allows evil but is not the author of it.

upon humanity as sinners when he made his choices? Did God choose to love some people and reject others and then bring about the fall in order to damn those he rejected? Or did he ordain the fall and then from fallen humanity choose to save certain ones?

The position called *supralapsarianism* (*supra*—"before" and *lapse*—"fall," hence "before the fall") argues that God's decrees to save some and to damn others logically occurred prior to his decision to ordain the fall. *Infralapsarianism* (*infra*—"after," "after the fall") contends that logically God's decree to save came after his decree to allow the fall.[55] In the discussion of the order of the decrees, one must remember that God is omniscient, so he never goes through the thought processes of arriving at a conclusion. The logical order, not the chronological order, of the decrees is under consideration.[56]

Supralapsarianism is sometimes called "high Calvinism." The original Reformers held to this position as did several at the Synod of Dort; however, it is a minority view within Calvinism today. Supralapsarianism contends that God is the ultimate cause of the choices of both types of individuals—those who accept Christ and those who reject him. God decided (or ordained) to choose certain ones to eternal life (the elect) and to reject others to eternal condemnation (the reprobate). God logically made this decision before all other decisions, and his subsequent choices are simply the logical outcome of this first double decree.

Advocates for supralapsarianism base their arguments on the infinite attributes of God. Since God is omniscient, omnipotent, and omnipresent, then by necessity all events must happen according to his will. Supralapsarianism clearly understands God to be the cause of all things—including evil. This means that God's relationship both to the elect and the reprobate is symmetrical (i.e., his sovereign will, equally and in the same way, is the cause of the salvation of some and the damnation of others).[57]

Critics point out a number of problems with supralapsarianism, particularly noting how the position creates serious moral difficulties and calls into question the character of God. First, some supralapsarians do not hesitate

---

[55] This approach often is called *decretal theology* because it operates with God's decrees as the starting pointing of studying theology.

[56] One must keep in mind that attempts to discern the order of the decrees are highly speculative. As Mouw states, "The infra- versus supra- debate functions in perceptions of Reformed theology in much the same way as the 'angels on the head of a pin' discussion does for medieval scholasticism. For many within the tradition it is an embarrassing example of how their own patterns of theologizing can run amok; for external critics of the tradition it provides the basis for a *reductio ad absurdum* of the system's basic premises." See Richard Mouw, "*Scholia et Homiletica*: Another Look at the Infra/Supralapsarian Debate" *CTJ* 35 (2000): 138.

[57] For a clear advocacy of supralapsarianism, see Robert Reymond, "A Consistent Supralapsarian Perspective on Election," in *Five Views on Election,* ed. Chad Owen Brand (Nashville: Broadman & Holman, 2006), 150–205.

to make God the author of evil and the cause of sin.[58] These supralapsarians present God's all-encompassing decree in such a way as to have little difference with the fatalism of Islam.[59] For the Muslim, Allah's will is the cause of all things, including sin and evil.[60] Therefore, the occurrence of wickedness is good because Allah mysteriously wills it.

Second, supralapsarianism makes God's hatred for the reprobate an attribute equal to his love. Just as God eternally loves the elect, in a parallel fashion he has always hated the reprobate.[61] If God has a symmetric relationship with the two classes of people, then this has disturbing consequences for our understanding of the nature of God.

A third criticism is that historically supralapsarianism has had the effect of stifling evangelism and missions. Staunch supralapsarians, such as Primitive (or "hardshell") Baptists, argue that since God decreed salvation only for the elect, then they are the only ones for whom Christ died. They then reason that the gospel is not really offered to all but is genuinely available only for the elect. Therefore, the gospel should be presented only to those who show evidence of being regenerated.[62]

John Gill, a leading Baptist of the seventeenth century, directed many Baptists to adopt supralapsarianism. The great preacher Charles Spurgeon,

---

[58] For example, in his discussion on the origin of evil, Sproul states, "Of course it's impossible for God to sin. He can't sin. This objection, however, is off the mark. I am not accusing God of sinning; I am suggesting that he created sin." R. C. Sproul, *Almighty over All: Understanding the Sovereignty of God* (Grand Rapids: Baker, 1999), 54. Arminius found supralapsarianism an easy target. He pointed out that if God is the ultimate cause of sin, then God is the only sinner, which in turn means that sin is not really sin at all. See James Arminius, "A Declaration of Sentiments," in *The Works of James Arminius* (1608; repr., Grand Rapids: Baker, 1986), 630.

[59] Boettner tries to distance supralapsarianism from Islam but also acknowledges their similarities. See Lorraine Boettner, *The Reformed Doctrine of Predestination* (Grand Rapids: Eerdmans, 1932), 2, 13–14, 318–23.

[60] In Sura 32:13 of the Qur'an, Allah declares, "Had we willed, we could have given every soul its guidance, but it is already predetermined that I will fill Hell with jinns and humans, all together."

[61] Some supralapsarians, such as David Engelsma, admit this freely. He states, "It is not at all surprising that advocates of the free offer oppose the Reformed doctrine of reprobation, for reprobation is the exact, explicit denial that God loves all men, desires to save all men, and conditionally offers them salvation. Reprobation asserts that God eternally hates some men; has immutably decreed their damnation; and has determined to withhold from them Christ, grace, faith, and salvation." See David Engelsma, *Hyper-Calvinism and the Call of the Gospel* (Grand Rapids: Reformed Free Publishing Association, 1994), 58.

[62] Articles 24–26 of *The Gospel Standard Articles of Faith* declares, "We believe that the invitations of the Gospel, being spirit and life, are intended only for those who have been made by the blessed Spirit to feel their lost state as sinners and their need of Christ as their Saviour, and to repent of and forsake their sins." See http://www.pristinegrace.org/media.php?id=313 for the full statement of the Gospel Standard (Baptist) Churches. Many decretal theologians reject using the word *offer* to describe the presenting of the gospel. Preaching is not an offer of salvation or an attempt to persuade the hearer to respond. Rather it is the instrument by which faith is activated in the elect. Any effort to persuade the hearers to repent and believe is viewed as interfering with the work of the Holy Spirit. This clearly is a sub-biblical view of preaching and is incompatible with the practice of the early church (Acts 2:40; 14:1; 2 Cor. 5:11).

who became the pastor of Gill's church in the nineteenth century, assessed Gill's hyper-Calvinism by stating, "The system of theology with which many identify his name has chilled many churches to their very soul, for it has led them to omit the free invitations of the gospel, and to deny that it is the duty of sinners to believe in Jesus."[63] The history of the influence of supralapsarianism in Baptist life is not an edifying one.

Though the Reformers—Luther, Zwingli, and Calvin—adhered to the supralapsarian paradigm of unconditional election in no small part due to the influence of Augustinian theology, Augustine himself held to *infralapsarianism*. And though both infralapsarians and supralapsarians were present at the Synod of Dort, the canons adopted only the infralapsarian position.[64] Like the Synod, most Calvinists break with Calvin concerning his supralapsarianism and opt for Augustine's infralapsarianism.

Rather than two equal decrees of election and reprobation, infralapsarianism argues that God ordained only one decree—the decree to elect. After God determined to create human beings and permit them to fall, he decided to save some of them (the elect). Last, he decreed to send Christ to provide salvation only for the elect.[65]

In order to avoid some of the moral conundrums of supralapsarianism, infralapsarianism uses a much more complex logic. Specifically, infralapsarianism's reasoning hinges on the concept of *divine permission*. God allowed the fall, and he would have been entirely just even if he had decided to save no one. However, God actively chose certain ones to be saved to the glory of his grace. Those whom he passively allowed to be eternally lost are entirely responsible for their sinful condition, so God is not the cause of their eternal damnation.

According to infralapsarianism, God has an asymmetric, or unequal, relationship with the two classes of people: he actively chooses the elect but passes over the reprobate. The reprobate are not ordained for hell but are omitted from heaven. Therefore, election is unconditional while reprobation is conditional. It is generally agreed that supralapsarianism has fewer logical problems while infralapsarianism attempts to have fewer moral ones.

Whether considering supralapsarianism or infralapsarianism, there is much about decretal theology to commend itself. First, decretal theology intends to present an entirely gracious salvation. Calvinism takes uncondi-

---

63 Charles Spurgeon, *Autobiography*, vol. 1 (Edinburgh: Banner of Truth, 1973), 310.

64 See the Synod of Dort, "The Canons of the Synod of Dort, 1618–19," article 6.

65 Most infralapsarian Calvinists hold to limited atonement as firmly as their supralapsarian brethren. However, Schreiner and Ware's book defending infralapsarianism conspicuously omits a defense of limited atonement. See Thomas Schreiner and Bruce Ware, eds., *Still Sovereign: Contemporary Perspectives on Election, Foreknowledge, and Grace* (Grand Rapids: Baker, 2000).

tional election as its starting point because it argues that a conditional salvation is inevitably man-centered and meritorious. Calvinists understand exercising faith to be a human work; therefore, if salvation is entirely by grace, then there is no room for any conditions.[66]

Second decretal theology strives to uphold God's sovereignty. In order to affirm that God's sovereign will is always done, Calvinists generally have to distinguish between what they call God's revealed will and his secret will. God's revealed will is the Scriptures, with his commandments against sin and his expressions of desire for the salvation of all. His secret will is his decisions to use the wickedness of responsible creatures and his decree to save only the elect. God's revealed will often is not done while his sovereign, secret will is always accomplished because this undisclosed will is the ultimate cause of all that happens.[67] Because infralapsarians embrace the concept of divine permission, they affirm the distinction between the two wills of God more readily than supralapsarians.

Third the goal of decretal theology is to magnify God's glory. More than once the Apostle Paul declared that we were predestined to salvation "to the praise of His glory" (Eph. 1:12). The ultimate purpose of all things and the final outcome of all ages will be the glory of God.

Despite Calvinism's commendable aspirations, its use of decretal theology leaves itself open to four weighty criticisms. First, decretal theology is highly speculative about issues on which the Bible gives little or no information. Detractors point out that trumpeting the humility of "the doctrines of grace" while divining the mind of God by discerning the logical order of the decrees can be seen as an act of inconsistent hubris. Thus decretal theology is actually a philosophy masquerading as theology. However, opponents should not be too eager to cast stones since alternative positions are also dependent on philosophical presuppositions and assumptions.[68] When working with the doctrine of election, exploring various options, assumptions, and implications is inevitable. We believe God sovereignly chooses individuals to eternal life because this is what the Scriptures plainly teach. But beyond that, the Bible tells us little on the subject; therefore humility is in order.

---

[66] In this regard the TULIP acronym is misleading. In order to spell the flower, the "T" of total depravity is listed first. However, the canons of the Synod of Dort begin with unconditional election and argue that the first point logically requires the other four points. The order presented by the canons is actually ULTIP. See the Synod of Dort, "The Canons of the Synod of Dort, 1618–19." Humpherys and Robertson also make this point; see Fisher Humpherys and Paul Robertson, *God So Loved the World: Traditional Baptists and Calvinism* (New Orleans: Insight, 2000), 16.

[67] Erickson distinguishes between God's revealed will and his secret will by calling the former "God's wish." See Erickson, *Christian Theology,* 387.

[68] For example, two alternatives to Calvinism, Molinism and Thomism, are primarily philosophical constructs. At best they can be found to be compatible with Scripture but not derived from Scripture.

A second criticism is that decretal theology is a logical system that ultimately fails logically. Thomas Schreiner, like many other thoughtful Calvinists, acknowledges this when he states, "The scandal of the Calvinist system is that ultimately the logical problems posed cannot be fully resolved."[69] When dealing with this subject, all theological systems must eventually appeal to mystery; the challenge is locating the proper place of mystery. It appears that, in the name of logical consistency, decretal theology has sometimes run roughshod over certain clear teachings of Scripture, particularly in the areas of the extent of the atonement and God's universal salvific desire.

The third problem is corollary to the previous one: decretal theology leaves the moral problems of predestination unresolved. Unfortunately, this is as true of infralapsarianism as it is of supralapsarianism. In the final analysis, Calvinism teaches that the ultimate reason a person dies lost is because God decides against him, not the other way around.[70]

Decretal theology teaches that even though God could save all, he chooses not to in order for his glory to be fully displayed. John Piper explains, "What does God desire more than saving all? . . . The answer given by Calvinists is that the greater value is the manifestation of the full range of God's glory in wrath and mercy (Rom. 9:22–23) and the humbling of man so that he enjoys giving all credit to God for his salvation (1 Cor. 1:29)."[71] Critics accuse Reformed theology of allowing a philosophical understanding of God's glory to cause them to fail to maintain a biblical view his glory.[72] In other words, opponents accuse decretal theology of sacrificing the glory of God's righteousness on the altar of God's sovereignty.

A fourth criticism brought against decretal theology is that it reduces Christ to the mere instrument by which the decrees are accomplished. Both

---

[69] Thomas Schreiner, "Does Scripture Teach Prevenient Grace in the Wesleyan Sense?" in *The Grace of God, the Bondage of the Will*, vol. 2, ed. Thomas Schreiner and Bruce Ware (Grand Rapids: Baker, 1995), 382. Calvinist theologian Paul Jewett concurs, stating, "In any case, when all is said and done, the problem of reprobation remains unresolved and, it would appear, irresolvable." See Paul Jewett, *Election and Predestination* (Grand Rapids: Eerdmans, 1985), 99–100.

[70] Calvin, recognizing the implications of decretal theology, conceded, "The decree, I admit, is dreadful." See Calvin, *Institutes,* 3:23:7.

[71] John Piper, "Are There Two Wills in God? Divine Election and God's Desire for All to Be Saved," in *The Grace of God, the Bondage of the Will*, ed. Thomas Schreiner and Bruce Ware (Grand Rapids: Baker, 1995), 123–24. Sproul makes the same point when he states, "It was his desire to make his wrath known. He needed, then, something on which to be wrathful. He needed to have sinful creatures. . . . All of this serves his eternal and ultimate desire, to glorify himself." See R. C. Sproul, *Almighty over All,* 57. The moral problems of decretal theology were not lost on the skeptic David Hume. "The grosser pagans contented themselves with divinizing lust, incest, and adultery; but the predestinarian doctors have divinized cruelty, wrath, fury, vengeance, and all the blackest vices." David Hume, *Principal Writings on Religion* (1757; repr., Oxford: Oxford University Press, 1993), 192.

[72] Jerry Walls and Joseph Dongell, *Why I Am Not a Calvinist* (Downers Grove: InterVarsity, 2004), 65.

supralapsarianism and infralapsarianism assume that God logically begins his plans with us and then decides to send his Son to be our Savior. This highly questionable assumption seems to have the effect of making Christ an afterthought and commits the mistake that decretal theology strives to avoid—it puts man at the front and center of attention. The Bible never reduces Christ to the role of mere instrument; rather Jesus Christ is the locus and sum of salvation, including election (Eph. 1:4; 2 Tim. 1:9).

One attempt within Calvinism to address the problems relating to decretal theology is sublapsarianism, or *Amyraldianism,* named after its proponent, Moses Amyraut, the most influential Reformed theologian of the seventeenth century.[73] In Amyraut's proposal for the logical order of the decrees, God determined to provide redemption sufficient to save all humanity through the blood of Christ before he decided to choose some people to receive this salvation. Amyraldianism is sometimes called four-point Calvinism because it rejects limited atonement but holds to the other four points of TULIP (total depravity, unconditional election, irresistible grace, and perseverance of the saints).

Amyraut saw his position as a corrective to the decretal theology of Dort and believed his view to be more faithful to the position of Calvin himself.[74] Jewett summarizes Amyraut's argument in six points.[75] First, we must begin with Christ. If we begin our study of the doctrine of election by asking what God ordained before the foundation of the world, then we are led into a hopeless labyrinth.[76] We must begin with what God has revealed in Jesus Christ. Second, we must not deny God's revealed will by appealing to his hidden will. In Amyraut's mind, claiming to know what God has not revealed is at best heresy and perhaps blasphemy. Third, election must be considered under the heading of salvation, not God's sovereignty. To begin with God's sovereignty as decretal theology does run the danger of making predestination appear arbitrary and capricious. Fourth, we must let the economy of salvation guide our investigations. Therefore, we must put

---

[73] See Brian G. Armstrong, *Calvinism and the Amyraut Heresy: Protestant Scholasticism and Humanism in Seventeenth-Century France* (Madison: University of Wisconsin Press, 1969).

[74] Whether Amyraut or Beza was truer to Calvin is still an ongoing debate. Armstrong sides with Amyraut while Nicole considers Amyraldianism a corruption of Reformed doctrine. See Roger Nicole, *Moyse Amyraut: A Bibliography with Special Reference to the Controversy on Universal Grace* (New York: Garland, 1981).

[75] Jewett, *Election and Predestination,* 101.

[76] This same warning was made by Calvin, though it seems he did not always follow his own advice. "The predestination of God is truly a labyrinth from which the mind of man is wholly incapable of extricating itself. But the curiosity of man is so insistent that the more dangerous it is to inquire into a subject, the more boldly he rushes to do so. Thus when predestination is being discussed, because he cannot keep himself within the proper limits, he immediately plunges into the depths of the sea by his impetuosity." John Calvin, *The Epistles of Paul the Apostle to the Romans and the Thessalonians,* 202.

more emphasis on the revealed will of God than the secret will. Fifth, we must focus on God's conditional will to save all rather than on his absolute will to redeem the elect.

Amyraut's last point is that we must view the work of salvation in trinitarian terms. He sees in the Father a universal will to save, a universal work of atonement provided by the Son, but a limited work of calling the elect by the Spirit. In other words, Amyraut understands election to be a decision of the Holy Spirit. Amyraut's modifications to decretal theology do not solve all the problems associated with Reformed soteriology, but they have been adopted by a sizable percentage of Calvinists.[77]

Conditional Election

The hallmark of classic Arminianism is the doctrine of *conditional election*.[78] Jack Cottrell defines conditional predestination as "the view that before the world ever existed God conditionally predestined some specific individuals to eternal life and the rest to eternal condemnation, based on his foreknowledge of their free-will responses to his law and to his grace."[79] In James Arminius's presentation of the logical order of the decrees, God first determines to provide Christ as Savior. Then he decrees to save those who believe and damn those who do not. God's third determination is to provide sufficient grace for all to believe. Fourth, he chooses to save and damn particular individuals according to his foreknowledge of their foreseen faith. Similar to Calvinism, Arminianism believes in the election and reprobation of individuals to salvation—with one crucial difference—Arminianism holds that predestination is conditional.[80] God has sovereignly determined to ratify the freewill choices of individuals.

The linchpin argument for the conditional election position is that election is according to foreknowledge. Several biblical texts, such as "for whom He foreknew, He also predestined to be conformed to the image of His Son" (Rom. 8:29) and "elect according to the foreknowledge of God the Father" (1 Pet. 1:2), clearly appear to support this assertion. In addition to the biblical support, Arminians point out that the early church fathers held to election according to foreknowledge, that it has always been the po-

---

[77] Bruce Demarest is a leading proponent of Amyraldian Calvinism. See Demarest, *The Cross and Salvation.*

[78] James Arminius, "A Declaration of Sentiments," 654.

[79] Jack Cottrell, "The Classical Arminian View of Election," in *Five Views on Election,* ed. Chad Owen Brand (Nashville: Broadman & Holman, 2006), 135–94.

[80] Arminians are split on whether conditional election is corporate or for individuals. Some Arminians, such as Robert Shank, contend that election always refers to communities of individuals, namely Israel and the church, while others, such as Robert Picirilli, see the predestination of individuals also being taught in the Scriptures. See Robert Shank, *Elect in the Son* (Minneapolis: Bethany House, 1989), and Robert Picirilli, *Grace, Faith, and Free Will* (Nashville: Randall House, 2002). Arminius himself held to the conditional predestination of individuals.

sition of Eastern Orthodoxy, and that it is the majority opinion of Catholics and Protestants today.

Calvinists generally respond by arguing that when the Bible speaks of God's foreknowledge of the elect, it is referring to more than mere advance awareness. Erickson sees a link between the Old Testament's use of the word *yada*, "to know," to indicate the intimate nature of the sexual relationship (e.g., Gen. 4:1, "Now Adam knew [*yada*] Eve his wife, and she conceived"), and the New Testament word for foreknow, *proginōskō*.[81] In this light, "to foreknow" means "to forelove," so foreknowing is essentially synonymous with choosing.

Cottrell presents a four-point rebuttal to the Calvinist argument.[82] First, he points out that in extrabiblical Greek literature, the use of *ginosko* in a noncognitive way is "virtually non-existent."[83] Second, the Bible's use of "know" as a euphemism does not help the Calvinist position since this speaks of the sexual act and not to any expression of love. In fact, the euphemism bolsters the foreknowledge view because it signifies an intimate type of knowledge rather than the making of a choice.

For his third argument Cottrell concedes that there are places in the Bible where *know* indicates care or love (e.g., Exod. 2:25; Hos. 13:5). However, this affection is generally stated in conditional terms (e.g., "But if anyone loves God, this one is known by Him," 1 Cor. 8:3). And fourth, in the over eighty times where the New Testament uses the word *know* with a person as its object, not once does it denote choosing. In addition, to make *foreknow* mean "choose" in Romans 8:29 ("For whom He foreknew, He also predestined") renders the statement redundant and destroys the logic of Paul's argument. In short, Cottrell concludes that the Calvinist position of *foreknowing* meaning "foreloving" is a case of special pleading.

The conditional election view has no problem affirming the universal salvific will of God. Based on the assertions of Scripture (Ezek. 33:11; John 3:16; 1 Tim. 2:3–4; 2 Pet. 3:9) and the nature and character of God ("God is love," 1 John 4:8), Arminians believe that God desires the salvation of all. Since coerced love is not really love at all, God gives individuals the genuine ability to reject him, which means that his salvific will may not be done.

Obviously, adherents of the conditional election position believe all persons are capable of responding to the gospel message. There is disagreement within the Arminian camp as to why sinful people are able to respond to God's call.[84] On the one hand, liberal Arminians hold to something close

[81] Erickson, *Christian Theology*, 382.
[82] Cottrell, "The Classical Arminian View of Election," 84–93.
[83] Ibid., 88.
[84] Ibid.

to Pelagianism, that this is a natural ability untouched by the fall. On the other hand, conservative Arminians accept the doctrine of total depravity and argue that God does a work of prevenient grace which negates the effects of the fall to the point that all persons are able to respond to the offer of grace.

The problem with conditional election is that it reduces God's decision to the ratification of what man decides. Arminians are correct when they assert that God can sovereignly cede over to humanity whatever he chooses, but Scripture teaches that God is not merely passive in the matter of election (Eph. 1:3–14). As Spurgeon observes, "Arminianism marries Christ to a bride he did not choose."[85]

In addition, if God has exhaustive knowledge of all future events, then conditional election does not really remove the unconditional nature of God's decisions. If God knows that a certain person will freely accept the gospel while that person's brother freely will not, and yet God decides to create both of them anyway, then this is a mysterious, sovereign, and unconditional determination on the part of God.

Some who hold to conditional election recognize that the question of why God creates those he foreknows will not accept the gospel is a problem for their view. Thomas Oden quotes the solution given by John of Damascus (ca. 676–754): "Had God kept from being made those who through His goodness were to have existence, but who by their own choice were to become evil, then evil would have prevailed over the goodness of God."[86] But this answer is unsatisfactory because it implies that God creates persons out of necessity. Certain Arminians recognize the full implication of God's foreknowledge and therefore deny he has exhaustive knowledge of all future events and decisions.[87] Arminianism has powerful and appealing arguments, yet in the end some type of unconditional choice on the part of God has to be acknowledged.

Concurrent Approaches to Election

A number of approaches can be grouped under the heading of *concurrence* or, as it is sometimes called, *congruism*.[88] The concurrent position contends the Bible teaches both that God sovereignly and unconditionally chooses the elect for salvation and that each individual person freely decides to accept or reject Jesus Christ as Savior. In other words, Scripture presents predestination and human freedom as twin truths in tension. Bernard of

---

[85] Charles Spurgeon, quoted by Jewett, *Election and Predestination,* 63.

[86] Oden, *The Transforming Power of Glory,* 144–45.

[87] Arminians who deny God has exhaustive foreknowledge argue for what they call "open theism." See Richard Rice et al., *The Openness of God* (Downers Grove: InterVarsity, 1994).

[88] Erickson, a proponent of congruism, quotes B. B. Warfield as calling congruism "the mildest form of Calvinism." See Erickson, *Christian Theology,* 385.

Clairvaux (1090–1153) expressed this tension when he observed, "Take away free will and there will be nothing left to save; take away grace and there will be no means left of salvation."[89] The goal of the concurrence positions is to affirm a high view of God's sovereignty while avoiding the mechanical reductionism of a causal determinism which in turn diminishes free will decisions to the level of a line of falling dominoes.

Calvinism and Arminianism both have compelling arguments because the Bible repeatedly presents divine and human choice side by side as parallel truths, often in the same context. As Paul and Barnabas preached during their first missionary journey, the Scriptures state they "spoke so effectively that a great number of Jews and Gentiles believed" (Acts 14:1 NIV). But just five verses earlier the text declares, "And as many as had been appointed to eternal life believed" (Acts 13:48). The Bible so congruently interweaves divine and human actions that it is a mystery where one ends and the other begins (cf. John 6).

The medieval scholastic Thomas Aquinas (1225–1274) based his argument that predestination and free will are concurrently true on two tenets of classical theism: God's simplicity and God's timelessness. Classical theism holds that God is simple in the sense that his essence is undivided and without parts. It also contends that time is a part of creation. Therefore God resides outside of time in the eternal now, and all parts of time—past, present, and future—are equally before him.

Aquinas reasoned that since God's essence is simple (i.e., undivided), then his foreknowledge and his predetermination are the same thing. Norman Geisler, an advocate of the Thomistic position, speaks of God "*knowingly determining* and *determinately knowing* from all eternity everything that happens, including all free acts."[90] Since what God knows and what he decides are indivisible, then there is no logical priority to either one.

If divine simplicity ensures there is no logical priority to God's foreknowledge and his decisions, then divine timelessness necessitates there is no chronological priority between his knowledge and his choices. If all moments are equally present to God, then God's election of a person and a person's free choice to accept the gospel occur "at the same time," so to speak.[91]

---

[89] Bernard of Clairvaux, "Divine Grace and Human Freedom," 1.2, in *Bernard of Clairvaux: Essential Writings,* ed. Dennis Tamburello (New York: Crossroad, 2000), 39–40.

[90] Norman Geisler, "God Knows All Things," in *Predestination and Free Will: Four Views of Divine Sovereignty and Human Freedom* (Downers Grove: InterVarsity, 1986), 70–72 (emphasis original). Geisler has written an entire book arguing for the Thomistic version of concurrence with a title that sums up his position: *Chosen, but Free.* See Norman Geisler, *Chosen, but Free* (Minneapolis: Bethany House, 2001).

[91] Koons argues that, because of God's timelessness, God's determination to elect and a person's decision to believe are equivalent events and therefore have the same "truth-maker." Since God's decisions are free, then our freedom "piggybacks" on his freedom. See Robert Koons, "Dual Agency: A Thomistic Account of Providence and Human Freedom," *Philosophia Christi* 4 (2002): 403–6.

This means God's choice does not cause the choice of free creatures, but because of God's timelessness, all free choices are eternally predetermined.[92]

While Thomism assumes God is outside of time, Molinism begins with the assumption that God operates within time, and when the Bible speaks of God's foreknowledge, it refers to his ability to perceive the future, not that future events are literally unfolding before him. Luis Molina (1535–1600), a Jesuit priest, argued that God predetermines human decisions in such a way that does not violate free will because he uses *middle knowledge*.

Instead of starting with a logical order of decrees as decretal Calvinism does, Molinism begins with a logical order of God's knowledge, which Molina sees occurring in three steps or moments.[93] First, God knows everything that *could* happen. Such infinite possibilities are beyond us but not God. This first moment is called his *natural knowledge* because God knows everything due to his omniscient nature. Second, from the set of infinite possibilities, God also knows which scenarios *would* result in persons freely responding in the way he desires. This crucial moment of knowledge is between the first and third moment, hence the term *middle knowledge*. From the repertoire of available options provided by his middle knowledge, God freely and sovereignly chooses which one he will bring to pass. This results in God's third moment of knowledge, which is his foreknowledge of what certainly *will* occur.[94]

The third moment is called God's *free knowledge* because it is determined by his free and sovereign choice. By using these three phases of knowledge, God predestines all events yet not in a way that violates genuine human freedom and choice. God meticulously "sets the table" so that humans freely choose what he has predetermined.[95] Molinism, with its use

---

Think of watching a recording of a sporting event in which you already know the final score. The outcome is certain but is not caused by your knowledge of the outcome. The Thomistic position posits that God's eternal ability to observe an event operates in a similar manner.

[92] Geisler concludes that God's predestination is confluent to his foreknowledge. He states: "There is a third alternative. It postulates that God's election is neither *based on* his foreknowledge of man's free choices nor exercised *independent of* it. As the Scriptures declare, we are 'elect *according to* the foreknowledge of God'" (emphasis original). Geisler, "God Knows All Things," 53. As one can see, the Thomistic version of concurrence is a philosophical argument based on some highly speculative assumptions about God's nature. Divine simplicity and timelessness are extremely difficult concepts to grasp and are viewed with skepticism by a number of theologians. Carson observes that the Thomistic view attempts to solve the obscure by appealing to the even more obscure. See D. A. Carson, *Divine Sovereignty and Human Responsibility* (Atlanta: John Knox, 1981), 207.

[93] Remember, due to God's omniscience, these are logical moments rather than moments in time.

[94] The verbs *could, would,* and *will* highlight the distinctions in the moments of God's knowledge. From knowledge of what *could* happen (first moment), God knows which ones *would* bring about his desired result (second moment), and he chooses one possibility, which means he knows it *will* come about (third moment).

[95] According to Molinism, our free choice determines how we would respond in any given setting, but God decides the setting in which we actually find ourselves. As Craig states, "It is up to God whether we find ourselves in a world in which we are predestined, but it is up to us whether

of middle knowledge, provides a unique way to approach the concurrence of divine and human choice.[96]

Perhaps we should entertain the possibility we are dealing with an intractable problem or an inscrutable *antinomy*.[97] The way the infinite God interacts with finite human beings is always a fundamental mystery. The inspiration of Scripture and the incarnation of Christ present us with examples of such mysteries. How did the Holy Spirit superintend the biblical writers without overwhelming their personalities? How did the divine nature of Christ unite with his human nature without rendering superfluous the limitations of his humanity? We affirm these doctrines because the Bible teaches them, but we do not pretend to understand these transcendent mysteries.

We should not appeal too quickly to mystery because such appeals can be a cover for incoherent thinking or mental laziness. However, we also must be able to recognize a theological antinomy when it appears, and this seems to be one of those times.

Biblical mysteries should not be ignored or abandoned. Though they cannot be explained, they still should be explored. In the same way we approach the mystery of the hypostatic union of Christ, we begin with an affirmation of the truthfulness of the divinely revealed mystery of concurrence and then search out the subsequent implications. The dissatisfaction with most Calvinist or Arminian presentations is that starting either with divine sovereignty or human freedom often results in one excluding the other. However, these twin truths are so inextricably interwoven that removing either thread results in the garment of the gospel falling apart.

The incarnation provides a particularly helpful analogy to the question of the interaction of divine sovereignty and human choice, especially in the matter of the two wills of Christ. Jesus Christ is one person with two natures—fully human and fully divine. The will is an essential part both of a human being and the divine nature of God so this means our Lord has two

---

we are predestined in the world in which we find ourselves." See William Lane Craig, "'No Other Name': A Middle Knowledge Perspective on the Exclusivity of Salvation Through Christ," *Faith and Philosophy* 6 (April 1989) 2:172–88. For Craig's defense of Molinism written at a popular level, see William Lane Craig, *The Only Wise God* (Grand Rapids: Baker, 1987).

[96] The distinctive difference between Calvinism and Molinism is that Calvinism sees God accomplishing his will through his omnipotent power while Molinism understands God using his omniscient knowledge. This leaves Molinism open to some of the same charges brought against Calvinism. See Jerry Walls, "Is Molinism as Bad as Calvinism?" *Faith and Philosophy* 7 (1990): 85–98.

[97] Packer, an advocate of the antinomy position, defines a theological antinomy as "an *apparent* incompatibility between two apparent truths. An antinomy exists when a pair of principles stands side by side, seemingly irreconcilable, yet both undeniable [emphasis original]." See J. I. Packer, *Evangelism and the Sovereignty of God* (Downers Grove: InterVarsity, 1961), 18. Another proponent, D. A. Carson, calls this position "tension theology." See Carson, *Divine Sovereignty and Human Responsibility,* 220.

wills—human and divine—and the Bible presents these two wills always working together freely in perfect congruence. Similarly, God's sovereign will and our human free choice occur in a confluent manner.[98]

Affirming a congruence of divine predestination and human freedom, we assert that Scripture teaches five corollaries. First, *salvation is a sovereign work of God from beginning to end* (Pss. 3:8; 37:39). A truly gracious redemption originates with God, is accomplished by God, and will be completed by God (Rom. 11:6). The entire Godhead is active in all aspects of our deliverance, but at various points in salvation history we see the different persons of the Trinity come to the forefront (Eph. 1:3–14). The Father figures preeminently in the planning of redemption, the Son pays the redemptive price upon the cross, and the Holy Spirit bestows the benefits of salvation through the preaching of the gospel.

Second, in a real and genuine way, *God desires the salvation of all humanity.* The passages of Scripture that assert God's universal salvific will can be affirmed at face value without detracting from God's sovereignty (e.g., Ezek. 18:23; John 3:16; 1 Tim. 2:4; 2 Pet. 3:9). However, the desire on God's part for the salvation of all is not fully met. The two leading explanations for this—that God has an even greater desire to glorify himself or that he has determined to save only those who freely believe in the gospel—are not necessarily in conflict. That God antecedently wills the salvation of all but consequently decrees the condition of faith is the overwhelming testimony of Scripture (e.g., John 3:16; Mark 16:15–16).

Third, *God purposes the salvation of the elect but only permits the damnation of the unbeliever.* The elect are saved by God's unconditional grace; the lost are condemned because of their unbelief. God is not the author of sin. He sovereignly chooses to allow unbelievers to go the way of perdition, but he does not desire it, nor does he cause it. God's choice of the elect is not conditioned upon any foreseen merit on the part of believers. We choose him and love him because he first chose and loved us (John 15:16; 1 John 4:19).

The fourth corollary is that *each person has the freedom to choose or reject salvation.* For this reason everyone is responsible for his decision and will give an account to God (John 3:18; Rom. 14:12; 2 Cor. 5:10–11).

Last, *election originates, is accomplished, and will be consummated in Jesus Christ* (Eph. 1:3–14). When we keep this truth in mind, it becomes

---

[98] The concurrence position does not attempt to find a compromise between divine sovereignty and human responsibility; rather it claims none is possible (or necessary). In a famous sermon Spurgeon made the case for congruism when he stated, "Some one said to me the other day, that he thought the truth lay somewhere between the two extremes. He meant right, but I think he was wrong. I do not think the truth lies between the two extremes, but in them both." Charles Spurgeon, "Sovereign Grace and Man's Responsibility," *New Park Street Pulpit,* available http://www.spurgeon.org/sermons/0207.htm.

clear that the Scriptures teach the doctrine of election for our assurance and comfort (Rom. 8:26–30). The biblical doctrine of our election in Christ gives no reason for fear or fatalism. We may not know all the secret counsels of God, but because of Christ, we know his will for us.

The Call to Salvation

From Genesis to Revelation, the Bible presents God as calling and inviting fallen humanity back to himself (Gen. 3:9; Rev. 22:17). A central motif in the Gospel record is Jesus as the Good Shepherd who searches out the lost sheep (Luke 15:1–7; 19:10).

Thiessen defines God's call as "that act of grace by which he invites men to accept by faith the salvation provided by Christ."[99] God calls externally through communication of the Word of God and internally as the Holy Spirit speaks inwardly to those who hear that communication. The external and internal calls operate together to deliver salvation to everyone who repents and believes.

God uses a variety of means to communicate the message of salvation. First, he providentially orchestrates the circumstances in which the good news is presented. The blessings and good things of life are gifts from God intended to call us to repentance (Rom. 2:4); and if we ignore his goodness, then even his judgments are gracious acts done for the purpose of drawing us to himself (Isa. 26:9).

Second, God communicates his call through human instruments—"how will they hear without a preacher?" (Rom. 10:14–15 NASB). When an angel appeared to Cornelius in Acts 10, he did not present the gospel to the centurion. Rather, he directed Cornelius to a human messenger, the Apostle Peter. God calls through the preaching of the gospel, and he reserves this task for the church (Matt. 28:18–20).

In addition to rendering humanity guilty before God, sin also affects the nature of persons. Because of human depravity, no one naturally desires God or holiness, and no one has the ability to respond to the gospel call. The world lives in a state of blindness that can be described as a severe case of spiritual autism or, worse yet, spiritual insanity (2 Cor. 4:4). This presents a tremendous problem for the preaching of the gospel. How are people in such condition able to respond to the gospel and receive salvation? The Bible teaches that the Holy Spirit oversees and accompanies the communication of the gospel, working in the unbeliever's heart while the messenger is speaking to the unbeliever's ears (1 Cor. 2:1–5). This internal

---

[99] Henry Clarence Thiessen, *Lectures in Systematic Theology* (Grand Rapids: Eerdmans, 1949), 350.

work of the Spirit convicts the hearer of sin (John 16:8–11) and enables him to respond (John 12:30–32).

The Holy Spirit's convicting ministry characterizes his relationship to the unbelieving world. Jesus spoke of this work when he explained: "And when He has come, He will convict the world of sin, and of righteousness, and of judgment: of sin, because they do not believe in Me; of righteousness, because I go to My Father and you see Me no more; of judgment, because the ruler of this world is judged" (John 16:8–11). The word "convict," *elegchein,* means "to cross-examine for the purpose of convincing or refuting an opponent" (generally in legal settings) or "to rebuke, to shame, or to expose."[100] For the believer the Holy Spirit is an advocate, but to the unbelieving world he is a prosecuting attorney. Our Lord teaches that the Holy Spirit will irrefutably reveal three truths: humanity's sin (16:9), God's righteousness (16:10), and the coming judgment (16:11).

When he convicts of sin, the Holy Spirit unmasks the true nature of man's problem—unbelief. Failure to believe God is the basis of sin, and failure to believe in Christ is the ultimate sin (John 16:9). Conviction is a gracious work because unless we are convinced of our true standing before God we will not believe. The Spirit's work is seen in the response of the hearers of Peter's sermon on the day of Pentecost: "Now when they heard this, they were cut to the heart, and said to Peter and the rest of the apostles, 'Men and brethren, what shall we do?'" (Acts 2:37). People often speak of "feeling convicted," but conviction is a state of awareness, not an emotional feeling of guilt. However, realizing our true standing before God is often emotionally difficult.

The Holy Spirit convinces us of our sinful state by revealing God's righteousness (John 16:10). In this the Spirit's ministry continues and parallels the ministry of Christ. When Peter realized who Jesus is, his first response was, "Depart from me, for I am a sinful man, O Lord!" (Luke 5:8). The Holy Spirit's work produces a similar reaction in us, which is to despair of our own righteousness.

This despondency is further accentuated as the Holy Spirit reveals the unbeliever's future punishment. God's judgment will certainly come, and his judgment upon Satan is proof (John 16:11). The message of salvation is good news, and the convicting work of the Spirit shows the hearer why it is imperative to respond to the message.

In addition to testifying to the truth, the Holy Spirit's internal work also enables the recipients of the gospel message to respond. Why, then, do many of those who hear not also believe? It seems that there are only three possible explanations: God's Spirit provides limited *irresistible grace,* universal *preve-*

---

[100] Leon Morris, *The Gospel According to John,* rev. ed., *NICNT* (Grand Rapids: Eerdmans, 1995), 619; and *TDNT,* 2:473–74.

nient grace, or sufficient *overcoming grace.* First, the proponents of *irresistible grace* argue that the Holy Spirit provides enabling grace only within the elect and that this work always accomplishes the task of drawing his chosen to himself. Schreiner and Ware advocate this position when they state:

> We contend that Scripture does not teach that all people receive grace in equal measure, even though such a democratic notion is attractive today. What Scripture teaches is that God's saving grace is set only upon some, namely, those whom, in his great love, he elected long ago to save, and that this grace is necessarily effective in turning them to belief.[101]

The problem with this view is that it freely accepts the notion that God offers salvation from eternal damnation while at the same time withholding the ability to accept it. The irresistible grace position ensures a purely gracious salvation but does so at a high cost. The logical conclusion is that those who reject the gospel remain lost because God wants them lost.[102] Generally starting with Titus 2:11 ("For the grace of God that brings salvation has appeared to all men"), proponents of *prevenient grace* argue God has done a preemptive universal work of enabling grace. Theissen is representative of the prevenient grace position when he states:

> Since mankind is hopelessly dead in trespasses and sins and can do nothing to obtain salvation, God graciously restores to all men sufficient ability to make a choice in the matter of submission to him. This is the salvation-bringing grace of God that has appeared to all men.[103]

The difficulty with this position is that, as a practical matter, it seems to render the doctrine of total depravity irrelevant.[104]

---

[101] Thomas R. Schreiner and Bruce A. Ware, "Introduction," in *The Grace of God, The Bondage of the Will* (Grand Rapids: Baker, 1995), 12. "Irresistible grace" comes from the TULIP acronym, but many Calvinists regret the term because it gives the impression that God compels a person to believe against his will. Most modern Reformed theologians prefer the expression "efficacious grace" and argue that God changes a person's will via regeneration so that a person freely but effectually believes.

[102] The issue at hand is not why the lost are lost but why the lost are not saved. All orthodox Christians affirm that the unsaved are lost because of their own sin. But if believers are saved by an irresistible work that is limited in scope, then the inevitable corollary is that the lost remain lost because God wants them in hell. Several who hold to irresistible grace accept this conclusion. See David Engelsma, *Hyper-Calvinism and the Well-Meant Offer of the Gospel* (Grandville, MI: Reformed Free Pub. Assoc., 1994), 58.

[103] Theissen, *Lectures in Systematic Theology,* 344–45.

[104] Arminian theologian Jack Cottrell acknowledges this when he states, "In the Arminian system it does not really matter whether this free-will ability to accept or reject the gospel is regarded as

A third position, *the overcoming grace view*, attempts to be a mediating option between the two previous models.[105] The overcoming grace position sees the convicting and enabling work of the Holy Spirit accompanying the preaching of the gospel and believes this work is accomplished in every believer. Unlike the prevenient grace position, the overcoming grace view does not see this work of the Spirit as universal or permanent. The Scriptures repeatedly warn that God's Spirit will not always strive with men and caution the recipients not to harden their hearts (Gen. 6:3; Ps. 95:8). The Bible also exhorts all to seek the Lord in the day of salvation while he may be found (Isa. 55:6; 2 Cor. 6:2). The special, saving work of the Spirit is limited and temporary, but every hearer of the gospel has "a window of grace" opened to them.

The same call is delivered to the elect and to the reprobate, with two different results. Tragically, God's grace can be successfully resisted; however, for those who believe, his grace is overcoming rather than irresistible. Granted, the overcoming grace position presents a logically less tidy argument than the previous two views, but it appears to be more in keeping with the tensions within the biblical record.[106]

There are at least three advantages to the overcoming grace position. First, it accounts for the passages that speak of God's offer of grace being rejected. Stephen declared to the inhabitants of Jerusalem, "You stiff-necked and uncircumcised in heart and ears! You always resist the Holy Spirit; as your fathers did, so do you" (Acts 7:51; see also Matt. 23:37; Acts 13:46).

Second, the overcoming grace position sees God's offer of salvation as genuine and full.[107] There is no dividing or distinguishing between the

---

natural (as in Pelagianism), or as *restored* for all at conception via original grace, or as restored for all at a later time through the Holy Spirit's intervention in an act of prevenient grace" (emphasis original). Jack Cottrell, "The Classical Arminian View of Election," 2006.

[105] The Formula of Concord adheres to the overcoming grace position, so Demarest labels the view as the Lutheran position. See "The Formula of Concord, 1577," article 11, in *Creeds and Confessions in the Christian Tradition*, 2:198; Demarest, *The Cross and Salvation*, 206–8. As George states, "I like the term *overcoming grace* because it conveys the truth witnessed by so many Christians: Despite their stubbornness and rebellion, they say, God did not give up on them. Like a persistent lover, He kept on wooing until, at last, His very persistence won the day" (emphasis original). Timothy George, *Amazing Grace—God's Initiative, Our Response*, 74.

[106] Some Calvinists recognize the weaknesses in the irresistible grace position and postulate a solution close to the overcoming grace view. Timothy George states, "The term *irresistible grace* is misleading because it seems to suggest that sinners are drawn to God in a mechanical, impersonal way, as a piece of metal is to a magnet. When pressed very far, this image eliminates human free agency and moral responsibility altogether. In the Bible, not only *can* grace be resisted—it invariably is." Timothy George, *Amazing Grace—God's Initiative, Our Response*, 74. Calvinist theologian Terrance Tiessen proposes a position he calls "universally sufficient enabling grace." See Terrance Tiessen, *Who Can Be Saved? Reassessing Salvation in Christ and World Religions* (Downers Grove: InterVarsity, 2004) 230–258, 493–98.

[107] As Henry Thiessen observes, "God does not mock men. If he offers salvation to all, then he also desires to save all, and to extend the same help to all who choose him. Man's will is the only

grace offered to those who believe and those who do not. The Bible does not present the convicting work of the Holy Spirit as limited merely to the elect. Jesus declared that when the Spirit comes he will "convict the *world* of sin, and of righteousness, and of judgment" (John 16:8, emphasis added). God's call may not be irresistible, but it is unavoidable (Acts 17:30–31).

The third advantage to the overcoming position is that it clearly places the responsibility for rejecting the gospel on the unbeliever. Evil is a mystery, and rejecting Jesus Christ as Lord and Savior is the ultimate evil. Therefore, there will always be an element of mystery why some people say no to the free offer of salvation. But it is important that we locate the mystery of unbelief in the proper place. The cause of unbelief resides in the human heart and not in the actions, or rather inactions, of God.

Regrettably, the lost spend eternity separated from God, but they do so of their own free choice. It is a solemn truth that everyone who is in hell is there because he chose to be. Undoubtedly, no one is glad to be in perdition, but its inhabitants chose sin and its consequences over the Son of God (2 Thess. 2:10–12).

Presently, there are inmates who are serving life sentences in maximum security prisons. Assuming they are guilty of the crimes for which they were convicted, then their incarceration is a sad fact—but not one that creates a crisis of conscience. This is because the criminal chose prison when he decided to commit crime. When the guilty are punished appropriately, then we may have sympathetic feelings of sorrow and regret but not outrage because justice is being done. So it is concerning the culpability and eventual punishment of those who reject the gospel. We grieve, even lament, over each person who rejects Jesus Christ, but we do not blame God for the unbeliever's choice. The gospel is genuinely available to all, including those who ultimately turn it down.

The Conditions to Salvation

God's choice of us is unconditional, but our receiving salvation is not. We are required to repent and to believe—twin decisions which when taken together are called conversion. Repentance and faith are not the same thing, but they are "joined at the hip."

Along with conversion this section will also discuss regeneration, because at the time a person believes, he is also regenerated. Conversion is a condition for salvation while regeneration is not; regeneration is a work of God (Titus 3:5). However, since regeneration occurs simultaneously with

---

obstacle to the salvation of anyone. God does not give one man the will to do good and leave the other without any help in this respect." Thiessen, *Lectures in Systematic Theology,* 350.

conversion and since there is great debate about which one is logically prior, we will consider regeneration in this section also.

Conversion and regeneration also highlight the principle that salvation is union with Christ. When a person is converted, he is united with Christ. In this way conversion is analogous to taking marriage vows, for both involve entering into a covenant relationship before and with God (cf. 2 Cor. 11:2; Eph. 5:23–32). If conversion is our uniting with Christ by faith, then regeneration is the manifestation that Christ has come to live within us ("that Christ may dwell in your hearts through faith," Eph. 3:17; cf. Eph. 2:5; Col. 1:27).

Though conversion is a graciously enabled action, it still is a decision made by the hearer of the gospel. In contrast, regeneration is entirely a work of God. Repentance and faith are gifts from God, and it is only by his grace that a person converts, but God does not repent and believe for us. Conversion is something we do; regeneration is a work accomplished in us by the Holy Spirit. Just as we did not birth ourselves, we do not enact our new birth either. We convert; God regenerates. ☆

Conversion

Grudem defines *conversion* as "our willing response to the gospel call, in which we sincerely repent of sin and place our trust in Christ for salvation."[108] Conversion is made up of two distinguishable yet inseparable parts: repentance and faith. True repentance and true faith are like the two sides of a coin—it is impossible to have one without the other. Repentance and faith are the conditions for salvation. They occur simultaneously, and taken together they make up the act of conversion. Mark tells us that when Jesus began preaching, his message was "repent, believe" (Mark 1:15). Paul highlighted the two components of conversion when he reminded the church at Thessalonica how they "turned to God from idols to serve the living and true God" (1 Thess. 1:9). In faith they turned to God while at the same time they repented from idols.

At times the Bible speaks only of the need for repentance (e.g., Matt. 4:17; Luke 13:3–5; Acts 2:38) while at other times it presents only the requirement of faith (e.g., John 3:36; Acts 16:31; Eph. 2:8–9) since one implies the other. In some wedding ceremonies, couples pledge vows which include the phrase "forsaking all others" while in other ceremonies the partners do not. However, even when the phrase is not stated explicitly it is obviously meant implicitly. To say yes to one is to say no to all others.

So it is with conversion. Like marriage, converting to Christ is entering into a covenant relationship with God. When we place our faith in the Lord Jesus Christ as Savior, we are implicitly repenting of all other spiritual

---

108 Grudem, *Systematic Theology,* 709.

masters. Repentance and faith are not the same thing, but one cannot exist without the other.[109] If one truly believes on Christ for salvation, then he has truly repented of sin and vice versa.

So then, what exactly are repentance and faith? First we will define *repentance* and examine its components and then do the same with faith. Repentance *is a change of mind that leads to a change of action.* Repentance is one's heartfelt willingness to have Jesus Christ save him from his sins. A full and true apprehension of what it means to be lost, of the nature of sin, and of the inevitable coming judgment will lead a person to renounce his sins and turn away from them.

In our understanding of repentance, two extremes are to be avoided. The first extreme is the view that repentance is merely a mental activity that does not involve the will. This position sees repentance only as a change of mind, namely, that one changes his mind about Jesus Christ—either who Jesus is or whether one wants to be saved by Jesus. Charles Ryrie argues for this understanding of repentance in his discussion of why Peter called for his Jewish hearers to repent on the day of Pentecost. He states:

> The content of repentance which brings eternal life, and that which Peter preached on the day of Pentecost, is a change of mind about Jesus Christ. Whereas the people who heard him on that day formerly thought of Jesus as a mere man, they were asked to accept Him as Lord (Deity) and Christ (promised Messiah).[110]

According to Ryrie's definition, repentance is not just a complement of faith, but actually faith itself, because one is repenting of his unbelief.

A lexical study of "repent" does not support Ryrie's position. The word used most often in the New Testament that is translated "repent" is *metanoeō,* and it does mean "a change of mind" but also more than that. Louw and Nida define *metanoeō* as "to change one's way of life as the result of a complete change of thought and attitude with regard to sin and righteousness."[111] The other word in the New Testament for repentance, *epistrephō,* means "to change one's belief" in such a way as "to change one's way of living as God would want."[112] Two words in the Hebrew,

---

[109] Demarest argues that it is "psychologically impossible" to believe in the biblical sense without loathing sin or to repent genuinely without embracing the truth of God's Word. See Bruce Demarest, *The Cross and Salvation,* 264.

[110] Charles Ryrie, *Balancing the Christ Life* (Chicago: Moody, 1969), 176.

[111] Johannes Louw and Eugene Nida, *Greek-English Lexicon of the New Testament* (New York: United Bible Societies, 1989), 41.52.

[112] Ibid., 31.60; 41.51. A third word, *metamelomai,* is sometimes translated "repent." It primarily means "to regret afterwards" and speaks of an emotional state that does not necessarily lead to repentance. The word is used of Judas in Matthew 27:3, which the KJV translates as "repent" but newer versions (NIV and NASB) translate as "remorse."

nicham and *shub,* are translated "repent." *Nicham* refers to "lamenting or regretting one's own doings."[113] *Shub* means "to turn or return."[114] From a lexical study of the words translated "repent," it is evident the position that views repentance merely to be a change of mind is incomplete and therefore deficient.[115]

The second extreme to avoid is understanding repentance as a work of penance. A distinction needs to be made between repentance and penance, for the two are not the same thing. In Roman Catholic theology, penance is an act of contrition that earns forgiveness.[116] The person attempting penance does a deed or series of works that are meant to display a genuine sorrow for the sins committed. Penance is supposed to obtain the right to receive grace.

Repentance, by contrast, is a rejection of the sins themselves. It does not involve any attempt to atone or repay for the misdeeds. Repentance is a change of attitude toward sin; penance is an attempt to be worthy of forgiveness. As H. A. Ironside states, "Repentance is a recognition of the need of grace, not an act of merit opposed to grace."[117] Penitence is not penance.

Each component of the human personality—intellect, emotions, and will—is involved in repentance. Our Lord provides the classic illustration of how repentance engages the whole person in the parable of the prodigal son (Luke 15:11–24 NASB). Jesus describes the young man's repentance in three ways. First, he tells us that when the younger son grew weary of his life with the pigs he repented with his mind: "But when he *came to his senses,* he said, 'How many of my father's hired men have more than enough bread, but I am dying here with hunger!'" (v. 17 NASB). The lightbulb came on for the young man when he saw the foolishness of his dilemma, and his thinking changed.

Second, the prodigal not only repented mentally but also evidenced a change in his emotions when he said, "I am no longer worthy to be called your son; make me as one of your hired men'" (v. 19 NASB). It is important to note that the Bible distinguishes between two types of sorrow

---

[113] J. R. Soza, "Repentance," in *Dictionary of the Old Testament: Pentateuch,* ed. T. Desmond Alexander and David W. Baker (Downers Grove: InterVarsity, 2003), 684. The Old Testament writers generally use *nicham* in reference to a change in God's dealings with humanity (cf. Gen. 6:6; 1 Sam. 15:11,35) and only occasionally in reference to human repentance (cf. Jer. 8:6).

[114] Ibid.

[115] Some who support Ryrie's position, such as Zane Hodges, recognize that repentance in the New Testament does refer to a change of attitude toward sin. Therefore, Hodges argues that repentance is required to have fellowship with God but is not necessary to be saved. See Zane C. Hodges, *Absolutely Free* (Grand Rapids: Academie Books, 1989), 145.

[116] See "Penance" in *The Catholic Catechism* (New York: P. J. Kenedy and Sons, 1932), 174–84.

[117] H. A. Ironside, cited in Gordon R. Lewis and Bruce A. Demarest, *Integrative Theology,* vol. 3 (Grand Rapids: Zondervan, 1994), 100.

(2 Cor. 7:9–10). In itself, regret has no healing power. There is a type of sorrow that merely laments the unhappiness of the situation or that one's deeds have caught up with him but a sorrow that truly repents is a genuine remorse for the sins committed. This young man demonstrated a change both in his thinking and in his attitude.

Third, the younger son repented with the center of his being—the will. His mind could be convinced and his emotions stirred, but until he yielded his will (i.e., his heart), he would remain with the swine. He stated, "I *will* get up and go to my father, and *will* say to him, 'Father, I have sinned against heaven, and in your sight'" (v. 18 NASB, emphasis added). The prodigal revealed a willingness, a change of heart. Once he hated his father and loved what his father hated; now all that changed. Repeatedly, the Scriptures invite sinners by stating, "Whoever will, let him come" (e.g., Rev. 22:17), and highlight the necessity of the will's participation in repentance. Our Savior's vivid parable teaches that true repentance involves the intellect, emotions, and will.

As we can see, repentance is not just a mental activity involving only the mind. Nor is repentance an attempt to curry forgiveness by doing acts of penance. Mere regret or the stirring of emotions does not meet the biblical criteria of repentance. Repentance is more than embarrassment, shame, regret for being caught, or fear of punishment. Repentance focuses on the sin itself and not just its consequences. The truly repentant person does not want to be saved *in* his sins but *from* his sins.

Lewis and Demarest list a number of distinguishing characteristics of repentance, three of which we note here.[118] First, repentance is a repudiation of good works for self-justification. Some of the most difficult areas for missions and evangelization are those regions dominated by the world's major religions, generally because the adherents do not see themselves in need of a savior. All must repent of their sins, but the religious person must also repent of his self-righteousness.

Second, repentance is a renunciation of all other spiritual masters. Missionaries recount that many times when the gospel is first presented in a polytheistic culture, there are those who want to respond by adding Jesus to the pantheon of gods they already worship. They want to receive Jesus as one lord among many. However, as Paul explains, to accept Jesus as Christ and Lord is to abandon the claims of all other gods (1 Thess. 1:9; also Rom. 10:9; 1 Cor. 12:1).

Third, repentance requires a submission to God's revealed truth and a commitment to radical honesty about oneself. This is the point of 1 John 1:9, where John says we are forgiven if and only if we "confess" our sins.

---

[118] Ibid., 100–1.

To confess, *homologeō,* is to agree with God's assessment of our spiritual condition.[119] God has some hard things to say about us, and repentance necessitates the spiritual candor to admit he is right. The demand for repentance allows no room for negotiating, minimizing, or rationalizing sin. "Good" people cannot be forgiven, because they do not believe they need pardoning (Mark 2:17). Only when we acknowledge we are as guilty as God says we are can there be cleansing.

Saving faith is being convinced that God's promises are true to the point that one places his trust in Jesus Christ for salvation (e.g., John 3:16,36; 11:25–26; Acts 16:30–31; Rom. 4:3).[120] Thus defined, faith has two components—an intellectual element ("being convinced") and a volitional element ("placing trust"). When we are persuaded by God's Spirit of the truthfulness of the gospel, we then act on that confidence by relying on Jesus Christ and the work he accomplished through his death, burial, and resurrection.

Some aspects of the intellectual component of faith are passive because faith requires being convinced of the gospel (the passive element) before one can place trust in the Son of God for salvation (the active element). When we recognize the gospel to be true (the passive aspect), we wholeheartedly depend on Jesus Christ to save us (the active aspect). The passive component of faith is mental; it is a matter of being intellectually convinced and refers primarily to the mind. The active component of faith is volitional; it is a matter of choice and refers primarily to the will (what the Bible often calls the "heart," as in Rom. 10:10). However, being convinced of the gospel requires receptivity to the truth, a disposition of openness. Responding to the good news is a moral decision, and for this reason we are responsible for the passive element of faith (of being convinced) just as much as we are accountable for the active element of faith (of placing trust).

Believing that God is telling the truth has always been the first criterion for a relationship with him (Gen. 15:6; Heb. 11:6). Unbelief produced the fall in the garden when our original parents determined that the serpent was more honest than God (Gen. 3:4–5). Admittedly, placing one's faith in the gospel is a difficult thing to do, so difficult that it requires the work of the Holy Spirit. But exercising saving faith is not an unreasonable act and is available to anyone who desires it (John 7:16–17). Unbelief is sin because the decision to believe or not believe is ultimately a moral choice. In fact, unbelief is the ultimate sin because it results in damnation (John 3:18).

---

119 *NIDNTT,* 1:344.

120 Erickson defines faith as the "laying hold of the promises and work of Christ." See Erickson, *Christian Theology,* 951. For Grudem, saving faith is "personal trust in Jesus Christ as a living person for forgiveness of sins and for eternal life with God." See Grudem, *Systematic Theology,* 710.

Faith is the instrument by which we accept salvation. In Romans, Paul establishes that salvation must be by grace because no one has the moral standing to be declared righteous or has the ability to earn merit before God (Rom. 1:18–3:27). The apostle then declares that faith alone must be the condition to receive salvation for redemption to be completely gracious (Rom. 3:28–4:16).[121] As such, faith is the instrument or vehicle by which we receive God's grace (Rom. 5:1; Eph. 2:8–9).

When considering the biblical terms for faith, it becomes evident that one will have a difficult time finding the word *faith* in an English translation of the Old Testament.[122] Because the Old Testament authors understand faith primarily as a verb rather than a noun, the English verb "trust" is used much more often than the noun "faith" (e.g., Pss. 37:3; 56:3; Prov. 3:5; Isa. 12:2). To express the concept of trust, the Hebrew writers primarily employ two words. The first, *'aman,* means "to believe, trust in, to regard as true,"[123] while the second, *batach,* means "to lean upon, confide in."[124] In the Old Testament, faith primarily is not something one has; it is something one does.

The Greek New Testament, in contrast to the Hebrew Old Testament, makes frequent use of both the noun form (*pistis*) and the verb form (*pisteuō*) of the word *faith.*[125] The English language does not have a corresponding verb form of "faith," so generally *pisteuō* is translated as "believe" (e.g., John 3:16,36; Acts 16:31). The New Testament calls upon us to "faith" Jesus, but we have no proper way to say this in English.[126] → Belief = mental / faith = mental + volitional

The lack of an English verb for faith is extremely unfortunate because belief and faith are not synonyms. Belief is mental, but faith adds the volitional element. We may believe without involving the will, but we cannot exercise faith without the will. Belief operates in the sphere of thought while faith operates also as an action. Faith substantiates belief (giving substance, reality, or activity to belief). Faith puts belief into action; faith acts on what you believe.

At this point it is important to note that faith is an action but not a work. Works are a subset of actions, so all works are actions. But the converse is

---

[121] Salvation is by faith alone, yet repentance is also a condition to salvation. This is because both are part of the same action of conversion. Demarest states, "The Reformational distinctive of *sola fides* does not exclude the godly sorrow for sin and the turning therefrom that constitutes biblical repentance." See Demarest, *The Cross and Salvation,* 264.

[122] The KJV of the Old Testament uses the word *faith* only twice (Deut. 32:20 and Hab. 2:4).

[123] Erickson, *Christian Theology,* 951–52.

[124] Ibid.

[125] Ibid.

[126] German, like biblical Greek, has the same root for the verb and noun forms of faith (*glauben, Glaube*). Latin and French have the same problem as English (believe, faith) in that they use words with different roots (Latin—*credere* and *fides*; French—*croire* and *foi*). See Garrett, *Systematic Theology,* 2:233.

not necessarily so; not all actions are works, and faith is an example of this. Exercising faith is something we do, but it is not a meritorious work.[127] The Scriptures frequently contrast faith and works, such as when Paul states, "But to him who does not work but believes on Him who justifies the ungodly, his faith is accounted for righteousness" (Rom. 4:5); or again, "For by grace you have been saved through faith, and that not of yourselves; it is the gift of God, not of works, lest anyone should boast" (Eph. 2:8–9).

Like a drowning man accepting being rescued or a pauper allowing a benefactor to pay his debt, the sinner receives the redemption offered by Christ. Accepting the gift of salvation requires a decision on the part of the sinner, but the merit is incurred by the giver of the gift, not the receiver.[128]

A number of theologians explain faith using a threefold heading: knowledge, assent, and appropriation.[129] This approach sees knowledge as an understanding of the content and object of faith, assent as an agreement with the claims made by the gospel, and appropriation as the application of the truth of the gospel to oneself. We will define the three terms similarly, but will combine the first two components, *knowledge* and *assent,* so as to explore the nature of saving faith under only two headings. Faith is thus understood to have two parts: *the intellectual aspect—assent,* and *the volitional aspect—appropriation.*[130]

First, as we have noted, the intellectual component of faith, *assent,* is to be persuaded or convinced of the message of the gospel. This means one assents to or agrees with the biblical claims that Jesus Christ, the incarnate Son of God, gave his sinless life as a sacrifice for his sins and then rose from the grave three days later. Matthew presents an example of this assenting type of faith when he records the Savior asking two blind men before he healed them, "Do you believe that I am able to do this?" (Matt.

---

127 See Norman Geisler, *Systematic Theology,* vol. 3 (Bloomington, MN: Bethany House, 2004), 198, 488–89.

128 Garrett states, "Repentance and faith are not acts to be performed by human beings on the basis of which or by virtue of which these people come to have a right relationship with God. Hence they are not 'works' in the classic theological meaning of that term." See Garrett, *Systematic Theology,* 2:249.

129 E.g., Murray, 137–38; A. H. Strong, *Systematic Theology* (Valley Forge: Judson, 1907); Thiessen, *Lectures in Systematic Theology,* 355–60, 837–49; Grudem, *Systematic Theology,* 709–12; and Lewis and Demarest, *Integrative Theology,* 102.

130 In this approach the first element of the traditional three-part definition, knowledge, is the necessary prerequisite of a biblical faith. It seems simpler to understand knowledge as an element of assent since assent is accepting the truth of what one has learned about the gospel message. So we will examine faith in terms of its intellectual and volitional components in hope that the twofold nomenclature provides clarity without oversimplification. Erickson gives a similar twofold taxonomy of faith's components. He states, "On the basis of the foregoing considerations, we conclude that the type of faith necessary for salvation involves both believing that and believing in, or assenting to facts and trusting in a person." See Erickson, *Christian Theology,* 953.

9:28–29). When the men replied, "Yes, Lord," they affirmed they were convinced of Jesus' ability, and he in turn called this persuasion "faith" (v. 29). An assenting faith requires two factors: a disposition of openness to the truth and an adequate knowledge of the truth.

As we said before, to be convinced of the claims of the gospel is a passive experience (i.e., it is something that happens *to* a hearer of the truth). At first, this would seem to absolve the unbeliever of responsibility for his unbelief since his lack of faith appears to be a failure on the part of the gospel to convince him. However, openness to the truth is an attitude or disposition that every person should have, and the Bible promises that anyone receptive to the truth can know the gospel is true. Jesus declared, "If anyone chooses to do God's will, he will find out whether my teaching comes from God or whether I speak on my own" (John 7:17 NIV). So even though being persuaded is a passive experience, it requires the active decision of the hearer to be receptive to the good news. In order to have an assenting faith one must be teachable.

Since assent is a mental or cognitive activity, then clearly it requires a certain amount of knowledge. One must know about the good news of Jesus Christ in order to trust in him. As Paul asked, "How shall they believe in Him of whom they have not heard?" (Rom. 10:14). In order for faith to be informed or have knowledge, it must have two things: content and an object. The content of assenting faith is the gospel and the object of that faith is Jesus Christ. Paul states that salvation comes through "belief in the truth" (2 Thess. 2:13), so we must know the truth in order for it to set us free. The Bible sometimes refers to this saving body of truth as "the faith" (e.g., Gal. 1:23; Eph. 4:5; Jude 3).

The fact that knowledge is an essential component of faith brings up an important question: how much knowledge is required for a biblical faith? In other words, what is the minimum amount of knowledge necessary for a person to exercise saving faith? This question takes on particular importance in matters such as the evangelization of children and the fate of unreached people groups.

A quick answer to the above question would be that, according to the Apostle Paul, one must at least know about the death, burial, and resurrection of Jesus Christ in order to believe on him and what he has done (cf., 1 Cor. 15:1–4). But the gospel account is based on additional truths that seem to be equally essential for an informed faith. Surely one also needs an adequate understanding of why Jesus came and who he is. The sacrificial death of Christ makes sense only in the context of understanding the sinful state of humanity and the uniqueness of his person.

The book of Acts provides insights to this question, for it recounts a number of occasions in which the gospel is proclaimed to those who are hearing it for the first time (e.g., Acts 8:26–37; 10:34–44; 13:16–41; 14:14–17; 17:22–31). A survey of the messages preached reveals three recurring themes. First, the apostles explain why the gospel is necessary: God exists, he is holy, and we are sinful (Acts 14:14–17). Second, they proclaim Jesus of Nazareth as the Christ and unique Son of God who came to address the guilt of our sin (Acts 8:26–37). And third, the apostles present the death, burial, and resurrection of Jesus as the means by which he obtained our salvation (Acts 17:22–31).

The hearers are then called upon to respond to the message with repentance and faith. The apostolic model indicates that the minimal information necessary for a saving faith is twofold: knowledge of the gospel and sufficient prerequisite information to understand its significance.[131]

If biblical faith has the gospel for its content, then it must have the Savior, the Lord Jesus Christ, as its object (Rom. 10:8,17). Faith is only as strong as the object it is trusting. For example, by faith one may believe he is taking the correct medicine, but if the prescription was filled incorrectly, then this faith is misplaced and will not help. A skydiver puts his complete faith in a parachute, but his faith is effective only if the parachute opens. We must be cautious not to place our faith in faith because believing of itself has no power. The power of faith resides in its object and is only as efficacious as its focus.[132] The object of our faith, Jesus of Nazareth, is the one who saves; faith operates merely as the vehicle by which we receive his gracious benefits.

The fact that knowledge is a part of belief means that saving faith is not merely a "blind leap into the dark," nor is it irrational. Faith rests on credible evidence (Rom. 10:8,17) and complements reason rather than opposing it.[133] Some, such as Schleiermacher, set faith against knowledge and view faith to be merely a noncognitive attitude or a feeling of complete dependence.[134] Similarly, Pinnock points out that the dis-

---

[131] What knowledge was necessary for saving faith during the Old Testament era is not as clear. The central Hebrew text concerning the role of faith in salvation is Genesis 15:6: "And he [Abraham] believed in the LORD, and he accounted it to him for righteousness." Evangelical theologians disagree concerning the content of Abraham's faith and the faith of subsequent Old Testament saints. Ryrie and Piper take different approaches to the question but come to the same conclusion: though the content of faith was different for the Old Testament saints than it is for those living in the New Testament era, today a knowledge of the gospel is required for a faith that saves (John 14:6). See Charles Ryrie, *Dispensationalism Today* (Chicago: Moody, 1965), 123; and John Piper, *Let the Nations Be Glad! The Supremacy of God in Missions* (Grand Rapids: Baker, 1993), 140–41.

[132] At times the Bible recognizes that faith is the instrument of salvation, as when Paul states, "Therefore, having been justified by faith, we have peace with God through our Lord Jesus Christ" (Rom. 5:1, see also Eph. 2:8–9). But even in these instances, the Scriptures are quick to point out that salvation is accomplished "through our Lord Jesus Christ." Faith saves when it has the proper object, the Son of God.

[133] Erickson, *Christian Theology,* 953.

[134] Friedrich Schleiermacher, *On Religion: Speeches to Its Cultured Despisers* (1799; repr., Cambridge: Cambridge University Press, 1997), 45–47.

tinguishing characteristic of saving faith is not so much its object as its reverent attitude, and he thus argues it is unnecessary to hear the gospel in order to be saved by Christ.[135] He concludes that as long as a person has a sincere, humble, and reverent faith, then the proper object of faith is not essential.

In response we would agree that saving faith does display a different attitude from a nominal faith but that Pinnock bases his argument on a false contrast. The opposite of faith is not knowledge; the opposite of faith is unbelief.[136] In fact, as we will see, faith is a type of knowledge.

The second component to saving faith is the active component, appropriation, which Evans defines as "the consent of the will to the assent of the understanding."[137] There is a difference between believing about Christ and relying on him. The Apostle John states, "He came to His own, and His own did not receive Him. But as many as received Him, to them He gave the right to become children of God, to those who believe in His name" (John 1:11–12). Here the apostle equates saving faith ("believe in His name") with the act of receiving, or trusting him for salvation ("as many as received Him"). While assent is a mental activity that involves the understanding which believes that Jesus Christ is Savior, the volitional component of faith, appropriation, is trust in him for salvation and requires the acceptance of the will. A full-orbed biblical faith is made up both of belief (the intellectual component) and trust (the volitional component).

Appropriation, or trust, has at least five characteristics. Trust acknowledges dependence on God, expresses itself in response to his call, requires commitment to him, involves affection for him, and enters into a relationship with him. First, trust is an act of dependence. Jesus declared, "Assuredly, I say to you, unless you are converted and become as little children, you will by no means enter the kingdom of heaven" (Matt. 18:3). When the Savior likened the citizens of heaven to little children, he emphasized how saving faith has the quality of a humble, depending trust.

Second, trust involves a response of obedience. The Bible refers to the act of trusting Christ for salvation as "obeying the gospel" (e.g., 2 Thess. 1:8; 1 Pet. 4:17). We respond to the gospel by obeying its command to repent and believe.

This obedient, saving faith in Christ is manifest by our faithful obedience to his other commands. A faith that does not produce good works is not

---

[135] Clark Pinnock, *A Wideness in God's Mercy: The Finality of Jesus Christ in a World of Religions* (Grand Rapids: Zondervan, 1992), 157–58.

[136] Erickson observes that there seems to be a correlation between one's understanding of revelation and whether one views knowledge of the gospel as a necessary aspect of saving faith. Holding to a nonpropositional definition of revelation leads naturally to a noncognitive understanding of faith. See Erickson, *Christian Theology*, 953.

[137] William Evans, *The Great Doctrines of the Bible*, rev. ed. (Chicago: Moody, 1974), 146.

a saving faith at all. This seems to be the point of the Apostle James when he distinguished between a faith that merely assents to the truth and a faith that appropriates the truth. He stated, "What good is it, my brothers, if a man claims to have faith but has no deeds? Can such faith save him? . . . But someone will say, 'You have faith; I have deeds.' Show me your faith without deeds, and I will show you my faith by what I do" (James 2:14,18 NIV).[138]

The apostle continued with the warning that mere mental assent is dangerous. Since it is a type of faith, some may think of it as sufficient for a right relationship with God. He cautioned the reader with the reminder that "the demons also believe, and shudder" (v. 19 NASB). Satan's angels believe the gospel is true—in fact, they know it is true—but that does not mean they have saving faith. Faith without works saves, but a trusting, saving faith is demonstrated by its works.

The second point leads naturally to the third which is that trust involves commitment. A faith that merely agrees with the gospel message but does not act on that belief fails to meet the biblical criteria for saving faith. Mental assent is a nominal faith, but if it does not affect the will, then it is a deficient, false faith. Demarest points out that "faith is not only the initial response by which one is saved; it is also a mode of living before God that should grow extensively and intensively (2 Cor. 10:15; 2 Thess. 2:13)."[139] When one trusts Christ for salvation, he is committing to a walk of faith with him.

A fourth characteristic of trust, or an appropriating faith, is affection. The Apostle Peter declared that, for those of us "who believe, He is precious" (1 Pet. 2:7). The Bible describes saving faith as a type of love, and when we trust Christ, we turn our hearts to him. On the one hand the Apostle Paul warned that those who do not love the truth will not believe the truth and as a result are not saved (2 Thess. 2:10–11). On the other hand, he described true faith in Christ as "faith working through love" (Gal. 5:6). Trust is an attitude of love and affection, and all who trust the Savior discover he loved them first and they then love him in return (1 John 4:7–21).

Fifth, since trust depends upon, commits to, obeys, and loves the Savior, then clearly to trust Christ is to enter into a relationship with him. This relationship of trust is an experiential knowledge of him. Often, trusting Christ is described as "knowing him" (e.g., Matt. 11:27; John 8:19; 10:14; and 2 Tim. 1:12) and, in this sense, faith is a very real type of knowledge (Heb. 11:1).[140]

---

138 Garrett cites Leon Morris's suggestion that James viewed works as something analogous to what Paul referred to as the fruit of the Spirit (Gal. 5:22–23). See Garrett, *Systematic Theology,* 239.
139 Demarest, *The Cross and Salvation,* 261.
140 Calvin stated, "Now we shall possess a right definition of faith if we call it a firm and certain knowledge of God's benevolence toward us, founded upon the truth of the freely given promise in

When examining the nature of saving faith, the question often comes up as to how much faith is required in order to be saved. This is an especially serious issue for those struggling with assurance of salvation, and sometimes for weak believers the listing of the qualities of true faith heightens their anxieties. The point to remember is that the *quality* of faith is much more important that the *quantity* of faith. A weak, struggling faith saves, as long as its object is the Son of God. Consider this: in Noah's day, how much faith was required to be saved? The answer, of course, is that if one had enough faith to get into the ark, he had enough faith. So how much faith is required to be saved today? Similarly, the answer is, enough faith to come to the cross. Everyone who trusts in Jesus Christ and his atonement is saved and can have full assurance of his salvation.

Regeneration

The historian Plutarch (ca. AD 45–125) tells about a man who tried to make a dead body stand upright. When he finally had the corpse propped up, the man observed, *"Deest aliquid intus"* (There's something lacking inside.)[141] The Bible declares that in a real sense every unsaved person, no matter how propped up by his attempts at ethical behavior, is in a similar state of spiritual death (Eph. 2:1–3). The only remedy for this condition is for a person to be spiritually born again—*regeneration*. The purpose of the gospel is not merely to make bad men good or even make good men better but to bring dead men back to life.[142]

Regeneration is *the act of God whereby the Holy Spirit imparts eternal life to the believer.* When the Bible speaks of the gift of eternal life, it refers to much more than an existence of infinite duration because even the condemned exist forever. Rather, eternal life signifies the quality of our new life in Christ. The Scriptures present five new qualities that regeneration conveys to the believer.[143] A person regenerated receives new life (John 3:5–7; 1 John 5:11–12), partakes of a new nature (2 Pet. 1:4), receives the spiritual circumcision of a new heart (Jer. 24:7; Ezek. 11:19;

Christ, both revealed to our minds and sealed upon our hearts through the Holy Spirit." See Calvin, *Institutes,* 3.2.7.

In the context of the above quote, Calvin refuted the Roman Catholic notion of "implicit faith." Implicit faith, the Catholic Church argued, is the pious and reverent attitude a worshipper may have even if he is clueless about what he is worshipping. In this way the medieval church authorities justified keeping parishioners ignorant by forbidding the publishing of the Scriptures.

[141] Cited in Strong, *Systematic Theology,* 813.

[142] Gordon B. Hinckley, president of the Church of the Latter Day Saints, often states that the purpose of the Mormon gospel is "to make bad men good and good men better" and thereby change human nature. See http://www.lds.org/newsroom/showrelease/0,15503,4044-1-3837,00.html. By contrast, the Apostle Paul teaches that human nature first must be transformed before there can be a true change in behavior (Eph. 2:1–10).

[143] Thiessen, *Lectures in Systematic Theology,* 367; Demarest, *The Cross and Salvation,* 293–94.

36:26, cf. Col. 2:11), becomes a new creation (2 Cor. 5:17; Eph. 4:24), and enjoys a new purity (1 Cor. 6:11; Titus 3:5).

Jesus spoke of the necessity of regeneration when he told Nicodemus, "You must be born again" (John 3:7). Sin kills every person who commits it because sin severs the offender from God, who is life. Since all have sinned (Rom. 3:23), the imperative of the new birth is directed to all. A sinner can continue to exist separated from God, but he cannot *live,* at least not in any meaningful understanding of the word, and certainly not in the way for which he was created. Regeneration provides the believer with the necessary nature of holiness in order for fellowship with God to be restored.

Like all other components of salvation, regeneration is to be understood as an aspect of uniting with Christ. Strong stated, "As we derive our old nature from the first man Adam, by birth, so we derive a new nature from the second man Christ, by the new birth. Union with Christ is the true 'transfusion of blood.'"[144] When Christ's Spirit makes a person his habitation, he communicates new life to that person. The Holy Spirit, who is the bond of our union with him, ensures that the righteousness of Christ continues its transforming work in us. The Bible emphasizes that each person of the Trinity takes an active part in our new birth. Regeneration is an activity of the Holy Spirit (John 3:6–8), originates in the will of the Father (John 1:13; James 1:18), and is based on the death, burial, and resurrection of Christ (1 Pet. 1:3).

One might think that regeneration is a minor doctrine because of the few times the word is found in the Bible. The word for regeneration, *palingenesia,* occurs only twice in the New Testament, and one of those times refers to something other than the new birth (Matt. 19:28).[145] The one instance where *palingenesia* denotes personal salvation is when Paul stated, "Not by works of righteousness which we have done, but according to His mercy He saved us, *through the washing of regeneration* and renewing of the Holy Spirit" (Titus 3:5, emphasis added). However, when we also consider terms synonymous to regeneration such as "born again" (John 3:3–8), "born of God" (John 1:12–13; 1 John 2:29; 5:1,4), "begotten" (1 Pet. 1:3), and "made alive" (Eph. 2:5), it becomes apparent that the doctrine is a major theme of the Scriptures.

The Holy Spirit acts as the agent of regeneration, and the Word of God is the instrument he uses. John's Gospel repeatedly teaches that the new birth is from above (John 3:3–8) (i.e., it is of divine origin rather than human achievement [John 1:12–13]), and that it is the Holy Spirit who imparts life to a soul which is dead in trespasses and sins (John 6:63; cf.

---

[144] Strong, *Systematic Theology,* 804.

[145] Jesus used *palingenesia* to describe the cosmic sense of transformations that will happen as a result of his second advent.

2 Cor. 3:6). However, the Holy Spirit uses means, and the instruments he employs to achieve regeneration are the gospel (James 1:18,21; 1 Pet. 1:23) and the messengers who share it (1 Cor. 4:15). If the gospel is the means by which the Holy Spirit regenerates, then where the gospel is not available, the saving, regenerating work of the Holy Spirit is also absent. This disturbing truth gives urgency to the missionary mandate of the Great Commission.

A number of churches and denominations teach that water baptism is the instrument by which the Holy Spirit regenerates.[146] Without a doubt, the Bible associates the new birth and baptism. (Rom. 6:3–5). However, the Scriptures present baptism as the sign or testimony that points to the new birth, not as the means that accomplishes regeneration. As such, baptism presupposes that regeneration has already occurred (e.g., Acts 10:47–48).[147]

Are those who believe in turn born again, or does a person believe because he has been regenerated? Which happens first? And if they occur simultaneously, which one is the logical cause of the other? Evangelicals agree that a saved person is both converted and regenerated, but there is wide disagreement as to which occurs first, either chronologically or logically. There are good arguments for either position, but the biblical texts seem to come down on the side of conversion resulting in regeneration. Regeneration is instantaneous; it is not a process drawn out over a period of time. An expectant mother may experience a protracted labor, but there will finally come a point when the child is delivered. Similarly, those who come to Christ often first go through the great spiritual travail of the Holy Spirit's conviction (John 16:8). The process of wrestling with God is not the new birth, but rather regeneration is the outcome of the effectual calling of God. Erickson makes the point that the Bible never presents regeneration as a progression.[148] Scripture describes believers as having been born of God but not in a state of being reborn (e.g., John 1:12–13; 2 Cor. 5:17; Eph. 2:1; 1 Pet. 1:3; James 1:18; 1 John 2:29; 5:1,4).

---

[146] See J. A. Jungmann and K. Stasiak, "Baptism, Sacrament of," in *NCE*, 2nd ed., ed. Bernard L. Marthaler (Washington, DC: Catholic University of America, 2003), 2.65.

[147] See Strong, *Systematic Theology*, 820–21.

[148] See Erickson, *Christian Theology*, 957. In contrast, Calvin presented regeneration as an ongoing process that continues throughout the believer's life. This is because he equated regeneration with the restoration of the image of God and saw this as a work accomplished by the Holy Spirit throughout the Christian's walk of faith. See Calvin, *Institutes*, 3.3.9. However, consider an analogy from natural birth: the fact that you, the reader, are alive obviously implies that at some point in the past you were born. But it does not mean you are constantly in the process of being born. This is similarly true about the new birth. Calvin's point that regeneration manifests itself in holy living is well taken, but we would make a distinction between sanctification and regeneration and understand the former to be the fruit of the latter. For further discussion, see Demarest, *The Cross and Salvation*, 286.

Certain Reformed and Presbyterian churches teach that regeneration precedes conversion chronologically and a number of covenant theologians connect regeneration with infant baptism. W. G. T. Shedd, for example, is careful not to attribute regenerating power to the rite of baptism, but he does consider baptism to be a sign that the infant has been regenerated. He states, "The baptism of the infant of a believer supposes the actual or prospective operation of the regenerating Spirit, in order to the efficacy of the rite. . . . The actual conferring of the Holy Spirit may be prior to baptism, or in the act itself, or subsequent to it."[149]

Shedd equates New Testament baptism with the Old Testament rite of circumcision, and he sees both as signs that one has been born into the covenant, and he contends that just as the male children of a Hebrew family were circumcised as infants, so today the children of believers also should be baptized. He concludes, "The infant of the believer receives the Holy Spirit as a regenerating Spirit, by virtue of the covenant between God and his people."[150]

However, as we have seen, the Scriptures point to the Word of God, not baptism, as the means by which the Holy Spirit imparts the new birth. In addition, Shedd's association of baptism with circumcision is not supported by the New Testament. Rather, the teaching of Scripture is that regeneration is concurrent, or coincident, with conversion. This means that conversion and regeneration, as events, occur at the same time.[151] For example, John stated that those who "receive him" are also those have been "born of God" (John 1:12–13).

Among those who agree that the two aspects of salvation are simultaneous, there is debate as to which is logically prior. Many Reformed and Covenant theologians reject Shedd's argument for chronological priority but still contend for the logical priority of regeneration.[152] Conversion is the willing response to the gospel call, but how does one who is totally depraved and dead in sins turn to God? The inability of a lost person to respond to the gospel seems to necessitate that something must happen to the person to make him receptive, and regeneration is seen to be that transforming event. Even those who do not hold to this position acknowledge its logical appeal.[153]

---

149 William G. T. Shedd, *Dogmatic Theology*, vol. 2 (New York: Charles Scribner's Sons, 1891), 575.

150 Ibid., 576.

151 Strong makes the point about the coincidence of conversion and regeneration by asking, "Which of the spokes of a wheel starts first?" See Strong, *Systematic Theology*, 793.

152 One could argue that the priority of regeneration, rather than the five points of Dort (TULIP), is the distinguishing doctrine of Calvinism. Among those who argue that regeneration causes conversion are Strong, *Systematic Theology*, 809; Murray, *Redemption Accomplished and Applied*, 106; and Grudem, *Systematic Theology*, 700.

153 Erickson concedes that "from a logical standpoint, the usual Calvinistic position makes good sense." See Erickson, *Christian Theology*, 945.

However, there are three strong biblical arguments for understanding conversion to precede the new birth.[154] First, the many appeals in the Bible calling sinners to respond to the gospel imply that conversion results in regeneration.[155] The Scriptures are presented as the seed the Spirit of God uses to bring about new life (1 Pet. 1:23; James 1:18,21; 1 John 3:9). That the Word of God is the Spirit's instrumental means indicates that faith leads to regeneration. Second, the Bible presents conversion as the condition to salvation, not the result of being saved (John 1:12; 3:16,18,24,36,40; Acts 13:39; Rom. 3:22,26; 4:3,5; 5:1).[156] The apostles repeatedly promise their hearers that, *if* they will repent and believe, *then* they will be saved (Acts 2:38; 16:30–31). The Apostle John put special emphasis on the necessity of the new birth, but he presented faith as the condition to becoming a child of God (John 1:12–13) and to receiving eternal life ("By believing you may have life in his name," John 20:31).[157]

And third, Geisler makes the point that if regeneration is prior to conversion, then salvation is no longer by faith. If one is already regenerated before he believes, then faith is not a condition to salvation but the evidence of having been saved.[158] However, *sola fide* is the testimony of Scripture (Rom. 10:9–10).

In order for a person to answer the gospel call, there indeed must be a special work of the Holy Spirit, but we conclude that this enablement is not regeneration but the inward call of the Spirit.[159] The convicting work of the Holy Spirit and the effectual call that accompanies the preaching of the gospel enable a sinner to believe. The order that seems to be the testimony of Scripture is that those who are converted are born again.

The transformed nature of the new birth manifests itself as a changed life. As we will see, in many ways sanctification is the ongoing process

---

[154] Rejecting limited atonement and holding to the priority of conversion are distinguishing characteristics of what is often called moderate or modified Calvinism. Lewis and Demarest describe their position as a "moderately Reformed *ordo salutis*." See Lewis and Demarest, *Integrative Theology*, 104. Other representatives of those who hold to the order of "conversion then regeneration" are Thiessen, *Lectures in Systematic Theology*, 352; Erickson, *Christian Theology*, 945; and Geisler, *Systematic Theology*, 477.

[155] See Erickson, *Christian Theology*, 945; Geisler, *Systematic Theology* 480.

[156] See Geisler, *Systematic Theology*, 477–78.

[157] See Lewis and Demarest, *Integrative Theology*, 104.

[158] See Geisler, *Systematic Theology*, 475–77. Many Reformed theologians are less than clear on this issue. R. C. Sproul, whom Geisler cites, states, "A cardinal point of Reformed theology is the maxim: 'Regeneration precedes faith.'" However, in his discussion on John 3:16 two paragraphs later, Sproul says that "everyone who believes in Christ will be saved. Whoever does A (believes) will receive B (everlasting life)." But according to Sproul's *ordo salutis*, it would seem that the regenerated person who believes already has everlasting life. See R. C. Sproul, *Chosen by God* (Wheaton: Tyndale, 1986), 72–73.

[159] Both Erickson and Demarest understand this work to be the effectual call of the Holy Spirit. See Erickson, *Christian Theology*, 945; Demarest, *The Cross and Salvation*, 219–29.

of experiencing the power of regeneration. Regeneration does not change our physical or psychological makeup, but it does change our dispositions and affections. As Mullins stated, "Man's personality remains when he is regenerated, but it is now a transformed personality. Paul the apostle was the same as Saul the persecutor. Yet the change in him was so great that he describes himself as an entirely new creature."[160] The Bible gives at least four characteristics that distinguish a regenerated person.

First, *the new birth imparts a new comprehension of spiritual truth.* Paul stated, "But the natural man does not receive the things of the Spirit of God, for they are foolishness to him; nor can he know them, because they are spiritually discerned" (1 Cor. 2:14). The "natural man," i.e., an unbeliever, can comprehend the facts of the gospel and perhaps even affirm their truthfulness, but what he cannot do is appreciate their value. The bondage of sin has the effect of blinding the unsaved person to matters of eternal worth, and, therefore, they are foolishness to him (2 Cor. 4:4). The unregenerate person can be aware of what the Bible teaches, but he is unable to "see" the truth. In contrast, one who is spiritually alive has the ability to discern God's revealed will (1 Cor. 2:15) and so possesses a spiritual wisdom no amount of natural knowledge can provide.

Second, *regeneration provides a new affection for God and the things of God.* The reason we have a new comprehension for the truth is that we have a new love for it. When we are born again, we are given a new disposition: now we love God and loathe the sin and self-righteousness we used to hold so near and dear (Eph. 2:1–5). The Bible specifically states that those who are born of God will love God (1 John 4:19; 5:2), the Word of God (1 Pet. 2:2), and the people of God (1 John 5:1). A regenerate person also exhibits a distinct attitude toward the world and its inhabitants: he does not love the world and its systematic opposition to God (1 John 2:14–16), but at the same time he loves his enemies (Matt. 5:44–45) and desires the salvation of the lost (2 Cor. 5:14).

The third effect of regeneration is *a new power over temptation and sin.* An unsaved person is controlled by his sinful nature (Eph. 2:1–3) so that he inevitably produces the fruit of sin (Matt. 7:16–20), and therefore he cannot live in a way that pleases God (Rom. 8:8).

For the regenerate, sin is not eradicated, but it is dethroned (1 John 3:9; 5:4,18).[161] As Strong states, "The sinful nature is not gone, but its power is

---

[160] E. Y. Mullins, *The Christian Religion in Its Doctrinal Expression* (Nashville: Baptist Sunday School Board, 1917), 380.

[161] John bluntly states, "Whoever abides in Him does not sin. Whoever sins has neither seen Him nor known Him. . . . Whoever has been born of God does not sin, for His seed remains in him; and he cannot sin, because he has been born of God" (1 John 3:6, 9). The verses are interpreted in a variety of ways: some see John teaching perfectionism while others understand him to be teaching only that the new nature within the believer cannot sin. While no interpretation is without difficulties, it seems clear

broken; sin no longer dominates the life. It has been thrust from the centre to the circumference."[162] When we were unsaved we were dead to righteousness but alive to sin, which was a type of "living death." Now that we are regenerate the exact opposite is true: we are alive to God but dead to sin (Rom. 6:1–11). We experience this new reality when we mortify, i.e., "put to death" (Rom. 8:13), our old desires and embrace our new, godly desires (Rom. 6:11). Paul calls this process of transformation the "putting off of the old man" and the "putting on of the new man" (Eph. 4:22–24; Col. 3:9–10). Sanctification is the distinct outcome of regeneration.

Fourth, *the new birth instigates a new relationship with God.* The Scriptures declare that the redeemed are "born of God" and are the "children of God" (1 John 3:1–2). This new relationship goes beyond our being pardoned or being made the servants of God, for it speaks of our inheritance as joint heirs with Christ (Rom. 8:16–17). The new birth means that Christ has more than restored what we lost in Adam, for he freely gives to us all that is his (1 Cor. 3:21–23).

The Components of Salvation

At the moment of conversion we are united by faith with Christ, and it is through our union with Christ that we receive the benefits of the atonement.[163] By our participation in Christ, we enjoy a twofold righteousness: *justification* and *sanctification.* Viewing us as in him, God declares us righteous, and this declaration is called *justification.* In addition to justifying believers, God also sets Christians apart as his possession and begins a lifelong development transforming believers into the likeness of Christ. This process of separating the Christian from the world and consecrating him to God is called *sanctification.* Like repentance and faith, these two aspects of salvation—justification and sanctification—are distinct but inseparable.

Justification

The believer enjoys a new legal standing before God as a result of his union with Christ, and as such "there is now no condemnation for those who are in Christ Jesus" (Rom. 8:1 NASB). The importance of a proper understanding of justification can hardly be overstated. Luther declared justification "the doctrine on which the church stands or falls,"[164]

John is declaring that the regenerate no longer live under the power of sin. For further discussion, see Daniel L. Akin, *1,2,3 John, NAC* (Nashville: Broadman & Holman, 2001), 142–51.

[162] Strong citing Stern, *Systematic Theology,* 809–10.

[163] Strong states, "Union with Christ . . . is begun in regeneration, completed in conversion, declared in justification, and proved in sanctification and perseverance." See Strong, *Systematic Theology,* 795.

[164] Martin Luther, quoted by McGrath, *Iustitia Dei,* 367.

while Calvin described justification as "the main hinge on which religion turns."[165]

Since only the righteous can enjoy a relationship with God, then how can we, who are sinners, be in right standing with him? In other words, how can the unjust ever be just before a holy God? Throughout church history the doctrine of justification has been understood in three different and competing ways. To be justified by God a person must be either (1) *found* righteous, (2) *made* righteous, or (3) *declared* righteous.

The first position was held by the followers of Pelagius, who taught it is possible to live such a holy life that one will be found righteous by God on the day of judgment. Roman Catholicism advocates the second position when it rejects the Pelagian notion that we have the ability to please God and instead teaches that justification is a process which makes us righteous. Rejecting both Pelagianism and Catholicism, the Reformers recovered the New Testament truth that we receive the righteousness of Christ by faith alone. We will argue the Reformers were correct in their position that justification is a declared righteousness and define justification as *the act of God by which he credits the righteousness of Christ to the believer and declares him just.*

How a person understands the effects of the fall and the work of the atonement will go a long way in determining his understanding of justification. If the only impact Adam's sin has upon us is that he provides a bad example, then we probably have it within our power to obey God, and the purpose of Jesus' death was to provide us with a contrasting good example. However, if the depraving effects of Adam's fall are passed on to his offspring, then we have no hope of pleasing God, and the cross was accomplished to provide a payment for our sins and to bestow his righteousness upon us.

According to Pelagianism, the person who follows Christ's example is justified in God's sight. Pelagius, a fifth-century monk, opposed what he perceived to be the antinomian tendencies of Augustine's teachings on grace. Man is born spiritually neutral, Pelagius argued, and with the assistance of grace he can obey the demands for righteousness and holiness presented in the Scripture. Compared to traditional Christian doctrine, the Pelagian view of justification supposes a person's abilities are elevated and God's expectations are lowered.

Though officially condemned by the church at the Second Council of Orange (529), Pelagianism has been advocated by a number of proponents. Pelagian doctrine can be traced from the views of Peter Abelard (1079–1142) through the Socinians of the sixteenth century and up to the

---

[165] Calvin, *Institutes,* 3.11.1.

theological liberalism of Friedrich Schleiermacher (1768–1834), Shailer Matthews (1863–1941), and Harry Emerson Fosdick (1878–1969). Foundational to theological liberalism and modernism are the Pelagian notions that all humanity seeks for God, that God is not wrathful toward humanity's sin, and that Jesus' death is merely an example intended to influence us morally.[166]

For example, liberal Catholic theologian Karl Rahner (1904–1984) understands all persons to possess a "supernatural existential" which makes everyone open to the divine.[167] In Rahner's thinking, if a person is true to his own belief system, whether that system is Christianity, Islam, or even materialism, then on account of that person's integrity, God views him as just and enjoying a state of grace. This is why Rahner calls sincere atheists "implicit believers"[168] and labels adherents of other religions "anonymous Christians."[169] Everyone is just, except for those persons who deliberately choose not to be.

The Scriptures present a very different picture of the human condition. According to Paul, no one is naturally oriented toward God or has the ability to meet his righteous demands (Rom. 1–3). A naive version of Pelagianism is the predominant religious belief of the typical "man on the street," however the Pelagian position on justification either redefines or ignores the biblical teachings concerning sin, righteousness, and judgment.

2. Roman Catholic theology understands justification to be a lifelong process of the believer becoming just by the infusion of Christ's righteousness. This is because Catholic theologians interpret the New Testament word for "to justify," *dikaioō*, to mean "to make righteous" rather than "to declare righteous."[170] Such an understanding views justification to be something that happens in and to the believer rather than for him: the righteousness of Christ is imparted to the believer. A person is just (or righteous) when, by grace, he is made just. In other words, Catholicism sees justification and sanctification as synonyms: God views as righteous the person who becomes righteous.[171] In this regard, Pelagianism and Catholicism are similar; however Pelagianism believes we have the natural ability to obey God sufficiently while Catholicism sees this ability to be a gift of grace.

---

[166] For more information concerning liberal views of the atonement such as the moral influence theory and the example theory, see chapter 10.

[167] Karl Rahner, "Anonymous Christians," in *Theological Investigations,* trans. Karl H. and Boniface Kruger (Baltimore: Helicon, 1969), 6:392–93.

[168] Karl Rahner, "Observations on the Problem of the 'Anonymous Christian,'" in *Theological Investigations,* trans. David Bourke (London: Darton, Longman, and Todd, 1976), 14:284.

[169] Ibid.

[170] See George Eldon Ladd, *A Theology of the New Testament,* rev. ed. (Grand Rapids: Eerdmans, 1993), 480.

[171] Council of Trent, "Dogmatic Decrees of the Council of Trent," sixth session; chapter 10, in *Creeds and Confessions in the Christian Tradition.*

In Catholicism, justification is accomplished through the "merit of worthiness," i.e., the merit wrought by free moral acts performed in a state of grace. The person who, by grace, obeys the will of God earns more grace, and thus continues the upward climb toward full justification. The Council of Trent stated that believers are to "grow and increase in that very justness they have received through the grace of Christ, by faith united to good works."[172]

To most evangelicals the notion of "merited grace" seems to be an oxymoron; however, if justification is a process of becoming more and more just, then in order to be seen as completely righteous before God it is necessary to earn additional grace. Even though Catholic theology teaches that a person is justified by works, Catholicism also claims that it holds to a completely gracious salvation because it understands the good works a Christian does to be accomplished through God's grace.

Roman Catholicism explicitly rejects the evangelical view that salvation is by faith alone. In fact, at Trent the Catholic Church anathematized any who held to the Reformed view of justification.[173] According to the Catholic understanding of justification, faith is essential to salvation, but one is not saved by faith alone. Justification usually starts with works rather than faith because generally the first justifying event that occurs in an adherent's life is when he is baptized as an infant.[174] The primary condition for justification is understood to be love rather than faith, because justification comes through a faith which works by love (Gal. 5:6).[175]

Evangelicals often find bewildering the Catholic doctrines of purgatory and prayers offered to the saints, but these teachings are consistent with and perhaps necessitated by the Catholic belief in progressive states of justification. If justification is a process performed within a Christian, then what happens to the believer who dies before the process is complete? The Roman Catholic answer is that a Christian is made perfect in purgatory, where his remaining sins are purged.[176] Those extraordinary Christians who are perfected (or sanctified) in this life achieve sainthood and earn a surplus of merit, which are called "works of supererogation."[177] Catholics believe these saints are free to transfer this merit to others in response to prayers, and the greatest saint of all is Mary, the mother of Jesus.

---

[172] Ibid.

[173] Ibid., canon 9: "If anyone says that the sinner is justified by faith alone, meaning thereby that no other cooperation is required for him to obtain the grace of justification . . . let him be anathema."

[174] Ibid., chapter 4. Roman Catholicism understands baptism to wash away the guilt of original sin, which is one reason Catholics believe that it is important that an infant is baptized as soon as possible.

[175] Ibid., chapter 7.

[176] See The Catholic Church, "The Forgiveness of Sins," in The Catholic Catechism, 112–13.

[177] See J. Hennessey, "Supererogation, Works of," NCE, 13:616.

Roman Catholics are not the only ones to understand sanctification as a part of justification; certain Arminians, generally called Wesleyan Arminians, argue for a similar position.[178] Interpreting justification in the light of the governmental theory of the atonement, Wesleyan Arminians hold to three beliefs that distinguish them from most evangelicals: they reject the doctrine that Christ's righteousness is imputed to the believer; they understand faith itself to be the basis of justification; and they see sanctification as an essential component of justification.[179]

First, Wesleyan Arminians do not believe that Christ paid for our sins or that his righteousness is imputed to us when believe in him. Rather, as proponent Kenneth Grider explains, Christ died for *us*, not our sins, and God accepted his death instead of the righteous demands of the law.[180] The purpose of Jesus' death was to demonstrate to us the seriousness of sin, but it was not a payment for our sins. The idea that Christ's righteousness is credited to the believing sinner's account is rejected as a "legal fiction."[181] For God to declare someone righteous whom he knows in fact to be wicked goes against his own character. Wesleyan Arminians see the doctrine of imputed or credited righteousness as a misunderstanding of Paul's use of

---

[178] Many make a distinction between Reformed Arminianism and Wesleyan Arminianism. Reformed Arminians align themselves with the teachings of James Arminius, particularly with his adherence to the penal substitutionary view of the atonement, while Wesleyan Arminians follow more closely to the theology of John Wesley. Whether Wesley himself advocated the governmental theory of the atonement is a matter of debate; it is the position of most Wesleyan Arminians. See Stephen B. Ashby, "A Reformed Arminian View," in *Four Views on Eternal Security,* ed. J. Matthew Pinson (Grand Rapids: Zondervan, 2002), 137–84. For another proponent of Reformed Arminianism, see Robert Picirilli, *Grace, Faith, and Free Will* (Nashville: Randall House, 2002).

[179] See Demarest, *Integrative Theology,* 353–55. Once again, we see how one's theory of the atonement and his doctrine of justification are interconnected.

[180] Grider states, "Many Arminians whose theology is not very precise say that Christ paid the penalty for our sins. Yet such a view is foreign to Arminianism, which teaches instead that Christ suffered for us. . . . Arminianism teaches that Christ suffered for everyone so that the Father could forgive those who repent and believe; his death is such that all will see that forgiveness is costly and will strive to cease from anarchy in the world God governs. The view is called the governmental theory of the atonement." See J. Kenneth Grider, "Arminianism," in *EDT,* 2nd ed., ed. Walter Elwell (Grand Rapids: Baker, 2001), 97–98.

[181] In his denunciation of the "legal fiction" involved in the doctrine of the imputed righteousness of Christ, Wesley explained, "Least of all does justification imply that God is deceived in those whom he justifies; that he thinks them to be what, in fact, they are not; that he accounts them to be otherwise than they are. . . . The judgment of the all-wise God is always according to truth. Neither can it ever consist with his unerring wisdom, to think that I am innocent, to judge that I am righteous or holy, because another is so. He can no more, in this manner, confound me with Christ than with David or Abraham." John Wesley, "Justification by Faith," quoted by Ashby, 184. Charles Finney echoed Wesley when he also argued for a governmental view of justification by stating, "But for sinners to be forensically pronounced just, is impossible or absurd. . . . The doctrine of an imputed righteousness, or that Christ's obedience to the law was accounted as our obedience, is founded on a most false and nonsensical assumption." Charles Finney, *Finney's Systematic Theology,* abridged, J. H. Fairchild, ed. (1846; repr., Minneapolis: Bethany Fellowship, 1976), 320–21. See also W. Sanday and A. C. Headlam, *Romans, ICC* (Edinburgh: T and T Clark, 1900), 36; Dale Moody, *The Word of Truth* (Grand Rapids: Eerdmans, 1981), 325–28.

the courtroom metaphor (Rom. 3–5), which in turn reduces salvation to simple bookkeeping.

Second, some such as Robert Gundry argue that, rather than Christ's righteousness being imputed to us, it is our faith itself that God counts as righteousness. Gundry interprets texts such as Romans 4:5 ("But to him who does not work but believes on Him who justifies the ungodly, his faith is accounted for righteousness.") and Romans 5:1 ("Therefore, having been justified by faith, we have peace with God through our Lord Jesus Christ.") to be teaching that God counts our faith as righteousness instead of our works.[182] According to this viewpoint, faith is not the instrument by which we receive the righteousness of Christ but the basis of our justification itself.

A third distinctive of the Wesleyan Arminian view of justification is that it sees sanctification as a part of justification, or more precisely, sanctification as necessary to remain justified. Since the governmental theory holds that only one's past sins are forgiven and that there is no positive imputation of righteousness, then the believer must maintain this state of grace through holy living and confession of sin. Arminians conclude that it is possible for a Christian to lose his salvation.[183]

Many proponents of the "make righteous" view of justification, both Roman Catholic and Wesleyan Arminian, add two additional beliefs: a denial of full assurance of salvation and perfectionism. First, adherents reason that since a believer's continued obedience is necessary for complete justification, then no one knows for sure he will persevere. In fact, the Council of Trent considered assurance of salvation a sign of spiritual arrogance and condemned anyone who claimed to know for sure he was going to heaven.[184] Second, the "make righteous" view of justification does not just imply that a Christian can perfectly fulfill God's expecta-

---

[182] See Robert H. Gundry, "The Non-imputation of Christ's Righteousness," in *Justification: What's at Stake in Current Debates,* Mark Husbands and Daniel J. Treier, eds. (Downers Grove: InterVarsity, 2004), 17–45.

[183] Wesleyan Arminians and Reformed Arminians disagree about what can cause a believer to fall from grace. Wesleyan Arminians believe unconfessed sin will damn a Christian but generally are vague about how much or how serious sin must be in order to cause such spiritual shipwreck. Since Reformed Arminians affirm that Christ paid for our sins through a penal substitution, they do not believe that a believer can lose his salvation because of sin. However, they do hold that a Christian can apostatize, or deliberately cease to believe, and thereby cease to be redeemed. See Scot McKnight, "The Warning Passages of Hebrews: A Formal Analysis and Theological Conclusions," *TJ* 13 (1992): 21–59.

[184] Council of Trent, sixth session, canon 16: "If anyone says with absolute and infallible certitude (unless he shall have learned this by special revelation) that he will certainly have that great gift of final perseverance: let him be anathema." Calvin replied that the Word of God is sufficient special revelation for one to know he is eternally saved. John Calvin, "Acts of the Council of Trent with the Antidote," in *Selected Works of John Calvin,* vol. 3 (Grand Rapids: Baker, 1983), 155. He asked, "What else, good Sirs, is a certain knowledge of our predestination than that testimony of adoption which Scriptures makes common to all the godly?"

tions of him; it seems to necessitate it. For this reason many Arminians embrace perfectionism—that Christians can achieve in this life complete Christlikeness—a belief we will examine more closely when we survey the doctrine of sanctification.

As we have seen, the first two views—the "found righteous" position of Pelagianism and the "made righteous" position of Roman Catholicism—argue that God declares as righteous those who *really are* righteous. The third view, the "declared righteous" position of the Reformers, contends that the righteousness of Christ is credited to us when we are united to him by faith. Justification is the legal act of God by which he declares the sinner righteous on the basis of his relationship to Jesus Christ and his finished work.

The terms used by the biblical authors support the "declared righteous" view. In the Old Testament the Hebrew word *tsiddek,* in the hiphil form of the verb, means "to declare righteous, to vindicate, or to justify."[185] The New Testament word, *dikaioō,* means "to pronounce, accept or treat as righteous."[186] Contrary to the Roman Catholic view, there is virtually no lexical support to interpret "to justify" to mean "to make righteous."[187] Leon Morris explains, "The verb is essentially a forensic one in its biblical usage, and it denotes basically a sentence of acquittal."[188] As a declaration, justification is the antithesis of condemnation ("It is God who justifies. Who is he who condemns?" Rom. 8:33–34).

In Romans 3:19–4:9, Paul explained how God can be both "just and the justifier of the one who has faith in Jesus" (Rom. 3:26). The apostle made the provocative claim that God "justifies the ungodly" (Rom. 4:5) and that Calvary enabled God to justify sinners while at the same time remaining true to his holy nature. The work of Christ accomplishes what otherwise would be impossible: it simultaneously upholds God's righteousness and reveals his grace (Rom. 3:25–26). Paul drove home the principle of justification by faith by using two Old Testament examples: Abraham and David (Rom. 4:1–9). Abraham demonstrated that the best man still must be saved by grace (Rom. 4:3) while David showed that grace can save even the one who has committed the worst of sins (Rom. 4:5–8).

---

[185] J. I. Packer, "Justification," in *EDT,* 2nd ed., ed. Walter A. Ewell (Grand Rapids: Baker, 2001), 644.

[186] Ibid.

[187] Ibid. Packer states unequivocally, "There is no lexical ground for the view of Chrysostom, Augustine, and the medieval and Roman theologians that 'justify' means, or connotes as part of its meaning, '*make* righteous' (by subjective spiritual renewal)." Ladd is slightly less adamant, but concurs with Packer: "But it is almost universally agreed that the word justify *(dikaioō)* does not mean 'make righteous.' Rather, it designates the status—the relationship of righteousness." Ladd, *A Theology of the New Testament,* 484.

[188] Leon Morris, *The Apostolic Preaching of the Cross* (London: Tyndale, 1965), 290.

The biblical witness concerning justification presents three truths: justification is an objective declaration; this declaration is an acquittal; and this acquittal is based on the Savior's righteousness being credited to the believing sinner's account. The believer's union with Christ by faith establishes a covenant relationship with him that has legal ramifications. Christ fulfilled the righteous demands of the law, and along with him we also are viewed as just. Our union with Christ is the basis of our justification.[189]

First, justification is a forensic, or legal, declaration. This means justification deals with how God sees us in Christ, not with the transformation Christ is doing within us. It refers objectively to what Christ has done for us and to the position we enjoy in him, not to his work of sanctification we are subjectively experiencing.

Second, justification is an acquittal. This is the content of the legal declaration God makes about us. Two objections against the "declared righteous" position must be answered: God does not acquit the sinner simply by forgiving his sin, nor is objective justification a legal fiction. Some explain that to be justified means God views the sinner "just-if-I'd never sinned." The saying is quaint but incorrect because we are not declared innocent but forgiven. And justification is not simply the ignoring of our transgressions. Though our sins are forgiven, they are not *merely* forgiven because Christ, our substitute, paid for them in full. God judged us in Christ so that positionally, when Christ died on the cross, God looked upon us as if we died with him (Rom. 6; Gal. 2:20; Col. 3:3). When Jesus rose from the dead, from God's perspective we rose with him (Eph. 2:5–6). We are found righteous because in Christ we have already been judged for our sins.

Pioneers of the Great Plains protected their settlements from oncoming prairie fires by burning the grass around their homes because flames pose no danger to an area already burned. Similarly, the Scriptures warn that Calvary is the only safe place from the coming fiery judgment that will someday engulf the world (2 Thess. 1:7–9; 2 Pet. 3:7) because it is the one place God's judgment has already been. We are safe from the coming judgment because God already has dealt with us in Christ upon the cross. Justification is not predicated on God ignoring our sins but on his judging us in Christ.

Our union with Christ prevents justification from being merely a legal fiction. If a wealthy man or woman marries a poor spouse, then from that point on both are rich. So it is when the believing sinner is united with Christ; from that point forward, God deals with them collectively. As Erickson points out, "God always sees the believer in union with Christ and measures the two of them together. Thus, he does not say, 'Jesus is righteous but that

---

[189] Packer states, "For Paul union with Christ is not fancy but fact—the basic fact, indeed, in Christianity; and the doctrine of imputed righteousness is simply Paul's exposition of the forensic aspect of it (see Rom. 5:12–21)." Packer, "Justification," 645.

human is unrighteous.' He sees the two as one and says in effect, 'They are righteous.'"[190] Justification is not a legal fiction but a legal reality.

Third, justification is *crediting, or imputing, to our account the righteousness of Christ.* In Romans 4:4–5, Paul used a bookkeeping metaphor to describe how the debt of our sins was imputed to Christ while his righteousness was credited to us.[191] The apostle repeatedly explained that our righteous standing before God is due entirely to the gracious exchange Christ made with us (Phil. 3:8–9). He declared in 2 Corinthians 5:21 that Christ has taken the sinner's sin—and paid for it at Calvary ("He made Him who knew no sin to be sin for us") while the sinner has received the riches of Christ's righteousness ("that we might become the righteousness of God in him"). It is a glorious exchange, and we are getting an infinitely better bargain.

In summary, the *essence* of justification is that God accepts, regards, and declares the believer as righteous. It is not a process but an act of God. Justification has two elements; negatively, the believer's debt to the law is paid; positively, believers are reinstated into a position of divine favor and privilege. The *basis* of justification is Christ and his work ("Being justified freely by His grace through the redemption that is in Christ Jesus," Rom. 3:24; see also Rom. 5:9a). The *condition* for justification is faith ("But to him who does not work but believes on Him who justifies the ungodly, his faith is accounted for righteousness," Rom. 4:5). Faith is not the ground of justification, but it is the instrument by which we receive God's justifying grace. The *result* of justification is peace with God ("Therefore, having been justified by faith, we have peace with God through our Lord Jesus Christ," Rom. 5:1).

Sanctification

Believers belong to God (1 Cor. 6:19–20), and those who have been justified and regenerated are his possessions. Positionally, we are righteous in Christ, and sanctification is the work of God by which he brings our experience into conformity with our position. Just as the doctrine of justification deals with how through Christ the unrighteous is restored to a right relationship with him, so the doctrine of sanctification addresses how by Christ the unholy is made pure.[192] Like justification, sanctification is the act of God, but just as we receive God's justifying work by faith, so also we must exercise faith to receive God's sanctifying work. Our experience of spiritual transformation wrought by our sanctification "justifies" God's act of positionally

---

[190] Erickson, *Christian Theology,* 965.
[191] John Piper, *Counted Righteous in Christ* (Wheaton: Crossway, 2002), 55–57.
[192] Garrett states, "What the righteousness of God is to justification the holiness of God is to sanctification." Garrett, *Systematic Theology,* 356.

declaring us righteous because it demonstrates that God has not merely saved us *in* our sins but *from* our sins (Matt. 1:21; cf. James 2:14–26).

Roman Catholicism reserves the term *saint* for those believers who enjoy "the beatific vision," i.e., those who are in heaven and in the presence of God.[193] However, the Bible refers to all redeemed persons as saints and not just those who achieve a state of spiritual perfection (Rom. 1:7; 15:25–26; 2 Cor. 1:1; Eph. 1:1). Every believer is called a saint and is called to be saintly (1 Cor. 1:2).

Whether Hebrew or Greek, the terms for "sanctify," "saint," and "holy" derive from the same word group in their respective languages. In both testaments the words translated "to sanctify" basically mean "to separate." The Old Testament term *qadesh*, rendered "to be consecrated" or "be holy," comes from the root *qad*, which means "to cut" or "to separate."[194] The New Testament word *hagiazō* basically means "to separate" or "to set apart."[195] Sanctification is God's work of consecrating us: he separates us from sin and sets us apart to himself. A number of times the Old Testament presents sanctification as an act of self-consecration ("Sanctify yourselves," Josh. 3:5; 1 Chron. 15:12; cf. Lev. 21:8; Num. 3:13), but the New Testament emphasizes that sanctification is a work that God does on behalf of a Christian (John 17:19; Acts 20:32; 1 Thess. 5:23; 1 Pet. 1:2).

We define *sanctification* as *God's claiming and subsequent purifying of the believer as his possession*. Note the two parts of sanctification according to this definition: God first claims the believer by setting him apart for himself, and then God cleanses the believer from sin by a persistent and progressive work of the Holy Spirit. Because we belong to him and his Spirit resides within us, God requires that we exhibit godly character and behavior.

The array of positions advocated about sanctification can be grouped under two headings: *the perfectionist view* and *the progressive view*. What the various perfectionist views of sanctification have in common is a belief that a Christian's sanctification can be perfect (even though they differ in their definition of perfection). We will advocate the progressive view of sanctification, which argues that though the believer's positional sanctification in Christ is perfect, his experience of this reality is an ongoing and imperfect process.

When considering the experiential side of sanctification, two questions become apparent: how quickly (or gradually) is a Christian sanctified and how thoroughly is he made holy? The first question addresses whether a believer should seek or expect a sudden experience which dramatically transforms him

---

[193] K. I. Rabenstein, "Saints and Beati," in *NCE,* 2nd ed., ed. Bernard L. Marthaler (Washington, DC: Catholic University of America, 2003), 12.65. According to the Catholic understanding of justification, it is possible that most departed Christians are still in purgatory.
[194] Erickson, *Christian Theology,* 980–81.
[195] Ibid.

spiritually or if experiential sanctification is a gradual process that occurs over the entire course of a believer's lifetime. Adherents of the perfectionist position generally believe that sanctification occurs in a definite experience after conversion while advocates of the progressive position do not.

The second question concerns the thoroughness of sanctification and asks if it is possible for a Christian to cease sinning, and if not, why not. This issue is particularly acute for many who hold to the perfectionist view, such as Roman Catholics and Wesleyan Arminians, who see sanctification as a part of justification. These perfectionists teach that a believer must arrive at some type of perfection before salvation can be complete. In contrast, most Protestants, such as Calvinists and Lutherans, advocate the progressive view because they do not believe that sinless perfection is necessary for salvation or that such an achievement is possible in a Christian's earthly lifetime.

Proponents of the perfectionist view believe that a Christian can achieve a state of complete spiritual perfection but generally disagree with one another about what this state entails. Some understand entire sanctification to be a condition of sinless perfection while others see it as a state of perfect surrender.

Adherents of the sinless perfection position believe that, just as Christians are justified at conversion, they also must be sanctified by a distinct, subsequent event that is as definite as the initial conversion experience. Some understand this second work of grace either to remove the sin nature or to subdue the power of the flesh so that a believer ceases to sin. Proponents of the sinless perfection position generally are from the Wesleyan Arminian tradition, such as the Nazarene and Pentecostal Holiness churches.

Nazarene theologian J. Kenneth Grider describes sanctification in these words: "In the grace of entire sanctification, sin, as a malady, is *removed,* so that the heart is pure. In the nature of the case, the eradication of sin in principle from the human heart completes the Christian character" (emphasis original).[196] According to his understanding of sanctification, every believer is capable of living a perfectly sinless life because the eradication of the sin nature is available to all. Similarly, the statement of faith of the Pentecostal Holiness denomination affirms, "We believe that entire sanctification is an instantaneous, definite second work of grace, obtainable by faith on the part of the fully justified believer."[197] Pentecostals generally equate this second work of grace with their understanding of the baptism of the Holy Spirit.

Perfectionists who hold that it is possible for a Christian to live above sin point to places in the Bible which seem to require perfect consecration. For example, Jesus commanded, "Be ye therefore perfect, even as your

---

[196] J. Kenneth Grider, *A Wesleyan-Holiness Theology* (Kansas City: Beacon Hill, 1994), 387.

[197] *Discipline of the Pentecostal Holiness Church* (1925), 2.4. Available at http://www.pctii.org/arc/1925.html.

father which is in heaven is perfect" (Matt. 5:48 KJV), while the author of Hebrews exhorted the reader to "pursue . . . holiness, without which no one will see the Lord" (Heb. 12:14). In addition, John declares, "Whoever has been born of God does not sin, for His seed remains in him; and he cannot sin, because he has been born of God" (1 John 3:9). These texts clearly present the expectation that believers live holy lives.

However, the word translated "perfect," *telios,* also can (and often does) mean "mature" or "complete" and does not carry with it the connotation of sinless perfection.[198] None of the passages cited by proponents of the sinless perfection position teach that the sin nature is eliminated in the Christian. Also, the Bible recognizes that the struggle with sin is an ongoing reality for Christians and promises that provision is made for forgiveness and victory (1 Cor. 10:13; 1 John 1:8–10).[199]

Most adherents of the perfectionist perspective disagree with the sinless perfection viewpoint and do not believe that the believer's sanctification destroys inbred sin or enables a sinless life. They instead interpret Christian perfection to be a state of perfect surrender or a level of extraordinary spiritual ability. However, like other perfectionist proponents, they also understand the Holy Spirit's work of sanctification in the believer to be a clear, crisis event similar to the conversion experience. Pentecostal and charismatic groups generally interpret the sanctifying event to be the baptism of the Holy Spirit, which empowers the believer to holiness otherwise not possible.[200] Typically, Pentecostalism teaches that the baptism of the Holy Spirit manifests itself with the phenomenon of speaking in tongues.[201]

---

[198] *TDNT*, 8:54–57.

[199] Whether or not Romans 7:7–24 describes the experience of a regenerate person is a matter of debate. For a representative argument that Paul is describing his experience as a Christian, see David Peterson, *Possessed by God: A New Testament Theology of Sanctification and Holiness* (Grand Rapids: Eerdmans, 1995), 103–9. For an opposing argument, see Ben Wirtherington III, *The Problem with Evangelical Theology* (Waco: Baylor University, 2005), 21–38. For a helpful survey of the arguments for both positions, see Thomas Schreiner, *Romans, ECNT* (Grand Rapids: Baker, 1998), 379–92.

[200] For example, a position paper adopted by the Assemblies of God denomination states, "All believers are entitled to and should ardently expect and earnestly seek the promise of the Father, the baptism in the Holy Ghost and fire, according to the command of our Lord Jesus Christ. . . . This experience is distinct from and subsequent to the experience of the new birth. . . . With the baptism in the Holy Ghost come such experiences as an overflowing fullness of the Spirit (John 7:37–39; Acts 4:8), a deepened reverence for God (Acts 2:43; Heb. 12:28), an intensified consecration to Him and a dedication to His work (Acts 2:42), and a more active love for Christ, for His Word, and for the lost (Mark 16:20)." The General Council of the Assemblies of God, "Fundamental Truth 7," in *The Baptism in the Holy Spirit: The Initial Experience and Continuing Evidences of the Spirit-Filled Life,* a position paper adopted by the General Presbytery, 11 August 2000. Available at http://ag.org/top/beliefs/position_papers/4185_spirit-filled_life.cfm.

[201] Ibid. "Fundamental Truth 8: The baptism of believers in the Holy Ghost is witnessed by the initial physical sign of speaking with other tongues as the Spirit of God gives them utterance (Acts 2:4)."

Noncharismatic adherents of the perfectionist view of sanctification may or may not label the subsequent experience as the baptism of the Holy Spirit, but they also believe that through a decisive act of surrender to Christ, the believer experiences the power to live a life of perfect victory.[202] Sometimes labeled the *Keswick view* of sanctification, this position argues that the Christian passively experiences victory by yielding to the fullness of the Holy Spirit.[203] According to Keswick teaching, the believer does not exercise the disciplines of prayer, fasting, and Bible reading in order to be spiritual. Rather, the truly spiritual Christian will naturally manifest spiritual discipline as the fruit of the Spirit. When a believer completely dies to self, then he experiences the victory of perfect surrender.

An example of Keswick perfectionism taken to a logical extreme is the teachings of the Chinese martyr, Watchman Nee (1903–1972). Nee taught that the believer enters a condition of complete and total surrender when, by faith, he mystically experiences death to self by identifying with the cross. At that time the personhood of the believer disappears into a Christian version of nirvana. The self ceases—with all its desires, conflicts, and temptations—and the believer walks in the perfect victory of the Christ-life. Nee explained:

> When a believer has experienced the practical treatment of the Cross he finally arrives at a pure life. All is for God and in God, and God is in all as well. Nothing is unto self. Even the tiniest desire for pleasing one's self is crucified. Self-love has been consigned to death. . . . This is a pure walk. Although God affords him peace, comfort and bliss, he does not enjoy them for the sake of gratifying his desire. He from now on views everything with God's eye. His soulish life has been terminated and the Lord has granted him a pure, restful, true and believing spiritual life.[204]

According to Nee, sanctification is a mystical experience by which a believer can enjoy the bliss of complete, absolute spiritual perfection.

To recap, three traits characterize perfectionist theologies: (1) the belief that a Christian can attain the spiritual ideal in this lifetime, (2) the belief that a Christian experiences sanctification instantaneously (generally this

---

[202] One noncharismatic who rejects the practice of speaking in tongues but who nonetheless advocates seeking the baptism of the Holy Spirit is R. A. Torrey. See R. A. Torrey, *The Holy Spirit* (Old Tappen, NJ: Revell, 1927).

[203] This understanding of sanctification is called the Keswick view because of its association with an annual Bible conference held in Keswick, England. See Demarest, *The Cross and Salvation,* 396–98; Garrett, *Systematic Theology,* 363–64; and Robert McQuilkin, "The Keswick Perspective," in *Five Views on Sanctification,* ed. Melvin E. Dieter (Grand Rapids: Zondervan, 1987), 152–67.

[204] Watchman Nee, *The Spiritual Man,* vol. 2 (New York: Christian Fellowship, 1968), 256.

experience is labeled the baptism of the Holy Spirit), and (3) the belief that a Christian can discern the moment of sanctification (generally by speaking in tongues). The desire expressed by perfectionist theology to obey Christ completely and to live in holiness and purity resonates deeply with all who love the Savior, but we believe the Bible teaches that the practical experience of sanctification is a lifelong, ongoing process.

The progressive view understands the Bible to present sanctification in a twofold way: sanctification is an objective, positional reality and a subjective, ongoing experience. At conversion God positionally sets the believer apart as holy, and the Christian experiences the liberating power of his sanctification when by faith he lives by this truth. We can experience the relative perfection of a progressing maturity while striving for the ideal perfection modeled for us by our Lord (Phil. 3:12–16).

The biblical teaching concerning sanctification can be summed up under five headings: sanctification has both a positional and an experiential aspect; sanctification is the inseparable twin to justification; sanctification is the manifestation of regeneration; sanctification is compatible with full assurance of salvation; and sanctification is the focal point of the "now—not yet" reality of salvation.

First, sanctification has two aspects: *positional and experiential*. The positional aspect is the initial setting apart of the believer by God. When the New Testament speaks of sanctification, by far the preponderance of references is to the objective, positional component.[205] Sanctification is primarily "a once-for-all, definitive act" accomplished by Christ on the cross, which benefits are applied to the believer at conversion.[206] Paul reminded the Corinthian church of their positional sanctification when he stated, "And such were some of you. But you were washed, but you were sanctified, but you were justified in the name of the Lord Jesus and by the Spirit of our God" (1 Cor. 6:11). At conversion, a believer comes under the ownership of a new Lord, and he is to act accordingly.

Sanctification is a definitive event that has ongoing effects. The experiential aspect of sanctification is the continual process of purification, transformation, and progress that comes as a result of God taking possession of what belongs to him, i.e., the church, the people of God. Paul referred to the sanctification of the church as a progressive process when he spoke of Christ's work to "sanctify and cleanse her with the washing of water by the word" (Eph. 5:26). The apostle made clear that this ongoing development of spiritual growth has ethical and moral implications when he exhorted the church at Thessalonica, "For this is the will of God, your sanctification:

---

[205] Some, like Peterson, argue that sanctification is entirely positional. See David Peterson, *Possessed by God.*
[206] Ibid., 24.

that you should abstain from sexual immorality; that each of you should know how to possess his own vessel in sanctification and honor, not in passion of lust, like the Gentiles who do not know God" (1 Thess. 4:3–5).

Our positional sanctification enables our experiential sanctification. Positionally, we died with Christ ("For you died, and your life is hidden with Christ in God," Col. 3:3); therefore, experientially we are to die to sin ("Therefore put to death your members which are on the earth: fornication, uncleanness, passion, evil desire, and covetousness, which is idolatry," Col. 3:5). Similarly, positionally we rose with Christ ("[He has] made us alive together with Christ . . . and raised us up together," Eph. 2:5–6), so therefore we are to live in righteousness ("Just as Christ was raised from the dead by the glory of the Father, even so we also should walk in newness of life," Rom. 6:4). Our union with Christ sums up the two components of sanctification and how these two components relate: positionally we are sanctified because we are holy in Christ, so experientially we are to live out this new reality through Christ, who dwells within us in the person of the Holy Spirit.

Purity in life is the experiential manifestation of the positional reality of our union with Christ. For example, Paul dealt forcefully with the members of the Corinthian congregation who were involved in immorality with prostitutes (1 Cor. 6:13–20) but not in a way one might expect. Though he could have, he neither appealed to Moses' seventh commandment nor to Jesus' instructions in the Sermon on the Mount (Matt. 5:27–32). Rather, Paul reminded the Corinthian believers that they were in Christ (1 Cor. 6:15a) and pointed out that when they engaged in illicit behavior they were committing the intolerable sin of uniting Christ with immorality (1 Cor. 6:15b–16). For Paul, union with Christ is the basis of our sanctification. Our objective position in Christ provides the pattern and power for our subjective experience of living for him.

Second, sanctification is *the inseparable twin of justification.* Critics fear that the teaching of justification by faith alone will lead to a lax attitude within the church toward the desire for holiness. However, the Bible couples forensic justification with a dynamic understanding of sanctification. Christ, who protects us from the condemnation of sin, also purifies us from sin's pollution (Phil. 1:6). As Calvin stated, "Christ justifies no one whom he does not at the same time sanctify. These benefits are joined together by an everlasting and indissoluble bond."[207]

Third, sanctification is *the manifestation of regeneration.* The new life imparted to the justified and regenerated believer inevitably manifests itself, and the progressive manifestation of this new life is the experiential

---

[207] Calvin, *Institutes,* 3.16.1.

component of sanctification. Regeneration is the starting point of a believer's sanctification, and the two are so interrelated that one could say that regeneration is simply looking at sanctification from the angle of the believer's first moment of salvation. Both are descriptions of the reality of the new, eternal life a Christian enjoys in Jesus Christ.

Fourth, *the objective and experiential aspects of sanctification are compatible with full assurance of salvation.* In 2 Timothy 1:12, Paul expressed a twofold confidence concerning his salvation: he knew he was saved ("for I know whom I have believed"), and he knew he would continue to be saved ("and am persuaded that He is able to keep what I have committed to Him until that Day"). His expression of security is generally called the *assurance of salvation,* and this assurance is available to every believer. Our objective position in Christ ensures redemption; the subjective reality of Christ dwelling in us ensures that the experience of our salvation will continue until it is complete (Phil. 1:6).

The New Testament teaches both the *preservation* and the *perseverance* of the saints. The preserving of the believer means he is eternally secure (this is sometimes called the doctrine of *eternal security,* or "once saved, always saved"). This confidence derives from texts that speak of the believer's preservation as the active task of God ("And I give them eternal life, and they shall never perish; neither shall anyone snatch them out of My hand. My Father, who has given them to Me, is greater than all; and no one is able to snatch them out of My Father's hand," John 10:28–29; see also Rom. 8:31–39; 1 Pet. 1:5; Jude 24).

The doctrine of perseverance teaches that the work of regeneration and sanctification eventually and inevitably manifests itself in the life of every believer. Christians are capable of tragic spiritual and moral failure (the Bible is replete with cautionary examples—consider Lot, Samson, and David), but the faith of a genuinely saved person remains. This faith compels the believer to eventual repentance and restoration (Matt. 26:74–75). A Christian may fail totally but not finally.[208]

The Scriptures never present the believer's security as an excuse for sin (Rom. 6:1–2), and they warn about the consequences of spiritual disobedience (Gal. 6:7–9). Sin in a Christian's life may result in divine chastening (Heb. 12:5–7), being rendered unfit for service (1 Cor. 9:27), loss of rewards (1 Cor. 3:13–15), and perhaps premature death (1 Cor. 11:30). The indwelling of the Holy Spirit guarantees that no happy backslider exists (Ps. 32:3–5), and an indifference to spiritual matters could indicate that no real conversion has occurred (Heb. 12:7–8; 2 Pet. 2:22). Our sanctification

---

[208] See Ken Keathley, "Does Anyone Really Know If They Are Saved? A Survey of the Current Views on Assurance with a Modest Proposal," *JGES* 15 (Spring 2002), 28:37–59. Available at http://www.faithalone.org/journal/.

means that, as God's possession, we are secure. But this also means that God jealously purges his own from whatever detracts from his purpose and glory (John 15:1–3).

Fifth, sanctification is *the focal point in the life of the believer of the "now—not yet" reality of salvation.* Often the Bible presents the initial and the continual senses of sanctification as a tension—a tension that is very real to Christians. Paul highlighted both aspects of sanctification when he greeted the Corinthian church as "those who are sanctified in Christ Jesus, called to be saints" (1 Cor. 1:2). As we noted before, "sanctified" and "saint" come from the same root word for "holy," *hagios,* so the apostle described the Corinthian believers as positionally sanctified, but he also declared they are called to become sanctified experientially.

No Scripture illustrates the "now—not yet" reality of the positional and experiential aspects of our salvation, and by extension our sanctification, better than Paul's letter to the Ephesians. The first three chapters comprise the first half of the epistle and emphasize what Christ accomplished for us. Positionally and objectively, our salvation is a finished task. The second half, the last three chapters, gives ethical and practical instruction that make clear that, experientially and subjectively, our task is far from over. For example, the first half declares that when Christ rose from the dead, he triumphed over the hierarchy of spiritual beings (Eph. 1:20–22). However, the second half warns that we are still struggling against that same spiritual armada (Eph. 6:12).

The "now—not yet" of sanctification means that believers live within the realms of two realities that interact as two opposing inclinations—the flesh and the Spirit (Rom. 8:4–17; Gal. 5:13–25).[209] Our spiritual advancement comes about in a context of *"effort* (1 Cor. 9:24; 1 Tim. 4:10; Heb. 12:1), *struggle* (Rom. 7:15–23; Gal. 5:17), *warfare* (Eph. 6:10–18; 1 Tim. 6:12), *suffering* (Rom. 5:3; Heb. 10:32–34), and *divine chastening* (Ps. 119:71; Heb. 12:5–11)."[210] Sanctification is evidenced not by self-righteousness but by a hunger for righteousness and spiritual formation that are essential components of every believer's life. In Christ, we are now more than conquerors (Rom. 8:37); yet while we are in the world, we still have intense spiritual conflict (2 Cor. 7:5).

So how is sanctification manifested within the believer? The Bible teaches that the Christian life is one of battle (Eph. 6:10–18) and growth (2 Pet. 3:18). A good illustration of the believer's progress is to think of a ball bouncing down a stairway: though it goes up and down, its general direction is down. The Christian's pilgrimage is similar, but in the opposite

---

[209] Sometimes the conflicting inclinations are cast as the "old man" versus the "new man" (Col. 3:5–11). See David S. Dockery, "New Nature and Old Nature," in *DPL,* 628–29.

[210] Demarest, *The Cross and Salvation,* 402 (emphasis original).

direction: our progress may go up and down, but the overall direction is up. Positional sanctification is a promise of what eventually will be an experiential reality at the end of this age (Eph. 5:26–27). Therefore, "everyone who has this hope in Him purifies himself, just as He is pure" (1 John 3:3).

How Does This Doctrine Impact the Church Today?

In Christ we enjoy a multiplicity of benefits. However, the blessings that redemption gives to us are penultimate, for the greatest blessing of salvation is the glory it gives to God. In the brief space left, let us examine how the truth of the doctrine of redemption applies to the individual, the church, the world, and the Lord.

Salvation and the Individual

For the individual, salvation is a matter of ultimate concern, and the weight of eternity overwhelms the scales of priorities. Jesus asked, "For what will it profit a man if he gains the whole world, and loses his own soul? Or what will a man give in exchange for his soul?" (Mark 8:36–37). The importance of salvation not only achieves total significance, but it also addresses the universal need because humanity is under the all-encompassing curse of sin (Rom. 1:18–3:20, esp. 3:9–12). Everyone needs to receive Jesus Christ as Lord and Savior, and all need him more than anything else.

Contrary to popular misconceptions, salvation enables, not hinders, the "good life." The American Declaration of Independence calls life, liberty, and the pursuit of happiness "unalienable rights," but these are actually gifts of grace found only in Christ. Jesus declared, "I have come that they may have life, and that they may have it more abundantly" (John 10:10), and he gives true freedom (John 8:36) and joy (1 Pet. 1:8).

The Scriptures promise the Christian that he is accepted by God (Rom. 8:1,31–39) and that every believer can clearly know he is saved (2 Tim. 1:12; 1 John 5:12–13). The person who enjoys new life in Christ now walks by faith (Eph. 4:1) in fellowship with the Lord (Rom. 5:1). This confidence grants him the freedom to pray with boldness (Eph. 3:12) and serve the Lord—not to earn or keep his salvation, but for the pure and simple reason of pleasing and glorifying God (1 Thess. 4:1; 1 Cor. 10:31).

Salvation also addresses the matter of final purpose. Even though one's eternal destiny has ultimate stakes, redemption cannot be reduced to the mere escaping of punishment. Salvation restores the believer's relationship with the one for whom he was created, and this enables him to fulfill the purpose for which God created him. And what is this final purpose? "Man's chief end is to glorify God, and to enjoy him forever."[211]

Salvation and the Church

The biblical doctrine of salvation necessitates that the local church be a body of baptized believers and that the church have a regenerated membership. When the believer trusts Christ for salvation, he is spiritually baptized into the universal church, the body of Christ (1 Cor. 12:13; Eph. 2:16). Since the local church is the visible representation of the universal church, this clearly indicates that only believers should be baptized and brought into the fellowship. The New Testament presents the model of a believer's church.

In addition to being an assembly of the redeemed, the church also has a task in relation to redemption. The mission of proclaiming the message of salvation to the world belongs to the church (Matt. 28:18–20; Mark 16:15–16; Acts 1:8). Parachurch organizations and denominational structures help to facilitate evangelism, but the Great Commission was given to the church, and it has the responsibility of preaching the good news to the entire world.

Salvation and the World

The Bible generally distinguishes between creation and the world with the former term referring to the physical heavens and the earth (2 Pet. 3:4) and the latter referring to humanity in its collective opposition to God (1 John 2:15–17). As for creation, the death, burial, and resurrection of Jesus Christ have cosmic significance (Eph. 1:20–23; Col. 1:15–17). According to the Bible, Adam's fall affected creation by subjecting it to the curse of sin, but it also promises creation's restoration at the return of Christ (Rom. 8:18–22) and describes the heavens and the earth as eagerly anticipating its deliverance. As for the world, God judged it for its unbelief during Jesus' earthly life (John 16:8–10), and he will execute this judgment in the last day (2 Thess. 1:7–10).

The kingdom of God invaded this world with the arrival of Christ at his first coming (Matt. 12:28; Luke 17:21). At the time of salvation, God places the believer in "the kingdom of his beloved Son" (Col. 1:13 NASB). Until Christ returns, every local church is a visible manifestation of the kingdom, a precursor to his rule and reign over all creation (Rev. 20:1–8). A believer is an example and ambassador of the kingdom to the world, and this responsibility should guide his conduct accordingly (2 Cor. 5:16–20).

---

[211] Westminster Assembly, "The Westminster Shorter Catechism, 1648, Question 1," in *Creeds and Confessions of Faith in the Christian Tradition,* vol. 2, ed. Jaroslav Pelikan and Valerie Hotchkiss (New Haven: Yale University, 2003), 652.

Salvation and God

Salvation is according to the goodness of God and is an expression of his grace (Eph. 2:4–5). Because he loves us, he saves us (John 3:16; Rom. 5:8; 1 John 3:1). Undoubtedly, one of the most influential theologians of the twentieth century was Karl Barth (1886–1968). Near the end of his life, the German neoorthodox theologian was asked at a panel discussion to sum up his life's work. He replied, "Jesus loves me, this I know, for the Bible tells me so."[212]

God is glorified by every aspect of salvation. Election is according "to the praise of the glory of His grace" (Eph. 1:5–6); the death of Christ procures God's glory (Heb. 2:9–10); the conversion of the lost glorifies God (Acts 21:19–20); the believer's present enjoyment of salvation brings to God "glory in the church" (Eph. 3:20–21); and God will ultimately be glorified in the final day (Phil. 2:11).

In sum, salvation is in Jesus Christ, and we are saved when we are united with him by faith. Everything about salvation we enjoy in the Lord Jesus Christ—redemption's origin, the gospel call, our justification and sanctification, and the bestowing of the benefits of salvation—all are graciously given to us in Jesus Christ to the glory of God (1 Cor. 15:24–28; Eph. 1:10–12).

---

[212] Roger Olson, *The Story of Christian Theology,* 579.

SECTION 7

THE DOCTRINE OF THE CHURCH

CHAPTER 13

The Church

Mark E. Dever

Need for Studying the Doctrine of the Church

The doctrine of the church is of the utmost importance. A theology for the church would be incomplete without a theology *of* the church. Though many earlier systematic theologies have largely omitted ecclesiology,[1] the doctrine of the church is a crucial component of Christian truth. It is the most visible part of Christian theology, and it is vitally connected with every other part. A distorted church usually coincides with a distorted gospel. Whether such a distorted church results from misunderstandings of the gospel or leads to them, serious departures from the Bible's teaching about the church normally signify other, more central misunderstandings about the Christian faith.

This is not to say that all differences in ecclesiology are tantamount to differences over the gospel itself. Honest Christians have long differed over a number of important issues in the church. But such ongoing differences are not necessarily unimportant. Nonessential does not mean unimportant. The color of church signs or the time of Sunday morning services are nonessential to the Christian faith, as are the practices of Scripture reading or believer's baptism. But all would agree these different matters vary greatly in importance.

Perhaps the popular disinterest in ecclesiology results from the understanding that the church itself is not necessary for salvation. Cyprian of Carthage may well have said, "No one can have God for his father, who has not the church for his mother," but few would agree with this sentiment today.[2] Even the Church of Rome recognized in the Second Vatican Council that a normally competent and self-conscious adult participation in the church is not necessary for salvation. And emphasizing salvation

---

[1] From the nineteenth-century theologies of J. L. Dagg, J. P. Boyce, C. Hodge, R. Dabney, and W. G. T. Shedd to the early twentieth-century theology of E. Y. Mullins, separate sections on ecclesiology have often been omitted from systematic theologies.

[2] Cyprian, *De Ecclesiae Catholicae Unitate* (Oxford: Clarendon, 1971), ch. 6.

by faith alone, evangelical Protestants certainly have even less use for the church, much less for studying the doctrine of the church.

However, the church should be regarded as important to Christians because of its importance to Christ. Christ founded the church (Matt. 16:18), purchased it with his blood (Acts 20:28), and intimately identifies himself with it (Acts 9:4). The church is the body of Christ (Eph. 1:23; 4:12; 5:23–32; Col. 1:18,24; 3:15; 1 Cor. 12:12–27), the dwelling place of his Spirit (Rom. 8:9,11,16; 1 Cor. 3:16–17; 6:11,15–17; Eph. 2:18,22; 4:4), and the chief instrument for glorifying God in the world. Finally, the church is God's instrument for bringing both the gospel to the nations and a great host of redeemed humanity to himself (Rev. 5:9).

More than once, Jesus said love for him would be demonstrated by obedience to his commandments (John 14:15,23). Such obedience not only requires individual commitment and action from Christians; it requires a committed corporate obedience. Together individuals in churches will go, disciple, baptize, teach to obey, love, remember, and commemorate his substitutionary death with bread and the fruit of the vine.

The enduring authority of Christ's commands compels Christians to study the Bible's teaching on the church. Present-day errors in the understanding and the practice of the church will, if they prevail, still further obscure the gospel. Christian proclamation might make the gospel audible, but Christians living together in local congregations make the gospel visible (see John 13:34–35). The church is the gospel made visible.

Today many local churches are adrift in the shifting currents of pragmatism. They assume that the immediate felt response of non-Christians is the key indicator of success. At the same time, Christianity is being rapidly disowned in the culture at large, as evangelism is characterized as intolerant and portions of biblical doctrine are classified as hate speech. In such antagonistic times, the felt needs of non-Christians can hardly be considered reliable gauges, and conforming to the culture will mean a loss of the gospel itself. As long as quick numerical growth remains the primary indicator of church health, the truth will be compromised. Instead, churches must once again begin measuring success not in terms of numbers but in terms of fidelity to the Scriptures. William Carey was faithful in India and Adoniram Judson persevered in Burma not because they met immediate success or advertised themselves as "relevant."

As in other sections in this book, the doctrine about the church will be considered first biblically, then historically, then systematically, and finally practically.

What Does the Bible Say?

Nature of the Church

The church is the body of people called by God's grace through faith in Christ to glorify him together by serving him in his world.[3]

People of God in the Old Testament: Israel

In order to understand the church in the full richness of God's revealed truth, both Old and New Testaments must be examined. Though some Christians use the phrase "a New Testament church," the shape of the visible church today bears a clear continuity—though not identity—with the visible people of God in the Old Testament.

God's eternal plan has always been to display his glory not just through individuals but through a corporate body. In creation, God created not one person but two, and two who had the ability to reproduce more. In the flood, God saved not one person but a few families. In Genesis 12, God called Abram and promised that Abram's descendents would be as numerous as the stars in the sky or the sand at the seashore. In the exodus God dealt not only with Moses but with the nation of Israel—twelve tribes comprised of hundreds of thousands of people yet bearing one corporate identity (Exod. 15:13–16). He gave laws and ceremonies that should be worked out not only in the lives of individuals but also in the life of the whole people.

In the Old Testament, Israel is called God's son (Exod. 4:22), his spouse (Ezek. 16:6–14), the apple of his eye (Deut. 32:10), his vine (Isa. 5:1–7; Nah. 2:2), his flock (Ezek. 34). In each of these names, God foreshadows the work he will eventually do through Christ and his church.

Etymologically, a connection exists between the Old Testament word for "assembly," qahal,[4] and the New Testament word from which "church" is translated—ekklēsia.[5] The Greek translation of the Old Testament, the

---

[3] A great definition of the church was given by Robert Barrow in 1589: "This church as it is universally understood, containeth in it all the elect of God that have been, are, or shall be. But being considered more particularly, as it is seen in this present world, it consisteth of a company and fellowship of faithful and holy people gathered together in the name of Christ Jesus, their only king, priest, and prophet, worshipping him aright, being peacably and quietly governed by his officers and laws, keeping the unity of faith in the bond of peace and love unfeigned." *A True Description out of the Word of God of the Visible Church* (London: 1589). For a typical Baptist definition of the church, see the definition given by the Charleston Association: "A particular gospel church consists of a company of saints incorporated by a special covenant into one distinct body, and meeting together in one place, for the enjoyment of fellowship with each other and with Christ their head, in all his institutions, to their mutual edification and the glory of God through the Spirit." In "A Summary of Church Discipline," in *Polity,* ed. Mark Dever (Washington: Center for Church Reform [9Marks Ministries], 2001), 118.

[4] קהל

[5] ἐκκλησία

LXX, translates *qahal* in Deuteronomy 4:10 and elsewhere with *ekklēsia* (Cf. Deut. 4:10 and Acts 7:38).

This word for assembly, *qahal,* is closely bound up in the Old Testament with the Lord's distinct people—Israel. The rich association between the assembly of God and the distinct people of God then carries over to the New Testament by the word now translated in the New Testament to describe God's distinct people—the church. The church is, literally, an assembly (see Heb. 10:25). It is God's assembly because God dwells with the church. And the church is comprised of people who are beginning to know the reversal of the effects of the fall. So members of both Israel and the church receive a glimpse of the glory which awaits God's people.

Isaiah saw and heard seraphim calling to one another, "Holy, holy, holy is the LORD Almighty; the whole earth is full of his glory" (Isa. 6:3).[6] John then encountered what appeared to be the same heavenly assembly when he heard the angels, living creatures, and elders singing, "Worthy is the Lamb, who was slain, to receive power and wealth and wisdom and strength and honor and glory and praise!" (Rev. 5:12). Though Isaiah and John's visions were unique, Paul told the Corinthians that unbelievers will perceive this same God at work among them: "God is really among you" (1 Cor. 14:25). Heaven appears on earth in God's assembly, the church.

Christians divide over how closely Israel should be identified with the church.[7] The New Testament explicitly identities Israel and the church with each other in one place only. In Galatians 6:16, Paul referred to "all who follow this rule" in the Galatian church with the title "the Israel of God." While some suggest that "Israel of God" refers specifically to the Jews who belonged to the predominantly Gentile churches in Galatia, others are convinced that in the same letter Paul referred to all Christians, Jew and Gentile, as "Abraham's seed" (Gal. 3:29), indicating that the link between Israel and the church is deliberate.

Distinctions between the Old and New Testament people of God are obvious. God's people in the Old Testament are ethnically distinct; in the New Testament they are ethnically mixed. In the Old Testament they live under their own government with God-given laws; in the New Testament they live among the rulers of the nations. In the Old Testament they are required to circumcise their male offspring; in the New Testament they are required to baptize all believers.

Continuities between Israel and the church are more debated. Acts 15 is a particularly significant passage on this question. At the Jerusalem

---

[6] Unless otherwise noted, all Scripture citations in this chapter are from the New International Version (NIV).

[7] This distinction is fundamental to the theology and eschatology of dispensationalism; e.g., John F. Walvoord, *The Millennial Kingdom* (Grand Rapids: Zondervan, 1959).

Council, James quoted a prophecy from Amos (9:11–12) which promised that David's fallen tent would be restored and that Israel would come to possess the nations which bore the Lord's name. James affirmed that this prophecy points toward the church's present circumstances and the recent influx of Gentile believers. The "apostles and elders" (Acts 15:6), meeting to consider precisely the question of the Gentile believers, seemed to accept the recent influx of Gentile believers into the church as a fulfillment of the prophecy about Gentiles coming to Israel.[8]

Though Israel and the church are not identical, they are closely related, and they are related through Jesus Christ (Eph. 2:12–13). Israel was called to be the Lord's servant but was unfaithful to him. Jesus, on the other hand, was a faithful servant (Matt. 4:1–11). The temples of Solomon and Ezra, as well as Ezekiel's vision, all point toward Jesus Christ, whose body constitutes the supreme earthly tabernacle for God's Spirit. We also find that the land of Israel, especially the city of Jerusalem, points toward the redemption of the whole earth. Heaven itself is referred to as the new Jerusalem. The multinational church fulfills the promises given to the twelve tribes of Israel (see Rev. 7). And the law of the Old Testament finds its fulfillment in Christ (Matt. 5:17). Christ is the fulfillment of all that Israel points toward (2 Cor. 1:20), and the church is Christ's body.

At the very least it must be said that God has consistently had a plan to glorify his name through groups of people that he specially chooses and takes as his own.[9] "The story of the church begins with Israel, the Old Testament people of God."[10]

People of God in the New Testament: Church

At one particularly low point in the moral degeneration of Israel, the writer of Judges describes the nation as "the people of God" (Judg. 20:2; cf. 2 Sam. 14:13).[11] The Greek equivalent of this phrase[12] is used by the writer of Hebrews to describe the people of Israel with whom Moses identifies himself instead of Pharaoh's household (Heb. 11:25). This same phrase had been used earlier (Heb. 4:9) to refer to Christians. Writing to some early

---

8 This would also be similar to the way the writer to the Hebrews in Hebrews 8 appears to regard the prophesy in Jeremiah 31 concerning the houses of Judah and Israel as fulfilled in the church.

9 See George Eldon Ladd, *The Gospel of the Kingdom* (Grand Rapids: Eerdmans, 1959), 120. For contrasting views, see the traditional dispensationalist position represented by Walvoord, *The Millennial Kingdom*. For the progressive dispensational position, see Craig Blaising and Darrell Bock, eds., *Dispensationalism, Israel and the Church* (Grand Rapids: Zondervan, 1992) and Robert Saucy, *The Case for Progressive Dispensationalism* (Grand Rapids: Zondervan, 1993). For the Reformed position, see O. Palmer Robertson, *The Israel of God* (Phillipsburg: Presbyterian and Reformed, 2000) and Robert Reymond, *A New Systematic Theology of the Christian Faith* (Nashville: Thomas Nelson, 1998), 503–44.

10 Edmund Clowney, *The Church* (Downers Grove: InterVarsity, 1995), 28.

11 עַם הָאֱלֹהִים

12 τῷ λαῷ τοῦ θεοῦ

Christians, Peter also employed this phrase, telling his readers, "Once you were not a people, but now you are the people of God"[13] (1 Pet. 2:10).

In the New Testament the English word *church* can be used to describe both a local congregation or all Christians everywhere. In contemporary use, the word is also used to describe buildings and denominations. In these latter ways the English word *church* does not exactly parallel the Greek word in the New Testament.[14]

The word from which "church" is translated, *ekklēsia,* occurs 114 times in the New Testament.[15] No other word translates into the English word *church.* But the Greek word *ekklēsia* was used in the New Testament period to describe more than the gatherings of Christians. The word was often used in Greek cities to refer to assemblies called to perform specific tasks. In Acts 7:38 and Hebrews 2:12, *ekklēsia* is used to describe Old Testament assemblies. Luke used *ekklēsia* three times in Acts 19 to describe the riot which gathered in an amphitheater in Ephesus to deal with Paul (Acts 19:32,39,41). The remaining 109 uses of the word in the New Testament refer to a Christian assembly.

Jesus Christ founded his own assembly, his own church. According to the Gospels, Christ first named his people "my church" in Matthew 16:18. As Adam named his bride, so Christ named the church. In his recorded teaching, Christ referred to the church twice—in Matthew 16:18 and 18:17. Since Jesus understood that he was the Messiah, his references to his church almost certainly contain the Hebrew idea of *qahal* or "assembly."[16] The Messiah was expected to establish his messianic assembly, and so throughout the Gospels Christ marked out those who were faithful to recognize and follow him.

In the book of Acts, Luke usually referred to specific local gatherings with the word *ekklēsia.*[17] This is how he designated the assemblies in Jerusalem, Antioch, Derbe, Lystra, and Ephesus. These churches met and sent missionaries (e.g., Acts 15:3). Luke also quoted Paul as describing the church as bought with God's "own blood" (Acts 20:28).

Paul often referred to the church (or churches) of God (e.g., 1 Cor. 1:2; 10:32; 11:16,22; 15:9; 2 Cor. 1:1; Gal. 1:13; 1 Thess. 2:14; 2 Thess. 1:4) or the church (or churches) of Christ (e.g., Rom. 16:16; Gal. 1:22). He

---

[13] Gk. *laos theou* (λαὸς θεοῦ).

[14] William Tyndale regularly translated *ekklēsia* as "congregation."

[15] Three times in Matthew, forty-six times in Paul's writings, twenty-three in Acts, twice in Hebrews, once in 3 John, once in James, and twenty times in Revelation.

[16] The Septuagint translates the Hebrew word *qāhāl* (קָהָל) with the Greek word *ekklēsia* (ἐκκλη-σία) seventy-seven times.

[17] The one exception to this may be in Acts 9:31. But because this usage is unique, perhaps this is the result of the one church of Jerusalem, which had been scattered, still being referred to as a unit.

identified himself as being a former persecutor of the church (Phil. 3:6; cf. 1 Cor. 15:9). And his apostolic ministry centered on planting churches and building up churches. Paul's letters (particularly to the Corinthians) are filled with instructions to the early Christians about their behavior in their assemblies. "When he speaks of ἐκκλησία, he normally thinks first of the concrete assembly of those who have been baptized at a specific place. . . . Ecclesiological statements that lead beyond the level of the local assembly are rare in Paul's letters."[18] In Ephesians and Colossians, Paul intimately related and identified Christ with the churches (Eph. 2:20; 3:10–12; 4:15; Col. 1:17–18,24; 2:10), particularly by using the language of husband/wife and head/body to describe Christ's relationship to the church (Col. 3:18ff; Eph. 5:22–33). God's intention "was that now, through the church, the manifold wisdom of God should be made known to the rulers and authorities in the heavenly realms, according to his eternal purpose which he accomplished in Christ Jesus our Lord" (Eph. 3:10–11).

The book of Hebrews mentions the church once (Heb. 12:23), referring to an earthly assembly with a heavenly destiny.[19] James, too, referred to a local church and its elders in James 5:14. The third letter of John presents a picture of a particular congregation and their struggles with a false teacher and leader. Outside of Paul and Acts, the book of Revelation has more occurrences of *ekklēsia* (or its plural) than any other book in the New Testament. Except for one reference in the last chapter of Revelation, these all occur in the first three chapters. The word is used fourteen times in these opening chapters in a formula format to either begin or conclude a separate letter to each of the seven churches (Rev. 2:1,7–8,11–12,17–18,29; 3:1,6–7,13–14,22). The word is not used again until 22:16, where Jesus states that he has sent his angel "to give you this testimony for the churches." So the message of this book from chapters 4 through 22 is meant for the local churches.

Much of the New Testament's teaching about the nature of the church itself can be derived from the images used for the church. Paul Minear in his classic work *Images of the Church in the New Testament* points to ninety-six images for the church in the New Testament.[20] While the number ninety-six may not be precisely correct, says Roman Catholic theologian Avery Dulles in his more recent work *Models of the Church*, he agrees the New Testament authors use a large number of images.[21] God has inspired multiple images, each of which offers a different perspective and none of which should so dominate our conception of the church that the depth and

---

[18] J. Roloff, "ἐκκλησία," in *NIDNTT* (Grand Rapids: Eerdmans, 1990), 1:412–13.

[19] Hebrews 2:12 as a reference to an Old Testament assembly was mentioned earlier.

[20] Paul S. Minear, *Images of the Church in the New Testament* (Philadelphia: Westminster, 1960).

[21] Avery Dulles, *Models of the Church*, 2nd ed. (New York: Image, 1987).

texture of understanding is lost. Though all are inspired, they are not interchangeable, nor are they all as comprehensive in their presentation of the nature and mission of the church. The great images are familiar: the church as the people of God, the new creation, the fellowship or communion in faith, and of course, the body of Christ.

None of these images negates the institutional aspects of the church, but their number and variety point to a degree of mystery in the nature of the church. The church is the herald of the gospel (as in Acts). The church is the obedient servant (drawing from Isaiah). The church is the bride of Christ (as in Rev. 19–20). The church is a building (Eph. 2:21; 1 Pet. 2); the church is the temple (1 Cor. 3:16). The church is the community of people who live in the last days inaugurated by Christ's earthly ministry and the coming of the Spirit. Many other minor images of the church could be listed, such as "salt of the earth" (Matt. 5:13) or "letter from Christ" (2 Cor. 3:2–3). But particular consideration should be given to four major image clusters.[22]

First, the church is *the people of God.* This image has already been considered in the discussion of Old Testament background. It is also present in the New Testament. Peter used the title to encourage the readers of his first epistle (1 Pet. 2:9–10; cf. Rom. 9:25–26; Hos. 1:9–10; 2:23). These young Christians were struggling with the at-times painful distinction being made between their identity in Christ and others around them. Peter's language of a temple, constituted by the living stones of Christian lives and Christ himself as cornerstone (1 Pet. 2:4–6), reminded these discouraged Christians that they were the people of God, the product of God's gracious creation of them into an integrated reality—a single people. The people of God are based upon him and his act, deriving their identity from him uniquely. Many connections made with the Old Testament—the seed of Abraham (Gal. 3), the holy nation (1 Pet. 2), Israel (Rom. 9–11)—confirm the status of the church as the people of God.

Another major image describes the church as *the new creation.* Many evangelical Christians think of the new creation in connection with the explicit language of Paul in 2 Corinthians 5:17: "If anyone is in Christ, he is a new creation; the old has gone, the new has come!" They immediately associate this with the conversion of an individual believer. But the new-creation image is corporate as well as individual. In the New Testament, Christ's resurrection is presented as the firstfruits from among the dead

---

22 Another common way to categorize the various New Testament images of the church has been to use the trinitarian structure of the people of God, the body of Christ, and the dwelling of the Spirit. So Hans Küng, *The Church,* trans. Ray and Rosaleen Ockenden (Tunbridge Wells, England: Search Press, 1968), 107–260; Dale Moody, *The Word of Truth* (Grand Rapids: Eerdmans, 1981), 440–48; Clowney, *The Church,* 27–70; Millard Erickson, *Christian Theology,* 2nd ed. (Grand Rapids: Baker, 1998), 1044–51.

(e.g., 1 Cor. 15:20–23). And in his resurrection, the great final resurrection has begun. In these references, all the kingdom of God images come as well. God is granting a new beginning, a new creation through Christ.

A third major image cluster used for the church is centered on the idea of *fellowship*. The salutations in Paul's letters present the Christians whom he is addressing as sharing particular points of distinctiveness from the world around them. So in 1 Corinthians 1:2, Paul wrote, "To the church of God in Corinth, to those sanctified in Christ Jesus and called to be holy, together with all those everywhere who call on the name of our Lord Jesus Christ—their Lord and ours." The Corinthian Christians, like Christians everywhere, shared the status of being set apart for God's special purposes. Likewise, Christians everywhere are all called together to holiness. Jesus prayed for his followers to know such a fellowship (John 17), and such a fellowship we find throughout Acts and the letters. Much of the material in the letters represents the working out of this common life, as the authors attempted to encourage the believers to interact in a way that brings glory to God and reflects their shared status as Christ's followers, Christ's disciples, and Christ's friends (John 15:15; Luke 12:4).

Ultimately, fellowship among Christians in the church is based on the Christian's union with Christ. According to the New Testament, therefore, Christians live with Christ, suffer with Christ, are crucified with Christ, die with Christ, will be raised with Christ, and are glorified with Christ.

The final, and perhaps best known, image used to characterize the church is *the body of Christ*. Paul wrote in 1 Corinthians 10:17, "Because there is one loaf, we, who are many, are one body, for we all partake of the one loaf." He used the image at great length in 1 Corinthians 12–14 to describe the diversity of gifts within the one body of the church. In Ephesians 3, Paul argued that Jewish and Gentile believers belong to the same body. Did Paul invent this image? No, it was given to him in his conversion, when the risen Christ asked him, "Saul, Saul, why do you persecute me?" (Acts 9:4).

One other image in the New Testament worth considering briefly is the *kingdom of God*, a metaphor that refers to God's rule or reign. Jesus Christ taught his followers to pray, "Our Father in heaven, hallowed be your name, your kingdom come" (Matt. 6:9–10). The question that naturally arises in our context is whether the kingdom is identical with the church. Is it one more image like the others? Though Roman Catholic theology tends to identify church and kingdom, in Scripture a distinction is made between the reign of God (present and coming) and the church. The kingdom of God refers more specifically to God's rule or dominion. As George Eldon Ladd puts it,

> The Kingdom is not identified with its subjects. They are the people of God's rule who enter it, live under it, and are governed by it.

The church is the community of the Kingdom but never the Kingdom itself. Jesus' disciples belong to the Kingdom as the Kingdom belongs to them; but they are not the Kingdom. The Kingdom is the rule of God; the church is a society of man.[23]

In the book of Acts, the apostles do not preach the church; they preach the kingdom—God's reign.[24]

The church then is the *koinōnia,*[25] or fellowship, of people who have accepted and entered into the reign of God. This reign is not entered into by nations, or even families, but by individuals (Mark 3:31–35; cf. Matt. 10:37). According to Jesus' parable in Matthew 21, the kingdom of God was taken from the Jews and given to a people, as Jesus said, "who will produce its fruit" (Matt. 21:43; cf. Acts 28:26–28, 1 Thess. 2:16). The relationship between the kingdom and church can therefore be defined as follows: The kingdom of God creates the church. True Christians "constitute a Kingdom in their relation to God in Christ as their Ruler, and a Church in their separateness from the world in devotion to God, and in their organic union with one another."[26]

Matthew 16:19 presents a particularly important text for understanding the relation between the kingdom and the church. Jesus promised to give his disciples "the keys of the kingdom of heaven" (Matt. 16:19). Whatever he precisely meant by promising the keys of the kingdom, the power of the kingdom was certainly being entrusted to the church. "The kingdom is God's deed. It has come into the world in Christ; it works in the world through the church. When the church has proclaimed the gospel of the kingdom in all the world as witness to all nations, Christ will return (Matt. 24:14) and bring the kingdom in glory."[27]

Attributes of the Church: One, Holy, Universal, Apostolic

The Niceno-Constantinopolitan Creed, fashioned by the Council of Constantinople in AD 381, affirms that Christians believe in "one, holy, catholic, and apostolic church." These four adjectives (*notae ecclesiae*) have been used historically to summarize biblical teaching on the church.[28]

---

[23] George Eldon Ladd, *A Theology of the New Testament,* rev. ed. (Grand Rapids: Eerdmans, 1993), 111. Cf. Roman Catholic theologian Hans Küng's criticism of his church's teaching on this point in his book *The Church,* 92–93.

[24] See, for example, Philip's preaching in Acts 8:12 and Paul's in Acts 19:8; 28:23.

[25] κοινωνία

[26] Louis Berkhof, *Systematic Theology* (Grand Rapids: Eerdmans, 1938), 569.

[27] George Eldon Ladd, "Kingdom of God," in *EDT,* 2nd ed., ed. Walter Elwell (Grand Rapids: Baker, 2001), 611; cf. Berkhof, *Systematic Theology,* 568–70.

[28] For more on this, see Richard D. Phillips, Philip G. Ryken, Mark E. Dever, *The Church: One, Holy, Catholic and Apostolic* (Phillipsburg: Presbyterian and Reformed, 2004).

The church is *one* and is to be one because God is one. Christians have always been characterized by their unity (Acts 4:32). The unity of Christians in the church is to be a property of the church, and a sign for the world reflecting the unity of God himself. Thus, divisions and quarrels are a peculiarly serious scandal. Paul wrote to the Ephesians, "There is one body and one Spirit—just as you were called to one hope when you were called—one Lord, one faith, one baptism; one God and Father of all, who is over all and through all and in all" (Eph. 4:4–6). In 1 Corinthians 1, Paul argued for the unity of the Christians based on their unity in Christ. In Romans 12 and 1 Corinthians 12, Paul taught there is one body. And in Galatians 3:27–28, Paul said that Christians are all one in Christ, regardless of ethnicity. Paul's teaching reflects Christ's own teaching that there is one flock (John 10:16). So Christ prayed in John 17:21 for his followers to be one.

The church, Hans Küng has stated, is one, though divided.[29] This unity is not visible at the organizational level; it is a spiritual reality, consisting in the fellowship of all true believers sharing in the Holy Spirit. It becomes visible when believers share the same baptism, partake of the same supper, and look forward to sharing one heavenly city. The church on earth experiences this unity only as they are united in God's truth as it is revealed in Scripture.

The church is *holy* and is to be holy because God is holy (Lev. 11:44–45; 19:2; 20:7; 1 Pet. 1:14–16). The holiness of the church describes both God's declaration concerning his people and the Spirit's progressive work. After all, the church is the dwelling place of the Holy Spirit, and it is composed of saints set apart for God's special use (1 Cor. 1:2). So the church's holiness is fundamentally Christ's holiness; at the same time, Christ's holiness will be reflected in the church's holiness (Rom. 6:14; Phil. 3:8–9). Christ "loved the church and gave himself up for her to make her holy, cleansing her by the washing with water through the word, and to present her to himself as a radiant church, without stain or wrinkle or any other blemish, but holy and blameless" (Eph. 5:25–27).

In this present age the church will never attain ethical holiness perfectly. "The Lord is daily at work in smoothing out wrinkles and cleansing spots. From this it follows that the church's holiness is not yet complete. The church is holy, then, in the sense that it is daily advancing and is not yet perfect."[30] But the holy status the church possesses by virtue of God's declaratory act also separates the church from the world for God's service. Hence, both Old and New Testaments emphasize the importance of holi-

---

[29] Küng, *The Church*, 320.
[30] John Calvin, *Institutes of the Christian Religion*, ed. J. T. McNeil, trans. Ford Lewis Battles, LCC (Philadelphia: Westminster, 1960), 4.1.17.

ness among the people of God so that they might accomplish the service to which they are called (Deut. 14:2; 1 Cor. 5–6; 2 Cor. 6:14–7:1). Certainly a church that resigns itself to evil fails dismally. This holiness of status is a being set apart, not a being cut off, which status results in holiness of action in the world.

The church is *universal* and is to be universal because God is the "Lord of all the earth" (Josh. 3:11,13; Ps. 97:5; Mic. 4:13; Zech. 4:14; cf. Jer. 23:24) and "King of the ages" (Rev. 15:3). The church is universal then in that it stretches across space and time. Universality alone among these four attributes is not actually found in the New Testament. Rather this description developed from later reflection upon the true church. *Catholic* is the older English word used to describe this attribute. But because of that word's association with the Church of Rome, *universality* provides a better translation of the Greek word originally used in the creeds, *katholikēin*.[31] Universality is not the domain of any one group of true Christians. In Ignatius of Antioch's letter to the Smyrneans in the early second century AD, he wrote that "where Jesus Christ is there is the universal church." From the third century AD, the word came to be used synonymously with "orthodox," as opposed to "heretical," "schismatic," and "innovative."

While every true local church is part of this universal church and is an entire church itself, no local church can be said to constitute the entire universal church. Therefore, Christians must exercise care in their assumptions about the correctness of doctrines or practices that may, in fact, be peculiar to their own time or place. Ever since the initial inclusion of Gentiles into the first-century church, the church has obeyed Christ's mandate to spread his gospel to all nations, so that the church will finally be composed of people from all nations. "You are worthy to take the scroll and to open its seals, because you were slain, and with your blood you purchased men for God from every tribe and language and people and nation" (Rev. 5:9). The continuity of the church across space and time prevents the church from being held captive to any one segment of it. The church, in both its local and universal manifestations, belongs to Christ and Christ alone.

The church is *apostolic* and is to be apostolic because it is founded on and is faithful to the Word of God given through the apostles. Early in Jesus' public ministry, Jesus "called his disciples to him and chose twelve of them, whom he also designated apostles" (Luke 6:13). Toward the end of his ministry, Jesus then prayed "for those who will believe in me through their [the apostles'] message" (John 17:20). From the apostles until the present day, the gospel that they preached has been handed down. There has been a succession of apostolic teaching based on the Word of God. Paul told the

---

[31] καθολικὴν

Ephesian Christians that they had been "built on the foundation of the apostles and prophets, with Christ Jesus himself as the chief cornerstone" (Eph. 2:20). The succession that followed the setting of this foundation may not always have involved a person-to-person transmission, but there has been a succession of faithful teaching of the truth. Writing to the Galatians, Paul emphasized that their allegiance to the gospel message he had already given them superceded any allegiance to him personally (Gal. 1:6–9).

What does that mean for today since the apostles are long gone? Edmund Clowney put it succinctly: "To compromise the authority of Scripture is to destroy the apostolic foundation of the church."[32] The physical continuity of a line of pastor-elders back to Christ's apostles is insignificant compared to the continuity between the teaching in churches today and the teaching of the apostles.[33] Only with the apostle's teaching is the church, as Paul describes it to Timothy, "the pillar and foundation of the truth" (1 Tim. 3:15).

These four attributes have long been used to express the Bible's teaching about the church. They are the church's gifts and tasks.

> The church is already one, but it must become more visibly one . . . in faith and practice. The church is already holy in its source and foundation, but it must strive to produce fruits of holiness in its sojourn in the world. The church is already catholic, but it must seek a fuller measure of catholicity by assimilating the valid protests against church abuse . . . into its own life. The church is already apostolic, but it must become more consciously apostolic by allowing the gospel to reform and sometimes even overturn its time-honored rites and interpretations.[34]

Marks of the Church

Over the centuries, the four attributes of the church have been joined and often replaced by two marks which define a local church.[35] These two marks are the right preaching of the Word of God and the right administration of baptism and the Lord's Supper. In fact, a biblical ecclesiology can largely be organized and presented under these two marks, since in them both the creation and the preservation of the church are accomplished. Here

---

[32] Clowney, *The Church,* 76.

[33] Robert Reymond comments: "Just as the true seed of Abraham are those who walk in the faith of Abraham, irrespective of lineal descent, so also the apostolic church is one which walks in the faith of the apostles, irrespective of the issue of 'unbroken succession,'" *New Systematic Theology,* 844.

[34] Donald Bloesch, *The Church* (Downers Grove: InterVarsity, 2002), 103.

[35] For an interesting comparison of the function of the classic four attributes (unity, holiness, universality, apostolicity) and the two marks of a true church, see Küng, *The Church,* 267–69.

is the fountain of God's truth that gives life to his people, and here is the lovely vessel to contain and display this glorious work. The church is generated by the right preaching of the Word. The church is distinguished and contained by the right administration of baptism and the Lord's Supper. It should also be noted this latter mark presumes and implies the practice of church discipline. The rest of this section will be devoted to an investigation of the Bible's teaching on the church organized under these two heads: first, the right preaching of the Word; second, the right administration of the ordinances. Several implications of the right administration of the ordinances will also be considered, including membership, polity, discipline, mission, and purpose of the church.

Right Preaching as a Mark of a True Church

God's people in Scripture are created by God's revelation of himself. His Spirit accompanies his Word and brings life.

The theme of "life through the Word" is clear in both the Old and New Testaments. In the Old Testament, God created life in Genesis 1 by his breath. God spoke, and the world and all living beings were created. In Genesis 1:30, the living creatures are described as having the "breath of life"[36] in them. So in Genesis 2:7, God breathed this same *breath of life* into those creatures made specially in his image—men and women.

After this first man and woman fell away from God, rebelling against him, God sustained them and their descendants by his Word. So a word of promise was given to them in Genesis 3:15. Again in Genesis 12, his word called Abram from Ur of the Chaldees to become the progenitor of God's people. In Exodus 3:4, God called upon Moses with his word to bring his people out of Egypt. In Exodus 20, God gave his people his ten "words," and throughout the Pentateuch, God's word was the shaping influence on his people. Throughout the Old Testament, God ministered to his people by his Word. He created them and re-created them through the priests' teaching of the law and the prophets' inspired guidance.

Ezekiel 37 presents a dramatic picture of re-creation in particular. The people of Israel were in exile, depicted as an army so devastated that only their bones remained. God commanded the Prophet Ezekiel to preach to these bones. As Ezekiel did, the Spirit of God accompanied Ezekiel's words, and the bones were brought to life.

> And as I was prophesying, there was a noise, a rattling sound, and the bones came together, bone to bone. I looked, and tendons and flesh appeared on them and skin covered them, but there was no breath in them. Then he said to me, "Prophesy to the breath;

---

[36] נֶפֶשׁ חַיָּה

prophesy, son of man, and say to it, 'This is what the Sovereign LORD says: Come from the four winds, O breath, and breathe into these slain, that they may live." So I prophesied as he commanded me, and breath entered them; they came to life and stood up on their feet—a vast army (Ezek. 37:7–10).

Moving to the New Testament, God's Word again plays the central role as bringer-of-life. So the eternal Word of God, the Son of God, becomes incarnate for the salvation of God's people (John 1). Jesus came to preach God's Word, to uniquely embody it, as well as to accomplish God's will through his perfect life, atoning death, and triumphant resurrection. He founded his church and taught his followers to go into all nations, preaching the message of reconciliation to God through faith in him (Matt. 28:18–20). Paul can therefore write that "faith comes from hearing the message, and the message is heard through the word of Christ" (Rom. 10:17). The consistent message of Scripture is that God creates his people and brings them to life through his Word.

The right preaching of the Word of God that creates the church is not only the Word from God; it is the Word about God. As the call to hear, the *shema,* puts it, "Hear, O Israel: The LORD our God, the LORD is one" (Deut. 6:4). Immediately following this statement about God is the command indicating the response required of God's people: "Love the LORD your God with all your heart and with all your soul and with all your strength" (Deut. 6:5). When asked which command was most important, Jesus pointed to this one (Mark 12:29–33; Matt. 22:37; Luke 10:27). Not only is it echoed throughout the Old and New Testaments (e.g., 2 Chron. 15:12; Isa. 44:6–8; John 17:3; 1 Cor. 8:5–6; James 2:19); it summarizes the whole law and fundamentally marks out the identity of those who belong to God. When God's people hear about God and what he requires, they *will* respond.

In that sense, a right understanding of God provides the right framework for right preaching. Everything a preacher says must be placed within and shaped by the grid of biblical theology that teaches both preacher and congregation about God and what he requires of humanity. After all, a right understanding of God is the only true foundation for the church. And God has always revealed himself through his Word—his written Word, his incarnate Word, and his preached word. That is the church's task—to proclaim God's Word.

An earlier section of this book has already dealt extensively with the nature and attributes of God, yet it is appropriate to review God's character in light of his foundational role in preaching and the existence of the church. According to the Bible, the church has as its Creator and Lord, and as its center, the God of the Bible. This God is creating, holy, faithful, loving, and sovereign. This God of the Bible is recognized as the great initiator. That means he is the Creator of the world and the giver of everything. It also means he is the author of the church's salvation (Heb. 2:10). The salvation offered inside the church through the preached Word is not originally from the church. The church merely acts as the means, or the instrument, through which the great creating and electing God calls his people to himself. God's people exist because of his pleasure (Eph. 1:9–14).

The God of the Bible is also the holy God. Holiness is an attribute of God's own character, his nature, and the nature of all of his works. Of course, God's holiness is a problem for sinful people because it separates all humans from God. Yet it characterizes God's unique self and his unique loveliness. Without this holiness—his utter moral purity—God would not be God. And he has created a people who are called to reflect his holy character through lives marked by holiness (Lev. 11:44–45; 19:2; 20:7; 1 Pet. 1:16).

The God of the Bible is a faithful God. He keeps his promises. When he promises to make a people his own, they will be made his own. The Old and New Testaments are a grand, sometimes elaborate account of God making promises to his people and then keeping his promises to his people. From the promise to forgive (Exod. 34:6–7) to the promise to provide a prophet like Moses (Deut. 18:15–19), God's Old Testament promises were fulfilled to his people in the New Testament through the person and work of Jesus Christ. Jesus is the ransom and the lamb, the prophet and the priest, the second Adam and the faithful Son. In all these ways, God's faithfulness makes a people for himself.

The God of the Bible is a loving God. But his love can be understood maximally only when counterpoised to his holiness because his love provides what his holiness requires. Apart from God's holiness the church *need* not exist. That is, if God is not set apart, his people need not be set apart. But apart from God's love, the church *would* not exist. Only God himself can set his people apart, and why would God set them apart unless he loved. So the whole message God brings to his people can be summarized as judgment and grace, holiness and mercy, human sin and divine forgiveness through Christ. For God loved the world in this way—"he gave his one and only Son, that whoever believes in him shall not perish but have eternal life" (John 3:16).

And the God of the Bible is a sovereign God. So Jesus taught his disciples to pray by approaching God as the sovereign King: "Your kingdom come, your will be done on earth as it is in heaven" (Matt. 6:10). The God who is the Creator and Lord of the church is also the Creator and Lord of all that has been made. His rule will be acknowledged by all people at the end—in one way or another. Some will greet his coming with shouts of joy and gladness, others with fists and teeth clenched in resentment. But all will acknowledge that he is sovereign. In that sense, the church is an inbreaking of his rule into this present age, a foretaste of heaven.

This is the God whom his people are commanded to love. All other gods are a creation of the human mind and will share in the vanishing fate of every other illusion. The God of the Bible must be the foundation and framework of all teaching and preaching in the church.

If a right theology of God provides the framework, or grid, for right teaching, then a focus on the gospel provides the center, or point, of right teaching. As we have seen, false teaching about God separates God's people from him and builds a community around a being who does not exist. Furthermore, if the "god" preached is not offended by sin and does not judge sinners, then the gospel itself is short-circuited. People are lied to in a manner that imperils their salvation. The right teaching of the true church, therefore, centers itself on a right understanding of the gospel.

Right teaching about the gospel, in turn, requires a right understanding not only about God but about humanity. If a church's teaching depicts people as spiritually sick, not spiritually dead, the gospel has been distorted. If congregants are regarded as consumers rightly expectant of a spiritual upgrade, not as rebels before a holy judge, then the gospel has probably been forgotten. Such churches build community around something other than the gospel. Any unity they experience is a unity based on a false message.

Right teaching about the gospel also centers the church upon Christ's work of atonement and not only on his teaching or life example. The true church is cruciform, not necessarily in its architecture but in its teaching. Jesus' life does provide an example for Christian living. So say both Christ and the apostles (Mark 8:34; Matt. 10:25; 1 Pet. 2:21). But what sets Christian teaching apart from every other major religion is that its figurehead acts as both example and redeemer. Christ came not only to preach but also to be a ransom for his people (Mark 10:45). Thus when the church gathers, it gathers not simply as an instructed or edified people but as a ransomed and saved people.

Finally, right teaching about the gospel centers the church not on human actions but on receiving by faith and repentance the rewards of God's actions in Christ. Paul wrote to the Corinthians, "God made him [Christ] who had no sin to be sin for us, so that in him we might become the righteousness of God" (2 Cor. 5:21). Sinful humanity has earned God's judgment. But through repentance and faith, sinners are made God's own people. Churches must not err by neglecting either repentance or faith. Without the former, a mental-assent-only faith that is dead follows (see James 2). Without the latter, faith and reliance on Christ vanish behind demands of obedience to the law (Rom. 2–3). A gospel-centered church teaches the need both to turn from sin and turn to Christ. By itself, a searching exposition on human sin is not enough. By itself, the proclamation of God's love in Christ's atoning death is not enough. Both are necessary. A cross not taken up by repentance or affirmed by faith is a cross that does not save. The right preaching of the Word of God is central to the church and is the basis and core of it.

Right Administration of the Ordinances

Jesus Christ has given two visible signs of his special presence to his people. These signs are baptism and the Lord's Supper. Sometimes these signs are referred to as "ordinances," emphasizing the fact that they were ordained by Christ. Other times they are referred to as "sacraments," emphasizing the fact that they set forth the mystery of the gospel.[37] Some evangelicals are hesitant to use the latter term, thinking it suggests the signs are effective for conveying grace apart from a believer's faith.[38] Therefore, the term *ordinances* will be used here.

Christ himself ordained these practices both by example and by command. He was baptized by John the Baptist, and he commanded his disciples to make disciples and baptize in all nations (Matt. 3:15–16; 28:19; Mark 1:9; Luke 3:21; cf. John 1:29–34). Based upon Acts and the letters, it seems this was the universal practice of New Testament Christians. Christ also established the Lord's Supper and commanded his disciples to "do this in remembrance of" him (Matt. 26:17–30; Mark 14:12–26; Luke 22:7–20; John 13–17; 1 Cor. 11:17–34; also Luke 22:19; 1 Cor. 11:24–25). From the rest of the New Testament, it seems clear that Christians regularly partook of what Paul calls the Lord's Supper (1 Cor. 11:20).[39]

When a church practices baptism and the Lord's Supper, it obeys Christ's teaching and example. In so doing, it portrays Christ's death and resurrection, the testimony of every believer's own spiritual rebirth, as well as the church's collective hope for the final resurrection. These two practices, in short, proclaim the gospel. Thus, even congregations that have long forsaken biblical doctrine regarding regeneration, Christ's substitutionary death, or the hope of heaven, still proclaim these truths in their liturgies as they reenact these signs. The new birth may be ignored, but baptism portrays it. Christ's atonement may be denied in the sermon, but the Lord's Supper proclaims it. In such cases, tradition at the table speaks more truth than the preaching from the pulpit. Practicing baptism and the

---

[37] The word *sacrament* is derived from the Latin term for mystery; e.g., see the Vulgate for Eph. 1:9; 3:3; 5:32. Louis Berkhof defined a sacrament as an ordinance (*Systematic Theology*, 617).
[38] "Let it be regarded as a settled principle that the sacraments have the same office as the Word of God: to offer and set forth Christ to us, and in him the treasures of heavenly grace. But they avail and profit nothing unless received in faith," Calvin, *Institutes*, 4.14.17.
[39] κυριακὸν δεῖπνον

Lord's Supper demonstrates obedience to Christ, and these practices are intended to complement by visible sign and symbol the audible preaching of the gospel.

Conversely, a church fails to obey Christ's command when it neglects either of these two signs.[40] Such failure removes that church from a submission to the larger teaching of Scripture. And it separates a congregation from the apostolic and universal practice of Christ's followers. Scripture acts as a counterweight against anyone—whether congregation or person—who decides to be a Christian and yet neglects baptism or the Lord's Supper. This neglect, or denial, separates those who truly follow Christ. While neither baptism nor the Lord's Supper is salvific, a deliberate neglect of either puts a question mark on any profession of faith. In this sense, baptism and the Lord's Supper act as the marks of a true church. They are the outward signs, or visible boundaries, that distinguish a particular people from the world. Yet matching that outward message is an inward message. The ordinances remind Christians of the fellowship that they enjoy with God and one another.

Some have taught that other ordinances or sacraments mark the true church. The Roman Catholic Church teaches that confirmation, confession (penance), ordination, marriage, and extreme unction (last rites) are also sacraments.[41] Yet due to the Roman Catholic Church's teaching about the authority of the church and the role of tradition, they need not convincingly maintain that these are all ordained of Christ during the time of his earthly ministry.[42] In the early sixteenth century, however, the Protestant Reformers recognized the Bible alone as authoritative for establishing church practice, resulting in the claim that only baptism and the Lord's Supper had sufficient

---

[40] Some organized bodies of confessing followers of Christ deliberately reject these practices (e.g., the Quakers and the Salvation Army). Many contemporary evangelical congregations could also be said to neglect baptism or the Lord's Supper in practice, if they are evaluated by either frequency or understanding.

[41] The Council of Trent finally determined seven as the number of sacraments that faithful Roman Catholics should accept. The other five with their biblical bases are confirmation (Acts 8:17; 14:22; 19:6; Heb. 6:2), confession (James 5:16), ordination (1 Tim. 4:14; 2 Tim. 1:6), marriage (Eph. 5:32), and extreme unction (James 5:14). See paragraph 1113 in *Catechism of the Catholic Church,* in *Libreria Editrice Vaticana* (Liguori: Liguori Publications, 1994). At some length, Calvin rejected these five additional practices as sacraments (*Institutes,* 4.19). Berkouwer concludes his consideration of the five "extra" Roman Catholic sacraments by gently stating that "this brief review of the five special sacraments makes it clear that Roman Catholic theology fixes the number of sacraments on the basis of its view that they constitute a series of supernatural acts that infuse supernatural grace into all of life from beginning to end, rather than upon an indubitable foundation of biblical exegesis." G. C. Berkouwer, *The Sacraments,* trans. Hugo Bekker (Grand Rapids: Eerdmans, 1969), 36.

[42] Modern Roman Catholic theology has spoken of the entire church as being a sacrament. E.g., "the Church, in Christ, is in the nature of sacrament—a sign and instrument, that is, of communion with God and of unity among all men." "Dogmatic Constitution of the Church," in *Vatican Council II,* ed. Austin Flannery (Northport, NY: Costello, 1975), 350.

warrant to be regarded as sacraments that were binding upon churches.[43] Among some Baptists and other Protestant groups, foot-washing has been treated as a church ordinance, following Christ's example and words in John 13:14. Yet neither churches in the New Testament nor in the immediate subapostolic period give evidence of having understood foot-washing in this way.[44] The ordinance of Christ in John 13 seems rather to teach a becoming humility.

1. Baptism. In the Old and New Testaments. Though Paul speaks of "one baptism" shared by all Christians (Eph. 4:5), Scripture surely recounts more baptisms than one.[45] The Christian church is commanded to practice baptism by immersing in water a person who both professes and evidences conversion. This baptism is performed in obedience to Christ as a confession of sin, a profession of faith in Christ, and a display of hope in the resurrection of the body. It is performed only once. The proper mode, subjects, and significance of baptism will now be considered.

Proper Mode. Baptism is generally understood to have been practiced by immersion in the New Testament church. The Eastern Orthodox churches have always understood *baptizein*[46] to mean "to immerse" and therefore have always practiced baptism by immersion. The Roman Catholic Church and most Protestant churches admit the antiquity of immersion, but they deny that a particular mode is essential for valid baptism.[47] While it is

---

[43] E.g., article 26 of the 39 Articles of Religion of the Church of England.

[44] See John L. Dagg, *Treatise on Church Order* (1858; repr., Harrisonburg: Gano, 1982), 226–31. Dagg lays out five arguments against taking the command to wash one another's feet as a lasting ordinance for the church.

[45] The Old Testament contains many ceremonial washings (cf. Heb. 9:10). Paul used the image of baptism to explain the people of Israel's submersion into the law of God (1 Cor. 10:1–2). John the Baptist distinguished his baptism from Jesus' (John 1:24–27,33; cf. Luke 3:3). Paul, too, explained the difference between the two baptisms in Ephesus (Acts 19:1–6). Jesus taught that his disciples would be baptized by the Holy Spirit (Acts 1:5). Jesus referred to his own death metaphorically as a baptism (Luke 12:50). And among the Corinthian Christians there was even a practice of baptism for the dead (1 Cor. 15:29). For more on the historical background of baptism in the first century, see George R. Beasley-Murray, *Baptism in the New Testament* (Grand Rapids: Eerdmans, 1962), 1–92.

[46] βαπτίζειν

[47] Thomas Aquinas wrote: "In the sacrament of Baptism water is put to the use of a washing of the body, whereby to signify the inward washing away of sins. Now washing may be done with water not only by immersion, but also by sprinkling or pouring. And, therefore, although it is safer to baptize by immersion, because this is the more ordinary fashion, yet Baptism can be conferred by sprinkling or also by pouring, according to Ezekiel 36:25: 'I will pour upon you clean water' . . . . And this especially in cases of urgency: either because there is a great number to be baptized, as was clearly the case in Acts 2 and 4, where we read that on one day three thousand believed, and on another five thousand: or through there being but a small supply of water, or through feebleness of the minister, who cannot hold up the candidate for Baptism; or through feebleness of the candidate, whose life might be endangered by immersion. We must therefore conclude that immersion is not necessary for Baptism." *Summa Theologica* (CD-ROM: AGES Software, 1997) Question 66, Answer 7. John Calvin, writing in the *Institutes,* recognized the antiquity of immersion, but not its necessity for valid baptism: "Whether the person being baptized should be wholly immersed, and

difficult to maintain that *baptizo*[48] could only mean "immerse" in the New Testament era,[49] immersion does seem both to be the most straightforward meaning of the word itself (thus the unbroken practice of immersion among Greek-speaking churches) and to best fit the uses of the word in the New Testament.[50] No other form of baptism dramatically displays the death, burial, and resurrection of Christ like immersion. As Millard Erickson writes, "It is not possible to resolve the issue of the proper mode of baptism on the basis of linguistic data alone. . . . While [immersion] may not be the only valid form of baptism, it is the form that most fully preserves and accomplishes the meaning of baptism."[51]

Proper Subjects. As an adult, Jesus Christ was himself a proper subject of baptism. Though circumcised as a descendant of Abraham, Jesus said the purpose of his baptism was "to fulfill all righteousness" (Matt. 3:15). By accepting John's baptism, Jesus indicated his acceptance of the will and plan of the Father to begin his public ministry. Additionally, Jesus' baptism was a profound display of his own death, burial, and resurrection.

---

whether thrice or once, whether he should only be sprinkled with poured water—these details are of no importance, but ought to be optional to churches according to diversity of countries. Yet the word 'baptize' means to immerse, and it is clear that the rite of immersion was observed in the ancient church." *Institutes,* 4.15.19. For a representative Lutheran consideration of the issue, see David P. Scaer, *Baptism* (St. Louis: Luther Academy, 1999), 91–101.

[48] βαπτίζειν

[49] So, for example, in chapter 7 of *The Didache* (dating most likely from the late first or early second century), we read: "Now concerning baptism, baptize as follows: after you have reviewed all these things, baptize 'in the name of the Father and of the Son and of the Holy Spirit' in running (ζῶντι) water. But if you have no running water, then baptize in some other water; and if you are not able to baptize in cold water, then do so in warm. But if you have neither then pour (ἔκχεον) water on the head three times 'in the name of the Father and Son and Holy Spirit.'" *The Didache,* in *The Apostolic Fathers,* 2nd ed., trans. J. B. Lightfoot and J. R. Harmer (1891; repr., Grand Rapids: Baker, 1992), 258–59. *The Didache* is, of course, not Scripture, and is in no way normative for the practice of Christians today. But it is lexically significant that, in this document, first- (or early second-) century Greek-speaking Christians could refer to ἔκχεον as a βαπτίσματος (baptism).

[50] One of the most recent defenses of pouring as baptism argues that Romans 6:3–6; Hebrews 9:10–19; Titus 3:5–6; and Ezekiel 36:25–27 demonstrate that baptism symbolizes the Holy Spirit's being poured out in connection with the Christian's being washed from sins as part of union with Christ, none of which require immersion, and any of which may more normally been signified by pouring, e.g., Joseph Pipa, "The Mode of Baptism," in *The Case for Covenantal Infant Baptism,* ed. Gregg Strawbridge (Phillipsburg: Presbyterian and Reformed, 2003), 112–26. Overarguing for immersion makes for arguments like Pipa's, which are perhaps overarguings in the opposite direction (i.e., for pouring or sprinkling). It is not disputed that βαπτίζειν means "to wash" fully and completely, at least when used for symbolic purposes. For a recent defense of immersion, see Tom Wells, *Does Baptism Mean Immersion?* (Laurel, MS: Audubon Press, 2000). See also Wayne Grudem, *Systematic Theology* (Grand Rapids: InterVarsity, 1994), 967–68. For an example of a historical defense of immersion, see John Gill, *A Body of Doctrinal and Practical Divinity,* new ed. (London; Mathews & Leigh Co., 1839), 909–14. The nineteenth-century denominational debates had thousands of pages published investigating every side of this controversy, e.g., John L. Dagg, *Church Order,* 21–65.

[51] Millard Erickson, *Christian Theology,* 1113–14; cf. Robert Saucy, *The Church in God's Program* (Chicago: Moody, 1972), 209.

According to the Scriptures, Christian baptism is exclusively meant for those who believe in Christ and follow him. Four reasons support this statement. First, those who evangelize are only commanded to baptize those who repent and believe (Matt. 28:18–20; cf. John 4:1–2). Second, the only clearly recorded subjects of baptism in the book of Acts are individuals who have repented and believed (Acts 2:37–41; 8:12–13,36–38; 9:18; 10:47–48; 16:15,33; 18:8; 19:5). Third, Paul's letters demonstrate the twin assumptions that those who have believed have been baptized and that those who have been baptized believe (Rom. 6:1–5; Gal. 3:26–27; Col. 2:11–12). Finally, Peter associates baptism with salvation, not as a cause of salvation but as a roughly contemporary occurrence (Acts 2:38; 1 Pet. 3:21). Through direct command, examples of obedience, Paul's assumptions, and Peter's associations, the Scriptures teach that baptism is for believers.

Baptism functions as both a confession of sin and a profession of faith for the believer. Faith is professed in Christ and the objective realities of Christ's death, the gift of the Spirit, and the final resurrection, all of which are depicted in baptism. Furthermore, it testifies to the subjective experiences of confession and forgiveness, spiritual regeneration, and the newly discovered resurrection hope. Baptism portrays the Christian's union with Christ, and therefore with other Christians and the church (see Rom. 6:1–14).

Water baptism does not create the reality of saving grace or faith in the person being baptized. Rather, it testifies to the presence of such grace and faith.[52] In Acts 2:38, Peter exhorted his hearers to "repent and be baptized . . . in the name of Jesus Christ for the forgiveness of your sins."[53] Baptism does not cause sins to be forgiven. Rather, faith apprehends the forgiveness of sins and responds to the commands for repentance and obedience in baptism. In his first letter Peter mentioned the waters of the flood in Noah's day, saying, "This water symbolizes baptism that now saves you also—not the removal of dirt from the body but the pledge of a good conscience toward God. It saves you by the resurrection of Jesus Christ, who has gone into heaven and is at God's right hand" (1 Pet. 3:21–22). Christians have a good conscience through God's grace by the resurrection of Jesus Christ. This salvation is not created but is symbolized by baptism. "It is a seal, not merely of an offered, but of an offered and accepted, that is, of a concluded covenant."[54] As Calvin said, "It is the mark by which we publicly profess that we wish to be reckoned God's people."[55]

---

[52] Such testimony should occur in the context of a believing community, whose responsibility it is to test the credibility of the profession.

[53] ἐπὶ τῷ ὀνόματι Ἰησοῦ Χριστοῦ εἰς ἄφεσιν τῶν ἁμαρτιῶν ὑμῶν.

[54] Berkhof, *Systematic Theology*, 632. Cf. his comments on proper recipients of the Lord's Supper on page 657.

[55] Calvin, *Institutes*, 4.15.13.

Though everyone has always agreed the Bible teaches believers should be baptized, the practice of baptizing infants has long been a matter of debate. Some have suggested that infants should be baptized because baptism itself is the instrument God's Spirit uses to regenerate the infant.[56] But as stated above, the New Testament in no way teaches that baptism is salvific. Others have suggested that an infant born into a Christian family belongs to Abraham's seed and that baptism declares the infant to be a recipient of the promises God made to his people through Abraham (see Gen. 12:7; 17:7; Acts 7:5; Gal. 3:16). Christian baptism in the New Testament is treated as parallel to Old Testament circumcision. But the Scriptures do not clearly support this latter view either. Not only is baptism expressly said to be for those who believe, as was considered above, but the promises to Abraham's seed are explicitly fulfilled in Christ (Gal. 3:16).

Furthermore, baptism with water is expressly said in the New Testament not to be analogous to physical circumcision but to circumcision of the heart (see Col. 2:11–12). Both the Abrahamic covenant and the new covenant are covenants of grace. Yet God promised the Israelites a change would occur in the spiritual solidarity of the physical family in the coming new covenant. Jeremiah wrote, "Everyone will die for his own sin" (Jer. 31:30). In the new covenant, "The covenantees are not those who are *born* into the covenant, those whose father and mother have the law 'written upon their hearts,' but those who *themselves* have had this experience, having been born again by the Spirit of God. This subjective, inward, existential, experiential, spiritual change is the hallmark of the new covenant."[57]

While the topics of children and baptism occur in the New Testament, the two never occur together in either explicit teaching or example. Whether construed as a matter of salvific cause or covenantal promise, any teaching that separates baptism from saving belief misrepresents Scripture and potentially confuses the gospel itself.

While Scripture clearly reserves baptism for believers, it does not directly address the *age* at which believers should be baptized. Nor does the command to baptize forbid raising questions about the appropriateness of a baptismal candidate's maturity. The fact that believers are commanded to be baptized does not give a church license to baptize indiscriminately, especially where maturity-of-life issues make it difficult to assess the credibility of a profession of faith. New Testament baptisms largely appear to have occurred shortly after conversion, but every specific individual mentioned

---

[56] E.g., *Catechism of the Catholic Church*, 319, 323. Also Acts 2:38; 22:16; 1 Peter 3:21.

[57] Paul K. Jewett, *Infant Baptism and the Covenant of Grace* (Grand Rapids: Eerdmans, 1978), 228; cf. Fred Malone, *The Baptism of Disciples Alone: A Covenantal Argument for Credobaptism versus Paedobaptism* (Cape Coral, FL: Founders, 2003).

was an adult coming from a non-Christian context, two factors which make the church's job of attesting to the credibility of a profession of faith simple and straightforward.

As a matter of Christian wisdom and prudence, therefore, the normal age of baptism should be when the credibility of one's conversion becomes naturally discernable and evident to the church community. A legitimate secondary concern is the effect of the child's baptism on other families in the church. The least spiritually discerning parents—with the best intensions—have too often brought pressure upon their compliant children to be baptized. Such children have thereby been wrongly assured of their salvation and have been further hardened to hearing the gospel later in life. Tragically, the hope they most need may be hidden by the very act meant to display it.

Proper Significance. The Bible's teaching on baptism is clear in institution, command, and fulfillment. People enter the new covenant by God's grace, and the means God has graciously chosen to use is faith. Faith is not caused or created by baptism. Rather, baptism is the public confession of faith. It symbolizes a commitment by both God and the believer (1 Pet. 3:21). The submission of the believer to the water of baptism represents his or her humble request to God for a conscience cleared of guilt because of Christ's atoning blood (cf. Heb. 10:22). Baptism is an act of confession and utter dependence. In summary, baptism in the Bible is neither elevated to be the cause of conversion nor diminished to be a mere marker of inclusion in a nonsalvific covenant. Rather, baptism is a public profession of God's saving work in the life of the believer.

2. The Lord's Supper. Christians celebrate the Lord's Supper in obedience to Christ's command, "Do this in remembrance of me" (Luke 22:19; 1 Cor. 11:24). Jesus said the bread was his body and the cup was the new covenant in his blood. While the command to take the bread and cup "in remembrance" of him does not appear in Matthew, Mark, or Luke, the Supper itself is recorded in all four Gospels (Matt. 26:17–30; Mark 14:12–26; Luke 22:7–38; John 13:1–17). The night before he was betrayed and crucified, Jesus shared a meal with his disciples. The exact relationship of this meal to the Old Testament Passover meal has long been debated, but few would question the larger typological relationship between the Passover meal and the death foreshadowed by the Last Supper.[58] Jesus clearly referred to the celebration as a Passover feast in Matthew 26:18–19. Paul referred to Christ as the Passover Lamb (1 Cor. 5:7) and called the

---

[58] See Exodus 12; cf. Exodus 24:8. See also D. A. Carson, *Matthew,* EBC (Grand Rapids: Zondervan, 1984), 528–32 on this question. Carson concludes that the Last Supper was a Passover meal.

church to keep the Passover feast (metaphorically) by living together in lives of holiness, thereby expressing unity in love (see 1 Cor. 10:17).

The Lord's Supper evidences the companionship Christians share in Christ and his Spirit as well as in holiness and mutual love.

> The new rite Jesus institutes has links with redemption history. As the bread has just been broken, so will Jesus' body be broken; and just as the people of Israel associated their deliverance from Egypt with eating the paschal meal prescribed as a divine ordinance, so also Messiah's people are to associate Jesus' redemptive death with eating this bread by Jesus' authority.[59]

This witness is to continue until Christ returns (1 Cor. 11:26).

The Bible does not provide an exact form (protocol and words spoken while distributing the elements) for the celebration of the Lord's Supper. This reticence, combined with the widespread nature of the practice, suggests the Lord's Supper should probably remain simple in form. Elaborate rituals would require careful written instructions, like those associated with Old Testament feasts. But no such instructions are given in the New Testament.[60]

The elements presented by the New Testament for the Lord's Supper are bread and wine ("the fruit of the vine," Matt. 26:29; Mark 14:25; Luke 22:17–18). Although wine in the first century was fermented, the degree to which it was diluted is unknown. Certainly, the Corinthians were able to get drunk from the wine reserved for the Lord's Supper, for which Paul rebuked them (1 Cor. 11:21). Other aspects of the celebration include a prayer of thanks (Matt. 26:27; Mark 14:23) and a hymn (Matt. 26:30; Mark 14:26). Beyond this, the accounts specify nothing about spoken words or means used while distributing the bread and wine.

As with baptism, the question of who should participate in the Lord's Supper (the subjects) is more important than the question of how to participate in the Supper (the mode or form). Instructing the Corinthians, Paul taught that participating in the Supper testifies to participating in Christ's body and blood. It is the believer's personal identification with Christ's saving work, represented objectively by the elements on the table. The person who takes the bread and the cup testifies to sharing in the fruits of Christ's death, including a communion with both God and fellow Christians through

---

[59] Carson, *Matthew*, 536.

[60] The first indications of the form of the Lord's Supper observances are found in late first- and early second-century sources—*The Didache,* Clement's *Letter to the Corinthians,* Ignatius's *Letter to the Smyrneans.*

the Spirit. Clearly, then, "the church must require of all those who desire to celebrate the Lord's Supper a credible profession of faith."[61]

As Paul says poignantly, anyone who eats and drinks at the Lord's table without this faith "eats and drinks judgment on himself" (1 Cor. 11:29). Because faith is required for those who celebrate the Lord's Supper, the table must be reserved for those who have been baptized. Furthermore, excluding a church member from its communion meal is one visible sign that an individual is under the church's discipline (hence the term, *excommunicate;* cf. section on discipline).

While no passage in the New Testament spells out a comparative time line for the believer's participation in both ordinances, baptism should probably occur near the time of conversion—and then only once—whereas the Lord's Supper should be repeated regularly as a continuing symbol of participating in Christ by faith. Those who look by faith to the body and blood of Christ for salvation are called to participate in this feast, and to do so in remembrance of him and in expectation of that final day when, Jesus said, "I drink it anew with you in my Father's kingdom" (Matt. 26:29). Jesus referred here to the marriage supper of the Lamb (Rev. 19:9). The Lord's Supper then is a regular rehearsal of this great celebration in which all Christians will share the table with their heavenly host, the Lord Jesus Christ.

Membership. In today's world the concept of membership makes one think of clubs and other voluntary associations. Such organizations exist in the world of the Bible, too.[62] But the idea of membership is even more basic to humankind. Households and families have members. Races and tribes and clans have members. So, also, do communities and parties and elite groups like orders, guilds, and councils. An even more basic meaning of *member* refers to the human person. Our bodies have members (Rom. 6:12–19; 7:23; 12:4–5; 1 Cor. 6:15; 12:12–27; Eph. 4:16; James 3:6; 4:1). The Bible uses the concept of "member" and "membership" in all these varieties.

The Bible also represents churches as composed of members. Combining the collective images of families, parties, and communities with the even more integrated image of an individual body and its various parts, the Bible presents the local church as an entity made up of multiple individuals yet so highly integrated they are identifiable as a unit. They are even said to

---

[61] Berkhof, *Systematic Theology,* 657.

[62] The synagogue of the Freedmen in Acts 6:9; the Pharisees and Sadducees; various courts, councils and guilds. In the Old Testament, there were members of brotherhoods of warriors (e.g., David's thirty men) or prophets.

be a part of one another (Rom. 12:5). When Jesus instructed his follow-ers to seek out the brother who had sinned (Matt. 18:15–21), he was pre-supposing such an integrated conception of body membership. Actions of reproach and, ultimately, exclusion are to occur within the arena of a spe-cific and identifiable group of people. In many other places in the New Testament, a church appears to be composed of a specific and identifiable group of people (e.g., Acts 9:41; 12:1; 15:3,22; Eph. 2:19; 3:6; 4:25; 5:30; Col. 2:19; 3:15; 3 John 9).

From the earliest of times, local Christian churches were congregations of specific, identifiable people. Certain people would be known to make up (or belong to) a particular assembly, while everyone else would be known to be outside of (or not belonging to) the assembly. So the censure Paul en-joined in 1 Corinthians 5, like Jesus in Matthew 18, envisions an individual being excluded not from a political community but from a particular kind of social community. None are extant, but physical lists of members may well have existed in the earliest Christian churches. Clearly, the keeping of lists was not unknown in churches. The early church kept lists of widows (1 Tim. 5:9). God himself keeps a list of all who belong to the universal church in his book of life (Rev. 20:12). And Paul assumed the Corinthians had identified a "majority" of a particular set of church members who were eligible to vote (2 Cor. 2:6).

The idea of a clearly defined community of people is central to God's action in both the Old and New Testaments. As demonstrated with Noah and his family, Abraham and his descendants, the nation of Israel, and the New Testament church, God has chosen to maintain a distinct and separate people for the purpose of displaying his character. God has always intended for a sharp, bright line to distinguish those who trust in him from those who do not. The lives of Christians together display visibly the gospel they proclaim audibly.

If the church, in fact, presents a glorious climax in God's plan, several questions arise: How does an individual know he or she belongs to the church? How can one become a part of it? What does membership entail?

The responsibilities and duties of members of a Christian church are simply the responsibilities and duties of Christians.[63] Church members, like Christians, are to be baptized and to regularly attend the Lord's table. They are to hear God's Word and to obey it. They are to regularly fellow-ship together for mutual edification. They are to love God, one another, and those outside their fellowship, and they are to evidence the fruit of the

---

[63] For the teaching on the duties of church members by Benjamin Keach, Benjamin Griffith, the Charleston Association, Samuel Jones, W. B. Johnson, Joseph S. Baker, and Eleazer Savage, see Mark Dever, ed., *Polity*, 65–69, 103–5, 125–26, 148–51, 221–22, 276–79, 510–11.

Spirit (Gal. 5:22–23). They are to worship God in all the activities of their home, work, community, and life.

Christians also have particular duties in relation to the congregation. "Christianity is a corporate matter, and the Christian life can be fully realized only in relationship to others."[64] The most fundamental duty Christians have in relation to the congregation is the duty to regularly attend gatherings of the congregation (Heb. 10:25; cf. Ps. 84:4,10; Acts 2:42). In general, membership duties can be divided into duties toward other members and duties toward pastors.

The duties and responsibilities church members have toward one another summarize the life of the new society that is the church. As followers of Jesus Christ, Christians are obliged to love one another (John 13:34–35; also John 15:12–17; Rom. 12:9–10; 13:8–10; Gal. 5:15; 6:10; Eph. 1:15; 1 Pet. 1:22; 2:17; 3:8; 4:8; 1 John 3:16; 4:7–12; cf. Ps. 133). Christians are members of one family, even of one another (1 Cor. 12:13–27). Without a life of love for one another, what other duty of church members is satisfying or worthwhile? Love obligates the members of the church to avoid anything that "tends to cool love."[65] By this love, the nature of the gospel itself is demonstrated.

Church members are also obliged to seek peace and unity within their congregation (Rom. 12:16; also Rom. 14:19; 1 Cor. 13:7; 2 Cor. 12:20; Eph. 4:3–6; Phil. 2:3; 1 Thess. 5:13; 2 Thess. 3:11; James 3:18; 4:11). The desire for peace and unity should follow naturally from the obligation to love (Rom. 15:6; 1 Cor. 1:10–11; Eph. 4:5,13; Phil. 2:2; cf. Zeph. 3:9). Further, if Christians share the same spirit and mind—the Spirit of Christ—then unity is a natural expression of that Spirit. Given the sin that remains in believers in this life, however, unity often requires effort. Thus Christians "stand firm in one spirit, contending as one man for the faith of the gospel" (Phil. 1:27). Strife should be avoided (Prov. 17:14; Matt. 5:9; 1 Cor. 10:32; 11:16; 2 Cor. 13:11; Phil. 2:1–3).

Love is expressed and unity is cultivated when church members actively sympathize with one another. As Paul exhorted the congregation in Rome, "Rejoice with those who rejoice; mourn with those who mourn" (Rom. 12:15; cf. Job 2:11; Isa. 63:9; 1 Cor. 12:26; Gal. 6:2; 1 Thess. 5:14; Heb. 4:15; 12:3). Other duties follow: to care for one another physically and spiritually (Matt. 25:40; John 12:8; Acts 15:36; Rom. 12:13; 15:26; 1 Cor. 16:1–2; Gal. 2:10; 6:10; Heb. 13:16; James 1:27; 1 John 3:17; cf. Deut. 15:7–8,11); to watch over one another and hold one another accountable (Rom. 15:14; Gal. 6:1–2; Phil. 2:3–4; 2 Thess. 3:15; Heb. 12:15; cf. Lev. 19:17; Ps. 141:5); to work to edify one another (1 Cor. 14:12–26;

---

[64] Erickson, *Theology,* 1058.

[65] Samuel Jones, *Treatise of Church Discipline* in *Polity,* ed. Mark Dever (1805; repr.), 150; cf. 2 Corinthians 12:20; 1 Timothy 5:13; 6:4; James 4:11.

Eph. 2:21–22; 4:12–29; 1 Thess. 5:11; 1 Pet. 4:10; 2 Pet. 3:18); to bear with one another (Matt. 18:21–22; Mark 11:25; Rom. 15:1; Gal. 6:2; Col. 3:12; including not suing one another, 1 Cor. 6:1–7); to pray for one another (Eph. 6:18; James 5:16); to keep away from those who would destroy the church (Rom. 16:17; 1 Tim. 6:3–5; Titus 3:10; 2 John 10–11); to reject evaluating people by worldly standards (Matt. 20:26–27; Rom. 12:10–16; James 2:1–13); to contend together for the gospel (Phil. 1:27; Jude 3); and to be examples to one another (Phil. 2:1–18).

Church members also have particular responsibilities toward the leaders of the church. As Paul said to the Corinthians, "Men ought to regard us as servants of Christ and as those entrusted with the secret things of God" (1 Cor. 4:1). Such men should be respected, held in the highest regard, and honored (Phil. 2:29; 1 Thess. 5:12–13). If Christians expect their pastor to fulfill his biblical responsibilities, church members must make themselves known to him. They must regard him as a gift from Christ sent to the church for their good.[66] The minister of the Word is a steward of God's household and an undershepherd of God's flock. He serves willingly and eagerly (1 Pet. 5:1–3). His reputation can and should be defended, his word believed, and his instructions obeyed unless Scripture is contradicted or facts are plainly distorted (Heb. 13:17,22; 1 Tim. 5:17–19). The faithful minister should be so regarded simply because he brings God's Word to his people; he does not replace it with his own.

Church members should remember their leaders and imitate their life and faith (1 Cor. 4:16; 11:1; Phil. 3:17; Heb. 13:7). Good preachers and teachers are worthy of being doubly honored, according to Paul in 1 Timothy 5:17, which includes material support.[67] And church members should give themselves both to praying for their ministers and to assisting them in every way they can (Eph. 6:18–20; Col. 4:3–4; 2 Thess. 3:1; Heb. 13:18–19). Ministers of the Word have been given the task of bringing God's Word to God's people. As Paul said to the Corinthians, "We are therefore Christ's ambassadors, as though God were making his appeal through us. We implore you on Christ's behalf: Be reconciled to God" (2 Cor. 5:20). More important work could hardly be conceived.

In the New Testament local congregations realized they had particular responsibilities that could not be delegated to groups outside of themselves. The local congregation was responsible for ensuring a qualified minister of the Word preached to them, insofar as it was in their power.[68] The congrega-

---

[66] Similar to the way the apostles were to be regarded as delegates of Christ; Luke 10:16; cf. 1 Corinthians 16:10.

[67] The word used in 1 Timothy 5:17 for "honor" has a clear financial connotation. See, too, Acts 6:4; 1 Corinthians 9:7–14; Galatians 6:6.

[68] We see this by inference from Galatians 1:8 and 2 Timothy 4:3, also Jude 3–4.

tion was ultimately responsible for ensuring converts were baptized and the Lord's Supper was duly administered to those giving credible evidence of regeneration. And the congregation was ultimately responsible for protecting and defining the membership of a church, both in admitting and dismissing members.[69] Thus Paul assigned these responsibilities to the Corinthian congregation in 1 Corinthians 5 and 2 Corinthians 2.

The entire congregation is also responsible for the faithful stewardship of the gifts entrusted to it. Foremost among these is the gospel, which must be preached in the church's own building, across the city, and around the world. Finally, the congregation is responsible for ensuring the gospel message reaches out across these different spheres (Gal. 1:6–9; Phil. 1:5; Col. 1:3–4; 1 Thess. 1:8).

The congregation's responsibilities finally cannot be delegated. Though congregations may substitute the judgment of a body of leaders—whether inside or outside their number—the responsibility it bears is inescapable. Just as the people who paid the false teachers were threatened with God's judgment along with the teachers themselves (2 Tim. 4), just as the Corinthian church was held accountable along with the sinning members (1 Cor. 5), and just as the church envisioned in Matthew 18 was held accountable by Christ to exclude the unrepentant, so congregations today cannot evade responsibility before God for fulfilling their biblically assigned duties.

What company is so obliged to worship God, as those who have been not only created but redeemed? What group is so concerned with the task of proclamation of God's Word and evangelism as those who have themselves been saved through hearing the Word? What body will be so involved in making visible signs—in baptism and the Lord's Supper—of God's saving action in Christ? From the ministry of the Word to the management of the church's own affairs, what other group is so charged with responsibility as the church of Jesus Christ?[70]

Polity. The fundamental responsibility under God for the maintenance of all aspects of public worship of God belongs to the congregation. Whether in settling disputes between Christians (Matt. 18:15–17; Acts 6:1–5), establishing correct doctrine (Gal. 1:8; 2 Tim. 4:3), or admitting and excluding members (2 Cor. 2:6–8; 1 Cor. 5), the local congregation has the

---

[69] Matthew 18:17. Note the involvement of the whole church as the final court and as the executors of the discipline.

[70] A good example of this is found in the details of Acts 15. Commenting on Acts 15:4, Jürgen Roloff has written that "the full congregational assembly in Jerusalem comprises its own governing body, to be distinguished from the apostles and the elders as a governing body leading the Church. The apostolic decree concluded by them is determined by the entire congregational assembly." Roloff, "ἐκκλησία," 413–14.

duty and obligation to ensure the continuance of a faithful gospel witness among themselves. No body outside of the whole congregation has this same degree of responsibility. While leaders within the congregations have their own special responsibilities before God, the smallest of congregations which takes upon itself the task of providing and listening to the regular preaching of God's Word, and of practicing baptism and the Lord's Supper, necessarily takes upon itself responsibility for the right practice of membership and discipline, even over those who are called to be its leaders (1 Tim. 5:19–20).

While congregations may and do err in fulfilling these responsibilities, the responsibilities do not cease to belong to them. No other body, either within or outside the local church, may finally remove these obligations of duty from the congregation as a whole. Toleration of erroneous teaching, particularly in regards to the gospel, neglect of baptism or the Lord's Supper, and carelessness in admitting or dismissing members are all the responsibility of the local congregation.

As with any gathered body of people, the church must be led. Universally and locally, the head and chief shepherd of the church is Christ (Eph. 4:1–16; Heb. 13:20; 1 Pet. 5:4). Christ did not establish any sort of leadership structure, explicit or implicit, for the universal church during his earthly mission. Thus, between congregations of Christians relationships are purely voluntary in nature.[71] Inside the local congregation, however, the New Testament's teaching is different. The church is established with a simple order of leadership. Before turning to the specific offices established for the church in the New Testament, five biblical principles of such leadership should be considered for those who desire or feel called to serve in leadership.[72]

Church leaders should be *explicitly qualified.* Not all Christians are qualified to serve as leaders or overseers in the church. In Acts 20, 1 Timothy 3, Titus 1, and 1 Peter 5, characteristics are laid down for undershepherds or elders of the flock. Distinctive among these qualifications is the requirement that those who serve as overseers be "able to teach" (1 Tim. 3:2). Furthermore, as representatives of Christ, ministers have a special obligation to reflect the character of Christ. Such character will include a care for the flock, a willingness to serve, a lack of greed for money, a refusal to

---

[71] This voluntary nature of relationships between congregations, however, does not mean that decisions made concerning one congregation's relations with another are simply indifferent matters.

[72] Historically, Christians have spoken of two aspects of the call to full-time ministry, the internal and the external. The external call is provided by an individual's church, which confirms the individual's gifts. The internal call refers to the individual's own subjective sense of a responsibility for and desire to minister God's Word. For more on this, see Charles Bridges, *The Christian Ministry* (1830; repr., Edinburgh: Banner of Truth, 1980), 94–102; see also, Basil Manly Jr., *A Call to the Ministry* (Philadelphia: American Baptist Publication Society, [no date cited]).

lord it over the flock, an exemplary life, blamelessness, being the husband of only one wife, and the ability to manage a household well. A minister is not overbearing, quick tempered, or given to much wine. And a minister should not be violent or willing to pursue dishonest gain. In these, and other ways listed in Scripture, the leader in the congregation should be explicitly qualified.

Church leaders should be particularly *reputable with outsiders.* Those who lead the church should not be men who bring the gospel into disrepute, but men whose lives hold the gospel up as the glorious light of hope and truth in the world. God's heart of love for the world shines most clearly through pure lives. In order for the whole church to be oriented to its mission and purpose, its leaders' interactions with the authorities, with neighbors, and with employers should commend the gospel to them. Overseers should not be lovers of money, Paul says in 1 Timothy 3, but lovers of strangers (which is the meaning of the word he uses, "hospitable"). In order to faithfully represent the Lord of the church, church leaders must have both God-centered and other-centered lives.

Church leaders should also possess a keen *sense of accountability,* knowing that they are under authority themselves. Their lives as public leaders leave them open to public rebuke and correction (1 Tim. 5:19–20). The shepherds of the flock must realize they are stewards, not owners. Therefore they serve as undershepherds of God's flock, subject to his rule. This includes a realization of an ultimate accountability, and of a more immediate accountability to Christ. James promised that teachers will be judged more strictly in the end (James 3:1), while the author of Hebrews promised that church leaders will give an account to God for their work (Heb. 13:17). As John Brown said to one of his ministerial pupils newly ordained over a small congregation:

> I know the vanity of your heart, and that you will feel mortified that your congregation is very small, in comparison with those of your brethren around you; but assure yourself on the word of an old man, that when you come to give an account of them to the Lord Christ, at his judgment-seat, you will think you have had enough.[73]

This eschatological reality should have present implications in a minister's life and work. Those who lead others well must themselves first follow well. They must be submitted to Christ so that they can say, like Paul to the Corinthians, "Follow my example, as I follow the example of Christ" (1 Cor. 11:1). Peter also reminded the church's undershepherds of

---

[73] Cited by Alexander Grossart in *Works of Richard Sibbes,* ed. Alexander Grossart (1862–1864; repr., Edinburgh: Banner of Truth Trust, 1979), 294.

their future appearance before Christ, bringing to mind the reward and the accounting they will give one day for their present work (1 Pet. 5:4).

Church leaders should exercise *authority*. While this observation may seem obvious, some dislike using words like "leader" or "authority" in the context of a local church. Perhaps they assume it implies a Diotrophes-like love to be first, or they associate it with unchristlike boasting (3 John 9; 1 Cor. 1–3). Yet Paul explicitly told Timothy that "if anyone sets his heart on being an overseer, he desires a noble task" (1 Tim. 3:1). He told the Romans that those who are set over others (*proistamenos*)[74] should use their gifts and abilities for the church (Rom. 12:8). He also exhorted Timothy to honor those "who direct the affairs of the church" (1 Tim. 5:17). The writer to the Hebrews spoke about the "leaders."[75] All these words imply both the responsibility and initiative that should mark the actions of church leaders.

Finally, church leaders should *edify* the church. Genuine leadership not only requires a leader to act with initiative and responsibility in an attempt to effect good; leadership requires the accomplishment of that good. The ability to achieve the intended ends corroborates an individual's gifts and calling to leadership in the church. Leadership does not fundamentally depend upon a self-proclaimed leader's own sense of internal calling and purpose. In 1 Corinthians 14, Paul repeatedly submitted the putative gifts of the Spirit to the simple test of edification. He asked whether good fruit had been born in the church. Is the fruit of this person's action, a church being built up? If this is the fruit of his actions, then he should be regarded highly, for the sake of the church and ultimately for the sake of Christ. All these characteristics should be present in those who lead a congregation.

Scripture provides for two specific offices in the local congregation: deacons and elders.[76]

1. *Deacon*. In modern translations of the New Testament, the word *diakonos* is usually translated "servant," sometimes "minister," and occasionally "deacon." The word can refer to service in general (Acts 1:17,25; 19:22; Rom. 12:7; 1 Cor. 12:5; 16:15; Eph. 4:12; Col. 4:17; 2 Tim. 1:18; Philem. 13; Heb. 6:10; 1 Pet. 4:10–11; Rev. 2:19), to God's servants in particular (Rom. 13:4), and to caring for physical needs (Matt. 25:44; Acts 11:29; 12:25; Rom. 15:25,31; 2 Cor. 8:4,19–20; 9:1,12–13; 11:8). Women clearly served diaconally in the New Testament (Matt. 8:15; 27:55; Luke 10:40; John 12:2; Rom. 16:1). Angels also served in this way (Matt. 4:11). Sometimes the word refers specifically to waiting tables (Matt. 22:13; Luke 10:40; 17:8; John 2:5,9; 12:2), and though such service was despised in

---

[74] προϊστάμενος
[75] ἡγουμένοις; Hebrews 13:17,24.
[76] See Mark Dever, *A Display of God's Glory* (Washington, DC: 9Marks Ministries, 2001), 5–30.

the Greek world, Jesus regarded it differently. In John 12:26 Jesus said, "Whoever *deacons* me must follow me; and where I am, my *deacon* also will be. My Father will honor the one who *deacons* me." Again in Matthew 20:26 (cf. Mark 9:35) Jesus said, "Whoever wants to become great . . . must be your *deacon*." And in Matthew 23:11 (cf. Mark 10:43; Luke 22:26–27) he said that "the greatest among you will be your *deacon*."

Jesus presented himself as a type of deacon (Matt. 20:28; Luke 12:37; Rom. 15:8). Christians are presented as deacons of Christ or his gospel. The apostles are similarly depicted (Acts 6:1–7), and it is how Paul regularly referred to himself and to those who worked with him (Acts 20:24; 1 Cor. 3:5; 2 Cor. 3:3,6–9; 4:1; 5:18; 6:3–4; 11:23; Eph. 3:7; Col. 1:23; 1 Tim. 1:12; 2 Tim. 4:11). He especially referred to himself as a deacon among the Gentiles, the particular group he was called to serve (Acts 21:19; Rom. 11:13). Paul called Timothy a deacon of Christ (1 Tim. 4:6; 2 Tim. 4:5), and Peter said the Old Testament prophets were deacons to Christians (1 Pet. 1:12). Angels are called deacons (Heb. 1:14). Even Satan has his deacons (2 Cor. 11:15; Gal. 2:17).

The clearest picture of the diaconal work in practice is found in Acts 6, where the first recorded official congregational deacons were set aside. Based on that account, three levels or aspects of the deacon's ministry may be noted.[77] First, deacons must care for physical needs. Some of the Christians "were being overlooked in the daily distribution of food" (Acts 6:1). In Acts 6:2, the apostles characterized this service as "waiting on tables," or literally, "deaconing tables." Caring for people, especially for other Christians and most especially for other members of the congregation, contributes not only to their physical well-being; it benefits their spiritual well-being. It encourages the recipients of the care, it embodies God's care, and it acts as a witness to those outside the church. As Jesus said, "This is how the world will know that you are my disciples, by the love you have for one another" (John 13:35). The physical care presented in Acts 6 demonstrates that kind of Christlike love.

Behind the physical care lies a second aspect of a deacon's work, one which benefits not just those in need, but the whole body: deacons must strive for the unity of the body. By caring for these widows, the deacons helped make the food distribution among the widows more equitable. This was important because the *physical* neglect was causing a *spiritual* disunity in the body (cf. Acts 6:1). One group of Christians was complaining against another group, and this seems to be what drew the attention of the apostles. The apostles were not just interested in rectifying a problem in the church's benevolence ministry. They wanted to prevent a fracture in church unity,

---

[77] Thanks to Buddy Gray, pastor in Birmingham, Alabama, for pointing this out to me in the text.

and a particularly dangerous fracture—between one ethnic group and another. The deacons were appointed to head off disunity in the church. Their job was to act as the shock absorbers for the body.

At a third level, the deacons were appointed to support the ministry of the apostles. In Acts 6:3, the apostles seem to acknowledge that caring for physical needs is a responsibility of the church. In some sense, therefore, they themselves owned this responsibility. But in verse 3 they determined to turn this responsibility over to another group within the church. These deacons, then, were not only helping the widows and the body as a whole; they were helping support the apostles/elders, whose main obligations lay elsewhere. By their ministry to widows, they supported the teachers of the Word in their ministry. In this sense, deacons are fundamentally encouragers and supporters of the ministry of the elders.

By the time Paul wrote his first letter to Timothy, he could instruct Timothy on the qualifications for what had explicitly become the office of deacon. When Paul's list of qualifications in 1 Timothy 3:8–13 is combined with the qualities of the individuals selected in Acts 6, it becomes apparent that deacons should be known for being full of the Holy Spirit. They minister to physical needs, but their ministry is a spiritual ministry. Deacons should be known as full of wisdom. They should be chosen by the congregation and have the congregation's confidence. They should willingly and diligently take on responsibility for the needs of their particular ministry. They should be worthy of respect, sincere, not indulgent in much wine, not interested in dishonest gain, and steadfast in the deep truths of the faith with a clear conscience. Deacons should be tested and approved servants who are the husband of only one wife. And they should be individuals who manage their own children and household well.

2. *Pastor/Bishop/Elder.* In addition to the office of deacon, the New Testament provides for the office of pastor, elder, or bishop. Most fundamentally, the elder is a minister of the Word. The *presbeut*[78] root occurs seventy-five times in the New Testament. Nine occurrences refer to people of chronologically advanced age (Luke 1:18; 15:25; John 8:9; Acts 2:17; 1 Tim. 5:1,2; Titus 2:2–3; Philem. 9). Four times it refers to ancestors of the Hebrew nation (Matt. 15:2; Mark 7:3,5; Heb. 11:2). John used words with this root twelve times in Revelation to refer to the heavenly elders (Rev. 4:4,10; 5:5–6,8,11,14; 7:11,13; 11:16; 14:3; 19:4). Twenty-nine times (all in the Gospels and Acts) the word refers to the Jewish nonpriestly leaders in the Sanhedrin, or in local synagogues. The remaining twenty uses refer to elders in churches: in the Jerusalem church (Acts 11:30; 15:2,4,6,22–23; 16:4; 21:18); in Lystra, Iconium, and Antioch (Acts 14:21,23); in Ephesus

---

[78] πρεσβύτ

(Acts 20:17); in the towns of Crete (Titus 1:5); and other general references (1 Tim. 5:17,19; James 5:14; 1 Pet. 5:1,5). John also referred to himself twice as "the elder" (2 John 1; 3 John 1). The Jews of Jesus' day had lay members of the Sanhedrin in Jerusalem called elders. Local synagogues also had bodies of ruling men called elders.

In the New Testament, the words *elder, shepherd* or *pastor,* and *bishop* or *overseer* are used interchangeably in the context of the local church office. This is seen most clearly in Acts 20 when Paul met with the "elders"[79] of the church in Ephesus, as he called them in verse 17. In verse 28, Paul said to these elders: "Keep watch over yourselves and all the flock of which the Holy Spirit has made you overseers [or bishops].[80] Be shepherds [or pastors][81] of the church of God, which he bought with his own blood." Then in Ephesians 4:11, Paul said that Christ "gave some to be apostles, some to be prophets, some to be evangelists, and some to be pastors and teachers." The word Paul used for "pastor" is *poimenas,*[82] which is related to the word for "shepherd."

Similarly, in 1 Peter 5:1–2, Peter addressed the elders, telling them to pastor or shepherd God's flock, serving as overseers or bishops. In 1 Peter 2:25, Jesus is called the "Shepherd and Overseer of your souls." The root of the word translated "overseer" here (*episkop*)[83] occurs eleven times in the New Testament. In Titus 1, Paul provided a list of qualifications for a particular office similar to the one he gave to Timothy in 1 Timothy 3. In both places the officer described is called an *episkopon,* that is, a bishop or overseer. But in Titus 1:5, Paul also said that he left Titus in Crete in order to ensure *presbuterous* (elders) were in every town. Then in verse 7, he referred to the same person as an *episkopon.* Clearly, the New Testament refers to elders, shepherds or pastors, and bishops or overseers in the context of the local church interchangeably.[84]

Paul laid out the qualifications for elders in 1 Timothy 3:1–7 and in Titus 1:5–9. Elders are to be blameless and above reproach, not overbearing, temperate, self-controlled, respectable, hospitable, able to teach, not given to much wine, not violent but gentle, not quarrelsome, well-reputed (particularly among outsiders), upright, holy, and disciplined. He is the husband of

---

[79] πρεσβυτέρους

[80] ἐπισκόπους

[81] ποιμαίνειν

[82] ποιμένας

[83] ἐπισκοπ

[84] So concluded R. B. C. Howell, pastor of First Baptist Church, Nashville, Tennessee: "The only officers appointed by God to preach, and administer ordinances, and whose commission has come down to our times, are called indifferently, elders, bishops and presbyters; all of which names, when referring to office, convey the same idea." R. B. C. Howell, "Ministerial Ordination," in *The Baptist Preacher,* ed. Henry Keeling (Richmond: H. K. Ellyson, 1847), 137.

only one wife, not a lover of money, not a pursuer of dishonest gain, a good manager of his family (his children obey him), and not a recent convert. He loves what is good, holds firmly to the gospel, and is eager to serve.[85]

All of the qualifications listed here are repeated elsewhere in Scripture as applicable for all Christians, except one—the ability to teach. The essence of the elder's office lies with ensuring the Word of God is well understood, evidenced by the commitment to teaching one's particular flock this Word. Anyone serving as an elder should have a better-than-average grasp of the basics of the gospel as well as the great truths of Scripture, especially those that are under assault in one's own day. An elder should also have a particularly solid grasp of those truths that distinguish his own congregation from others (e.g., baptism for Baptists). And he should be an example of care and concern for the congregation as a whole.

The qualification to be "the husband of but one wife" and to "manage his household well" does not mean that an elder must be married or have children.[86] Rather it appears that Paul assumed most men would be married and have children, and that those family relations provided a natural ground for assessing a man's ability to lead. Paul also assumed the elders would be men. Inherent in creation, Paul argued in 1 Timothy 2, there exists a divine order that precludes a woman from being called to "teach or to have authority over a man" in the church.[87]

A common discussion about New Testament elders is whether each local congregation was governed by only one elder or multiple elders.

Before Jesus established the church, the Jewish towns of Palestine were accustomed to being governed by multiple elders. Thus, in Luke 7, the centurion sent several elders of the local Jewish community in Capernaum to Jesus to plead on his behalf for help. Deuteronomy also refers to multiple elders in the context of their role as town leaders, whether that involves retrieving people from cities of refuge, solving murders, or dealing with disobedient children (Deut. 19:12; 21:1–9,18–21). Jewish synagogues similarly followed a pattern of plural leadership. Arising during the Babylonian exile, synagogues functioned as the religious and civil gathering for teach-

---

[85] For this last qualification, see 1 Peter 5:2.

[86] It would be odd that any qualification for elder would rule out (possibly) Paul himself—and the Lord Jesus!—from serving as an elder.

[87] Much helpful material on this has been published by the Council on Biblical Manhood and Womanhood. See John Piper and Wayne Grudem, eds., *Recovering Biblical Manhood and Womanhood* (Wheaton: Crossway, 1991; rev. 2006); Wayne Grudem and Dennis Rainey, eds., *Pastoral Leadership for Manhood and Womanhood* (Wheaton: Crossway, 2002); J. Lyon Duncan and Susan Hunt, *Women's Ministry in the Local Church* (Wheaton: Crossway, 2006); Wayne Grudem, *Countering the Claims of Evangelical Feminism* (Colorado Springs: Multnomah, 2006); Wayne Grudem, *Evangelical Feminism and Biblical Truth* (Colorado Springs: Multnomah, 2004); and Wayne Grudem, *Evangelical Feminism: A New Path to Liberalism?* (Wheaton: Crossway, 2006). See also www.cbmw.org.

ing God's law and, consequently, leading the community. Ten adult males were required to have public worship at a synagogue. Various offices facilitated the work of synagogues, including the office of ruler.[88]

In the New Testament, the book of Revelation features not one but twenty-four elders. References to the Jewish elders uniformly indicate a body of men. As for the Christian churches, Paul would typically do his work of establishing churches with the help of several people, yet as an apostle he clearly played the lead role. Also, multiple elders in the young churches certainly could not all have been financially supported fully. And Paul did not write to the elders of the church in Ephesus but to Timothy alone. Finally, the Lord Jesus addressed his letters for the seven churches in Revelation 2 and 3 to the "angel" or "messenger" (singular) of each church.

Does this mean the New Testament conceives of only one elder per church? On the contrary, the evidence suggests New Testament congregations were generally led by more than one elder. Five New Testament authors referred to the office a total of twenty times. John alone referred to the office exclusively in the singular. He referred to himself as "the elder" in his second and third letters. Apparently, he was known by this title. Assuming he was writing to people outside of his own congregation, the title may have suggested not so much an office as his wide recognition.

James, Peter, Paul, and Luke also referred to the office of elder in the church, and each of them appears to presume a plurality of elders per congregation. James instructed his Christian reader to "call the elders [plural] of the church [singular] to pray over him" (James 5:14). Peter wrote as an elder to the "elders [plural] among you" (1 Pet. 5:1–5). Unless Peter was saying, "From one old man to others," then he assumed that a plurality of elders sits within each congregation. Paul greeted the bishops (plural) in the church (singular) at Philippi (Phil. 1:1). And he exhorted the elders of the church at Ephesus to be "bishops" or "overseers" (plural) to the "flock" (singular) to which God had called them (Acts 20:28). Writing to Timothy and Titus, Paul again mentioned elders in the plural. He reminded Timothy of the body of elders who laid their hands on him (1 Tim. 4:14). A little later he referred to the elders (plural) who directed the affairs of the church (singular) (1 Tim. 5:17). And then he referred to accusations not against "the elder," but against "an elder" (*presbuterou*, without an article), which would be consistent with the assumption that Timothy had multiple elders in his one congregation.

---

[88] Examples of the "rulers" of synagogues mentioned in the New Testament are Jairus in Mark 5:22 [plural rulers], Acts 13:15 [plural], and Crispus in Acts 18:8 [singular].

Paul also left Titus in Crete in order to "appoint elders [plural] in every town [*kata polin*,[89] read distributively, "in each town"]" (Titus 1:5), again meaning Paul intended for each church in Crete to have a plurality of elders. Finally, Luke's narrative in Acts gives evidence for a plurality of elders in each local congregation. The church (singular) in Ephesus had multiple elders (Acts 20:17). At the end of Paul's first missionary journey, Paul and Barnabas "appointed elders [plural] for them in each church [singular]" (Acts 14:23). And references to the elders of the Jerusalem church always occur in the plural.[90]

The direct evidence in the New Testament indicates that the common and even expected practice was to have a plurality of elders in each local congregation.[91]

Another question that naturally arises these days is whether the New Testament supports the position of a senior or sole pastor. While no direct New Testament evidence points to this distinction, four glimpses can be found for a leading teacher among the elders, even in these early congregations. First, some men in the New Testament, like Timothy or Titus, moved from place to place yet served as elders. Other men would have remained in one location, perhaps like the men appointed by Titus in every town (Titus 1:5). In other words, Timothy sets a precedent by coming from outside of the community to act in a leadership role, even while other leaders were already set in place. Apparently, outsiders were not excluded from joining a community in order to assume primary teaching responsibilities.

Second, some men were financially supported for full-time work with the flock (e.g., Phil. 4:15–18; 1 Tim. 5:17–18), while other men simultaneously remained in their vocations and performed their work as elders. Paul often did this when establishing the gospel in a new area. And not every

---

[89] κατὰ πόλιν.

[90] Acts 11:30; 15:2,4,6,22–23; 16:4; 21:18. While a plural number of leaders are referred to in a single congregation, never in the New Testament are multiple congregations referred to as being a part of a single local church. The idea that there can be one bishop or presbytery with authority over various congregations is the essence of either an Episcopalian or Presbyterian understanding of church polity; it is the opposite of Congregationalism, which understands that each gathering that has preaching and the administration of baptism and the Lord's Supper should have its own, independent leadership. One local church having multiple services or even locations raises serious questions about traditional congregational understandings of ecclesiology. Even if such innovations are accepted, it is responsible to carefully consider them first. W. B. Johnson, the first president of the Southern Baptist Convention, provided a typical observation on this point: "The term church indicates one church, one body of the Lord's people, meeting together in one place, and not several congregations, forming one church." W. B. Johnson, "The Gospel Developed," in *Polity*, ed. Mark Dever, 171.

[91] The Anglican scholar and pioneer missiologist Roland Allen came to this same conclusion. "St. Paul was not content with ordaining one Elder for each Church. In every place he ordained several. This ensured that all authority should not be concentrated in the hands of one man." Roland Allen, *Missionary Methods: St. Paul's or Ours* (London: Robert Scott, 1912), 138–39.

elder appointed by Titus on Crete, one would think, could have been paid full-time.

Third, Paul wrote to Timothy alone with instructions for the Ephesian church, even though the book of Acts clearly points to a plurality of elders in the Ephesian church. Apparently, Timothy played a unique role among them.

Finally, Jesus addressed his letters to the seven churches in Revelation 2 and 3 to the messenger (singular) of each of these churches.

None of these examples presents an explicit command, but they describe the common practice of setting aside at least one individual from among the elders potentially from outside the congregation's community, supporting that individual, and giving him the primary teaching responsibility in the church. Nevertheless, the preacher, or pastor, is fundamentally one of the elders of his congregation. Working together with that senior pastor, the plurality of elders aids both him and the church by rounding out the pastor's gifts, making up for his shortcomings, supplementing his judgment, and creating support in the congregation for decisions, leaving leaders less exposed to unjust criticism.

A plurality also makes leadership more rooted and permanent and allows for more mature continuity. It encourages the church to take more responsibility for the spiritual growth of its own members and helps make the church less dependent on its employees. As the elders lead and the deacons serve, the congregation is prepared to live as the witness God intends his church to be.

Discipline. In the Old Testament, God called Abraham and his descendants to be his special people. However, God's holy presence with this people required a special holiness on their part (Exod. 33:14–16). "The LORD said to Moses, 'Speak to the entire assembly of Israel and say to them: "Be holy because I, the LORD your God, am holy"'" (Lev. 19:1–2; cf. Lev. 11:44–45; 20:26). Their holiness should reflect his own. God continued to preserve this witness for himself to the nations through the establishment of the covenant at Mt. Sinai—detailed in Exodus, Leviticus, Numbers, and Deuteronomy—and into the time of the writing prophets.

During the centuries between Moses and Ezra, Israel existed as a testimony of God's faithfulness to his promises to Abraham. During this time individuals were excluded from the community by means of the Levitical code if their lives became too polluted. Gordon Wenham summarizes the purpose of the Levitical code: "The unclean and the holy are two states which must never come in contact with each other."[92] An individual could

---

[92] Gordon J. Wenham, *The Book of Leviticus,* NICOT (Grand Rapids: Eerdmans, 1979), 19–20.

be temporarily excluded from God's people for a number of different actions (see Lev. 11–15; 18; Num. 35:33). For other more serious sins, capital punishment could be required (Lev. 17:10; 20:3–5), as could a divine severing from the Abrahamic promises (e.g., being "cut off from his people," Exod. 30:38; Lev. 7:20–21; Num. 15:30–31). It is an honor to belong to God's people, and membership has both obligations and privileges.

Ultimately, the nation's sins became too great for God to tolerate, and so he judged the whole nation. First, the nation was divided. Then, after more centuries of disobedience, the northern tribes fell to Assyria, and later still, the southern tribes fell to Babylon. If his people would not live distinctly from the nations—if instead they adopted the immorality and idolatry of those nations—then his people would be dispersed among them. God would not allow them to continue forever bearing his name in vain. In Ezekiel, God summarized the history of his faithfulness despite the people's unfaithfulness:

> The people of Israel rebelled against me in the desert. They did not follow my decrees but rejected my laws—although the man who obeys them will live by them. . . . So I said I would pour out my wrath on them and destroy them in the desert. But for the sake of my name I did what would keep it from being profaned in the eyes of the nations in whose sight I had brought them out (Ezek. 20:13–14).

In the New Testament, the church is also to exercise discipline because an expectation of holiness remains upon God's people. "As obedient children, do not conform to the evil desires you had when you lived in ignorance. But just as he who called you is holy, so be holy in all you do; for it is written, 'Be holy, because I am holy'" (1 Pet. 1:14–16, quoting Lev. 11:44–45; 19:2; 20:7). The church was founded by Christ, and its success is promised and ensured by him (Matt. 16:17–19). He commits to form holiness in his people through his Spirit. Yet Christ's Spirit uses the local body of believers to form and maintain the special holiness of God's people. The writer to the Hebrews reminded young Christians about the importance of discipline in the Christian life (Heb. 12:1–14). Part of that discipline occurs through the interaction of the people, as one member of Christ's body cares for another.

So Paul wrote to the Galatians, "Brothers, if someone is caught in a sin, you who are spiritual should restore him gently. But watch yourself, or you also may be tempted. Carry each other's burdens, and in this way you will fulfill the law of Christ" (Gal. 6:1–2). He also warned the Thessalonians,

> Keep away from every brother who is idle and does not live according to the teaching you received from us. . . . If anyone does not obey our instruction in this letter, take special note of him. Do not associate with him, in order that he may feel ashamed. Yet do not regard him as an enemy, but warn him as a brother (2 Thess. 3:6,14–15; cf. 1 Tim. 1:20; 5:19–20).

And to Titus, Paul instructed, "Warn a divisive person once, and then warn him a second time. After that, have nothing to do with him" (Titus 3:10).

This concept of church discipline, which can culminate in exclusion from the church, originated in the teaching of Christ himself. In Matthew 18, Jesus taught on the nature of following him, instructing about love that seeks the lost, and mercifulness toward others. In the same context, he also raised the matter of what should be done when one of his followers sins against another.

> If your brother sins against you, go and show him his fault, just between the two of you. If he listens to you, you have won your brother over. But if he will not listen, take one or two others along, so that "every matter may be established by the testimony of two or three witnesses." If he refuses to listen to them, tell it to the church; and if he refuses to listen even to the church, treat him as you would a pagan or a tax collector (Matt. 18:15–17).

Christ laid out three steps for confronting someone who claims to be a follower of his and yet refuses to repent of sin—first private confrontation, then small group confrontation, finally congregational confrontation. While these steps may be more suggestive than exhaustive, the desired outcome at each stage of confrontation is the same: the disciple's repentance.[93] However, should the one sinning even refuse to listen to the church, then the individual should be treated as "a pagan or a tax collector." He has demonstrated that he does not belong in the assembly because the church assembly is characterized by holy repentance.

Discipline is inextricably bound up with the church Jesus envisioned. But that discipline should not occur alone. Rather, it should occur as one part of a larger commitment by the entire church to pray and work for one another's formation in Christ. A rejection of such fashioning must be met by the lamentable rejection from the community that is defined by it.

Perhaps the most cited text on the practice of excommunication or church discipline is 1 Corinthians 5. In this passage Paul specifically

---

[93] E.g., "Hand this man over to Satan, so that the sinful nature may be destroyed and his spirit saved on the day of the Lord" (1 Cor. 5:5).

directed the entire congregation to "expel the wicked man from among you" (v. 13). Paul took these words from Deuteronomy, where the Lord instructed his people through Moses to expel those who worshipped other gods, who gave false witness, and who practiced premarital sex, adultery, or certain kinds of slavery (Deut. 17:7; 19:19; 22:21,24; 24:7). In ancient Israel such exclusion might be carried out through capital punishment. Paul, in his exhortation to the Corinthian congregation, simply meant the offender should be expelled from their community, similar to Jesus' commands for the unrepentant sinner to be treated as a pagan or a tax collector in Matthew 18:17. Though the offender claimed to be a Christian, his claim held no credence given his evident lack of repentance. Such judging inside the church is actually a part of the work of the church, said Paul. "What business is it of mine to judge those outside the church? Are you not to judge those inside?" (1 Cor. 5:12). "Yes," of course, is the answer Paul presumed to this second rhetorical question.

The nature of the exclusion Paul enjoined is excommunication, which typically means excluding the parties in question from communion (the Lord's Supper). In essence, this is a removal from church membership. While other disciplinary situations might call for a gradual approach, with something like a warning followed by a temporary suspension from certain privileges of membership, Paul contemplated no such middle steps in 1 Corinthians 5. The crime was heinous and public, and the church's response needed to be equally public and decisive.[94] Hence, Paul took excommunication in this circumstance beyond a mere denial of the Lord's Supper to the unrepentant.

Paul wrote, "I am writing you that you must not associate with anyone who calls himself a brother but is sexually immoral or greedy, an idolater or a slanderer, a drunkard or a swindler. With such a man do not even eat" (1 Cor. 5:11). He reacted strongly because the sinner's unrepentant life contrasted so starkly with his claim to be a Christian. As long as the church allowed him to remain in membership, it affirmed his claim to be a Christian and simultaneously provided the world with a deeply distorted picture of what a Christian is. The original sin belonged to the sinning couple. But the sin which drew Paul's ire and sharp rebuke was the inaction of the congregation. Their failure to act was potentially disastrous to their gospel witness and amounted to neglect of the gospel, which was

---

[94] Traditionally Christians have made a distinction between public and private offenses. Public offenses have been addressed with Paul's counsel in 1 Corinthians 5, in which no private rebukes preceded the public one. Private offenses have been addressed with Jesus' words in Matthew 18, in which a series of private appeals are made before being brought to public attention. For more on this distinction, see P. H. Mell and Eleazer Savage (among others) in their teaching reprinted in Dever, *Polity,* 422–26, 485–86, 520.

itself a serious sin. Church discipline done correctly might bring a sinner to repentance, but it will always faithfully represent the gospel to the surrounding community.[95]

Finally, church discipline should be practiced in order to bring sinners to repentance, a warning to other church members, health to the whole congregation, a distinct corporate witness to the world, and, ultimately, glory to God, as his people display his character of holy love (see Matt. 5:16 and 1 Pet. 2:12).

Mission and Purpose of the Church. The topics already covered within this chapter cannot be fully appreciated apart from a concrete understanding of the mission and purpose of the church. The church's mission and purpose lie at the heart of its nature, attributes, and marks; and right practices of membership, polity, and discipline serve those purposes. To summarize, the proper ends for a local congregation's life and actions are the worship of God, the edification of the church, and the evangelization of the world. These three purposes in turn serve the glory of God.

The collective worship of God occurs in the context of the assembled congregation, while individual worship of God occurs in the context of one's day-to-day life. Shaping and encouraging both corporate and individual worship are significant aspects of the church's purpose.

The worship of God in the public assembly consists of particular elements prescribed by God and the circumstances in which those elements occur. As David Peterson writes, "The worship of the living and true God is essentially an engagement with him on the terms that he proposes and in the way that he alone makes possible."[96] Ligon Duncan summarizes what elements should be included in corporate worship with the motto, "Read the Bible, preach the Bible, pray the Bible, sing the Bible and see the Bible."[97] By "seeing" the Bible, Duncan means the celebration of baptism and the Lord's Supper, which depict the gospel. Since this aspect of corporate worship is considered above, the remaining elements of corporate worship to

---

[95] "Beware of an ambition for mere numbers: a small body of well-instructed, earnest disciples is worth far more to the cause of Christ than a heterogeneous multitude undistinguished in spirit and life from the world." H. Harvey, *The Pastor: His Duties and Qualifications* (Philadelphia: American Baptist Publication Society, 1879), 66.

[96] David Peterson, *Engaging with God* (Downers Grove: InterVarsity, 1992), 20. Cf. D. A. Carson's much longer definition, in D. A. Carson, ed., *Worship by the Book* (Grand Rapids: Zondervan, 2002), 30.

[97] J. Ligon Duncan, "Foundations for Biblically Directed Worship," in *Give Praise to God: A Vision for Reforming Worship,* ed. P. G. Ryken, D. W. H. Thomas, and J. L. Duncan III (Phillipsburg: Presbyterian and Reformed, 2003), 65. A strong case can also be made for regarding financial giving as an element of public worship because of Paul's instructions to the Corinthian church (1 Cor. 16:1–2; 2 Cor. 9:6–7). It is clear that the early Christians gave benevolently toward those in need (Matt. 5:42; 6:3; Luke 6:38; 21:1–4; Acts 4:34–35; 11:29; 20:35; Rom. 12:8). What is unclear is the association of this act of Christian worship with the public gathering of the assembly.

be considered here are reading the Bible, preaching the Bible, singing the Bible, and praying the Bible.

Christians are commanded to read the Bible when assembled for worship. Paul exhorted Timothy, "Devote yourself to the public reading of Scripture."[98] But God's Word must not only be read; it must also be explained and applied. Hence, right preaching of God's Word is central to the church's worship, forming its basis and core. Since faith comes by hearing God's Word (Rom. 10:14–17), Scripture must be explained with precision and passion. So Paul exhorted Timothy to "preach the Word; be prepared in season and out of season; correct, rebuke and encourage—with great patience and careful instruction" (2 Tim. 4:2).

The duty of singing God's praises is enjoined upon Christians by both example and command. Mark and Matthew recorded, for instance, the fact that Jesus and the disciples sang a hymn after the Last Supper (Eph 5:19–20). Paul instructed the Ephesian congregation to "speak to one another with psalms, hymns and spiritual songs. Sing and make music in your heart to the Lord, always giving thanks to God the Father for everything, in the name of our Lord Jesus Christ" (Eph. 5:19–20). Ultimately, the praises of the Christian assembly on earth foreshadow the praise that will be offered in heaven (Rev. 5:9–14).

Another element of gathered Christian worship is prayer. In prayer, Christians glorify God in a number of ways: by making known their reliance on him, by demonstrating obedience to his command to pray, by remembering his faithfulness to answer previous prayers, and by presuming on his kindness by asking for still more. In corporate prayer, God is magnified, while the church is edified and encouraged. Jesus taught his followers to pray in a corporate fashion, beginning with "Our Father" (Matt. 6:7–15; Luke 11:1–4). James urged early Christians to "confess your sins to each other and pray for each other so that you may be healed" (James 5:16; cf. Eph. 6:18; Phil. 4:6; Col. 4:2; 1 Thess. 5:17; 1 Tim. 2:8; James 5:13). The book of Acts is also full of prayer. The early Christians "devoted themselves to the apostles' teaching and to the fellowship, to the breaking of bread and to prayer" (Acts 2:42; cf. 1:14; 4:24–31; 12:5,12). Reading and preaching God's Word, singing his praises, and praying to him are the required elements in the weekly gathering of Christians.

Behind the assertion that Christian worship must consist of these elements is the Protestant understanding of the sufficiency of Scripture, the idea that the Scriptures sufficiently reveal everything God's people need for salvation, perfect trust, and perfect obedience. The sufficiency of Scripture has many implications, including the conviction that Scripture should regu-

---

[98] 1 Timothy 4:13; cf. Ezra's ministry of reading the law publicly, recorded in Nehemiah 8.

late the way God's people should approach God in worship. This principle has often been called the regulative principle. The regulative principle applies the Protestant belief in the authority of God's Word to the particular doctrine of the church. And it is most often referenced in discussions of public worship.

Many people have debated what specific applications should be drawn from the regulative principle for the weekly gathering of the saints. For example, does the principle require or forbid taking an offering during a service? having a choir? using drama in lieu of a sermon? and so forth. Yet before the particular points of application are tackled, the basic principle should be clearly and firmly set in place: God has revealed what basic components of worship are acceptable to him. Left to themselves, humans do not worship God as they should, not even those who are blessed by him. One needs only to think of the unacceptable sacrifice of Cain or the golden calf of the Israelites.

In response to humanity's lack of knowledge and inclination for worshipping rightly, God graciously grants humanity his Word. The first two of the Ten Commandments show God's concern for how he is worshipped.[99] Jesus condemned the Pharisees for aspects of their worship (Matt. 15:1–14). Paul instructed the church at Corinth on what should and should not occur in their assemblies (1 Cor. 11–14). In short, recognizing the regulative principle amounts to recognizing the sufficiency of Scripture applied to assembled worship.[100] In the language of the Reformation, it amounts to *sola scriptura.*

The time and place for assembled, Christian worship are not clearly prescribed in the New Testament. Both public places, like the temple or a riverside, and private spaces, like homes, were used (Acts 2:46; 4:31; 5:42; 16:13; Rom. 16:5). Having said that, the church through its history has deemed it appropriate to meet on Sunday for several reasons. First, Christ was raised on a Sunday (Matt. 28:1–2; Mark 16:2–5; Luke 24:1–3; John 20:1). Second, the risen Christ first met the disciples on a Sunday (Matt. 28:8–10; John 20:13–19; cf. Luke 24:13–15). Third, the pattern of the first Christians in the New Testament points toward Sunday as the weekly time for a worship gathering, even though Sunday would not have been a day of rest for them (Acts 20:7; 1 Cor. 16:1–2). Fourth, this pattern was quickly enshrined in language with references to Sunday as "the Lord's day" (Rev. 1:10). According

---

[99] Exodus 20:2–4; Deuteronomy 5:6–10. These commands were violated many times throughout the Old Testament (e.g., Lev. 10:1–3; Deut. 4:2; 12:f32; 1 Sam. 15:22; 2 Sam. 6; Jer. 19:5; 32:35). All of these stories (Nadab and Abihu, Saul, and Uzzah) show that right intention by itself is insufficient for right worship.

[100] For more on the regulative principle, see the first two chapters in Ryken, Thomas, and Duncan, *Give Praise to God,* and D. A. Carson's introduction to his *Worship by the Book.*

to early sources in the Christian church, this was the universal custom of Christians.[101] Finally, Christians throughout history have deemed it appropriate to give the firstfruits of the week to God in order to acknowledge his ownership of the whole, just as they do with income.

In addition to promoting and regulating the corporate worship of God by the assembly, the church's mission and purpose include fostering the individual's worship of God. Worship occurs not only in public services and assemblies. It should occur in the Christian's day-to-day living. So Paul exhorted the Christians in Rome, "Offer your bodies as living sacrifices, holy and pleasing to God—this is your spiritual . . . worship."[102] Theology lived out in responsible action and obedience is worshipping God. When performed in faith, all the duties of the Christian life commanded in Scripture are means of worshipping God. "And whatever you do, whether in word or deed, do it all in the name of the Lord Jesus, giving thanks to God the Father through him" (Col. 3:17; cf. 1 Cor. 10:31). Worship of God is the supreme end of the Christian church, whether considered locally or universally, or in the individual lives of its members.

In addition to looking up, the church exists in order to look across. Put another way, the church's vertical purpose to worship God mandates its horizontal purpose: working to evangelize and edify those made in God's image. The church itself then is a means of grace, not because it grants salvation apart from faith but because it is the God-ordained means his Spirit uses to proclaim the saving gospel, to illustrate the gospel, and to confirm the gospel. The church, then, is the conduit through which the benefits of Christ's death normally come.

The purpose of the church, in part, is to encourage individual Christians in their faith and relationship with Christ. With this goal in mind, Paul prayed that the Ephesian congregation "will in all things grow up into him who is the Head, that is, Christ. From him the whole body, joined and held together by every supporting ligament, grows and builds itself up in love, as each part does its work" (Eph. 4:15–16). When the writer to the Hebrews exhorted his readers to assemble regularly, he pointed to the purpose of giving mutual encouragement: "Let us consider how we may spur one another on toward love and good deeds. Let us not give up meeting together, as some are in the habit of doing, but let us encourage one another" (Heb. 10:24–25).

The whole congregation's life together is pointed to this end of corporate edification. God created a people in the Old Testament who were to

---

[101] Didache 14:1 (see *Apostolic Constitutions* 7:30:1); Ignatius, *Magnesians* 9:1; *Gospel of Peter* 35, 50. See R. J. Bauckham, "The Lord's Day" and "Sabbath and Sunday in the Post-Apostolic Church," in D. A. Carson, ed., *From Sabbath to Lord's Day: A Biblical, Historical and Theological Investigation* (Grand Rapids: Zondervan, 1982), 221–98.

[102] λογικὴν λατρείαν, Romans 12:1.

be a people specially blessed by God's presence, by his promises, and by his power. He desired to have a people who would display his faithfulness to his promises, his character by following his laws, and his lordship by looking forward to the promised day of his coming. The nation was to be a people marked by holiness.

In the New Testament the people of God are the church. In a local congregation, the fellowship as a whole is to display the holiness of God in their own holiness. God's love is to be reflected in the love they show. The unity of God is to be reflected in their own unity.[103] The fellowship that believers are to know in a congregation is a partnership in laboring for mutual edification and for faithfulness in evangelism.

Another purpose of the local congregation is to bring God's Word to those outside the church. Jesus commanded the disciples to "go and make disciples of all nations, baptizing them in the name of the Father and of the Son and of the Holy Spirit, and teaching them to obey everything I have commanded you" (Matt. 28:19–20). He also told his disciples that forgiveness of sins would be preached in his name "beginning at Jerusalem" (Luke 24:47). "You will be my witnesses," Jesus said to his disciples, "in Jerusalem, and in all Judea and Samaria, and to the ends of the earth."[104]

---

[103] 1 Corinthians has all of these themes.

[104] Acts 1:8. Protestant pastors and theologians like Jonathan Edwards and C. H. Spurgeon have referred in a general fashion to the "spirituality of the church." When used by these authors, the phrase is roughly equivalent to the purity and holiness of the church. But the phrase has also been given a more technical use in the context of conversations about political establishment and compromise, particularly among southern Presbyterians like J. H. Thornwell and R. L. Dabney. Here, the phrase "spirituality of the church" refers to the need for keeping the proper concerns of the church in focus and eschewing worldliness. The church should not concern itself with affairs of the state, say advocates of the spirituality of the church. And it should guard its own purity by its own authority, rather than asking the state to protect it (see James Bannerman, *The Church of Christ,* [1869; repr., Edinburgh: Banner of Truth Trust, 1974], 1:148–59, and R. L. Dabney, *Lectures in Theology,* 4th ed. [Richmond: Presbyterian Committee of Publication, 1890], 873–87). After all, advocates of "the spirituality of the church" drew a connection between the independent authority of the church from the state to the proper focus of the church's concerns being distinct from the proper focus of the state's concerns. "The church is to teach men the way to heaven and to help them thither. The state is to protect each citizen in the enjoyment of temporal rights. The church has no civil pains and penalties at command; because Christ has given her none and because they have no relevancy whatever to produce her object—the hearty belief of saving truth. (See John 18:36; 2 Cor. 10:4)." Dabney, *Lectures in Theology,* 874–75. Two crucial proponents of the doctrine were Stuart Robinson, *The Church of God* (Philadelphia: Joseph M. Wilson, 1858), esp. 84–93, and Thomas E. Peck, *Notes on Ecclesiology* (Richmond: Presbyterian Committee of Publication, 1893), esp. 119–55. Against the idea that this was a solely southern doctrine, see Charles Hodge's comments on the floor of the 1861 general assembly of the Presbyterian Church: "The doctrine of our church on this subject is, that the state has no authority in matters purely spiritual and that the church has no authority in matters purely secular or civil. That their provinces in some cases overlie each other . . . is indeed true. . . . Nevertheless, the two institutions are distinct, and their respective duties are different." "The General Assembly," *Biblical Repertory and Princeton Review,* 33 (1861): 557; cf. 561; cf. J. H. Thornwell, *Collected Writings of James Henley Thornwell* (1875; repr., Edinburgh: Banner of Truth Trust, 1974), 4:448–51; B. M. Palmer, *Life and Letters of James Henley Thornwell*

Opportunities for ministry to others naturally arise in the neighborhood and city where a congregation lives. The good news will spread most naturally not only where the congregation holds its assembly, but also where its members spend their days. Their lives are known to others. Their witness is improved by the constant observance of their conduct.

Christians are called to live lives of love toward others. Scripture in no way *denies* the right or ability of a congregation to care for the physical needs of non-Christians in their area. Neither does Scripture *require* the local congregation to alleviate the physical needs of non-Christians in our community. Rather, congregations have a call to preach, display, model, and express the good news of Jesus Christ. And in obedience to *that* call Christian congregations have both the liberty and responsibility to prudently take such initiatives in our community.

But the outward purpose of the church is not limited to evangelizing a congregation's own city. A congregation's prayers and plans should stretch beyond the narrow horizons of familiarity. Jesus' command to go "to the ends of the earth" reminds believers that Christ is Lord over all, that he loves all, and that he will call all to account on the great day. Therefore, Christians today have a responsibility to take the gospel around the world. That responsibility lies not just with individual Christians but with congregations. Christians together can pool wisdom, experience, financial support, prayers, and callings and direct them all to the common purpose of making God's name great among the nations.

In many urban churches today, this outward purpose might require restructuring life so that members of the congregation naturally intersect with

---

(1875; repr., Edinburgh: Banner of Truth Trust, 1974), 501. Similar to Abraham Kuyper's "sphere sovereignty" ideas, the spirituality of the church in this more refined usage restricts the church's concerns to matters of the gospel and issues directly related to the gospel. Cf. also Calvin, *Institutes*, 2.15.3–4; 4.20.1. Other matters (like a concern for education, politics, and mercy ministries for those beyond the church's membership) are proper concerns for Christians to have, but the church itself is not the structure for addressing such concerns. They are the proper concern of Christians in schools, governments, and other structures of society. In fact, if such concerns came to be the focus of the church, they could potentially distract the church from its main and unique responsibility, that of incarnating and proclaiming the gospel. "To the church is committed the task of proclaiming the whole counsel of God and, therefore, the counsel of God as it bears upon the responsibility of all persons and institutions. While the church is not to discharge the functions of other institutions such as the state and the family, nevertheless it is charged to define what the functions of these institutions are. . . . To put the matter bluntly, the church is not to engage in *politics*. Its members must do so, but only in their capacity as citizens of the state, not as members of the church." John Murray, "The Relation of Church and State," in *Collected Writings of John Murray* (Edinburgh: Banner of Truth Trust, 1976), 1:255. A helpful summary of the discussion in the 19th century is Daryl G. Hart, *Recovering Mother Kirk* (Grand Rapids: Baker, 2003), 51–65; cf. Preston D. Graham Jr., *A Kingdom Not of This World: Stuart Robinson's Struggle to Distinguish the Sacred from the Secular during the Civil War* (Macon, GA: Mercer University Press, 2002). For a contemporary treatment of at least the implications of this, see Brian Habig and Les Newsom, *The Enduring Community: Embracing the Priority of the Church* (Jackson, MS: Reformed University Press, 2001).

unbelieving populations in the metropolitan areas. In all churches this outward purpose means praying and planning to send resources and people to those people groups who have not yet heard the gospel of Jesus Christ. Witnessing the glory of God proclaimed around the globe in the hearts of all his people should be an end and purpose for every local church.

The final, and most important, aspect of the church's purpose is the glory of God. In the Old Testament, the people of God are created for the glory of his name.[105] Even when he saves them from the results of their own sin, he saves them for the glory of his own name. Speaking through Ezekiel, God said,

> It is not for your sake, O house of Israel, that I am going to do these things, but for the sake of my holy name, which you have profaned among the nations where you have gone. I will show the holiness of my great name, which has been profaned among the nations, the name you have profaned among them. Then the nations will know that I am the LORD, declares the Sovereign LORD, when I show myself holy through you before their eyes (Ezek. 36:22–23, see also Isa. 48:8–11).

The same is true in the New Testament. The church ultimately exists for the glory of God. Whether pursuing missions or evangelism, edifying one another through prayer and Bible study, encouraging growth in holiness, or assembling for public praise, prayer, and instruction, this one purpose prevails. The church is the unique instrument for bringing God such glory. According to the Bible, God's "intent was that now, through the church, the manifold wisdom of God should be made known to the rulers and authorities in the heavenly realms, according to his eternal purpose which he accomplished in Christ Jesus our Lord" (Eph. 3:10–11). No lesser matters are at stake in the church than the promulgation of God's glory throughout his creation. As Charles Bridges expressed it, "The Church is the mirror, that reflects the whole effulgence of the Divine character. It is the grand scene, in which the perfections of Jehovah are displayed to the universe."[106]

---

[105] For example, see the Lord's reasoning for the plagues in Exodus 9–12.

[106] Bridges, *Christian Ministry*, 1. Cf. J. L. Reynolds's majestic statement about Christ's kingdom: "When Christ uttered, in the judgment hall of Pilate, the remarkable words—'I am a king,' he pronounced a sentiment fraught with unspeakable dignity and power. His enemies might deride his pretensions and express their mockery of his claim, by presenting him with a crown of thorns, a reed and a purple robe, and nailing him to the cross; but in the eyes of unfallen intelligences, he was a king. A higher power presided over that derisive ceremony, and converted it into a real coronation. That crown of thorns was indeed the diadem of empire; that purple robe was the badge of royalty; that fragile reed was the symbol of unbounded power; and that cross the throne of dominion which shall never end." J. L. Reynolds, "Church Polity, of the Kingdom of Christ," in *Polity*, ed. Dever, 298.

Culmination of the Church

In the Bible, God's people begin in a garden (Gen. 2–3) but end in a city (Rev. 21–22). The garden is Eden, and God created it to be the perfect environment for those made in his image. It had everything humans would need, from food to work to companionship. Most of all, the garden enjoyed God's own presence, and God enjoyed unbroken fellowship with his people in the garden.

Sin destroyed the fellowship between God, man, and creation. But the destruction made way for an even grander display of God's glory in the church. In another garden Christ faced Adam's choice—to follow his own will or the will of his heavenly Father. In God's mercy and grace, Christ, the second Adam, chose to follow God's will, and to take him at his word. What followed was the most terrible suffering by the only person ever undeserving of such suffering. Then, after he had borne the sins of his people as a substitute, and after he had exhausted the claims of God's wrath against them, Christ was raised in victory over sin and death. He then poured out his Spirit, creating his church.

From there, God's people have spread around the world sharing the good news of Jesus Christ. The culmination of history is pictured in the end of Revelation as a heavenly city, an eternal society of light in which God himself is personally present. The fellowship of Eden has been restored. Only this time the number of inhabitants has been multiplied many millions of times over, as has the intimacy of fellowship, since God's own Spirit inhabits all those who trust in Christ alone for the forgiveness of their sins. The garden has become the city. Faith gives way to sight. God's glory is magnified as the eternal love between the three persons of the Trinity is reflected forever in the interpersonal love shared between the bride and the bridegroom, the church and Christ.

Christ's prayer for his disciples in John 17:26 is answered: "I have made you known to them, and will continue to make you known in order that the love you have for me may be in them and that I myself may be in them." In that city Christians will enter fully and eternally into the love of God. The church on earth today presents the glimmering and growing picture of this coming reality.

What Has the Church Believed?

History of the Idea of the Church

The topic of the church itself has been of intermittent interest in the history of the church. In the fourth century the church's struggle with the Donatists was intense, a controversy which focused significantly on the nature of the church. In the Middle Ages the struggle over the bishop of Rome's authority helped separate East and West and caused great struggles among theologians in the West. Later, John Hus, John Wycliffe, and other medieval nonconformists pressed a doctrine of the invisible church in which Christ, not the pope, was head. Even as discussions on the topic of the church came and went over the ages, a number of important issues gradually gained more and more clarity.

The assemblies of Christians, or local churches, mentioned in the New Testament are examples of visible churches. God has designed the church to be an apparent and visible testimony to him to the watching world. But is *visible* the only way the church can be described? After all, Jesus professes that weeds have been sown among the wheat, but that the two will be separated on the last day (Matt. 13:20–23). Can one then also speak of the "invisible" church, that is, the church as God sees it, or as it will appear on the last day? The *invisible church* then is the church composed of all true believers, whether or not they are in the visible church, and excluding those in the visible church who are not genuinely converted. There are not two separate churches, one visible and one invisible; these are two aspects of the true church.[107]

Historically, Protestants have championed the distinction between the invisible and visible church. This distinction has been used to explain the absence of the visible unity for which Christ prayed in John 17. By its nature, the invisible church is united; the visible church is sadly mixed and divided. While it is not accurate to say that the idea of the invisible church began with the Protestant Reformation, since the idea is found in Wycliffe, Hus, and even Augustine, the Protestant Reformers made particular use of the idea.[108]

Another dichotomy with a significant history of theological consideration in the church has been the distinction made between the *local church* and the *universal,* or catholic, *church.* That church which is composed of all Christians throughout history is the universal church. While the universal church has never assembled, one day it will, and Christians currently are regarded by God as a part of that elect body. On the other hand, the local church is simply the local assembly of Christians. With one possible exception (Luke's interesting use in Acts 9:31), the word *church* found in English translations of the New Testament always refers either to a local

---

[107] "This Church is said to be invisible, because she is essentially spiritual and in her spiritual essence cannot be discerned by the physical eye; and because it is impossible to determine infallibly who do and who do not belong to her." Berkhof, *Systematic Theology,* 566–67. Cf. Westminster Confession, chapter 25.

[108] Calvin, *Institutes,* 4.1.7; cf. Benjamin Keach's catechism, Questions 105–06, reprinted in Tom J. Nettles, *Teaching Truth, Training Hearts* (Amityville: Calvary, 1998).

assembly (the great majority of usages) or to the universal church (a handful of usages).[109] Christians have historically accepted that both of these usages are found in the New Testament. Two significant disputes, however, have raged concerning this dichotomy.

First, and most significant for the church around the world, has been the dispute about whether there is a prescribed order and polity for the universal church, as there is for the local church. The Roman Catholic Church maintains a universal order exists. The Greek Orthodox Church and many Protestant groups maintain that there are structures that have developed that are allowed and are useful, though not mandated in Scripture, such as national assemblies, conventions, archbishops, and so forth. On the other hand, Congregationalists, like Baptists, have maintained that the New Testament prescribes no structure for the universal church. All cooperation between congregations is understood to be voluntary and consensual.

A second controversy of particular concern to Baptist Christians has surrounded the question of whether one can legitimately refer to something as a church if an order or structure for it has not been prescribed. Ironically, some nineteenth-century Baptists and their heirs agreed with this aspect of Roman Catholic thought. However, they joined this to the conclusion that the universal church is never discussed in the New Testament. This controversy was known by the name Landmarkism, after Proverbs 22:28: "Remove not the ancient landmark, which thy fathers have set" (KJV). This was the text for a sermon by J. M. Pendleton and the basis of J. R. Graves's book, *Old Landmarkism: What Is It?* (1854). This book became a manifesto for the movement and exercised great influence among Baptists in certain parts of the United States.[110]

Still another dichotomy which has been used to describe different aspects of the church is the *church militant* and the *church triumphant*.[111] The church militant refers to Christians alive now, who therefore remain engaged in battling the world, the flesh, and the devil.[112] The church triumphant, meanwhile, refers to Christians now in heaven, removed from the combat of spiritual warfare and fully victorious.[113] The Roman Catholic Church also speaks of the *church suffering,* by which they mean both the

---

[109] On Acts 9:31, see F. F. Bruce's comments, in Bruce, *Acts,* NICNT (Grand Rapids: Eerdmans, 1983), 208–9; cf. A. H. Strong, *Systematic Theology* (Valley Forge: Judson, 1907), 891.

[110] One can get something of an idea of the seriousness of the controversy when it is noted that Basil Manly Jr.'s 1859 Abstract of Principles written for the Southern Baptist Theological Seminary lacked any affirmation of the existence of the universal church—a matter which would have been uncontroversial among Baptists two or three decades earlier.

[111] Such language can be found in Aquinas and in Wycliffe.

[112] See the classic Puritan treatment of the militant nature of the church's life in this world in William Gurnall, *The Christian in Complete Armor* (1662–1665; repr., Edinburgh: Banner of Truth, 1964).

[113] See Berkhof, *Systematic Theology,* 565.

church now on earth and those who are redeemed but are still being purified in purgatory.

The topic of the church became the focal point of formal theological debate in the Reformation. Here, as in so much of the church's theological development, the question of how to distinguish the *true* from the *false* led to a clearer definition of the true.

Before the sixteenth century, the church was more assumed than discussed. It was regarded as a means of grace, a reality that existed, and a presupposition for the rest of theology. Roman Catholic theology commonly refers to "the mystery of the church," by which it means the inexhaustible, imponderable depth of this reality of the church. Thus in the Vulgate, Ephesians 5:32 refers to the union of Christ with his church as a *sacramentum* (mystery). Practically, the Church of Rome argued it was the true, visible church according to Petrine succession through the bishop of Rome, based upon Jesus' words to Peter in Matthew 16.

With the advent of the Reformation, discussion of the church's nature became inevitable. To the Protestant Reformers, "not the pretended chair of Peter, but the teaching of Peter was the real mark of apostolicity. The Reformation made the gospel, not ecclesiastical organization, the test of the true church."[114] Calvin criticized Rome's claims to be a true church on the basis of apostolic succession. "Especially in the organization of the church nothing is more absurd than to lodge the succession in persons alone to the exclusion of teaching."[115] Believing that the attributes of the church (one, holy, universal, and apostolic) had become insufficient to distinguish between a true and a false church, the Reformation introduced the *notae ecclesiae,* the marks of the church: the right preaching of God's Word and the right administration of the ordinances.

Beginning with the Reformation, then, Protestants have believed that an individual, local congregation should be regarded as a true church when the Word of God is rightly preached and the ordinances of Christ are rightly followed. The right preaching of the Word of God is the *formative discipline* that shapes the church (as opposed to *corrective discipline,* which includes measures like excommunication). The ministry of the Word, therefore, is central and defining. The way to distinguish between a true church and a false church then is to ask whether the church's public worship consists of right preaching of God's Word and the right administration of the ordinances. If both are present, a true church has been found.[116] The Word

---

[114] Clowney, *The Church,* 101.

[115] Calvin, *Institutes,* 4.2.3. Also in 1536 edition in 2.29.

[116] It should be noted that true churches can be divided between those true churches that are regular and those that are irregular, that is, between those that are according to the rule (*regula*) and those

being rightly taught should lead the church to rightly administer the ordinances of Christ (which would also imply discipline being exercised).[117]

Closely related to the idea of the church's universality is the idea of
the church's unity. In the early church Christians presented their unity as
a bulwark against heretics and schismatics. But mutual excommunica-
tions over issues like Nestorianism, Monophysitism, or papal supremacy
tore the visible unity of the church. The church was further divided during
the Reformation both by the Protestant understanding of the gospel and
by their method of understanding that gospel—through the perspicuous
and sufficient Scriptures rather than the mediation of the church. Roman
Catholics have insisted on a visible unity of the church. Protestants have
insisted instead on the primacy of a unity in doctrine and spirit.

Denominations, as they are known today, arose largely in the seventeenth century, though their roots are earlier. Protestants did not look
upon dividing the visible church lightly, but the Protestant principles
of Scripture's clarity (perspicuity) and authority gave them warrant, or
even required them, to divide from false teaching. As Calvin said, "We
acknowledge no unity except in Christ; no charity of which he is not
the bond; and . . . therefore, the chief point in preserving charity is to
maintain Faith sacred and entire."[118] This meant that the Reformers recognized that the cost of unity at the price of truth was a bad bargain.
Correct division should be preferred over corrupt unity. For these reasons
various groups on the European continent struggled free from the control
of established churches and began pursuing their own understanding of
faithfulness to Scripture.

Most of the denominations popularly known in America today initially
grew up in the United Kingdom (although their roots stretch back to the
continent). Presbyterianism, Congregationalism, and a belief in believer's
baptism are all derived from Queen Elizabeth I's England (1558–1603).
However, no recognized toleration was given to anyone beyond the established church until the late seventeenth century, almost one hundred years
later. Denominations may have solidified divisions in the church, but they
also eased the pinched consciences of many careful Christians in the seventeenth century. Freedom to meet together and to worship according to one's

---

that are not. Thus various Protestant churches may recognize each other as true churches but irregular (depending on their differences).

[117] The Reformation, understandably, led to changes in physical church structures: architectural
changes, changes in the service (more time for congregational singing, for the sermon), and changes
in the minister's role. He changed from being a priest offering sacrifices to being a minister of the
Word and a pastor of the people.

[118] John Calvin, in his preface to *Psychopannychia*, in *Selected Works of John Calvin: Tracts and
Letters,* vol. 3, ed. and trans. Henry Beveridge and Jules Bonnet (1851; repr., Grand Rapids: Baker,
1983), 416.

conscience were fundamental steps in the development of denominations as they are known today.

The three "old denominations," as they were called, were the Presbyterians, the Congregationalists, and the Baptists. These three joined the establishment Episcopalians and the eighteenth-century denomination, the Methodists, to comprise the British-born religious landscape of early America. Once other significant ethnic groups were added, such as the Dutch and French Reformed churches or the German and Scandinavian Lutheran groups, America became the primary laboratory for the coexisting scores of denominations of Christian churches.

These groupings of churches largely retained their doctrinal and practical distinctives, and new ones have emerged since then. In short, the rise of denominations represents the increasing desire for faithfulness in purity rather than in unity.[119] Every congregation decides which matters members must hold in common before they can in good conscience experience and express unity with them.

History of the Ordinances of the Church

It is sadly ironic that the very actions that Christians are commanded to share commonly—acknowledge "one baptism" (Eph. 4:5); celebrate the Lord's Supper together (1 Cor. 11:18,21,33)—have been the focus of so much dispute and division through the church's history. Disputes have centered on both the number and the nature of the ordinances to be practiced by the church.

Among theologians between Augustine in the fifth century and Hugo of St. Victor in the twelfth century, there was not an agreed-upon number of sacraments.[120] Numbers ranged from two all the way to thirty or more. Since the thirteenth century, the Roman Catholic Church has acknowledged seven sacraments. The theologians of the twelfth and thirteenth centuries, especially Hugo of St. Victor, Peter Lombard, Alexander of Hales, and Thomas Aquinas, largely brought the Roman Church to its current understanding of the number and nature of the sacraments. Along with baptism and the Eucharist, the Roman Catholic Church also teaches that confirmation, confession and penance, marriage, ordination to the priesthood, and extreme unction (last rites) are sacraments to be observed by Christians as God's ordained means of grace.

---

[119] Cf. "For the New Testament unity is in order to preserve the faith, not something which can exist irrespective of doctrinal purity." Iain Murray, *Evangelicalism Divided* (Edinburgh: Banner of Truth Trust, 2000), 140.
[120] Eastern Orthodox churches today are still less uniform in establishing a specific number of sacraments.

While arguments might be made for the biblical basis of these latter five, the Roman Catholic Church does not hold to the sufficiency of Scripture. Instead, it teaches that the tradition of the church, along with Scripture, preserves God's revealed will for his people. Therefore, the development of any of these sacraments succeeding the New Testament writings is, in and of itself, no embarrassment to Roman Catholic theology.

Other groups, such as the Quakers and the Salvation Army, have maintained that no ritual ordinances should be observed today, not even baptism and the Lord's Supper. They teach these actions were meant for the first believers only and were never intended as continuing observances for the church. What must continue, however, are the spiritual realities of entering into new life in Christ and communing with God who has now come. Both of these things were signified by baptism and the Lord's Supper.

Speaking about George Fox, founder of the Quakers, Rufus Jones has written:

> His house of worship was bare of everything but seats. It had no shrine, for the *shekinah* was to be in the hearts of those who worshipped. It had no altar, for God needed no appeasing, seeing that he himself had made the sacrifice for sin. It had no baptismal font, for baptism was in his belief nothing short of immersion into the life of the Father, Son and Holy Spirit—a going down into the significance of Christ's death and a coming up in newness of life with him. There was no communion table, because he believed that the true communion consisted in partaking directly of the soul's spiritual bread—the living Christ.[121]

Certainly, Fox's eschewal of baptism and communion is consistent with his prioritization of the inner light (taken from John 1:9) over and above the written Word of God.

Some Christians have maintained that foot-washing should be regarded as a third ordinance. Among these are a number of Old Regular and Regular Baptists, Primitive Baptists, Grace Brethren, and a few other groups.[122] Citing evidence from John 13:13–15, they construe Jesus' example not just as a lesson about humility; instead, they have taken this to mean Jesus intends the ritual to be continued by Christians. No historical records suggest the early Christians practiced foot-washing as a church ordinance. Still, several of these groups in the post-Reformation period have reinitiated the practice.

---

[121] Rufus Jones, "Introduction," to *George Fox: An Autobiography*, ed. R. Jones (London: Headley Bros., 1904), 22.

[122] See H. Dorgan, "Foot-Washing, Baptist Practice of," in *Dictionary of Baptists in America*, ed. Bill J. Leonard (Downers Grove: InterVarsity, 1994), 119–20.

All the discussion concerning the number and nature of Christ's ordinances might seem far removed from the concerns of evangelical churches today. Christ's command to baptize is either ignored or minimized in the teaching of many churches, in the books written and read by evangelicals generally, and in the membership requirements of those churches. Also, the Lord's Supper is seldom celebrated in many congregations. Through all of this, the Reformation doctrine *sola fide* ("faith alone") has been exploited for ill purposes, being used to relegate anything not directly necessary for salvation to the status of unimportant. But surely if Christ has commanded something, his followers have no authority to alter his command—either by adding to it or by ignoring it.

Historically, Baptists were never in danger of ignoring Christ's ordinances. From name to practice, Baptists have been shaped by a particular understanding of baptism. Yet it has never been the practice of baptizing professing believers that has prompted controversy between different denominations. Rather, the baptism of infants has caused many of the debates and divisions in the history of Christian churches.

Considerable debate has raged around the question of when infant baptism was first practiced. Recent practitioners almost universally argue that first-century Christians performed infant baptism though they must admit the New Testament evidence is inferential. Others have been less apt to find its origins in the earliest history of the church. From William Wall's *History of Infant Baptism*, the monumental seventeenth-century Anglican defense of the antiquity of infant baptism, to the famous mid-twentieth century debate between New Testament scholars Joachim Jeremias and Kurt Aland, consensus has continued to elude scholars.[123] The *Didache, Letter of Barnabas*, and *The Shepherd of Hermas*, second-century documents that all reflect church practice in that time, know nothing of infant baptism. In fact, their statements on baptism all presuppose the baptism of believers. Tertullian's statement in *De Baptismo* (written between AD 200 and 206) attacking the baptism of infants "constitutes the earliest express mention of infant baptism in the history of the church."[124]

Later in the first half of the third century AD, Origen referred to the baptism of infants.[125] At this point it could hardly be called a universal

---

[123] William Wall (1647–1728), *The History of Infant Baptism* (London: J. Downing et al., 1705); Joachim Jeremias, *Infant Baptism in the First Four Centuries,* trans. David Cairns (London: SCM Press, 1960); Kurt Aland, *Did the Early Church Baptize Infants?* trans. G. R. Beasley-Murray (London: SCM Press, 1961); Joachim Jeremias, *The Origins of Infant Baptism: A Further Reply to Kurt Aland* (Naperville: A. R. Allenson, 1963). Aland holds the interesting position that infants today should be baptized, even though, he says, no evidence exists for infant baptism before the third century.

[124] Jewett, *Infant Baptism,* 21.

[125] See Origen's *Homilies on Luke*, chap. 14; *Homilies on Leviticus,* chap. 8; *Commentary on Romans,* chap. 5.

practice. The practice of infant baptism seemed to originate with the rise of an *ex opere operato* understanding of its effects; it was thought that baptism would secure forgiveness of sins without fail for the one being baptized. When Christianity became legal and established, pressure followed for extending church membership to the whole community. By the Council of Carthage in 418, anyone who taught against infant baptism was anathematized.[126] In the sixth century the emperor Justinian made infant baptism mandatory throughout the Roman Empire.

While Roman Catholic, Orthodox, and various dissenting groups continued to practice believer's baptism in the case of converts, there was no general recovery of the practice of baptizing *only* believers until the early sixteenth century, when some people, particularly the evangelical Anabaptists, began to reject the validity of infant baptism.[127] It is no accident that the nature of true conversion began to be clarified at the same time the gospel of justification by faith alone began its recovery. Before the Reformation, most Christians called themselves Christians largely to affirm the family, the parish, the town, and even the nation to which they belonged. The Reformation led to a new appreciation of the radical nature of Christian conversion. Conversion did not result from a rite of infancy or from membership within a particular political entity. It resulted from a self-conscious profession of faith in God's justifying work in Christ.

The reaffirmation of the authority of Scripture and the clarity of the gospel led to a surprisingly wide rejection of the bishop of Rome's authority. As the gospel of justification by faith alone spread, the impossibility of justification without faith quietly challenged the practice of indiscriminately administering baptism and the Lord's Supper to everyone who belonged to a particular political entity, whether city, nation, or parish. Naturally, this meant the millennium-old, Constantinian relationship between church and state was itself being challenged. Yet only the Anabaptists and the Baptists were at first willing to rethink ecclesiology and so reconceive the relationship between church and state, as will be examined further in a moment.

In Christian Europe, to reconsider what it meant to be a Christian required a reconsideration of what it meant to be a citizen of a city or a nation. Previously, a Christian could probably imagine other Christians living outside of one's own nation. Now, by virtue of a Baptist ecclesiology, it became possible to imagine citizens in one's own nation who were not

---

126 Though even here, David Wright suggests that infant baptism may not have become the norm in practice until the sixth century. See D. F. Wright, "At What Ages Were People Baptized in the Early Centuries?" *Studia Patristica*, ed. E. A. Livingstone (Leuven: Peeters, 1997), 30:389–94. For a review of the evidence concerning the earliest date of infant baptism, see Jewett, *Infant Baptism,* 13–43. Cf. Peter Leithart, "Infant Baptism in History: An Unfinished Tragicomedy," in Strawbridge, ed., *Covenantal Infant Baptism,* 246–61.

127 See William Estep, *The Anabaptist Story* (Nashville: Broadman, 1963).

Christians, or at least were not members of the same church. From the beginning, ecclesiology has set Baptists apart from other evangelicals. The doctrine of a visible church composed of only the baptized regenerate is the hallmark of Baptists.

Recapturing the New Testament picture of a believers' church challenged the assumptions most Christians had made since Constantine, namely, that the state is responsible to provide for the church, and the church is responsible for guiding the state. The strongest connection of this sort between church and state continued among Constantine's heirs and others in the Eastern Orthodox areas. In the East, what has been called *caesaro-papism* treated the church as the responsibility of the ruler; in effect, to see Caesar as the pope, thus the name. In the West, a less centralized and more varied relationship has existed between church and state. Whereas the state typically held the dominant position in the East, especially since the rise of Islam, the church typically had predominance in the West, given its more centralized organization and tradition of enforcing episcopal jurisdiction over rulers. At times, emperors were excommunicated and entire cities were interdicted—unthinkable in the East.

During the Protestant Reformation, the leading theologians continued to affirm the traditional Western understanding of the relationship between church and state. Whether a somewhat more passive (Lutheran) or aggressive (Calvinist) stance was taken toward the magistrate's authority, the various reformations effected little immediate change in the church-state relationship. A nation facing a reformation would focus on the questions of which church to recognize and what structure to adopt, two questions about theology and leadership that did not disrupt the basic unit of the European parish. Protestant nations varied in their answers to these questions. But in no magisterial reformation was the local parish dissolved or replaced.[128]

As we have seen, the Baptist denial of infant baptism crucially imperiled the Constantinian church-state settlement in Western Europe.[129] The Baptist belief in regenerate church membership made the relationship between citizens and their church, and thus between church and state, voluntary. This would have been unimaginable in the early and mid-sixteenth century. Ultimately, the Baptist ecclesiology provided the seed for the birth of modern notions of freedom of religion, in which no one church is established, and the rights of citizens of every religion are secured. As Christians

---

[128] The magisterial reformations were those reformations in which the politically established churches were reformed by the political authorities (e.g., the Lutheran, the Anglican, the Calvinist).

[129] This was so much the case that Anabaptists and Baptists throughout the sixteenth and seventeenth centuries repeatedly needed to publicly disavow anarchism.

tried to answer the simple question, "Who should be baptized?" they found their answer to that question had tremendous effects. If they concluded that only believers should be baptized, that would preclude having a membership that was coextensive with the general population and so effectively would preclude having an established church.

The Roman Catholic Church teaches that baptism in and of itself conveys God's grace, remitting all sin, both original and actual. The Lutheran Reformation taught that baptism was as certainly effective.[130] Luther in his catechism said, "Baptism works forgiveness of sins, delivers from death and the devil, and gives eternal salvation to all who believe this, as the words and promises of God declare."[131] Calvin, echoing Augustine, called baptism "the visible Word."[132] The Council of Trent (1545–1563) anathematized anyone who taught that baptism conferred grace only to those who had faith and not *ex opere operato*. The Presbyterian and Reformed understanding has treated baptism as a sign and seal of God's grace.[133]

Among Baptists, baptism has never been treated as an essential conduit for God's grace. Rather, they have regarded it as a command given to new believers and, therefore, the normal means for marking and celebrating their salvation. Baptism is a visible sermon, entirely dependent upon God's Spirit to create the spiritual reality it depicts. In the baptism of a believer, "There is the blessing of God's favor that comes with all obedience, as well as the joy that comes through public profession of one's faith, and the reassurance of having a clear physical picture of dying and rising with Christ and of washing away sins."[134]

Baptism has not been the only ordinance beset by controversy in the history of the church. The Lord's Supper in its nature and effects has been variously construed. These various interpretations have helped distinguish Roman Catholic theology from Protestant and have also led to differences among Protestants. At its center the discussion has settled on the question, What is the relation of Christ to his Supper?

Fully developed by Thomas Aquinas and confirmed at the Fourth Lateran Council (1215), the doctrine of *transubstantiation* describes the Lord's Supper as a representation of the sacrifice of Christ. Aquinas ar-

---

[130] When pressed in conversation about historical Lutheran statements affirming the necessity and saving power of baptism and how those statements can be squared with justification by faith alone, some Lutheran theologians recently told this author that one may be saved without baptism, but one may not be saved without faith.

[131] See John Theodore Mueller, *Christian Dogmatics* (St. Louis: Concordia, 1955), 494–95.

[132] See Calvin, *Institutes,* 4.14.6.

[133] The Belgic Confession (article 33) says that baptism and the Lord's Supper "are visible signs and seals of an invisible thing, by means whereof God works in us by the power of the Holy Spirit." Cf. Charles Hodge, *Systematic Theology* (1871; repr., Grand Rapids: Eerdmans, 1952), 3:582.

[134] Grudem, *Systematic Theology,* 980–81.

gued the substance of the bread in the celebration of the Eucharist changes into Christ's physical body, while the substance of the wine changes into his physical blood.[135] Why then do the bread and wine not change in appearance? Aquinas's response depended on a philosophical distinction, drawn from Aristotle, between the accident, or the outward form, and substance, or inner essence, of a thing. Only the substance of the bread and wine change, said Aquinas, thus the word *transubstantiation.* The accidents, or those characteristics that impress themselves upon human senses, remain unchanged.

The Eucharist is understood to be a real and effective "unbloody sacrifice." All who partake of it, aside from those who have committed a mortal sin, receive God's grace. Merely witnessing a mass counts as a participatory act worthy of that grace. More often, communicants will receive the consecrated wafer, which is understood to be the transubstantiated body of Christ. Since Vatican II (1962–1965) laypersons have more often been allowed to participate in the cup. Proponents of transubstantiation often apply Christ's promises in John 6:53–57 to the Lord's Supper, even though Christ had not yet established the Supper.[136]

Consubstantiation denies the literal and essential transformation of the bread and wine into Christ's essence, but it proposes the body and blood of Christ join together with (*con* being the Latin prefix for "with") the substance of the bread and wine at the Lord's table. Lutheran theologians have described the body and blood of Christ as "in, with and under" the physical bread and wine.[137] As Luther's Small Catechism teaches, "What is the Sacrament of the Altar? It is the true body and blood of our Lord Jesus Christ, under the bread and wine, for us Christians to eat and to drink, instituted by Christ himself."[138] Luther's view allowed him to continue holding a deep reverence toward the elements (and one should never underestimate the effect of popular piety on theology), while also ridding himself of a logical problem of Rome's view, namely, that something appears to be what it is not (its accidents and substance no longer agree). This doctrine of consubstantiation continues to be the teaching of Lutheran theologians.[139]

John Calvin taught that Christ really is present in his supper; but his presence is not physical, as the Roman Catholics and Lutherans taught, but spiritual.[140] This *spiritual presence* is perceived and profited from by faith,

---

[135] Aquinas, *Summa Theologica,* part 3, questions 75–77.

[136] Joseph Pohle, *The Sacraments: A Dogmatic Treatise,* ed. Arthur Preuss (St. Louis: B. Herder, 1942), 2:25.

[137] See Mueller, *Christian Dogmatics,* 510.

[138] Cf. Augsburg Confession, article 10.

[139] E.g., Mueller, *Christian Dogmatics,* 509–20.

[140] Calvin, *Institutes,* 4.17.9–12. Cf. Berkhof, *Systematic Theology,* 653–54. Calvin received serious criticism on this point from later Reformed theologians like William Cunningham, Charles

not by the physical senses. Apart from faith, then, the Supper is not effective. According to this understanding, "In exchange for a personal claim on and actual possession of all this wealth [in Christ], believers express faith in Christ as Savior and pledge obedience to him as Lord and King."[141] As the Westminster Confession puts it, Christ's body and blood are "really, but spiritually, present to the faith of believers." They "really and indeed, yet not carnally and corporally but spiritually, receive, and feed upon, Christ crucified, and all the benefits of his death."[142]

Of the four views of the Lord's Supper detailed here, only the Supper as *memorial* is universally accepted. Advocates for the other three positions go beyond the Supper as memorial, but no one denies this is an aspect of the Lord's Supper. First Corinthians 11:26 is unambiguous: "For as often as you eat this bread and drink the cup, you proclaim the Lord's death until He comes" (HCSB). Unsurprisingly, then, memorialist language is found frequently in the history of the church, from Clement of Alexandria to Origen, from Cyril of Jerusalem to John Chrysostom. Even Augustine frequently used such language. This view came to prominence in the Reformation along with a denial of the physical presence of Christ in the Supper.

Huldrych Zwingli taught that the Lord's Supper is a representation of Christ's sacrifice but only in the symbolic sense of proclaiming it again.[143] Zwingli pointed to Paul's words in 1 Corinthians 11:25 as the clearest biblical testimony for how the Supper should be understood. Since Zwingli, many Protestants, including most Baptists, have adopted this memorial understanding, primarily because it is indubitably biblical and secondarily (perhaps) because it avoids any hint of the sacramentalism of the Roman Catholic position. That said, Baptists have historically used language so rich about Christ's presence in the Lord's Supper for those who come by faith that little difference is perceptible between their position and the Reformed idea of Christ's spiritual presence.[144]

Hodge, and Robert Lewis Dabney.

[141] Erickson, *Christian Theology*, 1127.

[142] Westminster Confession, 29.7.

[143] Cf. Strong, *Systematic Theology*, 538–43. Charles Hodge saw little difference between Zwingli and Calvin on this point. See Hodge, *Systematic Theology*, 3:626–31. The present author agrees with Hodge.

[144] In fact, Wayne Grudem represents these two views together as the view of "The Rest of Protestantism" in his *Systematic Theology*, 995–96. Cf. Ligon Duncan, "True Communion with Christ: Calvin, Westminster and Consensus on the Lord's Supper," in *The Westminster Confession into the 21st Century* (Rosshire, Scotland: Christian Focus, 2003), 2:429–75; W. G. T. Shedd, *Dogmatic Theology*, 3rd ed., ed. Alan W. Gomes (Phillipsburg: Presbyterian and Reformed, 2003), 814. So, too, Lutheran theologian Mueller, *Christian Dogmatics*, 509. "Calvin's doctrine was nothing but a polished form of Zwingli's crude teaching, couched in phrases approaching the Lutheran terminology as closely as possible." F. Bente, cited in Mueller, *Christian Dogmatics*, 514.

The chief division about the way in which the Lord's Supper is a means of grace in the lives of Christians is the same division that is found in understanding baptism. The basic dividing question is, what is the relation of faith to the ordinance? Does the participant's faith make the ordinance a means of God's grace, or does the ordinance bestow grace regardless of faith? Among Baptists, the Lord's Supper has not been regarded as an essential conduit for God's grace. Rather, it has been regarded as a command given to new believers, and therefore the normal means of marking out those who have been separated from the world and given fellowship with Christ. Like baptism, the Lord's Supper presents a visible sermon and is entirely dependent on God's Spirit to create the spiritual communion between God and believers it depicts.

C. H. Spurgeon's mid-nineteenth-century catechism well represents this view. In answer to Question 80, "What is the Lord's Supper?" Spurgeon wrote:

> The Lord's Supper is an ordinance of the New Testament, instituted by Jesus Christ; wherein, by giving and receiving bread and wine, according to his appointment, his death is shown forth (1 Cor. 11:23–26), and the worthy receivers are, not after a corporeal and carnal manner, but by faith, made partakers of his body and blood, with all his benefits, to their spiritual nourishment, and growth in grace.[145]

Baptists have disagreed about what faithfulness to Paul's exhortation in 1 Corinthians 11:27–31 implies. Indeed, there has been a wide spectrum among Baptist Christians about who are proper participants in the Lord's Supper.[146] These can be generally summarized in three positions

---

[145] Spurgeon echoes emphases of the Second London Confession (1689), which says in chapter 30, paragraph 7: "Worthy receivers, outwardly partaking of the visible Elements in this Ordinance, do then also inwardly by faith, really and indeed, yet not carnally, and corporally, but spiritually receive, and feed upon Christ crucified and all the benefits of his death: the Body and Blood of Christ, being then not corporally, or carnally, but spiritually present to the faith of Believers, in that Ordinance, as the Elements themselves are to their outward senses." In this, the Baptist ministers adopted the language entirely of the Westminster Confession (from 1646) in chapter 29, paragraph 7, except for changing the word "sacrament" to "ordinance," and omitting the description of how the body of Christ is not corporally present "in, with, or under the bread and wine."

[146] See Peter Naylor, *Calvinism, Communion and the Baptists: A Study of English Calvinistic Baptists from the Late 1600s to the Early 1800s,* in *Studies in Baptist History and Thought* (Carlisle, U.K.: Paternoster, 2003). The classic defense of the Southern Baptist position was penned in 1846 by R. B. C. Howell, at the time the pastor of Second Baptist church, Richmond, Virgina, later the pastor of First Baptist, Nashville, Tennessee. Howell articulated a non-Landmarkist position of close communion that is still instructive for Baptists today wondering why they should exclude from membership or participation in the Lord's Supper paedo-Baptists. See Howell's *The Terms of Communion at the Lord's Table* (Philadelphia: American Baptist Publication Society, 1846). There is a vast literature of nineteenth-century Baptist works on proper terms for admission to the

(though there are almost an infinite number of variations). The first position is called "strict," or "closed," communion. Many Baptists, particularly in the seventeenth and eighteenth centuries and among Landmarkists in the nineteenth and twentieth centuries, have taught that only members of a local congregation should be allowed to partake of the Supper when celebrated by its church. "Close" communion has usually referred to a position advocated throughout Baptist history but advocated more widely in the late-eighteenth and early-nineteenth centuries in the wake of the evangelical revivals that would say that all of those believers who have been baptized as believers are welcomed to the Lord's table. "Open" communion, again a position advocated throughout Baptist history (for example by John Bunyan) but becoming dominant only in the twentieth century, advocates that all who know themselves to be trusting in Christ for salvation, regardless of whether they had been baptized as believers, are welcomed to the Lord's table.

History of the Organization of the Church

Other than the role of the ordinances, the main ecclesiological disputes throughout the history of Christianity have occurred over matters of the church's organization. In particular, three areas have drawn much of the disagreement: membership, government, and discipline. The third area is so intertwined with the first two that in times past, a written work that dealt with all three topics might simply be called a "discipline." Someone must determine who is in and who is out of earthly communities (if corrective discipline is to be practiced); and that necessarily involves coming to conclusions about who has that right and responsibility, what processes determine inclusion in and exclusion from the community, and what the requirements of being "in" are.

Membership

Given that the New Testament restricts baptism to believers, Baptists have concluded that church membership is restricted to individuals who have made a credible profession of faith. The profession of faith should include submitting to believer's baptism and making oneself accountable to a particular local congregation with whom the professing believer regularly communes. These conclusions led both European Anabaptists in the early sixteenth century and various English separatists in the sixteenth and seventeenth centuries to separate themselves from the established churches. They instead espoused a "gathered" congregation, which was a revolutionary idea. Not everyone born in a certain geographic area, they said, should

---

Lord's table that would be a fruitful field of study for Christians today wanting to understand church membership better.

be baptized and confirmed in church membership. Rather, congregations should be composed of the faithful who gather together voluntarily upon their own profession of faith, desiring to unite with others in the same area and form a Christian congregation.

In connection with these new voluntary gatherings, church covenants began to be used. Christians had certainly made pledges to one another before the sixteenth century, but the situation brought about by the Protestant Reformation created a fresh need for such pledges.[147] If the boundaries of a parish could no longer define who should be included in a congregation's membership, what could? For many Christians, the answer became subscription to a church covenant. Charles Deweese has defined a church covenant as "a series of written pledges based on the Bible which church members voluntarily make to God and to one another regarding their basic moral and spiritual commitments and the practice of their faith."[148] Sixteenth-century Protestants, particularly the continental Anabaptists, the Scottish Reformers, and the English separatists and Congregationalists, began using church covenants. Even the 1527 Schleitheim Confession of the Anabaptists contains an element of covenanting.[149]

By the seventeenth century, church covenants continued in use not only among independent congregations in England and America, but Baptists adopted their usage, especially Particular Baptists. From the seventeenth to the nineteenth centuries, church covenants, often accompanied by a statement of faith, acted as the most basic document of a Baptist congregation. As recently as the late nineteenth century, Baptist congregations commonly gathered several days before celebrating communion in order to prepare for the Lord's table by reaffirming their covenant together. Over the last century, however, church covenants have had little role in the life of most Baptist congregations. Expectations of members (whether expressed in covenants or by the practice of church discipline) seem out of character in an age in which congregations vie with one another for members.[150]

If a church covenant represents the agenda (things to be done) of a local congregation, statements of faith or confessions represent their credenda (things to be believed). From the earliest times, Christians have practiced summarizing the content of their faith. Peter made the first Christian

---

[147] Writing in AD 112, Pliny refers to Christians making certain moral pledges to one another. Such covenants were also practiced by the followers of Jan Hus. See Charles W. Deweese, *Baptist Church Covenants* (Nashville: Broadman, 1990), 19–23.

[148] Ibid., viii.

[149] See Daniel L. Akin, "An Expositional Analysis of the Schleitheim Confession," *CTR* 2 (1998): 345–70.

[150] Deweese suggests a number of factors that have led to the decline in the use of the church covenant among Baptists in America. See *Baptist Church Covenants,* 88–91.

declaration of faith when he said, "You are the Christ" (Mark 8:29). Paul wrote to the Corinthian Christians, "What I received I passed on to you as of first importance: that Christ died for our sins according to the Scriptures, that he was buried, that he was raised on the third day according to the Scriptures, and that he appeared to Peter, and then to the Twelve" (1 Cor. 15:3–5). In the early church, simple formularies like the Apostles' Creed were developed for dealing with baptismal candidates. And Christians were shepherded away from heretical teachings with more complex and careful statements like the Christological definitions of the Nicene Creed (AD 325/381) and the Definition of Faith at Chalcedon (AD 451).

The Protestant Reformation spawned numerous confessions: the Augsburg Confession (Lutheran), the Thirty-nine Articles (Church of England), the Westminster Confession (Reformed), and many more. Baptists also produced confessions of faith. In fact, Baptists produced more than any other group because of their decentralized, congregational polity. In 1611, for example, Thomas Helwys, one of the first Baptists in England, led a number of Christians to write a confession of faith. From the seventeenth century on, it has been common for Baptists to summarize the content of their faith in a confession, both for making their beliefs clear to outsiders and for having an explicit common ground of unity for the members of their own congregation.[151] Confessions of faith have played a vital role in the history of Baptist congregations.[152] As J. L. Reynolds concluded, "The use of a confession of faith, so far from disparaging the authority of the Bible, as a standard, really exalts it."[153]

Polity

A second aspect of the church's life that has developed over its history has been its polity or organization. Every group must determine how it will be governed. Churches, likewise, must have procedures for determining who is a member and who is not; and who is the final earthly judicatory under God to give leadership, settle controversies, and so forth. To these questions several different answers have been given.

One of the earliest answers to the question of who should govern was "the bishop." As demonstrated earlier, the word "bishop" (*episkopos*) in the New Testament is used interchangeably with the words for elder and pastor. The sayings in the New Testament that underscore the authority

---

[151] Standard collections of Baptist confessions of faith have been assembled by W. J. McGlothlin, *Baptist Confessions of Faith* (Philadelphia: American Baptist Publication Society, 1911) and William L. Lumpkin, *Baptist Confessions of Faith* (Valley Forge, PA: Judson Press, 1959). For a defense of the use of confessions among Baptists, see Reynolds, *Church Polity,* 334–42.

[152] See, for example, the Second London Confession (1689), the New Hampshire Confession (1833), and the Baptist Faith and Message (1925, 1963, 2000).

[153] Reynolds, *Church Polity,* 340.

of church leaders (e.g., Heb. 13:7,17) point to the pastor as one who possesses responsibility and authority in the church. By the second century, the pastors of leading cities and towns had accrued increased authority, sometimes including over churches in nearby, newly evangelized areas.[154] From the second through the fourth centuries, the diocese (taken from the Latin word for a district in Roman civil administration) developed as an ecclesiastical area with a single bishop as its head. Though their duties and responsibilities vary, bishops in this sense are recognized by most churches, including the Eastern Orthodox churches, the Roman Catholic Church, Lutheran churches, Anglican churches, and Methodist churches. The Eastern Orthodox and Roman Catholic churches regard this office as divinely established.

The Lutheran, Anglican, and Methodist churches, on the other hand, simply recognize the office as useful and expedient. In the last two centuries, many Episcopalian churches have democratized their structures, even submitting bishops to decisions made by representative bodies of clergy and laity. At the same time, collections of congregations in many Pentecostal and Charismatic circles began to recognize extracongregational authority for some bishops. Whole "apostolic networks" have grown up around the ministries of particular individuals.

The Roman Catholic Church is distinguished from other Christian communions by its submission to and dependence upon the bishop of Rome, the pope. While pope (*papas*) was a common way to address certain bishops in the early church, it was increasingly restricted to the bishop of Rome between the sixth and the eighth centuries, particularly in the West. Rome, the former capital of the Roman Empire, was regarded as the central and principal see. The Eastern and Western churches broke communion in 1054 over the Western church's (and especially Gregory VII's) insistence that the bishop of Rome be recognized as the supreme head of the universal church. The West maintained (and maintains) that Christ declared Peter the first among equals and the chief of the apostles upon Peter's confession in Matthew 16:18–19. Peter became the first bishop of Rome, and those who succeed him in that see inherit his authority as well. Thus the Roman Catholic Church recognizes the pope as the vicar of Christ, the head of the church on earth.

With the advent of the Protestant Reformation, fresh interest was shown in the Bible's teaching on the structure of the church. The New Testament evidence for the plurality of elders (cited above) was rediscovered. And groups of ministers (called consistories) were put forward as appropriate replacements for bishops in the Swiss cantons that were reforming in the

---

[154] A good example of this would be the authority that Ignatius had as a bishop. He advocated that this authority legitimately belonged to the bishop.

early and mid-sixteenth century. Following the work of Heinrich Bullinger in Zurich and John Calvin in Geneva, others began to organize according to a Presbyterian system. Reformed congregations sprang up in the Netherlands, Scotland, Hungary, Germany, Poland, and France. In Scotland, John Knox took on the challenge of reforming the established church of an entire nation along the lines of this system. The nationwide general assembly became the final arbiter recognized in the Church of Scotland. Thomas Cartwright at Cambridge, England, began teaching presbyterianism in 1570 in his lectures on the book of Acts.

Though Presbyterianism was a strong force for reforming the established church in England throughout the seventeenth century, it never became the polity of the Church of England. Presbyterian structures came to North America with the European settlers from Scotland and the Netherlands, where they have flourished. They have also flourished around the world from Korea to Africa. Most Presbyterian bodies are connectional. In the United States, the (national) general assembly of any Presbyterian body usually functions as the final arbiter in ecclesiastical matters, with regional synods and/or presbyteries ruling beneath them and with sessions (boards of elders) of a local congregation below them. Some independent churches are Presbyterian in the sense that they are ruled by a board of elders, but they have no court of appeal outside of that congregation's own elders. Presbyterians generally teach that the principles of their organization, not the particulars, are taught in Scripture.[155]

At the time of the Reformation, churches that were gathered not by a ruler or magistrate but by the shared convictions of individual Christians began to organize, recognizing themselves as their own final earthly authority in religious matters. In England, advocates of a congregational polity arose in the 1580s. Robert Browne's *A Treatise of Reformation without Tarrying for Any* (1582) and Henry Barrow's *A True Description out of the Word of God of the Visible Church* (1589) laid out a doctrine of polity that was not reliant on structures above the local congregation. In the 1630s, as many Christians began to regard the structures of the Church of England as incorrigible, Congregationalism found new and prominent advocates.

John Cotton, John Owen, and Thomas Goodwin advocated "the congregational way." In 1658, the Savoy Declaration (an adaptation of the Westminster Confession) laid out congregational principles of church government. By the time of the American Revolution, two out of every five Christians in the American colonies were in some kind of congregational

---

[155] For an exception to their general posture, see Robert Reymond, "The Presbytery-Led Church: Presbyterian Church Government," in Chad Brand and R. Stanton Norman, eds., *Perspectives on Church Government: Five Views of Church Polity* (Nashville: Broadman & Holman, 2004), 87–138.

church, whether Congregationalist or Baptist. Today many independent churches are congregational in structure. Baptist churches are also congregational. Such congregational churches have often joined together voluntarily in local associations and national unions or conventions.

Advocates of Congregationalism understand that the Bible teaches the local congregation is ultimately responsible for its discipline and doctrine. Disputes between members (Matt. 18:15–17), as well as matters of doctrine (Gal. 1:8; 2 Tim. 4:3), church discipline (1 Cor. 5), and membership (2 Cor. 2:6–8), are all recognized as congregational matters. No other authority may obtrude itself into the position of giving final correction to the congregation or overruling them on such matters. Nor may the congregation delegate this authority to an elder or bishop or any other structure, thereby deferring their own accountability before God for doctrine or discipline.

Practice of Discipline

Historical data on the life of the church immediately after the New Testament period is only intermittent and partial. The church was, after all, a small and sometimes illegal group. Written sources multiplied greatly after the Christian church was legalized throughout the empire under Constantine. For the twelve hundred years between Constantine and the Protestant Reformation, church discipline, whether by individual excommunication or interdict (withholding the sacraments from the population of a political entity), was often used more to protect the church's corporate interests against the claims of the state than to reclaim Christians from sin and protect the gospel's witness.

When the leaders of the Reformation began to recover a more biblical understanding of preaching and administrating the sacraments as the two marks of the true church, the recovery of church discipline as a consequent mark followed. Implied in the right administration of the sacraments was the correct practice of church discipline. After all, if marking out the church from the world is one function of the sacraments, then discipline becomes the mechanism for enforcing that mandate. The right discipline of the church became so significant that it began to be presented as a third mark of a true church.[156]

The twenty-ninth article of the Belgic Confession (1561) said:

> The marks by which the true Church is known are these: If the pure doctrine of the gospel is preached therein; if she maintains the pure administration of the sacraments as instituted by Christ; if church discipline is exercised in punishing of sin; in short, if all

---

[156] For an example of a modern popular treatment, see D. Martyn Lloyd-Jones, *The Church and the Last Things*, vol. 3, *Great Doctrines of the Bible* (Wheaton: Crossway, 1998), 13–18.

things are managed according to the pure Word of God, all things contrary thereto rejected, and Jesus Christ acknowledged as the only Head of the Church.[157]

In our own day, Edmund Clowney has summarized these marks as "true preaching of the Word; proper observance of the sacraments; and faithful exercise of church discipline."[158]

While some Anabaptist groups like the Mennonites practiced banning, or social exclusion, this was exceptional. The most well-known example of church discipline in American history—the scarlet "A" sewed on Hester Prynne's clothes—was a product of novelist Nathaniel Hawthorne's historical imagination and not an accurate record of either a historical event or of the general practice of church discipline in colonial New England. In the vast majority of cases, whether in Presbyterian, Congregational, Baptist, or Methodist churches, congregational exclusion meant barring the sinner from communion and, ultimately, membership until repentance occurred.

Baptists, being committed to regenerate membership in the visible church, were vigorous practitioners of church discipline. Greg Wills's research shows that in Georgia, pre-Civil War "southern Baptists excommunicated nearly 2 percent of their membership every year," and yet at the same time the membership in Baptist churches grew at twice the rate of the general population.[159] Though fruitful and beneficial to the gospel, the work of confronting and disciplining was never easy. Basil Manly Jr. expressed his own "profound grief" over one case of discipline in the church he pastored.[160]

So why did this practice end? Wills has convincingly argued that discipline among Baptists

> declined partly because it became more burdensome in larger churches. Young Baptists refused in increasing numbers to submit to discipline for dancing, and the churches shrank from excluding them. Urban churches, pressed by the need for large buildings and the desire for refined music and preaching, subordinated church discipline to the task of keeping the church solvent. . . . They lost the

---

[157] So, too, the Scotch Confession (1560), Article 18: "The trew preaching of the Worde of God. . . . the right administration of the sacraments of Christ Jesus. . . . Ecclesiastical discipline uprightlie ministered."

[158] Clowney, *Church*, 101. In this book Clowney has a good summary of the marks of the church considered biblically, historically, and in context of current questions of church versus parachurch; see 99–115. See also John Hammett, *Biblical Foundations for Baptist Churches: A Contemporary Ecclesiology* (Grand Rapids: Kregel, 2005).

[159] Greg Wills, *Democratic Religion: Freedom, Authority and Church Discipline in the Baptist South, 1785–1900* (New York: Oxford University Press, 1997), 22.

[160] Ibid., 119.

resolve to purge their churches of straying members. No one publicly advocated the demise of discipline. No Baptist leader arose to call for an end to congregational censures. No theologians argued that discipline was unsound in principle or practice. . . . It simply faded away, as if Baptists had grown weary of holding one another accountable.[161]

And what was the result? John Dagg put it well: "When discipline leaves a church, Christ goes with it."[162]

By the twentieth century, the absence of church discipline was generally assumed and only occasionally observed as a problem.[163] In 1944, Greek scholar H. E. Dana observed that

> the abuse of discipline is reprehensible and destructive, but not more than the abandonment of discipline. Two generations ago the churches were applying discipline in a vindictive and arbitrary fashion which justly brought it into disrepute; today the pendulum has swung to the other extreme—discipline is almost wholly neglected. It is time for a new generation of pastors to restore this important function of the church to its rightful significance and place in church life.[164]

It is questionable whether the generation of pastors in the 1940s heeded Dana's call. However, as the surrounding culture has become more overtly immoral, twenty-first-century churches show some signs of recovering practices that promote the purity of the church, including the practice of corrective church discipline.

Through all the changes of the centuries, Christians can be confident that the survival of the church is not ultimately based upon human faithfulness. In both the parable of the growing seed, in which Christ taught that whether the sower sleeps or gets up "the seed sprouts and grows" (Mark 4:27), and in Christ's promise that "the gates of Hades will not overcome [the church]" (Matt. 16:18), Christ has given a sure pledge of his church's success. In everything from the church's obedience to its life and organization, the span of church history is a demonstration of Christ's faithfulness to his promises.

---

[161] Ibid., 9. Cf. "Church discipline presupposed a stark dichotomy between the norms of society and the kingdom of God. The more evangelicals purified the society, the less they felt the urgency of a discipline that separated the church from the world" (p. 10). "Activism became the crowning virtue of Baptist piety in the twentieth century" (p. 133). On documenting the decline, see Stephen Haines, "Southern Baptist Church Discipline, 1880–1939," *BHH* 20 (1985): 14–27.

[162] Dagg, *Church Order,* 274.

[163] E.g., Josef Nordenhaug, "Baptists and Regenerate Church Membership," *R&E* 60, no. 2 (1963): 135–48. James Leo Garrett Jr., *Baptist Church Discipline* (Nashville: Broadman, 1962).

[164] H. E. Dana, *Manual of Ecclesiology* (Kansas City, KS: Central Seminary Press, 1944), 244.

How Does It All Fit Together?

In order to be faithful to what the Bible teaches about the church's nature, shape, and outline, we must consider both what Christians have said in the past and what systematic conclusions have been established over the course of the church's history. And we do this always in the context of holding these findings up to the light of our own study of Scripture. Ultimately, we find that the various challenges which confronted the church through history have led to a clearer, more defined set of affirmations and entailments. By affirming the sufficiency of Scripture and the requisite role of faith in participating in the ordinances, we can conclude that a biblically faithful church is a Protestant church. By affirming the necessarily voluntary and consensual nature of membership in a local congregation, we can conclude that a biblically faithful church is a gathered church. By affirming the nature and polity of a local congregation, we can conclude that a biblically faithful church is a congregational church. And by affirming Christ's command to baptize only those who believe and obey, we can conclude that a biblically faithful church is a Baptist church. In this section each of these descriptions will be examined in turn in order to see how the Bible's teaching fits together in the life of a local church.

A Protestant Church: Putting Together the Marks of the Church

If in fact the Bible teaches God creates a people for himself through his Word, then preaching will take a central role in the life of the church. And if in fact the Bible teaches that baptism and the Lord's Supper mark off the visible church from the world, then their correct administration will be linked to faith in God's promises. Both of these understandings find expression in the biblical teachings of the Protestant Reformers.

The center and source of the congregation's life is the Word of God. God's promises to his people in Scripture create and sustain his people (Gen. 15:4–6; Rom. 10:8–11). Therefore the congregation is responsible to ensure, as much as lies within its power, that the Word of God is preached at its regular meeting.

By the sixteenth century the centrality of the Word had long been displaced by the sacraments, especially by the sacrament of the Eucharist. In the face of this near universal distortion, the Reformers correctly returned to Scripture to find a canon, or rule, against which to measure the Roman Church's current teaching. The central role played by the Word in the New

Testament church (Acts 2:40–47; 5:42; 2 Tim. 4:2) was recovered in the teaching and lives of the Protestant Reformers.

If the Scriptures are "the word of life," as Paul called them in Philippians 2:16, they should both generate and regulate the church's life. Christians gather in congregations to hear one who stands in the place of God by giving his Word to his people. Through preaching Christians come to know and understand God and his Word. It is a word to which Christians contribute nothing, other than hearing and heeding. A Christian sermon is—even in its very method—a picture of God's grace. Since faith comes by hearing (Rom. 10:17), hearing God's Word rather than seeing the mass is appropriately placed at the center of the congregation's public assembly. Christians rely on God's Word, so preaching of the Word must be absolutely central. And the preaching which most exemplifies this is expositional preaching—preaching in which the point of the passage of Scripture is the point of the message. Scripture is both authoritative and sufficient, and that should be evident in Christian gatherings.

The Protestant rediscovery of the biblical truth of justification by faith alone was a recovery of the biblical gospel. As Protestant congregations replaced sacramental ritualism with gospel preaching, the sacraments, or ordinances, themselves took on another purpose, or really, their original biblical purposes—marking out the church from the world and providing a visible picture of the gospel message accepted by faith. As a result, the church became defined not by individuals who were baptized and who witnessed the mass, but by individuals who personally believed the promises set forth in baptism and the Lord's Supper, and therefore participated in those rituals. Even Protestants who practiced infant baptism did not teach baptism effected salvation. They taught it reflected salvation, and that salvation would only come to pass if the person baptized believed, whether before or after his or her baptism. Faith, then, became the essence of what separated the church from the world. This faith was given visible form in the ordinances.

Faith's role in distinguishing the visible church from the world, then, makes the Protestant church what it is. Faith shows itself initially in the believer's submission to baptism, and then repeatedly in his or her participation in the Lord's Supper. Whereas obedience and submission to the visible church were also emphasized in the Roman Catholic Church, the Protestant churches were marked by adherents who expressed personal faith in Christ, apart from which baptism and the Lord's Supper would be useless.

The Protestant impulse to place faith at the center of the ordinances has shown itself in many ways, from the presence of numerous Baptist movements, to American colonial minister Jonathan Edwards's adoption of believer's-only Communion.

In summary, Christianity requires a conscious belief in the gospel. When God's authoritative Word is taught, it must be consciously believed and trusted. This trust, or faith, is what distinguishes God's people, who have made an initial confession in baptism, and a continuing confession through participation in the Lord's Supper. When the sufficiency of Scripture and the necessity of faith in practicing the ordinances are affirmed, it becomes clear that a biblically faithful church is a Protestant church.

A Gathered Church: Putting Together the Membership of the Church

In addition to being a Protestant church, a biblically faithful church is a gathered church. It is a voluntarily assembled congregation and not one bound together by nationality, ethnicity, or family alone. No circumstance of birth should determine the membership of a biblically faithful church. Rather, a profession of faith in Christ and a willingness to submit to the teaching and discipline of a particular church should regulate a congregation's membership.

The Protestant Reformation was carried out by both magisterial and nonmagisterial reformers. The magisterial Reformers were those who used the offices of the state, or the magistrate, to bring doctrinal reform to the churches, since political jurisdiction overlapped with ecclesiastical jurisdiction (with exceptions for groups like immigrants or Jews). Essentially, political citizenship not only entitled one to but normally entailed membership in the established church. The magisterial Reformers, in both their Lutheran and Reformed elements, began movements within established state churches. But once the true gospel of justification by grace alone through faith alone in Christ alone was recovered, forces were unleashed which acted to undermine the doctrine of an established church itself.

If participating in the ordinances was not saving in and of itself, a baptized communicant could remain unbelieving and unsaved. This dawning realization brought about more concern for the salvation of the individual. The nature of evangelism and missions moved from incorporating individuals into the community through ritual and education, as much Roman Catholic mission work had done, to persuading and calling for a deliberate commitment. Eventually, nonmagisterial groups like the Anabaptists covenanted together to form congregations not necessarily sanctioned by the state. Indeed, they were *often illegal.* Yet even in legally sanctioned Protestant churches, sermons were used to exhort the gathered to examine the self to ensure one's profession of faith was true.

Biblically faithful congregations are not shaped so much by geographical parish bounds as by people's beliefs and commitments. An individual must decide to join a congregation, and then he or she must make the continual decision to participate through attendance, prayer, acts of service, financial support, and submission to the discipline of the congregation. Ultimately, the church is gathered by the action of God's Spirit. As Luke wrote of the early church, "The Lord added to their number daily those who were being saved" (Acts 2:47). Yet this divine action is met with a human response. "Repent and be baptized" (Acts 2:38), commanded Peter. Those who are truly saved have repented of their sins and trusted in Christ. As the New Hampshire Confession puts it, repentance and belief are the "inseparable graces wrought in our heart by the Holy Spirit of God."

Yet the decision to repent and believe is then expressed by publicly affirming one's faith and covenanting together with a specific congregation. The congregation, too, must affirm the credibility of an individual's profession of faith. It is not merely the decision of an individual to join or leave a church; rather, the decision to join or leave a church requires mutual consent between individual and congregation (except, of course, in the case of death).[165] Through the preached Word and the response of faith, congregations gather. When the voluntary and consensual nature of membership in a local congregation is affirmed, it is clear that a biblically faithful church is a gathered church.

A Congregational Church: Putting Together the Structure of the Church

Nowhere does the Bible prescribe a polity for the universal church, that body of all Christians everywhere. The only other definition for *church* in the New Testament is of the local assembly. While no church constitution is included in the New Testament documents, the Bible has principles which inform a congregation's life. And the New Testament has explicit teaching on church structure. Both the officers and polity described in the New Testament have led many Christians to conclude that the church should be structured congregationally. This has implications for how one congregation relates to other congregations and to other connections of Christians outside their number. And it has implications for how leadership is exercised within the congregation.

A congregational church recognizes the congregation as the final earthly court of appeal in matters of dispute. Members' meetings are held where decisions are made by voting. Naturally, a higher degree of consensus is needed than in churches of other polities. More responsibility rests on each member and more authority resides in them.

---

[165] This seems to be clearly implied in Paul's words to the Corinthians in 2 Corinthians 2:6–7.

Such congregations have sometimes been called "independent" as opposed to "connectionalist," with Presbyterian and Episcopalian churches being examples of the latter. Congregationalist churches are not, however, independent of one another in affection, care, advice, or cooperation. Both in Scripture and in history, congregations have cultivated care and concern for one another. In the New Testament period, collections were taken and given, missionaries and teachers were sent, and recommendations and cautions were shared between congregations. This pattern has repeated itself among Anabaptist and Baptist congregations, as well as among many other congregational churches.

Traditionally Baptists have used associations between churches to help ministers and congregations take counsel with one another, reach joint conclusions, stop controversies, and draw doctrinal boundaries. And congregations have freely come together to accomplish work that would generally exceed the resources of one congregation, such as ministerial education and missionary support. Congregational churches are in one narrow sense "independent," but in other ways they are more accurately described as voluntarily interdependent.

Voluntary connections of congregations like the Southern Baptist Convention, the American Baptist Churches, and the National Baptist Convention long ago settled into the popular American consciousness as denominations. Many if not most other denominations are connectional churches, where final decisions on matters of doctrine and discipline cannot be handled by the local assemblies but must be decided by regional, national, or even internationally recognized assemblies, courts, or bishops. In that sense denominations of congregational churches are far different than other denominations.

One can speak in the singular of the Presbyterian Church in the United States of America or of the United Methodist Church in a way one could never correctly speak of "the National Baptist Church" or "the Southern Baptist Church." While it is commonly understood what such expressions mean, they belie an ignorance about the nature of the churches they mean to describe. Even if members of congregational churches sometimes exhibit great "tribal loyalty" to their denomination, they are actually only members of local churches that themselves in turn only voluntarily and never necessarily cooperate with regional and national bodies. Their congregations need not continue to affiliate with any particular convention in order to continue being a true church.

None of the aforesaid teaching on congregationalism should be mistaken as advocating leaderless anarchy in churches. Recognizing the congregation as the final court of appeal for matters of dispute is hardly inimical to the exercise of authority within the church. And other noncongregational polities, including Presbyterian, Episcopalian, and even Roman Catholic, have demonstrated a certain inevitability of congregationalism by recognizing representative bodies at various levels, and even advising congregational assent for many decisions to be enacted.

The most coherent way to understand the New Testament's presentation of local church polity is to recognize the role both of individual leaders and the congregation as a whole. Some recommend a pastor should govern the church almost like a CEO. But this gives inadequate attention to Scripture's teaching on both the plurality of elders and the role of the whole congregation. Others recommend the church should be governed by elders. This position is rightly distinguished from Presbyterianism because it does not simultaneously envision submitting to a hierarchy of authority outside the local congregation's body of elders.

But while this position helpfully discerns what the New Testament says about a plurality of elders, it also discounts the scriptural evidence for both congregational responsibility and the special recognition of a lead teaching elder, like Timothy in Ephesus—what might today be described as a "senior pastor." Still others recommend a vigorous congregationalism that is exercised at the expense of any other authority, whether corporate (a plurality of elders) or individual (a lead pastor).

Too often these varieties of congregationalism are pitted against one another.[166] But all three aspects of authority seen in the New Testament (individual, corporate, and congregational) should be enjoyed in every congregation, allowing for some variation between them congregation to congregation. One elder supported by the church and responsible for the ministry of the Word could well be recognized as having a senior position in order to give leadership to the church's vision and direction. At the same time, a plurality of elders, whether paid or unpaid, can together lead the congregation in matters of doctrine and discipline. And at the same time, the congregation can, in humility, shoulder the responsibility for acting as the final court, under God, in all matters of discipline and doctrine which rise to that level of significance. Which matters are dealt with at what level may vary from congregation to congregation.

The New Testament does emphasize the significance of congregational assent both for which doctrines must be taught and believed (Gal. 1:6–9), and for who is admitted and dismissed from membership (1 Cor. 5). However, none of these aspects of teaching, leadership, or final judgment may be finally delegated to any body outside of the local congregation, and the congregation still remain a church.[167] Whichever way all the parts are

---

[166] See, for example, Brand and Norman, *Perspectives on Church Government.*

[167] One obvious qualification of this statement is that times of a church's beginning and ending may well bring with them exceptional circumstances that call for temporary measures in which one or

combined, the New Testament's teaching on the nature of the congregation and the role of its leaders clearly indicates that a biblically faithful church is a congregational church.

A Baptist Church: Should We Have Baptist Churches Today?

One outstanding question for Christians today is, if agreement on a particular matter is not essential for salvation, should agreement upon it be regarded as essential for church membership? If the question springs from a receding grasp on the truth or at least a declining willingness to define and defend the truth—a mere essentialism—then more basic and dangerous issues than a misunderstanding of baptism are at stake. If, on the other hand, the question emerges from a sincere desire for the unity of the body of Christ, then the question is a noble one and deserves serious consideration. Whichever the reader may conclude, Christians from John Bunyan to D. Martyn Lloyd-Jones have pled for liberty on this point. They have advocated that agreement on the legitimacy or illegitimacy of infant baptism not be required for church membership.[168]

This position of neutrality over a matter not essential for salvation is gaining in popularity. The question essentially is, or at least very nearly is, Should we continue to have Baptist churches? If the question is posed as one of love versus dogmatism, the answer is easy, but the real issues at stake may be obscured. Two matters in particular cannot be overlooked. First, some things are not essential for an individual's salvation, yet agreement on them is essential in order for a church to function. One thinks of questions surrounding church government, qualifications for membership, or women serving as pastors and elders. But finally, each congregation must do one thing and not the other. A congregation will recognize women as elders or not, an outside bishop as an authority or not, and infants as viable subjects of baptism or not. If then a decision must be made one way or another, do we decide against Scripture on the issue of requiring believers to be baptized?

This brings us to the second and more important matter that must not be overlooked—fidelity to Scripture. If baptism is not essential for communion and church membership, it effectively becomes a matter of individual judgment. The desire for doctrinal inclusiveness and unity in the Spirit ironically reduces obedience to a matter of subjective preference. Some, like John Bunyan, have argued that disobedience to a command of Christ,

---

more of these aspects of leadership are not yet fully realized.
[168] The controversies about terms of admission to communion among nineteenth-century Baptists provide a rich resource for more biblical thinking on these matters. For example, see R. B. C. Howell, *Terms of Communion.*

especially when done in ignorance, represents a mere lack of light to be borne with more than it represents a disciplinable offense, or a sin.

A sin can consist of either an action or an intention. Certainly the intention to disobey God is sin. But a disobedient action toward God is also a sin even if the individual does not intend to sin. The Bible teaches clearly that there are unintentional sins (Lev. 4–5; Num. 15). Intentions are an important consideration in the nature and gravity of a sin, but they are not the only consideration. One of the effects of sin is to stupefy the sinner, to dull and darken the faculties. So those dwelling in sin are said to dwell in darkness, but that darkness does not ameliorate one's guilt. In the parable of the sheep and the goats in Matthew 25, Jesus teaches with stark clarity that obedience to God does not lie in the eye of the beholder, unless the beholder is God himself. Many goats thought they had lived righteous lives, but Jesus says they had not.

How then do we know what God considers obedience? By his own self-revelation. There is no other sure and certain guide! If Christ has commanded Christians to be baptized, then countermanding that instruction, or substituting mere intention, even sincere intention, does not serve him best. His glory is most displayed in the church when baptism guards both the regeneracy of church membership and the consistency of the church's corporate witness. If we understand that Christ commands the church to baptize only those who repent and believe, then it seems clear that a biblically faithful church is a Baptist church.

How Does This Doctrine Impact the Church Today?

What significance does a right ecclesiology have for the church today? A right ecclesiology matters for the church's leadership, membership, structure, culture, and even character. Ultimately, a right ecclesiology touches on God's glory itself. The church is not only an institution founded by Christ; it is his body. In it is reflected God's own glory. How will theology, the Bible, and even God himself be known apart from the church? What community will understand and explain God's creation and providence to the world? How will the ravages of sin be explained, the person and work of Christ extolled, the Spirit's saving work seen, and the return of Christ proclaimed to coming generations if not by the church? The theology expounded in every chapter of this book presses outward to be known, and it presses outward through the church. Therefore, getting the doctrine of the church right becomes a benefit to people, as the truth about God and his world is more correctly known, taught, and modeled.

This Matters for the Church's Leadership

Pastors in churches today must recover the understanding that their primary role is to preach the Word of God. This must happen both for the sake of the flock and for the sake of reaching those outside the flock.

The purpose of preaching God's Word to God's people is to build up, or edify, the church, which is God's will for the church. Whether numerical growth results from biblical preaching in any given congregation at any given time, Christ's church will experience true growth and edification through teaching and instruction. To this end pastors must also lead the church toward a recovery of corrective church discipline. This will be accomplished only when the leadership itself understands the Bible's teaching about the church and then gives itself to patiently teaching the congregation in these matters.

Whenever pastors recover the centrality of preaching in their ministry, beneficial effects follow. Congregations are better fed and healthier, and then they become better witnesses in their communities. Too often leaders promote church growth exclusively through evangelism, but they fail to consider that an untaught and unhealthy church is a poor witness. And a poor church witness will undermine the evangelistic ministries of the congregation. The pastor who recommits himself to feeding the congregation well will best prepare his congregation for evangelism and growth. Healthy organisms naturally grow.

God's Spirit creates believers through the preaching and hearing of the Word, yet God also intends for those believers to be collected together in congregations that are pure and protected. To this end, pastors must take greater care in scrutinizing candidates for baptism and in encouraging the congregation to scrutinize themselves before partaking of the Lord's Supper. If baptism functions as the watery moat separating church and world and if the Lord's Supper manifests the ongoing appearance of the church, then pastors today must recover the sense of gravity each ordinance requires.

Hebrews 13:17 promises that leaders will give an account for those under their charge. Will today's leaders give an account for carelessly admitting wolves into baptism or the Lord's Supper? Will the condemnations heaped on Israel's shepherds in Ezekiel 34 be repeated upon undershepherds of the church today who have left Christ's sheep to wander scattered and unprotected? The leaders of our congregations must be reminded that the right preaching of God's Word and the right administration of baptism and the Lord's Supper form the basic calling of their lives.

This Matters for the Church's Membership

A right ecclesiology also has implications for the church's member-ship.[169] Therefore, the reasons and requirements for membership should be widely and clearly understood. Most evangelical Christians today seem to treat their church as one more thing to help out their Christian life, perhaps along with this Bible study, that music, those authors, this retreat, and keep-ing a journal. In other words, the Christian conceives of his or her spiritual life as fundamentally one's own business, managed by selecting among various helps. This approach contrasts with an older and more biblical way of thinking about the Christian life that is congregationally shaped, where the demands of the gospel are made concrete in a particular local church (cf. 1 John 4:20).

Being a member of a local church should be made to seem normal for the Christian. Lives lived in regular accountability make the gospel clear to the world. Jesus said that Christians' love for one another would en-able the world to recognize Christians as those who follow Christ (John 13:34–35). In that sense a vigorous practice of church membership helps a congregation's evangelism. It also helps Christians gain a proper assur-ance of their own salvation. As Christians observe, teach, encourage, and rebuke one another, the local church begins to act as a cooperative that corroborates assurance of salvation. Church membership is good for weak Christians because it brings them into a place of feeding and accountability. Church membership is good for strong Christians because it enables them to provide an example for what a true Christian life is like.

Committed church membership is also good for the leaders of the church. How will God's work go forward if Christians do not organize together to serve him? And how will Christians receive the gifts God gives them in their leaders if there is no flock marked out for those leaders to steward? Finally, practicing church membership glorifies God. As Christians gather together to form the body of Christ, his character is reflected and expressed. Recovering this understanding of church membership should be one of the chief desires of congregations today.[170]

Before one quickly points to the parachurch as accomplishing the same objectives, remember that the parachurch neither has the same commit-ment to systematically proclaiming the whole counsel of God, nor does it have the mechanisms of baptism, the Lord's Supper, and church discipline

---

[169] For one thing, if this were widely understood among the members, congregations would be able to consider carefully the delicate question of the relation of children of church members to the church.

[170] For more on this, see Mark Dever, *Nine Marks of a Healthy Church,* 2nd ed. (Wheaton: Crossway, 2004); also Mark Dever, *A Display of God's Glory,* and Mark Dever, "Regaining Meaningful Church Membership" in *The Integrity of the Local Church in a Seeker-Sensitive World,* ed. Thomas White, Jason Lee, and Jason Duesing (Grand Rapids: Kregel, forthcoming 2007).

for drawing a clear, bright line that says to the world, "Here are the people of God." The parachurch is and always means to be a particular subset of the church, centered on a shared task.

The idea that membership in a local church should only require a profession of faith in Christ is an idea that is both common and destructive to the life and witness of the church. Historically, Baptists have realized that any profession of faith should be tried and deemed as credible. After all, a saving profession of faith includes repentance. A Christian life will be revealed not only by participation in baptism and the Lord's Supper but also by regular attendance at the congregation's gatherings, and a submission to the discipline of the congregation. This includes regularly praying for the congregation and tithing. When congregations do not give attention to lifestyles of repentance, nominal Christianity quickly comes to characterize the church to the world, hurt its witness, and lie about the character of God. Every congregation has the responsibility for deciding what membership standards are appropriate for their own church.

One of the areas in most need of reexamination in today's churches is the relation of the children of church members to the church. In non-Baptist Protestant congregations, this relationship begins with infant baptism and is usually completed by confirmation around age twelve. In Baptist churches traditionally, children were recognized as having an important role. They were regarded as the objects of all natural affections, but they were also recognized as specially entrusted to Christian families for training in the Lord. Conversions could occur at early ages, of course, but it was generally thought most wise to delay baptism until maturity tested the reality of their conversion.[171] Earlier Baptists understood that time is necessary for

---

[171] Much historical work remains to be done in this area, but the following facts are suggestive. Consider the noted Baptist ministers of the eighteenth and nineteenth centuries. John Gill was brought up in a Baptist home and was baptized at age nineteen in 1716 (just three weeks shy of his twentieth birthday). Samuel Medley was brought up in a Baptist home and was baptized at age twenty-two in December 1760. Richard Furman was brought up in a non-Christian home and was baptized at age seventeen in 1772. John Dagg was baptized in Middleburg, Virginia, at age eighteen in the spring of 1812. J. Newton Brown was baptized in Hudson, New York, at age fourteen in 1817. J. M. Pendleton was baptized near Pembroke, Kentucky, at age eighteen in 1829. P. H. Mell was brought up in a strong Christian home and was baptized at age eighteen in 1832 (according to his biography by his son). J. R. Graves was brought up in a strong Christian home and was baptized at age fifteen in 1835 (O. L. Hailey, *J. R. Graves: Life, Times, Teachings* [Nashville: n.p., 1929]). Sylvanus Dryden Phelps (author of the hymn "Something for Thee") was brought up in a Christian home and was baptized at age twenty-two in 1838 (William Cathcart, *The Baptist Encyclopedia* [Philadelphia: Lewis A. Everts, 1881], 916). John A. Broadus was brought up in a strong Christian home and was baptized at age sixteen in 1843 (A. T. Robertson, *Life and Letters of John A. Broadus* [Philadelphia: American Baptist Publication Society, 1901], 34–35). Charles Fenton James was baptized in 1864 at age twenty in the trenches near Petersburg, Virginia, while he was a Confederate soldier (see George B. Taylor, *Virginia Baptist Ministers* [Lynchburg, VA: J. P. Bell, 1915], 38). C. H. Spurgeon baptized his two sons when they were eighteen (Arnold A. Dallimore, *Spurgeon: A New Biography* [Edinburgh: Banner of Truth, 1984], 181). John R. Sampey

seeing a Christian profession lived out, especially in those who are not yet mature.[172] There seems to be little doubt that, at least in Southern Baptist churches, the last century has seen an increase in nominalism while the average age of baptism has been decreasing. It seems likely the two statistics are not unrelated.

Moreover, concerns with false baptisms (leading to a growing number of rebaptisms) should not be limited to the adverse effects a local church bears when pagans are welcomed into membership and called saints, as serious as those effects are.[173] The effects borne throughout eternity by those unbelievers to whom pastors and churches gave false assurance of salvation beggars the imagination and at the very least discourages haste.

This Matters for the Church's Structure

A right doctrine of the church should affect not only a church's leadership and membership; it should also affect its structure.

Too many in the last generation have derided authority. Authority may well be, as one book title suggested a few years ago, "the most misunderstood idea in America." "Americans do not distinguish authority, which is something good, from authoritarianism, which is something bad."[174] A suspicion of all power because of the abuse of some power holders has created a whole strain of misshapen Christian piety in which the powerlessness of Christ on the cross is viewed as the sole paradigm for all who exercise authority. While a humility should inhere in all Christian exercise of authority, God has also placed leaders within the body to teach, give direction and guidance, be examples, and make decisions (Gal. 6:1; Eph. 4:11; Heb. 13:17). Exercising trust in almost every sphere, whether marriage, family, work, the state, or the church, is for the Christian ultimately a reflection of trust in God.

---

was brought up in a Christian home and was baptized at age thirteen in 1877 (*Memoirs* [Nashville: Broadman, 1947], 7). He had already worked on his father's farm. E. Y. Mullins was brought up in the home of a Baptist minister in Texas and was baptized at age twenty in 1880. The above pastors all had jobs by the time they were baptized. H. Wheeler Robinson was brought up by a Christian mother in Northampton, England, and was baptized at age sixteen in 1888. This delay is still typical among most Baptists in Africa, Europe, and elsewhere overseas. Consider, for example, the practice in France. "Positioned in the middle of the service, it [baptism] serves as the centerpiece of worship. Baptism in France tends to come at a later age—sixteen is the youngest—and candidates always testify in the service before being baptized. While these traditions and practices seem a bit strange, the result is a vibrant and dynamic faith that puts Baptists on the cutting edge of the evangelical movement in France and Europe." C. Frank Thomas in Cecil P. Staton Jr., ed., *Why I Am a Baptist* (Macon, GA: Smyth & Helwys, 1999), 170.

[172] See Dennis Gunderson, *Your Child's Profession of Faith* (Amityville: Calvary, 1994) and Jim Elliff, *Childhood Conversions* (Parkville: Christian Communicators Worldwide, 1997).

[173] See "Adults Baptized in Southern Baptist Churches, 1993" *RR* (Winter 1995).

[174] Eugene Kennedy and Sara Charles, *Authority: The Most Misunderstood Idea in America* (New York, Free Press, 1997), 1.

Denominational battles within the Southern Baptist Convention in the last century have spawned a virulent strain of novel and naive Baptist history which suggests it is the essence of Baptist identity to be individualistic, cantankerous, and divisive. The rich Protestant doctrine of the priesthood of all believers,[175] originally formulated to oppose a mediatorial class of ordained Roman Catholic priests, has been transfigured into the optimistic and simplistic early twentieth-century phrase (by E. Y. Mullins) "soul competency." A biblically faithful emphasis on the sole mediatorship of Christ (the Reformation emphasis) has been traded (wittingly?) for a mistaken defense of human ability.

At best, the idea of soul competency simply restates one implication of the fact that humans are created in the image of God—that we are made spiritual beings who are able to have a relationship with God. At worst, the idea degenerates into a semireligious humanism in which proclaiming Christ's work becomes unnecessary. Following in the train of this misused doctrine, every locus of theology is reshaped—from the atonement to the inspiration of Scripture. In ecclesiology it tends to undermine ideas of authority and leadership in the church. But leadership is a gift from God and should be received by churches as a gift. Rejecting leadership deprives the church of Christ's gift, impoverishes the body, and hinders the church in its life and work.

One factor that has led many local congregations either to adopt an elder-led model or to avoid such model, has been the increasing controversy in popular culture over gender-based distinctions. After all, the New Testament is relatively clear on reserving the office of elder for men. But a society that has dismissed gender as an appropriate boundary marker for marriage is a society that has long ago lost any sense of gender roles in the church. Historically, the church took the New Testament's teaching on male eldership at face value. But that position was slowly abandoned in twentieth-century America. In 1924, the Methodist Episcopal Church voted to ordain women. They were followed by the main body of northern Presbyterians in 1956, and then the Episcopalians in 1976, and finally the main Lutheran body in 1979.[176] Among the new Pentecostal movements, Aimee Semple McPherson, Kathryn Kuhlman, and other women had prominent teaching ministries.

Among Baptist churches, the movement toward female ordination has been slower, but the process has undoubtedly been aided by extrabiblical structures such as committees, church councils, and staff positions, which

---

[175] For an excellent treatment of this doctrine, see Timothy George, "The Priesthood of All Believers and the Quest for Theological Integrity," *CTR* 3 (1989): 283–94.

[176] See Mark Noll, *A History of Christianity in the United States and Canada* (Grand Rapids: Eerdmans, 1992), 513.

are neither mandated nor described in Scripture, and which have, therefore, been more easily filled with women—even in otherwise biblically conservative churches. Moving to a plurality of elders brings clear biblical passages to bear that support male leadership in the congregation.[177]

This Matters for the Church's Culture

Not only are matters of leadership, membership, and formal structure affected by a doctrine of the church; so too are matters of the church's culture.

Along with the hard and defined skeletal structure of a church, there is also the more subtle, changeable, variable, and enveloping culture of a church. The culture of a church is constituted by the combination of peculiar expectations and practices that do not make the church a church but that do in fact typify a particular congregation. Suppose then that a congregation is marked by graciousness, a concern for truth, and a zeal for missions. These qualities are certainly appropriate and consistent with the scriptural presentation of a church, but they are not specifically required of every congregation in order to be recognized as a true church.

That said, the soundness of a church is greatly improved when the congregation cultivates a culture of discipleship and growth in which individual Christian growth is normal, not exceptional. One indicator of growth, moreover, is an increasing level of concern for the spiritual state of others. A concern for others should include non-Christians around the world (thus an emphasis on missions), in the congregation's own local area (thus an emphasis on evangelism), and especially for other members of the congregation (thus an emphasis on discipling one another). A culture of discipling, evangelism, and missions will best encourage the church to be what God has made it to be—a reflection of his own character.

Ranged against this radiant vision of the church is a large and growing nominalism in many evangelical churches today. Congregation after congregation is marked by membership roles filled with nonattending "members." Even among those members who do attend, too many live lives indistinct from the nonbelievers around them. This nominalism dulls and undercuts Christian evangelism; it pushes the church and individual Christians toward disillusionment, apathetic discouragement, or division;

---

[177] See Grudem and Rainey, *Pastoral Leadership.* It should be noted that genuinely biblical leadership is consensual, not coercive, and is concerned with guiding and serving, not "lording it over" others in pride. Should more secularly conceived questions of power be raised, it must be remembered that in most congregations women comprise the majority of members, so women could organize as women (along with men who agreed with them) at any time and change their church's practice, if they became convinced that the positions laid out in this chapter, and traditionally practiced by Christians, were in error.

and ultimately it dishonors God.[178] Surely if ecclesiology is to have any relevance today, this situation must be addressed. Evangelicals have advanced various answers to today's decline in churches. Space here permits a brief mention of only a few.

Since the beginning of the twentieth century, the rise of Pentecostalism has arguably been the most significant sociological development in world Christianity. The Christian landscapes in Africa and South America have been transformed, and more established churches in Europe and North America have been affected. Many of these Christians think the answer to the church's problems lies in rediscovering the biblical teaching of the baptism of the Holy Spirit. Many Pentecostals say this experience, which includes speaking in unknown tongues, signifies conversion. Many newer charismatics say the baptism of the Holy Spirit is a second experience intended for every believer after conversion. They believe that Christians invigorated by this baptism would replace the lamentable and dull witness of too many Christians and their congregations.

Other groups of Christians have suggested that the answer to nominal Christianity lies in recovering the dynamic of smaller groups, in which no function exists for inactive members. This has been variously advocated through the use of small groups, the cell church structure, and the house church movement.[179] Some have even advocated setting low quantitative limits on congregations, saying that anything beyond the set limit turns churches into mere "preaching points" and undermines the ability of the pastor to pastor as well as the ability of members to meaningfully involve themselves with other members in ministry.

Still other Christians have given up on the traditional local and heterogeneous congregation. This despair or rejection can be observed in the growth philosophy that recommends forming whole congregations around a single vision statement. It is also seen in some "purpose-driven" models. The rejection of heterogeneity is even more pronounced in congregations who set their mission on one homogeneous group, whether defined eth-

---

[178] Surveying the state of the churches in the mid-nineteenth century, John L. Dagg wrote, "Much that has existed, and that now exists, among the professed followers of Christ, cannot be contemplated by one who sincerely loves him, without deep distress," *Church Order,* 11. A century and a half later, John Piper reflected on the disturbing state of many churches today. "The injustice and persecution and suffering and hellish realities in the world today are so many and so large and so close that I can't help but think that, deep inside, people are longing for something weighty and massive and rooted and stable and eternal. So it seems to me that the trifling with silly little sketches and breezy welcome-to-the-den styles on Sunday morning are just out of touch with what matters in life. . . . I doubt that a religious ethos with such a feel of entertainment can really survive as Christian for too many more decades." *Counted Righteous in Christ* (Wheaton: Crossway, 2002), 22–23.

[179] Mark Dever, "The Priesthood of All Believers: Reconsidering Every Member Ministry," in *The Compromised Church,* ed. John H. Armstrong (Wheaton: Crossway, 1998), 85–116.

nically, generationally, sociodemographically, or otherwise. The homogeneous unit principle lies behind this approach—the recognition that in mission settings, like reaches like. Members of one caste in India, for example, will have more difficulty reaching individuals from a different caste. Yet the homogeneous unit principle has reordered the ecclesiology of many churches in the name of evangelism. Its logical conclusion is the rejection of the whole congregation in exchange for a missional parachurch subgroup, though they may continue referring to themselves as a church.

Still others who call themselves Christians have perceived the doleful state of many congregations and have concluded the organized congregation should simply be rejected. This rejection can occur publicly, as with radio preacher Harold Camping's pronouncement that Christians should desert the churches because the church age has ended.[180] Or it can occur more quietly, as when individuals simply desist in church participation. Yet in both cases, self-defined Christians will emphasize something like Jesus' teaching on the heart or doctrines like justification by faith alone in order to justify their rejection of the congregation's role in the Christian life. In short, nominalism and hypocrisy in churches are used to justify noninvolvement.

Others place the church's hope for recovery in re-creating excitement. Many authors and pastors appeal to a convert's experience of newness, a historical church's experience in a time of revival, or even the young church in the book of Acts in order to argue the best way forward is to replicate such excitement. While specific diagnoses of problems vary, most solutions tend toward a "give them what they want" pragmatism. Evangelism begins to resemble marketing, and church membership begins to resemble consumerism.

Still others believe the problems in the churches stem from a wrong (or at least unnecessary) focus on the subjective appropriation of the Christian faith by individuals. In response, they advocate refocusing on the objective ordinances, or sacraments, of the church, not on individual responses of piety. Such sacramentalist responses can be found in great variety. Some multiservice congregations are offering alternative high-church services. Some in the Emerging Church movement are re-engaging with pre-Reformation (and in some cases pre-Christian) practices of spirituality without fully comprehending the pre-Reformation understanding of the gospel often latent in such practices.[181]

---

[180] Though it must be noted with amazement that this elderly radio preacher has announced the church age has been succeeded by the "radio age." See J. Ligon Duncan and Mark Talbot, *Should We Leave Our Churches? A Biblical Response to Harold Camping* (Phillipsburg: Presbyterian and Reformed, 2004).

[181] For further discussion of the emerging church, see D. A. Carson, *Becoming Conversant with the Emerging Church* (Grand Rapids: Zondervan, 2005).

Among the Reformed, some are calling for an objectivism in the Christian life and profession that seems to deny any role for personal piety and subjective response to the gospel. Instead, they are promoting a "federal vision" built specifically in opposition to what they regard as problematic evangelical pietism.[182] More generally, many Protestant evangelicals are increasingly rejecting whatever is specifically evangelical or Protestant and replacing such distinctives with "the Great Tradition."[183]

To these and many other putative solutions to current problems in the churches, recourse must be relentlessly taken to Scripture. A clear understanding of the gospel is foundational for any genuine renewal in evangelical churches. Solutions treated as normative but that are not found in Scripture must be rejected as latter-day tradition that lacks the authority of the apostles. Ecclesiology cannot be reduced either to evangelism or to self-enhancement. In the Christian church the reigning consumer must become the repenting sinner, and the Christ-ordained sacraments are better not received than being received without personal faith (1 Cor. 11:30). God creates his church by his Spirit through his Word. All other answers to the lack of discipleship in too many of today's churches compound the problems they intend to address.

This Matters for the Church's Character

The culture of the church, like the life of an individual, simply reflects the church's character. If the doctrine of the church enunciated in this chapter is to be applied, the practice of corrective church discipline must be recovered.

The recovery of church discipline will require viewing it as a natural part of church membership. It should be taught in new members classes. It should be addressed in sermons, testimonies, and newsletters. And books on the topic can be recommended. Too many people treat this topic apologetically and act as if admitting to the practice of discipline is regrettable. While the sin and its tragic consequences requiring discipline

---

[182] See, for example, the works of Douglas Wilson. See also *The Auburn Avenue Theology Pros and Cons: Debating the Federal Vision,* a Knox Theological Seminary Colloquium on the Federal Vision (Ft. Lauderdale: Knox Theological Seminary, 2004).

[183] For appeals to the Great Tradition's attempt to recapture the essence of Christian unity before the schisms of the Middle Ages and Renaissance, see InterVarsity's Ancient Christians Commentary series, *Touchstone* magazine, and frequent allusions in Richard John Neuhaus's *First Things.* Sadly, too many of the so-called Protestant advocates of the Great Tradition take the Roman Catholic position in the Reformation-era debates about the apostolicity of certain practices and doctrines. Concern for the teachings of the church fathers is nothing new among evangelicals. It was prominent in the work of Martin Luther, John Calvin, Thomas Cranmer, John Jewel, and other Reformers across Europe. But today's disputants lack the Reformers' experience of having lived in a Roman Catholic church that was unchallenged by Scripture and loaded down with centuries' worth of doctrinal accretions, accretions that had not been sifted by apostolic teaching.

are of course regrettable, the attempt to correctively discipline unrepentant sin is not. When done in humility, prayer, and love, it edifies the body and glorifies God.[184]

One caution is in order here. Church discipline will seem odd and even offensive if introduced into a congregation not marked by a culture of mutual care, a desire to be involved in one another's lives, and a passion for discipling in the faith. A pastor may desire to be obedient to Scripture, but congregations will feel the deep involvement in their lives required by the practice of discipline is unnatural and wrong if things like church covenants and membership expectations have not been clearly taught. The first step toward practicing church discipline in a congregation is simply teaching the people to pray and care for one another. Learning to love and disciple one another—truly practicing the priesthood of all believers—is a prerequisite to introducing corrective discipline. Formative discipline must precede corrective discipline.

Church discipline provides one part of the necessary response to the nominalism prevalent in churches today. Pastors must consider that following biblical instructions in every area of church life—including their practices of membership admission and discipline—may be the key to health lacking in their churches. If pastors desire sinners to repent, they must realize that discipline is a biblical way to pursue that. If church leaders want their congregations to be characterized by thankfulness of heart and holiness of life, they should reexamine their practice of church discipline. The health of the whole church would be radically improved in many congregations by excommunicating those members who are committed to sins like nonattendance, divisiveness, adultery, or fornication more than they are committed to God's glory. The action of excluding the unrepentant enables the church to give a clear witness of the gospel to the world. And it ultimately brings glory to God, as his people more and more display his character of holy love.

This Matters for God's Glory

John L. Dagg concluded his introduction to his *Treatise on Church Order* with this appropriate admonition:

> Church order and the ceremonials of religion, are less important than a new heart; and in the view of some, any laborious investigation of questions respecting them may appear to be needless and unprofitable. But we know, from the Holy Scriptures, that Christ gave

---

[184] For good practical instructions on carrying out church discipline, see Jay Adams, *Handbook of Church Discipline* (Grand Rapids: Ministry Resources Library, 1986) and Dever, *Polity*.

commands on these subjects, and we cannot refuse to obey. Love prompts our obedience; and love prompts also the search which may be necessary to ascertain his will. Let us, therefore, prosecute the investigations which are before us, with a fervent prayer, that the Holy Spirit, who guides into all truth, may assist us to learn the will of him whom we supremely love and adore.[185]

Many Protestants have begun to think that because the church is not essential to the gospel, it is not important to the gospel. This is an unbiblical, false, and dangerous conclusion. Our churches are the proof of the gospel. In the gatherings of the church, the Christian Scriptures are read. In the ordinances of the church, the work of Christ is depicted. In the life of the church, the character of God himself should be evident. A church seriously compromised in character would seem to make the gospel itself irrelevant.

The doctrine of the church is important because it is tied to the good news itself. The church is to be the appearance of the gospel. It is what the gospel looks like when played out in the lives of people. Take away the church and you take away the visible manifestation of the gospel in the world. Christians in churches, then, are called to practice "display evangelism," and the world will witness the reign of God begun in a community of people made in his image and reborn by his Spirit. Christians, not just as individuals but as God's people bound together in churches, are the clearest picture that the world sees of the invisible God and what his will is for them.

Jesus said, "By this all men will know that you are my disciples, if you love one another" (John 13:35). Paul would add, "His intent was that now, through the church, the manifold wisdom of God should be made known to the rulers and authorities in the heavenly realms, according to his eternal purpose which he accomplished in Christ Jesus our Lord" (Eph. 3:10–11).

---

[185] Dagg, *Treatise on Church Order,* 14.

SECTION 8

THE DOCTRINE OF LAST THINGS

CHAPTER 14

Personal and Cosmic Eschatology

Russell D. Moore

A Christian's eschatology does not consist in his prophecy charts but in his funeral service. At a funeral the church is perhaps at its most theological. Our crying reminds us that death is not natural but a horrible curse to be abhorred. Our recitation of Psalm 23 and John 11 reminds us that in Christ we have already been delivered from the power of death—that his story is our story. Our placing the body in a casket reminds us of the metaphor of sleep used often in Scripture to convey to us that one who sleeps will also wake. Our burying the body in the earth reminds us that we are only creatures, formed from the clay—but creatures who will one day be called forth from the dust once again. At a funeral our hymnody is the most theological, the most resistant to the fads and trends of Christian music. We sing of looking across "Jordan's Stormy Banks," of understanding things better "By and By, When the Morning Comes." That's because all of Christian theology points to an end—an end where Jesus overcomes the satanic reign of death and restores God's original creation order.

This overarching story—with a beginning, a middle, and an end—makes sense of the smaller stories of each of our individual lives. In Scripture the eschaton is not simply tacked on to the gospel at the end. It is instead the vision toward which all of Scripture is pointing—and the vision that grounds the hope of the gathered church and the individual believer. In the face of death, we see faith, hope, and love. This is what we mean when we speak of Christian eschatology—the study of the last things or ultimate matters.

What Does the Bible Say?

Perhaps clearer than any other set of doctrines, eschatology reminds us that the Bible is one coherent story, with one author and one theme. The story line begins in an innocent garden and ends in a glorious garden city, with a bloody and violent war in between. All along the way the Scripture speaks of God's purpose to build a kingdom for his anointed, incarnate Son as the firstborn among many brothers. Eschatology, then, is inherently messianic—in both Old and New Testaments. Thus, one cannot understand

God's ultimate purposes unless one understands that God's purposes find their goal and content in Jesus Christ.

The Old Testament

Eschatology as Cosmic

The opening passages of Scripture reveal something of God's eschatological purposes since they present God's pleasure in the creation of the entire cosmic order, both the heavens and earth. Man's image-bearing vice-regency under the Creator is "over the fish of the sea and over the birds of the heavens and over the livestock and over all the earth and over every creeping thing that creeps on the earth" (Gen. 1:26).[1] The curse that comes about as a result of the Adamic fall is likewise cosmic in its extent—resulting in a disruption of the natural order, a degradation of the animal creation, a frustration of human labor, spiritual alienation from God, a conflict between the human and demonic realms, disharmony between the sexes, and a bloody reign of death extending eastward from Eden (Gen. 3:14–23). The judgment of God on the creation at the Noahic flood typifies God's final judgment—one that is cosmic in its extent and is followed by a new creation (Gen. 6:9–9:17; 2 Pet. 3:4–13).

The promises of God of a restoration of the creation include material blessings, the inheritance of land promised to the descendants of Abraham, the defeat of all enemies, and *shalom* for the people of God in a new order. God typifies these promises by bringing Abraham's seed into the land of Canaan but always with another horizon before them of a permanent, cosmic restoration in which all their enemies are under their feet and all is set right with the creation. Throughout the prophets, the Spirit points to a final order in which the curse on creation is reversed: animal predation is no more (Isa. 11:6–9), nature itself will be in harmony with humanity (Isa. 60:19–22), the demonic order is crushed (Isa. 27:1; Hab. 3:13), and all the nations stream to Israel bringing their wealth into her gates (Isa. 60:1–14; Micah 4:1–5).

The picture then is not of an eschatological flight from creation but the restoration and redemption of creation with all that entails: table fellowship, community, culture, economics, agriculture and animal husbandry, art, architecture, worship—in short, *life* and that abundantly.

Against this hope lies the reality of cosmic death—a reality rooted in the persistence of human death. The Old Testament affirms the inevitability of human death in the post-Eden epochs. "We must all die," says a woman to King David. "We are like water spilled on the ground, which

---

[1] Unless otherwise noted, all Scripture citations in this chapter are from the English Standard Version (ESV).

cannot be gathered up again" (2 Sam. 14:14). The psalmist speaks of the life of a man as "an evening shadow" that withers "like grass" in contrast with the immortality and covenant faithfulness of Israel's God (Ps. 102:11–12). He speaks of the frailty of human existence in the face of death, a brief time for those whose frame is but dust (Ps. 103:13–19). In Ecclesiastes, Solomon finds only vanity in light of a certain death; a death that wipes away all intellectual insight, bodily pleasure, or economic achievement and that comes to all whether great or trivial, righteous or wicked (Eccl. 9:1–10). But even here Solomon's despair turns to trust in the God whose purposes alone make sense of the seeming vanity of human existence (Eccl. 12:1–14).

Contrary to the claims of most contemporary biblical scholarship, the Old Testament never concludes that human life ends at the grave, nor does the text assume that the "afterlife" is a shadowy land of despair.[2] The Old Testament teaches that personal consciousness survives death. This is seen in relatively mysterious passages such as King Saul's hiring of the witch at Endor to summon the dead Prophet Samuel from the beyond (1 Sam. 28:8–19). Even the Preacher of Ecclesiastes ended his discourse on the shortness of life and the inevitability of death with the warning that there is a judgment coming in which God will bring "every deed into judgment, with every secret thing, whether good or evil" (Eccl. 12:14).

Moreover, the Old Testament Scriptures teach not only personal consciousness after death but also the resurrection of the body. Job hoped for the day when, in his flesh, he would see the Creator in whom he trusted (Job 19:25–27). The Prophet Daniel foresaw a day of cosmic tumult, followed by the judgment of humanity. On that day, he revealed, the graves will be opened, and God's people will be resurrected in honor and glory and God's enemies will be resurrected in defeat and judgment (Dan. 12:1–3).

But this hope of resurrection is about more than personal survival after death (although it is certainly not about less than that). It is about the cosmic purposes of a Creator God. The prophetic Scriptures point to the day when death itself, human and animal, is wiped away from the cosmos (Isa. 25:6–9; Ezek. 37:1–14). But, before this final order, the Old Testament prophets pointed to a Day of the Lord, a time of cosmic disturbance in which the heavens and the earth are tossed about and come under the fearful judgment of Israel's God (Joel 3:14–16). The Prophet Elijah will return to point the nation of Israel toward her king, before the "great and awesome day of the LORD" (Mal. 4:5–6). Then—and only then—comes the peace of the final messianic order.

---

2 For a fairly typical contemporary rendering of the idea of Hebrew development toward the idea of an afterlife, see Alan F. Segal, *Life after Death: A History of the Afterlife in Western Religion* (New York: Doubleday, 2004).

Eschatology as Covenantal

God's cosmic purposes are also intensely personal and particular, seen in the way God has chosen to bring about these purposes through covenant promise and fulfillment, mediated through the line of Abraham. After demonstrating God's creational origin of the whole universe—and his salvation of all animal and human life through the Noahic flood, God builds a vision of the end of all things through covenant promises with a chosen people, beginning with Abraham. The Abrahamic covenant promised material land, a name of great renown, and a multitude of offspring (Gen. 12:1–7; 17:1–14).

Thus, faith itself is defined as forward-looking and eschatological from the beginning—as Abraham offered up the promised son, knowing God could raise him from the dead (Gen. 22:1–19; Heb. 11:17–19) and as Joseph pleaded with his brothers to carry his bones into the promised land, knowing that his death could not annul God's covenant purposes for Israel (Gen. 50:25; Josh. 24:32; Heb. 11:22).

With the foundation of the Abrahamic promise, God further reveals the contours of biblical hope. Through the Mosaic covenant he outlines the blessings of an obedient nation and the curses of a disobedient people. In the Davidic covenant he promises a son to David who will build a dwelling place for God, defeat God's enemies, and rule the people in the wisdom of the Spirit (2 Sam. 7; Pss. 2; 73; 89). In the prophesied new covenant God promises to unite the fractured nations of Israel and Judah into one people, a people who all know Yahweh, are forgiven of their sins, and are restored as a nation in the promised land (Jer. 31:31–40).

The covenants look forward—past Israel's then-present disobedience—to the day when the vine of God bears fruit (Ps. 80:8–19; Isa. 5:1–7; 27:6; Ezek. 15:1–8; 17:1–24; 19:10–14; Hos. 10:1–2), the harlot of God's people is a faithful bride washed of all uncleanness (Isa. 54:5–6; Jer. 3:20; Ezek. 16:1–63; Hos. 2:1–23), the exiled refugees are returned to a secure homeland, and the flock of God is united under one Davidic shepherd who will feed them and divide them from the goats (Jer. 3:15–19; 23:1–8; Ezek. 34:1–31; Micah 5:2–4; 7:14–17). In this coming future Israel will be what she is called to be, the light of the world, a light that the darkness cannot overcome (Isa. 60:1–3). In this future God's favor on Israel is clear to the nations because he is present with his people. The repeated promise of the covenants is: "I will be your God and you will be my people." As Joel prophesies: "You shall know that I am in the midst of Israel, that I am the LORD your God and there is none else" (Joel 2:27).

With this in view, the covenants picture their fulfillment not just in terms of inheritance blessings but also in terms of a restoration of Eden (Ezek. 36:33–36; 37:22–23), the building of a glorious temple (2 Sam.

7:13; Ezek. 40:1–47:12), the return of a remnant from exile (Isa. 11:12–16), and the construction of a holy city of Zion in which Yahweh dwells with his people in splendor (Pss. 48:1–14; 74:2; Isa. 18:7; Lam. 5:17–22; Ezek. 48:30–35).[3] The covenants will come to their goal when Israel is judged for sin, raised from the dead, and anointed with the Spirit of Yahweh—a public act in the face of the hostile nations (Ezek. 20:21, 35–49; 37:11–27). These eschatological covenant promises are then inherently eschatological and messianic—a truth seen in the fact that the patriarchs themselves died and rotted away without seeing the realization of the promises (Heb. 11:13–16).

Eschatology as Kingdom

The cosmic and covenantal aspects of biblical eschatology are realized through kingship—specifically the establishment of the kingdom of God. Although the "kingdom of God" is not referenced by name in this way in the Old Testament, the concept is present throughout—a concept that Jesus and the apostles point to constantly in the New Testament. The kingdom is not seen in the Old Testament as simply the general sovereignty of God, although such divine kingship is everywhere affirmed (Ps. 103:19, for example). The kingdom of God is instead the reign of God through his human mediator-king over a world in submission to his righteous rule. This envisions the restoration of the Edenic order when God ruled through a human vice-regent, Adam, and put "all things under his feet" (Ps. 8:5–8).

This human rule is now disrupted, as the king and queen of the cosmos listened to a beast (over whom they were to rule) rather than to the Word of God. Thus, in animal predation, decay, natural disturbances, and death, we hear the universe asking, with its Creator: "Adam, where are you?" (see Gen. 3:9).

The prophecies speak, however, of this God-anointed human rule resumed, as a human warrior-king from Abraham's line defeats the satanic usurper, offers atonement for the human sin, and reclaims the kingdom for the sons and daughters of Adam. Moments after the Edenic fall, God warns the serpent that the seed of the woman would crush his reptilian head (Gen. 3:15). This kingdom promise is further seen as God typifies a prophet-leader in Moses but tells us there is another prophet like him who is yet to come (Deut. 18:15–19). Joshua typifies a warrior-leader who, routing his enemies before him, leads the people to the land of promise. In both the cases of Moses and Joshua, God listens to the voice of his human mediator, in interceding for the people's sins (Exod. 32:11–14) and in

---

[3] For an excellent discussion of an Old Testament eschatology of temple and presence, see Gregory K. Beale, *The Temple and the Church's Mission: A Biblical Theology of the Dwelling Place of God* (Downers Grove: InterVarsity, 2004).

commanding the natural order for the purpose of Israel's victory in battle (Josh. 10:1–14).

Along the way the Old Testament demonstrates graphically the lack of restraint and the moral chaos that come with no kingship (the book of Judges), with wicked or inept kingship (Saul, the narratives of 1 and 2 Kings), and with tyrannical foreign dictatorship (the Assyrians and the Babylonians). The text demonstrates the promise for the future, however, in the kingship of the shepherd-warrior David and in his son Solomon. David is anointed with the Spirit, a mighty defender of Israel, and one who points to the ways in which the coming King will suffer for the nation before Israel's enemies while seeking final vindication from God (Pss. 22; 69). David, however, is not the final messianic king. He ends shivering weakly beneath his bedcovers (1 Kings 1:1–4).

For one brief, shining moment, Solomon has his enemies under his feet, is anointed with the Spirit, builds a glorious temple, and sees the nations stream into the city of the great king (1 Kings 2–10). And yet he too is seen not to be the long-expected Son of David, as he too falls for the serpent's snares (sexual immorality, idolatry) and also succumbs to the curse of death. The whole history of Israel then is one of failing kings and a divided, then vanquished kingdom.

Throughout all of this, Zion's coming king and his kingdom are revealed. Jacob himself prophesies that one from the tribe of Judah will have preeminence and will rule over the other tribes (Gen. 49:9–12). The soothsayer Balaam sees through the revelation of God one coming from Judah who will exercise dominion and defeat the enemies of God (Num. 24:15–19). God tells David that his coming son will build a temple for God and that God will build a house for the king (2 Sam. 7:8–17). God promises to rescue the king from death and his enemies and seat him on a throne forever. The king will be an anointed one, a "Christ," anointed with the Spirit of God himself, which has always been the divine mark of legitimate kingship.

As with David and Solomon, this Spirit anointing will grant the coming Christ wisdom to judge the people of God and power to defeat the enemies of God (Isa. 11:1–5; 42:1–2; 61:1–11). The Spirit that rests on the Messiah will be his forever, but the prophets also speak of the Spirit being poured out on all flesh (Joel 2:28–32)—hinting at the coming reality of a head-body relationship between the Christ and his people. In the same vein the Prophet Isaiah speaks of a Spirit-anointed Root of Jesse who also has a fruit-bearing branch (Isa. 11:1–2), imagery later used of Jesus for the Spirit relation between himself and his ecclesial body (John 15). This messianic kingdom will rout the defiant spirits and nations, will serve as a model for God's creation purposes, will vindicate Israel's covenant claims, and will restore shalom to the universe in both its human and nonhuman aspects.

The messianic king will come with humility and lowliness, but his glorious rule will extend to the ends of the earth (Zech. 9:9–10). Coming from Galilee, this "light of the nations" shall inherit the Davidic throne and rule the earth in justice and with permanence (Isa. 9:1–7). The Prophet Daniel summarized the Israelite messianic eschatology when he surveyed the risings and fallings of human nations and then prophesied that kingdom will be given to a "son of man" from the Ancient of Days (Dan. 7:13–14). Again, here is language of human rule over creation ("son of man," Ps. 8), and yet this rule is clearly more than simply human. The kingdom of this Christ, Daniel foresaw, will crush the other kingdoms, and it will remain forever (Dan. 7:14).

The New Testament

Eschatology as Already

The kingdom of God dawns in a peasant Jewish virgin's uterus. The kingdom of God prophecies of the Old Testament find their goal in Jesus of Galilee, who is himself the promised King and the bearer of the kingdom and who inaugurated the kingdom two thousand years ago. The New Testament repeatedly emphasizes that Jesus is the descendant of Abraham and of David (Matt. 1:1–17; Luke 3:23–38). As the angel Gabriel put it to the young girl of the house of David: "He will be great and will be called the Son of the Most High. And the Lord God will give to him the throne of his father David, and he will reign over the house of Jacob forever, and of his kingdom there will be no end" (Luke 1:32–33), evoking both Abrahamic and Davidic promises.

When he is conceived, Mary sings a song of the triumph of the kingdom that echoes the song of Hannah over a thousand years earlier in view of the coming Davidic kingdom (1 Sam. 2; Luke 1:46–55). Like Hannah, Mary is convinced that God will keep his promises to the patriarchs and that he exalts the humble and humbles the exalted.

The Gospels apply the covenant fulfillments to Jesus directly, equating him with Israel itself. Indeed Jesus recapitulates the life of Israel. Like Israel under pagan rule, he escapes from a baby-murdering tyrant and is brought out of Egypt. "Out of Egypt I called my son," says Hosea, referencing the exodus of God's "son" Israel from Egypt, and yet Matthew applies this prophetically to the young Jesus (Matt. 2:15; Hos. 11:1). The nations, represented by eastern magi, stream to Jesus and give him gifts of frankincense and myrrh (Matt. 2:1–12), exactly as Isaiah had promised (Isa. 60:1–6). Jesus is identified as the messianic King by a prophet who is spiritually, Jesus says, the fulfillment of Malachi's promise of a returning Elijah (John 1:19–34). Jesus is then anointed by the Holy Spirit and is pronounced the regal Son of God, as he passes through the Jordan River and immediately takes on the enemy of God's people (Matt. 3:13–4:1).

In the temptation accounts, Jesus wanders for forty days in the wilderness, where he is tempted (1) with food, (2) with proving God's vindication of him, and (3) with grasping for the kingdom promises (Matt. 4:1–11; Luke 4:1–13). He explicitly ties these events to Israel's wilderness wanderings when Israel believed their present plight annulled their revealed eschatology. Jesus, however, overcomes. Advancing forward God's kingdom, Jesus applies temple language to himself—to his own body (Matt. 12:6). Like Ezekiel's eschatological temple, the living water of the Spirit flows from Jesus bringing life as it streams toward the tree of life (Ezek. 47:1–12; John 7:37–39).

Jesus applies the vine language of Israel to himself—and to his disciples as branches sharing the blessings with him. He speaks of himself as the Davidic shepherd-king who will fight the wolves and establish the flock of Israel under one head (Mark 14:27; John 10:1–21). Like the prophecy of Israel's latter-day glory, Jesus announces that he is the "light of the world" in whom the nations will see God (John 8:12–20). Jesus applies Israel's language of the coming restoration of the nation by the Spirit to personal regeneration and entrance into the kingdom itself. He confronts a teacher of Israel inquiring why he would not know that only the regenerate remnant of the nation can enter the promised kingdom (John 3:1–13). When Jesus is rejected by Israel, he announces that the prophets of old foresaw this aspect of the kingdom as well (John 12:36–43).

In his teaching, Jesus explicitly announces the onset of the kingdom of God. He applies Isaiah's prophecy of the anointing of the Spirit and the onset of the Day of the Lord to himself (Luke 4:16–21). He teaches the ways in which the new kingdom realities sharply change the ways God's people are to live with one another and with the world (Matt. 5–7; Luke 5:17–6:49). He applies the inheritance language of Israel (the meek inheriting the land, Ps. 37:11,22) directly to his followers now (the meek shall inherit the earth, Matt. 5:5). Jesus demonstrates that, unlike for Adam, nature itself is "under his feet," as his voice itself commands tumultuous winds and waves to be still (Matt. 8:23–27; Mark 4:35–41). He has authority over death as he turns back disease and raises those who have died, just as the prophets promised would happen in the last days (Luke 7:1–23; 8:40–56). He casts out demons through his Spirit anointing and announces to the religious authorities of Israel, "But if it is by the Spirit of God that I cast out demons, then the kingdom of God has come upon you" (Matt. 12:28). When asked by the Pharisees when the promised kingdom would come, Jesus tells them, "The kingdom of God is in the midst of you" (Luke 17:2–22). When followers mention the eschatological day of resurrection, Jesus says, "I am the resurrection" and "I am the way" (John 11:24–25; 14:6). Jesus speaks of his inauguration of the kingdom as signaling the judgment and eviction of Satan as the "ruler of this world" (John 12:31; 14:30; 16:11), as God is once again restoring his rule through a human mediatorial King. This is seen in Jesus' triumphal entry into the holy city Jerusalem when he fulfills the Prophet Zechariah's promise of a humble messianic King riding on a donkey, foreshadowing the global rule that is to follow (Matt. 21:1–11).

At his crucifixion Jesus relives the attack of the nations and the abandonment by God typified by his ancestor David. The curses of the Mosaic Law come upon Israel there. With Day of the Lord imagery, the sky turns dark and the earth quakes. As David was warned, the kingly son of David is beaten with rods as the discipline of God, though not for his own sins but the sins of the world (2 Sam. 7:14–15; Ps. 89:32–33; Matt. 27:29–30; Mark 15:19). The Gentile nations mock him—even gambling for the faux royal garments with which they had mocked his claimed kingship (John 9:16–24).

He is a hanged man and thus, according to Deuteronomy, exempt from the inheritance promises of Israel—and indeed the sight of such a cursed man imperils the nation's inheritance of the land (Deut. 21:22–23). He must be removed and buried immediately. Jesus speaks prospectively of this crucifixion as a fiery baptism he must undergo in order to receive his kingdom (Matt. 3:11–12; Mark 10:35–40; Luke 12:49–50), evoking the language used by the prophets of the coming fiery judgment of God upon his people Israel (Ezek. 20:48).

By his resurrection Jesus marks the cataclysmic onset of the new kingdom order. As Israel was promised, the righteous remnant—one man—is raised from the dead through the Spirit in view of the nations. Upon his resurrection Jesus identifies his disciples as his "brothers" (John 20:17)—language used in the Old Testament to identify the parameters of the inheritance, the people of Israel (Lev. 25:46; Deut. 17:15, 20). He eats with his disciples and commands Peter to "feed my sheep"—royal imagery that speaks of the coming of the last days of glory of Jerusalem in a restored Israel (Jer. 3:15–18). When Jesus' disciples ask him if he plans now to restore the kingdom to Israel, Jesus points to the coming of the Holy Spirit and the apostolic authority to proclaim the kingdom to the nations (Acts 1:6–8).

In Jesus' resurrection from the dead, the apostles see the onset of the last days—the enthronement of the promised messianic king. At Pentecost, the disciples proclaim that the long-awaited eschatological Spirit has now been poured out on Jesus' disciples, thus signaling that God has vindicated him as the true Israel, the righteous Son of David, and the faithful King whom God will not abandon to the grave (Acts 2:14–41; Rom. 1:1–4). The coming of the Spirit is seen as a sign that God's anointing was upon Jesus, an anointing he has now poured out on those who identify with him (Acts 2:34). This means that Jesus is the Davidic Messiah whose enemies will be made a footstool for his feet, in keeping with the ancient prophecies.

Peter identifies the coming of the Spirit with the Prophet Joel's promise of the last days and the climactic Day of the Lord (Acts 2:16–21). In the resurrection the apostles preach God is keeping his promises to Abraham and to David, and through it God will bring about the promised restoration of Israel (Acts 3:17–26).

The Apostle Paul joins with the other apostles in hailing the missionary task of the early church as grounded in the dawning kingdom of Christ. Paul explains that the resurrection of Jesus is inherently eschatological; indeed it is the hoped-for, last-days resurrection of the dead anticipated for centuries by the twelve tribes of Israel (Acts 26:6–8). Paul sees those among the Gentile nations turning to Christ as a fulfillment of the Abrahamic promise to bless all peoples through Abraham's seed (Rom. 15:8–13; Gal. 3:7–4:7). The apostles, meeting at the Jerusalem Council, identify the Gentile conversions as evidence that God, as promised, has granted the Davidic throne to Jesus in a global, indisputable latter-day reign (Acts 15:1–29).

For the apostles, this inbreaking kingdom is focused exclusively on Jesus Christ—and only derivatively to those who are united to Jesus by faith, hidden in him before God (Col. 2:3–4). In baptism, the church pronounces that such believers have already been through judgment, and they have also already been vindicated through resurrection, in Christ (Rom. 6:1–14; 8:1–11). They also share a guarantee—the Spirit of Christ—that they will one day be raised personally and physically along with him (Rom. 8). Believers have a pioneer who has already been through the veil of death and returned to tell us about it (Heb. 6:10–20). Because they are united with the Spirit-anointed Messiah, they all share the anointing of the Spirit (1 John 2:20).

This is why, for the new covenant apostles, Jew-Gentile unity is pivotal to the early church. It is about more than human relational harmony. Instead, it acknowledges that God's kingdom purposes are *in Christ*. He is the last man and the true Israel, the bearer of the Spirit. A Jewish person who clings to the tribal markings of the old covenant acts as though the eschaton has not arrived, as though one were still waiting for the promised seed. Both Jews and Gentiles must instead see their identities not in themselves or in the flesh but in Jesus Christ and in him alone. Jesus is the descendant of Abraham, the one who deserves the throne of David. He is the obedient Israel who inherits the blessings of the Mosaic covenant. He is the propitiation of God's wrath. He is the firstborn from the dead, the resurrection and the life.

Those who are in Christ—whether Jew or Gentile—receive with him all the eschatological blessings that are due to him. In him, they are all, whether Jew or Gentile, sons of God—not only in terms of relationship with the Father but also in terms of promised inheritance (Rom. 8:12–17). In Christ, they all—whether Jew or Gentile—are sons of Abraham, the true circumcision, the holy nation, and the household and commonwealth of God (Gal. 3:23–4:7; Eph. 2–3; Col. 2:6–15; 3:3–11; 1 Pet. 2:9–10).

The "already" of the kingdom then has everything to do with the church. The church is where Jesus rules *now* (Eph. 1:22–23). The kingdom is veiled in the present age since Jesus is ascended to the heavenly places and is invisible to the world order. It is manifested in this era in the church, which is mysteriously the body of Christ. The kingdom of God is seen within the assembly, not through demonstrations of power or through rule over the nations but in "righteousness and peace and joy in the Holy Spirit" (Rom. 14:17). The gifts of the Spirit within the church signal Jesus' resurrection victory over the principalities and powers (Eph. 4:8), a reality that also evokes the psalmist's earlier exultation in the warrior authority of the Davidic throne (Ps. 68:18).

In the church the eschatological temple is built, this time with "living stones" indwelled by the Spirit of Christ (1 Pet. 2:4–5; 1 Cor. 3:16–17; 2 Cor. 6:16–18). The church now experiences what Israel longed for; the "ends of the ages" have come upon them (1 Cor. 10:11). The church is the Israelite vine that bears the promised "fruit" of the eschaton, that of a dawning age of the Spirit as opposed to the collapsing age of the flesh (Gal. 5:15–24). The apostles constantly warn Christians to focus their hopes not on temporal wealth or national alignments but on the kingdom of Christ— of which the church is a colony—a kingdom that will one day displace every rival empire (Phil. 3:20–21), including the seemingly invincible *pax Romana* of Caesar.

It is not simply the blessings of the eschaton that have been inaugurated in the present age, however. The Apostle John sees the tumult of the present age as the fury of a defeated dragon god who "knows that his time is short" (Rev. 12:12). The church experiences the hostilities of the demonic principalities and powers precisely because the "Spirit of glory" that anoints the Davidic king now belongs to them in union with Christ (1 Pet. 4:13–14). The clatter of Armageddon battle is initially fulfilled in the now as the people of Christ struggle against the evil angelic rulers who are being deposed by the resurrection triumph of Jesus. Jesus speaks then of "birth pains" of the end—earthquakes, wars, false religion (Matt. 24:3–14). And

John warns us that the Evil One apes the "already/not yet" structure of biblical eschatology.

In these last days the spirit of antichrist is already at work as many "antichrists" appear in anticipation of the final antichrist figure (1 John 2:18; 4:3). Even the judgment of hell itself is prefigured in the present era as God gives over sinful humanity further and further to idolatry, depravity, and self-absorption in anticipation of the final throne of justice in which rebels are finally given over to the awful finality of their selves (Rom. 1:18–32).

Eschatology as Not Yet

The New Testament makes clear that the kingdom arrives in two stages, and that one of them is not yet here. Jesus announces, "An hour is coming, and is now here, when the dead will hear the voice of the Son of God, and those who hear will live" (John 5:25). The writer of Hebrews points out the obvious reality that, though God has promised to put all things under the feet of the Son of Man, "at present, we do not yet see everything in subjection to him" (Heb. 2:6–9). The New Testament thus constantly warns believers (and unbelievers, for that matter) not to assume that the kingdom is here in its fullness but to be ready for its sudden and cataclysmic arrival.

Jesus does not give exhaustive details about the end of the age, telling his disciples that the Father himself sets the timetable for such events by his own authority (Acts 1:7; Matt. 24:36). Jesus does, however, reveal the existence of a heaven and a hell, in one or the other of which all humans will find themselves immediately upon death (Luke 16:19–31). He affirms unequivocally the resurrection of the body, along with the Old Testament witness, against Sadducees who deny it (Mark 12:18–27). When asked about the end times, he looks to the coming destruction of Jerusalem in Rome, and then beyond it, to the final tumult of earth history that climaxes in the realization of the Prophet Daniel's vision, "the Son of Man coming on the clouds of heaven with power and great glory" (Matt. 24:30; Dan. 7:13–14).

Jesus speaks of the "birth pains" of tribulation but counsels his disciples not to think the end is here until they see this visible and glorious coming of the Son of Man in the eastern skies (Matt. 24:24–50). He affirms through stories that the kingdom, though almost invisible in the present age, will one day stand majestically over every rival (Matt. 13:1–52; Mark 4:21–33). Those with eyes to see, therefore, will seek this kingdom—not its temporal counterfeits (Luke 12:13–21, 31).

Jesus speaks of the Lord's Supper he institutes at the onset of the new covenant as pointing to another meal that he will eat with his disciples when "it is fulfilled in the kingdom of God" (Luke 22:16,18), a promise of a messianic banquet rooted in Old Testament eschatology (Isa. 25:6; Ps. 23:5).[4] At this Passover table—and throughout his ministry—Jesus promises his disciples that the kingdom they seek is in some aspect yet before them. "I assign to you, as my Father assigned to me, a kingdom," Jesus tells them, "that you may eat and drink at my table in my kingdom and sit on thrones judging the twelve tribes of Israel" (Luke 22:29–30). Jesus commands his disciples not to seek greatness or prominence in this life since their glory and rule will come in the resurrection, at the "regeneration" of the universe, when Jesus and his coheirs rule over all things (Matt. 19:28). Sharing this glorious rule with Jesus in the future, however, means also sharing "the cup," his "baptism," the suffering he endures in the present (Matt. 20:22–23; Mark 10:27–39).

On this last day, Jesus tells his disciples, they will face judgment and be rewarded according to their faithfulness through trials. In keeping with his role as Davidic king, Jesus will judge all humanity, separating the "sheep" of Israel's flock from the "goats" of the unbelieving world. The criterion will be whether they know Jesus, a knowledge that is seen in the way they treat his ignominious "brothers" in this life (Matt. 25:31–46). At this judgment those whom Jesus endorses will share in the kingdom; those he indicts will "go away into eternal punishment," into "eternal fire prepared for the devil and his angels" (Matt. 25:41,46). He warns that national identity or religious self-righteousness will not save. Some of the sons of Israel will find themselves in hell, while Gentiles celebrate at the messianic banquet table with Abraham, Isaac, and Jacob (Luke 13:27–29). The judgment of hell, Jesus warns, is final and irrevocable (Luke 16:26).

Jesus commands his followers to be ready for his return, even as they scatter across the world proclaiming the kingdom through the power of the Spirit. The "already/not yet" structure of his advent is seen even in the days following his resurrection. Jesus tells the disciples to wait for the Spirit, but he then ascends to the Father's presence. An angelic messenger tells the witnesses to the ascension that Jesus—this same Jesus—will return from the skies in the same manner (Acts 1:10–11).

The Apostle Paul counsels churches confused that the Day of the Lord has arrived, by pointing out that an antichrist must arise (2 Thess. 2:1–12) and that the day of the resurrection will be unmistakable (1 Cor. 15:12–56; 1 Thess. 4:13–5:10). For Paul, the present age is one of suffering and crucifixion, as we wait for the coming of the Son of Man. He sees the trajectory of history as downward—with apostasy and demonic deception growing

---

[4] For a fuller discussion of the eschatological nature of the Lord's Supper, see Russell D. Moore, "Christ's Presence as Memorial: The Baptist View," in *Table That Unites or Divides? Four Views on the Lord's Supper,* ed. John H. Armstrong (Grand Rapids: Zondervan, forthcoming).

(1 Tim. 4:1–5; 2 Tim. 3:1–9). Moreover, this longing for the coming of Christ, this agony in the face of present evil, is not limited to sentient creatures. Paul notes that the entire cosmos "groans" under the curse, longing for the "sons of God" to be revealed, a revelation that takes place at the final resurrection from the dead, when the creation is then liberated from the Adamic curse (Rom. 8:18–25).

This day of resurrection, Paul argues, is prefigured by the resurrection of Jesus, who is the firstborn among many brothers to come forth from the grave. Our future resurrection life will mean being conformed fully to the resurrection life Jesus now experiences (1 Cor. 15:49). Those who deny the bodily resurrection, Paul argues, deny the central truth of the Christian claim: the resurrection of Jesus. And those who deny the resurrection of Jesus deny the basis for Christian hope, thereby cutting themselves off from the hope of redemption (1 Cor. 15:1–58). The day of Christ brings with it also the fulfillment of God's promises to Israel. Paul sees the vine of Israel having "wild branches" of Gentiles grafted on to it in the present era, but he also sees Jewish believers grafted back on in the future. In this way, Paul argues, "All Israel will be saved," and God will keep his irrevocable promises (Rom. 9–11).

For Paul, resurrection is the ultimate hope of the believer. It is this hope of the second advent of our Messiah that keeps us from grieving "as others do who have no hope" (1 Thess. 4:13). Since we are convinced of the resurrection of Jesus, we must also be convinced that Jesus will, at his coming, resurrect those who belong to him—catching up in the air both resurrected dead and the translated living (1 Thess. 4:14–17). But those who are "asleep" in Jesus are not unconscious or forgotten, even on this side of the resurrection. Paul is convinced that, at his death, he is immediately in the presence of his Christ (Phil. 1:21–26). To be away from the body is to be "at home with the Lord" (2 Cor. 5:8). This heavenly state is always in view of the ultimate day of history, however, when bodies are raised and death is overturned forever (1 Cor. 15:50–57).

Like Jesus, Paul counsels against the temptation to love the present age above the future realization of the kingdom of Christ (2 Tim. 4:10). The present situation of the believer should be one of discomfort—a cry of the church for the coming of her righteous King. Also like Jesus, Paul places the present in the context of a future day of judgment. Paul warns believers that they must appear before the judgment seat of Christ, where their fidelity and service will be tested by the one who sees all (Rom. 14:10–12; 2 Cor. 5:10). He also warns that unbelievers will find the throne of judgment a horrifying experience of finality, as their unrepentant sins disqualify them from entrance into the kingdom of Christ (1 Cor. 6:9–10).

The Apostle Peter confronts false teachers in the early church with a warning that judgment never comes gradually. Peter points out that God has typified the Day of the Lord in previous epochs: the Noahic flood, the destruction of Sodom and Gomorrah, the sentencing of the rebel angels. In all of these instances, "scoffers" did not believe such judgment would come, until it was upon them (2 Pet. 3:2–3). Peter compares the coming cosmic conflagration with the Genesis flood. Just as God destroyed the creation with water, bringing safely through the righteous remnant, he at the eschaton will destroy the creation with fire, bringing believers safely through, to a new creation, a "new heavens and a new earth in which righteousness dwells" (2 Pet. 3:13).

The Apostle John, exiled by Caesar on the island of Patmos, receives from the ascended Jesus a vision, explaining the future reign of Christ and how this reign makes sense of the ongoing Caesar-Christ conflict that results in the persecution of the Christian communities.[5] This revelation encourages hard-pressed churches in the first century and throughout the ages to persevere. The one "who conquers," Jesus promises, will receive eschatological blessings: to eat from the tree of life, to eat hidden manna, to be named with a new name, to be a pillar in the holy temple of Yahweh. Christians should hold fast to the deposit of faith, even under imperial persecution since for the one who does so, "to him I will give authority over the nations, and he will rule them with a rod of iron, as when earthen pots are broken in pieces, even as I myself have received authority from my Father" (Rev. 2:26b–27).

John sees all of history as culminating in the kingship of Jesus as the Lion of Judah, the Root of David (Rev. 5:5–6). He sees the angelic armies and the disembodied redeemed in heaven praising the atonement of Christ and crying out for his vengeance on evildoers. He sees the covenant promises of God fulfilled in Christ as 144,000 from the twelve tribes of Israel bear the mark of Christ. In Revelation 12, John sees the sweep of cosmic history as the struggle between the dragon of Eden who seeks to devour a child born of the woman, hearkening back to the gospel of Genesis 3. He sees this serpent defeated through the blood of Christ, as his accusations no longer hold on a people whose sins are forgiven in Jesus.

In this revelation John is also shown the judgment of Christ on a rebellious world system. He sees a beast rising out of the seas that sets himself in opposition to Christ—even employing the power of the state to persecute Christ's people (Rev. 13:1–10). He sees a false prophet who

---

[5] There is debate within evangelical circles as to the dating of the Apocalypse, whether in the reign of Nero before the destruction of Jerusalem or after. For an examination and assessment of the alternatives, see Gregory K. Beale, *The Book of Revelation: A Commentary on the Greek Text*, NIGTC (Grand Rapids: Eerdmans, 1999), 4–27.

deceptively lures people away to worship this figure, who is mysteriously numbered "666" (Rev. 13:11–18). He sees mighty Babylon, standing proudly against the kingdom of Christ (Rev. 17–18), and Gog and Magog waging war against the Lamb. And he sees all of these enemies of the Messiah destroyed, as God pours out his wrath on them—first through plagues evocative of the exodus (Rev. 6–11; 15–16) and then through the return of Jesus himself as a glorious and triumphant warrior-king (Rev. 19:11–21).

The vision of the future triumph John receives is that of a restored cosmos, freed from the power of satanic occupation. He sees a "thousand year" reign of Christ, in which those resurrected rule over the earth (Rev. 20:1–6). This millennium ends with a revolt by a released Satan and his human and demonic minions, a revolt that is put down by fire from the heavens (Rev. 20:7–10). After this comes the resurrection and judgment of the unrighteous, with their final consignment to the lake of fire (Rev. 20:11–15). And then comes the eternal state, with a new Jerusalem coming down from the heavens to a transformed and regenerated new earth (Rev. 21–22). This new earth includes all of the covenant promises of God fulfilled. God dwells with his people, in Christ. He welcomes them to the tree of life. The city of Jerusalem is rebuilt and glorious, with the wealth of the nations streaming into it (Rev. 21:22–26).[6]

The story ends there—or perhaps begins again there—tying together all the plot lines of the millennia before. God's creation purposes are fulfilled as humanity is fruitful and has multiplied, filling the earth (and perhaps beyond). The cultural mandate is fulfilled, with a glorious civilization built to the pleasure of God. And, through it all, Jesus of Nazareth reminds his people that God's promises were kept through him: "I am the root and the descendant of David, the bright morning star" (Rev. 22:16).

What Has the Church Believed?

Eschatology in Patristic Theology

The centuries after the apostolic era were aglow with controversy, not the least of which centered on articulating a Christian view of the future. While confronting heresy, engaging philosophy and world religions, and interpreting tumultuous political changes, the church fathers wrestled with the development of a Christian eschatology that was biblically faithful and theologically coherent. The eschatological controversies during this era in-

---

[6] For an excellent discussion of the themes from Isaiah 60 in Revelation 21–22, see Richard J. Mouw, *When the Kings Come Marching In: Isaiah and the New Jerusalem* (Grand Rapids: Eerdmans, 2002).

cluded debates over bodily resurrection, the new creation, millennialism, and the nature of damnation.

At the root of these discussions, however, were more fundamental questions about the relationship between heaven and earth; between the kingdom of God and history. The eschatological discussion in the Patristic era was multivalent and ongoing, but the basic contours of the discussion may be seen in the theological contributions of Irenaeus of Lyons, Justin Martyr, Origen of Alexandria, and Augustine of Hippo.[7]

Irenaeus of Lyons

The eschatology of Irenaeus was developed in controversy with Gnostic teachers whom the bishop of Lyons believed threatened the heart of the Christian faith itself. The Gnostics believed a "secret knowledge" to be the key to understanding reality, a "knowledge" that led them to value the "spiritual" over the material and to degrade the material creation—including the human body—as inherently wicked. Irenaeus rejected anything that denied the corporeality of the resurrection body—of Jesus at the garden tomb or of his followers at the last day. In this Irenaeus saw himself in continuity with the Apostle John's struggles against the antimaterialism of his era. In his controversy with the Gnostics, Irenaeus quoted from disciples of Polycarp, who was said to have remembered that when John saw the proto-Gnostic Cerinthus in a bathhouse, the apostle exclaimed: "Let us fly, lest even the bath-house fall down, because Cerinthus, the enemy of the truth, is within."[8]

The materiality of redemption applied, for Irenaeus, not just to human bodies but also to the creation itself, an emphasis seen in Irenaeus's decidedly material vision of the kingdom. When it comes to the millennium, Irenaeus rooted his understanding again in what he learned from the testimony of those who learned eschatology directly from the Apostle John.[9] Irenaeus described this future millennial reign this way, purportedly from the teaching of Jesus himself:

> The days will come, in which vines shall grow, each having ten thousand branches, and in each branch ten thousand twigs, and in each true twig ten thousand shoots, and in each one of the shoots ten thousand clusters, and on every one of the clusters ten thousand grapes, and every grape when pressed will give five and twenty me-

---

[7] For an in-depth examination of patristic eschatology, see Brian E. Daley, *The Hope of the Early Church: A Handbook of Patristic Eschatology* (Peabody, MA: Hendrickson, 1991).

[8] Irenaeus, *Against Heresies* 3.3.4.

[9] For an argument that the millennialism of Asia Minor was due to the influence of the Apostle John in the region, see Larry V. Crutchfield, "The Apostle John and Asia Minor as a Source of Premillennialism in the Early Church Fathers," *JETS* 31 (1988): 411–27.

tretes of wine. And when any one of the saints shall lay hold of a cluster, another shall cry out, "I am a better cluster, take me; bless the Lord through me."[10]

Irenaeus further described the millennium as including the harmony of the animal kingdom along with an end to predation and bloodshed, so that all things are once again in subjection to human rule.[11] He acknowledged incredulity toward such an earthly millennium; but he attributed this incredulity, in the discourse described with Jesus, to Judas.[12]

Irenaeus's millennialism was not merely an isolated exegesis of passages from Revelation and the Old Testament prophets. It fit with his more overarching vision of God's purposes as holistic: a new creation in Christ that includes the entire universe, both spiritual and material. It is here that he was most at odds with his Gnostic interlocutors. Against any heretical suggestion that the flesh is evil, Irenaeus held to a real and corporeal resurrection. Against any suggestion that the physical world is transitory or wicked by virtue of its materiality, Irenaeus pointed to God's glory in creation and in re-creation. He denied that the "world would end," in the sense of complete annihilation: "For neither is the substance nor the essence of the creation annihilated (for faithful and true is He who has established it) but 'the *fashion* of the world passeth away': that is, those things among which transgression has occurred, since man has grown old in them."[13]

Irenaeus likewise denied that the kingdom described in the Scriptures referred merely to "super-celestial matters" but to a renovation of this present earth.[14] For Irenaeus this had everything to do with Christ's "recapitulation" of the Edenic task of Adam.[15] As Adam was assigned to rule a terrestrial order—and failed—Christ is assigned to demonstrate his human kingship over a terrestrial order. "It is fitting, therefore, that the creation itself should without restraint be under the dominion of the righteous," he wrote, drawing explicitly from the Pauline teaching in Romans 8:19ff.[16]

Irenaeus held to a restoration of Israel, but, like virtually every other Patristic thinker, he identified "Israel" with those who are in Christ. He asserted that "the church is the seed of Abraham; and for this reason, that we may know that He who is in the New Testament 'raises up from the

---

[10] Irenaeus, *Against Heresies* 5.33.

[11] Ibid., 5.3.4.

[12] Ibid.

[13] Ibid., 5.36.1.

[14] Ibid., 5.35.2.

[15] For Irenaeus's magisterial description of how all of redemptive history flows toward and coheres in Christ, see his *On the Apostolic Preaching,* trans. John Behr (Crestwood, NY: St. Vladimir's Seminary Press, 1997).

[16] Irenaeus, *Against Heresies* 5.32.1.

stones children unto Abraham,' is He who will gather, according to the Old Testament, those that shall be saved from all the nations."[17] The land promises of the old covenant were literal and material, he argued, but they applied to those whom the New Testament defines as "sons of Abraham," namely those of faith.

Justin Martyr

Justin Martyr's eschatology is seen chiefly through his *Dialogue with Trypho,* an apologetic encounter with a Jewish skeptic toward Christianity.[18] Here Justin considered and refuted his opponent's claim that the prophecies of the Old Testament, applied by the New Testament to Jesus, have not been fulfilled. Justin argued that the New Testament apostles did not simply mine the Old Testament Bible for "proof texts." Instead Justin demonstrated a hermeneutic that was Christocentric and typological—seeing the entire old covenant fulfilled in Christ.

Justin appealed to Trypho—and to Jewish readers "overhearing" the dialogue—to see the Bible as an organic unity, in which Jesus makes sense of all of the Old Testament promises. In so doing, Justin employed an "already/not yet" understanding of inaugurated eschatology—almost two millennia before such terminology was used. The reason Trypho could not see the fulfillment of Old Testament eschatology in Jesus, Justin argued, is that the kingdom is coming in two stages with one of them, including with it the promises of global peace and an Israelite theocracy, yet to come.

In laying out his understanding of the future kingdom, Justin carefully explored the meaning of "Israel"—a meaning that is found in the church's union with the Jewish Messiah, not in genetic bloodlines. As Patristic scholar Robert Lewis Wilken points out, a turning point in the dialogue between Trypho and Justin came when the Jewish thinker realized that they had two divergent views of Israel.[19] While Trypho assumed "Israel" refers only to descendants of Abraham, according to the flesh, he asked Justin, "What is this? Are *you* Israel and is he speaking these things about *you*?" To this, Justin answered in the affirmative.[20] Justin identified Israel with Jesus, literally translating "Israel" as the one who overcomes in power, a name merited by Jesus alone.[21]

---

[17] Ibid., 5.33–34.

[18] One scholar argues that passages from Justin's *First Apology* suggest "conclusively that Justin was either amillennial or postmillennial in his eschatology," but his *Dialogue with Trypho* gives a clearly premillennial picture. Art Marmorstein, "Eschatological Inconsistency in the Ante-Nicene Fathers?" *Andrews University Seminary Studies* 39 (2001): 127–28.

[19] Robert L. Wilken, "*In novissimis diebus*: Biblical Promises, Jewish Hopes, and Early Christian Exegesis," *Journal of Early Christian Studies* 1 (1993): 15.

[20] Justin Martyr, *Dialogue with Trypho* 123.

[21] Ibid., 125.3.

This does not mean, however, that Justin "spiritualized" the Old Testament promises. Indeed, he argued forcefully for the cosmic, material, and political aspects of the redemption of the world. Thus, he considered the idea that salvation means a heavenly, disembodied existence to be "blasphemy" against the God of Abraham, Isaac, and Jacob. Justin presented the implications of the Christian hope of bodily resurrection, and argued, like Irenaeus, for a literal and "earthly" understanding of the Apostle John's vision of the thousand-year reign of Christ.

Origen

Origen of Alexandria was, arguably, the most intellectually brilliant theologian of the Patristic era. His thought focused frequently on questions of eschatology, and his conclusions often could not be more different than those of Irenaeus and Justin. As Eastern Orthodox theologian George Florovsky puts it, Origen's attempts to integrate hellenic philosophical thought—especially Platonism—with fledgling Christian theology constituted in many ways an "abortive birth" of a Christian systematic eschatology but represented tendencies that later would find more doctrinally orthodox expression in the thought of Athanasius and Augustine.[22] Origen thoroughly rejected an earthly millennial reign of Christ and with it a more "material" understanding of the resurrection body and the life to come.

Origen was not the first amillennial Christian theologian; both amillennialism and premillennialism were present in the early church.[23] As New Testament scholar Thomas Lea points out, Origen's objections to millennialism were rooted less in exegesis than in his theological aversion to such ideas as "sensual" and "material."[24] As Origen described it, some Christians sought "the indulgence of their own desires and lusts" and saw in the eschaton

> bodily pleasure and luxury; and therefore they especially desire to have again after the resurrection such bodily structures as may never be without the power of eating, and drinking, and performing all the functions of flesh and blood, not following the opinion of the Apostle Paul regarding the resurrection of a spiritual body.[25]

Origen held to a resurrection body that is ethereal and heavenly and to a millennial reign that represents the rule of the saints in Christ from heaven

---

[22] George Florovsky, "Eschatology in the Patristic Age: An Introduction," *Greek Orthodox Theological Review* 2 (1956): 35.

[23] Daley, *The Hope of the Early Church*, 5–64.

[24] Thomas D. Lea, "A Survey of the Return of Christ in the Ante-Nicene Fathers," *JETS* 29 (1986): 176.

[25] Origen, *De Principiis* 2.11.2.

in the present era. The body is raised from the "germ" of this "earthly and animal body" a "spiritual one capable of inhabiting the heavens."[26] He held that, for the redeemed, the blessings of the eternal state are to be found in heaven and that these include spiritual blessings radically discontinuous from earthly existence.[27] Origen's understanding of a "spiritual" eschatology took root in Christian eschatology and eventually supplanted the more "earthly" eschatologies of the millennialists.

Origen was less successful in winning early Christianity over to his views of hell and final judgment.[28] Origen did not deny the existence of hell, nor did he deny its agonizing punishment. But from such biblical passages as Paul's teaching that at the end "God may be all in all" (1 Cor. 15:28), he posited a view of *apocatastasis,* the idea that all things will be ultimately reconciled to God through Christ—including the damned in hell and even Satan and his demons. Origen's view of eternal punishment was built on his understanding of God's goodness, and his strong view of libertarian human freedom.[29] God uses punishment to redeem humans and angels without coercing their wills. The church at the Second Council of Constantinople rejected Origen's view of universal salvation definitively in AD 553.[30]

Augustine of Hippo

Augustine, perhaps the most influential theologian of the early church, systematized what theologian Craig Blaising calls a "spiritual vision" model of eschatology as opposed to a "new creation" model of a restored earth and continuity between bodily life now and in the eschaton.[31] For Augustine, the hope of the Christian was not earthly but heavenly. He held to a resurrection of the body but described heaven in terms of the beatific

---

[26] Ibid., 2.10.3.

[27] Ibid., 2.2–32. Origen believed the resurrection body to be like that of an angel, a view he based on Jesus' remark to the Sadducees that there will be no marriage in the resurrection because humans will be "like angels" (Mark 12:25). For an analysis of the exegetical and philosophical presuppositions behind this idea, see Lawrence R. Hennessey, "Origen of Alexandria: The Fate of the Soul and the Body after Death," *The Second Century* 8 (1991): 176–78. Hennessey concludes that Origen's view so severs this body from the next that it jeopardizes any real identity between the two.

[28] Again, Origen was neither the first nor the last to articulate such a view of universal redemption and a redemptive purpose for hell. As John Sachs points out, Clement, Origen's predecessor in Alexandria, articulated similar ideas and, for a time, some of these themes were found in the writings of Gregory of Nyssa and Gregory of Nazianzus. John Sachs, "*Apocatastasis* in Patristic Theology," *Theological Studies* 54 (1993): 617–40.

[29] Graham Keith, "Patristic Views on Hell—Part 1," *Evangelical Quarterly* 71 (1999): 229–30.

[30] The ninth anathema against Origen at the Second Council states: "If anyone says or thinks that the punishment of demons and of impious men is only temporary, and will one day have an end, and that a restoration will take the place of demons and of impious men, let him be anathema." Henry R. Percival, ed., "The Seven Ecumenical Councils of the Undivided Church: Their Canons and Dogmatic Decrees," in *NPNF²*, 14.320.

[31] Craig A. Blaising, "Premillennialism," in *Three Views on the Millennium and Beyond,* ed. Darrell L. Bock (Grand Rapids: Zondervan, 1999), 160–76.

vision when the purified soul apprehends the vision of God. Augustine's view of heaven provided the template for a Christian theology of future hope extending to the medieval and Reformation eras and beyond. This spiritual eschatology had no place for an earthly millennium. Like his amillennial patristic forebears, Augustine saw the idea of an earthly millennium as "leisure of immoderate carnal banquets, furnished with an amount of meat and drink such as not only to shock the feeling of the temperate, but even to surpass the measure of credulity itself."[32]

For Augustine, the kingdom of Christ is now the church, both on earth and in heaven, ruling with Christ in the "thousand years" between his first and second comings.[33] Augustine's mistrust of "chiliasm" (the belief in a literal thousand-year reign) became codified by the Western Catholic church, which marginalized millennialism almost universally after Augustine. Augustine retained the orthodox Christian view of hell and judgment, rejecting any suggestion of universal redemption.[34]

Another important Augustinian contribution to Christian eschatology was his model of tying a Christian view of the kingdom to current social and political events. Faced with the fall of Rome, Augustine laid out the reality of the spiritual kingdom of Christ, "the City of God," which exists in the present era along with the kingdoms of this world, "the city of man." In a monumental work, *The City of God,* Augustine sought to demonstrate to his Roman contemporaries how these two kingdoms have been in conflict since the creation and how the City of God will ultimately triumph in the new Jerusalem of the heavenly eternal state. In this way Augustine's eschatology provided a crucial pastoral and practical function in an age of upheaval.

Eschatology in Medieval Theology

The medieval era solidified the Augustinian "spiritual vision" eschatology. There were uprisings of popular millennialism, especially among the peasant class in the Middle Ages.[35] But the mainstream of Christian thought was decidedly amillennial, equating the kingdom of God with the spiritual blessedness found through the church. Moreover, the eternal state was seen increasingly as an everlasting heaven in the spiritual realm rather than a renovated creation. Medieval thinkers such as Peter Lombard and Thomas Aquinas set forth detailed theologies about the states of blessedness and

---

[32] Augustine, "The City of God," in *A Select Library of the Nicene and Post-Nicene Fathers of the Christian Church,* vol. 2, *St. Augustine's City of God and Christian Doctrine,* ed. Philip Schaff (Grand Rapids: Eerdmans, 1983), 426.

[33] Ibid., 426–31.

[34] Ibid., 420.

[35] Norman Cohn, *The Pursuit of the Millennium: Revolutionary Millenarians and Mystical Anarchists of the Middle Ages* (New York: Oxford University, 1957).

damnation in eternity, along with speculations about, among other things, the nature of rewards in heaven and the souls of unbaptized babies in limbo (a realm between heaven and hell specifically for those infants who had not experienced a washing away of original sin through the waters of baptism).

Thomas was especially influential in setting forth the meaning of eschatological blessedness in heaven, which he defined as consisting in "nothing else than the vision of the Divine Essence."[36] Poets such as Dante, with his "Divine Comedy," fired the medieval imagination about the possible geography and populations of heaven, purgatory, and hell with biblically evocative literature that often shaped the popular mind about eternity, a phenomenon that continues to the present day.

During the Middle Ages the doctrine of purgatory, which existed in the Patristic era to varying degrees, became especially important to the life of the Roman Catholic Church. The church was the mediatorial dispenser of the "treasury of merit" of Christ and the saints. The sacramental system was the means by which sinners could be made pure enough to see the beatific vision in heaven. The church taught that those who did not die in mortal sin (sin worthy of immediate damnation) but were not sanctified sufficiently for heaven would be cleansed beneath the "refiner's fire" of purgatory.[37] The church appealed to passages such as 1 Corinthians 3:15 ("saved, but only as through fire") to demonstrate that eschatological purgation is part of God's purpose to make his people fit for heaven, and to passages such as Jesus' granting of "keys of the kingdom" to Peter to argue that the church could "bind and loose" such things (Matt. 16:19).

Pious people prayed then for shorter sojourns in purgatory for loved ones, a discipline the church formalized into a system of "indulgences." Believers could, through some act of spiritual discipline, gain for themselves, or for a loved one, reprieve from time in purgatory. This practice became a key facet of popular piety and of the Catholic understanding of the communion of the saints.

Eschatology in Reformation and Post-Reformation Theology

Reformation

The Magisterial Reformers did not contest the basic Augustinian "spiritual vision" eschatology of the medieval church. Martin Luther, John Calvin, Ulrich Zwingli, and their contemporaries in the Reformation movement maintained, with all orthodox Christians, the physical resurrection

---

[36] Thomas Aquinas, *Summa Theologica,* First Complete American Edition, vol. 1 (New York: Benziger Brothers, 1947), 2.1.Q.3.8.

[37] Jacques Le Goff, *The Birth of Purgatory,* trans. Arthur Goldhammer (Chicago: The University of Chicago Press, 1984).

from the dead. But for virtually all of them the hope of the church was essentially spiritual, heavenly, and amillennial. In keeping with the church fathers, the Magisterial Reformers identified Israel with the "spiritual Israel," the church. They also conserved the orthodox doctrine of hell as everlasting, conscious punishment of the wicked.

When it came to eschatology, the Reformers' protest against the Roman Church centered on the church's claim to the "keys" of heaven and purgatory through indulgences. Martin Luther, for instance, wondered why, if the pope had the ability to free any souls from purgatory, he did not free them all.[38] Included in the Reformers' charges against the church was the idea that purgatory itself is an unbiblical doctrinal innovation, one that is dependent on an unbiblical view of justification that sees the sinner's righteousness infused within him rather than united to him in Christ. From the Reformers' point of view, the doctrine of justification by faith alone in Christ alone took a hammer to any idea of purgatory.

Controversies over last things were not limited to those with the Roman Catholic Church, however. The radical wing of the Reformation—the so-called "Anabaptists"—often challenged the Augustinian consensus itself. Some of them recovered the chiliasm of some of the early church fathers, but with a more apocalyptic edge to it. Thus, millennial fanaticism of the time led to socially tumultuous enthusiasm in, for instance, Thomas Müntzer and the Peasants' Revolt.[39] The Magisterial Reformers rejected such millennialism, and not simply the more extreme, political streams of it. Instead, Calvin and Luther particularly denounced the idea of a physical, material, historical manifestation of the kingdom of God to be "carnal" and "Jewish"—unfit for a Christian understanding of a spiritual kingdom.

Some Anabaptists also sought to modify Christian thought on the intermediate state. Instead of the soul immediately going to heaven or hell upon death, they argued, the person remained unconscious until the resurrection from the dead. This idea of "soul sleep" was especially pernicious to Calvin. According to Karl Barth, Calvin saw this idea as "simply a metaphysical version of the attitude to life that by passivity, renunciation of all things, abandonment of all thinking, willing and doing, finally thinks that by the mystical death of the soul in God it can attain to the supreme summit of human striving."[40]

Calvin agreed that a final judgment takes place at the resurrection, but he just as vigorously argued that Scripture teaches immediate blessedness

---

[38] Martin Luther, "The Ninety-five Theses," in *Martin Luther: Selections from His Writings,* ed. John Dillenberger (New York: Doubleday, 1962), 498.

[39] For a description of this interaction between the magisterial and radical wings of the Reformation, see Diarmaid MacCulloch, *The Reformation: A History* (New York: Viking, 2003), 154–58.

[40] Karl Barth, *The Theology of John Calvin,* trans. Geoffrey W. Bromiley (Grand Rapids: Eerdmans, 1995), 151.

or punishment upon death. Ever the lawyer, Calvin explained the intermediate state of hell in terms of the legal system. The damned sinner's soul, "being departed from the body, is like a malefactor who has already received his sentence of condemnation and now awaits only the hour when he shall be led to the gallows for execution."[41] For Calvin, the intermediate state for the believer is "the 'joy' that the faithful soul has after death, when it sees itself delivered from all weakness, warfare, wicked lusts, and the dangers of daily temptations, having a clearer and firmer comprehension of its blessed state and immortal glory."[42]

Post-Reformation Development

The eschatological contours of the Magisterial Reformers shaped the Reformed and Lutheran confessions in the sixteenth and seventeenth centuries, as well as the Reformation streams of Protestant Scholasticism and English Puritanism. The Lutheran Augsburg Confession of Faith (1530) condemned both the "Anabaptist" view that "there will be an end to the punishments of condemned men and devils" and "certain Jewish opinions, that before the resurrection of the dead the godly shall take possession of the kingdom of the world, the ungodly being everywhere suppressed."[43] The primary Reformed confessions—including the Belgic (1561), Westminster (1646), and Savoy Declaration (1658) confessions—acknowledged an intermediate state of the soul, the resurrection of the dead, the nonexistence of purgatory, and the eternality of both heaven's blessedness and hell's torment.

Reformed confessionalism and Scholasticism systematized Calvin's view of the relationship between Israel and the church into a coherent doctrinal order known as "covenant theology." Covenant theology saw redemptive history in terms of one overarching covenant of grace—with the various biblical covenants as administrations of the one covenant, "I will be their God, and they will be my people." This theology saw a basic continuity between old covenant Israel and the church. The church "replaces" Old Testament Israel, inheriting her promises of land and rest from enemies as the spiritual blessings of peace, forgiveness of sins, the indwelling Holy Spirit, and eternity in heaven.[44]

Among Reformed Christians, significant doctrinal development occurred among the Puritans in the eighteenth century, especially those on

---

41 John Calvin, *Treatises against the Anabaptists and against the Libertines,* trans. Benjamin Wirt Farley (Grand Rapids: Baker, 1982), 136.

42 Ibid., 137.

43 Augsburg Confession, Article 17, in *Creeds of the Churches: A Reader in Christian Doctrine from the Bible to the Present,* ed. John H. Leith (Louisville: John Knox Press, 1982), 73.

44 For a discussion of the development of covenant theology, see Peter A. Lillback, *The Binding of God: Calvin's Role in the Development of Covenant Theology* (Grand Rapids: Baker, 2001).

the American continent. While many Puritans held an amillennial view of the future, some held fervently to a postmillennial vision—the idea that the Spirit will convert the nations to Christ resulting in a thousand years of peace and harmony *before* the return of Jesus. Some American Puritans believed themselves to be on the precipice of this "latter day rain" and believed the new world would play a crucial role in the eschaton. Thus, John Winthrop, for instance, could speak in 1630 of his New England as a shining "city on a hill" with an unparalleled optimism for the triumph of Christianity in the world.[45]

Perhaps the most significant Puritan proponent of postmillennialism was Jonathan Edwards, whose view of the last days fueled a renewed fervor for world missions among Christians who believed the world was on the verge of seeing the kingdom of God realized on earth.[46] Edwards preached a postmillennial hope but also constantly pointed his hearers to heavenly glory and to the varying states of heavenly reward. Edwards is, of course, perhaps best remembered for his vivid descriptions of everlasting punishment in his 1741 sermon "Sinners in the Hands of an Angry God."[47]

Eschatology in Contemporary Theology

Protestant Liberalism

In the modern age Western civilization increasingly replaced the kingdom of God with the evolutionary idea of "progress."[48] At the same time, with the "material" reality of biblical theism threatened by Darwinism, some liberal Protestants adopted a more subjective, interior meaning for Christianity. Thus, the attempted rapprochement between Christianity and Enlightenment modernism, led by theologian Friedrich Schleiermacher, saw the cast of Christian theology turning toward the internal life of the individual in a way that left broader historical forces to the prevailing evolutionary progressive ideologies. Such necessitated, then, a revision in the understanding of Christian hope.

German scholarship, especially the "quests for the historical Jesus," alternated between seeing Jesus as an apocalyptic visionary or as an ethical teacher; but both visions neglected the possibility that Jesus and the apostles might have been right about a coming supernatural kingdom order. In the early twentieth century, Protestant liberals forced the fundamental-

---

[45] John Winthrop, "A Model of Christian Charity," in *Puritan Political Ideas 1558–1794,* ed. Edmund S. Morgan (Indianapolis: Bobbs-Merrill, 1965), 75–93.

[46] Jonathan Edwards, "Thoughts on the Revival of Religion in New England," in *The Works of Jonathan Edward,* vol. 1, ed. Edward Hickman (Edinburgh: Banner of Truth, 1974), 380–83.

[47] Jonathan Edwards, "Sinners in the Hands of an Angry God," in *The Works of Jonathan Edwards,* vol. 2, ed. Edward Hickman (Edinburgh: Banner of Truth, 1974), 7–11.

[48] Robert Nisbet, *History of the Idea of Progress* (New York: Basic Books, 1980).

ist-modernist controversy between traditionalists and progressives within
the American denominations by questioning, among other things, whether
a return of Jesus "in the clouds" was tenable in a modern scientific cosmology. Harry Emerson Fosdick of New York's Riverside Church wrote: "I believe in the victory of righteousness upon this earth, in the coming kingdom
of God whereon Christ looking shall see of the travail of his soul and be
satisfied, but I do not believe in the physical return of Jesus."[49]

For Fosdick and the modernists, the kingdom was Jesus' way of speaking of internal, spiritual realities—"abiding experiences" of trust in God,
not a revelation of God's cosmic future purposes. Protestant liberalism often also dismissed the traditional Christian view of hell as outmoded and
unreflective of the fatherly goodness of God toward all his creatures.[50]

The Social Gospel movement sought to reclaim Jesus' emphasis on the
kingdom of God while still rejecting apocalypticism and supernaturalism.
Walter Rauschenbusch, the pioneer of the Social Gospel, reinterpreted a
Puritan postmillennialism in decidedly modern and liberal terms. The kingdom, in his assessment, was the triumph of Christian principles of peace,
love, and justice in the structures of human government, economics, and
society. The kingdom of God did not come with Jesus in the eastern skies,
but in Christians asserting the "fatherhood of God and the brotherhood
of man" through fair labor legislation, redistribution of wealth, racial reconciliation, and the "Christianization" of the world through international
diplomacy and peacemaking efforts.[51] Social Gospel advocates saw "hell"
as the agony of oppressive social structures, rather than as the punishment
of God in an afterlife. Hell, for them, was more reflected in conditions such
as that in Rauschenbusch's "Hell's Kitchen" tenement section of New York
than in a burning lake of fire.

Neoorthodoxy

Neoorthodoxy broke with more traditional liberalism over a variety of
issues, including the nature of the kingdom. Theologians such as Karl Barth
and Dietrich Bonhoeffer saw in the rise of Hitler's Germany a counterfeit
eschatology that could not be opposed by the "God-consciousness" king-

---

[49] Harry Emerson Fosdick, *The Modern Use of the Bible* (New York: Macmillan, 1942), 104.

[50] For a history of Protestant liberalism and the doctrine of hell, see R. Albert Mohler, Jr., "Modern
Theology: The Disappearance of Hell," in *Hell under Fire: Modern Scholarship Reinvents Eternal
Punishment,* ed. Christopher W. Morgan and Robert A. Peterson (Grand Rapids: Zondervan, 2004),
15–42.

[51] Wrote Rauschenbusch: "Our chief interest in any millennium is the desire for a social order in
which the worth and freedom of every human being will be honored and protected; in which the
brotherhood of man will be expressed in the common possession of the economic resources of
society; and in which the spiritual good of humanity will be set high above the private profit interests of all material groups." Walter Rauschenbusch, *A Theology for the Social Gospel* (New York:
Macmillan, 1917; reprint, Louisville: Westminster/John Knox, 1997), 224.

dom of Protestant liberalism. Hitler's "thousand-year Reich" was a thinly veiled pagan reinterpretation of the "thousand-year reign" of Christ pictured in the Apocalypse. In the Barmen Declaration of 1934, Barth opposed the "German Christian" movement that sought to co-opt Christian churches for the Nazi state. The declaration maintained that the true focus of the kingdom is Jesus Christ, displayed now in his church, and that any state that claimed ultimate allegiance had overstepped its bounds of authority.[52]

After World War II, Reinhold Niebuhr led the neoorthodox effort to relate the kingdom of God to the present age. Against the threat of totalitarianism, Niebuhr called the church to see that the kingdom was not yet fulfilled, so Christians must always be aware that they live in the midst of an "immoral society" of sinful individuals and structures. Niebuhr's eschatology, shorn of the naive optimism of both traditional liberalism and the Social Gospel, provided a theological basis for his "Christian realism," a key ideological component of the tough Cold War foreign policy of the United States and its allies. Niebuhr recognized that what was at stake in the struggle with Marxist communism was not simply an alternative political vision, but an alternative eschatology since Marxism was "a secularized but still essentially religious version" of the millennial hope of Isaiah and the Apocalypse.[53]

Revisionist Theologies

After World War II, eschatology gained new interest in Christian theology, largely through the pioneering scholarship of theologians such as Wolfhart Pannenberg and Jürgen Moltmann. Moltmann was especially influential through his "eschatology of hope," which blended Christian themes of the kingdom with those of the Marxist utopianism of philosopher Ernst Bloch.[54] Moltmann's view of the kingdom as a "magnet" drawing humanity toward an eschatological vision of social justice and liberation was influential on the burgeoning "liberation theology" movement of the Third World. Liberation theology saw the kingdom in similar structural, this-worldly terms as the Social Gospel, but with a less westernized, more Marxist and revolutionary orientation.[55] Liberation theology agreed with much of Karl Marx's critique of Christian views of future reward and punishment as "pie in the sky," designed to quell the longings of the oppressed for justice in the here and now.

---

[52] The Barmen Declaration (1934), in John H. Leith, ed., *Creeds of the Churches: A Reader in Christian Doctrine from the Bible to the Present* (Louisville: John Knox, 1982), 518–22.

[53] Reinhold Niebuhr, *Moral Man and Immoral Society* (New York: Scribner's, 1932, 1960), 61.

[54] Jürgen Moltmann, *A Theology of Hope: On the Ground and the Implications of a Christian Eschatology,* trans. James W. Leitch (Minneapolis: Fortress, 1967).

[55] Gustavo Gutierrez, *A Theology of Liberation: History, Politics, and Salvation* (Maryknoll, NY: Orbis, 1973).

Other developments in contemporary theology likewise shifted eschatology to fit systems of revision to the system of doctrine. The "death of God" movement of the 1960s was forced to articulate a vision of Christian hope for a "post-Christian" framework.[56] Some, such as theologian Harvey Cox, saw secularization itself as an almost millennial outworking of the kingdom of God.[57] Roman Catholic theologian-paleontologist Pierre Teilhard de Chardin sought to integrate Christian eschatology with Darwinian evolution, proposing that humanity is evolving toward an "Omega point," the image of Christ.[58]

Likewise, process theology sought to fit theology within evolutionary ideas of progress, a project that did away with the possibility of much traditional Christian eschatology, dependent as it is on a God who is somehow able to providentially govern history.[59] Feminist theology increasingly indicted some aspects of orthodox Christian eschatology, such as the language of "kingdom" and the notion of "rule" as too "masculine" in cast.[60]

Evangelicalism

In opposition to liberalizing denominational theologies, conservative Protestantism—dubbed "fundamentalism" because of its adherence to the fundamental doctrines of the Christian faith—maintained a vigorously supernatural eschatology. In the classic series *The Fundamentals,* an interdenominational band of conservatives argued for a future, bodily, and visible second coming of Christ along with historic Christian teachings about the dual destinies of heaven and hell.[61] The fundamentalist coalition included virtually every popularly held orthodox view on the millennium—with the streams of covenant theology and dispensationalism especially prominent within the movement.

Covenant theology remained vibrant in American Protestantism due to the Princeton tradition of confessional Presbyterianism and to the Dutch Reformed churches' influence. Dispensationalism, first systematized by Anglican clergyman John Nelson Darby in the mid-nineteenth century, was a form of premillennialism built on a fundamental distinction between Israel and the church in God's redemptive purposes. Dispensationalists argued that God's program with Israel was interrupted when the nation

---

[56] John A. T. Robinson, *In the End God* (New York: Harper and Row, 1968).

[57] Harvey Cox, *The Secular City: Secularization and Urbanization in Theological Perspective* (New York: Macmillan, 1966).

[58] Pierre Teilhard de Chardin, *The Future of Man* (New York: HarperCollins, 1964).

[59] Joseph A. Bracken, ed., *World without End: Christian Eschatology from a Process Perspective* (Grand Rapids: Eerdmans, 2005).

[60] See, for instance, Mary Daly, *Beyond God the Father: Toward a Philosophy of Women's Liberation* (Boston: Beacon, 1973) and Rosemary Radford Ruether, *The Radical Kingdom: The Western Experience of Messianic Hope* (New York: Harper and Row, 1970).

[61] *The Fundamentals,* vols. 1–4 (Los Angeles: Bible Institute of Los Angeles, 1917).

rejected Jesus as Messiah. The kingdom offered was now postponed, with the church serving as a "parenthesis" in God's prophetic program. At the end of the age, dispensationalism contended, God will "rapture" the church from the earth before seven years of tribulation falls on the world. During this time, God will convert the nation of Israel—144,000 Jewish persons. At the end of the tribulation, Jesus will return and initiate his millennial reign from Jerusalem during which Israel will inherit all her promises, including that of the land of Canaan promised to Abraham.

This system of prophetic thought was highly influential in American fundamentalism due to the influence of publications such as *Scofield Reference Bible,* educational institutions such as Moody Bible Institute and Dallas Theological Seminary, ministries such as Niagara Bible Conferences, and the person of evangelist Billy Graham. While covenant theology remained largely within Presbyterian and Reformed circles, dispensationalism took hold within the burgeoning fundamentalist parachurch infrastructure. It became so influential that some dispensationalist ideas—such as a pretribulational rapture—became in some circles associated with orthodoxy itself.

Dispensationalism further gained ground thanks to the establishment of Israel as a state in 1948, a move many believed to be part of the end-time scenario. Writers such as Hal Lindsey and Tim LaHaye popularized dispensationalism through best-selling nonfiction and fiction books, presenting a dispensational premillennial view of the apocalypse, often with rather speculative correlations between biblical prophecies and current events.[62]

After World War II, a group of "neoevangelicals," represented by theologians such as Carl F. H. Henry, institutions such as Fuller Theological Seminary, and publications such as *Christianity Today* magazine, sought to overcome eschatological tensions within the fundamentalist coalition and to overcome what they perceived to be the negative effect on Christian social action of dispensationalism's "pessimism" about the flow of history.[63] While calling for diversity within the evangelical coalition on matters such as the millennium and the timing of the rapture, evangelical theologians called for more serious doctrinal reflection on the meaning of the kingdom of God and its relation to the present age. Evangelical New Testament theologian George Eldon Ladd, a nondispensational premillen-

---

[62] For discussions of the impact of these books on American culture, see Paul Boyer, *When Time Shall Be No More: Prophecy Belief in Modern American Culture* (Cambridge: Harvard University Press, 1992) and Amy Johnson Frykholm, *Rapture Culture: Left Behind in Evangelical America* (New York: Oxford University Press, 2004).

[63] See, for instance, Carl F. H. Henry, *The Uneasy Conscience of Modern Fundamentalism* (Grand Rapids: Eerdmans, 1947).

nialist, called on evangelicals to adopt an "already-not yet" understanding of the kingdom—a view which argued that the kingdom was inaugurated at the first advent of Christ but still awaited its consummation at the eschaton.[64]

In the 1970s and 1980s such doctrinal development took off in earnest as both dispensationalists and covenant theologians moved closer together. Covenant theologians emphasized the material, cosmic nature of the kingdom—a redemption fulfilled in the new earth.[65] A younger group of "progressive dispensationalists" led by Dallas Seminary professors Craig Blaising and Darrell Bock modified dispensationalism in shocking ways: abandoning the idea of Israel and the church as "two peoples" of God, adopting an "already-not yet" model of kingdom fulfillment and casting aside the notion of the church as a "parenthesis" in God's timetable while retaining a pretribulational rapture and a future restoration of political, ethnic Israel.[66] Remarkably, evangelical theology came as close as it ever has to a consensus on matters of the kingdom of God.[67]

At the same time, however, evangelical Christianity's eschatological consensus faltered as revisionist theologies questioned orthodoxies that had lasted millennia within orthodox Christianity. This was nowhere as evident as in evangelical debates over hell, which came into focus in the 1980s. Some evangelical theologians, including the highly influential Clark Pinnock, suggested that hell might not be everlasting conscious punishment but instead annihilation of the wicked.[68]

Others, such as the "open theist" theologians, revised their understanding of prophecy to fit with a future in which God does not know all of the choices that will be made by his free creatures. Ironically, this "open" view of God led some on the evangelical left to revert to some ideas—such as a postponed kingdom and the church as a kind of "parenthesis"—reminiscent of most widely rejected facets of classical dispensationalism.[69] Some

---

[64] George Eldon Ladd, *Jesus and the Kingdom: The Eschatology of Biblical Realism* (New York: Harper and Row, 1964).

[65] For perhaps the most influential of such, see Anthony Hoekema, *The Bible and the Future* (Grand Rapids: Eerdmans, 1979).

[66] Craig Blaising and Darrell Bock, *Progressive Dispensationalism* (Grand Rapids: Baker, 1993); Robert L. Saucy, *The Case for Progressive Dispensationalism* (Grand Rapids: Zondervan, 1993).

[67] Russell D. Moore, *The Kingdom of Christ: The New Evangelical Perspective* (Wheaton, IL: Crossway, 2004).

[68] Clark H. Pinnock, "The Destruction of the Finally Impenitent," *Criswell Theological Review* 4 (1990): 243–59. While Pinnock's views on hell represented a flight from evangelical orthodoxy almost across the board, some who were otherwise orthodox, such as John R. W. Stott, also suggested the possibility of the ultimate annihilation of the wicked. Stott explains his view in a dialogue with liberal David Edwards in *Essentials: A Liberal-Evangelical Dialogue* (London: Hodder and Stoughton, 1988), 313–20.

[69] Russell D. Moore, "Leftward to Scofield: The Eclipse of the Kingdom in Post-Conservative Evangelical Theology," *JETS* 47 (2004): 423–40.

liberalizing voices within the evangelical movement suggested doing away with "kingdom" language altogether since it is outmoded in a world more accustomed to democratic republics than to monarchs. "Emerging church" guru Brian McLaren, for instance, proposed the "revolution of God" as a more descriptive term.[70]

Eschatology in Baptist Theology

A Baptist church is itself an affirmation of a particular eschatology. In the seventeenth century, the "Anabaptists" coming out of the English churches did so because they believed the fulfillment of the new covenant necessitated a believers' church, which, unlike old covenant Israel, was to be made up only of the regenerate. Baptists in England and in colonial America resisted the idea of state churches claiming prerogatives from Old Testament Israel for marking out "covenant children" as members of the visible kingdom of God. They opposed civil governments claiming the rights of the Israelite theocracy to enforce penalties against religious practices or ideas. For the Baptists the problem with these churches was that they didn't know what time it was; that is, they failed to see where the new covenant church fit in God's redemptive time line, between the first and second comings of Jesus.

The primary Baptist confessions of the seventeenth century reflected something of the covenant theology of English Puritanism, while holding forth a particularly baptistic understanding of the new covenant. The First London Confession of Faith (1644) identified the "spiritual kingdom" of God on earth with the church (article 33), and ends with a prayer for the quick coming of Jesus. In keeping with the Westminster Confession from which it was based, the Second London Confession (1689) affirmed an intermediate state, bodily resurrection of both saved and lost, future judgment, and the permanent eternal states of heaven and hell. These same eschatological patterns were broadly retained in later Baptist confessions, such as the New Hampshire Confession and the Baptist Faith and Message statements of 1925, 1963, and 2000.

For much of Baptist history, the millennial viewpoint of the working theologians tended toward amillennialism, perhaps as a result of the Reformed communions from which Baptists came and on whom many of them relied for theological guidance. In the American South, theologians such as John L. Dagg and James P. Boyce were decidedly amillennial. In the twentieth century, E. Y. Mullins and W. T. Connor continued the amillennial tradition. Mullins conceded that, if taken literally, Revelation 20 "certainly seems to teach the premillennial view in part."[71] Nonetheless, Mullins objected that the visions of Revelation "are symbolic in the highest degree," and, furthermore, that a strict premillennial view of Revelation 20 would limit the reign of believers

---

[70] Brian E. McLaren, "Found in Translation," *Sojourners* (March 2006): 14–19.

[71] Edgar Young Mullins, *The Christian Religion in Its Doctrinal Expression* (Nashville: Broadman, 1917), 470.

with Christ to martyrs.[72] In the later twentieth century, pastor-theologian Herschel Hobbs, a "convert" from historic premillennialism, popularized amillennialism within the Southern Baptist Convention. Nonetheless, there was always diversity within Baptist life when it came to interpretation of the millennium and of the precise pattern of future events.

In England, the Baptist missionary movement was propelled by a postmillennialism derivative from the thought of the Congregationalist Jonathan Edwards. Theologians such as Andrew Fuller and missionaries such as William Carey believed the mission task was crucial partly because, through it, God would convert the nations and usher in the thousand-year kingdom of Christ. Postmillennialism would remain one option within Baptist eschatology until the mid-twentieth century. Northern Baptists such as Augustus H. Strong and Southern Baptists such as B. H. Carroll held to a postmillennial understanding of the future, a view Carroll strongly advocated especially against pre-millennialism.[73]

Carroll, the first president of Southwestern Baptist Theological Seminary, did not see the millennium as having yet arrived in his day, convinced that it could not come with "human governments constituted as they are now."[74] Nonetheless, Carroll saw the millennium as imminent. "The world was four thousand years old when Christ came, and it is nearly two thousand years since he came," Carroll wrote. "The devil's time is nearly out; events are moving rapidly, ocean and air are navigated, telegraph wires long rusted with commercial and political lies shall shine with the transmission of messages of mercy and salvation."[75]

Postmillennialism even contributed to Baptist hymnody, as Southern Baptists grew more and more optimistic about the triumph of the Great Commission in the twentieth century. Thus, one gospel song, popularized by the SBC Woman's Missionary Union, proclaims: "We've a story to tell to the nations, That shall turn their hearts to the right/ A story of truth and mercy, a story of peace and light, a story of peace and light/ For the darkness shall turn to dawning, and the dawning to noonday bright; And Christ's great kingdom shall come on earth, the kingdom of love and light."[76]

Premillennialism has had strong representation in Baptist eschatology. The British Baptist preacher Charles H. Spurgeon was a historic premillennialist.[77] In the mid-twentieth century, neoorthodox Southern Baptist theologian Dale Moody championed an historic premillennialist view of the kingdom, while remaining highly critical of dispensational-

---

[72] Ibid.

[73] See, for instance, B. H. Carroll, *Interpretation of the English Bible, the Book of Revelation* (New York: Revell, 1916), 200–33.

[74] Ibid., 223.

[75] Ibid., 219–20.

[76] David S. Dockery observes that this WMU theme song is a postmillennial song that all evangelicals can sing, though postmillennialism itself may be faulty. David S. Dockery, *Our Christian Hope: Biblical Answers to Questions about the Future* (Nashville: LifeWay, 1998), 72.

[77] Dennis Swanson, "The Millennial Position of Spurgeon," *Master's Seminary Journal* 7 (1996): 183–212.

ism. "If the importance of belief in a thousand-year reign of Christ upon the earth were measured by the space it occupies in the Bible, it would be a footnote to discussions on the Kingdom of God," Moody wrote. "But if the influence of the idea on the history of the church, both negative and positive, is our guide, then a major role must be assigned to such belief or unbelief."[78]

Moody aligned himself with the historic premillennialism and "already-not yet" structure of eschatology articulated by evangelical New Testament theologian George Eldon Ladd, a view he found most reflective of the Bible's placing of Christian hope within human history.[79] He expressed frustration that Southern Baptist publishing efforts were overwhelmingly amillennial, while Southern Baptist preaching at the popular level was overwhelmingly dispensationalist.[80]

Prominent figures within the nineteenth century's Baptist Landmark movement, most notably J. R. Graves, held to a kind of dispensational premillennialism. Northern Baptists on the conservative side of the fundamentalist-modernist controversy were often strongly premillennial and often also dispensationalist. For Southern Baptists the premillennialist viewpoint became most influential through the ministry of W. A. Criswell, longtime pastor of Dallas's First Baptist Church. Criswell led the prominent Dallas congregation to revise its statement of faith to reflect a dispensationalist premillennialist view of the kingdom of God. When some church members objected that Criswell's predecessor, George W. Truett, a postmillennialist, could not sign the statement, Criswell retorted: "That, brother, is absolutely correct. When Dr. Truett, the far-famed pastor of this illustrious congregation was here, he could not have signed this. But he can now!"[81]

Dispensational premillennialists were dominant within the conservative resurgence in the SBC, a movement led by Paige Patterson and Paul Pressler—both dispensational premillennialists. In fact, of the conservative SBC presidents elected since the conservative movement began, at this writing all of them but one have been pretribulational and premillennial.[82] While Southern Baptist conservatives insisted that the details of eschatological time tables were not a measure of orthodoxy, moderates within the Convention were not so sure. Conservatives such as Jerry Vines pointed out that the supposedly "broad tent" of the moderates did not include room for dispensational premillennialism, which Southwestern Seminary president Russell Dilday called a "heresy" in the 1980s, while one of his New Testament faculty members called dispensationalism "a cult."[83] Some Southern Baptist conservatives equated amillennialism with liberalism since so many of the SBC moderates held

---

[78] Dale Moody, *The Word of Truth: A Summary of Christian Doctrine Based on Biblical Revelation* (Grand Rapids: Eerdmans, 1981), 548.

[79] Dale Moody, *The Hope of Glory* (Grand Rapids: Eerdmans, 1964).

[80] Moody, *Word of Truth*, 551.

[81] This anecdote is related by Paige Patterson in "Forum: Eschatology," *SBC Life*, June/July 1994, 6.

[82] The exception is James Merritt, who served as SBC president in 2001 and 2002 and who is a historic premillennialist.

[83] Jerry Vines, "Eschatology: Premillennial or Amillennial?" *Theological Educator* 37 (1988): 135.

this view. The real issue, however, was that the Convention liberals held an "a" position on many more things than the millennium.

Though particular millennial or tribulational views have never been a measure of orthodoxy, the primary confessional issues of eschatology—such as the reality of judgment and the second coming of Christ—are and always have been. Millennial controversies are so pronounced precisely because, on the most important aspects of Christian eschatology, there has been little controversy among Baptists. While some in Baptist life, such as modernist Harry Emerson Fosdick, have opposed orthodox views of the eternal state, Baptist theology has been overwhelmingly traditional in affirming eternal blessedness for the redeemed and eternal torment for those outside of Christ. Baptist views of heaven have often resonated with the "spiritual vision" model of future hope—a resonance seen perhaps most clearly in Baptist John Bunyan's 1676 *The Pilgrim's Progress* allegory of Christian's journey to the Celestial City, an otherworldly spiritual abode.[84]

Baptist hymnody has reinforced an emphasis on heaven, especially in the revivalist gospel song tradition with songs such as "When the Roll Is Called Up Yonder" and "When We All Get to Heaven." Baptist preaching typically has joined calls for individual repentance with warnings of the terrors of eternal judgment—thus, the reputation for "hellfire and brimstone" preaching has coincided with Baptist revival and outreach efforts throughout the centuries, especially in America. Indeed, burden for the unevangelized facing hell has been a major incentive for Baptist missionary efforts, to the occasional consternation of more liberal critics within the Baptist tent.[85]

In the late twentieth century, some Baptist theologians, such as Dale Moody and Molly T. Marshall, sought to revise Baptist eschatology to include, for instance, "postmortem" opportunity for the unevangelized to receive the gospel after death.[86] Most Southern Baptists rejected such proposals as not consonant with a biblical message that "it is appointed for men to die once and after this comes judgment" (Heb. 9:27 NASB). Thus, Baptists continued their longstanding confessional belief that both salvation and damnation were everlasting realities, conditioned upon one's faith response to God through Jesus Christ during the span of this life.

How Does It All Fit Together?

The future has a name: Jesus of Nazareth. Like all doctrines of the faith, eschatology is an outworking of Christology. God's final purpose with his

---

84 John Bunyan, *The Pilgrim's Progress: From This World to That Which Is to Come* (Edinburgh: Banner of Truth, 1977).

85 Alan Neely, "Baptists and Peoples of Other Faiths," *Perspectives in Religious Studies* 17 (1990): 233.

86 Molly T. Marshall, *No Salvation Outside the Church? A Critical Inquiry* (Lewiston, MD: Edwin Mellen, 1993), 223–51. Marshall acknowledges her debt to Moody's exegesis of 1 Peter 3:19 and 4:6 in establishing this view. Moody, *Word of Truth*, 496.

creation is to "bring everything together in the Messiah, both things in heaven and things on earth in Him" (Eph. 1:10 HCSB). This means that all of reality is about a clash of kingdoms. The rule Adam once had over Eden, a husbandry that was to extend to the ends of the earth, is now overtaken because Adam's heirs do not image God but another ruler, Satan. Humans may pretend to be autonomous, but they live and move as subjects in a kingdom—either the kingdom of the god of this age or the kingdom of the Christ of God. The message of Christian eschatology is that the tumult of this present warfare between the people of Christ and the principalities and powers is not eternal. Armageddon has been on the horizon since Eden. And, in the end, "the kingdoms of this world are become the kingdoms of our Lord, and of his Christ; and he shall reign for ever and ever" (Rev. 11:15 KJV).

The Kingdoms of This World

Darwinian naturalism, along with most non-Christian philosophies, assumes that death is the natural ending point to life. Christian eschatology insists otherwise, seeing death as an alien invader of the cosmic order, a curse from the Edenic fall, and a strategy of an enemy spirit to crush God's image-bearing humanity (Heb. 2:14–15). Death is personified as itself an enemy, indeed the final enemy to be placed under the feet of a triumphant King Jesus (1 Cor. 15:24–26). Death is not limited to human beings, but animal predation, natural disasters, agricultural frustration—these all point to the cold truth that God is not ruling the cosmos through his human mediator in the way he intended at the start. In this present age, all people—including the redeemed—still grow old, get sick, and die. At physical death, there is a sundering of the body from the soul, a violent act that tears at God's original creational purpose of breathing his life into the man of dust (Gen. 2:7). When a person dies, his flesh reverts back to the dust of the earth—a seeming contradiction of God's creation.

There is one man, however, who does not owe death as the wages of sin, who cannot be accused by the ruler of this age. The resurrection of Jesus is the first wave of a counter revolution that will turn back death's tyranny and satanic rule forever, but those who defy him are warned of a death that never ends. The reign of death is not simply the expiration of individuals. It is a deceptive and destructive kingdom of Satan that leads to a final confrontation, a final judgment, and a final defeat.

The Great Tribulation

Like the "already-not yet" structure of the rest of Christian eschatology, tribulation is part of the present experience of every believer throughout the ages. Tribulation is seen in the slaughter of Abel, the despotism of Pharaoh, the invasions of the Canaanites, the beheading of the disciples, and so forth. Since the fall of Adam, the creation heaves in torment, thrashing about for its ruler. Since the cunning of the serpent took down the primeval humans, cultic deception and false messianic claims have been afoot. Throughout the ages, believers have cried out to God for justice on a world order that militates against them. The promise of a Day of the Lord, in which God hands over the cosmos to its own iniquity and calls down judgment upon it, is a pivotal aspect of Christian eschatology.

Jesus pointed his disciples to earthquakes, false religions, and violent bloodshed as signs of the end of the age. It is not as though, however, we can catalog increases in, for instance, seismological activity or the frequency of military engagements in order to track out the unfolding of prophecy. Jesus specifically warned that these aspects of the tribulation are but "birth pains" of the end and will be present in every epoch until the end (Matt. 24:3–14). These birth pains culminate, however, in a final time of unparalleled distress, the time Christian theology calls the great tribulation. The Old Testament prophets and the Apocalypse of John present the tumult of these days in vivid detail: the intensification of warfare against the people of God, signs in the atmosphere, and the pouring out of God's judgments on his renegade creation.

Those who hold to *preterism,* the idea that most or all of Christian eschatology was fulfilled in the first century, argue that the tribulation came to pass in the fall of Jerusalem in AD 70.[87] Jesus did conflate the AD 70 tribulation with the final time of trouble. Preterists do not adequately account for, however, the typological fulfillment of the Day of the Lord, a pattern in history in which the judgment of God falls partially and repeatedly, pointing to the ultimate Day of the Lord at the end of the age.

We can see the tribulation woes of Matthew 24, for instance, as teaching, in the words of one biblical scholar "that the signs of the times *began* with Jesus and his generation, especially the fall of Jerusalem, but will not be complete until the return of Christ."[88] The fall of Jerusalem, like the exile of Israel before it, is a type of the coming Day of the Lord, a day that will end in the final unveiling of the Messiah.

Dispensationalists and some others see this great tribulation as a literal period of seven years, a figure drawn from Daniel's vision of seventy weeks of seven. Whether this period is literally seven years or an unspecified amount of time, it does not follow that people will discern immediately the apocalyptic nature of the tribulation. Rather it is seen as an

---

[87] See, for instance, Kenneth L. Gentry Jr., *Before Jerusalem Fell: Dating the Book of Revelation* (Tyler, TX: Institute for Christian Economics, 1989).

[88] C. Marvin Pate, "A Progressive Dispensationalist View of Revelation," in *Four Views on the Book of Revelation,* ed. C. Marvin Pate (Grand Rapids: Zondervan, 1998), 148.

enormous intensification of woes already at work, which then spills over into an obviously supernatural demonstration of God's judgment. Like the hardening of Pharaoh's heart through the plagues on Egypt, the great tribulation results in a backlash of lost humanity against the Creator, with a final battle, Armageddon, marshalling the armies of this age against the armies of heaven.

The Antichrist

The coming tribulation age will see a final human personification of wickedness, a figure the Scriptures call the "man of lawlessness" (2 Thess. 2) or "the beast" (Rev. 13) or the "antichrist" (1 John 2; 4; 2 John 7). The antichrist is one more example of the satanic aping of God's redemptive purposes. Just as God saves the world through a Spirit-anointed human Messiah, the god of this age unveils a human ruler, anointed with his spirit. Just as Jesus' Spirit poured out on his disciples is the guarantee of his future appearance (Rom. 8:23), the spirit of antichrist at work now in the world guarantees his eventual coming (1 John 4:3). Just as Jesus is typified in the millennia before his coming by other "anointed ones" who point to his coming rule, many antichrists appear throughout the ages, all pointing to the one who is to come. Just as the Messiah is announced by the prophet of God as the one worthy of worship, the counter-messiah raises up a "false prophet" to promote the worship of the beast (Rev. 13:11–18).

The Messiah refuses to conquer the world's kingdoms through the worship of Satan or through the sword; the counter-messiah is given his kingdoms by Satan and rules them through bloodshed. The Messiah counts worship of God as more important than food; the counter-messiah demands worship of his power and enforces it through controlling access to bread (Rev. 13:17). The Messiah speaks liberating truth (John 8:31–32) while the counter-messiah deceives through signs and wonders (Rev. 13:13–14). The Messiah builds a holy temple, his church, of which he is the cornerstone (Eph. 2:20–21), while the counter-messiah stands in this temple, falsely proclaiming himself as god (2 Thess. 2:4). As Jesus is presented as the final prophet, priest, and king, this antichrist claims prophetic authority and claims dominion over both the church and the state.

The antichrist is a figure shrouded in prophetic mystery. Much speculation has focused on what John sees as the "mark of the beast" borne by all who claim allegiance to him, and the "number of the beast" (666), which those with minds to discern are called to contemplate. Some Christians have sought through numerological codes to decipher a man's name in 666, ranging from the more plausible (Nero Caesar) to the almost laughable (the six letters in each word of "Ronald Wilson Reagan"). The mark of the beast has been equated with supermarket scanner UPC codes to microchips placed in dog's ears to enable owners to find lost pets. These speculative endeavors are not totally without merit. It could be that the number John received is a numerological code, perhaps only understood in the tumult of the tribulation to come. It is more likely, however, that Jesus is showing us the true identity of the antichrist in a way that applies to every age of the church. Though he claims to be god, he is only a man (Ezek. 28:2). He is one less than seven, the number of completion—and this number is repeated three times, another aping of the trinitarian glory of God (the redeemed cry "holy, holy, holy").

The mark of the beast could be a physical mark, a tattoo, or even a microchip, which sets apart citizens as those who belong to this evil emperor. It is possible, however, that the mark is spiritual and not physical—an indelible mark that corresponds to the mark on the foreheads of the people of God signaling their allegiance to Christ (Rev. 7:3).

We must be careful to evaluate every claim to state and ecclesial authority, but we must also be careful not to rule out that the mark of the beast may be more subtle and indelible than we can imagine. What if the mark is an attitude of the heart, a yielding to mammon and to personal security and to human autonomy? What if such a mark could be borne in the heart, even by those who would never countenance a state-sponsored microchip in their bodies?

As with the tribulation, preterists are partially right to argue that the beast of Revelation is to be identified with Caesar.[89] The beast texts of Revelation are set within the context of the Caesar-Christ conflict, a conflict that threatened the lives of the early Christian communities. But the Bible clearly presents the antichrist figure—a figure who is described in precisely the same terms as the beast of Revelation 13—as a future man of the last days who is defeated personally by the returning Messiah Jesus "with the brightness of His coming" (2 Thess. 2:8 HCSB). Early Roman Christians could rightly identify Caesar as antichrist because he met all the criteria—persecution with the sword, self-exaltation as a god, control of commerce, etc. This does not mean that the antichrist has already come.

Instead, John revealed that "many antichrists have come" even as he insists that "Antichrist is coming" (1 John 2:18 HCSB). Anytime Christians see a rejection of Jesus as the human mediator between God and humanity, we see the spirit of antichrist (1 John 4:3). Anytime Christians see a state that turns a sword given for the punishment of evildoers against the people of God, we see a beast state. Identifying such antichrists is perhaps more important—for every age of the church—than identifying *the* antichrist.

---

[89] Kenneth Gentry Jr., *The Beast of Revelation* (Tyler, TX: Institute for Christian Economics, 1989).

Hell

Christian theology faces a theodicy problem, but not the typical one posed by skeptics of the faith. The question for God's reputation is not why do some people go to hell, but rather why do the guilty seem to go unpunished? From Job to David to Solomon to the martyrs of Revelation, the cry of believers through the ages is a plea for God's justice to be displayed, for the rebellion of the wicked to end. Christian eschatology answers this question after the dust has settled from history, when, as John saw, the nations are brought before a great white throne to give an account to the King of the universe (Rev. 20:11–15). Though unbelievers tell themselves that God does not see their actions (Ps. 94:1–7; Ezek. 8:12), every idle word, thought, and deed will be brought before the throne and judged by the criterion of God's own righteousness (Matt. 12:36–37). Moreover, God has implanted knowledge of this coming judgment in the psyches of all humans (Rom. 2:15–16), knowledge they seek to deny and suppress.

As with other aspects of eschatology, damnation has facets that are "already" and others that are "not yet." Judgment does not begin in the afterlife but during life as God hands the impenitent unbeliever more and more over to his own depravity, idolatry, and self-absorption (Rom. 1:18–32). This "giving over" is seen as "the wrath of God . . . revealed from heaven" (Rom. 1:18), pointing to the awful day when God will remove all common grace and abandon the sinner to who he really is. As C. S. Lewis put it, the man who loves only the self is finally removed from all external grace toward what he desires: "And what he finds there is Hell."[90]

The sinner's judgment does not come suddenly upon him at death but is revealed even now as he loves the darkness and hates the light of Christ Jesus (John 3:21). This is one reason we can have confidence that all infants dying in infancy are redeemed through the blood of Christ. We do not merely speculate that these infants have been spared judgment. We *know* that they have been spared this initial aspect of judgment: the giving over to the outworking of the sin nature through volitional deeds in the body. We have every reason to assume—based on other biblical evidence—that God also spares them from the ultimate end of such judgment, hell.[91]

Upon death, the sinner immediately finds himself in torment, as Jesus made clear in his account of the rich man and Lazarus. The unbelieving soul, sundered from the body, faces punishment; but it is, as Calvin understood it, a temporary holding place—the waiting of a criminal for his

---

[90] C. S. Lewis, *The Problem of Pain* (New York: Macmillan, 1962; reprint, New York: Simon and Schuster, 1996), 110.

[91] For a full defense of universal salvation of infants dying in infancy, see Ronald H. Nash, *When a Baby Dies: Answers to Comfort Grieving Parents* (Grand Rapids: Zondervan, 1999). This issue is also addressed in this book, *A Theology for the Church,* in the sections on sin and salvation.

day in court. This experience of hell is frightful and imaginably horrific, but it is not the final sentence to the lake of fire, a sentence that awaits the day of judgment at the resurrection of the unrighteous (Rev. 20:11–15). In this sense the intermediate state for unbelievers parallels that of the angels who "left their proper dwelling" and who are thus presently "kept in eternal chains under gloomy darkness until the judgment of the great day" (Jude 6).

The final judgment focuses on the kingship of Christ. Jesus pointed to this judgment throne as a crucial aspect of his kingly role as Son of David when he will distinguish between the sheep and the goats (Matt. 25:31–46; Ezek. 34:17–24). The criteria for judgment include individual sins—all summoned as evidence for damnation—but the ultimate criterion for judgment is the sinner's response to Jesus himself. This is why John speaks of judgment as having to do with a book, a record of names written in the "Lamb's Book of Life." In Jesus' teaching of the judgment seat, humans are judged by their actions toward "the least of these," but these actions point beyond themselves to whether the judged ones *know Christ*—a relational knowledge seen in how they treat his "brothers" (Matt. 25:40,45; cf. 1 John 3:14–18).

The final judgment results in the condemnation of sinners—both human and angelic—to hell, a place of indescribable torment. John referred to it as a "lake of fire" (Rev. 20:14), and Jesus compared it to a Middle Eastern trash heap (Mark 9:42–50). God did not design this place of eschatological exile for human beings, but, in the words of Jesus, "for the devil and his angels" (Matt. 25:41). Because rebel humans choose the headship of Satan as their god and because they share his nature, they will join him in their inheritance, unless they are hidden in Christ. All human beings, however, unlike angels, are invited and commanded to flee the wrath to come (Heb. 2:16). This understanding of hell is in sharp contrast to a supralapsarian Calvinism that sees God predestining human beings to hell logically prior to the fall, in order to display his wrath. God sincerely invites all human beings to seek refuge from the wrath to come.

As the New Hampshire Confession of Faith puts it, "Nothing prevents the salvation of the greatest sinner on earth except his own voluntary refusal to submit to the Lord Jesus Christ, which refusal will subject him to an aggravated condemnation." Revelation brings with it responsibility. The greater the revelation, the greater the responsibility.

Unlike the rebel angels, human sinners suffer hell corporeally as well as spiritually. They are resurrected, after the millennial reign of Christ, to face judgment as bodily creatures. This too reinforces the justice of God. The sentence comes upon them for deeds "done in the body" (2 Cor. 5:10). They are indicted as those who have stored up wrath by "carrying out the desires of the body and the mind" (Eph. 2:3). The prototype of hell can be seen in the curse borne by Jesus at his crucifixion, a curse in which he suffered both physically and psychically. In hell, the whole person is handed over to the judgment of God.

The Scriptures seem to indicate that there are degrees of punishment in hell, based on the findings of the tribunal of God at the resurrection. Jesus can speak in parabolic terms of some being "beaten with few stripes" and some with "many stripes" (Luke 12:47–48 KJV). The difference between these punishments in the parable rests on the difference in knowledge of the master's will between the two servants. Hebrews can speak of punishment of death coming upon the disobedient while at the same time asking; "How much worse punishment, do you think, will be deserved by the one who has spurned the Son of God, and has profaned the blood of the covenant by which he was sanctified, and has outraged the Spirit of grace?" (Heb. 10:29). All people will be judged for sin—and will face the wrath of God for such sin, if they are outside of Christ. And every unbeliever's experience of hell is worse than anything we can imagine in this life. But, it would appear, those with access to the light of the gospel, who reject it anyway, face, as again the New Hampshire Confession puts it, "an aggravated condemnation." Revelation brings responsibility. Greater revelations bring greater responsibility.

Hell weighs heavily on the regenerate heart, as the Spirit prompts us to groan for those who will be lost. Hell is also an affront to the unregenerate sense of justice, since no person except through the conviction of the Spirit deems himself worthy of condemnation. Because of this, the history of Christian eschatology is a blur of heresies seeking to evade the clear teaching of conscious, everlasting punishment of unrepentant men and angels in hell. Origen could find proof texts to support his vision of universal reconciliation; the idea that hell is purgatorial in function and that all passing through it will be redeemed. Contemporary Catholic intellectual Richard John Neuhaus can extend the hope (though not the certainty) that hell will one day be empty.[92] Others can ponder the billions of unevangelized who die without Christ and wonder whether they will have an opportunity after death to respond to the gospel.

These hopes are misplaced and unbiblical. Christian eschatology maintains that the "day of salvation" is *now* (2 Cor. 6:2), during this lifetime's temporary suspension of doom. After this, the grace of God is not extended—only his justice, and that with severity. Jesus does indeed triumph over all things, making peace through the blood of his cross (Col. 1:20), but

---

[92] Richard John Neuhaus, *Death on a Friday Afternoon: Meditations on the Last Words of Jesus from the Cross* (New York: Basic, 2000), 42–64.

this peace does not mean the redemption of each individual. Instead, Jesus triumphs over his enemies—as they are all consigned to damnation beneath the feet of his sovereign kingship. Yes, every tongue confesses Jesus as lord eschatologically—even Satan himself (Phil. 2:9–11). This does not mean that every tongue calls out to him for salvation. Instead there is the universal recognition that Jesus has triumphed over every rival to his throne. The redeemed will love this truth; the impenitent will lament it.

Another alternative offered to the orthodox view of hell is that of *annihilationism,* the idea that those sentenced to hell eventually are consumed by the fire and cease consciousness. This view has been held by cultic groups, such as the Jehovah's Witnesses, and offered as a possibility in more recent years by otherwise orthodox evangelical Christians such as John R. W. Stott.[93] Annihilationism has some proof texts that seem to support it: hell is spoken of as a "second death" and as "destruction." Hell is contrasted with "everlasting life." Annihilationism also seems to maintain the justice of God. Sins committed over a finite span of time are punished in a finite span of time, and then the suffering is over. The author of this chapter has found himself wishing that he could believe in annihilationism. It would remove the overwhelming burden of thinking of so many lost, forever, without Christ. But Scripture leaves this burden intact. The "death" and "destruction" pictured in the lake of fire refers to a place where "they will be tormented day and night forever and ever" (Rev. 20:10).

In hell, God triumphs over the kingdoms of this world, the old order of the flesh. Why then must this punishment be eternal? There are at least two reasons. The revolt against God is more than a sin against one's neighbor. It is instead a reproach to an infinitely worthy Creator, itself worthy of an infinitely worthy punishment. Human justice reflects this when we sentence a man to one punishment for threatening to kill his coworker and another man to a much more severe punishment for threatening to kill the president of the United States. More significantly is the nature of the judgment itself. The sinner in hell does not become morally neutral upon his sentence to hell. We must not imagine the damned sinner displaying gospel repentance and longing for the presence of Christ. The damned indeed are longing for an escape from punishment, but they are not "new creations." They do not, in hell, love the Lord their God with heart, mind, soul, and strength. Instead, they are now handed over to the full display of their natures apart from grace, natures that are satanic (John 8:44). Thus, the condemnation continues forever and ever and ever, with no end in view either for the sin or the punishment thereof.

---

[93] For a defense of annihilationism, see Edward William Fudge, *The Fire That Consumes: The Biblical Case for Conditional Immortality* (Carlisle: Paternoster, 1994). For a convincing refutation of annihilationism, see Robert Peterson, *Hell on Trial: The Case for Eternal Punishment* (Phillipsburg, NJ: Presbyterian and Reformed, 1995).

Attempts to navigate around the truth of hell as everlasting punishment are indicative finally of the original Edenic sin, the substitution of human wisdom and human justice for the authority of God. Yes, hell is horrifying. God deems it so. Our response to such horror should not be denial, but the fervent evangelism of the nations. As C. S. Lewis writes: "In the long run the answer to all those who object to the doctrine of hell is itself a question: 'What are you asking God to do?' To wipe out their past sins and, at all costs, to give them a fresh start, smoothing every difficulty and offering every miraculous help? But He has done so, on Calvary. To forgive them? They will not be forgiven. To leave them alone? Alas, I am afraid that is what He does."[94]

The Kingdom of Christ

"If heaven ain't a lot like Dixie, I don't want to go," sings country music songwriter Hank Williams Jr. The sentiment that eternal reward shouldn't intrude too much on life is culturally popular and is not all that unusual even within the church. Theologian Jerry Walls traces two understandings of eternal blessedness in the history of Christian theology: a theocentric view and an anthropocentric view. In the theocentric view, eternity is "a timeless experience of contemplating the infinitely fascinating reality of God in all of his aspects," without much element of human fellowship. The anthropocentric view, by contrast, emphasizes "being reunited with family and friends" and sees eternity as the continuation of life without the mar of sin and suffering.[95]

In biblical eschatology, however, the eternal state is strikingly anthropocentric but not in the ways found in much of popular piety. Eternity can be said to be anthropocentric so long as we understand that the *anthropos* referenced is Jesus of Nazareth. Eternity is not a timeless beatific vision or an endless choir practice. But neither is it merely a family reunion in which the circle is seen to be unbroken after all. Eternity means Jesus (and, by extension, those who are in him) finally receives his promised inheritance: everything.

Heaven

Heaven is defined in Scripture as the dwelling place of God, a place inhabited by the angelic armies, the redeemed of all the ages, and the ascended Jesus himself as he awaits the consummation of his kingdom. At

---

[94] Lewis, *Problem of Pain,* 114. We must be careful to understand the way in which God "leaves the sinner alone." God is not absent from hell, but is present in his wrath and justice. He is, however, absent relationally. He abandons the sinner, in a real sense, to himself.

[95] Jerry Walls, *Heaven: The Logic of Eternal Joy* (New York: Oxford University, 2002), 7. Walls here acknowledges his dependence on a taxonomy developed by Colleen McDannell and Bernhard Lang, *Heaven: A History* (New York: Vintage, 1990), 228, 265.

the moment of death, the believer is ushered into the presence of Christ in heaven. Since Jesus is now in heaven, this is where the inheritance of the church waits for us, where our mother, the heavenly Jerusalem, is located. Our inheritance, our Jerusalem, and even our Christ do not stay in heaven though—and neither do we.

Many Christians think of their future existence as heaven, in the kind of disembodied, unearthly abode they know awaits them immediately after death. And yet the time between death and resurrection—what theologians call the *intermediate state*—is far from permanent. It is itself a time of waiting for the full blessings of salvation—the resurrection of the body and the coming of the kingdom. Karl Barth describes John Calvin's vision of this heavenly interlude for the dead in Christ with perfect clarity. Believers in heaven are conscious and active "but with the rest and assurance of conscience that comes with physical death, contemplating God and his peace, from which they are still at a distance, but of which they are sure."[96] These believers are "not yet in possession of the kingdom of God" but they can nonetheless "see what we here can only believe in hope."[97]

For believers, the intermediate state is blessedness, to be sure. But in heaven there is yet eschatology. The ultimate purpose of God is not just the ongoing life of believers but that his kingdom would come, his will would be done "on earth as it is in heaven" (Matt. 6:10). That awaits the end of all ends, the return of Jesus and the final overthrow of death.

Second Coming

There is a reason the bodily return of Christ is rejected by heretics, from first-century Gnostics to the twentieth-century Jesus Seminar. The idea of Jesus of Nazareth triumphantly returning as a warrior-king to reclaim his cosmic inheritance is anchored to a thoroughgoing supernaturalism and an orthodox Christology. Proudly unorthodox retired Episcopal Bishop John Shelby Spong suggests that the second coming reinforces the idea of Jesus as "rescuer" rather than merely an inspiring "spirit being."[98] Spong argues that one cannot have his liberal vision of "Christianity without theism" without getting rid of the premodern notion of a physically returning Messiah from heaven.

While all orthodox Christians everywhere have affirmed the physical, bodily return of Jesus at the end of the age, contemporary evangelicals have disagreed—sometimes sharply—over the timing of this event, especially as it relates to the tribulation and the rise of the antichrist.

---

[96] Barth, *Theology of John Calvin,* 146–47.

[97] Ibid., 147.

[98] John Shelby Spong, *Why Christianity Must Change or Die: A Bishop Speaks to Believers in Exile* (San Francisco: HarperCollins, 1998), 83–117.

The emergence of dispensationalism in the nineteenth century fueled the idea of a *pretribulational rapture*. This is the view that the second coming arrives in two stages: a secret, unexpected "catching away" of believers before the tribulation, and a public, visible coming of Christ with his church at the end of this time of Jacob's trouble.[99]

Amillennialists, postmillennialists, and historic premillennialists maintained the more common view in church history of a *posttribulational rapture*. In this view the second coming texts all refer to one event in which Jesus returns, the believing dead are raised, living believers are translated into glorified bodies, and the church meets Jesus in the air to return with him in triumph and glory.

A distinct minority of evangelicals has articulated a *midtribulational* or *prewrath rapture* in which the church is called to heaven sometime during the tribulation, before the final outpouring of God's wrath.

A pretribulational rapture makes perfect sense within the context of a dispensationalist hermeneutic. The doctrine rests on several considerations: a sharp distinction between Israel and the church, the church as a parenthesis in God's prophetic timetable, God's promise that he will deliver his people from judgment, and the imminent return of Christ. The pretribulational rapture initially was argued by dispensationalists such as Darby and Scofield most significantly as the end of the "church age"—when God restarts his prophetic timetable with Israel, the onset of Daniel's seventieth week, which has been on "pause" since the rejection of Jesus by the Jews in the first century. At the rapture, the "times of the Gentiles" are fulfilled and God turns again to his earthly people, Israel. "The mystery program (the church), which was so distinct in its inception, will certainly be separate at its conclusion," dispensationalist theologian J. Dwight Pentecost argues. "This program must be concluded before God resumes and culminates his program for Israel. This mystery concept of the church makes a pre-tribulation Rapture a necessity."[100]

Dispensationalists still hold to a distinction between the church and Israel, but the idea of two peoples and two programs, as Pentecost calls the "mystery program," is almost wholly abandoned by contemporary dispensationalist theologians, evacuating the primary theological reason for a pretribulational rapture.

---

[99] Not all dispensationalists hold to a "secret" rapture. Some, especially progressive dispensationalists, see a public, visible rapture as a sign of the coming unveiling of Christ and judgment. Most dispensationalists, however, have interpreted the "thief in the night" aspect of the rapture to include not just its unexpected coming but also the confusion the event leaves in its wake. Thus, popular dispensationalist Bible teachers will sometimes speculate on how the unbelieving world will "explain" the rapture, be it through claims of alien abductions or other more or less fantastic rationalizations.

[100] J. Dwight Pentecost, *Things to Come: A Study in Biblical Eschatology* (Grand Rapids: Zondervan, 1964), 200–1.

The second important reason for a pretribulation rapture remains in place for most dispensationalists: in prophetic passages in the New Testament the church is said to be "not destined . . . for wrath" (1 Thess. 5:9). But the question is whether this passage speaks of "wrath" in terms of the tribulation or of ultimate wrath—condemnation and hell. It would seem to speak of the latter, since Paul contrasts this wrath with "salvation through our Lord Jesus Christ, who died for us" (1 Thess. 5:9b–10a). God does promise that believers are exempt from wrath (Rom. 8:1), but he does not promise that they are exempt from tribulation; indeed he guarantees it for all who will live godly in Jesus (Rom. 8:17; Phil. 1:29; 1 Pet. 4:12–19). In the Revelation, Jesus does promise the church at Philadelphia that he will keep it "from the hour of trial that is coming on the whole world" (Rev. 3:10). It does not suggest, however, that he will do so by removing the church from the world.

Indeed, the pattern of God's provision for his people, as he is pouring out judgment around them, is to bring them safely through such a disturbance—not to "rapture" them out of it. Thus, as the plagues fall on Egypt, for example—plagues that are repeated and intensified during the Apocalypse—God "makes a distinction between Egypt and Israel" (Exod. 11:7) by protecting Israel from the judgments, but he does not remove Israel until after the plagues are ended. Moreover, the "salvation from wrath" argument is internally inconsistent. If even one redeemed person goes through the tribulation—and dispensationalists insist some will, Gentiles who turn to Christ after the rapture and the redeemed Jewish remnant—then this argument does not work. *Someone* who belongs to Christ is passing through the wrath of God in the tribulation.

The strongest argument for a pretribulational rapture is the case from imminence. The Scriptures call on believers always to be ready for the coming of Jesus, an unexpected event that will hit like a "thief in the night" (1 Thess. 5:2). A signless rapture certainly does preserve the unpredictability of an anytime coming of Christ. And yet this argument assumes that the tribulation is a time wholly and obviously incongruous with the present era. It assumes that an observer could read the newspaper and say, "Well, since the antichrist is on the move and Israel is converting, we have about six and a half years left until Jesus comes." As we have noted above, the tribulation is an intensification of God's judgments already being poured out on the cosmos; an explosion of persecutions that are already at work. How does one know that an antichrist on the scene now is *the* final antichrist?

To believers in some Islamic terrorist states, it may seem as though the great tribulation is now in full force. They may see the materialism and opulence and spiritual apathy of the West as a clear fulfillment of the great Babylon of the Apocalypse. Jesus does tell us his coming could be at any time, but the Bible also tells us *not* to let the day surprise us like a thief (1 Thess. 5:4). It does not make much sense that the Apostle Paul would comfort the Thessalonians that the coming of Christ has not yet occurred because the antichrist has not yet been unveiled (2 Thess. 2), if in fact the coming for believers is *before* the antichrist comes to power anyway. We are to be looking to the signs of the times, always understanding that, like those of first-century Galilee, we could be mistaken about whether God is fulfilling prophecies all around us. As missionary-theologian Benjamin Merkle has written, believers should "admit that the precise fulfillment of many verses of Scripture is ambiguous to us" right now, an ambiguity that just may be God's design.[101]

Just because these arguments for a pretribulational rapture are not conclusive, this does not mean that the second coming *could not* come in two stages, one of them being before the tribulation. The Bible nowhere precludes a pretribulational rapture, and God has in times past fulfilled in stages prophetic events (such as the coming of the Messiah, after all). This author certainly hopes he is wrong about the timing of the rapture and will gladly concede this point to his pretribulational friends while flying through the atmosphere. Moreover, all conservative evangelicals—especially Southern Baptists—owe a debt to pretribulational premillennialists who held tenaciously to orthodox Christianity when few others did. It is difficult to think of anyone in the history of the church who held to a pretribulational rapture and yet denied a central tenet of the Christian faith.

Believers who disagree about the timing of the rapture but who hold in common the blessed hope of the second coming of Christ do not disagree on anything of central importance. A different opinion on this issue should never be an issue of concern in a church, a Sunday school class, or even in a marriage. Posttribulational Christians can remind their pretribulational brothers and sisters that, even if the church is exempted from the great tribulation, the church is never exempt from tribulation itself. Pretribulational Christians can remind their posttribulational brothers and sisters that the "blessed hope" should always be on our hearts—and that Jesus could surprise us all *at any time* in the eastern skies.

It would seem that the second coming of Christ is a singular event, posttribulational, in which Jesus appears visibly in the eastern skies to call forth his people to meet him in the air. The rapture texts seem to signify the public nature of the event—a shout, a trumpet call, the tribes of the earth mourning as they see the Son of Man in the heavens (Matt. 24:29–31; 1 Thess. 4:16). The rapture of the church is intentionally public—a vindication of Jesus'

---

[101] Benjamin L. Merkle, "Could Jesus Return at Any Moment? Rethinking the Imminence of the Second Coming," *Trinity Journal* 26 (2005): 292.

people before the watching world. Moreover, the rapture signals the new kings and queens of the earth, as the translated church meets Jesus outside "the gates" of the atmosphere to join him in his march to victory.

Like the triumphal entry into Jerusalem, the rapture of the church is a kingly act. The Bible makes clear that Jesus calls the dead and the living to him in the air with a *shout*. Just as God the Creator calls all things into existence by his *word* and just as Yahweh showed his sovereignty by whistling for the nations and they come to him speedily from the ends of the earth (Isa. 5:26), Jesus demonstrates his regal authority by calling his people forward, and even those in the graves come to him (John 5:25–29). The second coming is one further example that the sheep hear the voice of the Shepherd, and they follow him (John 10:3)—even into the air itself. The simultaneous explosion of cemeteries across the globe is a globalization seen in Jesus' calling of Lazarus from his grave. Just as then, in Jesus' death-defying voice we see the glory of a God who always hears his Son (John 11:40–42).

Restoration of Israel

All Christians everywhere believe in a future for Israel. Christians disagree on exactly who *Israel* is. Dispensationalists insist that Romans 9–11 reaffirms the Old Testament covenant promises to Abraham's genetic descendants—promises of a rebuilt temple, a restored theocracy, and reclaimed geography. For dispensational premillennialists, this is a primary purpose of the millennium—ethnic Israel is reconstituted as a political state and serves as a mediator of God's blessings to the rest of the nations. Some dispensationalists further argue that this future for Israel demands current support for Israeli claims to all of what once was Canaan—along with virtual *carte blanche* support for Israeli policies since "I will bless those who bless you, and whoever curses you I will curse" (Gen. 12:3 NIV).[102]

Covenant theologians argue that the future restoration of Israel will be fulfilled—but fulfilled in the church, a largely Gentile body that has "replaced" the Jewish theocracy since the nation rejected her Messiah at Jesus' first advent. Covenant theology then (quite wrongly) sees great continuity between Old Testament Israel and the new covenant church—both are mixed bodies of regenerate and unregenerate members (believers and their children), and the sign of circumcision is replaced with the sign of baptism (and, like circumcision applied to new converts and to covenant children).

Both covenant theology and dispensationalism, however, often discuss Israel and the church without taking into account the Christocentric nature of biblical eschatology. The future restoration of Israel has *never*

---

[102] For a survey of evangelical attitudes toward the current state of Israel, see Timothy P. Weber, *On the Road to Armageddon: How Evangelicals Became Israel's Best Friend* (Grand Rapids: Baker, 2004).

been promised to the unfaithful, unregenerate members of the nation (John 3:3–10; Rom. 2:25–29)—only to the faithful remnant. The church is not Israel, at least not in a direct, unmediated sense. The remnant of Israel—a biological descendant of Abraham, a circumcised Jewish firstborn son who is approved of by God for his obedience to the covenant—receives *all* of the promises due to him.

Israel is Jesus of Nazareth, who, as promised to Israel, is raised from the dead and marked out with the Spirit (Ezek. 37:13–14; Rom. 1:2–4). *All* the promises of God "find their Yes in him" (2 Cor. 1:20), as Paul puts it, and this yes establishes a Jew like Paul with Gentiles like the Corinthians "in Christ, and has anointed us, and who has also put his seal on us and given us his Spirit in our hearts as a guarantee" (2 Cor. 1:21–22). The Spirit guarantees what? It guarantees that all who share the Spirit of Christ are "joint heirs with Christ" of his promised inheritance (Rom. 8:17 NKJV).

This is the radical nature of the gospel in the New Testament. Dispensationalists are right that only ethnic Jews receive the promised future restoration, but Paul makes clear that the "seed of Abraham" is singular, not plural (Gal. 3:16). Only the circumcised can inherit the promised future for Israel. All believers—Jew and Greek, slave and free, male and female—are forensically Jewish firstborn sons of God (Gal. 3:28). They are *in Christ.* Circumcision is not irrelevant. Instead, both Jews and Gentiles in Christ *are* "the circumcision" because they have "the circumcision of Christ" (Col. 2:11–12). In Christ, I inherit all the promises due to Abraham's offspring because I am "hidden" in Abraham's promised offspring so that everything that is true of him is true of me. As Paul puts it, "Christ is all, and in all" (Col. 3:11). It is not that God changes his mind about a rebuilt temple. He fulfills it in the temple of Christ's body, a temple Jesus builds with living stones.

The future of Israel then does belong to Gentile believers but only because they are in union with a Jewish Messiah. Paul speaks of a future conversion of Jewish people, but he is careful to denote this salvation as the growth of a single olive vine with a Jewish root—with a grafting on now of Gentiles and a future grafting on of more Jews. The church, as Israel was promised, does now "bear fruit"—the fruits of the Spirit (Gal. 5)—but it does so only because Jesus is the vine of Israel. We share his inheritance because we are the branches, united to him by faith (John 15:1–11). Is there a future for Israel? Yes. Does this future mean material and political blessings? Yes. Does this future mean the granting of all the land promised to Abraham in Canaan? Yes, along with the entire rest of the cosmos (Rom. 4:13). Does this promise apply to ethnic Jews? Yes, one ethnic Jew whose name is Jesus. Do Gentile believers share in this inheritance? Yes, if they are in Christ, one-flesh with him through faith (Eph. 5:22–33), they receive the inheritance that belongs to him (Eph. 1:11).

Millennium

Few things have been as divisive in Christian theology as the question of whether there will be a thousand years of peace. Christian theologians of the past and present have offered three broad categories of interpretation—amillennialism, postmillennialism, and premillennialism. There have been orthodox, faithful Christians who have held to each of these views. Nonetheless, premillennialism seems best to fit the witness of the Old and New Testaments, a witness consistent with the ancient expectation of the church for a visible manifestation of Christ's glory in this present age.

Amillennialism interprets Revelation 20 as a recapitulation of the church age from the resurrection of Jesus to the end of the age. Satan is bound at the cross and resurrection of Jesus. His power to deceive the nations is restricted as the Great Commission goes forward to the ends of the earth. The first resurrection is spiritual (regeneration or physical death with the soul ascending to heaven), while the second resurrection is physical (the general resurrection of believers and unbelievers at the coming of Jesus). The reigning of believers with Christ for "a thousand years" takes place now, as either the church on earth or the disembodied spirits in heaven rule with Jesus in his resurrection victory.

Amillennialists are right that Satan was defeated at the place of the skull and the emptied tomb. This does not prove, however, that he has been "sealed in an abyss," so that he cannot deceive the nations, as Revelation teaches will happen in the millennium. Earlier in the vision, John sees the defeat of Satan at the Christ event, but he certainly does not see him chained. Rather, he sees Satan falling onto the earth and sea, where he is seething with great wrath and persecuting the people of the Christ (Rev. 12:12–17). It is likewise difficult to see how the present era is a time when the nations are not deceived when the New Testament clearly teaches that now is the time when this age is deceived by its usurping god (2 Cor. 4:3–4).

Yes, individuals are freed from this deception through the gospel, but the fact remains that there is such a deception at work in the nations right now. Satan is pictured in this time between the times not as a chained and exiled dragon but as a prowling lion "looking for someone to devour" (1 Pet. 5:8 NIV). John sees this entire present world system as one that "lies under the sway of the wicked one" (1 John 5:19 NKJV). Yes, Satan's deception is not ultimately invincible, and, yes, Satan's bounds are conscribed by God. But this has always been the case, even before the coming of the Messiah (Job 1:12). Something more than this is revealed in this text about the future of satanic activity.

It is possible—though not likely—that John, as amillennialism holds, uses the wording of "came to life" in two different senses (one spiritual and one physical) with no clue in the context that he is doing so. It is difficult to see, however, how—if the "first resurrection" is regeneration—"the rest" (those who were not regenerated) can be said to "come to life" in any analogous sense after the thousand years have concluded.

More problematic, however, is the amillennial understanding of the reign of the saints. Ruling with Christ is never described in the Scriptures as the activity of disembodied souls. Rather, the New Testament ties the rule of believers as "sons of God" specifically to the resurrection of *their bodies* (Rom. 8:18,23). Moreover, the Revelation does not leave the promised rule of the saints in the category of the vague and abstract. Instead, Jesus specifically defines the rule promised to believers as a coercive rule "over the nations" in which the believer "will rule them with a rod of iron, as when earthen pots are broken in pieces" (Rev. 2:27).

Believers do not yet experience this kind of rule over the world. As a matter of fact, the Apostle Paul ridicules the Corinthian church believing themselves to be "kings" in the present era: "And would that you did reign, so that we might share the rule with you!" (1 Cor. 4:8). Instead, the present era is one of suffering and tribulation (1 Cor. 4:9–13). The church is specifically denied ruling authority over the world in the present age. Thus, Paul calls believers to judge between themselves in the church but not to govern the world (1 Cor. 5:12–13). Such ruling authority is yet future.

As mentioned in the historical overview, early amillennialism was not based primarily on exegetical considerations but on an aversion to the "carnality" and "sensuality" of the material blessings of a millennium. Contemporary amillennialists often eschew any hint of crypto-Platonism by locating the material blessings promised in the Old and New Testaments in the new earth. As amillennialist Vern Poythress puts it, everything the premillennialist has in the millennium, he has in the new earth, except better since all evil is gone.[103]

This is an improvement over earlier forms of amillennial thought, but therein is a problem. The prophets do speak of a time of messianic reign and global shalom in which all evil is not, in fact, gone. Isaiah, for instance, foresees a time of a reversal of the curse—with even an end to animal predation (Isa. 11:7–8; 65:25)—in which there is still a need for the king to decide disputes between the peoples, rule with a rod over the nations (Isa. 11:3–4). This messianic age still sees death, albeit at a very old age (Isa. 65:20), and sinful nations will be coerced into offering tribute to Jerusalem's Messiah (Zech. 14:16–21). Moreover, the prophets foresee an era when the Messiah and his people rule over and in the midst of his

---

[103] Vern Poythress, *Understanding Dispensationalists*, 2nd ed. (Phillipsburg, NJ: Presbyterian and Reformed, 1994), 133; cf. 47–51.

enemies (Pss. 23:5; 110:2–7; Rev. 2:27). In the new earth all enemies are gone—banished to the lake of fire.

Postmillennialism is a distinct minority view in the broad sweep of Christian theology, though there have been times when it predominated. This view of the thousand-year reign of Christ sees the rule commencing as the nations are converted to Christ through the Great Commission. The conversion of much of the world brings about an era of peace and tranquility, as Jesus rules through the Spirit over the nations. After this epoch of global harmony, Satan is released and leads a rebellion, which is quickly put down (Rev. 20:7–10), and the eternal state is ushered in.

Postmillennialists have many of the same critiques of amillennialism that premillennialists do—pointing, for instance, to material messianic blessings promised in an era when sinners still sin, babies are still being born, and the elderly are still dying.[104] They see the earthly rule of Christ as being the gradual outworking of Christ's kingdom, an outworking foreseen in the gradual deepening of the living waters flowing from Ezekiel's temple (Ezek. 47:1–12)—waters Jesus equates with the Spirit and a temple he equates with his body (John 7:37–39). Postmillennialists also see this pattern of kingdom fulfillment in the parables of Jesus in which a small invisible reign gradually grows into a mighty empire (i.e., Matt. 13:31–33). And postmillennialists remind us, Jesus conditions the end coming on the gospel being preached to the nations (Matt. 24:14).

There are many aspects of postmillennialism that are true generally, especially in its emphasis on the cosmic nature of God's saving purposes in history. It does not seem, however, that the millennium of Revelation 20 fits this pattern of prophetic expectation. The kingdom does indeed grow from a tiny flock into a global empire, but the trajectory laid out in Scripture is that this kingdom overcomes the other kingdoms of the world, not gradually through the Spirit but cataclysmically at the coming of Christ himself at the end of the age (Dan. 2:44; Matt. 13:38–43). Biblical eschatology does not reveal a trajectory of history that is gradually getting better but a time of tribulation and apostasy growing, as the Apostle Paul puts it, "from bad to worse" (2 Tim. 3:13). At the same time, postmillennialism keeps all of the problems of amillennialism when it comes to understanding the two resurrections mentioned in Revelation 20.

Premillennialism is the view that Jesus at his return inaugurates a one-thousand-year reign with his resurrected disciples over the rest of the universe. This premillennialism does not necessarily entail the later dispensationalist modifications to the system. *Historic premillennialism* affirms the future, literal, global reign of Christ and his followers over the earth,

---

without insisting that this reign includes a restored Israelite theocracy, a rebuilt temple, or renewed animal sacrifices. Premillennialism maintains that the human longing for utopia, or a golden age at the end of history, is a legitimate longing—though one that can never be fulfilled until the reign of the Messiah.

In the historic premillennialist view, Jesus at his coming resurrects those who have trusted in Christ, commencing their promised rule with him. The armies fighting against the returning Messiah at Armageddon are destroyed, but, presumably, this does not mean that every unconverted person is killed. The survivors of the nations—who submit to the rule of Christ—continue to live, marry, and repopulate the earth. The curse is rolled back though not completely reversed. The nations no longer war against one another since King Jesus rules in peace. Open rebellion is nowhere seen since Jesus has all of his enemies under his feet. One could assume that resurrected believers, who now have authority over the nations, are given specified spheres of governance over the universe. At the end of this epoch, Satan is released and initiates an insurrection of human subjects against the kingdom of Christ. This rebellion, as all rebellions against the anointed of God, is defeated and the judgment of men, angels, and nations ensues.

Historic premillennialism fits best with a natural exegesis of Revelation 20; the first and second resurrections are both bodily—one of the righteous at the beginning of the millennium and one of the unrighteous at its end, a resurrection identified with the second death (Rev. 20:6,14). It fits the flow of Revelation, coming after the climax of the book with the coming of Christ and before the eternal state.[105] Premillennialism makes sense of the decidedly future hope given to potential martyrs from the beginning of the vision—if you overcome, you will be raised from the dead, and you will rule over the nations (Rev. 2:26–27; 3:21; 12:5).[106] This millennial hope is a stimulus to those facing tyrannical Rome in the first century, a tyrannical antichrist at the end of the era, and everyone in between. Caesar may know how to lop off heads, but Jesus knows how to fit them on again. A premillennial view also fits best with the Old Testament prophetic hope of a messianic rule in an era in which there is still (although subdued) death, sin, and enemies.

The millennium is not neatly divided from the eternal state. Instead, it seems to be an overlapping of the ages, an interlude between this age and the age to come. As Craig Blaising puts it, just as it was not initially clear in the prophets that the Messiah would come in two stages as Suffering

---

[105] For a defense of why Revelation 20 is not a recapitulation of salvation history, see George Eldon Ladd, *A Commentary on the Book of Revelation* (Grand Rapids: Eerdmans, 1972), 260–61.

[106] It is important to note that John does not restrict the millennial reign to martyrs. He sees the martyrs among those "to whom the authority to judge was committed" (Rev. 20:4).

Servant and conquering King or that he would be raised far in advance of the general resurrection, the progressive revelation of Scripture pictures the kingdom coming in stages—the kingdom ministry of Jesus, the reign of Christ over his church, a reign with his church over the world, and then his eternal rule in a new creation.[107]

What is the purpose of this intermediate millennial reign of Christ? It seems that God's glorification of Christ entails a public vindication of his rule specifically in the presence of his enemies, a final, visible subjugation of the rivals of Christ's throne (Ps. 110; 1 Cor. 15:24–28). Irenaeus had it right, in this context, when he presented the work of Christ as a recapitulation of Adam's task. As Adam at the beginning of this age's history fails to guard the terrestrial paradise from the Dragon, the Second Adam fulfills this warrior-priest duty at the end of this age's history. The millennium showcases, again in the presence of Christ's enemies, the social and political aspects of kingdom rule, aspects that are obscured in the present age. The futurity of the millennium reminds us that a rod of iron to rule over the nations will belong to us one day—but not yet.

New Earth

The point of the gospel is not that we would go to heaven when we die. Instead, it is that heaven will come down, transforming and renewing the earth and the entire universe. After the millennium, the final judgment, and the condemnation of the lost, John sees a new Jerusalem coming down from the heavens *to earth* (Rev. 21:2). He then describes an eternal order that, consistent with the rest of biblical eschatology, is surprisingly "earthy." Eternity means civilization, architecture, banquet feasting, ruling, work—in short, it is eternal *life*. The new earth is not the white, antiseptic, hyperspiritual heaven some Christians expect as their eternal home. Nor is it simply the everlasting family reunion with calorie-free food and super powers, as some hope.

The hope of the new earth is often surprising to Christians. Doesn't the Bible tell us to focus our minds on heavenly things, not earthly things? Yes. The question is, why are we to have a focus on heaven? Because our inheritance is there—in Christ, seated at the right hand of God (Eph. 1:20–21). Paul contrasts the Christian mind-set with the appetite-driven mind-set of "enemies of the cross" who have "minds set on earthly things" by reminding the church at Philippi that "our citizenship is in heaven" (Phil. 3:18–20). But he does not stop there. Of heaven, Paul writes: "And from it we await a Savior, the Lord Jesus Christ, who will transform our lowly body to be like his glorious body, by the power that enables him even to subject all things to himself" (Phil. 3:20b–21). We lay up treasures in heaven, but the treasure

---

[107] Blaising, "Premillennialism," 200–4.

does not stay in heaven. We focus our minds on heaven, but heaven comes down to earth. Ultimately our hope is in new creation: transformation and glorification of our bodies and, with them, the cosmos itself.

The new earth means the triumph of Christ *in the restoration of creation.* There really is no such thing as "the end of the world." God does promise to destroy this present creation, but he speaks of this destruction as analogous to a previous "end of the world," the flood—only this time with fire rather than water (2 Pet. 3:1–13). The pre-flood creation indeed was destroyed—the old order was wiped out. But God does not completely wipe out the earth. There is both continuity and discontinuity with the pre-flood order. The same is true of the new heavens and the new earth. Jesus' resurrection body is glorified and transformed, but it is still *his body,* the same body that was placed in the tomb. A regenerate person is "a new creation" in Christ, the old is passed away (2 Cor. 5:17), but he is still the same man, just transformed and redeemed.

Indeed, personal regeneration is key to understanding God's plans for the earth and the heavens. It is the inbreaking of God's new creation (2 Cor. 4:6) in the present order. God demonstrates in individual lives what he one day plans to do with the entire universe, the age of the Spirit. This is why Jesus speaks of the consummated kingdom in the age to come as the *regeneration* (Matt. 19:28), and why he insists that personal regeneration is necessary to see the kingdom of God (John 3:3). God redeems individuals, transforming them through the Spirit because through redeemed human rulers, the sons of God, he will transform the creation itself, freeing it from its bondage to decay (Rom. 8:18–23). This is why the redeemed groan along with the creation itself for the consummation of the kingdom (Rom. 8:23). It is here in the regeneration that the personal and the cosmic aspects of eschatology meet.

In the beginning God created the heavens and the earth and declared it "good." God does not surrender this good creation to Satan but wins it back through the blood of Christ, which frees creation's rulers from the sentence of death for sin (Col. 1:19–21). God restores and recreates a world that vindicates his original creation purposes. This means not just a heavenly city of refuge for flown-away souls, but an entire universe of rocks and trees and quasars and waterfalls—everything created in which he takes delight.

The prophetic vision of Scripture is insistent, for instance, that nonhuman life is a part of God's eternal purposes, with Isaiah seeing a restoration of the original harmony of the animal order. Christians do not believe that individual dogs or cats or other animals are resurrected from the dead since they do not bear the image of God. But at the same time we must insist that the new earth will contain animals. This does not mean every known species or breed of animal. God, after all, probably did not have Chihuahuas or poodles in the garden of Eden. But we have every reason to believe that every created kind that was present from the beginning will be represented in the new earth with perhaps even new forms of biological diversity as well.[108] These animals will be under the dominion of human beings, chiefly the Son of Man himself, and will be restored to their original nonpredatory vegetarian diets (Isa. 11:7; 65:25). In the restoration, humans will have no reason to fear even the most primal predator, the serpent (Isa. 11:8).[109]

The material universe—including the galaxies never seen by human eye—was designed to declare the Creator's glory. In the new creation the heavens will declare this glory with unimagined brilliance, now freed from the bondage to decay.

The new earth means the triumph of Christ *in the cultural mandate*. It is significant that Jesus triumphs in redemption as a man, as the Second Adam, as the preeminent image of the invisible God (Col. 1:15). In the new earth, the mandate given to Adam is fulfilled indisputably by his greater son. Jesus "hands over the kingdom" to God the Father, Paul tells us. This does not mean that Jesus ceases to rule as king—that rule is everlasting (Luke 1:33). Instead it means that he delivers the kingdom, a triumphant warrior who has completed the task given to him. Jesus is fruitful and has multiplied, filling the earth with a number no person can count (Gen. 1:28; Heb. 2:13; Rev. 7:9).

Through Christ the people of God enter into creation's Sabbath rest (Heb. 4:9). Often we think of eternal rest as an everlasting "RIP," a cessation of activity, a dreamy gazing into a light. Biblical rest is hardly idleness but rest from the warring of one's enemies. The Israelites were promised *rest* in the land of promise, not because they would sit in inactivity there but because they would be free from the guerilla warfare of the Canaanites. Solomon was given "rest from all of enemies" in his kingdom, precisely because all his rival nations were placed "under the soles of his feet" (1 Kings 5:3–4). John saw no more sea in the new earth (Rev. 21:1)—not because there was an absence of water necessarily but because the sea represented for Israel the realm of danger and the dead, the hostile forces against which God wars in the present age (Isa. 27:1).

The eternal state is hardly inactivity for the redeemed but instead *work*—work that is joyously freed from the frustration of a cursed earth. The new earth is not simply a restoration of Eden but a glorious civilization with a *city*, and the glory of the nations redeemed and brought into it. One

---

108 For a discussion of the "created kinds" of Genesis and how they relate to animal life today, see Kurt P. Wise, *Faith, Form, and Time: What the Bible Teaches and Science Confirms about Creation and the Age of the Universe* (Nashville: Broadman & Holman, 2002), 99–139.

109 I realize that the Isaiah passages apply specifically in some instances to the millennial reign. As discussed earlier, however, it does not seem that the millennium and the new earth are two radically separate administrations, but instead one cosmic restoration coming in two stages.

can expect that the new earth would be abuzz with culture—music, painting, literature, architecture, commerce, agriculture, and everything that expresses the creativity of human beings as the image of God.[110] We can also expect in the eternal state, of all things, politics. Believers are promised a reigning function with Christ that is everlasting.

Significantly, this rule is conditioned upon Christ's judgment on faithfulness in this present life. The mother of James and John asked Jesus to grant that one sit on his left and one on his right in the kingdom (Matt. 20:20–23). She was not asking that they would have a good view but rather that they be given roles of significant authority. Jesus did not take issue with her concept but with how it is achieved—through suffering, self-denial, and becoming a servant to others (Matt. 20:23–28). In the eternal kingdom of Christ, the humble in this life will be exalted—as is always God's design. Those who were faithful in small things are given responsibility over many things (Luke 16:10).

This rule explains the rewards given to believers at the judgment seat of Christ. Christians tend to think of these "crowns" (2 Tim. 4:8; Rev. 4:4,10) as tiaras that are displayed as trophies. Instead the "crowns" bestowed on the redeemed signify glory and ruling authority. Jesus is "crowned" as the Son of Man, with all things under his feet (Heb. 2:7), and is crowned with glory and honor through his triumph in the cross (Heb. 2:9). The person who endures shares in this rule and is crowned with the responsibility to rule with the Messiah (James 1:12; 1 Pet. 5:4; Rev. 2:10).

Just as the "principalities and powers" of this age seem to have a ruling hierarchy, the sons of the kingdom will have varying levels of responsibility for the governance of the cosmos. The pious public school janitor—who scrubbed toilets to the glory of Christ—may find himself honored by Christ with a greater and more glorious realm of responsibility than the megachurch pastor who basked in the acclaim of the crowds but who has already received his reward (Matt. 6:2,5,16). Those who "network" with the powerful have a vaporous reward now, but those who care for the marginalized and the wounded "will be repaid at the resurrection of the just" (Luke 14:14).

Finally, the new earth means the triumph of Christ through *covenant community*. All of the covenants of promise reveal a twofold hope: you will be my people and I will be your God. In the new heavens and new earth, John sees the ultimate fulfillment of these promises: "Behold, the dwelling place of God is with man. He will dwell with them, and they will be his people, and God himself will be with them as their God" (Rev. 21:3). This

---

[110] For the best work written on culture in the new Jerusalem, see Mouw, *When the Kings Come Marching In.*

fulfillment draws together the God-centered and relational human-centered aspects of Christian longing for eternity in Christ. John sees "no temple in the city" (Rev. 21:22) because the presence of God is now fully with his people. He sees the city as Jerusalem, the city of peace where God promised to place his name and his presence, "prepared as a bride adorned for her husband" (Rev. 21:2).

Imagine the joy of our Old Testament ancestors seeing what they glimpsed from afar. The God who promised to tabernacle with them is now with them, ruling over them as their brother, a man with skin, fingernails, eyelashes, and a blood type. Imagine the tears of happiness in our resurrected eyes when we think of Jesus' words to us, "I will not leave you as orphans; I will come to you" (John 14:18)—and there he is.

Sometimes Christians ask, "Will we know one another in heaven?" That question is a symptom of an impoverished Christian hope. Of course! The end does not end relationships or isolate us from one another. Instead it invites us to a messianic banquet, a wedding party (Rev. 19:6–10). "I assign to you, as my Father assigned to me, a kingdom," Jesus tells us. "That you may eat and drink at my table in my kingdom and sit on thrones judging the twelve tribes of Israel" (Luke 22:29–30). The fellowship we have now around the Lord's table should point us to the inexpressible joy of eating bread and drinking wine with our triumphant King Jesus. We relish being with our loved ones but not simply because of some long-ago ties. Eternity is not the equivalent of old college roommates who catch up, only by telling "remember when" stories and asking about what acquaintances are up to these days. Love among the brothers is the love of Christ (1 John 3:15–17). We can expect this only to deepen and broaden in the new Jerusalem.

Relationships begun in this life continue in the new creation. Jesus, after all, tells his disciples that he will drink wine "new with *you* in my Father's kingdom" (Matt. 26:29, emphasis added). We can expect to live life with friends, family members, mentors, and disciples forever; and we have forever to build new friendships as well. Jesus does tell us that "giving in marriage" (Mark 12:18–27) will not be a part of eternity the way it is in the present life, presumably because the reproductive mandate is now fulfilled; but this doesn't mean that our future relationships with our spouses will be that of cold, distant strangers. The truth is, we do not know what such relationships will look like in the new creation. But we do know that God perfects and blesses our relationships, and that joyful intimacy now is not replaced with cool civility in eternity. God is love, and love never dies.

How Does This Doctrine Impact the Church Today?

A Middle Eastern terrorist on the verge of execution understood well what eschatology is about. The thief on the cross looked to Jesus, in all of his weakness and shame, and made the most profound statement of Christian eschatology ever uttered: "Jesus, remember me when you come into your kingdom" (Luke 23:42). This is the faith of every believer who has ever looked to the crucified Christ for salvation. A person's eschatology, then, has everything to do with the way he lives life now—whether one trusts Jesus for a future kingdom, or whether one grasps at the passing securities of this present age. Our understanding of the future informs our Christian hope, our personal ethics, our social action, and our corporate witness. Eschatology then should be at the forefront of our evangelism, discipleship, worship, counseling, spiritual formation, and vocational activity.

Eschatology and Christian Hope

Grief

Christians do not stoically suppress our emotions through the death of a loved one. We hate it. Because we know that death is an enemy to be conquered, we should hate death more than our secular neighbors. This means we ought to see every death as a tragedy, and mourn. Often Christians believe it is more "spiritual" to treat a funeral service as a "celebration." But a funeral is no celebration. It is a reminder that the one in the casket before us is a sinner, and the wages of sin is death. The Scripture tells us that the Spirit does not just give us peace and joy and comfort, but the Spirit causes us to "groan inwardly" with the rest of creation (Rom. 8:23). The more we are conformed to the image of Christ, the more we are frustrated to live in a world of funeral homes and electric chairs and abortion clinics. Our cry should be with genuine anguish: "Come, Lord Jesus!" (Rev. 22:20).

But, as the Scriptures tell us, we do not grieve as "others do who have no hope" (1 Thess. 4:13). Interestingly, the Apostle Paul tells us to "encourage one another" with eschatology (1 Thess. 4:18). When we are standing by the casket of an unconverted father, in the hospital emergency room waiting room where we've heard of the death of a godly teenage girl, in the family room when a young expectant mother just learns that she's miscarried her baby—at all of these times let's preach the gospel to one another, a gospel of resurrection hope. We cry with one another, knowing that one day our tear ducts will flow no more—all because we are convinced a grave in Jerusalem is empty now.

Burial

Our eschatology has everything to do then with how we "dispose" of the "remains" of our dead loved ones. Since we believe in the resurrection of the body, we do not see a corpse as "garbage." From the time of our earliest ancestors in the faith, we have buried our dead, committing them to the earth from which they came with the conviction that they will one day be summoned from it once more. The image of sleep is useful—not because the dead are unconscious but because they will one day be awakened (Luke 8:52–55). God deems as faith Joseph committing his bones to his brothers for future transport into the land of promise (Heb. 11:22). In the same way the act of burial is a testimony of the entire community to the resurrection of the body. Cremation is a horrifying testimony of the burning up of the flesh and bones, a testimony that is decidedly pagan in both origin and in practice. Of course, God can resurrect a cremated Christian (or a Christian torn to pieces by lions, etc.), but how we deal with the body of a Christian teaches us—and the watching world—what we really believe about the gospel. Cremation ought then to be shunned by those who hope in Christ.[111]

Fear of Death

We live in a culture in which people idolize youth. There is a reason hair dyes, liposuction, cosmetic surgery, and erectile dysfunction drugs are multibillion dollar industries. Like all people everywhere in all times, contemporary people are afraid of death (Heb. 2:14–15)—precisely because they know deep within that there is a judgment coming. We have been freed from such anxiety, knowing that life doesn't end with a flat-lining EKG screen. A Christian hypochondriac, constantly fearful of getting brain tumors or heart disease or leukemia, is a Christian who fundamentally lacks a robust eschatology and betrays mistrust in God. Sicknesses and bodily weaknesses, aging—these are all evidences that we are dying; that is true. But we know that these are reminders from God of eschatological hope. The doctor's nervous voice telling us, "It's cancer and it doesn't look good" is, for the Christian, a gift "to make us rely not on ourselves but on God who raises the dead" (2 Cor. 1:9).

Moreover, unlike popular culture, we ought not to make a fetish of youth but should honor and respect the elderly. Older men and women in our congregations should be high profile and listened to with reverence. We should expect our elderly to grow more and more joyful as they age, knowing they are closer and closer, not further away, from the primes of their lives. In a

---

[111] For a discussion of the tie between cremation and the rejection of bodily resurrection among early American proponents of the practice, see Stephen R. Prothero, *Purified by Fire: A History of Cremation in America* (Berkeley: University of California Press, 2001).

culture that values women only when they have youthful sexual appeal to men, a Christian husband should tell his wife how beautiful she is to him even as her hair is turning gray and wrinkles appear on her face.

Our triumph over death in Christ ought also to give us boldness and courage. Eastern Orthodox theologian Patrick Henry Reardon writes about how a lack of danger and courage in contemporary society leads to vacuous exploits of fake courage—bungee jumping or "extreme sports," for instance.[112] The same is true in church life. We think we can create the dangerous ambience of the catacombs by darkening rooms and lighting candles in the "emerging" worship services of safe, white, middle-class suburban churches. We should cultivate instead real courage in the face of death, especially among young boys and men. Any generation of Christians should be raised to face heroically persecution from enemies—from Caesar, terrorist Islam, mammon-worshipping American culture, or perhaps even from the final antichrist himself. Only a robust eschatology can give us such fearlessness.

Eschatology and Personal Ethics

Forgiveness

Jesus says that the alternative to forgiving one's enemies is hell. This is difficult for many Christians because we too often believe forgiving a trespasser means allowing an injustice to stand. At its root, though, this attitude betrays a defective eschatology. At the Lord's arrest (Matt. 26:47–54), Jesus told Peter to put his sword back into his sheath not because Jesus did not believe in punishing evildoers (think Armageddon). Jesus told Peter he could have an armada of angelic warriors at his side (and one day he will). But judgment was not yet, and Peter was not judge. This is precisely the point. When we forgive, we are confessing that vengeance is God's (Rom. 12:19). We do not need to exact justice from a fellow believer because justice has already fallen at Golgotha. We do not need to exact vengeance from an unbeliever because we know the sin against us will be judged in hell or, more hopefully, when the offender unites himself to the one who is "the propitiation for our sins, and not for ours only but also for the sins of the whole world" (1 John 2:2).

A prisoner of war who forgives his captor, a sexually abused woman who forgives her cretin of a father, a terminated pastor who forgives an obstinate congregation—these people are not overlooking sin; they are confessing that judgment is coming and that they can trust the one who will be seated on that throne. One who will not forgive is an eschatological liberal

---

[112] Patrick Henry Reardon, "Homer, Sex, and Bungee Jumping," *Touchstone* (October 2003): 19.

just as surely as any universalist or annihilationist; it doesn't matter what the prophecy charts at the back of his Bible say.

Humility

Christians tend to look down on the mother of James and John for insisting that her sons sit on the left and right hands of Jesus in his kingdom. But at least she was looking for kingdom greatness. Too often we are as competitive as she, but for a more pitiable inheritance: temporal wealth, fame, or power. So much disappointment among believers comes from those who expected more recognition or approval: a pastor who ministers in a small, rural church and wishes he could headline a denominational pastor's conference; a young sales representative who seethes when he sees his coworker's "employee of the month" plaque in the office next door; a middle-aged woman who insists that everyone know about her daughter in medical school; and so forth. The tendency behind all of this is, at root though not in degree, the same as an assassin's desire to make the history books by shooting the queen of England. It is the evil one's temptation to grasp the kingdoms of this world by force now, even if the kingdoms we want are only a higher reputation in the office cubicles around us.

Cultivating humility does not mean negating the desire for glory, even glory for ourselves. It is instead cultivating a desire for greater glory, the glory that comes in Christ at the eschaton. If we understand this, we can gladly have ignominy now, for ruling splendor later in Christ. We humble ourselves not because we are craven but because we know in due time God will exalt us (Prov. 15:33; Matt. 23:12; Luke 18:14; James 4:10; 1 Pet. 5:6). If one really believes in the judgment seat of Christ and his future rule over the entire universe, then who really cares how he is esteemed by coworkers around the office coffeepot?

Bodily Integrity

Because we believe in the resurrection of the body, we know our bodies are not expendable vehicles for our souls, and they are certainly not playthings for our amusement. Our eschatology of a resurrected, glorified body can save us from two dangerous extremes. We cannot idolize our bodies and their appetites, say for food or sex, because we know these bodies are not ultimate but will be destroyed by death and then resurrected to a life beyond these urges (1 Cor. 6:14). Neither can we believe our bodies unimportant to our spirituality. Such an attitude always leads to immorality.

Instead we see ourselves as embodied persons, now and in the age to come. We care for our bodies, but we do not allow them to tyrannize us. Fasting is a helpful spiritual discipline to remind us that the kingdom of God does not consist of eating and drinking (Rom. 14:17). Bodily exercise is "of some value" (1 Tim. 4:8) as it maintains proper stewardship over the body. A Christian who walks briskly each morning or plays basketball in the afternoon is communicating one thing about his priorities while the sedentary person in front of the television and the obsessive person slavishly working out for hours each day are both communicating something quite different.

Parenting

Parents spiritually form their children in all sorts of ways, but parenting itself uniquely pictures Christian eschatology. A father disciplining his child, for instance, communicates to the child the discipline and judgment of God in ways deeper and more resonant than any Sunday school lesson (Heb. 12:5–11). A parent who will not discipline a child for disobedience is teaching that child not to expect consequences for behavior. In short, a parent who will not discipline is denying the doctrine of hell. A parent who disciplines in rage or with inconsistency or with harshness teaches a judgment of God that is capricious and unjust. An abusive parent ingrains in a child's mind a picture of God as a ruthless devil who cannot be trusted to judge justly. Parental discipleship and discipline ought always to have repentance and restoration in view, picturing a God who is both just and justifier. Discipline should be swift and fair with quick reconciliation between parent and child. Long periods of "time out" do not communicate the discipline of God; they communicate the isolation and exile of hell.

Parents who spend time with their children—especially at meals—demonstrate something of the harmony they want their children to long for beyond this life, a longing to eat at another Father's table in the kingdom of Christ. Moreover, we should teach children to respect and acknowledge authority—attributes necessary for citizens of a democracy for a short time but for a kingdom forever. Teaching children to refer to adults as "Mr. Smith" or "Mrs. Jones" or "Pastor Cook" and to say "sir" and "ma'am" is about more than politeness; it is training them to recognize proper hierarchy and authority. In short, it is teaching them Christian eschatology.

Vocation

Too many evangelicals believe that only preachers and ministers of music do work that is of any eternal value. The rest of the church works to make money to tithe and support the annual Christmas mission offering and, perhaps, to find opportunities to witness to unbelievers. New creation eschatology, however, reminds us that the eternal state means the restoration of *work*. The faithful truck driver, secretary, plumber, artist, accountant, filmmaker, or peanut farmer can see in his labors the kind of thing God values, and will value forever in a redeemed world. Joy in our work should be seen as a spiritual discipline, designed to prepare us for eternity.

Eschatology and Social Action

Dignity of Work

The sanctified labor of God's cosmic rulers in the millennium and the new earth likewise ought to tell us something about public policy. Human beings are designed, from alpha to omega, to find meaning in work. Care for the poor is a mandate for any just society. But any social welfare system that gives incentives to people or communities not to work will soon find these people or communities adrift in despair, depression, substance abuse, and the like. As Christians, we should encourage the honoring of hard work at every level of society, always nudging our non-Christian neighbors to ask why they find such meaning in a novel written, a row hoed, a budget balanced.

Care for Creation

God will not wipe out the physical universe, but he will redeem it. We cannot therefore share an economic libertarian's purely utilitarian view of the earth and its resources. Nor can we share a radical environmentalist's apocalyptic scenarios of the world's end "if we don't act now" or his view of human beings as a parasitic presence on the planet. Instead, we ought to seek ways to protect the natural creation because we know God values it and always will. Our understanding of the final state as a garden-city ought to explain for us why people are unhappy with urban and suburban sprawl. We do not worship trees, but we know that we cannot be happy when they are cleared away to make room for one more chain discount store.

Since we see God's eschatological purpose to restore the animal creation, Christians ought to encourage stewardship of animals. An insistence on vegetarianism betrays an overly realized eschatology; we still live in a fallen world of bloodshed and carnivorousness. But we can agree that cruel practices of inhumane factory farming, for instance, or the inflictions of useless suffering on animals to test cosmetic products are at cross-purposes with the ultimate priorities of our God.[113] In all of our care for creation, we must maintain the limits of environmental action, knowing that the ultimate liberation of creation has everything to do with our resurrection and the resumption of human rule through Christ over this universe.

Love for the Jewish People

Dispensationalists have served the church by pointing us to our responsibility to support the Jewish people and the nation of Israel through a century that has seen the most horrific anti-Semitic violence imaginable. We need not hold to a dispensationalist view of the future restoration of Israel

---

[113] Matthew Scully, *Dominion: The Power of Man, the Suffering of Animals, and the Call to Mercy* (New York: St. Martin's, 2002).

to agree that such support is a necessary part of a Christian eschatology. Novelist Walker Percy pointed to the continuing existence of Jewish people as a sign of God's presence in the world. There are no Hittites walking about on the streets of New York, he remarked.[114] There does appear to be a promise of a future conversion of Jewish people to Christ (Rom. 9–11). The current secular state of Israel is not the fulfillment of God's promise to Abraham; Jesus is. Nonetheless, the state of Israel is the guardian of post-Holocaust world Judaism. This does not necessitate that we support every political decision of the Israeli government. It does mean that we stand with Israel against every form of anti-Semitic violence because we know that these are the kinsmen according to the flesh of our Messiah.

Respect for Life

Wisdom warns that "all who hate me love death" (Prov. 8:36). This is evident amid the cultural necrophilia of the present age. Since we believe in the resurrection of the body, our responsibility in our communities is to encourage a seemingly obvious truth: life is better than death. Since the kingdom of our Christ is one that honors all human life and protects the lifeblood of the innocent (Ps. 72:14), we should keep this kingdom priority ever before us. We should work through persuasion, legislation, and community service to end abortion, euthanasia, and unjust wars. We should insist that the state execute only those murderers who are proven to be guilty. We should seek to rescue unborn babies and "unwanted" elderly people by adopting children, financially supporting others who can adopt, manning crisis pregnancy centers, and taking in the lonely aged into our own homes.

Rejection of Utopianism

Since we know the kingdom of Christ is fully consummated only at the resurrection, we must be careful to avoid making a Messiah out of any ruler or state between now and the eschaton. Augustine would have cringed to hear President Lyndon B. Johnson glory in the possibilities of the "city of man" or President Ronald Reagan deem the United States of America a "shining city on a hill." With a vision of the kingdom before us, we should be skeptical of every other claim to "end poverty" or "wipe out tyranny across the world." We should be active as much as possible in political solutions, but we should always keep a certain emotional and ideological distance, knowing that the ultimate political solution to every human problem will be riding a white horse (Rev. 19:11), and he will not need the "evangelical vote."

---

[114] Walker Percy, *The Message in the Bottle: How Queer Man Is, How Queer Language Is, and What One Has to Do with the Other* (1975; repr., New York: Picador, 2000), 6.

Eschatology and Corporate Witness

Church Membership

Christian eschatology starts in the baptistry. In the act of baptism, the church declares that the candidate has already passed through the waters of God's wrath and has been raised from the dead with Christ. The church further announces that this man, woman, or child will one day be a corpse, buried beneath the earth, but will be raised by the power of the Father (Rom. 6:3–9). Baptism ought then to be taken very seriously and handled with joy and reverence. A local church's baptismal service is itself a prophecy conference, telling the congregation and the world what we believe about the Christian hope.

In the same way the church as a colony of the kingdom testifies through its membership those whom the community counts as citizens of the new heavens and the new earth. When we allow an unrepentant sinner to remain unchallenged on our church rolls, we are lying to him with the lie of the serpent of Eden himself: "You will not surely die" (Gen. 3:4). Our church membership must also testify to the reconciliation of the coming kingdom, a reconciliation that overcomes the "age of the flesh" that will be judged and put behind us. A segregated—whether officially or unofficially—church denies the multiethnic shalom of the new earth. And racial or economic or geographic bigotry is a problem of eschatology. Indeed, it is a problem of a rebellious heart that loves the idols of skin pigmentation or DNA or bank accounts more than the kingdom of God and his Christ. It is the constant temptation of the church to give greater attention to the more financially established members of the congregation and of the community. We can even justify this spiritually, as stewardship of funds for missions and church growth. God abhors it.

Instead, we are to recognize the impoverished among us as future kings and queens of the universe (James 2:1–5), royalty in exile waiting for the kingdom of Christ. A church that gives more heed to a corporate executive than to a hotel housekeeper has already settled its eschatology, and done so in the reverse direction of Scripture. This reconciliation ought to be seen in the way we make decisions within the congregation. The Corinthian congregation's divisions were pitiful precisely because they would one day rule the cosmos and yet could not even decide how to govern a little mission church (1 Cor. 6:2–3). Our decisions in the church ought never to be made on the basis of power structures or party disputes or manipulation. Our business meetings ought to show the world something of the marriage supper of the Lamb, not something of the curses of the damned.

Corporate Worship

When the church worships, she experiences eschatology. According to Hebrews, the worshipping church approaches Mount Zion, the heavenly city—a fact the text says should create "reverence and awe" among the community (Heb. 12:22–29). Worship ought to reflect the already/not yet tensions of Christian hope, as we teach one another Christian truth in worship (Eph. 5:19). Our worship should include triumphant songs of victory, signaling our march to Zion through the resurrection of Christ. It should also include our groaning together as we pass through this present darkness. So much of Christian worship is either dirgelike, which is not consonant with a people who will soon inherit the universe, or sentimental and syrupy, which is not consonant with a band of warrior-priests who are traveling through a dangerous wilderness on the way to Canaan's land.

Global Missions

The moment missions and evangelism are severed from eschatology, the global mission task becomes a denominational bureaucracy and evangelism becomes a public service program. When we understand that the Father has given "all authority" to Jesus (Matt. 28:18–20) and that he has promised him the "ends of the earth" as his inheritance, we cannot help but be impassioned for the evangelization of all nations. When we sense that we are in the last days, the era of the Spirit's power, we are unafraid of the persecutions that may come. Eschatology informs missions because we understand that a Sudanese merchant praying the sinner's prayer or a Haitian voodoo priestess walking away from idolatry is about more than an increase in Christian converts; it is yet another sign to the demonic powers that the kingdom of Jesus is global, massive, and on its way.

If we truly believe that our Hindu coworker or our Muslim next-door neighbor or our unregenerate Southern Baptist husband is hurtling toward eternal darkness and condemnation, how can we then let a fear of social awkwardness stand in the way of warning him to flee the wrath to come? If the kingdom of God will repay me for everything I have walked away from in this life (Matt. 19:29), then how can I refuse a call to serve as a missionary in a faraway land simply because I do not want to be more than driving distance from my parents or to do without the techno-gadgetry of American consumer culture? Or, worse yet, how can I begrudge my son or daughter going as a missionary to the nations just because I want the grandchildren nearby?

Conclusion

Not many churches have graveyards anymore, and that is a shame. This book, like all systematic theology texts, will one day wither away into mold and dust. The Library of Congress will be swept away like refuse. If one really wants to see a theology for the church in action, one might walk into an old church graveyard at night. Walk about and see the headstones weathered and ground down by the elements. Contemplate the fact that beneath your feet are men and women who once had youthful skin and quick steps and hectic calendars but who are now piles of forgotten bones. Think about the fact that the scattered teeth in the earth below you once sang hymns of hope—maybe "When the Roll Is Called Up Yonder I'll Be There" or "When We All Get to Heaven." They are silent now.

But while you are there, think about what every generation of Christians has held against the threat of sword and guillotine and chemical weaponry. This stillness will one day be interrupted by a shout from the eastern sky, a joyful call with a distinctly northern Galilean accent. And that's when life really gets interesting.

CONCLUSION

The Pastor as Theologian

R. Albert Mohler, Jr.

Every pastor is called to be a theologian. This may come as a surprise to some pastors who see theology as an academic discipline taken during seminary rather than as an ongoing and central part of the pastoral calling. Nevertheless, the health of the church depends on its pastors functioning as faithful theologians—teaching, preaching, defending, and applying the great doctrines of the faith.

The transformation of theology into an academic discipline more associated with the university than the church has been one of the most lamentable developments of the last several centuries. In the earliest eras of the church, and through the annals of Christian history, the central theologians of the church were its pastors. This was certainly true of the great Reformation of the sixteenth century. From the Patristic era, we associate the discipline and stewardship of theology with names such as Athanasius, Irenaeus, and Augustine. Similarly, the great theologians of the Reformation were, in the main, pastors such as John Calvin and Martin Luther. Of course, their responsibilities often ranged beyond those of the average pastor, but they could not have conceived of the pastoral role without the essential stewardship of theology.

The emergence of theology as an academic discipline coincides with the development of the modern university. Theology was one of the three major disciplines taught in the medieval university. Yet, so long as the medieval synthesis was intact, the university was always understood to be in direct service to the church and its pastors.

The rise of the modern research university led to the development of theology as merely one academic discipline among others—and eventually to the redefinition of theology as "religious studies" separated from ecclesiastical control or concern. In most universities, the secularization of the academy has meant that the academic discipline of theology has no inherent connection to Christianity, much less to its central truth claims.

These developments have caused great harm to the church, separating ministries from theology, preaching from doctrine, and Christian care from conviction. In far too many cases the pastor's ministry has been evacuated of serious doctrinal content and many pastors seem to have little connection to any sense of theological vocation.

All this must be reversed if the church is to remain true to God's Word and the gospel. Unless the pastor functions as a theologian, theology is left in the hands of those who, in many cases, have little or no connection or commitment to the local church.

The Pastor's Calling

The pastoral calling is inherently theological. Given the fact that the pastor is to be the teacher of the Word of God and the teacher of the gospel, it cannot be otherwise. The idea of the pastorate as a nontheological office is inconceivable in light of the New Testament.

Though this truth is implicit throughout the Scriptures, this emphasis is perhaps most apparent in Paul's letters to Timothy. In these letters Paul affirmed Timothy's role as a theologian—affirming that all of Timothy's fellow pastors were to share in the same calling. Paul emphatically encouraged Timothy concerning his reading, teaching, preaching, and study of Scripture. All of this is essentially theological, as is made clear when Paul commanded Timothy to "retain the standard of sound words which you have heard from me, in the faith and love which are in Christ Jesus. Guard, through the Holy Spirit who dwells in us, the treasure which has been entrusted to you" (2 Tim. 1:13–14).[1] Timothy was to be a teacher of others who would also teach. "The things which you have heard from me in the presence of many witnesses, these entrust to faithful men, who will be able to teach others also" (2 Tim. 2:2).

As Paul completed his second letter to Timothy, he reached a crescendo of concern as he commanded Timothy to preach the Word, specifically instructing him to "reprove, rebuke, exhort, with great patience and instruction" (2 Tim. 4:2). Why? "For the time will come when they will not endure sound doctrine; but wanting to have their ears tickled, they will accumulate for themselves teachers in accordance to their own desires; and will turn away their ears from the truth and will turn aside to myths" (2 Tim. 4:3–4).

As Paul makes clear, the pastoral theologian must be able to defend the faith even as he identifies false teachings and makes correction by the Word of God. There is no more theological calling than this—guard the flock of God for the sake of God's truth.

---

[1] Unless otherwise noted, all Scripture citations in this chapter are from the New American Standard Bible (NASB).

Clearly this will require intense and self-conscious theological thinking, study, and consideration. Paul made this abundantly clear in writing to Titus when he defined the duty of the overseer or pastor as one who is "holding fast the faithful word which is in accordance with the teaching, that he may be able both to exhort in sound doctrine and to refute those who contradict" (Titus 1:9). In this single verse Paul simultaneously affirmed the apologetical and polemical facets of the pastor-theologian's calling.

In reality there is no dimension of the pastor's calling that is *not* deeply, inherently, and inescapably theological. There is no problem the pastor will encounter in counseling that is not specifically theological in character. There is no major question in ministry that does not come with deep theological dimensions and the need for careful theological application. The task of leading, feeding, and guiding the congregation is as theological as any other vocation conceivable.

Beyond all this, the preaching and teaching of the Word of God is theological from beginning to end. The preacher functions as a steward of the mysteries of God, explaining the deepest and most profound theological truths to a congregation that must be armed with the knowledge of these truths in order to grow as disciples and meet the challenge of faithfulness in the Christian life.

Evangelism is a theological calling as well, for the act of sharing the gospel is, in short, a theological argument presented with the goal of seeing a sinner come to faith in the Lord Jesus Christ. In order to be a faithful evangelist, the pastor must first understand the gospel and then understand the nature of the evangelist's calling. At every step of the way, the pastor is dealing with issues that are irrefutably theological.

As many observers have noted, today's pastors are often pulled in many directions simultaneously—and the theological vocation is often lost amidst the pressing concerns of a ministry that has been reconceived as something other than what Paul intended for Timothy. The managerial revolution has left many pastors feeling more like administrators than theologians, dealing with matters of organizational theory before ever turning to the deep truths of God's Word and the application of these truths to everyday life. The rise of therapeutic concerns within the culture means that many pastors, and many of their church members, believe that the pastoral calling is best understood as a "helping profession." As such, the pastor is seen as someone who functions in a therapeutic role in which theology is often seen as more of a problem than a solution.

All this is a betrayal of the pastoral calling as presented in the New Testament. Furthermore, it is a rejection of the apostolic teaching and of the biblical admonition concerning the role and responsibilities of the pastor.

Today's pastors must recover and reclaim the pastoral calling as inherently and cheerfully *theological*. Otherwise pastors will be nothing more than communicators, counselors, and managers of congregations that have been emptied of the gospel and of biblical truth.

The Pastor's Concentration

The pastor's stewardship of the theological task requires a clear sense of pastoral priority, a keen pastoral ear, and careful attention to the theological dimensions of church life and Christian discipleship. This must be foundational to the ministry of the local church, and ministry must emerge from a fundamentally theological foundation.

In a real sense, Christians live out their most fundamental beliefs in everyday life. One essential task of the pastor is to feed the congregation and to assist Christians to think theologically in order to demonstrate discernment and authentic discipleship.

All this must start with the pastor. The preacher must give attention, study, time, and thought to the theological dimensions of ministry. A ministry that is deeply rooted in the deep truths of God's Word will be enriched, protected, and focused by a theological vision.

The pastor's concentrated attention to the theological task is necessary for the establishment of faithful preaching, God-honoring worship, and effective evangelism in the local church. Such a theological vision is deeply rooted in God's truth and in the truth about God that forms the basis of Christian theology.

The pastor's concentration is a necessary theological discipline. Thus, the pastor must develop the ability to isolate what is most important in terms of theological gravity from that which is less important.

I call this the process of *theological triage*. As anyone who visits a hospital emergency room is aware, a triage nurse is customarily in place in order to make a first-stage evaluation of which patients are most in need of care. A patient with a gunshot wound is moved ahead of a sprained ankle in terms of priority. This makes medical sense, and to misconstrue this sense of priority would amount to medical malpractice.

In a similar manner, the pastor must learn to discern different levels of theological importance. First-order doctrines are those that are fundamental and essential to the Christian faith. The pastor's theological instincts should seize upon any compromise on doctrines such as the full deity and humanity of Christ, the doctrine of the Trinity, the doctrine of atonement, and essentials such as justification by faith alone. Where such doctrines are compromised, the Christian faith falls. When a pastor hears an assertion that Christ's bodily resurrection from the dead is not a necessary doctrine, he must respond with a theological instinct that is based in the fact that such a denial is tantamount to a rejection of the gospel itself.

Second-order doctrines are those that are essential to church life and necessary for the ordering of the local church but that, in themselves, do not define the gospel. That is to say, one may detect an error in a doctrine at this level and still acknowledge that the person in error remains a believing Christian. Nevertheless, such doctrines are directly related to how the church is organized and its ministry is fulfilled. Doctrines found at this level include those most closely related to ecclesiology and the architecture of theological systems. Calvinists and Arminians may disagree concerning a number of vital and urgently important doctrines—or, at the very least, the best way to understand and express these doctrines. Yet both can acknowledge each other as genuine Christians. At the same time these differences can become so acute that it is difficult to function together in the local congregation over such an expansive theological difference.

Third-order doctrines are those that may be the ground for fruitful theological discussion and debate but that do not threaten the fellowship of the local congregation or the denomination. Christians who agree on an entire range of theological issues and doctrines may disagree over matters related to the timing and sequence of events related to Christ's return. Yet such ecclesiastical debates, while understood to be deeply important because of their biblical nature and connection to the gospel, do not constitute a ground for separation among believing Christians.

Without a proper sense of priority and discernment, the congregation is left to consider every theological issue to be a matter of potential conflict or, at the other extreme, to see no doctrines as worth defending if conflict is in any way possible.

The pastor's theological concentration establishes a sense of proper proportion and a larger frame of theological reference. At the same time this concentration on the theological dimension of ministry also reminds the pastor of the necessity of constant watchfulness.

At crucial points in the history of Christian theology, the difference between orthodoxy and heresy has often hung on a single word, or even a syllable. When Arius argued that the Son was to be understood as being of a *similar* substance as the Father, Athanasius correctly understood that the entirety of the gospel was at risk. As Athanasius faithfully led the church to understand, the New Testament clearly teaches that the Son is of the *same* substance as the Father. In the Greek language the distinction between the word offered by Arius and the correction offered by Athanasius was a single syllable. Looking back, we can now see that when the Council of Nicea met in AD 325, the gospel was defended and defined at this very point. Without the role of Athanasius as both pastor and theologian, the heresy of Arius might have spread unchecked, leading to disaster for the young church.

The Pastor's Conviction

As a theologian the pastor must be known for what he teaches as well as for what he knows, affirms, and believes. The health of the church depends on pastors who infuse their congregations with deep biblical and theological conviction. The means of this transfer of conviction is the preaching of the Word of God.

We will be hard pressed to define any activity as being more inherently theological than the preaching of God's Word. The ministry of preaching is an exercise in the theological exposition of Scripture. Congregations that are fed nothing more than ambiguous "principles" supposedly drawn from God's Word are doomed to spiritual immaturity, which will become visible in compromise, complacency, and a host of other spiritual ills.

Why else would the Apostle Paul command Timothy to preach the Word in such solemn and serious terms: "I solemnly charge you in the presence of God and of Christ Jesus, who is to judge the living and the dead, and by His appearing and His kingdom: preach the word; be ready in season and out of season; reprove, rebuke, exhort, with great patience and instruction" (2 Tim. 4:1–2).

As we have already seen, this text points to the inescapably theological character of ministry. In these preceding verses Paul specifically ties this theological ministry to the task of preaching—understood to be the pastor's supreme calling. As Martin Luther rightly affirmed, the preaching of the Word of God is the first mark of the church. Where it is found, there one finds the church. Where it is absent, there is no church, whatever others may claim.

Paul had affirmed Scripture as "inspired by God and profitable for teaching, for reproof, for correction, for training in righteousness" (2 Tim. 3:16). Through the preaching of the Word of God, the congregation is fed substantial theological doctrine directly from the biblical text. Expository preaching is the most effective means of imparting biblical knowledge to the congregation and thus arming God's people with deep theological conviction.

In other words, the pastor's conviction about theological preaching becomes the foundation for the transfer of these convictions into the hearts of God's people. The divine agent of this transfer is the Holy Spirit, who opens hearts, eyes, and ears to hear, understand, and receive the Word of God. The preacher's responsibility is to be clear, specific, systematic, and comprehensive in setting out the biblical convictions that are drawn from God's Word and that, taken together, frame a biblical understanding of the Christian faith and the Christian life.

The Pastor's Confession

All this assumes, of course, that the pastoral ministry is first rooted in the pastor's own confession of faith—the pastor's personal theological convictions.

The faithful pastor does not teach merely that which has historically been believed by the church and is even now believed by faithful Christians; he teaches out of his own personal confession of belief. There is no sense of theological detachment or of academic distance when the pastor sets out a theological vision of the Christian life.

All true Christian preaching is experiential preaching, set before the congregation by a man who is possessed by deep theological passion, specific theological convictions, and an eagerness to see these convictions shared by his congregation.

Faithful preaching does not consist in the preacher presenting a set of theological options to the congregation. Instead, the pastor should stand ready to define, defend, and document his own deep convictions, drawn from his careful study of God's Word and his knowledge of the faithful teaching of the church.

Our model for this pastoral confidence is, once again, the Apostle Paul. Paul's personal testimony is intertwined with his own theology. Consider Paul's retrospective analysis of his own attempts at human righteousness, coupled with his bold embrace of the gospel as grounded in grace alone.

"But whatever things were gain to me, those things I have counted as loss for the sake of Christ," Paul asserted.

> More than that, I count all things to be loss in view of the sur-passing value of knowing Christ Jesus my Lord, for whom I have suffered the loss of all things, and count them but rubbish in or-der that I may gain Christ, and may be found in Him, not having a righteousness of my own derived from the Law, but that which is through faith in Christ, the righteousness which comes from God on the basis of faith, that I may know Him and the power of His resurrection and the fellowship of His sufferings, being conformed

to His death; in order that I may attain to the resurrection from the dead (Phil. 3:7–11).

In other words, Paul did not hide behind any sense of academic neutrality from the doctrines he so powerfully taught. Nor did he set before his congregation in Philippi a series of alternate renderings of doctrine. Instead, he taught clearly, defended his case, and made clear that he embraced these doctrines as the substance of his life and faith.

Of course, the experiential nature of the pastor's confession does not imply that the authority for theology is in personal experience. To the contrary, the authority must always remain the Word of God. The experiential character of the pastor's theological calling underlines the fact that the preacher is speaking from within the circle of faith as a believer, not from a position of detachment as a mere teacher.

The pastor's confession of his faith and personal example add both authority and authenticity to the pastoral ministry. Without these the pastor can sound more like a theological consultant than a faithful shepherd. The congregation must be able to observe the pastor basing his life and ministry upon these truths, not merely teaching them in the pulpit.

In the end every faithful pastor's theological confession must include an eschatological confidence that God will preserve his work to the end. As Paul confessed, "For this reason I also suffer these things, but I am not ashamed; for I know whom I have believed and I am convinced that He is able to guard what I have entrusted to Him until that day" (2 Tim. 1:12).

In the end, every preacher receives the same mandate that Paul handed down to Timothy: "Retain the standard of sound words which you have heard from me, in the faith and love which are in Christ Jesus. Guard, through the Holy Spirit who dwells in us, the treasure which has been entrusted to you" (2 Tim. 1:13–14).

In other words, we are the stewards of sound words and the guardians of doctrinal treasure that has been entrusted to us at the very core of our calling as pastors. The pastor who is no theologian is no pastor.

Contributors

Daniel L. Akin
President
Southeastern Baptist Theological Seminary

Mark Dever
Senior Pastor
Capitol Hill Baptist Church

David S. Dockery
President
Union University

Timothy George
Dean of Beeson Divinity School of Samford University and
Executive Editor of *Christianity Today*

John S. Hammett
Professor of Systematic Theology
Southeastern Baptist Theological Seminary

Kenneth Keathley
Senior Associate Dean
Southeastern Baptist Theological Seminary

R. Albert Mohler, Jr.
President
The Southern Baptist Theological Seminary

Russell D. Moore
Senior Vice President for Academic Administration and
Dean of the School of Theology
The Southern Baptist Theological Seminary

David P. Nelson
Senior Vice President for Academic Administration and
Dean of the Faculty
Southeastern Baptist Theological Seminary

R. Stanton Norman
Vice President for University Development
Southwest Baptist University

Paige Patterson
President
Southwestern Baptist Theological Seminary

Peter R. Schemm, Jr.
Dean of the College
Southeastern Baptist Theological Seminary

Gregory Alan Thornbury
Dean of the School of Christian Studies
Union University

Malcolm B. Yarnell, III
Assistant Dean for Theological Studies and
Director of the Center for Theological Research
Southwestern Baptist Theological Seminary

Name Index

Subject Index

Scripture Index

Proverbs

Mark

Galatians

Ephesians